MW01292410

The Great Libraries

From Antiquity to the Renaissance (3000 B.C. to A.D. 1600)

The Great Libraries

From Antiquity to the Renaissance
(3000 B.C. to A.D. 1600)

by Konstantinos Sp. Staikos

Preface by
HÉLÈNE AHRWEILER

Translated by
TIMOTHY CULLEN

OAK KNOLL PRESS &
THE BRITISH LIBRARY
2000

Second impression

Published by **Oak Knoll Press**
310 Delaware Street, New Castle, Delaware, USA
and **The British Library**
96 Euston Road, St. Pancras, London NW1, UK

ISBN: 1-58456-018-5 (USA)
ISBN: 0- 7123-0661- 7 (UK)

Title: The Great Libraries
Author: Konstantinos Sp. Staikos
Translator: Timothy Cullen
Printed in Athens, Greece, by M. Toumbis S.A.
Photographer: Nikos Panayotopoulos
Editor: K. Sp. Staikos
Director of Publishing: J. von Hoelle
Editorial Board Reader: Nicholas Basbanes

Copyright © 2000 by Konstantinos Sp. Staikos

Originally published in Greek in 1996, under the title *ΒΙΒΛΙΟΘΗΚΗ.*

Library of Congress Cataloging-in-Publication Data

Staikos, K.
[Vivliotheke. English]
The Great Libraries: From Antiquity to the Renaissance / Konstantinos Sp. Staikos.
p. cm.
Includes bibliographical references and index.
ISBN 1-58456-018-5
1. Libraries - Europe - History - To 400. 2.Libraries - Europe - History - 400-1400. 3.Libraries - Europe - History - 1400 - 1600. 4.Library architecture - Europe - History - To 1500. 5.Library architecture - Europe - History - 16th century. I. Title

Z723.S7313 2000
027.04-dc21 99-087263

British Library Cataloguing-in-Publication Data
A CIP Record is available from the British Library

Dust jacket (Front): The Prunksaal or Great Hall of the Nationalbibliothek in Vienna.
(Back) The Theological Hall of the Strahov Abbey Library, Prague.
Printed endpapers: Preliminary drawings of the Royal Library in Paris
by Étienne-Louis Boullée.

ALL RIGHTS RESERVED:
No part of this book may be reproduced in any manner without the express written
consent of the publisher, except in the case of brief excerpts in critical reviews
and articles. All inquiries should be addressed to:
Oak Knoll Press, 310 Delaware Street, New Castle, DE 19720, USA.

Wisdom should be sought
for its own sake.

Lupus de Ferrières

Foreword

It is unusual for a publisher to write a foreword to one of his own titles, but this book and author are special. For me, this work brings back fond memories of a life-long love affair with books and their great depositories. I was once told that, *Libraries are the memory of mankind.* These immortal words of Goethe still whisper in my subconscious. They are true now as they were thirty years ago when a Cambridge don first tried to enlighten me to their usefulness. As a young American student I haunted the stacks and archives of British Library, the Bodleian and the magnificent libraries of my adopted Cambridge. I loved the quiet majesty of their lofty rooms and the aroma of ancient, leather-bound paper that held the stored knowledge of the ages. I was surrounded with the august words of pharaohs, prophets, kings and poets. Caesar, Shakespeare, Plato and Erasmus were my company for the asking. I was in awe and soon fell in love with the written and printed word.

Over the years books became my profession and I made it a point to visit as many of the old libraries of Europe as possible. They bacame the central focus of my holiday expeditions. However, my deep appreciation for these treasure houses extended beyond buildings and books. I would also meet some of the most unforgettable people I have ever known. These unsung heros of our society make libraries the vibrant, living caldrons for research, entertainment and tomorrow's new ideas.

I believe libraries are one of civilization's most unique institutions. They are monuments to the human condition, containing our wisdom, our folly, our fears and our dreams. They remember our past, serve the present, and are the launching pads to our future.

In this beautifully-written book, Konstantinos Staikos has captured the rich heritage and wonder of Western civilization's most notable ancient and medieval libraries. His magnificent color photographs are second only to the richness of his text. To read this book and savor its illustrations, is to know a labor of love from an important and serious scholar. In this singular endeavor the author shares with us his passion for the subject. This treasure belongs on the shelf of every true bibliophile. Mr. Staikos has created a masterpiece that celebrates one of humanity's greatest achievements, the library, and we here at Oak Knoll are proud to be part of it.

J. Lewis von Hoelle

Preface

At the time of writing these words, all I have read of this book by Konstantinos Staikos is a sample, a relatively small proportion of the total, dealing with the period which is my own particular field of study. However, I have no hesitation in commending the whole work highly, without fear of contradiction: first, because I know the author and his passion for anything to do with books and reading, as well as his wholehearted commitment to art and beauty; and secondly because I believe that the subject of this book (which must have taken years to complete) – libraries and their history, a story affording tangible proof of intellectual co-operation and the reciprocity of cultural achievement, which every nation passes on from generation to generation – is the foundation of the memory of mankind, which obeys the Greek principle of memory that sets out to be unfailing, in other words 'a possession for ever', like truth. *Bibliotheke*, which in one form or another is the word for library in almost every European language except English, is a Greek word, and libraries themselves are of Greek origin, yet not enough research has been done on libraries in their native country. Mr. Staikos's profound knowledge of the history of Greek books, already demonstrated in his *Charta of Greek Printing*, and his work on the design of the libraries in the Monastery of St. John on Patmos and the Oecumenical Patriarchate in Constantinople, afford the best possible guarantee of the scholarly value of his new book, *The Great Libraries: From Antiquity to the Renaissance (3000 B.C. to A.D. 1600)*.

The author is a gifted man who has expended a great deal of time and hard work on his researches on the 'cathedrals of the mind' (as libraries have aptly been called), keeping one fundamental principle always in mind: to avoid digressing too far from the point and so betraying the mystical atmosphere of learning that reigns in every library, bonding the readers with their books and, through them, with the literary and intellectual achievements of every age in history.

The hallmark of every library is its accumulation of knowledge, to which the humble reader applies his mind. Perhaps that is what those students of European history had in mind who defined a European as one who, wherever he may be – in Prague, Moscow, Paris, Athens or any other corner of the continent –finds the same books, the same library, so that he can read and admire the writers who have laid the foundations not merely of the national identity but of the sense of cultural brotherhood that characterizes all Europeans. This was the point Paul Valéry was making so strongly when he said that wherever the names of Plato, Aristotle, Cicero and St. Paul have significance and arouse reverberations, that is where Europe is. Moreover, it is only in that sense that Europe, by which I mean the European spirit, can be said to include the American continent in its embrace. We should also remember that libraries are the places where the intellectual heritage of past ages is preserved for posterity: for example, the *Bibliotheca* of Patriarch Photios, the founding father of the first Byzantine Renaissance, contains passages from works of ancient literature, now lost, which were then still available for him to read. In the same way, manuscripts in the possession of great libraries, many of them still unpublished, keep alive the memory of bygone eras.

A book may be in manuscript form – an autograph or an illuminated copy – or it may be a beautifully printed volume in an edition of few or many copies; it may be lying forgotten on a library shelf, perhaps with marginal annotations by readers known or unknown; but in every case it epitomizes the expression of an original thought, an invitation and a challenge to explore a new way of looking at the world. To a careful reader every book is a utopia, a journey to that new world which possesses the fundamental characteristics of the European critical spirit: a spirit that has its origins in Greece and is not afraid even to confront the possibility of its own self-negation – though always by means of a disquisition that continues an intellectual dialogue.

A book, whether in the form of a roll that is easy to read aloud in public, a manuscript codex that allows the reader to approach the text in his own way by enabling him to skip back and forth through the pages, a printed volume bound in a format of any shape and size, a film, video or television production, or a piece of high-tech electronic wizardry – a book in any form follows the history of the world through the ages. Civil powers, the Church, schools, individual human beings, groups of people and nations all, in their own several ways, apply their minds to 'the Book of the Fathers' (as the Armenians call history), which always remains open and is forever opening up new vistas thanks to the ceaseless creative activity of mankind. Every library, then, is a repository of wisdom, and the history of each individual library attests to the continuity of intellectual endeavour, which reinforces all education and learning through the unbroken heritage of knowledge. In this way the Romans, for example, who were well-known book-lovers and bibliomanes, attest to their familiarity with the Greek past. Being a living heritage, every library is enriched in order to enrich: it is a place dedicated to the preservation and propagation of everything that really matters. General libraries, specialized libraries, libraries of purely local interest and private libraries all bespeak their commitment to a body of achievement, to a past which, as Fernand Braudel has said, is never entirely past. They also proclaim the need for all members of the human community, choosing the reading matter they prefer, to take part in the everyday creative process of our times.

Libraries today face numerous problems, and librarians would do well to acquire a thorough knowledge of how libraries evolved whenever and wherever similar difficulties confronted them in the past. This is where the real value of Mr. Staikos's book lies: let no critic dismiss it as a mere narrative of a now useless tradition, for on the past that they embody we may be able to build a better future. Nor should we forget that tyrants and enemies of liberty have always sought to cling on to power by burning books and libraries. Autos-da-fé was what they called those acts of mindless violence. Respect for books and care for libraries is humanity's answer to all such barbarity: that is the lesson we learn from the historical memory of past and present civilizations which libraries have stored within them.

Let me conclude with a footnote. I was lucky enough to be able to look through the whole of this book, giving it more than passing attention, before it finally went to the press. What struck me was that the breadth of learning displayed in its pages, implicit in the enormous historical scope it covers (from earliest antiquity through the Middle Ages to the Renaissance), and the depth of research into great civilizations involved in its compilation, command not only the admiration but also the gratitude of every thoughtful reader. And by 'thoughtful reader' I mean anyone – specialist or non- specialist, researcher or member of the general public – who respects matters of genuine importance and is prepared to evaluate what he reads without being swayed by doctrinaire prejudice.

Hélène Ahrweiler
President
of the
European University

Author's Introduction

The scope of this book may be summed up under three main headings. First, it analyses the motives that prompted the peoples of the Mediterranean and the West to establish and maintain libraries, that is to say special buildings or parts of buildings designated as repositories of their oral traditions, their literary works and their accumulated knowledge in every branch of human learning, recorded on tablets or in books, from 3000 B.C. to the beginning of the sixteenth century A.D. Secondly, it outlines the development of libraries through the ages and the ways in which their evolution was affected by intellectual trends and historical circumstances in general. Thirdly, it examines the factors that influenced not only the spread of libraries through the civilized world but also their design and layout, by which I mean their furniture and fittings as well as their overall architectural style. Two points should be made clear at the outset: archives are deliberately excluded except in the chapter on Mesopotamia, where no clear-cut dividing line can be drawn between archival and literary collections; and there are no chapters on Jewish libraries or those in Persia and the Islamic world, which I hope to cover in a separate book.

Bibliotheke is a Greek word which, as Pompeius Festus informs us, was used by both the Greeks and the Romans to denote either a large collection of books or a room or building in which books were kept. The Sumerians spoke of a 'House of Tablets' and the Egyptians a 'House of Books' to mean a place used for the collection, classification and storage of written accounts of historical events (the happenings dealt to them by the gods, as Homer put it) and of their knowledge gained from the observation of nature, human conduct and human creative enterprise.

This accumulated knowledge – inscribed on commemorative stelae or tombstones, written in books made of papyrus, parchment or paper, or later printed on paper, and expressed in thousands of different languages and dialects – is the repository of all the fruits of human intellectual endeavour. Whether it is to be found in a humble fragment of an anonymous written work or in a sumptuous parchment codex, it is an irreplaceable part of an ageless book such as the *Book of Mankind* said to have been compiled by Hermes Trismegistus, which, according to the priests of Thoth, was composed of 36,525 separate books.

In the pages of this book, this 'world library' acquires an aura of the supernatural through the presentation of such a vast wealth of material. Every book ever written is shown to be connected with every other, so that all together form a colossal pyramid of knowledge founded on the work of some ordinary, anonymous person who piously sifted through the records left by his ancestors in order to study their achievements.

The first person in the history of books and libraries who encouraged his fellow-men to respect the words and deeds of their forefathers was Aristotle. If he takes the credit for according due recognition to the authors of creative work, it is because he was moved more by what he considered a moral imperative than by his thirst for knowledge as such. This led him to institute a roll of honour on which every author of work that contributes to the advancement of knowledge has a rightful place. Following Aristotle's example, his beloved pupil Theophrastus set out to record the beliefs of earlier philosophers so as to ensure that their names would not be forgotten by posterity. Aristotle himself, rejecting the contention of Socrates and Plato that the written word does nothing to promote constructive dialogue, spent his life rereading and revising his own philosophical and scientific works: as Theophrastus remarked, 'Reading begets corrections.' What is more, on reading Aristotle's work one has the feeling that he was trying to determine the parameters of a planned world beyond the grasp of the human mind, a world susceptible to any number of different interpretations.

This moral dimension of the transmission of knowledge from generation to generation obeys an unwritten universal law and is clearly discernible in the world of libraries, as it transcends time, national and cultural differences and peculiarities, longitude and latitude, social, political and economic conditions and even linguistic differences. It brings into being a worldwide company of men and women with a common interest, a company whose members are constantly multiplying, and thus it accords absolutely with Mallarmé's dictum: 'The world exists to end up in a book.'

Of the anonymous 'Scribe of the House of Books', who lived in Egypt around 2400 B.C., practically nothing is known, and the same is true of the author of the Creation epic written probably in the second millennium B.C. Nor do we know the identity of the scribes whom Assurbanipal sent out to the farthest corners of his empire to record any information that was not to be found in his extensive library at Nineveh. Very little is known even about Callimachus, the librarian of the Great Library of Alexandria and the only person of whom it is fair to say that he had almost all the books in the world through his hands and catalogued them. On the other hand, we do know that his catalogue entitled 'Tables' (*Pinakes*) long remained unsurpassed in its field: it laid the foundations of scientific librarianship and prompted Cicero to comment that happiness was to be found there (i.e. in Callimachus's well-organized library) and nowhere else. We also know that the German humanist Johannes Cuno kept a collection of proofs from the press of Aldus Manutius, even including bad copies, as he believed that every written or printed document could be of use in seeking out philosophical truth. We know, too, that August, Duke of Saxony in the sixteenth century, collected in his library all the printed works available in Europe and spent much of his time writing the particulars of every book in his possession on the spine, in his own hand. Lastly, we know about the Emperor Maximilian II's librarian Hugo Blotius, who, despite his extreme poverty, refused to betray the 'sacred trust' reposed in him and did all he could to ensure that the priceless treasures in his care should not be lost through carelessness, wear and tear or the over-generous lending policy of the imperial court.

All these, from Assurbanipal to Aristotle, Tyrannio, Ptolemy, Cicero, Libanius, Tychicus, Photios, Cosimo de' Medici, Palla Strozzi, Aldus Manutius and Johannes Cuno, and many others from all walks of life whose names are mentioned in the pages that follow, are the principal characters in the history of books and libraries: they are the members of the worldwide company mentioned above. The mystical bond that unites them was perfectly summed up by Léon Bloy (in *L'âme de Napoléon*) when he wrote that every human being has contributed by his or her work to the composition of a vast book of the history of mankind, in which commas and accents have the same value as chapters and clauses – a value that is hidden out of sight and can never be proved.

In conclusion, I wish to express my gratitude to Hélène Glykatzi-Ahrweiler for honouring me with a foreword to this volume. I must also put it on record that the English edition of this book would probably never have seen the light of day had it not been for the personal interest taken by Mr. Robert Fleck and Mr. J. Lewis von Hoelle, to whom I wish to express my gratitude once again. Their enterprise in publishing the fascinating story of libraries in the lingua franca of our time, thus making it accessible to readers all over the world at the dawn of the new millennium, is yet another example of the humanistic philosophy that makes books such an irreplaceable and inexhaustible source of knowledge. Lastly, I should like to express my enormous appreciation of the support given to me by Mr. Dimitri Contomina, a friend and now a comrade-in-arms in my writing projects and indeed in anything relating to cultural activities with a broader social dimension.

Konstantinos Sp. Staikos

Acknowledgements

During the ten years that it has taken me to write this book I have been fortunate enough to enjoy the support of many friends and acquaintances, who have helped me a great deal in my endeavours to make it as accurate as possible. The acknowledgements below are in chronological order.

First of all I should like to thank Chryssa Maltezou, both for spending so much of her precious time listening carefully to my ideas about the book throughout the time it was being written and for telling me about useful source works which I would not otherwise have been able to consult. I am sure I would have remained in ignorance of many important works about archaeological finds relevant to libraries if they had not been drawn to my attention by Evi Touloupa, and to her too I express my sincere thanks. I am grateful to my friend Linos Benakis, not only for his valuable advice and help with the indexing and translation of material from M.-I. Macdonald's *Treasury of the Greek Language*, but also for his authoritative assistance with the translation of numerous passages of ancient literature. My thanks are due to Georgios Babiniotis for his advice on the structure and form of some of the main chapters, and for the time he spent discussing various aspects of the work. I should like to thank Alkistis Spetsieri-Horemi, who was kind enough to take me round the ruins of Hadrian's Library, telling me about the recent work on the site and the available literature on the subject. I am indebted to Haralambos Bouras for his comments on some of the more complex chapters and his invaluable advice on architectural matters. Michalis Sakellariou was good enough to read a large part of the book in manuscript and gave me useful advice on the historical background, for which I am most grateful. Thanos Markopoulos very obligingly read the chapter on Byzantium and drew my attention to recent research findings on a number of topics, thus saving me from many potential pitfalls.

A special debt of gratitude is owed to Nikos Petrochilos, who read the chapter on the Roman period and, although working under acute pressure of time, was able to give me vital guidance on terminology, dating and bibliographical references in the field of Latin literature.

I should like to mention the great help I have received from my conversations with Cyril Mango, which have given me a better insight into many aspects of the complex character of the Byzantines, and also from his comments on the chapter about the Byzantine world. I deeply appreciate his assistance.

My sincere thanks are due to those who have worked most closely with me on the production of this book: Nikos Panayotopoulos, who was my sole collaborator and adviser in the work of photographing the libraries and preparing the photographs for publication, and Anna Hadjiandoniou, who saw all the material through the press, right down to the stage of final pagination. A special word of acknowledgement goes to Timothy Cullen, who has not only produced an excellent translation that faithfully conveys the atmosphere of the original but has taken great pains to discover and correct errors that had slipped through in the text and footnotes. I am most grateful to him. Lastly, I should mention that the Greek edition of *The Great Libraries* was dedicated to the memory of Frank E. Basil and that in my research for this book I received every assistance from Manos Mavridis and Karen Basil-Mavridi whom I should like to thank again publicly in print.

Methodology

The literature I have used for general and specialized reference in writing this book is of various kinds, and so some clarification is perhaps needed to explain my working method.

First of all I must point out the fundamental difference between the kinds of works used for Book I, entitled 'From Antiquity to the Renaissance', and for Book II, entitled 'Selected Monastic and Humanistic Libraries'.

In Book I my aim has been to evaluate every item of evidence supplied by the primary and secondary sources and the latest archaeological discoveries. In Book II it is my intention that the chronicle of each library should illuminate the personality of its founder and his particular interests in the world of books, on the basis of the relevant literature both old and new.

With regard to the working method I have used in writing Book I, a rather more detailed explanation is called for. Each chapter in this part of the book is based on certain specific works that have enabled me to depict the historical background to the developments occurring in the world of libraries and the book trade generally. Those works are listed below.

For the history of the peoples of Mesopotamia I have relied chiefly on by the works by G. Maspero (*The Dawn of Civilization*) and G. Perrot and C. Chipiez. For the Sumerians I have relied on the works by S.N. Kramer, and on the literature of the Mesopotamian peoples I have used C.F. Jean, *La littérature des Babyloniens et des Assyriens*.

On the Egyptians in general and their literature in particular I have read G. Maspero's classic *Les contes populaires de l'Égypte ancienne*; also the works by E.A.W. Budge on the various editions of the Book of the Dead and by E. Posner on 'archival libraries'.

On the Greek world from the Archaic to the end of the Hellenistic period I have used the books by R. Pfeiffer and A. Lesky on the history of classical literature and scholarship, and on papyrology the works by E.G. Turner and F.G. Kenyon. On the history of Alexandria under the Ptolemies I have used P.M. Fraser's book, and on the architecture of libraries of that period I have consulted A. Conze, K. Dziatzko and W. Hoepfner. In writing about that period, which extends to the early centuries of the Byzantine Empire, I have consulted the *Treasury of the Greek Language* (*Θησαυρὸς τῆς Ἑλληνικῆς Γλώσσας*) by Marianna-Irini Macdonald, now available on CD-ROM. On searching for all entries including the word *biblion* ('book') or any of its derivatives, I found over ten thousand references, which were subsequently indexed and perused.

For the chapter on the Roman period I have used J.H. Rose's *Handbook of Latin Literature*. On the book trade in that period I have used the works by T. Kleberg and G. Cavallo and, more specifically, Cicero's *Letters to Atticus*, *Noctes Atticae* by Aulus Gellius and the writings of the elder and younger Pliny. On the architecture of Roman libraries I have consulted V.M. Strocka, Elzbieta Makowiecka and J. Tøsberg.

For the chapter on Byzantium I have relied on the historical works by A.A. Vasiliev, P. Lemerle and C. Mango. On Byzantine libraries I have used the works by K.A. Manafis, N.G. Wilson and I. Ševčenko, and on general matters relating to book production and distribution the works by J. Irigoin and H. Hunger respectively.

On the history of books and libraries in the West during the Middle Ages I have relied on *The Medieval Library*, edited by J.W. Thompson, as well as B. Bischoff's works on monastic libraries and their manuscripts and the works by L.D. Reynolds and N.G. Wilson. On particular aspects of the subject, such as the history of Greek studies in the West, I have consulted P. Courcelle and A. Momigliano. On medieval university manuscripts I have relied on the seminal work by J. Destrez and the writings of those who followed in his footsteps.

For the chapter on the Renaissance I have relied on Vespasiano da Bisticci's *Lives* in the edition by A. Greco, with the editor's informative notes and bibliographical references, and the three volumes by G. Cammelli on Byzantine scholars in the West. On printing, publishing and libraries in the time of Aldus Manutius I have consulted the books by M.J.C. Lowry and Lotte Labowsky, and on the leaders of the Greek contribution to the Renaissance I have revisited my own *Charta of Greek Printing*.

Finally, a standard work on libraries through the ages is the series of treatises by C. Wendel, collected and completed in 1955 by W. Göber and others and now included in the series of volumes edited by F. Milkau and G. Leyh under the overall title of *Handbuch der Bibliothekswissenschaft*.

CONTENTS

Foreword by the Publisher i
Preface by Hélène Ahrweiler iii-v
Author's Introduction vii- ix
Acknowledgements xi
Methodology xii

BOOK ONE: CHAPTERS ONE TO ELEVEN

CHAPTER ONE. THE PEOPLES OF MESOPOTAMIA 3-17

I. The Sumerians 3-9
1. The first schools and the first school libraries 4-6
2. The first public record offices 6-7
3. The Epic of Gilgamesh 7-8

II. The age of Hammurabi 8-12
1. Public record offices and literary libraries 9-11
2. How the tablets were classified and arranged 11-12
3. The first library catalogue 12

III. Assurbanipal's library 12-16
1. What the library contained 13
2. The royal scribes 13-16

CHAPTER TWO. EGYPT 19-27

From the Pharaohs to the Ptolemies
1. The papyrus roll 19-20
2. Egyptian writing: Hieroglyphics 20-21
3. The Book of the Dead 21-23
4. Popular reading matter 23-26
(a) Subject matter 23-25
(b) Readership 25-26
5. Libraries 26-27

CHAPTER THREE. THE HELLENIC WORLD 29-55

From the Pre-Socratics to the end of the Classical period

I. The Pre-Socratic period 29-31
1. Public libraries 29-30
2. The first private collections 30-31

II. The Classical period 31-55
1. How the sophists helped to popularize books 33-37
2. Private libraries 37-41
3. The book trade in the Hellenic world 41-43
4. Aristotle 43-45
5. The eventful subsequent history of Aristotle's library 45-49
6. What books were made of 49-52
7. Library architecture 52-55

CHAPTER FOUR. THE HELLENISTIC PERIOD
THE GREAT LIBRARY OF ALEXANDRIA 57-89
1. The foundation of the Museum 60-63
2. The Library 63-66
3. The directors of the Library 66-69
(a) Arrangement by literary genre 67-68
(b) Architectural layout 68
4. The Library's stock of books 69-74
5. The destruction of the Library 74-80
6. A chronicle of the Library's history 80-81
7. Postscript 88-89

CHAPTER FIVE. OTHER LIBRARIES
IN THE HELLENISTIC PERIOD 91-96

I. Pergamum 91-94
1. The foundation of the library 91-92
2. The library at its zenith 92
3. Expansion of the library 92-93
4. The problem of pseudepigraphy 93-94
5. Architecture 94

II. Ai Khanoum 94-96

CHAPTER SIX. LIBRARIES IN THE ROMAN PERIOD 97-121

I. The world of Latium 97-109
1. The beginnings of Roman literature 97-100
2. The first libraries 100-101
3. Education 101-102
4. Private libraries 102-104
5. Authors and public recitation 104-105
6. Promotion of books by their authors 105
7. Relations between author and publisher 105
8. Publishers 105-106
9. The antiquarian value of old books 106
10. Booksellers 106-109

II. Public libraries 110-121
1. Pollio's library 110
2. Augustus's library (the Palatine Library) 110-111
3. Tiberius's library 111
4. Vespasian's library 111
5. Trajan's library 111-112

III. Architecture 112-121
1. Pollio's library 112-113
2. Augustus's library 113-114
3. The Library of the Temple of Peace 114
4. The Bibliotheca Ulpia 114

5. Libraries in bath-houses 116-117
6. Private libraries 117-120

CHAPTER SEVEN. LIBRARIES IN THE ROMAN PROVINCES 123-130

I. The library of Pantaenus 123

II. Hadrian as a patron of art and learning 123-130
1. Hadrian's library in Athens 125
2. Hadrian's library at Tibur 125-130

CHAPTER EIGHT. THE EARLY CHRISTIAN WORLD 131-134

I. The first Christian libraries 131-134
1. Parish libraries 132
2. Private libraries 132-133

II. Architecture 133-134

CHAPTER NINE. BYZANTIUM 137-187

I. From Constantine to early Byzantine humanism 140-154
1. The first 'imperial' library 141-143
2. Education 143
3. The crisis in the sixth century: from Justinian I to Leo IV 143-146
4. Monasticism and monastic libraries 146-149
5. Private libraries 149-153
6. Booksellers 153-154
7. The changeover to lower-case script 154

II. Byzantine humanism in the ninth century 154-165
1. Three humanistic libraries 154-162
2. Monasteries and centres of monasticism 162-164
3. A general library in the imperial palace. 164-165

III. From Constantine VII to the capture of Constantinople by the Crusaders 165-167

IV. The Empire of Nicaea 167-170
1. Higher education: Nikephoros Blemmydes 168-169
2. Theodore II Laskaris 169-170

V. The last Byzantine renaissance: from 1261 to 1453 170-182
1. The shortage of parchment 170-172
2. Libraries of the *literati* 172-175
3. University libraries 175-177
4. Byzantine libraries in the West: from 1400 to 1453 177-182

VI. Architecture 182-187
1. Secular libraries 182-184
2. Monastic libraries 184-186

CHAPTER TEN. THE MIDDLE AGES 189-212

I. The Dark Ages 190-198
1. Book production in the Late Roman period 190-192

2. The Greek world at the service of monastic learning: The Vivarium 192-196
3. Schools in the Middle Ages 196
4. The decline of Latin scholarship 196-197
5. The Celtic and Anglo-Saxon worlds 197-198

II. The Carolingian renaissance 202-205
1. Alcuin: Educational reforms and the revival of libraries 202-203
2. Libraries during the Carolingian renaissance 203-205

III. Books and libraries at the universities 205-212
1. The foundation of the first universities 205-209
2. The *pecia* system 209-210
3. University libraries 210-212

CHAPTER ELEVEN. THE RENAISSANCE 215-238

I. Humanism 215-226
1. The first humanist libraries. Lovati and his circle 215-218
2. The revival of the bilingual library 218-221
3. Court libraries 221-224
4. Academies and scriptoria 224-226

II. The achievements of the early printers 226-235
1. Humanist presses 229-232
2. The impact of printed books on the growth of libraries 232-235

III. Architecture 235-238
1. Three-aisled libraries 236-237
2. Libraries with painted decoration 237-238

BOOK TWO: CHAPTERS TWELVE TO TWENTY-FIVE

Ch. 12. The Library of the Oecumenical Patriarchate 244-265
Ch. 13. The Library of the Monastery of St. John on Patmos 266-283
Ch. 14. The Vatican Library 284-303
Ch. 15. The Biblioteca Malatestiana at Cesena 304-319
Ch. 16. The Biblioteca Marciana 320-337
Ch. 17. The Biblioteca Laurenziana 338-357
Ch. 18. The St. Gall Library 358-377
Ch. 19. The Library of Beatus Rhenanus at Sélestat 378-391
Ch. 20. The Herzog August Library at Wolfenbüttel 392-407
Ch. 21. The Bibliothèque Nationale in Paris 408-427
Ch. 22. The Nationalbibliothek in Vienna 428-445
Ch. 23. The Corvinian Library 446-463
Ch. 24. The Library of Strahov Abbey 464-483
Ch. 25. The Bodleian Library 484-501

ABBREVIATIONS 503-504

BIBLIOGRAPHY 507-539

INDEX 543-563

BOOK ONE

From Antiquity to the Renaissance

1. Sargon before the sacred tree. Drawing by Saint-Elme Gautier.

CHAPTER ONE

THE PEOPLES OF MESOPOTAMIA

The practice of using a special room or building for the storage and classification of written matter in order to preserve cultural traditions and improve social organization can be traced back to the peoples of Mesopotamia, starting with the Sumerians early in the third millennium B.C., or possibly earlier. The Sumerians developed a cuneiform script in which they wrote on clay tablets: not only factual records giving an insight into their daily life but also a considerable body of 'literature', which had an enormous influence on their education and their cultural activities generally. The rooms where they stored these tablets were 'libraries' of archival records and their 'books' were epigraphic in character, even though the Mesopotamian peoples were very keen on oral literature and established a great many libraries. Libraries consisting entirely of clay tablets went on developing, with new ones continually being created, from about 3000 B.C. to the conquest of Mesopotamia by Alexander the Great. During this period the Tigris and Euphrates basins were inhabited by many different peoples (Sumerians, Elamites, Akkadians, Assyrians, Hittites, Chaldaeans, Babylonians) with common cultural, religious and social attributes, the most striking of these being their script and their practice of keeping 'books' in 'libraries'.

I. The Sumerians. The Sumerians, who lived in organized city-states in the Euphrates basin from the beginning of the third millennium B.C., are a people whose existence would have remained completely unknown but for the discoveries of the archaeologists, as there is no mention of them in any Egyptian, Hebrew or Greek source.[1] The hub of a Sumerian town was usually a large and imposing temple which was the focal point of community life. The temple was not used only for religious worship: it was the nucleus of the local administration and the central point of reference in town planning. The public archives were kept in the temple compound, the civil servants had their offices there, the shops, law courts and schools were there and it was the meeting-place for townspeople from all walks of life.

At a very early date, almost certainly near the beginning of the third millennium B.C., educated Sumerians started keeping records of laws, by-laws, and important events inscribed on clay tablets, and from the closing centuries of the millennium they also wrote down a large number of literary works handed down by oral tradition. From the thousands of tablets that have been preserved we can now find the answers to all sorts of questions about the Sumerians and their way of life. We know which of their religious beliefs were the first to be recorded in writing. We know about their earliest decisions on political and social matters and their philosophical ideas. We know where their hymns, epics and myths originated. We know the form of words used in their first judicial rulings. We know who was their first political reformer, when taxation was first introduced, when their legislative assembly had its first meeting. Lastly, we know how their first schools were run, a matter of immediate relevance to the subject of this book since their curriculum dictated which books were kept in early Sumerian school libraries.[2] The picture of the

1. See C.F. Jean, *Šumer et Akkad: Contribution à l'histoire de la civilisation dans la Basse-Mésopotamie*, Paris 1923; S.N. Kramer, *L'histoire commence à Sumer* (orig. published as *History Begins at Sumer*, London 1958), Paris 1986, 22.

2. See Kramer, *op. cit.* 22.

3. Writing was developed in Mesopotamia for the sole purpose of recording commercial transactions. When the towns were organized into city-states, their high officers of state felt it was necessary to keep records of the quantities of goods stored or in transit through their warehouses. This made it possible for all commercial activity to be monitored and gave every citizen access to reliable proofs of his commercial dealings, his wealth, his obligations and his rights; and this in turn led to the formation of 'archival libraries' or public record offices. In its most primitive form the script was ideographic, but quite soon – in the early centuries of the

2. Gudea 'the architect'.

Sumerians that emerges from the tablets is of a people with a highly-developed 'humanistic' ethos, whose territory extended from the cities of Mari, Sippar and Kish in the north to Ur, Uruk, Nippur, Fara and Jemdet Nasr in the south.[3]

1. The first schools and the first school libraries. One of the most striking facts one learns about the Sumerian civilization is that the introduction of writing and the foundation of the first schools went hand in hand, seemingly as a matter of course. In contrast to other ancient cultures, where the oral tradition was the principal medium for the dissemination of literary works for many centuries, the Sumerians wrote down their first epic, the Epic of Gilgamesh, during its author's lifetime.[4] This difference of approach is clearly apparent in their educational system, for their schools were so carefully and efficiently organized that the curriculum seems to have been virtually the same at all of them.

In the middle of the third millennium there were almost certainly schools in Sumer where the main subjects taught were the language and calligraphy. In 1902-1903 a considerable number of 'school books' dating from about 2500 B.C. were discovered at ancient Shuruppak.[5] However, the most impressive finds relating to ancient Mesopotamian schools date from the second half of the second millennium: tens of thousands of inscribed tablets have been discovered to date, and there are almost certainly hundreds of thousands more still lying buried.[6]

The first schools were started for the purpose of training young scribes, who then taught their skills to the next generation of students and thus helped to perpetuate the literary tradition. Before long these teachers of writing branched out into other specializations and the

3. A teacher and his pupils, as depicted in an Assyrian relief.

4. Dudu the scribe.

third millennium – the ideograms evolved into cuneiform characters. It is sometimes known as the Sumero-Akkadian script after the peoples who first used it, and sometimes as Assyro-Babylonian, as the Assyrians and Babylonians continued to use it for a long time thereafter.

On the evolution of cuneiform characters from ideograms, see: B. André-Leickman and C. Ziegler, *La naissance de l'écriture: cunéiforme et hiéroglyphes*, Paris 1982; J. Bottéro, *Mésopotamie: L'écriture, la raison et les dieux*, Paris 1989; G.R. Driver, *Semitic Writing from Pictograph to Alphabet*, London 1976; A. Curris, *Ugarit (Ras Shamra)*, Cambridge 1985; J.G. Février, *Histoire de l'écriture*, Paris 1984, 99 ff.

4. See Kramer, *op. cit.* 33-38.

5. The French Archaeological School's excavations at Mari uncovered a room in King Zimri-Lim's palace containing rows of what seem to be desks, made of clay. Many scholars are convinced that this was probably a schoolroom: see M. Parrot, *Mission archéologique de Mari*, II: *Les palais: Architecture*, Paris 1958. Alternatively it may have been a scriptorium, or the clay structures may perhaps have been stands for 'bookcases' for

schools were reorganized into a graded educational system going from primary to college level, with provision for the training of high public officials. Later, as the curriculum was broadened, the schools came to be used as meeting-places for the educated classes – cultural centres, as we might call them now. There scholars and experts on one subject or another such as theologians, zoologists, geographers, botanists, mathematicians, grammarians and linguists would gather to further the advance of learning, which led in turn to the enrichment of the temple libraries. There were also literary centres where men of letters would not only copy out, study and comment on the works of earlier generations but also write new works of their own: in other words, they were what one might call public scriptoria. Most graduates of the Sumerian educational system probably ended up as scribes in the local temple or palace, but not a few went on to spend their lives in study and research. In any case, the point that needs to be emphasized is that the Sumerians, from the very dawn of their literature, regarded scholarship, the written word and 'books' as being related in accordance with a mathematical equation.

The head of a school, who had the title of *ummia* ('specialist' or 'teacher'), was also sometimes known as the 'father of the school', while the pupils were the 'sons of the school', and the two most important members of the staff were the drawing master and the teacher of Sumerian. The teacher's job was to prepare a tablet with a fair copy of the exercise to be copied by his pupils. As regards the syllabus, no detective work is needed because of the great number of writing tablets unearthed in school buildings:[7] excavators have found countless tablets inscribed with classroom work, from the simplest exercises done by the youngest primary school children to advanced studies of the upper grades, showing not the slightest variation from the teachers' own fair copies.[8]

Not much is known about the teaching methods employed in the upper grades, but we do have the text of a composition dedicated by a teacher to some of his pupils which gives an account of school life in termtime.[9] This chronicle is moralistic in tone and was evidently very popular, to judge by the fact that over twenty copies of it have survived. It opens with a question: 'Where did you go as a small child, young one?' And the pupil answers, 'I went to school.' Then follows a description of the start of the day, with the pupil snatching a hurried breakfast so as to get to school on time and escape a caning from his teacher or another member of the staff.[10] However, having avoided the first pitfall of unpunctuality, the unfortunate child incurs one punishment after another, for standing up in class without permission, being caught talking in class or running through the Great Gate in an unseemly manner. Then, as if all this were not enough, his teacher takes him to task for carelessness in copying out his exercise and he receives another beating. When he goes

the storage of inscribed tablets.

6. See Kramer, *op. cit.* 33-34.

7. The first things children had to learn at school were how to make a clay tablet and how to hold the stylus correctly: see C.B.F. Walker, 'Le cunéiforme' in Larissa Bonfante et al., *La naissance des écritures: Du cunéiforme à l'alphabet* (= *Reading the Past: Ancient Writing from Cuneiform to the Alphabet*, London 1990, tr. Christiane Zivie-Coche), Paris 1994, 62.

8. See Kramer, *op. cit.* 39-41 (= 'Vie d'un écolier: le premier exemple de "lèche"'). We know that the school curriculum, from primary up to college level, consisted of two main courses of study. The lower course was concerned with general knowledge and was largely a matter of learning by rote: its aim was not to teach the children to search out the truth as such, but rather to turn out scribes with a good mastery of the language and the script. The advanced course was more creative and literary in character. It is

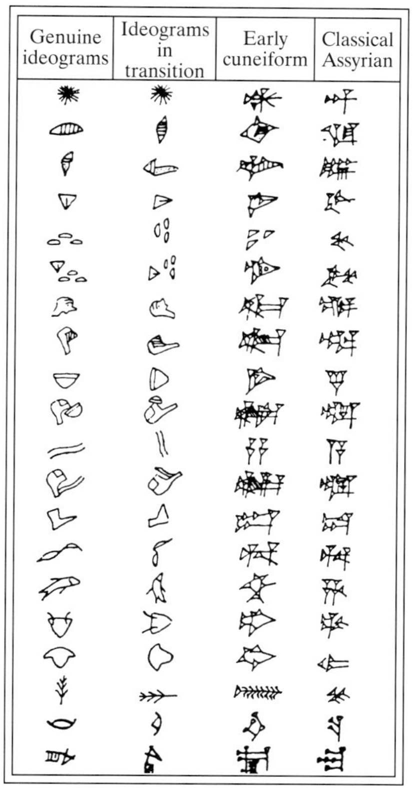
Genuine ideograms
Ideograms in transition
Early cuneiform
Classical Assyrian

5. The evolution of the cuneiform script.

home he tells his father about the events of the day, and father and son decide to invite the teacher to their house in the hope of winning his favour. All goes according to plan. The teacher accepts the invitation and goes to the pupil's home, where he is ushered into the chair of honour in the living-room and presented with gifts: clothes, food, even a ring. Won over by the family's generous hospitality, he makes a flowery speech to the future scribe: 'Young fellow, because you have listened to my words you can rise to the position of scribe. You can be your brothers' guide and your friends' leader, and you can attain to the position of highest honour among your fellow-pupils. You have acquitted yourself well in your duties as a pupil, you are now a scholar.' The chronicle ends with a fulsome envoi. Its anonymous author, who was satirizing the way things were done in his own time, could of course never have had the slightest idea that his words would turn out to have a prophetic relevance to future generations, right down to the present day.

Clearly the basis of a young Sumerian's schooling was constant practice in writing, which presupposed – or rather went hand in hand with – the existence of a school library, which was renewed every term. At the same time, the homework done by the aspiring scribe or civil servant would have hammered home to him the importance of building up a private library of his own.

2. The first public record offices. Although enormous numbers of inscribed tablets from the Sumerian period have been found, our knowledge of the way their libraries were run comes from evidence dated to the end of the third millennium. Nevertheless it is practically certain that all the big libraries of the Sumerian period were archival collections containing records of each city's political organization, civil administration and commercial activities: accounting ledgers, records of purchases and sales of goods and slaves, official correspondence and other equally interesting 'books'.[11] Nikolaus Schneider, in an article on the filing system used by the Sumerians and Akkadians in their libraries under the Third Dynasty of Ur (*c.* 2100 B.C.),[12] informs us that the Sumerians looked after their archives intelligently and methodically and kept them readily accessible for everyday transactions. This shows that the kings and the ruling class attached great importance to honest government and the administration of justice. Schneider also tells us about the contents of these 'archival libraries' and the principles governing their arrangement:-

(a) They contained anything that might be useful for future reference and almost anything connected with the fiscal administration;

(b) All this material was kept in a special room, arranged in such a way that it was possible to tell at a glance the identity of each tablet, the precise nature of its contents and the length of the work to which it belonged.

The Sumerian written tradition comes chiefly from two large towns,

6. A tablet of the Fara type, c. *2600* B.C.

worth mentioning here that the first dictionaries were compiled by Sumerian schoolteachers. When the Akkadians conquered the Sumerians they borrowed their script and maintained their cultural and oral tradition, which they continued to study and imitate long after the Sumerian language had died out. For this they needed dictionaries giving the Akkadian equivalents of Sumerian words and phrases.

9. See Kramer, *op. cit.* 39.

10. Corporal punishment was normal practice in Sumerian schools: see Kramer, *op. cit.* 39.

11. On the public record offices of the Sumerian period see J. Schawe, 'Der alte Vorderorient' in *HBW* I 1-50; A.A. Kampman, *Archieven en bibliotheken in het oude Nabije Oostern*, Schoten-Antwerpen 1942; and, more generally, E. Posner, *Archives in the Ancient World*, Cambridge Mass. 1972.

12. N. Schneider, 'Die Urkundenbehälter von Ur III und ihre archivalische Systematik', *Orientalia* 9 (1940) 1-16. See also G. Goossens, 'Introduction à l'archivéconomie de l'Asie Antérieure', *Revue d'Assyriologie* 46 (1952) 98-107.

13. More than 11,000 tablets were found in the excavations at Lagash (the modern Tello): see F. Thureau-Dangin, H. de Genovillac and L. Delaporte, *Inventaire des tablettes de Tello conservées au Musée Impérial de Constantinople*, Paris 1910-1914.

14. See esp. E. Chiera, *List of Personal Names from the Temple School of Nippur*, Philadelphia 1916;

Lagash and Nippur.[13] The tablets found at Lagash were nearly all to do with commercial transactions, with a few on historical and religious subjects, but the library of the older temple at Nippur contained at least 20,000 tablets covering a remarkable variety of subjects: there were works on linguistics, register books written in an ideographic script, grammar exercises (in Sumerian and Akkadian), gazetteers with names of mountains and states, lists of gods and temples, reference works on minerals, plants and functional articles made of wood and bronze, medical formulae, forms of words for the exorcism of spirits that cause headaches and paralysis, ritual texts and much else besides.[14] It is beyond the scope of this book to assess the significance of this material, but it is worth devoting some space to a literary work which originated in the early period of the Sumerian civilization, and from which we can draw some useful conclusions about the extent to which philosophical thinking and the spread of knowledge by means of the written word were supported by the Sumerian kings.

3. The Epic of Gilgamesh. Probably the first epic ever composed by man was the so-called Epic of Gilgamesh.[15] According to the narrator, it was composed by the hero of the work himself: King Gilgamesh, who ruled the city of Uruk *c.* 2700 B.C. What interests us here is not so much the literary and dramatic merit of the work, but rather the information that the minstrel who composed it wrote it down on tablets (or stelae) which he built into the foundations of the city walls where they could be read by passers-by.[16]

We do not know exactly what was included in the first written version of the Gilgamesh Epic, as the surviving portions of the text are too fragmentary for us to be able to reconstruct the whole plot until we come to the Third Dynasty of Ur, *c.* 2000 B.C.[17] Nor do we have the complete text in any of the later versions: in fact only about half of the 3,000 lines have survived. The fullest version that has come down to us is inscribed on eleven tablets dating from the first millennium, which were in Assurbanipal's library at Nineveh in the seventh century B.C.[18] It is based on an earlier version dating from the Early Babylonian period (1800-1600), since when it had enjoyed great popularity and been rewritten many times in new editions. The epic is also known from finds from the Neo-Assyrian period at Assur, Nineveh, Nimrud and Sultantepe and from the Late Babylonian period at Babylon and Uruk.[19]

The Gilgamesh Epic stands on its own as the most mature Babylonian work of literature, whose great popularity was due to its exceptional dramatic power. The hero is a real human being: he has his loves and his hates, he weeps and rejoices, fights bravely and gives way to moments of weakness, goes through periods of hope and of despondency. One is aware of an element of divinity underlying the story: in fact, to judge by the language used and the mythological portion of the

T.B. Jones, 'Bookkeeping in Ancient Sumer', *Archaeology* 9 (1956) 16-21; A. Deimel, *Sumerische Tempelwirtschaft zur Zeit Urukaginas und seiner Vorgänger*, Rome 1931; J. Papritz, 'Archive in Altmesopotamien: Theorie und Tatsachen', *Archivalische Zeitschrift* 55 (1959) 12-13; and the review of Papritz's article by A. Pohl, 'Der Archivar und die Keilschriftforscher', *Orientalia* 29 (1960) 230-232.

15. See R. Campbell Thompson, *The Epic of Gilgamesh*, Oxford 1930; W.G. Lambert, 'Gilgamesh in Literature and Art: The Second and First Millennia' in Ann Farkas et al., *Monsters and Demons in the Ancient and Medieval Worlds*, Mainz 1987, 37-52; J.H. Tigay, *The Evolution of the Gilgamesh Epic*, Philadelphia 1982; Kramer, *op. cit.* 219-234; Maureen Gallery Kovacs, *The Epic of Gilgamesh*, Stanford 1989; Avra Ward, *Tό "Επος τοῦ Γκίλγκαμες*, Athens 1994.

16. See Kovacs, *op. cit.* XIX.

17. *Ibid.* XXIII.

18. See Kramer, *op. cit.* 221. The most complete copy in Assurbanipal's library takes up twelve tablets, and

7. Gilgamesh strangling a lion.

plot, Gilgamesh himself is a person 'two-thirds divine' who yields to human weaknesses. Yet the overriding impression one has of him is of a human being, as the gods and their activities and interventions in human affairs are kept in the background. What makes this early work of literature outstanding is its concern with human preoccupations and weaknesses that are common to all peoples and all ages: the need for friendship, the sense of faith, the craving for adventure, the pursuit of glory, ambition for high office, agonizing over the prospect of death – the *leitmotif* running through the whole story – and the unquenchable desire for immortality. But enough of the literary merits of the great Gilgamesh Epic: let us return to the subject of libraries and their development in the post-Sumerian era, to assess the magnitude of the heritage bequeathed by the Sumerians to posterity.

8. The slaying of Khumbaba. Relief on a cylinder roll with scenes from the Epic of Gilgamesh. From the period of the Mitanni, c. *1500-1400 B.C.*

II. The age of Hammurabi. Round about 2475 B.C. the Sumerian people started mingling with the Akkadians, a race living between the Tigris and the Euphrates who, according to Sumerian tradition, had first achieved statehood under their king Sargon I (2900 B.C.). In the end, however, it was not the Akkadians who were destined to prevail in the area but the Semites, who spread and multiplied rapidly in the region of Sumer and Akkad. One of the Semites developed the little village of Babylon into his seat of government and founded a dynasty with virtually no opposition. His name was Hammurabi.[20]

Much earlier, under the First Dynasty of Babylon, commerce had been growing by leaps and bounds: the cities were no longer mere market towns for the sale of local produce but centres of a trade network

most versions are written in Assyrian: see C.F. Jean, *La littérature des Babyloniens et des Assyriens*, Paris 1924, 179. There are three published editions of the epic: R.C. Thompson, *op. cit.*; one by A. Heidel in his book *The Gilgamesh Epic and Old Testament Parallels*, Chicago 1949; and one by E.A. Speiser in J.B. Pritchard, *Ancient Near Eastern Texts relating to the Old Testament*, 3rd edn., Princeton 1969. See also the French translation with introduction and notes by R. Labet in *Religions du Proche-Orient asiatique*, Paris 1970, 145-226.

19. See Kovacs, *op. cit.* XVII. It has been established beyond doubt that Gilgamesh (whose real name was Bilgamesh) was the fifth king of Uruk, where he ruled towards the end of the First Dynasty (*c.* 2700-2500 B.C.). Although his name has yet to be found in any inscription, another person mentioned in the epic has been identified from contemporary sources. The Sumerian epic was entitled 'Gilgamesh and Agga' and deals with the war between Gilgamesh and Agga, King of Kish: see A. Falkenstein, 'Gilgameš' in *Reallexikon der Assyriologie,* 1957-1971, III 361.

20. See Jean, *La littérature...* 61-136 (= 'Époque Hammurabienne'). The First Dynasty of Babylon started with Hammurabi in 1762 and ended in 1162 B.C. with the invasion of the Elamites into Babylonia. Hammurabi was very well aware that no one could rule successfully by force of arms alone, so he secured peace and justice for his subjects by promulgating a code of laws known as the Code of Hammurabi. The 282 laws comprising the Code were inscribed on stone slabs built into the temples in the main cities and towns of the region under Babylonian control, and also on clay tablets that were circulated in schools not only by the teachers but also by the students of the 'law schools'. One such tablet was found at Nippur: see V. Scheil, *Les nouveaux fragments du Code de Ḥammurabi sur le prêt à intérêt et les sociétés*, Paris 1918.

21. The libraries at Sippar evidently kept tablets of historical interest from earlier periods, to judge by

that covered the whole country and extended even beyond its frontiers. From about 2500 B.C. the temple of the god Enlil at Nippur had wielded more influence, cultural as well as purely religious, than any other temple in Babylonia. However, during the reign of Hammurabi (1792-1750), a reformist monarch who welded the city-states of the Sumerians and Akkadians into a united empire, the situation changed radically. Babylon developed into a great capital city and the Babylonian god Marduk ousted Enlil and took over his following. Yet Hammurabi had no doctrinaire commitment to centralization and he respected the cultural traditions of other cities, such as Sippar with its splendid libraries.[21] The awesome religious rites performed regularly in the monumental temple of Marduk often served as the inspiration for both religious and secular works – such as the Hymn to Marduk[22] and the Epic of the Creation[23] – which exerted a strong influence on the Babylonians' intellectual life and were very widely read, copied, commented on and used as teaching aids.

1. Public record offices and literary libraries. Unless the phrase 'House of the Tablets' has some allegorical significance, perhaps denoting a school, it must have been the name the Sumerians gave to their libraries, rather as the Egyptians did.[24] As excavation proceeds in Mesopotamia, more and more evidence is coming to light to support the view that the ability to read and write was widespread and perhaps even a basic requirement for everyday life. This conclusion is borne out by the large number of libraries that have been discovered. Admittedly, most of the 400,000 surviving tablets were clearly intended for archival use, as ninety per cent of their content is concerned with financial and business matters. And although there are certain political centres – such as those of the Mitanni and those of Elam and Urartu – about which we have very little information for long stretches of time because no written material of any importance has been found there,[25] there is no reason to believe that fresh information coming to light about these blank periods will alter our view of the libraries of Mesopotamia. It is generally agreed that no distinction was made between archival and literary libraries, though this does not mean that there were no libraries belonging exclusively to one category or the other: such specialized libraries are known to have existed in the palace at Mari and in certain temples associated with schools.[26] Presumably the libraries of the Sumerians and other Mesopotamian peoples reflected the social conventions and the level of cultural attainment of the various regions and cities, as they contained writings of every kind, from records of transactions (deeds of sale of real property, deeds of gift, marriage deeds, accounting ledgers) to literary works (epics and myths) and orders of service for religious ceremonies. There were palace libraries, state libraries, large collections of documents in the temples, which usually supervised the running of the schools; and

9. Assyrian scribes, protected by a bodyguard, collecting taxes on merchandise.

the case of a scribe who went there to compare a worn or badly-written inscription with an old copy: see V. Scheil, *Une saison de fouilles à Sippar*, Paris 1902; H.V. Hilprecht, *Old Babylonian Inscriptions, chiefly from Nippur*, Philadelphia 1895; see also Jean, *La littérature...* 62. More than 60,000 tablets have been found in the libraries of Sippar: see Posner, *op. cit.* 46.

22. This was a litany intended to provide justification for Marduk's ascent to the summit of the divine

10. The ziggurat at Dur-Sharrukin (Khorsabad). Drawing by Faucher-Gudin.

there were small private libraries as well as impressively large collections belonging to high-ranking public officials, priests and 'book-collectors'. One of the most exciting finds in this last category was made by the Belgian Archaeological School at Tell ed-Der, where excavators discovered a private library of nearly three thousand tablets dated to about 1635 B.C.[27]

It is obviously not possible here to detail the contents of all the archival libraries, especially as this book is not primarily concerned with such collections. But some finds, such as those from Mari and Ugarit (Ras Shamra), tell us a good deal about the way libraries were organized and run, and it may well be that some or all of those practices were adopted later by the Greeks and Romans for use in their libraries. At Mari the French archaeologist André Parrot unearthed the ruins of a huge palace that had been an important centre of government in the early part of the second millennium.[28] There excavators have found a total of about 20,000 tablets, the earliest dating from the period of Assyrian domination under

11. Assyrian scribes recording the spoils from one of the campaigns of Tiglath-Pileser III (744-727 B.C.).

King Shamshi-Adad (1813-1781). The importance of this find is that the tablets were classified and kept in separate rooms according to the nature of their contents: in other words, here we have an integrated record office. Room 115, for example, contained the diplomatic archives of the last two governors of Mari, and other rooms were found to contain only

hierarchy and hence for the fact that his temple claimed precedence over all others: see Jean, *La littérature...* 95.

23. See below, p. 13.

24. See C.L. Woolley, *Excavations at Ur: A record of twelve years' work*, London 1954, 142-144.

25. See H. Schmökel, 'Mesopotamien' in H. Schmökel (ed.), *Kulturgeschichte des alten Orient*, Stuttgart 1964, 46; Posner, *op. cit.* 26.

26. See M. Weitemeyer, 'Archive and Library Technique in Ancient Mesopotamia', *Libri* 6 (1956) 217-238.

27. In the majority of cases, the material found in private libraries testifies to the thriving trade carried on by the Mesopotamian peoples and the ubiquitous reach of the huge bureaucracy that was established to control it. Most houses had a special room where the business records were kept, usually in an unfrequented corner of the building so that customers or business associates could come and go without being observed. A typical example was found at Nuzi, a provincial town in Assyria inhabited by people of the Hurri race, where excavators discovered the private archives of the Tehiptilla family containing about a thousand tablets with records of the business dealings of three generations. The room where they were kept had originally been used as a bathroom. See R.F.S. Starr, *Nuzi*, I, Cambridge Mass. 1939, 333-347; also M. Weitemeyer, *Babylonske og assyriske arkiver og biblioteker*, Copenhagen 1955, 39, on the excavations carried out by Sir E.A.W. Budge. On the bureaucracy of the Mesopotamian peoples see M. Lambert, 'La naissance de la bureaucratie', *Revue Historique* 224 (1960) 1-26; Id., 'Le premier triomphe de la bureaucratie', *Revue Historique* 225 (1961) 21-46.

28. On the finds from Mari see Kampman, *op. cit.* 35-37; Weitemeyer, *Babylonske og assyriske arkiver...* 40-43; Papritz, *op. cit.* 26-28; Parrot, *op. cit.* 80-81, 102, 162-163, 217-218, 288-292; M. Parrot, *Mari, une ville perdue ... et retrouvée par l'archéologie française*, Paris 1936.

29. Ras Shamra was excavated by a French team led by Claude Schaef-

business records, or payrolls, contracts and other documents relating to the administration and organization of the palace.

While Mari illustrates an attempt to decentralize administrative responsibilities and the corresponding archival facilities so as to avoid muddle and confusion, Ras Shamra tells us about the methods used in classifying and arranging the material. On the evidence of the finds from there we can work out how the tablets were classified and stored, either in separate rooms or in rooms used for more than one category of archives.[29]

2. How the tablets were classified and arranged. Two different methods were commonly used for storing the tablets: (a) on wooden shelves, and (b) in earthenware storage jars or baskets.

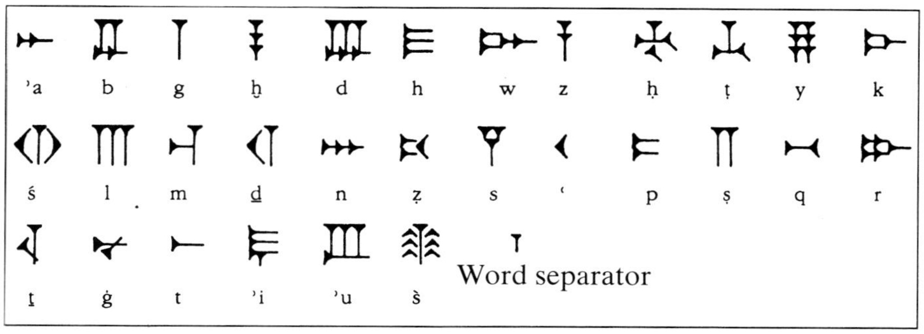

13. The alphabetic script in use at Ugarit (Ras Shamra).

(a) The discovery of the library at Ras Shamra revealed not only the classification system that had probably been worked out centuries earlier by the inventors of this type of 'book' but also the principles of librarianship in use, which were taken seriously form that time on.[30] The bookcases consisted of a low ledge built of clay, often along the walls, supporting tiers of wooden shelving. The tablets were stored standing on end, at right angles to the wall, and so it is quite likely that skilled bookcase-makers devised an integrated system of vertical partitions that could be moved to form large or small compartments, to prevent the tablets from falling over.[31]

(b) Where this storage system was not practicable, either because there was not enough room or for some other reason, the tablets were kept in clay storage jars or large baskets labelled with clay tags indicating the contents. Such tags attached to baskets full of literary works have been found from the Sumerian period.[32] Sometimes, too, tablets were kept in boxes made of wood, bronze or some other relatively costly material, as we know from a literary work: an epic of the Old Babylonian period, with Naram-Sin as its hero, begins with the words, 'You open the box of tablets and read the inscription.'[33]

It is thought that each 'book', that is the bundle of tablets constituting

12. A Chaldaean temple with a double ramp. Drawing by C. Chipiez.

fer: see C.F.A. Schaeffer, 'La première tablette', *Syria* 33 (1956) 161-168; Kampman, *op. cit.* 45-48; A. Pohl, 'Bibliotheken und Archive im alten Orient', *Orientalia* 25 (1956) 105-109; Posner, *op. cit.* 31 ff. See also P. Bordreuil (ed.), *Une bibliothèque au sud de la ville: Ras-Schamra-Ougarit VII*, Paris 1991.

30. See Schaeffer, *op. cit.* XI; Posner, *op. cit.* 32 ff.

31. See Schaeffer, *op. cit.* XI-XV; K. Bittel, 'Untersuchungen auf Büyükkale', *Mitteilungen der Deutschen Orient-Gesellschaft* 91 (1958) 57-61. In the library at Ras Shamra, which was part of a small palace, 3,600 tablets were discovered during excavations in 1931. A method of storing tablets in pigeonholes was used in the temple of Nabu at Khorsabad and nowhere else, as far as I know. There the excavators found a group of niches arranged in three horizontal tiers: the niches, each 25-30 cm. square and 40-50 cm. deep and separated by 10-cm. partitions, contained fragments of inscribed blocks and tablets. See C.B. Altman, *Khorsabad: The Citadel and the Town*, Chicago 1938, 46 and Pl. 96.

32. See Weitemeyer, *Babylonske og assyriske arkiver...* 222; S. Langdon, *Excavations at Kish*, I, Chicago 1924, 90.

a complete work, was tied up with string to make it easier to handle and to prevent the tablets from being separated when they were replaced in the basket, box or bookcase. Since there were no identification marks on the edges of the tablets, as there are on the spines of books, the scribe would add a colophon at the end of the text on each tablet, giving the title and the serial number of the tablet or chapter. In the Epic of Gilgamesh, for example, the colophon at the end of the eleventh tablet (which contains the story of the great flood) reads: 'He who saw all things, eleventh tablet,' where the words 'He who saw all things' are the chapter title. To make sure that the reader did not read the tablets in the wrong order, the colophon often gave the first words of the following tablet as well. In large general libraries, or in specialized libraries where the documents were all of a kind but covered a long period of time, there must have been some way of labelling and arranging the bookcases either in chronological order or by subject to save the librarian or archivist from having to waste time searching through itemized catalogues. This may be the reason why only a few library catalogues have been found.[34] Those that have survived, however, are interesting enough to be worth a brief look.

3. The first library catalogue. A catalogue may be a librarian's tool to help him to run the library more efficiently, or it may be simply a list of its contents. One small tablet unearthed by excavators, scarcely more than 6 cm. long by 3 cm. wide and in excellent condition, was found by Samuel Kramer to be part of a library catalogue.[35] It was evidently written by a highly skilled scribe, who managed to fit no less than sixty-two works on to the two sides of the tablet, in two columns on each side. Of these sixty-two, at least twenty have been identified. In accordance with normal practice, the works were listed not by their titles but by the first line (or, more often, the first few words) of the text. This makes it impossible to identify any works of which only fragments have survived. Kramer's studies of other library catalogues[36] and the finds from more recent excavations have enabled modern scholars to draw firm conclusions about the method of classifying and arranging tablets in the libraries, as we shall see.

Having briefly considered the main points concerning the subject matter and the organization and running of these libraries, and having seen how very seriously the people took the business of training young people to become scribes or teachers of reading and writing, let us turn our attention to the greatest bibliophile brought into the world by the Mesopotamian civilizations, the man who may be described as the pioneer of private libraries of literary works: King Assurbanipal.

III. Assurbanipal's library. The victorious military campaigns of the Hittites destroyed the power of Babylon and fuelled the ambition of the Assyrians, whose rise was made easier by the Babylonians' decline. The Assyrian king Tiglath-Pileser III crushed or annexed the lesser states that stood in his way and was eventually proclaimed King of Babylon in 728 B.C. Assyria was now at the zenith of its power, with dominions stretching from the frontiers of Egypt in the south-west to Urartu in the north and the old empire of Elam in the east. Sargon II (721-705) and his successors were at war with these three neighbouring states for more than a century before finally triumphing over them. And so Assurbanipal (668-628), known to the Greeks as Sardanapalos, established himself as the absolute master of the Middle East.[37]

Assurbanipal was a man of inexhaustible energy, who was capable of great cruelty yet at the same time had a deep love of literature and did all he could to raise the educational standards of his subjects. His predecessors Sargon II, Sennacherib and Esarhaddon had supported earlier endeavours to create a library in the Assyrian capital, but Assurbanipal put so much energy into the organization and enrichment of the library that he may fairly regarded as its founder. All the evidence suggests that it was his ambition to have in his library every written text that had any bearing on the social, cultural and religious traditions of his vast empire, and so he set out to bring to Nineveh copies of all the most important literary works of the Babylonians and Assyrians.

Accordingly, he sent agents out to every corner of the empire with instructions to list the contents of all public and private libraries in the big cities[38] and established a scriptorium for the purpose of copying and annotating earlier works of literature.

Assurbanipal's library contained some 25,000 tablets and was divided into two sections: correspondence, diplomatic documents, business accounts and contracts were in one section, and literary, historical, religious, scientific and scholarly works in the other.[39] His personal interest in systematically tracking down, collecting and evaluating the entire written tradition of the Mesopotamian peoples gave him every justification for his proud boast: 'I obtained the hidden treasures of the sum of the scribes' knowledge.... I solved the knotty problems of division and multiplication that were not set down with clarity. I have read the artistic script of the Sumerians and the obscure script of the Akkadians and I have deciphered the inscriptions that were carved in the rock some time before the Flood.'[40]

1. What the library contained. Assurbanipal's library contained any kind of material that might enlarge the fund of knowledge of the Mesopotamian peoples' history, social structure and religion. There were chronicles and works on chronology, such as the 'Chronicle of the First Kings of Babylon', the 'Synchronic History', a narrative of events covering the period from 1600 to 800, and the 'Canon of the Eponyms', a list of high-ranking officials giving their titles, a summary of their duties at the court of Nineveh and particulars of their chief claims to fame. In addition to the historical works there were great numbers of letters and official reports written by the king himself or his high officers of state, contracts for the purchase of slaves, houses, farmland and animals, and so on.[41]

Then there was a section of the library devoted to religious writings and ritualistic texts: prayers to Ishtar, Anu, Sin, Tashmetum and other deities, a large number of hymns to the gods and texts of the rites and ceremonies performed at the great festivals in honour of the gods or to celebrate the new year.[42]

Another important section contained lexicographical works: lists of cuneiform characters with notes on their uses and values in the various genres of literature, lists of names (i.e. vocabularies) and lists of ideograms with their values.[43]

The literature section was one of the most complete that had ever existed. It contained several different editions of the Epic of Gilgamesh, 'The Descent of Ishtar into the Underworld', legends and myths (such as the Myth of Etana) and the ever-popular verse epic of the Creation, which ran to a thousand lines, beginning with the cosmogony: 'When the heavens on high had no name, and the earth below had no name....'[44]

The biggest section of Assurbanipal's library consisted of works on astrology, medicine and religion, concentrating especially on what the Assyrians called 'omens' or 'signs', that is to say descriptions of human beings, animals and inanimate objects, their habits and distinctive features. The area of knowledge coming under the heading of 'signs' was encyclopaedic in its scope: facts about the birth of humans and animals, particulars of the eyes, mouth, nose, heart and blood, the differences between horses, lions, dogs and birds, the man-made environment (towns, roads) and the natural environment (rivers, farmland). Of particular interest are two long rows of texts dealing with astrological predictions, written on astrolabes.[45]

2. The royal scribes. Although scribes were in the habit of signing their tablets from the Fara period (*c.* 2600 B.C.) onwards, nothing is known about most of them. However, some of their names are of great interest, as they can be identified as persons of high social standing, sometimes even of royal blood: one such was Enheduanna, who was the daughter of King Sargon I and high priestess of the moon god Nannar at Ur.[46] A catalogue found at Nineveh gives us the names of some authors or editors of long epic poems, including Sin-liqi-unninni, the editor of the Epic of Gilgamesh, and Lu-Nanna, the author of the Myth of Etana.[47]

The royal scribes commissioned by Assurbanipal to organize and expand his library would have been specialists in a variety of fields, with varying levels of ability. The work required of them was not simply a matter of copying out texts that had become worn and difficult to read: sometimes they added explanations and glosses on the Assyrian and Sumero-Akkadian texts, and sometimes short epigraphs written on clay tablets to guide the sculptors of statues and reliefs.[48]

The scribes won great renown and were much respected in court circles, so much so that soon it was not enough for them to put only their own names in the colophons of the tablets they had written, and they took to adding the names of their father, their ancestors, the founder of the family or dynasty of scribes to which they belonged. Many of them were also authors in their own right, which lent added lustre to their profession.[49]

Assurbanipal's reign can fairly be described as a 'golden age' of books which paved the way for the establishment of an all-embracing library of the Mesopotamian lands. What is more, if any credence is to be given to Armenian tradition, it was the sight of Assurbanipal's library that gave

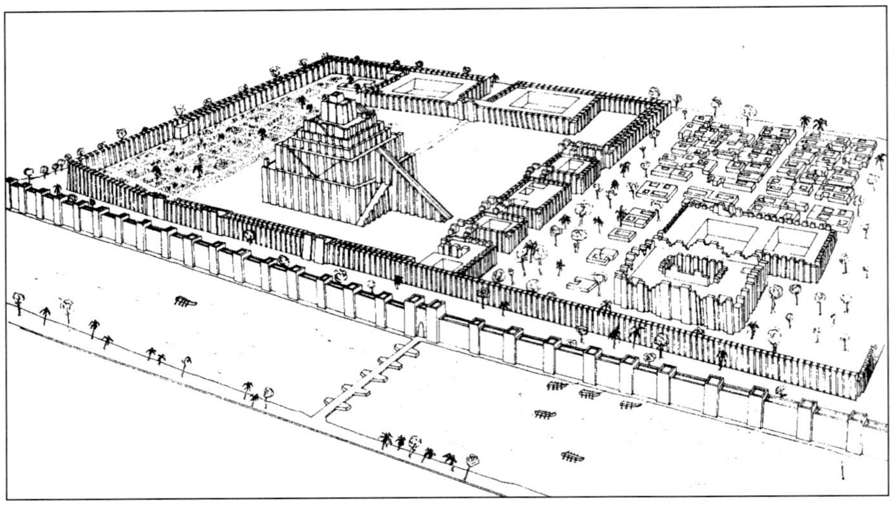

14. Reconstruction of the Great Temple of Marduk at Babylon.

Alexander the Great the idea of forming his own Great Universal Library, and in fact he decided to locate it at Nineveh, Assurbanipal's capital.

In this brief look at the clay tablet 'libraries' we have seen how methodically the descendants of the Sumerians, Akkadians and Assyrians organized their society through efficient use of their archives. The surprising thing is that they appear not to have realized how much more convenient it would have been to use papyrus rolls from Egypt for writing long texts, especially epics. Was it that the strongly-held local tradition of the peoples of the Tigris and Euphrates basins reduced the use of papyrus to a minimum, or could it have been that the Egyptians periodically banned its export? That is something we may never know.[50]

33. See Schneider, *op. cit.* 15; Posner, *op. cit.* 59 ff.

34. On cataloguing methods see Weitemeyer, *Babylonske og assyriske arkiver...* 23, 74-76; Id., 'Archive and Library Technique...' 223; Posner, *op. cit.* 61.

35. See Kramer, *op. cit.* 251-253, 'Les premiers "catalogues" de bibliothèque'.

36. See S.N. Kramer, 'A New Library Catalogue from Ur', *Revue d'Assyriologie* 55 (1961) 169-176.

37. See M. Streck, *Aschurbanipal und die letzten assyrischen Könige bis zu Untergange Niniveh's*, Leipzig 1916.

38. See Jean, *La littérature...* 161 ff. (= 'Époque Assyrienne'). A striking illustration of the Mesopotamian peoples' profound respect for the written word is provided by the fact that an Assyrian local governor in the thirteenth century was able to supply all the most important dates in the history of a temple at Assur that had been built 580 years earlier.

39. When Sir Austen Henry Layard excavated the palace of Assurbanipal's grandfather Sennacherib at Nimrud, a city abandoned in 612 B.C. which he mistakenly identified as Nineveh, he found two large rooms full of clay tablets: see his book *Discoveries among the Ruins of Nineveh and Babylon*, New York 1856.

40. See L. Waterman, *Royal Correspondence of the Assyrian Empire*, Ann Arbor 1930, 6. The quotation comes from a letter found amongst the royal correspondence in which Assurbanipal gives instructions to one of his agents named Shadanu, probably a scribe, on the collecting of tablets: 'The day that you receive my letter, take these three men and the artists from Borsippa and collect the tablets, as many as there are in the Ezida temple.'

41. See Jean, *La littérature...* 162-163; and see esp. A.T. Olmstead, *Assyrian Historiography*, Columbia 1916.

42. See Jean, *La littérature...* 164, 211-217.

43. See F. Delitzsch, *Assyrische Lesestücke*, Leipzig n.d.; Id., *Assyrische Grammatik*, Berlin 1906.

44. See P. Jensen, *Kosmologie der Babylonier*, Strasbourg 1890; Jean, *La littérature*... 164. Assurbanipal's copy of the Epic of the Creation was made specially for his library at Nineveh in the seventh century, but the work itself was originally Babylonian, as the gods whose praises it sings are not those of Nineveh but of Babylon, with Marduk in the central role: see Jean, *La littérature*... 92-94; L.W. King, *The Seven Tablets of Creation*, London 1902. There is a French translation of the Creation Epic by P. Dhorme in his book *La religion assyro-babylonienne*, Paris 1920. Some interesting additional information about the Babylonian cosmogony, drawn from the priests of Babylon in the third century B.C., is provided by Berossus in his *Babyloniaca* (see below, p. 73). According to him, in the days before the dawn of history the earth was ruled by ten demigod-kings, who helped the human race to raise itself from semi-barbarism to civilization. Their names, in the Hellenized forms in which Berossus gives them, were Aloros, Alaparos, Amelon (Amillaros), Ammenon, Megalaros (Megalanos), Daonos (Daon), Euedarachos (Euedoreschos), Amempsinos, Otiartes and Xisourthos (Sisouthros, Sisithros), and they were traditionally said to have ruled for a total of 423,000 years. See Jean, *La littérature*... 271-274.

45. See Jean, *La littérature*... 163, 297-313; E.F. Weidner, *Handbuch der babylonischen Astronomie*, I, Leipzig 1915. Even as early as the Sumerian and Babylonian periods, planetary observations and weather forecasts were associated with occurrences on earth and human activities. In the Assyrian period, and especially in Assurbanipal's reign, the astronomer-astrologers banded together into groups to copy out the earliest writings on astronomy. At the same time they compiled lists of the names of stars, classified the planets into groups and wrote down countless observations on the behaviour and characteristic features of the heavenly bodies. Unfortunately nothing is known about the nature of the works on astronomy

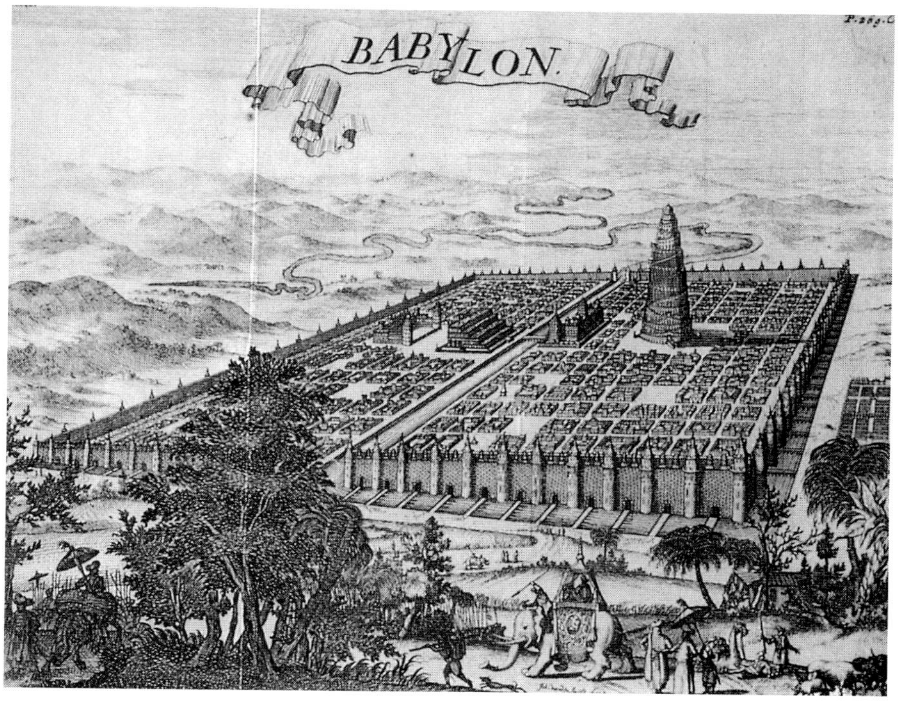

15. Babylon. Engraving from Q. Curtius Rufus, Alexander Magnus, *Utrecht 1693 (Pl. 24).*

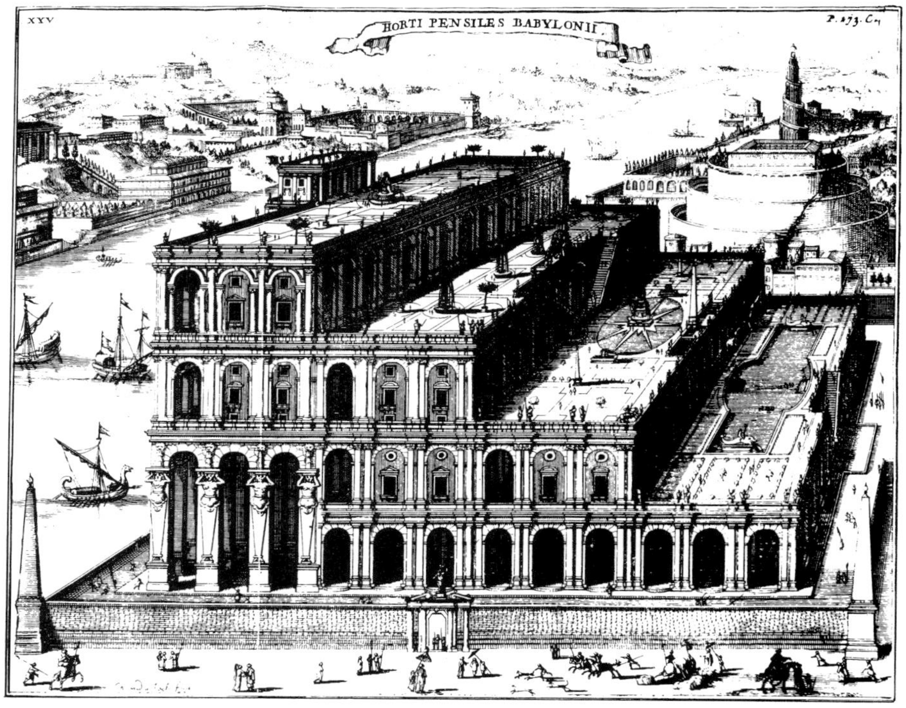

16. Babylon and the River Euphrates. Engraving from Q. Curtius Rufus, Alexander Magnus, *Utrecht 1693 (Pl. 25).*

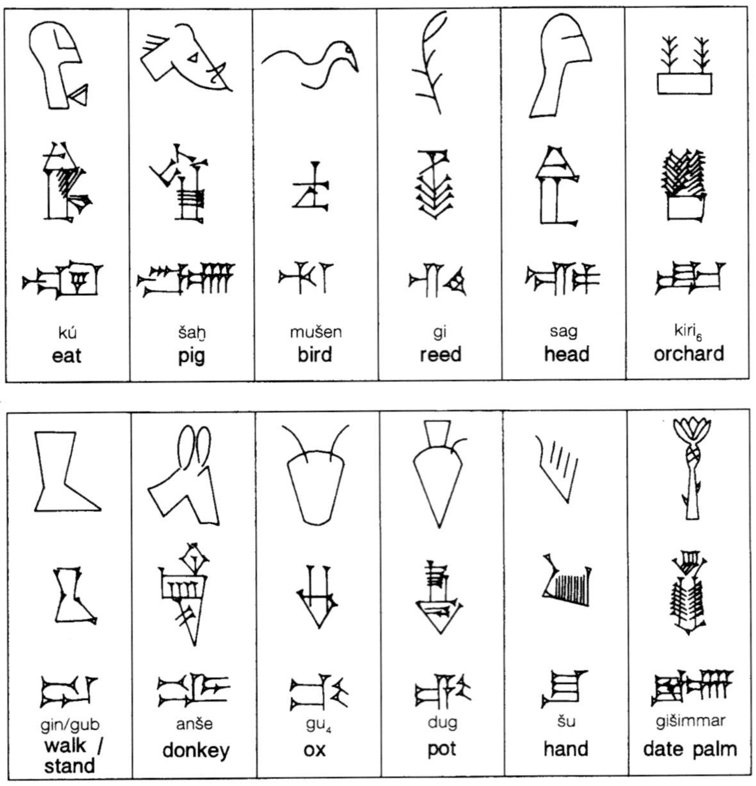

*17. Table of cuneiform symbols, showing for each one its pictographic form (*c. *3000* B.C.*), an archaic cuneiform representation (*c. *2400) and its form in late Assyrian (*c. *650) where it has rotated through 90°, with its phonetic value in Sumerian and its meaning.*

18. Assurbanipal carrying offerings to the gods. Drawing by Boudier.
19. Archaic tablet from Ur recording deliveries of barley and flour to a temple, c. *2900-2600* B.C.

written before Assurbanipal's time, but it is quite clear that those early astronomers were most interested in the connection between the stars and earthly occurrences.

46. See E.A. Speiser, 'Scribal Concept of Education' in C.H. Kraeling and R.M. Adams (ed.), *City Invincible*, Chicago 1960; A. Leo Oppenheim, 'A Note on the Scribes in Mesopotamia' in *Studies in Honor of Benn Landsberger*, Chicago 1965, 253-256; C.B.F. Walker, 'Le cunéiforme' in Bonfante et al., *La naissance des écritures*... 61-70.

47. See Walker, *op. cit.* 66.

48. See Jean, *La littérature*... 162.

49. See Walker, *op. cit.* 66.

50. Parchment was fairly widely used in Mesopotamia, side by side with clay tablets, from the eighth to the second century B.C., in other words during the Assyrian, Neo-Babylonian, Persian and Greek periods: see R.P. Dougherty, 'Writing upon Parchment and Papyrus among the Babylonians and Assyrians', *Journal of the American Oriental Society* 42 (1928) 109-135.

Besides clay tablets and parchment, two other materials that were widely used for writing on were ivory and wood. The wooden writing-boards were often coated with a thin film of wax, on which the scribes wrote with a stylus. It is impossible to say exactly when this method of writing was invented: all that is known at present is that the oldest tablets of this type were discovered in a well in the north-west wing of the palace at Nimrud. See D.J. Wiseman, 'Assyrian Writing-Boards', *Iraq* 17 (1955) 3-13.

20. Winged genie in a ritual pose. Drawing by Saint-Elme Gautier of a relief from the north-west side of the palace at Nimrud. Musée du Louvre, Paris.

21. Seti I. Bas-relief at Abydos.

CHAPTER TWO

THE EGYPTIAN WORLD

In antiquity it was as rare for Egypt to be at war as it was for Mesopotamia and the Greek states to be at peace. This fact goes a long way to explain the static nature of the Egyptian civilization, which spanned a period of over three thousand years. One of the great achievements of this mysterious civilization was to develop the book in the form in which it was taken over by other peoples, especially the Greeks and Romans, a form which greatly facilitated the production of multiple copies and their dissemination around the Mediterranean basin over a period of more than eight hundred years. It was on papyrus rolls that the great works of Greek and Roman literature were written, and papyrus rolls formed the basis of the first public and large private libraries, leading to the establishment of a practice of librarianship that has lasted without major changes to the present day. This historical survey of the evolution of libraries – or rather of books – in the Egyptian world therefore has to start with a few words about the raw material of which those rolls were made: papyrus.

From the Pharaohs to the Ptolemies

1. The papyrus roll. Herodotus was the first traveller to Egypt to leave a written account which has survived to our own time. At the beginning of it he sums up his impressions of that remarkable land in a memorable sentence: Egypt, he says, is a gift of the Nile.[1]

Along the banks of the Nile grows the papyrus plant (*Cyperus papyrus*), first described by Theophrastus in his *Enquiry into Plants*.[2] Papyrus, a tall, sedge-like reed that flourishes in hot, wet climates, was cultivated all along the Nile valley, but especially in the delta and the district around Arsinoe. A stylized representation of its flower-head was adopted at a very early date as the emblem of Lower Egypt. The most reliable description we have of the treatment of papyrus to make cylindrical rolls comes from Pliny the Elder (*Natural History*, XIII.11 ff.), but he does not reveal all the secrets of the process: no doubt they would have been learnt by trial and error and passed on by word of mouth from one generation of specialist craftsmen to the next.[3]

The process of treating the papyrus reed to make a flat sheet suitable for writing on in ink was as follows. First of all the cortex was removed from a freshly-cut length of the lower part of the triangular stem, to expose the pith. Skilled craftsmen then sliced the pith very carefully into wafer-thin vertical strips, making them as long as possible. The strips of pith were laid side by side, just touching or just overlapping, on a hard wet surface, with all the fibres lying in the same direction. The a second layer of strips of pith was laid on top of the first and at right angles to it. A few taps with a broad-headed hammer were enough to stick the two layers of pith together without the need for any adhesive. When dried and rubbed with pumice stone to make it smooth, durable and flexible, the sheet of papyrus was ready for use. The sheets were then glued together, edge to edge, to make a continuous roll.[4]

The papyrus industry was virtually an Egyptian monopoly, although

1. Herodotus, II.7. Herodotus devotes the entire second book of his *Histories* to Egypt. For a few comments on his work see G. Maspero, *The Dawn of Civilization: Egypt and Chaldaea*, tr. M.L. McClure, London 1894, 378. See also G. Perrot, *A History of Art in Ancient Egypt* (with illustrations by C. Chipiez), tr. W. Armstrong, 2 vols., London 1883.

2. Theophrastus, *Enquiry into Plants*, IV.VIII.3.

3. On Pliny's description of the papyrus see D. Cirillo, *Il Papiro*, with intro. by M. Gigante, Naples 1983 (a collector's edition, printed on Carta Amatruda di Amalfi, of *Dominici Cyrilli Medicinae Doctoris, etc. etc., Cyperus Papyrus*, originally printed by Bodoni at Parma in 1796). On the manufacture of papyrus rolls, the organization of the market in ancient Egypt and the different qualities available, see: J. Černý, *Paper and Books in Ancient Egypt*, London 1952; A. Lucas, *Ancient Egyptian Materials*

22. The flower-head of the papyrus reed. Drawing from D. Cirillo, Il Papiro, *Naples 1983.*

the plant did grow in some other places as well, such as Ethiopia.[5] In Egypt papyrus had been used as a writing material from a very early date, perhaps even before the third millennium: the earliest papyrus sheet so far discovered, though not written on, dates from the First Dynasty, that is around 3000 B.C.[6] The oldest extant papyrus with writing on it is a passage of text written in hieroglyphics dating from the reign of King Djedkare-Isesi of the Fifth Dynasty (*c.* 2400): it almost certainly came from a temple near Abusir, where some other papyrus fragments were found in excavations by the German Archaeological School.[7]

2. Egyptian writing: Hieroglyphics. Of all the ancient oriental scripts, the Egyptian is unquestionably the clearest example of a system of writing 'words' using nothing but pictorial representations of persons and things or easily recognizable symbols. This script, which the ancient Greeks called *hieroglyphika*, was subdivided by Clement of Alexandria, in the second century A.D., into three categories:[8] (a) hieroglyphic (used mainly for religious texts), (b) hieratic (used mainly by priests), and (c) epistolographic or demotic (used for everyday purposes). This classification was valid in Clement's time but had not always been so, as the hieroglyphic script was in use with only very slight modifications and variations from 3000 B.C. until the third century A.D. The invention of hieroglyphics was attributed to Thoth, the great god of Lower Egypt,[9] and they were used in the first books ever written. The principal characteristics of the three types of script are as follows:-

(a) The *hieroglyphic* or *monumental* script took shape as an 'alphabet' in the third millennium B.C. or thereabouts.[10] For this the scribes devised a set of ideograms and phonetic symbols based on a signary of twenty-four characters, with which in theory there was nothing that could not be written. A variant of this script was the *linear hieroglyphic* (as it was called by Jean-François Champollion), a set of simplified hieroglyphics used exclusively for inscriptions painted in ink on wooden sarcophagi and on papyri that were interred with mummies.[11]

(b) The *hieratic* script is so called because it was used chiefly by priests. It was written in black and red ink, mainly on papyri, and examples have been found from as early as the First Dynasty.[12] Since it was designed for everyday use it was very widely adopted, but rather surprisingly it never ousted hieroglyphs, which continued to be carved on monuments and public buildings with very little change over the centuries. The hieratic script evolved progressively until it was very different from what it had been originally. The latest surviving specimen is on a short strip of cloth that was wrapped round a mummy in the third century A.D.[13]

(c) The *epistolographic* or *demotic* was derived from the hieratic script and made its first appearance early in the seventh century B.C.[14] Designed to make writing simpler for everyday secular purposes through

and Industries, 4th edn. revised by J.R. Harris, London 1962. On the manufacture of papyrus from the Ptolemaic period onwards see N. Lewis, *L'industrie du papyrus dans l'Égypte gréco-romaine*, Paris 1934.

4. Besides describing the manufacturing process, Pliny lists the standard sizes of papyrus roll with the names by which the various sizes were known in his own time. The biggest was the *charta augusta*, or simply *augusta*, with a width of thirteen fingers (about 24 cm.), while the smallest was the *emporetica*, a mere six fingers (about 10 cm.) wide. The usual number of sheets in a roll was twenty. See D. Diringer, *The Book Before Printing: Ancient, medieval and oriental*, New York 1982, 113-169.

23. Amenhotep III with offerings to the god Amen. Relief from near Thebes.

the addition of new material, it was used for legal, administrative and commercial documents and also by letter-writers and writers of literary works. The simplification was effected by reducing the number of homophones and introducing numerous ligatures and abbreviations. The latest surviving demotic text is dated to A.D. 476.[15]

These three scripts were used not only to adorn monumental buildings and the walls of the ancient Egyptians' huge tomb complexes but also by writers of literary works: contrary to earlier belief, these early written works were not intended solely to prepare human beings for the great journey into the next world but formed the basis of a charming and original body of literature in prose and verse, with profound philosophical overtones, which was very popular with the ordinary people as well as the educated classes.

3. The Book of the Dead. The earliest written work, which was continually being revised and rewritten, was the Book of the Dead.[16] It first appeared about 4500 B.C., became available in book form from the third millennium and was still in circulation in the early centuries of the Christian era. The Book of the Dead is a compilation of shorter works about burial rites, with instructions and guidance on the way to prepare oneself for death and the afterlife.[17] It was a sort of guide to eternity, showing the way to the gates of Amenti and furnishing the departed soul with magical formulae and prayers which would enable him to come safely through the ordeals of the demons and stand before the judges of the afterworld. The title 'Book of the Dead' is usually given by Egyptologists to the editions that appeared in book form from the Eighteenth Dynasty (*c.* 1650) onwards, as until then the texts had generally been written on sarcophagi.[18]

The origin of the writings that make up the Book of the Dead is lost in the mists of time, and modern theories on the subject are inevitably speculative and are bound to remain so until the last ancient cemetery in Egypt has been excavated. It has been suggested that these prayers and hymns originated with the indigenous inhabitants, or with early Asian tribes that came and settled in Egypt, or that they represent the oral traditions of the peoples who lived on the banks of the Nile.[19]

The evidence brought to light in excavations of mastabas (private tombs) and pyramids, as exhaustively analysed by Gaston Maspero, proves that the writings in the Book of the Dead date from long before the reign of Menes or Narmer, the first historical king of Egypt; and the internal evidence of the writings themselves indicates that they had been in circulation since long before Menes came to the throne. Judging by many of the passages of text carved in hieroglyphics on the pyramids of Unas (the last king of the Fifth Dynasty, *c.* 2333), it would appear that even at that early date the scribes did not know the meaning of what they were writing.[20] According to Sir J.G. Wilkinson, one of the chapters was

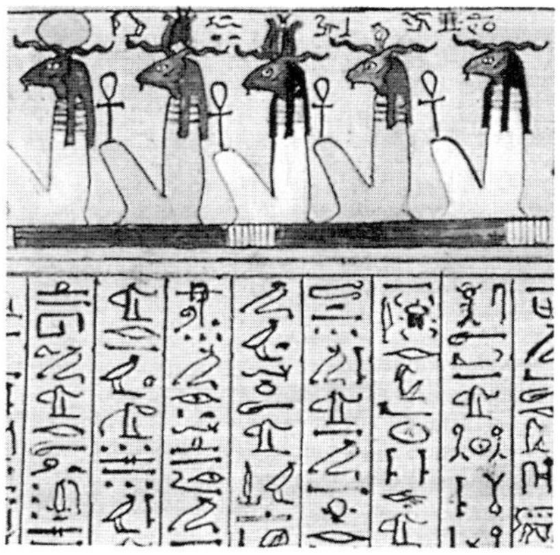

24. Cursive hieroglyphics from a Nineteenth-Dynasty copy of the Book of the Dead. Hunefer papyrus (British Museum 9901,8).

5. The best papyrus processing workshops were in Alexandria, and *papyrus alexandrinus* was highly reputed in the Graeco-Roman period. On the other places where papyrus was cultivated in small quantities see Diringer, *op. cit.* 126-127.

6. See E.G. Turner, *Ἑλληνικοί Πάπυροι: Εἰσαγωγή στή μελέτη καί τή χρήση τῶν παπυρικῶν κειμένων* (= *Greek Papyri: An Introduction*, Oxford 1968, tr. G.M. Parasoglou), Athens 1981, 17.

7. See G. Posener, P. Krieger and J.-L. de Cenival, *The Abu Sir Papyri*, London 1968.

8. Clement of Alexandria, *Stromateis*, v.4. Out of the very extensive literature on the subject, some useful works are: G. Lefebvre, *Grammaire de l'égyptien classique*, Cairo 1955; A.H. Gardiner, *Egyptian Grammar, being an introduction to the study of hieroglyphs*, Oxford 1957; J.G. Février, *Histoire de l'écriture*, Paris 1984, 119-133; Larissa Bonfante et al., *La naissance des écritures: Du cunéiforme à l'alphabet* (= *Reading the Past: Ancient Writing from Cuneiform to the Alphabet*, London 1990, tr. Christiane Zivie-Coche), Paris 1994.

9. See Février, *op. cit.* 125. Thoth, to whom the Greeks of late antiquity gave the name Hermes Trismegistus, is referred to in ancient Egyptian writings as 'lord of the divine books' and 'scribe of the company of the gods': see E.A.W. Budge, *The Egyptian Book*

discovered in the reign of Hesep-ti, the fifth king of the First Dynasty (*c.* 4266 B.C.).[21]

Modern scholarly convention distinguishes four versions of the Book of the Dead dating from different periods:-

(a) The Heliopolitan version produced by the priests of the college of Annu (called On in the Bible, Heliopolis by the Greeks), based on texts that are now lost. There is good evidence that numerous editions, all written in hieroglyphics, were made over a period starting in the Fifth Dynasty (*c.* 2400). The only four surviving copies of this version are inscribed on the walls of chambers and passages in the pyramids of the kings of the Fifth and Sixth Dynasties at Sakkara. Passages recognizable as coming from this version have been found on tombs, sarcophagi, stelae and papyri from the Eleventh Dynasty down to A.D. 200.[22]

(b) The Theban version, which was usually written in hieroglyphics on papyrus. Its distinguishing feature is that it is divided into sections, each with its own title but no definite place in the series. This version was current from the Eighteenth to the Twentieth Dynasty (1500-1100).

(c) Another version similar to the Theban, written sometimes in hieroglyphics and sometimes in the hieratic script, which first appeared in the Twentieth Dynasty.

(d) The so-called Saite version, in which, at some time before the Twenty-fifth Dynasty (700 B.C.), the chapters were arranged in a definite order. It was current from 700 B.C. until the end of the Ptolemaic period, in both the hieroglyphic and hieratic scripts.

25. Scribes recording the harvest. Drawing by Bourgoin after a representation on a tomb at Sakkara.

The Book of the Dead had an enormous readership. Given the strength of religious devotion among the ruling classes and common people alike, and their preoccupation with preparing themselves for the journey into the kingdom of the dead and their life in the next world, it is reasonable to assume that it was as popular and as widely-read as the Bible among the Christians. What is more, the Egyptians held the writers of their holy books almost equal respect with the books themselves, for the scribes, in the performance of their sacred duty, came to know many of the secrets of the tradition embodied in those writings. The story is told of the wise Kheti, son of Duauf, who took his son Pepi to the school for royal scribes and admonished him, 'I shall make thee love

of the Dead (The Papyrus of Ani): Egyptian text, transliteration and translation (London 1899), new edn., New York/London 1949, XXVI.

10. See Février, *op. cit.* 120-132.

11. See Février, *op. cit.* 132; W.V. Davies, 'Les hiéroglyphes égyptiens' in Bonfante et al., *La naissance des écritures...* 124.

12. See Février, *op. cit.* 132.

13. *Ibid.* 132.

14. *Ibid.* 133; Davies, *op. cit.* 127-128.

15. See Davies, *op. cit.* 128.

16. See C.H.S. Davies, *The Egyptian Book of the Dead*, New York 1895; Budge, *loc. cit.*

17. These writings, which the Greeks called the Hermetic books, were probably among the forty-two books which, according to Clement of Alexandria, constituted the holy scriptures of the Egyptians: see Iamblichus, *De Mysteriis*, ed. Parthey, Berlin 1857, 260-261.

18. See Budge, *op. cit.* XI.

19. *Ibid.* XII.

20. See G. Maspero, 'La mythologie égyptienne', *Revue de l'Histoire des Religions* 19 (1889) 12. The dating of the First Dynasty and the periods immediately preceding and following it has been drastically revised since the time of Budge and Maspero: I have followed the dating given in the *Chronologie de l'Égypte* published by the Louvre.

21. See Budge, *op. cit.* XIII.

22. See É. Naville, *Das Aegyptische Todtenbuch der XVIII. bis XX. Dynastie*, Berlin 1886, 39; Budge, *op. cit.* IX. The oldest carved monuments and human remains prove that the ancient Egyptians attached great importance to the preservation of the dead body, for which they used a variety of methods. The interment of the body in the tomb was accompanied by rites of symbolic significance, during which priests or relatives of the deceased recited prayers containing references to the afterlife for the repose of the departed soul.

23. See A. Flocon, *L'univers des livres. Étude historique des origines à la fin du XVIIIe siècle*, Paris 1961, 74.

24. See G. Maspero, *Les contes populaires de l'Égypte ancienne* (Paris

writing more than thy own mother: (thus) I shall make beauty enter before thy face.'[23]

4. Popular reading matter. Maspero, writing about the excavations at Deir el-Medina in the middle of the ruins of Thebes, describes the discovery of a Coptic monk's tomb containing two papyrus rolls for the dead man to take with him into the next world. As Maspero says, in this context one might have expected to find excerpts from the Book of the Dead, or at least some historical poems or collections of magic spells, but never a work of popular fiction.[24] That was in 1864, and since then more such works have been discovered, written in a more highly developed literary style and showing us another side of Egyptian society about which we would otherwise know nothing. What interests us here is to see how popular these books were and what class of person they were addressed to, which will tell us something about the conditions that gave rise to the growth of interest in acquiring and collecting books for private reading.The first step is to see what sort of books these popular readers were. In contrast to Greece, where storybooks were used mainly as teaching aids in schools, in Egypt they were regarded as standard works of literature, besides being common sources of reading and writing exercises for students studying to be scribes.[25] Another difference is that these stories were not set in the world of imagination and legend, like the fables of Aesop and Babrius and the prose romances full of thrilling adventures that were written in the Greek world: in general they are about real events, or at least the narrative has a historical basis, as in 'The Story of Sinuhe', 'The Misfortunes of Wenamun', 'The Story of the Eloquent Peasant' or 'The Tale of the Shipwrecked Sailor'.[26] Besides popular fiction and children's stories, there were elegiac love poems with profound philosophical undertones. These were not popular ballads, odes or verses intended for a mass readership: they were written round about 1500 B.C. by a class of scribes with a strongly-developed bent for literary composition.[27]

Before going on to discuss the dating of the works of popular fiction and their distribution, it is worth dwelling for a moment on certain salient features of this type of literature.

a. Subject matter. It is not known for certain whether these stories were authentic products of the Egyptians' own imagination or whether they were derived from the popular traditions of other peoples with whom the Egyptians came into contact.[28]

One of the earliest stories is 'The Tale of the Shipwrecked Sailor', dated to the Middle Empire (*c.* 2000 B.C.),[29] which describes the fantastic adventures of an Egyptian who sailed through the Red Sea to the mining country in the Sinai Desert. On his way he is shipwrecked and cast ashore on a wonderful island ruled by a monster in the form of a talking

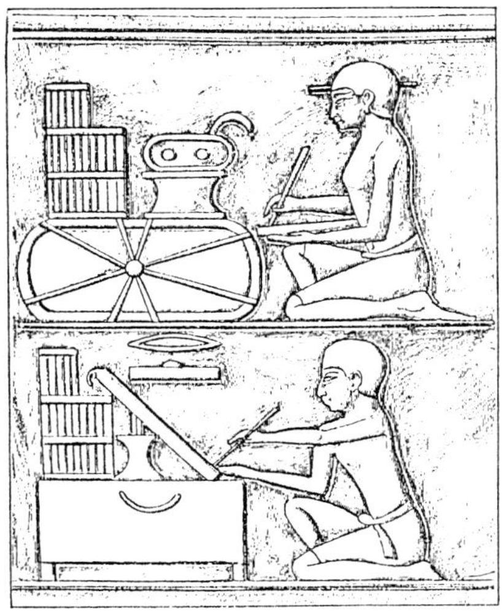

26. Scribes at work in a government office in the period of the Memphite Dynasties. Drawing by Faucher-Gudin, from a wall-painting in the tomb of Khûnas.

1882), repr. Paris 1988; A. Erman, *Die Literatur des Aegypter*, Leipzig 1923 (Eng. trans. by A.M. Blackman, London 1927); A.H. Gardiner, *Late Egyptian Stories*, Brussels 1932; G. Lefebvre, *Romans et contes égyptiens de l'époque pharaonique*, Paris 1988.

25. See Lefebvre, *Romans et contes...* VII.

26. Lefebvre has translations of and notes on sixteen of these stories: The Story of Sinuhe, The Story of the Eloquent Peasant, The Tale of the Shipwrecked Mariner, The Stories from the Westcar Papyrus, The Prophetic Tale, The Legend of the God of the Sea (The Legend of Astarte), The Tale of the Doomed Prince, The Capture of Joppa, The Quarrel of Apophis and Seknenre, The Tale of the Two Brothers, The Blinding of Truth by Falsehood, A Ghost Story (Khensemhab and the Spirit), The Contendings of Horus and Set, The Misfortunes of Wenamun, The Princess of Bakhtan.

27. See S. Schott, *Les chants d'amour de l'Égypte ancienne*, Paris 1956. Schott's book contains nine collections of poems, out of which I have chosen one that seems worth reprinting here in full (translated from the free rendering into French by P. Krieger on pp. 160-162).

serpent, which welcomes him and treats him very well. On his return to Egypt the Pharaoh bestows honours on him and appoints him to positions of civic dignity. 'The Tale of the Shipwrecked Sailor' is the only story that is purely imaginary and also has an allegorical significance, in this case connected with the deification of animals in Egypt. Another popular tale in the time of the Thirteenth Dynasty (*c.* 1700 B.C.) was 'The Story of the Eloquent Peasant', which must also have been widely read during the Middle Empire (2000-1800), to judge by the fact that four manuscripts – with different titles – have survived from that period.[30] It consists of 430 lines of verse telling the story of a man named Khunanup from the Oasis of Salt (Wadi Natrun), who travels down the Nile valley to sell his wares and buy supplies, and falls into the hands of a ruffian who gives him a severe beating and robs him of all his belongings. Khunanup appeals to the local ruler for satisfaction, and by his nine eloquent pleas he not only wins compensation but attracts the attention of the Pharaoh himself. The nine pleas (nine was a magic number for the Egyptians) are moralistic and philosophical in tone, one example being 'Justice is for eternity and descends into the grave with him who puts himself at its service.'[31]

Of all ancient Egyptian literary works, 'The Eloquent Peasant' is one of the three (the others being 'The Story of Sinuhe' and 'The Contendings of Horus and Set') that were copied and recopied most often. Written in the language of the Twelfth Dynasty (1900), it is an inexhaustible source of information for lexicographers and grammarians.

The all-time best seller of ancient Egyptian literature was 'The Story of Sinuhe', which existed in a great many copies and remained popular for a period extending from the Twelfth to the Twentieth Dynasty, in other words from about 2000 to 1100 B.C.[32] The hero was not an imaginary character but a real person who lived in the reigns of Amenemhet I (2000-1970) and Sesostris I (1970-1936). The extraordinary series of adventures that befell him fired the imagination of those who read the story to such an extent that the narrative was continually being revised and edited over the centuries to suit the readers' demands. In its original form the story may actually have been Sinuhe's autobiography, which he would have dictated to a scribe to be carved on the walls of his tomb, as Egyptian noblemen almost invariably did. The events described in the story take place after Amenemhet's death and are connected with the machinations between Sesostris and one of his brothers over accession to the throne, in which Sinuhe becomes involved. Fearing that Sesostris's brother will prevail, Sinuhe flees to escape the punishment he expects to be meted out to him. After a period of wandering hither and thither he falls in with Bedouin tribesmen who make him welcome, and eventually he becomes their chieftain. Towards the end of his life the royal family invites him back to Egypt, and so he can die and be buried in his native land, which was the dearest wish of every Egyptian. The nar-

THE WRITER'S FAME

The wise scribes of the time that came after the gods,
they whose prophecies come true:
their names endure forever.
They have departed for the land far away,
they have come to the end of their time.
All their contemporaries are forgotten.
They built no bronze pyramids
nor stelae of stone to go with them.
They chose not to leave children [of their own flesh]
to be their heirs and perpetuate their names:
they appointed as their heirs
the books they wrote and the precepts therein.

They made their books their priests,
the scribe's tablet they made their beloved son;
their precepts are their pyramids.
To them the stylus was a son,
the writing tablet a wife:
all things, from the greatest to the smallest,
are their children,
because the scribe is in their minds.

Colonnades and houses have been built, but they have fallen down;
gone are the priests who speeded them to the next world.
Their stelae lie buried in the sand,
their graves are forgotten.

Their names live on, thanks to the books
they wrote when they were alive.
The memory of their writings remains beautiful,
lasting forever, unto the end of time.

Be a scribe! Set your heart on being one,
so that your name will be like theirs.
A book is better than a painted stele
or a wall covered with inscriptions.
A book builds houses and pyramids in the hearts
of those who speak their name.

In truth, a name that lives on men's lips
is worth something in the necropolis.
Man vanishes, his body is buried in the ground,
all his contemporaries depart this earth,
but the written word puts the memory of him
in the mouth of any person who passes it on to the mouth of another.

A book is better than a house
or the tombs in the West.
It is more beautiful than a castle
or a stele in a temple.
Is there a man here comparable to Hardedef?
Is there a man here comparable to Imhotep?
In out own time there has been no man like Nefri
or Kheti, the greatest of them all.

I give you the name of Ptah-Djehuti
and of Kha-Kheperre-Seneb.

Is there a man comparable to Ptah-Hotep
or Kares?

Wise men foretold the future
and their words came true.
We keep discovering that something is a saying
and is to be found in their writings.
They were given the children of others to be their heirs
as if they were their own children.
So now, even though they are lost and gone,
their magical power touches those who read their writings.
They have departed for the far distant land
and their names would have been forgotten,
but the letters they wrote
have preserved their memory.

28. Contrary to earlier belief, the Egyptians travelled a good deal. Even as early as the Twelfth Dynasty (*c.* 2000 B.C.) they sailed the length of the Red Sea and up the Nile as far as Ethiopia, where the Pharaoh had his mines. They also made frequent voyages in the Mediterranean, especially to Crete, with which they had close trading links. See Maspero, *Les contes populaires*... LXVII-LXXI.

29. *Ibid.* 139-152; Lefebvre, *Romans et contes*... 29-40.

30. See Lefebvre, *Romans et contes*... 41-69. The original manuscripts are reproduced in A.H. Gardiner, 'Die Klagen des Bauern' in *Literarische Texte des Mittleren Reiches*, I, Leipzig 1908.

31. See Lefebvre, *Romans et contes*... 45.

32. See Maspero, *Les contes populaires*... 99-138; Lefebvre, *Romans et contes*... 1-28.

33. See Lefebvre, *Romans et contes*... VII.

34. See P. Newberry, *The Amherst Papyri*, London 1899.

35. Fifteen of the stories mentioned in n. 26 are to be found in their entirety in a total of at least twenty-six papyrus rolls, in addition to fragments on a large number of ostraka. For 'The Princess of Bakhtan' there is a single surviving source, carved on stone in hieroglyphics. See Lefebvre, *Romans et contes*... 221.

36. See Lefebvre, *Romans et contes*... XX.

37. *Ibid.* XX-XXI.

38. For a conspectus of the 'wis-

rative style betrays the touch of a gifted writer: the descriptive passages are remarkably vivid and the story is full of interesting information about life at court and the official mourning following the death of Amenemhet.[33] The oldest extant copy, known as the Amherst papyrus, dates from the Twelfth Dynasty (*c.* 2000).[34]

b. Readership. These books were evidently extremely popular, even among the lower classes, to judge by their unsophisticated subject matter and the large number of copies of them that have survived, not only on papyrus but sometimes also on ostraka (sherds of pottery, which in Egypt

27. Scribes holding papyrus rolls and styli. Relief on stone, Eighteenth Dynasty.

were used for memoranda, business accounts, writing exercises, etc.), which would certainly have been much cheaper. The extant stories have come down to us in twenty-six papyrus rolls and a large number of ostraka: complete copies of 'The Story of Sinuhe' are to be found in six papyrus rolls, and fragments of it on eleven ostraka.[35]

It is quite likely that the first reader of any new novel was often the Pharaoh himself. This was certainly true of Sneferu (*c.* 2550), who summoned his 'Companions' and asked them to find somebody 'capable of regaling me with fine words and well-chosen phrases suitable for the delectation of our Majesty'. And Sneferu's son Cheops (Khufu) used to tell his children wonderful stories from the collection now known as the Westcar Papyrus.[36] Groups of 'Companions' and court officials, with the Chief Minister almost invariably among them, would gather round the Pharaoh to entertain him with literary and philosophical discussions.[37] Outside the confines of the court, too, books were widely read not only by government officials, priests and scribes (many of whom were themselves writers) but also by ordinary people who wanted to broaden their own minds and educate their children, especially those of them who were studying for the civil service.[38]

5. Libraries. An inscription on the tomb of a senior official who was born in the reign of Shepseskaf (2472-2467) and was active in the reign of Neferirkara (2462-2426) refers to him as the 'Scribe of the House of Books'. As far as I know this is the earliest extant allusion to the practice of building a special room (or house) for the storage of books and the first time a name is given to the place where written documents are kept.[39] At first the House of Books was most probably a room used for the storage of official documents such as state revenue accounts, correspondence between the court and provincial governors and local administrators (such as Rensi), copies of private individuals' wills with bequests to temples, and all sorts of other state papers including international treaties. Doubtless there would also have been copies of the liturgical texts and hymns officially authorized for use in the religious ceremonies that played such an important part in Egyptian life under the Pharaohs: prayers and anthems for use in divine worship and funeral rites already existed in writing in the time of Menes, the first historical king, as well as mystical meditations from the Book of the Dead and the Rite of Burial. Besides these, the House of Books would presumably have been used as a repository for magic spells, which were held in high regard by kings and commoners alike,[40] as well as history books, treatises on scientific subjects (mathematics, astronomy, medicine) and official and private copies of literary works in prose and verse, such as the copy of 'The Tale of the Two Brothers' that belonged to Prince Seti Minephtah, who later ruled Egypt as Seti II.[41]

From to the time of the 'Scribe of the House of Books' to the time of Diodorus Siculus, who went to Egypt in the first century B.C. and described Ramses II's library, which he called Ψυχῆς Ἰατρεῖον ('Sanatorium of the Soul'),[42] we have no information at all about any literary library in the Pharaonic age.[43] The Greek philosophers who visited Egypt from the sixth century B.C. onwards, including Solon, Pythagoras and Plato,[44] talked to Saite priests and obtained valuable information from them about the Egyptian civilization, yet not one of them has anything to say about libraries or even makes any oblique allusion to their existence. Manetho, writing in the third century B.C., is also silent on the subject, although he acknowledges that in researching for his *Aegyptiaca* he found a good deal of useful material in rare books written in hieroglyphics.[45] Even the ruins of the library built by Ptolemy Euergetes II (part of the Temple of Horus) at Apollonopolis (Edfu), which is thought to have been modelled on an earlier Egyptian library, lead to no definite conclusions.[46]

Perhaps we should not expect the archaeologist's spade to turn up any spectacular finds shedding new light on Egyptian libraries, as all

dom literature' of the Near East see M.L. West, *Hesiod: Works and Days*, Oxford 1978, 3-15.

39. See Maspero, *The Dawn of Civilization*... 398.

40. Ancient Egyptian literature is full of passages dealing with magic, while spells and supernatural remedies are to be found in Egyptian books on medicine, where there is an element of magic in most of the treatments prescribed. These prescriptions, though scientifically worthless, provide us with valuable information about the script and the language. The Egyptians, who believed that life on earth was a period of preparation for eternity, had a great respect for magicians, whose fantastic tales were enjoyed by everyone from paupers to princes (cf.

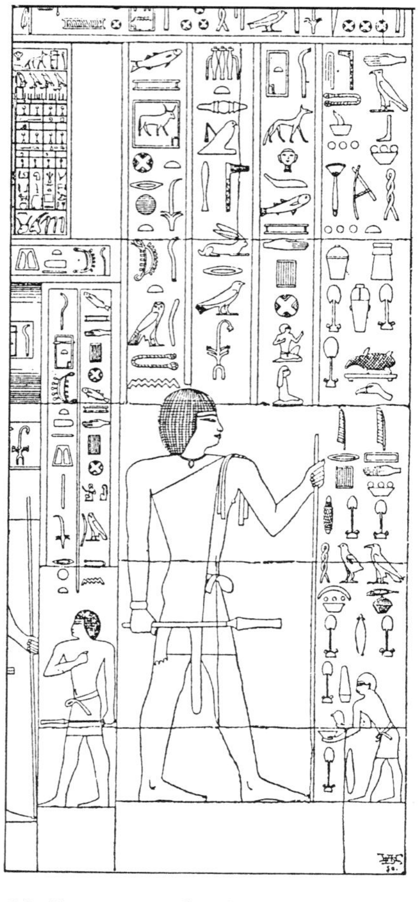

28. Funerary stele of Amten, a high-ranking official and governor of important provinces, who died in the reign of Sneferu, the first king of the Fourth Dynasty. Drawing by Faucher-Gudin.

Prince Dedefhor in the stories from the Westcar Papyrus: Lefebvre, *Romans et contes...* 80). On papyrus rolls of writings on magic see F. Lexa, *La magie dans l'Égypte antique*, 3 vols., Paris 1925.

41. See Maspero, *Les contes populaires...* 4. The copy in question is a papyrus signed by Ennana, who also wrote the Anastasi Papyrus IV. Ennana lived in the reigns of Ramses II, Minephtah and Seti II, which means that the document is well over 3,000 years old.

29. The obverse of the Metternich tablet with writings on magic, dating from the reign of Nekhtharehbe.

42. See p. 375. For a brief note on the libraries of Egyptian temples see C. Wendel, *Kleine Schriften zum antiken Buch- und Bibliothekswesen*, Köln 1974, 166-167.

43. Nor is there much extant information about the archival libraries of ancient Egypt, even though the Egyptians were a very bureaucratic people: see K. Preisendanz, 'Papyruskunde' in *HBW* I 192-196; E. Posner, *Archives in the Ancient World*, Cambridge Mass. 1972, 71-90 (= 'Pharaonic Egypt').

44. See R. Godel, *Platon à Héliopolis d'Égypte*, Paris 1956, 27.

45. See p. 73.

46. See Wendel, *loc. cit.*

30. Portrait of Ramses II as a child. Relief on stone. Musée du Louvre, Paris.

the evidence so far suggests that the Egyptians saw no need for special decoration for their 'Houses of Books': quite possibly they felt that the books themselves were fascinating enough without having to be placed in an ornamental setting. Another reason is that the libraries were probably kept locked and only the intellectual élite were allowed into them. But it is worth reiterating that Western thought owes a great debt to the Egyptians, who invented books in the form of papyrus rolls. It was this invention that made it possible for books to be reproduced and disseminated on a scale hitherto undreamt-of, leading to the creation in the Pharaonic era of an educated public whose like was not to be seen again until the Renaissance.

31. A view of Plato's Academy. Mosaic floor from Pompeii, 1st c. A.D. *Naples, Museo Nazionale.*

CHAPTER THREE

THE HELLENIC WORLD

From the Pre-Socratics to the end of the Classical period.

All the evidence points to the fact that the history of private and public libraries as we know them, and of the free movement of books as an essential prerequisite for the development of intellectual activity, really starts in the Hellenic world, even though collections of written documents and 'closed' school libraries had existed in the Middle East at least as early as the third millennium B.C.

I. The Pre-Socratic period. If we evaluate the evidence of the sources, going back to the beginning of the sixth century B.C., concerning the ancient Greeks' attempts to describe the nature of the world and the purpose of human existence – bearing in mind what we know of the huge output of poetical and (on a slightly smaller scale) philosophical works produced in Athens in the Classical period – we may conclude that it is not far from the truth to say that books, the book trade and the systematic reproduction of books were already much more widespread than they are generally thought to have been. Even in the Classical period there were bookshops, scriptoria for copying books, and individuals who used books to assist the sophists in their proselytizing campaigns or the philosophers and poets in their pursuit of knowledge or, of course, the general public in the indulgence of their love of serious reading, which was so characteristic of all the Greeks.

Just when the Greeks first had the opportunity to hold philosophical and literary works in their hands in the form of papyrus rolls is a matter of conjecture, but the origins of Greek books can be traced with reasonable certainty to Ionia, the Aegean coastal region of Asia Minor.[1] There, a combination of material prosperity and contact with the peoples of the Near East – especially Egypt, where the papyrus roll had been in use since the third millennium B.C. – encouraged the development of a cultural and literary tradition going right back to the time of Orpheus and Homer.[2] But we cannot be sure what materials were used by Thales of Miletus, the first Greek scientist-philosopher, and his fellow-townsmen Anaximander and Anaximenes, to write down the fruits of their studies in the sixth century; nor do we know in what form Heraclitus deposited his writings in the temple of Artemis at Ephesus.

1. Public libraries. It may have been the papyrus rolls containing works by philosophers of the Eleatic school that inspired Polycrates, the ruler of Samos, to found a public library in the island's chief town, as Athenaeus mentions in his *Deipnosophistai*.[3] Herodotus tells us that Polycrates was a very powerful ruler who extended his dominion over many of the nearby islands and cities on the mainland and concluded a pact of friendship with the Egyptian king Amasis. Wishing to enhance the beauty and fame of his native island, Polycrates erected fine public buildings, patronized the arts and gathered around him a brilliant court frequented by the most brilliant poets of the day.[4]

1. Not enough prominence has been given to the pre-Socratic philosophers' role in the development and dissemination of books in the Greek-speaking world, especially Athens. If more of their writings had survived we might know more about the form of 'book' in which the earliest works of Greek literature, such as Hesiod's *Theogony* and the Orphic hymns, were handed down to succeeding generations. On this period see: H. Diels, *Doxographi Graeci*, Berlin 1879; Id., *Die Fragmente der Vorsokratiker*, ed. W. Kranz, Berlin 1951; W.K.C. Guthrie, *A History of Greek Philosophy*, 6 vols., Cambridge 1962-1981; G.S. Kirk, J.E. Raven and M. Schofield, *Οί Προσωκρατικοί Φιλόσοφοι* (= *The Presocratic Philosophers*, 2nd edn., Cambridge 1983, tr. D. Kurtovik), Athens 1988 (= *KRS*).

2. Works attributed to Orpheus and his pupil Musaeus were circulating in book form as early as the sixth century B.C., and the text of a theogonic

32. Heraclitus. Engraving from M. Meibonius, Diogenes Laertius, *Amsterdam 1698, 548.*

Athenaeus also informs us that at about the same time another ruler, Pisistratus, who seized power in Athens for the first time in 560 B.C., founded the first public library there.[5] It may well be that the need for a public library arose from the practice of holding competitions for rhapsodists, instituted in the sixth century as part of the Panathenaea festival. Rhapsodists were bards who recited epic poems: in the competitions they took it in turns, each one taking over where the last one had left off, in accordance with a fixed procedure. This implies that there must have been an established text to follow, from which it is reasonable to conjecture that the Homeric epics were perhaps kept in a repository which developed into the first public library.

Although Diogenes Laertius, writing in the third century A.D., credits Solon (late seventh to early sixth centuries B.C.) with having conceived the idea, it is quite likely that Pisistratus took it up and dusted it down half a century later, establishing a tradition that endured. It has been suggested that Pisistratus was also responsible for the idea of subjecting the Homeric epics to critical revision, but this is an error arising from a misinterpretation of the words of the historian Dieuchidas of Megara.[6]

The first public library in Athens, founded by Pisistratus, met with an enthusiastic public response, but it was destined to have an eventful history. After nearly a century of peaceful existence it was pillaged by the Persians in 480 B.C., when Xerxes sacked Athens and burnt the whole city. He is said to have taken the contents of the library back to Persia with him and kept them in one of his palaces. Eventually, in the third century B.C., Seleucus I Nicator conquered Persia and returned the papyrus rolls to Athens.[7]

2. The first private collections. 'From the lips of wandering minstrels the people learnt the heroic poems of Homer and Hesiod,' Aelian remarks, and the implication of his statement is that the rhapsodists must have played a vital role in the development of libraries. It is hard to believe that they could have met the growing demands of their public if they did not have access to manuscript copies of the text in order to learn the words. Furthermore, the oldest Greek manuscript after the Derveni papyrus[8] was discovered in a context that seems to support this hypothesis: in a tomb at Abusir, near Memphis, a papyrus containing a fragment of *The Persians* by Timotheus, dating from the second half of the fourth century B.C., was found in a sarcophagus with the mummy of a man who had evidently been a wandering minstrel, for his knapsack and staff were also buried with him. Exactly when the rhapsodists first began to feel the need for a private library we can only guess, but on the evidence available it is reasonable to suppose that this happened at about the time when the first public library was formed (mid sixth century), if not earlier.

poem attributed to Epimenides had apparently been written down by then (*KRS* 38). These written texts had nothing to do with the well-known series of gold plates found in southern Italy and Crete, which actually carried instructions for the dead and were connected with Bacchic, Orphic and Pythagorean burial rites. See I.M. Linforth, *The Arts of Orpheus*, Berkeley 1941; W.K.C. Guthrie, *The Greeks and Their Gods*, London 1950. Guthrie takes the view that the Orphic hymns had already been written down in a sacred book by the sixth century.

3. The oldest – in fact the only – extant list of founders of public, private and royal libraries in the ancient Greek world is given by Athenaeus in the *Deipnosophistai* (I.3), a miscellany of literary table-talk written in Rome between A.D. 193 and 228. The central figure of Athenaeus's book is one Larnesius, who is said to have had so many Greek books that 'He outdoes all those who were renowned for their collections in the past, such as Polycrates of Samos, Pisistratus the ruler of Athens, Euclides of Athens, Nicocrates of Cyprus, the kings of Pergamum, Euripides the poet, Aristotle the philosopher, Theophrastus and lastly Neleus, who preserved the books of those I have mentioned.'

Useful information on libraries and Greek books in the Classical period is to be found in the following works: K. Dziatzko, *Untersuchungen über ausgewählte Kapitel des antiken Buchwesens*, Leipzig 1900; J.W. Clark, *The Care of Books: An essay on the development of libraries and their fittings from the earliest times to the end of the eighteenth century*, Cambridge 1901, 5; J.W. Thompson, 'Libraries of Ancient Greece' in *Ancient Libraries*, Berkeley 1940, 17-25; H.L. Pinner, *The World of Books in Classical Antiquity*, Leiden 1948; C. Wendel, 'Das griechisch-römische Altertum' (completed by W. Göber) in *HBW* III.1 51 ff.; E.G. Turner, *Athenian Books in the Fifth and Fourth Centuries B.C.*, London 1952; F.G. Kenyon, *Books and Readers in Ancient Greece and Rome*, Oxford 1951; E. Bethe, *Buch und Bild im Altertum*, Amsterdam

And what of the scholars? Do we know which of the Greek pre-Socratic philosophers had private libraries? The earliest known fact with any bearing on the subject is that at the end of the sixth century Heraclitus deposited a copy of his work *On Nature* (*Περί φύσεως*) in the temple of Artemis at Ephesus: about 150 years later this copy found its way into Aristotle's private library.[9] At about the same time two emigrants from Ionia, Xenophanes and Pythagoras, started teaching philosophy in the Greek cities of Magna Graecia (southern Italy), inaugurating a new period in which scholarly studies were largely based on the written tradition. Although Pythagoras did not write anything himself, and although his school of philosophy was characterized by inwardness and mysticism, he inspired others to write a number of works based on his teaching, which were later gathered together in a book which was reproduced in numerous copies and before long was circulating beyond the confines of Magna Graecia.[10] Pythagoras emigrated to Croton in Magna Graecia between 540 and 522 B.C.: by an irony of fate he was sent into exile by the very man who founded the first public library on Samos, Polycrates. A disciple who carried on his written tradition was Philolaus of Croton, the teacher of Simmias of Thebes and Cebes, two young philosophers who subsequently studied under Socrates and thus form a connecting link between the Pythagorean tradition and the Athenian school. A considerable body of literature was written about Plato's efforts to acquire the works of Pythagoras that Philolaus had published.[11]

In Athens, it was the influence of the philosophy schools in Ionia and Magna Graecia that prompted scholars to start taking an interest in books and forming private libraries in the early part of the fifth century, that is around the time of Socrates's birth (*c.* 470). Though it is impossible to trace the course of events in detail, we know that by the closing decades of the century books were already an issue in Athens. One of the Athenians' earliest contacts with books was in about 450, when Socrates and many others wished to listen to Zeno the Eleatic reading from his work on the occasion of his first visit to Athens with his teacher Parmenides.[12]

II. The Classical period. Socrates himself left no written work. What is more, he had something of an aversion to books and held them in scorn, regarding them as mere substitutes for productive oral dialogue, even though he acknowledged their beneficial role in the education of the young and the dissemination of knowledge generally. Yet these views of his did not, in the end, prevent him from building up a library of his own.

However, let us take first things first and see what Xenophon has to say in his *Memorabilia* on his mentor's attitude to books. This exchange between Socrates and the bookish Euthydemus is an example of what is called the maieutic method of dialogue:

1964; J. Platthy, *Sources on the Earliest Greek Libraries with the Testimonia*, Amsterdam 1968; M. Burzachechi, 'Ricerche epigrafiche sulle antiche bibliotheche del mondo greco', *Rendiconti dell' Accademia dei Lincei* 18 (1963) 75-97 and 39 (1984) 307-331; H.A. Thompson, 'The Libraries of Ancient Athens' in *Contributions to Aegean Archaeology: Studies in Honor of William A. McDonald,* Minneapolis 1985, 295-297; T. Kleberg, 'La Grecia e l'epoca ellenistica' in G. Cavallo (ed.), *Libri editori e pubblico nel mondo antico*, Rome/Bari 1989, 27-39; H. Blanck, *Tó*

33. Homer. Engraving from H. Spoor, Medici et Philosophi Favissae, utriusque antiquitatis tam Romanae quam Graecae, *Utrecht 1707, 119.*

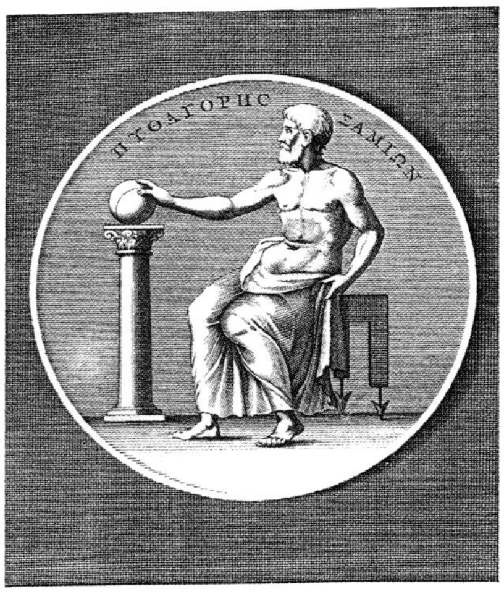

34. Pythagoras. Engraving from Spoor, Medici et Philosophi..., *487.*

'Tell me, Euthydemus,' he said, 'have you really collected a lot of books written by men famed for their wisdom?'

'Yes, Socrates,' said Euthydemus. 'I have, by Zeus, and I am still collecting and will go on until I have got as many as I can.'

'By Hera,' said Socrates, 'I congratulate you with all my heart because you have not chosen to amass treasures in preference to wisdom. For you obviously believe that silver and gold coins do not improve men in any way, while the opinions of wise men enrich with virtue those who hold them.'

And Euthydemus was pleased to hear this, because he believed that Socrates thought he was going the right way about endeavouring to acquire wisdom.[13]

35. A symposium at Agathon's house. Leaflet, probably 19th c.

Euthydemus took Socrates's congratulations at their face value, but Socrates, who was well aware of his interlocutor's inflated opinion of his own intellect, was using this dialogue with the simple-minded book-lover to satirize the bibliomania that was then rife. His barbs were intended to puncture the pomposity of the rich young pups who thought that possessing books was an adequate substitute for true knowledge.

If Socrates had reservations about the mindless proliferation of books, it was probably because he did not believe books were capable of generating constructive dialogue, as Plato explains in *The Sophist*. But he certainly did not deny that books had their uses, even if in *Phaedrus* he does give a warning against excessive dependence on them when he reports the god Ammon as saying to the inventor of writing, 'What you have discovered is a recipe for reminding yourself, not for remembering.'[14] On the other hand, Euclides of Megara is said to have heard Socrates encouraging a slave to read aloud to his friend, which shows that he recognized that reading is of greater value when one's hearing is also brought into play. It is a fact that people in ancient Greece were in

βιβλίο στὴν ἀρχαιότητα (= *Das Buch in der Antike*, Munich 1992, tr. D.G. Georgovasilis and M. Pfreimter), Athens 1994, 176-204.

4. Polycrates came to power probably in 532 and died in 522 B.C. Among those in regular attendance at his court were the physician Democides and a number of poets including Ibycus and Anacreon. See H. Berve, *Die Tyrannis bei den Griechen*, II, Munich 1966, 107-114.

5. See R. Pfeiffer, *Ἱστορία τῆς Κλασσικῆς Φιλολογίας. Ἀπό τῶν ἀρχῶν μέχρι τοῦ τέλους τῶν ἑλληνιστικῶν χρόνων* (= *History of Classical Scholarship: From the beginnings to the end of the Hellenistic age*, Oxford 1968, tr. P. Xenos et al.), Athens 1972, 6 ff.; A. Lesky, *Ἱστορία τῆς Ἀρχαίας Ἑλληνικῆς Λογοτεχνίας* (= *Geschichte der griechischen Literatur*, Bern 1957/58, tr. A.G. Tsopanaki), Thessaloniki 1983, 73; Berve, *op. cit.* 41-63.

6. See Pfeiffer, *op. cit.* 7.

7. Aulus Gellius, *Noctes Atticae* VII.17.1.

8. The oldest extant Greek manuscript is one that was found at Derveni, near Thessaloniki, in 1962. It contains an allegorical commentary on a theogony attributed to Orpheus, evidently written by an anonymous grammarian familiar with the thinking of Anaxagoras and Diogenes of Apollonia. It was discovered half-burnt in a grave of 330 B.C. and is to be published by K. Tsantsanoglou and G. Parasoglou. Cf. W. Burkert, 'La genèse des choses et des mots: Le papyrus de Derveni entre Anaxagore et Cratyle', *Études Philosophiques* 25 (1970) 443-455. The papyrus found by L. Liangouras in 1981 (*Archaiologikon Deltion* 36 (1981) 47) in a cist grave known as the musician's grave, because wooden tools for making musical instruments were buried with the body, has still not been dated or even read.

9. Diogenes Laertius, IX.6; Turner, *op. cit.* 17. The end of Heraclitus's active life is usually dated around 480 B.C. *On Nature* had the reputation in antiquity of being written in a crabbed style, so much so that Diogenes Laertius (IX.13) comments that not even those most conversant with literature

the habit of reading out loud, even when they were studying on their own: 'And if anyone else happens to be near the person reading, it will not be heard.'[15]

When Socrates once heard someone reading some interesting passages from the work of the philosopher Anaxagoras of Clazomenae (said to have been the first teacher of 'natural philosophy' in Athens, for perhaps thirty years from 460 B.C.), he went out to buy Anaxagoras's books, but his initial interest soon turned to disappointment with the intellectual capacity of their author. According to Plato (*Apology* 26d-e), Socrates dismissed Anaxagoras's work with the mocking remark that his books were very cheap, as they could be bought for one drachma apiece.[16] Plato admitted that the sophists played a leading part in Athenian intellectual life in the last few years before the outbreak of the Peloponnesian War (431 B.C.) and singled Anaxagoras out for praise as the last of the 'natural philosophers' (*Hippias Major* 281c).

As already mentioned, Socrates's declared opposition to the written tradition and his doubts about the usefulness of books did not prevent him from forming a library of his own. What is more, according to Xenophon, 'He was in the habit of unrolling the treasures of wise men of the past – autograph works of theirs, in fact – and studying them with his friends, making notes as he did so.'[17] All the evidence points to the conclusion that systematic book production got under way in Athens around the middle of the fifth century. During the next few decades it mushroomed to such an extent – mainly as a result of the sophists' activities and with their encouragement – that their opponents became seriously concerned. We also know that Socrates was not alone in being strongly opposed to the bibliomania stirred up by the sophists: he was supported by Aristophanes and Plato, among others, as well as many of their disciples including Antisthenes and Oenopides the mathematician.[18]

1. How the sophists helped to popularize books. The great battle over the value and proper function of the written word was provoked not so much by the flood of new books pouring on to the market as by the sophists' shameless exploitation of the medium. The sophists, who came from all parts of the Greek world and were in a way the successors of the itinerant rhapsodists, presented themselves as sages, interpreting the ancient epics and other archaic poetry and commenting on the language in the manner of the earlier philosophers. Their primary aim, however, was to give the people an 'education'. They were not interested in humanistic values, but only in the technicalities of the structure of the language and a proper understanding of the words and concepts they used themselves, so they seized upon books as the most effective means of propagating their educational philosophy. Books were their main teaching aid.

In the event, the sophists are rightly credited with having been chiefly

could understand what it really meant. Hieronymus of Rhodes records that in the fourth century B.C. the satirical poet Scythinus of Teos undertook to summarize Heraclitus's doctrines in verse. Heraclitus was the subject of many epigrams, one of which satirizes the style in which *On Nature* was written: 'Do not be in too great a hurry to get to the end of the book written by Heraclitus of Ephesus: the path is hard to travel' (Diogenes Laertius, IX.16).

10. The unwritten 'doctrines' of Pythagoras, as they are described by Plato in *Timaeus* and *Philebus*, left a gap which was filled by numerous works containing references to his life and teaching: see W.D. Ross, *Plato's Theory of Ideas*, Oxford 1951, Chs. 9-16. Most of those works are unreliable and owe much to their authors' imagination, the only reliable ones being those published by Philolaus and Archytas: see *KRS* 221-245. Josephus, writing in the first century

36. Socrates. Engraving from Spoor, Medici et Philosophi..., *93.*

A.D., states in his treatise *Against Apion* (I.163) that the most notable of those who wrote about Pythagoras was Hermippus of Smyrna: see *KRS* 478.

11. See Lesky, *op. cit.* 671-727. On Plato's library see pp. 37-39. A text showing an affinity to the Pythagorean tradition, or at least some similarities, is a written doxography of earlier date attributed to Orpheus, which was in use in the time of Pythagoras's pupils. Orpheus was generally believed to

responsible for a useful change in the way literary works and official documents were written – for it was they who introduced the Ionic alphabet in place of the ancient Attic script in the archonship of Euclides (403 or 402 B.C.) – and with having done much to raise awareness of the vital importance of books to the spread of knowledge. As professional teachers they had to provide their pupils with textbooks: these were mostly the works of the great poets, but the sophists also took the opportunity to promote their own writings by offering them as models for imitation, in an attempt to make polymaths of their students.[19] In the closing decades of the fifth century there was a general shift from the oral to the written tradition, and for the first time scholars now started making written compilations of facts of all kinds: one of the earliest was Hellanicus of Lesbos, whose *Attic History* is in some sense a precursor of the encyclopaedic works of Aristotle, Theophrastus and others of their circle.[20]

Protagoras. Around the middle of the fifth century the leader of the professional sophists, Protagoras of Abdera (*c.* 490-420 B.C.), a prolific writer who was considered subversive, arrived in Athens, where he practised his profession with great success for forty years, making many firm friends but many enemies as well. It may have been through the influence of Protagoras that Pericles, one of his friends, first started reading his speeches in court from a prepared text instead of speaking without notes, which until then had been the universal custom.[21]

Protagoras's most important contribution to philosophy was his doctrine that man is the measure of all things, but his most controversial work, regarded by the ancients as sophistry at its most dangerous, was *On the Gods*. He is said to have read out this discourse for the first time at the home of either Euripides or Megaclides; but according to another informant one of his pupils, Archagoras the son of Theodotus, read it for him at the Lyceum.[22] Be that as it may, the public readings evidently created an enormous furore and exposed him to grave accusations. At the beginning of the book he says he is unable to form any firm conclusions about the gods and cannot even decide whether they exist or not, so, according to Diogenes Laertius, the Athenians sentenced him to exile, sent a herald round the city to collect all the copies of his books they could find, and burnt them in the Agora.[23] If this is true, it is the first recorded case of censorship in ancient Greece.

Aristophanes. At that time the arch-critic of the sophists and their exploitation of books was Aristophanes, who was sufficiently disturbed by the unending spate of book-copying to comment wryly in *The Frogs* (line 1083) that Athens was suddenly 'swarming with clerks'. However, that did not stop him telling the Athenians that tragedies, although undoubtedly written down originally for the purposes of staging a

have lived before Homer, and the Orphics based the authenticity of their doctrines on the written tradition ('books'): see *KRS* 228, 478.

12. Plato, *Parmenides* 127-128; Diogenes Laertius, IX.21-23. Parmenides, a brilliant pupil of Xenophanes, is extolled by Plutarch (*To Colotes* 1114b) for the soundness of his book on ancient 'natural philosophy' (i.e. natural science) and the fact that he did not plagiarize other writers' works. See *KRS* 246-270.

13. Xenophon, *Memorabilia* (*Ἀπομνημονεύματα*) IV.2.8-10. Euthydemus, the son of Diocles, is mentioned in the *Symposium* (222b). The maieutic

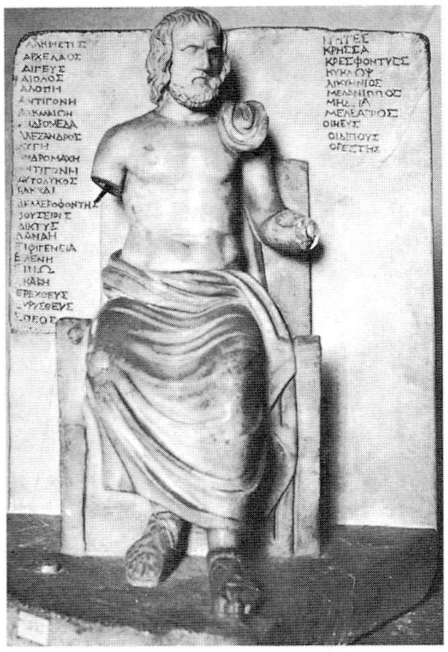

37. A relief. Reproduction from Gisela M.A. Richter, The Portraits of the Greeks, *I, London 1965 (Nos. 760-761).*

method of inquiry is intended to bring out latent thoughts and ideas and is so called because Socrates regarded himself as 'a midwife (*maia*) to men's thoughts'.

14. Plato, *Phaedrus* 275a; Kenyon, *op. cit.* 13. Xenophon tells us in his *Symposium* (III.5) that his father had urged him to learn the whole of the *Iliad* and the *Odyssey* by heart, and that years later he was still able to recite them from memory.

15. Plato, *Theaetetus* 143a-b; Xeno-

phon, *Symposium* IV.27. The change from reading aloud to reading silently would not have taken place overnight. It may perhaps have been Aristotle who made silent reading the norm (cf. Kenyon, *op. cit.* 21), but I believe it had probably been standard practice since about the beginning of the fourth century.

16. Plato asserts (*Phaedo* 97-99) that Socrates grasped all of Anaxagoras's beliefs at a single reading. According to the calculations of A.H.M. Jones (*KRS* 489), the drachma was equal in value to a day's work by one slave. This means that a book selling at one drachma (= 6 obols) took less than a day to copy out, since the slave's owner had to defray the expenses of one day's board and lodging for the slave, amounting to four obols, which would leave him two obols to cover the cost of the papyrus plus his profit. The cost of papyrus in

38. Vase-painting by the Cartellino painter. Neuchâtel, private collection.

production, were also useful in book form for private reading and discussion.

Apparently the bookshops of Classical Athens were well-known haunts of literary men. In *The Birds*, produced in 414 B.C., the Athenians are portrayed as voracious readers who rush out to the bookshops straight after breakfast to browse, catch up on the latest publications and talk to their friends about the literary merits and defects of the books they have been reading. There were two words in use to denote a bookseller: one was the neutral *bibliopoles*, first used by Aristomenes in *The Wizards* and then again by Theopompus in *Peace*, but Julius Pollux uses the rather more disparaging term *bibliokapelos* (a 'hawker' or 'peddler' of books). Their shops were in the Agora, at least from 425 B.C.[24] According to the comic playwright Eupolis, who refers to the place where books were sold, and to Xenophon in the *Apology*, in 399 B.C. all the bookshops were concentrated in the area known as the Orchestra, a semicircle of level ground in the centre of the Agora, at the foot of the Acropolis, watched over by statues of the tyrannicides Harmodius and Aristogeiton, which might be seen as symbolic of the role of books in the service of democracy.[25]

There was a story about Alcibiades and his thirst for books that was current in Aristophanes's time and must have remained in the repertoire of literary anecdotes for centuries thereafter, as it resurfaces in Aelian's *Historical Miscellany (Ποικίλη Ἱστορία)* in the second century A.D. Aelian found the story in the work of his contemporary Julius Pollux, who quoted it to illustrate the close relationship between book-lovers and booksellers in ancient Greece: 'Alcibiades, that depraved playboy, went to a bookshop to get a copy of Homer but was told it was out of stock, whereupon the unfortunate bookseller received a stinging slap in the face from his irate customer.' The story had been slightly altered in the telling, but the gist of it was true: the slap in the face had actually been given to a well-known teacher, who his pupils said was earning money on the side by copying books, and the customer was presumably angry with him because he had ordered a book and the copyist had not finished it in time.[26] Aristophanes quarrelled with Alcibiades in or about 410 B.C., and it is very likely that he himself spread this story to show up the selfish greed of which he was always accusing Alcibiades, as in the *Tagenistai*.

Aristophanes drew a sharp distinction between the sophists' books and the written texts of plays. It was his belief that the Athenians would never be in danger of lapsing into ignorance because the theatre was frequented by military servicemen and enlightened 'readers of books able to understand the right points' (*The Frogs* 1114), the implication being that most members of the audience came to the theatre armed with a copy of the play (cf. *The Birds* 471: 'You must be very unobservant, or very uneducated; you don't even know your Aesop').[27] Some plays were not intended for performance in competition, and in those cases copies may well have been put on to the market for publicity purposes.

While performances of tragedy were big events in Athenian social and political life, their texts were hunting-grounds for literary and philosophical critics. In *The Frogs* of Aristophanes, Aeschylus criticizes two lines of Euripides's *Antigone* for failing to give an accurate description of the fate of Oedipus. Such fault-finding would hardly have been possible without a written text available for consultation, especially as it would not have been the only case of its kind. In any case, there is good evidence that the tragedians did indeed have private libraries: in *The Frogs* Aristophanes ridicules Euripides for his book-learning, poking fun at him also for his fine library and for employing a private scribe-cum-publisher: 'And next a dose of chatterjuice, distilled from books, I gave her.'[28]

The atmosphere conveyed by Aristophanes has been re-created in a 'period piece' by N. Hourmouziadis, who vividly and imaginatively recaptures the mood of a theatrical performance in the time of Socrates, as seen through the eyes of an Athenian by the name of Anthemocritus.[29] The only point I should like to add is that on his way down from the Hill of the Nymphs to the Theatre of Dionysus it is more than likely that Anthemocritus came across some itinerant vendors, perhaps including a bookseller or two. The passage already quoted from *The Frogs* (line 1114) confirms that theatregoers did have copies of the plays to read, but nothing whatever is known about the process of putting those written texts on the market. One thing we may be sure of is that it would have been no easy matter to follow the text while the play was in progress without having done some fairly thorough homework beforehand, as it took a good deal of practice to be able to follow the dialogue. The punctuation, if any, was rudimentary; words were still not separated by a space; and the system of accentuation, which would have made it much easier to tell where one word ended and the next began, was not devised until much later, in the Hellenistic period. In the written texts of the plays there was nothing to show which lines were spoken by which characters, extraordinary though that seems to us nowadays: usually the only indication of a change of speaker was a dash or colon at the beginning of the line. The confusion thus created was often compounded through repeated copying by careless copyists, as in the case of the only surviving manuscript of Menander's *The Misanthrope* (*Δύσκολος*).[30]

Aristophanes believed that Athens was being corrupted by the sophists' teaching practices and by indiscriminate book publishing, and he expressed his fears in the *Tagenistai* (fr. 490 K.), where books and sophists are held to be as bad as each other: 'This man has been corrupted either by a book or by Prodicus.' By bracketing the two together in this way he is alluding to the sophists' way of using books for propaganda purposes, and it is no accident that he chooses to mention Prodicus

the fifth century can only be calculated approximately: it is known that the commissioners of the Erechtheum kept their accounts on papyrus rolls for which they paid one drachma and two obols each, but we do not know the length of the rolls. See Turner, *op. cit.* 21; R. Flacelière, *Ὁ Δημόσιος καί Ἰδιωτικός Βίος τῶν Ἀρχαίων Ἑλλήνων* (= *La vie quotidienne en Grèce au siècle de Périclès*, Paris 1959, tr. G.D. Vandorou),

39. Aristophanes. Engraving, 18th c.

40. Alcibiades. Engraving from Spoor, Medici et Philosophi..., *45.*

by name, possibly because of his verbosity and his somewhat suspect teaching methods but mainly because of the enormous proliferation of his books on the market, especially the *Horae*.[31]

Prodicus. Prodicus of Ceos, perhaps the most able disciple of Protagoras, was admired by his contemporary Socrates, who regarded him as an authority on the differences between related words. In fact Prodicus was excessively fussy about drawing distinctions between words of similar meaning, but what earned him the mockery of Socrates's circle was the exorbitant fee he charged for a single lesson – his 'fifty-drachma lecture', as Plato put it.[32] In Plato's *Protagoras* Prodicus is portrayed giving a lesson while 'reclining with some sheepskins and other coverings thrown over him'. His treatise entitled *Horae* appeared in book form not later than 416 B.C.[33] Prodicus and his *Horae* are mocked again in the *Symposium*: 'Or take our good professional educators, the excellent Prodicus for example; they write prose eulogies of Heracles and others – that is perhaps not so surprising – but I once came across a book by a learned man in which the usefulness of salt was made the subject of a wonderful panegyric, and you could find plenty of other things that have received similar treatment.'[34] The 'learned man' to whom Prodicus is likened may be Polycrates, a sophist who later wrote a savage attack on Socrates, for Polycrates was the author of panegyrics on cooking-pots, mice and pebbles.

2. Private libraries. Although Plato was the most outspoken critic of the sophists and missed no opportunity for sarcasm at the expense of their opinions and their attitude to books, he never questioned the importance of books as aids to the thinking person's self-knowledge and the proper education of the young; in fact he may be described as the first book-collector as such in the Greek world. That Plato had a fine library which he used in his teaching and the running of the Academy is not in doubt; indeed, it may well have contained not only books by his contemporaries but also the writings of the pre-Socratic philosophers. But we have to remember that much of the relevant information derived from later sources, especially with regard to his collection of papyri with the theories of Pythagoras, is unreliable because it was put about by people whose primary concern was to blacken his name.

Plato. Plato is known to have been introduced to Pythagoras's theories on his first visit to Magna Graecia, at a time when Pythagoreanism was enjoying a revival led by Archytas of Tarentum,[35] and their influence coloured his own views on metaphysics. Plato went to Sicily when Syracuse was ruled by Dionysius I (405-367), then at the zenith of his power. He had an extremely stressful time with Dionysius, with whom he got on very badly, and the only advantage he may be said to have

Athens 1990, 151 ff. On bookshops see n. 25.

17. Xenophon, *Memorabilia* I.6.14. Another testimony to the existence of private libraries is Plato's statement (*Critias* 113b) that his grandfather had had copies of Solon's writings in his house and that he, Plato, had read them as a boy.

18. See Turner, *op. cit.* 23.

19. Out of the extensive literature on the early sophists, some of the most important works are: R. Pfeiffer, 'Die Sophisten, ihre Zeitgenossen und Schüler im fünften und vierten Jahrhundert' in C.J. Classen (ed.), *Sophistik*, Reinbeck 1970, 170-219; Jacqueline de Romilly, *Les grand sophistes dans l'Athènes de Periclès*, Paris 1988; N.M. Skouteropoulos, *Ἡ Ἀρχαία Σοφιστική: Τά σωζόμενα ἀποσπάσματα* (fragments edited, translated into Modern Greek and annotated by –), Athens 1991; W.K.C. Guthrie, *Οἱ Σοφιστές* (= *The Sophists*, Cambridge 1971, tr. D. Tsekourakis), Athens 1991.

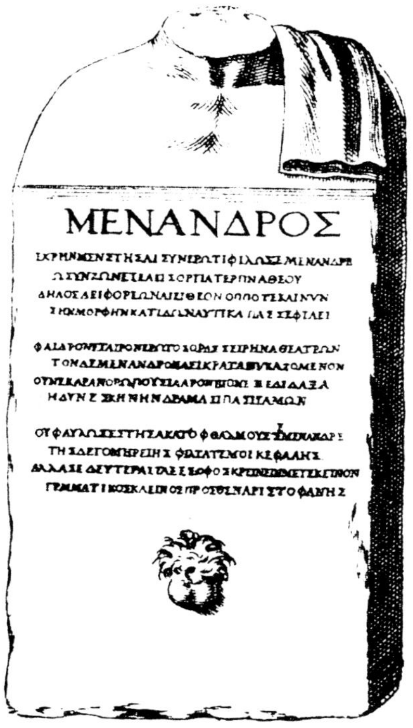

41. A mutilated herm of Menander, new lost. Reproduced from Richter, The Portraits..., *II.*

gained from his stay in Syracuse was the very generous stipend he received as long as he was in favour.

The principal source of information on Plato's library is Diogenes Laertius, who, citing the testimony of Satyrus and others, says that Plato wrote to Dion (Dionysius I's brother-in-law) in Sicily, asking him to buy from Philolaus three books by Pythagoras priced at 100 minae (10,000 drachmae). It was said that he could afford this sum because Dionysius had given him more than eighty talents (480,000 drachmae).[36] However, according to the Alexandrian historian Hermippus, as recorded by Diogenes Laertius, Plato bought these books himself in Sicily from relatives of Philolaus, paying forty Alexandrian minae for them; and a third version of the story has it that Plato was given the books as a reward for persuading Dionysius to release one of Philolaus's pupils from prison.[37] In Syracuse Plato was introduced to the work of Sophron, a writer of mimes who had been active there in the middle of the fifth century and had won great renown. It seems that he bought copies of Sophron's works and took them back with him to Athens, where they aroused great interest: Aristotle, who discusses them in his *Poetics*, thought so highly of them that he placed them on the same level as the words of Socrates. It has been suggested that Plato may have modelled some of the characters in his dialogues on characters from Sophron's mimes, but this is probably an exaggeration, and Diogenes Laertius's story that Plato kept a copy of the mimes under his pillow is thought to be apocryphal. Proclus informs us that Plato commissioned Heraclides Ponticus to procure for him the poems of Antimachus of Colophon.[38]

Plato's attitude to books and the proper way of educating the young is summed up in the *Laws* (809e-810a), where he says that a child should study literature first and then music: 'About three years will be a reasonable time for a child of ten to spend on literature, and a further three years, beginning at the age of thirteen, should be spent on learning the lyre.' This method is described more clearly in *Protagoras* (325e): 'When boys have learnt their letters and are capable of understanding the written word as until then they understood only the spoken, [the teachers] put the works of good poets before them on their desks to read.' Here Plato draws an analogy between the obligation on the young to study the law and live in accordance with its precepts and the work done by the language teacher, who traces faint outlines of the letters on the writing tablets for his pupils to follow in their writing exercises. The result was that schoolchildren not only improved their calligraphic skills but also developed a real awareness of the role of books in education and the acquisition of knowledge.[39]

Plato himself, however, following the example of Pythagoras and Socrates, did not teach from a written text. In *Phaedrus* he belittles the importance of the written word, and in his seventh Epistle he confirms that he has never used written lecture notes: his teachings were, as

20. See Pfeiffer, *Ἱστορία* 35; Lesky, *op. cit.* 467.

21. *Souda* ('Suidas') s.v. 'Protagoras of Abdera'; Guthrie, *Οἱ Σοφιστές* 38. Protagoras must have been in Athens in 443, for in that year Pericles commissioned him to draft the constitution of Thurii, a colony in Magna Graecia founded in 444/443 B.C. See K.M. Dietz, *Protagoras von Abdeira: Untersuchungen zu seinem Denken* (doctoral dissertation), Bonn 1976.

22. See Turner, *op. cit.* 18. According to Plato (*Protagoras 313d*), Protagoras was the first teacher to demand money from his pupils and was therefore known as 'the bill-collector'. It was he who classified the branches of learning into two groups, one comprising arithmetic, astronomy, geometry and music and the other grammar, rhetoric and logic, constituting respectively the quadrivium and the trivium of the seven 'liberal arts' of the Middle Ages. See H.-I. Marrou, *Ἱστορία τῆς Ἐκπαιδεύσεως κατά τήν Ἀρχαιότητα* (= *Histoire de l'éducation dans l'antiquité*, Paris 1948, tr. Th. Fotinopoulos), Athens 1961, 89, 97.

23. Diogenes Laertius, IX.51. The sentence of exile on Protagoras and the burning of his books are said to have been part of a campaign against atheism launched in Athens in the mid fifth century, aimed initially at Socrates, in the course of which Anaxagoras and Diagoras of Melos

42. Plato. Engraving from Spoor, Medici et Philosophi..., *137.*

were also prosecuted for impiety: see E. Derenne, *Les procès d'impiété intentés aux philosophes au Vème et au IVème siècles*, Liège 1930. However, serious doubts have been cast on the accuracy of Diogenes Laertius's facts: see C.W. Müller, 'Protagoras über die Götter', *Hermes* 95 (1967) 140-159; Skouteropoulos, *op. cit.* 41.

Eusebius, in his *De Evangelica Praeparatione* (XIV.3.7), records the testimony of Porphyry (3rd cent. A.D.) that books by Protagoras were available in his time even though the works of other pre-Platonic writers were very scarce: see Skouteropoulos, *op. cit.* 100-101.

24. See Kleberg, *op. cit.* 27-28.

25. Archaeological evidence concerning the purposes for which the Orchestra was used in the fifth century, brought to light by the Agora excavations, suggests that John Camp's hypothesis regarding the construction of the bookshops is almost certainly correct: namely that they were little more than roofed wooden stalls, perhaps built by scaffolders, not unlike the bookstalls on the Left Bank in Paris or at the Monastiraki flea market in Athens. They may have been either permanent or temporary, and in fact it is quite likely that when theatrical performances were put on for the Dionysia or other festivals the bookstalls were moved bodily to the theatre. See H.A. Thompson and R.E.

43. Archytas. Engraving from Meibonius, Diogenes Laertius, *540.*

Aristotle said, 'unwritten doctrines'. So it was left to his pupils to preserve his works for posterity in books, about which he himself had had such reservations. One of Plato's pupils, the mathematician Hermodorus, whose main interest – and the principal subject of his treatise *On Science* (*Περί Μαθημάτων*) – was astral religion, nevertheless spent a great deal of time writing out numerous copies of Plato's dialogues for publication. These books were sold even in far distant outposts of the Greek world such as Sicily, at a time when Plato's works were banned there, which meant that the profits were high.[40]

The concept of copyright was unknown in ancient Greece and piracy was rife, which largely accounts for the amount of textual corruption in the surviving manuscripts. Another of Plato's pupils, Philip of Opus, set up as a publisher in much the same way as Hermodorus: he produced an edition of the *Laws* (and possibly other dialogues too) from the rough notes he had taken 'on wax' at Plato's lectures. Not content with merely reproducing Plato's words, Philip took it upon himself to divide the work into twelve books and added a work of his own entitled *Epinomis*, which serves as an appendix to the *Laws*. In the light of Plato's known objections to the publication of his works and the incontrovertible evidence of Philip of Opus, it seems clear that Plato's own pupils, including Aristotle, Speusippus, Heraclides Ponticus and Xenocrates, were responsible for immortalizing his work in books.[41]

Isocrates. Isocrates was born in 436 B.C., when Athens was at the height of her power. One of the most distinguished pupils of Gorgias the sophist, he was a man of astute intellect who did much to promote the growth of book production by using books in his school of rhetoric and his new educational system. Although he was never in favour with philosophers and pursued an 'anti-philosophical' line in his school, he was highly regarded for his genuine love of the language and his great skill in the use of words.

Born into affluent circumstances, Isocrates lost his fortune and was forced to earn his living as a *logographos* (one who wrote speeches for litigants to deliver in court). He soon realized that his voice was too weak and he himself too diffident to succeed as an orator, so he would have to find another way of fulfilling his ambitions. Books were the obvious medium: he fought harder than anyone else for public recognition of their worth and backed his convictions in every way possible. At the age of about forty-six, in 390 or thereabouts, he opened a school which was destined to become extremely influential. The speeches written for use in his rhetoric classes are models of polished prose embodying his rhetorical principles: they were composed with the object of demonstrating the power of words, which it was the purpose of his school to instil in its students.[42] Isocrates himself never denied the debt he owed to books: he describes his speech *On the Antidosis* as 'an oration intended to be read [to an actual audience]', and in it he acknowledges that when his works had been written out and distributed his reputation grew and students flocked to him.[43]

Isocrates far outdid his predecessors Protagoras and Prodicus and chose to use books as one of his main tools in imparting his rhetorical skills. Aristotle's remark (as reported by Dionysius of Halicarnassus) about the parcels of Isocrates's courtroom speeches to be found in the bookshops may not have been so far from the truth, though one has to allow for a touch of irony due to the rivalry between their two schools.[44]

44. Schoolroom scene from a red-figure goblet by Duris.

His belief in the value of books is stated most clearly in his discourse *Against the Sophists*, a sort of manifesto in which he explains his views on the philosophers, the improvisation characteristic of courtroom oratory and the false assertions of his opponents: 'I wrote and published a discourse,' he states explicitly, and he urges his followers 'to distribute my discourse among those who wish to have it'.[45] His speeches are not as blatantly propagandistic as those of the sophists, and Plato (*Phaedrus* 279a) recognized his qualities as a philosopher: unlike his opponents, Isocrates was primarily concerned to educate healthy individuals capable of making a contribution to Athenian society.

Demosthenes. The other great ancient Greek orator, Demosthenes, was born in 384 B.C. Like Isocrates, he came from a wealthy family but was soon faced with the harsh realities of life. He trained his mind with the same self-discipline that helped him to overcome his physical infirmities:

Wycherley, *The Athenian Agora*, XIV, Princeton 1972, 126-127.

26. See Kleberg, *op. cit.* 28.

27. See Turner, *op. cit.* 31; Kenyon, *op. cit.* 23; Pfeiffer, *Ἱστορία* 32-33.

28. *The Frogs* 943. Here Aristophanes may have been mocking Euripides not only for his bookishness but also for having studied under Gorgias: see Aulus Gellius, *Noctes Atticae* XV.20.4.

29. N. Hourmouziadis, *Ἕνας Ἀθηναῖος θεατής στά ἐν ἄστει Διονύσια*, Athens 1988.

30. See E.G. Turner, *Ἑλληνικοί Πάπυροι: Εἰσαγωγή στή μελέτη καί τή χρήση τῶν παπυρικῶν κειμένων* (= *Greek Papyri: An Introduction*, Oxford 1968, tr. G.M. Parasoglou), Athens 1981; L.D. Reynolds and N.G. Wilson, *Ἀντιγραφεῖς καί Φιλόλογοι: Τό ἱστορικό τῆς παράδοσης τῶν κλασικῶν κειμένων* (= *Scribes and Scholars: A guide to the transmission of Greek and Latin literature*, 2nd edn., London 1975, tr. N.M. Panayotakis), Athens 1981, 19. Yet another difficulty was created by the fact that the old alphabet – in which, for example, the letter *ε* was also used for *ει* and *η* – was still in use right down to 403 B.C.

31. See Pfeiffer, *Ἱστορία* 47. On the sophists' teaching methods see Marrou, *op. cit.* 84 ff.; Pfeiffer, 'Die Sophisten'; Guthrie, *Οἱ Σοφιστές* 55-56. The world of the sophists forms the background to Aristophanes's *Tagenistai* ('the Fryers'), a comedy of which only fragments survive and which seems to be about various well-known Athenian rakes, notably Alcibiades: see Jacqueline de Romilly's recent monograph *Alcibiadès*, Greek trans. by Athina-Babi Athanasiou and Katerina Miliaressi, Athens 1995, 51, 107. On the *Horae* by Prodicus see n. 33.

32. Plato, *Hippias Major* 282: 'Our friend Prodicus has often come here in a public capacity, and the last time he came here in a public capacity from Ceos, just lately, he made a great reputation for himself by his speaking before the Boule [Senate]; and in his private capacity he made an astonishing amount of money by giving exhibi-

according to Cicero (*Brutus* 121), he studied Plato without ever going to any of his lessons. He was greatly influenced by Thucydides, who instilled in him his passionate devotion to the greatness of Athens, and that may have been the reason why he copied out the whole of Thucydides's *History*, either for friends or to order. Cicero's testimony chimes with that of Lucian, who said that Demosthenes himself had copied out most of the books in his possession and had made eight complete copies of Thucydides.[46] It is not known whether he was a talented calligrapher or whether he made money from his work as a copyist, but we do know that he gave lessons in rhetoric and worked as a paid *logographos*.By the time Alexander came to the Macedonian throne (336), Demosthenes was no longer delivering his own speeches: *For Phormio* and the speeches occasioned by the litigiousness of an Athenian named Apollodorus were delivered by advocates acting for him. The fact that he polished his prose for publication is evident from his two speeches *On the Embassy (Περί τῆς παραπρεσβείας).*[47] Exercises in rhetoric designed to show off the orator's skills, as well as philosophical and historical works, tragedies and comedies, were available from the booksellers in the Agora, and even Aristotle made room for rhetoric in his course of studies from the time when he found himself in competition with the school of Isocrates.

3. The book trade in the Hellenic world. Athens was the intellectual driving force of the Greek world, 'an education to Greece', as Pericles put it in his funeral oration (Thucydides, II.41). And without a doubt it was the centre of the book trade in Greece, at least until near the end of the fourth century, though that does not mean it was the birthplace of papyrus books or of the idea of the private library. From the beginning of the fifth century philosophers flocked to Athens in ever-increasing numbers from all the places where Greeks were settled, from southern Italy to the coastlands of Asia Minor, from the Black Sea to Rhodes. This great influx of scholars led to the accumulation of an immense fund of learning in Athens; and what better way of storing that knowledge than in books? Moreover, there is every reason to believe that there was a considerable trade in those books between Athens and the rest of the Greek world.

Xenophon in the *Anabasis*, describing the gruelling return journey of the Greek army from Persia, over the mountains to the Black Sea and then down through the Bosporus, mentions that near Salmydessus they came across a wrecked ship laden with crates containing household utensils and books: evidently those who had been studying in Athens liked to take home something of the bookish atmosphere they had become accustomed to.[48] Memnon, in his lost *History* (extracts from which are preserved by Photios in his *Bibliotheca*), records that the Bithynian ruler Clearchus, on his return home after studying in Athens

tions and associating with the young.' In Plato's *Theaetetus* (151b) Socrates explains the difference between his own educational method and the passive teaching of the sophists and sends to Prodicus any would-be student who appears to have no embryonic ideas in his mind waiting to be 'delivered' (see n. 13 on the maieutic method). In *Cratylus* (384b) Socrates acknowledges the importance of learning about words but remarks ironically that if only he had attended Prodicus's

45. Isocrates. Engraving, 18th c.

'fifty-drachma lecture' he would have had a thorough understanding of the correct meaning of words, but unfortunately he has heard only the 'one-drachma lesson'. Another leading sophist notorious for his exorbitant fees was Gorgias (*c.* 483-376), from Leontini in Sicily, who was said to charge his pupils a hundred minae (= 10,000 drachmae!) per lesson.

33. The *Horae* deals with the birth of religion as mankind's reaction to living conditions on earth, culminating in the dilemma confronting Heracles when Virtue and Pleasure appeared before him and invited him

under Plato and Isocrates, founded a library in his own country not later than 364 B.C. A rather curious story is told of a certain Bion, a man from the Dnieper valley region north of the Black Sea, who was sold into slavery with all his family when his father was convicted of some kind of tax fraud. On the death of the orator who had bought him, Bion inherited his property and decided to go to Athens to study philosophy, but before he left he burnt all the books bequeathed to him by his late master.

Zeno. Zeno was born at Citium in Cyprus in 334 or 333 B.C. His father Mnaseus, who often went to Athens on business, used to bring him manuscripts of works by various pupils of Socrates. When Zeno grew up he went into his father's business, but on his first voyage overseas with a cargo of purple cloth from Phoenicia his ship was wrecked off the coast of Attica and was a total loss. He then made his way to Athens and started working in a bookshop, where he spent his free time listening to the bookseller reading aloud from Xenophon's *Memorabilia*. He was very struck by what Xenophon said about Socrates and asked if such men were still to be found. Just at that moment Crates, the Cynic philosopher, happened to be passing and the bookseller introduced him to Zeno, who became his pupil.[49]

Having had his eyes opened to the importance of philosophical thought in human life, Zeno gave up the pursuit of money in order to pursue knowledge instead. The Stoic school that he founded (so named after the Painted Stoa in Athens, where he taught) exerted a profound influence on later generations of philosophers and attracted students in large numbers from many parts of the world. It would seem that the teaching there was based on the written tradition, for Cleanthes, who succeeded Zeno as the head of the school, was said to have taken notes on his predecessor's lectures using oyster shells and the shoulder blades of oxen to write on, as he had no money to buy paper.[50] Zeno, unlike his successor, had a sizable private library, which he built up by having books copied for him not only by scribes sent to him by the Macedonian king Antigonus Gonatas, an ex-pupil of his, but also by slaves acquired after the Peloponnesian War, owing to the increased demand for books.[51]

Faced with all this evidence, one can only conclude that from the middle of the fifth century there must really have been 'as many private libraries as there were Athenian citizens'. This unlikely-sounding assertion is corroborated by Polybius, who says that in the third century B.C. there were so many private and public (i.e. school) libraries that the Sicilian historian Timaeus – whom Polybius mocks for his book-learning – spent fifty years listing them all after being sent into exile by the Syracusan ruler Agathocles.[52] One result of the tremendous demand for the plays of the three great tragedians was that there were a great many corrupt copies in circulation. The problem became so acute that in 330

to choose between them: he opted for the arduous path of Virtue in preference to the transient delights of Pleasure. The *Horae* must have come out not later than 416 B.C. as it is mentioned in Plato's *Symposium*, which is set in that year.

34. Plato, *Symposium* 177d.

35. According to Diogenes Laertius (VIII.81), Plato wrote two letters to Archytas in which references are made to certain *hypomnemata* ('memoirs' or 'commentaries') sent to Archytas by an unnamed writer from Myra. The inference to be drawn from these letters is that Archytas supplied Plato with books by earlier

46. Demosthenes. Engraving, 18th c.

writers for his library. The form in which these *hypomnemata* were written – on papyrus rolls or clay tablets – is not known.

36. Diogenes Laertius, III.9. Cf. II.81, where we are told that Aristippus of Cyrene also received a sum of money from Dionysius, who was keen to attract philosophers to his court. When criticized for his conduct, Aristippus replied, 'Well, I need money, Plato needs books.'

37. Diogenes Laertius, VIII.85.

38. Diogenes Laertius, III.18 (on Sophron); Proclus, *Commentary on 'Timaeus'* 21C (on Heraclides Ponticus).

39. On ancient Athenian education and upbringing and the innovations introduced by the sophists, see: Marrou, *op. cit.* 69-147; M.A. Manacorda, 'Scuola e insegnanti' in *Oralità, scrittura, spettacolo*, Turin 1983, 187 ff.

40. Zenobius, v.6; J.W. Thompson, 'Libraries of Ancient Greece' 19; Kleberg, *op. cit.* 30.

41. Diogenes Laertius, III.37; Lesky, *op. cit.* 744.

47. Thucydides. Engraving, 18th c.

48. Zeno of Citium. Engraving from Meibonius, Diogenes Laertius, *564.*

B.C. Lycurgus, the State Treasurer, carried a decree that official copies of their works were to be kept in the Athenian state archives.[53]

4. Aristotle. Although Athens was plunged into a socio-political crisis after her crushing defeat by the Spartans in 404, two schools of philosophy that have exerted an enduring influence on human thought were founded during that period. In 388 or soon after, Plato established his school in a grotto sacred to the Muses and the hero Academus or Hecademus, after whom it was named the Academy (*Akademia*): it was originally a religious confraternity, and as a school it lasted for more than nine hundred years. The most famous alumnus of the Academy was Aristotle, who studied there from 368 until Plato's death in 348 and in 335 opened another school to give Plato's Academy some healthy competition. Aristotle's establishment, which lasted until A.D. 425, was at first called the Lyceum and later, at least from the time of his successor Theophrastus, the Peripatetic school. At its peak, under Theophrastus and down to the middle of the fourth century, it was said to have had two thousand students. These two schools between them were responsible not only for preserving many of their founders' treatises and lectures, as well as earlier works of literature, but also for promoting awareness of the importance of books and private libraries to scholarly writing. Their teachers, and their students too, made a practice of collecting, filing and publishing their works on a scale that has never been equalled since by any philosophical school or movement in either the West or the East.

From the middle of the fourth century the champion of the cause of books was Aristotle. It goes without saying that the immense body of learning generated by the Lyceum, thanks to the peripatetic teaching method that Aristotle employed and the pursuit of all-round knowledge that he enjoined on his pupils, could hardly have come into existence and could certainly never have been bequeathed to posterity without the aid of the book. And so, by an irony of fate, it was books – about whose value Plato had had reservations – that kept his own work alive through the ages.

Aristotle's library. According to Strabo, the first great private library in ancient Greece was that of Aristotle, most of which was handed down to his successors in the Peripatetic school to provide an infrastructure for its teaching programme.[54] The point Strabo wanted to make was that Aristotle's private library enjoyed historical continuity: it contained the basis of his thinking on education and scholarship, it was full of pearls of wisdom on every branch of knowledge and at every level, and having survived an eventful history it was still 'alive' in Strabo's own time (the first century B.C.), so that Cicero had been able to marvel at its riches as represented by copies of the same books in the great houses of Rome. Aristotle was unrivalled for the comprehensiveness of his knowledge and, unlike the sophists, he was able to classify and codify an enormous quantity of material on the basis of his own philosophical principles and his regular collaboration with his pupils. He was the first philosopher to produce scholarly editions of his work. A natural outcome of – and also a prerequisite for – the orderliness of his thoughts and the research methods that he instituted was a library, that indispensable aid to scientific thinking.

The titles of Aristotle's own works, which formed the major part of his library, are known to us from a catalogue preserved by Diogenes Laertius.[55] They were divided into two categories, 'exoteric' and 'esoteric' (see (a) and (b) below),[56] and were contained in 400 books with a total of 445,270 lines. Of these, 106 books comprised the *Corpus Aristotelicum*, that is the texts of the school lectures. Even on its own that is an impressive collection, without counting in the books by other authors that he owned, and Strabo is right in describing him as the greatest book-collector in antiquity. Alexander the Great, for whom Aristotle had prepared an edition of the *Iliad*,[57] had settled on his former tutor an annual stipend of eight hundred talents; and on his all-conquering march to the Middle East he sent back a great deal of valuable material for Aristotle's magnum opus on the constitutions of 158 cities. The greater part of his *Constitution of Athens*, a work about which little had been known, was discovered in 1891. Besides the books sent to him by Alexander, Aristotle had plenty of money with which to buy books for himself: he is known to have spent three talents on the works of Speusippus, Plato's successor as head of the Academy, totalling 43,475 lines.[58]

The contents of Aristotle's library can be divided into three main groups: (a) his 'exoteric' works, (b) his 'esoteric' works, and (c) writings by other authors.

(a) The 'exoteric discourses', as Aristotle himself called them, are his writings intended for the general public outside the school. As such they were edited and written up as literary pieces for publication. Among the outstanding works in this category are the *Protrepticus*, a literary 'exhortation to philosophy', the dialogue *Eudemus*, a work entitled *Alexander, or For the Colonists*, a series of treatises including *Reply to the Pythagoreans*, *To Zeno* and *To Gorgias*, and the first two books of the *Rhetoric*.

(b) The 'esoteric' works, which chiefly concern us here, were those prepared for use at the Lyceum: they are, in fact, outlines or notes for lectures that Aristotle delivered to his pupils or to those cultivated outsiders who attended his afternoon sessions. They include the *Analytica priora* and *Analytica posteriora*, the *Physics*, the *Nicomachean Ethics* and *Eudemian Ethics* and, most important of all, the *Organon*, a name given much later to the treatises on logic which were the basic textbooks for use in the school. The books in this category formed the nucleus of Aristotle's library, and he edited and revised them constantly.

(c) Lastly we come to the books by other writers, which Aristotle had

42. On Isocrates's teaching methods see Marrou, *op. cit.* 130 ff.; W. Jaeger, *Παιδεία: Ἡ μόρφωσις τοῦ Ἕλληνος ἀνθρώπου* (= *Paideia. Die Formung des griechischen Menschen*, tr. G.P. Verrios), III, Athens 1974, 128 ff.

43. See Turner, *Athenian Books* 19-20 (Isocrates, *On the Antidosis* 12).

44. Aristotle's disparaging comment led Cephisodorus, a loyal pupil of Isocrates, to take up the cudgels in defence of his teacher: see Dionysius of Halicarnassus, *Isocrates* 18.

45. See Turner, *Athenian Books* 19 (Isocrates, *On the Antidosis* 193, *Panathenaicus* 233).

46. Lucian, *To the Ignorant Book-Collector*, 4. Zosimus, a historian from Ascalon or Gaza who lived in the fifth and early sixth centuries A.D., writes about the life of Demosthenes and mentions a great library that existed in Athens in his time. According to Zosimus, the library burnt down and what was thought to be the only copy of Thucydides was destroyed with it; but fortunately Demosthenes had made a copy, the only one in existence, and so the *History* survived (*Oratores Attici*, ed. C. Müller, Paris 1848, II 523).

47. See Lesky, *op. cit.* 833-834.

48. Xenophon, *Anabasis* VII.5.14; Kenyon, *op. cit.* 23-24. On Bion see

49. Aristotle. Engraving from Meibonius, Diogenes Laertius*, 268.*

Diogenes Laertius, IV.46-47.

49. Diogenes Laertius, II.3.31.

50. Diogenes Laertius, VII.174. Cleanthes the Stoic philosopher, who came from Assus in Asia Minor, was the subject of the following anecdote. An acquaintance remarked to him one day that he was looking old. 'Yes, I too am willing to go,' Cleanthes answered, 'but seeing that I am in the best of health and still able to write and read, I am content to wait.'

51. Diogenes Laertius, VII.36; J.W. Thompson, 'Libraries of Ancient Greece' 18.

52. Polybius, XII.25: see Lesky, *op. cit.* 1060.

53. Pseudo-Plutarch, *Lives of Ten Orators* VII.841F. In 334 Aristotle started collecting transcripts of the versions of plays used in performance. Lycurgus, a friend his from the time when they had been students together, was in charge of the public finances of Athens from 338 to 326, and it was in that capacity that he issued his decree, which also compelled actors to follow the official texts.

54. Strabo, XIII.1. See also Athenaeus, *Deipnosophistai* I.3.

50. Theophrastus. Engraving, 18th c.

bought or otherwise obtained in order to acquire a solid grounding for his own philosophical and scientific investigations, to familiarize himself with the work of his predecessors and contemporaries and to back up the tuition he gave his pupils in other areas of knowledge. One of the books in his library was the only known copy of Heraclitus's work usually known as *On Nature* (*Περί φύσεως*), of which Heraclitus himself had deposited a copy in the temple of Artemis at Ephesus about 150 years earlier.[59] Aristotle was always advising his pupils to study the works of the pre-Socratics thoroughly and take notes on them, presumably using the copies in the Lyceum library, and he set specific projects for some of his followers: Eudemus was instructed to write a history of mathematics and astronomy, Menon to do the same for early medicine, and Theophrastus to publish his massive encyclopaedic work *Doctrines of Natural Philosophers (Φυσικῶν δόξαι).*[60]

Aristotle was generally regarded as pro-Macedonian, so on Alexander's death in 323, to avoid the risk of reprisals from the anti-Macedonian party, he decided to leave Athens and went to live in his mother's house at Chalcis, in Euboea. There he spent the last months of his life in solitude, apart from the company of a few select pupils, and died in October 322 at the age of sixty-three. In drawing up his will he was primarily concerned to provide for his housekeeper Herpyllis and made no provision at all for the future of his library.[61] There is no evidence that he took any of the books from his private library with him to Chalcis. It is fair to assume that he did, simply because of the sense of loss he would have felt if he had been parted from something that had been so much a part of his inner life, but this can only be a conjecture: after he left Athens, the story of what happened to his books moves from the realm of fact to that of myth.

5. The eventful subsequent history of Aristotle's library. Aristotle left for Chalcis not knowing how long he would be away from Athens. It is therefore reasonable to suppose that he took a good many books with him, starting with the original manuscripts of his teaching books, which he went on revising with the help of his pupils. This does not mean, of course, that he stripped the Lyceum library bare of the Aristotelian textbooks, reliable copies of which would certainly have been available, at least in the Lyceum. The authentic versions of the 'esoteric' works, that is to say the autograph manuscripts, probably went on his death to his two favourite pupils, Theophrastus and Eudemus. Eudemus may have taken a few of his teacher's books and gone back to Rhodes, while Theophrastus carried on Aristotle's work in what came to be called the Peripatetic school in Athens.[62]

Theophrastus. Theophrastus, born *circa* 370 B.C. at Eressus on the island of Lesbos, was Aristotle's most gifted pupil and became a bosom friend of his. When Aristotle went into voluntary exile Theophrastus stayed on in Athens and, though not an Athenian citizen, managed with the help of Demetrius of Phalerum to take over the title to the school premises. He was head of the Lyceum from Aristotle's departure until his own death in about 287, and in his will he bequeathed 'the gardens, the walk (Peripatos) and all the buildings adjoining the gardens' to all who wished to study literature and philosophy there together.[63] The Lyceum, which Aristotle left in Theophrastus's hands, was said not to have had its own library as it was a private school. What can this mean? Since the library was by this time an essential study facility, one has to assume that Aristotle could not possibly have stripped it of all its text-books, reference books and other teaching aids. Later evidence casts no further light on the matter, so we can only accept that this assumption is correct, especially as it seems to be corroborated by the subsequent course of events.

Theophrastus's high public standing, which was enhanced by the confidence that Aristotle reposed in him, made his name well known in Alexandria, the great new centre of Hellenism. However, he declined an invitation from Ptolemy I to go and teach at the Museum there and act as a link between the Alexandrian and Athenian schools, preferring to stay in Athens and carry on his teacher's work. His own writings alone amounted to 232,808 lines, and in his private library he would have had not only his own books and those he had inherited from Aristotle but also all the sourcebooks and reference works he had obtained to assist him in his researches for the books he wrote on a wide variety of subjects. Unlike his teacher, he left a will (preserved by Diogenes Laertius) with a clause stipulating exactly what was to be done with his library: 'All the books [I leave] to Neleus.'[64]

Neleus. Neleus, who came from the small town of Scepsis in the Troad, became the owner of the libraries of both Theophrastus and Aristotle: in fact, if his name were not connected with Aristotle's books we might know nothing at all about him. All that is known about his family is the name of his father, Coriscus. Neleus was a student at Plato's Academy at the same time as Aristotle, and when Speusippus succeeded Plato he went with Aristotle to the court of Hermeias, a eunuch who had been a slave and had made himself ruler of the cities of Assus and Atarneus. Hermeias, a man of dubious morals but generous of heart, who had connections of some kind in the Macedonian court, became a close friend of Aristotle's and treated him very well during his stay at Assus. On Hermeias's death Aristotle wrote a beautiful commemorative hymn in his honour starting with the words, 'Virtue in man is a hard-won acquisition, a precious object of living.'[65]

But what was it that led Theophrastus to bequeath all his books, including those entrusted to him by Aristotle, to Neleus, a man of his

55. Paul Moraux takes the view that this was a catalogue belonging to the Peripatetic school, compiled by Aristion of Ceos, who was head of the school in 226-225 B.C. The main works on Aristotle's library are: P. Moraux, *Les listes anciennes des ouvrages d'Aristote*, Louvain 1951; I. Düring, *Aristotle in the Ancient Biographical Tradition*, Göteborg 1957; Id., *῾Ο ᾿Αριστοτέλης: Παρουσίαση καί*

51. Strabo. Engraving, 18th c.

῾Ερμηνεία τῆς Σκέψης του (= *Aristoteles. Darstellung und Interpretation seines Denkens*, tr. P. Kotzia-Panteli), I, Athens 1991, 86, 91.

56. Düring, *῾Ο ᾿Αριστοτέλης: Παρουσίαση* I 86 ff.

57. The copy of Homer that Alexander always carried with him on his campaigns was kept in a precious casket looted from the Persian emperor's sumptuous palace at Persepolis, and was therefore known in antiquity as 'the casket Homer' *(ἡ ἐκ τοῦ νάρθηκος)*: see Strabo, 594; Callisthenes, *FGrHist* 124 T 10. The evidence for the existence of a copy of the *Iliad* comes from Onesicritus: see Düring, *Aristotle in the ... Tradition*, 285.

58. Diogenes Laertius, IV.4.

own age who was not a professional scholar and whose ability as a teacher – certainly at the level of the Peripatetic school – was open to question?[66] Perhaps the answer is to be found in the friendship that had developed between Neleus and Aristotle at Assus and the support that Neleus enjoyed from Demetrius of Phalerum, the ruler of Athens. When Neleus inherited Theophrastus's library he expected to be appointed head of the Peripatetic school, but he was disappointed in his hopes; and when Demetrius Poliorcetes seized power in 307 he found himself out of favour with the powers that be. He retired in dudgeon to his native town, taking with him many of the books that had been in Aristotle's private library.

52. *An imaginative reconstruction of the gardens of Plato's Academy. Engraving from C. Frommel,* Dreissig Ansichten Griechenlands zu den Werken griechischen Autoren, *Karlsruhe 1830.*

Precisely which books Neleus took with him and which of them survived are questions that cannot be answered. It is said that in the reign of Ptolemy II Philadelphus (285-247) he sold or gave away to the Alexandrian Library Aristotle's original manuscripts, or copies of them. Be that as it may, there is no doubt that some of the books from Aristotle's library were left to Neleus's heirs, who hid them in a cave when King Eumenes II of Pergamum started collecting books for his own great

59. See pp. 29, 31.

60. Theophrastus had undertaken to write a history of philosophy from Thales to Plato as part of his contribution to the encyclopaedic activity organized by his master: see *KRS* 19.

61. Aristotle's will has come down to us in two versions: one in Greek, as recorded by Diogenes Laertius, and one Arabic translation. The Greek version is based on the Alexandrian historian Hermippus, who used the archives of the Peripatetic school, while the Arabic translation can be traced back to Andronicus Rhodius by way of a certain Ptolemy whom the Arabs nicknamed el-Garib ('the unknown'): see Düring, *Ὁ Ἀριστοτέλης: Παρουσίαση* I 59.

62. See Düring, *Ὁ Ἀριστοτέλης: Παρουσίαση* I 90.

63. Diogenes Laertius, v.52; Düring, *Ὁ Ἀριστοτέλης: Παρουσίαση* I 56.

library, because they were afraid they would be forced to hand them over to the royal collection.[67] The heirs themselves never retrieved them and there they remained, forgotten and mouldering away.

Apellicon. In the first century B.C. a curious figure appeared on the Athenian intellectual scene: this was Apellicon, born at Teos in Asia Minor, who became a naturalized Athenian citizen. Apellicon was a whimsical and fickle man who described himself as a Peripatetic philosopher (although the Peripatetic school was not functioning at the time) and enjoyed giving his money to writers in the hope of being remembered as a patron of literature, though in fact, as Strabo (VIII.1.54) remarks, he was more interested in books than in philosophy. To gratify his ambitions he went so far as to steal some original Attic decrees from the public archives, an offence for which he could well have been condemned to death. He managed to escape this penalty through the intervention of the city's ruler Athenion, whose friendship he had won by appealing to the bond of their shared interest in Peripatetic philosophy, and as a result he was merely condemned to a brief period of exile from Athens.[68]

Across the Aegean in the coastlands of Asia Minor, the last king of Pergamum, Attalus III Philometor, had bequeathed his kingdom to the Roman Senate on his death in 133 B.C. The strife that ensued, owing to the inability of the Romans to impose their rule on Pergamum, reduced the kingdom to a state of near-anarchy. When the Romans had eventually won control and Pergamum had become a Roman province, certain descendants of Neleus remembered the cache of Aristotle's books and retrieved them with a view to selling them. Somehow Apellicon heard about this and lost no time in buying the books, for which he paid a handsome sum of money.[69] And so what was left of Aristotle's manuscripts, and perhaps some other books too, found their way back to Athens. Apellicon was now able to set himself up as the fount of all knowledge, and to impress the Athenians he himself edited and published a work by Aristotle from an imperfect manuscript, using his own imagination to fill in the missing parts. His vanity did have one positive effect, however, for he preserved Aristotle's manuscripts and, as Strabo informs us, he had new copies made so that they became available once again to the Peripatetic school and the Academy.[70]

But this was not to be the end of the story of Aristotle's books. During the First Mithradatic War the Athenians rose in rebellion against the Romans and Apellicon was elevated to high office. In 86 B.C., after a long siege, Sulla captured Athens, Apellicon was killed and the spoils that Sulla carried off to Rome included Apellicon's library, in other words those that were left of Aristotle's authentic manuscripts.[71]

Tyrannio. In Rome, the fate of Aristotle's books was initially bound up with another Greek. Tyrannio the Elder, born at Amisus on the Black Sea coast of Asia Minor, studied under the celebrated grammarian Dionysius the Thracian. In the Second Mithradatic War he was taken prisoner, but fortunately for him his captor was Lucullus, a philhellene, who treated him kindly and took him under his wing in Rome so that he was able to move freely in the most illustrious Roman literary circles. Lucullus was a great book-lover who had gathered round him a coterie of Greeks with intellectual and artistic interests, and thanks to him Tyrannio won the friendship and patronage of a number of prominent Romans including Julius Caesar, Cicero and Atticus. Tyrannio was an Aristotelian and an avid bibliophile who is said to have amassed a collection of 30,000 rolls, and by cultivating the friendship of Sulla and his librarian he was even allowed to borrow Aristotle's manuscripts.[72]

Besides collecting books for himself, Tyrannio made a serious effort to classify, edit and publish Aristotle's works. He also monitored all the big book collections brought to Rome as spoils of war and put his knowledge to good use as an adviser on book publishing. He worked in close co-operation with Cicero on the organization of the latter's library, as we shall see, and gave him valuable advice on various writing projects including the great book on geography, based on Eratosthenes, which Cicero started but never finished.[73] When Sulla died and all his books and other possessions were inherited by his son Faustus, Aristotle's autograph manuscripts were returned to Sulla's library. Faustus refused to lend out any of his books: anyone who wished to consult them had to go to Faustus's villa in person, with the result that his library became one of the centres of Roman intellectual life. It was there, many years later, that Cicero had perhaps his first opportunity to read Aristotle's 'esoteric' writings, some of them in manuscripts written by Aristotle himself.[74]

Strabo, who was proud of the fact that he had attended Tyrannio's lectures in Rome in about 40 B.C., has nothing further to say about the books that had belonged to Aristotle. For some reason Tyrannio abandoned his plan of classifying and publishing Aristotle's works and delegated it to a brilliant literary scholar, Andronicus of Rhodes.[75] Andronicus embarked on this daunting project after Cicero's death and was engaged on it between 40 and 20 B.C., overlapping with the period when the great biographer of the ancient world, Dionysius of Halicarnassus, was at work in Rome. Once Andronicus had completed the publishing programme there was a renewed surge of interest in Aristotelian studies, and with the help of Atticus, who supported the copying of the manuscripts, Rome became a centre from which Aristotle's thinking was carried to all the Greek-speaking provinces of the Roman empire. Unfortunately for the original books, Faustus was reduced to bankruptcy by his megalomania and extravagant lifestyle and had to sell off all his possessions, including his books: Aristotle's autograph manuscripts, and perhaps those of Theophrastus too, have never been heard of since.[76]

At this point, having outlined the circumstances that led to the formation of the first private libraries and the part played by those libraries in furthering the advance of scientific and philosophical thinking at the schools, it is worth devoting a little space to a short satire of much later date which is the only ancient Greek work exclusively devoted to the subject of books. Though not written until the second century A.D., it keeps alive the traditions of the Classical period in Greece and is strongly reminiscent of Socrates's dialogue with Euthydemus as immortalized by Xenophon. Entitled *To the Ignorant Book-Collector*, it was written by that mordant satirist of all human follies, Lucian (A.D. 130-200), who presented it to a young man who had refused to lend him a book he had asked for.[77] Lucian derides his victim for being unable to distinguish between valuable ancient books and others being 'pushed' by booksellers, taunts him that he will never be able to call himself an educated man even if he buys all the autograph manuscripts of Demosthenes and the books looted from Athens by Sulla (after all, as the saying goes, an ape is an ape even if he has birth-tokens of gold) and sneers at him for being unable to see through sycophancy and not realizing that his friends are laughing at him behind his back for his vanity in always carrying about with him a beautiful roll with a gold roller and purple case. He compares the ignorant young book-collector with the tyrant Dionysius of Syracuse, who wanted to write tragedies and bought the writing tablet that Aeschylus had used in the belief that it would make him a great poet. Since you own so many copies of Homer, Lucian continues, why not read them: you will find they have practically nothing to say that applies to you, but let your mind dwell on that caricature of a man, the ugly and deformed Thersites, who thought that by putting on Achilles's armour he would be transformed into a handsome hero. Lucian also compares the foolish young man with Bellerophon, who carried with him a letter containing his own death sentence, and reminds him of the story of Demetrius the Cynic, who came across an ignorant man reading Euripides's *Bacchae* aloud in Corinth: when the reader reached the point where the messenger recounts Pentheus's horrible fate, Demetrius snatched the book away and tore it up in fury, exclaiming, 'It's better for Pentheus to be torn to pieces once and for all by me than over and over again by you!'

6. What books were made of. Enough has now been said about people who supported or opposed the use of books as a medium for promoting the spread of knowledge, and it is time to consider the materials on which all these notes and books were written. The earliest reference to anything resembling a book in Greece occurs in the *Iliad* (VI.169), where Proetus gives Bellerophon a 'folded tablet' with a letter written on it. At first the Greeks used the writing tablet (*deltos*) as a substitute for the book and continued to do so even after the papyrus roll had been introduced into their lives.[78] A tablet consisted of a wooden board with a frame to keep the writing surface (a thinly-spread mixture of wax with pitch or thick grease) in place, and the stylus used for writing on it was a sharpened reed.[79] Two or more tablets bound together with cords or leather thongs made a notebook of a few 'pages', which Euripides calls *polythyroi diaptychai* ('many-leaved tablets').[80]

Writing tablets were widely used by scholars, teachers and schoolboys and were the principal material employed by civil service clerks for keeping notes for the public records.[81] Literary commentaries probably appeared first in Ionia in the form of unpublished lecture notes circulated among small groups of philosophers and students. We have seen how Philolaus published the teachings of Pythagoras from his own lecture notes, and how Philip of Opus produced an edition of Plato's *Laws* from the notes he had taken 'on wax'.[82] Socrates evidently thought it was the duty of every author to 'store up aids for recollection for the time when he will be overtaken by the forgetfulness of old age' (Plato, *Phaedrus* 276d). Tablets may also have been used for the notes which Archytas sent to Plato to broaden his knowledge of the 'natural philosophers' (i.e. natural scientists) and their beliefs.[83] Aeschylus mentions writing tablets *(μνήμοσιν δέλτοις φρενῶν)*, as does Sophocles *(θές δ' ἐν φρενός δέλτοισι τούς ἐμούς λόγους).*[84] Rough-and-ready bibliographies or book lists were written on tablets, as we know from Diogenes Laertius (VII.188) in his Life of Chrysippus: 'Moreover, this story is not mentioned anywhere by the bibliographers who wrote about the titles of books.' The same author (IX.114) also records a conversation between the philosopher-poet Timon of Phlius (*c*. 320-230 B.C.) and the orator Zopyrus, which implies that notes written on tablets were copied out later on to papyrus rolls, but often with no attempt to reduce them to order: we are told that Timon, wishing to read a certain poem to Zopyrus, had to unroll a whole papyrus, reading out whatever he found, until he came to the lines he wanted.

Exactly when papyrus 'books' were introduced into the Greek world is a matter of conjecture. Probably Naucratis, a Milesian colony in Egypt, was the trading centre from which the first papyrus rolls were exported to the Greek-speaking countries in the sixth century B.C., but the question remains open, at least as far as the use of papyrus rolls for official documents is concerned. No papyrus rolls have been found from Bronze Age Crete, where all that is known for certain is that records were written on clay tablets in the Linear A and B scripts, but that does not necessarily mean that papyrus was not used for literary works. Some of the clay seals found at Knossos and elsewhere bear traces of papyrus fibre, which suggests that fibre had been used to attach the seals to papyrus rolls.[85] The earliest known pictorial representation of a person reading a papyrus book is by the Attic painter Onesimus and dates from *c*. 490 B.C.

When Plato uses the word *biblos* or *byblion* he means a papyrus roll. The manuscript was written in successive columns from left to right across the length of the roll. Each of the sheets of which the roll was composed was known as a *kollema* (from the verb *kollao*, to glue, because the sheets were glued together). The width of the columns varied according to the nature of the text: narrower for oratory, broader for philosophical and historical works and commentaries. The length of the rolls made for the Greek market was usually between seven and ten metres, but some surviving rolls – including one with a copy of Plato's *Phaedrus* and one with the second book of Herodotus's *Histories* – are up to seventeen metres long. When the copyist reached the end, a slender rod (the *omphalos*) was attached to the margin to the right of the last column to serve as a roller. Each end of the roller was decorated with an ornamental knob, and for *éditions de luxe*, especially in the Roman period, the roller was often made of precious metal inlaid with gems. Attached to the roller there was often a small parchment label (*sillybos*), perhaps triangular, on which the title or some other indication of the book's contents was written.[86]

Besides writing tablets and papyrus rolls, there were times when the Greeks were reduced to writing

64. Diogenes Laertius, v.52. The catalogue of Theophrastus's writings recorded by Diogenes Laertius (v.42-50) lists 221 works each taking up from one to twenty-four books, making a corpus of 466 papyrus rolls in all.

65. See Düring, Ὁ Ἀριστοτέλης: *Παρουσίαση* I 55.

66. Aristotle mentions Neleus in the *Magna Moralia*, remarking that Neleus and Lamprus had been fellow-students of his when they learnt 'the art of writing'. Neleus must have been in his sixties when he inherited the library of the Peripatetic school

53. Lucian. Engraving, 18th c.

from Theophrastus: see Düring, *Ὁ Ἀριστοτέλης: Παρουσίαση* II (1994) 217.

67. Strabo, 609; see also Düring, *Ὁ Ἀριστοτέλης: Παρουσίαση* I 55.

68. See the fictional account by J. Bidez, *Un singulier naufrage littéraire dans l'antiquité*, Brussels 1943; Düring, *Aristotle in the ... Tradition*, 382-395; Id., *Ὁ Ἀριστοτέλης: Παρουσίαση* I 94.

69. Strabo, XIII.1.54.

70. See Düring, *Ὁ Ἀριστοτέλης: Παρουσίαση* I 94-95.

71. Strabo, XIII.1.54.

72. The information given by Strabo about the size of Tyrannio's

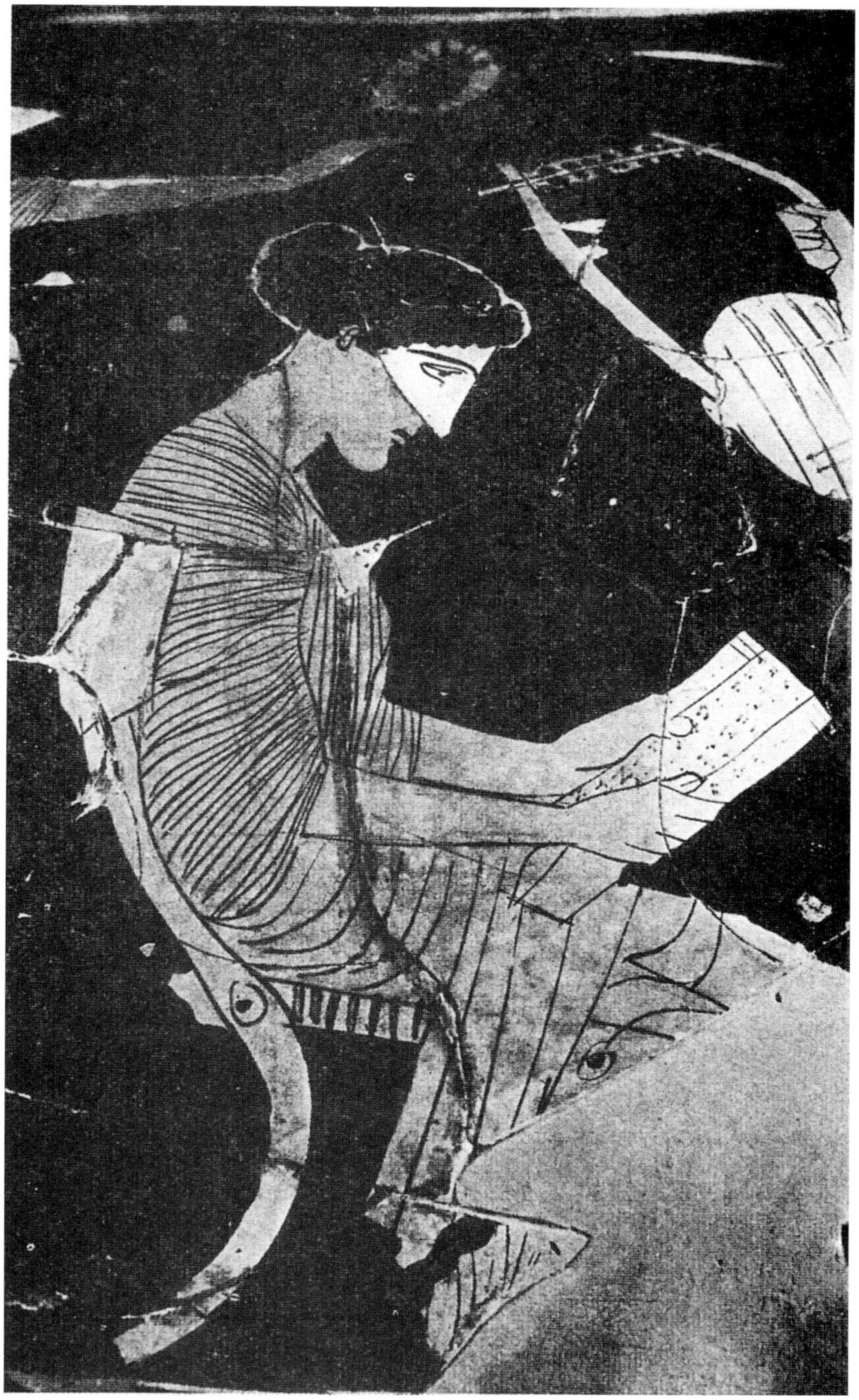

54. Sappho reading. Painting on a red-figure hydria, c. *440* B.C.

on treated animal skins. Herodotus (v.58) says that the Ionians had always used the word 'skins' (*diphtherai*) to mean 'books', because in bygone times, when papyrus had been hard to obtain, they did actually use goat and sheep skins to write on, as many foreign peoples still did in his own time.[87] His statement is more significant for what it implies about the causes of the papyrus shortage in Ionia than for the information that skins were used to take its place. The inference to be drawn from the words he uses is that at some time in the past the supply of papyrus rolls to Ionia had dried up as a result of political disturbances, and that for some time thereafter papyrus had been replaced by animal skins. The events he is alluding to should perhaps be dated to the early decades of the fifth century. The statement of Diodorus Siculus (II.22.4) that Ctesias of Cnidus, the author of the *Persica*, had educated himself by reading Persian books written on sheep and goat skins is not relevant to the present discussion.[88] Whatever the truth of the matter may be, there is no doubt that parchment books were known in Athens, and Euripides – who had a big library himself – commented on the fact, describing them as 'skins with black writing on them'.[89]

55. Vase-painting by the Eretria Painter. Paris, Louvre.

7. Architecture. Nothing whatever is known about library architecture in ancient Greece. There exists a fragment of the comedy *Linus* by Alexis (early third century B.C.) in which Linus urges his pupil Heracles to go through the titles in his library and pick out any book he wants from among the works of Orpheus, Hesiod, Homer, Epicharmus and Choerilus. One might have hoped that the playwright would have given a description of the room where the books were kept, or the bookcases. His silence on the subject comes as a disappointment, just as Linus was disappointed when Heracles, whom he calls 'a true philosopher', passes over the great poets and chooses a cookery book by Simus.[90]

collection of books is the earliest extant statistic concerning a private library in antiquity. On Lucullus, his library and his circle, see p. 101.

73. See Düring, *Aristotle in the ... Tradition* 412-413; Id., *Ὁ Ἀριστοτέλης: Παρουσίαση* I 95-96; Cicero, *Epistulae ad Atticum* II. 6.

56. Schoolroom scene from a red-figure goblet by Duris.

57. A papyrus roll.

74. It was in 45 B.C. that Cicero first came across the 'esoteric' writings of Aristotle, whom he described as 'a river of golden prose', and he wrote in his dialogue *Hortensius*: 'You have to have your mind at full stretch when reading and interpreting Aristotle.' See Düring, *Ὁ Ἀριστοτέλης: Παρουσίαση* I 96.

75. On the circulation of Aristotle's works in Rome see P. Moraux, *Der Aristotelismus bei den Griechen von Andronikos bis Alexander von Aphrodisias*, IV: *Die Renaissance des Aristotelismus im 1. Jhr. v. Chr.*, Berlin/New York 1973. Strabo visited Rome in about 40 B.C. and attended Tyrannio's lectures with Andronicus

58. Sophocles. Engraving, 17th or 18th c.

and his assistant Boethus.

76. Cicero, *Sulla* 54; Plutarch, *Cicero* XXVII.3.

77. Loeb Classical Library, *Lucian*, vol. III pp. 173-211.

78. Writing tablets served as notebooks or exercise books, being used by students for note-taking at lectures and by younger children for exercises in reading, writing and calligraphy, and they were also the usual medium for short letters and notes, public

59. Herodotus. Engraving, 18th c.

> *Both among the Greeks and among ourselves, the word 'bibliotheca' is used to mean either a large number of books or the place where those books are kept.*
>
> Sextus Pompeius Festus

It is clear from the excavated library on the acropolis of Pergamum that even in the Hellenistic period the Greeks usually kept their libraries in modest-sized premises of no particular distinction, with nothing much in the way of decoration and no character of their own, which were designed solely for the practical purpose of keeping papyrus books safe and in good condition. We may assume that the libraries maintained by the philosophy schools for study purposes were within easy reach of the lecture halls and reading rooms and were either situated in a separate building or else opened on to the courtyard of the main building or some other inner courtyard. Even though Aristotle's Lyceum is known to have had a well-stocked library, there is no mention anywhere of a special room where the books were kept.[91] The only descriptions we have of the facilities of the Lyceum refer to the altar, the shrine of the Muses and the classrooms, which were used not only for classes and lectures but also for symposia (one inventory even lists their crockery).

It is my belief that both private and public libraries, at any rate in the Classical period, were modelled on the architectural forms and fashions prevailing in the rooms used for similar purposes in earlier periods, that is to say in archival libraries. In the absence of firm evidence on the subject, it seems most likely that Classical Greek libraries followed the Eastern tradition, with different storage and classification systems in use according to the type of material and the ingenuity of the architect. Wall recesses of various sizes with wooden or marble shelving, as well as shelves supported on bronze brackets along the walls, would be just what was needed for the orderly storage of papyrus rolls.[92]

According to Cicero (*Epist. ad familiares* X. 3, 25, 27), Demosthenes was one who agreed with this idea of what a library is for and what the 'feel' of it should be. Unlike the scholars and men of letters of the Roman period, Demosthenes thought the ideal environment for reading, thinking and writing was a secluded room, if possible with no windows and no natural light, where there was nothing visible or audible to distract him.[93] There, working by lamplight, usually in the tranquillity of the night, he found the peace of mind and inner strength he needed to write his speeches. No doubt this utterly impersonal room was the place where he kept his books.

As far as I know, the earliest reference to a bookcase in the Classical period occurs in an account of the sale of Alcibiades's personal possessions in 415 B.C. One of the lots for sale was 'a chest with two and four doors', presumably a wooden cupboard in which Alcibiades kept his papyrus rolls.[94]

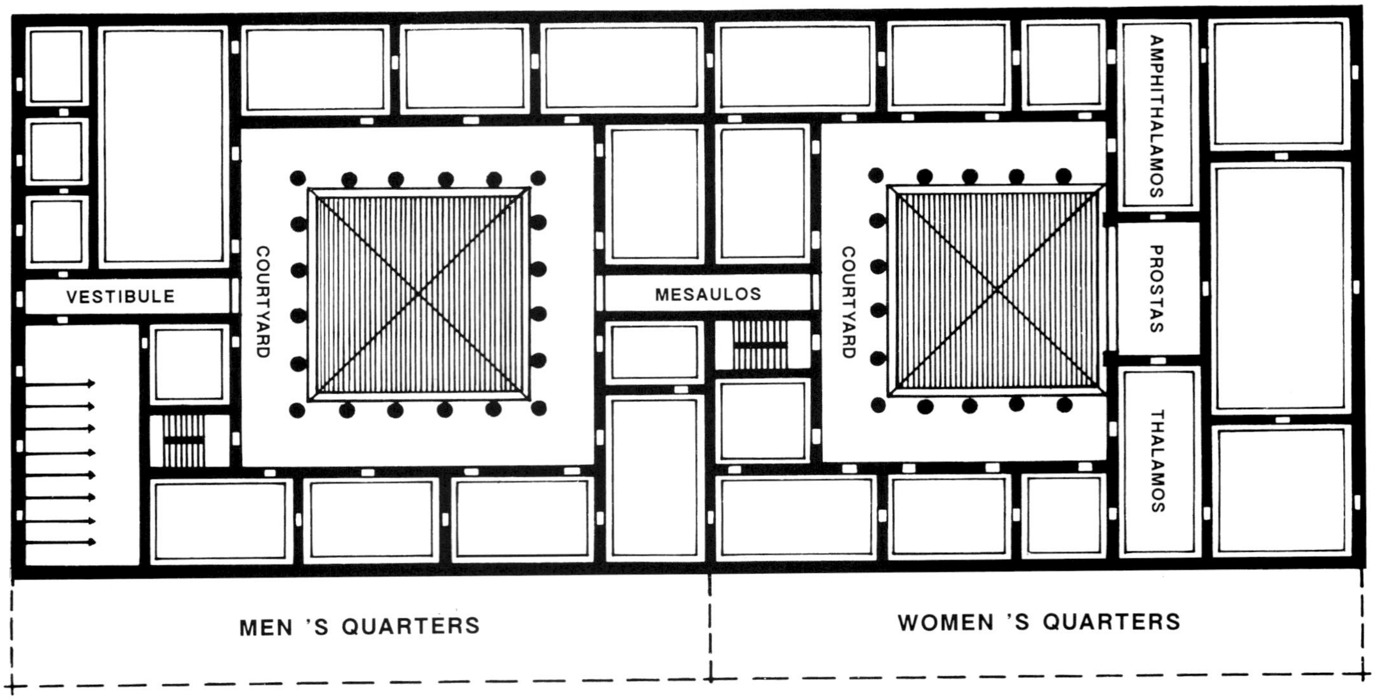

60. Plan drawn by W.A. Becker from Vitruvius's description of a Greek house. Thalamos: matrimonial bedchamber. Prostas: antechamber. Amphithalamos: women's sitting-room? Mesaulos: corridor between men's and women's quarters.

records and perhaps wills: see Turner, *Athenian Books* 12-15.

79. Turner, *Athenian Books* 10.

80. Euripides, *Iphigenia among the Tauri* 727. See Blanck, *op. cit.* 67 ff.; G. Cavallo, 'Le tavolette come supporto della scrittura: qualche testimonianza indiretta', *Bibliologia,* XII, Turnhout 1992, 97-105.

81. The bibliography on this subject is very extensive, but I should like to single out for special mention the attractive theory regarding the identification of three clerks put forward by Ismini Triandi in her paper *«Παρατηρήσεις σέ δύο ὁμάδες γλυπτῶν τοῦ τέλους τοῦ 6ου αἰώνα ἀπό τήν 'Ακρόπολη»* in W. Coulson et al. (ed.), *The Archaeology of Athens and Attica under Democracy*, Oxbow Monograph 37, 1994, 83-91.

82. Diogenes Laertius, III.37.

83. Diogenes Laertius, VIII.81.

84. Aeschylus, *Prometheus Bound* 789; Sophocles, *Triptolemus*, fr. 540 N^2.

85. S. Marinatos, 'Some general notes on the Minoan Written Documents', *Minos* 1 (1951) 40; M. Pope, *BSA* 55 (1960) 201. Finds from the excavations at Tell el-Dab'a suggest that the Egyptians were probably in contact with the Minoan world from the early years of the Thirteenth Dynasty (about the first half of the 18th c. B.C.): cf. M. Bietak, 'Connections between Egypt and the Minoan World: New results from Tell el-Dab'a/ Avaris' in *Egypt, the Aegean and the Levant: Interconnections in the second millennium B.C.*, London 1995, 19-28.

86. Cicero, *Epistulae ad Atticum* IV.4a. See also Kenyon, *op. cit.* 38-74; Blanck, *op. cit.* 104-113.

87. See Turner, *Athenian Books* 13; R.R. Johnson, *The Role of Parchment in Greco-Roman Antiquity* (dissertation), Los Angeles/Ann Arbor 1988.

88. Ctesias says that the Persians used 'royal skins' *(βασιλικαί διφθέραι)* for their historical records, and his statement has been confirmed by the discovery of the archives of the satrap Arsames (5th c. B.C.) written on treated skins: see G.R. Driver, *Aramaic Documents of the Fifth Century B.C.*, Oxford 1954.

89. Euripides, fr. 627: see A. Nauck, *Tragicorum Graecorum Fragmenta*, Leipzig 1889.

90. Alexis, *Linus* 135.

91. See H. Jackson, 'Aristotle's Lecture-room and Lectures', *Journal of Philology* 35 (1920) 191-200.

92. On the evolution of the storage systems used for books from the earliest times, see C. Wendel, *Kleine Schriften zum antiken Buch- und Bibliothekswesen*, ed. W. Krieg, Köln 1974, 64 ff.

93. Vitruvius (VI.7.1-5), describing a Greek house, puts the library near the so-called 'Rhodian courtyard', which was adjacent to the dining-room and the 'picture gallery'. See W. Schubart, *Das Buch bei den Griechen und Römern*, Heidelberg 1962; Blanck, *op. cit.* 55 ff.

94. See E.G. Bude, *Armarium und Κιβωτός*, Berlin 1939.

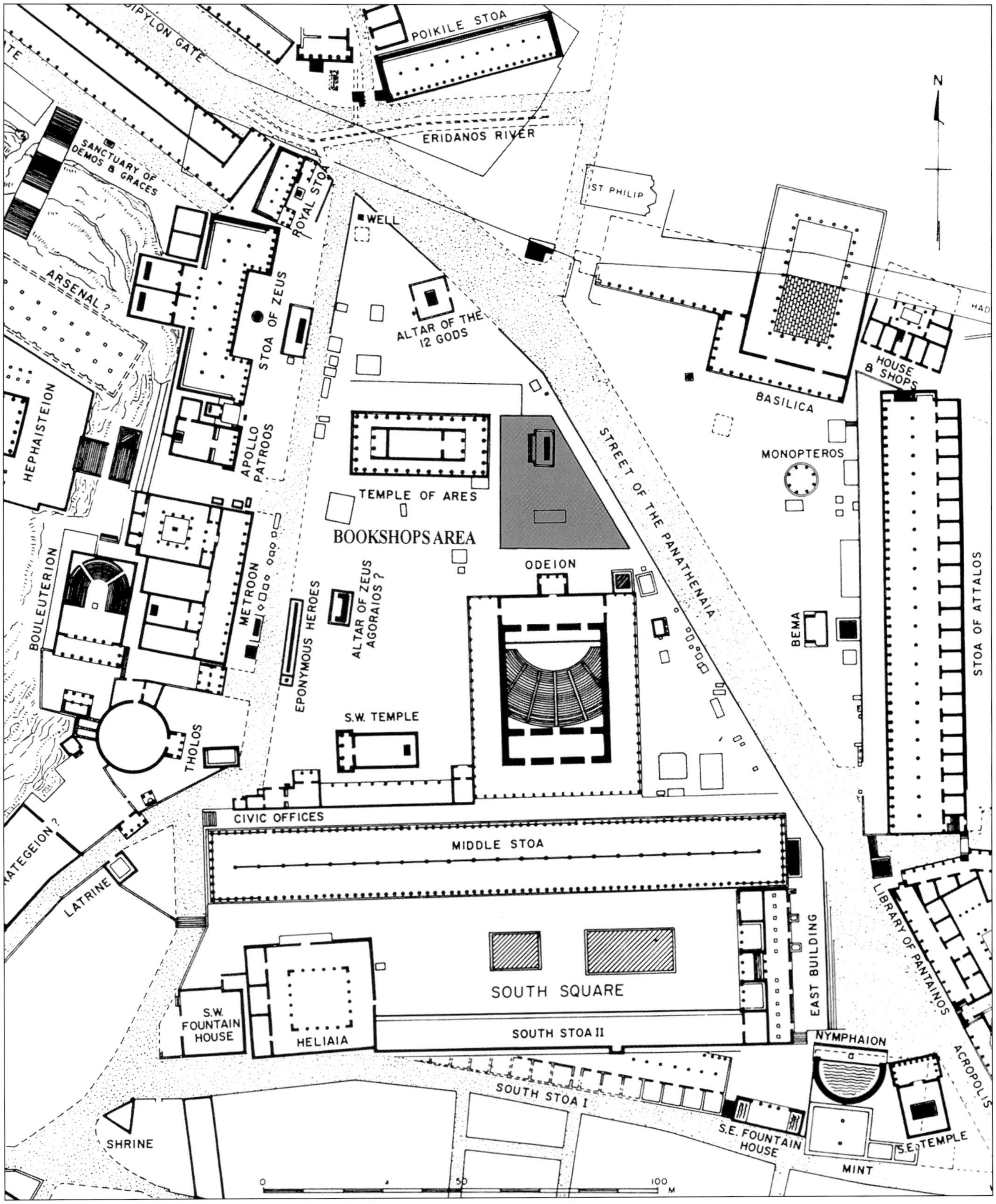

61. Plan of the Athens Agora in the 2nd c. A.D. *From J.M. Camp,* The Athenian Agora, *London 1986.*

62. Imaginary reconstruction of the Museum, from the title page of Meibonius, Diogenes Laertius, *Amsterdam 1698.*

CHAPTER FOUR

THE HELLENISTIC PERIOD

THE GREAT LIBRARY OF ALEXANDRIA

The foundation of the Great Library at Alexandria was a natural consequence of the enormous growth of book production and the book trade, in which Athens had taken the lead from the fifth century B.C. onwards. At the mention of the Hellenistic period the first thing that comes into most people's minds is the Alexandrian Library, a symbol of the Greeks' intellectual supremacy in the then known world and a unifying factor that helped to bind the Greeks together in a sort of commonwealth of independent states. Curiously enough, although the project was so grandiose both in conception and in execution, the Alexandrian Library was never run as a public library, as one might have expected: its status was peculiar to itself and its users belonged to an exclusive élite. There were three main reasons that led to its accumulating such an astonishing number of books: the opening-up of relations between the Greek world and the East, the introduction of the new literary discipline of textual criticism and the love of books displayed most particularly by the first kings of the Ptolemaic dynasty.

On the untimely death of Alexander the Great in 323 B.C., just a year before the death of his teacher Aristotle, many Greeks gradually awoke to the awesome truth that the supremacy of Hellenism now extended almost to the furthest limits of the known world. Brought up on the idea of the Classical Greek city-state, and firmly believing that everything should be adapted to the human scale, they found the vastnesses of the East quite bewildering to contemplate. The familiar old order – the 'unity' of the Greek world, the Greek way of life – was rapidly falling apart. Fortunately the struggle for supremacy among the *diadochi* (the successors of Alexander the Great) did not have catastrophic consequences and did not completely break the underlying cohesion of the vast Greek empire.[1] However, the establishment of Hellenism in countries with a philosophical approach so very different from that of the Greeks created a new framework for intellectual activity. The Greek literary and philosophical tradition now found itself confronted by a way of thinking, particularly prevalent in Babylonia, Judaea and Egypt, in which mysticism and often symbolism featured largely, in contrast to the lucid and incisive thinking of the Greeks.[2] To ensure untroubled continuity in the everyday life of such a mixture of races it was essential for the Greeks to show a measure of understanding and respect for the literary traditions of the Near Eastern peoples, and the creation of a 'world library' seemed an obvious course of action.

It was on the linguistic level that the contact between the Greeks and the indigenous peoples worked most fruitfully, for the Greek language spread to all parts of the Near East and soon established itself as the region's lingua franca. Moreover, the Ptolemies not only despised the Egyptian language (Plutarch, *Antony* XXVII.5) but refused to use their own Macedonian dialect and made a policy of promoting the 'pure' strain of Greek. One consequence of this Hellenizing policy was that large cultural centres were built around huge libraries. Another was that

1. On the history of the struggle between the *diadochi* I have consulted the pioneering work by J.G. Droysen, *Ἱστορία τῶν Διαδόχων τοῦ Μεγάλου Ἀλεξάνδρου*, tr. and annotated by R.I. Apostolidis, 2 vols., Athens 1992 (a new edition updated by I.R. and S.R. Apostolidis to include the latest findings of historical, archaeological and literary research). On the historical background to the Hellenistic period and the transition from the fourth to the third century, see M. Rostovtzeff, *Social and Economic History of the Hellenistic World*, Oxford 1941.

63. Alexander the Great. Engraving by J. Chapman.

2. J.G. Herder, in the eighteenth century, was one of the first to draw attention to the influence of Oriental epic poetry and philosophy on Greek thought. Since then the decipherment of the great Sumerian, Egyptian and Babylonian epics and theogonies has cast light on many of the probable points of contact. Martin West has pointed out certain elements in He-

a number of major works on the history of the Near Eastern peoples were written in Greek (two cases in point being the histories of Berossus and Manetho) to provide a new historical basis for the Eastern tradition in a widely used and understood language. It was even said that the first move in this direction had been made by Alexander the Great, for there was an old Armenian tradition to the effect that the archives at Nineveh had contained a book starting with the following words (in Greek): 'This book, translated from Chaldaean into Greek on Alexander's orders, tells the true history of our ancestors.' Whether or not this initiative should be seen as a first step towards establishing a world library at Nineveh is not clear.[3] Another story from the same source reflects an attitude directly opposed to this: it is said that when Seleucus I Nicator mounted Xerxes's throne in Babylon the first thing he did was to burn all the books he found there, in all the languages of the world, so that thenceforward time would be reckoned as starting with him. The idea is a monstrous one, and the story is contradicted by another tradition, according to which Seleucus rescued the contents of the first Athenian public library, which Xerxes had carried off in 484.[4]

By the time he died in 322, Aristotle had single-handedly reduced a vast body of human knowledge to order and codified it all, discipline by discipline. By then, too, the sophists and their methods had shaken off the mistrust engendered by the hostility of Socrates and Plato. All in all, it was now high time for the works of the Classical period to be reappraised so as to lay new foundations for the verbal expression of ideas. This new trend first made its appearance in the south-eastern corner of the Greek world and its leading exponents tended to congregate in Alexandria, which the Ptolemies had made their capital in 320. Literary studies, which drew on the traditions of the Ionian and Attic Greeks, found in Alexandria ideal conditions for their further development as a new academic discipline. Before long this new branch of learning, with its emphasis on criticism, had added greatly to the already large body of Classical literature, and these commentaries in turn gave rise to a second generation of critical writings. Then again, literary scholars who set out to reappraise the written tradition found that they needed new and accurate texts of the works of Greek literature, and so the number of books required to enable the world library to serve its intended purpose swelled to a total far beyond all expectations.

Ptolemy I Soter. The first of the Ptolemies, known as Soter, respected and espoused the ideals of Alexander the Great and was well aware of the part played by Aristotle in forming the character of the great Macedonian conqueror. These may have been the main reasons why he decided to make his kingdom the intellectual and cultural centre of the 'Greek empire' and, in the process, to implement Alexander's decision to found a world library. The Museum, the Alexandrian Library, the

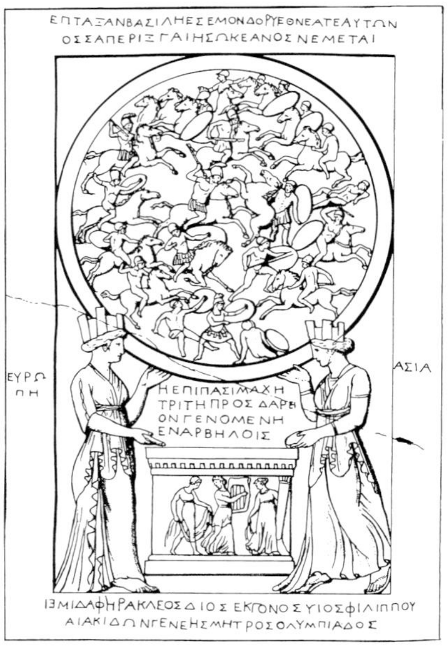

64. Drawing of a relief of the battle of Abdera, from Examen critique des anciens historiens d'Alexandre le Grand, *Paris 1804, 768-769.*

siod's work that appear to be drawn from the Sumerian 'Moral Precepts' of Shuruppak, the Egyptian 'Moral Precepts' and the Babylonian 'Counsels of Wisdom', which would place Hesiod in this current of Oriental literature: see M.L. West, *Hesiod: Theogony*, Oxford 1966, 74; Id., *Hesiod: Works and Days*, Oxford 1978, 172-177. It is thought that experts from the Near East may have helped the Alexandrians to classify works of literature by introducing them to the 'Babylonian methods': see G. Zuntz, *The Text of the Epistles: Corpus Paulinum*, London 1953, 270 ff.

3. The background to this tradition is that round about 150 B.C. a certain Chaldaean named Mar Abas Katina was said to have gone to Nineveh on a mission for the first Armenian king, Valascase, to look through the archives there for material relating to the history of the Armenians. Mar Abas gleaned all the information he could about the ancient history of the Armenians and wrote it up using Greek and Syriac characters. See F. Macler, 'Extraits de la Chronique de Maribas Kaldoyo', *Journal Asiatique*, May-June 1903, 492 ff.

library of the Serapeum, the attempt to transfer the Peripatetic school to Alexandria and Ptolemy's policy of attracting the most prominent scholars and artists to his capital established a tradition which was followed, sometimes with enthusiasm and sometimes half-heartedly, by all subsequent kings of Egypt down to Cleopatra in the first century B.C.

The sources, the evidence and the various theories put forward concerning the establishment, growth and final destruction of the Alexandrian Library are confusing, contradictory and often (especially with regard to its destruction) verging on the realm of myth. The only possible approach to the subject is to identify all those in any way concerned in its foundation, to follow the progress of the Greek literary scholars who first put it into working order, to trace the course of its growth and, of

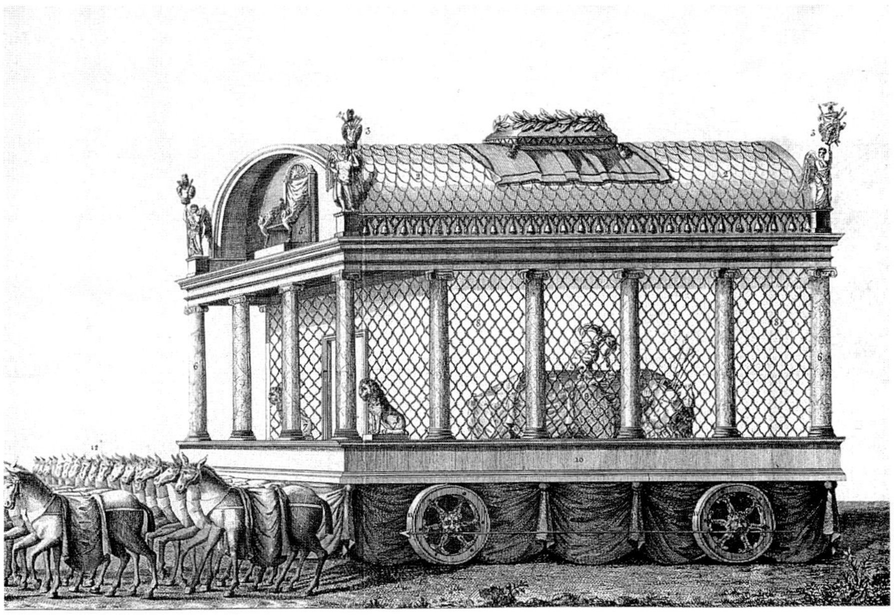

65. Reconstruction of the chariot carrying the bier of Alexander the Great. From Examen Critique des Anciens Historiends d'Alexandre-le-Grand, *Paris 1804.*

course, to inquire into the ultimate fate of its books. The first point that has to be made is that the Library was an integral part of the Museum. The principal sources for the foundation and initial organization of both these institutions are: a 'letter' written *circa* 160 B.C. by a man calling himself Aristeas; Strabo, who visited the Museum in the first century B.C.; Galen (second century A.D.), who relates all sorts of facts about the members of the Museum and the philosophy underlying the enlargement of the Library; the *Prolegomena to Aristophanes* by Ioannes Tzetzes (who wrote it in the twelfth century A.D. but may have obtained some of his facts from the tradition derived from Aristeas's letter, with only minor variations); and the *Lives* of the various directors of the Library. Let us start with the Museum, of which the earliest extant description is Strabo's.

That Alexander wanted his empire to be truly multi-cultural we know from his general Ptolemy (the future King Ptolemy I), who was present at the great reconciliation conference that Alexander called at Opis on the Tigris after the mutiny of the Macedonian troops had been put down. At that public banquet, which Arrian says was attended by a total of 9,000 Greeks and Persians (the term 'Persians' being used to mean Asians generally) who wished to offer sacrifices to the gods together, Alexander made a speech appealing for concord and unity between the Macedonians and the Persians, whom he called upon to live together as subjects of a multinational commonwealth. Arrian records Alexander's speech as it had come down to him from Ptolemy, and the same episode is recounted in different words by Plutarch (*On the Fortune or the Virtue of Alexander*) and Strabo, both of whom followed the account given by Eratosthenes of Cyrene, the scholarly director of the Library.

4. Macler, *op. cit.* 533. It is interesting to note that a similar story is told of a king in China, Si Huang Ti of the Ch'in dynasty, who united the Six Kingdoms under his rule. This first Emperor of China, in the period when the Great Wall was being built, is said to have given orders that all books written before his time were to be burnt. The event is dated to 245 B.C., that is to say during the reign of King Attalus I of Pergamum. See J. Delorme, *Παγκόσμια Χρονολογική Ἱστορία* (= *Chronologie des civilisations*, tr. and ed. K. Dokou et al.), I, Athens 1989, 130. A fuller account is given by J.L. Borges in *Διερευνήσεις* (= *Otras inquisiciones*, tr. A. Kyriakidis), Athens 1990, 11-114 (= *«Τό Τεῖχος καί τά Βιβλία»*). Borges took the story from Pope's *Dunciad*.

5. In the last years of his reign Ptolemy I started taking an interest in history and wrote the most reliable and circumstantial account of Alexander's exploits. Unfortunately only fragments of his narrative survive, and those only in the work of Arrian, who says little or nothing about the cultural

66. *From Gisela Richter,* Portraits of the Greeks, *2.*

1. The foundation of the Museum. The Museum and the Library were founded by Ptolemy Soter († 283 B.C.), a son of Lagus and Arsinoe who was said to have had some kind of connection with the Macedonian royal family, which may mean that he was an illegitimate son of Philip II. On Alexander's death Ptolemy transported his mortal remains to Alexandria and had a mausoleum built in his honour.[5] In the struggle between Alexander's would-be successors Ptolemy showed great circumspection and diplomatic acumen. He strengthened his own kingdom by acquiring a number of small territories of strategic importance, including Cyrene, Cos and Cyprus,[6] and he kept out of the fighting among his rivals, notably Perdiccas and Antigonus, each of whom hoped to emerge as sole inheritor of the whole of Alexander's empire.

This wise man, a general, diplomat and peacemaker, made it his aim to establish Alexandria as the cultural centre of the Greek world[7] and decided that it would be necessary to have at least one of Aristotle's pupils in residence there. Theophrastus refused to leave Athens, while Strato of Lampsacus stayed only a short time in Egypt before returning to take over from Theophrastus as head of the Peripatetic school.[8] By a stroke of good fortune, when Aristotle's pupil Demetrius of Phalerum fled from Athens he eventually sought asylum in Alexandria and settled down to live there (from 297) as a political refugee: he is widely regarded as the man who actually conceived the idea of founding the Museum and

aspirations that were so dear to Alexander's heart. See *FGrHist* 138, with notes by Jacoby (1930); see also H. Strasburger, *Ptolemaios und Alexander*, Leipzig 1934.

6. These new possessions of Ptolemy's, together with Samos (which Ptolemy II acquired in 280), were of more than merely military significance: their great cultural traditions did much to give Alexandria the universal status the Ptolemies wanted for it, at least on the cultural plane. Samos had been the centre of an influential circle of poets as early as the middle of the sixth century, when the great Polycrates was the island's ruler. Cos, where Ptolemy Philadelphus was born, was well known for its medical school and was also the birthplace of Philetas, a pioneer of literary studies, while Cyrene was the native country of Callimachus and Eratosthenes. Cyrene, Cyprus and Rhodes, which between them supplied Alexandria with some of its most prominent literary scholars, retained their political autonomy and served as places of refuge when the world of literary scholarship was shaken by its first crisis in 145 B.C.

7. There is no direct evidence of Ptolemy's ambitions for Alexandria as a centre of scholarship and culture, unless we count a passage in which Strabo compares the educational and philosophical institutions of Ptolemy's capital with those of Tarsus and other cities and notes that the people of

67. Demetrius of Phalerum, drawn from a bust (Florence).

was chiefly responsible for collecting the books that formed the nucleus of the Alexandrian Library, although this view is not corroborated by any authoritative evidence.[9]

Demetrius of Phalerum. Demetrius of Phalerum, a polymath with an incisive intellect and a genuine love of literature, was a strong believer in the importance of encouraging book-reading in any organized society. His father was a slave in Conon's household named Phanostratus, but he managed to rise above his lowly origins and ensure that they did not hamper his career.[10] He became a close friend of Theophrastus's and reached a high level of attainment in rhetoric and philosophy, according to Cicero. He made his appearance on the political scene in 325 B.C., by which time Attic orators had lost their ascendancy, and consequently he quickly won the fame he longed for. In politics he was something of an adventurer and fickle in his loyalties, for at the drop of a hat he switched from the anti-Macedonian democratic party and became a leader of the oligarchic faction. In this capacity he won favour with Cassander, the ruler of Macedonia, and governed Athens as his viceroy for ten years from 317. Cicero notes that his enlightened rule won him a large following in the city: his devotion to the ideals of the Peripatetic school and the innovations he introduced into the educational system made him extremely popular. He also breathed new vigour into the theatre, which had been in the doldrums because the state was no longer able to subsidize costly productions, and this was another reason why the Athenians idolized him. But the atmosphere of prosperity and well-being was rudely shattered in 307, when Demetrius Poliorcetes sailed into Piraeus harbour with his fleet and roused the Athenian democrats to rebellion, forcing the viceroy to flee to escape the death penalty.

Demetrius of Phalerum finally found asylum in Alexandria. It is beyond question that he was accepted into Ptolemy's innermost circle and quite possible that he too, like Strato, provided a link between the Lyceum in Athens and the Museum in Alexandria; but, important though his contribution to the Museum and the Library may have been, no reliable source tells us what he actually did. Neither of the two references to the work he put into the organization of the Library – the Letter of Aristeas and the *Prolegomena to Aristophanes* by the Byzantine scholar Ioannes Tzetzes – can be considered authoritative. We shall be returning to the subject of the traditional story of the foundation of the Library derived from Aristeas's letter, but first something must be said about the way the Museum worked, as compared with other educational institutions of a similar kind.

The Museum. The idea of opening a cultural centre to serve the Muses did not originate with Ptolemy I, for several similar centres existed in the Greek world, some of them with roots going back to Pythagoras and his

Alexandria did not leave their city to go and study elsewhere, whereas outsiders flocked to their city to complete their education there (Strabo, 673.4).

8. Diogenes Laertius, v.58, who also mentions that Ptolemy I's son (the future king Ptolemy II Philadelphus) paid Strato eighty talents for tutoring members of the royal family. After Theophrastus's death the atmosphere at the Peripatetic school changed considerably under Strato. Strabo thought its decline was due to the loss or disappearance of Aristotle's lecture notes and Theophrastus's books. This may not be the whole truth of the matter (and of course we have to remember that Strabo was writing two centuries after the event), but it is a fact that Strato, who was Ptolemy Philadelphus's tutor and acted as a link between the Athenian school and the Museum of Alexandria after his return to Athens, did find that the shortage of suitable textbooks severely hampered his efforts to keep the school's teaching standards up to the level maintained by Theophrastus. Strato was head of the school for eighteen years, from 286 to 268, and in his will he left his own books to Lycon, whom he named as his successor. Lycon was keen to broaden the school's curriculum, but in all the forty-four years that he was its principal he failed to revitalize Aristotelian studies. In his will he stipulated that after his death the school was to be run by a group of his friends (Amphion, another Lycon, Lycomachus and others), whom he exhorted to work together in harmony. The library started by Aristotle at the Lyceum is last heard of in connection with the will of the elder Lycon, who left all his published works to his namesake and his unpublished writings to Callinus, with instructions to edit and publish them. See F. Wehrli, *Die Schule des Aristoteles*, V, Basel 1950 (on Strato) and 1952 (on Lycon).

9. The source of this story is the Letter of Aristeas (see pp. 64-65), which states that Demetrius was still involved in the Library's affairs in the reign of Ptolemy Philadelphus, although he is known to have backed

circle.[11] The most highly-developed example was the *mouseion* in Aristotle's Lyceum in the form in which it existed under Theophrastus, that is to say a centre of specialized teaching and research equipped with lecture rooms and a library as well as courtyards, colonnaded galleries, garden walks and numerous statues of gods and mortals, and with the sanctuary and altar at the centre. Diogenes Laertius quotes a passage from Theophrastus's will which hints at its appearance: 'I should like the money entrusted to Hipparchus to be used as follows. First, work on the *mouseion* and the statues of the goddesses is to be completed, and anything else necessary for their embellishment is to be done. Secondly, the bust of Aristotle and the other votive offerings that used to be in the sanctuary are to be re-erected. The small stoa adjoining the *mouseion* is to be rebuilt, at least as handsomely as it was before, and the tablets with the maps of the world are to be replaced in the lower stoa. Lastly, the altar is to be repaired and made as beautiful and elegant as possible.'[12]

One reason why Ptolemy I wanted Theophrastus to come to Alexandria to run the Museum, and probably to set it going in the first place, was that he had been Aristotle's favourite pupil and was in a sense the continuator of his work, and would therefore confer enormous prestige on the new institution. A more important factor, however, was that the Peripatetic school had about two thousand students and auditors, and Ptolemy hoped that the whole school would move to Alexandria. His ambition was to establish a Panhellenic centre of education and scholarship, and with that object in view he invited eminent scholars from all over the Greek world: Strato from Athens, Philetas from Cos, Zenodotus from Ephesus and perhaps Demetrius of Phalerum, to name only a few. Demetrius of Phalerum, who had settled in Alexandria in 297, was well acquainted with the organization of the Peripatetic school and all that it involved. During his term as Cassander's viceroy in Athens he had helped the school to obtain legal recognition and Theophrastus to acquire some land of his own[13] (since resident aliens were normally forbidden to own land in Attica).

Unfortunately the historical sources for Ptolemy I's reign, such as Hecataeus of Abdera[14] and Manetho,[15] make only passing references to the Museum, while Herondas,[16] who does include the Museum among the sights of Alexandria, adds nothing to our knowledge of it. The only extant first-hand description of the Museum is that of Strabo, who visited Alexandria and studied in the library there in the first century B.C.[17]

The Museum was an institute of learning. The religious aspect of its character, attested by the fact that it was presided over by a priest appointed by the Ptolemies, may have been a survival from ancient Egyptian tradition.[18] The Museum, a splendid edifice in the palace grounds with colonnades and paved walks connecting it to the palace, appears to have been at the centre of a complex that also contained all sorts of auxiliary buildings such as boarding-houses for the staff and

Philadelphus's half-brother to succeed Ptolemy I and therefore incurred the enmity of the new king, which led to his death not long after Philadelphus's accession.

10. On Demetrius of Phalerum see E. Martini in *RE* 4 (1901) 2817-2841; E. Bayer, 'Demetrius Phalereus', *Tübinger Beiträge zur Altertumswissenschaft* 36 (1942) 105 ff.; F. Wehrli in *RE* suppl. 11 (1968) 514-522.

11. The term *mouseion* or *museum* was applied to a number of centres serving a variety of purposes. Some were shrines erected in memory of well-known poets, usually in their

68. Ptolemy I Soter.

birthplaces, like the *mouseion* in Homer's honour at Smyrna or the heroön of Archilochus on Paros (see N.M. Condoleon, «Ἀρχίλοχος καί Πάρος», *Ἐπετηρίς τῆς Ἑταιρείας Κυκλαδικῶν Μελετῶν* 5 (1965) 53-103); some were associated with burials, like the *mouseion* in honour of Andragoras (see C. Boyancé, 'Le culte des Muses chez les philosophes grecs', *Bibliothèque des Écoles Françaises d'Athènes et de Rome* 141 (1937) 329 ff.); and some were educational centres, the most obvious examples being the Peripatetic school and the *mouseion* at Stagira. In comparison with these last there was nothing new about the Alexandria Museum in conception, but only

students, as well as the 'exedra' (here a sort of amphitheatre) mentioned by Strabo.

The members of this unusual self-contained community received various privileges and substantial grants and amenities to enable them to concentrate on their work of serving the Muses without worrying about the necessities of everyday life. They were given free board and lodging, tax exemptions, high salaries and enough domestic servants to look after their needs.[19] Their extraordinarily privileged treatment provoked a good deal of comment all over the Greek world, and they often came in for scathing criticism and sarcastic gibes directed not only at their soft and easy lives but also at the poor quality of their work. Timon of Phlius (*c.* 320-230 B.C.), a Sceptic philosopher and pupil of Pyrrho, called the Museum 'the Muses' birdcage' and likened its philosophers to exotic birds; and he cast aspersions on the quality of Zenodotus's editorial work by advising Aratus of Soli, the author of a poem entitled *Phenomena*, to 'go back to the old copies of Homer instead of using the newly-corrected versions'.[20] In effect the members of the Museum lived in a gilded prison, because even when they went out of the building they were still in the palace grounds, which they were hardly ever allowed to leave.

Timon's words illustrate the general state of relations between scholars in the 'capital' of the Greek world, and especially between the members of the Museum and other intellectuals, who carried on much the same sort of learned but often heated arguments that so often erupted among Athenian scholars, the only difference being that the polemic of Socrates, Plato and Aristophanes against the sophists had been superseded by invective from the classicists against the adherents of the new-fangled literary studies, especially the scholars of the Museum. On a more specific level, however, although we know that the directors of the Library usually doubled as tutors to members of the royal family, nothing is known about their academic duties in the Museum and Library. For example, there is no evidence as to whether the literary scholars (*philologoi*) had fixed teaching hours, whether they had certain students under their own supervision or whether they gave regular lectures. The only thing that can be said with any certainty is that the bulk of their scholastic and literary work was concerned with arranging, evaluating and classifying the enormous number of books that the Ptolemies had obtained for their world library.

2. The Library. When we talk about the Alexandrian Library in the Ptolemaic period, we should not think of it in isolation from the Museum and the other facilities that supported its bibliographical and literary activities, as the Library was precisely what its name indicates: a place for keeping books.[21] We should also remember that there was another important library, the one attached to the Temple of Serapis (the Serapeum), which was at first directly dependent on the Great Library.

in the matter of its size and organization. There can be no doubt that Aristotle's Lyceum, as developed by Theophrastus, was the original on which it was modelled. On the various activities that went on in the Museum see Boyancé, *op. cit.*; and, more generally, see G. Parthey, *Das alexandrische Museum*, Berlin 1838; E. Müller-Graupa, «Μουσεῖον» in *RE* 16 (1933) 797-821; P.M. Fraser, *Ptolemaic Alexandria*, 3 vols., Oxford 1972, I 305-317.

12. Diogenes Laertius, V.51-57. On Theophrastus's will see U. von Wilamowitz-Moellendorff, *Antigonos von Karystos*, IV, Berlin 1881, 265; O. Regenbogen, 'Theophrastos' in *RE* suppl. 7 (1940) 1354-1562.

13. See Wilamowitz-Moellendorff, *op. cit.* 269.

14. Hecataeus of Abdera went to Egypt following the example of earlier Greek philosophers and historians such as Musaeus, Solon, Pythagoras and his namesake Hecataeus of Miletus. Fragments of a book of his entitled *On the Egyptians* are preserved in the *Bibliotheca* of Diodorus Siculus (I.48.5-49.3). If he wrote descriptions of the Museum and the Alexandrian Library they have perished, but we do have his guide to a Pharaonic 'library', the mausoleum of the great Ramses II, also known as Ozymandyas: 'Three doors lead into a hypostyle hall sixty metres long, which resembles an odeion in its construction. This hall is full of wooden statues of litigants, all looking towards the judge. Then there is an ambulatory lined with all sorts of rooms in which there are representations of the foods that people enjoy most. Along the way there are painted reliefs, one of which shows the king offering gold and silver from the Egyptian mines to the god. An inscription below the relief records the sum that was offered: thirty-two million silver minae. Next you come to the sacred library bearing the inscription *Ψυχῆς Ἰατρεῖον*, and immediately after that are images of all the gods of Egypt, to each of whom the king is offering the appropriate gifts, as if to prove to Osiris and the chthonian deities that he has lived a life of piety and justice to gods and men.' See G. Perrot and

In recounting the history of the Great Library, we have first to decide how much value to attach to Aristeas's letter and the account given by Tzetzes in his *Prolegomena*.

The 'Letter of Aristeas'. Aristeas's letter has to be approached with circumspection and its value assessed from two different angles: in relation to the Library and in relation to the Hellenized cultural tradition of the Jews during the Hellenistic period. The first point to note is that in antiquity this document was not presented as a letter: only later did it take that form. It was probably written between 180 and 145 B.C., perhaps *circa* 160, in the reign of Ptolemy VI Philometor. Its authenticity is disputed, but it is the oldest extant source of information concerning the thinking behind the enlargement of the Library, and all the indications are that the main facts stated in it are not far from the truth. The letter also attests to the first cultural contacts between the Greeks and the Jews and signals the birth of a substantial body of Hellenistic Jewish literature.[22]

Aristeas, who passed himself off of as a Greek at the court of Ptolemy II Philadelphus (285/3-247 B.C.), was a Jew who was perhaps deliberately setting out to glorify the Hellenistic tradition of Jewish literature in order to strengthen the cultural links between Greeks and Jews in Alexandria. According to him, Demetrius of Phalerum had been given *carte blanche* to manage the Library as he saw fit and reported regularly to the king, giving him lists of all new accessions and keeping him informed about the progress of the drive to enlarge the Library. At these meetings Ptolemy and Demetrius had concluded that 500,000 papyri would be needed if the Alexandrian Library were to have copies of all the books in the world. Ptolemy therefore entered into correspondence with all known kings and princes, asking them to send him copies of all the books and documents they had in their libraries and archives.

Ptolemy was particularly interested in acquiring entire libraries. In his reports Demetrius advised the king to extend his book search to the Jewish world: he reminded him of the authoritative standing of Hecataeus of Abdera (the author of *On the Egyptians*, which contained a good deal of information on Jewish history) and suggested that copies of all Jewish books in existence should be in the Library.[23] On one of Ptolemy's visits to the Library Demetrius told him that there were already 200,000 rolls on the shelves and pointed out that if the Library were to acquire works of Jewish literature – the king having by then agreed to the proposal – they would have to be translated into Greek from Hebrew and not (as the received wisdom was at that time) from Syriac.

The letter purports to have been written at the prompting of Aristeas, in such a way as to give the impression that he had been accepted into court circles and had used his contacts there to such good effect that he now had a say in the affairs of the Library.

According to Aristeas, the Pentateuch came to be translated by the Seventy in token of friendship between the Greeks and the Jews, as Ptolemy Philadelphus had recently freed more than a hundred thousand Jews who had been taken prisoner during his Syrian campaign and were living in exile in Alexandria. In return for this gesture of goodwill and clemency Ptolemy asked Eleazar, the high priest of Jerusalem, to send him a team of Jewish scholars to translate the scriptures. Eleazar gladly complied: Ptolemy made a special journey to Jerusalem to see about it, and the high priest nominated six scholars from each of the twelve tribes of Israel. Ptolemy welcomed the Jewish scholars with the utmost courtesy and entertained them to a banquet where he tested their scholarship by engaging them in penetrating discussions on a wide variety of topics. The Jewish translators were not accommodated in the Museum but in special quarters of their own on the offshore islet of Pharos. Demetrius visited them there regularly, taking his own grammarians along with him to check their work, which they finished in exactly seventy-two days.

When the Library was fully stocked (if the evidence of Aristeas is to be believed) it would have contained all the books in the known world both in their original languages and in Greek translation, or at least in abridged Greek versions, which were entrusted to foreign translators with a good knowledge of Greek.

The *Prolegomena* of Tzetzes. The other reference to Demetrius of Phalerum's role in the development of the Library occurs in the various versions of the *Prolegomena to Aristophanes* by Ioannes Tzetzes,[24] including an anonymous fifteenth-century Latin translation.[25] It is quite likely that Tzetzes got some of his information from the Letter of Aristeas, considering how hugely popular the letter had been in the Early Christian period. Another of his sources may have been a collection of scholia on Dionysius the Thracian.

In connection with the Library, Tzetzes gives us a piece of reliable information about three literary scholars who belonged to the famous group of seven tragedians known as The Pleiad,[26] formed for the purpose of classifying, cataloguing and commenting on the works of the ancient tragedians. Alexander of Pleuron[27] was commissioned to edit the tragedies and satyric dramas for publication, Lycophron of Chalcis[28] was to edit the comedies, and Zenodotus undertook the onerous task of editing Homer and other poets.[29] In his *Prolegomena* Tzetzes goes back to the tradition that Pisistratus conceived the idea of collecting and editing the Homeric epics and engaged four scholars, Onomacritus of Athens, Epicongylus, Zopyrus of Heraclia and Orpheus of Croton, to put it into effect. Demetrius of Phalerum, according to Tzetzes, was commissioned by Ptolemy II [*sic*] to collect copies of all the books in the world, which were to be kept in not one but two libraries in Alexandria. If this information is indeed taken from the Letter of Aristeas, it is the earliest reference to a second library, described as being 'outside the palace' and attached to the Temple of Serapis in the Rhachotis district of Alexandria. This much smaller library, which was open to the public, eventually contained only 42,800 papyrus rolls, whereas the Great Library in the palace grounds had 400,000 'composite' rolls (i.e. rolls containing more than one work each, by the same or different authors) and another 90,000 'unmixed' rolls (each consisting of a single work or part thereof). The information comes from Callimachus, the royal librarian, who had been entrusted with the colossal task of sorting, classifying and indexing the books. When the books, brought from many different countries and written in many different languages, had all been gathered together, Ptolemy had them translated by linguists well qualified in Greek and the other language involved in each case.

The Plautine Scholium. An excerpt from a fifteenth-century Italian humanist's Latin translation of the *Prolegomena* of Tzetzes, which appears in a scholium on Plautus,[30] has nothing new to say about the Library. The anonymous Italian omits all reference to the Jews and the translation of the Septuagint, but he does have the passage about Demetrius of Phalerum helping Ptolemy Philadelphus and the allusion to the second library which first occurs in Tzetzes. Nor is his translation always accurate: Callimachus, for example, is described as a man of the court and royal librarian (*aulicus regius bibliothecarius*).

Before going on to examine the reliable authorities and the known facts about the life and works of the Library's first organizers, let us take a look at the small collection of books attached to the magnificent Temple of Serapis.

The library of the Serapeum. The Great Library of Alexandria stood in the grounds of the palace and was not open to the public, but it was never the Ptolemies' intention that all the knowledge stored in the papyrus rolls should be reserved exclusively for royalty. They therefore founded a smaller library outside the palace grounds, attached to the Temple of Serapis in the Rhachotis district.[31] The existence of this library is known from the *Prolegomena* of Tzetzes and also from the writings of two fourth-century ecclesiastical authors, Epiphanius and Aphthonius, both of whom had been there. Epiphanius[32] states that the Septuagint was kept in the 'first library' and that a smaller library known as the 'subsidiary' (*θυγατρική*) was built later at the Serapeum.[33]

Excavation of the Temple of Serapis has shown that the original sanctuary was built by Ptolemy III Euergetes and not by Ptolemy II Philadelphus, although there may have been a small temple on the site in Philadelphus's time.[34] Aphthonius, who visited the temple in the middle of the fourth century, speaks of 'chambers' (*sekoi*) on either side of the 'stoas' and of 'treasuries' or 'storerooms' (*tameia*) full of books (in other words small book-lined rooms or carrels facing the stoas) accessible to 'those keen to study'.[35] The Serapeum library was probably opened in the reign of Ptolemy VIII Euergetes II and rebuilt in the Roman period, which would mean that Aphthonius's description refers to the Roman building.

It is a reasonable surmise that the Serapeum library was a public library containing copies of literary works in their final edited form and that, whether books were lent out or not, it was intended to serve the needs of scholars and other educated people who were not official scholars of the Museum and did not have access to the Great Library (which, as we shall see, was run as a literary research centre and scriptorium). Be that as it may, we have Aphthonius's word for it that the Serapeum library was still functioning in the fourth century A.D., and his evidence is supported by other Christian writers who refer to it as the place where the Septuagint and works of Biblical exegesis were kept.[36]

The story of the Alexandrian Library as told in the Letter of Aristeas came to be the generally accepted tradition, largely on his authority, while other more reliable sources and historical facts that really did affect what happened to it were consistently ignored by early chroniclers and historians. But let us go back to the beginning and examine the facts and the reliable sources, starting with the lives and works of the directors of the Library.

3. The directors of the Library. The first historical reference to the Library occurs in Strabo, who says that Aristotle advised the kings of Egypt on the formation of a library.[37] However, this can hardly be made to tally with the dates, as Aristotle died only eighteen months after Alexander the Great and before the Ptolemies had won power in Alexandria. So, apart from the Letter of Aristeas and occasional passing references to the Ptolemies' initiative in founding the Library, the clearest picture we have of the way it was run in the Ptolemaic period comes from biographies of the directors of the Library and of Callimachus.[38] One of the Oxyrhynchus papyri (No. 1241), which lists the directors, not only contradicts Aristeas's allegations about the position and contribution of Demetrius of Phalerum but also gives some interesting new information about Callimachus and Apollonius Rhodius.

Although Callimachus of Cyrene is the first name one thinks of in connection with the Library, he was never its director. The first holder of the post, Zenodotus, was succeeded by his pupil Apollonius Rhodius, who was followed by Eratosthenes, Aristophanes of Byzantium, Apollonius Eidographus, Aristarchus and Cydas in that order. Of the grammarians mentioned in the Oxyrhynchus papyrus – Ammonius, Zenodotus, Diocles and Apollodorus – nothing is said to indicate the nature of their connections with the Library.

C. Chipiez, *A History of Art in Ancient Egypt*, tr. W. Armstrong, 2 vols., London 1883, I 379-381; L. Canfora, *'Η Χαμένη Βιβλιοθήκη τῆς 'Αλεξάνδρειας* (= *La biblioteca scomparsa*, Palermo 1986, tr. F. Arvanitis), Athens 1989, 19-27, 156-174.

A word of explanation is needed about the significance of the inscription *Ψυχῆς 'Ιατρεῖον* (literally 'sanatorium of the soul'), which Hecataeus saw in a room that must have contained a statue of Ramses II. The word *ψυχή* (soul) refers to the *ka*, which in Egyptian religion was the life force that kept the souls of the king and a select few others alive after their death (J. Chevalier and A. Gheerbrant, *Dictionnaire des Symboles*, III, Paris 1974, 96; P. Kaplony, 'Ka' in *Lexikon der Aegyptologie*, III, 1980, 276). Therefore the room of the *ka* would have housed the life force of Ramses II, not his books. The phrase *Ψυχῆς 'Ιατρεῖον* was kept alive – but in connection with books – in two of the oldest and most important libraries in Europe, those of the Monastery of St. John on Patmos and the Abbey of St. Gall (see pp. 282, 375).

69. Aristeas. Engraving from Aristeae Historia, *Oxford 1692.*

Zenodotus. Zenodotus, born at Ephesus, was active in the second half of the third century B.C. After studying under Philetas he succeeded his teacher as tutor to the royal family and then became director of the Library with the title of 'Head of the Libraries [*sic*] in Alexandria'.[39] This was the title held by all the directors of the Library, as the term *bibliophylax*, which one would expect to mean 'custodian of the books', and which Tzetzes seems to have used in this sense, meant 'keeper of the government archives' in the Ptolemaic period.[40] According to *Souda* ('Suidas'), Zenodotus, who wrote epic poems himself, was the first Alexandrian scholar to undertake the daunting task of producing a critical edition of Homer, and he also did the same for Hesiod and Pindar.[41] Nothing is known about the work he did for the library. Before passing on to his immediate successor, Apollonius Rhodius, something must be said about the man who is associated with the Library more closely than anyone else: Callimachus.

Callimachus. Callimachus was born at Cyrene shortly before 300 B.C. Though he came from an aristocratic family, he was obliged to earn his living by giving lessons in Alexandria, while continuing his studies at the same time.[42] He was taken on to the staff of the Library with the backing of Ptolemy Philadelphus and worked there from 280 to 245. To him was assigned the difficult job of cataloguing the thousands of papyrus rolls in the Library; and, considering that in addition to his *Pinakes* ('Tables', i.e. catalogues), which eventually took up 120 books, he wrote over eight hundred other works, it is easy to see why he has always had the reputation of being an indefatigable literary scholar.[43]

It is not known whether the books that Callimachus took over from Zenodotus had been catalogued at all, apart from a few specific genres of literature that Zenodotus and his assistants Alexander of Pleuron and Lycophron had undertaken to index. In effect, Callimachus's approach to the problem was to rethink the architectural as well as the literary organization of the Library.

(a) *Arrangement by literary genre.* Quite possibly the 'philosophy' underlying the *Pinakes* was entirely Callimachus's own idea and owed nothing to the cataloguing methods employed by the Peripatetics at the Lyceum in Athens nor to the methods devised by the Babylonians for use in their great collections of archives.[44] Callimachus first made a division according to the main realms of literature (poetry, rhetoric, history, drama and so on). Then, within each of these divisions, he arranged all the authors in alphabetical order, separating the different genres in the work of an individual author which in turn were probably also arranged alphabetically. He also wrote a short biographical note on each author which he prefaced to each entry in his catalogue, to avoid confusion over the many authors of the same name, whom he distinguished by their place

15. Manetho was a Greek historian of the third century B.C., born at Sebennytus in the Nile delta. He was a high priest at Hierapolis and wrote a history of Egypt entitled *Aegyptiaca*, starting in the age of myth and legend and going down to the end of dynastic Egypt. This work, reputedly based on hieroglyphic lists of kings and obscure historical documents, was said by the Byzantine chronicler Georgios Synkellos to have been dedicated to Ptolemy II Philadelphus. Only fragments of it have survived (*FGrHist*, No. 609). Manetho was inspired to write his chronicle by the example of the Chaldaean writer Berossus, who wrote a similar book on the history of the Babylonians and dedicated it to Antiochus I.

16. Herondas or Herodas, who may have been of Dorian extraction, wrote a collection of mimes in the first half of the third century B.C., in which (according to the anthologist Stobaeus) he satirized the situation in Egypt and Ptolemy himself. See P.E. Easterling and B.M.W. Knox, *Ἱστορία τῆς Ἀρχαίας Ἑλληνικῆς Λογοτεχνίας* (= *The Cambridge History of Classical Literature*, I: *Greek Literature*, tr. N. Konomi, Ch. Grimba and M. Konomi), Athens 1994, 801-803, 1042.

17. Strabo, 793-794.

18. Apart from this piece of information about the priest at the top of the hierarchy, implying that there was a religious element in its constitution, Strabo tells us nothing about the way the Museum was organized. See Müller-Graupa, *op. cit.* 808.

19. The Museum had its own treasury and its funds came direct from the royal exchequer. The bursar may have had the title of '*Epistates* (Superintendent) of the Museum', or so it has been suggested on the evidence of a dedicatory inscription on Delos in honour of a certain Chrysermus, a member of a prominent Alexandrian family who is so referred to. His job would have been to collect taxes, make disbursements and monitor expenditure. See Fraser, *op. cit.* I 316. The main evidence for the members' free board and lodging comes from the

of birth. Then, since the title did not always identify the work with sufficient clarity, next to each title he wrote down the first words and the total number of lines in the book. The titles were written on parchment labels (which Cicero calls *sillyboi*) attached to the papyrus rolls, and the 'code numbers' on the labels were entered in the general Library catalogue, which was called the *Pinakes* ('Tables').[45] In this general catalogue the librarians often wrote notes in verse giving brief particulars of the works listed, like a sort of colophon.[46] Callimachus's *Pinakes* have never been surpassed and have served as the basis for all subsequent study and criticism at every level. They were expanded by Zenodotus's successors as director of the Library,[47] starting with Callimachus's pupil Apollonius Rhodius.

(b) ***Architectural layout.*** On the assumption that the main building of the Museum was a magnificent 'temple of the Muses' used mainly for ceremonies, symposia, lectures, discussions and reading, the only conclusion to be drawn is that there were other rooms where the books were classified prior to being allotted to their proper places in the Library. Quite possibly some of the books were kept in cupboards. There must have been an 'admissions room' to which all the newly-acquired papyrus rolls were taken on arrival, either for textual emendation and recension or for copying and translating or for immediate classification and cataloguing. When all this had been done, the librarian – in this case the person responsible for writing up the catalogue – sent them on to the storerooms, having first written their titles on identification labels. The Library was not a single large room, as most scholars believed until the early nineteenth century: it actually consisted of what Galen calls the 'book storerooms' and the *oikoi* (rooms or small buildings). Quite possibly there were separate storerooms or groups of storerooms for the various genres of literature defined by Callimachus, to make it easier for books to be found and also to leave room for future expansion, as no one could ever know how large each section would turn out to be when 'all the books in the world' had eventually been collected.[48]

Apollonius Rhodius. Zenodotus's immediate successor as director of the Library was Apollonius Rhodius, while Callimachus apparently continued to devote himself tirelessly to his work in the library. Apollonius was born in Alexandria between 295 and 290 B.C. and was called Rhodius because he spent most of his life on the island of Rhodes.[49] He is said to have been taught by Callimachus and was the greatest poet of his day, his best-known work being the *Argonautica*, the longest extant post-Homeric epic poem. He must have taken over as director of the Library between 270 and 260, and as holder of that post he tutored the future king Ptolemy III Euergetes (reigned 247-222). The pupil-teacher relationship he enjoyed for a time with Callimachus appears to have been rudely broken by the publication of the *Argonautica*, after which their feelings towards each other are said to have deteriorated into open antagonism. In fact this may have been the main reason for Apollonius's decision to leave Alexandria and settle in Rhodes.

Eratosthenes. Apollonius was succeeded by Eratosthenes, another former pupil of Callimachus who was born at Cyrene in 276 or 273 B.C. and lived to the age of eighty.[50] Before becoming director of the Library he had studied in Athens and may perhaps have attended Zeno's lectures. He was invited to take over the directorship of the Library by Ptolemy III in 246 and remained in the post without a break until the reign of Ptolemy V Epiphanes (204-180), combining his duties as librarian with those of tutor to the royal family. His versatility led him in different directions from Callimachus: he defined the field of study of the literary scholar as distinct from that of the grammarian, and in addition to his literary interests he was perhaps the first practitioner of the exact sciences.

Aristophanes of Byzantium. The appointment of Aristophanes of Byzantium confirmed the tradition whereby the director of the Library was tutor to the royal family and also a pupil of his predecessor: in fact he had studied not only under Apollonius Rhodius but under Callimachus and Zenodotus as well.[51] He was born between 258 and 255 B.C. and became director of the Library on the death of Eratosthenes (between 196 and 193), when Ptolemy V Epiphanes was on the Egyptian throne. He died *circa* 180 B.C.[52]

Aristophanes, who at the dawn of the second century B.C. inherited a great tradition going back to Philetas and Callimachus, produced important work in several fields. By the end of his life he had finished a complete textual recension of the works of the epic and lyric poets and the dramatists. He had an unbounded admiration for Menander, whom he ranked second only to Homer: in a witty reversal of the Peripatetic theory,[53] he often asked whether the comic poet Menander imitated life or life imitated Menander's comedy.

It is worth mentioning two incidents in the life of Aristophanes of Byzantium for the light they shed on the atmosphere prevailing in the Museum. One was quite serious: shortly after 197 Aristophanes was invited by King Eumenes II to go to Pergamum to be in charge of his new library, but as soon as the news of his plans to desert the Museum leaked out he was arrested and imprisoned to prevent his leaving.[54] The other was not so much an incident as a rather bizarre anecdote: it was said that Aristophanes and an elephant were rivals in love, because both of them were enamoured of a certain flower-girl in the city.[55] Preposterous though this sounds, there were apparently a lot of stories circulating in Alexandria about elephants being attracted by the fragrance of the flowers that were made up into wreaths and sold on the streets,[56] and Aristophanes himself tells a similar story in his book *On Animals*. He died at a time when Egypt had just started sinking into a social, economic and political decline.

Apollonius Eidographus. The person who took over the directorship of the Library when it fell vacant in 180 B.C. was Apollonius Eidographus,[57] about whom very little is known. The epithet Eidographus ('the Classifier') may perhaps have been given to him because he classified lyric poems according to the musical mode for which they were written (Dorian, Phrygian or Lydian).[58]

Aristarchus. The last librarian with a literary education was Aristarchus of Samothrace, who was born in 216 B.C. and lived in Alexandria in the reign of Ptolemy VI Philometor (180-145). It is not known when he was officially appointed director of the Library.[59] In accordance with the usual practice he was also tutor to the royal family.

Aristarchus was a popular teacher, and his writings won him a large following among the educated public.[60] He was regarded as an authoritative critic and interpreter of ancient poetry, but he made his biggest contribution to literary studies in the eight hundred or more *Commentaries* (*Ὑπομνήματα*) that he wrote on the works he edited, unlike most other editors who delivered their textual notes orally in the lecture room. In 144 Ptolemy VII was murdered on the orders of his uncle, who ascended the throne as Ptolemy VIII, and all who had been friends of the late king had to flee for their lives. Aristarchus went to Cyprus and is thought to have died there before the year was out.[61] After his departure there was an all-round decline in the standards of scholarship in Alexandria, typified by the appointment of an army officer named Cydas as director of the Library.[62]

After Cydas, the Oxyrhynchus papyrus listing the directors of the Library[63] mentions four grammarians who flourished under Ptolemy IX (Soter II), who reigned from 120 to 80 B.C. (including a period spent in exile). Their names are given as Ammonius, Zenodotus, Diocles and Apollodorus, but it is not clear whether they held any official position in the Library.[64] In any case, the last director of the Library was Onesander the son of Nausicrates. According to an inscription from Cyprus, Onesander backed Ptolemy IX during his exile in Cyprus and, when Ptolemy returned to Alexandria in 88 B.C., he rewarded Onesander by appointing him to be his personal priest and director of the Great Library.[65]

4. The Library's stock of books. As already mentioned, the only information we have about the size of the Library comes from the Letter of Aristeas, the lost sources that Tzetzes drew on for his *Prolegomena* and the *History* of Ammianus Marcellinus (4th c. A.D.). According to Aristeas, in the time of

Demetrius of Phalerum the Library already had 200,000 rolls and was aiming at a final target of 500,000. Tzetzes says that the palace library contained 490,000 rolls, of which 400,000 were 'composite' and 90,000 'unmixed'.[66] Ammianus maintains that the total eventually rose to 700,000 rolls: this is the figure given by Aulus Gellius (2nd c. A.D.) and repeated by Isidore of Seville (7th c. A.D.) and others, but it may have been arrived at by adding together the two totals given in the Letter of Aristeas. Whatever the truth of the matter, there is no doubt that the Library did have a stock of several hundred thousand rolls, and when all the reliable contemporary evidence is evaluated it is reasonable to suggest that the highest figure of all – 700,000 rolls – does not sound excessive and may even be an underestimate.[67]

The bibliomania of the Ptolemies, especially Soter, Philadelphus and Euergetes I, was without precedent in the history of books. Galen, born in A.D. 130 at Pergamum, the home of the library that was Alexandria's great rival, tells a number of stories that were still current in his time. The Ptolemies, he says, were so determined not only to collect as many thousands of manuscripts as possible but also to have nothing but first-class copies (he is probably referring to Euergetes I in particular) that on one occasion they borrowed the official copies of the Attic tragedians from Athens, putting down a deposit of fifteen talents to guarantee their safe return, but instead they chose to lose their deposit and sent back the copies they had made on best-quality parchment, keeping for themselves the historic copies which were probably those made in accordance with Lycurgus's decree of 330 B.C.[68] From then on a market came into being for books for which bibliophiles were willing to pay a premium, not only on account of their contents and their textual authenticity but also because of their origins. This trend became particularly pronounced in the Roman period: Galen tells us of forgers who made big profits by selling all kinds of spurious manuscripts containing adaptations of older books or works that were forgeries from start to finish.[69] Great expertise, a sharp mind and a good deal of time were often needed to unmask these forgeries because the authentic and spurious passages were woven together with great ingenuity, as in the case of the late scholiasts on Aristotle.[70]

Leaving the anecdotes aside, let us try to construct a working hypothesis as to the method of classifying and cataloguing and the running of the scriptorium. We know from reliable sources that the Library directors and their assistants classified the books in three main categories: (a) works of Greek literature, regardless of their place of origin, (b) miscellaneous works such as everyday correspondence, from which much useful information could be gleaned, and (c) books translated into Greek from other languages.

(a) It would seem that one of the first concerns of the organizers of the Library was to devise a method that would make it possible for scholars

Cornell papyrus of *c.* 220 B.C., published by N. Lewis in his paper 'The Non-Scholar Members of the Alexandrian Museum', *Mnemosyne* 16 (1963) 257-261.

20. Timon was well-known in antiquity for his *Silloi* (literally 'squint-eyed verses'), which were three books of poems in hexameters ridiculing all doctrinaire philosophers, including those who were at loggerheads with one another such as the scholars of the Museum: see H. Diels, *Die Fragmente der Vorsokratiker*, ed. W. Kranz, Berlin 1951, fr. 12. His disparaging description of the Museum is preserved by Athenaeus (*Deipnosophistai* I.22a): 'There are many people in populous Egypt who make a livelihood by scribbling on papyri and waging a constant war of words with each other in the Muses' birdcage.' On Timon's advice to Aratus see Diogenes Laertius, IX.113; Wilamowitz-Moellendorff, *op. cit.* 43.

21. The main works on the Alexandrian Library are: C. Wendel, 'Das griechisch-römische Altertum' (completed by W. Göber) in *HBW* III.1 62-82; E.A. Parsons, *The Alexandrian Library, Glory of the Hellenic World*, 3rd edn., New York 1967; Fraser, *op. cit.* I 312-335; Canfora, *op. cit.*; M.

70. Ptolemy I Soter, from an engraving.

El-Abbadi, *The Life and Fate of the Ancient Library of Alexandria*, Paris (UNESCO) 1990.

22. Eusebius, *De Evangelica Praeparatione* VIII.2.1-4. A full reading of Aristeas's 'letter' to his 'brother' Philocrates, who was probably not a real person, makes it clear that the account of the way the Library was organized was not the author's primary purpose in writing. Aristeas, who praises the Ptolemies for their initiative in making the literature and cultural traditions of the Near Eastern peoples better known by having them translated into an international language, Greek, takes the opportunity to discourse on the teachings of the Torah, preparing the ground for a comprehensive survey of the Jewish holy books with the object of making them known to the rest of the world. In the letter under discussion, which sets out the historical background of the links between Jews and Greeks, he discusses the whole question with the utmost diplomacy, first acknowledging the importance of Greek learning and ending with a glowing panegyric to Judaism. The subject is a large and complex one, and Aristeas's treatment of it testifies to the Jews' acceptance of Greek civilization as a powerful force in the world. See the standard work by E. Schürer, *Geschichte des jüdischen Volkes in Zeitalter Jesu Christi (175 B.C. - A.D. 135)*, new English edn. revised by Pamela Vermes, I-III, Edinburgh 1987-1995; V. Tcherikover, *Hellenistic Civilisation and the Jews*, Philadelphia 1959; M. Hengel, *Judaism and Hellenism: Studies in their encounter in Palestine during the Early Hellenistic period*, London 1974.

Given that the 'Letter of Aristeas' was not actually a letter written by one man to his brother, the presumption is that it was published in book form. Furthermore, considering how popular it was in the Christian era, it is fair to assume that it must have been widely read in the author's lifetime too, at least by Jews. If so, the events described by Aristeas cannot be fictitious, as they could easily be checked by the people in charge of the Library. The matters in dispute are two: Demetrius of Pha-

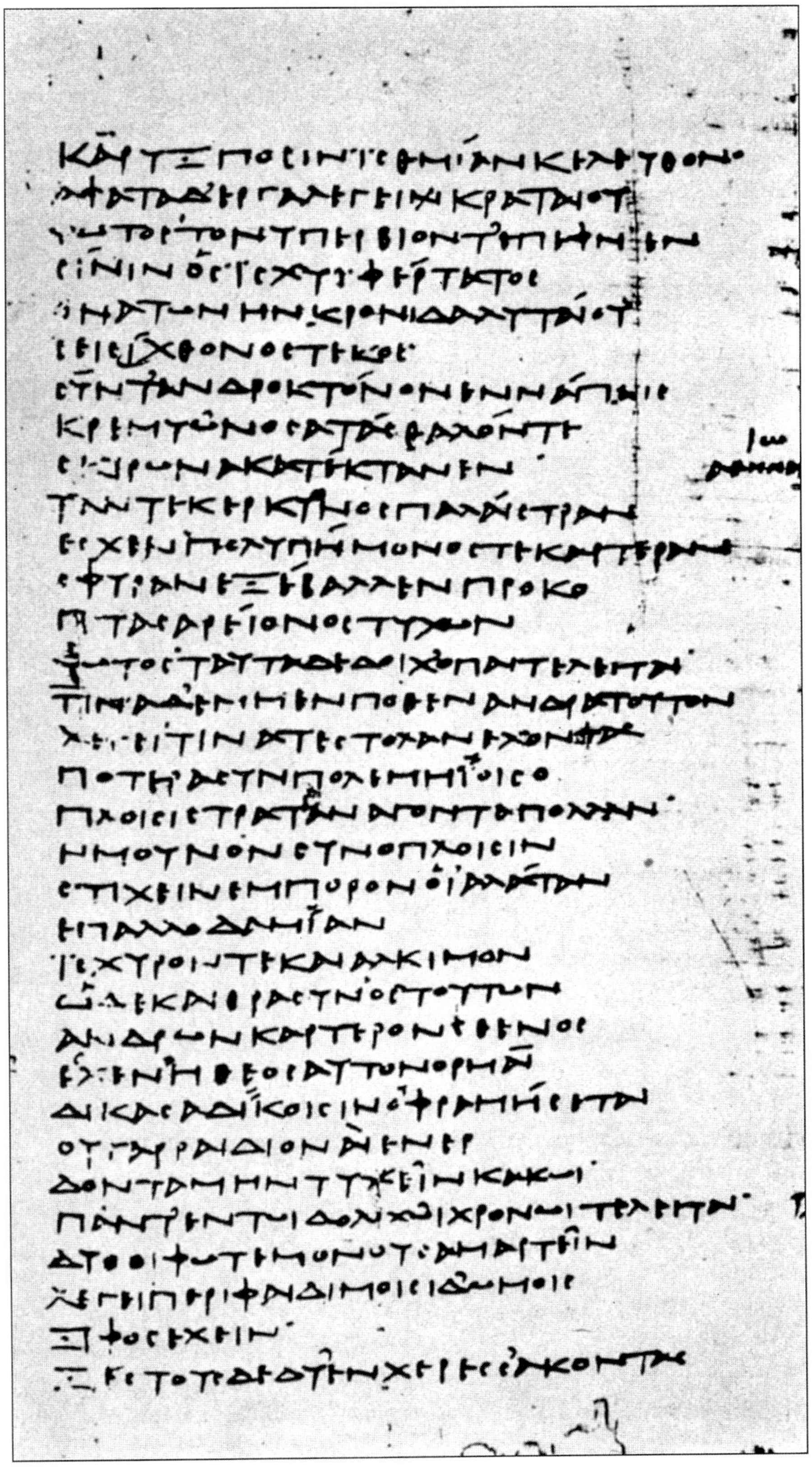

71. Bacchylides, XVIII.17-41. 2nd c. A.D. (Pap. Lond. 733).

to find their way about the vast stock of books and for future readers to consult the sources without too much difficulty. Since the texts often needed wholesale emendation, every copy was useful for historical comparison. About the state of the texts towards the end of the fourth century there can be no doubt: as already mentioned, Lycurgus found them so bad that he had to order new, 'official' copies of the Classical Greek tragedies to be made.[71] In any case, the director of the Library proposed that copies should be classified by city of origin: for example, there were copies of Homer known as the Chian, the Sinopic, the Argive and so on.[72] Another method of classification, 'by person', may have signified that the manuscript had belonged to the person named or been emended by him: thus there were copies labelled 'of Zenodotus' (*Ζηνοδότου* or *Ζηνοδότειος*) or 'emended by Mnemon of Side' (*κατά διοϱθωτήν Μνήμονα Σιδήτην*).[73]

Textual emendation was not the only reason for making new copies. The innovations introduced by Aristophanes of Byzantium in the way of writing Greek, with spaces between words and with accents, diacritics and punctuation marks (such as the obelus), made it necessary for the entire corpus of Greek literature to be written out afresh, in copies that were easier to read as well as being more reliable.[74]

(b) Galen informs us that one of the Ptolemies (perhaps Euergetes I) was so determined to maintain the Alexandrian Library's supremacy over its great rival at Pergamum that he decreed that every ship putting into the port of Alexandria was to be searched by a team of assessors, who were to appraise the worth of all the books they found (it is not clear whether the ruling applied to books in the passengers' baggage as well as those belonging to the shipmaster), confiscate those deemed to be of interest to the Library and give copies of the books to their owners in place of the originals. The 'books from the ships', as they were called, were not taken immediately to the Library proper but were stacked 'in heaps' in rooms set aside for the purpose, presumably to be inspected and evaluated by the Library staff.[75]

Galen's statement raises a number of questions and leaves the whole matter wide open to conjecture. In the first place, we have to accept that there existed a large staff of high-speed copyists who could copy books fast enough to avoid delaying the ships' departure – no easy task, especially as Alexandria was a busy port where more than one ship arrived every day. The purpose of setting aside special rooms for the 'books from the ships' was presumably threefold: to keep the new accessions separate from the rest of the books until they had been inspected and edited, to give time for the 'unmixed' papyrus rolls to be sorted from the 'composite' ones, and to label the books by place of origin (which one might reasonably suppose to have been frequently unspecified). Galen does not say whether the Library was interested only in literary works or whether it kept all kinds of written material in the form of diaries, ships'

lerum's position as official librarian and the statistics relating to the number of books in the Library. Obviously Aristeas was not particularly bothered about specifying Demetrius's precise position, and it may well be that he was commonly believed to have been director of the Library because of his association with Aristotle. About the size of the library there can be no argument, as the figure given by Aristeas is reasonable by the standards of the day. The first edition of the letter published in modern times was that of P. Wendland in *Aristeae ad Philocratem epistula*, Leipzig 1900. Wendland's edition was used as the basis for subsequent translations and commentaries: see, for example, the more recent edition by A. Pelletier in *Sources Chrétiennes* 89 (1962). The first person to challenge the authenticity of the letter was the Spanish humanist Ludovicus Vives in his notes on St. Augustine's *De civitate Dei*, which he edited and published in 1522 together with Erasmus's letter *To the Reader*.

23. See n. 14.

24. The Prolegomena to Tzetzes's *Commentary on Aristophanes* survives in three versions with slight variations between them: see G. Kaibel, 'Die Prolegomena Πεϱί Κωμωδίας', *Abhandlungen der Göttinger Gesellschaft der Wissenschaften*, n.s., 2.4 (1898) 4. See also the exhaustive discussion by C. Wendel, 'Tzetzes' in *RE* 7A$_2$ (1948) 1973 ff.; and the new edition by W.J.W. Kaster, *Scholia in Aristophanem* (in the series 'Prolegomena de Comoedia'), I, Groningen 1960, XX; and H. Hunger, *Βυζαντινή Λογοτεχνία. Ἡ λόγια κοσμική γραμματεία τῶν Βυζαντινῶν* (= *Die höchsprachliche profane Literatur der Byzantiner*, Munich 1978), II, Athens 1992, 446-447.

25. On the unidentified Italian humanist who made this adaptation see n. 30. On the scholia on Dionysius the Thracian see Wendel, 'Tzetzes' 1975-1976.

26. The earliest known use of the name 'Pleiad' in this connection is in Strabo (XIV.675): 'An excellent tragic poet, one of those numbered among the Pleiad.' The name recurs in literary

logs, maps, charts, letters and anything else that might help to expand the Alexandrians' encyclopaedic knowledge and the extensive notes they kept on the sorted books in the various *Pinakes*.

(c) Although there is no firm evidence from the Ptolemaic period that literary and other works of the Middle Eastern peoples were systematically collected and translated, it is quite possible – even quite likely – that such a project existed. The keenness of Ptolemy I and Antiochus I to learn about their subjects' history and culture is clearly apparent from the histories written for them by Manetho (*Aegyptiaca*) and Berossus (*Babyloniaca*) respectively.[76]

Of Manetho, the one who concerns us here, it is said that he compiled his *magnum opus* from sources not normally accessible to historians: papyri kept in temples, official Pharaonic records, literary works and other little-known religious, astrological and mathematical treatises, together constituting an unrivalled treasure-house of information about Egyptian history. In any case, it would have been unthinkable for the inquiring Greek mind to ignore the huge mass of written material stored in Middle Eastern libraries, which had traditionally been sought out and studied by Greek intellectuals visiting Egypt such as Pythagoras, Solon, Herodotus, Plato and many others. This assumption is supported by the evidence of Georgios Synkellos and Tzetzes (in his *Prolegomena*) concerning the summaries of Zoroaster's Persian verses that Hermippus compiled.[77] One incontrovertible fact is the translation of the Septuagint into Greek, an initiative undertaken as part of the project of translating foreign books in the reign of Ptolemy Soter or Philadelphus. Synkellos's statement (516.3) that Eratosthenes translated chronological tables from the Egyptian archives has been strongly disputed, as has the statement of Tzetzes that Latin literature was represented in the Library from as early as the reign of Philadelphus. And although there is no reason to doubt that Latin works were known in Alexandria towards the end of the Ptolemaic period, it would be rash, to say the least, to assume that the same was true in the third century B.C.

If all Greek literature written before the end of the first century B.C. were still extant – and Wilamowitz estimated that only a fifth of Classical literature had survived to modern times – the definition of the ideal size of a 'world library' might not perhaps be as Utopian as it is today. Let us consider some of the questions that arise and, on the strength of our findings, draw some tentative conclusions on the subject.

One work that shows up the paucity of our knowledge of Greek literature up to the time of Jesus Christ is the *Deipnosophistai* of Athenaeus, completed after A.D. 238 in thirty books, of which we have a tenth-century abridgement in fifteen books. In it Athenaeus mentions the names of about 700 authors and more than 1,500 titles of works now lost. It is reasonable to suppose that the number of books referred to in the original would have been considerably greater. What is more, Athenaeus is said

history centuries later to denote the group of French poets that formed round Ronsard in 1563, soon after the foundation of the Collège Royal, which Guillaume Budé dubbed 'the new Museum'.

27. Alexander, a native of Pleuron in Aetolia, worked for Ptolemy Philadelphus and was invited to the Macedonian court, with Aratus of Soli and others, by Antigonus Gonatas (276-240/39 B.C.). He wrote epics, elegiac poems, epigrams, mimes and plays. See R. Pfeiffer, *Ἱστορία τῆς Κλασσικῆς Φιλολογίας. Ἀπό τῶν ἀρχῶν μέχρι τοῦ τέλους τῶν ἑλληνιστικῶν χρόνων* (= *History of Classical Scholarship: From the beginnings to the end of the Hellenistic age,* Oxford 1968, tr. P. Xenos et al.), Athens 1972, 140-141; Easterling and Knox, *op. cit.* 1026.

28. Although Lycophron is known to have written a number of tragedies, mostly on mythological subjects, the few surviving fragments of his work nearly all come from a satyric drama lampooning the contemporary philosopher Menedemus of Chalcis and his circle. He was commissioned to write a treatise *On Comedy* as an aid to the arrangement of the comedies in the Library. See Pfeiffer, *op. cit.* 141-142; Easterling and Knox, *op. cit.* 1026-1027.

29. On Zenodotus see p. 67.

30. It was called the *Scholium Plautinum* by F. Osann, who discovered the Plautus manuscript in the Collegio Romano in 1819. It was Dindorf who first suggested that the mysterious author 'Caecius' was to be identified with Tzetzes: see W.J.W. Kaster, 'Scholium Plautinum plene editum', *Mnemosyne*, 4th ser., 14 (1961) 23 ff. On this worthless Latin adaptation see also Wendel, 'Tzetzes'.

31. On the literary evidence for the Serapeum library see esp. A.J. Butler, *The Arab Conquest of Egypt and the Last Thirty Years of the Roman Domination*, Oxford 1902, 402-426.

32. Epiphanius of Salamis, a Greek ecclesiastical writer from Judaea, lived in the fourth century. He entered the monastic life in Egypt at an early age, subsequently founded a monastery in his birthplace, of which he was the abbot, and from 367 was Bishop of

to have got his raw material from Alexandria, which makes one wonder what was the total output of those playwrights of the Middle and New Comedy for whom Athenaeus is our sole source. Another writer who tells us a good deal about the huge literary output of the Greeks is Galen, an important source even though he lived about three centuries after the period we are dealing with. Galen, a prolific writer who was extremely perceptive on all matters relating to books, compiled a catalogue of his own works (*On My Own Books*), in which he claims that his writings filled no less than five hundred papyrus rolls. Clitomachus, a pupil of Carneades and his successor at the Academy, is said to have written four hundred works, but it is not known how many rolls they filled.[78] The growth of literary and textual studies produced a flood of critical works, which in turn gave rise to a wave of further studies. Callimachus wrote more than eight hundred works filling at least two thousand rolls, and the 120 rolls of his *Pinakes* generated a fresh round of critical writings, such as Aristophanes of Byzantium's book *On the Pinakes of Callimachus*.[79] The most remarkable statistic of all concerns Didymus, a literary scholar of the first century B.C., whom the scholars of the Museum nicknamed *Chalkenteros* ('Brazen-guts') on account of his indefatigable industry and *Bibliolathas* ('Forgetter of books')[80] because he had written so many that he could not remember them all: his total output was said to have been between 3,500 and 4,000 rolls! So it is easy to see that the number of rolls in a 'world library', especially one with a great many duplicated titles, would have exceeded the figures given by the sources.

No evidence has come down to us concerning the existence of private libraries in the Ptolemaic period, let alone about their size; but from Strabo's time (first century B.C.) we have eye-witness accounts of private libraries that give food for thought. What is one to make of the report that in about 30 B.C. a Greek slave in Rome, Tyrannio, had a library of 30,000 rolls?[81] Or that a virtually unknown Roman named Serenus Sammonicus bequeathed his father's library of not less than 62,000 rolls to Emperor Gordian II in the third century A.D.?[82] Or that (according to *Souda*) one M. Mettius Epaphroditus had a private collection of 30,000 books? Or that (according to Athenaeus, *Deipnosophistai* I.3b) the library of Livius Larnesius was bigger and better than all other libraries renowned for their richness? These figures make one wonder how many books there were in the Alexandrian Library, which aspired to be a 'world library' and, as already mentioned, possessed two or more copies of a considerable number of books. Nor should we forget that the Library had been built up over a period of two and a half centuries, during which the Ptolemies had spent enormous sums of money on it.

5. The destruction of the Library. The other aspect of the Library's history that has generated as much controversy as the Letter of Aristeas

Constantia (Salamis) in Cyprus.

33. *PG* 43 255.

34. See A. Rowe, 'The Discovery of the Famous Temple and Enclosure of Sarapis at Alexandria', Appendix to the *Annales du Service des Antiquités de l'Égypte*, Cahier No. 12, 1946. On subsequent discoveries see P.M. Fraser, 'Two Studies on the Cult of Sarapis in the Hellenistic World', *Opuscula Atheniensia*, III, Lund 1960, 11.6.

35. Aphthonius, *Progymnasmata* 12 (H. Rabe, *Rhetores Graeci,* Leipzig 1926, X 40). Aphthonius's brief description is unambiguous architecturally: see pp. 94-95.

36. John Chrysostom (*PG* 47 851).

37. Strabo, 608. The most one can say about Strabo's testimony is that it may be true in spirit, in the sense that the Peripatetic philosophers – especially Strato, who spent some time in Alexandria working mainly as tutor to the royal family – advised Ptolemy I on the codification of Aristotle's works, probably following the methods that had been used in the library of the Lyceum.

38. The biographical notes on scholars and poets in the *Onomatologion* of Hesychius of Miletus and in *Souda* ('Suidas') were collected by A. Westermann in his book *Vitarum Scriptores Graeci*, Amsterdam 1845.

39. Westermann, *op. cit.* 369.

40. The problems arising in connection with the post of librarian and the use of the term *bibliophylax* are discussed at length in Fraser, *Ptolemaic Alexandria*, I 322 ff. See also E.G. Turner, *Ἑλληνικοί Πάπυροι: Εἰσαγωγή στή μελέτη καί τή χρήση τῶν παπυρικῶν κειμένων* (= *Greek Papyri: An Introduction*, Oxford 1968, tr. G.M. Parasoglou), Athens 1981, 180, 190-191.

41. See also p. 67.

42. See Pfeiffer, *op. cit.* 146-180; A. Lesky, *Ἱστορία τῆς Ἀρχαίας Ἑλληνικῆς Λογοτεχνίας* (= *Geschichte der griechischen Literatur*, Bern 1957/58, tr. A.G. Tsopanaki), Thessaloniki 1983, 968-991; Easterling and Knox, *op. cit.* 1029 (for up-to-date bibliography).

43. The source of the information that Callimachus compiled the *Pinakes* is once again Tzetzes, who says, '... and

Callimachus later wrote up the tables of [the books].' On the figure of 120 rolls of *Pinakes* see the biographical notes on Callimachus in Hesychius and *Souda*. His well-known dictum 'A great book is a great evil' occurs in a book, *To Praxiphanes*, attacking the Peripatetic philosopher of that name. Although on the face of it there seems to be no ambiguity about this saying, his real reasons for disliking big books were almost certainly practical ones connected with a librarian's preoccupation with shelf space and cataloguing, especially when one considers the length of some of his own works.

44. See C. Wendel, *Die griechisch-römische Buchbeschreibung verglichen mit der des vorderen Orients*, Halle 1949, 19 ff.; E. Posner, *Archives in the Ancient World*, Cambridge Mass. 1972.

45. On the *Pinakes* see F. Schmidt, *Die Pinakes des Kallimachos*, Kiel 1924; Wendel, *Die griechisch-römische Buchbeschreibung*... 69 ff.; O. Regenbogen, «Πίναξ» in *RE* 20 (1950) 1409-1482, esp. 1423-1438; also Turner, *op. cit.* 139-140, for a general survey of Alexandrian literary scholars and papyri. On Callimachus's subdivision of the realms of literature see Pfeiffer, *op. cit.* 152-158. On the specific *Pinakes* see *Souda*.

46. The earliest example of a colophon at the end of a papyrus roll giving the title and the number of lines of writing is in a copy of Menander's play *The Man from Sicyon*: see the edition by A. Blanchard and A. Bataille, *Recherches de Papyrologie* 3 (1964) 161 (Pap. Sorb. 2272 col. XXI, Pl. XIII).

47. Aristophanes of Byzantium, the fourth director of the Library, published a whole book entitled *On the Pinakes of Callimachus*.

48. See pp. 67-68.

49. Little is known for certain about Apollonius and his life. The romantic tales told about his initial 'failure' as a writer on the publication of his *Argonautica* in Alexandria, resulting in his self-exile to Rhodes and triumphant return later, are of particularly dubious authenticity. And the story of his famous quarrel with Callimachus, often described as a deadly feud that dominated his whole

72. Alexander the Great and Julius Caesar: 'Allegory of Victory'. Engraving by an unknown artist. Rome, Istituto Nazionale per la Grafica, Fe 91362.

concerns the circumstances of its destruction. The school of thought which holds that it was burnt down, either in the aftermath of the siege of Julius Caesar by Ptolemy XII and the army of Achillas in 47 B.C. or on the orders of Caliph Omar in A.D. 642, is not convincing.

Julius Caesar. Julius Caesar went to Alexandria in 48 B.C. at the invitation of the young King Ptolemy XII, brother of Cleopatra VII. His involvement in the dispute between Ptolemy and Cleopatra, the two children of Ptolemy XI Auletes (80-51 B.C.) who had succeeded their father as joint rulers, created such a furore in Ptolemy's entourage that the young king's all-powerful general Achillas and the eunuch Pothinus hatched a conspiracy against Caesar. Their plot was nipped in the bud and Pothinus was imprisoned and executed. However, Achillas managed to escape, raised a formidable army (including a number of Roman deserters) and besieged Caesar in the palace by land and sea. Caesar put up a stout resistance and went on to the counter-attack: from the top of the sea walls overlooking the harbour he set fire to sixty of Ptolemy's ships anchored there. The conflagration spread rapidly to the dockyard

73. An engraving of the Pharos at Alexandria.

installations and the buildings on the waterfront, with the result that (according to Dio Cassius, writing in the third century A.D.) about forty thousand books 'of excellent quality' perished in the flames.[83] It should perhaps be mentioned in passing that the only contemporary historian who wrote about the fire was Livy, who was twelve at the time. His statement that 40,000 (or, according to some accounts, 400,000) rolls were burnt was preserved by Seneca, from whom Dio Cassius and others got their information.

However the evidence is viewed, it is clearly wrong to say that the Library was destroyed in Caesar's time. In the first place, the description of the books as being 'of excellent quality' probably refers to the papyrus or parchment of which they were made, rather than their content, unless Livy had personally inspected the books (which had probably been intended for export) and meant that the standard of copying was excellent. In any case, even if Caesar had decided to ship out some of the Alexandrian Library's rare books in order to found the first public bilingual library in Rome (a project he is known to have put in hand on his return there),[84] the most reasonable supposition is that they would have been either duplicate copies that the Library could spare or new copies

life, is based mainly on contemporary anecdotes: see E. Eichgrün, *Kallimachos und Apollonios Rhodios*, Berlin 1961, 279.

50. Very little factual evidence survives concerning the life of Eratosthenes. Much of his writing was in the fields of mathematics and geography, and Archimedes dedicated to him a book on his method. Eratosthenes, who was a great polymath, liked to be called a man of letters (*philologos*) rather than a mere grammarian (*grammatikos*) in recognition of the breadth of his learning. He had several nicknames: 'Beta' (second-rater, because his rivals comforted themselves with the thought that he was active in too many fields to be of the first rank in any of them), 'Plato the Younger' and 'Pentathlete' (all-rounder). See Pfeiffer, *op. cit.* 181 ff.

51. See *Souda* s.v. 'Aristophanes of Byzantium'.

52. He was therefore about sixty when he was appointed Librarian and about seventy-seven when he died, though it is not known whether he held the post until his death.

53. Comedy was defined by the Peripatetics as 'the imitation of life': see Pfeiffer, *op. cit.* 227.

54. *Souda*: 'Intending [or wishing] to go to Eumenes, and having made the necessary preparations, he was thrown into prison.' It is in connection with this episode that the name of Pergamum makes its first appearance in the history of literary studies.

55. Pliny, *Natural History* VIII.13; Plutarch, *Moralia* 972 D.

56. Aelian, *On the Nature of Animals* VII.43, XIII.8. The Ptolemies were animal-lovers, and two of them (Philadelphus and Euergetes II) had their own private zoos, but whether that fact has any relevance to the story of the flower-loving elephants is hard to say. Diodorus Siculus (III.36.3) has a passage about the capture of a large snake for Ptolemy Philadelphus and adds that the king was always keen to obtain rare animals in order to study their habits.

57. *Μέγα Ἐτυμολογικόν*, ed. Fredericus Sylburgius, Heidelberg, Hieronymus Commelinus, 1594, col. 295.

specially ordered for Caesar. Unfortunately nothing is known about the book trade between Alexandria and Rome in the Ptolemaic period: our only definite information concerns the trade in papyrus, as Alexandria was the sole centre for the production and export of papyrus rolls throughout the ancient era and right down to the seventh century, when the city was taken by the Arabs. At all events – unless the Library had previously been systematically looted – the forty thousand rolls, even if abstracted from its stocks, represented so small a proportion of the total that their removal could not have altered its character or seriously affected its survival and future development. Most probably, in my opinion, the reason why so many books were burnt is that arrangements had been made on official authority, perhaps at the highest level, for the export of papyrus rolls to form the nucleus of a great library, probably the one in Rome whose organization Caesar entrusted to Varro.

The alternative account of the complete destruction of the Library, or rather of a collection of books that had belonged to the initial nucleus of the Library, is much later, dating from the middle of the seventh century, when Alexandria had fallen to the Arabs. It is worth dwelling for a moment on this delightful story. When Emir 'Amr ibn al-'Aç had captured Alexandria he wrote to Caliph Omar, 'I have taken the great city of the West and I have no words to describe its wealth and beauty. All I can say is that it has 4,000 villas, 4,000 public bath-houses, 400 theatres and places of entertainment, 12,000 greengrocers' shops and 40,000 Jewish subjects. The city was captured by force of arms, with no capitulation. The faithful cannot wait to enjoy the fruits of victory.'[85] 'Amr, however, was a cultivated man: he did not let his troops sack Alexandria, he refused to be stung into vindictiveness by the Byzantine army's repeated attempts to recapture the city, and he abided by his promise to keep Alexandria 'open to all comers, like a harlot's house', going so far as to demolish a large section of the city walls. On the very spot where he had managed to persuade his army to refrain from looting, he erected a mosque which he called the Mosque of Clemency.

Caliph Omar. When Alexandria fell to 'Amr, so we are informed by the chronicler Ibn al-Kifti, the eminent Aristotelian scholar John Philoponus was still living there at a ripe old age.[86] 'Amr, who had an insatiable thirst for knowledge and even took an interest in the doctrinal disputes taking place within the Orthodox Church, enjoyed talking to the elderly Greek scholar. At one of their meetings Philoponus mentioned that it was both annoying and worrying to have the books kept under lock and key in the royal treasury and asked 'Amr to make them freely available for study. 'Amr listened solicitously and asked Philoponus to tell him the history of the Library, as he was interested to learn more about it. Philoponus told him what he knew, basing his account on the Letter of Aristeas, which was still well-known and believed to be accurate, and 'Amr, being a

58. On the musical modes see Pfeiffer, *op. cit.* 220-221.

59. On the life and work of Aristarchus see: L. Cohn in *RE* 2 (1895) 862-873; Pfeiffer, *op. cit.* 251-278.

60. Athenaeus, *Deipnosophistai* II.71b: 'Ptolemy Euergetes ..., one of the pupils of Aristarchus the grammarian.'

61. According to *Souda*, Aristarchus had about forty pupils. No jokes or anecdotes about him have come down to us, apart from the fact that one Alexandrian scholar was strongly critical of the way he dressed (Athenaeus, *Deipnosophistai* I.21c).

62. *FGrHist* 234 F 11; *Souda* s.v. 'Aristarchos'. See also Pfeiffer, *op. cit.* 251-253.

63. P. Oxy. 1241, col. II, 16-17. See also M. Launey, 'Recherches sur les armées hellénistiques', *Bibliothèque des Écoles Françaises d'Athènes et de Rome* 169 (1949/50) 273, 1163; Fraser, *Ptolemaic Alexandria*, II 491.

64. P. Oxy. 1241, col. II, 17 ff. On the identity of these four grammarians see Fraser, *Ptolemaic Alexandria*, II 391-392. It is interesting to note that Diocles and Apollodorus are given as the names of the two benefactors who endowed a library on Cos, in an inscription of the second century B.C.: see p. 91 n. 1.

65. T.B. Mitford, 'The Hellenistic inscriptions of old Paphos', *BSA* 56 (1961) 40, No. 110. G. Pasquali described Onesander as 'anti-librarian', meaning that he did not perform his duties as Librarian in Alexandria but simply held the honorary title while living in Cyprus: see *Enciclopedia Italiana* s.v. 'Biblioteca', p. 943.

66. See p. 65.

67. G. Kaibel (ed.), *Comicorum Graecorum Fragmenta*, Berlin 1899, 19. The meaning of the terms 'composite' and 'unmixed' has been discussed at length by T. Birt in his book *Das antike Buchwesen*, Berlin 1882, 484, 490. F. Schmidt (*op. cit.* 37-38) arrived at a different conclusion from Birt, namely that a 'composite' roll was one containing more than one work (by the same or different authors), while an 'unmixed' roll contained a single work or part thereof: this seems a more

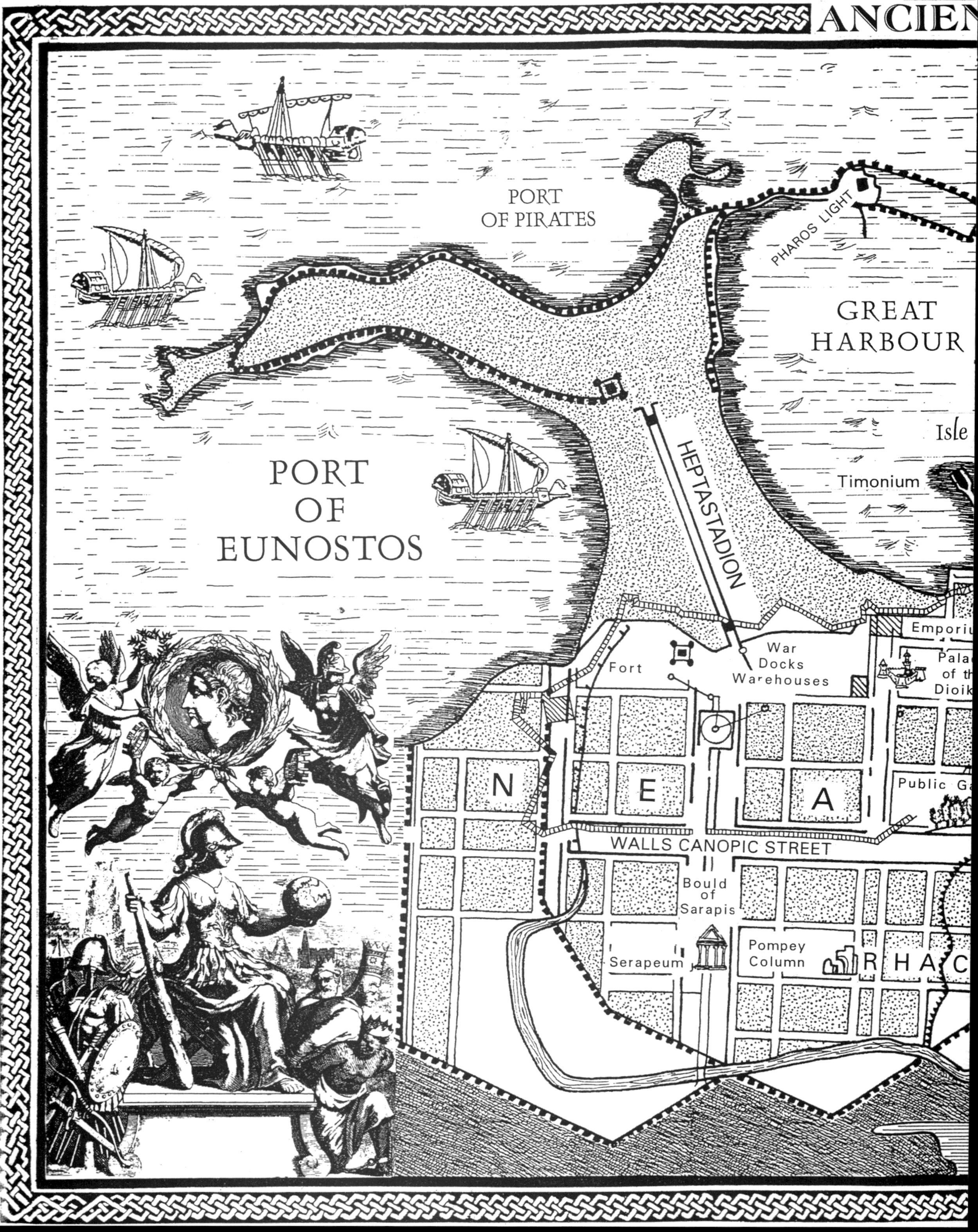

74. Ancient Alexandria, after the plan drawn by G. Botti (1898).

ALEXANDRIA

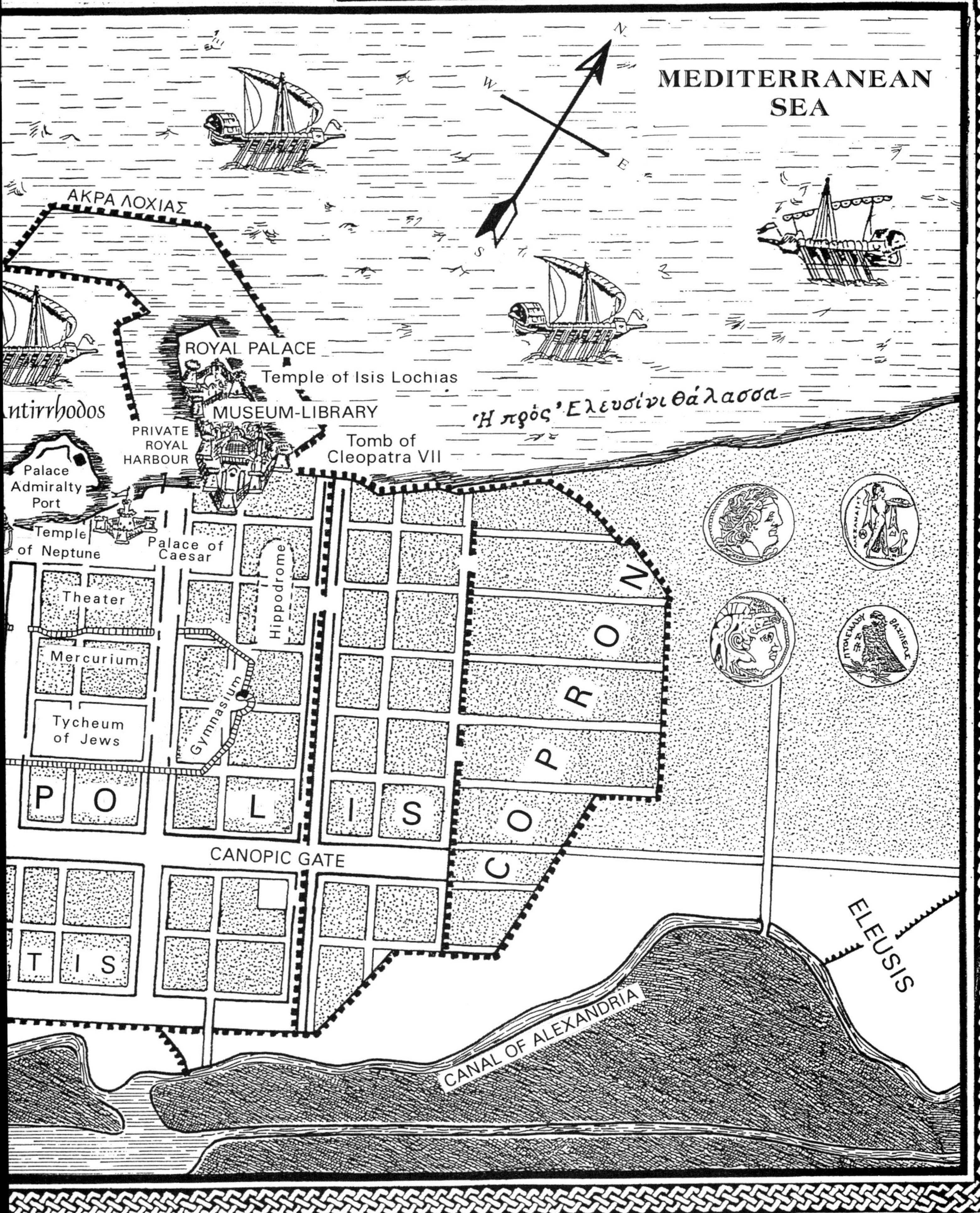
MEDITERRANEAN SEA
N
W
E
S
ΑΚΡΑ ΛΟΧΙΑΣ
ROYAL PALACE
Temple of Isis Lochias
ntirrhodos
MUSEUM-LIBRARY
Ἡ πρὸς Ἐλευσῖνι θάλασσα
PRIVATE ROYAL HARBOUR
Tomb of Cleopatra VII
Palace Admiralty Port
Temple of Neptune
Palace of Caesar
Theater
Hippodrome
Mercurium
Gymnasium
Tycheum of Jews
P O L I S
C O P R O N
CANOPIC GATE
T I S
ELEUSIS
CANAL OF ALEXANDRIA

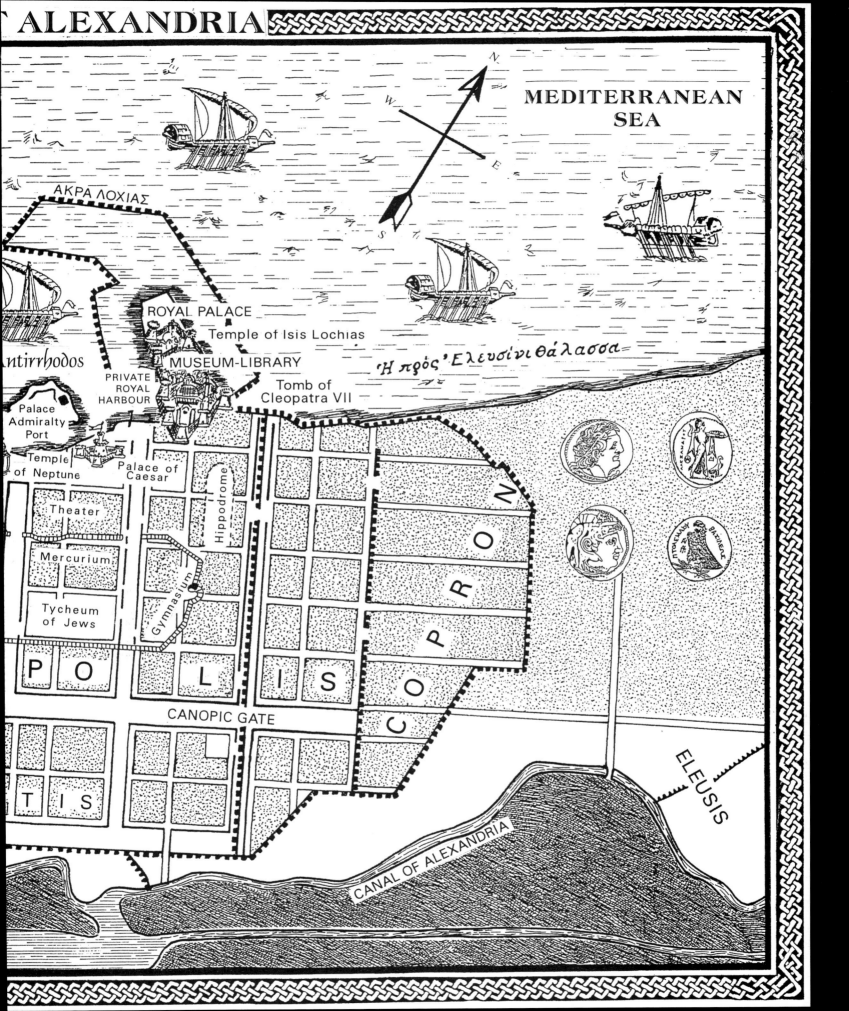

law-abiding and disciplined Muslim, promised to pass the request on to Caliph Omar.

This he did, but it took a while for Omar's reply to arrive. This gave 'Amr some time to find out more about the history of the Ptolemies' famous collection of books. Tradition relates that a Greek who had gone over to Islam complicated matters by asserting that the collection to which Philoponus was referring had been burnt before the Prophet was born. 'Amr decided to seek out the truth and went to the ruins of the Temple of Serapis, taking Philoponus and a Jewish doctor and historian named Philaretus with him. There they found some remains of the subsidiary library and of other pagan temples. Philaretus, a highly educated man, launched into a long lecture on the legends attached to the Alexandrian Library, doing his best to demolish the gross inaccuracies put about by Ammianus Marcellinus, who had blamed Caesar for destroying it by fire. The talk then moved on to later writers who had tried to uncover the true facts, such as Orosius. The Arab chronicler does not tell us whether 'Amr ever found any collection of books living up to the reputation of the Ptolemies' Great Library, or if so what state the books were in, but eventually a messenger arrived bearing Caliph Omar's answer.

Omar's verdict was terse and struck a note of finality worthy of the Koran itself, leaving no room for argument: 'If the contents of the books accord with the Book of Allah, we do not need them, because in that case the Book of Allah is more than enough. If, on the other hand, they contain anything contrary to the Book of Allah, there is no need to keep them. Proceed with their destruction.' 'Amr, of course, obeyed the Caliph's orders. He distributed the books – except the works of Aristotle – to all the public bath-houses in Alexandria (four thousand of them, according to the Christian Arab historian Eutychios) to be used as fuel for heating the water, and we are told it took six months to burn them all. If the involvement of John Philoponus is integral to the credibility of this version of events it is clear that the whole story is a fabrication, as he had died several decades before the fall of Alexandria.[87]

The burning of the Alexandrian Library in 47 B.C. and the burning of its books at Caliph Omar's behest in A.D. 642 are the two threads around which any number of legends and conjectures have been woven. However, the historical facts, the bibliophilic tradition, the upheavals caused in the intellectual world by the ascendancy of Christianity and consequent marginalization of Classical studies, and the emergence of the codex as the successor to the papyrus roll all show us that if we wish to draw any firm conclusions and uncover the truth we have to follow a different path from that of myth and tradition.

6. A chronicle of the Library's history. A glance at the history of any library, whether royal, public, monastic or private, is enough to show

reasonable interpretation. There is good evidence to suggest that by the Hellenistic period, if not before, there already existed papyrus rolls containing more than one complete work (cf. Diogenes Laertius, VI.15: 'The surviving works [of Antisthenes] are in ten volumes. The first contains: *On Expression, or Styles of Speaking*; *Ajax, or The Speech of Ajax*; *The Defence of Orestes*; etc., etc.'). See also E.G. Turner, *Athenian Books in the Fifth and Fourth Centuries B.C.*, London 1952, 15; F.G. Kenyon, *Books and Readers in Ancient Greece and Rome*, Oxford 1951, 50 ff.

68. See p. 43.

69. Galen, *Commentary on Hippocrates 'On Epidemics'* iii (xvi a 606-607).

70. Galen, *Commentary on Hippocrates 'On the Nature of Mankind'* ii (Introduction § 109). Galen states that *On the Nature of Mankind* was by a pupil of Hippocrates named Polybius, not by the master himself. Richard Bentley treated the question of forged works at length, in the light of Galen's comments, in his *Dissertation upon the Epistles of Phalaris*, London 1777; cf. Schmidt, *op. cit.* 92-93. It is worth quoting a passage from the *Prolegomena* of Olympiodorus (*CIAG* XII.1, p. 13): 'In the past spurious books came into existence in three ways: either through the vanity of kings, or through the benevolence of pupils (to their teachers), or through homonymy. But let us see how the vanity of kings came to be a cause of the existence of spurious books. It should be explained that in the old days kings loved the written word and so, out of vanity, they were eager to obtain books by ancient writers. For example, Iobates, King of Libya, was a great admirer of Pythagoras, the Ptolemy called Philadelphus admired Aristotle, and Pisistratus, the ruler of Athens, admired Homer; and so they offered good money to buy their works. Consequently there were many avaricious people who either wrote books themselves or acquired any books that happened to come their way, passing them off as the work of earlier writers, and offered them to the rulers in

that after the death of the founder, unless his heirs are possessed by the same passion for books, the decline and eventual dissolution of the library are simply a matter of time. We should therefore ask ourselves whether the successors of Ptolemy I and II, all the way down to Cleopatra VII, really were equally enthusiastic about building up the 'world library' or whether they merely tried to keep it going, often dragging their feet and with frequent spells of doing nothing at all.[88] As for the Roman period, there is no evidence to suggest that anything was done to enlarge and develop the Library.

As already mentioned, the founder of the Alexandrian Library and the man who originally conceived the idea of creating a 'world library' was Ptolemy I Soter. His son, who succeeded him as Ptolemy II Philadelphus in 283, kept up the good work with undiminished energy until his death in 247: in fact it was in his reign that perhaps the most important work was done in the Library, for this was the era of Zenodotus (its first director), Callimachus (the author of the *Pinakes*) and Apollonius Rhodius. From the accession of Ptolemy III Euergetes to the death of Ptolemy VI Philometor (144 B.C.) all we know about the history of the Library comes from the biographies of its directors, because the only person who recorded any information worth taking seriously was Galen, and he was chiefly interested in the way the books were classified. Galen apart, nothing has come down to us except a few anecdotes and legends mostly concerned with the writing of books and the general atmosphere surrounding the search for rare books. The downturn in the acquisition of new books and the activity of the Museum's scriptorium is probably to be dated to the middle of the second century B.C. The start of the decline is signalled by two events: the decision of Eumenes II of Pergamum (197-159 B.C.) to compete with the Alexandrian Library and the persecution of intellectuals in Alexandria by Ptolemy Euergetes II (*c.* 145-144 B.C.), coinciding exactly with the retirement of the last scholar-director of the Library, Aristarchus.[89]

Pergamum. The kings of Pergamum, having decided to create a library to rival that of Alexandria, not only erected a monumental library building[90] and other splendid edifices but went to great lengths to attract prominent scholars from the Museum, including Aristophanes of Byzantium, to their court. They then launched an all-out search for books, offering absurdly inflated prices, which led to the appearance on the market of a great many forgeries of real and imaginary works. The rivalry between the two cities became so intense, so we are told, that the Alexandrians eventually forbade the export of papyrus to their competitors.

The onset of the Alexandrian Library's real troubles is probably to be dated to the year 144 B.C., when Ptolemy VIII murdered Ptolemy VII and ascended the throne. The Alexandrians called Ptolemy VIII *Kakergetes* ('Malefactor') and *Physkon* ('Pot-belly'), the latter being an echo of the

order to claim the promised bounty. And that was how it happened, as already mentioned, that spurious books sometimes came into existence as a result of the vanity of kings.'

The sixth-century Byzantine philosopher John Philoponus, in his *Commentary on Aristotle's 'Categoriae'* (*CIAG* XIII.3, p. 7), gives three motives for the forging of Aristotle's works: (a) to create 'more Aristotles', (b) to increase the number of works ('They wrote "Categories" following their teacher's example') and (c) to get money from Ptolemy Philadelphus, who gave a handsome reward to anyone who brought him any work by Aristotle.

On the forgeries of works by Pythagoras and Socrates see Elias of Alexandria, *On the 'Categories'* (*CIAG* XVIII.1, p. 128): Elias mentions five ways of forging.

71. See p. 43.

72. See Wendel, *Die griechisch-römische Buchbeschreibung... 60.*

73. On Mnemon and the copy of *On Epidemics* by Hippocrates, which the Library acquired in the reign of Ptolemy Euergetes I (Galen, *Commentary on Hippocrates 'On Epidemics'* iii (xvii a 606-607), see Wendel, *Die griechisch-römische Buchbeschreibung...* 65-67. A very interesting piece of information is given in a manuscript of Homer's *Odyssey*, where the scholiast at XIV.204 has written *Καλλίστρατος ἐν τῇ ἐκ Μουσείου Κάστωρ* [...] *φησί γεγράφθαι*, where the words *τῇ ἐκ Μουσείου* ('the Museum copy') hint at a third category of books: perhaps these were the editions kept in the Great Library. See Wendel, *op. cit.* 60; Fraser, *Ptolemaic Alexandria*, I 328, II n. 166.

74. For a brief review of the subject see L.D. Reynolds and N.G. Wilson, *'Αντιγραφεῖς καί Φιλόλογοι: Τό ἱστορικό τῆς παράδοσης τῶν κλασικῶν κειμένων* (= *Scribes and Scholars: A guide to the transmission of Greek and Latin literature,* 2nd edn., London 1975, tr. N.M. Panayotakis), Athens 1981, 26-32; Turner, *'Ελληνικοί Πάπυροι* 152 ff.

75. Galen, *Commentary on Hippocrates 'On Epidemics'* iii (xvii a 606-607).

nickname given by Alcaeus to Pittacus, the ruler of Lesbos in the seventh century B.C.[91] Euergetes ('Benefactor') II, as the new king smugly called himself, was a licentious, violent and generally odious individual, though by no means an intellectual nonentity, as his *Memoirs* prove: indeed, Plutarch describes him as 'keen to expand his knowledge'. The Museum and the Library continued to function in his reign and we know the names of the persons involved in their administration. But the departure of the literary scholars for Rhodes or Athens, or above all for Pergamum, led to the steady decline of both institutions.[92]

The lessening of interest in books and the persecution of the Museum scholars did not imply total philistinism, for Plutarch tells us that Cleopatra herself had intellectual accomplishments unusual in a queen. Nor were these the only reasons for the downturn in the fortunes of the Library, for drastic political changes had also been taking place in the Mediterranean region. Since 168 B.C. Rome had been steadily extending her ascendancy over Egypt, in 146 Carthage had been conquered and destroyed, and in the same year Greece had become a Roman province. And although the new academic discipline of literary studies was not killed off by this first crisis in its history, its epicentre shifted from Alexandria and other Greek cities to Rome, which became the new centre of the book trade from the first century B.C. The last two Alexandrian historians, Andron of Alexandria and Menecleus of Barce, boasted of their city's pre-eminence (paraphrasing the well-known dictum of Pericles, who described Athens as an education to all of Greece) by saying that Alexandria had educated not only the Greeks but the barbarians as well, by which they presumably meant the Romans.[93]

Ptolemy IX Soter II, who reigned from 116 to 80 B.C., was unable to reverse the trend. Apollodorus of Athens, the author of a *Chronicle*, is thought to have left Alexandria for Pergamum, and an eminent former pupil of Aristarchus, Dionysius the Thracian, settled on Rhodes, where he attracted a large following from the surrounding area.[94] In 106 B.C. Cicero was born: he and his great friend Atticus greatly stimulated the book-reading habit and the growth of private libraries among the Romans, which helped to account for the westward shift of the centre of the book trade. And although the cultural policies of Julius Caesar, Mark Antony and Augustus were designed to preserve Alexandria's intellectual independence, in the end there were no foundations left on which to build a renaissance. After the siege of Caesar by Achillas, as we have seen, the royal library remained intact; but on Cleopatra's death in 30 B.C., when Egypt was annexed by Rome, the character of the Library was completely altered.

Egypt as a Roman province. Although Augustus wrote in the famous record of his career known as the *Res gestae* that he had 'added Egypt to the dominions of the Roman people', Egypt was never a Roman province in the same sense as all the other provinces but was administered more or less as the Emperor's private property. Broadly speaking, Roman Egypt was governed by a well-organized, centralized administration backed by an army strong enough to deal with marauding raids by the nomadic desert tribes and maintain law and order in the cities within the framework of a stratified society in which the Greeks, in particular, enjoyed special privileges at the expense of the indigenous Egyptians.[95] About the organization of the archival libraries (i.e. public record offices) a good deal is known, as it is also about the innovations introduced by the Romans into the Ptolemies' very highly-developed bureaucratic machine,[96] but the sources are silent on the subject of literary libraries. Nevertheless, it is possible to infer from indirect evidence that the Library and the Museum were turned into a sort of 'imperial foundation' (since even the priest who was the Principal of the Museum was appointed by the Emperor himself) and that the Museum kept its name and functioned as an educational establishment.[97]

On the inauguration of the Empire, the Romans made an important change in the organization of the library by creating separate sections for Latin and Greek books: in other words they introduced the concept of the bilingual library (*diplobibliotheke*), which was to remain the norm until the Early Byzantine period. The idea probably originated with Julius

Caesar but was not put into practice until after his death, by C. Asinius Pollio in 39 B.C.[98] The purpose of this innovation was to focus attention on the Romans' cultural background and history and to persuade the Greeks, a people noted for their intellectual curiosity, to learn the 'barbaric' Latin language and discover that Latin literature deserved respect. To remind the people of Egypt and visitors to Alexandria that the land of the Pharaohs and Ptolemies was now a Roman province, in 12 B.C. Augustus built a temple dedicated to Julius the God, with a bilingual library next to it.[99] The temple came to be known as the Sebasteion (from *Sebastos*, the Greek rendering of *Augustus*, the title given to the Roman emperors). It stood in a large precinct on a hill, surrounded by peristyle courtyards and extensive open spaces and adorned with statuary, and seems to have been intended to replace the public library of the Serapeum and Museum in accordance with the new cultural policy. The ultimate objective of this move was probably to erase from public memory the splendour and symbolism of the Alexandrian Library. Quite possibly thousands of papyrus rolls were moved to the new library, and in the course of time, as the enforcement of the library rules became more lax, it is probable that many rare copies found their way into the hands of booksellers.

Nevertheless, even in the first century A.D. it would seem that Alexandria still possessed the finest collection of Greek literature – and perhaps of Latin literature too, because when the Palatine Library was burnt down by Nero or Titus a team of experts was sent to Alexandria by Domitian to make new copies of the books that had been destroyed.[100] Suetonius, the source of this piece of information, also mentions that Emperor Claudius enlarged the Museum, but without making it clear whether Claudius was following the example of his predecessors.[101]

A significant point that should be mentioned before we go on to consider the interesting information about books revealed by the Oxyrhynchus papyri is that annexation by the Romans did not alter the linguistic tradition forced upon Egypt by the Ptolemies, which would have influenced the production and distribution of Greek books. Numerically, the Roman administrators in Egypt were a negligible minority, and so Greek was retained as the official language of the government. The use of Latin was compulsory for the Roman army and for all official documents (such as birth certificates and wills) relating to Roman citizens. And in spite of Caracalla's edict of A.D. 212 and Diocletian's attempts to bring Egypt into line with the administrative methods employed in other Roman provinces, Latin never managed to conquer more than a few strongholds of the Greek language: the rest held out until fully a century after the Arab conquest of 642.[102]

Incidental information about scholars of the Museum. There are innumerable papyri written during the Roman period in the form of letters, accounts and reports of various kinds which contain fascinating snippets of information about some of the scholars of the Museum and their bookish interests. In A.D. 155, for example, we learn that there was a piece of land at Euhemeria in the Faiyûm belonging to Julius Asclepiades, 'philosopher' (i.e. a member of the philosophy department of the Museum), which implies that the Museum was still functioning as an educational institution;[103] in the year 198 or 227 another scholar of the Museum, Valerius Titanianus, owned a property at Philadelphia; and an honorific inscription in the city of Antinoe, probably of the third century, promulgates a decree of the local council in honour of the Platonic philosopher Flavius Marcius Se[verianus?] Dionysodorus, one of the scholars maintained tax-free at the Museum.[104] From this it would appear that in the Roman period the Museum was still basically unchanged since the time of Ptolemy I and that its scholars were still being supported by the old system of 'royal' welfare. Even more interesting is a papyrus of A.D. 173 with a letter mentioning that a certain Valerius Diodorus, 'a former writer of commentaries and member of the Museum', had discussed books and the best way of obtaining them with two men named Polion and Harpocration.[105] Diodorus, Polion and Harpocration were Alexandrian literary scholars who were particularly interested in the Attic orators, Harpocration being best known as the compiler of the *Lexicon of the Ten Orators*.[106]

Letters written in Alexandria in the second century A.D. also provide invaluable information about the cost of copying manuscripts. A statement of account, probably from Oxyrhynchus, lists the fees paid to a scribe for copying books, including a sum of twelve drachmae for copying Aristophanes's *Plutus*, an unspecified work and *The Third Thyestes* by Sophocles. Other entries refer to two different rates of pay: one of 28 drachmae per 10,000 lines and a cheaper rate of 20 drachmae and 4 obols for the same number of lines.[107] These statistics are extremely interesting for the light they throw on the differences between Rome and Alexandria in the business of book production and marketing. In Rome the book trade relied on the services of a pool of highly-trained slaves and substantial export sales, whereas in Alexandria publishing was evidently not organized on a business footing, and books – or at least those that were not current 'best-sellers' – were to be found only in the homes of a few literary men.[108]

So much for the evidence to be gleaned from letter-writing in the early centuries of our era about the Museum and its scholars. It is also worth mentioning a story told by Dio Cassius (LXXVIII.7) which, whether true or not, is of interest for its implications about the many imponderables that may have helped to determine what was and was not in the Library. According to Dio, Caracalla was a passionate admirer of Alexander the Great: he used weapons and drinking goblets that were said to have belonged to him, erected statues of him in army camps and in Rome itself and formed a phalanx composed entirely of Macedonian soldiers. But even this was not enough to satisfy his obsession with Alexander, so he actually wrote to inform the Senate that Alexander had been reincarnated in the person of the Augustus (i.e. Caracalla himself) in order to live out the rest of his time on earth, which had been so cruelly cut short. Being particularly obsessed by the circumstances of his hero's death, for which he persuaded himself that Aristotle had been ultimately responsible, Caracalla determined to take revenge and threatened the Aristotelians of the Alexandrian school that he would burn all their books[109] and deprive the Museum scholars of their entitlement to free board and other privileges.

The event that had the most powerful impact on the world of books was the triumph of Christianity. The transition from paganism to Christianity was a complex process that lasted for more than four hundred years in the Eastern Mediterranean. The Christians of Egypt were always given to heretical tendencies with a pronounced leaning towards Gnosticism, and in the first century A.D., through the influence of Philo Judaeus, they developed a Judaic philosophy in the Greek language whereby Egypt came to be a centre for reconciliation between paganism and the new faith of Christianity. A typical instance of this coexistence is to be seen in the fact that the Museum continued to function side by side with the great Christian Catechetic School founded by Pantaenus, with which the illustrious names of Clement of Alexandria and Origen were closely associated.[110]

The first armed conflict in Alexandria after the siege of Caesar by Achillas in 47 B.C. was due to the protracted war waged by Queen Zenobia of Palmyra and her allies against Emperor Aurelian (*c.* A.D. 272-275). After capturing Alexandria, Zenobia naturally took an interest in the Museum and more especially in the Library, as she was noted for her learning: she was equally at home in Greek, Latin, Syriac and Egyptian and had written a brief history of the East. When Aurelian forced Palmyra into submission in 272, he recaptured Alexandria. In the course of the fighting the Bruchium quarter of the city, which included the palace with the Museum and the Library, was badly damaged: according to Ammianus Marcellinus (XXII.16.15), it was razed to the ground.

The accession of Diocles (who preferred to be known as Diocletian) to the Roman imperial throne marks the beginning of what one might call a Pre-Byzantine period, with many features characteristic of the Middle Ages. Diocletian's administrative reforms ushered in a formative period of history, and the redistribution of provincial power eventually worked to the advantage of the peoples of the East. But his reign was marred by persecution of the Christians and mutual suspicion between Christians and pagans. The rapid spread of Christianity did not proceed as peacefully in all the Roman provinces as it did in Alexandria. During this peculiar period the signals reaching Nicomedia, Diocletian's capital, were confusing and contradictory: the suspicion shown by the Christians for the pagans; the picture of desolation presented by the Gardens of Epicurus, the Stoa of the Stoics and the other philosophical schools; and the fact that the Romans went so far as to condemn the works of no less a person than Cicero, which were submitted to the Senate for censorship.[111] North Africa was up in arms from the banks of the Nile to the Atlas Mountains, and L. Elpidius Achillaeus seized control of Alexandria. Diocletian chose to start his campaign against the rebels in Egypt and in 296 he laid siege to Alexandria, which fell to him after holding out for eight months. No historical records survive to tell us whether or not the fall of the city resulted in further damage to its monuments and cultural treasures.

The Byzantine period. When the Roman Empire was finally divided the whole of Egypt went to the Eastern Empire without bloodshed, but the familiar atmosphere of classicism no longer existed even in the Ptolemies' old capital. And although Patriarch Cyril of Alexandria failed to have the city's school of philosophy closed down, the lasting influence of monasticism, combined with the agitation of the indigenous population against economic oppression, created a climate that posed a permanent threat to Hellenism. For the fourth century we are again without sources, apart from the accounts of their visits to the Serapeum library given by Epiphanius and Aphthonius, and so one can only hypothesize.

It goes without saying that whenever any new royal library is founded it tends to supplant all its predecessors, assuming that it covers the same range of subjects. Unfortunately we have practically no information about the books that went into the new 'imperial' library founded by Constantius II in Constantinople in 357 mainly for the purpose of collecting works of classical literature. The only point of which we can be fairly certain is that not all the necessary books were to be found in Constantinople, because only a few years earlier Constantine the Great, needing fifty copies of the Bible, had had to order them from Eusebius's scriptorium in Caesarea.[112] It seems likely that valuable books were taken from what remained of the Ptolemies' Great Library in order to build up the new 'imperial' library in Constantinople.

The Roman and Early Byzantine periods witnessed a major innovation in book production that was later to have a decisive impact on the interior architecture of libraries. This was the invention of the codex – a book in the form in which we know it today, consisting of quires of folded sheets – which eventually consigned the papyrus roll to oblivion. The changeover was a gradual process that took several centuries to complete, and during the second and third centuries the codex and the roll were both in common use.[113] It is worth spending a little time on this important development, because in my opinion it was one of the main factors affecting the fate of the innumerable papyrus rolls in the Library. Once the codex had finally come into its own, papyrus rolls were no longer used for copying literary works. Theological treatises, a new category of writing, were usually published in codex form from the outset. As more and more works of the ancient tradition were transferred to the newer and much more convenient format, even the rarest of the old rolls lost much of their value until at last they were of interest only as museum pieces. It may be no exaggeration to say that papyrus rolls containing classical writings eventually came to be worth no more than the material they were written on, or even less, because the papyrus needed to be processed before it could be reused. At the same time as the codex was superseding the roll, another new development in book production was taking place: this was the replacement of papyrus by parchment. The first signs of this change had been seen as early as the first century A.D., when education spread so rapidly in the Roman Empire that papyrus could no longer be produced in sufficient quantities to keep up with demand. At first parchment was used as a substitute for papyrus, but a great drought in the reign of Tiberius (A.D. 14-37) reversed their relative positions and paved the way for the general acceptance of parchment as a standard writing material.[114] Throughout this period the balance was steadily tilting from papyrus to parchment, as it was from the roll to the codex.[115]

These changes in book production followed very different patterns in Christian religious writing and in secular literature. When C.H. Roberts published his account of the development of the codex in 1955, he noted that not one of the surviving early texts of the Greek New Testament on papyrus was written on the recto of a roll. Of the 111 then known biblical manuscripts in Greek dating from before the end of the fourth century, 99 were codices; and those of them that were Christian in origin (in other words, those that did not contain the Old Testament only) and could be dated to the turn of the second to third centuries were all papyrus codices.[116] Roberts concludes: 'When the Christian bible ... first makes its appearance in history, the books of which it is composed are always written on papyrus and in codex form.' Although many more examples of early Christian literature have been found since then, Roberts's finding still holds good. In classical (i.e. pagan) literature the percentages are different, and only in the fourth century do we find a big swing in favour of the codex. This means that in Alexandria there was no systematic drive to copy the classics from papyrus to parchment before the fourth century, and therefore the Library's stocks remained unchanged.[117]

It must also be remembered that Egypt had a monopoly of papyrus, though this does not mean that everybody in Egypt could afford to use it: for instance, there is a copy of Aristotle's *Constitution of the Athenians* written on the back of some private farm accounts.[118] There is also evidence of people going to the trouble of rubbing out an entire document so as to reuse the papyrus:[119] such a twice-used papyrus is called a palimpsest, which literally means 'rubbed clean again'. Impecunious priests, Roman soldiers, civil servants and (of course) schoolboys in Egypt used all kinds of available material to write on, such as potsherds and even linen mummy wrappings.[120] These remarks about the change in the format of books and the availability of writing materials are relevant to our theme inasmuch as they may shed some light on the question whether the Great Library underwent a process of 'peaceful spoliation', with books being stolen simply for the value of the material of which they were made. However, isolated incidents, the general climate of the age and the attitude to books can only be matters of conjecture.

The last piece of historical evidence prior to the Arabs' capture of Alexandria that may be relevant to the Ptolemies' original collection of books concerns what was left of the public library in the Serapeum. In 415 Patriarch Theophilus of Alexandria galvanized the Christians into

76. See n. 15; also Josephus, *Jewish Antiquities* I.107.

77. Hermippus of Smyrna, a supporter of Callimachus, was the main source used by Diogenes Laertius in writing his lives of the Peripatetic philosophers: see Diogenes Laertius, V.78. The only authority for the allegation that Hermippus embarked on such a project is Pliny the Elder (*Natural History* XXX.ii.4).

78. Diogenes Laertius, IV.67.

79. Pfeiffer, *op. cit.* 152, 158.

80. The latter nickname was given to him by Demetrius of Troezen 'on account of the great number of works he had published' (Athenaeus, *Deipnosophistai* IV.139).

81. On Tyrannio see pp. 48-49.

75. Plutarch. Engraving, 18th c.

82. See *Scriptores Historiae Augustae*, 'Gordianus' XVIII.2.

83. Dio Cassius, XLII.38.2. On the siege of Caesar in the palace, see: Seneca, *De tranquillitate animi* IX.5; Orosius, VI.15.31; P. Graindor, *La guerre d'Alexandrie*, Cairo 1931, 53 ff.

84. See p. 109.

85. The letter from 'Amr to the Caliph is mentioned in the *Chronicle* of Eutychios (II.316, ed. Pococke). The earliest references to the subject

in Arabic literature are in the chronicles of 'Abd al-Latîf of Baghdad and Ibn al-Kifti, both of which were written around the year 1200 and became known in Europe in the seventeenth century.

86. John Philoponus was born in the late fifth century and studied under Ammonius Hermeiou in Alexandria. He developed into one of the intellectual giants of his age, who influenced Islamic as well as Byzantine thinking and whose legacy was invaluable to natural scientists throughout the Middle Ages and right down to the time of Galileo. The date of his death is unknown, but it could not have been later than 567, over seventy years before the fall of Alexandria to the Arabs. Ibn al-Kifti included the story about 'Amr in his *History of Wise Men*, and the whole matter is discussed by A.J. Butler, *op. cit.* 400 ff.

87. See n. 86.

88. The enthusiasm of the later Ptolemies is called in question by the fact that the chroniclers and historians and Galen always give the main credit for the development of the Library to Ptolemies I, II and VI (Soter, Philadelphus and Philometor).

89. See p. 69.

90. See pp. 91-95.

91. See also p. 69; cf. Pfeiffer, *op. cit.* 251-253.

92. See pp. 91-92.

93. J. Jüthner, 'Hellenen und Barbaren', *Das Erbe der Alten*, n.s., 8 (1923) 7 ff.

94. On Dionysius the Thracian see L. Cohn in *RE* 5 (1905) 977-983; Pfeiffer, *op. cit.* 316 ff.

95. H.I. Bell, *Egypt from Alexander the Great to the Arab Conquest*, Oxford 1948, 65 ff.

96. We know from Ptolemaic tradition that even in the first century of Roman rule every nome had its own public library or public records office. In A.D. 72 these regional record offices were divided into 'archives of public documents and records' and 'archives of property records': see Turner, *Ἑλληνικοί Πάπυροι* 182 ff.

97. See n. 101.

98. See pp. 110, 113-114.

99. C. Wendel, *Kleine Schriften zum*

76. 'Cleopatra's Needle' standing amid the ruins of the Library and Museum.

launching an unprecedented campaign against the pagans: great crowds swarmed through the streets of the Bruchium and Rhachotis districts of Alexandria and made their way to the Serapeum, which they stripped of everything connected with the city's glorious past. (It is worth mentioning that in the Roman period the Temple of Serapis was considered the most magnificent building in the empire outside the Capitol.) This frenzied outburst of hooliganism aimed at destroying all trace of the pagan tradition reached its climax with the murder of Hypatia, a philosophy teacher prominent in Alexandrian life who was the daughter of the Neoplatonist mathematician Theon, the last known member of the Museum.[121]

7. Postscript. One question remains. What eventually happened to the only library that ever set out to be a 'world library'? To sum up what has been said so far, no authoritative source mentions its total destruction or hints at any 'policy change' that might have caused it to slide gradually into oblivion. The Library remained intact throughout the Ptolemaic period. Not only was Julius Caesar not responsible for burning it down, but its magnificence so fired his imagination that he took steps to found the first public library in Rome on his return there.[122] What is more, Strabo, who is known to have been a great book-lover, went to the Library after Caesar had left Alexandria[123] and says nothing that even hints at any catastrophe in its recent or earlier history. Whether Augustus (who included a bilingual library among the build-

77. The Great Library of Alexandria in the Ptolemaic period, with Egyptian-style architectural elements. O. von Corven, Illustrierte Geschichte des Alterthums, *vol. 2, Leipzig/Berlin 1880, 91.*

antiken Buch- und Bibliothekswesen, Köln 1974, 149.

100. Suetonius, *Domitian* 20.

101. Suetonius, *Claudius* 42. Claudius was an educated man who wrote histories of the Etruscans and the Carthaginians. In his honour the Museum was enlarged and public readings from his two history books were instituted, to be held on fixed dates each year. Hadrian, a great book-lover and admirer of Greek scholarship, appointed his teacher L. Iulius Vestinus to be director of the Greek and Latin libraries in Rome and also Principal of the Museum in Alexandria (*IG* XIV 1085).

102. Turner, *Ἑλληνικοί Πάπυροι* 108.

103. P. Faiyûm 89. On the philosophers of the Museum see Dio Cassius, LXXVII.7.3.

104. Turner, *Ἑλληνικοί Πάπυροι* 121.

105. P. Oxy. 2471. After the postscript to this letter someone has added in a different hand: 'Harpocration says that Demetrius the bookseller has got them. I have instructed Apollonides to send me some of my own books, which you will hear about in due course from Seleucus himself. If you find any, apart from those I already possess, have them copied and send them to me. Diodorus and his friends also have some that I haven't got.'

106. The first edition of the lexicon was published at Lyon in 1683, with notes by P.J. Maussaci and with Latin translation.

107. See K. Ohly, 'Stichometrische Untersuchungen', *ZB*, Beiheft 61 (1928) 88-89.

108. See pp. 105-106.

109. Two earlier instances of book-burning had been recorded in the history of the Mediterranean peoples: once in the case of Protagoras's books (see p. 34) and once under King Seleucus I (see p. 58).

110. On Origen and his splendid library of theological books see p. 152.

111. E. Gibbon, *The History of the Decline and Fall of the Roman Empire*, II, London 1788, 462.

112. See p. 140.

113. Turner, *Ἑλληνικοί Πάπυροι*

ings attached to the splendid Temple of Julius the God) purloined any books from the Alexandrian Library is not known; nor is it known whether the Library was in any way affected when Claudius and/or any of his predecessors enlarged the Museum.

On the other hand Epiphanius and Aphthonius, who visited the Serapeum library, perhaps in the middle of the fourth century A.D., do not mention the Great Library at all, and the possibility that some of the books were transferred from there to the subsidiary library in the Serapeum is no more than a working hypothesis. Whatever damage may have been done to the city when it was besieged by Aurelian and then by Diocletian, there is no firm evidence of the destruction of the Museum or the Library buildings. The riots instigated by Patriarch Theophilus may perhaps have caused serious damage to the books kept there. However, the chronicler's reference to the burning of the books by Caliph Omar in or after 642 is probably a figment of the imagination. My personal view of the matter, assuming that there was no other catastrophe of which we have no historical record, is that the Great Library of Alexandria suffered the fate that sooner or later befalls every library when, through changing circumstances, it ceases to fulfil its original purpose, gradually becomes run down and depleted and finally succumbs to the inexorable law of nature: progressive decay leading to extinction.

78. Alexander the Great rescues the works of Homer. Etching by Marcantonio Raimondi. Paris, Bibliothèque Nationale, Cabinet des Estampes.

29-32; E. Mioni, *Εἰσαγωγή στήν Ἑλληνική Παλαιογραφία* (= *Introduzione alla Paleografia Greca*, Padua 1973, tr. N.M. Panayotakis), Athens 1977, 45 ff. On the origins of the codex see *Bibliologia*, IX: *Les débuts du codex*, Turnhout 1989, with introduction by Jean Irigoin. See also the bibliographical and critical article by J. Irigoin, 'Les manuscrits grecs 1931-1960', *Lustrum* 8 (1962) 287-302.

114. Pliny, *Natural History* XIII.13.

115. Turner, *Ἑλληνικοί Πάπυροι* 22-24; Mioni, *op. cit.* 47.

116. C.H. Roberts, 'Books in the Graeco-Roman World and in the New Testament' in *The Cambridge History of the Bible*, I, Cambridge 1970, 48-66.

117. Turner, *Ἑλληνικοί Πάπυροι* 30.

118. On the peculiarities of the script used in this document, see Turner, *Ἑλληνικοί Πάπυροι* 125, 130.

119. See W. Schubart, *Das Buch bei den Griechen und Römern*, Heidelberg 1962, 163 ff.; M. Norsa, *La scrittura letteraria greca,* Florence 1939, 23; Mioni, *op.cit.* 51-53.

120. For further information about the owners of papyri in Alexandria see Turner, *Ἑλληνικοί Πάπυροι* 107-132, esp. 124 ff.

121. Socrates of Constantinople, *Ecclesiastical History* VII.14.15.

Cyril of Alexandria failed to have the Alexandrian philosophy school closed down. An interesting philosophical memorandum of the second half of the fifth century, on papyrus, tells us a good deal about the social pattern of general education: see Bell, *op. cit.* 116.

122. As far as I know, the first person to acquit Caesar of responsibility for burning down the Library was L. Canfora (*op. cit.* 84).

123. Strabo spent about five years in Egypt *circa* 25-20 B.C., i.e. some twenty years after Caesar's death.

79. A bookcase containing Plato's works from the main room of the royal library at Pergamum. Reconstruction by W. Hoepfner.

CHAPTER FIVE

OTHER LIBRARIES IN THE HELLENISTIC PERIOD

The great Library of Alexandria symbolized the intellectual supremacy of the then known world, and it was undoubtedly there that the most important work was done in the field of literature and textual criticism down to the middle of the second century B.C. However, the founding of libraries and the growth of textual studies were characteristic features of several of the kingdoms ruled by Alexander the Great's successors and of other intellectual centres with traditions going back to the Classical period, many of which managed to remain administratively independent of the ambitious Macedonian kings.[1] In this chapter we shall take a look at two of those other libraries, which are of interest from both an architectural and a literary point of view: the library of the Attalid kings of Pergamum and the 'archival library' at one of the most remote outposts of the Greek world, Ai Khanoum in Bactria.

I. Pergamum. The kingdom of Pergamum, a city not far from the Aegean coast in western Asia Minor, was founded after the territorial war (282-281 B.C.) between Lysimachus and Seleucus I. Until then Pergamum had belonged to Lysimachus, whose right-hand man, Philetaerus of Tieum, was responsible for the royal exchequer. When Lysimachus was killed, Philetaerus surrendered to Seleucus with the 9,000 talents from the exchequer and by adroit wire-pulling managed to carve out an independent kingdom for himself. This kingdom, Pergamum, was enlarged by his successors Attalus I and Eumenes II, who drove off the marauding Celts and, with the assistance of the Romans, defeated the Seleucids in 190 B.C. Meanwhile a systematic drive had been launched to turn Pergamum into a major centre of scholarship and the arts: it proceeded successfully, gathering momentum especially in the first decades of the second century, and continued until 133 B.C., when the kingdom of Pergamum was bequeathed to Rome.[2]

1. The foundation of the library. It is not known whether Attalus I (241-197 B.C.) ever intended or took steps to set up a library to rival that of the Ptolemies, so the founder of the Pergamum library is generally considered to be Eumenes II, who reigned from 197 to 158. Like the Ptolemies in Egypt, the Attalid kings of Pergamum tried to dignify their project with greater prestige and ensure its success by associating it with a leading representative of the Peripatetic school. Lacydes and Lycon politely declined the invitation to Pergamum,[3] while Aristophanes of Byzantium was unable to go because Ptolemy V was determined to keep the scholars of the Museum in Alexandria, by force if necessary, and so the only prominent scholar that Eumenes II managed to attract to the Pergamene court was the Stoic philosopher Crates of Mallus.

To judge by the subsequent course of events, it would seem that the kings of Pergamum had no intention of competing with the Museum by setting up a school of poets and literary scholars to rival that of Alexandria. At Pergamum we do not find teachers being succeeded by their pupils, and it was as philosophers – predominantly orthodox Stoics – rather than as textual critics that Pergamene scholars approached the

1. Archaeological excavations in the Hellenistic kingdoms tend to confirm the rule that from the third century B.C. every major Greek city had its library. For a list of all the known libraries in the Graeco-Roman world see J. Tøsberg, *Offentlige bibliotheker: Romerriget i det 2. arhundrede e Chr.*, Copenhagen 1976, 9-12; see also below, p. 124. It is worth saying a few words about a foundation which was one of the earliest examples of a public library endowed by private benefaction, like the Gennadius Library in Athens today, and so started a tradition that lasted at least until the end of the Hellenistic period. It was on the island of Cos, and according to the inscription on a marble dedicatory stele it was endowed mainly by a certain Diocles and his son Apollodorus, who contributed the library building and a hundred books. Others followed their example and helped with gifts of money or books. See L. Robert, 'Notes d'épigraphie hellénistique', *BCH* 59 (1935) 421-425. It is a curious coincidence that the two main benefactors have the same names as two of the known Alexandrian grammarians of the reign of Ptolemy Soter II (see p. 70), though of course that does not necessarily mean that they were the same persons. Quite possibly the library in question was attached to a gymnasium. On gymnasium libraries see: J. Delorme, *Gymnasion*, Paris 1960; R. Nicolai, 'Le biblioteche dei ginnasi', *Nuovi Annali della Scuola Speciale per Archivisti e Bibliotecari* 1 (1987) 17 ff.; G.Ch. Papachristodoulou, «Τό ἑλληνιστικό Γυμνάσιο τῆς Ρόδου: Νέα γιά τή βιβλιοθήκη του» in *Akten des XIII Internationalen Kongresses für klassischen Archäologie*, Mainz 1990, 500 ff. A library in Philadelphia (modern Amman), excavated

literary tradition.[4] The achievements of Crates and his circle in the field of textual studies are of no concern to us here: after a brief look at some of the incidents in the literary world that punctuated the period of rivalry between the two great libraries, we shall go on to evaluate the archaeological evidence uncovered by excavators at Pergamum insofar as it relates to the architecture of the library.

2. The library at its zenith. The high point in the history of the Pergamene library, or rather the period about which we know most, is the reign of Eumenes II. It would seem that Crates was the person who did most to enlarge the library and was the prime mover in the field of textual studies at Pergamum, but the only evidence we have consists of stories connected with the growth of interest in books and the reasons that led to the appearance of a large number of spurious works.

Crates was born at Mallus in Cilicia and, according to *Souda*, was a contemporary of Aristarchus. Nothing is known about his studies or the name of his teacher. He adopted the allegorical approach to the interpretation of poetry, first advocated by the orthodox Stoics, and concentrated especially on Homer. He also followed the Stoic line on 'the irregularity of words'. The only one of his pupils to distinguish himself was the philosopher Panaetius.[5] Crates's greatest achievement was to have introduced the Romans to the study of grammar during his prolonged stay in Rome in 168 B.C. There is no evidence to suggest that he was in any way involved in writing the anonymous *Pinakes* of the Pergamene library, which bear no comparison with the *Pinakes* compiled by Callimachus in Alexandria.[6]

3. Expansion of the library. The only information we have about the size of the Attalids' library is a solitary reference in Plutarch's *Life of Antony*, and Plutarch himself expresses reservations about its reliability because its source, a certain Calvisius (Calvisius Sabinus?) was hostile to Mark Antony.[7] Antony is said to have given Cleopatra 200,000 volumes from the library at Pergamum, and many scholars take the view that the gift was directly connected with the loss of the Alexandrian Library when Caesar was under siege in 47 B.C. No other historian mentions the story of Calvisius – not even the great Galen, a very prolific writer who was a native of Pergamum, nor his fellow-citizen Telephus, a grammarian.

That the post of librarian existed at Pergamum is attested by only one source, Diogenes Laertius (VII.34, in his *Life of Zeno*). Discussing the authors who had written about the art of love, he asserts that the Stoic philosopher Athenodorus, who had been in charge of the books at the Pergamum library, had excised certain passages that displeased the Stoics, for which he had been arrested and tried. After that episode, in 70 B.C., Athenodorus – who was evidently close to Antipater of Tyre and

by the Egyptian archaeologist Fawz el-Faqarani, is described by him in his paper 'The Library of Philadelphia(?)', *Wissen-schaftliche Zeitschrift der Universität Rostock*, but I have been unable to lay my hands on a copy of it.

2. Strabo, XIII.623 ff.

3. Lacydes was Principal of the Academy in Athens from 241/240 to 216/215. Lycon, a native of Ilium (Troy) who had inherited the Peripatetic school from Strato, had a high reputation and received generous support from Eumenes and Attalus: see Diogenes Laertius, V.67.

4. See W. Kroll in *RE* 11 (1922) 1634-1641; R. Pfeiffer, *Ἱστορία τῆς Κλασσικῆς Φιλολογίας. Ἀπό τῶν ἀρχῶν μέχρι τοῦ τέλους τῶν ἑλληνιστικῶν χρόνων* (= *History of Classical Scholarship: From the beginnings to the end of the Hellenistic age*, Oxford 1968, tr. P. Xenos et al.), Athens 1972, 282 ff. Another branch of literary studies that was developed at Pergamum and received substantial backing from the Pergamene court was archaeology and antiquarianism, which chimed perfectly with the Attalids' interest in books and general knowledge. One of the first of the scholars who went to work at Pergamum was Antigonus of Carystus, whose works include a series of brief biographies of philosophers: these he wrote on the basis of personal interviews with his subjects, declining to use the biographical methods recommended by Hermippus: see U. von Wilamowitz-Moellendorff, *Antigonos von Karystos*, Berlin 1881.

5. See Kroll, *op. cit.* 1640.

6. See F. Schmidt, *Die Pinakes des Kallimachos,* Kiel 1924, 28.

7. Plutarch, *Antony* LVIII. See also F. Münzer in *RE* 3 (1899) 1411.

8. Many Stoic philosophers are known to have taught privately in Rome, some of them living in the luxurious villas of the aristocracy. The last of this line mentioned in the sources was Arius Didymus, whom Augustus appointed 'court philosopher'.

9. See Pfeiffer, *op. cit.* 300 ff. On the persecution of Alexandrian literary scholars, *ibid.* 253. See also above, p. 63.

Diodotus, both of whom belonged to Cicero's circle – went to Rome and became friendly with Cato of Utica.[8]

In about 145 B.C., when many intellectuals including Aristarchus, the director of the Library, had been driven out of Alexandria by Ptolemy VIII's persecution, a number of literary scholars decided to go and work with Crates. As we have seen, one of those who went to Pergamum as a result of this first crisis in the world of literary studies was Aristarchus's distinguished ex-pupil Apollodorus of Athens, and Menecleus of Barce may have been another.[9]

4. The problem of pseudepigraphy. The feverish haste with which the Attalids sought to obtain as many rare and valuable books as possible is attested by Strabo (609), who informs us that Neleus's heirs had had to hide the books formerly owned by Aristotle and Theophrastus in a cave to keep them out of the grasping hands of the kings of Pergamum.[10] The problem of forged and spurious works is treated at greater length by Galen, who was an expert on anything to do with books.[11] He informs us, for example, that the Pergamenes bought a manuscript of the *Orations* of Demosthenes which appeared to be more complete than the one in Alexandria since it contained a 'new' Philippic which Demosthenes had delivered a few months before the battle of Chaeronea and, even more remarkably, a letter from Philip to the Athenians. However, this last anomaly seems not to have aroused the Pergamene scholars' suspicions, and so the new Pergamene edition of the *Orations* was believed to be authentic until further examination of the books in the Alexandrian Library revealed that the 'new' Philippic was not new at all: it already existed in Book VII of the *Philippica* by Anaximenes of Lampsacus.[12]

A more extravagant example of the completely spurious work produced during this period was a 'literary-historical' composition by Cratippus, who claimed to have been a contemporary of Thucydides and to have compiled a chronicle of events that the latter had not considered worth mentioning in his *History*. He even wrote about Thucydides's tomb, a topic that had recently been receiving attention from writers with an antiquarian turn of mind such as Polemon of Ilium. Cratippus's works were not taken seriously in Alexandria and Didymus, an expert on such matters, described Cratippus and Zopyrus as 'foolish windbags'. Nevertheless, Dionysius of Halicarnassus and Plutarch were both taken in and used Cratippus as a reliable source.[13]

As Varro informs us, the jealous rivalry between the two great libraries was such that Ptolemy V prohibited the export of papyrus to Pergamum so as to frustrate Eumenes II.[14] It was said that the Attalids invented parchment at this time as an alternative writing material: be that as it may, Crates certainly assisted its development by devising a method of treatment that produced parchment of a finer quality and suggesting that an export market be sought for it in Rome.[15] It may be

10. On the books that Neleus had inherited, see pp. 46-47.

11. Others besides Galen who wrote about the problem of pseudepigraphy were Olympiodorus, John Philoponus and Elias of Alexandria: see pp. 80-81.

12. See *Didymus on Demosthenes*, Pap. Berl. inv. 9780. Didymus has his own comments to make on the commentators (cols. 15, 10 ff.).

80. Galen. Engraving from Diogenes Laertius, Vite de philosophi moralissime, *Venice, N. Zopino, 1521.*

13. Marcellinus, *Life of Thucydides* 31-34 (on Zopyrus and Cratippus). Thucydides' unfinished *History* was quickly followed by a rash of 'continuations' and imitations. Xenophon's *Hellenica* starts exactly where Thucydides leaves off, in 411 B.C., and was continued by Cratippus and Theopompus, whose works are lost: see P.E. Easterling and B.M.W. Knox, *'Ιστορία τῆς Ἀρχαίας Ἑλληνικῆς Λογοτεχνίας* (= *The Cambridge History of Classical Literature*, I: *Greek Literature*, tr. N. Konomi et al.), Athens 1994, 585, 605.

14. Varro, *On Libraries*(?) = Pliny, *Natural History* XIII.70. Perhaps the first person to write about book collections, long before Varro, was Artemon of Cassandreia (see Athenaeus, *Deipnosophistai* XII.515e, XV.694a), to whom two works are attributed: *Collection of Books* and *Song of the Symposium*. According to I.A. Fabricius (*Bibliotheca graeca*, Hamburg

true that the export of papyrus to Pergamum was forbidden, but it seems that there was not a total embargo on exports since the Pergamenes were still able to obtain papyrus via another country.[16]

The extant literary and historical evidence concerning the Pergamum library is very sketchy, but the results of the excavations on the acropolis of Pergamum make up for that deficiency and tell us a good deal about the library premises.

5. Architecture. The only Greek library for which we have firm evidence concerning the architecture, layout, fixtures and fittings is that of Pergamum. The recent study by Wolfram Hoepfner not only confirms the theories originally advanced by A. Conze and K. Dziatzko but also adduces new evidence and compels us to revise our mental picture of Hellenistic libraries once and for all.[17] Hitherto it had been believed that they were entirely composed of small, bare, impersonal rooms, an idea derived from Aphthonius's description of the Serapeum library in Alexandria.[18] Now, however, it seems clear that the main room of a big Hellenistic library, such as that of Alexandria or Pergamum, consisted of a monumental hall dominated by the statue of a god or goddess, usually Athena, standing on a pedestal directly opposite the main entrance. Along the back and side walls there ran a narrow stone platform on which stood the bookcases, closed cupboards[19] rising to a height of about two metres, with windows higher up in the walls to admit light. The hall would have been used as a reading room and also for debates, lectures and ceremonies. Only a very small proportion of the total stock of books would have been kept there, because it is obvious that there was not nearly enough room for the hundreds of thousands of rolls in the Library's possession.[20] Extra rooms – and these would have been austere, impersonal rooms of no architectural distinction – were therefore added on for the storage of catalogued books as the library expanded, as well as scriptoria and study rooms where manuscripts were catalogued and edited.

Ancient architects were faced with two fundamental problems, to some extent interrelated, in designing libraries: protection against the elements and the provision of adequate lighting. Humidity was and always has been one of the worst enemies of books, and that was the very reason why the papyrus rolls were kept in closed bookcases away from the walls: to prevent the wooden bookcases or the rolls from being damaged by rising damp from the foundations or humidity coming in through the open windows. And since there had to be windows to admit light, wide eaves or a roofed, open-fronted stoa were needed to protect the books from the rain and dust-laden air, as glass windows were not in use anywhere until the first century B.C.[21]

II. Ai Khanoum. The 'archival library' in the palace of Ai Khanoum has a section to itself not so much because it was the farthest-flung outpost

1790-1809), it was Artemon who was instructed by Demetrius of Phalerum to collect all Aristotle's works.

15. John the Lydian, *On the Months* I.28 (ed. R. Wuensch, 1898).

16. See p. 20.

17. W. Hoepfner, 'Zu griechischen Bibliotheken und Bücherschränken' in *Sonderdruck aus Säule und Gebälk zu Struktur und Wandlungsprozeß griechisch-römischer Architektur*, Mainz 1996, 25-36; A. Conze, 'Die pergamenische Bibliothek', *Sitzungsber. Berliner Akad. für Wissenschaft* 53 (1884) 1257 ff.; R. Bohn, *Altertümer von Pergamon*, II, Berlin 1885, 56 ff.; Wendel, 'Das griechisch-römische Altertum' 82-88; W. Radt, *Pergamon*, Köln 1988, 187 ff.

In the second century A.D. there was another big library just outside Pergamum, endowed by the wealthy Flavia Melitene. It was in the grounds of a healing centre dedicated to Asclepius, with which it was connected by a network of courtyards and colonnaded galleries. Architecturally there is nothing original about it: its design and layout simply follow the standard pattern of other Roman libraries. For the central recess in the back wall Flavia Melitene commissioned a statue of the deified Emperor Hadrian, which bore the inscription *ΘΕΟΣ ΑΔΡΙΑΝΟΣ* ('Hadrian the God'): see O. Deubner, *Das Asklepieion von Pergamon. Kurze vorläufige Beschreibung*,

81. Floor plan of the royal library at Pergamum showing the position of the bookcases, from a drawing by W. Hoepfner. Scale 1:500.

of the Greek world, in the heart of the Buddhist Orient, as because it is the oldest library in which Greek literary works have been found.

Ai Khanoum, in the north-east of Afghanistan (ancient Bactria), was one of the many kingdoms through which the Silk Road ran. French archaeologists excavated a city dating from the third century B.C. in which they discovered a gymnasium, a theatre and a sanctuary dedicated to the city's founder. There was even a stele with a large collection of Delphic sayings inscribed on its base by the Peripatetic philosopher Clearchus of Soli, proving that Ai Khanoum kept closely in touch with the traditional centres of the Greek world.

The 'archival library'[22] in the palace was founded by King Eucratides, a contemporary of the Parthian king Mithradates I (second century B.C.). The salient feature of the palace complex was a square peristyle courtyard with a door on one side leading into a smaller court: opening on to the latter were several rooms used as shops, some of them selling luxury goods, which led the French archaeologists to describe the shops collectively as 'the treasury'. Between the two courtyards there was a small oblong room used as an 'archival library': not a public library, nor yet a library for academic study and research, but a royal archive that was an integral part of the palace. There the excavators found many scattered pieces of papyrus and parchment inscribed with fragments of philosophical dialogues and one play. The most remarkable thing about

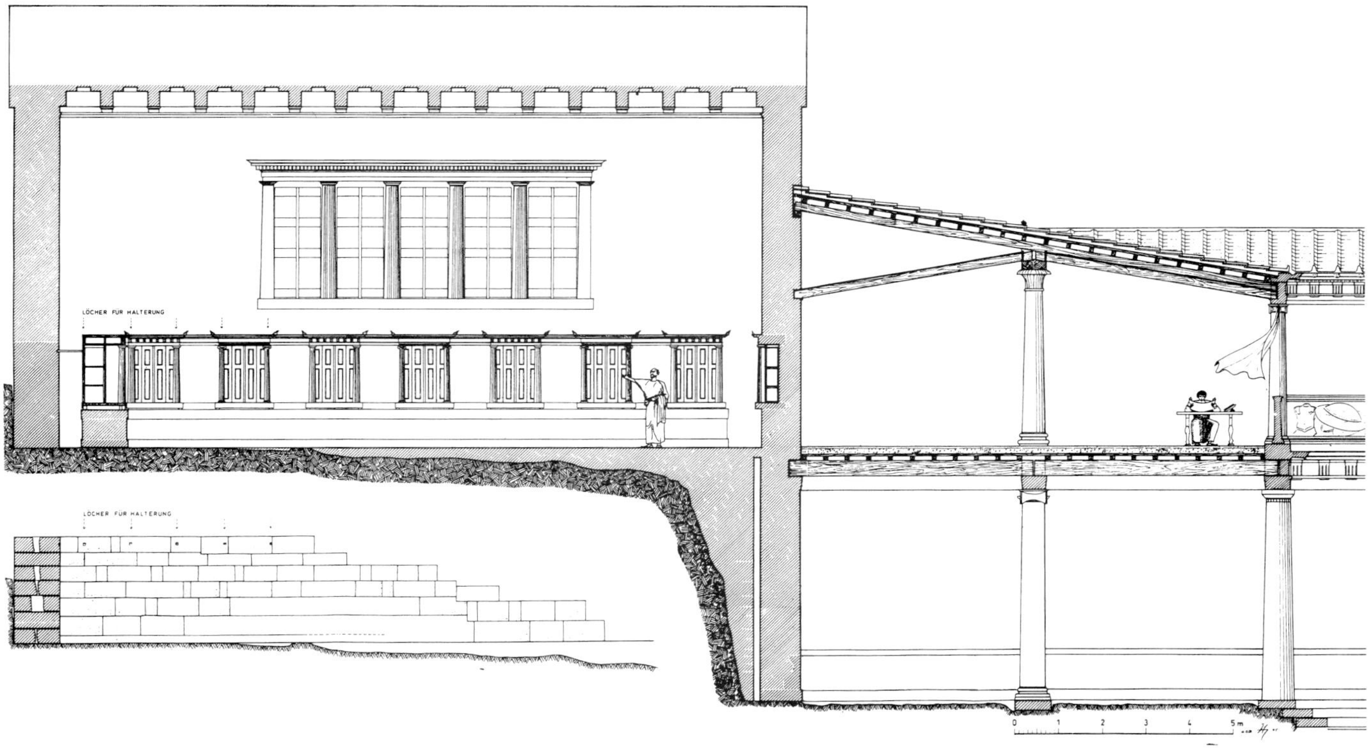

82. Longitudinal section of the royal library at Pergamum. Reconstruction drawing by W. Hoepfner. Scale 1:200.

Berlin 1938; V.M. Strocka, 'Römische Bibliotheken', *Gymnasium* 88 (1981) 320.

18. See p. 66.

19. The earliest reference to closed bookcases in a Greek library occurs in the introduction to Vitruvius's *De architectura* (VI.Intro.) in connection with the appointment of Aristophanes of Byzantium as director of the Alexandrian Library. Ptolemy V, to advertise his devotion to literature, organized a festival of competitions in honour of Apollo and the Muses, open to all comers, with prizes for the winners. Six men were picked to judge the contests and, as nobody suitable could be found to make up a panel of seven, the name of Aristophanes of Byzantium was suggested to the king. The festival began with a poetry competition that attracted a large number of entrants, one of whom was ranked first by judges and audience alike. When it came to Aristophanes's turn to give his verdict, he stated flatly that only one of the competitors was a real poet, as all the

this room was the method used for storing the documents, for there was no trace of bookcases of any kind attached to, or built into, the walls, but only sherds of earthenware storage jars strewn on the floor.[23] This shows that the librarians kept their papyrus rolls in jars of the kind that were used in 'archival libraries' in Egypt.[24]

83. Statue of Athena from the library at Pergamum. Berlin, Pergamonmuseum.

others had recited passages stolen from earlier writers, and to prove his point he fetched a lot of books out of the cupboards and showed the king the pirated passages, whereupon the would-be laureates broke down and confessed. Ptolemy gave orders for the plagiarists to be punished and rewarded Aristophanes by putting him in charge of the Library.

20. Hoepfner (*op. cit.* 33) estimates that the bookcases in the main hall would have held about 4,000 rolls.

21. See D. Baatz, 'Fensterglas, Glasfenster und Architektur' in A. Hoffmann and E.L. Schwandner (ed.), *Bautechnik der Antike*, Berlin 1991, 1 ff.

22. See C. Rapin, 'Les textes littéraires grecs de la trésorerie d'Aï Khanoum', *BCH* 111 (1987) 259-265.

23. *Ibid*. 263. For the way in which similar containers were used by the Egyptians for keeping archives, see E. Posner, *Archives in the Ancient World*, Cambridge Mass. 1972, 86-88; J. Černý, *Paper and Books in Ancient Egypt*, London 1952, 29.

24. The Egyptian document storage jars were just like the ones found at Ai Khanoum – oval-bodied, flat-bottomed, with or without handles – and identical to the jars used as coffers in public treasuries or for storing oil or perfumes: see C. Rapin, 'Les inscriptions économiques de la trésorerie hellénistique d'Aï Khanoum (Afghanistan)', *BCH* 107 (1983) 357-358.

CHAPTER SIX

LIBRARIES IN THE ROMAN PERIOD

The Romans inherited Greek civilization and cultivated it, but without ever surpassing it. The people of Latium, who never denied their debt to Greek learning, kept the Greek language alive not only in their Eastern provinces but in the West as well, in an attempt to bring their own literature up to the standards attained by earlier Greek writers. But it was an extraordinarily long time before books and private libraries, which the Greeks had accepted as indispensable tools of scholarship ever since the fifth century B.C., were recognized as essential to the intellectual life of Rome. Not until the dying years of the Republic, in the first century B.C., do we find books being regarded in Rome as familiar old friends, as they had long been in Athens and Alexandria. However, the Romans did introduce some important innovations in the architectural design of public libraries; they conceived the idea of the bilingual library with separate sections for Greek and Latin books; and they organized and expanded the book trade in all the provinces of the Empire.

I. The world of Latium. The Romans started to play a major political role in the Mediterranean around the middle of the third century B.C., chiefly as a result of their victory in the war (281-275) with Pyrrhus I, King of Epirus. In 273 they established diplomatic relations with the Ptolemies of Egypt, and after their conquest of Macedonia in 168 the area under their supremacy extended right up to the Egyptian frontier. In 146 Carthage was razed by the Romans, and in the same year Greece became a Roman province. These victories left the Romans in the same position as the Greeks had been after the death of Alexander the Great: they had conquered all the peoples and all the city-states in the Mediterranean basin. Meanwhile a well-organized, well-disciplined class of affluent citizens capable of administering all this wealth and these territories had come into being; but at the same time Rome had drifted away from the Latin way of thinking and the Latin religion and aligned herself more and more with the Greek world.

1. The beginnings of Roman literature. It was the Greeks who taught the Romans how to write, as the Etruscans had never managed to persuade the other inhabitants of Italy to adopt their alphabet. From those distant days of the sixth century B.C. we have only the sketchiest of information about Rome in the 'pre-book' period. According to the *Natural History* of Pliny the Elder, Cassius Eminas stated in his *Chronicle*, written in 146 B.C., that in the consulship of Cornelius Pompeius Cethegus and Baebius Pamphilius there was a scribe by the name of Terentius who discovered (at the foot of the Janiculum) the sarcophagus of the legendary early king Numa Pompilius with written papyri inside it.[1] Livy (I.26) also implies that writing was in use in Numa's time when he says that the instructions for religious ceremonies were written down by a high priest in his reign. According to Dionysius of Halicarnassus, the fourth king of Rome, Ancus Marcius, ordered all Numa's laws to be written down on oaken tablets and posted up in public places.[2] We know that in the fifth century the Romans sent a delegation to Athens to copy out Solon's

1. F.G. Kenyon, *Books and Readers in Ancient Greece and Rome*, Oxford 1951, 76. The Latins used a variety of writing materials, as is evident from a passage by the great jurist Ulpian (early 3rd c. B.C.): 'For official wills all kinds of material are to be deemed valid, whether they are written on wood or any other material or papyrus or parchment or the skin of any animal: all are valid documents.' For a general survey of ancient writing materials see H. Blanck, *Τό βιβλίο στήν ἀρχαιότητα* (= *Das Buch in der Antike*, tr. D.G. Georgovasilis and M. Pfreimter), Athens 1994, 55-85.

2. Dionysius of Halicarnassus, *Roman Antiquities* III.36.4.

84. Numa Pompilius. Engraving from Plutarch, Les vies des hommes illustres, *Paris 1694, 271.*

3. Kenyon, *op. cit.* 77.

4. On the history of Latin literature see R.W. Browne, *A History of Classical Literature*, II: *A History of Roman Classical Literature*, London 1851; Kenyon, *op. cit.* 77. On relations between Rome and Greece see N. Petrochilos, *Ρωμαῖοι καί Ἑλληνισμός. Μία διαλεκτική σχέση*, Athens

laws, and it is to be inferred from the *Myth* of Virginius Rufus that by then there was already a school (*litterarum ludi*) in the Forum.[3] The annalist C. Licinius Macer, a contemporary of Cicero's (1st c. B.C.), claimed to have read and edited some ancient chronicles written on linen (the *libri lintei*), from which he had obtained valuable information about the history of Rome.[4] But all this testimony is closer to legend than reality, and it was not until the third century B.C. that the earliest Latin literature came into being. At this point we are faced with a major problem, for we have no idea how Latin literature was passed on from generation to generation for the first two hundred years or so.[5]

Livius Andronicus. If any one person can be thought of as the father of Latin poetry, in the sense that his influence on succeeding generations was comparable to that of Homer on Greek literature, that person was a Greek from Tarentum, Livius Andronicus.[6] He was taken prisoner in the war against Pyrrhus (*c.* 275 B.C.) and brought back to Italy, where he was bought by a Roman belonging to the family of M. Livius Salinator, a general. He was manumitted in recognition of his contribution to the education of Livius's children and, in accordance with the usual custom, took the family name of his master, keeping Andronicus as his cognomen. He continued teaching after gaining his freedom and his method of education was widely adopted by the Romans. His teaching was based on the principle stated by Plato in his *Republic*, that children should learn the works of the great poets, especially Homer. But there was no Latin epic poem to compare in quality or importance with those of Homer, and so Andronicus took it upon himself to translate the *Odyssey* into Saturnians. It was this Latin version that Roman children were taught at school, right down to the time of Horace in the first century B.C.[7]

Livius certainly made his mark in Rome: he was officially recognized as a professional poet and, when the Romans felt that they had fallen out of favour with the gods and wished to woo them back, they commissioned him to write the propitiatory hymn they needed. This recognition made it possible for him to found a guild of writers and actors domiciled on the Aventine. His contribution to Roman intellectual life was immense. According to Cicero, in addition to his work as an educator and translator he introduced the Romans to drama in 240 B.C.: certainly he wrote several plays (with extensive musical accompaniment) based on Greek originals, in which he himself acted and sang the leading role on stage.[8] Knowing as he did how important books were in Greek culture, it is my belief that he was also the first systematic book-collector in the Roman world and raised public awareness of the paramount importance of books in the dissemination of knowledge.

The Hellenization of Rome. No evidence at all has come down to suggest how the book trade was run in Rome up to the middle of the first

1984. Flavius Vopiscus, in his 'Life of Aurelian' in the *Historia Augusta* (VI.1), probably written in the fourth century A.D., says that a friend of his, Junius Tiberianus, claimed to be able to supply him even then with the *libri lintei* from the Bibliotheca Ulpia.

5. Browne, *op. cit.*; H.J. Rose, *Ἱστορία τῆς Λατινικῆς Λογοτεχνίας* (= *A Handbook of Latin Literature*, London 1967, tr. K.Ch. Grollios), 2 vols., Athens 1978-1989.

85. L. Clodius Macer. Engraving from Spoor, Medici et Philosophi..., *83.*

6. Browne, *op. cit.* 50 ff.; Rose, *op. cit.* I 23ff. For a detailed study of Livius Andronicus's work see S. Mariotti, *Livio Andronico e la traduzione artistica*, Milan 1952; and, on the Hellenization of Latin literature generally, Petrochilos, *op. cit.*

7. Horace, *Epist.* II.1.69-71.

8. Rose, *op. cit.* I 23-24.

9. Browne, *op. cit.* 57; Rose, *op. cit.* I 29.

10. It is clear from what remains of Ennius's output that the Romans had access to Greek literary works, not only by Classical authors such as Euripides (from whom Ennius borrowed a lot of valuable material for his plays *Hecuba*, *Iphigenia* and *Medea exsul*) but also by Aristarchus of Tegea, by Euhemerus on the origins of religious beliefs, and by Sotades on Greek mythology (for his *Sota*). Ennius also wrote on philosophical subjects in his *Annales*, and some fragments of his poem *Epicharmus* have survived.

century B.C., but it is reasonable to suppose that the very numerous works of Livius Andronicus's successors circulated in book form among a fairly restricted readership. The fact that Greek plays exerted such a powerful influence on the development of Latin literature from the middle of the third century B.C. suggests that books were already being imported from Athens and Alexandria by that time. Naevius, for example, wrote a number of successful tragedies and comedies, adapting Greek metres to the Latin language,[9] while Ennius and his contemporaries, taking their inspiration from Greek literature, strove to refine the rather uncouth idiom of the Romans into a language that would bear comparison with the elegance and polished style of Greek.[10] This new literary output had many rich and powerful patrons, and there may have been a rather more organized market for books among the circles of Scipio Aemilianus and Laelius the Wise.

The Hellenization of Rome had started by the early decades of the second century B.C.: Homer's epics, the tragedies of Euripides and Sophocles and above all the comedies of Menander had been used as sources of material not only by Ennius (who had actually had a Greek education) but also by Caecilius Statius, Plautus and Terence, especially Plautus. Ennius borrowed from every area of Greek literature, which strongly suggests that he either had a large Greek library of his own or had access to one. Plautus, who had a genuine dramatic talent, adhered closely to Greek models: in nearly all the 130-odd comedies attributed to him the plots and characters are drawn from Philemon and Menander.[11] Since there was no public library in Rome at that time, nor indeed any organized library at all, we can only conclude that the Roman writers had their own private libraries containing works of early Roman literature as well as plays by the great Greek tragedians and the most important exponents of the New Comedy. No names of booksellers, copyists or publishers are known from that period, and so, in view of the provincialism of Roman writers and patricians, we have to assume that until Julius Caesar's time (mid first century B.C.) Greek books in Rome generally came from Athens, or perhaps from Alexandria.

It was Aristophanes (*The Frogs* 1114) who first suggested that plays were not written only for performance on stage but were also suitable objects of serious study, especially for educational purposes.[12] Clearly he recognized the close connection that existed between books and the theatre. Matters were different in Rome, however, at least until the end of the first century B.C., as the theatre was never such an integral part of life as it was in Athens and could not therefore be used as a springboard for the promotion of book-reading among the masses. In fact Rome did not even have a theatre until Pompey built one in 55 B.C.[13] Until then plays had been performed in temporary structures with two platforms of different heights and a wooden back wall with openings for the actors' entrances and exits. Two attempts to have a real theatre built, both in

11. Plautus's debt to Greek playwrights raises a good many questions about the availability of Greek books in the late third century B.C., as his own plays are all adaptations of Greek originals and he follows the structural conventions of the New Comedy. His *Asinaria*, for example, is based on the *Onagos* (*The Donkey-Driver*) by Demophilus, and his *Cistellaria* on the *Synaristosai* (*Ladies' Lunch Party*) by Menander. See Browne, *op. cit.* 87 ff.; Rose, *op. cit.* I 42 ff.

12. Cf. pp. 34-35.

13. Rose, *op. cit.* I 64.

14. Scipio Nasica came to prominence in his youth through the discovery by priests of a prediction in the Sibylline books foretelling that the Republic would never drive its enemies out of Italy until the image of the *Mater Idaea* (Mother of the Gods) was brought from Asia Minor to Rome by the most upright of its citizens. He was the person chosen to perform this office. See Livy, XXIX, XXXIV, XXXIX; Pliny, *Natural History* VII.34.

15. Nepos, *Cato* III.3; Cicero, *Brutus* 65.

16. The last scene of *Poenulus* provides another striking instance of the taking of liberties with the text, for it is given in several different versions in the various surviving manuscripts.

17. Plautus, *Amphitruo* 52.

18. Suetonius, *De grammaticis et rhetoribus* 62.

19. John the Lydian, *On the Months* I.28 (ed. R. Wuensch, 1898).

20. Plutarch, *Aemilius Paullus* 28. On Roman libraries see C. Wendel, 'Das griechisch-römische Altertum' (completed by W. Göber) in *HBW* III.1 113 ff.; Kenyon, *op. cit.* 75-85; T. Kleberg, 'Roma a l'epoca greco-romana' in G. Cavallo (ed.), *Libri editori e pubblico nel mondo antico*, Rome/Bari 1989, 40-80; R. Fehrle, *Das Bibliothekswesen im alten Rom*, Wiesbaden 1986; Blanck, *op. cit.* 204-216.

21. H.J. Rose, *Handbook of Greek Literature*, London 1948, 307 ff., 361, 371 (on Polybius, 31 ff.). One of the early authors who wrote about Pollio's library was Isidore of Seville (*Etymologiae* VI.5.1).

22. See p. 48.

about 179 B.C., were thwarted by Scipio Nasica and a philistine Senate, who held that the theatre tended to corrupt morals.[14]

The discontinuity of the Latin literary tradition is due not only to the absence of public libraries but also to the circumstances in which most such works were written and published. By Cicero's time, if not even earlier, the body of Roman literature had been eroded by large-scale losses and textual corruption. Works by Naevius, Ennius, Plautus and Cato the Censor had disappeared for ever. Cicero deplored the wastage, while boasting that he himself had saved 150 of Cato's speeches.[15] In contrast to Athens, where texts were liable to be corrupted by frequent and often careless copying, in Rome the texts of plays were more likely to be altered by theatre managers, who paraphrased them to suit the tastes of their audiences. Plautus, for example, who wrote for a theatre manager and publisher, gave him a free hand to make any alterations to the scripts that the actors might suggest. Successful plays were revived from time to time, as we learn from the prologue to *Casina*, which was staged in the late second century B.C., some fifty years after Plautus's death, in a new production with major cuts and alterations to suit the wishes of the public and the spirit of the times.[16] Comedy was certainly popular in Rome, but the plays were hardly remembered once the performances were over: they were not considered suitable material for literary research or intellectual inquiry into deeper issues. Tragedy failed to prosper in Rome because the audience there was not sufficiently cultivated for it. Plautus, in the prologues to his plays, had to cajole the audience to pay a bit of attention: 'You groaned when I mentioned the word "tragedy".'[17]

Crates. Towards the middle of the second century B.C., around the year 168, the untravelled scholars and literati of Rome had an opportunity to hear Crates talking about the wonderful libraries of Alexandria and Pergamum. Crates of Mallus, who had gone there as a member of a diplomatic delegation from Eumenes II of Pergamum, was said by Suetonius to have been the person who introduced the systematic study of grammar to Rome.[18] This came about because he had an accident in Rome and had to stay on there for some months, which he spent giving lessons and lectures on poetry and grammar. What interests us here is not so much his contribution to the schooling of the first generation of Roman grammarians as his extensive knowledge of Hellenistic libraries, which could hardly have failed to excite his listeners' wonder. Crates had accepted an invitation to the Attalids' court at Pergamum, where he organized and ran the library and devised methods of treating skins to produce parchment of a finer quality. It was he, too, who suggested that parchment might be exported to Rome, probably after his return from his prolonged stay there.[19]

2. The first libraries. The first libraries formed by Roman patricians contained only Greek books: these were the spoils they had carried away

86. Mithradates. Engraving from Spoor, Medici et Philosophi ..., *33.*

23. Isidore, *loc. cit.*; Kleberg, *op. cit.* 41.

24. Suetonius, *De grammaticis...* 15; Pliny, *Nat. Hist.* xxv.5-7. Mithradates's interest in medicine stemmed from practical considerations and was not entirely of his own choosing, for he wished to protect himself against his enemies who were intent on poisoning him. Pliny evidently believed the popular story that he made himself immune to all kinds of

87. M. Porcius Cato. Engraving.

88. Aemilius Paullus. Engraving.

from their victorious wars with various Greek states. In 168 B.C., when Crates was actually in Rome, Aemilius Paullus sacked the library of the Macedonian kings at Aegae and gave the contents to his sons, who were deeply immersed in Greek literature.[20] In this way his sons acquired an excellent collection of books representing a comprehensive cross-section of Greek literature. One of them, Publius Aemilius, was adopted by Publius Cornelius Scipio (the son of Scipio Africanus Major), taking the name of Scipio Aemilianus. His entry into Scipio's highly cultured household brought him into contact with the Greek philosophers and historians then residing in Rome. A fluent Greek speaker, he was an intimate friend of the Stoic philosopher Blossius of Cyme and of Polybius, and his favourite book was Xenophon's *Cyropaedia*. Nearly a hundred years after his death his collection of books became the nucleus of Rome's first public library, founded by Pollio shortly after 39 B.C.[21] In 86 B.C. Sulla captured Athens and carried off Apellicon's library, which included the books that had belonged to Aristotle and Theophrastus.[22] Lucullus, too, after his victorious campaign against Mithradates VI of Pontus, brought back with him the books of the Pontic kings as his spoils of war.[23] Among them was a case full of medical textbooks, which Pompey appropriated for himself and had translated into Latin.[24]

3. Education. The surest way of enlarging the reading public so as to broaden the appeal of books is by organizing education properly. The system prevailing in Rome, however, was not capable of supporting a 'book policy': although primary schools and private teachers had existed for centuries, the environment in which children picked up their elementary education was the family. The symbolic significance attached to this tradition is illustrated by the story of Coriolanus: when he rebelled and marched on Rome at the head of the Volsci, he remained inflexible in the face of entreaties from the Roman people and the priests, and only his mother's reproofs moved him sufficiently to make him call off his assault on the city.[25]

In his seventh year a boy was handed over into the sole care of his father, who from then on would take the youngster out with him when he went to work, even to closed sessions of the Senate. Plutarch devotes a whole chapter to Cato the Censor's upbringing of his son, a paternal duty which he took extremely seriously.[26] Boys were brought up by the family until they were nine or ten, when, as a general rule, they were taken in hand by friends of the family or men active in public life (Cicero records that his father sent him to study law with a member of the great Gracchus family, Quintus Mucius Scaevola 'the Augur'[27]). If they were bright enough to go on to higher education, there was no alternative but to send them to study with a private teacher, known in Rome by the Greek word *grammaticus*.[28] Following standard Greek practice, the teacher took his pupils through the major works of Greek and Latin lit-

poison by taking daily doses of small quantities of poison and antidotes. See H. Funaioli, *Grammaticae romanae fragmenta*, Leipzig 1907, 403-404.

25. See the classic work by H.-I. Marrou, *Ἱστορία τῆς Ἐκπαιδεύσεως κατά τήν Ἀρχαιότητα* (= *Histoire de l'éducation dans l'antiquité*, Paris 1948, tr. Th. Fotinopoulos), Athens 1961, esp. 325 ff. («Ἡ Ρώμη καί ἡ Κλασική Ἐκπαίδευσις»). For the story of Coriolanus see Livy, II.40.5-9.

26. Marrou, *op. cit.* 330 (Plutarch, *Cato the Elder* 20).

27. Marrou, *op. cit.* 331 (Cicero, *De legibus* 1).

28. *Ibid.* 351, 381 ff.

29. *Ibid.* 353, 355.

30. See p. 98.

31. Rose, *Ἱστορία* ... I 135.

32. Cicero, *Brutus* 104; Plutarch, *Tiberius Gracchus* VIII.17.20.

33. Cicero himself gives details of his studies in *Brutus* 315-316. Cf. Plutarch, *Cicero* 4.

34. Plutarch, *Cicero*. Plutarch's is the only extant ancient biography of Cicero: most of what we know about him comes from his own writings, especially his letters.

35. See T. Pütz, *De M. Tulli*

89. L. Cornelius Sulla. Engraving.

90. L. Licinius Lucullus. Engraving.

erature, especially poetry. Besides the *grammaticus* there were two other classes of specialized teachers active in higher education, for philosophy and rhetoric.[29] All this tuition was private and the state was not involved at all. Often the teachers were educated slaves like Livius Andronicus,[30] working for their masters.

Although a particularly able and gifted teacher might sometimes gather round him a group of pupils that could be called a school of a kind with its own academic standards, as in the case of Valerius Cato, these 'schools' were never influential enough to spread the reading habit to the masses.[31] But from Cicero's time all this changed and the aristocracy adopted the Greek system of education. As we have seen, Aemilius Paullus had highly-qualified Greek teachers for his sons. Cornelia, the mother of the Gracchi, had Tiberius educated by the famous rhetor Diophanes of Mytilene and the Stoic philosopher Blossius of Cyme.[32] Young Romans with the inclination and talent to pursue their studies still further went either to Athens, where they boarded at one of the renowned Athenian schools, or to the philosophy schools on the island of Rhodes (like Cicero and many of his contemporaries). A natural outcome of this Hellenizing tendency in education was that the book trade expanded enormously in the first century B.C.

4. Private libraries. The first century B.C. brings us to the golden age of books in Rome, for which we have more evidence than for any other period up to the Renaissance, not only about public and private libraries but also about the book trade and the methods used to promote sales. The first person to be so enamoured of books as to earn the title of the earliest real book-collector of antiquity was Cicero, a strong enough personality to break Rome's cultural dependence on Athens and Alexandria and to remould Latin literature in keeping with the trends of his time and the character of the people of Latium.

Cicero. Cicero was born in the small town of Arpinum in 106 B.C. and had a Greek higher education. He chose the celebrated Rhodian rhetor Apollonius Molo to teach him rhetoric, Phaedrus the Epicurean and Diodotus the Stoic to teach him philosophy. He also spent some time at Plato's Academy in Athens when Philo was its principal.[33] He fell in love with Athens and seriously considered spending the rest of his life there, but in the end his thirst for knowledge led him further afield. After making the acquaintance of some teachers of the Asiatic school, he visited the philosophy schools on Rhodes and then went back to Rome. His life was a long struggle to maintain a romantic ideological outlook in the face of the harsh realities of a political career punctuated by frequent conspiracies. His opposition to Julius Caesar led to his being exiled in 58 B.C., and when he returned to Rome a year later he found it impossible to re-establish himself at the top of the political tree. He incurred Mark

Ciceronis Bibliotheca (dissertation), Münster 1925. On Atticus's role in the literary world see R. Sommer in *Hermes* 61 (1926) 389-422; R. Feger in *RE*, suppl. 8 (1956) 517-520; and the methodical but rather biased study by J. Carcopino, *Les secrets de la correspondance de Cicéron*, II, Paris 1947, 305-329.

36. Atticus was born in 109 B.C., which made him three years older than Cicero. He inherited a huge fortune which he later increased by judicious investment and by capitalizing on his personal popularity, for he even managed to persuade people who were in no way related to him to leave him their property. Because of his family connections with the tribune Publius Sulpicius Rufus, he decided it would be more prudent to leave Italy and go to live in Athens until the troubles following the murder of Sulpicius should blow over. His long stay in Athens earned him the cognomen Atticus.

Atticus was one of the most consistent adherents of Epicureanism in history. He managed to reconcile his philosophy with his own egocentricity and great wealth, staying out of politics and living a simple but comfortable life. He used his money to help followers of all political parties: besides Cicero, his friends included Sulla, Hortensius, Cato, Mark Antony and Octavian. Developing and culti-

91. M. Tullius Cicero. Engraving from Spoor, Medici et Philosophi..., *34.*

Antony's wrath by speaking out against him and was murdered by his agents in 43 B.C.[34]

Atticus. To find out about ancient Roman book-lovers, their new ideas on the running of private libraries and the people who worked in the production and marketing of books, one need only read Cicero's *Letters to Atticus*.[35] Titus Pomponius Atticus was an exceptional person, an expert on grammar and a great admirer of Atticism. Besides being an intimate friend and trusted confidant to whom Cicero revealed his secret hopes and fears, he was also an excellent adviser on matters of literary style and content and was instrumental in putting Cicero's writings into good shape for publication. The correspondence between them covers a period from 68 B.C. to the last years of Cicero's life, during part of which Atticus was living in self-imposed exile in Greece, sometimes in Epirus but more often in Athens.[36] His boundless enthusiasm for books and his standing as an unquestioned authority on Greek and Latin literature made it possible for him to establish the book trade on a firm footing, even when he was not in Rome himself, and to raise the literary standards of editing and publishing. He possessed a fine private library, on which Cicero himself had designs (*Epistulae ad Atticum* I.4, 7, 10). Cicero's love of books is in any case well attested: for example, when he acquired the library of the literary scholar Servius Clodius in 60 B.C., he wrote to Atticus, 'I am longing to work my way through all the rolls, because my enthusiasm for these books grows at the same rate as my dislike of anything else' (*ibid.* I.20).

Atticus ran one scriptorium in his villa on the Quirinal and another in Athens, from where he regularly sent books to Cicero and other Roman book-lovers. In one of his letters Cicero thanks him for sending a copy of Serapis, adding that he has made arrangements for payment to be made immediately (II.4). Elsewhere (VIII.11a) Cicero asks Atticus to send him as soon as possible a copy of *On Concord* by Dionysius of Magnesia, which he knew had been given to Atticus. Atticus helped Cicero not only by obtaining new books for him but also by organizing his library. On the death of Cicero's 'reader' Sositheus, Atticus helped Cicero to arrange his books. It would seem that Tyrannio, the celebrated literary scholar and book-collector, was employed by Cicero to put his library in order and perhaps also to buy books for him, to judge by the complimentary remarks Cicero makes about him (IV.4a). In the same letter Cicero asks Atticus to send him two of his slaves trained as bookbinders (*glutinatores*) to help Tyrannio in his work of patching torn rolls and sticking on labels ('which you Greeks call *sillyboi*'). When these two slaves (Dionysius and Menophilus) had accomplished their task, Cicero wrote to Atticus to tell him that his house felt as if it had a soul now that Tyrannio had finished arranging the books (IV.8).[37] Atticus greatly influenced Cicero, who had absolute faith in his critical judgment and

vating his circle of friends and acquaintances may be described as one of his main hobbies, and he was also keenly interested in Roman history. His only piece of writing on current affairs was a monograph on Cicero's consulate, which he wrote in Greek. The remainder of his time he apparently spent on his editorial and publishing work. His household, which was entirely staffed by educated slaves, was in effect the first publishing house of its time, doing business over a vast geographical area that reached to the furthest corners of the Empire. There is good evidence to suggest that he published Greek as well as Latin books, which indeed is only to be expected, given his love of Greek and his profound knowledge of Greek literature. The main source of information about his life is the biography by Cornelius Nepos.

37. On Tyrannio's library see pp. 48-49. P. Oxy. 2450 gives us an idea of the sort of work done by *glutinatores*. Cf. Diogenes, *Epistles* XXXIII.1 (Hercher, *Epistolographi graeci* 247): 'I was sitting ... glueing books.'

38. Seneca the Elder, *Controversiae* 4, preface; Horace, *Satires* I.4.74-75. On Pollio see pp. 110, 112-113; also J. André, *La vie et l'oeuvre d'Asinius Pollion*, Paris 1949. A useful and well-researched study of books and the relations between writers, publishers and booksellers is Catherine Salles, *Lire à Rome*, Paris 1994, 94 ff.

39. Ovid was exiled at the age of fifty to Tomi, probably on the site of modern Constanța in Romania. Before leaving Rome he had burnt his manuscript of the *Metamorphoses*, but fortunately the work was saved because it was so popular that numerous copies were in circulation in book form. See Rose, *Ἱστορία* ... II 35 ff.; Salles, *op. cit.* 95.

40. Pliny the Younger, *Letters* I.13: for more on the subject see A.N. Sherwin-White, *The Letters of Pliny: A historical and social commentary*, Oxford 1966. Varro, who was very interested in the history of Roman literature, wrote a great many short treatises including three books entitled *On Readings* (*De lectionibus*):

allowed him to make any improvements he thought fit in his own writings, from the choice of title to the question of whether it was a good idea to publish the work at all (IV.14), not to mention points of style (I.19). Thanks to Cicero's inflated self-importance and overweening ambition, we know more than we otherwise would about the organization of the book trade. Not only did he boast to Atticus, 'I have astounded the Greek world with my writings,' but he asked him for information about the stocks of his books in bookshops in Athens and elsewhere, as he expected their publication to win him the sort of fame that the Philippics had earned for Demosthenes (II.1).

To sum up the information gleaned from the letters to Atticus, it seems clear that from Cicero's time the Roman patricians started spending a fair amount of time on reading and on philosophical symposia and dialogues, bringing the world of Socrates and Plato, Protagoras and Prodicus back to life. Educated Greek slaves took part in literary banquets, often reciting prose or poetry to the guests. And the Roman aristocracy, imbued with Greek ideals of beauty and Greek attitudes to the healthy development of the mind, lived in villas adorned with statues imported from Athenian studios and equipped with well-stocked libraries. Even Cicero, whose personal fortune did not begin to compare with those of Sulla and Lucullus, maintained no less than seven villas (at Antium, Arpinum, Tusculum and elsewhere), with his books divided between them. *Librarii* – a term that covers booksellers, publishers and copyists – used a wide variety of prepublication advertising techniques, including readings of excerpts from the new books at small private parties or big public meetings. The book trade was well organized, not only in Rome but in all the Greek-speaking areas of the provinces as well.

We know that books were first introduced into Rome from the Greek world, and it was from the Greeks, too, that the Romans learnt to regard private libraries as an essential tool for scholarly research. One thing we do not know, however, is precisely how books were distributed to the reading public in the Greek world, even in the Hellenistic period. It is quite likely that the relationship between Roman authors and their publishers and booksellers from the first century B.C. was also modelled on Greek practices. From the time of Cicero's death in 43 B.C. we have a good deal of information, either because the workings of the book trade had by then become settled practice or simply through a stroke of fortune. Enough evidence is therefore available for us to be able to follow the progress of a book from author to final buyer and the role of books in Roman intellectual life, with fuller and better documentation than for any other period up to the Renaissance.

5. Authors and public recitation. The most widely-used method of publicizing new books, the *recitatio*, was introduced into Roman intellectual life by the wealthy bibliophile Gaius Asinius Pollio. *Recitationes*, with their combination of public recitation and literary competition, were perfectly suited to the Roman character and soon became as popular as gladiatorial shows. Pollio, Virgil's patron and founder of Rome's first public library in 39 B.C., instituted the practice of reciting new literary works to audiences with varying levels of literary education.[38] Whatever his original motive may have been – whether personal vanity, a desire to give the government a means of controlling literary output or a genuine interest in spreading the benefits of education – the impact of his new idea very soon exceeded anything he could have expected. Well-to-do, educated Romans suddenly developed a craze for writing, with the sole object of winning public acclaim and hearing their names mentioned in the same breath as the great orators of the Republican age. Even Ovid, languishing in exile in the land of the Getae, translated extracts from his poems into the local dialect and recited them to a barbarian audience.[39] Most literary works written in the first century B.C. have something to say for or against *recitationes*, which always attracted large audiences, sometimes including the Emperor himself. Augustus showed his support for various literary circles by patronizing their *recitationes* regularly,[40] while Claudius paid an unscheduled visit to a recitation by Nonianus to see for himself what it was about the latter's 'performances' that roused the public to such wild demonstrations of enthusiasm.[41]

The fashion for recitation provided endless scope for exhibitionists interested only in self-advertisement, with the result that the public eventually became bored to death by the whole business, as Pliny the Younger testifies (*Letters* I.13): 'This year has brought a rich crop of poets: hardly a day passed in April without a public recitation by at least one of them. I am delighted that literary studies are flourishing and that fresh talents are emerging and producing good work. Needless to say, people go to hear them without enthusiasm. Most people stay in their shops and occupy themselves with inanities while the recitation is in progress, from time to time asking whether the master of ceremonies has come in, whether he has read the preface or whether he has nearly reached the end of the roll. Then they go in, though still reluctantly and dragging their feet, and they do not sit patiently but go out before the end, some of them slipping out furtively and others walking out boldly and openly.' The popularity of *recitationes* is of some importance in the history of Roman intellectual life because it did a great deal to make serious literature more widely read and appreciated, but that is beyond the scope of this book. At the same time, public recitations had a beneficial effect on the output and sales of books.

6. Promotion of books by their authors. Working a text into its final form for publication was no simple matter.[42] When an author decided that his book was ready to be published he would first try to promote it by self-advertisement before handing it over to a publisher-bookseller. This approach, which had become established practice by the early years of the Empire, was adopted even by the most respected writers. For orators and poets still trying to make their way, and for many Romans afflicted with the *cacoethes scribendi*, the surest path to success was of course to dedicate the book to a member of the aristocracy, or even to the Emperor himself, and even well-established writers were not above using the same tactics. Statius, a highly accomplished poet, dedicated the second book of his *Silvae* to Atedius Melior, with the following note: 'If you like these verses, such as they are, they will find a readership with your backing; otherwise, please send them back to me.'[43] Pliny the Younger used to send copies of his books to senators and other patricians. Vespasian's name is first on the list of dedicatees of Josephus's *History of the Jewish Wars*, which also includes his sons Titus and Domitian.[44] Martial gave copies of the fifth and eighth books of his *Epigrams* to Domitian, and to make sure that the Emperor actually received them he asked the imperial chamberlain Parthenius to put them on Domitian's table.[45]

The object of dedicating books to highly-placed personages was twofold: first, to make the work more widely known (since the dedicatee was usually someone with a following) and so enhance its prospects of commercial success, and secondly to improve the chances of its being read by educated men who might annotate the text and perhaps suggest corrections, which would help to increase the book's literary merit.

7. Relations between author and publisher. Roman literature tells us nothing about the contractual arrangements between author and publisher regarding publication rights.[46] Only Horace,[47] Quintilian and Martial mention their publishers by name, while Pliny the Younger refers to them simply as 'booksellers' (*bybliopolae*). Authors devised various ways of advertising their publishers and booksellers with the idea that this would also help to promote sales of their own books. Martial, in several of his epigrams, names the bookshops in Rome where his books were on sale, and Quintilian prefaced the first book of his *Institutio oratoria* with a testimonial to Tryphon, his publisher and bookseller.[48]

8. Publishers. Large-scale publishing certainly had a healthy effect on the dissemination of knowledge and the standards of scholarship, but it also led to widespread corruption of the texts. Some publishers, with an eye to quick and easy profits, resorted to a process of mass-production that virtually precluded the possibility of accurate copying: a typical 'printing house' of the Roman period was staffed by a team of slaves or freedmen all writing simultaneously to the dictation of a reader who might or might not be an expert on the subject.[49] Although it was not unknown for book copying to be treated seriously, with a conscientious scribe copying a roll from dictation for best results, books often reached the market without having been checked for accuracy, as Strabo informs us.[50] Cicero, for example, asked Atticus to look for the unsold copies of the *Orator* and replace the name of the Attic comic playwright Eupolis with that of Aristophanes (*Epist. ad Att.* XII.6.13). Similarly, Aulus Gellius (*Noctes Atticae* V.4) tells a story about a visit to a bookshop in Rome: there he saw for sale an edition of the early Roman annalist Fabius Pictor, whose accuracy the bookseller vouched for with a guarantee of a certain sum of money. Unfortunately, the proof-reader called in to certify the truth of the bookseller's statement found one small error: instead of *duodevicesimo* (eighteenth) the copyist had written *duoetvicesimo* (twenty-second). It need hardly be said that the publishers did not rely on the scribes alone to ensure the textual accuracy of their books: the manuscripts were checked by a proof-reader (*corrector*), on whose literary experience the reliability of the text largely depended.

9. The antiquarian value of old books. In the Ptolemaic period, and more particularly at the time of the great rivalry between the libraries of Alexandria and Pergamum in the second century B.C., we have seen how forgery was rife and old copies of books commanded a premium, either because they were considered authentic and textually reliable or because they were by famous authors. In the Roman period this trend became still more marked. According to Gellius (II.3), the grammarian Fidus Optatus owned a copy of the second book of the *Aeneid* which he had bought from a merchant in the Sigillaria market for no less than twenty aurei, believing it to have once belonged to Virgil. The huge sums of money that ignorant bibliophiles in Rome and elsewhere were willing to pay led many booksellers and other clever forgers to give manuscripts an artificial appearance of antiquity so that they would command a higher price. Dio Chrysostom, writing late in the first century A.D., has a passage (XXII.12) in which he exposes some of the sharp practices employed by these tricksters: 'They know very well that old books are in greater demand because they are better written and are on more durable papyrus. They therefore rub the defective copies of our own time in flour, to give them the colour of old manuscripts. In this way they damage them even more and pass them off as old copies.' The fashion for book-collecting led to the introduction of new marketing methods for old books, such as selling by auction or by pedlars hawking their wares to the farthest corners of the Empire.[51]

10. Booksellers. We know from Aristophanes (*The Birds* 1222) that bookshops in Athens had been regular haunts of literary men since the

presumably the *lectiones* of the title were public readings of the kind that the next generation called *recitationes*.

41. Pliny the Younger, *loc. cit.*

42. On the promotion of books by their authors see Salles, *op. cit.* 149 ff.

43. Statius, *Silvae* II, preface.

44. Salles, *op. cit.* 152.

45. *Ibid.* 152-153.

46. Up to a point, publishing practices in the ancient world were much

92. Seneca the Younger and Seneca the Elder, Opera omnia, *Leiden 1649.*

the same as they are today. When the author had finalized his text he gave it to a publisher-bookseller, who decided how many copies to have made according to the popularity of the author or the strength of public response to the recitations. He might then keep all the copies to sell at his own bookshop, or he might distribute them to other booksellers as well. Nothing whatever is known about the payment made to the author: probably each contract was negotiated individually.

47. Horace's publishers were the Sosius brothers (*Epist.* I.20.2, *Ars poet-*

93. *Cicero in his library. Engraving, 18th c.*

fifth century B.C. In the Roman period, when the book trade was firmly established, the same was true. Gellius informs us that bookshops were meeting-places for intellectuals, where poets lost no opportunity to boast of the popularity of their work.[52] Horace (*Odes* II.20.13-20) and Ovid (*Tristia* IV.9.15) both prided themselves on the fact that their books were read throughout the length and breadth of the Empire. Martial (VII.88, XI.3) made no attempt to conceal his pleasure at the favourable reception given to his poems in Vienna, while Pliny the Younger (*Letters* VIII.12.2) expressed his satisfaction with the sales of his books in Lyon. The illustrated edition of Varro's *De imaginibus* was available in all countries, as we are told by Pliny the Elder (*Natural History* XXXV.11), and a thousand copies were made of the obituary of the son of the orator Marcus Aquilius Regulus, to be distributed throughout the Italian peninsula (Pliny the Younger, *Letters* IV.7.2).

Cicero mentions a *taberna libraria* (bookshop) in the Forum, where Clodius took refuge from Antony.[53] The bookshops in Rome were concentrated in the Argiletum, the Vicus Tuscus and the Vicus Sandaliarius and the Sigillaria district.[54] From Martial we know the names of two shopkeepers who sold books. One of them, Atrectus, had his premises in the Argiletum, facing the Forum Caesaris, where he kept a stock of works by famous poets; he also allowed his customers to sell books of their own at his shop, charging them a commission of five denarii per copy.[55] The other, Secundus by name, had his shop behind the Temple of Peace and the Forum of Nerva.[56]

These bookstores are to be imagined as shops opening on to a street or perhaps an enclosed courtyard. Book lists or excerpts from the books on sale were often displayed on the doorposts,[57] and if there was space outside the shop front there might be stalls on the pavement with books set out on them to attract passers-by.[58] Inside the shop the books were kept either in *armaria* (closed bookcases or chests)[59] or on shelves. Horace, however, in his early days flatly refused to let his work be sold in bookstores, where it would be thumbed by all and sundry: 'No shop shall ever hang my books on its pillars to be soiled by the sweaty hands of common folk' (*Satires* I.4.71-72).

The dawn of the second century A.D. ushered in a great new chapter in the history of books. It is now possible to talk of a fairly homogeneous public of scholars and educated men in the provinces of the Roman Empire. And although it was the Greek element that predominated in that cosmopolitan mosaic, Latin books were sold on an equal footing in the Empire, which helped to create the literary unity that Julius Caesar had envisaged when he first conceived the idea of founding a bilingual library. Books by Greek and Latin writers were on sale in the bookshops of neighbouring France, in North Africa and Spain, and of course in the Hellenistic East. With justifiable pride Horace boasted that his poems were available in book form from the shores of the Bosporus to North

ica 345). A papyrus found in Egypt, containing a commentary by Apollonius of Athens ('the Grammarian') on the points of grammar raised by Book XVI of the *Iliad*, has the word ΣΩΣΥΟΥ ('of Sosyos') written after the title. This probably refers to the Sosii, who may well have had a market for their books in Egypt.

48. *Inst. orat.*, preface.

49. Martial, I.113. Educating an intelligent slave was a useful way of getting a good return on the funds invested in him, for the slave could make money for his master by giving lessons or copying manuscripts. A typical case in point is that of Lutatius Daphnis, whom Gaius Catullus bought for 700,000 sesterces and manumitted soon afterwards: see Suetonius, *De grammaticis...* 3; Funaioli, *op. cit.* XIII.

Some papyri have line numbers written in the margin every hundred lines, with the total number of lines at the end, for the purpose of calculating the copyist's wage. According to the Edict of Diocletian (301), which fixed prices for the whole of the Empire, the going rate for a copyist was twenty-five denarii per hundred lines for work of the highest quality or twenty for run-of-the-mill work (Edict *De pretiis*, VII.38-40). On the fees paid to copyists in Roman Alexandria see p. 84.

50. Strabo, XIII.609. See T.C. Skeat, 'The Use of Dictation in Ancient Book-Production', *Proceedings of the British Academy* 42 (1956) 179 ff. On publishing see Kleberg, *op. cit.* 47 ff.

51. T. Kleberg, 'Book Auctions in Ancient Rome?', *Libri* 22 (1973) 1 ff.; R.J. Starr, 'The Used-Book Trade in the Roman World', *Phoenix* 44 (1990) 148 ff. A papyrus found in Egypt contains a reference to a travelling bookseller: see J. van Haelst, 'Les origines du codex' in A. Blanchard (ed.), *Les débuts du codex*, Turnhout 1989, 13 ff., esp. 21 ff.

52. On Roman bookshops see Kleberg, 'Roma a l'epoca greco-romana', 45 ff.; Blanck, *op. cit.* 158-172; Salles, *op. cit.* 160-163.

53. See Salles, *op. cit.* 160.

54. Aulus Gellius, *Noctes Atticae* XVIII.4.1; Kleberg, 'Roma a l'epoca greco-romana', 54 ff.

Africa, from Colchis and the icy plains of the far north, through the basins of the Dnieper, the Danube and the Rhone to the Iberian peninsula in the far west.[60] Unfortunately, little is known about the organization of the book trade and the relations between publishers in Rome and booksellers in the provinces, though it seems clear that the provincial bookshops not only stocked new works but were also used as convenient dumping-grounds for 'remaindered' copies of books that had sold less well than expected and for old collections of books and even whole libraries. Gellius, for example, once visited a bookshop near the docks at Brundisium (Brindisi) and found a large assortment of Greek books being offered for sale at knockdown prices owing to their age and bad condition. Spotting a number of early copies of works by well-known authors among them, he bought most of the books on offer (Aulus Gellius, *Noctes Atticae* IX.4).

As a postscript to this section on Roman bibliophiles I have chosen a letter written by Pliny the Younger to his friend Baebius Macro, which tells us much about the part played by books in the everyday life of a great author such as his uncle, Pliny the Elder.[61] Young Pliny, after saying how pleased he is that Macro should want to acquire a complete list of his uncle's works, goes on to explain how it was that a busy man like his uncle, burdened with the pressing responsibilities of high office, managed to find time to read and write so many works on such a variety of subjects. The answer is that the elder Pliny was blessed with a keen intellect, an inquiring mind and an incredible appetite for work. He started staying up all night during the Vulcania, not to read omens but to study his books. Before dawn he would call on the Emperor, Vespasian, who also worked at night, and from there he would go wherever his duties called him. On returning home he would have a light lunch and then lie in the sun while a slave read to him, interrupting from time to time to make notes on points of interest. That was how he made time for his literary pursuits amidst the hurly-burly of city life. In the country, the only thing he permitted to interrupt his reading was his bath, and even while he was scrubbing and drying himself he had a slave reading to him or recited from his own work. When travelling and free of all outside claims on his attention he would spend all his time reading, and he was invariably accompanied by a secretary equipped with books and writing tablets. He always travelled by chariot so as not to lose valuable reading time. It was only by working so intensively that he managed to write such an enormous number of books, besides leaving his nephew 160 fragmentary commentaries. He himself used to say that when he was Procurator of Spain he could have sold these works to Larcius Licinius for 400,000 sesterces. Pliny the Younger sums up his uncle's erudition and creative energy in these words: 'Who of those who have devoted their lives to study, when compared with him, would not blushingly admit that they had been overcome by sleep and laziness?'

55. Martial, I.117.10.
56. Martial, I.2.
57. *Ibid*. I.117.10.
58. Horace, *Epist*. I.20.2.
59. Sidonius Apollinaris, *Epist*. II.9.4.
60. *Odes* II.20.13-20. See A.M. Guillemin, *Le public et la vie littéraire à Rome*, Paris 1937.
61. Taken from a Greek edition of Pliny the Elder's discursus on art in his *Natural History*, tr. T. Roussos and A. Levidis, Athens 1994, 487 ff.
62. According to Suetonius (*Caesar* 44), it was Caesar's intention that

94. Virgil. Engraving from Spoor, Medici et Philosophi..., *73.*

95. Cicero addressing the Romans.

II. Public libraries. As we have seen, the first person in the ancient world to conceive the idea of founding a public library (in the modern sense) was Julius Caesar.[62] Inspired by the immense prestige of the Alexandrian Library in the world of scholarship, Caesar set about establishing the first public library as soon as he returned to Rome and appointed Varro to be in charge of the project. Marcus Terentius Varro (116-27 B.C.) was a man of wide learning backed by good taste and an original mind. It is therefore hardly surprising that he undertook at the same time to write a book containing all he knew about libraries: *De bibliothecis*.[63] The library project never came to fruition: Caesar's death brought it to nothing, and Varro then went back to the quiet life of reading and writing books, as he was proscribed by Antony and only escaped with his life through the intervention of his friend Fufius Calenus. Unfortunately, one result of these tribulations was the loss of *De bibliothecis*, the only work written in antiquity about libraries.

1. Pollio's library. Caesar's cherished project was eventually brought to fruition by a close friend and follower of his, Gaius Asinius Pollio, who was indebted to him for his political advancement. Pollio proved to have a considerable talent as a writer, and as a personal friend of Antony's he was able to move about freely in those dangerous times. Such was his love of literature that he retired from public life to devote himself to writing. Using his spoils from a campaign against the Parthians in Dalmatia, he set about building the first public library in Rome shortly after 39 B.C.[64] Very little is known about this library, other than that it formed part of a complex of public buildings in the Atrium Libertatis[65] and consisted of separate Greek and Latin sections, as Caesar had wished. From that time on Rome always possessed fine public libraries worthy of their founders and of their beneficiaries, namely the Roman emperors and the Roman people.

2. Augustus's library (the Palatine Library). The first public library in Rome actually founded by an emperor was built by Augustus on the Palatine and opened probably in 28 B.C.[66] It was part of a large complex of buildings dominated by the majestic Temple of Apollo Palatinus. The library's official name, mentioned in some funerary inscriptions, attests to its dual character: *Bybliotheca Latina* [Templi] *Apollinis* and *Bybliotheca Graeca* [Templi] *Apollinis*.[67] It was situated near the Emperor's official residence and was organized by a Greek poet, Gnaeus Pompeius Macer (son of Theophanes of Mytilene), who had served as a provincial commissioner.[68] It was Augustus, too, who was responsible for the foundation of the third library in Rome, built for his sister Octavia in memory of her son Marcellus, who died in 23 B.C.[69]

There are grounds for believing that the Emperor was no mere figurehead but took an active interest in libraries. For one thing, he refused

the collection of books to be made available to the public should be as large as possible.

63. Suetonius, *Caesar* 44. The assumption that *De bibliothecis* was an encyclopaedic work and that it covered the great Hellenistic libraries and the way they were organized is based on the fact that Varro is known to have had an antiquarian bent. His *Antiquitates rerum humanarum et divinarum* was a similar work: like *De bibliothecis*, it has not survived, but we know that in it there was a mass of information that Varro had collected about his country's past history and traditions.

64. Pliny, *Nat. Hist.* VII.115, XXXV.10, XXXVI.33. On the public libraries in Rome and their architecture see J.W. Clark, *The Care of Books: An essay on the development of libraries and their fittings from the earliest times to the end of the eighteenth century*, Cambridge 1901, 12; V.M. Strocka, 'Römische Bibliotheken', *Gymnasium* 88 (1981) 298-329; Wendel, *op. cit.* 119-125; J. Tøsberg, *Offentlige bibliotheker: Romerriget i det 2. arhundrede e Chr.*, Copenhagen 1976; Elzbieta Makowiecka, *The Origin and Evolution of Architectural Form of Roman Library* (in the series 'Studia Antiqua'), Warsaw 1978; C.E. Boyd, *Public Libraries and Literary Culture in Ancient Rome*, Chicago 1915; Blanck, *op. cit.* 216 ff.

65. On the architecture of Pollio's library see pp. 112-113.

66. Suetonius, *Augustus* 29.3. See also G. Catrettoni, *Das Haus des Augustus auf dem Palatin*, Mainz 1983, 7 ff. On its architecture see pp. 113-114.

67. *Corpus Inscriptionum Latinarum* VI 5188, 5189, 5191.

68. Suetonius, *De grammaticis*... 21.

69. Plutarch, *Marcellus* 20. The Octavian Library, a bilingual library like its two predecessors, was one of a group of buildings (among which were the temples of Juno Regina and Jupiter Stator) comprising the Porticus Octaviae. Architecturally it is of interest in that it was housed in buildings separate from the portico. Its first librarian was Gaius Melissus, a freedman who was a confidant of Maecenas (Suetonius, *De grammaticis*... 21). The

96. M. Terentius Varro. Engraving.

to allow some of Julius Caesar's youthful poems to be put out on the shelves.[70] And later, when Hyginus had taken over as librarian,[71] Ovid, who had fallen into disfavour, complained from his place of exile that his works had been discarded by the keeper of the library (presumably Hyginus) on orders from the Emperor (*Tristia* III.1.59 ff.). The Palatine Library, like that of Pollio, was sometimes used for meetings of the Senate.[72] It was in use for about a hundred years before being destroyed by fire in the reign of Nero or Titus, and was later rebuilt by Domitian.[73]

3. Tiberius's library. Tiberius, who succeeded Augustus on the imperial throne in A.D. 14, decided that the Palatine Library and the small library in the Porticus Octaviae were not enough;[74] and so, when he founded the temple dedicated to the deified Augustus, he had a new library, the *Bibliotheca Templi Augusti*, built on to it.[75] The temple and the library, which stood in the Forum Romanum near the south side of the Basilica Julia, were inaugurated by Caligula but burnt down not many years later, in A.D. 79. According to Martial (IV.53, XII.3), both were rebuilt by Domitian.[76]

4. Vespasian's library. Another important public library, appropriately situated in an area where many booksellers had their shops, was founded in the year 75 by Vespasian, the first of the Flavian emperors.[77] It was in a group of buildings dominated by the Temple of Peace, east of the Temple of Faustina and the Basilica Aemilia, and was said to have been housed in two large rooms, the precise location of which is today a matter of conjecture.[78] In 191 both the temple and the library were burnt down in one of the great fires that broke out so frequently in Rome, and many of Galen's medical treatises perished in the blaze.[79] The whole complex of buildings was rebuilt in the reign of Septimius Severus and was admired as one of the glories of Rome down to the fourth century.[80]

5. Trajan's library. The library that best typifies the monumentality of Roman libraries in general was founded by Emperor Trajan but probably not opened until 123, in Hadrian's reign. Officially named the *Bibliothecae Divi Traiani*[81] (in the plural because it consisted of a Greek and a Latin library), it was generally known as the Bibliotheca Ulpia. It was built to a magnificent design by the Emperor's official architect, Apollodorus of Damascus,[82] near the Forum Trajanum, which came into being as part of the new city plan that swept away the Atrium Libertatis and Pollio's library. The new library was connected with the temple of the deified Trajan, and we know that in late antiquity it had a statue of Emperor Numerianus (A.D. 283-284) as an orator.[83] Trajan, whose circle of friends included writers such as Dio Chrysostom, appointed a certain Annius Postumus to be the librarian and gave him the title of 'Procurator of the Libraries of the God Trajan'.[84]

library and the many works of art adorning the portico were destroyed by fire in A.D. 80, in Titus's reign (Dio Cassius, LXVI.24). Cf. Boyd, *op. cit.* 8-10; Makowiecka, *op. cit.* 36 ff. On the location of the library see J.H. Middleton, *The Remains of Ancient Rome*, London 1892, 205; E. Nash, *Bildlexikon zur Topographie des antiken Rom*, Tübingen 1961, II 254.

70. Suetonius, *Caesar* 56.

71. Gaius Julius Hyginus, who was of Spanish descent, may have been the same Hyginus who studied in Alexandria under the polymath Cornelius Alexander, nicknamed Polyhistor. Hyginus was a most prolific writer: although none of his works have survived, many of their titles are known, giving us a good idea of the great breadth of his knowledge and interests. See Rose, *'Ιστορία* ... II 161; J. Christes, *Sklaven und Freigelassene als Grammatiker und Philologen im antiken Roma*, Wiesbaden 1986, 71 ff.

72. Suetonius, *Augustus* 29.

73. *Ibid*. 20.

74. Pliny, *Nat. Hist.* XXXIV.43; Suetonius, *Tiberius* 74. Suetonius refers to the Octavian Library as the *Bibliotheca Templi Novi*: cf. Makowiecka, *op. cit.* 41 ff.

75. Our information about another library, built in Claudius's reign and known as the *Bibliotheca Domus Tiberianae*, amounts to nothing more than speculation, as no trace of it has been found and not even its position

Apparently there were far more public libraries in Rome than one would ever imagine from the explicit and implicit evidence of the extant sources: a description of the various districts of Rome in the time of Constantine the Great (4th cent. B.C.) mentions no less than twenty-eight(?) public libraries.[85] This total presumably includes the libraries in public bath-houses (such as the Baths of Trajan and of Caracalla)[86] and the smaller libraries of the emperors and their relatives (such as the one built by Augustus for his sister), which were to some extent private.

The start of the decline of public libraries in Rome coincides with the rise of Christianity. In the middle of the fourth century Ammianus Marcellinus attributed the philistinism of Rome to the abandonment of classical education and the debasement of standards that was a feature of his time: 'The few houses that once were famous for their serious cultivation of learning are now full of tedious, idle games and echo to the sound of singing and the raucous scraping of stringed instruments. Nowadays people employ a singer rather than a scholar, and a comedian rather than an orator. The libraries are permanently closed, like tombs. The people construct hydraulic organs or gigantic, cart-sized lyres and flutes, and monstrous musical instruments for theatrical shows.'[87] Although Ammianus does not make it clear whether he is talking about public or private libraries, there is no doubt that the advent of Christianity created an enormous upheaval in the world of books and libraries,[88] with the result that by 450 the only one of the twenty-eight public libraries in Rome still in use was that of Trajan.

6. Architecture. The Romans introduced two main innovations in the architecture of their public libraries. In the first place, they often built an imposing edifice, with separate wings for the two languages, in which nearly all the books were kept, in contrast to the humble rooms (*oikoi*) where most of the books were kept in the great libraries of Alexandria and Pergamum. Secondly, the practice of integrating a library into an architectural complex of courtyards, colonnaded porticoes and temples fell into disuse. This change came about gradually, and it is safe to say that here the architects were responding to a change in the function of libraries.[89]

1. Pollio's library. The excavations carried out in the Atrium Libertatis have not yielded enough evidence for a complete reconstruction of Pollio's library.[90] It consisted of two fairly small rectangular rooms of equal size, one for the Greek and one for the Latin books. Abutting on the side walls was a colonnaded gallery which came up to the height of the top of the doors, making it possible for the rooms to be illuminated by windows above that height. All this suggests that the library was designed on much the same lines as Greek libraries and was linked by porticoes to the Temple of Apollo. The interior was adorned with portraits of great writers, all deceased with the exception of Varro.[91] We have to remember that

has been identified. See G. Lanciani, *Pagan and Christian Rome*, London 1892, 101; A. Langie, *Les bibliothèques publiques dans l'ancienne Rome et dans l'empire romain*, Fribourg 1906, 94.

76. Pliny, *Nat. Hist.* XII.94.

77. See Makowiecka, *op. cit.* 42-49.

78. Aulus Gellius, *Noctes Atticae* V.21.9, XVI.8.2.

79. Galen, *De comp. med.* I.1.13.

80. *Historia Augusta*, 'Tyranni trig.' XXXI.10.

81. Aulus Gellius, *Noctes Atticae* IX.17.1; cf. Makowiecka, *op. cit.* 52 ff. ('The Era of Trajan'). On its architecture see p. 114, 119-120.

82. Dio Cassius, LXIX.4.1.

83. *Historia Augusta*, 'Numerianus' XI.3.

84. *Corpus Inscriptionum Latinarum* XIV 5352. On Trajan's literary friends see Ovid, *Tristia* IV.10.90, IV.2.109.

85. For a description of Rome in Constantine's reign see *Reg. urb.* (ed. Richter, 1901) 37. On the Capitoline Library (of whose existence we know from Orosius and St. Jerome) and the library in the Temple of Aesculapius, see Boyd, *op. cit.* 19-20.

86. On the libraries in public baths see pp. 116-117.

87. Ammianus Marcellinus, XIV. 6.18. See also G.W. Houston, 'A Revisionary Note on Ammianus Marcellinus 14.6.18: When did the Public Libraries of Ancient Rome Close?', *Library Quarterly* 58 (1988) 258 ff.

97. The Emperor Nero. Engraving from Spoor, Medici et Philosophi..., *81.*

Pollio did not have the library built to his own specifications but adapted an existing building originally intended for a different purpose.

2. Augustus's library. The second library to be built in Rome, the one founded by Augustus on the Palatine in 28 B.C., caused dissension among archaeologists until it was identified with the ruins of a certain building.[92] Suetonius states that Augustus added 'porticoes with a Latin and Greek library' to the Temple of Apollo.[93] Its identification with the building in question, out of all the ones that it might have been, was deduced from a fragment of the marble city plan called the *Forma Urbis Romae*, on which the Palatine Library is marked. From this evidence we now know that Augustus's library consisted of two rooms of equal size (about 10-15 m. overall). Each was rectangular in outline but had an apsidal interior wall at the back, with regular rectangular niches along the interior of both side walls and the curved back wall. In the middle of the back wall, facing the entrance, was a larger rectangular recess for the statue of a god or goddess, perhaps the deified emperor himself. Although the entrance is not clearly identifiable on the *Forma Urbis Romae*, the likelihood is that both entrance doors faced on to a portico. Suetonius mentions the portico before the library, and archaeologists and historians have long wondered whether there is any special reason for this. Such a reversal of the natural order may sometimes be highly significant, as in the case of the peristyle of the Temple of Apollo mentioned by Pliny, but it may simply be due to the fact that the portico more or less enclosed the library.[94]

The interior of the Palatine Library marks the dawn of a new era in the layout and interior decoration of ancient libraries, and all the available evidence suggests that the innovations were due to architects then working in Rome. The niches were used for the storage of books, either on open-fronted wooden or marble shelves or in closed *armaria* with wooden doors, and this remained the standard form of bookcase in the East and the West (with a few exceptions, mainly in the Anglo-Saxon world) until the beginning of the Renaissance in Italy.[95] Immediately in front of the niches there was a raised platform following the line of the interior wall, reached by regularly-spaced flights of two or three steps. On the evidence of the *Forma Urbis Romae*, it would seem that the platform supported a row of columns, with two extra columns forming a small chamber in front of the apsidal recess. The positioning of the columns suggests that there was an upper floor, or rather a gallery running in front of the niches to double the amount of accessible bookshelf space: this arrangement came to be almost universal in Central European libraries, especially from the eighteenth century onwards. The Palatine and the Octavian were the first libraries to incorporate the new Roman design principle of separating the main library building from the porticoes and religious shrines around it.

88. See p. 131.

89. On the architecture of public libraries in Rome see C. Callmer, *Antike Bibliotheken* (= Opuscula Archaeologica, III), Lund/Leipzig 1944; Boyd, *op. cit.*; Tøsberg, *op. cit.*; Makowiecka, *op. cit.*

90. Boyd, *op. cit.* 4-5; Tøsberg, *op. cit.* 22 ff.; Makowiecka, *op. cit.* 28-29. On the position of the Atrium Libertatis, which remains uncertain, see R. Thomsen, *Studien über dem ursprungliche Bau des Caesarforums* (=Opuscula Archaeologica, II), Lund/Leipzig 1941, 209.

91. Pliny, *Nat. Hist.* VII.30.

92. On the history of the attempts to identify it, see C. Hülsen and H.

98. The Emperor Vespasian. Engraving from Spoor, Medici et Philosophi..., *59.*

99. The Emperor Trajan. Engraving from Spoor, Medici et Philosophi..., *175.*

All that is known about the other libraries built under the Julio-Claudian emperors from Augustus to Nero – including the library of Tiberius that was inaugurated by Caligula, the library in the Temple of the Divine Augustus (*Templum Divi Augusti*, also known as the *Templum Novum in Palatio*) and the second library built in Claudius's reign (the *Bibliotheca Domus Tiberianae*) – comes from literary references.[96] None of them have so far been identified in excavations and nothing is known about their architecture, so we shall move on to the library built by Vespasian in the Forum of Peace, which is well documented archaeologically and in literature, although the interpretation of the evidence is a matter of dispute.

3. The Library of the Temple of Peace. The *Bibliotheca Pacis*, as it was called, was one of a complex of buildings centred on a large quadrangle: the quadrangle was surrounded by a colonnade, with a row of buildings along its south side.[97] Attempts to identify the site of the library have led to different conclusions: some locate it on the site where the Church of SS. Cosma e Damiano now stands,[98] while others, following A. Colini, maintain that it was on the south side.[99] Colini, on the evidence of his own excavations and his interpretation of the *Forma Urbis Romae*, concluded that the temple was either an independent building in the middle of the quadrangle or else the central nucleus of the row of buildings on the south side of the forum, in which case the library must have been built in two sections, one on either side of the Temple of Peace, rather like Trajan's library in the Forum Trajanum.[100] Either way, it is quite possible that the Church of SS. Cosma e Damiano stands on the remains of one of the two sections of the library, as Colini believes.

4. The Bibliotheca Ulpia. Probably the most important library in Rome from the second century A.D. to the fall of the Roman Empire was the Bibliotheca Ulpia, built by Trajan in the redevelopment that included the Forum Trajanum and the Basilica Ulpia. The library was opened in 113 or 114, at about the same time as Trajan's Column was unveiled. It consisted of two rectangular rooms facing each other end to end across a peristyle courtyard, in the centre of which was the famous column with Trajan's statue at the top.[101] These two identical rooms, one for the Greek and the other for the Latin books, had exactly the same layout: in the middle of the wall facing the entrance there was a recess containing the statue of a god or goddess, with rectangular niches for storing books on either side.[102] Along the walls there was a platform reached by three steps, to facilitate access to the bookshelves. A row of column bases symmetrically placed at regular intervals along the platform suggests that there was a colonnade supporting a gallery, where there may have been an upper tier of shelving. Presumably the rooms were illuminated by windows above the bookcases.[103] The staircase to the upper gallery may have been in one of the small rooms at the back.

Jordan, *Topographie der Stadt Rom in Altertum*, Berlin 1907, 74; G. de Gregori, *Biblioteche d'Antichità, Accademie e Biblioteche d'Italia*, Rome 1937, 9-24.

93. Suetonius, *Augustus* 29.3.

94. Boyd, *op. cit.* 5-8; Tøsberg, *op. cit.* 37-38; Makowiecka, *op. cit.* 29-36.

95. On the types of bookcases used in the ancient world see C. Wendel, 'Die bauliche Entwicklung der antikes Bibliothek', *ZB* 63 (1949) 407-428 (on the Palatine Library: 412-413). On the Anglo-Saxon tradition of carrels in college and monastic libraries see pp. 490-494.

96. *Corpus Inscriptionum Latinarum* VI 4222; Suetonius, *Tiberius* 70; Martial, IV.3.2.

97. Boyd, *op. cit.* 16-17; Tøsberg, *op. cit.* 39-45; Makowiecka, *op. cit.* 42-49.

98. G. Lanciani, 'Degli antichi edificii componenti la chiesa di SS Cosma e Damiano', *Boll. della Comm. Arch. Communale di Roma* 10 (1882) 39 ff.; P.B. Whitehead and G. Biasiotti, 'La chiesa di SS Cosma e Damiano', *Rend. Pont. Acc. d. Arch.*, 3rd ser., 3 (1924-1925) 83 ff. Cf. T. Ashby and S.B. Platner, *A Topographical Dictionary of Ancient Rome*, London 1929, s.v. 'Forum'. Clark (*op. cit.* 22-23) tells how he went to Rome in April 1898 and there met Lanciani, who was brimming over with excitement at having at last discovered an ancient Roman library. Working from the measurements and notes taken by Lanciani and J.H. Middleton, Clark made a drawing of a wall relief found in the ruins of the library. The relief, the remains of which are now in the Museo del Orto Botanico in Rome, depicts Apollonius of Tyana, a Pythagorean philosopher of the first century A.D.

99. A. Colini, 'Foro del Pace', *Boll. della Comm. Arch. Communale di Roma* (1941) 30.

100. *Ibid*. 34.

101. Boyd, *op. cit.* 17-19; Tøsberg, *op. cit.* 45-51; Makowiecka, *op. cit.* 53-60; C.N. Amici, *Foro di Traiano: Basilica Ulpia e bibliotheche,* Rome 1982; G. Piazzesi, 'Le due biblioteche', *Archivio Classico 41 (1989)* 180 ff.; L. Messa and Lucrezia Ungaro, 'Rilievi

100. Stage set for a play of the New Comedy. Wall-painting from Boscoreale. 1st c. B.C. New York, Metropolitan Museum

5. Libraries in bath-houses. The other library associated with Trajan was located in the baths named after him and was the earliest example of a bath-house library.[104] From A.D. 109, when the Baths of Trajan (with their libraries) were officially opened, public baths occupied much the same position in Roman life as gymnasia had in Greece: they were equipped with training facilities for wrestling and all kinds of other athletic sports

101. Reconstruction of the Baths of Diocletian.

as well as bilingual libraries, to encourage the Romans to spend some of their leisure hours (which they would otherwise devote to physical fitness and hygiene) on intellectual and literary pursuits. The library in the Baths of Trajan was designed by Apollodorus of Damascus and consisted of two exedrae (semicircular structures) facing each other, with the Greek section in the east exedra and the Latin section in the western one. Architecturally it was no different from the other libraries in Rome, except as regards the floor plan. Here again we find two tiers of recessed bookcases with a colonnade supporting the upper gallery, the only difference being that the semicircular steps below were probably used as an amphitheatre for lectures and public recitations, and as a reading room. The ceiling of each exedra was a semidome with plaster coffers.

The next library to be built in an imperial bath-house was in the Baths of Caracalla. This one shows its Greek origins even more clearly.[105] The Greek and Latin sections were some distance apart and occupied a rectangular space instead of having a semicircular wall like the library in the

102. Mural decoration from a private library in Rome (drawing by G. Lanciani).

moderni e recostruzioni 1926-1986', *ibid.* 199-214.

102. See G. Hornsbostel-Hüttner, *Studien für römischen Nischenarchitektur*, Leiden 1979.

103. The question of how ancient libraries were lit is difficult to answer.

Baths of Trajan. That apart, the interior design followed the normal pattern of Roman libraries: at the back there was a space for a statue of a god or the Emperor, and the bookcases were on two floors. A row of small rooms served to insulate the wall with the bookcases.

6. Private libraries. The Romans' influence on the development of library architecture was not limited to great public edifices but was felt in the private sector as well. About the architecture of the rooms in

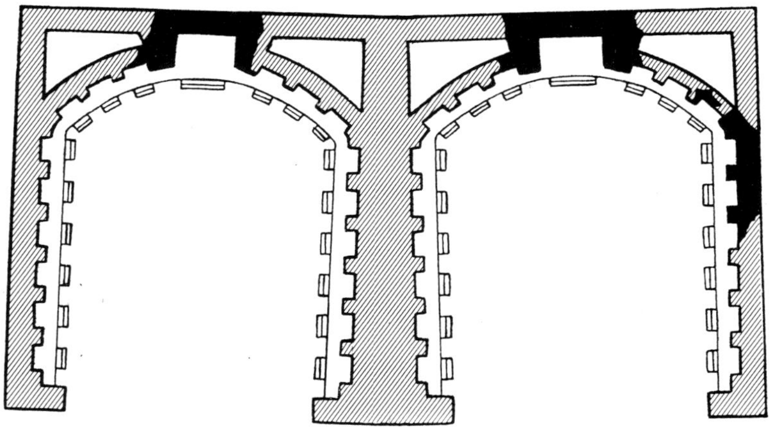

104. Plan of the Palatine Library, after a drawing by C. Callmer in Opuscula Archaeologica, *III, Lund/Leipzig 1944, 158.*

ancient Greek houses that were used for keeping and reading books we know absolutely nothing.[106] It is conjectured that Piso's villa (1st cent. A.D.) excavated at Herculaneum, with its well-stocked library, was modelled on Greek houses.[107] The discovery of the room Piso used as a library, with his fine collection of books still *in situ*, was unique in the annals of archaeology and is worth considering at some length.

On 24th August, A.D. 79, Herculaneum, a town on the Bay of Naples near Pompeii, founded by Greeks at a very early date, was wiped off the face of the earth by a fearsome eruption of nearby Mt. Vesuvius. In the 1750s the first excavators dug down through the layers of lava and rubble and brought to light a villa with not only its lavish decoration still well preserved but also a library with an estimated 1,814 papyri on its shelves.[108] The owner has never been positively identified, but the name of Lucius Calpurnius Piso, Julius Caesar's father-in-law, is often mentioned in this connection.[109] The central feature of the villa was a square atrium off which the various rooms opened. Some of the papyri were found in the garden courtyard, but most were in a room three metres square. The walls of this room were lined with bookcases about as tall as an average man (*c.* 1.70 m.), and in the middle there was a desk so large that there was only room for one person in the room at a time.[110]

Among the papyri in Piso's villa were many that were badly burnt, but even their contents are now coming to light thanks to the new methods

Although we know that in the Hellenistic period it was normal for library reading rooms to open on to a colonnaded portico, the form given to public libraries in Rome necessitated new design solutions for their proper illumination: cf. Makowiecka, *op. cit.* 55, 58. The advice given by Vitruvius (VI.4.1) was that libraries should face east, as the morning sun is good for it and helps to protect the books and bookcases from decay. South-facing libraries are at risk because the south winds bring moisture and create the right conditions for bookworms, with the result that the books are ruined by mildew and the damp breath of the worms.

104. Tøsberg, *op. cit.*; Makowiecka, *op. cit.* 60-62. On Roman baths see I. Nielsen, *Thermae et balnea*, Aarhus 1990, 163 ff.; K. De Fine Licht, 'Untersuchungen an den Trajansthermen zu Rom', *Analecta Romana* 7 (1974), suppl. 19, 1990.

105. Tøsberg, *op. cit.* 51 ff.; Makowiecka, *op. cit.* 91-92.

106. Vitruvius (VI.7.1), describing the layout of Greek houses, makes no mention of a special room where books were kept, and to the best of my knowledge no such room has been discovered in excavations of Greek

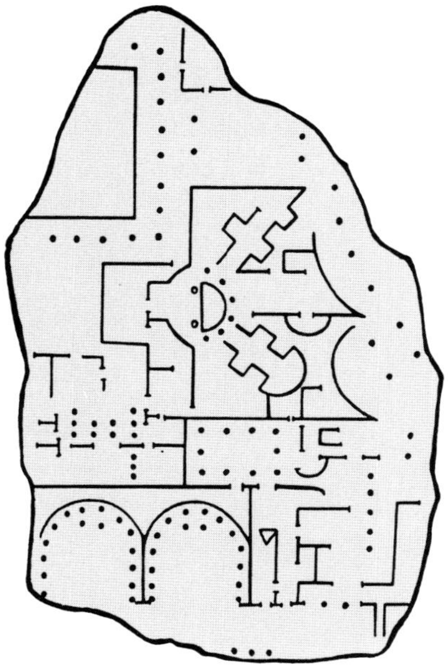

103. Fragment of the Forma Urbis Romae.

employed by the Centro Internazionale per gli Studi dei Papiri Ercolanensi (CISPE), which is studying and conserving them under the direction of Marcello Gigante.[111] They are all philosophical works written in Greek with the emphasis on Epicurean writings, which can be divided into two main groups: works by Epicurus and his followers written in the third and second centuries B.C., and a great many treatises by Philodemus of Gadara in multiple copies. Philodemus, an Epicurean philosopher who studied under Zeno of Sidon in Athens, went to Italy between 80 and 70 B.C., made friends with Piso at Herculaneum and became a philosophical counsellor. In time he and Siron, Virgil's teacher, came to be the leaders of the Epicurean movement in Italy, which was centred round Naples.[112] Philodemus was a most prolific writer, the author of works on rhetoric, logic and philosophy besides being a poet and composer. He had his own scriptorium in Piso's villa, employing Greek slaves as copyists, and from there he published his writings, most of which he sold in the Naples area. At the same time he supported the cause of philosophy (from the Epicurean standpoint) against the claims of the teachers of rhetoric.[113]

It is clear from the sources that even before the end of the Republican era, in the first century B.C., Roman aristocrats had adopted a style of architecture for their villas which strongly emphasized the beauty and genius of the Greek tradition, and that they imitated the Greek way of life to a considerable extent. Lucullus's villa at Tusculum, on the slopes of the Mons Albanus, is the most typical example of this trend. The palaestrae, porticoes and gardens, the spacious, lavishly-decorated rooms, the numerous colonnaded courtyards and the library containing the books Lucullus had looted from Mithradates, King of Pontus, must have created an effect that was thoroughly Greek. In these opulent surroundings Lucullus and his family lived like princes, and all the local people who had had a Greek education were invited to attend the cultural activities that took place there. Lucullus's love of books is attested by Plutarch, who describes his villa as 'a resort of the Muses'.[114] Cicero, writing after Lucullus's death, gives

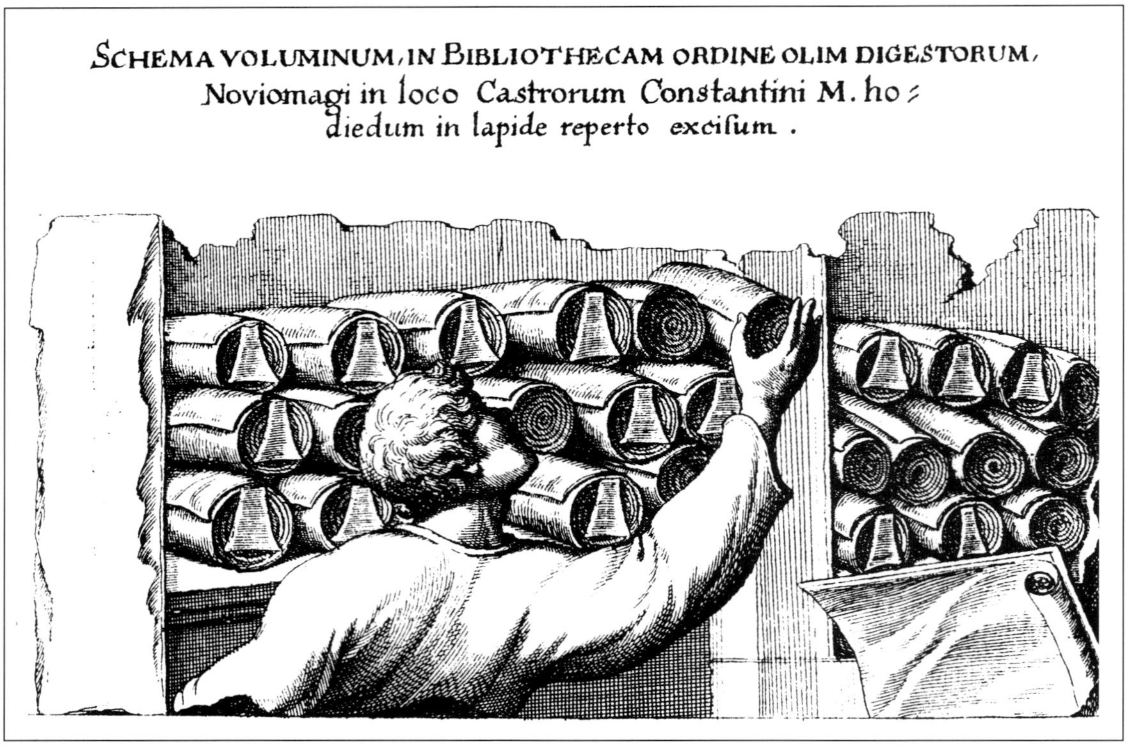

105. Engraving of a lost Roman relief from Neumagen, on the Moselle.

an idea of what it must have been like to visit the library there: in an imaginary dialogue with Cato of Utica he expresses a wish to consult Aristotle's works, as he is in the process of writing his philosophical essay on the concepts of good and evil.[115]

Cicero's correspondence with Atticus and others provides us with first-hand information about the reading rooms and libraries in his villas. For his libraries he uses the following terms: *gymnasium*, *palaestra*, *xystus*, *academia* and *bibliotheca*.[116] And he firmly believes that their interior decoration should be in keeping with the dignity expected of a library: he therefore eschews representations of such figures as Bacchus, Ares and Cronus in favour of Hermes, the Muses, Heracles and Demeter.[117] Unfortunately Cicero's references to his libraries never go beyond generalizations except when he talks about Tyrannio and his assistants attaching labels to his rolls, and his allusions to the *pegmata* (wooden fixtures, probably bookcases) and *structio* (structure) of his library are not at all enlightening. We know from another source (Seneca the Younger, *Dialogues* IX.9.4-7) that many Romans were more interested in what a library looked like than in what it contained, and so they lavished their attention on fitting it up with cedarwood and ivory bookshelves.

Pliny the Younger supplies some rather more interesting information about the rooms in which wealthy Romans read and worked on their books.[118] He, of course, was no ordinary book-lover and man of letters but perhaps the most passionate bibliophile in all the history of ancient Rome. The library in his villa at Laurentum was an apsidal room adjacent to his gymnasium. Here he kept his 'philosophical' books, by which he meant those that were not for light reading but for serious study. For his

private houses of the Classical and Hellenistic periods.

107. J.J. Winckelmann, *Sendschreiben von den Herculanischen Entdeckungen*, German edn., 1792, 63 ff.

108. This total includes fragments. Of the 1,814 papyri, 340 are intact and in excellent condition, 970 are damaged in many places and more than 500 exist only in fragments. Out of the extensive bibliography, see: D. Comparetti and G. de Petra, *La villa ercolanese dei Pisoni*, Turin 1883; C. Gallavotti, 'La custodia dei papiri nella villa suburbana ercolanese', *Boll. dell' Ist. di patologia del libro* 2 (1940) 53 ff.; Id., 'La libreria di una villa romana ercolanese', *ibid.* 3 (1941) 129 ff. For the publication of the texts see: Reale Accademia Ercolanese, *Herculanensium voluminum que supersunt*, Collectio prior, 9 vols., Naples 1793-1850, Collectio altera, 11 vols., Naples 1862-1876; *Herculaneum Fragments*, 9 vols., Oxford 1889, and Facsimiles, Oxford 1891.

109. On Piso, his possible identification with the addressee of Horace's *Ars poetica* and his relations with Cicero, see Rose, *Ἱστορία* ... I 288-289.

110. Clark, *op. cit.* 24 ff.; D. Diringer, *The Book Before Printing:*

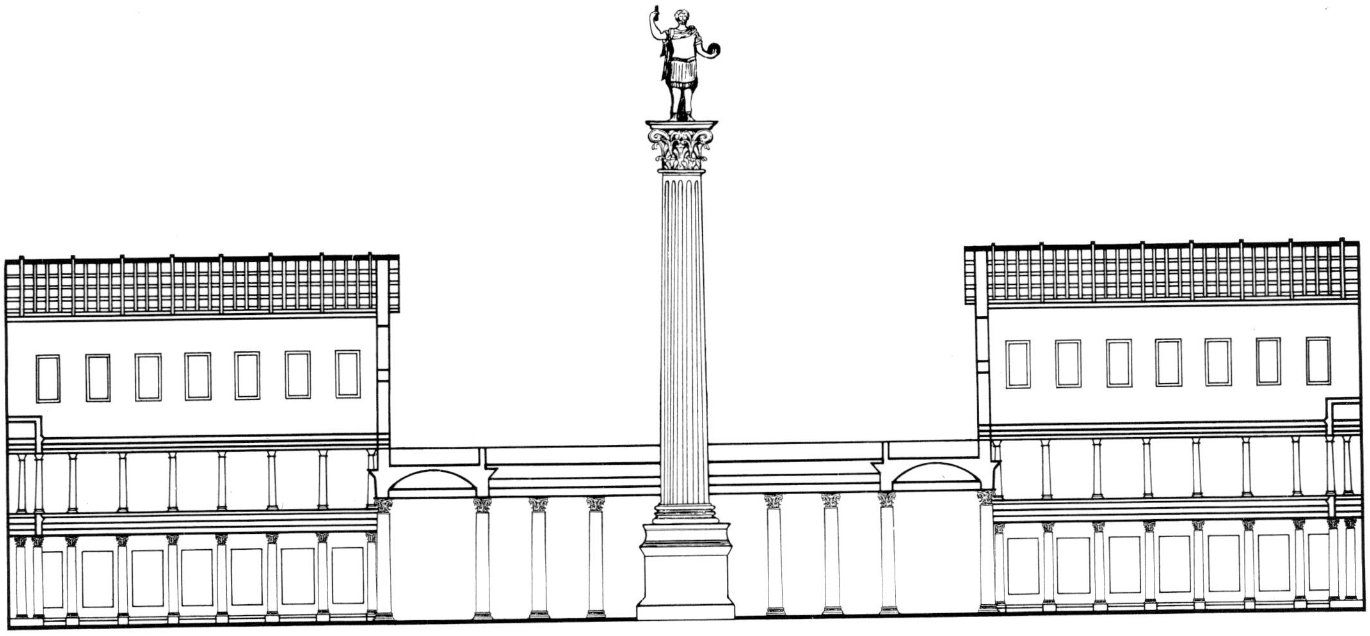

106. Vertical section of Trajan's library (the Bibliotheca Ulpia), after a drawing by Schuitt.

everyday reading (*diaeta*), which he called his 'silent and true passion', he had another apartment which he had fitted out and decorated himself. This was a sort of pavilion in a quiet position at the end of a vaulted passage (*cryptoporticus*) on the garden side of the villa. It consisted of

107. A Roman reading in front of an open cabinet. Drawing of a relief on a sarcophagus found in the garden of the Villa Balestra, Rome.

three main rooms and two smaller ones. In the middle was the 'sitting-room' (*cubiculum*) with folding doors to the vaulted passage and a window looking out over the sea. Opening off that, on the far side as you entered from the vaulted passage, was an attractive veranda (*zotheca*) which could be closed off from the *cubiculum* by glass partitions and curtains and was furnished with a couch and two armchairs: here Pliny could sit in seclusion, with the sea at his feet and behind him the little villages against the backdrop of the forest.

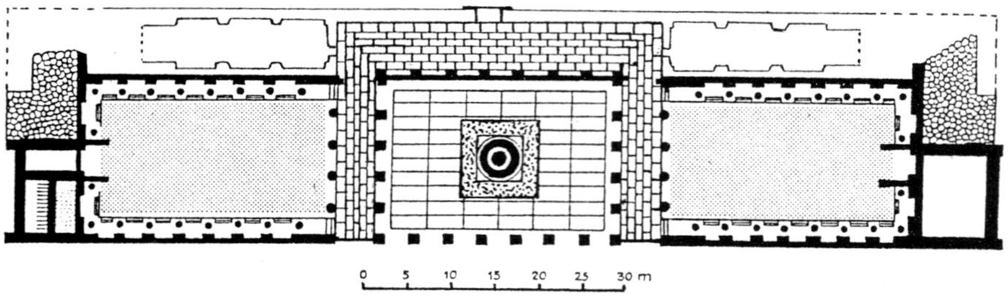

108. Plan of Trajan's Library, by C. Callmer in Opuscula Archaeologica, *III, 163.*

Ancient, medieval and oriental, New York 1982; Blanck, *op. cit.* 213-216. Winckelmann visited the excavations between 1758 and 1763, and in one of his long letters to Consigliere Bianconi, written in 1762, he gave a detailed description of the library, which he maintained was used only for storing books, not for reading or copying (Clark, *op. cit.* 25).

111. On the decipherment of the texts see M. Capasso, *Storia fotografica dell' officina dei papiri*, Naples 1983.

112. Cicero, in one of his two speeches criticizing Piso's conduct as governor of Macedonia, refers to a certain Greek Epicurean philosopher and poet who was a close friend of Piso's (*In Pisonem* XXVIII.68-72).

113. Philodemus gathered round him a circle of ambitious writers including Virgil, Gallus and perhaps Neoptolemus of Parium, whose work influenced Horace's *Ars poetica*.

114. Plutarch, *Lucullus* 42.

115. Cicero, *De finibus bonorum et malorum* 7 ff.

116. *Epist. ad Att.* I.10.3, I.4.3, I.1.5, I.6.2, I.8.2, I.9.2, IV.10.1; *Epist. ad familiares* VII.23.2, VII.9.4.

117. *Epist. ad fam.* VII.23.2; *Epist. ad Att.* I.4.3, I.1.5. In *Brutus* (VI.24) he also mentions a statue of Plato.

118. See W. Liebenwein, *Studiolo: Storia e tipologia di uno spazio culturale*, tr. A. Califano, Ferrara/Modena 1988, 3 ff.

109. Interior elevation of the central part of Trajan's bilingual library. Drawing based on the vertical section by I. Gismondi.

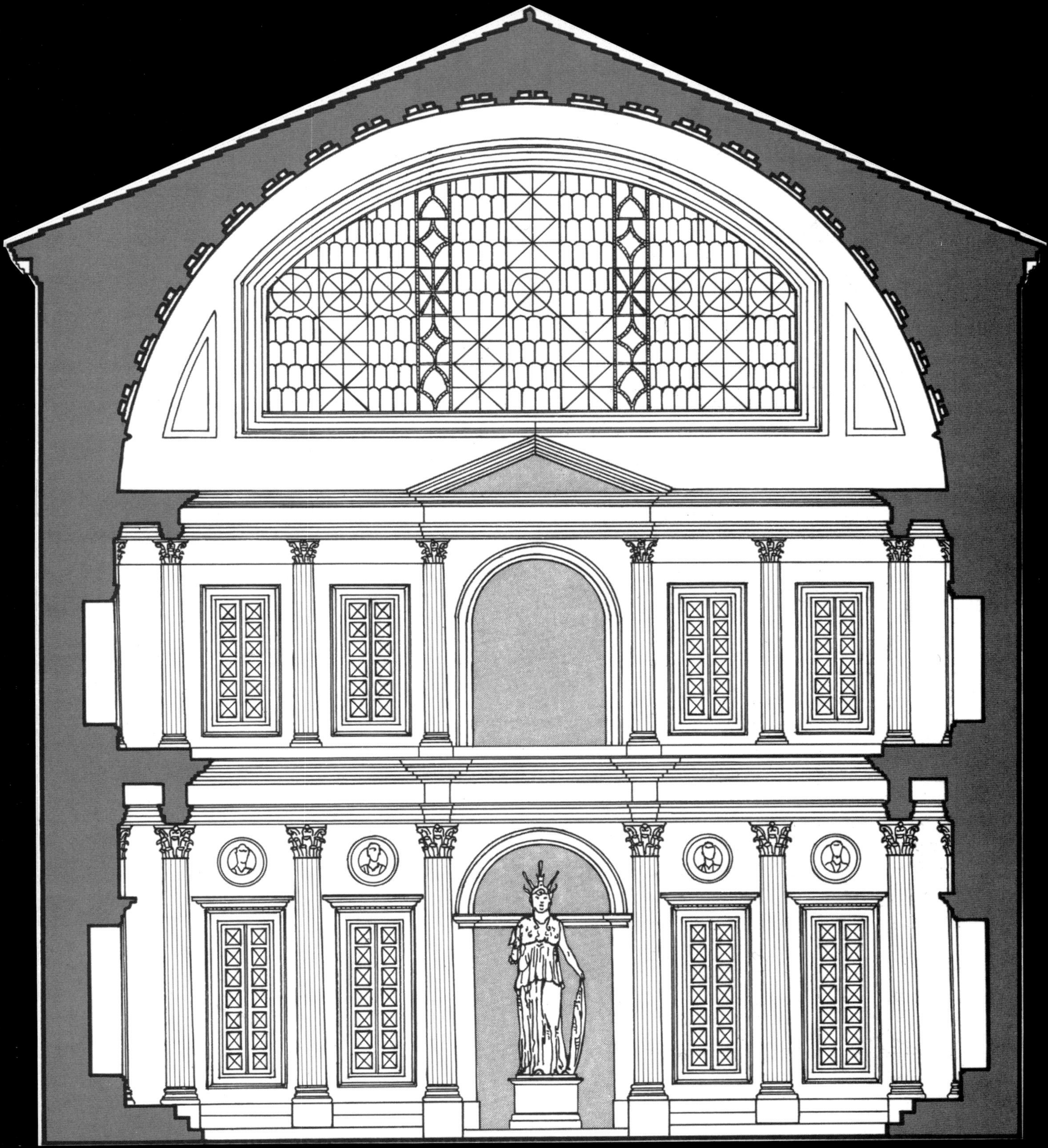

110. The reading room and library in the Capuchin friary that was built around the Monument of Lysicrates. Drawing by S. Pomardi in E. Dodwell, A Classical and Topographical Tour through Greece, *London 1819.*

CHAPTER SEVEN

LIBRARIES IN THE ROMAN PROVINCES

Public libraries were established not only in Rome but in all the provinces of the Empire. Many of the provincial libraries were magnificent buildings, sometimes surpassing most of the imperial libraries in Rome: among them were the Library of Celsus at Ephesus[1] and the Library of Marcus Iulius Quintianus Flavius Rogatianus at Timgad.[2] To tell the story of the foundation of all these libraries – which have been discovered in large numbers in practically every Late Roman city ever excavated, from Carthage in North Africa to Comum (Como) in Italy, Dyrrhachium (Dürres) in what is now Albania, Thessalonica, Piraeus, Delphi and Corinth in Greece, Ephesus and Nyssa in Asia Minor – is beyond the scope of this book.[3] However, a distinction that has to be made between them, apart from their architectural differences, is that some of them were bilingual while others contained Greek books only: evidently the Romans always had libraries with separate Latin and Greek sections, whereas the Greeks felt no need to fill their shelves with books in any other language than their own. In this chapter we shall take a closer look at just three of the libraries built outside Rome during this period, that of Pantaenus in Athens and those built by Emperor Hadrian in Athens and at Tibur, concentrating on the circumstances that led to their foundation.

I. The library of Pantaenus. At the end of the first or the beginning of the second century A.D. Titus Flavius Pantaenus, the son of Flavius Menander, gave the Athenians a library situated on the Panathenaic Way in the Agora, just south of the Stoa of Attalus,[4] which means that it was only a few yards away from the area where booksellers had had their stalls in the time of Aristophanes and Plato. The design of the library is of no particular interest and the building lacks the symmetry so characteristic of most libraries designed by Roman architects. The reason for making more than a passing reference to it here is that the excavators discovered two marble slabs with interesting inscriptions. One, a dedicatory inscription from the founder carved on the lintel of a door leading from the west stoa to a courtyard, reads as follows: 'To Athena Polias and the Emperor Caesar Augustus Nerva Traianus Germanicus and the city of Athens, the priest of the philosopher Muses Titus Flavius Pantaenus, son of Flavius Menander the principal of the school, donated the outer stoa, the peristyle and the library with its books and all its fixtures and fittings, out of his own funds, together with his children Flavius Menander and Flavia Secundilla.'[5] Even more interesting than the founder's inscription is a fragment of a stele with the library regulations laconically inscribed on it: 'No books may be removed from the premises. Opening hours six a.m. to twelve noon.'[6]

II. Hadrian as a patron of art and learning. Hadrian founded at least three libraries and may have been instrumental in restoring others as well. The first of his own foundations was in Athens, his 'adopted home', and the other two in his villa at Tibur (Tivoli), not far from Rome. There is little point in describing any of these libraries, as the one in Athens is

1. See W. Wilberg, M. Theurer, F. Eichler and J. Keil, *Die Bibliothek* ('Forschungen in Ephesos' 5.1), 2 vols., Vienna 1953; F. Hueber and V.M. Strocka, 'Die Bibliothek des Celsus', *Antike Welt* 6 (1975) 3 ff.; J. Tøsberg, *Offentlige bibliotheker: Romerriget i det 2. arhundrede e Chr.*, Copenhagen 1976, 89-94.

2. On the library at Timgad (Thamugadi) in Algeria, see esp. H.F. Pfeiffer, 'The Roman Library of Timgad', *Memoirs of the American Academy in Rome* 9 (1931) 157 ff.; also Tøsberg, op. *cit.* 106 ff.

3. For an early study of libraries in the Roman provinces see M.R. Cagnat, 'Les bibliothèques municipales dans l'empire romain', *Mémoires de l'Institut National de France* 38

ΒΥΒΛΙΟΝ ΟΥΚ ΕΞΕ
ΝΕΧΘΗΣΕΤΑΙ ΕΠΕΙ
ΩΜΟΣΑΜΕΝ ΑΝΥΓΗ
ΣΕΤΑΙ ΑΠΟ ΩΡΑΣ ΠΡΩ
ΤΗΣ ΜΕΧΡΙ ΕΚΤΗΣ

111. Inscription with the regulations of the Library of Pantaenus (width 32 cm.).

still being excavated and new evidence is continually coming to light, while the excavations carried out so far at the other two have yielded disappointing results and there seems little prospect of discovering anything more. What is particularly interesting about them is the personality of their founder, Hadrian.

Of all the emperors up to the time of Constantius II (337-361), the one who most distinguished himself in literature and the arts was Hadrian (117-138). Looking into his complex personality, one has the feeling that he was exceptionally interested in people and things, which may be explained by the fact that he saw himself as the protector of the intellectual and artistic heritage of Mediterranean civilization in all its manifestations. And this in turn explains why he founded his two monumental libraries.

Hadrian, born in A.D. 76, was related to Emperor Trajan. In his youth he showed an exceptional aptitude for his studies and a keen interest in all branches of knowledge, which led him to travel in later life to the farthest corners of the Roman Empire.[7] Not for nothing did Tertullian call him 'the investigator of all curiosities' (*curiositatum omnium explorator*). Such was his enthusiasm for Greek that he came to be nicknamed

112. Hadrian's Library in Athens as it was in 1844. Engraving by A. Gasparini.

Graeculus, and it may well be that his independent spirit as an adult owed much to his study of Greek literature. In contrast to most of his contemporaries, he made it clear that he preferred Antimachus to Homer, Ennius to Virgil and Cato to Cicero. Although he surrounded himself with philosophers and writers, he never aligned himself with any particular philosophical school: in fact, displaying remarkable self-assurance and independence of mind, he was equally at home with

LIBRARY	DATE
Aelia Capitolina (Jerusalem)	3rd c. A.D.
Ai Khanoum, Bactria	3rd c. B.C.
Alexandria, Egypt	
Great Library	3rd c. B.C.
Serapeum	1st c. B.C.
Sebasteion	1st c. B.C.
Antioch, Syria	
Temple of Trajan	4th c. A.D.
Aphrodisias, Asia Minor	2nd c. A.D.
Athens	
of Pisistratus	6th c. B.C.
Lyceum	4th c. B.C.
Ptolemaeum	2nd c. B.C.
of Pantaenus	1st c. A.D.
of Hadrian	2nd c. A.D.
Cnidus, Asia Minor	2nd c. A.D.
Corinth, Greece	2nd c. A.D.
Cos, Greece	
Gymnasium(?)	200-175 B.C.
Lyceum	3rd c. A.D.
Crete, Greece	1st c. A.D.
Delphi, Greece	1st c. A.D.
Dertona, Italy	22 B.C.
Dyrrhachium, Macedonia	2nd c. A.D.
Ephesus, Asia Minor	2nd c. A.D.
Epidaurus, Greece	2nd c. A.D.
Halicarnassus, Asia Minor	2nd c. A.D.
Heraclea Pontica, Asia Minor	4th c. B.C.
Kirbet Qumran	1st c. A.D.
Laodicea, Syria	4th c. A.D.
Mylasa, Asia Minor	3rd c. B.C.
Nîmes, France	2nd-3rd c. A.D.
Nyssa, Asia Minor	2nd-3rd c. A.D.
Oea (Tripoli), N. Africa	2nd c. A.D.
Patrae, Greece	2nd c. A.D.
Pergamum, Asia Minor	
Acropolis	2nd c. B.C.
Asklepieion	A.D. 132
Philadelphia (Amman, Jordan)	2nd c. B.C.
Philippi, Macedonia	2nd c. A.D.
Pompeii, Italy	1st c. A.D.
Prusa, Asia Minor	2nd c. A.D.
Rhodes, Greece	2nd c. A.D.
Rome	
Atrium Libertatis	1st c. B.C.
Temple of Apollo Palatinus	1st c. B.C.
Octavian	1st c. B.C.
Temple of Augustus	1st c. A.D.
Domus Tiberiana	1st c. A.D.(?)
Temple of Peace	1st c. A.D.
Forum Trajanum	2nd c. A.D.
Athenaeum	2nd c. A.D.
Capitoline	2nd c. A.D.
Baths of Caracalla	3rd c. A.D.
Baths of Diocletian	3rd-4th c. A.D.
Samos, Greece	6th c. B.C.
Smyrna, Asia Minor	1st c. A.D.
Soli, Cyprus	1st c. A.D.
Susa, Persia	A.D. 193
Thessalonica, Macedonia	2nd c. A.D.
Tibur, Italy	2nd c. A.D.
Timgad, N. Africa	2nd-3rd c. A.D.
Volsinii, Italy	not known

'natural philosophy' (i.e. the natural sciences) and with metaphysics. He was a prolific writer and left a large collection of poems to posterity. The grammarian Sosipater Charisius found his books in the libraries of Rome before they were destroyed by the Goths, and in the ninth century Patriarch Photios found some of his writings in libraries in Constantinople. But Hadrian's great love was architecture: it was he who adorned Rome with the Temple of Diana and that architectural marvel, the Pantheon, among many other buildings. To him, architecture was more than just a creative urge, for in the grounds of his villa at Tibur, outside Rome, he put up a complex of buildings to house all the achievements of the Graeco-Roman civilization. It was in the pursuit of these interests that he became involved in a long-running dispute with the great architect Apollodorus of Damascus.[8]

Hadrian came to the throne in A.D. 117 and a few years later set off to travel all over the Empire, spending the winter of 125-126 in Athens. Recognizing the fact that the city of Pallas Athene was the undisputed centre of literary life in his time, he decided to make a place for himself in the city's history, as attested by the inscriptions on the arch that bears his name: on one side, 'This is Athens, the ancient city of Theseus,' and on the other, 'This is the city of Hadrian, not of Theseus.'

Hadrian's contribution to the restoration and construction of monuments in all the countries of the Mediterranean basin is incalculable. He gave orders for the rebuilding of a large part of Jerusalem, which was in ruins, and he also gave that city a new name of his own, Aelia Capitolina; at Cyzicus, on the Sea of Marmara, he built a temple of Artemis which was generally considered an architectural masterpiece; at Antioch he restored the city wall and added a three-arched gate of unusual design; at Alexandria he erected various buildings and founded a new district called Antinoupolis; and he founded the city of Adrianople in Thrace.

1. Hadrian's library. Hadrian gave the Athenians a library – a centre of learning on the lines of the Museum at Alexandria – that is architecturally the most interesting ancient library known today.[9] From the dimensions of the rooms in which the books were kept it would appear that Hadrian's library was not particularly well stocked in comparison with those at Alexandria and Pergamum. When the rhetorician Aelius Aristides (*Panath.* XIII.306, ed. Dindorf) claimed that Athens could boast of libraries unrivalled anywhere else, which were among the city's great glories, he was probably thinking also of the library in the Lyceum, Zeno's library and perhaps the state archives as well. The design of Hadrian's library follows the pattern of the bilingual libraries in Rome, though quite possibly it only contained books in Greek.

2. Hadrian's library at Tibur. Hadrian's other monumental bilingual library was part of the huge complex of buildings collectively known as

113. Drawing of a coin of Hadrian's reign, showing the Emperor wearing a laurel wreath. Rome, Museo della Civiltà Romana.

(1909) 1-26. Tøsberg (op. cit. 9-11) gives a list of libraries in the Graeco-Roman world based on Cagnat's work but greatly expanded. An updated version of Tøsberg's list is given on p. 124.

4. The Library of Pantaenus was excavated by the American School of Classical Studies: see J.M. Camp, *The Athenian Agora*, London 1986, 187-191.

5. *Agora Inscriptions* I 848.

6. *Agora Inscriptions* I 2729.

7. See Noel des Verges, 'Adrien', NBU 1 (1852) 302-326; *Der Klayne Pauly* 907-911; Marguerite Yourcenar, *'Αδριανοῦ 'Απομνημονεύματα (=Mémoires d'Hadrien*, tr. Ioanna D. Hadjinikoli), Athens 1975.

8. Apollodorus of Damascus was one of the most famous architects of the Roman imperial era. His most important projects included the Odeum (Dio Cassius, lxix.4), the Baths of Trajan and the Forum Trajanum, the last of these being a masterpiece of architecture and planning and a splendid monument to his genius. On Hadrian's accession he fell out of favour and his caustic comments on Hadrian's architectural projects (Dio Cassius, lxix.4) infuriated the Emperor, who ordered him to be put to death (*Der Klayne Pauly* 440).

9. On Hadrian's library in Athens, see esp.: M.A. Sisson, 'The Stoa of Hadrian at Athens', BSR 11 (1929) 50-72 (Pls. XVII-XXVII); G. Knithakis and E. Soumbolidou, «Νέα στοι-

his 'villa' at Tibur. His library there was as large as the one in Athens and was surrounded by other buildings, stoas, courtyards and shrines like those of the Museum in Alexandria. There can be little doubt that Hadrian had visited the Museum, seen the Great Library and, like Julius Caesar, been fascinated by its history. It is reasonable to suppose that the Alexandrian Library was the model for his bilingual library at Tibur, which consisted of a peristyle courtyard with single-storey and two-storey buildings facing on to it. In the two main buildings, which housed the Greek and Latin libraries, there were a number of guest-rooms, scriptoria and reading rooms for scholars who came to study there.[10] Lastly, in the centre of a large open space known as the Great Peristyle there was a square building whose interior walls were lined from floor to ceiling with recesses to hold the boxes of books belonging to Hadrian's private library.[11]

χεῖα διά τήν Βιβλιοθήκην 'Αδριανοῦ», *'Αρχαιολογικό Δελτίο* 124.1 (1969) 107-117 (Pls. 54-57); J. Travlos, *Pictorial Dictionary of Ancient Athens*, Athens 1971, 244 (Pls. 314-324); Arja Karivieri, 'The So-called Library of Hadrian and the Tetraconch Church in Athens', *Papers and Monographs of the Finnish Institute at Athens* 1 (1994) 89-113; Alkistis Spetsieri-

This brief reference to Hadrian, the humanist emperor, gives some idea of the way in which the Graeco-Roman civilization received continual support at the imperial level, in his case chiefly through the establishment of bilingual libraries. Unfortunately we do not have enough evidence to draw conclusions about the way in which the whole corpus of Greek literature was evaluated and reproduced in order to stock those libraries. But we should not overlook the connection between these imperial trends and the colossal growth in the output of books from the Roman bookseller/publishers. It is reasonable to assume from this that the foundation of so many important centres of learning must have been fully in tune with an imperial policy of supporting literature in all its forms.[12]

To sum up, it is fair to say that from the first century B.C. Greek libraries generally formed part of educational institutions in which the dominant architectural features were colonnaded walks, peristyle courtyards and semicircular recesses, all integrally linked with the main buildings. The library itself consisted simply of a room or rooms used only for storing the books, as nearly all the reading, recitation, discussion and study took place out of doors in keeping with the Peripatetic philosophi-

114. The Library of Celsus at Ephesus. Photo: Dora Minaidi.

115. Reconstruction drawing of the façade of the Library of Celsus at Ephesus (2nd c. B.C.).

116. The central part of the façade of Hadrian's Library in Athens. Engraving from J. Stuart and N. Revett, The Antiquities of Athens, *2 vols. London 1762-1787.*

cal tradition. The most advanced form of this type of library may well have been the one in Aristotle's Lyceum in the time of Theophrastus. In the Hellenistic period a library was a monumental building, a sort of temple of the Muses, containing a statue of the presiding deity, a row of book-cases and perhaps alcoves as well, in other words a sort of academy in the modern sense. Small utilitarian rooms for book storage still existed, but mainly in the bigger libraries such as those of Alexandria and Pergamum, where there were far too many books for all of them to fit in the main hall.

117. Part of the façade of Hadrian's Library in Athens. Photo: T. Anagnostou.

With the introduction of bilingual libraries by the Romans, a different architectural design was devised and became standard in public and imperial libraries. These libraries were symmetrical in plan, as the only difference between the Greek and Latin sections was in their contents. The most conspicuous feature of the interior, as before, was the statue of the presiding deity or deified emperor, flanked by symmetrical rows of book cabinets which often occupied an upper gallery in addition to the ground floor. In its most highly-developed form, as in Trajan's Bibliotheca Ulpia, a bilingual library consisted of two buildings placed symmetrically on either side of the emperor's statue. In the early centuries of the Christian era monumental libraries were built by patricians and high-ranking officials across the length and breadth of the Empire. In them there was no architectural homogeneity: with the exception of the bilingual libraries, which conformed to what had become standard practice, their founders gave the architects carte blanche to use their imagination.

Horemi, 'Library of Hadrian at Athens: Recent finds', *Rivista di antichità* 4.1 (1995) 137-147.

10. See Marina de Franceschini, *Villa Adriana, mosaici, pavimenti, edifici*, Rome 1991, esp. 199-201, 487-591 ('Sala dei Filosofi'), 73-82, 380-385 ('Biblioteca Graeca'), 89-92, 386-390 ('Biblioteca Latina'), 93-97, 391-396 ('Cortili delle Biblioteche'); H. Kähler, *Hadrian und seine Villa bei Tivoli*, Berlin 1954.

11. A full-sized reconstruction of Hadrian's private library with all its fixtures and fittings is to be seen in the Museo della Civiltà Romana.

12. Juvenal, for example, writing in a.d. 117, says in a laudatory preface (*Sat.* 7-8.1 ff.), 'Caesar is our only hope for literature.'

118. The interior of Hadrian's private library.

CHAPTER EIGHT

THE EARLY CHRISTIAN WORLD

I. The first Christian libraries

To understand the reasons for the diminished importance of public and private libraries in both the East and the West in the Middle Ages and the simultaneous decline of the book trade, we have to consider certain events connected with the establishment of Christian literature in book form up to the year 312, when the first Christian emperor, Constantine the Great, issued a historic edict overturning Diocletian's laws and giving the Christians freedom to practise their religion. Ever since the time of the apostles the method of copying and disseminating Christian writings had been quite different from the practice current among the pagans, so much so that the ancient practice could be said to have been completely reversed. And, although we have plenty of reliable evidence as to how and why the Christian book trade came to diverge from the existing Graeco-Roman tradition, the issue is so complex that any generalization would be unsound. Let us look first at the social and linguistic situation in the West and particularly in Rome, where the biggest booksellers in the Empire were based.

Christianity arrived in the West as a sect with a wide following among people of the lower classes, most of whom were not from Italy: in fact the majority of them spoke Greek or a Greek dialect, and in any case not Latin. Even as late as two centuries after St. Paul's visit to the newly-founded church in Rome, most of the Roman church's records were still being written in Greek and relatively few in Latin. Little by little, however, the situation began to change, until eventually the Romanization of the Western Empire and the use of Latin by the early Christian apologists in the region around Carthage halted the triumphant progress of the Greek language. Meanwhile Christianity had started to attract members of the upper classes, who used Latin almost exclusively.[1]

With the progressive alteration in their living conditions, the Christians were able to devote more attention to their inner life and made greater efforts to present the arguments in support of their beliefs more cogently, which meant that history and literature became a necessary part of their reading. What hampered the growth of the Christian book trade and the formation of big public libraries containing Christian writings was not the bilingualism of the Empire or the competition between Latin and Greek for supremacy: the real obstacle was the authorities' suspicion of early Christian theology, which made booksellers and publishers throughout the Empire extremely loth to handle Christian books. Their unwillingness to become involved was to rebound against them, for the spread of Christianity greatly reduced the readership for books with a pagan content, causing a disastrous slump in their business; and the Christians' own attitude to book-buying[2] was influenced by the thought that the ownership of books was incompatible with their obligation to eschew personal wealth. It is also relevant to note that early Christian literature, with its profusion of polemical writings, was never likely to attract a wide readership: this explains why books were distributed through personal contacts, the recipients being mostly friends or

1. See A. Momigliano, *The Conflict between Paganism and Christianity in the Fourth Century*, Oxford 1963; M.L.W. Laistner, *Christianity and Pagan Culture in the Later Roman Empire*, Ithaca N.Y. 1951.

2. See pp. 150-151.

3. On Christian libraries see C. Wendel, *Kleine Schriften zum antiken Buch- und Bibliothekswesen*, ed. W. Krieg, Köln 1974, 178 ff.

119. Tertullian. Engraving from A. Thevet, Les vrais portraits et vies des hommes illustres, *Paris 1584.*

4. H.J. Rose has a chapter on Early Christian literature in his *Handbook of Latin Literature*: *Ἱστορία τῆς Λατινικῆς Λογοτεχνίας*, tr. K.Ch. Grollios, II, Athens 1989, 185-256 (on Tertullian, 192 ff.). For further reading see A.G. Amatucci, *Storia della letteratura latina cristiana*, Turin 1955. St. Jerome casts an interesting light on the state of the contemporary Christian book market when he states (*De viris illustribus*, 53) that he

opponents of the author. From this time down to about the end of the fourth century Christian libraries can be divided into two categories: parish libraries and private collections.

1. Parish libraries. From the very earliest times, the Christian communities needed libraries of some kind for their liturgical and catechetic books. These libraries usually started with a basic nucleus of the Pentateuch, the Psalter and the New Testament and were gradually expanded to include works of Christian literature (often of local interest) such as liturgical calendars, lives of martyrs, episcopal rolls, transcripts of synodical resolutions, letters, doctrinal treatises, works of apologetics and polemics.[3] In places where paganism was still relatively strong, parish priests and bishops needed to have access to the standard apologias and polemics against the Gnostics, especially in the period characterized by internecine persecutions within the Church and the spread of heresies. And so the larger parishes tended to build up parallel libraries composed not of liturgical books but of writings on theology and the defence of the catholic faith. There was plenty of material available for these non-liturgical libraries, as writers were busy turning out books laying down guidelines for Christian thought and action and other works – such as Tertullian's *Ad martyras* – intended to boost the morale of persecuted Christians held in prison awaiting the death sentence.[4] On the other hand there were numerous heretical writings, which were a thorn in the flesh to defenders of the catholic faith. One such defender was Tertullian, who, employing his talents as an able lawyer and orator, set out to define heresy in a polemic published around the year 200 under the title of *De praescriptione haereticorum*, in which he put forward a neat way for disputants to test the validity of their opponents' arguments without having to go into a lengthy investigation of their merits. Can the proponent prove that his opinion is derived from the apostles? If so, it is a catholic doctrine; if not, it is a heresy and that is the end of the argument.

Libraries containing books of these kinds must have existed in the parish of Rome in the early decades of the third century, when St. Hippolytus, a presbyter, was writing prolifically on a wide range of subjects. In Jerusalem Bishop Alexander had a fine collection of books in which Eusebius (*Ecclesiastical History*, VI.20) discovered some valuable information about the library that Origen built up when he was exiled from Alexandria and living in Palestine.[5]

2. Private libraries. The biggest libraries in the Early Christian period were those belonging to writers, who needed a good collection of books of their own for research purposes. There were no public libraries, parish libraries did not allow books to be borrowed, and theological writings were not generally available on the market. Consequently writers

knew works by Tertullian that were already lost.

5. On Origen and his library see p. 152.

6. Jerome, *Letters* V.2. Rufinus, the addressee of the letter, was a former pupil of St. Jerome's. Both had belonged to the small Christian community at Aquileia, which had been broken up in about 373, whereupon most of its members had emigrated to the Levant.

The most interesting of all Jerome's writings are his letters, in which he records events with a vividness matched only by Cicero. The sense of life permeating his descriptions comes not only from his style of writing but also from his character, as he was constitutionally incapable of discussing dispassionately any subject that really interested him: he conducted all his arguments on points of theology as if he were a personal enemy of those who held opposing views.

R.P.E. Arns, in his book about the production and distribution of books in the Early Christian period (*La technique du livre d'après Saint Jérôme*, Paris 1953), has a great deal of extremely interesting information based on St. Jerome's work as author and publisher. In the first place, he points out, the fact of writing or copying a piece of work did not necessarily mean that it was meant for publication, because when a text was intended to be an exemplar, i.e. a 'master copy' for future copyists, the author or editor

120. St. Ambrose, Opera, *Basel, J. Froben et al., 1506.*

worked in close collaboration with the scribe and checked the quality of his work. Unfortunately for the standards of textual integrity, however, the 'master copy' would come into the hands of *librarii* (a term that covers booksellers, publishers and copyists), with or without the author's consent, where it was liable to be corrupted as

121. St. Jerome. Fresco by Ghirlandaio. Florence, Cenacolo di Ognissanti, 1494.

122. St. Augustine. Fresco by Botticelli. Florence, Cenacolo di Ognissanti, 1444-1445.

operated a closed circle of book production and distribution, copying their books out themselves. No less a person than St. Jerome has given us a reliable account of the way this 'book trade' functioned.

St. Jerome was unquestionably the most erudite of the Christian scholars in the West. He studied in Rome, where he was taught by Donatus. Between 375 and 377, when he was living in a community of anchorites in the Syrian desert, he wrote a letter to Florentinus, a well-to-do priest in Jerusalem, which contained the following passage:

'You tell me in your letter that brother Rufinus has not reached you yet. But even if he had arrived it would not help me, as I would not be able to see him. He is so far away from me that he cannot come here, so I beg you to ask him – and I hope you will be able to press my request strongly – to lend me the commentary by the late Bishop Reticius of Autun, whose interpretation of the Song of Songs is so very well written, as I would like to copy it. A compatriot of the same brother Reticius, an elder named Paul, has written to tell me that he still has the codex of Tertullian in his possession. He would like it to be returned to him as soon as possible. In the brief postscript to this letter you will find a list of books I do not have: if you don't mind, please would you get a scribe to copy them out on papyrus. Please do another thing for me, too, and send me the sainted Hilary's exegesis of the Psalms of David and his long book about the synods, which I copied out with my own hand at Trier. If you could possibly do all that I have asked, you will be doing me a great favour. Since we have here, by God's help, a sacred library containing many codices, tell me what you would like me to send you in my turn. Don't be afraid that your request will be a burden to me. I have pupils who specialize in copying books.'[6]

This practice of lending books privately is confirmed by Libanius, an eminent Greek rhetorician about thirty years Jerome's senior, who lived near Antioch. In his *Orations* he mentions that authors not only lent their books to friends and admirers but allowed them to make copies.[7]

II. Architecture. When we talk about an early Christian library, what we are really referring to is the large or small collection of books often kept in a church or in the assembly room used by the local Christian community.[8] It need hardly be said that there was an integral connection between these 'libraries' and the churches they belonged to, as there had been between libraries and Hellenistic and Roman temples, because without the books it would obviously have been impossible to perform church services or instruct catechumens. The practice of keeping the books in an alcove or cupboard was not borrowed from Jewish synagogues, where the scriptures were kept in the ark of the Torah, but was simply the archetypal and most natural form of storage. When the books became more numerous they were moved to another room in the same building, and so the first parish libraries came into being. One such library is mentioned in the protocol of Minucius Felix, in connection with the search of the house of Bishop Paul of Cirta during the persecutions in Diocletian's reign: 'When entry had been gained into the library, empty cupboards were found there.'[9]

In the climate of oppression and intimidation then prevailing, church libraries could not be anything more than rooms in which books happened to be kept. The rooms were not designed for the purpose, of course, and the books were kept in ordinary cupboards which were positioned at random and were not attached to the walls. Nor was this state

123. 'Presentation of a book'. Woodcut from Jacopo da Cessole, Tractato degli scachi, *Florence, A. Miscomini, 1494.*

of affairs limited to those early years: it lasted for many centuries into the Christian era, in the East as well as the West, and even in large and important monastic libraries. Once religious tolerance had become the rule, the Christians started building churches to rival the great monuments of pagan antiquity, replacing their humble places of worship with grand basilicas surrounded by porticoes and colonnaded courtyards in imitation of secular buildings, and then they would move their archives and books to one of the outlying rooms. One library that was moved in this way was that attached to the Church of St. Lawrence in Rome, built by Pope Damasus shortly after 366 on a site inherited from his father.

a result of the copying methods in use. At this stage the integrity of the text was not always left to careful copyists and editors who respected the author's words: it was often corrupted by money-grubbing booksellers who employed *tachygraphi* or 'speed-writers'. The author himself had no control whatever over what was done to his work, and that is the main reason why a text varies from one copy to another.

7. On the book trade from the beginning of the fourth century see R. Schipke, *Untersuchungen zur Herstellung und Verbreitung des Buches im lateinischem Westen zwischen dem 4. und 6. Jahrhundert* (dissertation), Berlin 1976.

8. On the furnishing of early libraries in church buildings see Wendel, *op. cit.* 159-160.

9. Minucius Felix was one of the earliest Christian apologists. Born probably in Africa, he spent most of his life in Rome. His only extant work is the dialogue *Octavius*, in which he describes the conversion to Christianity of his friend and fellow-lawyer Caecilius.

124. Libanius. Engraving from A. Thevet, Les vrais portraits et vies des hommes illustres, *Paris 1584.*

125. Reconstruction of a library of Christian writings.

126. Senator Magnus. Engraving after an ivory triptych carved in Constantinople in 518. Reproduced from C. du Cange, De Imperatorum et Constantinopolitanorum..., *Rome 1755.*

CHAPTER NINE

BYZANTIUM

The inauguration of Constantinople as the capital of the Eastern Roman Empire and the adoption of Christianity as the Empire's official religion augured well for the future of books and libraries generally. The Eastern Empire had inherited not only the ancient Graeco-Roman civilization but a whole new literature as well, which was based on the Christian faith and was therefore the repository of a vast body of knowledge stored away in books. And so Constantinople obviously needed a great new library to house all this literature; but that was not to be. While the city of Rome boasted no less than twenty-eight public libraries at the beginning of the fourth century, not to mention the many monumental libraries in the provinces, in Constantinople we are hard put to find any trace of one large 'public' library, and even the existence of that one is conjectural. Nor was the situation any better where private libraries are concerned: to a scholarly bibliophile like Leo the Mathematician (9th c.) or his contemporary Patriarch Photios, stories of the private library of Tyrannio (a Greek slave in Rome who possessed 30,000 papyrus rolls) or of the Roman patrician Larnesius must have seemed like fables from the *Arabian Nights*.

There are many reasons to account for the fact that books were never so numerous as they had been in Graeco-Roman antiquity; that at times they were the somewhat recherché preserve of a few intellectual coteries, imperial foundations and monastic communities; that for long periods they were regarded with suspicion; and that there were occasions when books were suppressed by the ecclesiastical or civil authorities. However, before attempting to chronicle the course of events from the fourth century to the fall of Constantinople in 1453, it would be useful to examine the four main factors that worked against the large-scale production and distribution of books. These were: (a) the slump in the business of the Roman bookselling and publishing houses that had marketed books throughout the Roman Empire; (b) the Church's attempts to impose orthodox dogma on the population and curb the dissemination of pagan writings, including the whole corpus of classical learning, coupled with its unceasing efforts to challenge and suppress Christian theological works which it considered heretical; (c) the steep rise in book prices caused by the higher cost of parchment (which gradually superseded papyrus) and the exorbitant rates of pay demanded by copyists, owing to the shortage of slaves with a specialized training as scribes; and (d) the disapproving attitude of many monks to the ownership of books.

(a) In the brief chapter on early Christian libraries we saw that the production and distribution of Christian books was not taken over by the existing pagan copying and publishing firms: a new pattern set in, with the authors themselves copying their works and distributing them among their friends and acquaintances. This change deprived the old booksellers and publishers of a large part of their market, of course; and eventually, as more and more of the educated classes went over to Christianity, it led inexorably to the ruin of the book trade as such. The failure of Graeco-Roman literature to maintain the interest of the Roman reading public is attested by Ammianus Marcellinus (XIV.6.18),

1. P.J. Alexander, *The Oracle of Baalbek*, Washington D.C. 1967, 14; C. Mango, *Βυζάντιο: Ἡ Αὐτοκρατορία τῆς Νέας Ρώμης (= Byzantium: The Empire of New Rome, London 1980*, tr. D. Tsoungarakis), Athens 1990, 25-43.

2. Mango, *op. cit.* 109-114.

3. See p. 167. See also Polymnia Athanassiadi, 'Persecution and Response in Late Paganism: The evidence of Damascius', *JHS* 113 (1993) 1-29.

127. The Gospel book on the Sacred Throne at the Council of Constantinople (362), in the Emperor's presence.

4. *Codex Justinianus* I.1.1 (*Cod. Theod.* XVI.1.2).

5. John of Damascus, *On Heresies* (*PG* 94 677 ff.).

6. V. Laourdas, *Photios. Epistolae et Amphilochia*, 6 vols., Leipzig 1983-1988. Of the later heresies, one that deserves special mention for its subversiveness and hostility towards the Byzantine Empire is Paulicianism.

7. Mango, *op. cit.* 281; cf. pp. 161-162 herein.

8. John Chrysostom, *On Vanity and the Upbringing of Children*, ed. A.M. Malingrey, Paris 1972, para. 70.

9. See p. 33.

10. See H. Hunger, *Reich der neuen Mitte: Der christliche Geist der byzantinischen Kultur*, Vienna/Köln 1965,

who says that the libraries were 'permanently closed, like tombs'.

No large bookselling and publishing houses are known to have existed in Constantinople or any of the other principal cities of the Eastern Empire. From time to time it happened that a number of copyists banded together round an inspiring teacher, calligrapher or illuminator and fulfilled that function, but such enterprises never lasted. A great proportion of the books produced came from the imperial scriptoria and the new scriptoria run by the monasteries, though there is no real evidence that any of them had business dealings with the general public.

One of the biggest obstacles confronting anyone who might have thought of opening a bookselling and publishing house modelled on those of Rome was the language problem. Julius Caesar's decision in the first century B.C. to divide Roman public libraries into two separate sections reflected the linguistic dualism of the Roman Empire, where Greek and Latin were used side by side. But the bilingual library was not a practical solution in the new capital, Constantinople, whose heterogeneous population included foreigners speaking all seventy-two known languages and dialects, some of them permanently resident and others visiting the city regularly on commercial or administrative business.[1] Even in the reign of Justinian I, in the sixth century, there were Syrian, Mesopotamian and Egyptian monks who spoke little or no Greek flocking into the capital under the patronage of Empress Theodora.

(b) When Christianity was adopted as the official religion of the Eastern Empire in 334, scholars and other educated people may have been under the illusion that Graeco-Roman and Christian literature would generate a revival of business for publishers with ambitious plans. But here again the course of events ran far from smoothly. Orthodox fanatics always regarded idolaters as a permanent threat, and by their rigorous standards there were always idolaters to be found in the Byzantine Empire. Although there were not many pagans left by the end of the sixth century, the middle classes and some intellectuals kept up many idolatrous customs and practices, following the tradition of the Graeco-Roman civilization.[2] Then the persecution of pagans that lasted from 340 until the reign of Justinian I – with the closure of pagan temples in 391, the sack of the Serapeum, the hacking to death of the philosopher Hypatia by an enraged mob in 415 and the closure of the Athenian philosophy schools in 529 – created a climate of uncertainty and risk for would-be publishers. What is more, even as late as the eleventh century (by which time the danger of a pagan revival had ceased to exist), it still sometimes happened that people were convicted on charges of propagating theories tainted with paganism, as in the case of John Italos.[3]

Besides the risk of a relapse into paganism, the problem of heresies had been plaguing the Empire for centuries, with the Church repeatedly stepping in to censor or stifle suspect religious writings. In practice, the

242: 'Abbot Serapion admonished one of the monks because he had seen a lot of books in his cell, which was tantamount to stealing from widows and orphans. Likewise, Abbot Theodore of Pherme sold three books of his on the advice of the venerable Father Makarios and distributed the proceeds among the poor.' Many such stories are told of hermits.

11. Patriarch John of Antioch (11th c.) believed that the population of the world was divided equally between monks and the laity: see *PG* 132 1128A.

128. St. John of Damascus. Illumination from a manuscript of his works: Paris, Bibliothèque Nationale, Ms Gr. 1123λ, fol. 5v.

12. *Const. apost.* I.6 (F.X. Funk (ed.), *Didascalia et constitutiones apostolorum*, Paderborn 1905, 13-15): 'Shun all pagan books. What need is there of foreign writings, laws and false prophets that lead fools away from the faith? What do you hope to find in pagan myths that is not in the Divine Law? If you wish to read stories, there is the Book of Kings; if rhetoric and poetry, there are the prophets, Job, the Book of Proverbs, where you will find more wisdom than in any poetry or sophistics, for they are the words of the

Byzantines were required not merely to be Christians but to believe and obey a single dogma that defined the nature and structure of the Trinity. But not even the Emperor could be relied on to follow the precepts of this dogma consistently. For example, Justinian's decree of 390 declared: 'It is our desire that all the peoples under our imperial rule should practice the religion which the holy apostle Peter handed down to the Romans so that we should all believe in the indivisible divinity of the Father, the Son and the Holy Ghost in equal majesty and worshipful trinity. We therefore command that all persons who follow this law be called Catholic Christians. All others, whom we consider to be impious and possessed by mania, are to suffer the ignominy of heretical doctrine, their meeting-places are not to be known by the name of churches, and they are to be punished first by divine vengeance and then by the punishment of our own power, which we have received through divine favour.'[4] The imperial decree left no room for argument, yet it was repeatedly interpreted in different ways by the emperors themselves. Constantius II and Valens fought for Arianism, Anastasius I was a champion of the Monophysites, Heraclius tried to impose Monotheletism on the Empire, and the Iconoclastic views of several emperors in the eighth and ninth centuries consigned thousands of books to the flames. The result of this religious confusion was that the 'impious' subjects of the Empire came to outnumber the Orthodox Christians. It is astonishing to discover from the records of the Councils of the Church that in the eighth century John of Damascus listed over a hundred different heresies.[5] And although Patriarch Photios declared after the Council of 867 that religious doctrine had now been determined finally and irrevocably, the Empire continued to be riven by heretical doctrines and the authorities' often heavy-handed reaction to them.[6]

(c) The third obstacle to the formation of large private libraries was the cost of books. In the Byzantine period books were most commonly produced in the form of codices, not rolls. Until about the seventh century they were usually written on Egyptian papyrus, but the Arab conquest of Egypt put an end to papyrus exports. Parchment, which had started being used on a large scale in the fourth century and would eventually supersede papyrus altogether, made books too expensive for the general public, and it was only with the introduction of paper from the Arab world at the end of the eleventh century that they became affordable again. A remarkable but not untypical case in point is that of Arethas, Archbishop of Caesarea (early tenth century), who ordered a parchment codex of the fourth and fifth tetralogies of Plato, which cost him thirteen nomismata, roughly equivalent to $4,000 at today's prices.[7]

Even as early as the Classical period (fifth century B.C.) scriptoria were staffed with specially trained slaves, often prisoners of war, and this remained the normal practice down to the end of the Roman period.

Lord, the only repository of wisdom. If you want songs, there are the Psalms; if ancient genealogies, there is Genesis; if law books and legal precepts, there is the seventh Divine Law. Therefore be steadfast and shun all pagan and diabolical books.'

13. On Byzantine libraries and the book trade generally, see: P. Batiffol, 'Librairies byzantines à Rome', *Mélanges d'Archéologie et d'Histoire de l'École Française de Rome* 8 (1888) 297-308; S.K. Padover, 'Byzantine Libraries' in J.W. Thompson (ed.), *The Medieval Library*, Chicago 1939 (reprinted in 1965 with additions by B.B. Boyer), 310-329; C. Wendel, *Kleine Schriften zum antiken Buch- und Bibliothekswesen*, ed. W. Krieg, Köln 1974, 46; R. Devreesse, *Introduction à l'étude des manuscrits grecs*, Paris 1954; C.H. Roberts, 'The Codex', *Proceedings of the British Academy* (1954) 169-204; N.G. Wilson, 'The Libraries of the Byzantine World', *GRBS* 8 (1967) 53-80; K.A. Manafis, *Αἱ ἐν Κωνσταντινουπόλει Βιβλιοθῆκαι, Αὐτοκρατορικαί καί Πατριαρχική, καί περί τῶν ἐν αὐταῖς χειρογράφων μέχρι τῆς Ἁλώσεως (1453)*, Athens 1972; N.G. Wilson, 'Books and Readers in Byzantium' in *Byzantine Books and Bookmen: A Dumbarton Oaks Colloquium 1971*, Dumbarton Oaks 1975, 1-15; J. Irigoin, 'Centres de copie et bibliothèques', *ibid*. 17-27; C. Mango, 'The Availability of Books in the Byzantine Empire, A.D. 750-850', *ibid*. 29-45; H.-G. Beck, 'Der Leserkreis der byzantinischen Volksliteratur', *ibid*. 47-67; K. Weitzmann, 'The Selection of Texts for Cyclic Illustration in Byzantine Manuscripts', *ibid*. 69-109; G. Cavallo, 'Il libro come oggetto d'uso nel mondo bizantino', *XVI. Internationaler Byzantinisten-Kongress*, Vienna 1981, 395-423; P. Lemerle, *Ὁ πρῶτος Βυζαντινός οὐμανισμός* (= *Le premier humanisme byzantin*, tr. Maria Nystazopoulou-Pelekidou), Athens 1981, 59, 60, 64, 65; Mango, *Βυζάντιο* 140, 145, 148-149, 166, 281-283; H. Hunger, *Ὁ κόσμος τοῦ Βυζαντινοῦ βιβλίου: Γραφή καί ἀνάγνωση στό Βυζάντιο* (=*Schreiben und Lesen in Byzanz. Die byzantinische Buchkultur,* tr. G. Vasilaros), Athens 1995.

14. Wendel, *op. cit.* 46: 'You are to order fifty copies of the holy scriptures, easily legible and of convenient

However, this kind of treatment was contrary to the precepts of Christianity and the ostentatious exploitation of large numbers of slaves provoked fierce criticism. St. John Chrysostom considered it acceptable for a good Christian to employ one slave only, and exclusively for household chores.[8] Consequently the 'one-drachma editions' of Anaxagoras's works that had been obtainable in the fifth century B.C. were as dead as their author, and books now cost several gold nomismata.[9]

(d) Besides the above three reasons for the decline of large-scale book production, mention should be made of the attitude towards books held by a great many monks in the Byzantine world, mostly hermits and the older members of monastic communities, who followed the strict rules of asceticism and believed the ownership of books to be incompatible with their vow of poverty.[10] So the rapid growth of monasticism in the fourth, fifth and sixth centuries and the power it acquired through sheer weight of numbers (for there were thousands of monasteries all over the Empire) meant that, in effect, half the population was barred from buying books.[11] Furthermore, the Canons of the Apostles (4th c.) stated flatly: 'Shun all pagan books.'[12]

In all the centuries of the Byzantine Empire's existence, even though hundreds of thousands of manuscript codices were produced and a new type of library – the monastic library – came into being, books were never available on the market in the same numbers as they had been in late antiquity. The only large libraries were to be found in imperial institutions, patriarchates and monasteries. Private libraries, even those with imperial backing, never contained more than two hundred books, and the library of an educated man or scholar would usually have no more than about thirty.[13]

I. From Constantine to early Byzantine humanism. The earliest known official reference to books in New Rome concerns the Emperor Constantine the Great, who commissioned Eusebius, Bishop of Caesarea in Palestine, to have fifty copies of the Bible made by skilled calligraphers, on smooth vellum in codex form.[14] As scholars have frequently reiterated, these books were not to be the nucleus of a library in Constantinople: most probably the Emperor intended them for the use of churches and religious foundations. The fact that Constantine chose to order the codices from Caesarea comes as no surprise, because the necessary facilities did not exist in the capital, whereas in Caesarea there was a Christian library developed by Eusebius's teacher Pamphilus from Origen's collection, as well as a copying centre whose importance to Christian writings equalled that of the Museum in Alexandria to classical literature.[15] The brevity of Constantine's reign (324-337) gave him no time to make Constantinople the cultural as well as the administrative capital of the Empire, and he devoted more of his attention to beautifying the city than to developing its intellectual life.

size to be carried and used, to be written on prepared parchment by skilled calligraphers well versed in their art. As you know, it is necessary for these to be made and used for the purposes of the Church.' (Eusebius

129. Eusebius, Bishop of Caesarea. Engraving from A. Thevet, Les vrais portraits et vies des hommes illustres, *Paris 1584.*

of Caesarea, *The Life of the Blessed Emperor Constantine* IV.36: *PG* 20 118A-C.) Irigoin conjectures that the Codex Sinaiticus may have been one of these fifty Bibles: see *Lustrum* 1962 (Göttingen 1963) 57.

15. Devreesse, *op. cit.* 122 ff.; C. Wendel, 'Das griechisch-römische Altertum' (completed by W. Göber) in *HBW* III.1 131-133.

16. See G. Dagron, 'L'empire romain d'orient au IVe siècle et les traditions politiques de l'hellénisme: Le témoignage de Thémistios', *TM* 3 (1968) 1-242.

17. Wendel, *Kleine Schriften...* 50-51; Themistius, *Orations* IV 59b-61d (ed. Dindorf, Leipzig 1832, 70-73); Themistius, *Orations*, ed. G. Downey and F. Norman, 3 vols., Leipzig 1965-1974; Manafis, *op. cit.* 21-40.

18. For the sciences and other specialized branches of study inherited from ancient Greece the Byzantines compiled lists of standard school and university textbooks, of which fresh copies were made periodically. Manuscript copies of the textbooks used in the teaching of rhetoric, astronomy, mathematics

1. The first 'imperial' library. The development of books and libraries has always depended on education and the policies of those in power towards learning and scholarship. In the Byzantine Empire, the triumph of Christianity over paganism brought no correspondingly fundamental changes to the educational system: both the methods of teaching and the textbooks used in schools and higher educational establishments continued to follow the traditions of late antiquity. That was the reason why itinerant teachers, rhetoricians and philosophers who had divided their time between the intellectual centres of the Levant (Antioch, Alexandria, Gaza and Palestinian Caesarea) started flocking to Constantinople, forming scholarly coteries and opening schools and small academies to which they attracted large numbers of pupils and auditors. In this fertile climate Constantine's son, who became Emperor as Constantius II (337-361), decided that intellectual improvement was needed as well as economic growth. The man he chose to co-ordinate this campaign was Themistius, a most remarkable person: orthodox by upbringing, heretical in his views on the political Romanization of the Eastern Empire, and first and foremost an Aristotelian philosopher.[16]

Themistius very soon showed that the Emperor's faith in him was not misplaced: in a letter to the Senate, Constantius extols his achievement in turning the capital into 'an open hostelry of learning'. Returning the compliment, Themistius, in a speech delivered on 1st January 357, sings the Emperor's praises and congratulates him on his splendid initiative in forming the first collection of ancient literature in Constantinople. Carl Wendel, who first discovered this speech, is right in stressing its importance.[17] Yet Themistius leaves many questions unanswered with regard to the processes of book production and says nothing about the place where all these books were kept, not even specifying the official name of the library or its location. He mentions a scriptorium whose services Constantius used to 'resurrect Plato and Aristotle from Hades'; other authors he mentions include Demosthenes, Isocrates and Thucydides (all of whom he praises for their Attic style); the great poets Homer and Hesiod and their successors; the Stoic philosophers Zeno, Cleanthes and Chrysippus; and 'the children of the Muses', by which he means the whole legacy of ancient wisdom, even of the most arcane and unusual kind. It is odd that Themistius makes no reference whatever to Christian literature and is vague about the sort of library for which the output of this scriptorium was intended. It is reasonable to suppose that the phrase 'public wealth of wisdom' alludes to an educational library open to scholars and students. Quite possibly multiple copies were made of some of these works for other libraries too, in schools or colleges and perhaps also in the palace. Themistius expressly states that the original manuscripts from which copies were taken were papyrus rolls in an advanced state of disintegration; the copies were presumably written on parchment codices. In view of the Byzantines' known predilection for

and music have come down to us, annotated with a mass of scholia. See H. Hunger, *Βυζαντινή Λογοτεχνία. Ἡ λόγια κοσμική γραμματεία τῶν Βυζαντινῶν* (= *Die höchsprachliche profane Literatur der Byzantiner*, Munich 1978, tr. G.Ch. Makris et al.), 3 vols., Athens 1987-1994.

19. On the condition of libraries in the Roman provinces in the fourth century, see pp. 123 ff.

20. See *Oeuvres de Julien*, I.2: *Lettres et fragments*, ed. J. Bidez, Paris 1924; A. Piganiol, *L'empire chrétien (325-395)*, Paris 1947; Wendel, *Kleine Schriften*... 53 ff.

21. *Oeuvres de Julien*, I.2, No. 107.

22. *Ibid*. p. 98.

23. *Ibid*. Nos. 106-107.

24. Wendel, *Kleine Schriften*... 54.

25. *Ibid*. 54. St. Jerome informs us that there had been a chair of Latin Rhetoric at the Higher School of Constantinople since 360 (in Constantius's reign) and that it was occupied by Evanthius, the author of commentaries on Terence: see Wendel, *Kleine Schriften*... 55; Lemerle, *op. cit*. 62-63.

130. Emperor Constantius II.

26. Wendel, *Kleine Schriften*... 54.

27. Wendel, *Kleine Schriften*.... 56 (Zonaras XIV.2). According to Kedrenos (ed. I. Bekker, *CSHB*, Bonn 1838, I 616), the fire, which occurred early in Basiliscus's reign, destroyed 'both the stoas and all the adjacent buildings and the so-called basilica, containing a library of twelve thousand

form over substance in their studies, it may well be that the practice of writing summaries of long works started at this time.[18]

One question to which Themistius does not give or even hint at an answer is where all this material came from and how it was brought to Constantinople. There is no evidence to suggest that an official appeal was issued, as Ptolemy II had done to obtain books for the great Alexandrian library, or that agents were sent out to the traditional centres of book production, but we should not forget that nothing at all is known about the fate of dozens of libraries that existed throughout the Roman Empire from the Black Sea to Carthage, including those of Alexandria, Pergamum, Ephesus, Timgad, Nyssa, Rhodes, Thessalonica and Philippi and so many others that were closed by the Christians because they were considered suspect as being pagan survivals from antiquity – although one such library, having had its doors sealed, did continue to exist until the tenth century.[19] Most probably those libraries were ransacked for the books Themistius wanted; but, be that as it may, the greatness of Themistius's achievement lies in the fact that he created a library in Constantinople with a priceless collection of Greek and Latin literature, to judge by the decree of Valens.

Constantius II was succeeded on the imperial throne by Julian 'the Apostate',[20] who had been much influenced by Libanius, admired the ancient tradition and was an avid book collector. While still an adolescent he had borrowed books from his teacher George of Cappadocia and copied them out for himself.[21] When he was in Gaul the Empress Aurelia Eusebia sent him gifts of books by ancient Greek philosophers, orators and historians.[22] And after the Alexandrian uprising of 361, when his teacher George of Cappadocia was killed and his fine library pillaged, he gave orders for the looted books to be found and sent to Antioch.[23] Julian was the first Byzantine emperor to have a private library, which he kept in a room built specially for the purpose.

The location of Julian's library is uncertain: Wendel believes it was probably an extension of Constantius's library rather than a new building.[24] However, the real problem is different: assuming that Julian's private library was an extension of Constantius's library or adjacent to it, what sort of library was it? Was it for the use of the Emperor and the university or was it, as tradition has it, an imperial library open to the public, or at least to scholars who moved in court circles? The question remains unresolved: my own belief is that it was modelled on the great bilingual libraries of Augustus's and Trajan's reigns but had a different architectural design.

The emperors' desire to keep alive the tradition of the bilingual library and at the same time to fuse together the Eastern and Western intellectual traditions, for political and cultural reasons, is clearly apparent in the decree of Valens (372).[25] This decree, which was addressed to Clearchus, the Prefect of Constantinople and a friend of Themistius and Libanius, stipulated that four Greek and three Latin scholars were to be appointed, as well as a number of competent calligraphers to keep the books in good condition and repair damaged copies. It also laid down that librarians (*condicionales*) were to be employed to look after the library and ensure that all books were put back in their proper places.[26] The obvious implication is that here too there were separate Greek and Latin sections, as is known to have been the case in the Patriarchal Library.

After Themistius's eulogy of Constantius II for his action in saving so much of ancient literature in book form and the enterprise shown by Julian in forming an imperial private library, the next thing we hear about these collections is a report of a tragic event: during the brief period when the throne was occupied by Basiliscus (475-476) a sophist named Malchus, who taught in Constantinople, wrote in his *Byzantiaca* that a fire starting in the Chalcopratia district (the brassware market) devastated the so-called κεκλημένη basilica (a meaningless term), which housed a library containing 120,000 volumes.[27] It is remarkable that Georgios Kedrenos (11th c.) and Ioannes Zonaras (12th c.), who both used the same source, give no particulars of this library and in fact imply that it was a library adjacent to the basilica, not the great library of Constantinople.[28] It seems to me that the library destroyed by fire may perhaps have been Julian's. Though the number of books sounds excessive, it is not really so very remarkable, considering that tens of thousands of rolls of pagan writings were available in the mid fourth century and that Julian was a fanatical book collector. Be that as it may, the conclusion to be drawn from three epigrams in the *Anthologia Planudea* is that the basilica, including the room where the books were kept, was rebuilt in Zeno's reign (therefore before 491).[29] The fact that the basilica and the library built by Julian were reconstructed does not mean, of course, that the books lost in the fire were replaced, nor that the library ever functioned again in the same way as it had before the disaster.

2. Education. As already mentioned, the adoption of Christianity as the official religion in the fourth century did not lead to any reforms in the educational system that might have affected the role or the nature of books as teaching aids. In fact education in the Byzantine Empire did not veer away from the ancient Greek pattern, despite John Chrysostom's frequent exhortations (to desist from the study of pagan literature, for example), until the Church officially took over the education of the clergy in the tenth century; nor was any real provision ever made for the education of monks.[30] In other words, not even the Church made any serious attempt to replace the old school books.

The educational system comprised three levels: primary, secondary and higher. From the age of seven, boys – and sometimes girls too – were entrusted to the care of a teacher (*grammatistes*), who usually had only a limited education himself and taught elementary subjects: the alphabet, reading, writing and arithmetic. This private tuition at the primary level was all that most of the population ever had. In the secondary curriculum the emphasis was on Homer and certain other classical authors, mostly poets. The secondary teacher (*grammatikos*), whose education was far superior to that of the *grammatistes*, also taught philosophy, grammar (based on Dionysius the Thracian's textbook of about 100 B.C.), further arithmetic, geometry, astronomy and music.

The subjects taught up to the end of the secondary level were collectively known as *enkyklios paideia* (general education). Anyone who wanted to continue studying beyond that level had to have lessons with one of the rhetoricians or sophists who ran their own schools, often with great success. Where one went for one's higher education depended on one's chosen subject, and it often involved a long journey. Rhetoric was the principal branch of study, and it was satisfactorily taught in Constantinople, but for philosophy the most highly-regarded schools were in Athens and Alexandria, for medicine it was Pergamum, for law Berytus (Beirut). Antioch, Smyrna, Gaza and Nicomedia also developed into major centres of learning. Constantinople became the most important intellectual centre in the Eastern Empire as a result of Theodosius II's decree of 425, which conferred the title of 'public professor' on teachers at the higher schools (i.e. universities) as well as granting them tax concessions and in some cases a salary paid out of public funds.

3. The crisis in the sixth century: from Justinian I to Leo IV. It was Justinian who dealt the first major blow to the development of Greek-Christian education, the systematic preservation of the ancient literary heritage and the survival of the New Sophistic, because he wished to rule over an empire that was Christian in its whole approach to life.[31] Pagans were no longer to be employed in the public sector, nor would any honours or titles be conferred on them, and persons suffering from 'the sacrilegious madness of the Hellenes' were not allowed to teach (*Codex Justinianus* I.21.10). In line with this policy, a directive was sent to the Prefect of Athens, Flavius Decius the younger, instructing him to forbid the teaching of philosophy and interpretation of the law, which resulted in the closure of the Athenian school of philosophy in 529.[32] Nor was that the end of the matter, for in 546 and 562 teachers and men of letters were imprisoned and tortured and their writings were burnt in the capital itself, to celebrate the triumph of Orthodoxy.[33] In the face of this evidence it cannot be seriously argued that secular books continued to be copied or that Constantius II's 'classical library' continued to be enlarged – even assuming that it survived the fire. On the contrary, books were systematically suppressed. These episodes mark the end of the renaissance of learning initiated by Constantius, and there ensued a period of intellectual decline.

Justinian's death in 565 signalled the beginning of a period which, at least as far as books and libraries are concerned, can only be painted in the darkest colours. The fall of Alexandria to the Arabs in 642 and the dire blow dealt to Byzantium by Islam, which overran regions of the Empire where the Graeco-Roman tradition had been deeply rooted, sounded the death knell of the ancient world. Hardly any books, either secular or religious, have come down to us from the sixth to ninth centuries. This does not mean that all of a sudden no one was writing new books or copying old ones – for both authors and scriptoria were still at work, especially in the field of religious writing[34] – but political strife and the Iconoclastic controversy certainly had a disastrous impact on the world of books.

Practically nothing is known about the library in the stoa of the basilica until near the end of the eighth century, apart from the legend that Leo III burnt down an institution of higher education with its library in 726.[35] The story that this library was enlarged because certain emperors (such as Maurice and Heraclius) were keen to improve their minds through study is not based on good evidence. One thing that is certain, however, is that Constantinople did not have nearly enough educators qualified to teach at university level.

Matters went from bad to worse with the outbreak of the Iconoclastic controversy, which raged throughout the Empire from before the middle of the eighth century to 843 and caused most of the population to be labelled heretics, at least in theory. The veneration of images of Christ and the saints was a vexed question which Leo II set out to resolve in 730 by decreeing that all sacred images were to be removed from the churches, a decision he took without the consent of the Patriarch.[36] But it is not true that he attempted to have teachers burnt at the stake and their books consigned to the flames, as some chroniclers allege.[37] Thereafter a fog descends over the subject and nothing more is heard about books until the reign of Leo V the Armenian (813-820), when the imperial library is referred to once again, as we shall see.[38] According to Michael Glykas, writing in the twelfth century, the library founded by Constantius II was situated in the Octagon and contained 36,500 books.[39]

At this point a brief recapitulation would be useful, as the extant evidence concerning the history of Constantius II's and Julian's libraries over the years does not help us to form a clear picture. The facts are that

books'. It is worth mentioning that this passage gives us our third piece of evidence concerning the size of a royal public library in the Greek world, following the Alexandrian Library and that of Pergamum.

28. Zonaras, following Malchus, states that one of the books destroyed was an illuminated roll of Homer, 120 feet long, written in gold ink on 'dragon's gut' (cf. Kedrenos, ed. I. Bekker, *CSHB*, Bonn 1838, I 616). John Chrysostom, who also mentions books written in gold ink, inveighs

131. Ioannes Zonaras. Engraving from A. Thevet, Les vrais portraits et vies des hommes illustres, *Paris 1584.*

against owners of such books who do not know what they are reading (*PG* 59 187).

29. According to the *Eclogae historiae ecclesiasticae* of Theodore Anagnostes (*PG* 86^{1} 184B-C), there was also a library in the palace in Zeno's reign and the Emperor had a copy of St. Matthew's Gospel signed by the calligrapher Barnabas.

30. L. Bréhier, 'L'enseignement classique et l'enseignement religieux à Byzance', *Revue d'histoire et de philosophie religieuses* 21 (1949) 34-69; H.-I. Marrou, *Ἱστορία τῆς Ἐκπαιδεύσεως κατά τήν Ἀρχαιότητα* (= *Histoire de l'éducation dans l'antiquité*, Paris 1948, tr. Th. Fotinopoulos), Athens 1961, 428-465; W. Jaeger, *Early Christianity and Greek Paideia*, Cambridge Mass. 1961; Mango, *Βυζάντιο* 151-177.

31. Lemerle, *op. cit.* 65-70.

32. John Malalas, *Chronicle* XVIII (ed. L. Dindorf, *CSHB*, Bonn 1831, 451); A. Cameron, 'The End of the Ancient Universities', *Cahiers d'histoire mondiale* 10 (1966-1967) 653-673; Ead., 'The Last Days of the Academy at Athens', *Proceedings of the Cambridge Philological Society* 15 (1969) 7-29; H.J. Blumenthal, '529 and its Sequel: What happened to the Academy', *Byzantion* 48 (1978) 369-385; A. Frantz, *The Athenian Agora: Results of excavations conducted by the American School of Classical Studies at Athens*, XXIV: *Late Antiquity, A.D. 267-700*, Princeton 1988, 44-47, 84-92.

33. John Malalas, *Chronicle* XVIII (ed. L. Dindorf, *CSHB*, Bonn 1831, 451): see Lemerle, *op. cit.* 65-70 (n. 76). Cavallo (*op. cit.* 401) mentions a series of imperial decrees relating to the destruction of books: in 363/4 Jovian ordered all pagan books to be cast into the fire at Antioch; in 371 Valens issued a decree ordering the burning of books suspected of dealing with sorcery, again in Antioch; in 431 Nestorian writings were destroyed by Theodosius II; and in 455 Marcian gave orders for books dealing with the heresies of Apollinaris the Younger of Laodicea and Eutyches to be burnt. An interesting

132. Emperor Justinian I. Engraving by J. Pine.

Constantius founded a scriptorium that is believed to have supported a library which was probably open to the public and closely associated with an institution of higher learning. There is no evidence relating to this library: even its location is not known. It is thought to have been near the so-called 'Basilica of the Schools', which was probably the building otherwise known as the Octagon. Assuming that it followed the model of public libraries in Rome, it was an imperial library, open to the public but directly controlled by the Emperor or members of his court, who often practised censorship. The library built by Julian in the royal stoa to house his private collection was probably for the exclusive use of himself and the imperial household, and it would no doubt have contained a large number of classical books, as he was deeply interested in paganism and its works. In my opinion, there is no connection between this and the library of Constantius. The next item of information concerns the organization of the library and the promulgation of Valens's decree on the maintenance and restoration of damaged Greek and Latin manuscripts. From this decree it is possible to draw conclusions concerning the Emperor's supervision of the library and the continuance of the Roman institution of the bilingual library.

The stance taken by Theodosius II and Empress Eudocia with regard to books favoured the development of libraries.[40] In fact, considering that the Emperor himself sometimes copied out sacred writings in his own hand, it is reasonable to suppose that new sections devoted to Christian literature were opened in his time, both in the palace library and the one near the Basilica of the Schools.[41] Here a question of topography arises, as Theodosius II's reorganization of the educational system led to the extension of the buildings: in 425 the Higher School (i.e. the University) was moved from the Octagon to the Capitol, which in turn proved too small for the number of students attending it, and so podiums were built in the north stoa of the basilica for the teaching of law and philosophy.[42] The Octagon was burnt down in 532 (in Justinian's reign), but the Higher School is known to have moved back there, presumably after it was rebuilt. The library is not mentioned in the context of this move.

The next reference to the subject comes from the chronicler Michael Glykas, who states that there was a magnificent building near Hagia Sophia containing 36,500 books. At first sight it would appear that this 'great library' was much smaller than the one burnt down in 475/6 – three centuries earlier – with the loss of 120,000 books, but the seeming discrepancy is easily explained: it is simply a matter of comparing like with unlike. The library burnt down in 475/6, if it really was Julian's, would certainly have contained a great many papyrus rolls, whereas nearly all the books in use in the eighth century would have been in codex form, and it is an established fact that one codex equalled anything from ten to a hundred papyrus rolls of late antiquity. Therefore, if Glykas's figure is correct, it would seem that this library rivalled the Great Library of Alexandria. No comparison can be made with any other contemporary library, while even the biggest private collections numbered no more than a few hundred codices. We should remind ourselves that near the end of the fifteenth century the biggest library in the West, that of the Vatican, possessed barely two thousand manuscripts; yet on the threshold of the first period of Byzantine humanism we find a unique collection of books capable of supporting any humanist age.

4. Monasticism and monastic libraries. No other type or form of Byzantine library is so well documented as the monastic. Before considering this subject, the first point to note is that monasticism was a lay movement governed by very strict rules, started by groups of Christians living in Egypt.[43]

The father of monachism, St. Antony, states that there were no monasteries or hermits in Egypt around the year 270.[44] Withdrawal from the world was the first step towards the next form of monasticism, the cenobitic or communal religious life, which was inaugurated by Pachomius (†346) in Upper Egypt. What concerns us here is not the way in which monastic rules evolved but the fact that Pachomius, by the terms of his Rule, in effect instituted monastic libraries. The study of edifying writings was compulsory for all members of the community, tuition being provided for novices who were unable to read and write, and the monks spent a large part of the day meditating on their reading. Every morning the subprior would hand out a manuscript to each monk, to be returned to him at dusk for safe keeping. Strict regulations were laid down for the careful handling of books.[45] The *Typikon* (Rule) of Pachomius had a wide following and quickly spread from Egypt to Palestine, Syria, Mesopotamia and Asia Minor, with the result that a chain of good theological libraries came into being.

Monasticism came to Constantinople from Syria. The first monastery was founded there in 382, and monastic life reached its heyday in the fifth and sixth centuries with the support of the aristocracy and several emperors.[46] That period saw the establishment of the first Christian foundation connected with the name of Justinian the Great, St. Catherine's Monastery on Mt. Sinai. The Church often had reservations about monasticism, not only because of its origins in the laity but also because the monks frequently pursued an independent policy. Indeed, the conflict between the monasteries and the imperial and ecclesiastical authorities had disastrous consequences for the monastic libraries. In the first phase of the Iconoclastic controversy the monks put up an astonishingly strenuous resistance to the ban on sacred images and were fiercely attacked by the imperial administration. Constantine V dissolved some of the most famous monasteries in Constantinople, but in the second phase of Iconoclasm (815-842) the monastic communities were better prepared, thanks chiefly

relic attesting to the religious intolerance of this period is the manuscript of Zosimus's *Historia nova* (Vat. gr. 156) in which a chapter containing strongly anti-Christian views has been cut to pieces.

34. Devreesse mentions no dated manuscripts from before 800 apart from the Vienna codex of Dioscorides (*c.* 512). However, there exist fragments of illuminated manuscripts dating from the late fifth and early sixth centuries, such as the Cotton Genesis and the Vienna Genesis, written on purple vellum. The earliest illuminated Greek manuscript Gospel (6th c.) is in the treasury of Rossano cathedral in Calabria, southern Italy.

35. See n. 37 below.

36. A. Grabar, *L'iconoclasme byzantin. Dossier archéologique*, Paris 1957; A. Bryer and J. Herrin (ed.), *Iconoclasm*, Birmingham 1977.

37. This story, first put about in the chronicle of Georgios Monachos (9th c.), the *Life* of Patriarch Germanos I (715-730) and the *Patria* of Constantinople, was laid to rest once and for all by Lemerle, *op. cit.* 88.

38. Wendel, *Kleine Schriften...* 59; Michael Glykas (ed. I. Bekker, *CSHB*, Bonn 1836, 522); Konstantinos Manasses (ed. I. Bekker, *CSHB*, Bonn 1837, 4262-4263); O. Lampsidis, *Φιλολογικά εἰς τήν χρονικήν σύνοψιν Κωνσταντίνου τοῦ Μανασσῆ*, Athens 1951.

39. *Theophanes Continuatus* (ed. I. Bekker, *CSHB*, Bonn 1838, 35-36)

133. Emperor Leo III. Engraving from Portraits des empereurs d'Orient autrement dits de Grèce (= Atlas Historique), *Amsterdam 1714.*

to the indomitable courage of Theodore the Studite.[47] This latter period also saw the emergence of a man who was a maverick in both secular and ecclesiastical affairs, and whose name is connected with an enormous upheaval in the libraries of the monasteries and ecclesiastical centres in the capital: Patriarch John the Grammarian.[48]

John the Grammarian was probably born in Constantinople, it is not known when. After studying classics, at which he did brilliantly, he started working as a teacher, hence his nickname 'the Grammarian' (*Grammatikos*). After some time he entered the Church and eventually became Abbot of the Monastery of SS. Sergius and Bacchus. During the second phase of the Iconoclastic controversy, under Leo V, John came to the fore on the side of the Iconoclasts. After Pentecost in 814, he and some others began searching for old books that had been gathering dust in churches and monasteries: these were brought to the palace to be sifted for passages that condemned the use of sacred images.[49] We cannot be sure whether the books John brought to the palace were all theological or whether some secular works were included as well. The reference to 'books that had been gathering dust in the churches and monasteries of Constantinople' seems to imply that the libraries were in a state of dereliction and decay.[50] Be that as it may, it is beyond doubt that all these upheavals in the world of books reduced the capital's library stocks to a desperately low level and discouraged any thought of looking for books and reading them, let alone copying and publishing them.

It is impossible to cover the huge subject of monastic libraries at all fully in these pages.[51] There was no generally accepted rule governing their formation and operation, and the form taken by each library depended very largely on the following factors: the founder's intellectual interests and philosophy of life, the wealth of the monastery, the terms of its *typikon*, its geographical position, its history, the extent of its dependence on the capital, and whether it was an isolated community or one of a large group of monasteries. All we can do here is to note some of the distinguishing characteristics of various monastic libraries, which serves rather to highlight the problem than to answer any questions.

Each monastery usually had three different kinds of library: one attached to the katholikon or main monastery church, an archive collection and the private collections of the monks themselves. The katholikon library, which was the nucleus of every monastic library, contained the liturgical books, and its size varied enormously from one monastery to the next. It was often located in the sacristy, which was usually adjacent to the katholikon. The first archival collection of which anything is known for certain is the one in the Monastery of the Akoimetoi in Constantinople,[52] founded by Syrians in about 420, which was one of the first monasteries in the capital. By the time of Marcellus of Apamea (440-486) it already had a systematic collection of conciliar canons and

mentions an imperial library ('a Sibylline oracle in a book in the imperial library'), which Ioannes Zonaras locates in the palace. This is an allusion to the fact that Leo V is said to have been in fear of his life because of a prophecy in one of the books in the imperial library. From the seventh to the tenth century there was a Greek community living around the Palatine and Aventine hills in Rome, consisting of emigrants and a number of monks who had been expelled from Constantinople under Leo V and had sought refuge in Rome, bringing their books with them: see Batiffol, *op. cit.* 299.

40. Legend has it – and there may be an element of truth in the story – that Eudocia (formerly Athenais), the daughter of an Athenian rhetorician, was accompanied from Athens to Constantinople by seven philosophers: see *Scriptores originum constantinopolitanarum*, I, ed. T. Preger, Leipzig 1901, 61 ff.

41. Theodosius was keenly interested in works of Biblical exegesis, as is illustrated by the following story. According to the apocryphal Apocalypse of St. Paul, an officer living in what had been St. Paul's house in Tarsus dug down into the foundations, following the instructions of an angel of the Lord, and there found 'a marble *glossokomos* [a storage case for papyrus rolls] containing this Apocalypse'. The officer took his find to the governor of the city, who secured it with a leaden seal and sent it to the Emperor. In the Greek version of the story Theodosius copied out the text and sent the original to Jerusalem, while in the Latin version he kept the original and sent the copy he had made to Jerusalem. See W. Speyer, *Die literarische Fälschung im heidnischen und christlichen Altertum. Ein Versuch ihrer Deutung*, Munich 1971; Manafis, *op. cit.* 26-27. A *glossokomos* for keeping books is also mentioned by John Chrysostom (*In epistulam II ad Timotheum*: *PG* 62 656.19).

42. On the topography of the Higher School and the library, and their buildings, see A.M. Schneider, *BYZANZ*, Berlin 1936, 23-26; Wendel, *Kleine Schriften...46-59.*; R. Janin, *Constantinople Byzantine*, II, Paris 1964, 157 ff. Lemerle (*op. cit.* 325 n. 60) sums up the whole question and

an extensive bibliography of Christological writings. This we can deduce from the testimony of the deacon Rusticus (*c.* 564), who wished to compare the Latin translations of the records of the Councils of Ephesus and Chalcedon in the possession of the Roman Church and the Patriarchate of Constantinople against the originals, and found the most numerous and most reliable conciliar records in the Monastery of the Akoimetoi.[53] He also found there a large number of manuscripts supplementing the conciliar records and a collection of the letters of Isidore of Pelusium.[54] It should be added that the Monastery of the Akoimetoi was trilingual in Greek, Latin and Syriac, and the same may have been true of its library.

St. Catherine's Monastery, Mt. Sinai. One library that has been lucky enough to keep hold of its books since the time of its foundation is that of St. Catherine's Monastery on Mt. Sinai, and its archives provide valuable information about early monastic libraries. No monograph has been written about the Sinai library, but we know that in Justinian's reign it already had a nucleus of books whose influence is clearly apparent in the *Stairway to Paradise* (*Climax Paradisi*) of John Climacus (late sixth century).[55] And the *Guide* written by Anastasius of Sinai a hundred years later implies that the library contained heretical writings as well as works by pagan authors, such as Aristotle's *Categories*.[56]

Of paramount importance to the development of monastic libraries were the monasteries' own scriptoria, which not only kept them supplied with books but also served as teaching centres for the monks. Some of these scriptoria, especially in the principal cities, may also have taken orders from lay people who wanted manuscripts copied. The earliest scriptorium in Constantinople for which we have firm evidence was that of the Monastery of Studius, dating from the turn of the eighth to the ninth century.[57]

The Monastery of Studius. The dominant figure in the monastery was Theodore the Studite, who was born into a prominent and prosperous family in Constantinople in 759 and had an excellent education in a wide range of subjects, including non-Christian literature, in a period when Iconoclasm was at its height (under Constantine V). Theodore, a practical man who believed in strict discipline, found that monasticism had strayed from its original path and set out to reform the movement in accordance with the ideals of the founder of cenobitic life, Pachomius. He was able to put his ideas into practice when he became Abbot of the Monastery of Studius.[58] By the early years of the eighth century the Studite fraternity founded by Theodore's uncle, Platon of Sakkoudion, was represented by a number of monasteries reaching to the farthest corners of the Empire, with a total of about a thousand monks.[59]

Theodore, who believed in hard work, poverty and obedience, dis-

134. Emperor Constantine V. Engraving from the Atlas Historique.

refutes certain misinterpretations relating to the date of the library's return to the Octagon after the fire caused by the Nika riots.

43. For a general review of the subject see G. Bardy, 'Les origines des écoles monastiques en Orient' in *Mélanges J. de Ghellinck*, I, Gembloux 1951, 293-309; P. Brown, 'The Rise and Function of the Holy Man in Late Antiquity', *JRS* 61 (1971) 80-101; O. Meinardus, *Monks and Monasteries of the Egyptian Deserts*, Cairo 1962.

44. Mango, *Βυζάντιο* 12 (*Life of St. Antony*, Chs. 3-4 = *PG* 26 844-845).

45. A. Boon, *Pachomiana latina*, Louvain 1932, 3 ff.; Wendel, *Kleine Schriften...* 184. The traditional story is that the angel of the Lord revealed to Pachomius a *typikon* engraved on a bronze tablet. The fullest form in which the *Typikon* of Pachomius has come down to us is in a Latin translation made by St. Jerome in 404.

46. Wendel, *Kleine Schriften...* 184-186.

47. Mango, *Βυζάντιο* 140.

48. On John the Grammarian, known as 'the Sorcerer Patriarch', see L. Bréhier, 'Un patriarche sorcier à Constantinople', *Revue de l'Orient chrétien* 9 (1904) 261-268.

49. Joseph Genesius (ed. C. Lachmann, *CSHB*, Bonn 1834, 27), now also in a new edition by J. Thurn: *Corpus Fontium Historiae Byzantinae*, 14 vols., Berlin 1978. On the Emperor's decision to have the books gathered up and scrutinized, see *PG* 95 372; cf. Lemerle, *op. cit.* 120-128.

50. On the texts that John and his fellow-inquisitors were looking for, see P.J. Alexander, 'Church Councils and Patristic Authority: The Iconoclastic Councils of Hiereia (754) and St. Sophia (815)', *Harvard Studies in Classical Philology* 63 (1959) 493-505.

51. On monastic libraries in the East see Wendel, *Kleine Schriften...* 184-186; Wilson, 'The Libraries of the Byzantine World' 62-67; B.L. Fonkitch, 'La bibliothèque de la Grande Lavra du Mont-Athos aux Xe-XIIIe siècles', *Palestinskij Sbornik* 80 (1967) 167-175; Eleni Kakoulidi, «Ἡ Βιβλιοθήκη τῆς Μονῆς Προδρόμου-Πέτρας στήν Κωνσταντινούπολη», *Ἑλληνικά* 21 (1968) 3-39 (Pls. 1-5); F. Halkin, 'Manuscrits galésiotes', *Scriptorium* 15 (1961) 221-227 (Pls. 17-18, and a note by N.G. Wilson on pp. 217-220). On the libraries of the monasteries of Christos Akataleptos and the Chora in Constantinople, see pp. 175-177 herein; on that of the Monastery of St. John on Patmos, see Ch. XIII (pp. 267 ff.).

52. Wendel, *Kleine Schriften...* 184-186.

53. *Ibid.*

54. *Ibid.* When Nikephoros Kallistos Xanthopoulos wrote his *Ecclesiastical History* in the fourteenth century he used Isidore's letters, which were in the Patriarchal Library: see *PG* 146 1351A-B.

55. Wendel, *Kleine Schriften...* 186 (Krumbacher I 383).

56. Wendel, *Kleine Schriften...* 186 (Krumbacher I 121-124).

57. The Monastery of Studius was founded in 462 by Studius, the Prefect of the East. On the name of

135. Emperor Leo V. Engraving from the Atlas Historique.

couraged his monks from having slaves to work for them and attached great importance to systematic study and calligraphy. He founded a fully-equipped scriptorium, whose products set the standards of calligraphy for centuries to come and attested to his passion for books, and he made sure that the monks in the Studite fraternity were well educated. Eight of the articles in his disciplinary code[60] were concerned with discipline in the scriptorium, which was run by a *protokalligraphos* ('master calligrapher'). For example, punishments were laid down for anyone who made an excessive quantity of glue (leading to the risk of wastage), anyone who did not take proper care of the paper he was working on, anyone who made mistakes in the copying by relying too much on his memory, or anyone who put his own interpretation on the text instead of copying the original words.[61]

The books copied out by Theodore, his uncle Platon and the other Studites were intended first and foremost for the edification of the monks, and so they were kept in 'the book place', where the librarian (*bibliophylax*) was in charge. On major feast days the librarian would summon the brethren by beating the semantron (a wooden bar used instead of a bell in Orthodox monasteries) and each monk would take a book to read until the evening, when the semantron would be struck again and the books had to be returned, otherwise the borrower would be punished. Penalties were laid down for not taking good care of a borrowed book, taking a book without the librarian's permission, complaining about the book one had been given or hiding a book under one's mattress when it was due to be returned. The librarian, too, was liable to be disciplined if he left books piled in a heap or failed to keep them dusted and in their proper places.[62]

Many of the books acquired by monastic libraries came to them from the private libraries of members of the community. These were not the collections of ordinary monks but of scholarly abbots or high-ranking laymen – sometimes even emperors – who decided to take the habit for the last years of their lives and brought with them one or more of their favourite books, which nearly always went to the monastery library when they died. In later times, when printed books had superseded manuscripts, monastic libraries often acquired multiple copies of books from the monks' private collections, the Monastery of St. John on Patmos being a case in point.

From what is known of early Byzantine monastic libraries it is impossible to discern any standard pattern in the way they were formed and run, unlike monastic libraries from the tenth century onwards.

5. Private libraries. In the chapter on the Early Christian period we saw that the method whereby books were disseminated and the first libraries were formed followed the pattern that had been standard in the pagan world from a certain time on. Most probably the number of private libraries at that time was at least equal to the number of pagan and Christian writers put together, so I shall limit myself here to those book collectors who are of particular interest as regards either the philosophy underlying their choice of books or their aims and objects in forming a library.

Libanius. The first large library in which educational aims were combined with a collector's taste was perhaps that of Libanius.[63] Libanius (314-*c*. 393) was a distinguished man of letters, a sophist and the best teacher of rhetoric of his day, who was also a passionate book-lover and took great care over his library. Born at Antioch, he studied in Athens and in 340/1 founded a school in Constantinople which very soon won a fine reputation for itself. Among his pupils were Gregory of Nyssa, John Chrysostom and Basil the Great. However, his rivals intrigued against him and he was forced to close the school and move to Nicomedia in 346.

Libanius was perhaps the last rhetorician in late antiquity to publish his speeches and other work using the methods adopted by the great Roman orators and poets from Cicero onwards. The popularity of his speeches meant a great deal to him: he was in the habit of adapting them to suit his listeners' tastes, and he often launched a publicity drive to attract an audience to his public readings.[64] In any case, he had a wide circle of pupils and admirers, whom he could count on to want to read his work. He therefore set up a scriptorium in his library and employed scribes to copy manuscripts to order. The clerk whom he employed to manage the scriptorium – one of the occupants of this post was named Thalassius – was also responsible for seeing that manuscripts lent out to friends and public officials were returned promptly.[65] To promote sales of his books, Libanius used the same public relations gambit that had been employed by Statius and Martial in the first century, sending copies to highly-placed patricians in the hope of winning public commendation from them. But the depth and genuineness of his love of learning is attested by the fact that he also used to lend his works to friends of his and allowed them to make copies, reasoning that this was quite as good as publishing them in any other way.[66]

John Chrysostom. Let us turn now to John Chrysostom, not so much to reconstruct the contents of his library (for his own works alone make a very extensive collection) as to consider his attitude to religious and pagan books. Some of his views are summarized in the following paragraph.

A book is an all-powerful weapon that strikes fear even into the hearts of kings, which explains why rulers often mutilate books out of all recognition or have them burnt. To burn a sacred book is an affront to God.[67] It is a sin not to keep a copy of the Holy Scripture in one's house,[68]

the monastery see H. Delehaye, 'Stoudion-Stoudios', *Anal. Boll.* 52 (1934) 64-65.

58. N.X. Eleopoulos, *'Η βιβλιοθήκη καί τό βιβλιογραφικόν ἐργαστήριον τῆς μονῆς τῶν Στουδίου*, Athens 1967. Some ninth-century codices from the Monastery of Studius are still in existence: see Eleopoulos, *op. cit.* 36 ff. On Theodore the Studite see A.P. Dobroklonskij, *Prep. Feodor, ispovjednik i igumen Studijskij*, Odessa 1913; H.-G. Beck, *Kirche und theologische Literatur im byzantinischen Reich*, Munich 1959, 491-495; *Theodori Stoudites Epistulae*, ed. G. Fatouros, 2 vols., Berlin 1991.

59. The word 'Studite' was applied to other monasteries where Platon, Theodore and the Studite monks of Bithynia lived before their numbers started growing. With the rise of the Arabs the movement spread to the Greek islands and mainland Europe, until it came into conflict with the authorities and its members were driven into exile. On the significance of the term see Lemerle, *op. cit.* 359 n. 44.

60. *PG* 99 1740A-B.

61. *PG* 88 1713A-B.

62. *PG* 99 1740A-B.

63. For general reading on Libanius see P. Petit, *Libanius et la vie municipale à Antioche au IVe siècle après J.-C.*, Paris 1955; Id., *Les étudiants de Libanius*, Paris 1956. For a more detailed discussion of the role of the monasteries in education, see A.J. Festugière, *Antioche païenne et chrétienne, Libanius, Chrysostome et les moines de Syrie*, Paris 1959.

64. P. Petit, 'Recherches sur la publication et la diffusion des discours de Libanius', *Historia* 5 (1956) 479-507, esp. 489. Libanius usually read his works to his close friends before publishing them: 'I showed them [i.e. two songs] to four people, as I did not have time to arrange a public reading (οὐ γάρ ἦν ὁ καιρός μοι θεάτρου) (Petit, 'Recherches...' 487).

65. *Ibid.* 485. On one occasion Thalassius was bold enough to refuse to lend manuscripts to Eustathius, the Governor of Antioch, on the grounds that he never returned borrowed books but used them to build up a library of the most popular works at no expense to himself (Libanius, *Orations* XLII.3-4, LIV.63).

and every Christian should read from it before going to bed each night, while contemplating his misdemeanours.[69] Chrysostom criticizes those who deck themselves out with gaudy clothes instead of with books[70] and reminds them that at the Last Judgment they will have to defend their conduct by saying, 'I am poor and cannot afford to buy books.'[71] He is scathing about the fact that books are far outnumbered by sets of dice and other games of chance,[72] and he counsels devout Christians to improve their souls by reading books and writing short summaries and anthologies of sacred writings which they can carry with them when travelling.[73] In general he advises the faithful to possess books,[74] which he calls the medicines of the soul,[75] and to have private libraries to help them to comprehend the deeper meanings.[76]

John Chrysostom does not come out openly against all ancient Greek literature: he makes some scornful allusions to books written by those who crucified Jesus[77] and mentions various occasions when the faithful burnt 'books of magic' (i.e. pagan books).[78] To show how muddled was the thinking of the pagans, he points out that even those who boasted of having written great philosophical or rhetorical works failed to agree with each other and were for ever at loggerheads.[79] Of the Athenian philosophers, he said that their writings were sick.[80] He even goes so far as to assert that hardly anyone is interested in the books and other works of the 'Hellenes', which explains why they are now lost; and he adds with rueful irony that if some of them have survived it is because they have been rescued by the Christians.[81]

Tychicus. What we know about the library of Tychicus, a scholar who taught at Trebizond, comes from an autobiographical work by an Armenian, Ananias of Shirak, who was born in the late sixth or early seventh century and died after 667.[82] Ananias tells us that after studying Armenian literature and the Bible in his native country he decided to go on to philosophy and mathematics, but there was no properly qualified teacher in Armenia, nor any textbooks. So he travelled to 'the land of the Greeks' and, on the advice of a certain Eleazar, joined the class of a mathematics teacher named Christosatur in the Byzantine province of Armenia IV.[83] Dissatisfied with Christosatur's teaching, after six months he decided to go to Constantinople, but his compatriots dissuaded him from making such a long journey and advised him to go instead to Trebizond, where there was a wise and highly-regarded 'Byzantine teacher' named Tychicus, who spoke Armenian.[84] Ananias became a good friend of his teacher's and stayed with him for eight years, working hard at his studies, as Tychicus had an unusually large library which contained 'well-known and arcane books, secular books, scholarly and historical books, medical books and books about the calendar'.

According to Ananias, Tychicus's library covered seven branches of learning, and at a rough estimate it must have contained about a

66. Petit, 'Recherches...' 488. Libanius's bibliophilism, in the sense of his discriminating taste as a collector, is illustrated by the way he tells the story of the loss of a book by Thucydides and its eventual finding (*Orations* I. 148).

'I owned a copy of Thucydides, written in an attractive small script and so light and portable that I used to carry it about myself, even if I had a slave with me, because the very weight of it was a pleasure.... By extolling the merits of this book to so many people and showing that I took even more pleasure in it than Polycrates did in his ring, I aroused the greed of some bandits. I caught them red-handed, but the last one to leave burnt my belongings to destroy the evidence of his guilt. So I had to give up my researches, though I continued to brood. And I derived much less benefit from reading Thucydides than I would otherwise have done, because it irritated me to read him in books written in a different hand. However, Fortune eventually relieved me of this pain, albeit after a long time. In my sorrow over this loss I wrote again and again to all my friends, telling them the exact dimensions of the book, describing it inside and out and asking them, "Where could it be now, and in whose hands?" Then one day a local pupil came for a lesson, having just bought that very copy. The assistant teacher exclaimed, "That's it!" He had recognized it by its distinguishing marks, and he came to me to make sure he had not made a mistake. I took it from him and rejoiced as one would rejoice over a son who has suddenly returned after a long absence, and I left in high spirits.'

67. *In principium actorum* (*PG* 64 997.27, 64 1000.8).

68. *In psalmum 50* (*PG* 55 581.42).

69. *In psalmum 50* (*PG* 55 581.42, 55 581.46).

70. *De pseudoprophetis* (*PG* 59 556.39).

71. *De pseudoprophetis* (*PG* 59 560.64).

72. *Eclogae I-XIII ex diversis homiliis* (*PG* 63 611.43).

73. *In Matthaeum* (*PG* 58 669.30).

74. *In Ioannem* (*PG* 59 187.19).

75. *In epistulam ad Colossenses* (*PG* 62 361.51).

hundred volumes. On the face of it, in the light of what we know about contemporary conditions and the price of books, it would seem that this represented a very substantial outlay of money. Just how deceptive that picture can be, how far it disobeys rules and fails to match the known circumstances of a particular case, I shall now try to show.

No comparative figures exist for book prices during the period in question except for one solitary statistic concerning John Moschus, an itinerant monk from Palestine who lived in the sixth century. Moschus, who longed to possess a copy of the New Testament, had to work for two months as a labourer to get the money he needed for it.[85] This means that it would have cost him three nomismata, equivalent to nearly $400 at today's prices, which gives us an idea of the putative cost of Tychicus's hundred-odd books. But, to judge by what we know of the circumstances of his life, he was far from wealthy and could never have afforded such a large library at those prices.

Tychicus, born at Trebizond in about 560, started his adult life in the army. In 606 or 607, after a battle at Antioch, he lost everything he possessed.[86] He then set out to travel the world, supporting himself by teaching: first he went to Jerusalem, then to Alexandria, where he spent three years, then on to Rome and Constantinople before going home to Trebizond. How he came to acquire such a large library is not known, but there is enough evidence available for some conjectural conclusions to be reached, and they may apply in many other cases as well.

The changeover from the papyrus roll to the codex did not take place all at once in the third century A.D.: rolls did not go out of use overnight. The cartloads of books that Libanius tells us were brought to Nicomedia were papyrus rolls which in all probability had either been looted from the great libraries existing throughout the Roman Empire, from Carthage to Pergamum, or had been disposed of by Christians who had inherited large collections of books by pagan authors and sold them off for the price of the papyrus on which they were written.[87] Further opportunities arose for dealers in old books to replenish their stocks whenever papyrus rolls were replaced with parchment codices. St. Jerome states that Eusebius's successors on the episcopal throne of Palestinian Caesarea saved the books in the library created by Origen and expanded by Pamphilus, which were falling to pieces, by having them copied on to parchment codices.[88] Once this had been done, it is quite likely that the old rolls were acquired by itinerant teachers, who built up substantial libraries in this way and eventually recopied the tattered manuscripts themselves, thus adding to the stock of pagan literature in circulation and disseminating it more widely. It is a fair hypothesis that this was how Tychicus obtained his books; and the same may be true of Julian the Apostate's teacher, George of Cappadocia; of the presbyter Philip of Side,[89] who, according to Socrates of Constantinople, had 'countless books of all kinds' about A.D. 440; and of

76. *In Ioannem* (*PG* 59 296.31).
77. *Eclogae...* (*PG* 63 826.61).
78. *Eclogae...* (*PG* 63 790.34).
79. *In Matthaeum* (*PG* 67 171.31).
80. *In epistulam ad Romanos* (*PG* 60 419.9).
81. *De Babyla contra Julianum et gentiles* (ed. M. Schatkin, *Critical edition of, and introduction to, St. John Chrysostom's 'De Sancto Babyla', contra Iulianum et gentiles* (dissertation), Fordham Univ., N.Y., 1-106.
82. H. Berbérian, 'Autobiographie d'Anania Širakači', *Revue des études arméniennes*, n.s., 1 (1964) 189-194.
83. Nothing is known about Christosatur: he may have been of Greek origin.
84. Wendel, *Kleine Schriften...* 183-184.
85. Mango, *Βυζάντιο* 281 (Moschus, *The Spiritual Meadow*, Ch. 134 = *PG* 87^3 2997).
86. Berbérian, *op. cit.* 194, for the interpretation of the historical evidence.
87. Hunger, *Ὁ κόσμος τοῦ Βυζαντινοῦ βιβλίου* 34.
88. Wendel, *Kleine Schriften...* 183-184
89. *Ibid.*
90. *Ibid.* 251.
91. Agathias, *Historiae* II.29 (ed. R. Keydell, *Agathiae Myrinaei Historiarum libri quinque*, Berlin 1967, 70 ff.). Cf. J.-F. Duneau, 'Quelques aspects de la pénétration de l'hellénisme dans l'empire perse sassanide (IVe-VIIe siècles)', *Mélanges René Crozet*, Poitiers 1966, 13-22; Averil Cameron, *Agathias*, Oxford 1970, 101-102. On Constantinopolitan bookshops see the short article by Th.D. Yiannakopoulou, «Ἡ βιβλιοπωλία κατά τούς βυζαντινούς χρόνους», *Ὁ Βιβλιόφιλος* 8 (1954) 111-113.
92. G. Rallis and M. Potlis, *Σύνταγμα τῶν Θείων καί Ἱερῶν Κανόνων τῶν τε Ἁγίων καί Πανευφήμων Ἀποστόλων, καί Ἱερῶν Οἰκουμενικῶν καί Τοπικῶν Συνόδων, καί τῶν κατά μέρους Ἁγίων Πατέρων*, 6 vols., Athens 1852-1859. The list of books is in Canon 60 (*ibid.* I 225-226: 'Neither private psalms nor non-canonical books shall be sung or read in churches, but only the canonical books of the Old and New Testaments').
93. Canons of the Apostles, Canon 60 (Rallis and Potlis, *op. cit.* I 77).

Cosmas the Scholastic, who lived in Alexandria shortly before the Arab conquest.[90]

6. Booksellers. Did bookshops exist in Constantinople? The question is answered by the historian Agathias, writing in the sixth century: 'Often, passing in front of the Royal Stoa and sitting in the bookshops, he would argue and talk boastfully to the people gathered there.'[91] The clear implication is that, at least in Agathias's time, the bookshops were concentrated near the Higher School and the library founded by Julian to accommodate his books, and presumably very close to the scriptorium and library founded by Constantius II, which Themistius had opened with his speech of 1st January 357.

Nothing specific is known about booksellers and their shops, but it seems that their guild was a force to be reckoned with. Despite their recurring problems, they were sufficiently powerful to cause successive Ecumenical Councils to take notice of them. The Canons of the Apostles controlling the book trade placed tough restrictions on booklovers as well as booksellers, with penalties ranging from fines to confiscation of property and excommunication for offences against its provisions.

The Church's ceaseless efforts to stem the flow of heretical writings and prepare a list of books approved for reading in churches and in the home culminated in the Council of Laodicea (341-381), where an official list of permissible books was drawn up.[92] For by then the Bible had grown to include works which had been judged at one time or another to be spurious or contrary to orthodox Christian doctrine ('impious books'), such as the gospels of the Ebionites, apocryphal acts and letters of the apostles and pseudo-Clementine precepts. On the other hand, the Canons of the Apostles did accept other apocryphal works as canonical – the Books of Wisdom, Judith and Tobias (Tobit) and the Apocalypse of St. John among them – and exhorted the faithful to read them.[93] So there were long periods when Christians found that they possessed books containing heretical passages and had no option but to burn them. Buying and selling such books, or even cutting them into pieces, was expressly forbidden: all offenders incurred a fine, while clergymen were liable to be unfrocked and laymen to be excommunicated in addition.[94]

Nevertheless John Chrysostom, for example, attacks no pagan writers by name with the solitary exception of Porphyry, and him only for his polemical work *Against the Christians*.[95] One curious provision in force for long periods was that mathematicians who did not burn their books in the presence of the local bishop and (publicly?) embrace Orthodoxy were expelled from the towns.[96] Dealers in old books found another major source of supply in legacies, but here again the *Nomokanon* (a law manual attributed to Photios) expressly states: 'Books of magic [i.e. non-

136. St. John Chrysostom.

Commenting on this canon, Zonaras writes: 'Many books have been corrupted by impious persons, to the confusion of simpler folk, and so have the apostolic precepts written by the saintly Clement to the bishops.'

94. Canon 68 of the Concilium Quinisextum, otherwise known as the Trullan Council or Council in Trullo (Rallis and Potlis, *op. cit.* II 463-465). Zonaras explains that excommunication was the penalty for booksellers who showed disrespect towards sacred books, erased scriptural writings and copied others in their place, or used pages from the Bible or patristic writings as wrapping paper, unless they were already worm-eaten or ruined by damp. Zonaras also stresses that any person who sold or dealt in proscribed books was committing an offence.

95. Rallis and Potlis, *op. cit.* I 266-267.

96. Photios, *Nomokanon* (Rallis and Potlis, *op. cit.* I 266).

97. Rallis and Potlis, *op. cit.* I 267.

98. Hunger, *Ὁ κόσμος τοῦ Βυζαντινοῦ βιβλίου* 47-51.

99. *Ibid.* 49, 51.

100. In the Byzantine world the Biblical majuscule script was used, with only slight variations, until the ninth century, when the so-called liturgical majuscule script (used mainly for liturgical books) became the norm. See T.W. Allen, 'The Origin of the Greek Minuscule Hand', *JHS* 40 (1920) 1-12; G. Cavallo, *Ricerche sulla maiuscola biblica*, Florence 1967; E. Crisci, 'La maiuscola ogivale diritta.

canonical books] found in the property of a deceased person shall not be distributed among the heirs but shall be destroyed by order of the judge.'[97]

In these circumstances, with booksellers and their customers in danger of having all their property confiscated, any systematic copying or dissemination of books for private use was obviously out of the question. The word *bibliopoios* is sometimes found in the sources:[98] literally it means a maker of books, but it was actually used to mean one who repaired codices by replacing badly worn sections of parchment or making a new binding. Whether the booksellers (*bibliokapeloi*) doubled as book repairers I do not know, but the fact is that the services of the *bibliopoios* were used at the highest level, for example by Patriarch Gregory of Cyprus and Maximos Planoudes, who expressed his delight over the restoration of a codex of Diophantus.[99]

Before moving on to a period showing clear signs of the dawning of the humanist spirit, let us sum up what is known about the library of Constantinople in the previous centuries. Is it true that in the eighth century there was a large library in the capital containing the impressive number of 36,500 codices? Certainly there was a library in the palace, about which we know absolutely nothing but can only conjecture that it contained the emperors' own books. Nothing specific is known about monastic and private libraries, except that there was a scriptorium and some sort of collection of books at the Monastery of Studius. As regards education, which relied chiefly on the great library for which Themistius delivered the inaugural oration in the fourth century, the picture is unclear. The palace school did not exist, nor were there any state schools or other educational institutions with official support apart from the school of Sphoracius, which is believed to have been a law school.

7. The changeover to lower-case script. Around the end of the eighth and the beginning of the ninth century a revolution occurred in the world of books, with beneficial effects on prices and therefore on sales. The revolution was caused by two innovations: the changeover from majuscule to minuscule script and the introduction of paper as a substitute for papyrus and parchment.

The switch from capitals to lower-case letters had a major impact on the economics of the book trade, because it considerably reduced the number of pages required for a given text.[100] Furthermore, the practices of separating words and using punctuation marks, both of which had been rare in the old script, made it much easier to read what was written and take in the meaning. And so, from the ninth century, it became standard practice for all new books to be written in minuscule and a start was made on the gradual process of recopying the most widely used books: first the Bible and theological works, then books in everyday use such as textbooks of medicine and arithmetic, and finally literary works.[101]

Exactly when paper was first imported into Byzantium is not known.[102] It was the Arabs who learnt the technique of making paper from the Chinese, and they then introduced it into the Christian world.[103] The new material was at first called *bagdatikos* ('from Baghdad') or, more often, *bambykinos*, which probably denoted that it came from the town of Bambyce (Hierapolis) in northern Syria near the Euphrates. The earliest dated Arab manuscript written on paper is from 866, but we have to wait nearly two hundred years for its Byzantine counterpart, a chrysobull issued by Emperor Constantine Monomachos in 1052 to the Monastery of the Great Lavra on Mt. Athos.

II. Byzantine humanism in the ninth century

1. Three humanistic libraries. A man with humanist interests who went to great lengths to build up a collection of classical writings was Leo the Mathematician, also known as Leo the Philosopher.[104] Leo was born at about the beginning of the ninth century, perhaps in Constantinople, but after finishing his primary education he had to go to the island of Andros to find someone capable of teaching him what he wanted to know.[105] Even there, however, he did not find what he needed, and so he embarked on a grand tour of monasteries, searching through the books in their libraries and discovering much valuable and hitherto unknown material. He managed to persuade the monks to part with many of their books, which he took up into the mountains and read there in seclusion.[106] But he does not record the names of the monasteries nor the nature and number of the books he took away with him and probably brought back to Constantinople. What he does tell us is that he acquired a thorough grounding in philosophy and 'the sister sciences' (arithmetic, geometry, astronomy and music) and started giving private lessons in his humble home, suiting his tuition to the needs of his pupils.[107] From this he progressed to giving public lessons, in the course of which he had a pupil who was to be the central figure in a charming story concerning Leo and Caliph al-Mamûn.[108] From then on one has the feeling that it was the Arabs who did the most to promote his reputation for erudition. He was consecrated Archbishop of Thessalonika but deposed after a few years, whereupon he went to teach at an institution of higher education until his death.

Leo's is the first private library of whose classical contents anything specific is known:[109] they probably included Porphyry's works and perhaps Achilles Tatius's novel *Leucippe and Cleitophon*.[110] Rather more is known about the scientific books in his library, which included treatises on mechanics by Cyrinus and Marcellus, Apollonius of Perge's *Conics*, a work on astronomy by Theon of Alexandria and a geometry textbook by Proclus son of Xanthias, all bound together in one volume. Almost certainly he had the works of Euclid, judging by the story about his former pupil and Caliph al-Mamûn. Leo also possessed a copy of Ptolemy (Ms Vat. gr. 1594), which he may have had copied for him,[111] and his name is associated with the start of the manuscript tradition of Archimedes,[112] as there are two manuscripts in existence (of the thirteenth and sixteenth centuries) bearing the following inscription at the end: 'Fare well, Leo the Geometrician! May you be beloved of the Muses!'

We come now to one of the great figures of Byzantine civilization, who marks the beginning of the humanist period: Photios,[113] a man of many parts with a somewhat ambivalent attitude to the writings of pagan antiquity, a staunch champion of Orthodoxy and a true believer in the apostolic role of the Byzantine Empire. The side of his character that concerns us here is his passionate love of books, which found expression in his great work known as the *Bibliotheca*.

Photios was born into an aristocratic family in Constantinople, probably *circa* 807, and had an excellent education. The names of his teachers are not known, and indeed it is not unlikely, given his egocentric character, that he was largely self-taught. Following in the footsteps of his uncle, Patriarch Tarasios, he entered the imperial service: he was appointed *Protasecretes* (head of the imperial secretariat) in about 845 and was sent by the Emperor on some delicate diplomatic missions. He subsequently entered the Church and served two terms as Patriarch (858-867 and 877-886). His most important works are the *Bibliotheca*, the *Lexicon* and the *Amphilochia*, and it is on these that I shall concentrate.

The *Bibliotheca*[114] occupies an important place in the history of humanism. The two features that make it particularly interesting with reference to the history of books are, first, that it is the first lengthy annotated list of an important selection of works by various writers, and secondly that it is the only work of literary history to have come down to us from Byzantium. The mysterious circumstances of its compilation and publication, and the presence in it of a dedicatory epistle that does more to obfuscate than to illuminate the subject, have given rise to an extensive bibliography.

Myriobiblos and *Bibliotheca* were titles given to this work much later, probably in the fourteenth and sixteenth centuries respectively. The original title is: *An inventory and enumeration of the books I have read, of which my beloved brother Tarasios requested a summary: these being twenty-one short of three hundred*.[115] Photios prefaced the work with a letter to Tarasios, which was reproduced without revision or explanatory notes when the book was first published in manuscript in the tenth century.[116] The gist of the letter can be summed up briefly. When he was nominated to go on a mission to the Arabs, he says, Tarasios asked him to write down the 'particulars' or

ΙΩΑΝΝΗΣ
ΗΝ Ο ΛΟ
ΓΟΣ ΟΥ
ΤΟΣ ΗΝ
ΕΝ ΑΡΧΗ
ΠΡΟΣ Τ

summaries (ὑποθέσεις) of the books he had read, to console him in some measure for the sorrow of their separation and to give him a working knowledge of the books Photios had read. In response to this request Photios, with the help of a secretary (ὑπογραφεύς), wrote down everything he could remember in the random order in which it came into his mind. He explains that he devotes less space to the better-known works, as Tarasios is bound to have read them for himself, and states that he has read all these books since he developed a critical faculty. In conclusion, he adds that if by God's grace he returns safe and sound from his mission, he hopes to carry the work further.

The *Bibliotheca* is divided into 279 chapters ('codices', as Photios calls them) varying enormously in length, each being a set of notes on, or a summary of, a work of Christian or pagan literature, 122 of them being pagan works. He is thought to have read these books over a period of about fifteen years, and although he asserts that he wrote the whole of the *Bibliotheca* from memory, one can hardly believe that he had not taken notes while he was reading them.[117] Attempts by researchers to discover his method of working have yet to bear fruit, probably because he did not have one. He simply dictated what came into his head, concentrating on what he thought Tarasios might not know: for example, the secular authors covered in his book include historians, the Attic orators, the rhetorical writers of the second sophistic and novelists; of poetry there is none, and the philosophers are poorly represented, not one of Plato's or Aristotle's works being included.

So what conclusions can be drawn from what Photios himself wrote in his dedicatory epistle and from the internal evidence of the *Bibliotheca*? In the first place, we should bear in mind that no one has yet contradicted the statement made by the twelfth-century chronicler Michael Glykas and repeated by his contemporary Konstantinos Manasses, namely that there was in the eighth century a splendid library in Constantinople containing the impressive total of 36,500 books, most of them by non-Christian ancient writers. Therefore it is wrong to say that there was a shortage of books in Constantinople, even if it is true that the library was not yet open to the public at that date.

What we should really like to know is: on what basis did Photios select the books for inclusion in the *Bibliotheca*? As already mentioned, he may have been largely self-taught, and in his efforts to broaden his education he is known to have followed the example of Leo the Mathematician: that is to say, he made the rounds of the monasteries and other centres of learning in Constantinople and its environs, and all the other places he visited in the course of his career, reading voraciously and taking notes on everything he read. So quite possibly he started acquiring books of his own from the very beginning of these travels.[118] In any case it is clear from the *Bibliotheca* that he had read old copies of some works (Ch. 77),[119] that in some cases he had seen more

Origini, tipologie, dislocazioni', *Scrittura* 9 (1985) 103-115.

101. On the spread of the new script see A. Dain, *Les manuscrits*, Paris 1964, 121-122; Id., 'La transmission des textes littéraires classiques de Photius à Constantin Porphyrogénète', *DOP* 8 (1954) 33-47; J. Irigoin, 'Survie et renouveau de la littérature antique à Constantinople', *Cahiers de civilisation médiévale* 5 (1962) 287-302.

102. J. Irigoin, 'Les premiers manuscrits grecs écrits sur papier et le problème du bombycin', *Scriptorium* 4 (1950) 194-204; Id., 'Les débuts de l'emploi du papier à Byzance', *BZ* 46 (1953) 314-319.

103. On the introduction of paper to the West see J. Irigoin, 'Les origines de la fabrication du papier en Italie', *Papiergeschichte* 13 (1963) 62-67; and esp. G. Piccard, 'Carta bombycina, carta papyri, pergamena graeca. Ein Beitrag zur Geschichte der Beschreibstoffe im Mittelalter', *Archivalische Zeitschrift* 61 (1965) 46-75.

104. See Lemerle, *op. cit.* 129-153.

105. *Theophanes Continuatus* (ed. I Bekker, *CSHB*, Bonn 1838, 192). In this context it would be interesting to discover how many monasteries there were in mainland Greece and the Greek islands by careful scrutiny of the list of bishops and abbots who attended the Second Council of Nicaea in 787. See J.D. Mansi, *Sacrorum conciliorum nova et amplissima collectio*, Florence/Venice 1759-1798, XIII 150-156.

106. *Theophanes Continuatus*, *loc. cit.*

107. *Ibid.* 185.

108. This pupil was subsequently employed as secretary to a general and was taken prisoner in the war against the Arabs during al-Mamûn's caliphate (813-833). When the prisoner heard about the Caliph's keen interest in Greek science, he contrived to have himself introduced to the great man and proceeded to display his remarkable knowledge of geometry, in the presence of the Arab court mathematicians. Al-Mamûn was greatly impressed and asked who his teacher was, with the result that he invited Leo to his court, tempting him with the offer of a fabulous sum of money. (For further details see Lemerle, *op. cit.* 130 ff.) Al-Mamûn founded the 'House of Wisdom' in

139. St. Mark with the personification of Inspiration and St. Luke with his secretary. Illuminations from a New Testament, late 12th c. Pantokratoros Monastery, Mt. Athos, Cod. 234, folios 23β and 31a.

than one copy (Chs. 35, 224)[120] and that he was aware of the rarity of many of the books, such as those by Nicomachus of Gerasa (Ch. 187).[121]

About Tarasios, the dedicatee of the *Bibliotheca*, absolutely nothing is known. Presumably he lived in Constantinople, otherwise there would have been no 'sorrow of separation' when Photios went away. He too had scholarly interests and had sometimes gone with Photios to explore long-forgotten libraries. He must also have had a library of his own, whose contents would have been familiar to Photios. A problem arises here in connection with the phrase *φιλολογουμένους ἡμῖν καθ' ἑαυτούς* at the end of his dedicatory letter. What does it mean – that the *Bibliotheca* deals with books that Photios read when he was travelling on his own, or

Baghdad – comprising a university, a translation centre and an observatory – directed by al-Kind, an encyclopaedist, philosopher and prolific writer. See Olga Pinto, 'Le biblioteche degli Arabi nell' età degli Abbassidi', *La Bibliofilia* 30 (1928) 139-165, esp. 148.

109. Kedrenos (ed. I. Bekker, *CSHB*, Bonn 1839, II 168).

110. Lemerle (*op. cit.* 147-149) has attempted to reconstruct the contents of Leo's library.

111. Lemerle, *op. cit.* 148; C.

that Tarasios was a frequent visitor to Photios's house, where the two of them would read and discuss books together, or that the books covered by the *Bibliotheca* were works that Photios had read in Tarasios's absence?

On the assumption that Tarasios lived in Constantinople, it seems unlikely that Photios would have compiled the *Bibliotheca* when they were both in the city,[122] as the time spent dictating summaries and notes to his secretary he could have spent with Tarasios, either reading to him or advising him what to read. As to the suggestion that the books summarized in the *Bibliotheca* were all in Photios's private library, I am inclined to believe that the very opposite is true, for if Photios had had copies of all these books on his shelves Tarasios would have been able to read them when he was away. Assuming that the dedicatory letter is not misleading, the most plausible explanation seems to me that Photios left Constantinople to prepare the ground for his diplomatic mission, taking with him various books as well as his old notes and using these to compile the *Bibliotheca*. It is very likely that in its original form the *Bibliotheca* was not the book we know today, and that in its final form it was not exactly as Photios wanted it.[123] Whatever the truth of the matter, he obviously derived great pleasure from compiling the book, as he says at the end of the dedicatory letter that he is thinking of producing a second instalment.

Photios had a well-stocked library covering a wide range of subjects in which classical as well as Christian writers were well represented. Even his declared enemy Niketas David concedes as much in his biography of Patriarch Ignatios: 'In the matter of worldly wisdom and intelligence [Photios] was considered to be the most illustrious of all those engaged in affairs of state. So great were his accomplishments in grammar and poetry, rhetoric and philosophy, and indeed in medicine and nearly all the sciences of the ancient world, that he was said not only to excel almost all others of his generation but even to rival the ancients themselves. For in him everything was combined: natural talent, an industrious disposition, wealth, which he used for the acquisition of every book he wanted, and, above all, ambition, which caused him to spend sleepless nights poring studiously over his books. And when he was appointed – improperly – to a position in the Church, he applied himself to the study of ecclesiastical books as well.'[124]

Before going on to the third of the great humanistic libraries it is worth digressing for a moment to quote the account given by the Arab chronicler Ibn an-Nadim (in his *Kitâb al Fihrist*) of the desolate plight of a historic collection of classical books even at the end of the tenth century (987-988): 'Three days' journey from Constantinople, in the land of the Romans, there stands an edifice with a huge door that is always firmly closed. In the old days, when the Greeks worshipped idols and stars, this building was a far-famed temple. One day an Arab traveller

Giannelli, *Codices vaticani graeci, 1485-1683*, Vatican City 1950, No. 1594, p. 225.

112. J.L. Heiberg, 'Der byzantinische Mathematiker Leon', *Bibliotheca Mathematica* (Stockholm), n.s., 1887, 33-36.

113. See K. Ziegler, 'Photios' in *RE* 20 (1941) 684-724; Lemerle, *op. cit.* 154-183, with notes and bibliography; and, more generally, Margaret Mallett, 'Writing in Early Byzantium' in *The Uses of Literacy in Early Medieval Europe*, Cambridge 1990, 156-185.

140. Emperor Theophilos. Engraving from the Atlas Historique.

114. See esp. the preface in the first volume of R. Henry's edition of the *Bibliotheca* (*Photius, Bibliothèque, texte établi et traduit*, 9 vols., Paris 1959-1991); also S. Impellizzeri, 'L'umanesimo bizantino del IX secolo e la genesi della *Bibliotheca* di Fozio', *Rivista di Studi Bizantini e Neoellenici*, n.s., 6-7 (1969-1970) 9-69; Ziegler, *op. cit.*; A. Nogara, 'Note sulla composizione e la struttura della Biblioteca di Fozio', I, *Aevum* 49 (1975) 213-242; T. Hägg, *Photios als Vermittler antiker Literatur*, Uppsala 1975; Mango, 'The Availability of Books...'; W.T. Treadgold, *The Nature of the Bibliotheca of Photius*, Dumbarton Oaks 1980; N.G. Wilson, *Scholars of Byzantium*, Baltimore 1983, 93-111.

115. The first edition of the *Bibliotheca* was printed by J. Praetorius at Augsburg in 1601. It was edited by David Hoeschel (1556-1617), Principal of the School of St. Anne in that city, a pupil of Xylander's and a very prolific editor. He based his recension of

the text on four reliable manuscripts and had the good fortune to be assisted by J.J. Scaliger, who made corrections and supplied additions. See Henry, *op. cit.*

116. On the textual emendation of the letter see C. Coppola, 'Contributo alla restituzione del testo della lettera a Tarasio, proemiale della "Biblioteca" di Fozio', *Rivista di Studi Bizantini e Neoellenici*, n.s., 12-13 (1975-1976) 129-153.

117. N.G. Wilson believes that Photios really did write the whole of the *Bibliotheca* from memory: see his article 'The Composition of Photius' *Bibliotheca*', *GRBS* 9 (1968) 451-455. See also T. Hägg, 'Photius at Work: Evidence from the text of the Bibliotheca', *GRBS* 14 (1973) 213-222; Treadgold, *op. cit.* 81 ff.

118. It has been suggested that Photios himself possessed manuscripts of most of the books treated in the *Bibliotheca*. See J.B. Bury, *A History of the Eastern Roman Empire from the Fall of Irene to the Accession of Basil I (802-67)*, London 1912, 445; Treadgold, *op. cit.* 92-95.

119. *Εὐναπίου χρονικῆς ἱστορίας, τῆς μετά Δέξιππον νέας ἐκδόσεως.*

120. *Φιλίππου σιδέτου, χριστιανική ἱστορία.*

121. *Νικομάχου τοῦ Γερασηνοῦ, ἀριθμητικῶν θεολογουμένων.*

122. The problem of the date of the *Bibliotheca* remains unresolved: see Hélène Ahrweiler, 'Sur la carrière de Photius avant son patriarcat', *BZ* 58 (1965) 348-363. Ahrweiler believes that Photios was a young man when he wrote it; F. Dvornik

141. Emperor Michael III. Engraving from the Atlas Historique.

with an inquiring mind came there and wanted to see the interior of the monument. He therefore asked the Roman Emperor to open the door for him, but the Emperor refused, because the building had remained closed since the time when the Romans embraced Christianity. But the traveller persisted with his request, and eventually the Emperor agreed to grant his wish. On his orders the door was unlocked and the traveller entered the building. Inside, among inscriptions and marble reliefs the like of which had never been seen before, was an unimaginably large collection of ancient books, some of them in an excellent state of preservation while others were worm-eaten. When the Arab traveller left, the door was firmly closed behind him.'[125] I do not know how reliable the Arab chronicler's testimony is, but it is beyond doubt that many libraries and temples in the Eastern Roman Empire, if not burnt down and torn stone from stone by fanatical Christians, remained standing for centuries as burial monuments subject to the ravages of the elements, if nothing worse.

The third humanistic library is that of Arethas, which calls to mind the libraries that were supported by book-loving editors and publishers in antiquity, such as Atticus in first century B.C.

Arethas was born at Patrai around the middle of the ninth century.[126] Nothing is known about his studies, nor about what he did in his early years after moving to Constantinople. He entered the Church in 888 and was consecrated Archbishop of Caesarea (Cappadocia) in 902 or 903. Most of his life was spent in Constantinople because his duties as the *protothronos* (senior bishop of his province) required his almost constant presence there. The date of his death is unknown, but he was still alive in 932.[127] Arethas was no mere collector or editor: his interest in books was wide-ranging and his scriptorium was in some ways surprisingly far ahead of its time.[128] It is impossible to say how many of the books that passed through Arethas's hands ended up in his private library, how many were copied to order or how many were kept on the shelves of the scriptorium for sale to the public.

Although Arethas was not a great literary scholar, he was a good grammarian. He would have books copied for him by professional scribes, generally monks, who were paid for their work at market rates, and from the exquisite specimens of calligraphy that have survived it appears that he had excellent taste and demanded high standards. Many of these manuscripts have marginal notes written in his own hand, which he copied from reliable sources. Over twenty manuscripts have been positively identified as being items that Arethas ordered or annotated, or faithful copies thereof: they include works by Plato, Aristotle (the *Organon*), Euclid, Aelius Aristides, Pindar, Lucian, Dio Chrysostom and Marcus Aurelius, as well as three religious books.[129] Only two of the copyists who worked for him – John the Calligrapher (who was responsible for the Plato and the Euclid) and Baanes – are definitely known by name, and none of the customers who commissioned copies from him have been identified as yet.[130] However, we do know the cost of three of these codices: the Plato, the Euclid and a collection of writings by the Greek Christian Apologists. The Plato (424 leaves of parchment) was priced at twenty-one gold nomismata, of which eight went on the parchment and thirteen on the copyist's labour; the Euclid, which is in a smaller format and also shorter, at fourteen nomismata; and the book of apologetics was the most expensive at twenty-six nomismata.[131]

The conclusion to be drawn from Arethas's 'library' is that, hand in hand with the humanistic tendencies that started to develop early in the ninth century, there was at least a small-scale bibliophilic movement among wealthy grandees and high-ranking officials at the court, though their interest was largely confined to books with a high standard of calligraphy.

2. Monasteries and centres of monasticism. Of all the various types of Byzantine libraries, the ones about which we know most are those of the monasteries.[132] A number of monastic libraries are still in existence and still retain much of their original splendour. By the eighth century there were so many monasteries in the cities and towns in all parts of the Byzantine Empire that the monks took to establishing self-contained centres of monasticism. At first the most important of these was the group of monasteries on Bithynian Mt. Olympus, the spiritual home of St. Platon (uncle of Theodore the Studite, the great Abbot of the Monastery of Studius in Constantinople), St. Methodios and many others. The tenth century saw the rise of the group of monasteries on Mt. Latmos or Latros near Miletus, from where St. Christodoulos brought the books that formed the initial nucleus of the library of the Monastery of St. John on Patmos. Other centres of monasticism came into being on Mt. Galesion near Ephesus (which flourished in the eleventh century), at Meteora in central Greece and on a smaller scale in many other places; and in the second half of the tenth century on the peninsula of Mt. Athos, which eventually eclipsed all the other 'holy mountains'.

It would be impossible, even in a book very much larger than this, to deal fully with the bibliographical and bibliological tradition of all the monasteries and centres of monasticism that existed even in the remotest corners of the Empire. One reason is that the monasteries of the Eastern Church did not belong to monastic orders of the kind that exist in the West: each monastery had its own Rule, or *Typikon*. What can be said with certainty is that the great centres of monasticism and some individual monasteries had large and excellent libraries: of the thirty thousand or so Byzantine books that survive, the majority come from monastic libraries.[133] All I shall attempt to do, therefore, is to raise some questions and make some observations on points that seem contradictory.

('The Patriarch Photius in the light of recent research' in *Berichte zum XI. Internationalen Byzantinisten-Kongress*, Munich 1958, III.2 9 ff.) argues that it was written *circa* 855; while the theory that it was a product of Photius's later years is supported by F. Halkin, 'La date de composition de la "Bibliothèque" de Photius remise en question', *Anal. Boll.* 81 (1963) 414-417; K. Tsantsanoglou, *Τό Λεξικό τοῦ Φωτίου. Χρονολόγηση - Χειρόγραφη*

142. Patriarch Photios I. Drawing after an illumination in Codex 499 of the Monastery of the Great Lavra, Mt. Athos.

παράδοση (*Ἑλληνικά,* suppl. 17), Thessaloniki 1967, 11-35; and Mango, 'The Availability of Books...' 40, 42-43. See also A. Markopoulos, «Νέα στοιχεῖα γιά τή χρονολόγηση τῆς Βιβλιοθήκης τοῦ Φωτίου», *Σύμμεικτα* 7 (1987) 165-181.

123. Mango ('The Availability of Books...' 42-43) believes that after returning from his mission Photios went on expanding the *Bibliotheca*,

143. Emperor Basil I. Engraving from the Atlas Historique.

I think it is a mistake to extrapolate the number of monks in a monastery from the number of books in its library, and it is also wrong to generalize about philistinism and bibliophobia on the basis of isolated instances or even periods. I am thinking of the great bibliophile Eustathios, the twelfth-century Archbishop of Thessalonika, who tells the story of an abbot who sold a beautifully illuminated manuscript of Gregory of Nazianzos because the monastery no longer needed it. Eustathios, himself a fine scholar, also fulminates against the illiteracy of monks who leave books lying about in dusty corners and by so doing condemn them, too, to a 'monastic' life. He accuses monks of looking upon books as if they belonged to an unknown world and of selling them off below cost, without stopping to consider the resulting loss to the monastery.[134] Against this one has to set the touching and praiseworthy behaviour of the many anonymous monks who devoted their whole lives to preserving that priceless humanistic treasure, such as the twelfth-century Cypriot monk Neophytos.[135] Neophytos, the son of a poor farmer, entered the Monastery of Hagios Chrysostomos near Nicosia as an illiterate youth, but before long he had a good grounding in Greek ecclesiastical literature and had started acquiring books of his own. He eventually built up a collection of about fifty books, about a quarter of the number that the Monastery of St. John on Patmos had when St. Christodoulos founded its library with the Emperor's support.[136]

Libraries in the centres of monasticism and the great monasteries of the East should not be thought of as collections of exclusively religious writings. The way a library and its scriptorium were run was not always governed solely by the Rule of the monastery: more often it depended on the abbot's personality and attitude to books. And every monastic library contained secular books at one time or another. All of which may be summed up as follows: it was a tradition, established by the Rule of Pachomius and fervently supported by John Chrysostom, that monks should not be prevented from reading; it was a tradition that monks worked as copyists and indeed maintained a high standard of calligraphy in the monasteries, at least from the time of Theodore the Studite (8th-9th c.); monkish calligraphers sometimes copied books for lay patrons on a professional basis, as they did in Arethas's case; monastic libraries often received books as gifts from civil dignitaries and even from the Emperor himself; fine collections of books were sometimes brought to monastic libraries by noblemen and commoners who decided to retire to a monastery for the last years of their lives; sometimes monasteries ran public schools, as in the case of Hagios Georgios ton Manganon; and on the other hand there were monasteries – such as the Machairas Monastery in Cyprus[137] – whose *typikon* virtually prohibited all contact with laymen, secular education and secular books.

In view of all these variables, it would be a mistake to speak of general rules governing the working of monastic libraries in the Eastern

and he considers it quite likely that the book was put into its present form by subsequent editors, such as Arethas.

124. *Life of Ignatios* (*PG* 105 509B). According to Ignatios's biographer, Photios tried to curry favour with Emperor Basil I by claiming to be descended from Tiridates. He alleged that he had found the family tree in a book of prophecies which he said was entitled *ΒΕΚΛΑΣ* (*BECLAS*, from the initials of the members of the imperial family: Basil, Eudokia, Constantine, Leo, Alexander, Stephen), adding: 'It is kept in this great palace library.'

125. E. Arrigoni, 'Ecumenismo Romano-Cristiano a Bisanzio e tramonto del concetto di Ellade ed Elleni nell' impero d'Oriente prima del mille', *Nuova Rivista Storica* 55 (1971) 151.

126. The monograph on Arethas by S. Kougeas, *Ὁ Καισαρείας Ἀρέθας καί τό ἔργον αὐτοῦ*, Athens 1913, remains unsurpassed. See also Lemerle, *op. cit.* 184-216.

127. Lemerle, *op. cit.* 402-403 n. 9.

128. On Arethas's literary and humanistic activities, see esp. J. Bidez, 'Aréthas de Césarée, éditeur et scholiaste', *Byzantion* 9 (1934) 391-408; Eugenia Zardini, 'Sulla biblioteca dell'archivescovo Areta di Cesarea', *Akten des XI. Internationalen Byzantinisten-Kongresses, München 1958*, Munich 1960, 671-678.

129. On the contents of Arethas's library see Zardini, *op. cit.*; Lemerle, *op. cit.* 190-211.

130. Kougeas, *op. cit.*, Pl. II.

131. Enrica Follieri, 'Un codice di Areta troppo a buon mercato: Il Vat. Urb. Gr. 35', *Archeologica Classica* 25-26 (1973-1974) 262-279. Mango (*Βυζάντιο* 281) estimates that the cost of the Plato was equivalent to two years' wages for a manual labourer! It is also worth noting that Arethas sometimes bought papyrus from Egypt for his manuscripts: cf. his letter to a financial official named Stephanos (*Arethae scripta minora*, ed. L.G. Westerink, I, Leipzig 1968, 294 (Letter 38)). But whereas Arethas could afford to keep on enlarging his library by buying astronomically expensive books, life was by no means so easy for humbler scholars such as the so-called 'Anonymous teacher'. Thanks

Church. However, all the evidence leads to the conclusion that the monasteries showed greater reverence for the Byzantine literary heritage, including interpretations of Orthodox dogma that had subsequently been condemned as heretical and even works by pagan authors, which at various periods in the Empire's history had been suppressed.

3. A general library in the imperial palace. Little documentary ev idence has come to light concerning the three humanistic libraries mentioned above, but such evidence as there is enables much wider inferences to be drawn, on the basis of a noticeable trend in intellectual activity from the tenth century onwards: the move towards encyclopaedism. This time the movement in that direction was spearheaded by the Emperor himself, Constantine VII Porphyrogennetos (reigned 913-959). The available evidence concerns a new library started by him in the palace and a general upsurge in literary activity in which he was the prime mover.

The last documentary evidence to the palace library dates from the time of Photios and is connected with the fanciful story of the book entitled *ΒΕΚΛΑΣ*, already mentioned.[138] At about that time Emperor Theophilos built a number of pavilions, one of which, known as the Kamilas, Constantine VII turned into a library. We are specifically told that this library was on a mezzanine floor (*mesopaton*) and that it faced the banqueting chamber called the Chrysotriklinos or Ioustinianos Triklinos.[139] Though I cannot prove it, I believe that this was not an extension of the palace library nor a new room to which the palace library was moved, but the private study where Constantine VII did his reading and wrote his own books: it would have been the room to which the 'books of all kinds' were brought which the Emperor had demanded for use in his ambitious authorial projects. Nothing is known about the books that were kept there, nor do we know what eventually became of this library.

It might be thought that one way of trying to reconstruct the contents of the Kamilas library would be to list all the authors Constantine drew on in writing his own works, all of which – and especially his *Excerpta*, a selection of passages from ancient Greek and Byzantine writers – are invaluable sources of information on a wide range of topics. But such an approach would come to nothing, as it is estimated that the surviving portion of the *Excerpta*, which was composed of fifty-three sections divided according to their subject matter, represents no more than one thirty-fifth of the total. What is more, even if the whole work had survived we could not expect to learn a great deal from it, because the authors he quotes are believed to have been historians and chroniclers only, and the tone of the book was more moralistic than anything else.[140] Even so, it is worth looking closely at the preface to each section of the *Excerpta*,[141] because useful inferences can be drawn as to the purpose of

to the survival of one solitary tenth-century manuscript containing 122 letters, now in London, it is possible to gain some insight into the living conditions of a Constantinopolitan schoolteacher. The 'Anonymous teacher' probably came from Thrace. On completing his education, about which nothing is known, he started work at a secondary school in Constantinople and eventually became its headmaster. His teaching methods were not always to the liking of the pupils' parents, who made his life difficult, and he turned to his books for relief from his problems. In his spare time from teaching he wrote, he offered his services as an editor and publisher (one of his clients being Patriarch Nicholas [Nicholas the Mystic?]), he earned gifts from prominent figures in Constantinopolitan life such as the Lady Sophia (Letters 8, 98), and he borrowed, lent and dealt in books. In a word, he did what any scholar with a well-organized library of useful books would do. An annotated edition of the letters of the 'Anonymous teacher' is to be published shortly by A. Markopoulos in the series *Corpus Fontium Historiae Byzantinae*. See Lemerle, *op. cit.* 220-230.

132. On monastic libraries see the works cited in n. 51; also I. Ševčenko, 'Observations sur les recueils des Discours et des Poèmes de Th. Métochite et sur la bibliothèque de Chora à Constantinople', *Scriptorium* 5 (1951) 279-288; O. Volk, *Die byzantinischen Klosterbibliotheken von Konstantinopel...* (dissertation, Munich 1955), which as far as I know is still unpublished.

133. Hunger (*Ὁ κόσμος τοῦ Βυζαντινοῦ βιβλίου* 55-56) has estimated the total number of Byzantine codices now in existence and rates 600-900 of the illuminated manuscripts as being of an exceptionally high artistic standard.

134. *Eustathii opuscula* (ed. T.L.F. Tafel, Frankfurt 1832, 245): 'Do you equate the monastery's library with your own soul? Uneducated man that you are, you are emptying the library of the vessels of education!'

135. Mango, *Βυζάντιο* 147-149. On the life of Neophytos see C. Mango and E.J. Hawkins, 'The Hermitage of St. Neophytos and its Wall Paintings',

DOP 20 (1966) 122 ff.; Catia Galatariotou, *The Making of a Saint: The life, times, and sanctification of Neophytos the Recluse*, Cambridge 1991.

136. The size of St. Neophytos's library is all the more remarkable in view of the dearth of books in the surrounding country. Neophytos himself describes his fruitless thirty-year search for a copy of St. Basil's *Hexameron*, and in his Rule he enumerates his own writings: several of them have survived in unique copies which he donated to the monastery library, which sold them to agents of the French government in the seventeenth century. See Mango, *Βυζάντιο* 149.

144. Vatopedi Monastery, Mt. Athos. Engraving after an 18th c. drawing, from L. de Beylié, L'habitation byzantine, *Paris 1902, p. 65.*

137. I.P. Tsiknopoulos (ed.), *Κυπριακά Τυπικά*, Nicosia 1969, 1 ff.

138. See p. 163 n. 124.

139. *Theophanes Continuatus* III.43 (ed. I. Bekker, *CSHB*, Bonn 1838, 145). Janin (*op. cit.* II 114), Manafis (*op. cit.* 48) and Lemerle (*op. cit.* 430 n. 9) give their interpretations of the location of the library and the architectural significance of the word *mesopaton*.

140. *Excerpta de legationibus*, ed. C. de Boor, Berlin 1903-1905; *Excerpta de sententiis*, ed. V.P. Boissevain, Berlin 1906; *Excerpta de virtutibus et vitiis*, I, ed. T. Büttner-Wobst, Berlin 1906, II, ed. A.G. Roos, Berlin 1910.

141. The preface has been trans-

the Kamilas library. The preface (which is the same in each section) appears to have been written by a close associate of Constantine's, as the Emperor is lauded for his deep-rooted Orthodox faith, his penetrating mind, his humanistic ideals and his concern for his subjects' welfare. Constantine's aim in compiling the *Excerpta* was to summarize the whole course of history, because so many events had taken place over the centuries and history had become so complex that it was almost beyond the grasp of the human mind, with the result that people were beginning to look to falsehoods for the solutions to their problems. He therefore gave orders for 'books of all kinds', containing information on a variety of subjects, to be hunted down throughout the known world and brought to Constantinople. This, incidentally, is the earliest surviving written record of an appeal for books from all over the world, because the only evidence we have for the two previous appeals of this kind (by Ptolemy I and Constantius II) is second-hand.

It was probably the influence of Constantine's writings that led to the growth of encyclopaedism so characteristic of tenth-century Byzantine literature. The trend reached its peak in that quintessentially Byzantine reference book, the lexicon called *Souda* ('Suidas'),[142] which gives us a much better idea of what books were available in Constantinople than does the *Excerpta*. *Souda*, an anonymous work which may have been started at the prompting of Constantine VII himself, was completed in the second half of the tenth century. It contains several thousand entries, ranging from a single line to about a page in length, listed in alphabetical order. It was intended not as a scholarly reference work but as an aid to educated readers, and it seems to fit in perfectly with the Emperor's humanistic interests as set out in the preface to the *Excerpta*.[143]

III. From Constantine VII to the capture of Constantinople by the Crusaders. Following Constantine VII's conversion of the Kamilas for use as a library, we have no further material evidence concerning the libraries of Constantinople until 1204, the year of the Fourth Crusade. It is therefore easier to talk about the work of the various scriptoria and some of the books in circulation in the court than about libraries as such.[144] In my opinion, the erudition of certain prominent men of letters such as Michael Psellos owed more to the Emperor's reorganization of higher education than to the existence of a good public library.

Be that as it may, the fact is that in the middle of the eleventh century Emperor Constantine IX Monomachos (1042-1055) embarked on a programme of raising the standard of higher education, laying a high priority on the establishment of a law school and a school of philosophy.[145] The law school, founded in about 1047 to provide a proper training for judges, lawyers and notaries, was under the supervision of John Xiphilinos, a member of the circle of intellectuals surrounding Michael Psellos.[146] Its probable location was in the Monastery of Hagios

Georgios ton Manganon, where its library was situated.[147] Since the head of the law school was required to know Latin, it is reasonable to suppose that bilingual libraries were still sometimes in use. It is expressly stated in the regulations of the law library that it was open to the public. We do not know for certain whether the school of philosophy ever actually came to anything, or if so in what form: Michael Psellos is said to have been its principal, with the grandiose title of 'Consul of the Philosophers'.

The polymath Michael Psellos (1018-1078) was the intellectual giant of his age. Given the breadth of his interests, he could be said to have been the continuator of the encyclopaedic movement characteristic of the reign of Constantine Porphyrogennetos.[148] The point of interest in the present context is that the books he needed to satisfy his insatiable curiosity were to be found in Constantinople. In the funeral oration he wrote and delivered for his mother he tells us about his own studies. Having started with Aristotle and Plato, he went on to read Plotinus, Porphyry, Iamblichus and the 'most wonderful' Proclus, from whom he learnt something about every branch of knowledge. Then, turning to pure science, he studied first mathematics and then geometry, music and astronomy. On reading of the existence of learning that can never be proved, he read a number of non-canonical books; and even with his consuming passion for philosophy he found time to study rhetoric as well. Following the precepts of the great Church Fathers, he studied the philosophical foundations of the Orthodox faith. He was fascinated by the 'theories of the Chaldaeans', i.e. the occult sciences, and admits that he read books 'written by Orpheus or Zoroaster or Ammon the Egyptian'.[149]

The development of libraries and the book trade in the Komnenian period (1081-1185) is again a matter of inference only. The existence of certain books is to be deduced from our knowledge of the works that Anna Komnene drew on in writing the *Alexiad*,[150] and more particularly from the number and diversity of passages quoted by Ioannes Tzetzes. Tzetzes (*c.* 1110-1185), the headmaster of a school in Constantinople, liked to boast that had 'a library in my head': in his great work entitled *Histories* (or *Chiliads*) he gives excerpts from more than 270 ancient and Byzantine authors.[151]

While modern scholars search desperately for evidence enabling them to reconstruct the Byzantine literary scene and the capital's stocks of manuscripts, and while we know how difficult it was for intellectuals living on low incomes to buy or even borrow books,[152] the case of John Italos – an episode reminiscent of earlier times – must give us pause for thought. Italos went to Constantinople from southern Italy in about 1050, studied philosophy under Psellos and subsequently taught for several years as his successor.[153] In the year 1076/7 he was indicted on a charge of impiety, but the case against him was dropped. In 1082,

lated by Lemerle, *op. cit.* 255-256.

142. See Krumbacher II 311-315; 'Suidas' in *RE* 7 (1931) 675-717; and esp. Ada Adler, *Suidae Lexikon* (=*Lexicographi Graeci*, XI), Stuttgart 1971.

143. It occurred to me to try to estimate the number of books available in Constantinople by listing all the works that *Souda* seems to have used as its sources: the total came to no more than four hundred.

144. See O.I. Spatharakis, *Corpus of Dated Illuminated Greek Manuscripts*, Leiden 1981. For a general survey of the subject see Hunger, *Ὁ κόσμος τοῦ Βυζαντινοῦ βιβλίου* 55-96.

145. Ayiou Pavlou Monastery, Mt. Athos. Engraving from L. de Beylié, L'habitation byzantine, *Paris 1902, p. 64.*

145. See F. Fuchs, *Die höheren Schulen von Konstantinopel im Mittelalter*, Leipzig/Berlin 1926; Manafis, *op. cit.* 38-39.

146. The relevant Novel *(Νεαρά ἐκφωνηθεῖσα παρά τοῦ Φιλοχρίστου δεσπότου κυροῦ Κωνσταντίνου τοῦ Μονομάχου)* is in *Ioannis Euchaitorum metropolitae quae ... supersunt*, ed. J. Bolling and P. de Lagarde, Göttingen 1882, No. 187, pp. 195-202.

147. Michael Attaleiates, *Historia* (ed. I. Bekker, Bonn 1853, 48); Fuchs, *op. cit.* 25. On the monastery built by Constantine IX Monomachos see R. Janin, *La géographie ecclésiastique de l'empire byzantin*, Paris 1969, 70-76.

148. E. Kriaras, «Μ. Ψελλός», *Βυζαντινά* 4 (1972) 55-128. Anna Komnene called Psellos a boastful, brash barbarian and mocked him for 'taking his philosophy seriously':

Alexiad, v.8 (ed. B. Leib, Paris 1967, II 35 ff.).

149. Psellos, *Chronographia*, ed. E. Renauld, I, Paris 1926, 135-138.

150. On Anna Komnene's circle see R. Browning, 'An Unpublished Funeral Oration on Anna Comnena', *Proceedings of the Cambridge Philological Society* 8 (1962) 1-12.

151. *Ioannis Tzetzae Historiae*, recensuit Petrus Aloisius M. Leone, Naples 1968, 605-614. Tzetzes used to write out the first drafts of his work himself and send these out to his copyists. Being a blunt-spoken man, he called his copyists *koprophagoi* ('dung-eaters'); but he also called himself *phaulographos* ('a shocking writer'). In one of his prefaces he wrote: 'I am a book, a youthful work. Tzetzes first wrote me, though his writing is terrible. His features, familiar to everybody, you see before you.' See L. Massa Positano, 'Prolegomena et Commentarius in Plautum' in W.J.W. Kaster (ed.), *Scholia in Aristophanem*, IV/1 25, 92.

152. A certain Nikephoros asked his friend Petros if he could borrow a book by Dionysius of Halicarnassus which he needed urgently, promising to return it straight away: see J. Darrouzès, 'Épistoliers byzantins du Xe siècle', *Archives de l'Orient Chrétien* 6 (1960) 22.

153. See L. Clucas, *The Trial of John Italos and the Crisis of Intellectual Values in Byzantium in the Eleventh Century*, Munich 1981, 266; Mango, *Βυζάντιο* 173-175; L.G. Be-

146. Emperor Constantine VII Porphyrogennetos. Engraving from the Atlas Historique.

shortly after Alexios I had come to the throne, he was indicted again and brought to trial. One of the charges against him was that he had introduced pagan cosmological theories into his teaching, most notably the theory of the eternity of the world. The confession of faith that he made was deemed inadequate, whereupon he was anathematized, forbidden to teach and finally banished to a monastery. Five of his pupils, all deacons, were arraigned before a council of bishops, and to save themselves they had to denounce their former teacher.[154] Italos seems to have been used as a scapegoat, as the anathema covered a broad spectrum of philosophical teaching; and it is extraordinary to see the contradictions and hazards implicit in everything to do with the dissemination of pagan learning.

Constantinople on the eve of its capture by the Crusaders presented a sorry picture. Out of its population of about 200,000, the reasonably well-off merchant class accounted for barely twenty per cent, if that. The rest were such a motley assortment of people from the North and the coasts of Asia Minor that Tzetzes in one of his poems describes the city as a latter-day Tower of Babel. In August 1203, two months after the beginning of the siege by the crusading army, a disastrous fire raged out of control for eight days, razing half the city. When Constantinople finally fell to the Crusaders in April 1204, there followed days of merciless pillaging and vandalism, vividly described by Niketas Choniates;[155] and the treasures that remained in the capital were systematically looted by the conquerors during the fifty-seven years of their occupation. There is no doubt that incalculable damage was done to the books in the city: those that survived the conflagrations were stripped of their valuable bindings (many of which are now to be seen in the treasury of St. Mark's in Venice), and many others may have been used as fuel in domestic fireplaces. Not only did the Crusaders have no use for these books, as they did not know Greek, but they considered Orthodox religious books to be heretical. Michael Choniates (*c.* 1138-1222), a great book-lover who became Archbishop of Athens, wrote a letter giving an ironic description of the conquerors' ignorance and barbarousness: 'A donkey would be more likely to appreciate the sound of the lyre, or a perfume jar the fragrance of the unguent, than those men to appreciate the delights of harmony and words.'[156]

IV. The Empire of Nicaea. After the fall of Constantinople to the Crusaders in 1204, the territory remaining in Greek hands was divided into three states: the Empire of Trebizond, ruled by the Komnenos dynasty; the Despotate of Epiros; and the Empire of Nicaea. The last of these was deemed the lawful successor to the Byzantine Empire, in religious and cultural life as well as in politics.[157] The court of Theodore I Laskaris (1204-1222) at Nicaea, within easy reach of Constantinople, attracted growing numbers of teachers, scholars and intellectuals, who carried on the renaissance of literature and learning that had started in the reign of Constantine VII Porphyrogennetos in the mid tenth century. Niketas Choniates, for example, was appointed official orator to the imperial court;[158] Nikolaos Mesarites, a former deacon of the Great Church of Christ, was nominated by Emperor Theodore as leader of the Orthodox delegation in the talks with the papal legates;[159] and Theodore Eirenikos, who had been a high-ranking financial official before 1204, was appointed 'Consul of the Philosophers' and eventually became Patriarch in 1214.[160]

1. Higher education: Nikephoros Blemmydes. In spite of the problems facing the Empire of Nicaea and the lack of facilities and personnel, remarkable progress was made in the development of education and libraries. This was because the Emperor interested himself in the promotion of higher education and set the lead in acquiring and disseminating books, giving equal weight to classical and Christian literature. The life and times of Nikephoros Blemmydes afford a particularly striking illustration of this trend.[161]

Nikephoros Blemmydes was born in Constantinople around the year 1197/8 and moved to Bithynia with his family after the fall of the city in 1204. He spent four years studying scripture at Prusa under the direction of Monasteriotes, subsequently Metropolitan of Ephesus, and then took a course of general education at Nicaea. At the age of sixteen he aspired to go on to higher studies but was unable to find the right teacher, so he spent another four years studying and practising medicine, which was his father's profession. When he was about twenty-three he decided to visit the regions under Latin occupation and moved to the Troad, where he became a disciple of a hermit named Prodromos, whose fame had spread far and wide.[162] Not only was Blemmydes deeply influenced by Prodromos, but he was taught geometry, astronomy, logic and physics, which suggests that the hermit teacher's school may have possessed a good library. After at least three years in the Troad he spent some time studying scripture at Nymphaion and then returned to Nicaea aged about twenty-six.[163]

By this time the imperial throne of Nicaea was occupied by John III Doukas Vatatzes (1222-1254), who took a great interest in Blemmydes and instructed Demetrios Karykes to test him (with some others) on his level of academic attainment. The Emperor was impressed by Blemmydes's erudition and wanted to keep him at his court, but the young scholar preferred to live out of the limelight and asked to join the circle of friends of Patriarch Germanos II, who ordained him deacon and gave him the title of Logothete.[164] Meanwhile the Emperor had initiated a great drive to educate promising students to a high level of scholarship for the purpose of defending Orthodox dogma against the 'papist invasion', and also to raise the general standard of education by

147. Emperor Constantine IX Monomachos. Engraving from the Atlas Historique.

nakis, «Ἡ θεωρητική καί πρακτική αὐτονομία τῆς Φιλοσοφίας ὡς Ἐπιστήμης στό Βυζάντιο» *in Ἀφιερωματικός τόμος στόν Κ. Δεσποτόπουλο* Athens 1991, 239-243.

154. J. Gouillard, 'Le Synodicon de l'Orthodoxie', *TM* 2 (1967) 56-71.

155. Niketas Akominatos Choniates, *Ἱστορία*, ed. C.A. Fabrotus, Venice 1729, 305-307. For a more recent edition see *Niketas Choniates Akominatos, Historia*, ed. J.L. van Dieten, 2 vols., Berlin 1975.

156. S. Lampros, *Μιχαήλ Ἀκομινάτου τοῦ Χωνιάτου τά σωζόμενα*, II, Athens 1880, 296; Id., «Περί τῆς Βιβλιοθήκης τοῦ Μητροπολίτου Ἀθηνῶν Μιχαήλ Ἀκομινάτου (1182-1205)», *Ἀθήναιον* 6 (1877) 354-367.

157. On the Empire of Nicaea see A. Miliarakis, *Ἱστορία τοῦ Βασιλείου τῆς Νικαίας καί τοῦ Δεσποτάτου τῆς Ἠπείρου (1204-1261),* Athens 1898; Hélène Ahrweiler, 'L'histoire et la géographie de la région de Smyrne entre les deux occupations turques (1081-1317), particulièrement au XIIIe siècle', *TM* 1 (1965) 1-204; M. Angold, *A Byzantine Government in Exile: Government and society under the Laskarids of Nicaea (1204-1261)*, Oxford 1975.

158. See S. Lampros, *Μιχαήλ Ἀκομινάτου...*, I (1879) 345; Angold, *op. cit.* 149; C.N. Constantinides, *Higher Education in Byzantium in the Thirteenth and Early Fourteenth Centuries (1204 - ca. 1310)*, Nicosia 1982, 5-6.

159. See Angold, *op. cit.* 51, 53; Constantinides, *op. cit.* 6.

160. See Constantinides, *op. cit.* 6.

opening libraries and schools in many of the cities and towns under his rule. Presumably it was in this connection that Blemmydes was sent on official visits to monastic centres from 1227 to 1239 to list the books he found there, have copies made and bring back to Nicaea those that were needed.[165] He was the ideal person for the job since he, like Leo the Mathematician before him, had on his own initiative been to monasteries in and around the Aegean to look for manuscripts.[166] From 1227 he was on Lesbos,[167] in 1233 he spent some time in a monastery on Mt. Artamytos in Rhodes,[168] and in 1238 or 1239 he visited Samos[169] and then went on to Mt. Athos, where he stayed for four years.[170] From Athos he went to Thessalonika and Larissa,[171] thus rounding off a remarkable tour of great monasteries in the course of which he discovered numerous rare or even unique manuscripts, some of them not previously known to be in existence. Blemmydes's recognition of the role that these monasteries and their well-stocked libraries could play in the promotion of education may have been partly responsible for the Nicene emperors' efforts to revive monastic life.[172]

When Blemmydes returned from his travels his wish to live a modest life brought him into conflict with the court, and even with Emperor John III and Patriarch Manuel II (1243-1252). He refused to accept an appointment as principal of a higher school, even when threatened with excommunication, arguing spiritedly that secular office was not fitting for a cleric. He was supported in his stand by the Emperor's son, the future Theodore II, who had been one of his favourite pupils and corresponded with him regularly.[173] The school eventually opened in about 1246, not in Nicaea but some distance away, under the direction of a group of teachers including Georgios Babouskomites.[174] The fact that Babouskomites sent a copy of one of Aristotle's works to Ioannes Makrotos, a bookish friend of his who was a secretary in the imperial service, seems to imply that the school ran a public lending library.[175] In about 1248 Blemmydes himself opened a school for monks at Ematheia, near Ephesus, which he ran according to his own strict rules.[176] The school is known to have been flourishing in 1259, when George of Cyprus, the future Patriarch Gregory II, went there from Nicaea for further studies.[177]

2. Theodore II Laskaris. When Theodore II Laskaris (1254-1258) ascended the throne of Nicaea, the only change in the cultural situation was yet another infusion of fresh life. The new Emperor restored the Church of St. Tryphon in Nicaea and founded new public schools in its grounds, largely endowed by funds from the imperial exchequer. Theodoros Skoutariotes,[178] who knew the Emperor personally, gives details of his deep interest in education. Theodore II was a staunch champion of book learning, he had a private collection of books about the arts and sciences, and he founded libraries – public libraries – in

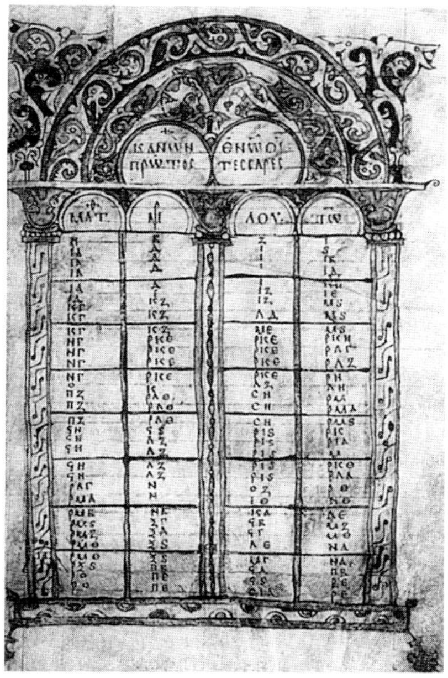

148. Concordance of the Gospels. Paris, Bibliothèque Nationale, Ms Gr. 63, fol. 10.

161. On Blemmydes see *Nicephori Blemmydae curriculum vitae et carmina*, ed. A. Heisenberg, Leipzig 1896; Constantinides, *op. cit.* 6.

162. This particular part of the Troad was sometimes called Skamandros: for more about the area and a school of the same name, see R. Janin, *Les églises et les monastères des grands centres byzantins*, Paris 1975, 212-213. Prodromos was still a youngster at the time of the calamity of 1204, and he probably crossed the Bosporus with a schoolfellow of his named Leo, who later entered the Church. He became a hermit in the Skamandros area and by 1220 was already renowned as a teacher. In a letter to Emperor Theodore II, Blemmydes mentions that his former mentor Prodromos subsequently became Bishop Kaloethes of Madytos: see Constantinides, *op. cit.* 8.

163. See *N. Blemmydae curriculum vitae*... 6.

164. *Ibid.* 60.

165. See Constantinides, *op. cit.* 13.

166. On Leo and his travels to monasteries on the island of Andros and elsewhere, see pp. 154-155. On Blemmydes's mission see A.A. Vasiliev, *History of the Byzantine Empire, 324-1453*, Madison Wis.

various cities and towns. It is worth noting that Skoutariotes's testimony is the first surviving record of the foundation of a public library in the Byzantine world since the time of Constantius II.[179]

Theodore II had had a classical education and openly admired the ancient world. He was proud of his descent from the ancient Greeks and referred to Asia Minor and Greece as 'Hellenikon' and 'Hellas'. He liked to compare Nicaea with the Athens of the Golden Age and actually considered his own birthplace to be superior, because there it was possible to study Christian as well as pagan philosophers.[180] It was in this climate of humanism, thoroughly favourable to books and libraries and with clear signs of a synthesis of Hellenic and Christian learning, that Michael VIII Palaiologos (1258-1282) recaptured Constantinople in 1261.

V. The last Byzantine renaissance: from 1261 to 1453. This revival of literary and academic studies in the Empire of Nicaea, with books being collected by emperors and private citizens and new schools and public libraries being founded, gathered pace with the recapture of Constantinople. In fact, by the time a small circle of scholars gathered round Lovato Lovati in Padua at almost exactly the same date (*c.* 1270) and showed interest in reviving Latin literature – which makes them the harbingers of the humanist movement – humanism in Byzantium already had a long history behind it, dating back to the tenth century and the initiatives of Emperor Constantine VII Porphyrogennetos.

In the last two centuries of the Byzantine Empire nothing more is heard of the great library last mentioned by the chroniclers Glykas and Manasses, nor of any other university-level or public library apart from those in monasteries such as Christos Akataleptos, the Chora and the Prodromos (the home of the Katholikon Mouseion, as the university was now called). And the only apparent mention of a palace library, in the memoirs of the fifteenth-century traveller Pero Tafur, probably refers to a room in the Blachernai Palace that was not actually a library at all.[181] On the other hand there are frequent references to private libraries belonging to scholars and imperial dignitaries: they were so numerous that Nikephoros Choumnos, describing the spirit of the age, declared that anyone who had no books was like an artisan with no tools.[182] Unfortunately this movement, which was to be paralleled and greatly surpassed in Italy from the early decades of the fifteenth century, was impeded by an insuperable obstacle: the Empire's dire economic plight, which meant that books were luxury items.

1. The shortage of parchment. We have seen that even in Arethas's time (early tenth century) parchment was already so expensive that it accounted for about forty per cent of the cost of a book; and although there is evidence from earlier periods that parchment used to be manufactured in Corinth and also at the Monastery of Studius in

1964, 550; A. Tuillier, 'Recherches sur les origines de la Renaissance byzantine au XIIIe siècle', *Bulletin de l'Association Guillaume Budé*, 4th ser., 3 (1955) 73-76. On the libraries in Nicaea and the emperors' policy towards them, see Padover, 'Byzantine Libraries' 328; Wilson, 'The Libraries of the Byzantine World' 78; Manafis, *op. cit.* 55.

167. *N. Blemmydae curriculum vitae...* 21.

168. *Ibid.* 61-62.

169. *Ibid.* 33.

170. *Ibid.* 36; Wilson, 'The Libraries of the Byzantine World' 78.

171. In Blemmydes's account of his visit to Larissa there is a hint that he may have visited the monasteries of the Meteora.

172. See J.B. Papadopoulos, *Théodore II Lascaris empereur de Nicée*, Paris 1908, 10; D. Deraedt, *La politique monastique des empereurs de Nicée (1204-1261)* (unpublished dissertation, Louvain 1952).

149. Emperor Alexios I Komnenos. Engraving from the Atlas Historique.

173. See *Lascaris Theodori, Ducae, Epistulae CCXVII*, ed. N. Festa, Florence 1898; Constantinides, *op. cit.* 14; A. Markopoulos, «Θεοδώρου Β΄Λασκάρεως, Ἀνέκδοτον ἐγκώμιον πρός τόν Γεώργιον Ἀκροπολίτην», *ΕΕΒΣ* 36 (1968) 104-118.

174. See V. Laurent, 'La correspondance inédite de Georges Babouscomitès' in the festschrift *Εἰς μνήμην Σπυρίδωνος Λάμπρου*, Athens 1935, 83-100.

175. Laurent, *op. cit.* 93.

Constantinople itself, nothing is known about parchment makers or dealers in the capital in the thirteenth century.[183] Apparently it was brought in from Asia Minor, so it was now difficult for supplies to reach Constantinople as the Turks were advancing through the regions where most of the sheep and goats were raised. The shortage may not have made a great difference to the emperors' projects of copying valuable illuminated codices, but scholars were not so well placed for purchasing the raw material. Ioannes Tzetzes, for example, in his commentary on Aristophanes (*Frogs* 843), mentions that writing material was hard to find.[184] About a century later Maximos Planoudes wrote and asked a friend of his to send him some parchment because all he could find where he lived (presumably in Constantinople) was of inferior quality.[185] What is more, as he informs us himself, it was only thanks to Alexios Philanthropinos's victorious campaign against the Turks in Asia Minor that he managed to finish his edition of Plutarch in about 1294-1296;[186] and even then parchment remained beyond the means of all but the moneyed classes by the time it reached the market. Nigel Wilson, in a paper on the dissemination of books, cites the case of a man in the thirteenth century who owned a theological book which he wanted to sell but could not afford to buy the parchment he needed to replace some lost pages.[187] Another problem was that the supply of parchment was now seasonal. George of Cyprus (the future Patriarch Gregory II of Constantinople) wrote to tell a customer of his that it would be a while before he could finish the copy of Demosthenes he was working on because no parchment would be available until the spring, when people started eating meat again.[188] Unfortunately, paper – which would have been an excellent substitute for parchment because it was neither so scarce nor so costly – was not available, or at least not until it started being imported on a relatively large scale from the West.[189] George of Cyprus actually asked his supplier to provide him with paper, even if it one side of it had already been written on.[190] This is reminiscent of the practice adopted by some booksellers, who used to buy books that were no longer in demand, erase the writing and reuse the parchment, just as they had done in Alexandria in the second century A.D., when papyrus was scarce.[191] The only factual information that has come down to us about the cost of parchment refers to an earlier period – the tenth century, when Arethas mentions some prices – and so it is impossible to draw any general conclusions. The figures mentioned by Arethas would have been irrelevant from the thirteenth century onwards, when the scarcity of parchment must have pushed the price up.

The cost of copying – the other input that determined the price of a book – would also appear to have been high on the whole, and the fees that Arethas paid to his scribes were not always attributable to the high standard of the calligraphy. In a Menologion for January, written in 1057, there is a note to the effect that the copyist was paid 150 nomis-

176. See Constantinides, *op. cit.* 24-25.

177. See W. Lameere, *La tradition manuscrite de la correspondance de Grégoire de Chypre, patriarche de Constantinople (1283-1289)*, Brussels/Rome 1937, 177.

178. See *Theodori Scutariotae additamenta ad Georgii Acropolitae Historiam*, ed. A. Heisenberg, I, Leipzig 1903, 512.

150. Emperor Theodore I Laskaris.

179. See *Theodori Scutariotae additamenta...* 297: 'He collected more books on all the arts and sciences than even Ptolemy, who boasted about [his library]; and he had them stored in the cities and towns and decreed that they were to be made available to anybody who wanted to read them and cultivate the learning contained in them.'

180. See Papadopoulos, *op. cit.* 86; Constantinides, *op. cit.* 20-21.

181. See p. 184.

182. See J.F. Boissonade, *Anecdota Nova*, Paris 1844, 93 (No. 77).

183. See Eleopoulos, *op. cit.* 23; Wilson, 'Books and Readers...' 1.

184. See Wilson, 'Books and Readers...' 4 (*Scholia in Aristophanem*, ed. W.J.W. Kaster, IV, Groningen/Amsterdam 1962, 932). Even before the fall of Constantinople in 1204 Michael Choniates was complaining, perhaps with a touch of

mata for seven copies, and a liturgical book dated 1166 cost twelve nomismata in copyist's fees.[192] In the Constantinople Synaxary, Paul Lemerle found a note of the following remarkable record: Athanasios the Miracle-Worker, a monk and calligrapher at a monastery in Bithynia, was struck blind but his sight was soon restored. Thereupon he made a solemn vow to share out the proceeds of his work among the poor and settled down to copying once again. In twenty-eight years of working every day except Saturdays and Sundays he managed to make nine hundred nomismata, which he gave to the poor: this is equal to thirty-two nomismata per year, an astonishing income for a monk.[193]

Clearly, then, writing materials were very expensive and copyists' fees very high, and one way for people without much money to acquire books was to copy them out for themselves. Obviously it would be foolish to assume that this state of affairs lasted for ever. With the contraction of the Empire and the influx of Western students into Constantinople from the beginning of the fifteenth century the market conditions must have changed, otherwise it is hard to explain the huge numbers of books purchased by Italian humanists such as Giovanni Aurispa, who went home from the East in 1423 with nearly 240 codices: at the prices that applied in Arethas's time, these would have cost him around 4,000 nomismata![194]

2. Libraries of the *literati*. The general attitude of scholars towards the ownership of books in the last two centuries of the Byzantine Empire exactly paralleled the situation in Italy during the Renaissance from the first decades of the fifteenth century to the middle of the sixteenth, that is to say even after the invention of printing had radically altered the whole concept of book production. This important movement was directly linked with higher education, where books were needed not only as class textbooks but also for private reading by teachers and students. Indeed, that was the purpose that Nikephoros Blemmydes had in mind when he went on his manuscript-hunting trip: to compile a list of works, mainly classical, to be used as a basis for writing the sort of books that he himself had written for his pupils, such as his *Abridged Physics* and *Summary of the History of the World*. Ihor Ševčenko has calculated that there were then about a hundred men of letters in the Byzantine Empire whose names are now known, and in his opinion the total number of people who had had a higher education was relatively small.[195] Robert Browning believes that the total number of *literati* was probably higher than Ševčenko's estimate, if we include people who were not members of the church hierarchy nor government officials but nevertheless had a good all-round education.[196] What concerns us here, however, is to show that nearly all these individuals owned books and were keen to build up large libraries of their own. It seems to me that we have more factual and circumstantial evidence concerning the world of books in these two centuries than in any other period of Byzantine history,

exaggeration, that there was no parchment available for books because whole shiploads of it had been sold to the Italians: see Lampros, *Μιχαήλ Ἀκομινάτου*...; Id., «Περί τῆς βιβλιοθήκης...» 355, where Choniates is quoted as saying that the Italians carried off books and took them abroad.

185. See *Maximi monachi Planudis epistulae*, ed. M. Treu, Breslau 1890, 115 (Letter 106).

186. See Constantinides, *op. cit.* 74-75, 136. When Planoudes was working on the first edition of Plutarch he lived in the Chora Monastery. In about 1299 he moved to the Monastery of Christos Akataleptos but did not take all his books with him: see A. Diller, 'Codices Planudei', *BZ* 37 (1937) 296.

187. See Wilson, 'Books and Readers...' 4.

188. See *Planudis epistulae*, ed. M. Treu, 261 (Letter 209).

189. See J. Irigoin, 'Les premiers manuscrits grecs...'. According to Irigoin, the oldest Greek book written on paper made in the West dates from 1255: see his paper 'Les débuts de l'emploi du papier...'.

190. See Constantinides, *op. cit.* 136 n. 18, where several similar cases are mentioned.

191. See Wilson, 'Books and Readers...' 2; also p. 86 herein.

192. See Wilson, 'Books and Readers...' 3-4.

193. Lemerle, *op. cit.* 363 n. 73.

194. See p. 179.

195. I. Ševčenko, 'Theodore Metochites, the Chora and the Intellectual Trends of his Time' in P.A. Underwood (ed.), *The Kariye Djami*, IV, Princeton 1975, 19-91. For more general information on the subject see Tuillier, *op. cit.* 71-76; R. Browning, 'Literacy in the Byzantine World', *BMGS* 4 (1978) 39-54; Id., 'Further Reflections on Literacy in Byzantium' in *Τό Ἑλληνικόν* (festschrift in honour of S. Vryonis), I, New Rochelle N.Y. 1990, 69-84; N. Oikonomides, 'Literacy in Thirteenth Century Byzantium: An example from western Asia Minor' in *Τό Ἑλληνικόν,* I 253-265.

196. Browning, 'Literacy...', where he draws attention to owners of books who were not professional scholars nor churchmen but military officers.

151. Headpiece of a Gospel. Gospel book, 3rd quarter of the 11th c. Athens, National Library of Greece, Cod. 57, fol. 108a.

as so much is known about the various preoccupations of everybody involved with books: writers, copyists, borrowers, booksellers, second-hand dealers, collectors, book-lovers, even out-and-out bibliomanes. The examples cited in the following paragraphs will, I hope, present a clear picture of this world, and I think they will also corroborate what has been said about financial constraints being the greatest obstacle to the ownership of books.

George of Cyprus, who described himself as a book-lover (*philobiblos*), started working as a copyist before the imperial court moved back from Nicaea to Constantinople.[197] He had a good collection of books

197. See Lameere, *op. cit.*, Letter 9.

198. See J. Eustratiades, «Ἐπιστολαί Πατριάρχου Γρηγορίου τοῦ Κυπρίου», *Ἐκκλησιαστικός Φάρος* 1-5 (1908-1910); Id., *Γρηγορίου τοῦ Κυπρίου οἰκουμενικοῦ Πατριάρχου ἐπιστολαί καί μῦθοι*, Alexandria 1910, Nos. 14, 38 and 110 respectively.

199. See Lameere, *op. çit.* 189; Immaculada Pérez Martini, 'Àpropos des manuscrits copiés par Georges de Chypre (Grégoire II) patriarche de Constantinople (1283-1289)', *Scriptorium* 46 (1992) 73-84.

200. See S. Fassulakis, *The Byzantine Family of Raoul-Ral(l)es*, Athens 1973. On her correspondence with George of Cyprus (still unpublished) see Constantinides, *op. cit.* 44 n. 68. Theodora probably had a team of calligraphers working for her at the Monastery of Hagios Andreas in Constantinople, which she founded. See H. Buchthal and H. Belting, *Patronage in Thirteenth-Century Constantinople: An atelier of Late Byzantine book illumination and calligraphy*, Washington 1978, 100-101.

201. See Lameere, *op. cit.*, No. 227.

202. See Constantinides, *op. cit.* 44. Planoudes was extremely interested in music, especially harmony, and kept a notebook in which he copied out everything that had been written on the subject up to about 1294. A monk in the Peribleptos Monastery named Georgios or Arsenios Autoreianos once borrowed a book on harmony from him and never returned it. When Autoreianos left the monastery, Planoudes and some of the other monks went to look in his cell, but, although Autoreianos had left some books behind, the one Planoudes was looking for was not there: see *Planudis epistulae*, ed. M. Treu, 78 (Letter 64), 79 (Letter 65), 86 (Letter 68).

203. See Constantinides, *op. cit.* 164.

204. See Eustratiades, *op. cit.*, No. 58.

205. *Ibid.*, No. 111.

206. See Constantinides, *op. cit.* 141: 'Reaching the upper floor of the building, he takes [the book] he is looking for from the chest.' The only previous reference to the use of a chest *(κιβωτός)* for storing books dates from the fifth century B.C., when Alcibiades's possessions were being auctioned off.

including classical authors such as Plato, Demosthenes and Aelius Aristides as well as numerous theological and liturgical books.[198] He states that he could not afford to buy books and considered himself a mediocre copyist, but because of his passion for the written word he copied more books for himself than anyone else in his day.[199] And, as we shall see, copying books for oneself was the commonest way for scholars – and others too – to enlarge their libraries. When George of Cyprus was on the patriarchal throne as Gregory II he shared his interest in books with his confessant Theodora Raoulaina, a niece of Michael VIII, who was known both for her collection of manuscripts and as a writer.[200] One of his letters to her refers to some books of hers which he had borrowed and was now returning, all except one manuscript of Demosthenes and Aelius Aristides, which needed emendation.[201] To judge by her correspondence, Theodora kept in touch with a wide circle of scholars, for she sent a book on harmony to Maximos Planoudes for him to correct[202] and a book on mathematics to Konstantinos Akropolites for him to evaluate for her.[203] One of the sources from which George of Cyprus borrowed books to copy for himself was the well-stocked library of Theodoros Skoutariotes, who was consecrated Metropolitan of Kyzikos in the last years of Manuel II's reign: George says that he used it constantly, borrowing another book every time he returned one.[204]

Two eminent scholars teaching in Constantinople who also had private libraries were Georgios Akropolites and Maximos Holobolos.[205] When Akropolites died he left a sum of money for his son Konstantinos to continue his studies and enlarge his library. Konstantinos spent a lot of the money on buying new books, as he tells us that that was the biggest item in the cost of higher education. Among the books he possessed were Plato's *Meno*, works by Heraclitus and Democritus, poems by George of Pisidia and philosophical writings by Plotinus. It is also very interesting to read what he says about the room where he did his reading and kept his books, which were not arranged in bookcases in any specific order but stored in a chest (*κιβώτιον*).[206]

From an anonymous collector related to the Xiphilinos family, who kept a register of all the books he lent over a period of twenty years (1268-1287), we learn of the existence of a circle of scholars holding high rank, who were regular users of his private library. The names listed in the register book are: Manuel Xiphilinos, (Ioannes) Penteklesiotes, Nikolaos Skoutariotes and (Michael) Iasites, all members of the Great Church of Christ. The books they borrowed were a copy of Homer, the commentaries of Doxapatres on Hermogenes, a book on arithmetic and one on music, Aristotle's *Organon* and, in the field of religion and theology, two copies of the Old Testament, works by John of Damascus and the *Ascetica* of Basil the Great.[207]

Others as well, besides scholars, were interested in books for their own sake: we hear of noblemen and government officials collecting,

207. See Constantinides, *op. cit.* 137.

208. Browning, 'Literacy...' 44; D.M. Nicol, *The Byzantine Family of Kantakouzenos*, Washington 1968, 34; D.I. Polemis, *The Doukai*, London 1968, 179-180.

209. Browning, 'Literacy...' 43.

210. See L. Levi, 'Cinque lettere inedite di Manuele Moschopoulos', *SIFC* 10 (1902) 61-63; I. Ševčenko, 'The Imprisonment of Manuel Moschopoulos in the year 1305 or 1306', *Speculum* 27 (1952) 134; R. Browning, 'Recentiores non Deteriores', *BICS* 7 (1960) 13.

211. See Browning, 'Literacy...' 44; S. Vryonis, 'The Will of a Provincial Magnate, Eustathius Boilas (1059)', *DOP* 11 (1957) 263-277.

212. See Constantinides, *op. cit.* 70. On the Monastery of Christos Akataleptos and its library see Janin, *La géographie ecclésiastique de l'empire byzantin*, I: *Le siège de Constantinople et le patriarcat oecuménique*, III: *Les églises et les monastères*, Paris 1969, 504-506; Volk, *op. cit.* 99-101.

213. See Constantinides, *op. cit.* 35; J. Gill, 'The Church Union of the

152. A parchment-maker's workshop. Illustration from Floriano da Villola, Chronique, *15th c. Bologna University Library, Ms 963, fol. 4.*

153. St. Luke the Evangelist. Illumination from a manuscript of the New Testament, 1125-1150. Oxford, Bodleian Library, Ms Anct. T. inf. 1.10 - Misc. 136.

copying and reading manuscripts on all kinds of subjects, not just in Constantinople but all over the Empire. The *megas stratopedarches* Ioannes Komnenos Synadenos used to boast that he had spent his entire fortune of precious stones and gold on books, and that he possessed a bigger and better library than any of his predecessors in the post or any living imperial official.[208] Another remarkable story concerns one Niketas, a *spatharios* and former commander of the imperial fleet, who copied out a whole manuscript of a work by Basil the Great when he was a prisoner of war in Africa in 971.[209]

This bookish activity was not confined to Constantinople and the three other big cities in the Empire (Nicaea, Thessalonika and Trebizond) that had traditions of scholarship and good libraries. Nikephoros Moschopoulos, Metropolitan of Crete (*c.* 1283-1315/6), evidently owned a great many books, for when he moved house in about 1305 he needed four horses to carry his personal possessions, most of which were books.[210] Eight codices have so far been identified as coming from Moschopoulos's collection. Eustathios Boilas, a large landowner who held the office of *protospatharios tou chrysotrikliniou* before retiring to the province of Armenia, almost certainly had an equally large collection.[211] From the fifty books of his that have been identified it would appear that his interest lay mainly in theology, though he also had works by Aesop, Achilles Tatius and George of Pisidia.

3. University libraries. From the time of the recapture of Constantinople in 1261, if not before, monasteries in the capital with good libraries were used more systematically as centres of higher education. One such 'university' with a very fine library was functioning in the Monastery of Christos Akataleptos as early as 1270.[212] Georgios Akropolites taught there, and he may have been succeeded by George of Cyprus in 1274, when Akropolites went abroad as a member of the imperial delegation to the Council of Lyon.[213] Maximos Planoudes was also teaching at that school in the last decades of the century, but it is not certain whether he succeeded George of Cyprus when the latter was elected Patriarch in March 1283.[214] The vigour of the monastery's intellectual life is attested not only by the excellence of its library but also by the number of students, literary scholars, copyists and

Council of Lyons (1274) Portrayed in Greek Documents', *OCP* 40 (1974) 5-45.

214. Planoudes lived in the Akataleptos Monastery and taught there at least from September 1299, and it was there that he copied two manuscripts in his own hand: his edition of the Greek Anthology (the *Anthologia*

book-lovers who frequented its premises. Georgios Akropolites, Planoudes and George of Cyprus – especially the last – are known for their valuable collections of books. George of Cyprus and Planoudes sometimes copied manuscripts in the monastery, sometimes they read the classics there and looked for epigrams for their collections; and they had a number of mutual friends who were interested in books, including Emperor Andronikos II, Ioannes Glykys, Ioannes Phakrases, Nikephoros Choumnos, Theodora Raoulaina and Theodoros Mouzalon, many of whom had been their pupils.

Another foundation with a very good library was the imperial monastery of the Chora, though we cannot be absolutely certain that it ran a fully-fledged school of higher education. Planoudes tells us that the Chora library had a long history, but at the time when he took it upon himself to reorganize it the books were in bad condition, as indeed was the whole monastery. In about 1292 or 1293 Planoudes wrote and asked Theodoros Mouzalon for financial assistance to enable him to reorganize the library and, in particular, to repair and restore the manuscripts. The Chora library was accommodated in a big building of its own and had a large collection of books from all over the Empire. It had been catalogued quite recently, probably after 1261, but in the meantime it had been allowed to go to rack and ruin: many of the books had been borrowed and never returned (as one can see by comparing the old with the new catalogue) and others had almost fallen to pieces through neglect. Planoudes came up with two proposals: that the librarian should report directly to the *protovestiarios* (a senior official of the imperial court) or to the Emperor in person, which would enable him to monitor outgoing and incoming books more effectively; and that books in urgent need of attention should be restored inexpensively, the cost to be borne by a member of the imperial court.[215] It is not known whether Planoudes's proposals came to anything: the renovation of the library is associated with the name of Theodoros Metochites, who was responsible for the restoration of the monastery buildings.[216]

Theodoros Metochites, born in Constantinople in 1270, came from an educated family and quickly rose to high office, eventually reaching the exalted position of *Megas Logothetes* (the Emperor's first minister).[217] In 1316 he decided to give serious attention to the restoration of the Chora Monastery, and the project was completed in 1321. Meanwhile he had been mulling over the idea of retiring from public life and going into the monastery himself, and he started making preparations for the move. However, the year 1328 turned out disastrously for him: in the aftermath of the civil war between Andronikos II and his grandson, who seized the throne as Andronikos III, his house was pillaged, his property was confiscated and he was exiled to Didymoteichon. From there he sent a letter to the monks of the Chora Monastery, after the death of his friend Abbot Luke, counselling them to preserve the

154. Emperor Michael VIII Palaiologos. Engraving from the Atlas Historique.

Planudea) and the paraphrase of St. John's Gospel by Nonnus of Panopolis: see Constantinides, *op. cit.* 70.

215. See C. Wendel, 'Planudes als Bücherfreund', *ZB* 58 (1941) 82-84. Planoudes, who considered himself an expert bookbinder, backed up his proposal by sending Mouzalon a tattered codex of the *Sphaerica* by Theodosius of Bithynia and another codex in which he had bound together the works of Diophantus, the *Arithmetica* of Nicomachus, Zosimus on harmony and an epitome of the canons of Euclid: see Wendel, *op. cit.* 80-81.

216. See Ševčenko, 'Theodore Metochites...' 25 ff.

217. On the Chora's status as an imperial monastery see C. Wendel, 'Planudes', *BZ* 40 (1940) 407; Ševčenko, 'Theodore Metochites...' 29 n. 75, with bibliography to date.

218. See I. Ševčenko, 'Observations sur les recueils des Discours et des Poèmes de Th. Métochite et sur la Bibliothèque de Chora à Constantinople', *Scriptorium* 5 (1951) 279-288. The library is known to have contained secular as well as theological books and to have been open to the public: see Ševčenko, 'Theodore Metochites...' 36 n. 139.

219. Ševčenko, 'Theodore Metochites...' 37.

220. On the Katholikon Mouseion see S. Lampros, *Ἀργυροπούλεια*, Athens 1910, 21-27; Fuchs, *op. cit.* 65-77; G. Cammelli, *I dotti bizantini e le origini dell' Umanesimo*, II: *Giovanni*

spirit of unity and adhere to the policy of their late superior; but what interested him most of all was to find out what had happened to his own books, as the monks owed it to the restorer of their monastery to keep his books safe and sound and treat them well. Evidently the matter preyed on his mind, for he also wrote a letter in verse to Nikephoros Gregoras for the sole purpose of asking him to look after his books in the monastery, and especially the manuscripts of his writings on astronomy, for posterity's sake.[218]

After two years in exile Metochites returned to Constantinople in 1330 and entered the Monastery of the Chora, where he found to his great joy that his admonitions to the monks had had the desired effect and the library was in good order. Thereafter nothing more is heard of this valuable collection. Metochites, who took the monastic name Theoleptos, died in 1332.[219]

The third and most important of the higher schools in Constantinople occupied a building erected as a hospice by the Serbian *Kral* (King) Stephen Uroš II (Stephen Milutin), adjacent to the Prodromos (or Petra) Monastery. Since all the faculties were together in one place – in what was to all intents and purposes a university campus – it was known as the Katholikon Mouseion. Francesco Filelfo informs us that Western humanists who studied there called it the *Universitas litterarum et scientiarum, publicus discendi ludus*.[220] Very little is known about the Katholikon Mouseion, though it is on record that Georgios Chrysokokkes, Ioannes Chortasmenos, Manuel Chrysoloras, Georgios Scholarios (who was Rector from 1425 to 1448), Ioannes Argyropoulos and Michael Apostoles all taught there at one time or another. But its greatest claim to fame is that, through the influence exerted by Chrysoloras during his years as a teacher at the Studium in Florence from 1396, young Italian classicists started flocking to Constantinople to attend the Katholikon Mouseion, making it the first international centre for the study of the humanities.

About the library attached to this university absolutely nothing is known. The list of manuscripts belonging to the Prodromos Monastery, compiled by Eleni Kakoulidi contains nothing to suggest that it was used as the university library:[221] from this list it would appear that the only book in the monastery library that could have been used as a university textbook was a manuscript of Dioscorides, written after 512, while Nigel Wilson also mentions copies of Plutarch and Polybius.[222] However, we do know that all the scholars who taught there had their own private libraries and that most of the Italian students – notably Aurispa, Guarino and Filelfo – went home from Constantinople laden with manuscripts.

4. Byzantine libraries in the West: from 1400 to 1453. I decided on this title for the final section of this historical review not only because it

Argiropulo, Florence 1941, 30-34; L. Bréhier, *La Civilisation Byzantine*, III, Paris 1950, 435-443; P. Speck, 'Die kaiserliche Universität von Konstantinopel', *Byzantinisches Archiv* 14 (1974); also *Charta* 178-180 for biographical notes on the Greeks and Italians who studied there.

221. Kakoulidi, *op. cit.*; Volk, *op. cit.*

222. Wilson, 'The Libraries of the Byzantine World' 64.

223. On intellectual life in Constantinople between 1261 and 1453, see B. Tatakis, *'Η Φιλοσοφία στό Βυζάντιο* (= *La philosophie byzantine*, Paris 1949, tr. Eva K. Kalpourdzi, edited and with bibliography updated

155. Emperor Manuel II Palaiologos. Engraving from the Atlas Historique.

by L.G. Benakis), Athens 1977; I. Ševčenko, *La vie intellectuelle et poétique à Byzance sous les premiers Paléologues*, Brussels 1962; Id., 'Theodore Metochites...'; I. Medvedev, *Βυζαντινός Οὐμανισμός, 14ος-15ος αἰ.* (unpublished translation from the Russian by G. Beveratos, Leningrad 1967); Wilson, *Scholars of Byzantium*; Hunger, *Βυζαντινή Λογοτεχνία* I 39-122; Sophia Mergiali-Falangas, *L'enseignement et les lettrés pendant l'époque des Paléologues*, Athens 1996.

224. On Plethon's school at Mistras see F. Masai, *Pléthon et le platonisme de Mistra*, Paris 1956; S. Runciman, *Mistra, Byzantine Capital of the Peloponnese*, London 1980, 53-56; C.M. Woodhouse, *Gemistos Plethon: The last of the Hellenes*,

reflects a historical reality but also because it seems to me that this last Byzantine renaissance – the Palaiologian renaissance – achieved its final flowering in the West, and more particularly in Italy, thanks to the contribution made by Greek scholars to the humanist movement and the spread of Greek learning, both by their teaching and by their propagation of the Byzantine manuscript tradition.

When the first representatives of Byzantine humanism went to Italy at the beginning of the fifteenth century they had very little option but to cut themselves off from their natural environment, while the new audience they found themselves addressing did not strike a chord with their Byzantine sensibilities. They had to forget their personal preoccupations and cherished dreams, and often even their ideology, and the only way left open to them, if they were to survive in an climate strongly in favour of church union, was to help to lay the foundations of Italian humanism. Realizing that any seeds they might sow for the flowering of the Byzantine renaissance in Constantinople would fall on stony ground, they chose to accept the leading roles offered to them in the West rather than endure the frustration that certainly awaited them if they stayed in Constantinople. To appreciate fully the contribution they made to classical studies in the West, one would have to study the historical map of printing in Italy up to the middle of the sixteenth century and to acknowledge the important influence exerted by those publications on the writings of humanists in every branch of learning. But such an approach is beyond the scope of this book, so I shall simply make a few observations on matters relating to books and their editors, publishers and readers (some of which will crop up again in the chapter on the Renaissance) to give some idea of the Byzantines' love of books in the last fifty years or so before the Turkish conquest.[223]

The myth of the mass exodus of Byzantine scholars with their manuscripts after the fall of Constantinople in 1453 needs to be exploded once and for all, as more than a thousand Byzantine codices were taken to Italy, mostly from Constantinople, between the beginning of the fifteenth century and the Turkish conquest. Nor were they all contemporary copies: some of them were of great importance as being among the earliest links in the manuscript tradition of classical and Byzantine texts. Nearly all the leading Byzantine scholars had private libraries and maintained close contact with centres of learning in Italy, and most were excellent Latinists: those who fled to the West after the fall of the Byzantine Empire were the last of their generation.

The most prominent representatives of that trend, some of whom spent some time at Mistras[224] before going on to Italy, were Manuel Chrysoloras, George of Trebizond, Georgios Gemistos Plethon, Theodoros Gazis (from Thessalonika), Cardinal Bessarion, Andronikos Kallistos, Ioannes Argyropoulos, Michael Apostoles, Demetrios Chalkokondyles, Konstantinos Laskaris, Ianos Laskaris, Georgios

Oxford 1986; W. Blum, *Georgios Gemistos Plethon: Politik, Philosophie und Rhetorik im spätbyzantinischen Reich (1355-1452)*, Stuttgart 1988.

225. For information about the Byzantine scholars who were active in the West see D.J. Geanakoplos, *Ἕλληνες λόγιοι εἰς τήν Βενετίαν: Μελέται ἐπί τῆς διαδόσεως τῶν ἑλληνικῶν γραμμάτων ἀπό τοῦ Βυζαντίου εἰς τήν δυτικήν Εὐρώπην* (=*Greek Scholars in Venice...*, tr. Ch.G. Patrinelis), Athens 1965; D. Zakythinos, *Μεταβυζαντινά καί Νέα Ἑλληνικά,* Athens 1978; *Charta*.

226. Geanakoplos, *op. cit.*; M. Manoussacas, «Ἡ ἀλληλογραφία τῶν Γρηγοροπούλων χρονολογουμένη (1493-1501)», *EMA* 6 (1956) 156-209; Id., «Ἀρσενίου Μονεμβασίας τοῦ Ἀποστόλη ἐπιστολαί ἀνέκδοτοι (1521-1534)», *EMA* 8/9 (1959) 5-56, 208.

227. See esp. R. Devreesse, *Les manuscrits grecs de l'Italie méridionale*, Vatican City 1955; A. Turyn, *Codices Graeci Vaticani saeculis XIII et XIV scripti annorumque notis instructi*, Vatican City 1964; Id., *Dated Greek Manuscripts of the Thirteenth and Fourteenth Centuries in the Libraries of Italy,* Urbana 1972; Id., *Dated Greek Manuscripts of the Thirteenth and Fourteenth Centuries in the Libraries of Great Britain*, Dumbarton Oaks 1980. The two contemporary historians who give an account of the years following the Turkish conquest – Doukas, *Historia Turco-Byzantina* XLII.1 (ed. V. Grecu, Bucharest 1958, 393) and Kritoboulos, *Historiae* (ed. V. Grecu, Bucharest 1963, 2) – have nothing specific to say about the destruction of books. At the same time, the allegation by Cardinal Isidore of Kiev that over 120,000 books were destroyed (*Ultra centum et viginti millia librorum devastata*) must be an exaggeration, perhaps connected with his dramatic flight to the West: see E. Jacobs, *Untersuchungen zur Geschichte der Bibliothek im Serai zu Konstantinopel*, Heidelberg 1919, 3.

228. Scarperia was one of the first foreigners to go to Constantinople to buy Greek manuscripts, but nothing is known about the nature and contents of his library: see Dorothe M. Robathan, 'Libraries of the Italian Renaissance' in J.W. Thompson (ed.), *The Medieval Library*, Chicago 1939, 516.

Hermonymos Spartiates and Michael Maroullos Tarchaniotes.[225] To these we should add the names of those who went to Western Europe from Crete and take an equal share of the credit for propagating Greek language and literature and teaching students who developed into able Greek scholars: among them were Emmanuel Adramyttenos, Arsenios Apostoles, Ioannes Gregoropoulos, Demetrios Doukas, Demetrios Kastrenos, Ioustinos Dekadyos, the great incunabular printer Zacharias Kallierges and the learned Markos Mousouros.[226]

To return to the subject of books and libraries, let us consider the implications of the finding that, according to the available evidence, the manuscripts bought by Italian humanists on their visits to Constantinople represented a very high proportion of the stock of books remaining in the city in the first half of the fifteenth century. Systematic research on this subject reveals that the majority of the manuscripts removed from Constantinople in this way were not recent copies but old and valuable.[227] Quite apart from the great manuscript-hunters such as Giovanni Aurispa (who went back to Italy taking 238 manuscripts with him), nearly all the eminent Greek teachers at the Katholikon Mouseion had sizable collections of Greek books in their libraries, as did their foreign pupils, including Jacopo da Scarperia,[228] Niccolò Niccoli,[229] Ermolao Barbaro the Elder,[230] Bernardo Michelozzi,[231] Francesco Filelfo,[232] Antonio da Massa,[233] Sassolo da Prato,[234] Gian Mario Filelfo,[235] Giovanni Tortelli[236] and Guarino da Verona.[237] What a contrast to the poignant picture painted by Emperor Manuel II Palaiologos to Demetrios Kydones: 'I have

156. St. Mark the Evangelist. Illumination from a Gospel book, 1300-1301. Pantokratoros Monastery, Mt. Athos, Cod. 47, fol. 114β.

229. See p. 340. Niccoli bought some of his manuscripts from Aurispa after his return from his first visit to Constantinople in 1417. The most noteworthy was a copy of Aristarchus's commentary on Homer.

230. See A. Diller, 'The Library of Francesco and Ermolao Barbaro', *IMU* 6 (1963) 253-262. One of the

Suidas in my hands, and in the poverty that now surrounds us it is something, at least, to be enriched by the treasury of his words.'[238]

Unfortunately it is impossible to say which particular manuscripts each of these Italians owned, because in most cases they changed hands, either by bequest or by sale, and many of them bear no owner's mark or name. Aurispa, for example, sold his books to various princes and noblemen, including his eleventh-century Demosthenes to Novello Malatesta, the ruler of Cesena;[239] and Chrysoloras's collection ended up in the library of the philhellene Palla Strozzi, as did that of Demetrios Skaranos.[240] Niccoli's collection is still recognizable as such, as it was bought by Cosimo de' Medici for the library of the Monastery of San Marco in Florence.[241] Theodoros Gazis's library went first to Demetrios Chalkokondyles, then to one of the latter's pupils, Giano Parrasio and then to Cardinal Seripandi before finally coming to rest in the Monastery of San Giovanni Carbonara in Naples.[242] Andronikos Kallistos's fine collection eventually came into the possession of Lorenzo de' Medici[243] through the agency of two Italian scholars working in Milan. Francesco Filelfo sold Greek manuscripts whenever the opportunity arose, while Ioannes Argyropoulos, in his old age in Rome, had to sell his books to make ends meet.[244]

Even if it were possible to reconstruct the contents of all these libraries, which would amount to no more than a list of titles, it is more interesting – and more to the point – to consider the part played by manuscripts from Byzantium in promoting the study of the humanities and spreading a wider knowledge of Greek literature. All those involved in the vital work done on manuscripts – editors, translators and commentators, printers, publishers and financial backers – formed a network of people and things that illustrates what is perhaps the most fascinating and heart-warming side of the whole story, namely the friendships that developed between the Byzantine scholars and their pupils and colleagues in the West.[245] Ptolemy's *Cosmographia*, which belonged to Chrysoloras before being acquired by Strozzi, was translated into Latin by Jacopo da Scarperia with Chrysoloras's help, and this version was used for the first six incunabular editions, of which four were printed in Italy and two at Ulm.[246] Aristotle's *Politics*, of which the only manuscript in existence in Italy was found when Chrysoloras was looking for texts to use in his classes at the Studium in Florence, was translated into Latin by Leonardo Bruni: it was published in Italy in 1492, in an edition of 1,500 copies, and then eight more times in northern Europe.[247] Strabo's *Geographia*, which also came from Strozzi's library, was translated by Guarino da Verona and Gregorius Tiphernas: it was first published in 1469 and then in six more editions, all in the same version.[248] The manuscripts used for the *editio princeps* of *Souda* ('Suidas') were bought by Chalkokondyles for 25 gold scudi as part of his contribution to the capital of a partnership

visitors to Barbaro's library was Ianos Laskaris: see K. Müller, 'Neue Mittheilungen über Janos Lascaris und die Mediceische Bibliothek', *Centralblatt für Bibliothekswesen* 1 (1884) 333-412.

231. See Fuchs, *op. cit.* 68. On Michelozzi's library see A. Della Torre, *Storia dell' Accademia Platonica di Firenze*, Florence 1902, 774-775.

232. See Fuchs, *op. cit.* 68. On Filelfo's library see *Charta* xxx.

233. See Fuchs, *loc. cit.* On Antonio da Massa's library see R. Pratesi, 'Antonio da Massa Maritima' in *DBI* 3 (1961) 555-556.

234. See Fuchs, *op. cit.* 69. Sassolo da Prato (Saxolus Pratensis) wrote a textbook of Greek grammar entitled *De accentibus ac diphthongis et formatione praeteritorum graecorum*, Milan, [Demetrios Damilas], *c.* 1481: see *Charta* 148.

235. See Fuchs, *op. cit.* 68-69.

236. *Ibid.* 69. Tortelli, who was the papal librarian under Nicholas V, wrote a Greek-Latin dictionary.

237. See G. Cammelli, *I dotti bizantini e le origini dell' Umanesimo*, I: *Manuele Crisolora*, Florence 1941, 137.

238. Manuel Palaiologos, *Lettres*, ed. É. Legrand, Paris 1893 (repr. Amsterdam 1962).

239. See pp. 305 ff.

240. See p. 224.

241. See pp. 342-344.

242. On Gazis's library see L. Dorez, 'Un document sur la bibliothèque de Théodore Gaza', *Revue de Bibliothèques* 3 (1893) 385-390. Parrasio married Chalkokondyles's daughter Theodora: see F. Lo Parco, *Aulo Gianno Parrasio*, Vasto 1899; G. Cammelli, *I dotti bizantini e le origini dell' Umanesimo*, III: *Demetrio Calcondila*, Florence 1954, 131.

243. Andronikos Kallistos sold his books in Milan to raise enough money to take him to Paris. They were bought by Buono Accorsi and Joachim della Torre: see E. Bigi, 'Andronico Callisto' in *DBI* 3 (1961) 162-163. On the sale of the books by della Torre to Lorenzo de' Medici, see A. Fabroni, *Laurentii Medicis Vita*, II, Pisa 1784, 286-287; V. Malaguzzi, *La corte di Ludovico il Moro*, IV, Milan 1923, 109.

244. On Argyropoulos's pitiful living conditions in Rome and the sale of his books, see the letter from Konstantinos Laskaris to Giovanni

Pardo published in É. Legrand, *Bibliographie Hellénique ... aux XVe et XVIe siècles,* I, Paris 1885, lxxx-lxxxi.

245. A first attempt to gather the texts together and to edit and emend them was made for the purposes of

formed to finance its publication: the only incunabular edition of this Byzantine lexicon was published at Milan in 1499, with a print run of eight hundred copies.[249] There is no need to say more here on this subject, as many of the facts testifying to the influence of Byzantine manuscripts on Western scholarship and their contribution to the Renaissance are recorded in Chapter 11.

157. St. Gregory of Nazianzos. Illumination from the Liturgical Homilies of Gregory of Nazianzos, *1136-1155. St. Catherine's Monastery, Mt. Sinai, Cod. 339, fol. 4β.*

In this brief survey of over 1,100 years of Byzantine history we have seen that there was a plan to establish a big public library of classical literature with the backing of Constantius II, though we are not told how much progress was made with the project and so it is impossible to say whether it ever came to fruition. A significant but uncorroborated piece of evidence is the statement by Michael Glykas that this library contained the astonishing number of 36,500 volumes in the eighth century; thereafter nothing more is heard of it. Private libraries, especially collections of parchment codices, were confined to a moneyed élite and rarely contained more than fifty volumes. But the thousands of monasteries in the Orthodox East developed into major centres of book production, besides having large libraries, and it was there that many rare or even unique manuscripts were preserved for posterity. When reading about the Byzantines, one often has the impression that there were two sides to everything they did, and that in order to understand how these two sides were reconciled one needs a deep insight into the Byzantine way of life and thinking. Be that as it may, in view of the way things went in the West, where Greek education died out and no Greek books at all were available until shortly before the fall of Constantinople, the Byzantines must be given credit for the fact that – allowing for the periodic reshuffling of priorities and the ebb and flow of religious thinking that altered their approach to classical studies and books as a whole – they were the custodians of classical literature and the standard-bearers of a humanist movement which historical circumstances prevented from maturing in its natural environment.

VI. Architecture. If the known facts about secular libraries in the 1,100 years of the Byzantine Empire are meagre, the evidence we have concerning their architecture, interior design, furniture and fittings is practically non-existent. It might be possible to deduce something about these libraries by studying monastic scriptoria and the libraries that went with them, since many of the most important of them still exist; but the problem here is that some abbots and other churchmen were opposed to the ownership of books, and it may be that the small size of the rooms used as libraries in monasteries reflects this attitude rather than the paucity of books. All one can do is to tackle the subject in brief, making the best use of the little evidence available. Secular and monastic libraries are treated separately.

1. Secular libraries. When I use the term 'secular libraries' I am referring to only two: the one founded in Constantinople in the mid fourth century, which served the needs of the institutions of higher education and the schools of law and philosophy that existed in the capital at one time or another, and an imperial library that apparently existed in the palace, often referred to as the Royal or Palatine Library.[250] The only documentary source that gives us any help at all in trying to form a picture of Constantius II's public library is the statement by Malchus that the library in the *κεκλημένη βασιλική* (sometimes spelt *κεκλιμένη βασιλική*, which means 'leaning basilica') was burnt down in 475 or 476.[251] This library, or rather the building in which it was accommodated, was rebuilt at some time before 491, as we have seen, though we do not know whether it was restored exactly as it had been.[252] The only further information we have about this library, which may have been open to the public, is connected with the Higher School, which was located in what was called the Octagon, where there was a library.[253] We know from Kedrenos's description that the octagonal main building was surrounded by eight stoas and that the whole complex functioned as a university.[254]

From the little direct and indirect evidence available it is impossible to tell whether, in the first centuries after the foundation of Constantinople, the Byzantines followed the usual Roman architectural pattern (at least in their bigger libraries) or whether they broke new ground: all we know is that bilingual libraries remained in use for a long time.[255] It would be interesting to know what sort of bookcases they used, but there does not seem to be an illustration of one in any of the numerous manuscript illuminations.[256] As far as I know, the only 'bookcase' depicted in the art of that period is the chest that appears in the mosaics

the great translation project initiated by Pope Nicholas V: see pp. 288-290. On the manuscripts on which the *editiones principes* were based, especially those of Aldus Manutius, see: J. Irigoin, *Histoire du texte de Pindare*, Paris 1952; A. Turyn, *Studies in the Manuscript Tradition of the Tragedies of Sophocles*, Urbana 1952; Id., *The Byzantine Manuscript Tradition of the Tragedies of Euripides*, Urbana 1957; M. Sicherl, 'Die Editio Princeps Aldina des Euripides und ihre Vorlagen', *Rheinisches Museum für Philologie* 118 (1975) 205-225; Id., *Handschriftliche Vorlagen der Editio Princeps des Aristoteles*, Mainz 1976; Id., 'Die Musaios-Ausgabe des Aldus und ihre lateinische Übersetzung', *IMU* 19 (1976) 260-262; Id., *Johannes Cuno, ein Wegbereiter des Griechischen in Deutschland. Ein biographisch-kodikologische Studie*, Heidelberg 1978; Id., 'Die Editio Princeps des Aristophanes' in Hallen, B. (ed.), *Das Buch und sein Haus*, I: *Erlesenes aus der Welt des Büches*, Wiesbaden 1979, 189-231; M.J.C. Lowry, *The World of Aldus Manutius: Business and Scholarship in Renaissance Venice*, Oxford 1979; *Charta* 371-373.

246. In the *editio princeps* of the *Cosmographia*, printed by Hermann de Liechtenstein (Levilapis) at Vicenza in 1495, Chrysoloras is obliquely referred to in the dedicatory preface addressed to the Greek Antipope Alexander V (Petros Philarges) by Jacopo da Scarperia: 'quam appellationem uir saeculi nostri erudentissimus MANVEL Constantinopolitanus, suauissimus litterarum graecarum ... dum in latinum eloquium id transferre ad uerbum...': see Legrand, *op. cit.* III 34-35. For the other editions see *Census* P 1081-1085; *GW* 7799.

247. See *GW* 2448.

248. The first ten books were translated by Guarino and the rest by Tiphernas. The *editio princeps* was printed by Sweynheim and Pannartz in Rome in 1469 (*Census* S 793; for the other editions see *Census* S 794-798, 15091). Tiphernas had studied Greek: we do not know where or with whom, but it must have been somewhere under the jurisdiction of the Byzantine Empire. Thereafter he worked in several centres of learning, mostly in Naples and Paris. He did

158. The High Admiral Apokaukos. From a manuscript of the works of Hippocrates: Paris, Bibliothèque Nationale, Ms Gr. 2144, fol. 11.

of the Mausoleum of Galla Placidia in Ravenna,[257] and there the distinctive superstructure of the chest may be derived from the Oriental tradition, that is from the design of the ark containing the scrolls of the Torah in a Jewish synagogue.[258] That apart, the only objects depicted in Byzantine art that can be identified as cases for books are the little chests of the kind used by scribes as a worktable and support for the bookstand; the boxes full of scrolls occasionally depicted with the rest of the evangelists' writing equipment; and the *glossokomoi* first mentioned by John Chrysostom.[259] There is also a description by a Spanish traveller, Pero Tafur,[260] who visited a palace in Constantinople (probably Blachernai or the Boukoleon) in 1437 and refers to a room containing books. At the entrance to the palace, below a set of rooms, there is an open-fronted marble loggia with stone stalls along the wall and stone tables, supported by colonnettes, running the whole length of the row of stalls. Here there are many books by historians and ancient writers, and on one side of the room there are gaming boards, because the imperial residence is always well-appointed.

2. Monastic libraries. I have been lucky enough to work on the interior design and furnishing of two historic libraries, those of the Oecumenical Patriarchate in the Phanar, Constantinople, and the Monastery of St. John on Patmos. In both cases I was faced with the same problem relating to the design of monastic libraries:[261] if one looks for evidence of a general rule, one is more likely to come up with unanswered questions than solutions. Documentary sources offer no help, for we have no written descriptions of libraries nor pictures of them in manuscript illuminations, where the artists adhered strictly to the traditional iconography. What we sometimes see are not copyists, whether laymen or monks, but evangelists writing their Gospel against a unvarying background: not a realistic setting but a 'stage set' dominated by secular and ecclesiastical buildings. The shape of their writing-tables and bookstands may vary, and the Gospel book symbolizes the library, as there are no other books to be seen in these miniatures.[262]

Western artists treat the matter altogether differently. When the central figures in their pictures are Church Fathers or humble monastic copyists, they are portrayed in their real surroundings. The architecture, furniture and fittings are drawn from life, with many features of interest. Writers and copyists are shown surrounded by books carefully arranged on shelves or chained to desks, with the precious bindings depicted in detail and even the words legible in some books, such as the copy of Euclid in St. Augustine's library. Evidently Western Europeans saw no reason to conceal any of the secrets of the bookman's world.[263]

To find out as much as one can about the design of monastic libraries in the East we have to go to another part of the world, which is dealt

some spells of teaching in Paris and Venice, was a protégé of Francesco Filelfo and the teacher of Giovanni Pontano, the future founder of the Neapolitan Academy. See L. Delaruelle, 'Une vie d'humaniste au XVe siècle: Gregorio Tifernas', *Mélanges d'Archéologie et d'Histoire de l'École Française de Rome* 19 (1899) 9-33.

249. The first members of the partnership were the printers Giovanni Bissoli and Benedetto Mangio, the Milan bookseller Alessandro Minucciano and Demetrios Chalkokondyles, who did all the editorial work. The selling price of the book was set at three gold ducats and it was agreed by all the partners that two copies of the book should be given to Taddeo Ugoletti, the first librarian of King Matthias Corvinus of Hungary. See A. Cioni, 'Bissoli, Giovanni' in *DBI* 10 (1968) 702.

250. Manafis, *op. cit.* 42 ff.; also pp. 144-145 herein.

251. See Zonaras, ed M. Pinder and T. Büttner-Wobst, *CSHB*, Bonn 1897, III 130-131. The phrase *κεκλημένη βασιλική* is meaningless: perhaps it should be amended to *καλουμένη βασιλική*, as Kedrenos has it (ed. I. Bekker, *CSHB*, Bonn 1838, I 616).

252. See pp. 145-146.

253. On the Octagon see p. 145.

254. See p. 145.

255. See p. 142.

256. A collection of miniatures of scholars at work is reproduced in *Oἱ Θησαυροί τοῦ Ἁγίου Ὄρους*, 4 vols., Athens (Ekdotike Athenon) 1973-1991. See also Anna Marava-Hadjinikolaou and Christina Toufexi-Paschou, *Κατάλογος Μικρογραφιῶν Βυζαντινῶν Χειρογράφων τῆς Ἐθνικῆς Βιβλιοθήκης τῆς Ἑλλάδος*, I, Athens 1978.

257. L. de Beylié has a clear reproduction of the mosaic in his book *L'Habitation Byzantine: Recherches sur l'architecture civile des Byzantins et son influence en Europe*, Grenoble/Paris 1902, 193.

258. See Wendel, *Kleine Schriften...* 266.

259. For the use of the word *glossokomos* see n. 41 above. A box of exactly the kind used for books in the Roman period is depicted in a miniature of St. John the Evangelist in Codex 43 of Stavronikita Monastery on Mt. Athos, a Gospel book

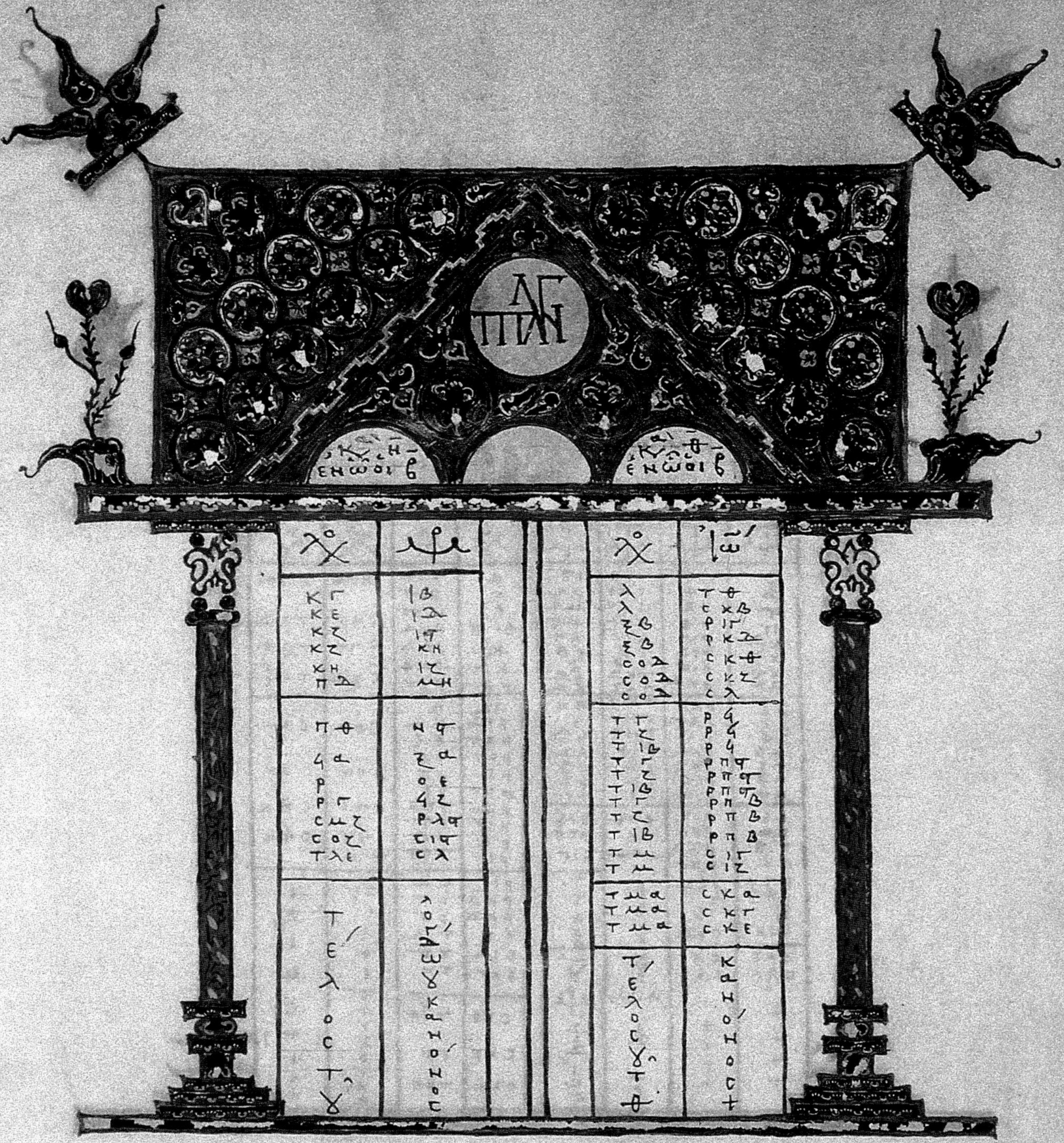

ΕΝ Ω ΟΙ Β
ΕΝ Ω ΟΙ Β
τέλος τοῦ
κανόνος
τέλος τοῦ θ
κανόνος

with in the next chapter. The most one can say here is that monastic libraries in the Byzantine world were designed in accordance with the Greek model of the Classical period: in other words, they were impersonal rooms used simply for the storage of books, with cupboards for bookcases.

dated 950-960, fol. 13α. It is reproduced in G. Galavaris, *Ζωγραφική Βυζαντινῶν Χειρογράφων,* Athens 1995, 63.

260. See A.A. Vasiliev, 'Pero Tafur: A Spanish traveler of the fifteenth century and his visit to Constantinople, Trebizond and Italy', *Byzantion* 7 (1932) 75-122.

261. In the Patmos library the manuscripts and printed books were kept in ordinary cupboards, while in the Phanar they were in ornate nineteenth- and twentieth-century bookcases donated or bequeathed (together with their books) by various Patriarchs.

262. Anastasios Orlandos has a brief note on monastic libraries in his book *Μοναστηριακή Ἀρχιτεκτονική*, Athens 1927, 65-66, as does Wendel in his *Kleine Schriften*... 194-195. Isabella Stone has nothing relevant to the subject in her short paper 'Libraries of the Greek Monasteries in Southern Italy' in Thompson, *The Medieval Library* 330-337. More generally, see G. Cavallo, 'La cultura italo-greca nella produzione libraria' in V. Scheiwiller (ed.), *I Bizantini in Italia*, Milan 1986, 495-612.

263. See, for example, the Codex Amiatinus, which shows Cassiodorus copying out the Pentateuch in front of a cabinet with five sloping shelves of books. The manuscript (Florence, Biblioteca Medicea Laurenziana, Amiatino 1) was written in about 700 at Jarrow or Wearmouth Abbey in England. See J. Glenisson (ed.), *Le Livre au Moyen Âge*, Paris 1988, 97 (and see p. 195 herein). A very realistic representation of St. Jerome's library is to be seen in a fresco by Tommaso da Modena in the Church of San Niccolò at Treviso: see G.P. Brizzi and J. Verger (ed.), *Le università dell' Europa. Le scuole e i maestri. Il Medioevo*, Milan 1994, 166. St. Augustine's library is depicted in a fresco by Botticelli in the Cenacolo di Ognissanti in Florence (Brizzi and Verger, *op. cit.* 162).

160. Reconstruction drawing of the interior of an imperial library in Constantinople conforming to the standard Graeco-Roman design.

CHAPTER TEN

THE MIDDLE AGES

If a book-lover of the Roman imperial age had been alive in Italy towards the end of the sixth century and investigating the opportunities for building up a library of Greek and Latin books, he would have been struck by three things in particular: the demise of bilingual libraries, the marginalization of Graeco-Roman literature and the decline of the *librarii* (a term covering booksellers, publishers and copyists), whose place had been taken by monasteries and the clergy generally. The days when any Roman citizen – or indeed any resident of the Empire, which included all the countries of the Mediterranean basin and more besides – could find any work of Latin literature and some books in Greek at an affordable price were gone for ever. Yet the process of decline was not universal, for throughout the Middle Ages there were places where Latin literature always continued to be read. Given that the spread of Christianity brought sweeping changes in the established methods of book production and distribution, it is almost impossible to work out the way in which many works of late Roman and Greek literature (mainly in the field of philosophy) were disseminated, for example among ecclesiastical writers in the West. A typical case in point is St. Augustine, whose writings show clear signs of having been influenced by Plotinus, through Porphyry:[1] this suggests that there must have been some kind of machinery for the dissemination of books, though we are still unable to discover how it worked. The matters that concern us here, however, are the similarities and differences between libraries (private, public and monastic) in the West and the East and the part played by books in the evolution of movements for a revival of learning.

With regard to the opportunities for building up a library in the West, it appears that the situation there generally paralleled that in the Byzantine world from the sixth century onwards. In the West, as in the East, book ownership was concentrated in the hands of the clergy, and monasteries not only had the best libraries but also developed into the main centres of book production. It is a remarkable fact that almost all the works of Graeco-Roman literature preserved in the Middle Ages were discovered by Renaissance manuscript-hunters in monasteries. Intellectual movements involving a renaissance-type reappraisal of classical literature, leading to a massive increase in book ownership among the laity, are discernible at both ends of the Mediterranean basin. But it is important to remember that there is an essential difference between the two worlds: Byzantium always kept the tradition of ancient Greek learning alive and consequently often created new ways of disseminating books, whereas in the West the process of civilizing so many semi-barbarian peoples and building up a generally accepted corpus of literature to form the basis of all elementary and higher education was an extremely long and complex one. In this respect the two worlds moved in opposite directions: in Byzantium almost all the institutions of higher learning that existed in the early centuries eventually came to be located in monasteries and totally dependent on the palace, while in the West the cathedral schools were superseded in the twelfth century by great universities which were controlled by laymen. Lastly, we must bear

1. See H.-I. Marrou, *Saint Augustin et la fin de la culture antique* (thesis), Paris 1938. On the influence of Plotinus on Augustine, see W. Theiler, *Porphyrios und Augustin* (= Schriften der Königsberger gelehrten Gesellschaft, 10), Halle 1933; P. Henry, *Plotin et l'Occident. Firmicus Maternus Victorinus, Saint Augustin et Macrobe*, Louvain 1934.

2. See N.E. Karapidakis, *Ἱστορία τῆς Μεσαιωνικῆς Δύσης (5ος-11ος αἰ.)*, Athens 1996, 57 ff.; Z.N. Tsirpanlis, *Εἰσαγωγή στή Μεσαιωνική Ἱστορία τῆς Δυτικῆς Εὐρώπης*, Thessaloniki 1996, 77 ff., 83.

3. See P. Riché, *Éducation et culture dans l'Occident barbare, VIe-VIIIe siècles* (= Patristica Sorbonensia, 4), Paris 1962; B. Bischoff, *Mittelalterliche Studien*, II, Stuttgart 1967, 312-

162. St. Augustine in his library. Painting by an anonymous artist, 15th c. Vich Museum.

161. St. Jerome at his writing-desk. Painting by Antonello da Messina, c. 1474. London, National Gallery.

in mind that the abandonment of the bilingual library tradition in the West led to the virtual extinction there of the Greek language and Greek literature, whereas in Constantinople it was not necessary to keep up that tradition after the seventh century because thereafter the last remaining bilingual inhabitants of the Empire all learnt Greek and had a Greek education. But before we go on to consider the changes brought about in the world of books by the collapse of the Roman Empire in the West, a few words must be said about political developments there and the demise of Graeco-Roman education.

I. The Dark Ages. After the death of Theodosius the Great in 395, the Roman Empire was divided into two, which led to serious problems of co-ordination. And, despite the best efforts of the Ravenna emperors to keep the barbarians out, when Valentinian III died in 455 his successors were powerless to deal with the threat. It was difficult to enforce the laws of the central government, and the inhabitants of the provinces sensed this weakness and sought protection elsewhere, abandoning the rural areas and going in search of a new way of life.[2] Large estates belonging to the aristocracy still existed, but one of the side effects of the shortage of labour and the gradual disappearance of slavery (with the strong backing of the Church) was that editors and publishers eventually found themselves working in a completely different environment from that of the Roman period.

1. Book production in the Late Roman period. Although the new intelligentsia that came into being with the spread of Christianity was hostile or at best indifferent to Latin literature, by the late fifth century it was still possible for anybody to buy books by such authors as Virgil, Cicero, Plautus, Lucian, Ovid, Livy and Pliny the Younger,[3] but not works of early Latin literature, some of which had already been lost in Cicero's time.[4] The evidence for this is to be found in the survival of some *éditions de luxe* dating from the fifth century A.D., including manuscripts of Virgil,[5] which supports the view that in certain places the book trade was still not completely defunct. To judge by certain magnificent codices of the sixth century, it would seem that the art of the manuscript and the character and quality of Roman books were by no means on the verge of extinction but had been smoothly absorbed into the Church's sphere of influence.[6] Most works of Latin literature were still in existence at that time (in and after the sixth century), but control over the choice of books to be reproduced and the marketing of books had passed from private enterprise to the superiors of monasteries and the heads of cathedral schools. And so the publishing policy of the *librarii*, which had been designed to suit the tastes of Roman society, gradually gave way to a different *modus operandi*, as the object now was to sell religious books for the use of Christian communities and religious houses.[7] Meanwhile a

327; E.A. Lowe, *Codices latini antiquiores*, 2 vols. (with suppl.), Oxford 1934-1971; B. Bischoff, Virginia Brown and J.J. John, 'Addenda to *Codices Latini Antiquiores*', *Medieval Studies* 54 (1992) 286-307.

4. By the first century B.C. works by Naevius, Ennius, Plautus and Cato the Censor had vanished for ever, and Cicero voiced his sadness at their loss: see p. 100.

5. For example, the Codex Romanus (Vat. lat. 3867); also the Corpus Agrimensorum Romanorum in the Herzog August Library at Wolfenbüttel (see p. 400).

6. The first period of book production, from the fourth to the sixth century, was followed by a period in which books reached an ever broader readership, lasting from the time of Gregory the Great (†604) to the time of Emperor Otto III (†1002) or even later. Many of the great libraries that had remained intact until the Lombards started their incursions in 567 were destroyed in the years that followed, and it was only in centres such as Rome, Ravenna and Campania that significant collections of books lived on. However, from the time when Gregory ascended the papal throne, not only were books in remarkably wide circulation by the standards of the day, but new monasteries were founded in which books of all kinds, including works of Latin literature, found a safe haven. At Bobbio Abbey, founded by the Irish missionary St. Columban in 613, Renaissance manuscript-hunters found codices dating from well before the founder's lifetime, which proves that manuscripts of earlier generations had been available and had usually come to rest in monastic libraries. See B. Bischoff, *Manuscripts and Libraries in the Age of Charlemagne*, tr. and ed. M. Gorman, Cambridge 1994, 9 ff.

7. See p. 196.

8. The changeover from the papyrus roll to the codex was an extremely slow process. According to Martial, the first codices appeared in the first century A.D. in Rome, in the form of several pages of parchment sewn together, which he called 'parchment

writing tablets' (*tabellae membranenses*). The book as we know it may well have been born in Rome between A.D. 84 and 86: see E.G. Turner, *The Typology of the Early Codex*, Philadelphia 1977; C.H. Roberts and T.C. Skeat, *The Birth of the Codex*, London 1983.

change also took place in the form of the book: gone were the handy papyrus rolls, superseded by bulky parchment codices, often containing more than one work, which were time-consuming to produce and therefore expensive.[8] This does not mean that Latin books were no longer read or reproduced, especially as there were many works on history, mechanics and other technical and general subjects that were in constant use everywhere as textbooks. And from the eighth century onwards more and more laymen, mostly members of the princely courts of northern Europe, started acquiring books of their own and building up small but worthwhile collections of Latin literature, in which some important classical works were preserved.[9]

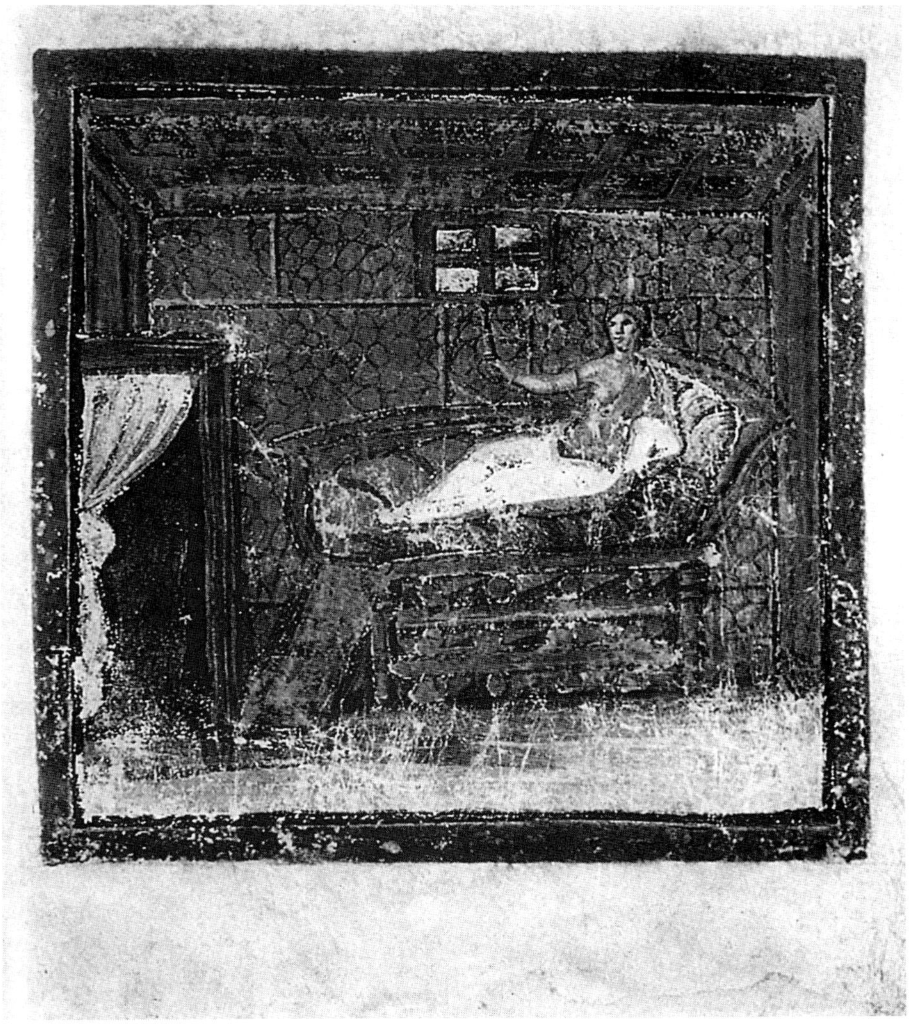

163. Dido's suicide. Illumination in a manuscript of Virgil, c. *A.D. 400 (Ms Vat. lat. 3225, fol. 40).*

But if Latin literature was reasonably well served during the early Middle Ages, the situation with regard to the publication of Greek books offered a clear foretaste of the atrophy that was to follow. By the sixth century, Greek had already fallen into disuse in Spain, Britain and France. When the Vandals had overrun North Africa, not only had the Greek language been wiped out there for good but the Church in Italy and theologians everywhere had been cut off from the vibrant centre of Christian thinking that had been active in Africa since the second century. And even in Italy, where bilingualism had prevailed until near the end of the fourth century, at least among the upper classes and in part of the machinery of state, the last generation of Greek speakers was that of Boethius (†525) and Cassiodorus.[10] By about 600 there was no one in Rome capable of reading the works of the Greek Church Fathers, and even Pope Gregory the Great (590-604), who had spent some time in Constantinople as papal nuncio, knew no Greek.[11] At Ravenna, the capital of the Byzantine exarchate, in the seventh century, no one could be found to write and translate the correspondence in

9. See Bischoff, *Manuscripts and Libraries*... 20-55 ('Manuscripts in the Age of Charlemagne'), 56-75 ('The Court Library of Charlemagne').

10. See P. Courcelle, *Les lettres grecques en Occident de Macrobe à Cassiodore*, Paris 1948, 389 ff.; E. Delaruelle, 'La connaissance du grec en Occident du Ve au IXe siècle', *Mélanges de la Société toulousaine*

Greek with the imperial court in Constantinople.[12] Although there were periods when Greek lessons were available either from private teachers or in monasteries, mainly in southern Italy, Greek was a closed book to the vast majority of scholars and educated people in the West – even to Petrarch, the pioneer of humanism[13] – until late in the fourteenth century.

2. The Greek world at the service of monastic learning: The Vivarium. Intellectual life in Italy during the transitional phase between the ancient era and the Middle Ages, that is towards the end of the fifth century, is epitomized by three nobly-born Italians: Boethius, St. Benedict and Cassiodorus. One of these tried to reconcile the Graeco-Roman intellectual tradition with Christian literature and theology and to establish an educational curriculum based on classical and Christian literature, and that was Cassiodorus.[14]

Cassiodorus was born at Squillace, southern Italy, in the year 468. When still only twenty years old he was taken into the service of Theodoric the Great, the powerful king of the Ostrogoths, and rose quickly to high office.[15] His father before him had been a member of Odoacer's court and he himself was appointed Governor of Sicily by Theodoric, in which position he amassed a huge fortune in landed property in Sicily and Calabria, to the extent that whole towns belonged to him. It was not long before Cassiodorus, with his broad education and diplomatic skills, became effectively Theodoric's chief minister, in sole charge of policy-making and the administration of the realm. He made it his business to implant in Theodoric his own love of the classics and instructed him in Platonic philosophy, so that the monarch would rule his kingdom in accordance with its precepts, and he also persuaded Theodoric's daughter Amalasuntha to take Latin lessons. The letters written by Cassiodorus as plenipotentiary of the Ostrogoth rulers prove that his efforts to raise the standard of education and introduce radical reforms, in collaboration with Boethius and Symmachus, had the support of the royal house. Unfortunately, however, Theodoric abandoned his allegiance to Byzantium and not only reversed these reforms but had Boethius and Symmachus judicially murdered.[16]

Nothing daunted, Cassiodorus pressed on with his campaign to reform the educational system, trying to force his proposals through from Rome. In collaboration with Pope Agapitus I, and taking as his model the Christian teaching practices adopted earlier in Alexandria, he founded a Christian 'university' in Rome in 535 or 536, an ill-chosen moment for enterprises of that sort. In the course of the war between the Ostrogoths and the Byzantine Empire, the Byzantine general Belisarius captured Rome in 536: the university was destroyed and the books collected by Cassiodorus were scattered far and wide.[17] Even after this grave setback, Cassiodorus, who had retired from public life and

d'études classiques 1 (1946) 207-226; J. Irigoin, 'La culture grecque dans l'Occident latin du VIIe au XIe siècle' in *Proceedings of the Settimana di Spoleto "La cultura antica nell' Occidente latino dal VII all' XI secolo" (1974)*, Spoleto 1975, 425 ff.

11. H. Steinacker, 'Die römische Kirche und die griechischen Sprachenkenntnisse des Frühmittelalters', *Mitteil. des Inst. für Oesterr. Geschichtsforschung* 62 (1954) 28-66.

12. See L.M. Hartmann, 'Johannicius von Ravenna' in *Festschrift für Theodor Gomperz*, Vienna 1902, 319-323.

13. See p. 215.

14. There is a vast literature on Cassiodorus and the Vivarium: see esp. Courcelle, *op. cit.*; A. Momigliano, 'Cassiodorus and the Italian Culture of his Time', *Proceedings of the British Academy* 41 (1955) 207-245.

15. See Courcelle, *op. cit.* 316.

16. Symmachus and Boethius were not prepared to admit that Rome's only remaining claim to fame was in the field of pillage and destruction. They had found a way of combining Christian faith with staunch devotion to all the practices of the ancient Roman pagan tradition: in fact Symmachus, the oldest of the advocates of the rebirth of learning, took Cato as his model and made a reputation for himself as the best orator of his day. See Momigliano, *op. cit.* 211-212; H.J. Rose, *Ἱστορία τῆς Λατινικῆς Λογοτεχνίας* (= *A Handbook of Latin Literature,* London 1967, tr. K.Ch. Grollios), II, Athens 1989, 245 ff. On Boethius see P. Courcelle, *La Consolation de Philosophie dans la tradition littéraire. Antécédents et postérité de Boèce*, Paris 1967.

17. See Courcelle, *Les lettres grecques...* 316; H.-I. Marrou, 'Autour de la bibliothèque du pape Agapit', *Mélanges d'Archéologie et d'Histoire de l'École Française de Rome* 48 (1931) 124-169.

18. On the school of Nisibis see N. Pigulevskaja, 'Istorija nisibijskoj Akademii, Istočiniki po istorii sirijskoj školy', *Palestinskij Sbornik* 17 (80) (1967) 90-109.

19. See A. van de Vyver, 'Cassiodore et son oeuvre', *Speculum* 6 (1931)

244-292; Courcelle, *Les lettres grecques...* 318 ff.

20. See A. van de Vyver, 'Les Institutiones de Cassiodore et sa formation à Vivarium', *Revue Bénédictine* 53 (1941) 59-88.

21. See Cassiodorus, *Institutiones*, ed. R.A.B. Mynors, Oxford 1937, 62, 13.

22. The fact that translations were made from Greek means that some of the monks at the Vivarium must have known Greek, and quite possibly it was spoken there on a par with Latin. The question whether the monastery was Greek-speaking or Latin-speaking remains open. See G. Rohifs, *Scavi linguistici nella Magna Grecia* in the series 'Collezione di studi meridionali', Halle/Rome 1933, 120-122; H. Pernot, 'Hellénisme et Italie méridionale', *Studi italiani di filologia classica* 13 (1936) 161-182; Courcelle, *Les lettres grecques...* 318 ff.

23. *Institutiones* I.30.1.

24. Very few manuscripts have been identified as having been written at the Vivarium or used there as prototypes for copying. One of these few is the famous Codex Amiatinus, containing the Bible, which has had an eventful history. It was written at the Vivarium, and one of its illuminations depicts Cassiodorus, probably in his library. Like many other manuscripts, it eventually found its way to Rome, where it was bought by the scholarly abbot Ceolfrid, perhaps in 678. When Ceolfrid returned to Northumbria he had this superb codex copied at Wearmouth or Jarrow. Later, when he was on his way back to Rome, he decided to present it to the Pope, but he died at Langres in 716 before reaching his destination. See R.L.S. Bruce-Mitford, 'The Art of the Codex Amiatinus' (Jarrow Lecture), *Journal of the British Archaeological Association,* 3rd ser., 32 (1969) 1-25.

25. An extant schoolbook embodying this approach to education is Ms Paris lat. 7530, probably written at the Abbey of Monte Cassino in the time of Paul the Deacon (during the eighth century). Among other things, the manuscript contains didactic poems and instruction on points of grammar.

164. Boethius in his library. Illumination in a fifteenth-century manuscript (Mâcon, Municipal Library, Ms 95, fol. 1).

switched his allegiance to the Byzantines, refused to abandon his original plan of founding a centre of learning in Italy, especially after being informed on a visit to Constantinople that just such a centre of Christian education existed at Nisibis in the Persian Empire.[18] But Rome, although now under Byzantine rule, was still under threat, so Cassiodorus decided to carry out his plan further south and established his school in the monastery called the Vivarium at Squillace, his birthplace, in 538.

Practically nothing is known about this monastery apart from its name and the fact that Cassiodorus did not impose the Rule of St. Benedict on the monks there. The Vivarium actually lasted as a monastery for only twenty-eight years, for it did not survive its founder's death.[19] However, we do know about its curriculum thanks to a treatise entitled *Institutiones divinarum et saecularium litterarum*, written by Cassiodorus in about 563 and based on the books in the monastic library.[20] It is clear from the introduction to the *Institutiones* that Cassiodorus was endowed with practical perceptiveness as well as visionary ideas, for he foresaw that in centuries to come, with the collapse of political institutions, monasteries would play an important part in preserving the Graeco-Roman tradition and would offer scholars and intellectuals a place of refuge. Although he had been influenced by Eastern thinking through Dionysius Exiguus, a pupil and dear friend of his who possessed an astonishing facility for translating from Latin into Greek and vice versa,[21] Cassiodorus had decided views of his own on what was the right kind of education for monasteries in the West. In his opinion, every monk who aspired to a thorough knowledge of the Scriptures had to be well versed in Graeco-Roman literature, and he was convinced that this familiarity could not be acquired from Latin literature alone: translations of Greek books on philosophy and other branches of learning were essential, too. Although opinions differ on what was the official language of the Vivarium monks, and although there cannot have been more than fifteen Greek manuscripts in the monastery library, it is an established fact that works by Origen, Clement of Alexandria, Epiphanius, Didymus, Socrates, Sozomenus, John Chrysostom and others were translated there.[22]

Cassiodorus was a great book-lover and liked books to be as encyclopaedic as possible: he did his best to see that this was true of his own books by binding together in one codex two or more works on related subjects, such as Cicero's *De Inventione*, Fortunianus's *Ars Rhetorica* and some of Quintilian's writings. He was also a stickler for accurate copying of manuscripts and often expressed his admiration for the work of those copyists – many of them anonymous – who lived up to his standards. As he said, 'Blessed is the intention and laudable the zeal of him who teaches men with his hand, opens their mouths with his fingers, offers salvation to mortals without speaking and fights the devil's false and iniquitous works with pen and ink.'[23]

See L. Holtz, 'Le Parisinus Latinus 7530, synthèse cassinienne des arts libéraux', *Studi Medievali*, 3rd ser., 16 (1975) 97-152. According to the educational philosophy and schooling system developed in late antiquity, grammar was the most basic of the seven 'liberal arts', the first step on the road leading to *divina sapientia*. Cf. p. 370.

26. See P. Lehmann, *Erforschung des Mittelalters*, III, Stuttgart 1960, 173-183 ('The Benedictine Order and the Transmission of the Literature of Ancient Rome in the Middle Ages'), 149-172 ('Deutschland und die mittelalterliche Überlieferung der Antike'). See also R. Pfeiffer, *Ausgewählte Schriften*, Munich 1960, 175-182 ('Humanitas Benedictina').

27. See Bischoff, *Manuscripts and Libraries*... 134-160 ('Benedictine Monasteries and the Survival of Classical Literature').

28. Isidore of Seville, the son of a Gothic king, was born at Cartagena in 570 and died at Seville in 636. Since the Goths had been in power in Spain for a century and a half before his birth, he was able to accomplish most of his plans from a position of power. His first concern was to found a school for the young. Then, in the course of his drive to promote Christian orthodoxy, he went to Rome to seek an audience with Pope Gregory the Great. He presided over the second Council of Seville in 619, and in 633 he attended the second Council of Toledo, where he argued strenuously against the Arian heresy. His most important written work, *Origines* or *Etymologiae*, can rightly be described as an encyclopaedia of medieval learning and one of the most significant works in the history of human knowledge. In it he explores the intellectual achievements of the most controversial period in the history of the Western world. In the sixth book he has a discursus on libraries (VI.3.3), in which he discusses Pisistratus and the library he founded in Athens as well

165. The Codex Amiatinus, a manuscript copied at Jarrow or Wearmouth Abbey, c. 700 (Florence, Biblioteca Laurenziana, Ms Amiatino 1).

When the monastery was closed, in about 575, its valuable collection of books was dispersed. Most of them probably went to the Lateran Library but subsequently vanished without trace through the negligence of some of the popes. Cassiodorus's *Institutiones* played a crucial part in shaping educational curricula during the Middle Ages, though higher education was less accessible than ever before. Cassiodorus was the last book-collector and private library owner of the Late Roman period in the West.[24]

3. Schools in the Middle Ages. With the disappearance of pagan schools and the failure of Cassiodorus's attempt to incorporate Graeco-Roman literature into the Christian school curriculum, education came to be entirely controlled by the Church. Such schools as were established, either in monasteries or attached to cathedrals, were regarded as training grounds for priests and monks. At first the number of pupils attending these schools was relatively small, but after a time the intake was enlarged by the admission of scions of the aristocracy and children of humble birth who wanted an elementary education. There were no standard textbooks, and so all teaching was based on such books as were available in each school's library or the teachers' private collections. It was the teachers, too, who decided on the syllabus, which was often structured around their own writings on the subjects that interested them. The children were taught to read and write, to memorize passages from the Psalms and other parts of the Bible, to explain the meaning of certain doctrinal writings – and that was all.[25]

The takeover of education by the Church did not augur well for the survival of classical studies. By the time St. Benedict drew up his Rule early in the sixth century, the classics were no longer being read – not even in Italy. All the books on the reading list for Benedictine monks had to do with the Bible and the religious life. That is one reason why so many works of Latin literature have been lost, as the Benedictine Rule was adopted by a great many monasteries in the West and had a formative influence on the Rules of later religious orders. We may be sure that St. Benedict's attitude to Latin literature was no accident: it came about as a result of a complex situation caused by historical circumstances.[26]

4. The decline of classical scholarship. In the seventh and eighth centuries the very survival of the classics was in danger except in northern Spain, where Catholicism survived the Arab invasion and what remained of Latin literature was passed on from generation to generation.[27] The rebirth of learning in the Visigothic kingdom was due mainly to the achievements of the greatest writer of that period in Spain, Isidore of Seville (*c.* 570-636), who not only exerted considerable influence on the transmission and interpretation of Graeco-Roman literature but was

as the Ptolemies' great library in Alexandria, drawing on Aulus Gellius, Athenaeus and probably Varro's lost work *De bibliothecis*. See J. Fontaine, *Isidore de Seville et la culture classique dans l'Espagne wisigothique*, 2 vols., Paris 1959. On the dissemination of his work see B. Bischoff, *Mittelalterliche Studien*, I, Stuttgart 1966, 174-194 ('Die europäische Verbreitung der Werke Isidors von Sevilla').

29. See Mirella Ferrari, 'Spigolature Bobbiesi', *IMU* 16 (1973) 23 ff.

166. Origen. Engraving from A. Thevet, Les vrais portraits et vies des hommes illustres, *Paris 1584.*

30. See E.A. Lowe, *Palaeographical Papers*, II, Oxford 1972, 480-519 ('Codices rescripti').

31. On the connection between the transmission of the stories of Alexander the Great and Apollonius of Tyre see M. Delbouille, 'Apollonius de Tyr et les débuts du roman français', *Mélanges offerts à Rita Lejeune*, II, Gembloux 1969, 1184 ff.

32. It is virtually impossible to determine just how knowledgeable the Irish were about Latin literature, with the result that opinions on the matter are often diametrically opposed. See, for example, E. Coccia, 'La cultura irlandese precarolina – miracolo o mito?', *Studi Medievali*, 3rd ser., 8 (1967) 257-420; L. Bieler, 'The Classics in Celtic Ireland' in R.R. Bolgar (ed.), *Classical Influences on European Culture, A.D. 500-1500*, Cambridge 1971, 45-49.

also a great book-lover, as one can see from the entry 'De Bibliothecis' in his *Etymologiae*.[28]

In the Merovingian kingdom, Gregory of Tours is the last writer whose works show traces of a classical education: after him we find no references to, or quotations from, any classical author. There are no surviving manuscripts of classical literature written during the period in question (the seventh and eighth centuries), whereas those on theological subjects are numerous. In Italy the situation was no different: the fact that works by Julius Valerius (*Res gestae divi Alexandri*) and Naucellius (epigrams) were copied at Bobbio around the year 700 is an exception to the rule.[29] It is significant that most palimpsests date from that period, that is from the late sixth to the early eighth century. As a result, numerous classical works – whole books as well as short works and fragments – were erased, including the 151 folios of Cicero's *De re publica* and the 194 folios of the work of Fronto.[30]

Evidently the predominant memory of ancient Rome that lingered in the minds of the people of pre-Carolingian Italy was of the Christians' persecution by the pagans, which forced them to seek refuge in monasteries. Their interest in classical literature was confined to certain works of practical usefulness and a few historical works, such as accounts of the life of Alexander the Great and the exploits of Aeneas (which appealed to the Franks because they believed they were descended from the Trojans) and the *Historia Apollonii regis Tyrii*.[31]

5. The Celtic and Anglo-Saxon worlds. Although conditions in Italy and in northern Europe were less favourable for the creation of private or public libraries than at any time before, a scholarly revival with a strong religious flavour which came into being, centred on Ireland, reinforced the connection between monasteries, scriptoria and libraries. A gradual re-evaluation of the ancient world occurred first among two peoples that had never been subject to Rome, the Irish and the British: in fact the Irish nation's proud tradition of scholarship invented a legend to explain how this happened.

When Rome was attacked by barbarian tribes such as the Huns, Vandals and Goths, so the story goes, the scholars from the regions under threat fled to Ireland, where they introduced the inhabitants to Latin literature. In the fifth century Christianity was brought to Ireland with the Latin language, which soon became indispensable to the leaders of the Irish church. Before long the monks there had progressed well beyond basic Latin grammar textbooks and were applying their minds to classical literature and the scriptures. The Irish were avid readers who devoured anything that might broaden their intellectual horizons and expand their general knowledge,[32] and they did not confine their activities to their own country: in their eagerness to visit other Christian countries, to win new converts to the faith and to carry their superb

33. See Bischoff, *Manuscripts and Libraries*... 14.

34. Columban's written works have been published in an edition by G.S.M. Walker, *Sancti Columbani Opera*, Dublin 1957. On the literary activity of the Irish see B. Bischoff, 'Il monachesimo irlandese nei suoi rapporti col continente' in *Settimane di studio del Centro italiano di studi sull'alto medioevo*, IV, Spoleto 1957, 121-138; Id., 'Wendepunkte in der Geschichte der lateinischen Exegese im Frühmittelalter', *Sacri Eruditi, Jaarboek voor Godsdienstwetenschappen* 6 (1954) 189-279. On Irish culture generally, see L. Bieler, *Irland, Wegbereiter des Mittelalters*, Olten 1961.

35. Luxeuil Abbey was one of the most influential monastic houses in the seventh century. The oldest extant manuscript from there, known as the Morgan Augustine, was written in 669, by which time the abbey's scriptorium had lost its Irish characteristics. See E.A. Lowe, 'The *Script of Luxeuil*: A title vindicated', *Revue Bénédictine* 63 (1953) 132-142. On St. Gall Abbey and its library see Ch. XVIII.

36. It is most interesting to note that Pope Vitalian appointed the Greek monk Theodore of Tarsus to be Archbishop of Canterbury, charged with the task of reforming the Anglo-Saxon church. Theodore's

167. A deacon teaching grammar, from N. Perottus, De disciplina scholarium, *Köln 1493.*

manuscript illumination skills further afield, they developed a fervent missionary zeal. In this way the Latin-based civilization of Ireland gradually spread to England and Scotland, and large monasteries were founded which became major centres of book production and did much to preserve the artistic and calligraphic traditions of manuscript copying: among them were the abbeys of Lindisfarne, Malmesbury and Iona, the last of which developed into one of the foremost centres of Celtic Christianity outside Ireland.[33] The man who spearheaded the movement to found monasteries with strong intellectual and artistic traditions was St. Columban (*c*. 543-615),[34] who left his mark not only on the island monasteries off the shores of Britain but on the continent as well, for he was responsible for the foundation of the abbeys of Luxeuil in Burgundy in 590 (the mother house of Corbie, founded a century later), Bobbio in Lombardy in 614 and St. Gall in Switzerland, which was founded by his pupil Gall (or Gallus) in about 613.[35]

Whereas the prevalent form of Christianity in northern England was that of the Irish, a different Christian culture with direct links to Rome sprang up in the south through the initiative of Pope Gregory the Great, who in 597 sent St. Augustine on a mission to Britain to convert the Anglo-Saxons. It was Augustine who made Canterbury the centre of Roman Christianity in Britain. About seventy years later Rome sent a second mission to Canterbury to reinforce its spiritual primacy over the whole of England. The missionaries, led by Theodore of Tarsus and Adrian of Niridanus, reached Canterbury in 668, having drawn up plans for a new educational system.[36] To judge by the number of books produced in England from then on, Theodore and his fellow-missionaries must have brought with them a good stock of works of Latin and Greek literature. Thereafter we find church dignitaries, and sometimes others, travelling to Rome and stopping on the way to buy manuscripts, which were then copied and recopied. Notable among them were Wilfrid (*c*. 634-709), Bishop of York and Abbot of Ripon; Aldhelm; and Benedict Biscop, the founder of the sister monasteries of Wearmouth (674) and Jarrow (682).[37]

The Irish passed on their missionary zeal to the Anglo-Saxons, who strongly favoured the creation of general libraries to provide the basis for the education of the clergy.[38] One consequence of this policy was the foundation and growth of important bishoprics in continental Europe, including those of Mainz and Würzburg, and of many new monasteries with libraries and scriptoria, such as Hersfeld, Reichenau, Murbach and Fulda.[39] And so, in the closing years of the eighth century – at the dawn of the first period of Byzantine humanism which was later to be dominated by Patriarch Photios – scholarship in the West was beginning to show signs of unity based on a common origin. Nor is there any doubt that in both the East and the West libraries, scriptoria and the book trade had been taken over by the clergy.

companion Adrian, too, had studied at Byzantine Carthage.

37. See Bischoff, *Manuscripts and Libraries*... 14; L.D. Reynolds and N.G. Wilson, *Ἀντιγραφεῖς καί Φιλόλογοι = Τό ἱστορικό τῆς παράδοσης τῶν κλασικῶν κειμένων*, (= *Scribes and Scholars: A guide to the transmission of Greek and Latin literature*, 2nd edn., London 1975, tr. N.M. Panayotakis), Athens 1981, 110.

38. See J.D.A. Ogilvy, *Books Known to the English*, Cambridge Mass. 1967.

39. On the libraries of these monasteries see Bischoff, *Manuscripts and Libraries*... 93-114. On the Anglo-Saxons' missionary activities in general see W. Levison, *England and the Continent in the Eighth Century*, Oxford 1946.

40. Charlemagne's biography (*Einhardi Vita Karoli Magni*, ed. G. Waitz, Hannover 1911) was written by Einhard, who taught at the school of the Frankish court and was also superintendent of the imperial buildings. It is Einhard who tells us, among other things, what provision Charlemagne made for the disposal of his library after his death (see pp. 409-410). The

168. Brother Lawrence, a monk of Durham, in a codex of 1149-1154.

169. The Irish manuscript Gospel book known as the Book of Durrow (Dublin, Trinity College, Ms A.IV.5, fol. 125v).

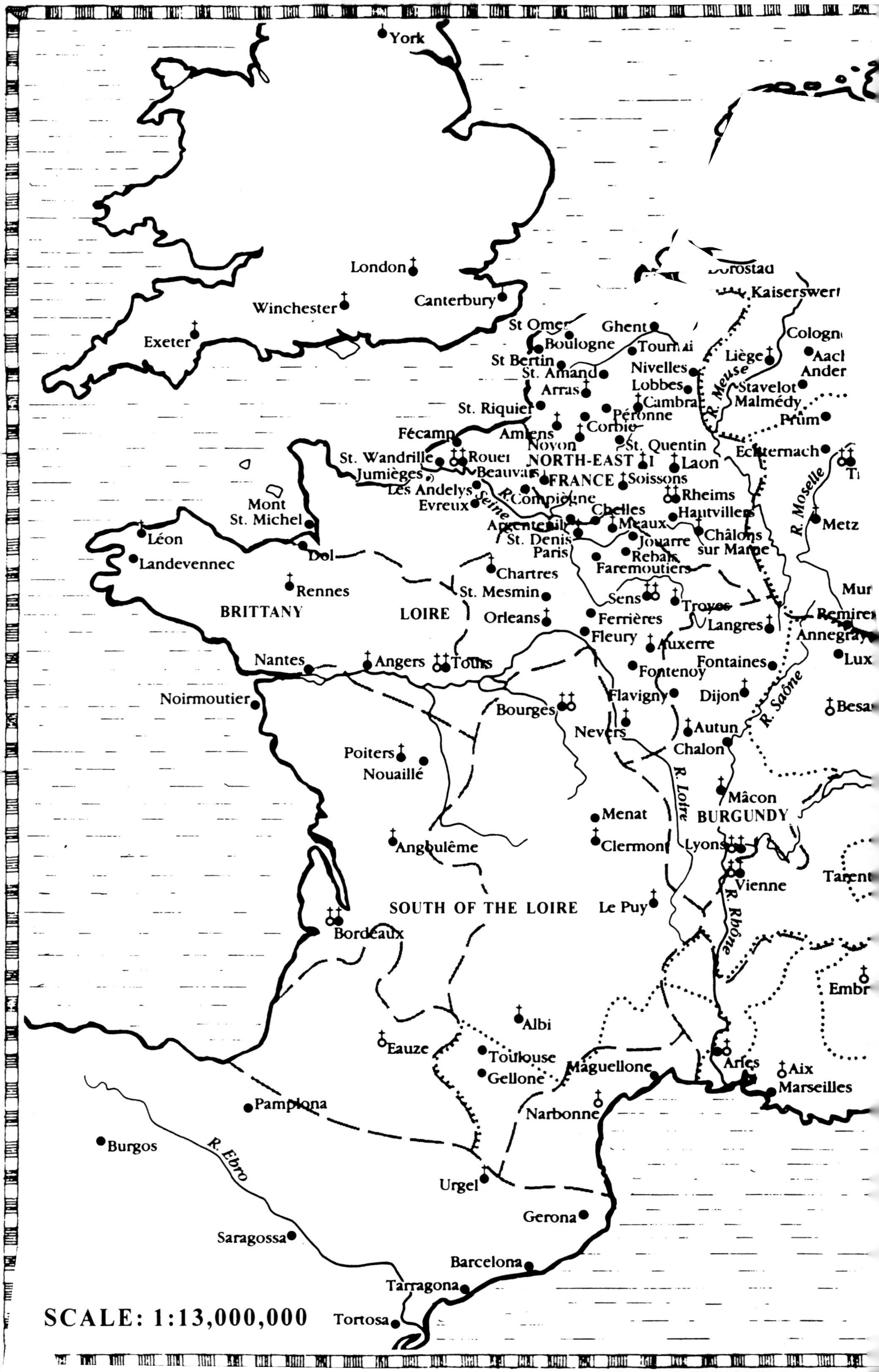
York
London
Winchester
Canterbury
Exeter
St Omer
Ghent
Boulogne
Tournai
St Bertin
Nivelles
St. Amand
Arras
Lobbes
Cambrai
St. Riquier
Péronne
Corbie
Amiens
Noyon
St. Quentin
Fécamp
St. Wandrille
Rouen
NORTH-EAST
FRANCE
Laon
Jumièges
Beauvais
Soissons
Les Andelys
Compiègne
Rheims
Evreux
Chelles
Hautvillers
Argenteuil
Meaux
St. Denis
Jouarre
Châlons sur Marne
Paris
Rebais
Faremoutiers
Mont St. Michel
Léon
Landevennec
Dol
Rennes
BRITTANY
LOIRE
Chartres
St. Mesmin
Orleans
Sens
Troyes
Ferrières
Langres
Fleury
Auxerre
Nantes
Angers
Tours
Fontaines
Fontenoy
Noirmoutier
Bourges
Flavigny
Dijon
Nevers
Autun
Chalon
Poiters
Nouaillé
Mâcon
Menat
BURGUNDY
Clermont
Lyons
Angoulême
Vienne
SOUTH OF THE LOIRE
Le Puy
Bordeaux
Albi
Eauze
Toulouse
Gellone
Maguellone
Arles
Aix
Marseilles
Narbonne
Pamplona
Burgos
Urgel
Gerona
Saragossa
Barcelona
Tarragona
Tortosa
Kaiserswert
Cologne
Liège
Stavelot
Malmédy
Prüm
Echternach
Metz
Annegray
R. Meuse
R. Moselle
R. Seine
R. Loire
R. Saône
R. Rhône
R. Ebro
SCALE: 1:13,000,000

MAP OF EUROPE
AT THE TIME
OF CHARLEMANGE
Archiepiscopal sees
Episcopal sees
N
Hamburg
R. Elbe
Bremen
Magdeburg
Hildesheim
Halberstadt
Corvey
Fritzlar
Hersfeld
Erfurt
Fulda
R. Main
Karlburg
Würzburg
Holzkirchen
Kitzingen
Lorsch
Ochsenfort
Amorbach
Tauberbischofsheim
Eichstätt
Regensburg
Niederaltaich
Weissenburg
Solnhofen
Schwarzach
Heidenheim
SOUTH-EAST
GERMANY
Passau
R. Danube
Honau
Augsburg
Freising
Chiemsee
Mondsee
Wessobrun
Salzburg
Staffelsee
Tegernsee
Kochel
Benediktbeuren
Reichenau
St. Gall
Kempten
Pfäfers
Chur
Disentis
NORTH-EAST
ITALY
Cividale
Aquileia
NORTH-WEST
ITALY
Milan
Verona
Novara
Venice
Cremona
Pavia
Tortona
R. Po
Bobbio
Nonantola
Ravenna
Genoa
Lucca
Florence
R. Arno
Ancona
Monte
Amiata
Perugia
Spoleto
R. Tiber
Farfa
Chieti
Rome
Monte
Cassino
Teano
Benevento
Capua
SOUTH ITALY
Naples
Salerno

II. The Carolingian renaissance. The term 'Carolingian renaissance' is generally taken to denote the period covering the last decades of the eighth century and the early decades of the ninth, roughly corresponding with the reign of Charlemagne (768-814).[40] Charlemagne succeeded in rebuilding an empire stretching from Rome to the far shores of France and from the Elbe to Spain, and, even though his successors proved unable to keep that empire intact, his cultural reforms lasted until the tenth century and the standardized educational system introduced in his reign remained unchanged until the time of the Italian Renaissance. His great love of books and writers sent the production and dissemination of books soaring to unimagined heights and led to the emergence of a scholar class with sizable private libraries. This revival of book learning had its origins in a programme of educational reforms decreed by Charlemagne, which was the brainchild of an unusually talented man, his adviser Alcuin.[41]

171. Illuminated initial copied by a Canterbury miniaturist in a Gospel book of c. *1130.*

1. Alcuin: Educational reforms and the revival of libraries. The springboard for any significant growth of the book-reading habit, which invariably leads to the creation of libraries, is the organization of education. Charlemagne had the brilliant idea of looking for the right person in York – even though it was far away in England – because it was the foremost educational centre at that time. Having found in Alcuin a man of great erudition with forward-looking ideas on education and the importance of libraries in that respect, in 782 he invited him to his court.

Alcuin, who liked to be known by his Latin name of Albinus and was nicknamed Flaccus at Charlemagne's court academy, was born at York in 735. He was educated at the York Minster school under the supervision of the renowned teacher Aelbert, with whom he later travelled to Rome to look for manuscripts. When his mentor was consecrated Archbishop of York in 766, Alcuin succeeded him as headmaster of the school. He made another journey to Rome in 780, and at Parma on his way home he met Charlemagne, who persuaded him to leave York and join his court, granting him the benefices of the two large abbeys of Ferrières and Saint-Loup (at Troyes). Charlemagne relied on Alcuin's ability and erudition to realize his ambition of raising the general standard of learning among the Franks by reorganizing the schools and introducing classical (especially Latin) literature to a wider readership. Alcuin undertook this task from 780 to 781. During that time he himself tutored the king, gave lessons to members of the royal family and the younger clergymen of the palace chapel, and was the inspirational leader of the so-called palace academy, as it is called in the *Dialogue* between Alcuin and Charlemagne's son Pépin.[42] Having acquired a good collection of books at Charlemagne's court, Alcuin went home to York in 781, but he did not stay long there because the king urgently needed him by his side to advise him on how to deal with the Autopianist heresy,

distinctive feature of the Carolingian renaissance is that it was spearheaded by churchmen: bishops and monks gladly fell in with the king's wishes, hoping to bring about a sweeping reorganization of diocesan schools, monasteries and presbyteries and so to raise the general standard of education among the clergy. Charlemagne himself dreamed of a unified Frankish kingdom, and that was why he threw

172. St. Matthew. The sole surviving leaf of a lost Irish Gospel book (St. Gall, Stiftsbibliothek, Cod. 1395, fol. 418).

173. *The Godescalc Evangelistary, copied for Charlemagne and his queen in 781. Paris, Bibliothèque Nationale, Ms Nouv. acq. lat. 1203, fol. 1r.*

which had a wide following in Spain. Alcuin brought a successful charge of heresy against Felix de Urgel and was rewarded by Charlemagne with the abbacy of the great Abbey of St. Martin at Tours. There, far from the bustle of the court, he spent the last years of his life transforming the abbey school into an exemplary scriptorium where highly skilled calligraphers produced manuscripts of rare beauty to his orders.

Besides imparting to the Franks his knowledge of the Latin literature that had survived in England from the time of Bede (673-735), the most learned man of his age, Alcuin was the author of a number of useful educational works. In addition to his letters and poems, some of the textbooks he used in his educational programme have survived to the present day, including a grammar and books on rhetoric and dialectics: the latter are written in the form of dialogues between Alcuin and the future King Charles. The influence that was exerted on Charlemagne's court by Alcuin and his pioneering work is apparent from the way libraries grew and developed during the Carolingian renaissance.

his weight behind the Pope and standardized the use of the Roman rite in the churches of the North. He ordered the churches and monasteries to renew their stocks of books and then to reform their schools, his objective being to revitalize non-Christian learning. This automatically created a demand for new books and meant that the rudi-

2. Libraries during the Carolingian renaissance. Charlemagne's keen interest in preserving the literary treasures of antiquity led to a revival of learning. Many new libraries came into being in his empire, while older collections of books in monasteries were thoroughly reorganized and expanded and their contents were evaluated afresh. In about 780 or a little earlier we find an unusual situation, with new libraries being opened and the well-known scriptoria being flooded with orders for more books. Charlemagne's policy of educational reform was not the only factor responsible for this trend, for by enlarging his own private library he set a personal example for imitation. Although the full catalogue of the court library has not survived, the list of manuscripts of Latin authors in the important grammatical codex Berlin Diez. B.66, compiled around 790, gives us a very good idea of what Charlemagne's library actually contained. Among the manuscripts listed were works by Statius, Lucian, Terence, Juvenal, Tibullus, Horace (*Ars Poetica*), Claudian (*De raptu Proserpinae*), Martial, Servius (*De finalibus*) and Cicero (*Ad Catilinam*, *Ad Verrem*, *Pro Deiotaro*). Besides serving the needs of the monarch and his court, these writings were used as exemplars for frequent copying, and thus there came into existence a corpus which was used for centuries thereafter by men of letters and students, and especially by teachers looking for reading matter for their pupils.[43]

It is a remarkable fact that three-quarters of all known Roman and early medieval grammar books have come down to us thanks to the educational programmes of Charlemagne's reign.[44] This means, of course, that the scriptoria remained active for about a hundred years after his death, as there were always some bishops in dioceses with cathedral schools, as well as high-minded abbots in monasteries, who maintained the level of interest in books.

Bernhard Bischoff came to the conclusion that it is almost impossible to deduce the exact contents of libraries in the Frankish and Lombard domains in the seventh and eighth centuries. Older libraries that had escaped destruction were not properly looked after, and the one that was started at Bobbio early in the seventh century – an extremely fine collection acquired at different periods, which contained 666 manuscripts by the tenth century – should be regarded as an exception.[45] The oldest library catalogue from northern Italy, perhaps dating from the seventh century, of which only a fragment survives, was probably the catalogue of an insignificant monastic library.[46] Consequently we are unlikely ever to know what was in the libraries founded on Charlemagne's initiative through the zeal of bishops and the abbots of so many monasteries in various parts of northern Europe.

Although a great deal could be written on this subject, there is only space here to take a brief look at some of the monastic libraries of the period. A point that is illustrated by the history of each one of them, as described in greater detail in the chapter on St. Gall (Chapter 18), is that the development of any monastic library depended mainly on the interests of individual abbots. Early examples of large monastic libraries are those of Corbie and Lorsch. Corbie,[47] which was administered by Charlemagne's cousin Adalhard (826), by 770 already possessed a considerable number of manuscripts dating from earlier centuries, some of which had been copied in its own scriptorium. The enterprising spirit of its library can be deduced not only from the fact that two different

mentary libraries in existence had to be transformed into dynamic centres for teaching and the dissemination of knowledge.

41. On Alcuin see G.J.B. Gaskoin, *Alcuin: His Life and His Work*, London 1903; on his relations with Charlemagne see L. Wallach, *Alcuin and Charlemagne*, Ithaca N.Y. 1959: this gives a good account of Charlemagne's aims in the field of education, which he himself set out clearly in a missive that he sent to Baugulf, Abbot of Fulda, between 794 and 800. On the role played by Alcuin's school in the palace see F. Brunhölzl, 'Der Bildungsauftrag der Hofschule' in B. Bischoff (ed.), *Karl der Grosse, Lebenswerk und Nachleben*, II: *Das geistige Leben*, Düsseldorf 1965, 28-41.

42. On Pépin's character see B. Simson, *Jahrbücher des fränkischen Reiches unter Ludwig dem Frommen*, II, Leipzig 1876.

43. See Bischoff, *Manuscripts and Libraries*... 56-75 ('The Court Library of Charlemagne'). See also pp. 409-410 herein.

174. A Premonstratensian monk. Illumination in a fourteenth-century manuscript (Besançon, Municipal Library, Ms 667, fol. 1).

175. The illustrious Dominicans Giovanni and Tommaso da Modena in their scriptorium. Fresco, 14th c. Treviso, Seminario Vescovile.

scripts were in use in the closing decades of the eighth century, but also from the presence there of works by Greek Church Fathers such as Basil the Great and Gregory of Nyssa, which attests to a renewal of the monks' interest in patristic writings.[48] Lorsch Abbey was founded much later than Corbie, in 764. The first group of copyists we can identify were active in the time of Abbot Richbod, who had been a pupil of Alcuin's at the court of Charlemagne around 780. Even though some manuscripts have probably been lost, at least twenty-five are known to have been written at the Lorsch scriptorium in Richbod's time.[49] Other important libraries of this period include those of Würzburg cathedral, whose catalogue of manuscripts dates from about 800, and of Reichenau Abbey, which had the most detailed catalogue of any medieval library. Mention should also be made of the libraries of St. Riquier, Murbach and Fulda abbeys: these, as well as other libraries of minor significance, played their part in preserving major works of classical literature and transmitting the tradition of manuscript writing and illuminating and the techniques of book production generally.[50]

From manuscripts in monasteries and cathedrals, let us turn now to a subject of great importance to the whole question of books and the formation of private libraries: the system devised for the production and distribution of university textbooks. This system, which had no precedent in the East, constitutes an essential difference between the otherwise similar paths taken in the development of libraries by the Byzantines and the peoples of Western Europe.

III. Books and libraries at the universities. The enormous growth of book production and the book trade in the last decades of the fifteenth century was due mainly to the fact that there existed in Western Europe a sizable section of the population for whom books were not merely a source of edification but a necessary tool of everyday living and often a person's sole livelihood. This phenomenon developed more or less simultaneously in Italy and the northern countries and was connected with the foundation of the first universities. One difference between the East and the West is that, although the Byzantine Empire had always had university-type institutions of higher education, mostly in Constantinople, we have no record of the way they were run, whereas there is no shortage of information about universities in the West. Much could be said about the universities' decisive contribution to the spread of learning and the flowering of the Renaissance, but there is only room to discuss certain aspects of the organization of the first universities, especially the new method of book production and distribution adopted in the universities, known as the *pecia* system.

1. The foundation of the first universities. The first independent institutions of higher education appeared in Western Europe in the late

44. Bischoff lists these manuscripts in *Manuscripts and Libraries*... 113-114.

45. On Bobbio Abbey see P. Collura, *Studi paleografici: La precarolina e la carolina a Bobbio* (= Fontes Ambrosiani, 22), Milan 1943, 143 ff.; P. Engelbert, 'Zur Frühgeschichte des Bobbieser Skriptoriums', *Revue Bénédictine* 78 (1968) 220-260; Ferrari, *op. cit.* 1 ff.

46. See W.M. Lindsay, *Notae Latinae*, Cambridge 1915, 489. On medieval libraries in Italy see J.W. Thompson, 'Libraries of Medieval Italy' in J.W. Thompson (ed.), *The Medieval Library*, Chicago 1939, 136-189.

47. See L. Delisle, 'Recherches sur l'ancienne bibliothèque de Corbie', *Mémoires de l'Institut National de France* 24 (1861) 267-342.

48. See Bischoff, *Manuscripts and Libraries*... 95-96.

49. See B. Bischoff, *Lorsch im Spiegel seiner Handschriften*, Munich 1974.

50. See Bischoff, *Manuscripts and Libraries*... 95 ff.

51. On the history of European universities see H. Rashdall, *The Universities of Europe in the Middle Ages*, ed. F.M. Powicke and A. Emden, 3 vols, Oxford 1936; J. Verger, *Les Universités au Moyen Âge*, Paris 1973; Id., 'Les universités françaises au XVe siècle', *Cahiers d'histoire* 21 (1976) 43-66; and the recent study edited by G.P. Brizzi and J. Verger, *Le università dell'*

twelfth and early thirteenth centuries. The transition from church-controlled to independent education was a process fraught with difficulties. In the early stages, these higher schools consisted of no more than small groups of students, with teachers who were neither paid a salary nor provided with accommodation, and with no library. The classrooms were usually rented by the teachers themselves, who relied on the money they were given by students from wealthy families, or on alms,[51] but sometimes rooms were offered to them by high-minded churchmen.

In the matter of university libraries there were even more difficulties to be overcome, as all the necessary books were in monastic libraries, which were firmly closed to the public and would never dream of lending out their precious manuscripts. There can be no doubt that the creation of an independent education sector proved very expensive to the originators of the idea; and although it was not long before teachers started enjoying certain privileges such as tax exemption, subsidized housing and a measure of legal immunity, those benefits were not enough to relieve them of the problems they faced in their everyday life.[52] However, once the universities established themselves on a firm footing they began to attract students from a wider spectrum of the lay population as well as substantial numbers of clerics wishing to acquire a scholarly grounding in theology and law.

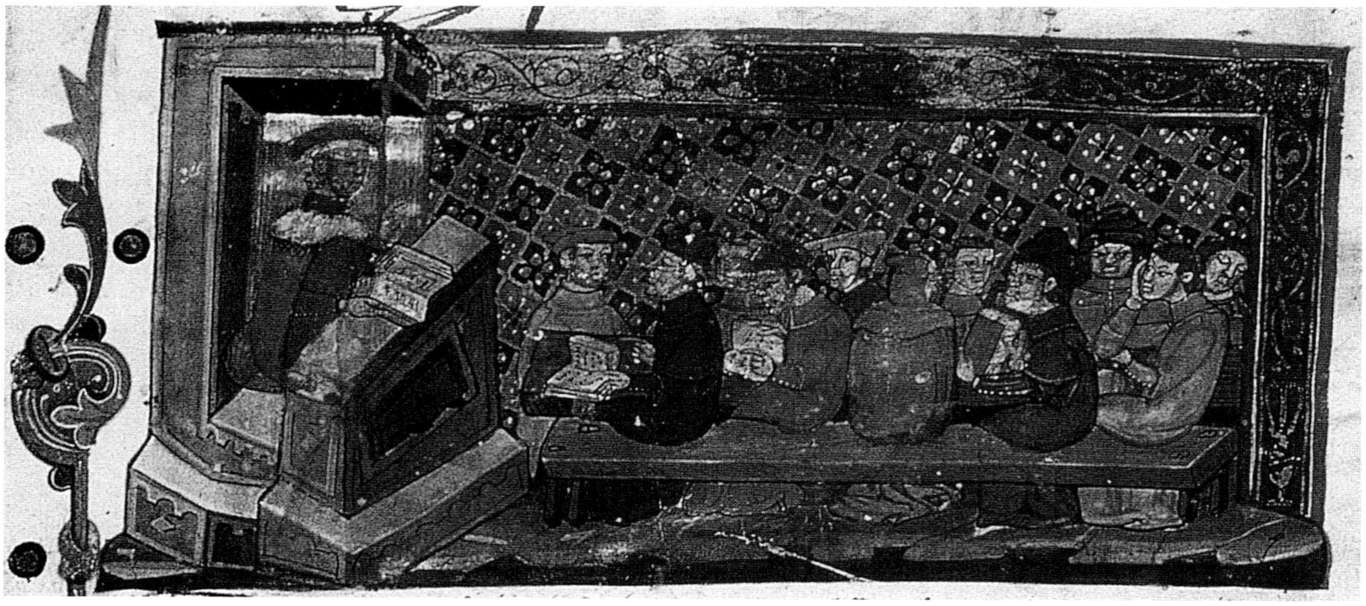

178. *A professor of law in his study. Illumination from a 14th-c. Bologna manuscript of the* Decretum Gratiani. *Leipzig, University Library, Ms Rep. 119b (CCXLIII), fol. 81v.*

176. St. Jerome in his study. Wall-painting by Tommaso da Modena. Treviso, Church of San Niccolò.
177. St. Augustine in his study. Wall-painting by Benozzo Gozzoli, 15th c. San Gimignano, Church of Sant' Agostino.

Europa. Le scuole e i maestri. Il Medioevo, Milan 1994.

52. See Marie-Henriette Jullien de Pommerol, 'Livres d'étudiants, bibliothèques de collèges et d'universités' in A. Vernet (ed.), *Histoire des bibliothèques françaises. Les bibliothèques médiévales du VIe siècle à 1530*, Paris 1989, 93-111.

53. See Jullien de Pommerol, *op. cit.* 93; M. Félibien and G. Lobineau, *Histoire de la ville de Paris*, V, Paris 1725, 690.

54. See M. Fournier, *Les Statuts et privilèges des universités françaises depuis leur fondation jusqu'en 1789...*, 4 vols., Paris 1890-1894, esp. II 614 (Jullien de Pommerol, *op. cit.* 93).

55. The standard work on the *pecia* system is J. Destrez, *La pecia dans les manuscrits universitaires du XIIIe et du XIVe siècle*, Paris 1935. For more recent research on the subject see L.J. Bataillon, B.G. Guyot and R.H. Rouse (ed.), *La production du livre universitaire au Moyen Âge. Exemplar et pecia (Actes du symposium tenu au Collegio San Bonaventura de Grottaferrata en mai 1983)*, Paris 1988. See also L. Gargan, 'Il libro per l'università' in Brizzi and Verger, *op. cit.* 73-97.

Would-be students who set their minds on improving their social status by getting a higher education at one of the universities needed enough money to cover not only their living expenses but also the necessary study aids, of which books were by far the most important: they had to have grammar books, textbooks of theology and law and, above all, a copy of the Bible. The regulations of the Collège de Séez in Paris, for example, required every student to possess a copy of the Bible from his first year and to obtain copies of the *Book of the Sentences* and the commentaries thereon in his second year.[53] It is true that the timetable for the acquisition of the books was so arranged that students who could not afford to buy them would be able to borrow them and copy them out, but the fact remains that books came to be high-priced necessities; and, as the universities expanded and grew more popular, the prices of books soon rose beyond the reach of many students. Fate has preserved some letters written by students to their parents, begging for money to buy a copy of the Bible or the *Corpus Juris Civilis*, or even *Grécisme* or the *Doctrinalis*.[54]

2. The *pecia* system. From the very outset, it was found that one of the biggest obstacles to the smooth running of the universities was the impossibility of ensuring that every student possessed all the necessary textbooks. A solution to the problem was devised almost simultaneously at the universities of Bologna and Paris, making it possible for books to be copied as cheaply, rapidly and flexibly as possible in conformity with strict specifications laid down by the university authorities.

It is known that bookshops (*stationes librorum*) existed in Bologna as early as the twelfth century, for a list of the city's inhabitants who accepted the peace treaty concluded in 1219

56. The indispensability of books to university students in the Middle Ages is illustrated by a story told by the great Odefred in the thirteenth century: according to him, the students of Alberico di Porta Ravegnana (known as the *antiquus doctor* of Bologna) used to invite their teacher to drinking parties in the hope of persuading him, when he was in his cups,

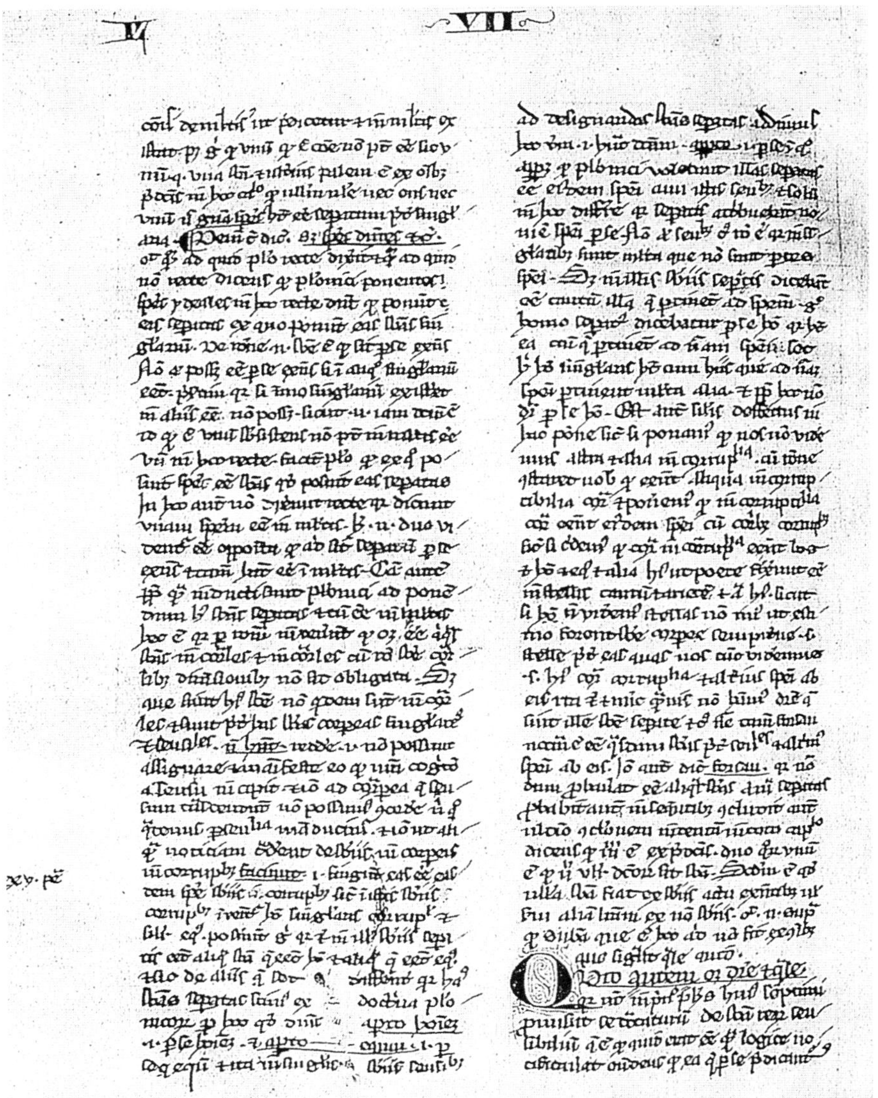

179. The Bible. Manuscript copied by a Dominican in Paris, 13th c. Paris, Bibliothèque Nationale, Ms Lat. 17232, fol. 752.

between Bologna and Pistoia contains the names of three booksellers (*venditores librorum*). Two of them had their shops in the San Procolo district of the city, where the law schools were situated. Bologna University had a number of booksellers officially attached to it: they were divided into two categories, *stationarii exempla tenentes* (or *stationarii peciarum*) and *venditores librorum*. The tradesmen in both these categories had the right to hire out fascicles of the various books on the university syllabus to any interested party – whether copyist, student or teacher – for a fixed charge. Those in the second category, the *venditores* or booksellers proper, were allowed by the university authorities to deal in books, in other words to act as middlemen finding buyers for old manuscripts or other educational books (*pecie*) which the owners wanted to sell.[55]

In 1275 or perhaps earlier, Bologna University decided to organize the *pecia* system and draw up a code of conduct to control its operation and the activities of the *stationarii*, and these regulations provided the model for those of the University of Paris.[56] The place where students and teachers could obtain the books they needed for their studies or their lectures was the scriptorium of the *stationarii*, which also functioned as a bookshop: in other words it was rather like a printing and publishing house, as university books were approved by the authorities of each university in accordance with the *pecia* system.[57]

So what exactly was the *pecia* system? Its *raison d'être* was to make university books affordable to students by breaking them down into their separate chapters, which were published as fascicles. In this way book prices were considerably reduced by the saving on parchment costs and copying expenses, with no loss of quality. To prevent confusion, each fascicle had the number of the next instalment written in the margin. What we have here is an admirable organization for the supply of university books, conforming to the highest academic standards and designed to even out social inequalities. In accordance with the best kind of humanist philosophy, it gave exactly the same opportunities to all, as every student or teacher could choose between buying the whole book in codex form, buying only the fascicle (*pecia*) that he needed for that term's syllabus, or borrowing the necessary fascicle to copy out for himself, with the option of selling it when he had finished with it.[58]

Having seen how the biggest problem facing the early universities – the publishing of university books – was resolved in the best possible way, and having examined the conditions governing the acquisition of books by medieval students, let us now consider how university libraries developed and to what extent they served the needs of the universities.

3. University libraries. The institution of the *pecia* system did not automatically result in the creation of a university library, because books were still extremely expensive, even though by this time the universities possessed the facilities necessary for book production. The few books that were actually owned by a university were usually handed over to the Rector or one of the professors for safe keeping. They were not the common property of all: they were assets belonging to the university. Eventually, with the development of the universities and the natural decline of colleges and other educational establishments with only rudimentary libraries, the situation altered, as philanthropists seeking a posthumous claim to fame began donating or bequeathing their books to universities. A typical example was the donation from Robert de Sorbon and Gérard d'Abbeville that led to the foundation of one of the richest libraries in Europe, that of the Sorbonne. This donation is worth discussing at greater length, as the information available about this particular case enables us to draw some general conclusions.[59]

Maître Robert de Sorbon (1201-1274), a clergyman at the court of Louis XI, had spent many years studying theology at the University of Paris, despite the sacrifices that he had to make because his family was not rich. Moved by his own experience of student life, he later founded the College of the Sorbonne with the aid of wealthy patrons. The College, dedi-

180. A Paris University manuscript showing the use of the pecia *system. 13th c. Paris, Bibliothèque Nationale, Ms 14706, fol. 122v.*

... hec glo. est de supplemento

... non sunt illa tempora ... legem ...

[F]uit missus est homo in testimonium ut lucas ... ipsa lux i. verbum factum caro qui nutritum in lac xpi parvulos. Sufficientia enim ... non possumus nostra a parvulis.

b. beda. In principio omnium creaturarum ut temporum i. cum inciperent omnes creature vel ipsa iam erat verbum.

In principio i. in patre qui est principium sine principio illius qui est principium de principio ... ab ipso omnia habent principium existendi.

Alii evangeliste describunt xpm natum temporaliter. Iohannes affirmat eum fuisse in patre ut in principio non fuerat an pater quin filius esset filius alia persona a patre una substantia cum patre.

Aug. Non est creatura per quam omnis creatura facta est. Malum non est factum per ipsum verbum quia nichil sunt et nulla sua natura subsistunt.

Ea que sunt per ipsum facta sunt. Alia autem sunt que a natura ipsa non recedunt ... divinitatis.

Sed ... ita distinguit: sine ipso factum est nichil quod factum est ...

faber prius facit archam in mente ... in mente est vivit cum artifice ... mutatur cum ipsa.

Ipsum dicit ut nec ... solem super se lucentem.

homo non angelus ut ... lucem missus a deo ideo non potuit dicere de deo.

Iohannes i. gratia dei qui vocatur a gratia ... predicat.

In principio erat verbum et verbum erat apud deum et deus erat verbum. Hoc erat in principio apud deum. Omnia per ipsum facta sunt et sine ipso factum est nichil. Quod factum est in ipso vita erat et vita erat lux hominum et lux in tenebris lucet et tenebre eam non comprehenderunt. Fuit homo missus a deo cui nomen erat Iohannes. Hic venit in testimonium ut testimonium perhiberet

Cum substantivum verbum duplicem habeat significationem. Aliquando enim qualitatem motus secundum analogiam aliorum verborum declarat. Aliquando substantiam uniuscuiusque rei de qua predicatur sine ullo temporali motu designat. Ideo et substantivum vocatur; tale est quod dicitur In principio erat verbum ...

Quater ponitur erat substantivum verbum ut intelligas omnia tempora precessisse eternum patris verbum.

Verbum non prolatum sed semper apud eum manens scilicet sapientia ...

... et deus erat verbum. Alii inter homines subito apparuisse, Iohannes dicit apud deum semper fuisse. Alii eum hominem, Iohannes verum deum asserit dicens et deus erat verbum. Alii eum hominem ... Iohannes apud deum manentem dicit: hoc erat in principio apud deum. Alii dicunt in ... que fecit homo in mundo; Iohannes omnia per ipsum facta testatur: Omnia per ipsum facta sunt. Ecce auctor bonorum; sine ipso factum est nichil: non est auctor malorum.

Aug. Si audis mutabilem creaturam per verbum factam non credas esse mutabilitatem voluntatis qui non subito aliquid voluit facere set omnia ab eterno ... in immutabili est ...

Post ... sublimi volatu ultra omnem naturam in altitudinem theologie ascendit quod verbum semper apud patrem fuisse contemplatus est. Mox ad humanitatem humane nature reparande ... descendit contra illos qui dicebant humanam naturam in primo parente perditam et ad nichilum redactam ita ut irreparabilis esset.

hic missus est hic venit in testimonium.

Omnis homo creatur illa natura in homine que ad ymaginem et similitudinem dei ...

... Supple quia ...

... verbum ... qui est res ... in principio ... glo.

cated by de Sorbon *aux maîtres en théologie pauvres*, opened its doors in 1275 and quickly outstripped all the other colleges, chiefly by virtue of its superior organization and mode of operation. It was run along the lines of an academy and the members of the theology faculty lived communally with their students, as in monasteries, the only difference being that they were subject to regulations rather than rules.[60]

From the very earliest years of the college's existence, the library played an important part in its life; and the first donations to enlarge its stock showed that the Parisians had come to appreciate the importance of books in education.[61] It is not known whether Robert de Sorbon bequeathed any books in his will to provide an initial nucleus of books for the use of the college, but if so there could not have been very many of them. At all events, by 1290, by which time we have a global picture of the College of the Sorbonne, the library contained one of the best collections of books in Europe and certainly the biggest in Paris. The fact that de Sorbon was a prominent member of Louis XI's court and that the college stood high in the King's favour attracted the notice of potential benefactors, such as Robert de Donai, Queen Marguerite's physician, who gave the college 1,500 livres to buy books for the students. Although we do not know exactly how many books the Sorbonne library contained at any given time, it is said to have doubled in size on the bequest of three hundred books by its co-founder, Gérard d'Abbeville, in 1272. About the same number of volumes was donated by the avid bibliophile Richard de Fournival, the author of *Bibliomania*.[62] The example of these two great benefactors was followed by many others, whose donations ranged from large collections to single volumes.

To sum up the developments that took place in the Middle Ages, we have seen how the *librarii* were superseded by churchmen, who monopolized book production and education; how in the early thirteenth century books, libraries and learning were taken back into the hands of the laity; and how the foundation of universities at about this time prepared the way for the Renaissance. And before closing this chapter I should like to revert to the subject of Richard de Fournival, who, in his book *Bibliomania*, presents an allegorical picture of the distinctive characteristics of every branch of knowledge – an approach that was the foundation of all higher studies during the Renaissance. In what is clearly intended as an admonition to his fellow-citizens, de Fournival describes secular literature and learning as an elaborately laid-out garden in which each branch of knowledge has its prescribed place. This elaborate garden described by de Fournival – a refuge of the kind that Cicero found essential to his peace of mind, and which Petrarch, who greatly admired that prince of Roman orators, tried to revive – is the common denominator demonstrating the feeling of love and respect for books and libraries that is to be found in every period.

to lend them his books to copy. See Gargan, *op. cit.* 82.

57. *Ibid*. 73, 75.

58. See R.H. and M.A. Rouse, 'The Book Trade at the University of Paris, ca. 1250-ca. 1350*' in Bataillon et al., *La production du livre universitaire...* 41-114, which answers a

181. Medical students attending a lecture. Illumination from an early 14th-c. Bologna manuscript of Guglielmo da Saliceto, Cyrurgia. *Paris, Bibliothèque Nationale, Ms Lat. 14731, fol. 2r.*

number of questions relating to disputes between *librarii* and *stationarii* and the university's supervision of the booksellers and publishers.

59. See R.H. and M.A. Rouse, 'La bibliothèque du collège de la Sorbonne' in Vernet, *Histoire des bibliothèques françaises* 113-123.

60. *Ibid*. 113.

61. See R.H. Rouse, 'The Early Library of the Sorbonne', *Scriptorium* 21 (1967) 42-71.

62. See P. Glorieux, 'Études sur la *Bibliomania* de Richard de Fournival', *Recherches de théologie ancienne et médiévale* 30 (1963) 205-231.

182. The Collegio Borromeo at Pavia. View of the inner court from the upper loggia.

CHAPTER ELEVEN

THE RENAISSANCE

The rediscovery and re-evaluation of the ancient world – a process that spread from one European country to another and has come to be known as the Renaissance – brought back the familiar atmosphere of books and libraries that had existed in ancient Athens, Alexandria and Rome. The achievements of the Renaissance produced two innovations in the field of books and libraries: in the first place, it again became possible for private individuals – and not only the rich – to acquire their own book collections; and secondly, the unprecedented scale of book production and distribution led to radical changes in the architectural design and style of public libraries. Both these innovations resulted from the revolutionary impact of printing on the traditional method of reproducing books. In this chapter we shall concentrate on the humanist world, because it is there that we can get the clearest insight into the contemporary conception of a library's role in society.

I. Humanism. The idea of acquiring collections of Graeco-Roman literature was first revived by humanists, whose admiration of the ancient world was heightened every time they discovered a lost or forgotten classical work. Petrarch, who rescued the great classical poets from oblivion in the mid fourteenth century, is generally considered to have been the first to instil a love of the classics in the Italians, but a group of lawyers with scholarly interests had made a move in this direction nearly a hundred years earlier.

1. The first humanist libraries. Lovati and his circle. The dominant figure in the group was Lovato Lovati (1241-1309), a judge from Padua,[1] who was an authority on Latin poetry and was highly regarded as a poet himself. Lovati had an extraordinary instinct for tracking down valuable manuscripts. By searching through the great medieval libraries of the cathedral cities around Padua, such as Verona and Pomposa, and elsewhere in northern Italy, he acquired manuscripts of Lucretius, Propertius, Martial and Catullus. Two others who shared Lovati's humanistic interests and spent much of their spare time editing works of Latin literature were the notary and poet Albertino Mussato (1262-1329) and the Vicenza notary Benvenuto Campesani (1255-1323), the procurator of Verona cathedral, who had direct access to the excellent diocesan library.[2]

Petrarch. From that early circle of humanists the path leads directly to Petrarch (Francesco Petrarca, 1304-1374), who in 1318, after learning all he could from the grammarian Convenole da Prato, went to Montpellier to study law and the classics.[3] At a time when manuscripts of Latin literature were hard to find, he managed to lay his hands on copies of works by Cicero and Virgil. When his father discovered the books that Francesco had secretly brought into the house, he threw them on to the fire in a rage, though in the face of the young scholar's heart-rending cries he relented just enough to let him keep two books: a copy of Virgil and one of Cicero's rhetorical works.[4]

1. See G. Billanovich, *I primi umanisti e le tradizioni dei classici latini*, Freiburg 1953; Id., 'Veterum vestigia vatum', *IMU* 1 (1958) 155-243.

2. See A.Ch. Megas, «Ὁ προουμανιστικός κύκλος τῆς Παδούης (Lovato Lovati - Albertino Mussato) καί οἱ τραγωδίες τοῦ Σενέκα», *Ἐπιστημονική Ἐπετηρίς Φιλοσοφικῆς Σχολῆς Πανεπιστημίου Θεσσαλονίκης* 11 (1967) 229-233 (English summary).

3. G.G. Forni, 'F. Petrarca scolare a Bologna', *Atti e Memorie della Academia Petrarca di Lettere, Arti e*

183. Petrarch at his writing-desk. Drawing, after a manuscript illumination by Francesco di Antonio del Chierico. 15th c.

Petrarch was so fascinated by the ancient Romans and so eager to emulate them that he set out to bring the ancient world back to life, taking his models from their own works and the accounts of their lives. His years spent in Avignon, which was the seat of the papacy from 1309 to 1377, played a formative role in the development of his internationalist outlook, for not only did the cultural barriers between North and South begin to crumble during that time, but it was then that the differences of intellectual outlook and orientation between the papal court and the prelates of the Church in France began to emerge.[5] Italian scholars seized the opportunity to find out about the manuscripts available in the intellectual and religious centres of the North and visited libraries, cathedrals and monasteries in France and Germany, where they sometimes discovered rare codices dating from Charlemagne's reign. Avignon served as their base for forays to illustrious abbeys such as Fulda, Hersfeld, Reichenau, Murbach and, of course, St. Gall. Some indication of the surge of interest in finding and collecting works of classical and Christian literature is given by the fact that the library built up by John XXII and Clement VI in the papal court at Avignon eventually contained no less than 2,400 codices.[6]

Petrarch's is the first large private library of this period of whose contents we have any record. Fortunately for us, the existence in Paris of a codex containing marginal notes written in Petrarch's own hand enables us to deduce his literary tastes – though this record covers only those works that he possessed as a young man, and quite possibly his interests changed as he grew older. Topping his list is Cicero, followed by Seneca the Philosopher (especially his *Epistulae Morales*) and the historians Valerius Maximus and Livy, while Aulus Gellius and Macrobius were also among the writers he took as his exemplars. Then come the poets – Virgil, Lucretius, Lucan and Statius – and last of all the grammarians, rhetoricians and astronomers. The only Greek work he mentions is Aristotle's *Ethica*, which he probably knew in a Latin version translated by one of the Averroists.[7] Petrarch must have written these notes before 1364, when Nikolaos Sigeros, an official envoy from the Byzantine Emperor to the papal court at Avignon, gave him a copy of the *Iliad*, which he kissed reverently (though he admitted that he could not read it in the original, saying, 'Homerus tuus apud me mutus').[8]

Petrarch, who had a boundless admiration for Cicero and had learnt from him that the Greeks were not only consummate writers but also a race that epitomized the concept of humanity or humanism (*genus humanissimum*), tried to give his reading rooms an atmosphere of learning similar to that of the great Roman orator's libraries. It was his belief – which he expounded in his book *De vita solitaria* (1346-1366) – that solitude was essential for any really worthwhile intellectual activity. Petrarch is known to have had a room that he used as a study in two of his homes: at Vaucluse, near Avignon,[9] and at Arquà, near Padua.[10] In

Scienze, n.s., 37, Anni 1958-1964 (1965) 83-96. On Petrarch's contribution to the humanist movement see M.P. de Nolhac's invaluable book *Pétrarque et l'Humanisme*, 2 vols., Paris 1907. The standard work on his life is E.H. Wilkins, *Life of Petrarch*, Cambridge Mass. 1961. For a literary evaluation of his work and much other useful information see R. Pfeiffer, *'Ιστορία τῆς Κλασσικῆς Φιλολογίας. Ἀπό τό 1300 μέχρι τό 1850* (= *History of Classical Scholarship: From 1300 to 1850*, tr. P. Xenos et al.), Athens 1980, 1-19.

4. De Nolhac, *op. cit.* I 221; B.L. Ulman, 'Petrarch's Favorite Books', *TAPA* 54 (1923) 21-38.

184. Petrarch at his writing-desk. Drawing, late 14th c. (Darmstadt, Hessische Landes- und Hochschulbibliothek, Ms 101, fol. 1v).

5. On the importance of Avignon in the transmission of manuscripts to Italy, see B.L. Ulman, 'Studies', *Philological Quarterly* 20 (1941) 213-217; W.B. Ross, 'Giovanni Colonna, Historian at Avignon', *Speculum* 45 (1970) 535-545.

6. The papal library at Avignon was situated on the fourth floor of the Tour des Anges, while the Pope's private study in the Tour de la Garde-Robe communicated with the papal

185. Aristotle reading his Logica. *Engraving from P. Gringore,* Les menus propos..., *Paris P. Le Noir, 1525.*

suite on the third floor of the Tour des Anges. The library, which occupied one half of the fourth floor, had built-in cabinets to hold the books, and the whole of this small room was decorated with naturalistic designs: see E. Müntz, *Les arts à la cour des papes pendant le XVe et le XVIe siècle: Recueil des documents inédits*, III, Paris 1878, 118-120. For further information about the library see J. Monfrin and M.H. Jullien de Pommerol, *La Bibliothèque pontificale à Avignon et à Peniscola pendant le Grand Schisme d'Occident et sa dispersion*, Rome 1989; Id., 'La bibliothèque pontificale à Avignon au XIVe siècle' in A. Vernet (ed.), *Histoire des bibliothèques françaises. Les bibliothèques médiévales du VIe siècle à 1530*, Paris 1989, 146-169.

7. Ulman, 'Petrarch's Favorite Books' 21-28. See also A. Petrucci, *La scrittura di Francesco Petrarca*, Vatican City 1967; B. Guillemain, *La cour pontificale d'Avignon (1309-1376). Étude d'une société*, Paris 1962.

8. See A. Pertusi, *Leonzio Pilato fra Petrarca e Boccaccio*, Venice/Rome 1979, 62 ff.

9. See *Francesco Petrarca, Prose*, ed. G. Martellotti, Milan/Naples 1955, 285-591. On Petrarch's house at Vaucluse see M. Mignon, 'La maison de Pétrarque à Vaucluse', *Études italiennes* 9 (1927) 215-235; W. Liebenwein, *Studiolo: Storia e tipologia di uno spazio culturale*, tr. A. Califano, Ferrara/Modena 1988, 32-37.

De vita solitaria he tells us that at Vaucluse he had two gardens – one formal and ornamental, dedicated to Apollo, and the other more or less in its natural state, dedicated to Bacchus – where he used to read, write and meditate. At Arquà his study was a room on the second floor with two windows looking out over the garden: its walls were decorated with

186. Petrarch's house at Arquà. Drawing by J.F. Tomasini, 1635.

naturalistic motifs and the books were kept in two alcoves, one on each side of his desk. His library, which he called the *biblioteca* or *armarium*, was the room where he used to entertain his official guests, and it was there that he died while writing a commentary on Homer.[11] Petrarch was the first humanist to envisage his private library as an asset belonging to the whole community: he intended it to form the nucleus of a future Venetian public library.[12]

Giovanni Boccaccio. Another man who did much to develop the idea of forming a humanistic library was a contemporary of Petrarch's, Giovanni Boccaccio (1313-1375). Born in Paris, the son of an Italian merchant, he abandoned a career in commerce and also gave up the study of canon law which he had started in Naples.[13] He then turned his hand to writing and became highly successful with his most famous collection of stories, published in one volume as *The Decameron*, as well as many other stories that were extremely well received by the merchants of Florence.[14] Boccaccio was a great collector of historical facts, especially those relating to ancient Roman literature, and his instructive treatises enjoyed great popularity throughout the Renaissance. He must have had a large private library, to judge by the fact that he bequeathed over a hundred manuscripts to the Monastery of Santo Spirito in Florence.[15] He also worked as a copyist and was one of the first people to be allowed into the library of the Abbey of Monte Cassino, which was very influential during the Middle Ages.[16] Boccaccio was instrumental in having the Monte Cassino library opened up to lay scholars: in it he discovered unknown works by Cicero, Varro and Apuleius, and saw to it that copies of them were sent to Petrarch.[17]

Leonzio Pilato. Before moving on from the early humanist period of renewed interest in books, a word should be said about Leonzio Pilato (†1364), a Greek from Calabria.[18] In about 1360, when he was passing through Florence on his way to Avignon, he received an offer from the Florentine authorities of an official post as a Greek teacher, which he found too tempting to resist; so he gave up the idea of going on to Avignon and stayed there, rendering sterling service to the cause of classical literature. Pilato evidently had a collection of books of his own, which he used in his teaching. He was the first person to translate the whole of Homer into Latin, which he did for Boccaccio; and he also translated Euripides's *Hecuba* and some of Plutarch's *Lives*. He and Boccaccio were the only two scholars in the West who knew Greek until 1396.

The year 1396 marks the dawn of a new era in the history of classical studies and libraries generally. It was then that Greek started to be taught systematically in Italy, preparing the way for a return to Caesar's cherished principle that every Latin library should be paired with a library of Greek books. From the beginning of the fifteenth century, scholars and princes embarked on a campaign for the propagation of the humanist ideals formulated by Greek philosophers and extolled in Latin literature. Manuscripts were hunted down and every work that was found, from the Pre-Socratic period to the end of the ancient era, was copied out and carefully stored away. This movement, which lasted for over a century in Italy and spread to the North from the early decades of the sixteenth century, led to the emergence of libraries of two kinds: those belonging to private individuals and those of the ruling princes. Between them, these largely superseded the monastic libraries.

2. The revival of the bilingual library. When the first large private humanist libraries were formed early in the fifteenth century, there were clear signs that bilingual libraries were on their way back into favour. It was equally clear that there were no booksellers or scriptoria to meet the needs of this trend. Initially, the gap was filled by the advent of a new

10. See A. Callegari, 'La casa del Petrarca in Arquà ed il suo ultimo restauro', *Atti e Memorie della R. Accademia di Scienze, Lettere ed Arti di Padova*, n.s., 11 (1924-1925) 211-257.

11. De Nolhac, *op. cit.* I 50, 70, II 167.

12. See p. 321.

13. For information on Boccaccio's life see N. Sapegno, 'Boccaccio, Giovanni' in *DBI* 10 (1968) 836-856; Pfeiffer, *op. cit.* 23-28.

14. The merchants of Florence made great efforts to improve their minds by reading the classics and contemporary literary works: see pp. 232-233 n. 86. Other popular works by Boccaccio, besides *The Decameron*, included *Corbacio*, *Filosofo*, *Fiammetta* and *Amorosa Visione*. Cf. V. Branca, *Tradizione delle opere di Giovanni Boccaccio*, Rome 1958.

15. Boccaccio actually bequeathed his books to a monk named Martino da Signa: see A. Goldmann, 'Drei italienische Handschriften-Kataloge s. XIII-XV', *Centralblatt für Bibliothekswesen* 4 (1887) 142-155. On the manuscripts of Boccaccio's that ended in Niccolò Niccoli's collection see O. Hecker, *Boccaccio-Funde*, Braunschweig 1902.

16. See Cornelia C. Coulter, 'Boccaccio and the Cassinese Manuscripts of the Laurentian Library', *Classical Philology* 43 (1948) 217 ff.

17. His pupil Benvenuto Ramboldi da Imola tells us that on Boccaccio's first visit to the Monte Cassino library he was so horrified by the

187. Sappho. Engraving from an edition of Boccaccio by Johann Zainer, Ulm 1473.

breed of scholar-publisher-bookseller not unlike those of bygone times, such as Hermodorus, who copied out works by his teacher, Plato, and sold them in places far away from Athens. During the Renaissance that role was taken chiefly by humanists who travelled all over Italy and northern Europe and even as far as Constantinople, to study Greek, and were able to make some money for themselves by peddling Latin and Greek manuscripts. Thus we have parallel paths for the formation of private humanistic libraries: aristocratic and other cosmopolitan libraries; humanistic libraries intended for private and/or educational use; and the libraries of booksellers and publishers intended for their professional use. We shall be looking at all three of these categories, paying attention to the personalities and activities of some prominent individuals in whom they are exemplified, starting with Coluccio Salutati and Niccolò Niccoli.

Coluccio Salutati (1331-1406) initiated a new pattern of social conduct, and in his capacity as Chief Secretary to the Signoria or Florence he made a great reputation for himself by the style of his letter-writing.[19] His position of power, which he held for about thirty years, gave him an opportunity to pursue his Latin studies systematically, and with the inauguration of regular Greek teaching in Florence in 1397 he gave to the humanist spirit the basic elements of classical literature. At the same time he supported the new merchant class, which in its turn formed a new social substructure that helped the humanist movement to become established.[20] It was on his initiative that Manuel Chrysoloras came to Florence to teach Greek at the Studium, while there, Chrysoloras introduced his own method of translating Greek literature into Latin.[21]

When not engaged on his official duties, Salutati found the time to study and copy manuscripts, for example Seneca's tragedies. Although his literary commentaries cannot be compared with Petrarch's marginal notes, his collection of manuscripts was important to the scholars of Florence. Among his possessions were copies of Cicero's letters, including the *Epistulae ad familiares*, which were unearthed at Salutati's prompting by Pasquino Cappelli, the Chancellor of Milan, in the library of Vercelli cathedral. So far more than a hundred manuscripts from Salutati's collection have been identified.[22]

Niccolò Niccoli. The first Renaissance man in whom we can discern a *modus vivendi* similar to that of the patricians in Cicero's time is Niccolò Niccoli (1363-1437),[23] a Florentine aesthete of exquisite taste. Niccoli lived in his own world, surrounded by all sorts of antiques and mementoes of the past, always busy copying manuscripts, collecting and collating, adding titles and paragraphs. Although he did not travel as much as Poggio, he was able to give the Medici family's agents invaluable information and guidance as to the whereabouts of manuscripts, especially in the monasteries of the North. He eventually amassed a collec-

appalling state in which he found the manuscripts that he broke down into uncontrollable sobbing: see Ramboldi's *Commentum super Dantis Comediam*, ed. J.P. Lacaita, V, 1887, 301 ff.

18. See Pertusi, *op. cit.* 17, 433 ff.

19. See B.L. Ulman, 'The Humanism of Coluccio Salutati', *MU* 4 (1963) 3-11. Cf. E. Kessler, 'Das Problem des frühen Humanismus: Seine philosophische Bedeutung bei Coluccio Salutati', *Humanistische Bibliothek* I (1968).

20. See pp. 232-233 n. 86.

21. On Chrysoloras's translating method see R. Sabbadini, *Il metodo degli Umanisti*, Florence 1922, 23-24; G. Cammelli, *I dotti bizantini e le origini dell' Umanesimo*, I: *Manuele Crisolora*, Florence 1941, 85-92; N.G. Wilson, *From Byzantium to Italy: Greek Studies in the Italian Renaissance*, London 1992, 8-12 ('Chrysoloras: Methods of Learning the Language').

22. Ulman, *op. cit.* 146 n. 14.

23. On Niccoli see pp. 340-342 herein; also Pfeiffer, *op. cit.* 35 ff.

24. See pp. 342-344.

25. The *Erotemata*, a work based on the *Art of Grammar* by Dionysius the Thracian, was the standard textbook of Greek grammar in Western

188. Dante, Petrarch and other humanists. Engraving from [Vasari], 'Questionario degli eruditi', La Bibliofilia *45 (1924) 342.*

tion of eight hundred manuscripts, which went to the Medici library on his death and formed the nucleus of what was to become the Biblioteca Laurenziana.[24]

An outstanding and, one might say, symbolic example of the second category of libraries mentioned above is that of Manuel Chrysoloras. Chrysoloras arrived in Florence from Constantinople very well prepared to teach Greek, as one of the items in his luggage was the *Erotemata*, a Greek grammar he had written specifically for the purpose of teaching Greek to Western Europeans.[25] The Italians only needed to go to one or two of Chrysoloras's lectures to realize what enormous gaps there were in their knowledge of Greek language and literature, since even the Aristotelian corpus had only been available to them in Latin versions by the medieval Schoolmen and needed to be retranslated. Chrysoloras had brought copies of some Greek classical works with him from Constantinople; but Palla Strozzi, a distinguished Florentine, realizing that Chrysoloras was unable to cover all the ground with the material he had, organized a mission to the East to buy more Greek manuscripts. Among the works brought back to Florence were Ptolemy's *Cosmographia*, Plato's *Republic* and Aristotle's *Politics*, all hitherto unknown in the West.[26] It is impossible to reconstruct the contents of Chrysoloras's library. When he was away on his travels his manuscripts had been looked after by Strozzi, and on his death a quarter of his collection was left to his pupil Cencio de' Rustici, while the remainder went to Niccoli, from whom they were subsequently acquired by the Medici.[27]

Another prominent humanist who was a member of Chrysoloras's wider circle was Poggio Bracciolini (1380-1459),[28] the most tireless manuscript-hunter of all. Although employed as a papal secretary, Poggio always found time for all kinds of literary pursuits: among other things, he translated the *Bibliotheca* of Diodorus Siculus and Xenophon's *Cyropaedia*.[29] He was given his first opportunity to demonstrate his talent at the Council of Konstanz (1414-1417), when the entire Curia took up residence there. As and when his official duties permitted, Poggio slipped away on a series of journeys in search of manuscripts. On the first of these, to Cluny Abbey in Burgundy in 1415, he found an old manuscript with some of Cicero's speeches, including *Pro Roscio* and *Pro Murena*, both hitherto unknown.[30] His next trip took him to the famous Abbey of St. Gall, where he discovered three very important works of Latin literature by Quintilian, Asconius and Valerius Flaccus. He continued his exploratory forays throughout the time the Council was in progress, with successful results, extending his range to more distant parts of France and Germany from the summer of 1417. Here we have a scholar who, while holding an official position as an Apostolic Secretary, built up a private collection of the classics and, by lending his manuscripts and sometimes buying on behalf of others, acted as a sort of open private library. The humanist world was also indebted to him for

189. Manuel Chrysoloras. Engraving from I. Bullart, Académie des sciences et des arts, *Amsterdam 1682, 625.*

Europe for at least a century and a half. It may fairly be called the first Greek contribution to the Renaissance in the field of language studies. See A. Pertusi, 'ΕΡΩΤΗΜΑΤΑ. Per la storia e le fonti delle prime grammatiche greche a stampa', *IMU* 5 (1962) 321-350. On the incunabular editions of the work see *Charta* 116-120.

26. See P.F. Galletti, *Capena municipio de' Romani*, Rome 1756, 81; Cammelli, *op. cit.* 184-185. On Strozzi's library see pp. 222-224.

27. It is worth noting that not all the people whom Chrysoloras inspired to collect Greek as well as Latin classics were fuure leaders of the humanist movement: some of them were men of relatively modest literary attainment. One such was Antonio Corbinelli, who was born in Florence in 1376 or 1377 and died in Rome in 1425. He came from a family prominent in politics and commerce and followed both those careers himself. In 1400 he joined Coluccio Salutati's circle of scholars and humanists and studied with Giovanni Malpaghini and Chrysoloras. In 1403 he went into politics and in 1416 he was taken on to the administrative staff of the Signoria. Of the fruits of his scholarly pursuits

creating italic handwriting, a more refined version of the Carolingian minuscule script.[31]

It is clear from all this that by the first decade of the fourteenth century the hunt for manuscripts had acquired a new dimension. No longer were the humanists content to look for lost works of Latin literature and buy Greek books in the East: they deliberately set out to strip monastic and cathedral libraries of their classical treasures, acting as merchants, at first on behalf of lesser noblemen and other private individuals and later for ruling princes, who usually kept their priceless possessions in big libraries.

The first person to set about acquiring manuscripts on an openly commercial basis was Giovanni Aurispa.[32] He spent two long periods in the East, from 1403 to 1413 and from 1421 to 1433, and acquired about 250 Greek manuscripts there altogether. In Constantinople, where he got most of his manuscripts, it was said that he used to sell his own clothes to scrape together enough money to buy Greek books. Among the manuscripts that came into his hands were: a copy of the *Iliad* with the commentary by Aristarchus (Venet. Marc. 454); a codex of the tenth or eleventh century, bought on Chios, containing works by Sophocles and Aeschylus and the *Argonautica* of Apollonius Rhodius (Laur. XXX 119); and the only known manuscript of the *Deipnosophistai* by Athenaeus, which was used for the Aldine *editio princeps* edited by Markos Mousouros and printed in 1514.[33]

Another cultured and highly talented humanist who bought and sold manuscripts, mostly Greek, was Francesco Filelfo (1398-1481).[34] Like Aurispa, Filelfo was a member of Chrysoloras's wider circle and was noted for his philhellenism. He was a charmer and adventurer who made many enemies, and whenever possible he lived in the lap of luxury by flattering the rulers of Italy's principalities and duchies. He spent seven years as an attaché at the Venetian embassy in Constantinople, from 1420 to 1427, and on his return he brought some forty rare Greek manuscripts back with him.[35] In Italy he spent much of his time travelling from court to court, living on the generosity of his patron of the moment, and writing epic poems such as the *Sforziade*, which won him the teaching post vacated by Ioannes Argyropoulos at the Studium in Florence. He never missed an opportunity to supply his patrons with Greek manuscripts, which he had copied for him by Greek scribes, one of those being Demetrios Sgouropoulos.[36]

3. Court libraries. The Renaissance in Italy saw a revival of large libraries housed in monumental buildings, of the kind that had existed in the Roman period, on the initiative of the ruling princes and dukes of the Italian states, high-ranking church dignitaries and above all the Popes themselves. The essential difference between the libraries founded by Roman emperors and those of the Renaissance princes was that the latter

nothing remains except his library, which was one of the biggest and best of its time, especially as regards Greek manuscripts: it contained 277 codices, of which 77 were Greek. He lived in Florence until shortly before his death, when he went to Rome. He died there on 14th August 1425. His collection of manuscripts was acquired by the Biblioteca della Badia in Florence: see R. Blum, *La Biblioteca della Badia Fiorentina e i codici di Antonio Corbinelli*, Vatican City 1951; *VBV* I 450. On Corbinelli's studies with Chrysoloras see *VBV* II 141; A. Molho, 'Corbinelli, Antonio' in *DBI* 28 (1983) 745-747.

190. Poggio. Woodcut from N. Reusner, Icones sive Imagines vivae, *Basel 1599.*

28. See E. Walser, *Poggius Florentinus. Leben und Werke*, Leipzig/Berlin 1914; A.C. Clark, 'The Reappearance of the Texts of the Classics', *The Library*, 4th ser., 2 (1921) 36.

29. See pp. 288, 290.

30. Poggio's trip to Cluny is of doubtful historicity: see T. Foffano in *IMU* 12 (1969) 113-128.

31. See L.D. Reynolds and N.G. Wilson, *'Αντιγραφεῖς καί Φιλόλογοι. Τό ἱστορικό τῆς παράδοσης τῶν κλασικῶν κειμένων* (= *Scribes and Scholars: A guide to the transmission of Greek and Latin literature*, 2nd edn., London 1975, tr. N.M. Panayotakis), Athens 1981, 165.

genuinely loved books and did not see their collections as mere symbols of cultural power, especially as most of them had been brought up in a scholarly environment where they had learnt to appreciate the indispensable part played by books in propagating the humanist movement. Some typical court libraries are dealt with at greater length in Book II: here there is room only to look briefly at a few of them and to trace the history of the first 'court' humanist library.

The main common factor linking the court libraries is their humanistic character, in terms of both the range of their contents and the purpose of their existence. These were not closed collections but were open for use by outsiders and in some cases actually functioned as lending libraries, in a manner of speaking, even before they officially became open to the public. Finding out about the court libraries of Renaissance Italy is a source of constant delights. What is one to admire first: the atmosphere created by Matteo Nuti in Novello Malatesta's library at Cesena[37] or the lovely *studiolo* of Federico da Montefeltro, Duke of Urbino, with that exquisite marquetry work on the cabinets containing his 1,120 books?[38] And where can one find words to describe the 'library' of Enea Silvio Piccolomini in Siena cathedral, with those magnificent frescoes by Pintoricchio soaring above the cardinal's music manuscripts?[39] Or the great library of the Aragonese kings of Naples, which was looted by the French when they captured the city?[40] Or the fine library of the d'Este family, notable among other things for the superb bindings of its books, still to be seen in the Biblioteca Nazionale at Modena?[41] Finally, one can hardly fail to be entranced by the library that Michelangelo designed for the Medici family, where, in an atmosphere redolent of the architect's genius, tribute is paid to the spirit of the bilingual library.[42]

The first person to found a court library with a classical bias – in which he demonstrated his commitment to humanistic ideals by ensuring that his books were available to all – was an illustrious citizen of Florence named Palla Strozzi (*c.* 1373-1462).[43] It was he who took the lead in organizing an expedition to obtain texts suitable for use by Chrysoloras in his teaching at the Studium.[44] Strozzi had had a Greek education himself, having studied with Ioannes Argyropoulos[45] and Andronikos Kallistos.

On Strozzi's death in 1462 his library contained about four hundred codices, according to a catalogue of 1431.[46] As already mentioned, his collection consisted mostly of classical works and was divided into two sections, one Latin and one Greek. By the time he died he had bought Chrysoloras's books and probably those of Demetrios Skaranos too.[47] In his library he had two or more copies of a number of works, which may have been because they were to be used for teaching purposes in several academies in Florence or else because he had bought up other scholars' entire collections. One documented fact is that he hoped to

32. Giovanni Aurispa was born at Noto, Sicily, in 1369 and was one of the first Italians to study in Constantinople: see F. Fuchs, *Die höheren Schulen von Konstantinopel im Mittelalter*, Leipzig/Berlin 1926, 68. On his return to Italy in 1414 he went to live in Savona, making trips from there to Pisa, Bologna and Florence to sell the codices he had brought back with him from the East. In 1421 he went to Constantinople again, this time on a mission from Gian Francesco Gonzaga to Emperor Manuel II Palaiologos, and was taken on as private secretary to Manuel's son John. In this capacity he accompanied John (by now Emperor John VIII) on a visit to Italy and spent the last years of his life in Rome, where he died in 1459. But it would be wrong to think of Aurispa as a mere book dealer, for he taught at the Studium in Florence and translated many Greek texts (including works by Aesop, Hierocles the Neoplatonist, Hippocrates and Lucian) into Latin. See E. Bigi, 'Aurispa, Giovanni' in *DBI* 4 (1962) 593-595; R. Sabbadini, *Biografia documentata di G. Aurispa*, Noto 1890; *VBV* I 42.

33. The discovery and preservation of the manuscript of Athenaeus is of great importance for the history of ancient libraries and books in general. On Mousouros's edition see *Charta* 347.

34. See C. Rosmini, *Vita di Francesco Filelfo da Tolentino*, 3 vols., Milan 1808; *VBV* II 53-58.

35. See A. Calderini, 'Ricerche intorno alla biblioteca e alla cultura greca di Francesco Filelfo', *Studi Italiani di Filologia Classica* 20 (1913) 204-224.

36. When Ianos Laskaris was on his travels in the East, locating, cataloguing and buying Greek manuscripts, he saw Demetrios Sgouropoulos's library: see K. Müller, 'Neue Mittheilungen über Janos Lascaris und die Mediceische Bibliothek', *Centralblatt für Bibliothekswesen* 1 (1884) 361. On Sgouropoulos's work

191. Enea Silvio Piccolomini's library at Siena.

found a public library in Florence. His plan was that it should be linked with the Church of the Santa Trinità, near his family's *palazzo*:[48] this would be in keeping with the tradition of having public libraries adjacent to a temple – a practice that was followed until the very end of the ancient era.

The provisions of Strozzi's will relating to his library are of great interest from a human as well as a humanistic point of view. Part of his collection he bequeathed to the Monastery of Santa Giustina in Padua, with admonitions to the monks to look after the books and not lend them out, and a note to the effect that the Greek books in his bequest were the only sources of truly scientific learning.[49] The rest of his books he left to his grandsons Barbo and Lorenzo and to two of his sons, Gianfranco and Onofrio: to his other son, Niccolò, he left two hundred ducats, the approximate value of the books he had left to Gianfranco and Onofrio, as Niccolò showed no interest in books.[50]

The human interest of Strozzi's testamentary dispositions lies in his choice of books for the various beneficiaries: each of them, he decided, was entitled to have any book he had copied out with his own hand, or had in his possession for a long time, or paid for out of his own savings. And in an effusion of humanistic idealism he urged his legatees to appreciate the worth of the rarer manuscripts and to sell them if they wished, to make them accessible to a wider public. It would appear that that is what they did, retaining only the unique copy of Ptolemy's *Cosmographia* that Chrysoloras had brought with him from Constantinople, as Strozzi felt that it should be kept as a family heirloom.[51] Provision was made in the will not only for books that belonged to the family, but also for some which were not Strozzi's but had found their way into his library. Here again he displayed his usual sensitivity to, and respect for, those who served the republic of letters. A typical case in point is that of Alberto da Camerino, his sons' tutor, who left some philosophy books behind for safe keeping before setting out on a journey to Hungary, from which he never returned. Strozzi insisted that these books were never to be disposed of, in case da Camerino's lawful heir should turn up and claim them.[52]

The facts noted here about Palla Strozzi's library are not necessarily of general application to all court libraries of the Renaissance. However, there are certain points that they have in common, and it would be fair to say that Strozzi's revival of the bilingual library, his appreciation of and respect for the role of books in education, and his policy of making his priceless collection open to all are features characteristic of all court libraries from the early fifteenth to the mid sixteenth century.

4. Academies and scriptoria. While the humanists were amassing private collections of books and the rulers of various Italian states were taking steps to fill their libraries with a good cross-section of Greek and

as a copyist see E. Mioni, 'Bessarione scriba e alcuni suoi collaboratori' in *Miscellanea Marciana di Studi Bessarionei*, Padua 1976, 263-318.

37. See Ch. XV, pp. 305-318.

38. See A. Bohmer and H. Widmann, 'Von der Renaissance bis zum Beginn der Aufklärung' in *HBW* III.1 526-527; L. Cheles, *The Studiolo of Urbino: An Iconographic Investigation*, Wiesbaden 1986; Liebenwein, *op. cit.* 66.

39. See A. Cecchi, *The Piccolomini Library in the Cathedral of Siena*, tr. A. McCormick, Siena 1991.

40. See T. de Marinis, *La Biblioteca Napoletana dei Rè d'Aragona: Supplemento*, 2 vols., Verona 1969.

41. See G. Beroni, *La Biblioteca Estense e la cultura ferrarese ai tempi del duca Ercole I, 1471-1505*, Turin 1903; D. Fava, *La Biblioteca Estense nel suo sviluppo, con il catalogo della mostra permanente*, Modena 1925.

42. See pp. 352-356.

43. Palla, the son of Noferi Strozzi, was born in about 1373 and won general admiration for his political and intellectual activities. In 1434 he was banished by the Medici to Padua, where he died in 1462. See *VBV* II 139-165.

44. See *VBV* II 140-141. Among the manuscripts brought back for this purpose were Ptolemy's *Cosmographia*, Plutarch's *Lives*, the works of Plato and Aristotle's *Politics*.

45. On Strozzi's library see V. Fanelli, 'I libri di messer Palla Strozzi (1372-1462)', *Convivium* 1 (1949) 57-73; G. Fiocco, 'La biblioteca di Palla Strozzi' in *Studi di Bibliografia e di Storia in onore di Tammaro de Marinis*, II, Verona 1964, 289-310.

46. Fiocco, *op. cit.* 289.

47. Fiocco, *op. cit.* 292.

48. See the letter from Ambrogio Traversari to Francesco Barbaro in R. Sabbadini, *Centotrenta lettere inedite di Francesco Barbaro*, II, Salerno 1884, 134.

49. Ioannes Argyropoulos had lived as Palla's guest in the Strozzi *palazzo* for some years: see Cammelli, *I dotti bizantini...* II: *Giovanni Argiropulo*, Florence 1941, 21-22; G.

Latin literature, and before shops selling printed books had made their appearance, the main centres for the production and distribution of books were the scriptoria.

The most notable privately-organized scriptorium in the Renaissance, as far as the reproduction of Greek books was concerned, was that of Cardinal Bessarion.[53] Bessarion, foreseeing that nothing would come of his efforts to stir the Christians of the West into mounting a crusade to liberate the Greek homelands from the Turks, decided that at least he would try to save the treasures of Greek literature. With this end in view he paid agents – some of them wholly employed by him, others working on a freelance basis – to make the rounds of the major Greek book centres and bring back as many manuscripts as they could lay their hands on, or copies of those they could not buy.

One of the most dynamic of these agents was Michael Apostoles, who went to live in Crete in 1455 and devoted all his energies to copying manuscripts for the Greek cardinal.[54] Little by little, and especially after the disintegration of the team of scholars working in the Curia under Pope Nicholas V, Bessarion's villa on the Quirinal Hill in Rome became the home of a sort of academy where Greek and Italian scholars were able to copy rare (sometimes unique) Greek and Latin manuscripts and to spend their time discussing matters of literary interest. Among them were Theodoros Gazis, Andronikos Kallistos, Athanasios Chalkiopoulos, Konstantinos Laskaris, Niccolò Perotti (who was Bessarion's private secretary), Flavio Biondo, Giovanni Antonio Campana (who, at Bessarion's instigation, went to work as a proof-reader at Ulrich Han's press), Giuliano Maffei, Lorenzo Valla, Giovanni Baptista Almadiano and many others.[55] To these we should add Johann Müller of Königsberg, who Latinized the name of his birthplace and called himself Regiomontanus. Regiomontanus, who went to Rome to study under Bessarion with the object of improving his Greek and making copies of Greek manuscripts for his own collection,[56] was one of the first links between Italian humanism and the North.

Elpidio Mioni, in an attempt to identify the copyists working in Bessarion's scriptorium and the agents employed by the cardinal to search for manuscripts, has published a preliminary study listing the names of twenty-three Greek scribes and Ciriaco d'Ancona.[57] The most productive of them were Michael Apostoles, Andronikos Kallistos, the hieromonk Kosmas, Ioannes Rossos, Demetrios Sgouropoulos, Metropolitan Theognostos of Perge and Demetrios Trivolis. Much interesting information about the conditions of work in the scriptorium is to be gleaned from their correspondence with Bessarion. In particular, we learn of the cardinal's great desire to lay his hands on hitherto unknown texts, a desire sometimes amounting almost to an obsession. We also learn that Georgios Trivizias and Kosmas the monk together copied the codex Marc. gr. 429, our only manuscript of the rhetorical works of

Fiocco, 'La casa di Palla Strozzi', *Memorie dei Lincei, Classe scienze morali*, ser. VIII, 5.7 (1954) 361-382.

50. Fiocco, 'La biblioteca...' 295; L.A. Ferrai, 'La biblioteca di S. Giustina di Padova' in G. Mazzatinti (ed.), *Inventario dei manoscritti d'Italia nelle bibliotheche di Francia*, II, Rome 1887, 569-573.

51. See Fiocco, 'La biblioteca...' 299.

52. *Ibid.* 305. Strozzi mentioned two other lots of books in his library which were not his: some belonging to a certain Francesco di San Biagio, of Volterra, and some belonging to an unnamed Florentine (*ibid.* 301-302).

53. On Greek copyists active during the Renaissance, see: Marie Vogel and V. Gardthausen, 'Die griechischen Schreiber des Mittelalters und der Renaissance', *ZB* (1909); Ch.G. Patrinelis, «Ἕλληνες κωδικογράφοι τῶν χρόνων τῆς Ἀναγεννήσεως», *EMA* 8-9 (1958-1959) 63-125; P. Canart, 'Scribes grecs de la Renaissance', *Scriptorium* 17 (1963) 56-82; K.A. de Meyier, 'Scribes grecs de la Renaissance', *Scriptorium* 18 (1964) 258-266.

54. See A. Diller, 'Three Greek Scribes Working for Bessarion: Trivizias, Callistus, Hermonymus', *IMU* 10 (1967) 404-410 and Pls. XXV-XXVI; Mioni, *op. cit.*

55. See H. Vast, *Le cardinal Bessarion*, Paris 1878, 306-311, 314, 320-321; L. Mohler, *Kardinal Bessarion als Theologe, Humanist und Staatsmann: Funde und Forschungen*, I, Paderborn 1923, 330-335; A. Kyrou, *Βησσαρίων ὁ Ἕλλην*, Athens 1947, II 135-161.

56. On Regiomontanus see pp. 328-329 n. 8.

57. It is worth noting that nearly all the scribes listed below had libraries of their own: see A. Oleroff, 'Démétrius Trivolis, copiste et bibliophile', *Scriptorium* 4 (1950) 260-263; E. Mioni, 'La biblioteca greca di Marco Musuro', *AV*, 5th ser., 93 (1971) 5-28. Their names are: Michael Apostoles, Leon Atrapes, Antonios Belhassim, Athanasios Chalkiopoulos, Ciriaco d'Ancona, Ioannes Dokeianos, Gedeon, Georgios Gemistos Plethon,

Dionysius of Halicarnassus and Apsinus. Both were extremely fast workers: Kosmas took only two days to copy the whole of the two chapters containing the treatises of Dionysius.[58] There is also a letter from Bessarion thanking Michael Apostoles for sending him (in 1454 or 1455) a codex of *De compositione verborum* by Dionysius of Halicarnassus, which again he had copied in only two days.[59] In this way Bessarion amassed his astonishing collection of 746 codices (482 in Greek and 264 in Latin), the biggest and best then in existence, which – as we shall see – he donated to the Venetian Senate as a symbol of the Graeco-Roman civilization and a lantern of Hellenism.[60]

II. The achievements of the early printers. It was chiefly due to the invention of printing, which gradually revolutionized the process of disseminating knowledge and deprived selfish 'bibliotaphs' of their monopoly of certain texts,[61] that classical studies became so firmly entrenched in the relatively few city-states of Italy. There is no point in trying to find out who bought the hundreds of thousands of classical and other books printed in Europe, and it is hardly possible to calculate the precise extent to which those books altered traditional modes of thinking and self-expression or helped to create a more broadly educated public. However, it is worth tracing the development of printing in Italy and the way in which scriptoria began to be superseded by humanistic and other printing houses.

The method of printing with movable metal types was invented by a German, Johann Gutenberg, who, with his close associates Johannes Fust and Peter Schöffer, started printing religious books at Mainz as early as 1455 (though the books themselves are not dated).[62] Before long printed books had reached the smaller towns in the vicinity, and meanwhile German printers were fanning out into all parts of Europe, from the Iberian peninsula to the Hungary of King Matthias Corvinus, carrying with them the secrets of the new craft and taking over much of the work previously done by copyists. To get some idea of the crucial impact of typography on social conditions and the spread of humanism through the medium of books and the private libraries of an ever-growing circle of scholars, one has only to consider the fact that in the three countries where printing developed most rapidly – Germany, Italy and France – about forty thousand editions were printed during the incunabular period (i.e. up to 1500). Assuming an average print run of five hundred copies, this means that the total number of copies printed up to the end of the fifteenth century was approximately twenty million. The books were of all kinds: Bibles, liturgical books, patristic writings, works in Greek and Latin by classical and postclassical writers, grammars and dictionaries, history books and novels, school books, theological works, moralistic fables and comedies, as well as broadsheets, leaflets and pamphlets on all kinds of subjects. Classical literature, a key

Charitonymos Hermonymos, Andronikos Kallistos, the hieromonk Kosmas, Manuel of Apollonia, Ioannes Plousiadenos, Ioannes Rossos, 'A. Scriba' [anonymous scribe], Demetrios Sgouropoulos, Ioannes Skoutariotes, Metropolitan Stephanos of Medeia, Theodoros (legal adviser and notary to the Oecumenical Patriarchate), Metropolitan Theognostos of Perge, Georgios Trivizias, Demetrios Trivolis and Georgios Tzangaropoulos.

192. Cardinal Bessarion. Engraving from J.B. Scioppalalba, In perantiquam sacram tabulam graecam..., *Venice, Modesto Fenzo, 1767.*

58. Mioni, 'Bessarione scriba...' 293.

59. See Mohler, *op. cit.*, III 485; E. Mioni, 'Bessarione bibliofilo e filologo', *Rivista di Studi Bizantini e Neoellenici*, n.s., 5 (1968) 61-83.

60. See p. 321.

61. The literature on this subject is very extensive: see C. McMurtie, *The Invention of Printing: A Bibliography*, New York 1936 (repr. 1962). For a rather more recent bibliography see Geldner I 17 ff.

62. To compile a complete catalogue of all incunabula is simply not possible. The standard reference works on the subject are still *BMC* I-XII; *GW*; *H*; Pr; and *Census*.

63. On the incunabular editions of Greek and Latin classics see M. Flodr, *Incunabula Classicorum*, Amsterdam 1973; *Charta* lii ff., 1-38.

element in the spread of humanism, is represented by a corpus of at least 1,750 editions (in the original or in translation), which means that by the end of the century scholars and educated readers had about 1,100,000 copies of classical works at their disposal. The 'best-seller' of the incunabular period was Aristotle: counting the books by his commentators as well as his own works, we have a total of 590 editions, of which 265 were printed in Italy.[63]

Although more than twenty million printed books were published in the incunabular period, the invention of printing did not have the same impact on the creation of private libraries by the general public in all the countries where the new craft was practised. In the first place, a clear distinction can be drawn between the subject matter of the books published in northern Europe and those published in Italy; secondly, there was a fairly long initial period when printed books tended to cost no less than good-quality manuscripts, and often the prices were prohibitive.

In Italy, from the time when printing was first introduced, there was a marked preference for works of Greek and Latin literature. These were intended to meet the needs of the humanist movement and to develop a new market among the people who came flocking to the great centres of learning in the Italian peninsula: Venice, Padua, Bologna, Rome, Naples, Milan and Florence. By contrast, printers in the North made no attempt to use typography as a means of changing the social and intellectual status quo: they pursued a more conventional and therefore safer publishing policy, their sole object nearly always being simply to replace manuscript codices with printed books. It was only in the first decade of the sixteenth century that the seeds of humanism started falling on fertile ground in the North and printing houses started employing teams of scholars, as they had done in Italy for some time. Not all printed books were offered for sale at affordable prices because there were all sorts of factors affecting their production costs, especially in the case of books dealing with the classics and most of all if the language was Greek. A typical, if perhaps extreme, instance is recorded by Antonio Urceo, who wrote to his friend Aldus Manutius that for eleven ducats, the price of his five-volume Greek edition of Aristotle, one could buy ten excellent Latin manuscripts.[64]

It is not possible to trace the movements of the thousands of editions that flooded Italy during this period and found their way on to the shelves of libraries large and small. Far more significant than that, in my opinion, is a surprising feature of the book market that endured from the dawn of printing in Italy until Aldus's death in 1516: contrary to what one might have expected, manuscripts not only lost none of their importance but were actually regarded as the cornerstone of any humanistic library. The reason for the coexistence of manuscripts and printed books has to do with textual studies: the scholars who worked as editors for the printing and publishing houses made a point of collating and

64. See M.J.C. Lowry, *The World of Aldus Manutius: Business and Scholarship in Renaissance Venice*, Oxford 1979, 106. Aldus seems to have had no problem with his Latin editions, but only with the Greek: evidently the cost of typesetting and proof-reading was prohibitive. His catalogues reflect the commercial failure of some of his Greek editions, which he was forced to sell off at greatly reduced prices (see A.A. Renouard, *Annales de l'imprimerie des Alde, ou Histoire des trois Manuce et de leurs éditions*, 3rd edn., Paris 1834, 329-338). For example, the official selling price of his 1503 edition of the *Anthologia Planudea* is believed to have been two ducats and ten marchelli, whereas in his own 1503 catalogue it was priced at a mere four marchelli (Renouard, *op. cit.* 334). In 1505 Aldus's partner Andrea Torresani d'Asola told Scipio Carteromachus that the publication of Greek books was being discontinued and Johannes Cuno reported that booksellers were refusing to take any more Greek books unless they came down in price (see *Charta* 354).

65. The word *bibliotaphos* ('burier of books') was coined by Michael

193. A printing house. Engraving from G. Budé, De asse, *Paris, Josse Bade, 1514.*

copying every doubtful passage they came across, to ensure that their editions would be as accurate as possible, with the result that the whole of Italy was transformed into a vast centre of textual scholarship, rather like the Museum founded in Alexandria by the Ptolemies to meet the needs of their great library. Classical scholars, mostly Greeks and Italians, moved about from city to city like political refugees, carrying with them

194. A printing house. Engraving by Abraham von Verdt.

195. A printing house. Engraving by Hans Merian in J.L. Gottfried, Historischer Chronik, *Frankfurt 1642. Early 17th c.*

Apostoles in a letter to Cardinal Bessarion in 1467, to describe a person who keeps his manuscripts hidden away. Ianos Laskaris also used it when on his travels in search of Greek manuscripts in Italy. See Firmin-Didot 80, 220-221.

66. On Sweynheim and Pannartz see Geldner II 25-30.

67. Giovanni de Bussi was born at Vigano in 1417 and died in Rome in 1476. In 1467 he was consecrated Bishop of Aleria. In 1468 he moved to Rome and embarked on the publication of the first corpus of Latin classical works. See M. Miglio, 'Bussi, Giovanni Andrea' in *DBI* 15 (1972) 565-572.

68. Bussi's studies with Vittorino da Feltre are to be dated to about 1440, when he was living in Mantua.

69. See *Charta* 71-72.

70. Bussi's first spell in publishing was extraordinarily productive, but the second lasted only a year (1475-1476) and produced only two books: the *Histories* of Herodotus and St. Jerome's *Letters*.

71. On the history of the publication and distribution of the petition, see D. Marzi, 'Giovanni Gutenberg e l'Italia', *La Bibliofilia* 2 (1900-1901) 81-135. On the result of the petition see V. Scholderer, 'The Petition of Sweynheim and Pannartz to Sixtus IV', *The Library*, 3rd ser., 6 (1915) 186-190.

72. See H.F. Brown, *The Venetian Printing Press*, London 1891; V. Scholderer, *Fifty Essays in Fifteenth- and Sixteenth-Century Bibliography*, ed. D.E. Rhodes, Amsterdam 1966, 74-89 ('Printing at Venice to the End of 1481'). The estimate of about 4,500 Venetian incunabular editions comes from V. Scholderer, 'Printers and Readers in Italy in the Fifteenth Century', *Proceedings of the British Academy* 35 (1949) 28-30.

73. On the manuscript used by the printer, see P. Scapecchi, 'New Light on the Ripoli Edition of the *Expositio* of Donato Acciaioli' in D.V. Reidy (ed.), *The Italian Book 1465-1800: Studies presented to D.E. Rhodes on his 70th birthday*, London 1993, 31-33. Argyropoulos and Acciaiuoli had been

their personal collections of rare and valuable books, many of which they had prised out of the hands of 'bibliotaphs' with the greatest difficulty and at considerable expense to themselves.[65]

1. Humanist presses. The readiness with which the Italians welcomed printed books can be gauged by the fact that the first serious venture in the field of printing and publishing classical books came just two years after the introduction of printing into Italy. The first printers to work in Italy were two Germans, Konrad Sweynheim and Arnold Pannartz, clergymen from the dioceses of Mainz and Köln respectively. They accepted an invitation from the Spanish Cardinal Johannes de Turrecremata, who had been Abbot of Santa Scholastica at Subiaco since 1455, and started working at the abbey in 1465.[66]

Giovanni de Bussi. In November 1467, in Rome, the two German printers entered into partnership with Giovanni Andrea de Bussi, Bishop of Aleria.[67] At that time the Roman scene was still dominated by the personality of Cardinal Bessarion, and Bussi, who had studied under Vittorino da Feltre (at the same time as Theodoros Gazis) and had served for a period as secretary to the humanist Cardinal Nicolaus da Cusa, undertook to set up the first humanist publishing house.[68] Accordingly he moved into Pietro Massimo's *palazzo* in Rome with Sweynheim and Pannartz, and the three of them started printing and publishing a representative selection of the Latin classics, working in close collaboration with Gazis, the eccentric antiquarian Pomponio Leto, Lampugnino Birago, Andronikos Kallistos and Niccolò de Valle, among others. In fact Bussi's publishing house was basically an 'academy', similar to the one founded by Aldus in Venice some thirty years later.[69] Between 1468 and 1472 the two printers produced at least twenty-three editions for Bussi, including works by Cicero, Livy, Lactantius, Ovid, Apuleius, St. Jerome, Suetonius, Gellius and Strabo.[70] A year before the dissolution of their 'academy' Bussi and his two printers, who were in financial straits, decided to appeal to Pope Sixtus IV for assistance, and a printed leaflet with a copy of their petition was inserted in every copy of Nicolaus de Lyra's book *Postilla super totam bibliam*. This document is of interest for what it tells us about books and libraries in general, as well as the history of printing. It lists all the books published by Bussi and, in a parallel column, the number of copies of each that were printed, ranging from 275 to 1,100. Altogether, in the four years that the press was in operation, it turned out (mainly for the Roman market) 13,095 books – an impressive number, even if some copies did remain unsold.[71]

The long-term effects of Bussi's pioneering endeavours were disappointing. Following Bessarion's death in 1472 and the dissolution of his academy, and a short-lived attempt by Bussi to re-establish his printing

friends for many years before the publication of the *Expositio*, in fact since 1454, when a group of keen young scholars in Florence formed a literary society with the object of studying Greek literature in depth. This society finally took the form of an 'academy' and was called the Chorus Achademiae Florentinae. Its members hoped to persuade Argyropoulos to come and live permanently in Florence and help them with their studies, and eventually their efforts bore fruit, for Argyropoulos was offered the Chair of Philosophy at the Studium and took up his appointment in 1456. On the foundation and objects of the Academy see A. Della Torre, *Storia dell'Accademia Platonica di Firenze*, Florence 1902, 354-366. On the humanistic outlook prevailing in Florence and its leading exponents

196. A printing house. Engraving, early 18th c.

see L. Martines, *The Social World of the Florentine Humanists, 1390-1460*, London 1963.

74. On this edition and the press where it was printed, see: *GW* 140; P. Bologna, *La stampa fiorentina del monastero di S. Jacopo di Ripoli e le sue edizioni*, Turin 1893.

75. *BMC* VI 678-679 (IB.27657a). On the history of the edition see R. Ridolfi, *La Stampa in Firenze nel secolo XV*, Florence 1958, 95-111; *Charta* 150-152.

76. *BMC* VI 666 (IB.27995). On the Plato (of which the first volume

HERODOTI HISTORICI INCIPIT.
Laurentii Vallen.conuersio de Græco in Latinum.

ERODOTI Halicarnasei historiæ explica-
tio hæc est: ut neq; ea quæ gesta sunt: ex rebus
humanis obliterentur ex æuo:neq; ingentia &
b admiranda opera: uel a Græcis edita:uel a Bar
baris golria fraudētur:cum alia: tum uero:qua
de re isti inter se belligerauerūt. Persarū eximii
memorāt dissensionū auctores extitisse Phœ-
nices qui a mari quod Rubrum uocatur:in hoc nostrum proficis-
centes:& hanc incolentes regionem:quam nunc quoq; incolunt:
longinquis continuo nauigationibus incubuerunt : faciendisq;
Aegyptiarum & Assyriarum merciū uecturis in alias plagas: præ-
cipueq; Argos traiecerunt. Argos &enim ea tempestate omni-

197. A copyist's and bookseller's shop. Engraving from Herodotus, Historiae, *Venice, J. and Gr. di Gregorii, 1494.*

house in 1475, there was no longer any future for humanistic pursuits in Rome. The humanist printing houses moved further north and Venice developed into the most productive centre of incunabular printing, with 150 print-shops producing more than 4,500 editions in the space of about thirty years.[72] Aristotle alone is represented by 172 separate Venetian editions, which is half of the total number printed in Italy. Yet classical studies did not take root in Venice until the last decade of the

was printed at the Dominican nuns' Ripoli press, while the second is signed by Alopa), see G. Galli, 'Gli ultimi mesi di vita della stamperia di Ripoli e la stampa del Platone', *Studi e ricerche sulla storia della stampa del Quattrocento* 20 (Milan 1942), repr. Nendeln, Liechtenstein (Kraus/Reprint) 1972, 159-184.

77. *BMC* V 465 (IB.23432).

78. Nothing whatever is known about the financial or editorial arrangements between Laskaris and the young printer: see Ridolfi, *op. cit.* 25-27; A. Mandolfo, 'Alopa, Lorenzo' in *DBI* 2 (1960) 523; *Charta* 278.

79. On Laskaris see B. Knös, *Un ambassadeur de l'hellénisme – Janus Lascaris – et la tradition gréco-byzantine dans l'humanisme français*, Uppsala/Paris 1945. On his part in organizing the French royal library see pp. 422 ff. herein.

80. 'Ubique libri imprimuntur, ubique bibliotheque aperiuntur': Knös, *op. cit.* 26.

81. On Laskaris's printing ventures in Florence see *Charta* 272-280.

82. Whereas it was customary at that time for printer's types to be modelled on either calligraphic or informal handwriting, Laskaris broke with tradition by designing (or having designed for him) a fount of majuscule Greek characters (large and small capitals) strongly reminiscent of the lettering in ancient Greek inscriptions: see Proctor 80.

83. The Biblioteca Nazionale in Florence has a number of copies of Laskaris's publications printed on parchment and illuminated in period style by Attavante degli Attavanti: see M. Cipriani, 'Attavanti, Attavante' in *DBI* 4 (1962) 526-530. For examples of such illuminations in the *Anthologia Planudea* and in the *Argonautica* of Apollonius Rhodius, see W.D. Orcutt, *The Book in Italy*, London 1926, 146, 149. On Attavanti's work for King Matthias Corvinus of Hungary see p. 462 herein. On the cost of producing a Latin book in fifteenth-century Florence see W. Pettas, 'The Cost of Printing a Florentine Incunable', *La Bibliofilia* 75 (1973) 67-85.

84. Angelo Poliziano, the greatest

fifteenth century, at about the time when the French army entered Florence and put an end to the rule of the Medici. Even Florence, which can claim to have been the unchallenged centre of humanist studies throughout the fifteenth century and an essential stopping-place on every scholar's itinerary, cannot begin to compare with Venice's record in the printing of the classics. The thirty presses founded there before 1500 were short-lived and did not have a reputation for efficiency. However, the humanists' close relationship with the printing houses and their efforts to encourage the formation of classical libraries is perhaps more clearly visible in Florence than anywhere else up to the time of Aldus in Venice.

We do not know whether Ioannes Argyropoulos or his favourite pupil, Donato Acciaiuoli, had any direct contact with the printing press at the nunnery of San Jacopo di Ripoli, where Acciaiuoli's *Expositio super libros Ethicorum Aristotelis* was printed:[73] that book, based on the Latin version of Aristotle's *Nicomachean Ethics* prepared by Acciaiuoli himself with the assistance of Argyropoulos, was published in 1478, when the learned Constantinopolitan scholar was again teaching in Florence.[74] But if the nature of the collaboration between author and printer remains uncertain in that case, in the monumental edition of Homer's *Collected Works* (*Σωζόμενα*) it is apparent for all to see. This, the *editio princeps* of Homer, jointly edited by Demetrios Chalkokondyles, Demetrios Damilas and Bernardo Nerli, was the first Greek book printed in Florence (in 1488). For this edition the editorial team collaborated so closely with the printer and did so much of the work, including helping with the typesetting and reading all the proofs, that in the end it was the printer's name that was not mentioned in the book.[75] Another equally important edition was Marsilio Ficino's Latin translation of the complete works of Plato, which was printed at the then small and obscure press of Lorenzo da Alopa in 1484-1485 and was therefore earlier than the Homer.[76] With regard to this edition we have no information about the collaboration between editor and printer, but the really remarkable thing about it is that 1,025 copies were printed and had evidently been sold out within six years, as it was reprinted at a Venetian press in 1491.[77] This shows what a heavy demand there was for classical books in the late fifteenth century.

The first purely humanistic press that clearly illustrates the relations between editors and printers is that of Lorenzo de Alopa, which produced Greek books for only three years (1494-1496) under the guidance and supervision of Ianos Laskaris.[78] Alopa's press could be described as the precursor of the printing and publishing house founded at about the same time by Aldus Manutius and his partners. It is worth saying something more about Laskaris, as he was one of the leading lights of the Renaissance and it was he who organized and catalogued the library of the Medici and that of the kings of France from Charles VIII to François I.[79]

Hellenist of the Italian Renaissance, who boasted that he knew Greek as well as any of the great Byzantine scholars, was so infuriated by the thoughtless alterations so often made to classical texts that he wrote a characteristically stern note to proofreaders: 'This is a manuscript that Angelo Poliziano, a member of the court of the Medici and protégé of Lorenzo, had copied for him from a

198. Theodoros Gazis. Engraving from N. Reusner, Icones, *Basel 1599.*

very old codex. Then he himself compared it with the original and corrected it with meticulous care, to make sure that it did not differ from the original in the slightest. Any corrupt passages he found he left as they were, never presuming to alter them according to his own judgment. If only our predecessors had been equally careful, we would now have manuscripts with far fewer mistakes. When you read this text, leave it as it is, and God be with you. Florence, December 1485.' (Reynolds and Wilson, *op. cit.* 173.)

85. Internal evidence of the dealings between proprietors of printing and publishing houses is to be found in the books they produced. In the fifteenth century there were no workshops specializing in the making of new types or woodcuts for book illustrations, and so the printers often cast the types themselves and lent or sold

Laskaris always maintained that the way to put Greek studies on to a firm footing and keep up the tradition of bilingualism that had been a mark of the educated classes in the Roman period was to introduce Greek literature to a wider readership. Printing presses could obviously help to achieve this, and he believed that they should flood the universities and schools with nothing but Greek books.[80] The Medici, who employed Laskaris to organize their library, espoused his belief in Greek printed books and financed his printing and publishing venture. Starting in 1494 with the *Anthologia Planudea* (the *Greek Anthology* as edited by Maximos Planoudes), Laskaris and Alopa produced a string of Greek *editiones principes* including the *Hymns* of Callimachus (*c.* 1495), *Γνῶμαι μονόστιχοι διαφόρων ποιητῶν* ('Quotations from Sundry Poets', *c.* 1495), the *Tragedies* of Euripides (1496), the *Pinax* of Cebes (*c.* 1495) and Lucian's *Dialogues* (1496).[81] The list of titles makes it clear that the publications were intended for educational purposes. Besides undertaking the textual recension, Laskaris himself, perhaps in collaboration with others, designed an original fount of majuscule Greek characters.[82] How successful his press was commercially, one can only guess. Although the Medici ordered copies printed on parchment for their own use and then had them illuminated by leading Florentine miniaturists, it would seem that the great majority of the voluminous tomes he printed remained unsold.[83]

These humanistic printing and publishing houses should not be imagined as mere print-shops, for they served other functions as well. They were used as meeting-places by scholars, teachers and printers, who would gather there to find out how the business was going and discuss all sorts of topics relating to books: in fact they were little 'academies'. The subject uppermost in the minds of these scholars was the emendation and restoration of corrupt and defective texts so as to produce an accurate edition.[84] They were constantly in touch with one another, not only on literary and textual matters but on technical problems as well, borrowing and lending printing equipment and sometimes even title pages.[85] Many presses also ran their own bookshops, on busy shopping streets wherever possible,[86] with handbills on the doors advertising their publications, and often with displays of books in wooden showcases on the pavement to attract customers. They must have borne a very close resemblance to the bookshops of ancient Ostia, as described by Martial and Horace.[87]

2. The impact of printed books on the growth of libraries. To assess the impact of printing on the growth of libraries – and private libraries in particular – in the latter part of the fifteenth century, we have only to look at the life and work of Aldus Manutius.[88] Aldus, who gave up an academic career to devote himself to typography, aspired to use the art of printing with movable metal types to supply the teachers of Italy (and eventually of other countries too) with all the tools they needed to

them (and other printing equipment) to other presses.

86. The organization of the book trade was not due solely to the huge number of books put on to the market by the printing houses, for the new presses were able to capitalize on the existence of a reading public that had been growing steadily since the earliest days of the humanist movement. It is in Florence, from the late 1370s onwards, that the distinctive characteristics of this movement are most clearly discernible. In the city of the Medici an unusual relationship developed between merchants and the rest of the population: the tradesmen, seeking to climb the social ladder, made great efforts to interest themselves in literature, reading classical and contemporary works and writing short historical pieces and chronicles. Before long the merchant class had established firm foundations on which scholars relied to large extent for the fulfilment of their humanistic ideals. One of the prime exponents of this symbiosis was Coluccio Salutati, who in his writings showed a proper regard for the value of practical pursuits and did much to allay the intellectuals' suspicion of those involved in commerce. It was the merchant class – whose members had acquired a knowledge of Roman law, read books

199. Demetrios Chalkokondyles. Engraving from N. Reusner, Icones, *Basel 1599.*

mould the human character in accordance with humanist ideals.[89] He remained faithful to this philosophy all his life and expressed it again and again in the fulsome dedicatory epistles of his magnificent editions, addressed not only to princes and dignitaries but sometimes to humble members of the teaching profession.[90] His passionate devotion to the cause of propagating Graeco-Roman literature throughout Christendom was astonishing. He did everything in his power to keep the prices of his books down and the products of his press were highly prized by noblemen, scholars and students alike. No one before or since has done as much as he did to promote the popularity of private libraries.

But let us take first things first and try to isolate those actions and initiatives of his that were the highlights not only of his own career but of the history of Renaissance scholarship in general and books in particular.

Aldus Manutius. Aldo (Teobaldo) Manucci or Manuzio was born at Bassiano, near Rome, in about 1450. He studied Latin with Gaspare da Verona and Domizio Calderini and perfected his Greek by taking lessons with Emmanuel Adramyttenos.[91] It was probably under Adramyttenos's influence that he developed such strong views on the importance of Greek, summed up in these words: 'How can anyone who does not know Greek possibly hope to emulate the Greek writers, who are the best educated in every branch of learning and from whom nearly everything of any note in the Latin language is derived?'[92] In about 1493 he decided to open a press in Venice, where he would print Greek books and nothing else. To start with, he had three Greeks working with him: Ioustinos Dekadyos, Arsenios Apostoles and Markos Mousouros.

201. The earliest picture of a printing house. Engraving from Mathias Huss, Danse Macabre, *Lyon 1499.*

in Latin and were thoroughly familiar with contemporary literature – that had kept the book trade going in the days of the manuscript codex. And so, when the printing houses started producing books in thousands of copies, there was already a well-established book distribution network that spread from Florence, hand in hand with the humanist movement,

200. The bibliomane. Engraving from Stultifera navis, *Augsburg, S. Brandt, 1497.*

to all the other cities and towns in Italy. See C. Bec, *Les marchands écrivains à Florence 1375-1434*, Paris 1967.

87. See p. 108.

88. The most important books and papers about Aldus, excluding monographs that deal with specific aspects of his work or are very specialized, are: Renouard, *op. cit.*; Firmin-Didot; R. Christie, *Selected Essays*, London 1902, 193-222 ('The Chronology of the Early Aldines'); Ester Pastorello, *L'Epistolario Manuziano. Inventario cronologico-analitico 1483-1597*, Venice/Rome 1957; G. Orlandi, *Aldo Manuzio editore: Dediche, prefazioni, note ai testi*, 2 vols., Milan 1976; and the excellent study by M.J.C. Lowry, *The World of Aldus Manutius: Business and Scholarship in Renaissance Venice*, Oxford 1979.

89. See *Charta* 314-315.

90. See Firmin-Didot.

91. *Ibid*. 7; Lowry, *op. cit.* 54. For a biographical note on Adramyttenos see *Charta* 359-361.

92. Aldus Manutius, *Musarum*

His first dated book, occupying the symbolic place of honour in the list of his publications, was Konstantinos Laskaris's *Grammar* (*Erotemata*), published in 1495.[93] Although Aldus had originally intended to print nothing but Greek books, he soon realized that the readership was too small to enable him to carry out the great plans he had in mind, so he started including Latin works in his list. Just after 1500 – by which time he had a string of great typographical achievements behind him, including the five-volume edition of Aristotle, the *Comedies* of Aristophanes, Hesiod's *Theogony* and numerous grammar books and dictionaries – he decided to give his customers an offering much better attuned to their needs and printed the *Tragedies* of Sophocles in a small-format edition of at least two thousand copies. From then on a print run of about two thousand copies was the norm for all his pocket-sized books.

Aldus published tens of thousands of books that were sold through-

202. A fifteenth-century copyist's and bookseller's shop. Woodcut from Ketham, *Venice, J. and G. di Gregorii, 1493.*

Panegyris (also known as *Epistola ad Catherinam Piam*), Venice 1489 (*Census* M 227).

93. *BMC* V 552 (IA.24383).

94. See B. Botfield, *Praefationes et Epistolae Editionibus Principibus Auctorum Veterum Praepositae*, Cambridge 1861, 254.

95. The manuscript of Hesychius originally belonged to Giacomo Bardellone of Mantua. After being edited by Mousouros and published, it probably remained in Aldus's possession; from him it was acquired by the Venetian nobleman Giuseppe Recanati, and finally by the Biblioteca Marciana: see Renouard, *op. cit.* 67.

96. Ognibene, who was related to Niccolò Leoniceno, was born at Lonigo between 1410 and 1419 and died in Venice in 1502. He studied under Vittorino da Feltre and taught at the School of St. Mark's in Venice. On his studies with Vittorino see Nella Giannetto (ed.), *Vittorino da Feltre e la sua scuola. Umanesimo, Pedagogia, Arti*, Florence 1981; R. Sabbadini, 'Nuove notizie e nuovi documenti su Ognibene de' Bonisoli Leoniceno' in *Antologia Veneta* 1 (1900) 12-26, 174-189.

His principal occupation was editing Latin and Greek texts for printers in Venice and elsewhere, which ran to a total of sixty-one editions. Of the Latin authors, he edited works by Cicero (37 editions), Sallust (1), Valerius Maximus (5), Lucretius (17), Horace (2), Donatus (1), Quintilian (1) and Lucan (8). Of works by Greek authors, two editions of Aesop and two of Xenophon are known. In addition to his translations, Leoniceno also wrote original works of his own: his textbooks of grammar and rhetoric were published in print and were popular with the public.

97. Conrad Celtis was one of the pioneers of textual studies in Germany, perhaps the very first to introduce into his country the method of working used in Italy. Influenced perhaps by the example of Aldus's Academy, when he moved to Vienna in 1497 he founded the Societas Danubiana and worked hard to promote the sales of the Aldine editions. See L. Spitz,

out Italy and in all the centres of learning in Europe; and to do this he enlisted the services of countless scholars for the sole purpose of evaluating and rehabilitating the Graeco-Roman and Byzantine manuscript tradition. When Thomas Linacre, the first Englishman to study at the humanist schools in Italy, went to Venice to work on the Aldine edition of Aristotle (1495-1498), he brought with him a rare manuscript of Prudentius that had been lost and gathering dust for centuries.[94] Giacomo Bardellone, the owner of what is still the only known manuscript of Hesychius's *Lexicon*, gladly lent it to Aldus to be used for the *editio princeps* of 1514, though he was well aware of its rarity value.[95] Similarly, Ognibene Leoniceno gave Aldus free use of all his valuable and reliable manuscripts of medical works, thanks to which the Aldine editions were much more authoritative than they would otherwise have been.[96] And while Aldus was expecting more rare codices to be sent from the North, as Conrad Celtis had promised him,[97] Erasmus came and joined his Academy to prepare a new edition of his encyclopaedic *Adagia* and soon had his own agents searching far and wide for manuscripts of all kinds. While at work, tirelessly correcting proofs as they came off the press, Erasmus spoke of being approached by Poles and Hungarians offering valuable manuscripts for sale.[98] Another of Aldus's associates was Urbano Bolzanio, whose unquenchable love of Greek literature had taken him on a tour of the Aegean islands in search of manuscripts of Homer, and while there he had managed to obtain rare codices for use in the school he subsequently opened in Venice.[99] Also available was Giorgio Valla's large library, which on being acquired by Alberto Pio, Prince of Carpi, was put into order by Mousouros and provided a mass of textual material for Aldus's editorial team.[100] The enormous prestige attached to the Aldine editions is indicated by the fact that Willibald Pirckheimer, a German lover of Greek literature, sent Albrecht Dürer to Venice to buy copies of all the Greek books Aldus had printed and make illustrations for them.[101] One last instance giving us a good idea of the size of some Renaissance libraries is the collection of Cardinal Domenico Grimani, which was enlarged in 1498 by the acquisition of 1,198 books from Pico della Mirándola and eventually contained no fewer than fifteen thousand volumes.[102]

III. Architecture. The architecture of public and court libraries during the Renaissance did not evolve to meet the fresh needs created by the invention of printing: the enormous expansion of book production, the book trade and book-collecting made no difference to library design, at least until near the end of the sixteenth century. One has the feeling that even after 1500, by which time printed books had taken over everywhere in Europe, the real *raison d'être* of the monumental libraries then being built was to celebrate the beauties of manuscripts rather than to signal the dawn of a new era in the propagation of learning. There is no such

Conrad Celtis, the German Arch-Humanist, Cambridge Mass. 1957; see also pp. 432-436 herein.

98. Aldus had established a close relationship with the University of Krakow: see Lowry, *op. cit.* 287-289.

99. Urbano Bolzanio was born at Belluno in 1443 and died in Venice in 1524. Having studied Greek in Constantinople and Messina, he loved the language and made a study of the rules of Greek grammar. He was the author of the first Greek grammar written in Latin: *Institutiones graecae grammatices*, Venice 1497 (Renouard, *op. cit.* 11-12). He had a fine collection of manuscripts, which Erasmus consulted for his *Adagia*. One of them had been given to him by Mousouros (see Mioni, 'La biblioteca...' 16-17), and it is also recorded that one of the manuscripts he brought back with him from Constantinople was a copy of Homer: see A. Castrifrancanus, *Oratio habita in funere Urbani Bellunensis*, Venice 1524, No. 38.

100. Alberto Pio's library contained 146 or 147 Greek manuscripts: see Lowry, *op. cit.* 59. On the eventual fate of Valla's library see J.L. Heiberg, 'Beiträge zur Geschichte Georg Valla's und seiner Bibliothek', *ZB* 16 (1896) 353-416.

101. Pirckheimer boasted that he

203. Aldus Manutius. A contemporary engraving.

thing as a standard typology of these libraries because, except in the case of monastic libraries, each architect drew up a design that met his own personal criteria. However, one thing they do have in common is the predilection for grand halls that were also used as reading rooms, a feature derived from ancient Rome. In this brief note on library architecture I shall not be referring to the *studioli* (private libraries) of the Italian princes,[103] nor to the great libraries that made their appearance in the North from about the middle of the sixteenth century, but only to certain types of libraries built in Italy which, both functionally and aesthetically, epitomize the Renaissance spirit. No absolute classification is possible, but two clearly recognizable types can be dealt with separately: three-aisled libraries and libraries with painted decoration.

1. Three-aisled libraries. Cosimo de' Medici's proposal that libraries should once again be open to all scholars, combined with a general move away from the restrictions of medieval architectural form, gave Michelozzo di Bartolommeo (1396-1472) an opportunity to design one of his finest pieces of work, the first public library to be built in Italy. Commissioned by Cosimo in 1441, it forms part of the Dominican Monastery of San Marco in Florence.[104] The main room, which occupies an area of 45 x 10.50 metres on the first floor, is divided into three aisles by two rows of eleven Ionic columns. The central aisle is roofed with a barrel-vault, the two side aisles with rib-vaults springing from elegant semi-capitals on the side walls. The distinctive appearance and atmosphere of the room are due to the proportions and the simple ornamentation: the columns, capitals and central arches are made of *pietra serena*, while the walls and ceilings are faced with the white stucco typical of Florentine Renaissance buildings. Light is admitted through two rows of windows in the side walls. The original furniture has not survived, but according to Vasari it consisted of two rows of thirty-two reading-desks flanking the central aisle, with the manuscripts (including four hundred from the celebrated collection of Niccolò Niccoli) chained to them.[105] So the only real innovation in the design of Renaissance libraries was the adoption of the basilica plan, as the furniture and fittings remained exactly as they had been in the Middle Ages.

By virtue of its design, this type of library was not susceptible to further evolution or modification, as it was based on an architectural form that ruled out the possibility of attaching bookcases to the side walls. Yet it remained the standard model for all monastic libraries, at least until the middle of the fifteenth century, and for some secular libraries too. The monastic libraries in which the influence of Michelozzo's style is most strongly apparent are those of San Domenico in Bologna (1461),[106] San Domenico in Perugia (1464),[107] Santa Maria delle Grazie in Milan (1469),[108] San Sepolcro in Piacenza (1508-1509)[109] and San Giovanni Evangelista in Parma (1523).[110] But few

had copies of 'all the Greek books ever printed in Italy': see E. Offenbacher, 'La bibliothèque de Willibald Pirckheimer', *La Bibliofilia* 40 (1938) 241-263.

102. See M. Sanudo, *Diarii*, XXXIV, Venice 1892, 407-408.

103. The most famous Renaissance *studioli* were those of Federico da Montefeltro at Urbino and of François I in the Palazzo Vecchio, Florence. See Liebenwein, *op. cit.* 66-77, 99.

204. Paolo Manuzio. Engraving from P. Manuzio, Epistolarum libri X, *Venice 1571.*

104. Still indispensable as a reference work on the architecture of medieval libraries is J.W. Clark, *The Care of Books: An essay on the development of libraries and their fittings from the earliest times to the end of the eighteenth century*, Cambridge 1901. See also: B.H. Streeten, *The Chained Library*, London 1939; E. Lehmann, *Die Bibliotheksräume der deutschen Klöster im Mittelalter*, Berlin 1957; G. Cecchini, 'Evoluzione architettonico-strutturale della biblioteca pubblica in Italia dal secolo XV al XVII', *Accademie e Biblioteche d'Italia* 35 (1967) 27-47; Id., *Sei biblioteche monastiche rinascimentali*, Milan 1960; A. Masson, *Le décor des bibliothèques du Moyen εge à la Révolution*, Geneva 1972; J.F. O'Gorman, *The Architecture of the Monastic Library in Italy, 1300-1600*, New York 1972. See also p. 342 herein.

would quarrel with the assertion that Michelozzo's model reached its peak of perfection in the library designed by Matteo Nuti for Novello Malatesta at Cesena, which remains to this day exactly as it was originally, even down to the furniture and fittings.[111]

2. Libraries with painted decoration. Before we move on to the libraries with painted decoration, something should be said about the

205. Carved panelling in the study of Federico da Montefeltro, Duke of Urbino.

105. On Niccoli and the fate of his library see pp. 340-344.

106. See P.V. Alce and A. d'Amato, *La biblioteca di S. Domenico in Bologna*, Florence 1961; O'Gorman, *op. cit.* 39-41.

107. See G. Cecchini, 'La quattrocentesca biblioteca del convento di S. Domenico di Perugia' in *Miscellanea di scritti vari in memoria di Alfonso Gallo*, Florence 1956, 249-254.

108. See A. Pica, *Il gruppo monumentale di S. Maria delle Grazie in Milano*, Rome 1937; O'Gorman, *op. cit.* 64-65.

109. See O'Gorman, *op. cit.* 71.

110. See A.I. Boselli, 'Le pitture della biblioteca dell'ex-convento dei benedettini in Parma', *Aurea Parma* 2 (1913) 167-172; L. Testi, 'I corali miniati della chiesa di S. Giovanni Evangelista in Parma', *La Bibliofilia* 20 (1918-1919) 1-30, 132-152; Masson, *op. cit.* 76-77.

111. On the Biblioteca Malatestiana see Ch. XV (pp. 305-318).

112. On the Biblioteca Laurenziana see Ch. XVII (pp. 339-356).

113. A library similar in many respects to the Vatican Library in style and appearance is that of the Escorial (1563-1584), which was built for King Philip II of Spain and was actually completed two years before the Vatican Library. See J.W. Clark, *The Care of Books*, 270, 274.

114. See Cecchi, *op. cit.*

Medici library in Florence, for two reasons: its unusual architectural style, which occupies the middle ground between the two types described here, and the fact that it is the only bilingual library on the ancient Roman model.[112] This library, designed by Michelangelo, differs in two respects from Michelozzo's model and that of Jacopo Sansovino and Domenico Fontana. Even though it was built as late as 1571, it has the traditional medieval furniture and fittings (two rows of reading-desks with an open space between them), but the architectural form is different: it is a large oblong room with no interior columns and with a flat ceiling. The most conspicuous decorative features are the architectural elements in natural stone against a background of white stucco, the ornate carved wooden ceiling and the imitation marquetry floor. Here the concept of the bilingual library is revived in perfect harmony with the ancient Roman model: the Latin books are in the desks on the left, the Greek books on the right. No other library ever recaptured the style of this one, which epitomizes the genius of Michelangelo and is the hallmark of the Medici family library.

Libraries with painted decoration were intended to bring the ancient world back to life in the frescoes on the walls and ceilings, which represented subjects drawn chiefly from Greek mythology. This was because most of these libraries contained works of Graeco-Roman literature, many of them illuminated or illustrated by some of the greatest artists of their day. But the subject matter of the paintings was not limited to mythological themes: compositions were often specially chosen to suit the personality of the library's founder or the principles on which it was based. In the Vatican Library, for example, in addition to frescoes of Heracles, Cadmus and ancient Greek philosophers such as Pythagoras and Epicharmus, there were scenes from the most important Ecumenical Councils and symbolical representations of the libraries of the patriarchates of the Eastern Church.[113] And in the library of Enea Silvio Piccolomini, in Siena cathedral, Bernardino Pintoricchio painted a series of splendid frescoes depicting scenes from the life of the founder when he was on the pontifical throne as Pius II.[114]

To sum up, the innovations in library design introduced during the Italian Renaissance (from the early fifteenth to the mid sixteenth century) were limited to the architectural form of the main hall, which served as library and reading room combined. The furniture and fittings were generally no different from those of medieval monastic libraries: here again the dominant features were the reading-desks, which often had the books chained to them. Only in a few cases were modifications made to the furniture, two of those being the Biblioteca Marciana and the Vatican Library, where the original reading-desks were replaced by wall cabinets. Besides the monumental dimensions of the public libraries in Italy and the court libraries founded throughout Europe, from Portugal to Prague, the one other feature they have in common is the pictorial decoration, consisting of frescoes on subjects taken from mythology and the struggles leading to the triumph of Christianity, to remind readers of the part played by books in perpetuating the achievements of the human mind.

206. The Hall of Sixtus V in the Vatican Library. Watercolour by Francesco Pannini, late 18th c.

BOOK TWO

Selected Monastic and Humanistic Libraries

1. Wood-carving of St. John the Evangelist holding a book. Strahov Abbey. Late 15th c.

The Library of the Oecumenical Patriarchate

CHAPTER TWELVE

The Patriarchal Library in Constantinople was founded to be a repository of theological learning and a storehouse of patristic, doctrinal and hermeneutical writings and refutations of heretical tendencies with which to defend the Orthodox faith against constant argument over the correct interpretation of the Bible. The Patriarchal Library is in fact as old as the Patriarchate of Constantinople and may well be the oldest theological library in Christendom.[1]

The inauguration of Constantinople as the new capital of the Empire (11th May 330) and the formal organization of its Church shifted the intellectual centre of gravity from the West to the East. The history of the Patriarchal Library may be said to date symbolically from Constantine the Great's decision to write to Eusebius, the Bishop of Caesarea in Palestine, asking him to send fifty manuscripts of the Bible.[2] Admittedly, these were probably intended for the use of the churches in the imperial capital, but it is quite likely that some of them ended up in a collection of books which later formed the nucleus of one of the great libraries of Constantinople.

There is very little documentary evidence concerning the Patriarchal Library from the fourth to the seventh century, and what is known about its contents and the way it was run is mainly a matter of conjecture. We cannot even be sure exactly where the library was, let alone how it was arranged, although it is known that in certain periods the books were kept in the Patriarch's residence – the *Episkopeion* (Episcopate) or *Hieron Anaktoron* (Holy Palace), as it was called – near the Church of Hagia Sophia.[3] From the seventh century, and more especially from the reign of Heraclius (610-641), the history of the Library is easier to trace. It was at about that time, probably under Patriarch Thomas I (607- 610), that a fine new building known as the Thomaitis Triklinos was erected to serve as the patriarchal residence,[4] and the library was probably located there until 791, when the Thomaitis was completely destroyed by fire. Patriarch Thomas's work was carried on, with perhaps even greater zeal, by his successor Sergios I (610-638), whom George of Pisidia praised for his great improvements to the Library in a poem entitled 'To the Library Built by Patriarch Sergios'.[5]

With perennial controversy raging over the knotty problems of theology involved in defining Christian orthodoxy, and with books of all sorts always needed to keep the patriarchal staff abreast of current developments, the Library came to be a very important institution. Nor was ideology the Church's only concern, for the Church had to be on the lookout not only for heretical writings but also for textually corrupt, unsigned and misattributed works used at various times by sects such as the Manichees, Donatists, Pelagians and Nestorians and many others. To guard against such works the Library needed

2. The sixteenth-century tower where the archives are kept.

reliable texts which convincingly refuted the heretical beliefs.[6]

Following the tradition which had grown up in the Roman period, the Patriarchal Library was bilingual, with separate Greek and Latin sections. The Latin section contained works by such writers as St. Augustine of Hippo and St. Ambrose of Milan. Quite possibly there was a librarian who specialized in Latin manuscripts, like the three employed in the Imperial Library under a law enacted by Emperor Valens (364-378).[7] Another feature of the Patriarchal Library was that the orthodox books were kept separately from the heretical and idolatrous. This was the usual practice in the Western Christian world as well as the East. At the monastery of Cluny in France, for example, any monk who read the work of an ancient writer in the library had to scratch his ear with his finger like a dog scratching itself with its hind leg, 'because the infidel is rightly compared with that animal.'[8] Patriarch Germanos I (715-730) tells us in his treatise *On Heresies*, written after his resignation in January 730 and addressed to Anthimos the Deacon, that in the Patriarchal Library the books by Eusebius of Caesarea were not shelved with the works of Orthodox writers but were kept separately at a distance, at the beginning of the heretical books, 'in the same box'. The implication is that there was a special cupboard or box in which the heretical books were kept.[9]

The size of the Patriarchal Library is hinted at in the Proceedings of the Sixth Ecumenical Council (Constantinople, 680-681). There we learn that the deacon Georgios, the archivist (*chartophylax*) of the Patriarchate,[10] brought from the library to the conference chamber such books as the papal delegates did not have with them, which shows that there had been close consultations between the Patriarchal and Vatican Libraries during the preparations for the council.[11] Among the numerous works mentioned in the Proceedings are treatises by Gregory of Nyssa, John Chrysostom, Cyril of Alexandria, Athanasius, Dionysius the Areopagite and Ephraim, Archbishop of Antioch.

The accession to the imperial throne of Bardanes Philippikos (711-713), an adherent of Monotheletism, marked the beginning of a period of great upheavals. The new emperor ostentatiously burnt the original Proceedings of the Sixth Ecumenical Council (which were kept in the Imperial Library) and wrought havoc with monastic libraries, but the Patriarchal Library was left almost unscathed: a few books were destroyed and pages with holy pictures or written evidence of the veneration of sacred images were ripped out of some others, but that was all.[12]

The existence of an official post of librarian (*bibliophylax*) is first attested in the Proceedings of the Seventh Ecumenical Council, where there is a reference to 'Stephanos, the devout monk and *bibliophylax*'. Nothing is known about the organization or the administrative hierarchy of the record office (*chartophylakion*) and the library, nor do we know who was responsible to the Patriarch for seeing that they functioned

1. The most comprehensive study of the Patriarchal Library from its beginnings to the fall of Constantinople is K.A. Manafis, *Αἱ ἐν Κωνσταντινουπόλει Βιβλιοθῆκαι, Αὐτοκρατορικαί καί Πατριαρχική, καί περί τῶν ἐν αὐταῖς χειρογράφων μέχρι τῆς Ἁλώσεως (1453)*, Athens 1972, 62-148.

2. See esp. C. Wendel, 'Der Bibel-Auftrag Kaisers Konstantins', *ZB* 56 (1939) 165-175; R. Devreesse, *Introduction à l'étude des manuscrits grecs*, Paris 1954, 124 ff.; P. Lemerle, *Ὁ πρῶτος Βυζαντινός οὐμανισμός: Σημειώσεις καί παρατηρήσεις γιά τήν παιδεία στό Βυζάντιο ἀπό τίς αρχές τοῦ 10ου αἰώνα* (= *Le premier humanisme byzantin...*, tr. Maria Nystazopoulou-Pelekidou), Athens 1981, 54; Manafis, *op. cit.* 22, 62. The ma-nuscripts sent to Constantine in response to his request were vellum codices, i.e. they were written on vellum (parchment) and bound in book form; copied by master calligraphers, they were easy to read and conveniently portable. See J.A. Heikel's edition of Eusebius of Caesarea, *Εἰς τόν βίον τοῦ μακαρίου Κωνσταντίνου βασιλέως*, I, Leipzig 1902, IV, 36, 131-132.

3. The firmest evidence for the existence of the Patriarchal Library was provided by the Proceedings of the First Council of Nicaea (325). The Proceedings have not survived, but they were still in the Library at least as late as the decade 1565-1575, when a catalogue of the Library was compiled: see R. Förster, *De antiquitatibus et libris manuscriptis Constantinopolitanis*, Rostock 1877, 21. To prepare for councils of the Church there had to be libraries in the various patriarchates: besides minutes of the proceedings of Church councils and synods, of which fair copies were made and sent to the other patriarchates, copies had to be made of other works as well, such as books which the organizing committee considered ought to be mentioned and were not to be found in the Library:

3. A view of the library.

4. General view of the library.

properly. The librarian had to sign the inventory (*brevium*) when he took over, enter all new accessions in it as they came in, and finally pass it on to his successor in the same way.[13]

John the Grammarian. The history of the Library in the first half of the ninth century is dominated by the figure of John the Grammarian, known as 'the Sorcerer Patriarch'.[14] John came close to being appointed as the successor to Patriarch Nikephoros I (806-815) to lead the renewed campaign against sacred images, but on that occasion it was Theodotos Melissenos (815-821), nicknamed Kassiteras ('the Tinsmith'), who was eventually installed on the patriarchal throne. In May 814 Emperor Leo V the Armenian (813-820), wishing to find documentary evidence in support of his iconoclastic policy, gave orders for all old books (by which he presumably meant old religious books) to be rounded up; and under the supervision of John the Grammarian a great many books that had been gathering dust in the churches and monasteries of Constantinople were brought to a room in the palace to be scrutinized by a special commission appointed to search for passages that condemned the use of sacred images.[15] Eventually they turned up the '*Synodikon* of Constantine Kaballinos the Isaurian' in the Proceedings of the first Iconoclastic Council, held at the Hiereia Palace in 754.

Photios. The Patriarch who really made the Byzantines aware of the importance of books and reading in their cultural life was Photios I. In his two nine-year terms as Patriarch (858-867 and 877-886) he did more than anyone else to promote the role of the Patriarchate's universal cultural policy, and in his own work he stressed the need for a return to the sources of 'Hellenizing Christianity'.[16] In the opinion of his contemporaries – even those who were openly opposed to him, such as Niketas David, the biographer of Patriarch Ignatios – Photios was so knowledgeable about grammar, poetry, rhetoric and philosophy, not to mention medicine and all the natural sciences, that he not only surpassed all other scholars of his own time but deserved to be compared with the ancients.[17] His bookish pursuits and his writings, especially his *Bibliotheca* and *Lexicon*, continue to engage the attention of historians and literary scholars to this day.[18] By the end of his life he must have had a complete picture of all the books that existed in Constantinople; after all, to a man in his position no library could afford to close its doors. His involvement in the work of the Patriarchal Library is purely a matter of inference, as there is no evidence for it in any of the sources, but he is known to have had a fine library of his own, and the time he spent reading his books with his friends was to him the greatest blessing life had to offer.

Although the ensuing period was one of great economic prosperity for the Byzantine Empire, accompanied by a splendid burgeoning of all

see Manafis, *op. cit.* 62-69.

4. See Nikephoros Kallistos Xanthopoulos, *Ἐκκλησιαστική Ἱστορία*, in *PG* 147 457B; R. Guilland, *Le Thomaïtès et le Patriarcat: Études de topographie de Constantinople byzantine*, 2 vols., Berlin/Amsterdam 1969, 14. See also Manafis, *op. cit.* 70 ff.; Lemerle, *op. cit.* 345.

5. George of Pisidia, the chronicler and poet, was a deacon, archivist and sacristan of Hagia Sophia. His work was a source of historical material for the chronicler Theophanes and was much used by Michael Psellos, and the compilers of the lexicon called *Souda* ('Suidas') drew on him for a good deal of their information. See Krumbacher II 621-625; L. Sternbach, 'Georgii Pisidae carmina inedita', *Wiener Studien* 14 (1892) 55; for his poem on Sergios see A. Pertusi, *Giorgio di Pisidia, poemi,* I: *Panegirici, epici* (= Studia Patristica et Byzantina, 7), Ettal 1960, 61.

6. On the problem of textually corrupt and forged writings at the first six Ecumenical Councils see W. Speyer, *Die literarische Fälschung im heidnischen und christlichen Altertum: Ein Versuch ihrer Deutung*, Munich 1971, 260-277.

7. On the growth of the tradition of bilingual libraries in Rome from about 39 B.C., soon after the death of Julius Caesar, see pp. 97-121.

8. Lemerle, *op. cit.* 344. One of the canons adopted at the Second Council of Nicaea, in 787, laid down that heretical books were to be kept in a special place: see J.D. Mansi, *Sacrorum conciliorum nova et amplissima collectio*, Florence/Venice 1759-1798, 430B ('Canon 9, XIII, on not hiding any anti-Christian heretical book').

9. See Manafis, *op. cit.* 90-91; Lemerle, *op. cit.* 344. The text of Patriarch Germanos's treatise is in *PG* 98 41D-44A.

10. On the deacon Georgios see Mansi, *op. cit.* XI 213E-216A. The post of archivist (*chartophylax*) is first

5. Ὁμιλίαι (Homilies) *of St. John Chrysostom. Parchment, 11th c. (Ms No. 2, fol. 30).*

τυχεῖν· χάριτι καὶ φιλανθρωπίᾳ τοῦ κυρίου ἡμῶν Ἰησοῦ Χριστοῦ· μεθ' οὗ τῷ πατρὶ ἅμα τῷ ἁγίῳ πνεύματι δόξα κράτος τιμή· νῦν καὶ ἀεὶ καὶ εἰς τοὺς αἰῶνας τῶν αἰώνων·

ἀμήν·

Καὶ εἶπεν ὁ θεός· γενηθήτωσαν φωστῆρες ἐν τῷ στερεώματι τοῦ οὐρανοῦ εἰς φαῦσιν ἐπὶ τῆς γῆς· τοῦ διαχωρίζειν ἀναμέσον τῆς ἡμέρας καὶ ἀναμέσον τῆς νυκτός· καὶ ἔστωσαν εἰς σημεῖα καὶ εἰς καιροὺς καὶ εἰς ἡμέρας καὶ εἰς ἐνιαυτούς.

Βούλομαι τῆς συνήθους ἅπτεσθαι διδασκαλίας. καὶ ὀκνῶ καὶ ἀναδύομαι· πάθος γὰρ ἀθυμίας ἔβαλε θόν. συνέχει τε καὶ συνταράσσει μου τὸν νοῦν ... μου δέδοικα θ...

the arts, little is known about the Patriarchal Library during that time except that it escaped unscathed in the terrible fire which destroyed the *cerularia* of the Great Church. It was still located in the Thomaitis, which was used for at least twelve council and synod meetings between 1089 and 1117. The Library is said to have been enlarged in accordance with the 'Renaissance' spirit that prevailed under the Komnenos dynasty in the twelfth century.

In 1166 a council was convened to resolve the theological dispute that erupted in the reign of Manuel I Komnenos (1143-1180) over the correct interpretation of a passage in the Gospel. The Patriarch at the time was Loukas Chrysoverghis (1156-1169), who led the way in condemning the heretical doctrines of Eirenikos (Irenicus). The proceedings of the council mention the titles of twenty-nine works which were cited against Eirenikos, and most probably they all came from the Patriarchal Library.[19]

The conclusion to be drawn from our researches on the history of the Patriarchal Library from its foundation to the conquest of Constantinople by the Crusaders in 1204 is that there was indeed a large theological library in the Patriarchate for about nine hundred years, and that the patriarchal archives were kept there too. But there is no way of knowing whether the original books survived intact or whether they (and the conciliar records in the archives) shared the fate of the Thomaitis, which was burnt down several times. Nor can we be sure what books it contained: whether there was a consistent stock renewal policy, what was eventually decided about the fate of the heretical books, or whether there were classical as well as theological books, since the only evidence we have to go on in most cases is the existence of one or two classical works which are known to have belonged to the Library. Nor do we know whether the Latin section was kept up throughout this period or whether it was closed abruptly after the breach between the Eastern and the Western Church; nor whether it functioned as a public theological library or was kept as a repository of knowledge for the use of the Patriarch's staff.

The appalling devastation done to Greek and Orthodox cultural treasures during the sack of Constantinople by the armies of the Fourth Crusade in 1204 was without precedent in the history of the European peoples. The Thomaitis was probably burnt down yet again – or so at least Niketas Choniates implies in his *History* – and unique and irreplaceable manuscripts were thrown into the flames in their hundreds, regardless of their contents, because they were 'incomprehensible'.[20] The sources tell us nothing about the fate of the Patriarchal Library, but the Thomaitis must have been rebuilt or repaired, as it was used in 1214 for negotiations between the emissaries of Emperor Theodore I Laskaris (1204-1222) and the Crusaders. The Patriarchal See was re-established in the new Byzantine capital of Nicaea, though its authority

attested in 536 and that of librarian (*bibliophylax*) in the Proceedings of the Seventh Ecumenical Council (787). On the office of *chartophylax* see J. Darrouzès, 'Recherches sur les ΟΦΦΙΚΙΑ de l'Église Byzantine', *Archives de l'Orient chrétien* 11 (1970) 337-351; Manafis, *op. cit.* 69, 73, 87, 102-103. On the offices of *chartophylax* and *bibliophylax* in general see A. Vernet, 'Du "Chartophylax" au "Librarian"' in *Vocabulaire du livre et de l'écriture au moyen âge* (Actes de la table ronde, Paris 24-26 septembre 1987), ed. Olga Weijers, Turnhout 1989, 155-167. The distinction between these two posts in the Patriarchal Library was due to the fact that, although the library proper and the record office (*chartophylakion*) were probably both in the same building, they were not in the same room (Manafis, *op. cit.* 86). Some books were also kept in the sacristy of the Patriarchate, as they are nowadays in all monasteries: usually it is the rarest and most valuable books that are kept there (Mansi, *op. cit.* XIII 8b, 184d). Several copies of the proceedings of Church councils and synods were kept in the *chartophylakion*, which contained no patristic or other theological writings but only conciliar and synodical records, correspondence between the Patriarch and the Pope and discourses by heretical writers (Manafis, *op. cit.* 86-87).

11. Bishops and delegates of the patriarchates attending councils of the Church would bring books of their own with them: at the Sixth Ecumenical Council, for example, the locum tenens of the Patriarchate of Jerusalem arrived bearing conciliar writings by Patriarch Sophronios of Jerusalem (Manafis, *op. cit.* 82). Cyril Mango gives some interesting insights into the preparation of the documentation for Church councils and tells how the *chartophylakes* presented selected texts (called *pittakia*, 'plain sheets') which were distributed to the delegates for discussion: see C.

6. An initial Χ in Ἡ Γέννηση τοῦ Χριστοῦ *(Ms No.16, fol. 76v).*

ἐρῶν τῶν καὶ ἀνυμνοῦμεν
τῷ, τῷ θεῷ τὴν τοσ-
αύτην δόξαν τε καὶ λαμπρό-
τητα. ὅτι αὐτῷ ἡ
δόξα καὶ ἡ τιμὴ καὶ
ἡ προσκύνησις, εἰς
τοὺς αἰῶνας τῶν
αἰώνων· ἀμήν +

τοῦ αὐτοῦ λόγος εἰς τὴν γενέθλιον ἡμέραν τοῦ κυρίου ἡμῶν Ἰησοῦ Χριστοῦ

Χριστὸς γεννᾶται, δοξά-
σατε· Χριστὸς ἐξ οὐρανῶν,
ἀπαντήσατε· Χριστὸς
ἐπὶ γῆς, ὑψώθη-
τε. ᾄσατε τῷ κυρίῳ
πᾶσα ἡ γῆ· καὶ ἵν᾽
ἀμφότερα συνελὼν
εἴπω· εὐφραινέ-
σθωσαν οἱ οὐρανοὶ καὶ
ἀγαλλιάσθω ἡ γῆ· διὰ
τὸν ἐπουράνιον, εἶ-

was questioned by the branch of the Komnenos family that settled in Trebizond and by the branch of the Angelos family that founded the Despotate of Epiros. When Constantinople fell, Patriarch John X Kamateros (1199-1206) fled to Didymoteichon in Thrace: he never formally resigned and he declined Laskaris's invitation to join him at Nicaea. For the Patriarchate, as for the Empire as a whole, these were troublous times. The Crusaders installed their own Patriarch of Constantinople, the Venetian Tommaso Morosini, while the Greeks refused to accept Laskaris's primacy and denied the legitimacy of Patriarch Michael IV Autoreianos, who had been elected Patriarchal Bishop at a council held at Nicaea in 1208. The full authority of the Patriarchate was eventually restored in 1261, when Constantinople was recaptured by the Emperor of Nicaea.[21]

The conquest of Constantinople by the Crusaders had not broken the cultural unity of the Empire, however. The Patriarchate was reinstalled in the Thomaitis and efforts were probably made to reconstitute the Patriarchal Library there, though not so much as an oblique allusion to its reopening is to be found in the sources. Patriarch Gregory II (Gregory of Cyprus) (1283-1289), a great bibliophile, helped to revitalize the scriptoria by commissioning manuscripts of Plato for himself, and it is fair to surmise that he worked equally hard to restore the fortunes of the Patriarchal Library.[22]

Nikephoros Kallistos Xanthopoulos, in the preface to his *Ecclesiastical History*, refers to the books he consulted 'in the Great Church of the Wisdom of the Word of God', implying that there was a library in the Church of Hagia Sophia.[23] However, it would be a mistake to attach too much importance to his testimony. One positive piece of information to emerge from his book is that the Patriarchal Library, wherever it was located, still contained the *Ecclesiastical Histories* of Cyrus, Hermeias and Eusebius of Caesarea, as well as a mass of letters, proceedings of Church councils and synods, chronicles, lives of saints, liturgical books and other valuable material which had always been kept there.[24]

From the beginning of the thirteenth century right up to the Turkish conquest in 1453 the Byzantines had many other problems on their minds besides the steady contraction of the Empire's boundaries. The question of the reunion of the churches divided the upper strata of Byzantine society down the middle, and fresh literary and theological disputes – most notably the controversy over the Hesychast movement – caused further headaches for the authorities. The alarming depletion of the Empire's resources inevitably had an impact on the production and supply of books. At the council held in Constantinople in 1351, where the teachings of Barlaam of Calabria were condemned, the clerics preparing the case against him seem to have been hampered by a serious shortage of documentation; and we learn from Silvestros Syropoulos

Mango, 'The Availability of Books in the Byzantine Empire, A.D. 750-850' in *Byzantine Books and Bookmen: A Dumbarton Oaks Colloquium 1971*, Dumbarton Oaks 1975, 31.

12. The pages of the various eighth-century chronicles are full of accounts of the destruction by the imperial army of sacred relics and books in churches, monasteries and nunneries, in hermits' caves in the mountains, in shops in the towns and any other places where 'heretical' or other undesirable books might be hidden: see, for example, Theophanes, *Chronographia* I 689; *PG* 95 372B. On John of Damascus's 'Letter to Emperor Theophilos concerning holy and venerable images' see Manafis, *op. cit.* 88-89.

13. On the *brevium* (βρέβιον or βραβεῖον) see: Darrouzès, *op. cit.* 317; Deacon Chrysostomos G. Florentis, *Βραβεῖον τῆς Ἱερᾶς Μονῆς Ἁγ. Ἰωάννου τοῦ Θεολόγου Πάτμου*, Athens 1980.

14. Men of high intelligence and independent spirit were commonly reputed to be magicians in the Middle Ages, both in the West and in the East: see L. Bréhier, 'Un patriarche sorcier à Constantinople', *Revue de l'Orient chrétien* 9 (1904) 261-268.

15. John and the other members of this commission, 'having gathered together all the books from the monasteries at the Emperor's behest', kept quiet about the real object of the exercise, telling inquirers that their search through the books was connected with a prophecy made to the Emperor about the length of his reign (*PG* 95 372). While rounding up the books it is very likely that John came across rare works of classical literature, some of which he probably took to the Palace, but this does not mean that he intended to make a collection of works of ancient Greek lit-

7. One of the rare early printed liturgical books bearing the printer's mark of Andreas Kounadis. Τυπικόν καί τά 'Απόρρητα, *Venice, (Andronikos Noukios) Nikolaos and Petros Savieon, 1525.*

ΤΥΠΙΚΟΝ ΚΑΙ ΤΑ
ἈΠΟΡΡΗΤΑ

Ἀνδρέου  Κουνάδου.

Con Priuilegio dello Illustrissimo Senato Veneto, che per anni dieci niuno ardisca la presente opera Greca intitolata Typicon, stampare, ne far stãpare, ne stampata uendere in tutti i luoghi del suo Dominio, sotto le pene in esso priuilegio contenute, come amplamente nel prefato appare.

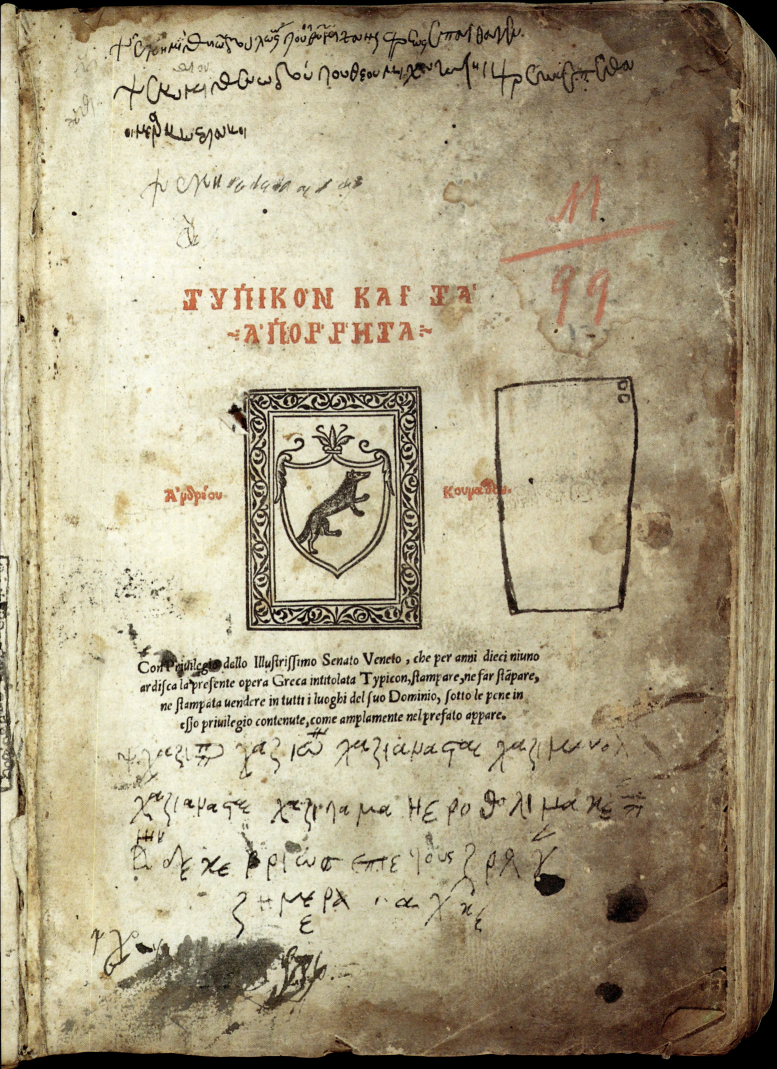

that many of the Greek delegates to the Council of Ferrara-Florence (1437-1439) had to scour the monasteries for the manuscripts they needed, from which it appears that the Patriarchal Library had not been able to maintain its stocks.[25]

Under the Ottomans, the privileges granted to the Orthodox Greeks of Constantinople evidently made it possible for the Patriarchal Library to be resuscitated. In the middle of the sixteenth century Theodosios Zygomalas, a patriarchal notary, compiled a catalogue of the manuscripts in its possession, of which only a fragment survives: 174 manuscripts are listed in this one fragment.[26]

After the fall of Constantinople the Patriarchate was accommodated in various places before finally settling in the Phanar, where it remains to this day. At first it occupied premises in the Pammakaristos Convent, where it stayed for 132 years, and it was then given the use of a building belonging to the Hospodars of Wallachia near the Church of the Panayia ton Palation. Nothing is known about what happened to the Patriarchal Library or how it was organized during the first century and a half of Ottoman rule. In 1599 Patriarch Matthaios II (1598-1602) moved the Patriarchate out of the Church of Hagios Demetrios tes Xyloportas and into the Phanar, which at that time contained the small parish church of St. George and – so it is said – a nunnery. The Library and archives were apparently housed in a tower, still standing, which formed the nucleus of the Library and, later, of the patriarchal press.[27]

The Patriarchal Press. While the East remained at a standstill as far as the manuscript tradition was concerned, in the West the invention of

8. The Pammakaristos Convent as it is today.

erature, as is implied by the canon (hymn) sung in Orthodox churches to celebrate the restoration of icons and other sacred images, where John is reviled for being 'on a par with the Hellenes': see V. Grumel, 'Jean Grammatikos et saint Théodore Studite', *Échos d'Orient* 36 (1937) 181-189; Lemerle, *op. cit.* 120-128.

16. See Lemerle, *op. cit.* 154 ff., with relevant bibliography.

17. The present biographical note on Photios is based on the description of him in the *Life of Ignatios*, first published in *PG* 105 488-581 (the passage about Photios is in col. 509). An interesting light is cast on Photios's character by a letter he wrote to Pope Nicholas I in Rome. In the spring of 861, some time after Photios had replaced Ignatios on the patriarchal throne, a synod held in the Church of the Holy Apostles in Constantinople, to which delegates were sent by the Pope, adopted a resolution condemning Ignatios. When the synod was over a Byzantine mission went to Rome bearing letters to Pope Nicholas from Emperor Michael III (842-867) and Photios. Photios in his letter told the Pope that he had been elected Patriarch against his own wishes and was to be pitied for having had to give up a peaceful life devoted to his studies, his books and his dear friends in answer to the call of duty, a renunciation which had caused him deep dis-

9. Georgios Scholarios, Σύνταγμα (Syntagma). *Printed by Nikodemos Metaxas (who later became the first Greek printer in Constantinople) at the Eliot's Court Press, London, 1627.*

10. Διαταγαί Γάμων. *[Constantinople,] Panayotis Kyriakidis, 1767.*

11. Ραντισμοῦ Στηλίτευσις. *[Constantinople, P. Kyriakidis,] 1756.*

12. Ἱερογραφική Ἁρμονία, *a collection of poems by George of Pisidia, Theodoros Ptochodromos and Nikephoros Xanthopoulos. Printed at the Patriarchal Press in 1802.*

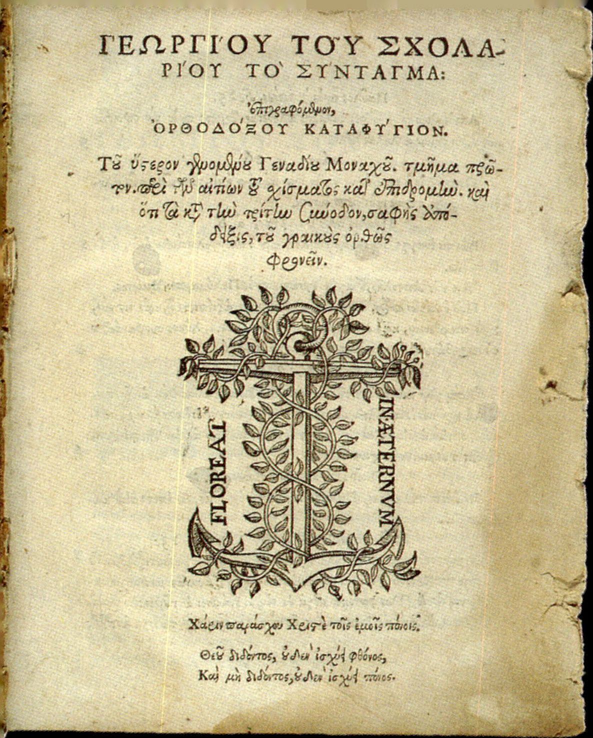

ΓΕΩΡΓΙΟΥ ΤΟΥ ΣΧΟΛΑ-
ΡΙΟΥ ΤΟ ΣΥΝΤΑΓΜΑ:
ἐπιγραφόμενον,
ΟΡΘΟΔΟΞΟΥ ΚΑΤΑΦΥΓΙΟΝ.

Τοῦ ὕστερον ὀνομασθέντος Γενναδίου Μοναχοῦ. τμῆμα πρῶτον. περὶ τῶν αἰτιῶν τοῦ σχίσματος καὶ ἐπιδρομῶν. καὶ ὅπως κατὰ τὴν τετάρτην σύνοδον, σαφὴς ἀπόδειξις, τοῦ γραικοὺς ὀρθῶς φρονεῖν.

Χάριν παράσχου Χριστὲ τοῖς ἐμοῖς πόνοις.

Θεοῦ διδόντος, οὐδὲν ἰσχύει φθόνος,
Καὶ μὴ διδόντος, οὐδὲν ἰσχύει πόνος.

Διαταγαὶ Γάμων.

Ἐν Ἔτει Σωτηρίῳ. αψξζ. ἐν μηνὶ φευρουαρίῳ.

παρὰ Παναγιώτῃ Κυριακίδῃ. τῷ εὐξαιτίῳ.

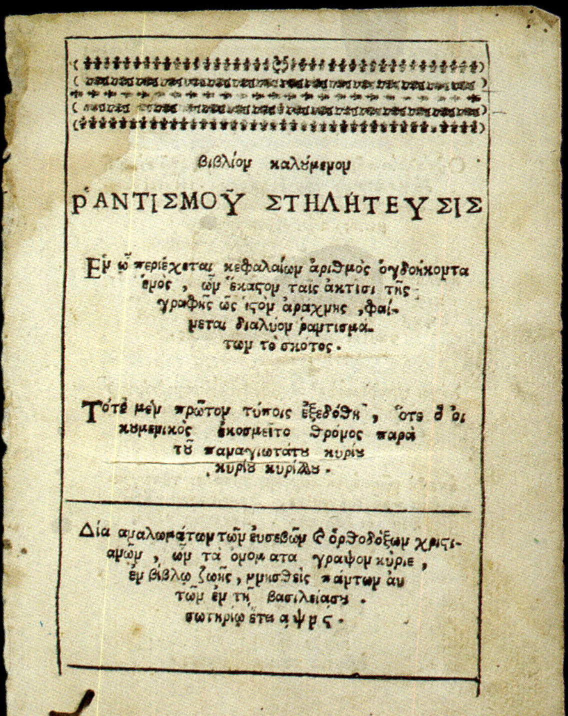

Βιβλίον καλούμενον

ΡΑΝΤΙΣΜΟΥ ΣΤΗΛΙΤΕΥΣΙΣ

Ἐν ᾧ περιέχεται κεφαλαίων ἀριθμὸς ὀγδοήκοντα ἕνος, ὧν ἕκαστον ταῖς ἀκτῖσι τῆς γραφῆς ὡς ἴσον ἀράχνης, φαίνεται διαλύον ῥαντισμάτων τὸ σκότος.

Τότε μὲν πρῶτον τύποις ἐξεδόθη, ὅτε δ' οἰκουμενικὸς ἐκοσμεῖτο θρόνος παρὰ τοῦ παναγιωτάτου κυρίου κυρίου Κυρίλλου.

Διὰ ἀναλωμάτων τῶν εὐσεβῶν καὶ ὀρθοδόξων χριστιανῶν, ὧν τὰ ὀνόματα γράψον κύριε, ἐν βίβλῳ ζωῆς, μνησθεὶς πάντων αὐτῶν ἐν τῇ βασιλείᾳ σου. σωτηρίῳ ἔτει αψμς.

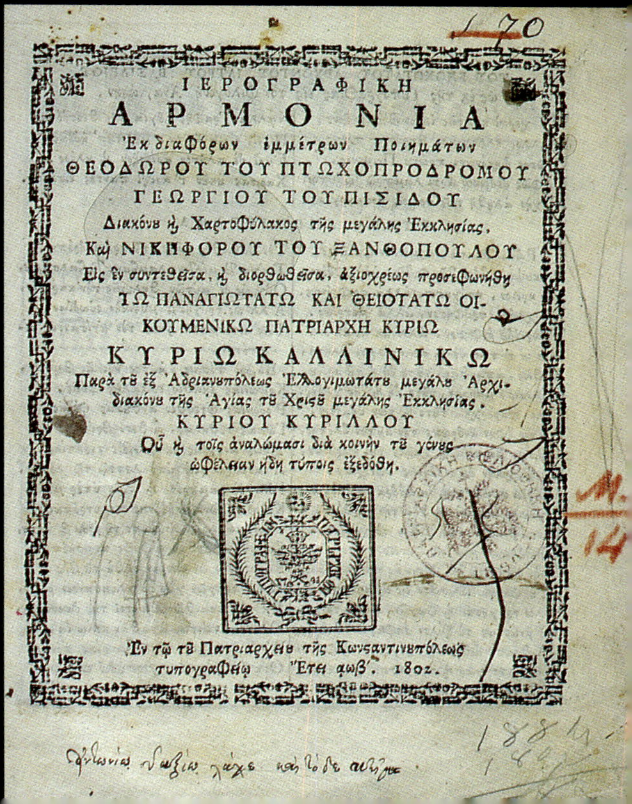

ΙΕΡΟΓΡΑΦΙΚΗ
ΑΡΜΟΝΙΑ
Ἐκ διαφόρων ἐμμέτρων Ποιημάτων
ΘΕΟΔΩΡΟΥ ΤΟΥ ΠΤΩΧΟΠΡΟΔΡΟΜΟΥ
ΓΕΩΡΓΙΟΥ ΤΟΥ ΠΙΣΙΔΟΥ
Διακόνου καὶ Χαρτοφύλακος τῆς μεγάλης Ἐκκλησίας,
Καὶ ΝΙΚΗΦΟΡΟΥ ΤΟΥ ΞΑΝΘΟΠΟΥΛΟΥ
Εἰς ἓν συντεθεῖσα, καὶ διορθωθεῖσα, ἀξιοχρέως προσεφωνήθη
ΤΩ ΠΑΝΑΓΙΩΤΑΤΩ ΚΑΙ ΘΕΙΟΤΑΤΩ ΟΙΚΟΥΜΕΝΙΚΩ ΠΑΤΡΙΑΡΧΗ ΚΥΡΙΩ
ΚΥΡΙΩ ΚΑΛΛΙΝΙΚΩ
Παρὰ τοῦ ἐξ Ἀδριανουπόλεως Ἐλλογιμωτάτου μεγάλου Ἀρχιδιακόνου τῆς Ἁγίας τοῦ Χριστοῦ μεγάλης Ἐκκλησίας.
ΚΥΡΙΟΥ ΚΥΡΙΛΛΟΥ
Οὗ καὶ τοῖς ἀναλώμασι διὰ κοινὴν τοῦ γένους ὠφέλειαν ἤδη τύποις ἐξεδόθη.

Ἐν τῷ τοῦ Πατριαρχείου τῆς Κωνσταντινουπόλεως τυπογραφείῳ. Ἔτει αωβ΄. 1802.

printing radically altered the whole pattern of intellectual activity and cultural interaction. The Sultan's steadfast refusal to allow printing presses in the Ottoman Empire stifled the 'wind of change' that was blowing the cobwebs away elsewhere, but it did not prevent the Catholics from extending their influence in the East, as they were allowed to distribute printed books of all kinds quite freely, and did so on a vast scale. In this context an important part was played by the great Patriarch Cyril I Loukaris (1620-1638). Perceiving the dangers posed by papal policy, and realizing that the Orthodox clergy in Constantinople were unable to do much to counter those dangers because they had to go to Catholic schools and universities, Loukaris decided to take matters in hand.[28]

Nikodemos Metaxas. The Jesuits, who had had a house in Constantinople since 1583, opened a seminary there in about 1601. Meanwhile the Catholic Church had launched a systematic campaign to win converts in the territories of the former Byzantine Empire: among other things they distributed school textbooks, theological books and tracts, often of dubious provenance, which were printed in Rome by the Congregation for the Propagation of the Faith and taken to the East by Catholic missionaries.[29] In 1616 Loukaris began corresponding with the Archbishop of Canterbury, George Abbot, to see if it would be possible for Orthodox clergymen to go to English universities for higher studies. One of those who took advantage of Loukaris's policy was Nikodemos Metaxas of Kefallinia, who had been taught by Theophilos Korydalleus in Athens. Metaxas studied in London from 1622 to 1626 and subsequently became the first Greek to work as a printer in the Greek homelands.[30] One of Loukaris's most cherished projects was to open a press in Constantinople to help keep the Orthodox faith alive and flourishing; and this probably explains why Metaxas studied printing in England in addition to his university course. After learning the trade at various print-shops in London he set up a press of his own at the Eliot's Court Press.[31]

In June 1627 Metaxas sailed from London for Constantinople in an English ship, the *Royal Defence*, taking with him books, a printing press, a stock of types and two assistant printers. With the help of Loukaris and the British and Venetian ambassadors, he obtained a permit to set up a press in a rented house near the British Embassy. After seven months in Constantinople he had published one book, the *Sermons* (*Ὁμιλίαι*) of Maximos Margounios, but on 22nd January 1628, on the orders of the Kaimakam (the Grand Vizier's deputy and Governor of Constantinople), the Turks raided Metaxas's house, confiscated his books, his press and all the rest of the printing equipment and took his employees off to prison. Metaxas himself was deported but was allowed to take all his printing equipment with him. Such was the inglorious end of the first

tress. The original text of the letter is in *PG* 102 597A-D, and there is a translation of perhaps the most heart-rending passage from it in Lemerle, *op. cit*. 175-176.

18. For more on the *Bibliotheca* see pp. 137-186, with footnotes and bibliographical references.

19. See Manafis, *op. cit*. 122-123.

20. See J.L. van Dieten (ed.), *Akominatos, Niketas Choniates,*

13. Woodcut by S. Schweigger, 'Ein neue Reyssbeschreibung auss Teutschland nach Constantinopel und Jerusalem', from Frühe Reisen und Seefahrten in Originalberichten, *III, Graz 1964, 118.*
14. Woodcut by S. Gerlach from M. Crusius, Turcograecica, *Basel 1584, 190.*
15. Nikodemos the Athonite, Ἐπιτομὴ Ψαλμῶν (Selections from the Psalms), *Constantinople, Patriarchal Press, 1799.*
16. Front page of the periodical Ἐκκλησιαστικὴ Ἀλήθεια (Ecclesiastical Truth), *Constantinople 1922.*
17. Nikodemos the Athonite. Engraving from Garden of the Graces, *Venice, Nikolaos Glykys, 1819.*
18. Front page of the periodical Ὀρθοδοξία (Orthodoxia), *issue of March-April 1947.*

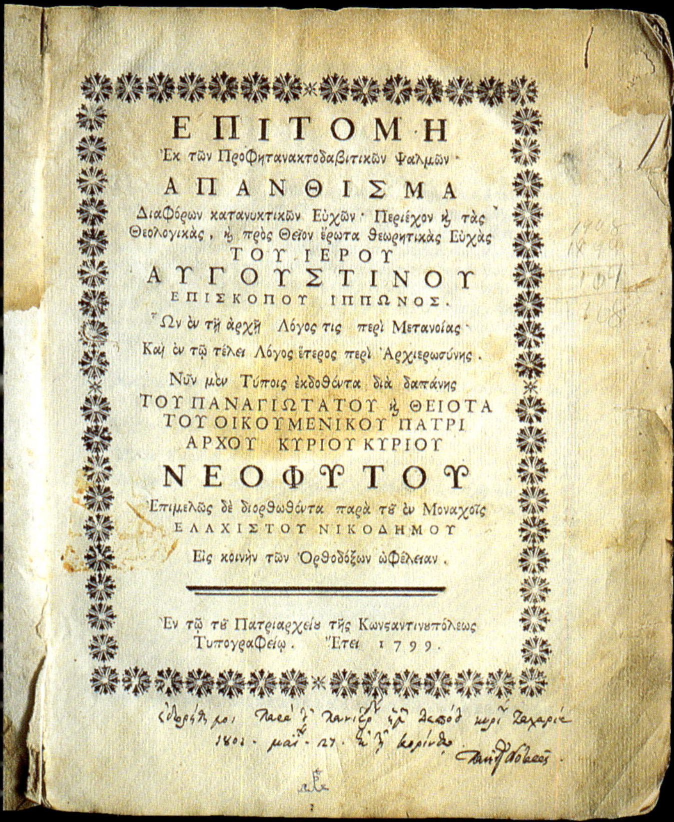
ΕΠΙΤΟΜΗ
Ἐκ τῶν Προφητανακτοδαβιτικῶν Ψαλμῶν
ΑΠΑΝΘΙΣΜΑ
Διαφόρων κατανυκτικῶν Εὐχῶν· Περιέχον καὶ τὰς Θεολογικὰς, καὶ πρὸς Θεῖον ἔρωτα θεωρητικὰς Εὐχὰς
ΤΟΥ ΙΕΡΟΥ
ΑΥΓΟΥΣΤΙΝΟΥ
ΕΠΙΣΚΟΠΟΥ ΙΠΠΩΝΟΣ.
Ὧν ἐν τῇ ἀρχῇ Λόγος τις περὶ Μετανοίας·
Καὶ ἐν τῷ τέλει Λόγος ἕτερος περὶ Ἀρχιερωσύνης.
Νῦν μὲν Τύποις ἐκδοθέντα διὰ δαπάνης
ΤΟΥ ΠΑΝΑΓΙΩΤΑΤΟΥ καὶ ΘΕΙΟΤΑΤΟΥ ΟΙΚΟΥΜΕΝΙΚΟΥ ΠΑΤΡΙΑΡΧΟΥ ΚΥΡΙΟΥ ΚΥΡΙΟΥ
ΝΕΟΦΥΤΟΥ
Ἐπιμελῶς δὲ διορθωθέντα παρὰ τοῦ ἐν Μοναχοῖς
ΕΛΑΧΙΣΤΟΥ ΝΙΚΟΔΗΜΟΥ
Εἰς κοινὴν τῶν Ὀρθοδόξων ὠφέλειαν.
Ἐν τῷ τοῦ Πατριαρχείῳ τῆς Κωνσταντινουπόλεως Τυπογραφείῳ. Ἔτει 1799.

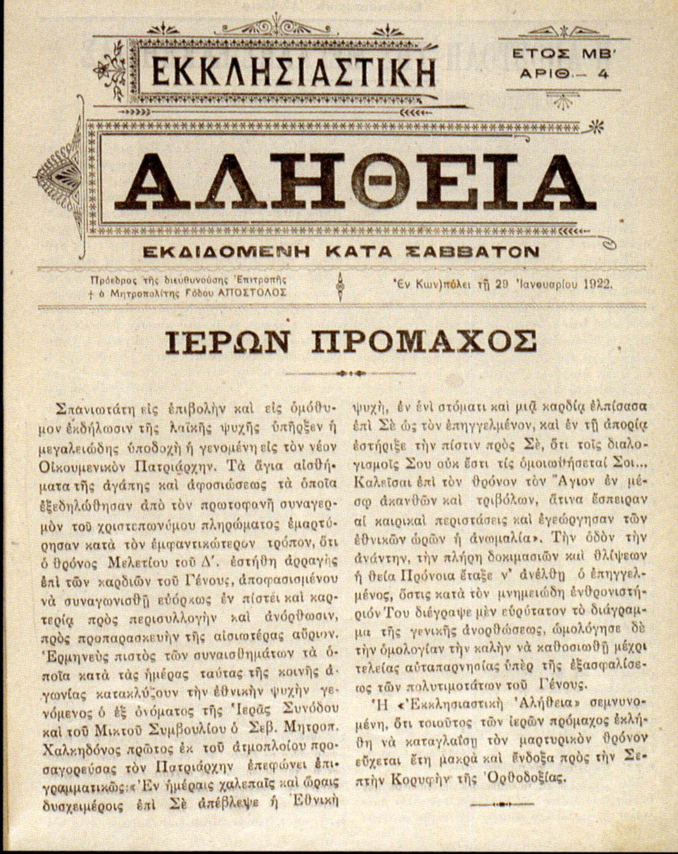
ΕΚΚΛΗΣΙΑΣΤΙΚΗ
ΕΤΟΣ ΜΒ'
ΑΡΙΘ. 4
ΑΛΗΘΕΙΑ
ΕΚΔΙΔΟΜΕΝΗ ΚΑΤΑ ΣΑΒΒΑΤΟΝ
Πρόεδρος τῆς διευθυνούσης Ἐπιτροπῆς
† ὁ Μητροπολίτης Ρόδου ΑΠΟΣΤΟΛΟΣ
Ἐν Κων)πόλει τῇ 29 Ἰανουαρίου 1922.

ΙΕΡΩΝ ΠΡΟΜΑΧΟΣ

Σπανιωτάτη εἰς ἐπιβολὴν καὶ εἰς ὁμόθυμον ἐκδήλωσιν τῆς λαϊκῆς ψυχῆς ὑπῆρξεν ἡ μεγαλειώδης ὑποδοχὴ ἡ γενομένη εἰς τὸν νέον Οἰκουμενικὸν Πατριάρχην. Τὰ ἅγια αἰσθήματα τῆς ἀγάπης καὶ ἀφοσιώσεως τὰ ὁποῖα ἐξεδηλώθησαν ἀπὸ τὸν πρωτοφανῆ συναγερμὸν τοῦ χριστεπωνύμου πληρώματος ἐμαρτύρησαν κατὰ τὸν ἐμφαντικώτερον τρόπον, ὅτι ὁ θρόνος Μελετίου τοῦ Δ'. ἐστήθη ἀρραγὴς ἐπὶ τῶν καρδιῶν τοῦ Γένους, ἀποφασισμένου νὰ συναγωνισθῇ εὐόρκως ἐν πίστει καὶ καρτερίᾳ πρὸς περισυλλογὴν καὶ ἀνόρθωσιν, πρὸς προπαρασκευὴν τῆς αἰσιωτέρας αὔριον. Ἑρμηνεὺς πιστὸς τῶν συναισθημάτων τὰ ὁποῖα κατὰ τὰς ἡμέρας ταύτας τῆς κοινῆς ἀγωνίας κατακλύζουν τὴν ἐθνικὴν ψυχὴν γενόμενος ὁ ἐξ ὀνόματος τῆς Ἱερᾶς Συνόδου καὶ τοῦ Μικτοῦ Συμβουλίου ὁ Σεβ. Μητροπ. Χαλκηδόνος πρῶτος ἐκ τοῦ ἀτμοπλοίου προσαγορεύσας τὸν Πατριάρχην ἐπεφώνει ἐπιγραμματικῶς:«Ἐν ἡμέραις χαλεπαῖς καὶ ὥραις δυσχειμέροις ἐπὶ Σὲ ἀπέβλεψε ἡ Ἐθνικὴ ψυχὴ, ἐν ἑνὶ στόματι καὶ μιᾷ καρδίᾳ ἐλπίσασα ἐπὶ Σὲ ὡς τὸν ἐπηγγελμένον, καὶ ἐν τῇ ἀπορίᾳ ἐστήριξε τὴν πίστιν πρὸς Σὲ, ὅτι τοῖς διαλογισμοῖς Σου οὐκ ἔστι τίς ὁμοιωθήσεταί Σοι... Καλεῖσαι ἐπὶ τὸν θρόνον τὸν Ἅγιον ἐν μέσῳ ἀκανθῶν καὶ τριβόλων, ἅτινα ἔσπειραν αἱ καιρικαὶ περιστάσεις καὶ ἐγεώργησαν τῶν ἐθνικῶν ὡρῶν ἡ ἀνωμαλία». Τὴν ὁδὸν τὴν ἀνάντην, τὴν πλήρη δοκιμασιῶν καὶ θλίψεων ἡ θεία Πρόνοια ἔταξε ν' ἀνέλθῃ ὁ ἐπηγγελμένος, ὅστις κατὰ τὸν μνημειώδη ἐνθρονιστήριόν Του διέγραψε μὲν εὐρύτατον τὸ διάγραμμα τῆς γενικῆς ἀνορθώσεως, ὡμολόγησε δὲ τὴν ὁμολογίαν τὴν καλὴν νὰ καθοσιωθῇ μέχρι τελείας αὐταπαρνησίας ὑπὲρ τῆς ἐξασφαλίσεως τῶν πολυτιμοτάτων τοῦ Γένους.

Ἡ «Ἐκκλησιαστικὴ Ἀλήθεια» σεμνυνομένη, ὅτι τοιοῦτος τῶν ἱερῶν πρόμαχος ἐκλήθη νὰ καταγλαΐσῃ τὸν μαρτυρικὸν θρόνον εὔχεται ἔτη μακρὰ καὶ ἔνδοξα πρὸς τὴν Σεπτὴν Κορυφὴν τῆς Ὀρθοδοξίας.

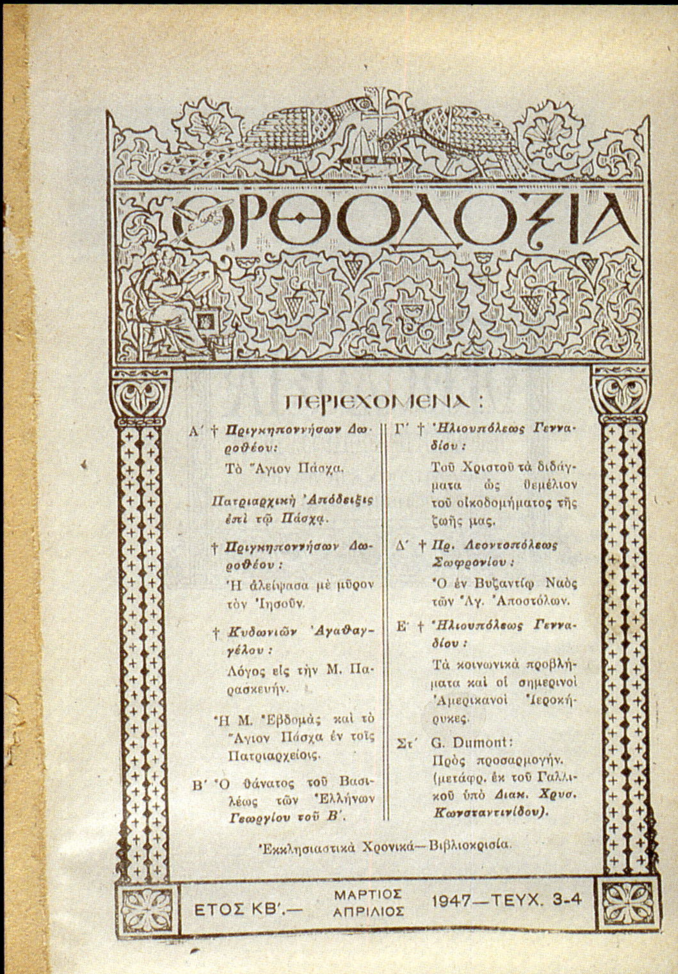
ΟΡΘΟΔΟΞΙΑ

ΠΕΡΙΕΧΟΜΕΝΑ:

Α' † *Πριγκηποννήσων Δωροθέου:*
Τὸ Ἅγιον Πάσχα.
Πατριαρχικὴ Ἀπόδειξις ἐπὶ τῷ Πάσχα.
† *Πριγκηποννήσων Δωροθέου:*
Ἡ ἀλείψασα μὲ μύρον τὸν Ἰησοῦν.
† *Κυδωνιῶν Ἀγαθαγγέλου:*
Λόγος εἰς τὴν Μ. Παρασκευήν.
Ἡ Μ. Ἑβδομὰς καὶ τὸ Ἅγιον Πάσχα ἐν τοῖς Πατριαρχείοις.
Β' Ὁ θάνατος τοῦ Βασιλέως τῶν Ἑλλήνων *Γεωργίου τοῦ Β'.*
Γ' † *Ἡλιουπόλεως Γενναδίου:*
Τοῦ Χριστοῦ τὰ διδάγματα ὡς θεμέλιον τοῦ οἰκοδομήματος τῆς ζωῆς μας.
Δ' † *Πρ. Λεοντοπόλεως Σωφρονίου:*
Ὁ ἐν Βυζαντίῳ Ναὸς τῶν Ἁγ. Ἀποστόλων.
Ε' † *Ἡλιουπόλεως Γενναδίου:*
Τὰ κοινωνικὰ προβλήματα καὶ οἱ σημερινοὶ Ἀμερικανοὶ Ἱεροκήρυκες.
Στ' G. Dumont:
Πρὸς προσαρμογήν. (μετάφρ. ἐκ τοῦ Γαλλικοῦ ὑπὸ *Διαν. Χρυσ. Κωνσταντινίδου).*
Ἐκκλησιαστικὰ Χρονικά—Βιβλιοκρισία.

ΕΤΟΣ ΚΒ'.— ΜΑΡΤΙΟΣ ΑΠΡΙΛΙΟΣ 1947—ΤΕΥΧ. 3-4

Greek printing venture in Constantinople or anywhere in the East.[32]

After this it was well over a century before the next step was taken in this direction by Patriarch Samuel I Chantzeris (1763-1768), who established the patriarchal press in the Phanar, opposite the Patriarchal Church, with Panayotis Kyriakidis of Byzantium as the first printer in charge. This was between 1764 and 1767. The Patriarchate had never given up the idea of setting up its own press. Greek books and leaflets had been printed at the Armenian press in Constantinople since 1718,[33] and it was there that the first of the so-called *karamanlidika* was printed, perhaps by Kyriakidis: the *Ἀπάνθισμα τῆς Χριστιανικῆς Πίστεως*

19. Patriarch Cyril Loukaris. Engraving from Collectanea, *1707.*

Historia, Berlin 1975, II 757-786.

21. A. Miliarakis, *Ἱστορία τοῦ Βασιλείου τῆς Νικαίας καί τοῦ Δεσποτάτου τῆς Ἠπείρου (1204-1261)*, Athens 1898, 98.

22. See Manafis, *op. cit.* 133.

23. See *PG* 145 609C. Foremost among the foreign travellers who visited Constantinople in the Middle Ages were the Arabs, not only because they were the most numerous but also because they recorded a considerable amount of information, much of which is still unpublished. In 1958 an edition appeared of a hitherto unpublished text by a merchant named 'Abd Allah bin Mohammad from Singar in Upper Mesopotamia, who went to the Byzantine Empire in the reign of Andronikos II Palaiologos (1282-1328) and visited Hagia Sophia, where he said there were several libraries: see M. Izeddin, 'Un texte arabe inédit sur Constantinople byzantine', *Journal Asiatique*, 1958, 453-457.

24. See Manafis, *op. cit.* 134-141.

25. *Ibid.* 142-144.

26. *Ibid.* 148. On the catalogue of manuscripts see G. Przychocki, 'Menander im Katalog der Patriarchalbibliothek zu Konstantinopel', *Bulletin International de l'Académie Polonaise des Sciences et des Lettres* 1-3 (1937) 28-34.

27. See A. Pasadaios, *Ὁ Πατριαρχικός Οἶκος τοῦ Οἰκουμενικοῦ Θρόνου*, Athens 1995, 144.

28. On Loukaris and the political and diplomatic background to the period see the comprehensive study by G. Hering, *Οἰκουμενικό Πατριαρχεῖο καί εὐρωπαϊκή πολιτική 1620-1638* (= *Ökumenisches Patriarchat und europäische Politik 1620-1638*, tr. D. Kurtovik), Athens 1992.

29. On the Greek publications of the Congregation for the Propagation of the Faith see *Sacrae Congregationis de Propaganda Fide Memoria Rerum (1622-1700)*, I, Rome/Freiburg/Vienna 1971; Z.N. Tsirpanlis, *Οἱ ἑλληνικές ἐκδόσεις τῆς "Sacra Congregatio de Propaganda Fide" (17 αι.):*

20. A monastic binding of the 18th c.

(*Anthology of the Christian Faith*) compiled by Neophytos Mavromatis.[34] The patriarchal press started with a set of types that had first been used by the Armenian press to print the *Ραντισμοῦ Στηλίτευσις* in 1756. In 1780 Abbot G. Toderini was told by Patriarch Neophytos VII (1789-1794, 1798-1801) that it had been closed down because it was too expensive to run, though it had not been destroyed.[35] It is interesting to note that although the Armenian press had been in operation since 1718, it was not until 1726 that the first Turkish press was founded, in the reign of Sultan Ahmet III. The Jews had had a press of their own since 1488.[36]

A third press was set up in the Patriarchate in 1793, under the auspices of Patriarch Neophytos VII. An Armenian, Ioannis Pogos, was appointed chief printer and was instructed by Patriarch Gregory V (1797-1798, 1806-1808, 1818-1821) to employ Greek apprentices and teach them the trade. Every book printed at the press had to be approved by a committee appointed by the Patriarch and the Holy Synod before it could be published. The first manager of the press (1798-1807) was a doctor by the name of Vasilios, and the first book printed there was *Διδασκαλία Πατρική* (*Paternal Exhortation*). It was followed by publications on a variety of subjects – liturgical books, *karamanlidika*, spelling primers, grammars and others – for the Greeks of Constantinople and Smyrna. It is worth noting that the standard of scholarship among the staff was so high that Hilarion Sinaitis, a later manager of the press, undertook to compile a lexicographical work entitled *Κιβωτός τῆς Ἑλληνικῆς Γλώσσης* (*Ark of the Greek Language*).[37]

The sixteenth century saw a change of policy in the Patriarchal Library as regards its *raison d'être* and therefore the type of books it needed: its role was expanded, for it was now expected to supply the religious and general educational needs of the whole Greek population of Constantinople. Even before the Turkish conquest there may well have been a tradition of patriarchs leaving their books to the Library on their death, though this is not known; but from the sixteenth century onwards it became common practice, and the Library now contains the collections of Photios II (1929-1935), Benjamin (1936-1946) and Athenagoras (1948-1972). Besides these, and besides the systematic purchases of books of various kinds (mainly those printed by Greeks of the diaspora), the Library has received generous donations over the years, mostly of books printed in Venice and Vienna. Consequently the Library proper, which now contains about 32,000 books, not only covers ecclesiastical and theological subjects but also includes a wide variety of educational and reference works and thus represents a comprehensive cross-section of Greek literary and academic achievement in the eighteenth and nineteenth centuries. Add to these the manuscripts – at least five hundred of them, dating from as far back as the fifth century – and the large collection of newspapers and periodicals, not to mention other

21. Printer's mark in Kallinikos, Νέον Ἐξομολογητάριον, *Constantinople 1837.*

22. Printer's mark in Διδασκαλία Εὐσύνοπτος, *Constantinople 1816.*

23. Printer's mark in Ἱερογραφική Ἁρμονία, *Constantinople 1802.*

Συμβολή στή μελέτη τοῦ θρησκευτικοῦ οὐμανισμοῦ, Athens 1974.

30. On the printing work of Nikodemos Metaxas see R.J. Roberts, 'The Greek Press at Constantinople in 1627 and its Antecedents', *The Library*, 5th ser., 22 (1967) 13-43; Evro Layton, 'Nikodemos Metaxas, the First Greek

Printer in the Eastern World', *Harvard Library Bulletin* 15 (1967) 140-168; Ead., «Ἡ τεχνική τοῦ βιβλίου» in *Τό Ἑλληνικό Βιβλίο (1476-1830)*, Athens 1986, 291-292; G. Hering, «Τό πρῶτο ἑλληνικό τυπογραφεῖο», *ibid*. 194-212.

31. See Layton, 'Nikodemos Metaxas...' 155, 159. On Metaxas's printer's mark see R.B. McKerrow, *Printers' and Publishers' Devices in England and Scotland, 1485-1640*, London 1913, 423. On his relations with Korydalleus see C. Tsourkas, *Les débuts de l'enseignement philosophique et de la libre pensée dans les Balkans. La vie et l'oeuvre de Théophile Corydalée (1570-1646)*, Thessaloniki 1967.

24. Preliminary sketch for the polychrome stained-glass windows overlooking the Golden Horn.

books of more general interest, and it can be seen that the Library is a veritable repository of the fruits of Greek scholarship in the East up to the middle of this century.

Architecture. The Patriarchal Library is now accommodated in a two-storey building added on to the tower which had been used as a record office and library since the end of the sixteenth century and is a typical specimen of the architecture of that period. The new building, which is in the same style as the tower, was erected at the beginning of the twentieth century. The ground floor contains miscellaneous books, periodicals and newspapers and the relics of the patriarchal press. All the manuscripts and a selection of early printed books are kept in the upper storey of the annexe, and the precious archives are in the upper storey of the tower.

THE RECONSTRUCTION OF THE LIBRARY OF THE OECUMENICAL PATRIARCHATE WAS BEGUN UNDER THE LATE PATRIARCH DEMETRIOS I IN 1991, THROUGH THE BOUNTY OF THE GENEROUS BENEFACTOR PANAYOTIS T. ANGELOPOULOS, ARCHON AND GREAT LOGOTHETE OF THE GREAT CHURCH OF CHRIST, AND HIS SONS THEODORE AND CONSTANTINE, AND WAS COMPLETED UNDER THE OECUMENICAL PATRIARCH BARTHOLOMEW IN 1994.

Although something is known about the architecture of monastic libraries, we have no information at all about the design, layout and style of any of the great libraries in Constantinople. The restoration of the Patriarchal Library has therefore been based on the Byzantine architectural tradition, adapted to take account of the radical alterations in library design necessitated by the invention of printing. The new main hall of the library, designed to these specifications by the present author, is used not as a reading room but as a museum of old books and manuscripts. It is 15 x 18 metres in size and has two large stained-glass windows overlooking the Golden Horn. The central dome, from which a large seventeenth-century wooden chandelier is suspended, is flanked by two vaults that effectively divide the room into three bays. The floor is of oak, painted purple and inlaid with rectangular panels of old Iznik tiles, which had covered the whole floor since the beginning of this century. The entrance to the Library is through two double doors, the outer one of steel and the inner one of carved wood. On either side of the doorway are the bookcases, which fill all the available wall space right up to the springing of the vaulted ceiling. They have carved wooden posts designed in the tradition of Byzantine church architecture, to support the movable shelves for the books and the drawers for the manuscripts. The bookcases, made of mahogany and beech, are painted a transparent purple and coated with a patina shot with gold, red and emerald green.

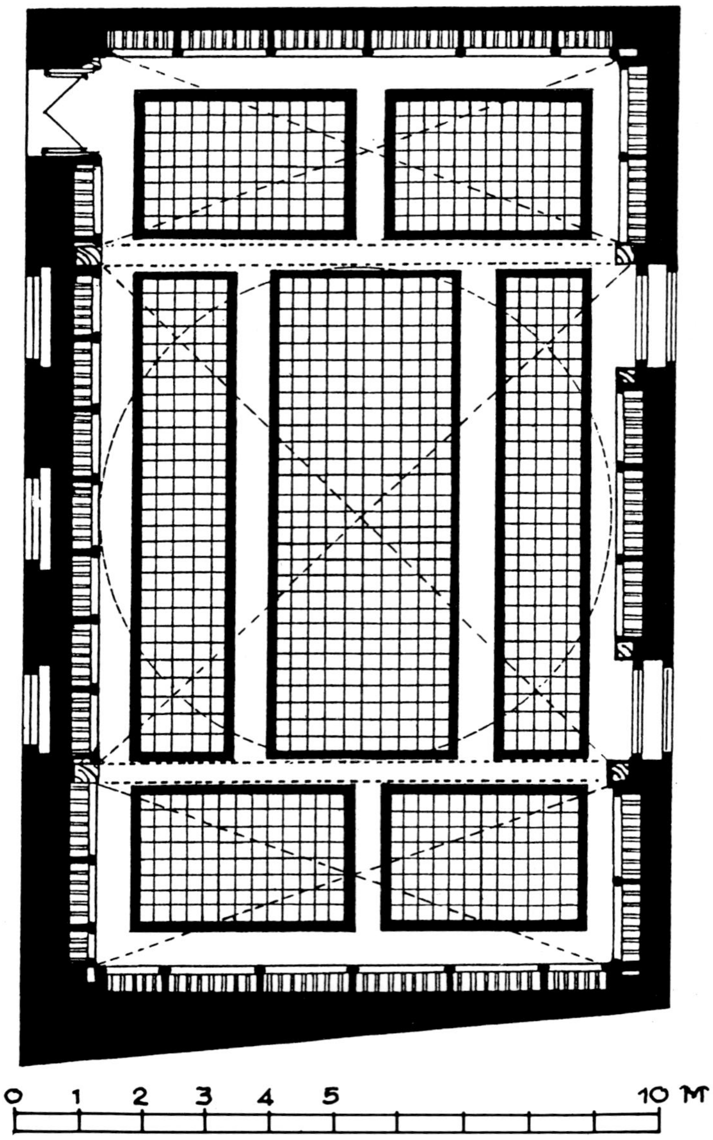

25. Plan of the library showing the wall shelving, the positions of the dome and the two ceiling arches, and the floor design.

32. See Layton, 'Nikodemos Metaxas...' 149, 150, 160.

33. The drive to establish a patriarchal press was stimulated by the simmering ideological crisis that finally came to a head in the years 1793-1805: see F. Iliou, *Προσθῆκες στήν Ἑλληνική Βιβλιογραφία: Α΄Τά βιβλιογραφικά κατάλοιπα τοῦ É. Legrand καί τοῦ H. Pernot (1515-1799)*, Athens 1973, 272-276.

34. See G. Ladas and A.D. Hadjidimos, *Ἑλληνική Βιβλιογραφία: Συμβολή στόν δέκατο ὄγδοο αἰώνα*, Athens 1964, 212.

35. *Ibid.*; Layton, «Ἡ τεχνική τοῦ βιβλίου», 331.

36. See A.K. Offenberg, 'The First Printed Book Produced at Constantinople (1493)', *Studia Rosentaliana* 3 (1969) 96-112.

37. See Ladas and Hadjidimos, *op. cit.* 212; Layton, «Ἡ τεχνική τοῦ βιβλίου», 331-332. On Pogos see *Les arméniens et l'imprimerie* (= Études sur la civilisation arménienne, 1), Constantinople 1920, 37, 58. The Greek books produced by the Armenian press in 1756 were printed with exactly the same types as the books produced in 1764-1767 by the patriarchal press, which had probably acquired the types from the Armenian press's stock. The same types were used again in 1797, when Pogos printed the *Πατρική Διδασκαλία* and simultaneously made new matrices in which he cast a fount for the third patriarchal press.

The patriarchal press, as an official organ of the Oecumenical Patriarchate, was founded at the end of the eighteenth century and operated until the end of the nineteenth century.

26. Preliminary sketch of the interior of the library: above, the original proposal for a galleried room; below, the final design.

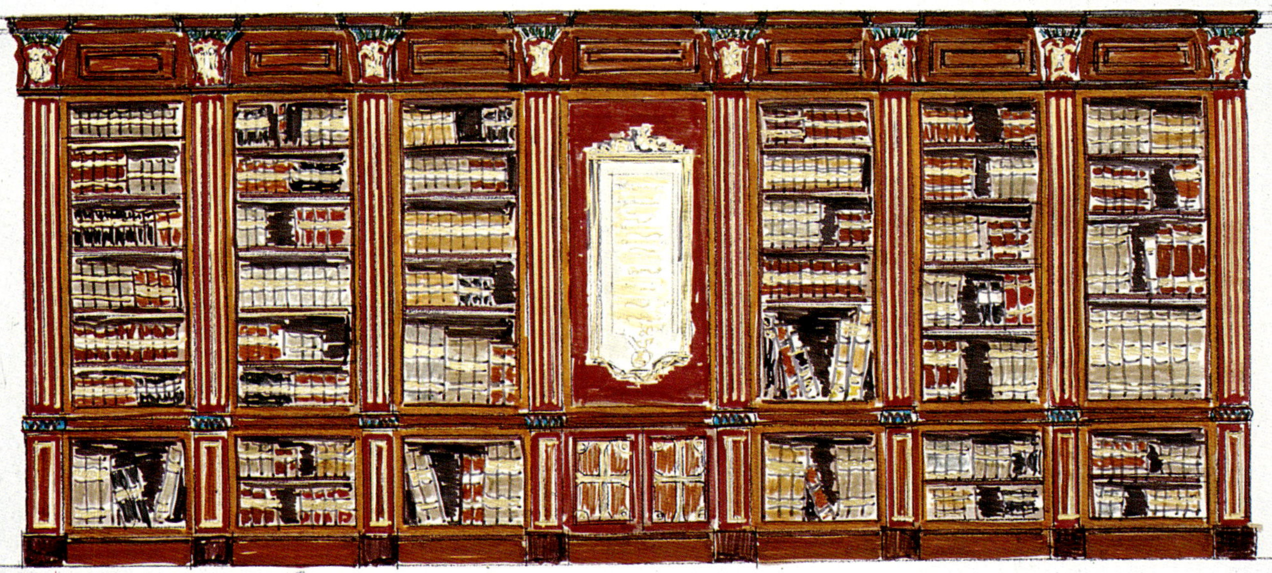

The Library of the Monastery of St. John on Patmos

CHAPTER THIRTEEN

The Monastery of St. John the Divine which crowns Patmos, the island of the Apocalypse, is one of the most imposing monuments of the Orthodox faith and Byzantine civilization. Deep in its heart lies its library, one of the oldest libraries in the world in terms of continued existence in one place, which still possesses a catalogue of the original nucleus of the library of its founder, St. Christodoulos.

St. Christodoulos, whose secular name was John, was active before and after the ascent of the Komnenos dynasty to the Byzantine imperial throne. Starting with Alexios I (1081-1118), these aristocratic soldier emperors endeavoured to restore order to the disorganized administration of the Empire and to secure its eastern, northern and western frontiers against the threats posed by the Normans, the Patzinaks and above all by the Turks. The Turks had managed to penetrate far into Asia Minor, founding several emirates there, and from their sultanates of Iznik (Nicaea) and Konya (Iconium) they ravaged the whole region right up to the shores of the Bosporus. It is quite likely that the frequent moves of St. Christodoulos from one place to another were entirely due to the turbulent state of the Empire's Asian provinces and the fact that the provincial governors, wishing to show their discontent with the policy being pursued in Constantinople, were unwilling to organize any serious resistance to the invaders.[1]

It was in these conditions that Christodoulos was born at a small town near Nicaea in Bithynia, perhaps in about 1025. His parents were devout Christians who gave him a good education, sending him to a private teacher from an early age.[2] Wishing to devote himself to religion, he left his parents and took himself off to a monastery on the Bithynian Mt. Olympus. There he stayed for about three years, practising the monastic life under the tutelage of a wise old monk. On his mentor's death Christodoulos decided to go back into the world.[3] He went first to Rome (1054), where he prayed at the tombs of SS. Peter and Paul, and then to the Holy Land, visiting Bethlehem and Jerusalem.[4]

When he was twenty-five he withdrew to the monasteries of the Palestinian desert and stayed there until the Turkish advance forced him to flee to the Monastery of Stylos near Miletus, one of the group of monastic communities on and around Mt. Latmos (Latros). There he subjected himself to a régime of fasting and self-denial, and his way of life quickly won him a following of disciples. In March 1079, when he was the abbot of Stylos, he went to Constantinople to settle various business matters and claims outstanding against the monastery, having first appointed two monks named Sabbas and Luke to act for him.[5] Following his talks with the Patriarch and other church dignitaries, judgment was found in his favour and he was appointed 'Archimandrite of the whole mountain' with the title of Primate (*Protos*) of Mt. Latmos and Protector of the Monastery of Stylos.[6]

27. The north side of the Monastery of St. John, overlooking some of the fine town houses.

The arrival of Turkish forces in the vicinity of Mt. Latmos compelled Christodoulos to seek safety elsewhere. With a number of other monks he fled first to Strobilos, where his friend Arsenios Skenoures installed him as abbot, but almost immediately they came under threat from the Turks yet again and moved on to Kos on the advice of Skenoures, who owned land on the island where it was hoped that a suitable site for a monastic community might be found. Christodoulos looked over the estates and chose a hill called Pelion for his new monastery. By this time Skenoures was away on a journey to Jerusalem, so Christodoulos had to set about building it on his own. He began with the church, which he dedicated to the Mother of God, and round it he built cells and an enclosure wall. In about 1079 the monasteries on Mt. Latmos were sacked by the Turks, and Christodoulos, safe in his refuge on Kos, could not stop worrying about what had happened to their religious and artistic treasures. Eventually he chartered a boat and mounted an expedition to Latmos for the express purpose of salvaging what remained, especially the contents of the monastic libraries. These books he sent to Patriarch Nicholas III in Constantinople, who deposited three quarters of them in Hagia Sophia for safe keeping and gave the rest to Christodoulos.[7]

Christodoulos made frequent journeys to Constantinople, where he was in contact with the Patriarch, the Emperor's mother Anna Dalassene and Emperor Alexios himself. He had decided to leave Kos, which he considered too worldly a place, with too many distractions, and on one of his trips to the capital he sought an audience with the Emperor to ask for the title to the uninhabited 'small islet' of Patmos. Alexios countered by offering him the position of 'Protector' of the monasteries in Thessaly, many of which had fallen into evil ways. Christodoulos agreed, on condition that the Rule he intended to draw up was accepted by the monks. But the monks eventually rejected his Rule and he left Constantinople armed with a chrysobull granting him the title to Patmos.[8]

On his arrival on Patmos Christodoulos demolished the statue of Artemis that dominated the goddess's sanctuary on the summit of the hill, and on the site of the sanctuary he built 'a humble house of prayer' dedicated to St. John the Evangelist. He then set to work on the construction of the monastery, which proceeded apace.[9] The foundation of the monastery made him famous: indeed, his reputation was such that his biographers credited him with miraculous powers. The book-loving abbot stayed on Patmos for about three years, but when the construction work was almost complete and only the outer wall was still unfinished he had to go into voluntary exile yet again to escape the Turks, who by now were poised to capture the Aegean islands. This time he went with his monks to Euboea, which turned out to be his last home, for he died there in 1093. His body was brought back to Patmos by the monks and

1. On the complex situation created in Asia Minor by the Turkish incursions and the difficulties of coexisting with the new immigrants, see esp. S. Vryonis, *The Decline of Medieval Hellenism in Asia Minor and the Process of Islamization from the Eleventh through the Fifteenth Century*, Berkeley/Los Angeles/London 1971. On ideological and political trends in general during the reign of Alexios I Komnenos, see Hélène Glykatzi-Ahrweiler, *Ἡ πολιτική ἰδεολογία τῆς Βυζαντινῆς Αὐτοκρατορίας* (= *L'idéologie politique de l'empire byzantin*, tr. Toula Drakopoulou), Athens 1977, 78-86.

28. St. Christodoulos. Engraving from the Ἀκολουθία τοῦ ὁσίου Χριστοδούλου (Holy Office of St. Christodoulos)*, Venice, A. Tzatas, 1755.*

2. The primary sources for the life and works of St. Christodoulos are a semi-autobiographical work entitled *Hypotyposis* (*Ὑποτύπωσις*, 8th March 1091: see n. 11), his will (*Διαθήκη*, March 1093) and the codicil to his will (*Κωδίκελλος*, 10th March 1093). After his death three short biographies of him were written, in the following order: (a) *Βίος καί πολιτεία*, by John, Metropolitan of Rhodes, (b)

29. The entrance to the passageway leading down to the library and archives in the crypt, showing the marble plaque with the inscription Ψυχῆς Ἰατρεῖον *('Sanatorium of the Soul').*

ΨΥΧΗΣ ΙΑΤΡΕΙΟΝ

has attracted large numbers of pilgrims ever since; and his supernatural powers are said to have been acknowledged even by many non-Christians.

In Euboea St. Christodoulos drew up a 'secret' will[10] (March 1093) and compiled a catalogue of the library which also includes an inventory of his own liturgical utensils and other valuable possessions, which he bequeathed to the monastery. The original catalogue has not survived, nor has the 'memorandum' listing the books given to him by Patriarch

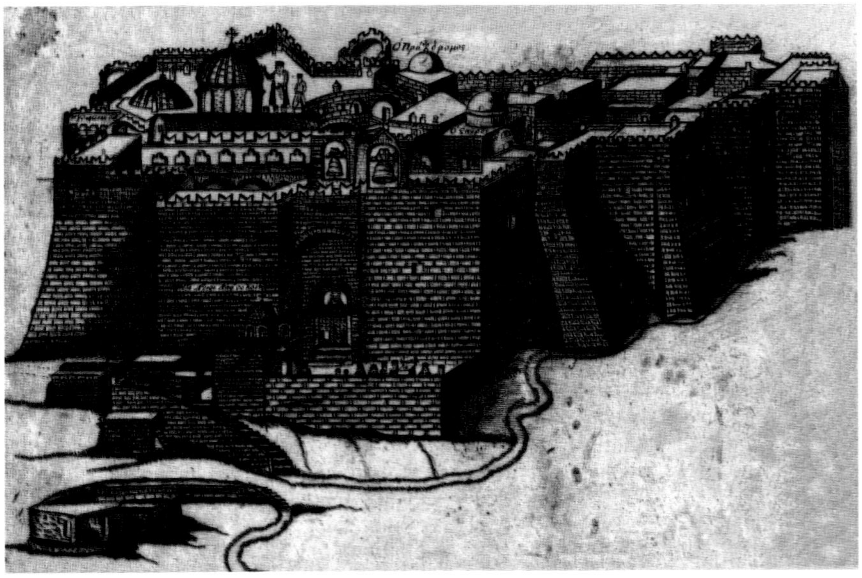

30. General view of the monastery. Engraving from the Ἀκολουθία τοῦ ὁσίου Χριστοδούλου, *Venice 1755.*

Nicholas III. We learn from the semi-autobiographical *Hypotyposis* that not all of his books came from the Patriarch, for he mentions that he had been a regular buyer of manuscripts with his own money: 'I bought most of the said books by my own efforts and at my own expense.'[11] The extant catalogue of books, valuable liturgical utensils and icons that had belonged to Christodoulos, compiled in 1200 under Abbot Arsenios, was copied from a synoptic catalogue of 1103, now lost. It gives the most comprehensive particulars of his library, as well as information about the monks' intellectual interests, the monastery's reputation in the Orthodox world and the library lending rules.[12]

At the beginning of the thirteenth century, according to the catalogue, the library's contents consisted almost entirely of theological works. Out of a total of 330 codices (267 written on parchment, 63 on paper), 109 were liturgical books, 107 are classified as 'moral and protreptic' treatises, and 31 were lives of saints: these constituted the theological core of the library. The rest were of various kinds, but only twenty were secular and there was only one classical work, the *Categoriae* of Aristotle.[13]

Ἀνέκδοτος βίος, by an unknown author, and (c) *Ἐγκώμιον εἰς τήν ἀνακομιδήν τῶν λειψάνων*, by Athanasios, later Patriarch of Antioch. See Era Vranoussi, *Βυζαντινά Ἔγγραφα τῆς Μονῆς Πάτμου. Α΄: Αὐτοκρατορικά*, Athens 1980, *3-*20.

3. See *Βίος καί πολιτεία*, published by I. Sakkelion in his book *Πατμιακή Βιβλιοθήκη*, Athens 1890; Vranoussi, *op. cit.* *9.

4. See Vranoussi, *op. cit.* *21.

5. See *Βίος καί πολιτεία*; Vranoussi, *op. cit.* *9 and (on his Latmos period) *22-*28.

6. See *Βίος καί πολιτεία*; Vranoussi, *op. cit.* *9-*27.

7. On the time spent by St. Christodoulos on Kos, see the *Hypotyposis*, the *Κωδίκελλος* and the *Βίος καί πολιτεία* (= Vranoussi, *op. cit.* *29-*31). The books he rescued from Latmos are mentioned by him in the *Κωδίκελλος*: see F. Miklosich and J. Müller, *Acta et diplomata graeca medii aevis sacra et profana*, 6 vols., Vienna 1860-1890, 87 (= Vranoussi, *op. cit.* *30-*31).

8. On Christodoulos's visit to Constantinople see Vranoussi, *op. cit.* *31-*32; also a document headed *Ἔνταλμα καί παραίνεσις* ('Ordinance and admonition'), *ibid.* *34.

9. See Vranoussi, *op. cit.* *35-*40. The two deities chiefly worshipped on Patmos in antiquity were Artemis Patmia and Apollo Karneios: see Johanna Schmidt, 'Patmos' in *RE* 18 (1949) 2174-2191. On the architecture of the monastery see A.K. Orlandos, *Ἡ ἀρχιτεκτονική καί αἱ βυζαντιναί τοιχογραφίαι τῆς μονῆς τοῦ Θεολόγου Πάτμου*, Athens 1970.

10. The will was called 'secret' because its contents were not to be disclosed until after his death: see Vranoussi, *op. cit.* *5.

11. On his purchases of manuscripts see Miklosich and Müller, *op. cit.* 87. The *Hypotyposis*, which Christodoulos wrote not long before he died, is not merely a monastic *typikon* or constitution laying down the rules for the running of the community, as the name usually implies, for it is also a mine of information about the founder himself. In fact it is more or less an autobiography, full of facts about his youth, his adventures, his

31. The third aisle of the library.

The Monastery of St. John was like most other monasteries in that it was the Abbot who decided on library policy. The catalogue of *c.* 1350 testifies to an impressive broadening of the monks' intellectual interests, but fifty years later the climate had changed and we see a steady decline in the quality of the library. In the middle of the fourteenth century a number of historical, literary and philosophical works were acquired and the monks were reading Xenophon, Diodorus Siculus and Plato.[14] But the Palaiologian renaissance, the growth of the great school of philosophy at Mistras, the contribution to classical studies made by Byzantine scholars at Italian centres of learning (from the late fourteenth century) and the widespread commerce in classical manuscripts all failed to arouse the interest of the Patmos monks. The spirit of the Renaissance, that life-giving 'wind of change' blowing from Constantinople to the West, left St. Christodoulos's library untouched: the number of books may have gone on increasing, but the emphasis was still overwhelmingly on theology.

The Patmos monastery also had a scriptorium, sometimes very busy and sometimes less so, which the *Hypotyposis* implies was already in existence in Christodoulos's time.[15] Problems were created for the library by the difficulty of enforcing the lending rules when books were lent to dozens of other monasteries and the Patmos monastery's own dependencies. By the fifteenth century the rules were no longer being strictly observed: it frequently happened that books were borrowed and not returned, and the number of classical works diminished in geometric progression. However, these losses were offset by handsome donations to the library, mainly from monasteries in Asia Minor which were trying to save their valuable possessions from the depredations of the Turks.[16]

The only information we have about the library in the Monastery of St. John comes from the catalogues and the various documents relating to the lending rules. We do not know, for example, whether the monks were set compulsory reading, as they were in some other monasteries, nor how the scriptorium was run, nor are the librarian's duties mentioned in the monastic rules and regulations. And although Western Europeans are known to have visited Patmos as early as the Komnenian period (1081-1185), the first systematic traveller being an English monk named Saelwulf (1103), their memoirs contain practically nothing of any real interest about the library.[17] Even scholar-travellers like Pierre Bellon du Mans (1546), Jean de Thévenot (1655) and J. Pitton de Tournefort (*c.* 1700), who wrote about the traditional customs of Patmos, were more impressed by the grotto of the Apocalypse than by the monastic library. The Comte de Choiseul-Gouffier, in his admirable and lavishly illustrated book about his travels in Greece in 1776, records an amusing conversation he had with an educated monk on Patmos: 'On the way down the hill this monk asked me in Italian where I was from, where I had just come from and what had been happening in Europe in

time spent in various monasteries and the monastic libraries he had known. The *Hypotyposis* survives in six manuscripts and five printed editions, all from Venice. The earliest of these, dating from 1756, was printed by A. Vortoli and published under the title of *Τυπική διάταξις*: see É. Legrand, *Bibliographie hellénique du dix-huitième siècle*, I, Paris 1918, 466 (494).

12. See Vranoussi, *op. cit.* *80-*82; Ead., «'Ανέκδοτος κατάλογος ἐγγράφων τῆς ἐν Πάτμῳ μονῆς (ΙΒ΄-ΙΓ΄αι.)», *Σύμμεικτα ΚΒΕ*, Athens 1966, 137-162; C. Astruc, 'L'inventaire dressé en septembre 1200 du trésor de la bibliothèque de Patmos. Édition Diplomatique', *TM* 8 (1981) 15-30; Id., 'Les listes de prêts figurant au verso de l'inventaire du trésor et de la bibliothèque de Patmos dressé en septembre 1200', *TM* 12 (1994) 495-499 (two plates).

13. See Vranoussi, *Βυζαντινά Ἔγγραφα...* *81. Charles Diehl, in his

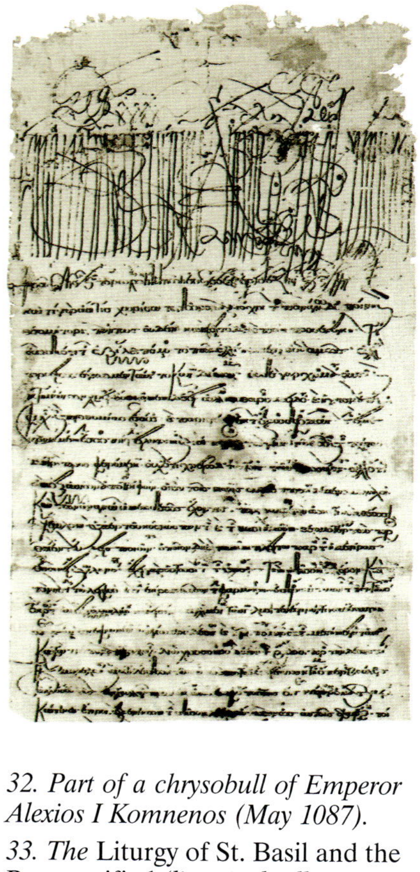

32. Part of a chrysobull of Emperor Alexios I Komnenos (May 1087).

33. The Liturgy of St. Basil and the Presanctified *(liturgical roll, Ms No. 707).*

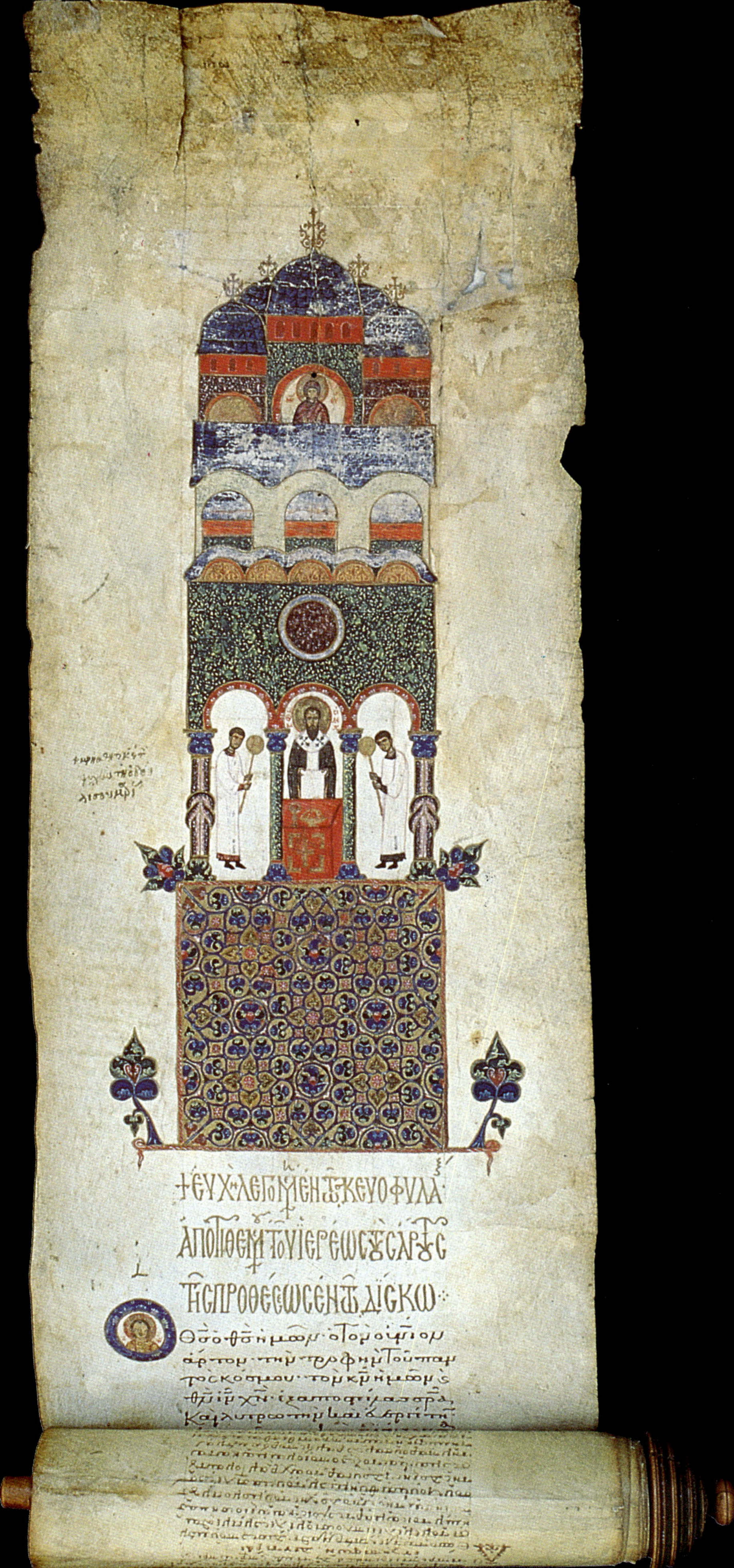

the seven years since the last ship had stopped at his rocky island. As soon as he discovered that I was French, he cried out, "Is Voltaire still alive?"' The monk then showed Choiseul-Gouffier the way to the library, where, with the Abbot's permission, he noted some particulars of the old manuscripts.[18]

Sad to say, the person who took the closest interest in the Patmos library during the Turkish period was one who carried off a number of valuable manuscripts, including a ninth-century codex of some of Plato's dialogues.[19] The future Cambridge professor Edward Daniel Clarke, son of a traveller and writer, set out in 1799 on a European tour from which he returned in 1804. At the beginning of his travels in the Aegean islands, before he reached Patmos, he had tried unsuccessfully to buy some old manuscripts from a fez-wearing shopkeeper on Kos whom he found reading the *Odyssey* amidst his piles of merchandise. The shopkeeper refused to sell any of the manuscripts because they were intended for his son, who was then studying at the school run by the monks of Patmos.[20] But when Clarke went to Patmos he got what he wanted: there, in the vaulted library where only the printed books were properly arranged and the manuscripts were lying about in disorder, he made his famous 'purchase'. According to Clarke's own account, the Abbot and the monks, none of whom could read ancient Greek, agreed to sell him a number of manuscripts on condition that the transaction should be kept secret from the islanders. The manuscripts were duly smuggled out in a basket full of bread. But the truth of the matter was not quite as Clarke had made it out to be, and as soon as the 'theft' became known uproar broke out both inside the monastery and out. In 1802 an inscription was carved over the entrance to the library, enjoining visitors to behave honourably:

ΨΥΧΗΣ ΙΑΤΡΕΙΟΝ
Δεῦρ' Ἄνερ, κεῖνται ὅσαι φαειναί χειρόγραφοι βίβλοι,
Ἀνδρί ρά φέρτεραι πινυτοῦ χρυσίου δοκέουσαι·
Ταῦτ' ἄρα τήρεε φύλαξ σεῖο μᾶλλον βιότοιο
Τῶν δόμος οὕνεκα ὅς νῦν τοι γίνατο φεγγόβολός γε.
ἐπί ἔτους ᾳωβ' Μηνός Αὐγούστου.

SANATORIUM OF THE SOUL
In this place splendid manuscripts are kept. To a wise man they are more valuable than gold. Look after them, therefore, more carefully than you would guard your own life, for it is thanks to them that this foundation has won lustre. August 1802.[21]

The historic library of Patmos is now one of the most important and most efficiently organized monastic libraries in Christendom. Its precious contents can be divided into three categories: (a) codices, (b) documents and (c) printed works.

article 'Le trésor et la bibliothèque de Patmos au commencement du XIIIe siècle', *BZ* 1 (1892) 488-525, identified more than seventy codices from the twelfth-century catalogue among those published by Sakkelion in 1890.

14. The catalogue of *c.* 1350 puts the number of books in the library at 380: see Diehl, *op. cit.* 507.

15. See Miklosich and Müller, *op. cit.* 75. The various catalogues compiled at different times frequently mention the name of the donor or the copyist, who was often a Patmos monk or even the Abbot himself (e.g. Arsenios).

16. Notes of borrowings were jotted on the back of the Catalogue: see Vranoussi, *Βυζαντινά Ἔγγραφα...* *82, *88-*89. It is not known for certain whether the librarian's duties were the same as at the Monastery of Studius in Constantinople (see pp. 148-149).

17. Most of the information about the history of the library comes from

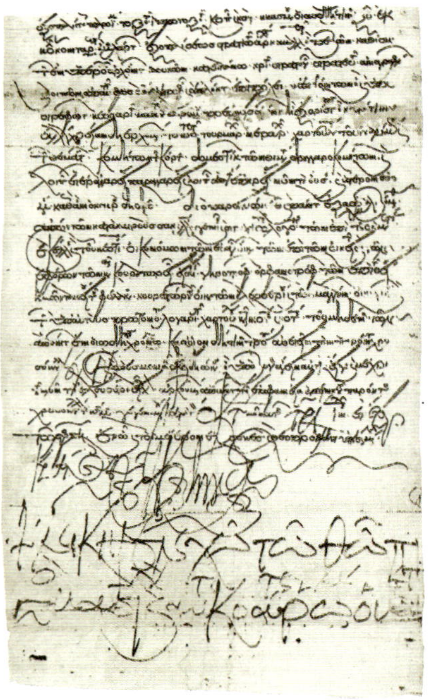

34. Part of a chrysobull of Emperor Nikephoros III Botaneiates (October 1079).

35. Tetraevangelion *(book of the four Gospels), 1st half of the 12th c. (Ms No. 274). The Nativity and St. Matthew (fols. 5v-6r), the Baptism and St. Mark (fols. 93v-94r).*

(a) By 1890, when Sakkelion published his *catalogue raisonné*, the nucleus of 330 manuscripts originally belonging to St. Christodoulos had increased to 855 (292 parchment codices, 563 paper codices and 35 rolls). Today there is a total of over a thousand manuscripts, mostly to do with religion. They include more than 180 liturgical books, i.e. evangelistaries, psalters, *euchologia* (formularies of services and prayers), *menologia* (monthly liturgical calendars) and books of music; at least a hundred works by the Fathers of the Church such as John Chrysostom, Basil the Great and Gregory of Nazianzos; and about fifty works on canon law. The remainder are books by various Byzantine writers, ascetics and works by post-Byzantine and modern Greek scholars.

Of the older (fifteenth-century or earlier) manuscripts of religious and secular works, the only ones that have survived are: Diodorus Siculus, *Bibliotheca* (10th c.), an *Anthology of Apophthegms* (11th c.), a codex of medical treatises by Paul of Aegina (14th c.), *Scholia* on Plato's *Timaeus* (14th c.), Euripides, *Hecuba* and *Orestes* (1442), and Sophocles, *Ajax* and *Electra* (15th c.). There are also several seventeenth- and eighteenth-century manuscripts of Lucian, Isocrates and Homer.[22]

The earliest manuscript, dating from the sixth century, consists of fragments of thirty-three crimson-dyed parchment folios with passages from St. Mark's Gospel: they form part of a codex which is now dispersed piecemeal in several major libraries in Europe, including St. Petersburg. This manuscript, which has the headings and holy names (such as Christ) written in silver and gold capitals, is notable for its attractive and majestic visual style. An important codex written in the early part of the eighth century, distinguished by the beauty of its calligraphy and the originality of its illuminations, is a large-format Book of Job with 44 illustrations (many of them occupying a full page) of scenes from the book, executed in a style showing the influence of Hellenistic art but with a certain naïveté of manner. Another outstanding work of art is the twelfth-century *Tetraevangelion* (book of the four Gospels) with its miniatures of the four evangelists sitting at their writing-desks, the luminous colours still undimmed. A roll dating from 1429, with the Liturgies of St. Basil the Great, is yet another artistic masterpiece: at the beginning of the text there is an elaborate headpiece depicting St. Basil celebrating the Divine Liturgy, surrounded by a mass of brightly-coloured decorative motifs. The library also has a continuous series of representative samples of handwriting and (in smaller numbers) manuscript illumination styles from the ninth to the fifteenth century.[23]

(b) An archive was formed more or less as soon as the Monastery of St. John was founded, in 1088, to house the documents that Christodoulos had collected during his time in various other monasteries. Among them were the chrysobulls (imperial edicts) granting the title to the land and other documents relating to the foundation

E.N. Frangiskos's preface to the catalogue of its printed books published by the Centre for Neohellenic Research: see Emmanuel N. Frangiskos and Deacon Chrysostomos G. Florentis, *Πατμιακή Βιβλιοθήκη. Κατάλογος τῶν Ἐντύπων (15ος-19ος αἰ.)*, I, Athens 1993, ιζ'-οβ'. On travellers in Greece see the comprehensive study by K. Simopoulos, *Ξένοι ταξιδιῶτες στήν Ἑλλάδα, 333 μ.Χ.-1700*, 4 vols., Athens 1970-1975; on Saelwulf see vol. I p. 195. The *Holy Office of St. Christodoulos* (*Ἀκολουθία ἱερά τοῦ ὁσίου Χριστοδούλου*) edited by Deacon Voinis, Athens 1884, contains the following injunction (p. 96): 'It is the duty of the sacristan in person to take delivery of the books and the title-deeds of the monastery and any other church property, subject to inventory, and to look after them with scrupulous care and attention.'

18. See Simopoulos, *op. cit.* II 381-383. It was just at this time that the French Enlightenment was beginning to make some impact in Greece as the name of Voltaire became more widely known, he being regarded as the embodiment of liberal thinking for almost the whole of the eight-

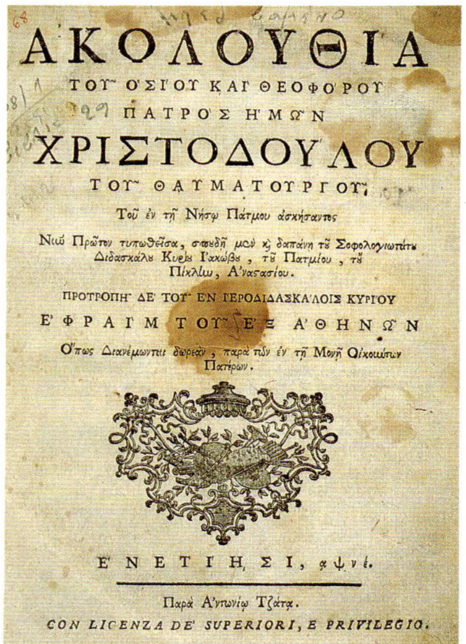
ΑΚΟΛΟΥΘΙΑ
ΤΟΥ ΟΣΙΟΥ ΚΑΙ ΘΕΟΦΟΡΟΥ
ΠΑΤΡΟΣ ΗΜΩΝ
ΧΡΙΣΤΟΔΟΥΛΟΥ
ΤΟΥ ΘΑΥΜΑΤΟΥΡΓΟΥ,
Τοῦ ἐν τῇ Νήσῳ Πάτμου ἀσκήσαντος
ΠΡΟΤΡΟΠΗ ΔΕ ΤΟΥ ΕΝ ΙΕΡΟΔΙΔΑΣΚΑΛΟΙΣ ΚΥΡΙΟΥ
ΕΦΡΑΙΜ ΤΟΥ ΕΞ ΑΘΗΝΩΝ
Πατέρων.
ΕΝΕΤΙΗΣΙ, αψνε.
Παρὰ Ἀντωνίῳ Τζάτᾳ.
CON LICENZA DE' SUPERIORI, E PRIVILEGIO.

36. The Holy Office of St. Christodoulos, *Venice, A. Tzatas, 1755.*

37. Gospel book. Crimson-dyed parchment codex written in majuscule, 6th c. (Ms No. 67, fol. 22v).

ΦΙΕΤΕ ΟΥΔΕ Ο
ΠΗΡ ΥΜΩΝ Ο ΕΝ
ΟΥΡΑΝΟΙΣ ΑΦΗ-
ΣΕΙ ΤΑ ΠΑΡΑΠΤΩ-
ΜΑΤΑ ΥΜΩΝ·
ΚΑΙ ΕΡΧΟΝΤΑΙ
ΠΑΛΙΝ ΕΙΣ ΙΕ-
ΡΟΣΟΛΥΜΑ ΚΑΙ
ΕΝ ΤΩ ΙΕΡΩ ΠΕ-
ΡΙΠΑΤΟΥΝΤΟΣ
ΑΥΤΟΥ ΕΡΧΟΝ-
ΤΑΙ ΠΡΟΣ ΑΥΤΟΝ
ΟΙ ΑΡΧΙΕΡΕΙΣ
ΚΑΙ ΟΙ ΓΡΑΜΜΑ-
ΤΕΙΣ ΚΑΙ ΟΙ ΠΡΕ-
ΣΒΥΤΕΡΟΙ ΚΑΙ ΛΕ-
ΓΟΥΣΙΝ ΑΥΤΩ·
ΕΝ ΠΟΙΑ ΕΞΟΥ-
ΣΙΑ ΤΑΥΤΑ ΠΟΙΕΙΣ·
ΚΑΙ ΤΙΣ ΣΟΙ ΤΗΝ
ΕΞΟΥΣΙΑΝ ΤΑΥ-
ΤΗΝ ΕΔΩΚΕΝ
ΙΝΑ ΤΑΥΤΑ ΠΟΙ-
ΕΙΣ·
Ο ΔΕ ΙΣ ΑΠΟΚΡΙ-
ΘΕΙΣ ΕΙΠΕΝ ΑΥ-
ΤΟΙΣ ΕΠΕΡΩΤΗ-
ΣΩ ΥΜΑΣ ΚΑΓΩ
ΕΝΑ ΛΟΓΟΝ ΚΑΙ
ΑΠΟΚΡΙΘΗΤΕ
ΜΟΙ ΚΑΙ ΕΡΩ ΥΜΙΝ
ΕΝ ΠΟΙΑ ΕΞΟΥ-

of the monastery, its possessions and its privileges. The archives now contain about 150 Byzantine and at least 13,000 post-Byzantine documents, many of them in languages other than Greek (Latin, Vlach, Turkish).[24]

(c) The printed books in the library go right back to the fifteenth century. The catalogue compiled by Emmanuel Frangiskos and Deacon Chrysostomos Florentis, the monastic librarian, besides being a most useful source of information about the original owners of the early printed books and the various scholars who read and annotated them, serves as a guide to the intellectual interests of the monks and the attitudes of successive abbots to books and book learning.[25]

The incunabula comprise ten Greek titles and one Latin. It is not known whether these books were acquired in the incunabular period (up to 1500) or much later, perhaps early in the seventeenth century. All the incunabula are either editions of classical texts or aids to humanist studies. Outstanding among them are two of the books that Ianos Laskaris edited and published in Florence, the *Anthology* (*'Ανθολογία,* 1494) and the *Argonautica* (*'Αργοναυτικά*) of Apollonius Rhodius (1496), as well as the *Grammar* (*Γραμμική Εἰσαγωγή*) of Theodoros Gazis (Venice, 1495) and the *Thesaurus Cornucopiae* (*Θησαυρός: Κέρας 'Αμαλθείας*) published by Aldus Manutius in 1496 with the assistance of leading Greek scholars of the Renaissance. Of the five-volume Aldine edition of the complete works of Aristotle in the original Greek, the library has two volumes, the *Acroases Physicae* (*Φυσική ἀκρόασις*) and the *Ethica ad Nicomachum* (*'Ηθικά Νικομάχεια*); and it also has a copy of the famous *editio princeps* of Aristophanes' *Comedies* (*Κωμωδίαι ἐννέα*) edited by Markos Mousouros and published in 1498.

There are 177 books published in the sixteenth century and about 280 from the seventeenth, representing a large proportion of the total output of Greek books in Italy and northern Europe during that time. Evidently the monks read the Neoplatonist philosophers Ammonius Hermeiou and Simplicius, as well as ancient Greek tragedies, poetry and anthologies of epigrams. Pindar is represented by the first annotated edition of his works, printed by Zacharias Kallierges in Rome in 1515. Also from Kallierges's press is the valuable *Lexicon* of Guarino Favorino (Rome, 1523), the last book produced by that great Greek printer. The oldest printed liturgical book in the library is a *menologion* for September (Venice, 1526), and there are many others – *typika*, evangelistaries, *pentekostaria*, *euchologia*, books of hours, etc. – printed from 1550 onwards, all of them in Venice. Venetian editions still predominate among the 550 books printed in the eighteenth century, although from 1756 onwards we find more and more from Vienna, the other great printing centre of the Greek diaspora.

Altogether the Patmos library contains about 1,200 books printed between the fifteenth and eighteenth centuries and a great many more

eenth century. Ten years before Choiseul-Gouffier's visit Evgenios Voulgaris had made Voltaire's thinking accessible to the Greek reading public for the first time with his verse translation of the short story *Memnon* (included in Voulgaris's edition of the *Bosporomachie* by Momars, published at Leipzig in 1766).

19. This manuscript of Plato, containing the first six tetralogies, was copied by John the calligrapher for Arethas, the future Archbishop of Caesarea (then still a deacon) in November 895. It is recorded that Arethas paid eight *nomismata* for the parchment and thirteen to the copyist for his work: see S. Kougeas, *'Ο Καισαρείας 'Αρέθας καί τό ἔργον αὐτοῦ*, Athens 1913, Pl. II.

20. The Patmian School was one of the oldest Greek educational institutions functioning in the Turkish period. Round about 1700 it was counted among the six most important Greek schools in the Balkans, together with those of Constantinople, Bucharest, Yannina, Athens and Mesolonghi: see K. Xanthopoulos, *Συνοπτική Ἔκθεσις τῆς πνευματικῆς 'Αναπτύξεως τῶν νεοτέρων Ἑλλήνων ἀπό τῆς ἀναγεννήσεως αὐτῶν μέχρι τοῦδε*, Constantinople 1880, 10; A. Vakalopoulos, *Ἱστορία τοῦ νέου Ἑλληνισμοῦ*, Thessaloniki 1973, 332. Adamantios Korais (1748-1833), the famous Greek intellectual nationalist, maintained that the schools of Patmos and Mount Athos were to blame for the pillaging of Greek manuscripts by foreigners: 'The two breeding-grounds of these well-educated men stripped all Greece of her valuable manuscripts and betrayed their ancestral heritage to a foreign nation, perhaps for a very few pieces of silver.' See the preface (entitled «'Ακολουθία τῶν αὐτοσχεδίων στοχασμῶν») to his edition of Isocrates, Athens 1840, κέ, also κγ́ for the list of books bought by Clarke.

38. Tetraevangelion, *early 13th c. (Ms No. 80). St. Luke (fol. 131v).*

39. Λόγοι (Orations) *of Gregory of Nazianzos. Parchment codex dated 941 (Ms No. 33, fols. 3r, 5r).*

Ο ΛΟΥΚΑϹ

2

·:· ΥΨΙΜΕ
ΔΩΝΗΜΑΚΑΡ
ΥΙΕΟΣΑΦ·Θ·Ι
ΤΟΥΓΕΝΗΠΗ
ΤΩΡ·ΚΗΝΕΥ
ΕΙΣΓΕ·Φ·ΣΤΑ
ΤΡΙΑΔΟΣΤΗΣ
ΗΜΕΤΕΡΗΣ
ΤΑΜΙΗΣΕΦΥ
ΤΑΝΣΕΝΕΟΡ
ΓΑΣΚΑΙΣΟΦΙΗΣΠΑΡΟΧΟΣΕΥΡΥ·Θ·ΜΟΥΓΕΛΟΓΟΥ·ΓΡΗΓΟΡΙΟΥΜΕΓΑ
ΛΟΙΟΑΓΓΗΙΣΙΓΕΟΥΙΕΡΗΟΣΟΥΧΑΡΙΣΕΚΧΕΙΛΩΝΠΡΟΥΡΧΕΤΑΙΟΙΑ
ΜΕΛΙΚΑΙΓΕΝΟΗΜΑΤΟΣΕΝΚΡΑΔΙΗΙΚΑ·Θ·ΟΣΑΠΛΕΤΟΝΙΣΧΕΙΠΑ
ΣΙΔΕΝΙΧ·Θ·ΟΝΙΟΙΣΟΥΝΟΜΑΣΕΙΟΤΡΑΝΟΙ·ΤΑΝΜΟΝΑΝΙΚΟΛΑ
ΟΝΜΟΝΑ
ΧΟΝΔΕΙΛΗ
ΜΟΣΙΝΕΝ
ΠΑ·Θ·ΕΕΣΣΙΚ
ΛΥΓΡΩΣΤΕΙ
ΡΟΜΕΝΟΝ
[illegible]ΛΥΚΕ
ΩΣΣΩΖΕ
ΣΗΝΕΠΑΡΕΙ
ΓΩΝΗΟΙΑΧΕ
ΡΑΠΑΝΣ·Θ·Ε
ΡΗΝΓΕΚΑΙ
ΤΑΡΕΤΕΖΕΝ
ΠΟ·Θ·ΩΕΥΦΡΟ
ΝΑΓΗΝΔΕΚΥ
ΒΑΡΝ ·:·

ἀρχὴ τοῦ πρώτου βιβλίου
ἔχει ὀλίγα δογματικά

printed in the nineteenth century in Venice, Vienna and the new centres of printing such as Ermoupolis (Syros), Nafplion and Athens.

Architecture. It is not known which room was originally used for Christodoulos's books, nor in which part of the monastery the archives and library were subsequently housed until the early seventeenth century, when Metropolitan Nikephoros of Laodicea gave his books to the monastery and had a room built for them next to the katholikon. Later, when more space was needed owing to the steady influx of new accessions, especially printed books, the library was moved to new premises next to the present-day Abbot's lodgings. The manuscripts and printed books were kept in cupboards decorated in a style typical of the popular wood-carving of the Turkish period.

The library has recently been relocated in the crypt below the new museum, reached by a winding ramp. Construction work on the new premises, designed and supervised by the present writer, was started in 1978 under Abbot Isidore and continued under Abbot Theodoretos.

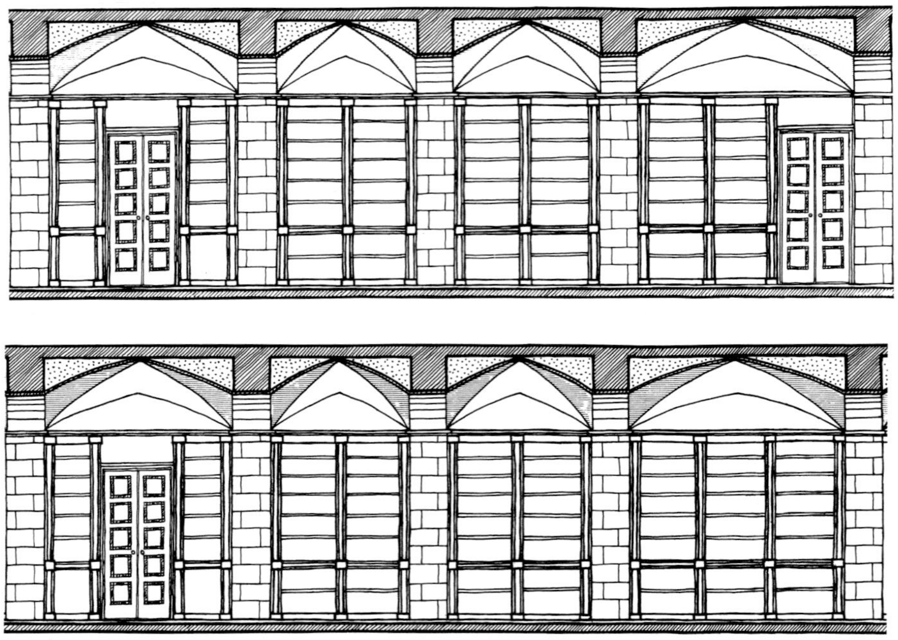

40. Partial side elevations of the library (scale 1:100).

The new library was completed in time for the celebrations of the ninth centenary of the monastery's foundation in 1988, when Abbot Isidore was again on the throne, and was officially opened by the Oecumenical Patriarch Demetrios I.[26]

The library – the 'sanatorium of the soul' (*ψυχῆς ἰατρεῖον*), as it is called in the inscription on a marble slab put up by Nikephoros of Laodicea in 1802 – consists of a central room with smaller rooms (where the archival

21. See Simopoulos, *op. cit.* III 63-65.

22. See esp. Sakkelion, *op. cit.*; also A. Kominis, *Πίνακες χρονολογημένων πατμιακῶν κωδίκων*, Athens 1968.

23. A full study of the Patmos manuscript illuminations has yet to be published. For a first introduction to the art of the miniature in Byzantine books see: K. Weitzmann, 'The Selection of Texts for Cyclic Illustration in Byzantine Manuscripts' in *Byzantine Books and Bookmen: A Dumbarton Oaks Colloquium, 1971,* Dumbarton Oaks 1975, 69-109; K. Weitzmann, W.C. Loerke, E. Kitzinger and H. Buchthal, *The Place of Book Illumination in Byzantine Art*, Princeton 1975. On the organization of manuscript illumination workshops in Constantinople see N.X. Eleopoulos, *Ἡ βιβλιοθήκη καί τό βι-*

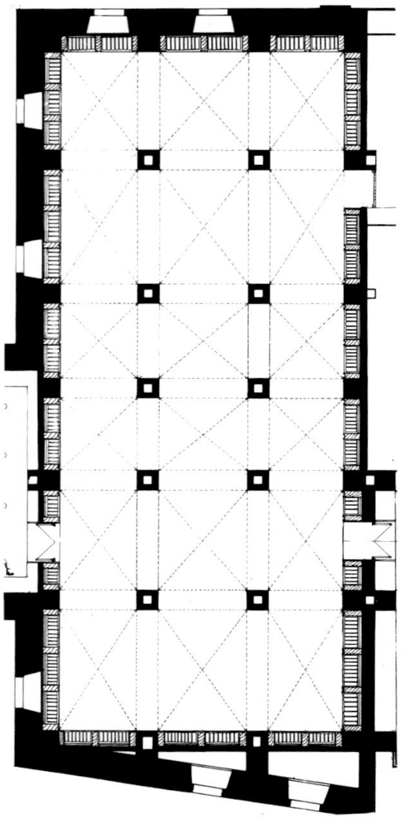

41. Plan of the main hall of the library (scale 1:200). Part of it is used as the reading room, where the manuscripts and early printed books are kept.

records and reference books are kept) opening off it on all sides. The central room has stone columns supporting gypsum cross-vaults – a characteristic feature of the monastery – dividing it into three bays, of which the middle one is equipped as a reading room. All the manuscripts and early printed books are kept in the central room, in specially made bookcases which cover all the walls. All the materials used for the interior décor, furniture and fittings are in walnut and have been left in their natural colours.

42. The inscription put up by Nikephoros of Laodicea in the outer treasury, where the manuscripts belonging to St. Christodoulos were originally kept.

βλιογραφικόν ἐργαστήριον τῆς Μονῆς τῶν Στουδίου, Athens 1967, 29.

24. See Chryssa Maltezou, «Τά λατινικά ἔγγραφα τοῦ πατμιακοῦ ἀρχείου», *Σύμμεικτα* 2 (1970) 349-378; Vranoussi, *Βυζαντινά Ἔγγραφα...* *19-*121; Maria Nystazopoulou-Pelekidou, *Βυζαντινά Ἔγγραφα τῆς Μονῆς Πάτμου*, Athens 1980. The monastic archive of Patmos is the only one on the islands off the Asia Minor coast with a virtually unbroken history from the time of its foundation. Besides the financial records of the monastery, which was one of the great landowners in the Aegean, it contains documents relating to its general organization, historical events, local laws and by-laws, even linguistic matters. In the fifteenth century its scope was extended to include papal documents and others issued by the Grand Masters of the Knights of St. John of Rhodes or by the dukes and lesser officials of the Venetian possessions in the region: see Miklosich and Müller, *op. cit.*

25. A catalogue of the incunabula in public, private, monastic and other libraries in Greece was compiled by D. Rhodes: *Incunabula in Greece: A first census*, Munich 1980. The Patmos library catalogue compiled by E.N. Frangiskos and Ch.G. Florentis (see n. 17) lists a number of earlier catalogues of the printed books: the earliest one mentioned is that of 1769, followed by those compiled by the Marquis of Sligo (*c.* 1810-1811) and Pothitos Nikolaidis (1829). Five old catalogues of the printed books in the library are still in existence: see Emmanuel N. Frangiskos, «Οἱ σωζόμενοι κατάλογοι τῶν ἐντύπων τῆς Βιβλιοθήκης τῆς Μονῆς Ἁγ. Ἰωάννου τοῦ Θεολόγου Πάτμου», offprint from the *Proceedings of the International Symposium on 'The Monastery of St. John the Divine: Nine hundred years of historical testimony (1088-1988)', Patmos, 22-24 September 1988*, Athens 1989, 311-330.

26. The whole project was completed within ten years with the invaluable assistance and co-operation of the librarian, Deacon Chrysostomos. I should like to take this opportunity to thank him once again in print.

TEMPLA DOMVM EXPOSITIS: VICOS FORA MOENIA PONTES:
VIRGINEAM TRIVII QVOD REPARARIS AQVAM.
PRISCA LICET NAVTIS STATVAS DARE COMMODA PORTVS:
ET VATICANVM CINGERE SIXTE IVGVM:
PLVS TAMEN VRBS DEBET: NAM QVAE SQVALORE LATEBAT:
CERNITVR IN CELEBRI BIBLIOTHECA LOCO.
270 MELOZZO DA FORLI

The Vatican Library

CHAPTER FOURTEEN

The Vatican or Apostolic Library is a product of the Renaissance, and the person mainly responsible for its foundation was Pope Nicholas V (Tommaso Parentucelli), a passionate admirer of ancient Greece. Under his guidance and supervision, what had been a small collection of manuscripts grew into the most important library of its time. Generally speaking, in fact, Nicholas V, from his position of supremacy, did more than any other Renaissance scholar to reconcile ancient Greek literature with 'Italian' learning.

Tommaso Parentucelli was born at Sarzana, near La Spézia, on 15th November 1397 and went to Bologna at an early age to study theology.[1] He then went to Florence, where shortage of money compelled him to earn his living as a tutor, first to the Albizzi and later to the family of Palla Strozzi, for whom he may have worked as a copyist. He went back to Bologna in about 1421 and soon afterwards was taken into the service of Niccolò Albergati,[2] becoming his closest confidant and working as his private secretary for fully twenty years. Albergati's contacts with other humanists, especially people like Francesco Filelfo and Poggio, opened up wider horizons for the young Tommaso, and when Albergati accompanied the Pope to Florence in 1434 Parentucelli went with him and met the leading figures at the foremost centre of humanist studies in Italy. His discussions with Leonardi Bruni, Giannozzo Manetti, Niccolò Niccoli, Giovanni Aurispa and others did much to form his remarkable character and stimulated his undying love of the classics.[3]

Parentucelli was a great lover of books. Quite early in life he decided to build up a library of his own, making every effort to track down writings of every kind and copying manuscripts with his own hand when he was unable to obtain a copy for himself. He started by looking for forgotten manuscripts in Lombardy and Emilia and then extended his researches to Germany and France, often in company with the indefatigable manuscript-hunter Aurispa. In the course of his travels, which took him to numerous cathedral and monastery libraries, he discovered the *Psalms* of Leo the Great and several copies of works by Irenaeus and Theophilus of Antioch then unknown in Italy.[4]

Parentucelli's immense knowledge of books was enough to win him, with Niccoli's backing, the sought-after post of first librarian at the public library founded by Cosimo de' Medici in the Monastery of San Marco in Florence. He was an extremely methodical worker, and his system for arranging the books was soon adopted by the greatest manuscript collectors, such as Federico da Montefeltro, Duke of Urbino, and Alessandro Sforza, for their own libraries.[5] He took part in the theological debates over the proposed union of the Eastern and Western churches at the Council of Ferrara-Florence (1437-1439), where his contributions to some of the discussions drew attention to his perspicuity and sharp reasoning power.[6] Pope Eugenius IV noticed his ability and, after Albergati's death, sent him on some delicate diplomatic missions to Germany. He was

43. Fresco by Melozzo da Forlì of the ceremonial opening of the library by Pope Sixtus IV. Vatican Museum.

SIXTVS·V

erre e cammini dell' Evangelizzazione

made Bishop of Bologna on his return to Italy and received his cardinal's hat soon after. At the conclave to elect a new Pope on the death of Eugenius, at which he was not a candidate for election, he was nominated by the Cardinal of Taranto and was elected.

The new Pope's first concern, after his enthronement as Nicholas V on 19th March 1447, was to heal the long-standing rift between the Catholics of Italy and those of northern Europe. He also conceived an ambitious plan for the reorganization of the papal library and the spread of humanistic writings. There had been a papal library in the old St. Peter's Church since the seventh century.[7] At the Council of 649 the Abbot of Taio, a monastery in Zaragoza,[8] consulted the works of Gregory the Great in the Pope's collection because the books in the Lateran Library were in such a muddle that he could not find them there.[9]

Most of the books in the papal library were theological works, chiefly patristic and doctrinal writings, which were used not only for research and as sources of documentation for conciliar deliberations but also as textbooks for the studies of the higher clergy. A number of liturgical books and Greek manuscripts were sent by Pope Paul I to Pépin, Charlemagne's father, between 761 and 763. In the fourteenth century the contents of Boniface VIII's library – 443 titles, including 32 in Greek – were dispersed. When the Holy See was moved to Avignon a new library was built up by John XXII and Clement VI: it grew at a spectacular pace, eventually reaching a total of 2,400 volumes. Oddly enough, however, when the Papacy returned to Rome the library was left behind. Two groups of books from this collection, together amounting to well under half the total, have survived by chance.[10]

Nicholas V was to all intents and purposes the founder of the Vatican Library, for he inherited only about 340 books which included several classical titles but only two in Greek.[11] His ambition was not merely to build up a fine library but also, more particularly, to establish Rome as the most important intellectual centre in Italy. He had the breadth of learning and the obsessive urge necessary for such a project, and in his short pontificate (1447-1455) he proved that he was capable of making his dream come true.

First he reorganized the Curia, turning it into a sort of open academy, and invited the leading Italian humanists and the most eminent Byzantine scholars living in Italy to his court. He gave them money and accommodation and set them to work translating Greek books into Latin, to the exclusion of all else. Among the Italians were Poggio, whom he had known since his youth, Aurispa, with whom he had travelled in search of manuscripts, Giannozzo Manetti, Umberto Decembrio, Lorenzo Valla, Giovanni Tortelli and Niccolò Perotti.

44. The Hall of Sixtus V in the Vatican Library.

1. The main sources of information on Nicholas V's life and works are three biographies by contemporaries of his: Vespasiano da Bisticci, *Commentario de la vita di papa Nicola composta da Vespasiano et mandata a Luca de gli Albizi* (in manuscript in the original), recently edited with a critical introduction and notes by Aulo Greco, 2 vols., Florence 1970-1976 (=*VBV* I 35-81); Bartolomeo Platina, *De vitis Pontificum Romanorum*, Köln 1573, 281-289; and Giannozzo Manetti, *Vita Nicolai V*, published in *RIS* III/2, 1734, 907-960.

2. Niccolò Albergati, born at Bologna in 1375, entered the Church and rose rapidly to become Cardinal of the Holy Cross of Jerusalem. In 1431 he was sent to France as papal legate, and the collector Niccolò Niccoli asked him to check all the manuscripts he had located in monasteries at Reichenau, Hersfeld, Fulda and Köln (R. Sabbadini, *Storia e critica di testi latini*, Catania 1914, 1-7). In 1413 he was present at the

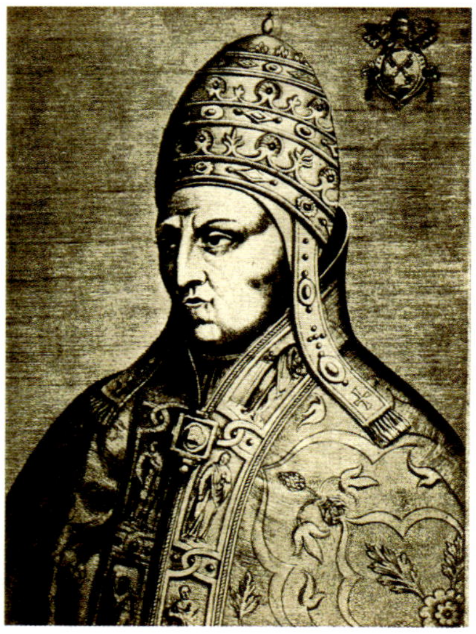

45. Pope Nicholas V: an engraving of the founder of the Vatican Library.

46. The Book of Job, 11th c. (Vat. gr. 749, fol. 6r). A majuscule manuscript containing 57 illuminations, from a Constantinople scriptorium.

ΟΛΥΜΠΙΟΔΩΡΟΥ ΔΙΑΚ

Η ΧΩΡΑ Η ΑΥϹΙΤΙϹ ΧΩΡΑ Η ΜΙΤΙϹ ΗϹΑΥ· ΑΠΟ ΓΑΡ ΗϹΑΥ· ΑΥϹΙΤΙϹ ΕΚΛΗΘΗ· Η ΤΟΙ ΑΠΟ ΑΥϹ ΕΝΟϹ ΤΩΝ ΥΙΩΝ ΗϹΑΥ· ΒΟΥΛΕΤΑΙ ΔΕ ΕΙΠΕΙΝ ΟΙΟΝ ΑΝΔΡΑ ΗΝΕΓΚΕΝ ΕΙϹ ΕΥϹΕΒΕΙΑΝ Η ΤΟΥ ΒΕΒΗΛΟΥ ΚΑΙ ΑΘΕΟΥ ΧΩΡΑ· ΑΥΤΗ ΔΕ Η ΑΥϹΙΤΙϹ ΕΝ ΟΡΙΟΙϹ ΙΟΥΔΑΙΑϹ ΚΑΙ ΑΡΑΒΙΑϹ· ΩϹ ΕΥϹΕΒΙΟϹ ΦΑϹΙ ΚΩΝ ΟΥ ΤΩΝ ΑΡΙϹΤΑΙΟΝ ΕΝ ΤΩ ΠΕΡΙ ΙΟΥΔΑΙΩΝ ΕΙϹ ΛΑΒΕΙΝ:—

ΝΟϹ ΤΙϹ ΗΝ ΕΝ ΧΩΡΑ ΤΗ ΑΥϹΙΤΙΔΙ. Ω ΟΝΟΜΑ ΙΩΒ

ΤΗΝ ΧΩΡΑΝ ΤΟΥϹ ΗΩΝ ΦΗϹΙΝ Η ΤΙϹ ΕΒΡΑΙϹΤΙ ΑΟΥϹ ΚΑΛΕΙΤΑΙ· ΚΑΤΑ ΦΥϹΙΝ ΜΕΝ ΕϹΤΙ ΤΩΝ ΠΟΛΛΩΝ· ΚΑΤΑ ΑΡΕΤΗΝ ΔΕ ΠΟΛΛΩΝ ΥΨΗΛΟΤΕΡΑ:—

ΤΟΥ ΑΓΙΟΥ ΙΩΑΝΝΟΥ ΤΟΥ ΧΡΥϹΟϹΤΟΜ

ΟΡΑ ΠΡΩΤΟΝ ΕΓΚΩΜΙΟΝ ΑΝΟϹ ΗΝ· ΟΥ ΓΑΡ ΔΗ ΜΙΚΡΟΝ ΕΓΚΩΜΙΟΝ ΤΟΥΤΟ ΤΟ ΑΝΟΝ ΕΙΝΑΙ ΦΗϹ ΕΝ ΧΩΡΑ ΤΗ ΑΥϹΙΤΙΔΙ· ΚΑΙ ΤΟΥΤΟ ΜΕΓΑ ΕΓΚΩΜΙΟΝ· ΤΟ ΓΑΡ ΕΝ ΑΡΑΒΙΑ ΕΙΝΑΙ ΕΝΘΑ ΑΠΑΝΤΕϹ ΔΙΕΦΘΑΡΜΕΝΟΙ· ΕΝΘΑ ΟΥΔΕΝ ΥΠΟΔΕΙΓΜΑ ΗΝ ΕΥΝΟΜΙΑϹ. ΤΟΥΤΟ ΗΝ ΤΟ ΘΑΥΜΑϹΤΟΝ:—

ΙΩΒ ΚΑΙ Η ΓΥΝΗ ΑΥΤΟΥ

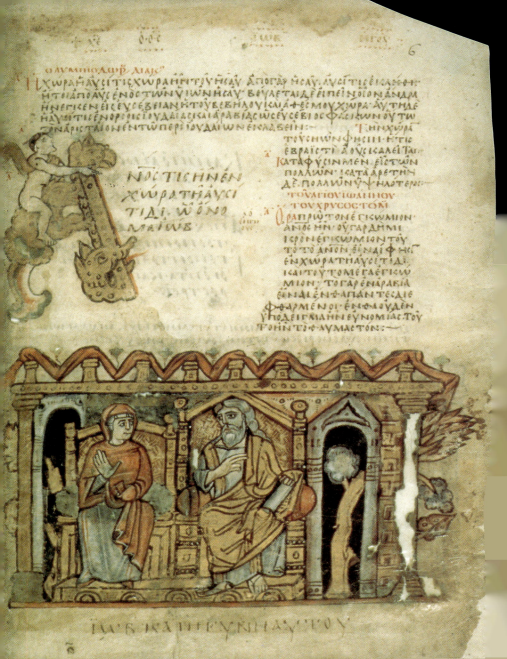

ō

The Greeks included Athanasios Chalkiopoulos, Theodoros Gazis, Andronikos Kallistos, Cardinal Bessarion and George of Trebizond, the last of whom shouldered the heaviest burden of the translation work.[12]

Since he had a special liking for the Greek historians, Pope Nicholas, a naturally methodical and sensible man, commissioned Lorenzo Valla to translate Thucydides and Herodotus. Valla had considerable experience in translating both Greek poetry and Greek prose, going back to 1428, when he had embarked on a prose rendering of the *Iliad*.[13] The translation of Xenophon's *Anabasis* and the *Bibliotheca* of Diodorus Siculus was entrusted to Poggio, who was greatly helped by George of Trebizond.[14] Perotti was commissioned to translate the *Histories* of Polybius.[15] Philo Judaeus, whose work had until then been unavailable in Latin, was given to Manetti to translate.[16] Theodoros Gazis, the preeminent Aristotelian, was commissioned to translate Aristotle's *Problemata* and *De Animalibus*.[17] Ambrogio Traversari, who was well versed in religious matters, was entrusted with the *Works* of Dionysius the Areopagite.[18] George of Trebizond had the greatest work load, for he translated Plato's *Republic* and *Laws* and many works by Aristotle, including the *Ethica*, *Rhetorica* and *Metaphysica*; he also took on the lion's share of the patristic writings, making translations of *De evangelica praeparatione* by Eusebius of Caesarea, the *Homilies* of John Chrysostom and works by Basil the Great and Gregory of Nazianzos.[19]

47. Pope Gregory IX. Woodcut from Decretates, *Paris, Thielman Kerver, 1507.*

Council of Konstanz, and while in the area he and Parentucelli discovered a large number of manuscripts, including one of Tertullian (R. Sabbadini, *Biografia documentata di G. Aurispa*, Noto 1890, 67). Filelfo dedicated to him his translations of Plutarch's *Lives* and two works by Xenophon (*VBV* I 129). He died at Siena on 9th May 1443. Albergati's funeral oration was composed and delivered by Poggio, and the first biography of him was written by Jacopo Zeno, Bishop of Feltre. See L. Bertalot and A. Campana, 'Gli scritti di Jacopo Zeno e il suo elogia di Ciriaco d'Ancona', *La Bibliofilia* 41 (1939) 356-376; on Zeno see *VBV* I 267-268.

3. On the humanists of Florence see pp. 220-222.

4. *VBV* I 46.

5. His system is embodied in his hand-list of the books that a fifteenth-century library ought to contain: see *VBV* I 47. Alessandro Sforza was born at Cotignola in 1409 and died in 1473. Though he made his career as a soldier, he was a great lover of literature and was particularly interested in theology. Libraries fascinated him, especially large ones like the great public libraries in imperial Rome. Besides theology, he loved to read Latin literature and Latin translations of Greek works. His library was burnt in 1512: see A. Vernarecci, 'La libreria di Giovanni Sforza, signore di Pesaro', *Archivio di storia patria per le Marche e per Umbria* (1886) 502, 518, 519; *VBV* I 421-427.

6. Parentucelli evidently knew Greek well enough to be made officially responsible for the translations from Greek into Latin, even on such delicate matters as these, and he performed the task with signal success. The Italians were unable to carry on a conversation in Greek, and Nikolaos Sekoundinos, whose Latin was excellent, was almost unique among

48. The Chronicle of Konstantinos Manasses, *1344-1345 (Vat. slav. 2, fol. 145r). Written in Bulgarian, probably by Simeon the monk, for Tsar Ivan Aleksandir.*

никифоръ црь иде на блъгары

крумъ кнѧзъ ухвати никифора црѣ и ѿсѣче главѫ его

Apart from anything else, the manuscripts of his translations are artistic masterpieces, with their beautiful calligraphy and illuminations by the leading miniaturists of the day. Textually, too, his versions served as the basis for most of the printed editions of these works that started coming regularly from Italian presses from 1469 onwards.[20]

Another who played an important part in the development of the

49. N. Perotti, Regulae, *Florence, Bartolommeo di Libri, c. 1490.*

library was Giovanni Tortelli, who was its Keeper (*Custode*) from 1449. His knowledge of grammar and the recent new accessions to the library made it possible for him to classify and catalogue the precious books in an exemplary manner. Tortelli dedicated to Nicholas V a product of his linguistic expertise, a major work on the spelling, meaning and etymology of words entitled *Orthographia*, which contains a comprehensive list of Latin words derived from Greek.[21]

Not content with his already impressive achievements, Pope Nicholas sent Enoch d'Ascoli to Germany, Denmark and Greece to buy as many manuscripts as he could find.[22] Enoch came back with a great many

the Greeks in that respect (*VBV* I 144).

7. On the Vatican Library see J.W. Clark, *The Care of Books: An essay on the development of libraries and their fittings from the earliest times to the end of the eighteenth century*, Cambridge 1901, 207-233; William Dana Orcutt, *The Magic of the Book: More reminiscences and adventures of a bookman*, Boston 1930, 69-193; Paolo de Niccolò, 'Profilo storico della biblioteca Apostolica Vaticana' in *Biblioteca Apostolica Vaticana*, Florence (Nardini) 1985, 19.

8. C. Wendel, *Kleine Schriften zum antiken Buch- und Bibliothekswesen*, ed. W. Krieg, Köln 1974, 182.

9. The Lateran Palace was built by Plautius Lateranus but confiscated by Nero on the discovery of Plautius' conspiracy against him. In the fourth century it was acquired by Fausta, the wife of Constantine the Great, who built a new church next to the original building and gave the entire complex to Pope Sylvester I. Sylvester took up residence there in about 320, and from then on the Lateran Palace was the home of the popes until about 1305, when the Holy See was moved to Avignon.

10. De Niccolò, *op. cit.* 20. On the papal library at Avignon see p. 216-217.

11. Bilingual copies of Boethius and the Psalms.

12. *VBV* I 65-69. For a detailed description and critical assessment of Nicholas V's circle see J. Monfasani, *George of Trebizond: A biography and a study of his rhetoric and logic*, Leiden 1976, 69-136.

13. Lorenzo Valla was born in 1407, probably in Rome, and died in 1457. After extensive travels in Italy and a period spent in the service of the king of Naples, he spent the last years of his life copying and translating manuscripts for the Pope. His command of Latin was masterly, and

50. Federico da Montefeltro, Duke of Urbino, the great bibliophile. From Cristoforo Landino, Disputationum Camaldulensium, *Books I-IV, 1475 (Urb. lat. 508, foglio di guardia).*

books, but perhaps the only ones previously unknown in Italy were the cookery book attributed to Apicius, *De re culinaria*, and the *Commentary on Horace* by Pomponius Porphyrion. Before long the library contained 1,200 codices, of which a third were in Greek, yet Nicholas still went on looking for new Greek manuscripts with undiminished zeal. To attain one of his most cherished projects, a translation of Homer into Latin hexameters, he appealed to all the humanists in Italy and promised Filelfo a fabulous fortune if he managed to complete the task.

A somewhat extreme illustration of the humanistic atmosphere prevailing in Rome is provided by Pomponio Leto's remarkable Academy. Leto, a passionate admirer of everything to do with the ancient world, contrived to have himself appointed to succeed Lorenzo Valla in his teaching post in Rome in 1457, and while there he founded his Academy. Wishing to revive the ancient Roman way of life, he persuaded large numbers of young men to give up their Christian names and surnames and adopt the names of famous Romans of the imperial period. Pope Paul II, who succeeded Pius II in 1464, was so alarmed by the eccentricities of Leto – one of whose foibles was to hold Latin and Greek classes in the ancient ruins, wearing a toga – that he not only disbanded the Academy but arrested and tortured several of its members.[23]

The untimely death of Pope Nicholas V did not disrupt the valuable work being done at the library. His immediate successor was Calixtus III (1455-1458), who in turn was soon succeeded by Enea Silvio Piccolomini, that great scholar, calligrapher and patron of humanists who was himself a book-collector. Piccolomini, who came from a noble Sienese family, occupied the papal throne as Pius II from 1458 to 1464. His splendid library can still be admired in Siena cathedral, with its magnificent frescoes by Pintoricchio depicting scenes from his pontificate. Paul II, born at Venice in 1418, was no great lover of the humanist movement, but he kept Tortelli on as librarian until his death in 1466. In 1476, after a gap of ten years, Tortelli was succeeded by a favourite pupil and friend of Cardinal Bessarion's, Bartolomeo Sacchi, known as Platina.[24] When Platina took over he engaged three copyists (*librarii*) named Demetrius, Salviatus and Johannes, and with their help he managed in the space of six years (1476-1481) to make the Vatican the most advanced library in the West: the 2,527 manuscripts (770 Greek and 1,757 Latin) which he had inherited had increased to a total of about 3,500 volumes.[25]

Most of the books in the Apostolic Library were humanist writings. The classical section, which was remarkably comprehensive, included numerous Greek manuscripts and a representative selection of scientific works. Although the books were chained to the desks in accordance with the usual medieval practice in monastic libraries, the lending rules were very liberal: besides cardinals, bishops, copyists and humanist members of the Curia, the borrowers included ordinary priests and even non-

51. Pomponio Leto. Woodcut from N. Reusner, Icones, *Basel 1599.*

he devoted much of his energy to restoring the purity of the language. The introduction to his *Elegantiae Latini sermonis* is a paean in praise of Latin. He is said to have studied Greek with 'the best Byzantine teachers', one of whom was probably Theodoros Gazis (*Charta* 32, 34, 67 ff.). For a bibliography of his translations see *VBV* I 66; and esp. F. Gaeta, *Lorenzo Valla: Filologia e storia nell' Umanesimo italiano*, Naples 1955; and S.I. Camporeale, *Lorenzo Valla: Umanesimo e teologia*, Florence 1972.

14. Poggio wrote to George of Trebizond in 1450, 'I am greatly indebted to you for giving me such invaluable assistance with my translations' (Monfasani, *op. cit.* 70). The Vatican Library still has the manuscripts of Poggio's Latin translations (Vat. lat. 3344, Vat. lat. 3422): *VBV* I 66-67. Poggio was born at Terranova, Valdarno, in 1380 and died there in 1459. He learnt Latin under the supervision of Giovanni Malpaghini (Giovanni da Ravenna) and Greek probably from Guarino da Verona. He travelled widely, searching for manuscripts with the enthusiasm of an explorer, but one journey that left a bitter taste in his mouth was his

52. Psalter, 13th c. (Pal. 381B, fol. IIr).

ϹΟΦΙΑ
ΠΡΟΦΗΤΙΑ

academic laymen, such as a certain Cola di Giovanni, who worked in Rome for the local agent of a Milanese merchant. The library became famous throughout Italy, so much so that towards the end of the century the brilliant scholar Angelo Poliziano, who controlled all the libraries in

53. Pope Sixtus IV visits the library. Fresco in the Santo Spirito Hospital, Rome.

Florence and was able to borrow all the books he wanted, set his sights on becoming the Vatican Librarian; but his untimely death in 1494 brought his plans to nothing. One of the most illustrious calligraphers working for the library was Demetrios Damilas, the pioneer of Greek printing, who lived in Rome from 1490, copying manuscripts for the Vatican Library and prominent Romans. Damilas quickly won a high reputation, and Pope Pius III (Francesco Todeschini Piccolomini) appointed him official copyist of Greek manuscripts to the Apostolic Library.[26] He was succeeded in 1515 by Giovanni Onorio de Maglie, a fine artist who designed the first Greek characters used at the papal printing press opened by Cardinal Ridolfi.[27]

The library enjoyed a second renaissance when Giovanni de' Medici, another humanist and lover of Greek literature, was elected to the papal throne as Leo X in 1513. The new Pope had been brought up on the humanistic ideals that had been cultivated continuously for a hundred years in Florence; he was a former pupil and personal friend of Ianos Laskaris and a book-lover (*philobiblos*) in the truest sense of the word; and he intended to make Rome once again the intellectual centre of Italy.[28] By that time printing had been flourishing for several decades, completely transforming the business of book production and distri-

long visit to England: after the Council of Konstanz he accompanied Henry Beaufort, Bishop of Winchester, back to his country, where he spent four profoundly depressing years living under grey skies among uncultured people. In a sour letter to Niccoli he bemoans the fact that he has found no classical manuscripts in England except for some short excerpts (*particula*) from Petronius.

15. *VBV* I 67. Niccolò Perotti was born at Sassoferrato in 1429. He spent several years living in the home of Cardinal Bessarion, whose protégé and friend he was, and died in 1480. He translated Polybius and Hippocrates and used his excellent knowledge of Latin to write an up-to-date Latin grammar entitled *Rudimenta grammaticae*. See G. Mercati, *Per la cronologia della vita e degli scritti di Niccolò Perotti, arcivescovo di Siponto*,

54. Pope Sixtus V. Engraving from W.D. Orcutt, The Magic of the Book, *Boston 1930.*

55. Theophylact, Commentary on the Epistles of St. Paul, *Latin translation by Cristoforo Persona, 1478 (Vat. lat. 263, fol. 1r).*

monastic lines and the books were chained to the desks. The library was built next to the Sistine Chapel and was divided into four rooms, one of which was reserved for the most valuable manuscripts. It was a public library, open to laymen as well as the clergy. Thanks to Platina's efficient administration, we are able to follow every step in the reorganization of the library. The register book he kept (Ms Vat. 5008), in which the first entry is dated June 1457, records full details of all transactions with the artists and craftsmen who worked on the library. The intention, quite clearly, was that the library building should be monumental and practical at the same time, and accordingly the top experts in their respective fields were engaged to carry out the work. The interior was adorned with portraits of the ancients and other paintings of standard Renaissance subjects, and the artists who worked on the frescoes included Melozzo da Forlì, Antoniazzo Romano and Ghirlandaio. Sadly, all that remains of this lavish decorative scheme is a fresco that shows the Pope appointing Platina to the post of librarian.[30]

The Vatican Library owes its present form to Pope Sixtus V (1585-1590), who commissioned Domenico Fontana to design a library in keeping with the dignity of the Papacy and its now vast wealth. An

59. Pope Leo X, oil painting by Raphael (1483-1520). Uffizi Gallery, Florence.

60. The New Gallery of the Vatican Library. Engraving by the architect Domenico Fontana (Paris, chez Maillet, rue St.-Jacques).

58. Niccolò Perotti. Woodcut from N. Reusner, Icones, *Basel 1599.*

20. On incunabular editions of works by Greek and Latin authors see M. Flodr, *Incunabula Classicorum*, Amsterdam 1973; *Charta* 7-23.

21. *VBV* II 61; G. Mancini, *Giovanni Tortelli cooperatore di Niccolò V nel fondare la Biblioteca Vaticana*, with supplement by Mgr. G. Mercati, Florence 1921. Giovanni Tortelli was born at Arezzo, *circa* 1400, and died in 1466. He studied under Gaspare Sighicelli in Siena before going to Florence in 1434. There he met Filelfo, with whose encouragement he went to Constantinople for three years of further studies. On his return to Italy in 1438 he lived first at Ferrara, then moved to Bologna to read theology and finally, after attending the Council of Ferrara-Florence, settled in Rome: see *VBV* II 61-64; *Charta* 194-195.

22. *VBV* II 51-52; de Niccolò, *op. cit.* 20. Alberto Enoch, to give him his full name, was born at Ascoli and died there in 1457. He studied Latin with Filelfo in Florence and was tutor to Giovanni and Piero, the sons of Cosimo de' Medici. See A. Reumont, 'Enoche d'Ascoli', *ASI* 20 (1874) 188-190; R. Sabbadini, 'Le scoperte di Enoche da Ascoli', *Studi italiani di filologia classica* 8 (1899) 119-131; G. Cantalamessa Carboni, *Biografia di Enoc d'Ascoli*, n.p. 1918.

imposing hall was erected overlooking the Cortile del Belvedere, with frescoes on the walls and the cross-vaulted ceiling. These fine paintings by Cesare Nebbia, Giovanni Guerra and a team of assistants, depicting ancient libraries, ecumenical councils and portraits of imaginary persons, convey an impression of the utmost grandeur.[31]

61. Partial side elevations of the library (scale 1:100).

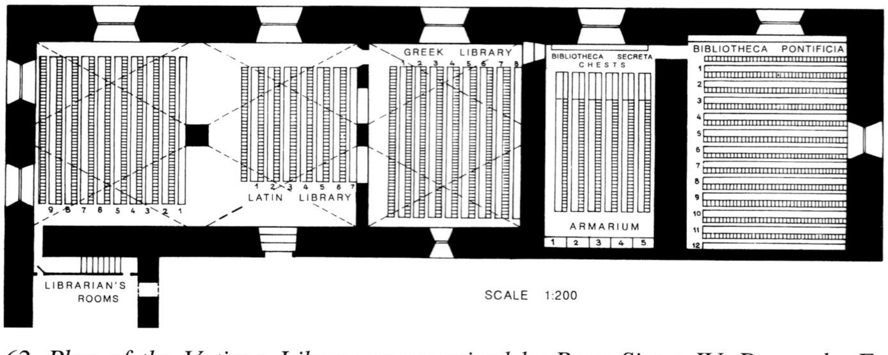

62. Plan of the Vatican Library as conceived by Pope Sixtus IV. Drawn by E. Wilson, Cambridge.

23. Pomponio Leto was born at Amendolara, Upper Calabria, in 1425 and died in Rome in 1497. He studied under the great grammarian Pietro de Monopoli in Rome, and then under Lorenzo Valla. The first biography of him was written by a pupil of his: M.A. Sabellico, *Vita Pomponii Laeti*, Strasbourg 1510. On his way of life and his teaching in Venice see J. Delz, 'Ein unbekannter Brief von Pomponius Laetus', *IMU* 9 (1966) 417 ff.

24. Platina was born at Piadena, a small town near Cremona, in 1421. He began his career as a soldier, but then went to study literature with Ognibene Leoniceno at Mantua and Greek with Argyropoulos at Florence (1457): see *Charta* 106.

25. Clark, *op. cit.* 208-209, 231.

26. *Charta* 138; P. Canart, 'Démétrius Damilas, alias le "Librarius Florentinus"', *Rivista di Studi Bizantini e Neoellenici,* n.s., 14-16 (1977-1979) 281-347.

27. The Greek section of the papal press was founded by Cardinal Niccolò Ridolfi, whose secretary, Matthaios Devaris, edited the first volume of Eustathius, Archbishop of Thessalonika, *Παρεκβολαί εἰς τήν Ὁμήρου Ἰλιάδα* (1544).

28. What Leo X had in mind was to turn Rome into another Venice. He supported the publication of Greek books, financed the Greek press on the Quirinal Hill and set up a Greek college for children from Greece: see *Charta* 270.

29. On the work of Laskaris as an editor and of Kallierges as a printer in Rome, see *Charta* 282-284 and 413-420 respectively.

30. The entrance to the library led from the courtyard into the Latin room; this and the Greek room together constituted the public part of the library (*Bibliotheca communis* or *publica*). Next to them were the *Bibliotheca secreta*, where valuable manuscripts were kept, and the *Bibliotheca pontificia*, which was used for the storage of the records – the *intima et ultima*, as they were called from 1512: Clark, *op. cit.* 211.

31. For fuller information on the

63. Platina (Bartolomeo Sacchi). Woodcut from N. Reusner, Icones, *Basel 1599.*

architecture, interior decoration and equipment of the library, and on Platina's catalogue (the *Inventarium Bibliothecae Platina*), see Clark, *op. cit.* 207-231; E. Müntz, 'Les arts à la cour des papes pendant le XVe et le XVIe siècle', *Bibliothèque des Écoles Françaises d'Athènes et de Rome*, 28 (vol. III) 1882; E. Müntz and P. Fabre, *La Bibliothèque du Vatican au XVe siècle*, Paris 1887.

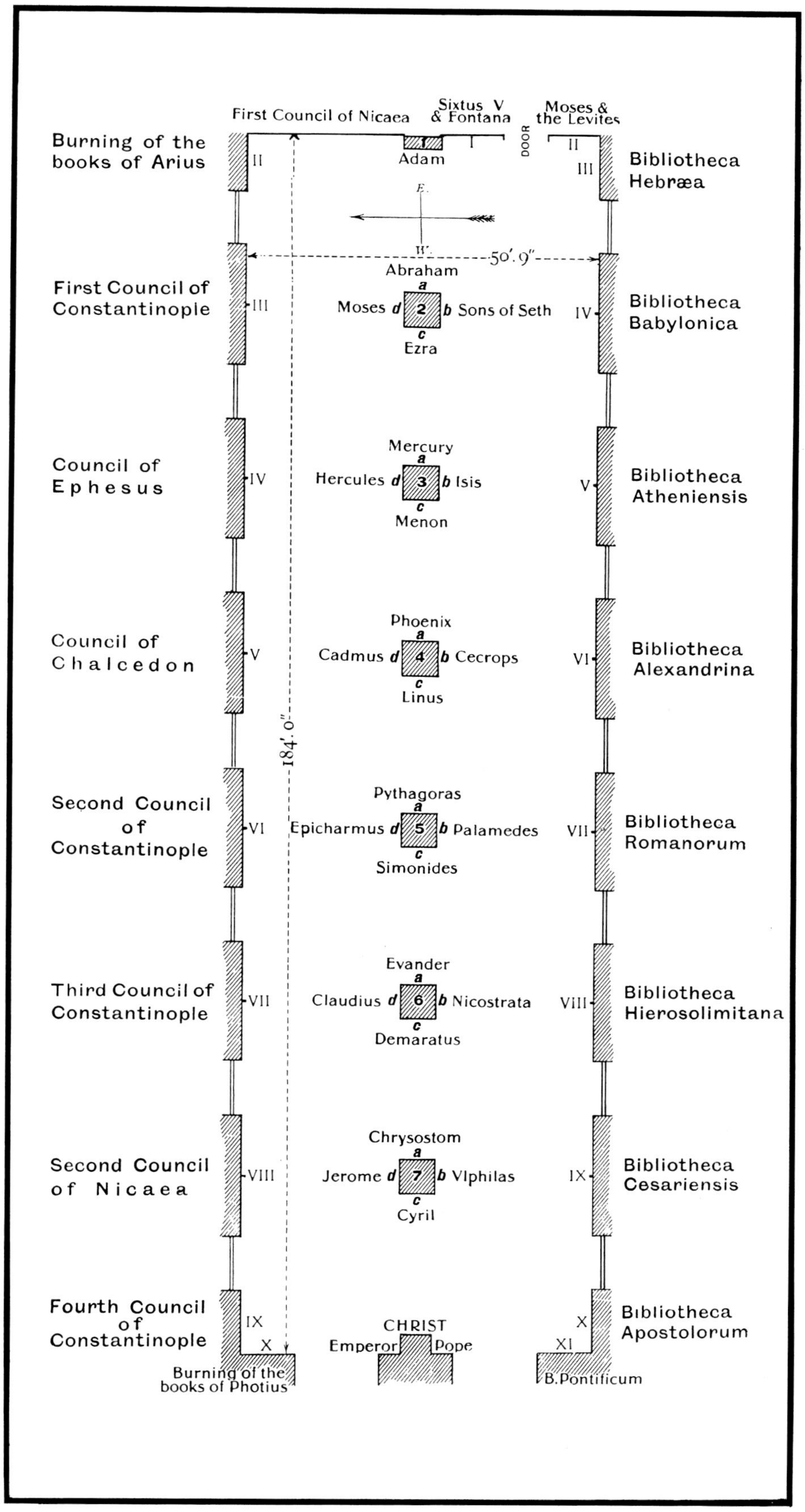

64. Plan of the Vatican Library showing the subjects of the painted decoration.

The Cesena Library

CHAPTER FIFTEEN

The small Italian town of Cesena is not where one would expect to find the oldest of all Renaissance libraries; yet that distinction belongs to the Biblioteca Malatestiana there, which has survived the centuries unscathed and still has its original furniture and fittings and most of its original contents. Designed in accordance with medieval practice, but with distinct overtones of Italian Renaissance aesthetics, the library owes its existence very largely to a young prince of Cesena, Novello Malatesta.

The Malatesta family ruled the region around Rimini, on either side of the River Rubicon, for about 250 years. On the death of Pandolfo Malatesta in 1429 the realm was divided between two brothers: Pandolfo's elder son, Sigismondo, became the ruler of Rimini while the younger son, Novello, inherited Cesena.

Sigismondo Malatesta had no academic education, was untroubled by humanistic preoccupations and spent his life fighting.[1] He was destined to go down in history for his initiative in rescuing the body of Gemistos Plethon, whom Cardinal Bessarion called 'the greatest Greek since Plotinus'.[2] When Venice set out to recover her lost possessions in the Peloponnese, Sigismondo was put in command of an expeditionary force sent out to conquer Mistras. He succeeded in capturing the town, but not the citadel, and when he was eventually obliged to raise the siege he returned to Italy taking with him Plethon's dead body, which was interred in the cathedral close at Rimini. It is fair to say that no more suitable resting-place could have been found for the Greek philosopher's mortal remains than the precincts of Rimini cathedral, described by Enea Silvio Piccolomini (the future Pope Pius II) as 'not so much a Christian church as a temple of daemon-worshipping pagans'.[3]

Novello Malatesta was a cultured and sensitive person. While still a young man he helped to finance the foundation of a public library at Cesena, and this at a time when 'open' libraries were rare even in the great centres of Italian humanism. The nucleus of his library had been formed in the thirteenth century by Franciscans who settled at Cesena after St. Francis's death in 1226.[4] There they built a church and a friary, and by the end of the thirteenth century the elementary school they started had developed into a small university. The natural sequel was that a small library came into being, not in the sense of a building or room set aside for the purpose, but simply a collection of books used for teaching. In the early fifteenth century a teacher of law named Fredolo Fantini was sufficiently impressed by this 'library' to bequeath to it all his books on canon law (1429). And about ten years later, in 1440, the friars began thinking seriously about building a special room for their collection of about fifty books.[5]

On 12th May 1445 Pope Eugenius IV issued a bull granting them permission to build their library and to raise funds for the purpose by good works and public appeals.[6]

65. The restored north wall of the library building.

Although the initiative had originally come from the Franciscans themselves, Novello Malatesta had also taken an active interest in their plans, and it was he who in 1447 commissioned the architect Matteo Nuti, a friend of the Malatesta family, to start work on the new library.[7] The building was completed in 1452, but it took two more years for it to be furnished and fitted out. Novello had developed a passion for books even before he involved himself in the Franciscans' library plans, and careful study of the manuscripts that belonged to him reveals not only

66. The Church of San Francesco. Drawing by Francesco Zarletti.

his love of books but also the depth of his humanist interests. In fact he was so keen to see his ideas come to fruition that in 1450, when the library was still under construction, he asked Pope Nicholas V to issue a bull ratifying his gift to the library of his collection of manuscripts, which he valued at five hundred florins.[8]

When Novello Malatesta started collecting manuscripts he did not limit himself to those that were available in Italy but patronized Francesco Filelfo and Giovanni Aurispa, who travelled to the East, especially Constantinople, in search of Greek manuscripts. As the little town of Cesena was not well placed for the book trade, Novello set up a scriptorium to copy manuscripts which he wanted but was unable to obtain.[9] Evidence of its existence is to be found as early as 1446, and about a year later Jacopo da Pergola was engaged as its first copyist. At least fifteen codices were written in his graceful italic script: most of them are dated and signed, including Pliny's *Natural History* and Plutarch's *Lives* in two volumes. Among the copyists who worked at the scriptorium were Jacopo Macario of Venice, Andrea Catrinello of Genoa and Matteo Contuggi of Volterra, a most accomplished calligra-

1. On the Malatesta family see G. Franceschini's recent monograph *I Malatesta*, Varese 1973, esp. 389-414 (on Novello Malatesta's character and personality); also N. Masini, *Vita di Domenico Malatesta signore di Cesena*, BCM, Ms 45188 (16th c.), published by G.M. Muccioli in *Catalogus Codicum Manuscriptorum Malatestianae Caesenatis Bibliothecae* II, Cesena 1784, 273.

2. Bessarion's verdict on Plethon was recorded by Demetrios Kavakes Ralles: see G. Mercati, 'Minuzie', *Bessarione* 38 (1922) 135-143.

3. Sigismondo's action in taking

67. Novello Malatesta. Drawing after a medallion by Pisanello.

Plethon's body under his protection was no spur-of-the-moment decision, for he had invited Plethon to his court at Rimini after the marriage of Cleopa Malatesta to Theodoros II Palaiologos. The impact of this initiative of his on the history of the Renaissance is noted by A. Chastel in his paper 'Le platonisme et les arts de la Renaissance' in *Congrès de Tours et Poitiers ... 1953*, Paris 1954, 392.

4. Legend has it that St. Francis, after his meeting in 1226 with the saintly hermit Giovanni Bono in a cave in the plain of Cesuola, decided to go and live at Cesena: see G. Conti, 'L'edificio: Architettura e dec-

68. A corner of the library, showing the wooden reading-desks and the painted coats of arms of prominent Cesena families.
69. General view of the library.

pher.[10] The result was that Novello's library soon became famous, so much so that the humanist Flavio Biondo, in his book *Italia illustrata* (mid 15th cent.), described it as 'on a par with the best in Italy' (*melioribus Italiae aequiparanda*).

In 1465 Malatesta had six copyists in his employ, and in the interim period since 1446 at least twenty more had worked at his scriptorium for longer or shorter spells. Often the manuscripts were started and finished by different hands. Most of the scribes were Italians, but three are known to have come from abroad. The most prolific of the foreigners was the French notary Jean d'Épinal, Novello's favourite, who came to live at Cesena before 1451, married a local girl, latinized his name to Johannes de Spinalo and died in 1467, two years after Novello. One of his manuscripts, a copy of St. Augustine's *Commentary on the Gospel of St. John* (1452), was sent to Ferrara to be illuminated by the great Taddeo Crivelli.[11] Two other experienced copyists from northern Europe who were employed in Malatesta's scriptorium were Tomaso da Utrecht (Thomas Blavart), who wrote a Gothic script and took seven months to copy the *Commentary* of Nicolaus de Lyra, and Mathias Kuler, a German who signed a codex of commentaries on Aristotle as follows: 'Written with the hand, not with the foot.... All the profits have been spent on good wine in the tavern in the company of women. *Venite exaltemus*.'[12] All these copyists worked permanently at Cesena, but they may well have accompanied Novello when he went to his castle at nearby Bertinoro for his summer holidays.

Before being accepted for the library, every new manuscript had first to be checked against the original by a scribe of Malatesta's court, any mistakes or omissions being marked with the words *Hic deficit* in the appropriate place. It was then sent for illumination, either to Crivelli's famous studio in Ferrara (as in the case of the Cicero and a translation of Plutarch by Filelfo) or to a local court artist. In most cases the only ornamentation consisted of the family arms or crest, with the initials of Novello Malatesta, on the front page.[13]

Besides having manuscripts copied in his own scriptorium, Malatesta built up his collection by purchases from other sources. His fourteen Greek codices, including copies of the *Odyssey* and Plato's *Republic* and *Dialogues*, may have been bought in a single lot from one of the big dealers such as Aurispa, Filelfo or Vespasiano da Bisticci. One manuscript of Demosthenes was copied by a Greek scholar in Italy, and another of his orations was bought in 1431 by a Genoese merchant in Constantinople from Niccolò Martinozzi, who later became Malatesta's Chancellor. Some manuscripts were copied in nearby cities and a collection of Hebrew codices was bought from the Cesena City Council. Lastly, the library received generous gifts from Cardinal Bessarion (such as a Latin translation of Aristotle's *Metaphysica* dated *c.* 1455) and, of course, from Francesco Filelfo, who was a liberal patron of all enter-

orazione' in *La Biblioteca Malatestiana di Cesena*, Rome 1992, 57.

5. See A. Domeniconi, *La Biblioteca Malatestiana*, Cesena 1982, 8. On Novello and the formation of his library see A. Campana, 'Le biblioteche della provincia di Forlì. I: Cesena' in D. Fava (ed.), *Tesori delle biblioteche d'Italia: Emilia-Romagna*, Milan 1931, 3-43; P.G. Fabbri, 'Il signore, la libreria, la città' in *La Biblioteca Malatestiana di Cesena* 15-54.

70. Francesco Filelfo and Flavio Biondo. Woodcuts from N. Reusner, Icones, *Basel 1599.*
71. Detail of the initial letter of the Gradual (Corale Bessarione 1) showing a kneeling monk. 15th c. (No. 2, fol. 1r).

prises of this kind in any of the centres of Italian humanism.[14]

Malatesta was familiar with the so-called 'ideal library catalogue' compiled by Tommaso Parentucelli for Cosimo de' Medici, and he corresponded with the Medici and Francesco Sforza, Duke of Milan, with a view to borrowing manuscripts which he wanted to have copied for himself. He set his copyists to work mainly on theological writings, including works by Augustine, Jerome, Gregory, Ambrose and other Church Fathers, and he was particularly keen to collect books by the great medieval scholars and commentators such as Albertus Magnus, Thomas Aquinas and William of Ockham. History was another of his great loves, and his collection included twenty-six manuscripts of historical works including the *History* of Polybius in Niccolò Perotti's translation. Of humanist writings he had none, nor were there any books in Italian in his library: Dante and Petrarch were not represented at all, and there seems to have been just one Latin translation of some of Boccaccio's works.[15]

Cardinal Bessarion. One of the Cesena library's proudest possessions is its collection of Cardinal Bessarion's choral manuscripts (*corali*) with lavish Late Gothic and Renaissance illuminations. It is not known how these came to be acquired by the Malatesta family. Bessarion commissioned three large-format graduals and four antiphonaries from Bologna scriptoria in 1451-1452, when he was the papal legate to that city, for the Franciscan friary of St. Antony of Padua in Constantinople. After the fall of Constantinople he changed his plans. In 1458 an Observancy (a community of the Observant Order, a branch of the Franciscans), similar to St. Antony's Friary in Constantinople, was founded in Cesena, and in the same year Bessarion was made Patron of the Franciscan Order. In 1459 the choral manuscripts were sent to the famous studios at Ferrara to have their illumination completed. In 1460 or 1461 Novello founded the Order of Minori Osservanti at Cesena, and in about 1462 Cardinal Bessarion decided to give the choral manuscripts to Novello or directly to his wife Violante.[16]

The sudden death of Novello Malatesta on 20th November 1465, at the age of only forty-seven, put an end to the systematic enlargement of the library, which by that time contained more than two hundred manuscripts. However, Novello had made provision for the future of the *libraria domini*, as he called it, by leaving to the Franciscans an annuity of a hundred ducats guaranteed by the Venetian Republic: the money was intended to cover the running costs of the library as well as the purchase of new books.[17]

The biggest gift ever made to the monastic library at Cesena was a bequest from Giovanni di Marco of Rimini, who died about nine years after Novello. Di Marco, who was chief physician to Pope Sixtus IV in Rome, was also Novello Malatesta's doctor and a personal friend of his, and it was Novello who introduced him to the pleasures of book-

6. Campana, *op. cit.* 8; Domeniconi, *op. cit.* 9; Conti, *op. cit.* 64.

7. Nuti was in Cesena in about 1445 for discussions about the library project, which he was to undertake in partnership with his brother Giovanni and in collaboration with Cristoforo Foschi: see Campana, *op. cit.* 6; Conti, *op. cit.* 64. On Foschi see C. Grigioni, 'Per la storia della scultura in Cesena nel secolo XV', *La Romagna* 7, 10 (1910) 392.

8. Campana, *op. cit.* 8; Domeniconi, *op. cit.* 9.

9. According to local tradition, Novello had to revise his plans for the library, making it smaller than originally intended, because a ship he had chartered to bring his newly-acquired manuscripts from the East was lost at sea: see Campana, *op. cit.* 10; Domeniconi, *op. cit.* 13-14.

Emmanuele Casamassima, the author of an unpublished paper in which he examines the circumstances of the copying of Novello Malatesta's manuscripts, is in no doubt as to the existence of the scriptorium, though he has been unable to determine its precise location: see Fabbri, *op. cit.* 39-40. For Domeniconi's reservations on the subject see C. Riva, 'Gli inediti di Antonio Domeniconi', *Studi Romagnoli* 30 (1979) 69-83.

10. Campana, *op. cit.* 9 ff.; Domeniconi, *op. cit.* 14-15; Fabbri, *op. cit.* 50. Macario was in Cesena on a brief visit: the Bible he copied for Novello is an outstanding example of contemporary italic writing. Catrinello's last work for Novello was a copy of Cicero's *Rhetorica ad Herennium* which he completed and delivered in 1465, the year of Novello's death.

11. Campana, *op. cit.* 10; Domeniconi, *op. cit.* 15-16; Fabbri, *op. cit.* 39, 42, 50. On Jean d'Épinal see A. Domeniconi, 'Ser Giovanni da Epinal, copista di Malatesta Novello', *Studi Romagnoli* 10 (1959) 261-282. Taddeo Crivelli, who was probably a native of Lombardy, is regarded as the origi-

72. Illuminated initials from Corali Bessarione 1 (Pentecost, 12v; Holy Communion, 41r; Eternal Father, 35v) and Bessarione 3 (Christ resurgent, 1r).

collecting. On his death in 1474 he bequeathed his entire collection of 119 manuscripts, mostly on medical subjects but with some literary and philosophical works as well, to the Cesena library. Fewer than seventy of these now remain.[18]

Novello Malatesta's collection has not survived intact in the Cesena library: many of his manuscripts have disappeared in one way or another over the centuries. Some may have been stolen, some may have been exchanged for works of which the library had no copy, some may have been lent out for copying and never returned. Novello himself evidently noticed that carelessness was leading to the loss of some of his stock, for in 1461 he introduced special security precautions and delegated the running of his library to the Franciscan friars and the Cesena City Council. Some years later, at the urging of Antonio Zanzolini, the Council – which by that time was responsible for the overall supervision of the library – started carrying out regular inspections and set to work on the compilation of a catalogue.[19]

Architecture. Matteo Nuti based his architectural plans on the style of the monastic library of San Marco in Florence, designed by Michelozzo di Bartolommeo for the Medici, which represented a departure from tradition. The standard medieval library consisted of an impersonal rectangular room with little in the way of architectural ornamentation and

73. The left-hand room of the library, designed and built by Domenico Fontana during the pontificate of Sixtus V.

with plain reading-desks that were also used for the storage of manuscripts. In contrast, Michelozzo's library at San Marco was a spacious hall rather reminiscent of a basilica, and the style he introduced there was adopted in nearly all Renaissance libraries in Italy. Some characteristic examples are to be seen today in Parma (San Giovanni Evangelista), Piacenza (San Sepolcro), Bologna (San Domenico) and Perugia (San Domenico).[20]

nator of the Ferrara style of Renaissance manuscript illumination. His regular patrons included the d'Este family (the rulers of Ferrara), the Church and local bibliophiles, and he is known to have worked for Novello Malatesta as early as 1451. See L. Eleen in *DBI* 36 (1988) 156-160.

12. Campana, *op. cit.* 13; Domeniconi, *La Biblioteca Malatestiana* 16; Fabbri, *op. cit.* 50.

13. Novello Malatesta's armorial bearings consisted of a linear composition surrounded by a laurel wreath. This was generally embellished with various decorative motifs in the artist's own style: see Fabbri, *op. cit.* 30, 31, 40, 41, 45.

14. Campana, *op. cit.* 17-18; Domeniconi, *La Biblioteca Malatestiana* 37-40; Fabbri, *op. cit.* 54.

15. See Muccioli, *loc. cit.*; R. Zazzeri, *Sui codici e libri a stampa della Biblioteca Malatestiana di Cesena*, Cesena 1887.

16. Cardinal Bessarion did a great deal for Bologna during his time there, in various ways: he paid for the upkeep and restoration of several churches in the city itself and the surrounding country, he advocated the construction of the first public clock tower and he reorganized the University, which had sunk to a shockingly low standard: see *Charta* 106.

On the history of the choral manuscripts see L. Baldacchini, 'Dalla "libraria domini" alla biblioteca publica' in *La Biblioteca Malatestiana di Cesena* 133-167; and esp. F. Lollini, 'Bologna, Ferrara, Cesena: I corali del Bessarione tra circuiti umanistici e percorsi di artisti' in P. Lucchi (ed.), *Corali Miniati del Quattrocento nella Biblioteca Malatestiana*, Milan 1989, 19-36.

Violante Malatesta was the daughter of Guido Antonio da Montefeltro and Caterina Colonna and sister-in-law of the famous book-collector Federico da Montefeltro, Duke of Urbino. Bessarion had many friends at the court of Urbino and

74. An illuminated initial in a manuscript of St. Augustine's De civitate Dei *(No. 1, fol. 15r).*

BEATISSIMI AVRELII AVGV

DE CIVITATE DEI LIB: PRIMVS

ad

LO

N

TA

SI

TE

CV

IN

PIO

GH

ex fide uiuens: siue in illa stabilitate sedis
nunc expectat per patientiam quoad usq: iust
tur in iudicium deinceps adeptura per excell
a ultima: & pace perfecta: hoc opere ad te ins

The Cesena library, situated on the second floor of the friary's new wing, is entered through a Greek-style Renaissance portal. To the right of this monumental entrance, with its double wooden door, is an inscription giving the architect's name and the date of completion of the library, and in the middle of the pediment there is a relief of the Malatesta family crest, an elephant, with the motto *Elephas indicus culices non timet* ('The Indian elephant fears not mosquitoes'). Another plaque on the right of the doorway has the dedicatory inscription *MAL. NOV. PAN. F. HOC DEDIT OPUS* ('Novello Malatesta, son of Pandolfo, financed this project'). The door opens on to an extremely elegant, airy, rectangular room with two rows of pseudo-Ionic marble columns forming an open aisle down the centre. The ceiling takes the form of a continuous vault in the middle section, over the aisle, with a series of uniform cross-vaults on either side. The column capitals, which are all different, incorporate Ionic elements, but the central feature of each of them is a coat of arms of the Malatesta family. Ranged at regular intervals along the side walls are the reading-desks, twenty-nine on each

76. The interior of the library.

75. The front door of the library: engraving by J.M. Muccioli.

was on close terms with Federico: see C.H. Clough, 'Cardinal Bessarion and the Greeks at the Court of Urbino', *Manuscripta* 8, 3 (1964) 160-171.

17. See Campana, *op. cit.* 15; Domeniconi, *La Biblioteca Malatestiana* 15-16; and esp. G. Bonfiglio Dosio, 'Il testamento di Novello Malatesta (9 aprile 1464)', *Romagna arte e storia* 8, 22 (1988) 11-18.

18. Campana, *op. cit.* 15-17; Domeniconi, *La Biblioteca Malatestiana* 17-18; Fabbri, *op. cit.* 34-36.

19. In 1469, more than three years after Novello's death, the Cesena Council of Ninety-Six decided, at the urging of Antonio Zanzolini, to institute a system of regular checks on the library and drew up plans for its organization and administration: see Fabbri, *op. cit.* 34. Actually, from the time when the library was founded (1451), Novello had always declared his intention that it should be under the Council's control and should be run as a public rather than a private library: see A. Domeniconi, 'I custodi della Biblioteca Malates-

77. A manuscript of the Orations *of Demosthenes, bought in Constantinople from a Genoese merchant in 1431 (fol. 344r).*

μένου τὸν ἔλεγχον ἐκ τῆς ἀνθρώπου περὶ τῆς αἰκίας
ὁπότερος ἡμῶν ἦρξε χειρῶν ἀδίκων· τοῦ
το γάρ ἐστιν ἡ αἰκία· πῶς οὖν καταγνοίημεν ἔτι
τούτοις τοὺς μάρτυρας τὰ ψευδῆ μεμαρτυ
ρηκέναι· οἱ γὰρ οὐδ' ἐμοῦ προκαλουμένου τὸ σῶμα
τῆς ἀνθρώπου παραδοῦναι κατ' αὐτὸ ἔφασαν προκα
λεῖσθαι τὸν Θεόφημον· καὶ ἐμαρτύρησ
αν αὐτῷ καὶ τὴν μαρτυρίαν δ' ἐγὼ ἐβεβαιώσα
σθαι ὡς ἀληθής ἐστι· καὶ τοὺς μάρτυρας ἀπη
λλάχθαι τοῦ ἀνθρώπου παραδόντας τὸ σῶμα
τῆς ἀνθρώπου· τὴν δ' ἄνθρωπον περὶ τῆς αἰκίας βασα
νίζεσθαι· ἐφ' ἧ ἀγωνιοῦσθαι δίκην τὸν Θεόφημον·
ἐπειδὴ τὸ ἴσον οὐ παρεῖχον· καὶ τὸν ἔλεγχον ἐ
ξὸν ὁ Θεόφημος ἔλεγε τοῦτο ἐξαπατᾶν ὑμᾶς τοὺς
δικαστὰς ἐκ τούτων γίγνεσθαι· ἔφη γὰρ ἐν
τῇ δίκῃ τῆς αἰκίας τοὺς μὲν μάρτυρας τοὺς
παραγενομένους καὶ μαρτυροῦντας τὰ γε
νόμενα ἐν γραμματείῳ κατὰ τὸν νόμον ψα
δρὲς εἶναι· καὶ [illegible] παρεσκευάσθαι τὴν
ἄνθρωπον τὴν παραγενομένην εὑρεῖν τἀ
ληθῆ· οὐκ ἐκ γραμματείου μαρτυροῦσαν·
ἀλλ' ἐκ τῆς ἰσχυροτάτης μαρτυρίας βασανιζο
μένην ὁπότερος ἦρξε χειρῶν ἀδίκων· ἀλ
λὰ δὴ λέγω τοῦτο καταχρώμενος· καὶ μάρτυσι
παρεχόμενος τούτων· ἐξηπάτα τοὺς δικασ
τὰς· νῦν ἐξελέγχεται ψευδῆ ὄντα· τῆς ἀνθρώπου γὰρ
τὸ σῶμα· οὐ τολμᾷ παραδοῦναι ὃ μεμαρτύρηκα

† κύριε Ἰησοῦ Χριστὲ ὁ [illegible] Κατὸ λουβι βλίον τοῦτο τὸ [illegible]
[illegible] ἀπὸ [illegible] ἀρχῆς μέχρι καὶ τέλους τοῦ βιβλίου τούτου [illegible]
[illegible] λόγον [illegible] καὶ [illegible] γράψας [illegible]
ἐκ μαρτυρίας [illegible] ὁ ἀναγνώστης τοῦ βιβλίου τούτου
ἐν [illegible] λόγον [illegible]

side, of standard medieval design. The ends of the desks facing the central aisle are adorned with the coats of arms of prominent Cesena families. Illumination comes from a row of windows closely spaced along one side wall and a circular window in the middle of the wall opposite the door.[21]

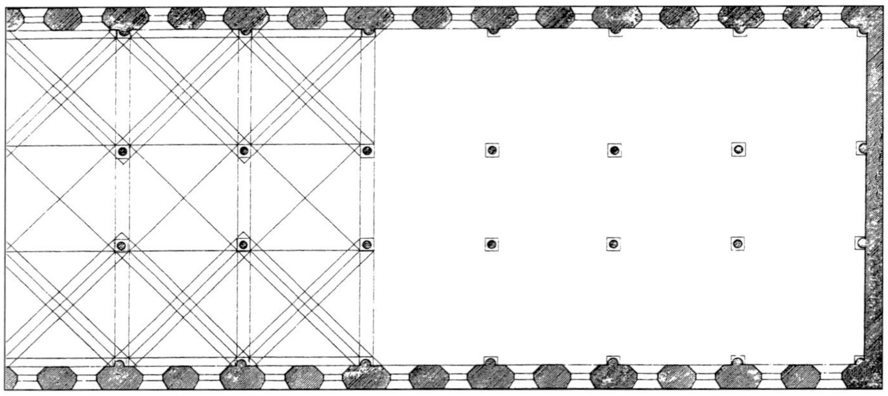

78. Side elevation of the library, drawn by Leonardo Santucci.

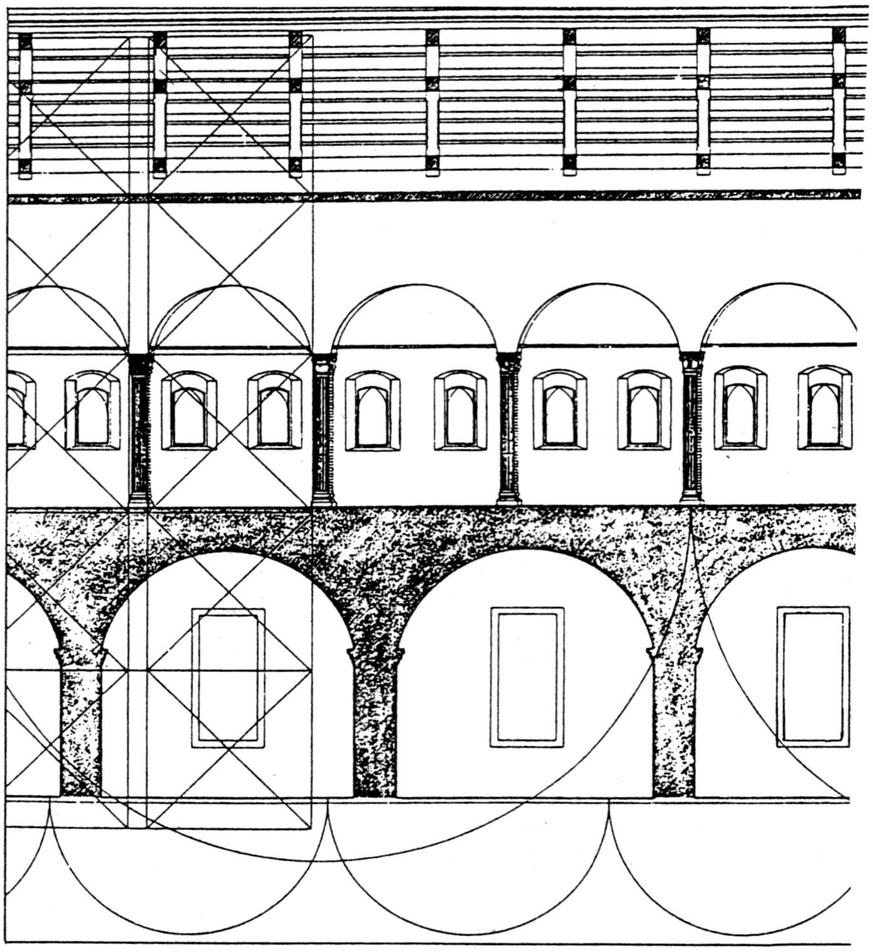

79. Longitudinal section of the library building, with squares, diagonals and semicircles showing how its proportions were calculated.

tiana di Cesena dalle origini alla seconda metà del Seicento', *Studi Romagnoli* 14 (1963) 385-396.

20. Campana, *op. cit.* 5-6. For more on the library of San Marco in Florence see the chapter on the Biblioteca Laurenziana herein. On monastic libraries in general see G. Cecchini, *Sei biblioteche monastiche*

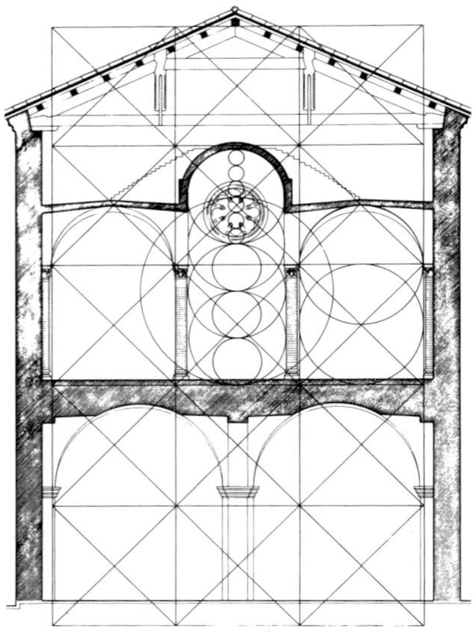

80. Lateral section of the building, overlaid with geometrical figures indicating the proportions.

rinascimentali, Milan 1960; J.F. O'Gorman, *The Architecture of the Monastic Library in Italy, 1300-1600*, New York 1972. On Nuti, who was born at Fano, see C. Grigioni, 'Matteo Nuti. Notizie bibliografiche', *La Romagna* 6, 8-9 (1909) 361-365; on his relations with Novello Malatesta see G. Volpe, *Matteo Nuti architetto dei Malatesta*, Venice 1989, 75-77.

21. On the architecture of the library see J.W. Clark, *The Care of Books*, Cambridge 1901, 199-203; Campana, *op. cit.* 6-8; Domeniconi, *op. cit.* 11-13; and esp. Conti, *op. cit.* 57-118.

*81. Drawing by J.W. Clark (*The Care of Books, *Cambridge 1901, 202) giving a close-up view of a reading-desk and showing how the books were chained.*

The Biblioteca Marciana

CHAPTER SIXTEEN

Cardinal Bessarion never ceased to hope that the Western Europeans would one day awaken to the necessity of liberating the Greek world so that it might regain its place as a bastion of the West against the expansionist designs of the Ottoman Empire. When he felt that he was nearing the end of his life he decided to donate his priceless collection of manuscripts to the Venetian Republic (which he described memorably as *quasi alterum Byzantium*), so that they would be seen as a symbol of the West's cultural heritage and as a beacon of Hellenism.[1]

The first person to have the idea of opening a public library in Italy – again in Venice, as it happened – was Petrarch. That great poet, who provided the initial impetus for the revival of classical literature and humanism through re-evaluation of the ancient world, had amassed a fine collection of books by searching in monasteries and cathedrals, mainly in the south of France, where he was living in exile. Musing on the Alexandrian Library and the great public libraries of Rome, as he often did, he formed the idea of bequeathing his 'daughter' (as he called his own collection of books) to the Venetian Republic to be the nucleus of a future public library. The Grand Council formally accepted his gift in 1362, but fate had a different destiny in store for his books: although a considerable number of them did stay together, eventually making their way to Paris by way of Pavia, the remainder were scattered far and wide, which was exactly what he had hoped to avoid.[2] Yet Petrarch's noble gesture did not come to nothing, for his dream of starting a public library was subsequently realized by one of the great luminaries of Byzantine scholarship who shared his humanistic ideas and was well versed in philosophy: Cardinal Bessarion.

Bessarion, whose baptismal name was Basil, was born in Trebizond on 2nd January 1403. His first teacher was Ignatios Chortasmenos, Metropolitan of Selymbria. He then studied rhetoric with Georgios Chrysokokkes in Constantinople at a time when considerable numbers of Italians were going there to study Greek, learn about the cultural achievements of the Eastern Empire and look for Greek manuscripts. Among his fellow-students in the imperial capital were Francesco Filelfo, Giovanni Aurispa and many others who later came to prominence as leading lights of the Renaissance. While still an adolescent he entered the monastic life on the advice of his patron, Patriarch Dositheos Dorieus. He was professed as a monk following the Rule of St. Basil on 30th January 1423 and took the name Bessarion. He took his solemn vows later that year, was ordained deacon in 1426 and set off almost immediately as a member of an imperial mission to his home town of Trebizond. Some years later he went to live at Mistras, capital of the Despotate of the Morea, where he completed his education.[3] Between 1431 and 1436 he was given tuition in philosophy, mathematics and astronomy by Georgios Gemistos Plethon, the sage of Mistras, and became both a disciple and a friend of his.[4] His thinking was moulded perhaps more strongly than anyone else's by his teacher's inspired and inquiring mind, and he later became the foremost champion of Platonic philosophy in the

82. The Biblioteca Marciana seen from the loggia of the Palazzo Ducale.

West. Bessarion firmly believed that if Christianity was to retain its influence on the humanist movement it needed to turn to Platonism for fresh ideas with which to defend itself against the pragmatism of the Averroists and Epicureans.

In 1437 Bessarion returned to Constantinople, where he was consecrated Metropolitan of Nicaea, and a year later he accompanied

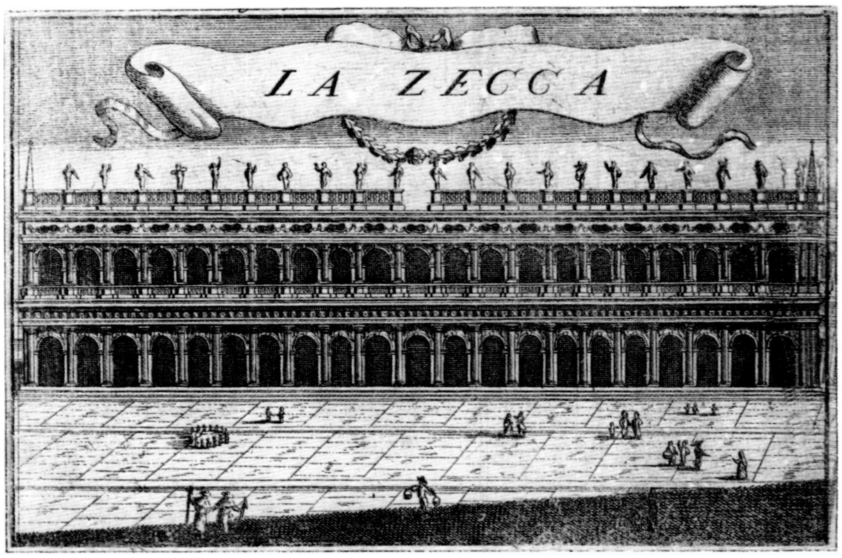

83. The St. Mark's Square façade of the library. Engraving, 18th c.

Patriarch Matthaios I to the Council of Ferrara-Florence. After the Council he went back to Constantinople, but there, being a fervent advocate of the reunion of the two churches and leader of the pro-union party among the Greeks, he found his career prospects obstructed by the prevailing climate of opinion. In 1440 he went back to Florence and in the autumn of 1443 he moved to Rome for good.[5]

On the election of Nicholas V to the pontificate in 1447, Bessarion moved rapidly up the hierarchy. In 1449, very soon after being consecrated Bishop of Sabina, he was made Cardinal Bishop of Tuscolo, and the following year he was sent on important political missions to Bologna, the Romagna and the Marca d'Ancona. In his capacity as a member of the Curia, he was a staunch supporter of Nicholas V's scheme of having the most important Greek literary works and patristic writings translated into Latin. He himself, however, had a much broader conception of what was needed: it was his intention that Greek scholars fleeing from the Byzantine Empire to Italy should be able to find a safe refuge there, and accordingly he transformed his own home near the Baths of Caracalla into a combination of scriptorium, open library and a sort of academy. Thus it became a temporary home from home for numerous humanists, not only from different parts of Italy but from northern Europe as well. There they studied and copied his priceless

1. A valuable recent work on the Biblioteca Marciana is Marino Zorzi's book *La Libreria di San Marco: Libri, lettori, società nella Venezia dei Dogi*, Milan 1987, which covers the whole period from the library's foundation to the present day, with comments on its priceless possessions, its librarians and its directors, and has a full bibliography.

2. Venice was Petrarch's great love: to him it was a city from another world, and as the years went by he became more and more enamoured of the idea of going to live there permanently. Concerned as he was about the fate of his manuscripts, he eventually decided to offer them to the Venetian Senate in return for the lifetime gift of a house for him to live in, on condition that the collection would be made open to the public after his death. See E.H. Wilkins, *Petrarch's Later Years*, Cambridge Mass. 1959; N. Vianello, 'I libri del Petrarca e la prima idea di una pubblica biblioteca a Venezia' in *Miscellanea Marciana di Studi Bessarionei*, Padua 1976, 435-451.

The greater part of Petrarch's library consisted of Latin manuscripts, as Greek was a closed book to

84. Francesco Petrarca. Woodcut from N. Reusner, Icones, *Basel 1599.*

85. The Sala Sansovino, the main room of the library.

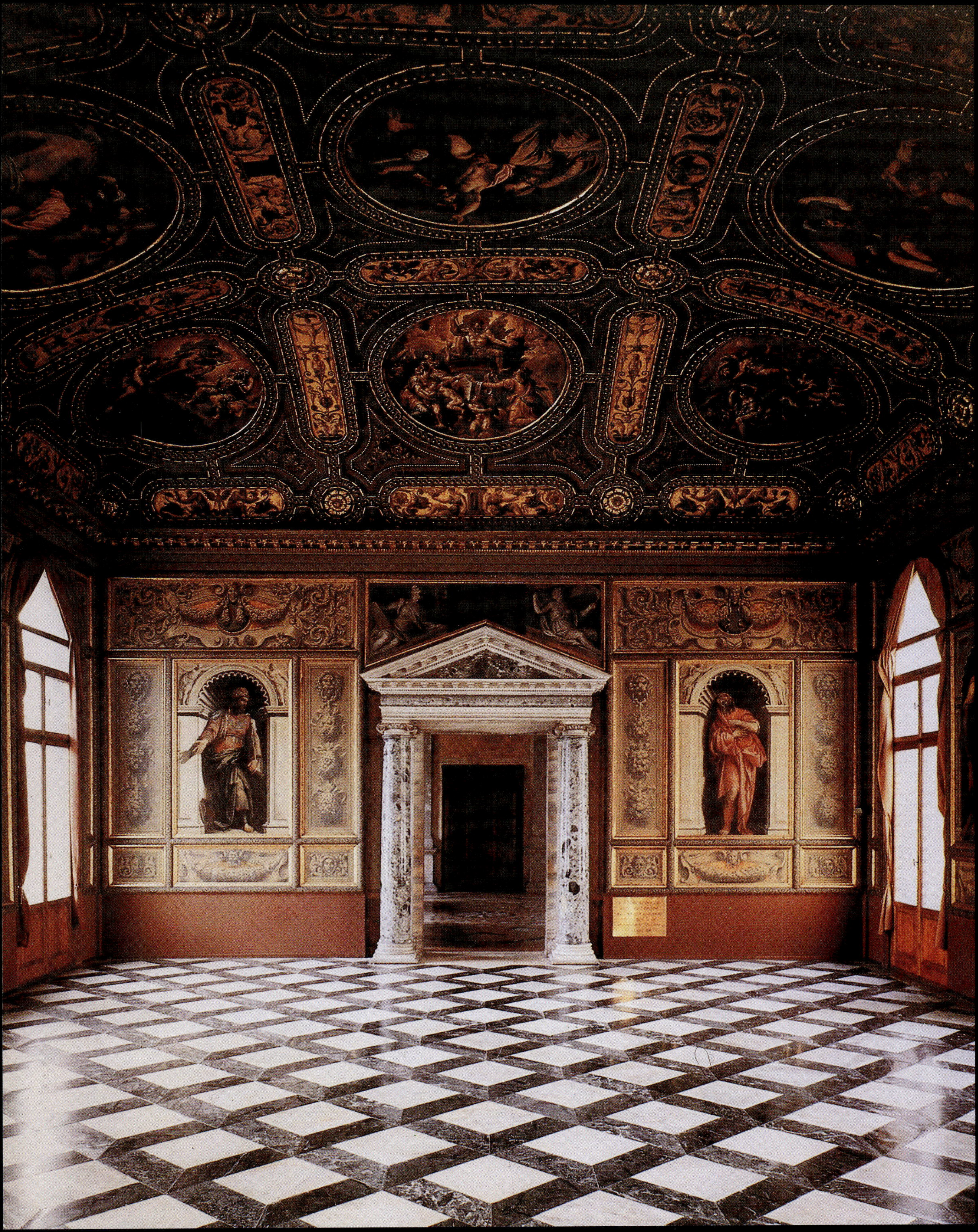

manuscripts, while others travelled to the East to look for new manuscripts to buy for his collection. This band of scholars evolved into a sort of academy, in the sense that they spent a good deal of time discussing all the literary and philosophical problems that arose while the manuscripts were being copied, edited and prepared for publication.[6] As early as 1468 the printing houses of Rome were already hard at work printing and publishing works of Greek and Latin literature.[7]

On Nicholas V's death in 1455, Bessarion was nominated for the pontificate but his election was blocked by the Archbishop of Avignon, who

86. Cardinal Bessarion. Woodcut from P. Giovio, Elogia virorum literis illustrium, *Basel 1577.*

denounced him hotly as a former schismatic. The new Pope, the Spaniard Alfonso de Borja, who took the name Calixtus III, had the greatest admiration and respect for Bessarion and encouraged the Greek cardinal in his plans to launch a crusade for the reconquest of Constantinople. The next Pope, Pius II, who was elected on 13th August 1458, deputed Bessarion to speak for him at the Convivium of Mantua about the peril threatening Europe from the East. At the insistence of the German princes, the conference was transferred from Mantua to Nürnberg and Vienna. At Nürnberg Bessarion spoke forcefully but failed to persuade all the delegates to adopt a resolution calling for action against the Turkish menace. He sent a message to the Pope informing him of the negative outcome of the discussions, and when the conference was over he set off from Nürnberg for Vienna. Once again his mission was political and diplomatic: to persuade Emperor Frederick

him, to his lasting sorrow. He went on trying to learn the language to the very end of his life but died with his ambition unfulfilled, having written a commentary on Leonzio Pilato's Latin translation of the *Iliad* and the *Odyssey*. We do not know exactly how many manuscripts Petrarch owned, but the number was probably around two hundred: see P. de Nolhac, *Pétrarque et l'Humanisme*, Paris (Honoré Champion) 1907; Vianello, *op. cit.*; R. Sabbadini, *Le scoperte dei codici latini e greci nei secoli XIV e XV*, new edn. by E. Garin, Florence (Sansoni) 1975.

3. Out of the extensive literature on Bessarion, see esp.: L. Mohler, *Kardinal Bessarion als Theologe, Humanist und Staatsmann: Funde und Forschungen*, Paderborn 1923-1942, which gives a comprehensive account of his life and work; A. Kyrou, *Βησσαρίων ὁ Ἕλλην*, 2 vols., Athens 1947; Lotte Labowsky, 'Bessarione' in *DBI* 9 (1967) 686-696. See also *Charta* 91-106.

4. On Bessarion's studies with Georgios Chrysokokkes see F. Fuchs, *Die höheren Schulen von Konstantinopel im Mittelalter*, Leipzig/Berlin 1926, 70. On the school of Mistras see Mohler, *op. cit.* 45, and F. Masai, *Pléthon et le platonisme de Mistra*, Paris 1956, 306-312. The subjects that Bessarion actually studied are not known, but the scope of his education must have been extremely broad, if we are to believe what he wrote in a letter to his friend Nikolaos Sekoundinos: 'When you read these lines, do not imagine they contain the slightest element of exaggeration. That man really was the embodiment of philosophy and all branches of learning, not only rhetoric. Everything to do with the movements of the heavenly bodies and the harmonious progression, geometric proportions and numerical measurement of those movements, everything there is to

87. Cardinal Bessarion's letter to Doge Cristoforo Moro and the Venetian Senate, informing them of the gift of his books (Cod. lat. 14, May 1468).

ILLVSTRISSIMO ATQVE INVICTISSIMO PRINCIPI DN̄O CHRISTOPHORO MAVRO DVCI ET INCLYTO VENETORVM SENATVI BESSARIO CARDINALIS & PATRIARCHA COSTANTINOPOLITANVS SAL.

EQVIDEM SEMPER á tenera ferè puerilíq; ætate omnem meum laborem: omnē opera curam: studium que adhibui: ut quotcūq; possem libros in omni disciplinarum genere compararem. propter quod nō modo plærosq; et puer et adolescens manu mea conscripsi: sed quicquid pecuniolæ seponere interim parca frugalitas potuit: in his coemendis absumpsi. Nullam enim magis dignā atq; præclaram supellectilem nullum

III to give up his aggressive designs on Hungarian territory. Frederick gave Bessarion a royal welcome and, in token of his admiration, asked him to be godfather to his only son, the future Emperor Maximilian I. While in Vienna Bessarion met Nicolaus da Cusa and was introduced to the astronomer Georg Peurbach and the ardent humanist Regiomontanus.[8]

Bessarion finally succeeded in making peace between Frederick and the Hungarians and then returned to Italy. After stopping off in Venice,

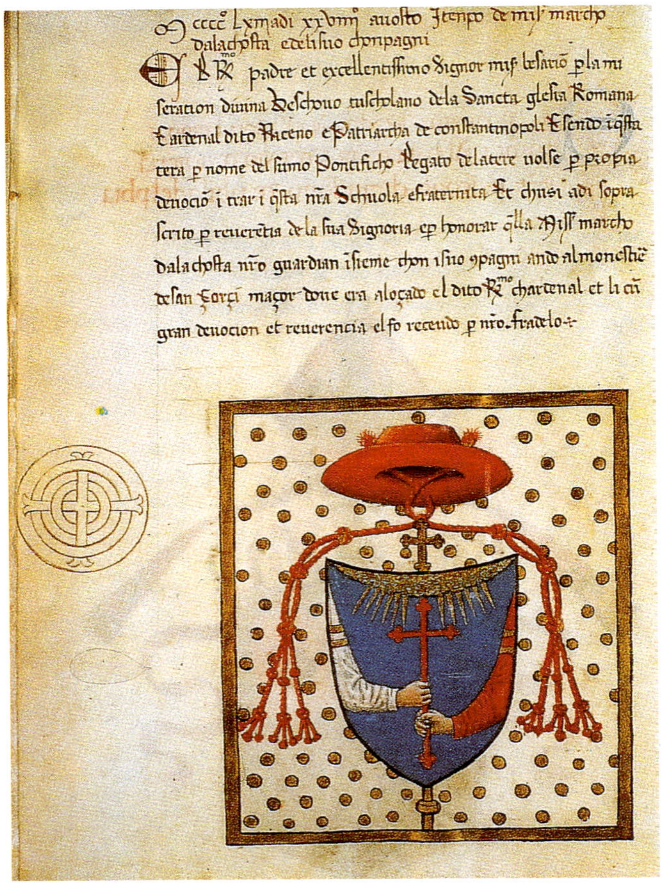

88. Cardinal Bessarion's coat of arms (Cod. it. VII 2700, fol. 2v).

where the Republic made him a member of the Grand Council, he arrived in Rome in November 1461. Further crises in ecclesiastical affairs awaited him there, and following the death of Isidore of Kiev in 1463 he was proclaimed Latin Patriarch of Constantinople. In 1472 he was nominated for the pontificate for the second time, but the intrigues of the College of Cardinals resulted in the election of Francesco della Rovere. The new Pope, who took the name of Sixtus IV, sent Bessarion to France to negotiate a reconciliation between King Louis XI of France and Charles the Bold, Duke of Burgundy, with the ulterior motive of organizing a new crusade; but the religious fanaticism of the Catholic

know about Plato and the other savants who sought the answers to divine problems, every aspect of research into natural phenomena – to all these matters he turned his mind, and all of them he studied with great precision. Such honour did he bring upon himself by his life that even Diogenes and his like, even the famous Stoics, were as nothing beside him. I have never known anybody who was so far removed from the false allure of sophistry, and although I have met so many wise men I have not met anyone who strove better than he did to discover the truth by philosophical inquiry. He was a man who towered above us in stature, a hero, to whom our astonished silence is a fitter tribute than words can ever be.' (Masai, *op. cit.* 310-311.)

5. Labowsky, *op. cit.* 688.

6. On Bessarion's academy see H. Vast, *Le cardinal Bessarion*, Paris 1878, 306-311, 314, 320-321; Mohler, *op. cit.* I 330-335; Kyrou, *op. cit.* II 135-161; *Charta* 92. On the copyists and assistants he employed in the development of his collection see A. Diller, 'Three Greek Scribes Working for Bessarion: Trivizias, Callistus, Hermonymus', *IMU* 10 (1967) 404-410; E. Mioni, 'Bessarione scriba e alcuni suoi collaboratori' in *Miscellanea Marciana di Studi Bessarionei*, Padua 1976, 263-318; Id., 'Bessarione bibliofilo e filologo', *Rivista di Studi Bizantini e Neoellenici*, n.s., 15 (1986) 61-83. On the choral manuscripts (*corali*) given by Bessarion to Novello Malatesta, see p. 312.

7. It was in Rome that printing with movable metal types was started on a regular basis by the German printers Konrad Sweynheim and Arnold Pannartz, who had previously run a press at the monastery of

89. Ψαλμοί μέ Σχόλια (Psalms with Commentary). *Parchment codex, 10th-11th c. (Gr. Z. 17, fol. IIIr-v). A manuscript from Bessarion's collection that originally came from the Peribleptos Monastery, Constantinople.*

† ἔνθα χρίεται Δα̅δ εἰς βασιλέα κέρατι ὑπὸ Σαμουὴλ τοῦ προφήτου †

† ἔνθα ἀναιρεῖ τὴν ἄρκτον ὁ προπάτωρ Δα̅δ ἐπελθοῦσαν κατὰ τῶν προβάτων †

ἔνθα σχίζει τὸν λέοντα Δα̅δ ἐπελθόντα κατὰ τῶν προβάτων

ἔνθα ἀναιρεῖ Δα̅δ τῇ σφενδόνῃ τὸν ἀλλόφυλον Γολιάδ

† ἔνθα καταπραΰνει Δα̅δ τῇ μελῳδίᾳ τῆς κιθάρας καὶ τῷ ῥυθμῷ τῷ βασιλεῖ Σαοὺλ ὑπὸ πν̅ς ἐνοχλουμένῳ †

† ἔνθα ἐλέγχεται Δα̅δ ὑπὸ τοῦ προφήτου Νάθαν. διὰ τὴν μοιχείαν καὶ τὸν φόνον· ὁ δὲ μετανοῶν. ἀποστρέφει τοῦ θ̅υ̅ τὴν ὀργήν †

Louis caused the talks to break down. Bessarion, embittered and disappointed, returned to Italy and went to live in Ravenna, where he died on 19th November 1472.

The negotiations between Bessarion and the Venetian Republic over the gift of his library started in March 1468. The Republic was represented in the talks by Ambassador Pietro Morosini, and on 14th May 1468 the deed of gift was drawn up:[9] written on parchment in an elegant italic script, and bearing Bessarion's coat of arms and the crest of the

90. Regiomontanus, Epitoma in Almagestum Ptolemaei, *Venice, Johannes Hamman, 1496.*

Republic, it was drafted on the Cardinal's instructions.[10] Thus was the Library of St. Mark born. With its 746 codices (482 in Greek and 264 in Latin), it was one of the largest and finest libraries of its time. The books were delivered over a period of time, starting with a batch of 466 codices in 1469, and when they were counted on completion of the handover in 1474 it was found that there were 1,024 volumes in fifty-seven boxes.[11]

Subiaco for two years (1465-1467) which may be termed their 'trial period'. The printing house they operated in Rome from 1468 to 1473 published a number of prestigious editions of the classics, with editorial assistance from a group of scholars living in Rome including Pomponio Leto, Lampugnino Birago, Andronikos Kallistos, Theodoros Gazis, Niccolò de Valle, Cardinal Bessarion and Giovanni Andrea de Bussi, who provided most of the financial backing. See *Charta* 73-77.

8. Labowsky, *op. cit.* 691; *Charta* 93.

Georg Peurbach, one of the first humanists in the North, was born near Linz in 1423 and died in Vienna in 1461. After studying in Vienna he travelled around Germany, France and (of course) Italy, to broaden his knowledge of mathematics and astronomy. He was a protégé of Nicolaus da Cusa and also of Giovanni Blancini, who eventually kept him on in Rome and invited him to teach astronomy at various Italian universities. On his return to Vienna he was appointed Professor of Mathematics: while there he applied himself to the study of astronomy, concentrating especially on Ptolemy, and invented several new instruments for observing the heavenly bodies. At Bessarion's suggestion he decided to learn Greek so that he could consult the original sources instead of having to rely on translations, which were often unreliable. See *NBU* 39 (1862) 772-773.

Johann Müller of Königsberg, who Latinized his name as Regiomontanus (or Monte Regio), was born in 1436 and took lessons with Peurbach from an early age. He carried on his teacher's work of emending the corrupt passages that had crept into ancient writings on astronomy and mathematics, starting, naturally

91. Claudius Ptolemaeus, Geographia. *Parchment codex, 15th c. (Gr. Z. 388, fol. 6v). A manuscript with illuminations of exceptional beauty and originality. Commissioned by Cardinal Bessarion from the calligrapher Ioannes Rossos.*

Ἐπίγραμμα ὅπερ ἔγραψε Πτολεμαῖος εἰς ἑαυτόν

ΟΙΔ᾽ ΟΤΙ ΘΝΗΤΟϹ ΕΦΥΝ ΚΑΙ ΕΦΗΜΕΡΟϹ, ΑΛΛ᾽ ΟΤΑΝ ΑϹΤΡΩΝ
ΜΑϹΤΕΥΩ ΠΥΚΝΑϹ ΑΜΦΙΔΡΟΜΟΥϹ ΕΛΙΚΑϹ
ΟΥΚΕΤ᾽ ΕΠΙΨΑΥΩ ΓΑΙΗϹ ΠΟϹΙΝ, ΑΛΛΑ ΠΑΡ᾽ ΑΥΤΩ
ΖΗΝΙ, ΘΕΟΤΡΟΦΕΟϹ ΠΙΜΠΛΑΜΑΙ ΑΜΒΡΟϹΙΗϹ

EPIGRAMA PTOLEMEI.
MORTALEM VITAM PERITVRA Q₃ MEMBRA DEDERE
FATA MIHI. & SVMVM PRESTITVERE DIEM.
SED IOVIS AMBROSIA VESCOR. TERRAM Q₃ RELINQVO.
INGENIO CVRSVS DVM NOTO SYDEREOS.

BIBLIOTHEQUE NATIONALE
BIBLIOTECA MARCIANA STAMPE

Besides Bessarion himself, at least twenty-two copyists, calligraphers, famous scholars, philosophers and manuscript hunters had a hand in the formation of this collection comprising a representative selection of extant works of classical literature as well as major treatises by Byzantine educators and the Church Fathers. Among the copyists whose signatures are found on the manuscripts are Bessarion's friend and protégé Michael Apostoles,[12] the great teacher and literary scholar Andronikos Kallistos (who lived and worked in Florence), Athanasios Chalkiopoulos, the outstanding calligrapher Ioannes Rossos, Bessarion's teacher Georgios Gemistos Plethon and Ciriaco d'Ancona. The collection comprises philosophical, poetic and literary works and books on rhetoric,

92. Aldus Manutius: engraving, 16th c. Markos Mousouros: woodcut from N. Reusner, Icones, *Basel 1599.*

history, geography, mathematics, astronomy, medicine and other subjects. Pride of place goes to philosophy: besides Plato and Aristotle, the authors represented include Theophrastus, Alexander of Aphrodisias, Simplicius, Plotinus, Hierocles and, of course, Plethon. Among the historians are Thucydides, Xenophon, Polybius and Herodotus. The medical treatises include numerous works by Galen and one by Paulus Aegineta. Homer is represented by the oldest surviving manuscript of the *Iliad*, the famous Codex Venetus A (10th century), and the poetry collection also contains works by Aeschylus, Sophocles, Euripides, Aristophanes, Pindar and Lycophron. Then there are works that fall into none of the above categories, such as the *Sphaera* by Proclus, the *Cynegetica* by Oppian (in an illuminated manuscript of the eleventh century) and *De Mysteriis Aegyptiorum* by Iamblichus. Finally, outstanding among the religious works are the *Ecclesiastical History* of Eusebius, the *Homilies* of John Chrysostom and a collection of ecclesiastical chants and psalms dating from the tenth or eleventh century.[13]

Contrary to what Bessarion had envisaged when he donated his

enough, with three standard authorities on these subjects: Pythagoras, Ptolemy and Euclid. On Peurbach's death in 1461 he followed Cardinal Bessarion to Rome, where he completed the work of editing Ptolemy's *Almagest*. He then devoted himself to the study of Bessarion's manuscripts and started buying Greek manuscripts for himself: whenever he found one on his travels around Italy that he wanted but could not buy – such as the manuscript of hitherto unknown works by Diophantus that he discovered in Venice – he had it copied. See E. von Zinner, 'Die wissenschaftlichen Bestrebungen Regiomontans' in *Beiträge für Inkunabelkunde*, n.s., 2 (1938) 89-103. For further information on Regiomontanus, his printing and editorial work in Nürnberg and his celebrated *Ephemerides*, see *Charta* 98-100.

9. Zorzi, *op. cit.* 82.

10. The final draft of the deed of gift, entitled *Index librorum utriusque linguae*, was prepared when Bessarion was living at Viterbo and had his close friend Niccolò Perotti at hand to help and advise him: see Zorzi, *op. cit.* 82-83.

11. See Marino Zorzi's introduction to *Biblioteca Marciana: Venezia*, Florence (Nardini Editore) 1988, 22.

12. Michael Apostoles played an important part in the formation of Bessarion's collection. He was born in about 1420, probably in Constantinople, and early in life he became an adherent of Neoplatonism. He studied under Ioannes Argyropoulos at the Katholikon Mouseion in Constantinople from 1448 and subsequently succeeded him in the same

93. Guillaume Fichet, Rhetorica, *Paris, M. Friburger, U. Gering, M. Crantz, 1471 (fol. 7r). Fichet, the Rector of the Sorbonne, founded the first printing press in Paris in collaboration with Johann Heynlin. One of the first books to be printed there was his own* Rhetorica, *which he dedicated to Bessarion in recognition of the cardinal's contribution to the spread of Platonism in northern Europe.*

manuscripts to the Venetian Republic, his collection was kept out of circulation for decades, with the result that many reliable manuscripts of classical works, some of them unique, could not be used by literary scholars engaged on the colossal project of preparing *editiones principes* for the Italian printing houses. The Venetian authorities kept these priceless treasures hidden away, allowing access to them very grudgingly if at all, and treated them with a cavalier unconcern that can only be described as outrageous. When making his gift, Bessarion had stipulated that his manuscripts should be made freely available to all for consultation and that anyone should be allowed to borrow them on payment of a returnable deposit equal to twice their value. In 1473, a year after Bessarion's death and about five years after he had given them to the Republic, they were still lying in boxes in the Sala di Scrutinio of the Palazzo Ducale, and ten years after that they were still in the same place. In 1485, because they were taking up precious space, the boxes were stacked on top of one another and boarded up behind a flimsy wooden partition at one end of the room. In these conditions no one could seriously claim that they were available for study, and Poliziano drew attention to the fact in his notes. For this he was barred from entering the library.[14]

It was not until 1488 that the first librarian was appointed to take charge of Bessarion's collection: he was Marco Antonio Coccio, known as Sabellico, who had met Bessarion when he was a student at Pomponio Leto's Academy in Rome. Sabellico, who was quite an authority on Greek literature, went to teach in Venice in 1484 but left for Verona after only a year to escape a cholera epidemic. In Verona he wrote a historical work of great importance, *Rerum Venetarum Decades*, which brought him back into favour with the Venetians, and consequently he was appointed to two posts there: Professor of Greek in succession to Giorgio Valla and curator of the Library of St. Mark's.[15]

On Sabellico's death in 1506 it was found that some manuscripts had been stolen. This so alarmed the Venetian authorities that from then on access to the library, which had always been difficult, became virtually impossible. Borrowing from the library was now prohibited and special permission was needed to consult the manuscripts. The official records show that the books were no longer even kept in Venice, as the terms of Bessarion's gift expressly stipulated they should be, and those who were lucky enough to borrow one were rarely made to pay the prescribed fee. The post of librarian remained vacant for nine years, a period of scandalous neglect and mismanagement, before being filled by Andrea Navagero in 1515. Markos Mousouros, who was then living in Rome, found some of Bessarion's manuscripts being offered for sale there and wrote to Navagero to tell him about this flagrant malpractice.[16]

Navagero was well qualified to take charge of Bessarion's library and a fitting person to succeed Sabellico. He had studied under Sabellico,

teaching post. After the Turkish conquest he was held prisoner for about a year, and on his release he went to live in Crete. In the autumn of 1454 he went to Bologna to meet Cardinal Bessarion, in the hope of gaining his support for the opening of a school in Crete or in Italy, but the only outcome of his visit was that he became one of the Cardinal's agents who were commissioned to acquire or copy manuscripts for him. He then settled permanently in Candia, where he worked as a copyist, mostly for Bessarion. The best known of Apostoles's works is his anthology of Greek proverbs entitled *Ἰωνιά*, which he presented to Bessarion's former secretary Gaspar Zacchi, Bishop of Osimo. See *Charta* 190-191; Mioni, *op. cit.* 263, 296.

13. Zorzi, *op. cit.* 45-61.

14. On the ban imposed on Poliziano, see I. del Lungo (ed.), *Prose volgari inedite, poesie latine e greche edite ed inedite di A.A. Poliziano*, Florence 1867, 79-80. On the chaotic administration of Bessarion's library see esp.: L. Labowsky, 'Manuscripts from Bessarion's Library Found in Milan', *Medieval and Renaissance Studies* 5 (1961) 109-131; Ead., *Bessarion's Library and the Biblioteca Marciana: Six Early Inventories*, Rome 1979; M.J.C. Lowry, 'Two Great Venetian Libraries in the Age of Aldus Manutius', *Bulletin of the John Rylands University Library of Manchester* 57 (1974) 128-166.

15. Zorzi, *op. cit.* 88, 94-97. Marco Antonio Coccio was born at Vicovaro, a town near Rome in what was the territory of the ancient Sabines (Sabelli), which prompted his teacher Pomponio Leto to dub him Sabellico. He studied in Rome under Leto until 1468, when Leto's Academy was disbanded, and then followed his teacher to Venice. In about 1475 he went to Udine to teach rhetoric, and while there he carried on with his own

94. Book cover with a representation of the Crucifixion. Byzantine work of silver-gilt, cloisonné enamel (demarcated with gold fillets), pearls and leather. Late 9th/early 10th c.

was proficient in Greek – which he had learnt under Mousouros's tuition at Padua – and had also attended Pietro Pomponazzi's philosophy lectures. He became a member of the Pordenone Academy, and the assistance he gave Aldus with his Latin editions was as valuable as was that of Mousouros on the Greek editions. Navagero also succeeded Sabellico as the official historian of the Venetian Republic. He travelled north of the Alps as a Venetian ambassador and died in 1529 at the court of King François I at Blois, where, appropriately enough, he was near the royal library of the kings of France which had been set to order by Ianos Laskaris.[17]

Navagero's death raised a problem of succession. Although the post of librarian should perhaps rightly have gone to Marino Sanudo, the author of the Sanudo Diaries, the Venetian authorities chose instead to give it to Pietro Bembo, a scholar highly regarded in all Italian centres

95. Andrea Navagero and Sabellico. Woodcuts from N. Reusner, Icones, *Basel 1599.*

of learning.[18] Bembo's first concern was to find suitable premises for the library, so that scholars would not be obliged to borrow them when they only wanted to check a passage in the text. In 1531 he secured the use of an upper room in the Basilica of St. Mark, and the books were transferred there from the Palazzo Ducale. By then it was obvious that this could be no more than a temporary solution: the time had come for the authorities to give serious attention to the construction of a library building worthy of Bessarion's benefaction.[19]

Venice was at this time going through a period of peace, and from 1515 her coffers were being refilled by the commercial enterprise of her people. After the sack of Rome in 1527, Venice became once again the intellectual centre of Italy and Vettor Grimani, son of the Doge Antonio Grimani, was appointed Superintendent of St. Mark's. With the library

studies in logic, mathematics and Greek literature. See *Sabellici Opera Omnia*, Basel 1560. On his contribution to Venetian historiography see: A. Pertusi, 'Gli inizi della storiografia umanistica nel Quattrocento' in A. Pertusi (ed.), *La storiografia veneziana fino al secolo XVI. Aspetti e problemi*, Florence 1970, 269-332; F. Gilbert, 'Biondo, Sabellico and the Beginnings of the Venetian Official Historiography' in *Florilegium Historicale* (Essays presented to Wallace K. Ferguson), Toronto 1971, 276-293.

16. On the storage of the manuscripts outside Venice see G. Coggiola, 'Il prestito di manoscritti della Marciana dal 1474 al 1527', *ZB* 25 (1908) 47-50. The text of Bessarion's letter to Navagero is published in C. Castellani, 'Il prestito dei codici manoscritti della Biblioteca di San Marco a Venezia nei suoi primi tempi e le conseguenti perdite dei codici stessi', *Atti del Imp. Reg. Istituto Veneto*, 7th ser., 8 (1896-1897) 367. Mousouros was offered two manuscripts stolen by a young Venetian who was the Grand Chancellor's nephew. He bought the first one, a codex of *De Medicina Equorum* by Apsyrtus, from a Rome bookseller. The second, a Greek copy of Bessarion's *In Calumniatorem Platonis*, was brought to him by a Roman barber whose son, a student of Greek, had bought it from the Grand Chancellor's nephew. See Labowsky, 'Il Bessarione...' 177.

17. Zorzi, *op. cit.* 97-105. See also: Firmin-Didot 465-466; M. Carmenati, 'Un diplomato naturalista del Rinascimento: Andrea Navagero', *NAV* 24 (1912) 164-205; *Charta* 368.

18. Bembo was born in Venice in 1470 and died in Rome in 1547. He frequented scholarly circles in Venice from an early age and went to live with Poliziano in 1491, a fact which presumably influenced his choice of studies. In 1492 he went to

96. Book cover with a representation of Christ. Byzantine work of silver-gilt, enamel, precious stones and pearls. Late 10th/early 11th c.

now in the hands of a family renowned for its support of art and culture – one of whose members was Cardinal Domenico Grimani, who possessed a huge collection of manuscripts – there was no question of Cardinal Bessarion's benefaction being treated with the same philistine indifference as in the past. After so many years, it was at last decided to house the library in a building of its own.[20]

Architecture. Under the personal supervision of Doge Andrea Gritti the aesthetic style of the city's historic buildings was subjected to thorough reappraisal, and Jacopo Sansovino, the architect and sculptor who had worked with Bramante and Michelangelo, was commissioned to design

97. A drawing of the Corte Dogale in Venice by Jost Amman, showing the Biblioteca Marciana under construction. 16th c.

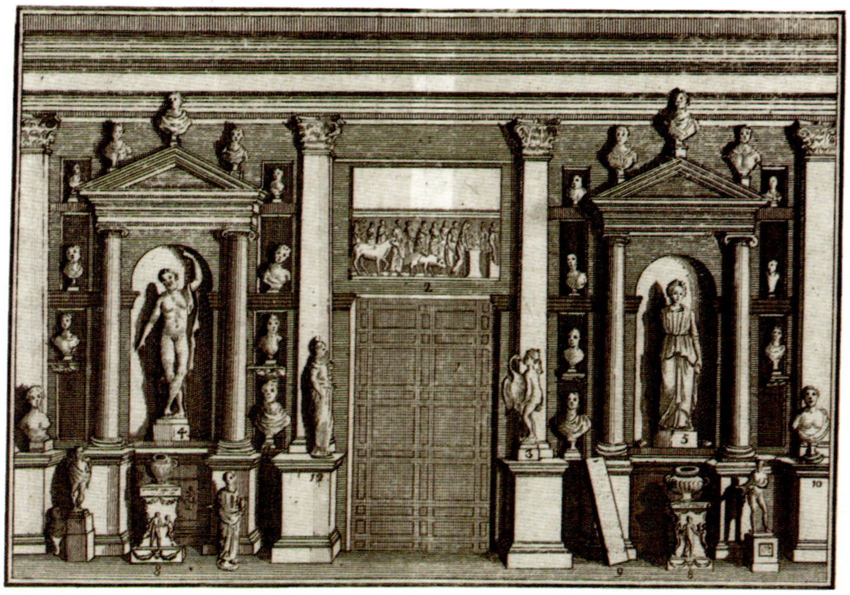

98. The entrance hall of the library. Engraving, 18th c.

Messina with his friend Angelo Gabrielli for the sole purpose of taking Greek lessons from Konstantinos Laskaris. In 1494 he was in Padua taking a course in philosophy, but he returned to Venice in time to deliver to Aldus the corrections Laskaris had made for the second edition of Aldus's *Grammar*, which came out in 1495. He worked for the Aldine press and learnt the art of printing when he

99. Pietro Bembo. Woodcut from N. Reusner, Icones, *Basel 1599.*

was co-editing its 1514 edition of Petrarch (*OAME* I 147-151). In 1497 he accompanied his father on a mission to Ferrara, where he took further lessons in philosophy with Niccolò Leoniceno, and from 1506 to 1512 he lived at Urbino. He then decided to enter the Church and was taken on as private secretary to Pope Leo X. In this capacity he assisted Leo in his efforts to revive classical studies in Rome and came into daily contact with the leading lights of the Pope's classical revival, notably Ianos Laskaris. He acquired a fine collection of books, which later went to the Vatican Library, and was sent by the Pope on several diplomatic missions. See C. Dionisotti, 'Bembo, Pietro' in *DBI* 8 (1966) 133-151. His contemporaries admired the elegance of his prose style and regarded him as the pioneer of the revival of Ciceronianism: see Zorzi, *op. cit.* 105-110.

100. The beautiful and widely-famed ceiling of the Sansovino staircase leading up to the library.

the library building. In March 1537 work began on the construction of the library in accordance with Vettor Grimani's wishes. The interior was richly ornamented with sculptures and frescoes in High Renaissance style, but marred by the over-ornate decorative designs intended to complement the frescoes. The building was ready in 1559, and at the beginning of July 1560 the manuscripts were finally moved to their new home, where they were stored in thirty-six reading-desks in two rows with a central aisle between them. This arrangement is no longer in use, but one can still admire Sansovino's original architecture and design: a fine staircase, beneath a ceiling decorated with painted reliefs of subjects inspired by Neoplatonist philosophy, leads up to the Sala Sansovino, where Bessarion's priceless treasures were kept.[21]

19. Zorzi, *op. cit.* 108.

20. Zorzi, *op. cit.* 99. The library of Cardinal Domenico Grimani played a prominent part in Venetian intellectual life and more particularly in the publishing programme of Aldus Manutius, who, with his team of editors, was always on the lookout for reliable manuscripts in Italy or elsewhere, in order to bring out textually accurate editions of the classics. The Grimani collection was enlarged in 1498 by the acquisition of 1,190 codices from Pico della Mirándola, including quite a number in Greek (mostly volumes of scholia on Aristotle). When Grimani died in 1523 it contained no fewer than fifteen thousand volumes and was the greatest library in the West. See M. Sanudo, *Diarii,* XXXIV, Venice 1892, 407-408.

21. For Bessarion's precious codices Sansovino designed a library in a style influenced by Greek Classical, Hellenistic and Byzantine architecture. A happy union of Plato and Neoplatonism, with allegorical paintings of the Olympian gods enclosed in raised rectangular frames, with geometrical motifs moulded in plaster against naturalistic decorative backgrounds, and with shimmering expanses of gold mosaics, creates a world of magical beauty. And at the centre of this world is the grand entrance to the Sala Sansovino: a piece of Early Hellenistic architecture with numerous statues, reminiscent of the homes of the great Renaissance collectors of antiquities: see F. Valcanover, 'Profilo Artistico' in *Biblioteca Marciana* 37-49. For fuller particulars see D. Howard, *Jacopo Sansovino: Architecture and Patronage in Renaissance Venice*, New Haven/London 1975; G. Romanelli, 'Il progetto di Sansovino e lo scalone' in *Da Tiziano a El Greco. Per la storia del manierismo a Venezia, 1549-1590* (exhibition catalogue), Milan, 277-285.

BIBLIOTECA MEDICEA LAURENZIANA

The Biblioteca Laurenziana

CHAPTER SEVENTEEN

The Biblioteca Laurenziana in its present form is perhaps better known for having been designed by Michelangelo than for its history as a typical humanist library. And in fact the construction of the present library only started on the initiative of Pope Clement VII in about 1524, by which time the Medici and the circle of humanists they gathered around them had long since done their finest work for the Italian Renaissance. We should not forget that the Medici kept their library private, and permission to read or borrow their manuscripts was given only to a few privileged humanists who were close friends of theirs.

Book-collecting for its own sake would seem to have begun in Florence, and the trend gathered momentum when Coluccio Salutati, a leading humanist who was Chancellor of the Florentine Republic, officially invited Manuel Chrysoloras to come and teach Greek at the Studium there in 1397.[1] Thereafter the eloquent advocacy of Petrarch and Boccaccio, the humanist teachings of Leonzio Pilato, who urged a reappraisal of the ancient world, and the introduction by Chrysoloras of hitherto unknown Greek works radically altered the Italians' view of themselves and opened up new horizons for Florentine intellectuals. Greek manuscripts were quite unknown in the West, Latin translations of Greek texts – even the works of Aristotle – were few and far between, and those that did exist needed drastic revision. Under these conditions it was vital to leave no stone unturned in the search for lost Latin and Greek writings if the humanist movement was to make any progress.[2]

In the fifteenth century the Medici patronized book production, giving extremely generous support not only to artists but to writers as well. Under their auspices Florence reigned supreme in the sphere of humanist studies in Italy for fully a hundred years. Giovanni di Bicci de' Medici (1360-1429), the father of Cosimo 'il Vecchio', bequeathed precisely three books to his son, all in Italian. But Cosimo showed a liking for literature from an early age, spent three years learning Latin and Greek and frequented the company of members of Roberto Rossi's academy, who opened his mind to the humanities.[3] Inspired by the passionate interest of Niccolò Niccoli and the great Venetian collector Francesco Barbaro, he planned a voyage to Palestine to look for Greek manuscripts. He was also friendly with Poggio, that insatiable manuscript-hunter, with whom he went on a tour to Grottaferrata, Ostia and other places in Italy, looking mainly for ancient Roman inscriptions. He often attended symposia with the indefatigable Giannozzo Manetti and other humanists at the Monastery of Santa Maria degli Angeli, where the assembled company would read such books as Xenophon's *Cyropaedia* under the guidance of Ambrogio Traversari.[4]

It is to Cosimo that the Renaissance is chiefly indebted for the foundation and princely maintenance of the Platonic Academy of Florence, which schooled a whole generation of Italians and northerners in the ideals of Platonism and served as the beacon for the spread

101. The staircase to the upper floor of the Biblioteca Laurenziana.

of Platonic and Neoplatonic philosophy throughout the West.[5] By 1418 Cosimo already had 63 manuscripts in his library, including a good many classical titles as well as a copy of the Bible, various textbooks and a representative selection of works by early humanists: Dante's *Canzoni*, Petrarch's *Sonnets*, Boccaccio's *Decameron*. It was said of him that he never went anywhere without at least one of his books.[6] In building up his collection he was guided largely by Niccolò Niccoli, one of the more remarkable figures on the Florentine humanist scene.

Niccoli lived a secluded life, devoting all his energies to the collecting and copying of manuscripts. When he heard about the discovery of a unique manuscript of Pliny the Elder's *Natural History* in a monastery at Lübeck, Cosimo bought it for himself.[7] Niccoli spared no expense in putting his collection together and eventually amassed a total of 800 manuscripts, an impressive number for those days. He did not travel himself, but on his advice friends of his and agents of the Medici went to monastery and cathedral libraries in the North and discovered lost works of Latin literature. By a lucky chance one of his catalogues has survived and makes fascinating reading for a bibliophile.[8] With the toleration of the Medici he borrowed recklessly beyond his means to buy books and other collectors' pieces, with the result that when he died in 1437 he was heavily in debt and his books became the property of the sixteen trustees

102. General view of the library. Engraving by G. Zocchi, 18th c.

of his estate, who included Cosimo and his brother Lorenzo de' Medici, Poggio, Leonardo Bruni, Traversari and Manetti. Cosimo (who was Niccoli's biggest creditor) managed to ensure that the collection was not dispersed. As he had started rebuilding the Monastery of San Marco for the Dominicans, he had other plans for Niccoli's books.[9]

Cosimo de' Medici envisaged an ideal monastic library containing a representative selection of theological and classical writings, and he commissioned Tommaso Parentucelli (the future Pope Nicholas V) to write a catalogue of the works it should contain.[10] Armed with this list,

103. Manuel Chrysoloras. Woodcut from P. Giovio, Elogia..., *Basel 1577.*

1. Coluccio Salutati (1331-1406) was neither a great writer nor even particularly knowledgeable about literature, but he did possess the energy, drive and practical turn of mind to put into practice the visionary ideas of Petrarch, with whom he corresponded in the last years of the latter's life. His political position allowed him to put humanist studies 'on the map' and also to inject a touch of realism into the humanist movement, which it needed if it was to survive. He was taught rhetoric by Pietro da Moglio, the greatest teacher of his day, and although he never discovered the beauty of the Greek language he had the insight to lay the foundations of Greek studies. He earned his niche in literary history with his letters, notable for their originality and style. See *Charta* 111, 125-126; and esp. R. Witt, *Coluccio Salutati and his Public Letters*, Geneva 1976. On the fine library of Salutati and Chrysoloras see pp. 219-220, 220-221. On Chrysoloras see G. Cammelli, *I dotti bizantini e le origini dell' Umanesimo*, I: *Manuele Crisolora*, Florence 1941; *Charta* 111-130.

2. For an introduction to Florentine humanism see E. Garin, 'Le tra-

104. The monumental main hall of the Biblioteca Laurenziana, showing the elaborate floor.

he had no difficulty in persuading his fellow-trustees to waive their claims in his favour, and thus the entire contents of Niccoli's library came into his possession. He kept most of them for himself, giving only a small number to the San Marco library; but at the same time, mindful

105. The entrance hall of the library before installation of the flat ceiling. Engraving by V. Spinazzi, 18th c.

of his plan to create an ideal monastic library, he undertook to repair many of San Marco's codices and chain them all to the reading-desks, and he put up a commemorative plaque.

The library of San Marco was designed by Michelozzo di Bartolommeo and is an architectural gem, an example of the Renaissance style marked by real originality and outstanding for its

duzioni umanistiche di Aristotele', *Atti e Memorie dell' Accademia Fiorentina di Scienze Morali* 8 (1950) 1-50; Id., *L'umanesimo italiano: Filosofia e vita civile nel Rinascimento*, Bari 1952; Id., *Educazione umanistica in Italia*, Rome/Bari 1971; P.O. Kristeller, *Renaissance Thought: The Classic, Scholastic and Humanist Strains*, New York/Hagerstown/San Francisco/London 1961; Id., 'Platonismo bizantino e fiorentino e la controversia su Platone e Aristotele' in A. Pertusi (ed.), *Venezia e l'Oriente fra tardo Medioevo e Rinascimento*, Florence 1966, 103-116.

3. *VBV* II 168, 405; on Cosimo de' Medici, 167-211.

Roberto Rossi was born at Florence in about 1355 and was on friendly terms with the most eminent scholars living there. He dedicated Flaminio's translation of Plutarch's *Lives* to Francesco Barbaro and Guarino da Verona, and the students at his academy included Domenico Buoninsegni, Bartolo Tebaldi, Luca degli Albizzi and A. Alessandri. He was a systematic collector of Greek manuscripts for his private library. See *VBV* II 141; on his library, 168, 405.

4. C. Gutkind, *Cosimo de' Medici il Vecchio*, Florence 1940, 99; *VBV* II 452.

Ambrogio Traversari (1386-1439), though a priest in the Camaldolese Order, became a devotee of the humanities early in the fifteenth century. He was taught Greek by Manuel Chrysoloras, although he later claimed to have learnt the language without the least help from a teacher (*absque miniculo praeceptoris*) from the Greek Psalter and later from the Gospels. On his experience of the humanists' methods of teaching Greek see R. Sabbadini, *Il metodo degli Umanisti*, Florence 1922, 17-27. On Traversari see *VBV* I 449-461; A. Dini Traversari, *A. Traversari e i suoi tempi*, Florence 1912; C. Somigli, *Un amico dei Greci*, Arezzo 1964.

5. On the Platonic Academy see the seminal work by A. Della Torre, *Storia dell' Accademia Platonica di*

106. The entrance hall, showing the striking wall decorations by Michelangelo.

light, graceful lines. Michelozzo's ideas served as a model for other Renaissance libraries: similar stylistic features are easy to discern in buildings at Cesena (Biblioteca Malatestiana), Parma (San Giovanni Evangelista), Perugia (San Domenico) and elsewhere.[11]

Cosimo passed on his passion for books to both his sons, Giovanni and Piero. Piero I de' Medici (1414-1469), whose talents lay mainly in the direction of politics and diplomacy, was interested in literature as such, and not only in book-collecting. He is known to have commissioned Donato Acciaiuoli, a favourite pupil and disciple of Ioannes Argyropoulos, to translate Plutarch's Lives of Alcibiades and Demetrios Poliorcetes for him.[12] About Giovanni di Cosimo de' Medici the Florentine ambassador to Milan, Nicodemi, remarked, 'He looked after his books as if they were rivers of gold,' and he added that when Giovanni was on his deathbed he had said to his court favourite Angelo Poliziano, 'I had hoped that death would wait at least until I had completed your library.' Both brothers had their books illustrated with elaborate miniatures by artists such as Francesco di Antonio del Chierico and Attavante degli Attavanti, some of the illustrations being portraits of luminaries of the humanist movement and historical figures from antiquity. Piero took particular care over the bindings of his books, which were extremely tastefully done in different colours for different subjects: blue for theology, yellow for grammar, purple for poetry and so on.[13]

But the most fertile period for the growth of the Medici library was when Lorenzo the Magnificent (1449-1492) was the city's ruler. It was during the Laurentian Age (1469-1492) that Florence was considered an essential port of call for every scholar visiting Italy from the West and the city's intellectual coteries and establishments of higher education recalled Classical Athens. The Studium was at the pinnacle of its prestige and its Chairs of Philosophy, Poetry and Literature were occupied by men of the calibre of Ioannes Argyropoulos, Demetrios Chalkokondyles, Francesco Filelfo, Cristoforo Landino and Angelo Poliziano. Small groups of scholars formed private 'academies', the Greek language and Greek philosophy were on the public educational curriculum, symposia and philosophical discussions on the ancient Greek pattern were held regularly and there were even open debates on philosophical and literary subjects in the back streets. The Platonic Academy of Marsilio Ficino, founded in 1469, numbered the most original thinkers in Italy among its members, and in 1471 a new intellectual and artistic movement was born with the foundation of the first Florentine printing presses.[14]

Florence was one of the major centres of printing in Italy. Nearly all the leading teachers at the Studium and the Platonic Academy did at least some work for the printing houses, working in close collaboration with their printers and publishers, and they produced some fine work which enriched the private libraries of humanists such as the Medici

Firenze, Florence 1902.

6. *VBV* II 183 ff.; F. Pintor, 'Per la storia della libreria medicea nel Rinascimento', *IMU* 3 (1960) 189-210.

7. *VBV* I 541, II 229. On Niccoli see p. 219; *VBV* II 238-239. On his library see B.L. Ulman and P.A. Stadter, *The Public Library of the Renaissance in Florence: Niccolò Niccoli, Cosimo de' Medici and the Library of San Marco*, Padua 1972.

8. The original of the *Commentarius Nicolai Niccoli* is in the Pierpont Morgan Library in New York. It has been published by R.P. Robinson in his paper 'De fragmenti

107. St. Augustine, Soliloqui, *Florence 1491.*

Suetoniani de grammaticis et rhetoribus codicum nexu et fide', *University of Illinois Studies in Language and Literature* VI 4 (1922).

9. *VBV* II 201-201, 230.

The old Sylvestrian Monastery of San Marco was given to the Dominicans by a bull of Pope Eugenius IV dated 21st January 1436, and within a month a group of Dominicans from Fiesole had settled in there. It was in a dilapidated state when they moved in, and so it remained for about two years until Cosimo and Lorenzo de' Medici paid for its restoration. The attribution of the library of San Marco to the architect Michelozzo is based on the testimony of Vasari, which has never been questioned. The only evidence as to the date when the library was opened is a statement by Francesco Lapaccini, the executor of Niccoli's will, to the effect that it was completed in 1443 (*VBV* II 419). When it was rebuilt after the catastrophic earthquake of 1457 an extra room was added to the north of the basilica to house the Greek codices: see R. Morçay, 'La cronica del convento fiorentino di San Marco', *ASI* 81 (1913) 1-29; A. Visani, 'La biblioteca del convento di San Marco in Firenze', *L'Archiginnasio* 35 (1940) 275-285.

10. Vespasiano da Bisticci described this catalogue as one of the *opere necessarie ad una libreria*: see *VBV* I 46-47; Pintor, *op. cit.* 209.

11. On the architecture of the San Marco library see G. Marchini, 'Il San Marco di Michelozzo', *Palladio* 6 (1942) 113; L. Gori-Montanelli, *Brunelleschi e Michelozzo*, Florence 1957. Vasari says that among the books shelved in the sixty-four cypress-wood desks, which were ranged in two rows, were four hundred volumes from Niccoli's collection.

12. *VBV* II 50.

13. Piero may have owned the superb manuscript of Aesop illuminated probably by Gherardo di Giovanni (1444-1497), a contemporary of Botticelli's, which is now in the Spencer Collection (New York Public Library, Spencer Ms 50): see *The Medici Aesop*, with intro. by Everett Fahy and trans. by B. McTigue, New York 1989. On Florentine manuscript illumination see P. d'Ancona, *La miniatura fiorentina*, Florence 1913; Mirella Levi d'Ancona, *Miniatura e miniatori a Firenze dal XIV al XVI sec.*, Florence 1962.

The catalogue of Piero's library, compiled in 1465, lists 150 volumes as compared with the seventy he had inherited from his father. The major source of his new acquisitions was the shop of Vespasiano da Bisticci, which supplied manuscripts to book-lovers in other countries besides Italy: see E. Barfucci, 'Vespasiano da Bisticci (1421-1498) e la sua bottega' in *Lorenzo de' Medici e la società artistica del suo tempo*, Florence 1964, 247-271.

14. For more on the teachers and

108. The library in the Monastery of San Marco, Florence, founded by Cosimo de' Medici and designed by Michelozzo.

family. Yet the output of incunabular editions of the classics was not very large, and in terms of productivity there is no comparison between the Florentine presses and those of Venice. The thirty printing houses that were founded in Florence up to 1500 (as compared with 150 in

109. C. Landino, Formulario, *Florence, Bartolommeo di Libri, 1490.*

Venice) were short-lived and not renowned for their efficiency. But it was in Florence that the Greek *editio princeps* of Homer was printed in 1488: the text was finally edited by Demetrios Chalkokondyles after years of hard work by the Italian humanists.[15]

The principal adviser to Lorenzo the Magnificent on the organization of his library, or at least the Greek section of it, was Ianos Laskaris, the most eminent representative of Byzantine scholarship after Bessarion's death, who played an important part not only in cultural life but also in the political and diplomatic affairs of Venice, Florence, Rome and France.[16] Laskaris made two journeys through Italy and to the Near East

students at the Studium, which was the foremost educational institution in Florence, see A.F. Verde, *Lo studio fiorentino 1473-1503: Ricerche e documenti*, 4 vols., Florence 1973 - Pistoia 1977. The Studium moved to Pisa in 1472 and ceased to be the 'university' of Florence, but some of its professors, such as Poliziano and Chalkokondyles, continued to teach in Florence under the patronage of the Medici. A little-known story is

110. Epistole*, Florence, Antonio di Bartolommeo Miscomini, 1481-1482.*

told by Landino in his *Dialogus de Vera Nobilitate* about one of the philosophical symposia organized by the Medici. In 1469 a certain Philotimos of Constantinople, a wealthy Byzantine nobleman living in Rome, went to Florence to offer his condolences to Lorenzo de' Medici on the death of his father, and Lorenzo arranged a symposium in his honour. Also present was an Athenian philosopher named Aretophilos, who was accompanying Philotimos, and all the most eminent scholars then living in Florence: Gentile Becchi, Landino, Poliziano, Argyropoulos, Donato Acciaiuoli, Alamanno Rinuccini,

111. Greek Gospel book. Parchment codex, 11th c. (Plut. 6.23, fol. 4v). Probably from the library of Lorenzo the Magnificent.

in 1490 and 1491, travelling as the Medicis' ambassador to Sultan Beyazit II, in order to compile a register of the ancient Greek and Byzantine manuscripts surviving in Italy, in Greek private libraries and in the Orthodox monasteries of the East, and to buy or copy for Lorenzo as many manuscripts as he could. Before setting out he drew up an inventory of the Greek codices in the Medici library and a list of the manuscripts he wanted to obtain, by authors ranging from the Attic orators to the Byzantines. He came back from his travels with about two hundred manuscripts, many of them rare works by ancient and early Byzantine authors which were unknown in the West.[17]

Laskaris was interested in old manuscripts not only in his capacity as agent for the Medici library but for himself as well, and he built up a valuable private library of his own. After his death a beloved and faithful pupil of his, Matthaios Devaris, collected all his papers, notes and books and made a list of all the books still in his possession. These included about 128 manuscripts, which Devaris sorted into twenty-two boxes.[18] The object Laskaris had in mind was to make a list of extant works for use in his publishing programme, whereby he aimed to produce printed editions of the classics and grammar textbooks to make the study of Greek accessible to a wider public. While he was in Crete on his second journey Lorenzo died, on 8th April 1492; but, fortunately for the future of Greek studies and scholarship in general, Laskaris found a new patron of literature in the person of his successor, Piero II de' Medici. In 1494, with financial assistance from the new Florentine ruler, he set up a 'Greek press' which in the space of three years brought out the famous *Anthologia Planudea* and seven other editions – mostly volumes of poetry or books for students – including the *editio princeps* of four tragedies by Euripides, the *Argonautica* of Apollonius Rhodius, the *Dialogues* of Lucian, the *Pinax* of Cebes and the *Erotemata* (a grammar book) of Chrysoloras. All his editions were illuminated at well-known studios in Florence, such as that of Attavanti, and special parchment copies of them were given to Piero de' Medici for his library.[19]

Another literary adviser to the Medici was Angelo Poliziano, a grammarian with a consuming interest in his subject, a textual emendator of the classics with a mania for perfection, and undoubtedly the greatest Hellenist of the Renaissance. Poliziano travelled round Italy, collating the manuscripts located by Laskaris in various cities and towns and buying as many as he could; in case he could not buy them, he had no less a calligrapher than Ioannes Rossos with him to copy them for him. But this unrivalled collection amassed by the Medici remained inaccessible to the public: the privilege of reading and copying the manuscripts was limited to close friends of the family. Poliziano, for example, who had free access to the library, kept some Medici codices in his house for years, and on one occasion he borrowed as many as thirty-five at once![20]

After the return of Laskaris from his travels, the Medici library con-

112. Lorenzo the Magnificent. Woodcut from N. Reusner, Icones, *Basel 1599.*

Giorgio Antonio Vespucci and many others. See A.M. Bandini, *Specimen litteraturae florentinae saeculi XV*, 2 vols., Florence 1747-1751, 110.

15. On the Florentine printing presses of the fifteenth century see esp. R. Ridolfi, *La Stampa in Firenze nel secolo XV*, Florence 1958; D.E. Rhodes (ed.), *La Stampa a Firenze 1471-1550: Omaggio a Roberto Ridolfi* (exhibition catalogue), Florence 1984; P. Kristeller, *Early Florentine Woodcuts*, London 1897. On Chalkokondyles' edition of Homer see *Charta* 150.

16. On Ianos Laskaris see the monograph by B. Knös, *Un ambassadeur de l'hellénisme – Janus Lascaris – et la tradition gréco-byzantine dans l'humanisme français*, Uppsala/Paris 1945; on his editorial work see *Charta* 257-309.

17. K. Müller, in his paper 'Neue Mittheilungen über Janos Lascaris und die Mediceische Bibliothek', *Centralblatt für Bibliothekswesen* 1 (1884) 333-412, published a series of letters (based on Cod. Vat. Gr. 1412)

113. Homer, Batrachomyomachia and Iliad. *Parchment manuscript, 15th c. (Plut. 32.1, fol. 17r). Written by Theodoros Gazis for Francesco Filelfo and illuminated by artists of the Lombardy school.*

ΙΛΙΑΔΟΣ ΑΛΦΑ
ΟΜΗΡΟΥ ΡΑΨΩΔΙΑΣ
ΑΛΦΑ ΛΙΤΑΣ ΧΡΥΣΟΥ. ΛΟΙΜΟΝ
ΣΤΡΑΤΟΥ ΕΧΘΟΣ ΑΝΑΚΤΩΝ.

tained a number of priceless treasures. Among them were the oldest extant manuscript of Paulus Orosius, containing the first six books of his *Historia adversus Paganos* (6th cent.) and a ninth-century manuscript of Cicero's *Epistolae ad familiares* discovered by Coluccio Salutati. Aristotle's *Nicomachean Ethics*, a widely-read work which Argyropoulos used in his teaching, was represented in the library by the earliest surviving manuscript (10th cent.); and the *History* of Thucydides, copied by an unidentified Greek named Petros, is of similar date. Another unique manuscript was the *Συλλογή χειρουργικῶν πραγματειῶν*

114. Ianos Laskaris. Woodcut from P. Giovio, Elogia..., *Basel 1577.*

(*Collection of Surgical Treatises*) (10th-11th cent.), which had belonged to one Niketas and was bought by Laskaris for Lorenzo at Candia, Crete. From Constantinople Laskaris brought an eleventh-century codex of the *Stromateis* by Clement of Alexandria, which was used for the *editio princeps* published by Pier Vettori in 1550. The famous Codex Etruscus (11th cent.) containing Seneca's *Tragedies* was purchased by the library from Pomposa Abbey, on Niccoli's advice. One last manuscript particularly worthy of note, among many others, was an eleventh-century codex of works by Sophocles, Aeschylus (*Choephoroi* and *Suppliant Women*) and Apollonius Rhodius, which Laskaris used for his *editio princeps* of the *Argonautica* (1496): it was bought by Giovanni Aurispa in Constantinople and belonged to Niccoli before being acquired by the Medici.[21]

which Laskaris wrote to the Medici, listing the manuscripts he had found on his travels through Italy and the Near East. See also Knös, *op. cit.* 30-55.

18. On Laskaris's library see the catalogue originally compiled by Müller, *op. cit.* 407-412; also M.P. de Nolhac, 'Inventaire des manuscrits grecs de Jean Lascaris', *Mélanges d'Archéologie et d'Histoire de l'École Française de Rome* 6 (1886) 251-272; J. Whittaker, 'Parisinus Graecus 1962 and Janus Lascaris', *Phoenix* (University of Toronto Press) 31 (1977) 239-244.

The scholar Matthaios Devaris, who was librarian to Cardinal Niccolò Ridolfi, catalogued Laskaris's manuscripts in collaboration with Nikolaos Sophianos. Lascaris was a friend of Ridolfi's: many of his manuscripts eventually went to the Cardinal's collection, while others went to the library of Fulvio Orsini. Apropos of Laskaris and catalogues, the existence of a book list written in Laskaris's handwriting poses an interesting puzzle, as we do not know which library it refers to. It is in the form of a diary which Laskaris kept while he was living in Rome, and it lists about a hundred Greek and Latin manuscripts and printed books that were borrowed by various scholars in Ridolfi's circle: see Nolhac, *op. cit.* 261-266; Id., *La bibliothèque de Fulvio Orsini*, Paris 1887; H. Omont, 'Un premier catalogue des manuscrits grecs du card. Ridolfi', *Bibliothèque de l'École des chartes* (1888) 309 ff.; R. Ridolfi, 'La biblioteca del card. Niccolò Ridolfi', *La Bibliofilia* 31 (1929) 174-193.

19. On Laskaris's editorial and publishing career in Florence see *Charta* 272-279.

20. Nearly all the Renaissance humanists' libraries have been dispersed, and Poliziano's is no excep-

115. Homer, Ἅπαντα (Complete Works). *Parchment manuscript, 15th c. (Plut. 32.4, fol. 43r). The manuscript was commissioned by the Medici and is lavishly illuminated by the Florentine artist Francesco Rosselli.*

Ὑπόθεσις τῆς α ὁμήρου ῥαψῳδίας

Κρύσης ἱερεὺς ἀπόλλωνος παραγίνεται ἐπὶ τὸν ναύσταθμον τῶν ἀχαιῶν, τὴν ἑαυτοῦ θυγατέρα χρυσηΐδα λυτρωσόμενος. τοῦ δὲ
ἀγαμέμνονος μὴ βουληθέντος ἀπολῦσαι αὐτήν, ἀλλὰ μεθ᾽ ὕβρεως ἀποπέμψαντος αὐτόν, αἰτιᾶται ἐπελθεῖν
τῷ ἀπόλλωνι λοιμὸν ἐπιπέμψαντος τοῖς ἀχαιοῖς. λοιμοῦ δὲ ἐνσκήψαντος καὶ τῶν ἀχαιῶν φθειρομένων, ὁ ἀχιλλεὺς τὸν
αἴτιον ἐκμαθών, ἢ μάντεως ... ἀξιοῖ τὴν χρυσηΐδα ἀποδοθῆναι· διὸ ἐφ᾽ ἔριν ἐλθὼν τῷ ἀγαμέμνονι
ὀργισθείς, ἀποπέμπει μὲν τῷ πατρὶ τὴν χρυσηΐδα· ἀφαιρεῖται δὲ τὸν ἀχιλλέα βρισηΐδα. ὁ δὲ ἀχιλλεὺς διὰ
τὴν ὕβριν, τῶν πολεμικῶν ἀφίσταται καὶ τὴν θέτιν τὴν μητέρα ἱκετεύει ... τὸν δία ... ἀγαμέμνονος
ὕβριν. ἀφικνεῖται δὲ ὀδυσσεὺς ... ἀπάγων τὴν αὐτοῦ ... τοῖς ἀχαιοῖς,
νίκην ... παρὰ τοῦ διὸς ... Τρωσί. ἐλεγχ... τοῦ δὲ ... ἐπαγγειλαμένου
αὐτοῦ ... ἀπελθούσης αὐτῆς, ἡ ἥρα ... πρὸς τὸν δία ... ἐν οὐρανῷ ... οἰνοχοῶν :~

ΙΛΙΑΔΟΣ Α ΟΜΗΡΟΥ ΡΑΨΩΔΙΑΣ·

Ἄλφα λιτὰς χρύσου λοιμὸν στρατοῦ ἔχθος ἀνάκτων.

Μῆνιν ἄειδε θεὰ πηληϊ-
άδεω ἀχιλῆος
οὐλομένην· ἣ μυρί᾽ ἀχαι-
οῖς ἄλγε᾽ ἔθηκε·
πολλὰς δ᾽ ἰφθίμους ψυχὰς
ἄϊδι προΐαψεν
ἡρώων· αὐτοὺς δὲ ἑλώ-
ρια τεῦχε κύνεσσιν
οἰωνοῖσί τε πᾶσι· διὸς
δ᾽ ἐτελείετο βουλή·
ἐξ οὗ δὴ τὰ πρῶτα δια-
στήτην ἐρίσαντε·
ἀτρείδης τε ἄναξ ἀνδρῶν καὶ δῖος ἀχιλλεύς·
τίς τάρ σφωε θεῶν ἔριδι ξυνέηκε μάχεσθαι·
λητοῦς καὶ διὸς υἱός· ὁ γὰρ βασιλῆϊ χολωθείς,
νοῦσον ἀνὰ στρατὸν ὦρσε κακήν· ὀλέκοντο δὲ λαοί·
οὕνεκα τὸν χρύσην ἠτίμησ᾽ ἀρητῆρα
ἀτρείδης· ὁ γὰρ ἦλθε θοὰς ἐπὶ νῆας ἀχαιῶν
λυσόμενός τε θύγατρα φέρων τ᾽ ἀπερείσι᾽ ἄποινα·
στέμματ᾽ ἔχων ἐν χερσὶν ἑκηβόλου ἀπόλλωνος
χρυσέῳ ἀνὰ σκήπτρῳ καὶ ἐλίσσετο πάντας ἀχαιούς·
ἀτρείδα δὲ μάλιστα δύω κοσμήτορε λαῶν·
ἀτρείδαι τε καὶ ἄλλοι ἐϋκνήμιδες ἀχαιοί·
ὑμῖν μὲν θεοὶ δοῖεν ὀλύμπια δώματ᾽ ἔχοντες
ἐκπέρσαι πριάμοιο πόλιν εὖ δ᾽ οἴκαδ᾽ ἱκέσθαι·
παῖδα δ᾽ ἐμοὶ λύσαιτε φίλην τὰ δ᾽ ἄποινα δέχεσθαι·

At the end of 1494, after a hundred years of making an outstanding contribution to the Renaissance, the Medici family was driven out of Florence, their palace was sacked by the army of Charles VIII of France and an unknown number of books was lost. The remaining 1,039 volumes were transferred to the library of San Marco, where their safety was again endangered during the riots provoked by the excommunication of Savonarola.[22] One third of the collection was then bought by the Florentine family of Salviati and the remainder by the Dominicans of San Marco. In 1508 the Dominicans made over their share to Giovanni de' Medici, the second son of Lorenzo the Magnificent who later became Pope Leo X. He took the books to Rome, where he allowed students to come and read them: being a highly educated man with an excellent command of Greek and Latin and the principal financial backer of the Greek press on the Quirinal Hill, it was only natural that he should want these precious sources of learning to be available to all.

Architecture. On the death of Leo X in 1521 Cardinal Giulio de' Medici was elected to the papal throne as Clement VII. It was he who gathered together all the books belonging to the family and commissioned Michelangelo to design a new library to house them. Although work on it did not begin until 1524, the first ideas and preliminary drawings had been under discussion since 1519. A fascinating series of letters between the Pope and Michelangelo has survived to the present day, making it possible to follow every step of their thinking with regard to the various architectural problems, leading up to the final plans.[23] The letters also attest to the excellent co-operation between the architect and the Pope, who was actively involved in seeing the project through to completion. The library was opened to the public in 1571.

The first plan to be submitted had the library divided into separate Latin and Greek sections. There followed a series of proposals and counter-proposals concerning the location of the library, its architectural style, the structural strength of the building to which it was to be added, the lighting, and the question of the staircase leading up to it. Eventually the Pope wrote to Michelangelo on 8th April 1524, giving him a free hand to position the library wherever he wanted, 'even next to the old monastery'.

Although the Biblioteca Laurenziana was planned at a time when the invention of printing necessitated a radical reappraisal of the furniture and fittings required for an up-to-date library, the philosophy underlying Michelangelo's design was firmly committed to the medieval and early Renaissance tradition. In effect, what he had in mind was a 'book museum' to house the manuscripts and incunabula which the Medici had collected in the fifteenth century. In style and form it ignores the precedent set by Michelozzo's library of San Marco, and although the reading-desks are retained and indeed are the sole items of furniture, the 'feel' of the library is totally unlike that of any previous Italian library.

tion. Unfortunately there is no contemporary documentary record of the manuscripts and annotated books that belonged to him. As it happened, Florence was in a state of turmoil at the time of his death (28th September 1494): only a few weeks later, on 9th November, Piero de' Medici was driven from power and, in the chaos that followed the entry of Charles VIII's army and the sack of the city by French soldiers and the Florentines

116. Angelo Poliziano. Woodcut from N. Reusner, Icones, *Basel 1599.*

themselves, no one was seriously concerned about rescuing Poliziano's priceless books and manuscripts.

An old book by E. S. Piccolomini, *Intorno alle condizioni e alle vicende della Libreria Medicea privata*, Florence 1875, gives precise particulars of the contents of the Medici library in 1495, taken from a catalogue compiled by a special commission on 28th October of that year. This catalogue was the first to list the thirty-five manuscripts borrowed by Poliziano.

Most of Poliziano's books are now in the Vatican Library: see Ida

117. Pausanias, Ἑλλάδος Περιήγησις (Description of Greece). *Parchment manuscript, 15th c. (Plut. 56.11, fol. 1r). Written by the famous Renaissance calligrapher Ioannes Rossos for Lorenzo the Magnificent in 1485.*

ΠΑΥΣΑΝΙΟΥ ΕΛΛΑΔΟΣ ΠΕΡΙΗΓΗΣΕΩΣ

ῆς ἠπείρου τῆς ἑλληνικῆς, κατὰ
νήσους τὰς κυκλάδας καὶ πέλαγος τὸ
αἰγαῖον, ἄκρα σούνιον πρόκειται γῆς
τῆς ἀττικῆς· καὶ λιμήν τε παραπλεύ-
σαντι τὴν ἄκραν ἐστί· καὶ ναὸς ἀθηνᾶς
σουνιάδος, ἐπὶ κορυφῇ τῆς ἄκρας· πλέ-
οντι δὲ ἐς τὸ πρόσω λαύριόν τέ ἐστιν, ἔνθα ποτὲ ἀθηναίοις ἦν ἀργύρου μέταλλα· καὶ
νῆσος ἔρημος οὐ μεγάλη, πατρόκλου κα-
λουμένη· τεῖχος γὰρ ᾠκοδομήσατο ἐν αὐτῇ,
χάρακα ἐβάλετο πάτροκλος· ὃς τριήρεσιν
ὑπέπλει ναύαρχος αἰγυπτίαις· ἃς πτολεμαῖος ὁ τοῦ λάγου, τιμωρεῖν ἔστειλεν ἀθηναίοις
ὅτε σφίσιν ἀντίγονος ὁ δημητρίου στρατιᾷ τε αὐτὸς ἐσβεβληκὼς ἔφθειρε
τὴν χώραν, καὶ ναυσὶν ἅμα ἐκ θαλάσσης κατεῖργεν· ὁ δὲ πειραιεύς, δῆμος μὲν
ἦν ἐκ παλαιοῦ· πρότερον δὲ πρὶν ἢ θεμιστοκλῆς ἀθηναίοις ἦρξεν, ἐπίνειον
οὐκ ἦν· φάληρον δέ· ταύτῃ γὰρ ἐλάχιστον ἀπέχει τῆς πόλεως ἡ θάλασσα·
τοῦτό σφισιν ἐπίνειον ἦν· καὶ μενεσθέα φασὶν αὐτόθεν ταῖς ναυσὶν ἐς
τροίαν ἀναχθῆναι· καὶ τούτου πρότερον, θησέα δώσοντα μίνῳ δίκας
τῆς ἀνδρόγεω τελευτῆς· θεμιστοκλῆς δὲ ὡς ἦρξε, τοῖς τε γὰρ πλέουσιν
ἐπιτηδειότερος ὁ πειραιεὺς ἐφαίνετό οἱ προκεῖσθαι, καὶ λιμένας τρεῖς
ἀνθ᾽ ἑνὸς ἔχειν τοῦ φαληροῖ, τοῦτό σφισιν ἐπίνειον εἶναι κατεσκευάσατο·
νεώς καὶ ἐς ἐμὲ ἦσαν οἶκοι· καὶ πρὸς τῷ μεγίστῳ λιμένι, τάφος θεμι-
στοκλέους· φασὶ γὰρ μεταμελῆσαι τῶν ἐς θεμιστοκλέα ἀθηναίοις· καὶ ὡς οἱ
προσήκοντες τὰ ὀστᾶ κομίσαιεν ἐκ μαγνησίας ἀνελόντες· φαίνονται
δὲ οἱ παῖδες οἱ θεμιστοκλέους, καὶ κατελθόντες καὶ γραφὴν ἐς τὸν παρ-

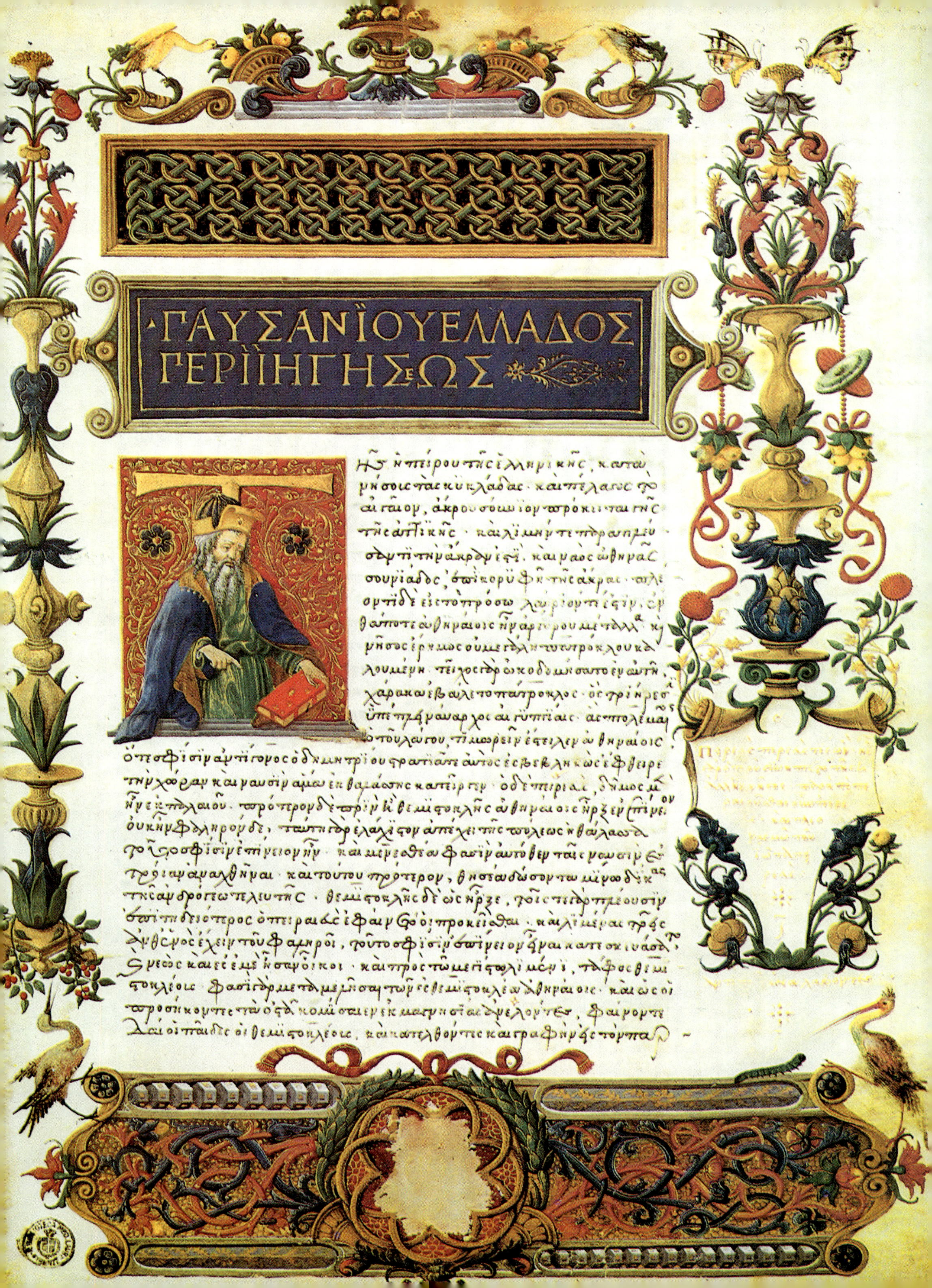

The library is reached by a superb triple stairway whose steps, balustrades and curves make it look more like a sculpture. It leads up from an entrance hall where pairs of columns stand like sentinels to right and left of harmoniously designed niches. The library itself is a rectangular room (46.2 x 10.54 m.) with its two side walls in the same style as the walls of the entrance hall, but without the columns. Some of the windows are of stained glass, adorned with heraldic devices: they were designed and made by Giovanni da Udine in 1567-68. The floor and ceiling are variations on more or less the same design, consisting of garlands and palmettes framed by rectangular panels with a conspicuous decorative design of linear and naturalistic motifs. The floor resembles a precious necklace of marble inlaid work, while the ceiling is of natural-coloured carved wood.

118. The frontispiece from G. Savonarola, Copia duna epistola, Florence, Bartolommeo Libri, c. 1490.

Pope Clement personally interested himself in the details of the planning, even to the extent of finding out how many books each reading-desk would hold. The desks were of walnut, ranged in two rows on either side of the aisle, and according to Vasari they were designed and made by Battisti del Cinque and Ciapino: it is generally agreed that they are probably not by Michelangelo, as sketches of desks have been found in the Buonarroti house in Florence. Their general style is similar to that of the desks in the Cesena library: each desk has a board attached to it, listing the books that are shelved there, and the books were attached to the desks with elaborate iron chains in the usual medieval fashion.

The Biblioteca Laurenziana (or Medicea) perfectly expresses Michelangelo's aesthetic philosophy and provides exactly the right home for the princely family's manuscripts and early printed books, even though it lacks something of the charm and atmosphere of earlier Renaissance libraries.[24]

Maïer, *Les manuscrits d'Ange Politien*, Geneva 1965, 5-10.

On the great Greek calligrapher of the Renaissance, Ioannes Rossos, see *Charta* 260-261, 321, 396, 411; on his contribution to the editorial and publishing work of Zacharias Kalliergès, *Charta* 391-449.

21. The manuscripts mentioned here are illustrated in *Biblioteca Medicea Laurenziana: Firenze*, Florence (Nardini) 1986.

22. The detailed inventory of the books, compiled in 1495 and entitled *Inventario de' libri di Piero o vero degli heredi di Lorenzo de' Medici*, is given in Piccolomini, *op. cit*. 65-108.

23. On the correspondence between Michelangelo and Clement VII see G. Milanesi, *Le lettere di Michelangelo Buonarotti*, Florence 1875; Berta Maracchi Biogarelli, *La Biblioteca Medicea-Laurenziana nel secolo della sua apertura al pubblico (11 giugnio 1571)*, Florence 1971.

24. On the Biblioteca Laurenziana see J.W. Clark, *The Care of Books*, Cambridge 1901, 234-240; R. Wittkower, 'Michelangelo's Biblioteca Laurenziana', *Art Bulletin* 16 (1934) 123-218; C. de Tolnay, 'La

119. Savonarola. Woodcut from De simplicitate christianae vitae, *Florence, L. Morgiani and J. Petri, 1496.*

120. Plotinus, Enneadi *(in the Latin translation by Marsilio Ficino). Parchment manuscript, 15th c. (Plut. 82.10, fol. 3r). This codex, dedicated to Lorenzo the Magnificent, was illuminated by Attavante degli Attavanti, the great Florentine miniaturist at the court of the Medici.*

SEMPER
PROHEMIVM MARSILII FICINI FLOREN
TINI IN LIBROS PLOTINI AD MAGNA
NIMVM LAVRENTIVM MEDICEM
PATRIAE SERVATOREM
MAGNVS
COSMVS
senatus consulto patrie pr. quo te
pore concilium inter Grecos atque la
tinos sub Eugenio Pontifice Flore
tie tractabatur phum grecum no
mine Gemistum cognomine Pletonem quasi Platonem alter de mysteriis
Platonicis disputantem frequenter audivit e cuius ore ferventi sic afflatus e pro
tinus. sic animatus: ut in academia quadam alta mete concepit: hac opor
tuno primu tempore pariturus. Deinde dum conceptum tantu Magnus ille
Medices quodammodo parturiret me electissimi medici sui Ficini filium ad
huc puerum tanto opi destinavit. Ad hoc ipsum educavit indies. Operam
preterea dedit ut omes non solum Platonis: sed et Plotini libros grecos haberem.
Posthec autem anno millesimo quadringentesimo sexagesimo tertio: quo ego
trigesimu agebam etatis annum mihi Mercurium primo ter maximu mox
Platone mandavit interpretandum. Mercuriu paucis mensibus eo vivete
peregi. Platone tuc & sum aggressus. Et si Plotinu quoque desiderabat: nullu tn de
hoc interpretando fecit verbum: ne graviore me pondere semel premere videret.
Tanta erat viri tanti erga suos clementia: in omes tanta modestia. Itaque nec
ego quidem qui nec vates aggredi Plotinu aliqn cogitavi. Verum interea Cosmus
quod vivens olim in terra reticuit tande expressit: ut potius ipressit ex alto.
Quo n. tempore Platone latinis dedi legendu: heroicus ille Cosmi avus heroica
Johanis Pici mirandulo mente. nescio quo instigavit: ut Florentia & ipe qi

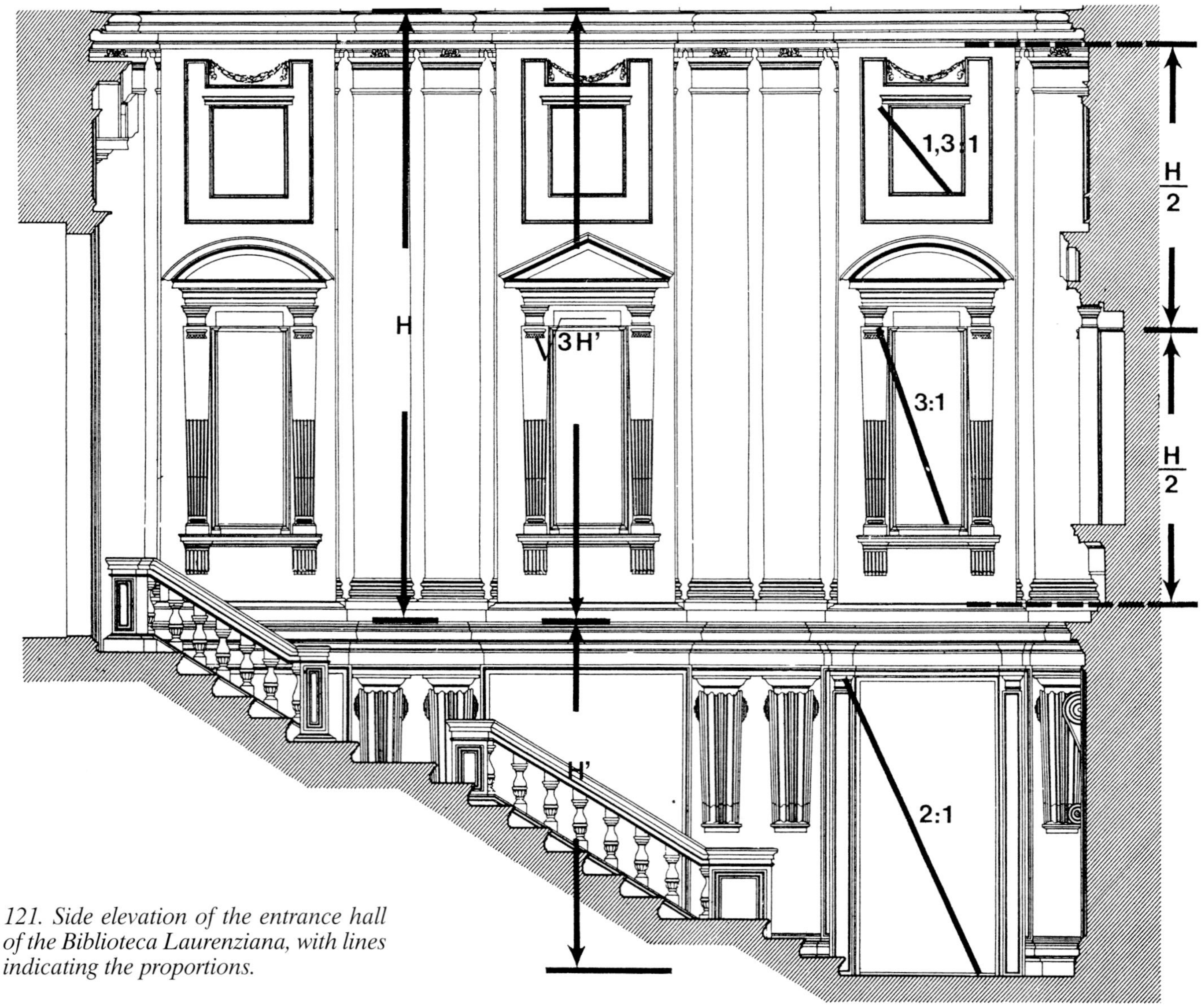

121. Side elevation of the entrance hall of the Biblioteca Laurenziana, with lines indicating the proportions.

122. Side elevation of the library. Note the architectural design, the proportions of the decorative elements and the overall aesthetic created by the alternation of the two typical materials of Renaissance Florence: pietra serena *and white stucco.*

bibliothèque laurentienne de Michel-Ange', *Gazette des Beaux-Arts* 14 (1935) 95-105; J.S. Ackerman, *The Architecture of Michelangelo*, London 1961, I 33-34, II 33-42; P. Portoghesi, 'La biblioteca laurenziana' in *Michelangiolo architetto*, Turin 1964, 209-350, 856-865.

123. Greek Gospel book. Parchment codex, 10th c. (Plut. 6.18, fol. 139v). From the library of Lorenzo the Magnificent.

SPISER·DAR·
BRVL·DAR·
BLATZ·DAR·
SCHIBEN·DAR·
MVOLTER·DAR·
MVLER·DAR·
DES ABTS·DAR·
GRVN·DVRN·
LADERA·DVRN
MICHAELS·DV
SCHV HVS
KIRCH HAF·
C
B
T

The St. Gall Library

CHAPTER EIGHTEEN

The library of the Abbey of St. Gall (St. Gallen) might be described as a by-product of the policy of proselytism carried on by the Western Church, which sent out missionaries to 'save' the world from what was left of paganism. Although it is one of the oldest libraries with an unbroken history in Europe, there is nothing about it now to suggest the period when it was founded – about the tenth century – because the present building, one of the most delightful examples of German baroque architecture, dates from the eighteenth century.[1]

The history of this abbey on the River Steinach in northern Switzerland goes back to the seventh century, when a group of Irish missionaries led by St. Columban made their way across the territories of various Germanic tribes until they reached the shores of the Bodensee (Lake Constance). One of them, named Gall, but usually known as Gallus, took himself off into the wilderness of the Arbon Forest nearby, and there he lived as a hermit with two local anchorites. He built a log cabin which he used for prayer, and before long he had attracted a number of disciples. After his death a church was built on the site, his bones were laid to rest in it, and pilgrims came to pray at his tomb. That church still stands as the nucleus of the Abbey of St. Gall.[2]

In about 720 the group of hermits that had grown up around Gallus organized themselves into a monastic community under the wise leadership of one of their number named Otmar. Abbot Otmar's monastery followed a mixed rule at first, until in 747 Carloman instituted the Rule of St. Benedict. Though always impoverished, it grew steadily, and it was coveted by certain powerful bishops, notably the Bishop of Konstanz, who resented its growing independence. Otmar was succeeded by a monk from Reichenau named Johannes, who was soon made a bishop, and under him the abbey made great progress.[3] Already in Otmar's time the monks had had a part of their day set aside for study and a scriptorium had been turning out copies of important manuscripts in considerable numbers, in the characteristic script of the region. The first copyist whose name is known was called Winithar, who from 760 onwards, with a team of fourteen other scribes, copied numerous theological and educational manuscripts.[4]

The year 770 marked the beginning of a period of steady achievement which strengthened the abbey's independence and helped to establish its reputation. Waldo, a monk of noble birth who was active in the archives, was made Abbot of St. Gall in 782 and Bishop of Reichenau in 786.[5] This most cosmopolitan of the St.Gall monks, who had previously been in Pavia and Basel, ended his career as Abbot of the prestigious imperial Abbey of St. Denis, near Paris, from 806 to 814. The abbey began to acquire political influence and power under Gozbert, who was abbot from 816 to 837.[6] In 818 the Frankish Emperor Louis the Pious granted immunity to the abbey and in 833 this privilege was extended by Louis the German, who gave the monks the right to elect their abbots without interfer-

124. The Abbey of St. Gall in 1596. Engraving from a drawing by Melchior Frank. Archives of the Municipality of St. Gall - Valiana.

ence. In 854 the abbey was granted full exemption from the tribute it had hitherto paid to the Bishop of Konstanz.

The ninth century – or, to be more precise, the 110 years from 816, when Gozbert became abbot, to the Hungarian invasion in 926 – is often described as the 'Golden Age' of the Abbey of St. Gall. Four of the abbots who guided its fortunes during this time – Gozbert, Grimald, Hartmut and Salomon – may be considered forerunners of the Renaissance.[7]

Gozbert radically reorganized the abbey and acquired new estates, mainly in the German lands to the north, which greatly increased its wealth and hence its independence. The scriptorium flourished: no fewer than a hundred copyists, working under the supervision of the calligrapher Wolfcoz, copied a large number of manuscripts, of which at least seventy have survived to the present day.[8] Major reforms were introduced in the organization of the abbey, most of them motivated and promoted by Louis the Pious and his adviser Benedict of Aniane: in fact the basic copy of the Rule of St. Benedict, which still exists in the abbey library, dates from this period. Another historic document dating from Gozbert's time is the only architectural plan (*c.* 825) of the new abbey buildings, showing the library above the scriptorium.

Grimald, a nobleman from distant Rheno-Franconia, was abbot from 841 to 872. In addition to the Abbey of St. Gall, he was also the superior of Weissenburg and one other monastery. His *Vademecum*, a personal prayer book and guide to good conduct, survives to this day. He won numerous honours and held more than one high office, including the post of Chancellor at the court of Louis the German, and because his duties kept him away from the abbey for much of the time he appointed Hartmut deputy abbot.[9]

Hartmut came from a local family, studied at Fulda and was a close friend of Otfried of Weissenburg. He became abbot in 872 and held office for eleven years before resigning voluntarily. A good administrator, he maintained fruitful relations with the imperial rulers, as a result of which the abbey acquired a reputation as a cultural centre and developed into an academy, with its own poets. One of these was Notker Balbulus, a man gifted not only with a flair for poetry but also with a perceptive eye for history, who wrote historical treatises many of which – such as the *Gesta Caroli Magni Imperatoris* – were dedicated to local rulers.[10] Among Notker's contemporaries were Tuotilo, who wrote tropes and hymns, and Ratpert, a historian who was also a poet and set hymns to music. Ratpert wrote the first part of the chronicle of the abbey, *Casus Sancti Galli*, ending with the visit of Emperor Charles III in 883.[11]

During this period the abbey ran a school of an extremely high standard, where the subjects taught included poetry, singing and church music, which played an important part in monastic life in the Middle

1. The literature on the Abbey of St. Gall, its library, its scriptorium and the political background to its history is enormous and stretches back at least two hundred years. However, a recent volume edited by James C. King and Werner Vogler, *The Culture of the Abbey of St. Gall*, Stuttgart/Zürich 1991, provides a good, informative introduction to the abbey and its history.

2. On the history of the abbey see W. Vogler, 'Historical Sketch of the Abbey of St. Gall' in King and Vogler, *op. cit.* 9-24. The earliest

125. Otmar, founder of the Abbey of St. Gall. Manuscript (the Stuttgart Passionale) from Zwiefalten, c. *1150. Stuttgart, Württemberg State Library (Bibl. fol. 58, fol. 118v).*

126. Notker Balbulus meditating. Zürich State Archives, AG 19 XXXV.

127. The interior of the library of St. Gall.

Ages. And the scriptorium turned out manuscripts which are superb specimens of calligraphy, written in the neat Carolingian minuscule script. The policy of the scriptorium was to copy works suitable for the monks' general education and to build up a corpus of theological textbooks.

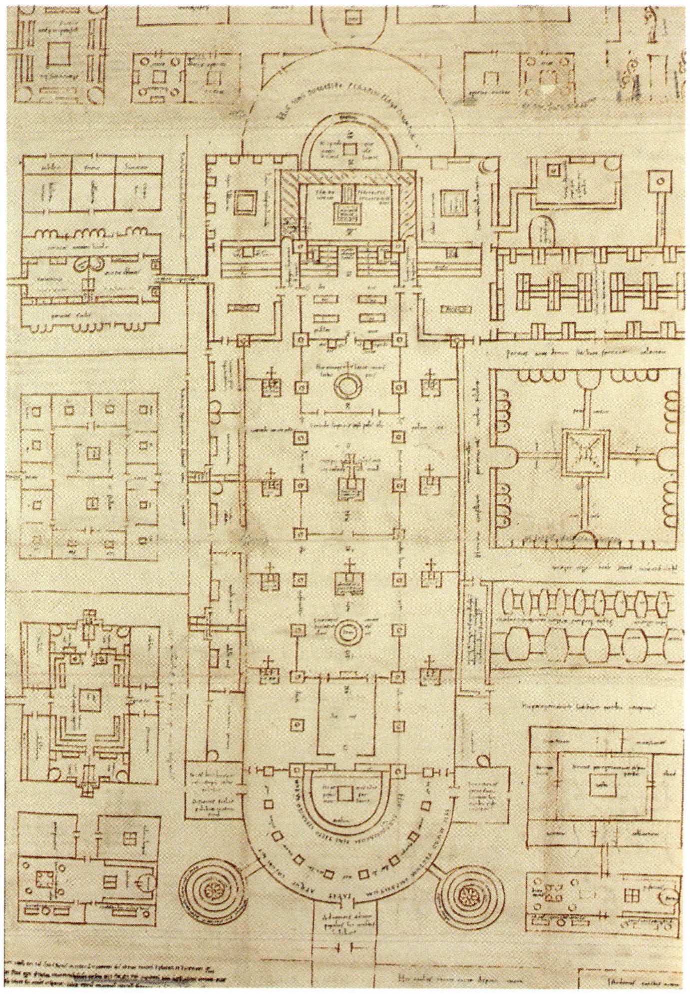

128. Ground plan of the Abbey of St. Gall drawn at Reichenau, c. 825. Cod. Sang. 1092.

The output of the scriptorium also reflects the strength of the abbey's cultural ties with southern Germany, especially Reichenau, and the British Isles.[12] It has to be remembered that although Ireland was a long way away, the monks of St. Gall kept in touch with the roving Irish missionaries, at least for the first three hundred years up to the tenth century. The Irish never forgot that the abbey had been founded by a compatriot of theirs and, as the chronicle *Casus Sancti Galli* attests, they invariably stopped there on their travels. These missionaries, to whom the nomadic life was second nature, followed the routes charted by their predecessors, travelling to Rome by way of the Low Countries and the Rhine basin, and they were to be found

source work on Gallus is the *Vita Sancti Galli vetustissima* (esp. p. 680), which was written a few decades after his death. For further information see J. Duft, *Die Lebensgeschichten der Heiligen Gallus und Otmar* (= Bibliotheca Sangallensis, 9), St. Gall/Sigmaringen 1988.

3. An original document dated 6th November 744, headed *Monasterium, monachi, abbas,* lists the names of the monks and abbots, so it is clear that we are already dealing with an organized monastic community.

4. Besides playing an extremely active part in the life of the abbey, Winithar copied and collected a large number of important manuscripts, and he also wrote a poem in hexameters about the intellectual trends of his age. In the nine manuscripts and one document written by him that have survived, we see him developing a graphic style of his own. See W. Berschin, 'The Medieval Culture of Penmanship in the Abbey of St. Gall' in King and Vogler, *op. cit.* 69-80.

5. On the lives of the abbots see J. Duft, A. Gössi and W. Vogler, *Die Abtei St. Gallen*, Bern 1986.

6. Vogler, *op. cit.* 13. It was during this period (830-837) that the massive Carolingian abbey church was built with the collaboration of the monks Winithar, Isenrich and Ratger. The plan of the abbey was drawn at Reichenau in about 825.

7. Vogler, *op. cit.* 13-14.

8. Vogler, *op. cit.* 14. The oldest extant psalter at St. Gall (Codex 20)

129. The Folchart Psalter (Ms No. 23): Psalm 39, Expectans expectavi Dominum.

130. The Folchart Psalter: Psalm 48, Audite haec, omnes gentes.

131. The Folchart Psalter: Psalm 131, Memento, Domine, David.

132. The Folchart Psalter: Psalm 148, Laudate Dominum de caelis.

133. Initial B (Beatus vir) *from the most famous manuscript of the St. Gall school, Ms No. 23, illuminated by Folchart for Abbot Hartmut between 865 and 872.*

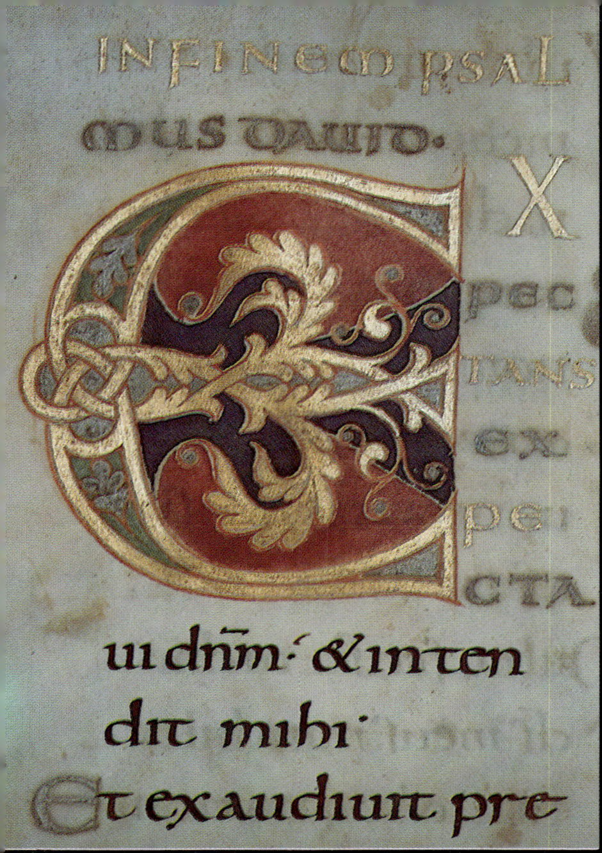
IN FINEM PSAL
MUS DAUID·
X
PEC
TANS
EX
PE
CTA
ui dn̄m· & inten
dit mihi·
Et exaudiuit pre

Quoniam hic est ds̄
ds̄ noster in aeter
num. & in saeculum
saeculi· ipse reget
nos in saecula·
IN FINEM FILIIS
CHORE PSALMUS
UDITE
HAEC OMS
GEN
TES AURIBUS per
pite om̄s qui habi

Sper& ist in dn̄o·
ex hoc nunc &
usq· in saeculum·
CANT· GRADUUM
ME
MENTO
DNE DAUID· ET
OMNIS MANSUE

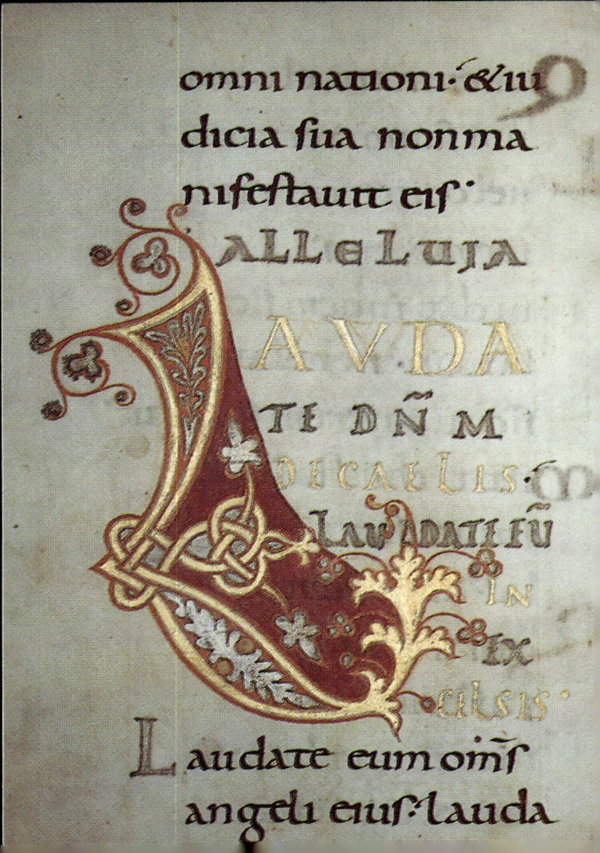
omni nationi· & iu
dicia sua non ma
nifestauit eis·
ALLELUJA
AUDA
TE DN̄M
DE CAELIS·
LAUDATE EU
IN
EX
CELSIS·
Laudate eum om̄s
angeli eius· lauda

N XPI
NOMIN
INCIPIT
PSAL
TERIV
DE TRANS
LATIONE
SEPTVA
GINTA
IN TER
PRETV
EMEN
DATVM
A SCO
HIERO
NIMO
PRBO IN
NOVO

BEATVS
VIR
QVI

everywhere. They were conspicuous by their outlandish appearance, for their eyes were brightly painted and the front part of the crown of the head was shaven. Often they brought valuable manuscripts with them as presents to the abbey: these were listed in a separate catalogue entitled *Libri scottice* scripti.[13]

The nature of the Irish missionaries' relationship with the abbey is illustrated by the case of Bishop Marcus and his nephew Moengal or Marcellus, who visited St. Gall in the ninth century and were so taken

134. 'The Poet', one of the putti in the St. Gall library.

with the way of life there that they decided not to go back to Ireland. They gave the books they had with them to the community, and Moengal started teaching grammar to the boys in the abbey school.[14] Even at that early date there is evidence of Greek studies at St. Gall. Moengal, who knew Greek, taught Notker, and he in his turn taught Abbot Salomon III. Notker actually speaks of a 'Greek brotherhood' in the abbey, presumably meaning a group of students, and an elementary Greek grammar written at St. Gall survives to this day. There is also a Gospel

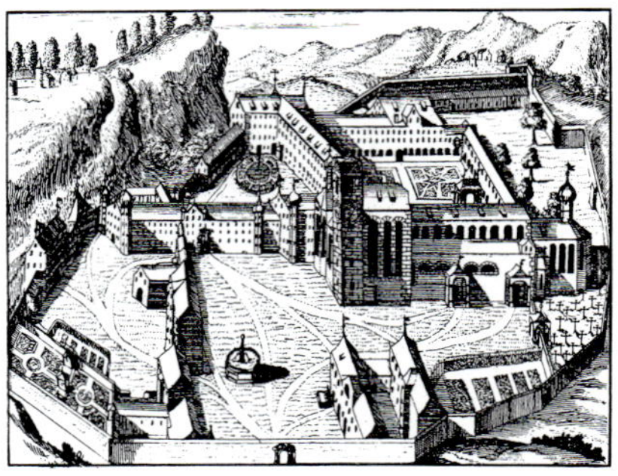

135. Perspective drawing of the abbey from the north. Engraved by Gabriel Hecht, 1702.

is by Wolfcoz: see C. Eggenberger, 'The Art of the Book in St. Gall' in King and Vogler, *op. cit.* 95, 99, 104.

9. Vogler, *op. cit.* 14.

10. Notker, who died in 912, modestly called himself Balbulus ('the Stammerer'), but nowadays he is unequivocally regarded as *the* poet of St. Gall. A prolific writer of verses that are among the great achievements of the abbey's Golden Age, he is best known for the sequences (hymns to be sung after the gradual at Mass) which he wrote for the abbey choir, notably *Natus ante saecula* (a Christmas sequence), *Festa Christi* and *Sancti baptistae Christi*: these and others found their way into numerous medieval manuscripts and early printed books of church music. See J. Duft, 'The Contribution of the Abbey of St. Gall to Sacred Music' in King and Vogler, *op. cit.* 57-62.

11. Ratpert (died *c.* 890), Notker and Tuotilo (died *c.* 913) were an inseparable trio. They were at school together, later they taught together at the abbey school, and they remained friends all their lives, each one being a source of inspiration to the other two. Their teacher, Moengal, encouraged them to study the seven 'liberal arts', especially music. On the Byzantine origin of the trope in Tuotilo's poetry and music see Duft, 'The

136. The ivory cover of the so-called Long Gospel (Cod. Sang. 53), depicting the Assumption of the Blessed Virgin and St. Gallus giving bread to a bear. Carved by Tuotilo, c. 894.

ASCENSIO SCE MARIE
S GALL PANE PORRIGIT VRSO

book with the Greek and Latin texts (the latter written in the pointed Irish script) on alternate lines: this was evidently written in an Irish community, perhaps in Liège.[15] It is also known that Notker borrowed a copy of the canonical Epistles (in Greek) from Liutward, Bishop of Vercelli, to improve his proficiency in the language, and succeeded in copying them 'with great pains'.

The curriculum of the St. Gall school was no different from that of other early medieval monastic schools: it was originally drawn up for the monks of Calabria by Cassiodorus soon after 554, the ultimate objective being to give them a proper understanding of the Bible and enable them to expound its teaching. The prerequisite for this was a general education in the seven 'liberal arts', namely grammar, rhetoric and logic (the trivium) and arithmetic, geometry, music and astronomy (the quadrivium). Armed with these skills, one could then progress to higher studies (*sacra eruditio*), which consisted in studying the scriptures with an exegesis.[16] But the most important part of the educational process was the teaching of Latin. A thorough mastery of Latin was essential for communication within the Church and, of course, for an understanding of the classics. We should not lose sight of the fact that the only basic instructional texts available in the West in the early Middle Ages were Latin versions of Aristotle's shorter works on logic, translated and annotated by Boethius.[17]

When Abbot Hartmut took over the library he inherited a motley collection which, incredible though it may seem, did not contain even the most fundamental works of theology – not even anything by Augustine, Jerome or Gregory. Instead there were only such books as the *Revelation of Methodios* by Tichonius, the lost commentary on the last book of the *Revelation* and the *Epistles* of Faustus, Bishop of Riez. Educational books were few and far between: some treatises on astronomy, law books and grammar textbooks, as well as a few historical romances such as the *History of the Franks* (to which Grimald and Hartmut added the *History of the Trojan War*) and works by Vegetius on military tactics. Hartmut excelled himself in his efforts to enrich the library: he edited the whole of the Bible and bequeathed to the abbey an eight-volume edition with an extremely reliable text, and it was in his time that the names of the librarians were recorded for the first time. The ninth-century catalogue (*Breviarium Librorum*) listing the 361 manuscripts in the library reflects the intellectual interests predominant in the abbey.[18]

Hartmut's successor as abbot was Bernhard (883-890), who in turn was succeeded by Salomon (890-919), a future Bishop of Konstanz. Salomon, a towering figure, came from a noble family and was related to all the top civil and ecclesiastical dignitaries in the surrounding country. Secular honours and titles were heaped upon him, yet in spite of the criticism levelled against him for his multiple involvement in worldly affairs he succeeded in holding on to his position as abbot of St. Gall and

Contribution...' 59-60. On Tuotilo see E.G. Rüsch, *Tuotilo – Mönch und Künstler. Beiträge zur Kenntnis seiner Persönlichkeit*, St. Gall 1953; J. Duft and R. Schnyder, *Die Elfenbein-Einbände der Stiftsbibliothek St. Gallen*, Beuron 1984.

Ratpert's poetical and musical talents are known to us from the Latin hymns he composed for prayers sung by the community. His authorship has been established for four such hymns, including *Ardua spes mundi*: see Duft, 'The Contribution...' 57-58; and esp. P. Stotz, *Ardua spes mundi. Studien zu lateinischen Gedichten aus St. Gallen*, Bern/Frankfurt 1972.

12. Vogler, *op. cit.* 15.

13. On the Irish monks see J. Duft, 'Irish Monks and Irish Manuscripts in St. Gall' in King and Vogler, *op. cit.* 119-128. On the Irish manuscript illuminations in St. Gall see J. Duft and P. Meyer, *The Irish Miniatures of the Abbey Library of St. Gall*, Olten/Bern/Lausanne 1954.

14. Duft, 'Irish Monks...', 120; W. Berschin, 'Latin Literature from St. Gall' in King and Vogler, *op. cit.* 150.

137. Initial B (Beatus vir) *from Notker's twelfth-century German translation of the psalter (Cod. Sang. 21, fol. 8).*

138. Johannes Hartlieb, Alexander, *c. 1468 (Ms No. 625, fol. 180).*

guetten ferde gepracht

Die kungin Candacis · vordert an den
kunig Alexandern · gar haymleich
vnd sprach zu jm · O wie salig ich
war · daz du alzeit vor meinen aug
en wærest · wann ich wolt dich lieb
er haben dann meinen Sun · ainem
wann wie mocht ich ymmer hoher
lobe vnd preys · ere · vnd wierde geh
aben · dann daz ich aines solleichen kchindes mueter wær
wann ich wær sunder zweyfel · daz ich noch ain kungin
aller werlt wær · vnd wierd · Darnach gab sy jm haim
leich · vnd in ainer grossen styll · die aller kostleichist ken-
klainot · so sy ye kain man gesehen hett · ain kunikleichen
gute ain reiche kchron · von edeln gestain · vnd ain gewant
daz was durch hefft mit gestain · vnd den aller schönist
en perlein · so man sy in allem Oriennt · finden mocht
Die kchlainat gab so mangen liechten schein vnd plicks
als der gestiernt hymel thuet in volmächtigem nacht
scheinen · Darnach fuert sy jn offenleich an den Sal · vnd
besannt jr Sun · vnd thett jm hertragen kostleiche presennt
vnd schanckung · als dann ainem posten zugeben zymbt
vnd gab jm vrlawb mit willen · Als nun Alexander
vrlawb nam von der kungin · er gieng zu Carator · vnd
sprach was ich euch versprochen hab daz laist ich ·

Nun was er auf dem selben Sal · da er versproch
en hett Alexandrum · zu antwurtten · daz
hett er auch gethan · vnd was seines herrenn
ydes den er bey seinen gotteren versprochen hett genug
ledig · damit schied er von dannen · Die kungin Cann
dacis · liess jn fueren in ain krufft · da die gotter maning
wierdtschafft ynne hetten · Als er nun fuer daz lock

brought three new dependencies under its sway: the monasteries of Pfäfers (in Chur-Rhaetia), Faurndau (near Göppingen, Württemberg) and Massino (on Lake Maggiore).[19]

Thereafter the abbey went into a gradual decline, and the buildings were completely destroyed by fire some years after the Hungarian invasion of 926. The outstanding feature of this first phase in its long history is the high artistic standard of the output of its scriptorium,

139. Notker Balbulus copying a manuscript. Illumination in the Minden Tropary, c. 1025 (Jagiellonska Library, Krakow, Theol. lat. quart. 11, fol. 144r).

which developed a recognizable book style that was all its own. The most typical example is the so-called Long Gospel, with calligraphy by Sintram and illumination in part by Salomon himself.[20]

A revival of the abbey's fortunes in the middle of the tenth century, under the scholarly guidance of Notker Labeo ('Broad-lipped'), proved to be short-lived. Notker made the monks study Latin literature and the emphasis of the scriptorium's work shifted accordingly: copies were

15. The bilingual manuscript of the four gospels was presumably brought to St. Gall by Marcus and Moengal, who has been identified as a scribe. It was written in about 850, with the Greek text in majuscule and

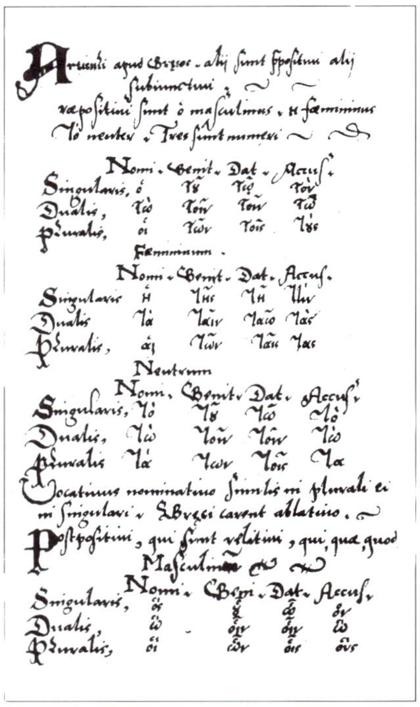

140. A page from a manuscript by Nicolaus Lindenmann giving the declension of the Greek definite article. Ms No. 1291, c. 1567.

the Latin in Irish minuscule, following the example of bilingual books from the circle of pupils of Sedulius Scotus. See S. Berger, 'De la tradition de l'art grec dans les manuscrits latins des évangiles', *Mémoires de la Société Nationale des Antiquaires de France* 52 (1891) 144-154; W. Berschin, *Griechisch-lateinisches Mittelalter. Von Hieronymus zu Nikolaus von Kues*, Berne/Munich 1980, 175 ff.; Duft, 'Irish Monks...' 119-128; A. Hobson, *Great Libraries*, London 1970, 31.

16. P. Ochsenbein, 'Teaching and Learning in the Gallus Monastery' in King and Vogler, *op. cit.* 137-139. For

141. The monumental door of the library with the inscription Ψυχῆς Ἰατρεῖον.

ΨΥΧΗΣ ΙΑΤΡΕΙΟΝ

ΨΥΧΗΣ ΙΑΤΡΕΙΟΝ

ΨΥΧΗΣ ΙΑΤΡΕΙΟΝ

made of many texts that had been unknown until then, including works by Horace, Ovid, Sallust and Lucian, Cicero's *Topica* and Seneca's *Apotheosis of the Emperor Claudius*.[21]

From the time of Notker Labeo's death until the middle of the fifteenth century the abbey was hardly recognizable as the place that had known such a flowering of scholarship and the arts under Gozbert and Hartmut. In the summer of 1416, when the Council of Konstanz was in progress and all the leading members of the Curia (as well as Manuel Chrysoloras) were in the neighbourhood, three of the secretaries in the papal delegation – Poggio, Cencio de' Rustici and Bartolommeo da Montepulciano – decided to go on a tour of the area with some friends of theirs, taking in the Abbey of St. Gall. All three were fanatical book-lovers, and they were appalled at the derelict state of the library in Hartmut's tower next to the abbey church. Cencio records that at the sight of those mildewed, worm-eaten books, all covered in dust, they wept with grief and inveighed against the abbot, Prince Heinrich von Gundelfingen, and the whole community: 'The abbot and monks of this monastery are strangers to all knowledge and to literature. O barbarous land, hostile to the Latin language! O vile dregs of humanity!' But the visit of the three humanists did at least bear fruit, for they discovered a complete manuscript of Quintilian's *Institutio Oratoria* (until then known only from an imperfect copy) and three other works unknown in Italy: the *Argonautica* of Valerius Flaccus and two volumes of commentaries on Cicero's speeches. They were allowed to borrow them, as well as a number of works by Silius Italicus, Marcus Manilius and other writers, to have them copied.[22]

Abbot Ulrich Rösch (1463-1491) is rightly credited with having given the Abbey of St. Gall a new lease of life: thanks to his prudent administration, inexhaustible energy and decisiveness, it quickly regained much of its former prestige. Rösch secured as many of the abbey's assets and estates as could be saved, revived the abbey school, sent a number of monks away for further studies and completed the reorganization of the library, a task he had begun before he became abbot. A new catalogue was compiled from scratch, many of the books were rebound and an annual grant of a hundred guilders was set aside for new acquisitions. Most of the money was spent on printed books and the emphasis was placed on theology, philosophy and law, but some of the new accessions were works of Latin literature, humanist writings and German folk tales, which were very popular at the time. In addition gifts were received from a number of benefactors, including a monk named Gall Kemly, who was a keen collector of rare specimens of early printing, with the result that the library almost doubled in size.[23]

The resuscitation of the library was followed by an unexpected revival of the scriptorium, which had been inactive for at least three hundred years. Early in the sixteenth century Abbot Franz von Gaisberg (1504-

further information see P. Riché, *Les écoles et l'enseignement dans l'Occident chrétien de la fin du Ve siècle au milieu du XIe siècle*, Paris 1979. On the liberal arts see J. Koch (ed.), *Artes liberales. Von der antiken Bildung zur Wissenschaft des Mittelalters*, Leiden/Köln 1959. On the school of St. Gall see G. Meier, 'Geschichte der Schule von St. Gallen im Mittelalter', *Jahrbuch für Schweizerische Geschichte* 10 (1884) 33-127.

17. Ochsenbein, *op. cit.* 139.

18. On the range of subjects covered by the library see Hobson,

142. A Roman orator (probably Cicero) in a Latin schoolbook, 7th or 8th c. Cod. Sang. 912, fol. 3.

op. cit. 27; Vogler, *op. cit.* 15. On Hartmut's calligraphic style see Berschin, 'The Medieval Culture of Penmanship...' 73-74.

19. Vogler, *op. cit.* 15-16.

20. Vogler, *op. cit.* 16; S. Sonderegger, 'German Language and Literature in St. Gall' in King and Vogler, *op. cit.* 173.

21. Hobson, *op. cit.* 31; Sonderegger, *op. cit.* 172-177.

22. On Cencio's record of the visit see Hobson, *op. cit.* 32. Poggio wrote to Guarino da Verona in 1417 to tell him about the discoveries they had made at St. Gall: see *VBV* I 542.

23. Hobson, *op. cit. 32.*

24. Berschin, 'The Medieval Culture of Penmanship...' 77; J. Holen-

1529) commissioned Leonhard Wagner, a Benedictine monk from Augsburg who was the most famous calligrapher in the Holy Roman Empire, to instruct two young monks in the art of calligraphy. Wagner, in collaboration with the miniaturist Nikolaus Bertschi of Rorschach, produced a splendid codex containing the sequences composed by Notker Balbulus the poet.[24]

The Reformation caused a temporary upheaval in the life of the abbey, but without halting its progress towards political, economic and religious independence. The number of monks began to grow again at a satisfactory rate, and soon St. Gall was the most important abbey in the Swiss Confederation. It is doubtful whether Gozbert's original plan for the library ever materialized, nor is it known where the manuscripts were kept before the end of the Middle Ages, when the printed books were put in the library and the old manuscripts were kept in Hartmut's tower. Gabriel Hummelberger, a humanist doctor from Swabia, wrote to Beatus Rhenanus, 'Few people, and they only selected friends, are allowed in [to the library].' And the Swiss historian Johann Strumpf, describing the tragic state of the library, records that manuscripts were strewn about like old bones in a vaulted room in the old tower.[25]

Abbot Diethelm Blarer laid the foundations of a new library in 1551. In 1758 Abbot Coelestin II Gugger von Staudach replaced this building with the present baroque library designed by Peter Thumb and his father.[26] The Greek words Ψυχῆς Ἰατρεῖον ('Sanatorium of the Soul') inscribed over the elaborately-wrought door of the library nearly two thousand five hundred years after their first appearance in Egypt, were chosen as the most suitable motto to put visitors to the library into the right frame of mind.[27]

Architecture. The outstanding feature of the St. Gall library is the lavish use of unpainted wood, treated in different ways and in a variety of shades of brown, both in the construction of the bookcases and the elaborate marquetry floor and for purely decorative purposes. All the walls at ground-floor and gallery level are lined with bookcases except where they are pierced by the seventeen windows, which admit ample daylight. Although the prevailing style is German Baroque, the forty unpainted wooden columns bordering the central aisle and supporting the gallery spring from a plain torus moulding and terminate in a gilt pseudo-Corinthian capital. One of the architect's most delightful touches is the series of twenty statuettes of putti, each about a foot tall, set in niches above the window recesses and at both ends of the room: they symbolize the arts, sciences and crafts, though their positions do not correspond to the arrangement of the books in the library. The Baroque ceiling consists of ornamental plaster mouldings framing frescoes of symbolic scenes from the Ecumenical Councils of Nicaea (325), Constantinople (381), Ephesus (431) and Chalcedon (451). The

stein, 'Zur Forschung über den Buchmaler Nikolaus Bertschi von Rorschach', *Zeitschrift für schweizerische Archäologie und Kunstgeschichte* 16 (1956) 75-98.

25. Hobson, *op. cit.* 34.

26. Diethelm Blarer of Wartensee (abbot 1530-1564), who became a bishop, was even more active and enterprising than Rösch had been before him, and he continued to support the art of manuscript illumination at St. Gall several decades after printing with movable type had become the norm. On Peter Thumb (1681-1766) and the baroque architecture of the abbey see H.M. Gubler, 'The Culture of Baroque Architecture at the Abbey of St. Gall' in King and Vogler, *op. cit.* 201-213.

27. It is not known whether the inscription Ψυχῆς Ἰατρεῖον existed on any of the earlier library buildings. A similar inscription was put up by Nikephoros of Laodicea over the library door at the Monastery of St.

143. Illumination from The Twenty-Four Elders *or* The Golden Throne of the Loving Soul, *manuscript by the calligrapher Otto von Passau, 14th c. (No. 987, fol. 93).*

smaller ceiling frescoes contain portraits of Greek and Latin Church Fathers.

The manuscripts are not kept in this lavishly-decorated large room but in a smaller room situated at a higher level, reached by a spiral staircase on the south side of the library proper. It is decorated in Rococo style, but with nothing like the gorgeous magnificence of the main room. The manuscripts are kept in marquetry cabinets with deep-grained veneers. The ceiling vaults, ornamented with naturalistic motifs, are out of keeping with the wall fixtures, making the impression of stylistic heterogeneity even more marked in comparison with the main room where the printed books are kept.

The manuscript room contains some two thousand manuscripts, most of them from the abbey's own scriptorium. When these are added to the 130,000 printed books and more than 1,650 incunabula, it is easy to appreciate the enormous importance of the St. Gall library, which can perhaps be said to possess the most representative collection of medieval writing in Northern and Central Europe.

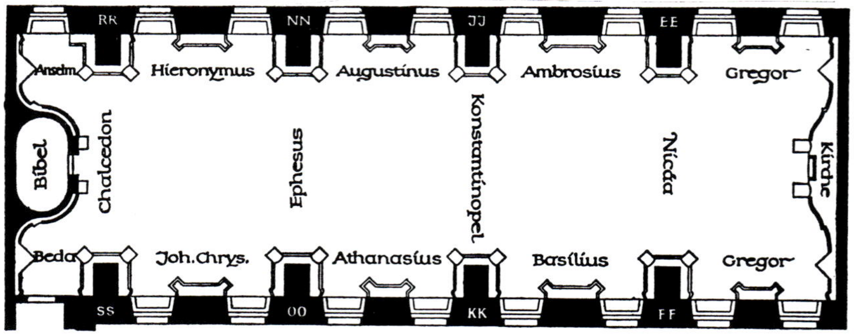

144. Floor plan of the library, showing the subjects of the ceiling frescoes and indications of the book classifications.

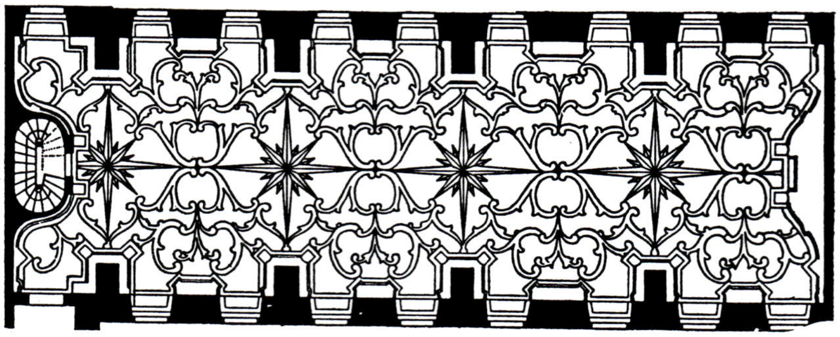

145. Floor plan of the library, showing the designs of the marquetry floor.

146. 'The Astronomer'.

John on Patmos in 1802, shortly after E.D. Clarke's 'purchase' of the manuscript of Plato (see pp. 274, 282). On the origin of the phrase 63, 67.

The first library building was erected in 1551-1552 under Abbot Diethelm on the north and west sides of the abbey, which was still quite small then, and was used for the storage of the archives as well as books. In 1758 Abbot Coelestin pulled down everything on this side of the precinct in order to incorporate the library in the new abbey building. The new library, designed by the two Thumbs, was built and roofed within six months. The interior wooden panelling was designed by craftsmen from the abbey under the direction of Brother Gabriel Loser. The ceiling frescoes, executed in 1762, are signed by Joseph Wannenmacher, and the plasterwork was done by the renowned Gigl brothers. The fixtures and fittings of the manuscript room were completed under Abbot Beda Angehrn (1767-1796).

147. 'The Sculptor' studying anatomy.

The Library of Beatus Rhenanus at Sélestat

CHAPTER NINETEEN

Perhaps the most typical of all humanist libraries during the Renaissance was that of Beatus Rhenanus[1] at Sélestat in Alsace: typical both for the wide range of subjects it covered, reflecting the proverbial breadth of learning of the 'Renaissance man', and also on account of its history, for after Rhenanus's death it became the public library of his native town, Sélestat, in accordance with his dying wish. The Renaissance practice of bequeathing personal libraries to the public was an excellent way of furthering the scholars' humanist ideals while simultaneously satisfying their human ambitions, because by such benefactions they not only promoted the spread of learning but also, through their books, left their mark on the intellectual life of the community.

The library of Beatus Rhenanus and the one donated by Johann Reuchlin[2] to his native town of Pforzheim are the only humanist libraries in northern Europe that have survived intact. In fact, apart from Cardinal Bessarion's incomparable collection of codices which formed the nucleus of the Biblioteca Marciana, the books belonging to all the other great pioneers of humanism – Erasmus, Markos Mousouros, Ianos Laskaris, Marsilio Ficino, Angelo Poliziano, Giovanni Battista Guarino, even Aldus Manutius – have been scattered far and wide.

Beatus Rhenanus. Born in 1485 at Sélestat (Schlettstadt), he received his primary education there at the hands of Crato Hofmann and Hieronymus Gebwiler.[3] His real name was Bild von Rhynow, which he changed to Beatus Rhenanus in accordance with the Renaissance humanists' habit of Latinizing or Hellenizing their names. From Sélestat he went for further studies, first to Paris,[4] where he read classics, philosophy, mathematics and astronomy, then to Strasbourg and finally to Basel, where his enthusiasm was aroused by the scholarly works being turned out in large numbers by the city's printing houses.

Rhenanus was in Paris for four years, from 1503 to 1507. In his first two years there he mastered Aristotle's great treatise on logic known as the *Organon*, took lessons in literature and then studied Aristotle's writings on ethics. The teacher who brought out the best in him, made him into a devoted Aristotelian and exercised a seminal influence on him was Lefèvre d'Étaples.[5] Rhenanus shared Lefèvre's conviction that the Stagirite was the definitive authority on all matters relating to human knowledge, he revered him as 'divine among philosophers' and regarded him as the father of Christian learning. In Paris he had his first Greek lessons from Georgios Hermonymos Spartiates,[6] who turned out not to be the inspiring teacher he was looking for. It was there, too, that he met Erasmus, who was also in Paris to learn Greek: later on, in Basel, their acquaintance ripened into a deep and lasting friendship.

148. The front of the Humanist Library at Sélestat.

Just when Rhenanus was seriously thinking of going to the great centres of humanist learning in Italy – Padua, Florence and Rome – to improve his Greek, he heard that Johannes Cuno,[7] a Dominican friar from Nürnberg who had studied with Markos Mousouros at Padua, was about to start giving regular lessons in ancient Greek at Basel. Without further ado he enrolled for Cuno's classes in July 1511.

In the second decade of the sixteenth century Basel was the centre of humanist studies in northern Europe, and its printing and publishing houses brought out an impressive number of first editions of classical and patristic works edited by some of the most brilliant and famous scholars of the Renaissance.[8] Rhenanus learnt all about the printing business by working as an editor and proof-reader for two of the best-known presses, those of Johann Amerbach[9] and Johann Froben.[10]

His religious principles were the same as those of Erasmus: he was opposed to Luther's reforms, which had precipitated a breakdown of ecclesiastical discipline, and an adherent of the Fratres Communis Vitae (Brethren of the Common Life), a religious movement which initially based its principles on the writings of the Church Fathers but later turned to ancient Greek literature for its inspiration.[11] But he never

149. A 17th c. print of Sélestat.

shared the ambition of his more famous mentor, preferring to live in relative obscurity, working tirelessly at his studies; and his natural modesty prevented him from seeking to win fame and glory as a scholar.

Rhenanus was not a writer of original, creative works on a scale to match his scholarly zeal. He was an avid student of the history of the late Roman Empire and the Germanic peoples, but most of his energies were spent on the editing of classical and patristic texts.[12] His achieve-

150. Beatus Rhenanus. Engraving by Théodore de Bry after a lost drawing from the Sélestat archives.

1. The best works on Rhenanus are: A. Horawitz, 'Beatus Rhenanus: Ein biographischer Versuch', *Wiener Akademie der Wissenschaften* 70 (1872) 189-244; *Annuaire 1985: Spécial 500*^{e} *anniversaire de la naissance de Beatus Rhenanus*, Sélestat (Les amis de la bibliothèque humaniste de Sélestat) 1985, esp. the articles by J. Sturm, 'Vie de Beatus Rhenanus' (pp. 17-18), and N. Holzberg, 'Beatus Rhenanus (1485-1547). Eine biographisch-forschungsgeschichtliche Bestandsaufnahme zum 500. Geburtstag des Humanisten' (pp. 19-32); P. Adam, *L'humanisme à Sélestat: L'école. Les Humanistes. La bibliothèque*, Sélestat (Imprimerie Stahl) 1987, 51-67.

2. Johann Reuchlin was born at Pforzheim in 1455 and died at Stuttgart in 1522. A scholar with an inquiring mind, he championed the dissemination of Greek literature in Germany. He studied with the most famous teachers of his day, mainly in France, acquiring a phenomenal knowledge of Latin, Greek and Hebrew, and was taught philosophy by Andronikos Kontovlakas. He was the first systematic teacher of Greek in Ger-

151. A corner of the Sélestat library, showing the rich bindings of the books.

Pro cristi laude lege libros postea claude 1862
MENTEL
DE
SCHLESTADT
INVENTEUR
DE L' IMPRIMERIE

ments in this field were considerable: they included a substantial number of recensions and the emendation of a great many corrupt passages. He also searched for manuscripts in obscure libraries in Alsace and the Oberrhein region, at the same time as Conrad Peutinger of Augsburg,[13] and in 1515 he discovered at Murbach Monastery in Alsace an unknown work by Velleius Paterculus which he edited for the *editio princeps*. The most important work written by Rhenanus himself was a book of German history entitled *Rerum germanicarum libri tres*, published in 1531.[14]

Once Luther's reforms had gained general acceptance (in 1520),

152. An engraving of Josse Bade's press in Paris.

Rhenanus left Basel and went home to Sélestat. There he spent the rest of his life pursuing his interests, immersed in his classical and philosophical studies and attempting to plumb the depths of human thought. He died while on a brief visit to Strasbourg, on 20th July 1547. A few days before his death he made his last wishes known to Gervais Gebwiler: among other bequests, his books were to be given to the Sélestat parish church.[15] Thus his books and manuscripts and all his other possessions of value came into the possession of the town of Sélestat and Rhenanus became the first humanist to bequeath his private library to his birthplace to form the nucleus of a public library.

many and had a large collection of Greek books printed in Italy. On Reuchlin's library see U. Christ, 'Die Bibliothek Reuchlins in Pforzheim', *ZB* 52 (1924), and for other books and papers on his life and work see *Charta* 201-202. On the libraries and collections of other humanists see *Charta* 317 (Mousouros), 272 (Laskaris), 326 (Aldus); on Cardinal Bessarion's library see pp. 321-337 herein.

3. Hieronymus Gebwiler (1473-1545) was born at Kayserberg and educated first at Basel and then in Paris, where he was taught by Lefèvre d'Étaples (see n. 5 below). He was profoundly influenced by Italian humanism and taught Greek at the humanist school at Sélestat from 1501 to 1509.

4. On Rhenanus's studies in Paris and his circle of friends there see: S. Musial, 'Beatus Rhenanus étudiant de philosophie à Paris (1503-1507)', *Annuaire 1985*, 271-279; C. Vecce, 'Il giovane Beato Renano e gli umanisti italiani a Parigi all' inizio del XVI secolo', *Annuaire 1985*, 134-140.

5. Jacques Lefèvre d'Étaples was one of the greatest luminaries of early French humanism. He was born at Étaples in Picardie in about 1460 and died in 1536. In the course of his studies at the great Italian university centres of Padua, Bologna, Florence and Rome he was initiated into Aristotelian philosophy by Ermolao Barbaro the Younger, espoused the philosophical doctrines of Marsilio Ficino and became a disciple of Pico della Mirandola. He was also lucky enough to study in Paris under Ianos Laskaris, whom he described as his 'praeceptor et singularis amicus'. In his search for the true meaning of life he combined Aristotelian philosophy with Christian faith and maintained that his scriptural studies and researches were guided by divine inspiration. On Lefèvre see *Charta* 297-299 and esp. G. Bedouelle, *Lefèvre d'Étaples et l'Intelligence des Écritures*, Paris 1976.

153. Erasmus, Adagia, *Basel, J. Froben, 1515.*

Sum Beati Rhenani. Nec muto dominũ. Basileae. M.D.XV. 1101

IO. FROBENIVS STVDIOSIS OMNIBVS S. D.

Accipito candide lector, Erasmi Roterodami, prouerbiorum Chiliadas, rursum ab ipso non æstimandis sudoribus recognitas, & ex probatissimis autoribus sic locupletatas, ut superioris æditionis summæ, fere quarta pars accesserit. Nos neq; sumptui, neq; labori pepercimus, ut tam eruditum opus, tam copiosum, ut uere flumen aureũ uocare possis, q̃ emẽdatissimum e nostra officina prodiret in lucem, plane nouum, & hactenus a nemine excusum. Eme, fruere, & Vale.

IN INCLYTA BASILEA

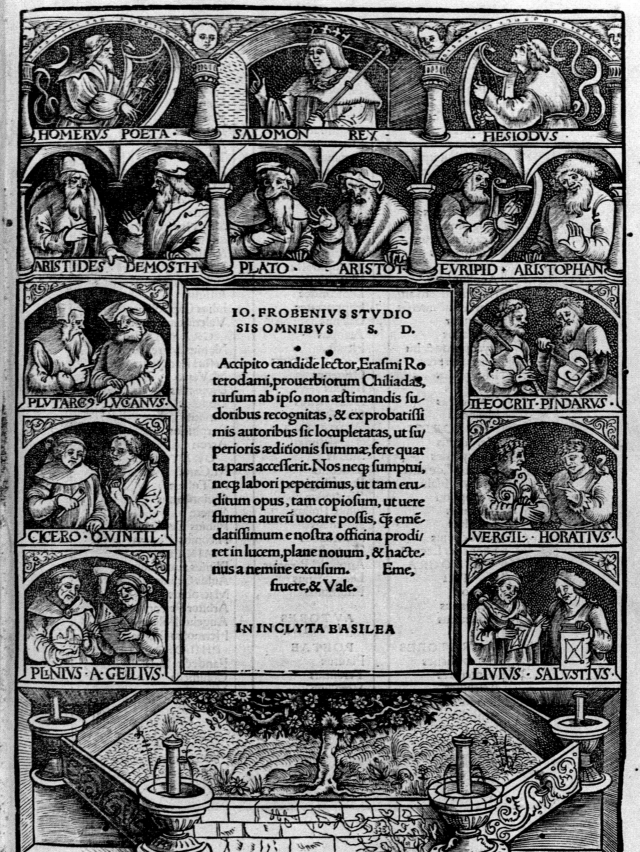

Beatus Rhenanus grew up in a town which played an important part in the revival of learning in northern Europe from 1471 to 1526 and was the home of the only humanist school in the western German states for more than a hundred years.[16] In time the Sélestat school became a link between the great schools of Italy and the Rhine valley and attracted steadily increasing numbers of prominent humanist scholars. It was influenced by Italian thinking, but most of all by the *philosophia Christi* of Erasmus. This was the atmosphere prevailing at the school when Ludwig Dringenberg[17] came to teach there at the urging of young disciples of the humanist movement studying at the school in Heidelberg. It was largely due to the inspired teaching of Dringenberg, as well as his successor Crato Hofmann and above all Hieronymus Gebwiler,[18] that the Sélestat school developed as it did.

In 1450 the school authorities realized that they could not do without a well-stocked library for Latin studies, which flourished at Sélestat, especially after Dringenberg started teaching there. The library was built up steadily from 1452 to 1526, thanks to a series of donations over the years. The biggest benefactors were Johannes de Westhuss (1452), Johannes Fabri (1470), Dringenberg (1477), Jakob Wimpfeling (1500) and Martin Ergersheim (1535).[19] Most of the books donated were theological works given by churchmen, but the humanist school needed books of a different kind to help the teachers with their lesson preparation and the pupils with their schoolwork, and so copies of the classics were bought to supplement them. Teaching was now based on the books in the library, many of which were first editions of classical works from Venetian printing houses. The books were carefully bound to protect them against wear and tear and were kept on tables, to which they were chained to prevent theft.

The flowering of intellectual activity soon spread beyond the confines of the little town, and in about 1515 the scholars of Sélestat formed a literary society (Stubengesellschaft) modelled on those that existed in Italy.[20] For about eighty years the parish library provided invaluable facilities for the humanists of Sélestat. It was visited regularly by pupils and teachers from the school and by other scholars as well, with the result that it became an established meeting-place for the literary society and soon developed into the intellectual centre of Alsace. However, opposition from the reformers put an end to the humanist movement in these parts: from 1525 the school's prestige declined and the members of the Stubengesellschaft stopped using its library.[21]

Beatus Rhenanus started taking an interest in books in 1500, when he was only fifteen,[22] displaying a critical faculty rare in one of his years. The first volumes he acquired were grammars and literary works. Being a methodical man and devoted to his books, he made a point of affixing his bookplate on the title page with a note of the date of acquisition, the purchase price and his now famous owner's mark: *Sum Beati Rhenani nec*

6. Georgios Hermonymos Spartiates was the first teacher of Greek in Paris and numbered among his pupils many illustrious French scholars and humanists from elsewhere in northern Europe, including Guillaume Budé and Erasmus. Hermonymos was a disciple of Gemistos Plethon. Nothing is known about his life prior to 1476, when he is heard of in Rome as a member of the Curia under Pope Sixtus IV. Before going to Paris he had led an eventful life, but once there his unrivalled knowledge of Greek and his skill as a copyist of Greek manuscripts won him a wide circle of intellectual friends. There is no monograph on his life and work, but for a full bibliography to date see *Charta* 293.

7. Johannes Cuno, also known as

154. The teacher with his pupils, from Beda Repertorium, *Köln, H. Quentell, 1495.*
155. Confessio fidei exhibita ... Carolo V Caesari Aug. in Comiciis Augustae, *Wittenberg 1530.*
156. Erasmus, Annotationes in Novum Testamentum, *Basel, J. Froben, 1518.*
157. Erasmus, De conscribendis epistolis, *Basel, J. Froben, 1522.*
158. Guillaume Budé, Annotationes (priores) in ... Pandectarum libros, *Paris, J. Bade, 1521.*

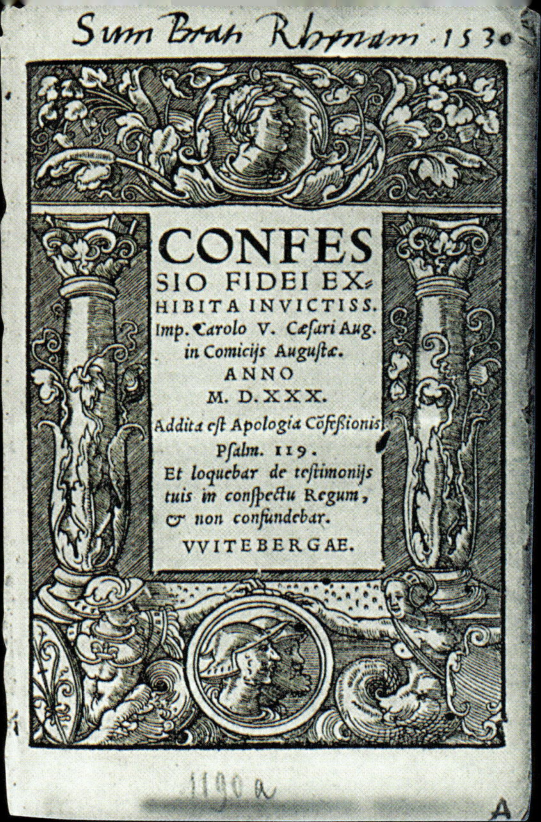
Sum Beati Rhenani 1530

CONFES
SIO FIDEI EX-
HIBITA INVICTISS.
Imp. Carolo V. Cæsari Aug.
in Comicijs Augustæ.
ANNO
M. D. XXX.
Addita est Apologia Cõfeßionis.
Psalm. 119.
Et loquebar de testimonijs
tuis in conspectu Regum,
& non confundebar.
VVITEBERGAE.

1190 a

A

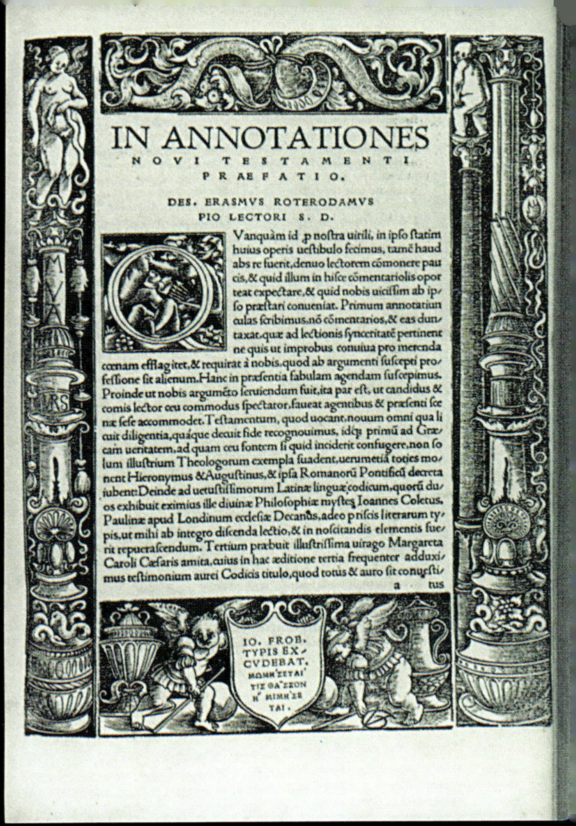
IN ANNOTATIONES
NOVI TESTAMENTI
PRAEFATIO.

DES. ERASMVS ROTERODAMVS
PIO LECTORI S. D.

Vanquàm id ꝑ nostra uirili, in ipso statim huius operis uestibulo fecimus, tamẽ haud abs re fuerit, denuo lectorem cõmonere paucis, & quid illum in hisce cõmentariolis oporteat expectare, & quid nobis uicissim ab ipso præstari conueniat. Primum annotatiunculas scribimus, nõ cõmentarios, & eas duntaxat, quæ ad lectionis synceritatẽ pertinent ne quis ut improbus conuiua pro merenda cœnam efflagitet, & requirat à nobis, quod ab argumenti suscepti professione sit alienum. Hanc in præsentia fabulam agendam suscepimus. Proinde ut nobis argumẽto seruiendum fuit, ita par est, ut candidus & comis lector ceu commodus spectator, faueat agentibus & præsenti scenæ sese accommodet. Testamentum, quod uocant, nouum omni qua licuit diligentia, quáque decuit fide recognouimus, idq; primũ ad Græcam ueritatem, ad quam ceu fontem si quid inciderit confugere, non solum illustrium Theologorum exempla suadent, uerumetiã toties monent Hieronymus & Augustinus, & ipsa Romanorũ Pontificũ decreta iubent: Deinde ad uetustissimorum Latinæ linguæ codicum, quorũ duos exhibuit eximius ille diuinæ Philosophiæ mystes, Ioannes Coletus, Paulinæ apud Londinum ecclesiæ Decanus, adeo priscis literarum typis, ut mihi ab integro discenda lectio, & in noscitandis elementis fuerit repuerascendum. Tertium præbuit illustrissima uirago Margareta Caroli Cæsaris amita, cuius in hac æditione tertia frequenter adduximus testimonium aurei Codicis titulo, quod totus & auro sit conuesti-

a tus

IO. FROB.
TYPIS EX-
CVDEBAT.

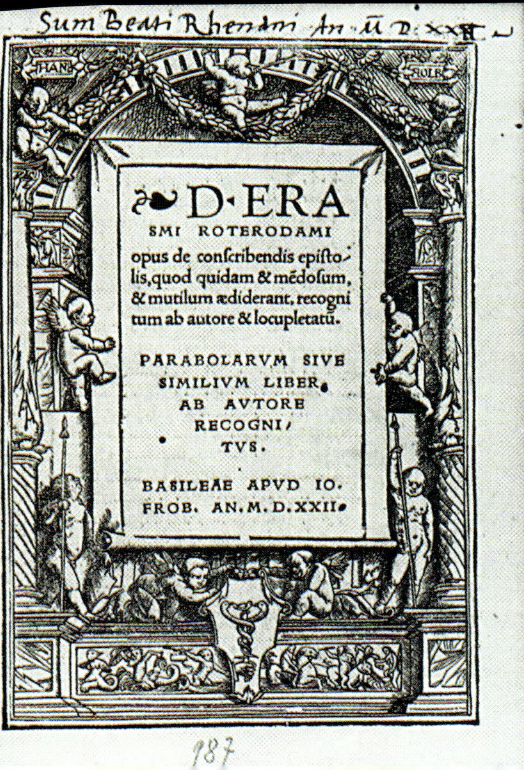
Sum Beati Rhenani An. M. D. XXII

D. ERA
SMI ROTERODAMI
opus de conscribendis epistolis, quod quidam & mẽdosum, & mutilum æediderant, recognitum ab autore & locupletatũ.

PARABOLARVM SIVE
SIMILIVM LIBER,
AB AVTORE
RECOGNI-
TVS.

BASILEAE APVD IO.
FROB. AN. M. D. XXII.

987

1211 a

Sum Beati Rhenani

ANNOTATA
in G. Budæi Epistolas tam Priores q̃ Posteriores præmisso indice.

Prelum
Ascensianũ

Væneundantur vbi & Epistolę in officina Io. Badii Ascensii.

muto dominum. The core of his collection now comprises some fifty-seven books, including about a dozen treatises on grammar and rhetoric and a number of works by Italian humanists such as Battista Guarino, Franciscus Niger and Augustinus Datus.[23] He was also a keen collector of the *editiones principes* of the classics coming from the best-known Italian printing houses: among the works he bought were first editions of Virgil, Lucretius, Suetonius and Pliny the Younger, as well as patristic writings.

159. J. Wimpfeling, Argentinensium Episc. Catalogus, *1508.*

The four years he spent as a student in Paris he put to productive use: during that period he bought at least 188 books, mostly works by Aristotle, including several edited by his teacher Lefèvre d'Étaples.

His departure from Paris marked the beginning of a long and fruitful period spent in Strasbourg, Basel and Sélestat. His experience of editorial work and the time he spent working for the best-known printing houses in northern Europe provided him with further opportunities to enlarge his library. Every time one of his editions was published he received a number of complimentary copies, which he then swapped with his friends and acquaintances. Beatus Rhenanus, a humanist in the fullest sense of the word, always amiable and willing to put his knowledge at the disposal of others if it would help to improve the quality and accuracy of the work in hand, was much loved and respected by his fellow-scholars: he would correct proofs for his friends and give up his time uncomplainingly to search for material in archives.

Norimontanus or Conon, was born between 1462 and 1467 at Nürnberg and died in 1513. An ardent Hellenist and a pupil of Ioannes Gregoropoulos, he was the only humanist from northern Europe who made any real impact in the Italian printing houses where Greek books were produced. He had been brought up on the régime prescribed by Aldus and his scholarly team of editors and proofreaders for the running of his printing house in Venice, and he always regarded the famous Aldine press as the model for the establishment of a similar academic circle in Germany. On Cuno see M. Sicherl, *Johannes Cuno, ein Wegbereiter des Griechischen in Deutschland. Ein biographisch-kodikologische Studie*, Heidelberg 1978; see also *Charta* 370-371.

8. Germany led the field in the development of typography, but it was in Italy that the intellectual climate was most conducive to the printing of first editions of the classics. Learned Greeks from Byzantium and their Italian pupils made recensions of large numbers of classical and patristic works for publication, and frequently they translated them into Latin as well. Several factors contributed to the decline of Italy's primacy in classical scholarship: among them were the political conditions in the peninsula, the natural cooling of humanist ardour in the Italian centres of learning after about a century and the intellectual vigour of the humanists of northern Europe. As a result, Paris and Basel developed into new centres of humanist learning.

9. Adam, *op. cit.* 56. On the relations between Rhenanus and Amerbach's son Bonifacius see Jean-Claude Margolin, 'Beatus Rhenanus et Boniface Amerbach: Une amitié de trente ans', *Annuaire 1985*, 157-175.

10. Adam, *op. cit.* 56. Froben was born at Hammelburg in Bavaria, perhaps in 1460, and died in 1526. He was one of the most important and most productive humanist printers in

160. John of Damascus, Theologia, *printed on parchment, Paris, Henri Estienne, 1507.*

SANCTI PATRIS IOANNIS DAMASCENI ORTHODOXE FIDEI ACCVRATA EDITIO INTERPRETE IACOBO FABRO STAPVLENSI.

¶Quod incomprehensibilis diuinitas/ ꝙ nichil
inquirendũ preter ea que nobis a sanctis prophe=
tis/apostolis/et euangelistis sunt tradita. Cap. I.

DEVM nemo vidit vnq̃: vnigenitus filius Ioan. 1.
qui est in sinu patris/ipse enarrauit. Ineffa=
bilis igitur diuinitas: atq; incõprehen=
sibilis. neq; eni vllus nouit patrẽ nisi fili= Math. 11.
us: neq; filiũ nisi pater. ceterũ spiritus sanctus ita no
uit ea que dei sũt: vt spiritus hominis ea nouit que i 1. Corin. 2.
illo sunt. Post diuinã itaq; beatissimãq; naturã/nul
lus vnq̃ deũ nouit: nisi cui ipse reuelauerit/nõ homi
num modo/sed ne supramũdanarũ quidẽ virtutũ/
supramundanarũ(aio) vt ipsorũ Cherubim atq; Se
raphim. Attamẽ haudquaq̃ nos deseruit deus om=
nimoda sui circũfusos ignorãtia: quinimo cũctis co
gnitio ꝙ deus sit/ab ipo naturaliter ĩsita est atq; ige
nita. Sed et ipa mũdi creatura/et eius coaptatio/pa
riter et gubernatio: magnitudinẽ diuine ĩsinuat na
ture. Et ipe primitus ꝑ legẽ et prophetas/deinde et
ꝑ vnigenitũ filiũ suũ et dominũ et saluatorẽ nostrũ
Iesũ Christũ(quantũ nostra capit ĩfirmitas) nobis
suiipsius cognitionis ĩdulsit cõsortiũ. Cũcta igitur
que tradita sũt et ꝑ legẽ et ꝓphetas et Apostolos et
euãgelistas: suscipimus/ cognoscimus/veneramur/
nichil vltra illa perquirẽtes. Nã bonus cũ sit deus/
omnis boni largitor est: nõ ĩuidie aut perturbatiõi
cuipiam obnoxius. procul eni a diuina natura(que

Before long this generosity of his brought its own reward in the further enlargement of his library through gifts from his friends, evidenced by the large number of his books inscribed with the words *Dono dat*, *Dono misit* or *Muneri mittit*. Many of them were sent to him by Johann Froben in return for the valuable work he had done for Froben's press.[24] Between 1508 and 1515 Michael Hummelberg, an old friend from his Paris days, sent him fifteen books from Rome, most of them in Greek. His former colleagues Johannes Kierher and Jodocus Badius (Josse Bade) each sent him two books and his beloved teacher

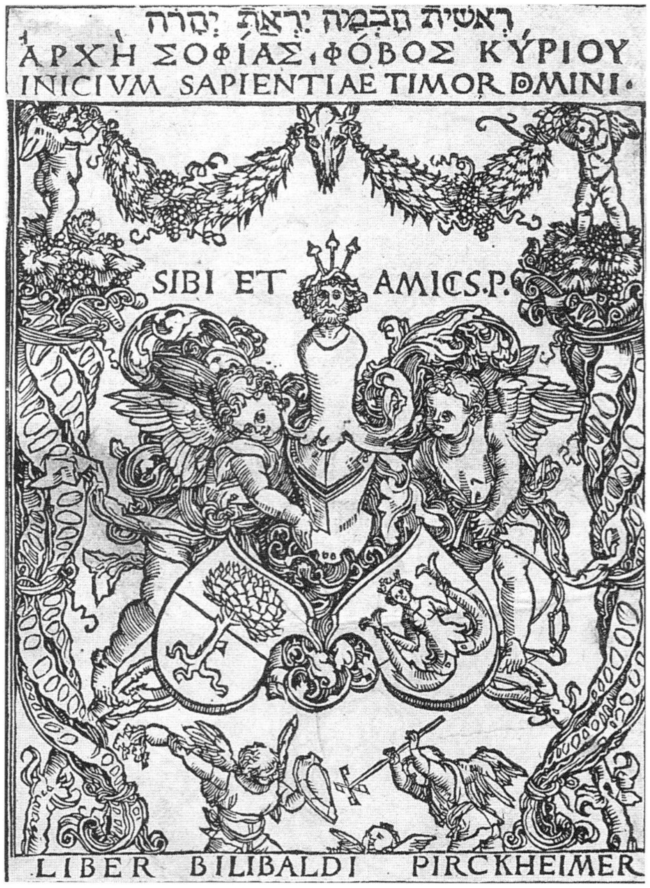

161. Willibald Pirckheimer's bookplate, designed by Dürer.

Lefèvre d'Étaples gave him three. But the biggest contribution to his library came from his Greek teacher, Johannes Cuno, in 1513.[25] While in Italy, and particularly during his time in the printing house of Aldus Manutius, Cuno had amassed a splendid collection of material to do with the work involved in preparing an edition for publication: rare editions of the classics, humanist writings, proof sheets, misprints with their corrections and pagination samples which were never actually used. All this mass of material, as well as other manuscripts and Cuno's lecture notes, was bequeathed to Rhenanus. In the same year, 1513, the

northern Europe. Froben took great care over the textual accuracy of his editions and organized his printing house along the lines of the Aldine press. It was he who gave German books their distinctive style, commissioning famous artists such as Holbein, Dürer and Urs Graff to do the frontispieces and illustrations for his editions. See C.W. Heckethorn, *The Printers of Basle in the XV and XVI Centuries*, London 1897, 84-112; P. Bietenholz, *Basle and France in the Sixteenth Century*, Geneva 1971; Geldner I 123-124.

11. The Fratres Communis Vitae, though a religious movement, had nothing to do with the Church or even with the Scholastic tradition. The Brethren based their philosophy on a view of the universe that was simpler in its outlook and came to be known as *devotio moderna*. The movement was founded by Geert Groote (1340-1384) at Deventer,

162. The printer's device of Johann Froben (C.W. Heckethorn, The Printers of Basle, *London 1897).*

which developed into a flourishing centre of the classical revival. Erasmus was educated at the Brethren's school there, whose headmaster, Alexander Hegius, was a firm believer in the value of learning Greek: one of his posthumous works was entitled *De Utilitate Linguae Graecae*. See *Charta* 371-372.

12. For a list of his works see A. Horawitz and K. Hartfelder (ed.), *Briefwechsel des Beatus Rhenanus*

great German bibliophile Willibald Pirckheimer sent him an edition of his translation of Plutarch with a frontispiece engraved by Dürer, who was a protégé of his.[26] And the following year further gifts arrived to enrich Rhenanus's collection: they came from Johannes Oecolampadius, from Johann Amerbach, the great printer of Basel, from the Alsatian scholars Johann Lapidus and Beatus Arnoaldus and

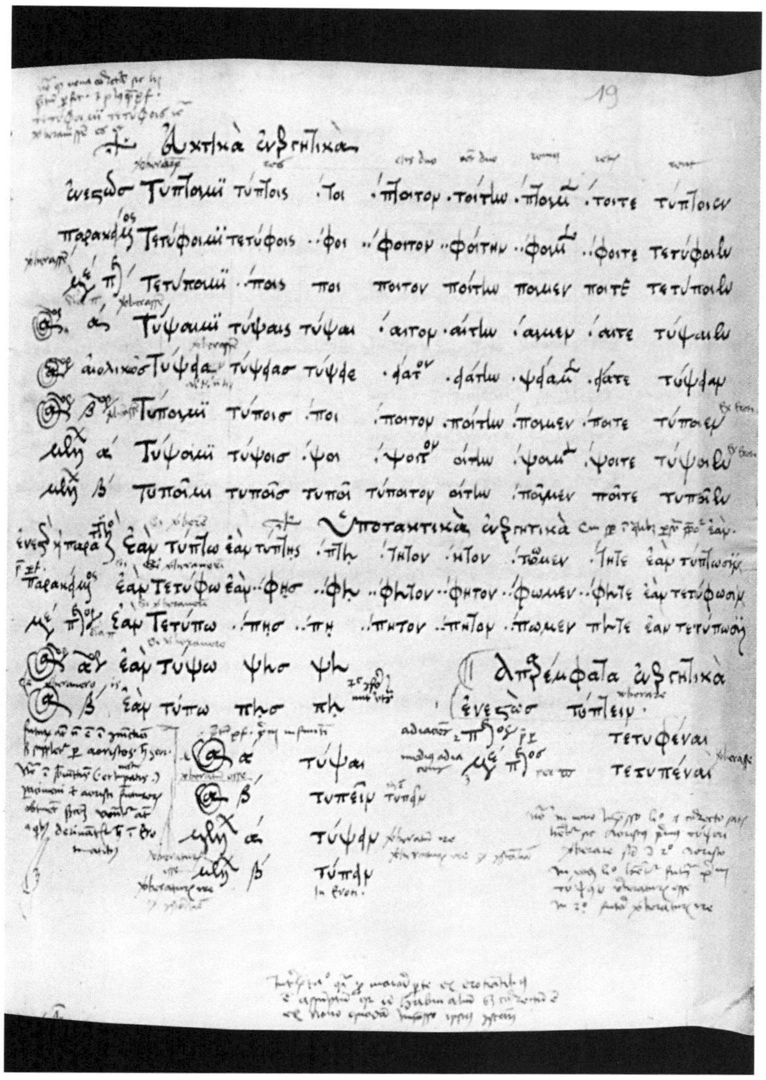

164. Greek grammar: a page from one of Johannes Cuno's school exercise books.

from the two printers working in Sélestat, Matthias Schürer and Crato Mylius.[27]

The Humanist Library of Sélestat, as it is now called, comprises not only the books from Beatus Rhenanus's personal collection but also those from the local parish library. Since 1760 all of them have been housed on the first floor of the old Halle-aux-Blés (Cornmarket), a building in early Renaissance style. The parish library was founded in

(Leipzig 1886), repr. Hildesheim (G. Olms) 1966, 592-618. See also Adam, *op. cit.* 59-67.

13. Conrad Peutinger was born at Augsburg in 1465 and died there in 1547. After a university education in

163. A bibliophile at his desk. Woodcut from Jakob Wimpfeling, Isidoneus germanicus, *Strasbourg 1497.*

Italy he stayed in that country for forty years, studying the classics – and more particularly the editing of manuscripts – with the temperamental and eccentric Pomponio Leto, who taught in Rome. Peutinger built up a large collection of ancient Greek and Roman relics ranging from coins to statues and inscriptions. See R. Pfeiffer, 'Conrad Peutinger und die humanistische Welt', *Augusta* (1955) 179-186.

14. Rhenanus's edition of Velleius Paterculus affords a characteristic example of his indefatigable efforts to produce reliable texts of the works he edited. The first manuscript he used, dating from the tenth century, was full of mistakes. He then borrowed another manuscript from a copyist friend of his, but that was no more helpful than the first and it took him countless hours of painstaking

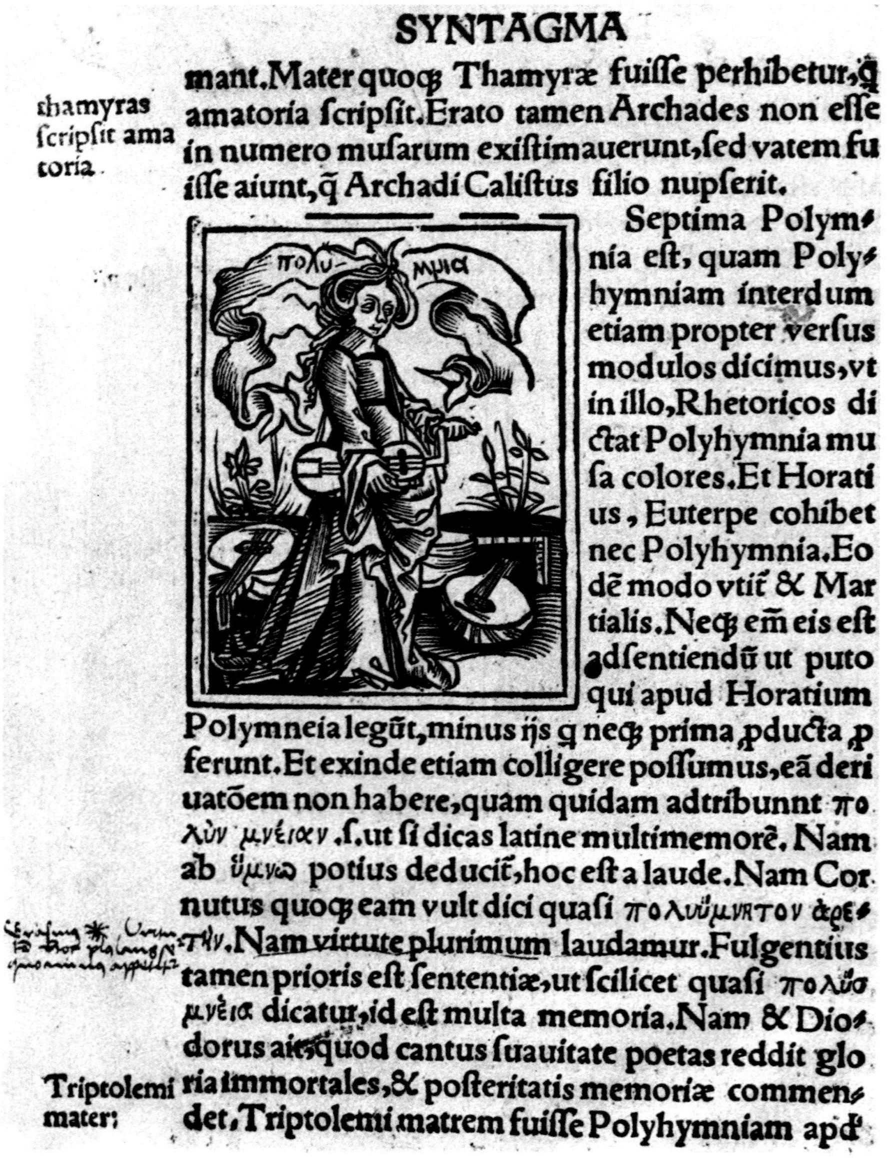

SYNTAGMA

mant.Mater quoq Thamyræ fuisse perhibetur,q̃
(thamyras scripsit amatoria) amatoria scripsit.Erato tamen Archades non esse
in numero musarum existimauerunt,sed vatem fu
isse aiunt,q̃ Archadi Calistus filio nupserit.

Septima Polym
nia est, quam Poly
hymniam interdum
etiam propter versus
modulos dicimus,vt
in illo,Rhetoricos di
ctat Polyhymnia mu
sa colores.Et Horati
us, Euterpe cohibet
nec Polyhymnia.Eo
dẽ modo vtit & Mar
tialis.Neq eñ eis est
adsentiendũ ut puto
qui apud Horatium
Polymneia legũt,minus ijs q neq prima ꝑducta ꝑ
ferunt.Et exinde etiam colligere possumus,eã deri
uatõem non habere,quam quidam adtribuunt πο
λὺν μνείαν.s.ut si dicas latine multimemorẽ. Nam
ab ὕμνω potius deducit,hoc est a laude.Nam Cor
nutus quoq eam vult dici quasi πολυύμνητον ἀρε
τὴν.Nam virtute plurimum laudamur.Fulgentius
tamen prioris est sententiæ,ut scilicet quasi πολύ
μνεία dicatur,id est multa memoria.Nam & Dio
dorus ait,quod cantus suauitate poetas reddit glo
(Triptolemi mater) ria immortales,& posteritatis memoriæ commen
det.Triptolemi matrem fuisse Polyhymniam apd

165. Gregorius Gyraldi, Syntagma de musis, *Strasbourg, Matthias Schürer, 1515. It was in this book that Schürer made his first attempt at printing Greek characters.*

1452 with a donation of manuscripts from Johannes de Westhuss and subsequently enlarged by further donations from Fabri, Dringenberg, Wimpfeling and Ergersheim. It would be wrong to think of this parish library as a humanist innovation, as there had been monastic libraries hereabouts since the eleventh century. The Benedictine Convent of Sainte-Foy, founded in 1094, had a library of sorts started by its first abbess, and other religious houses founded in the vicinity from the thirteenth century onwards – friaries of the Dominicans of Sylo (1245), of the Franciscans (1280) and of the Dominicans (1284) – carried on the tradition of keeping and copying manuscripts. A number of manuscripts from these houses are now in the Humanist Library at Sélestat.[28]

work to complete the *editio princeps*, published in 1522: see Adam, *op. cit.* 61-62. On *Rerum germanicarum* see Adam, *op. cit.* 65-67.

15. Adam, *op. cit.* 58; H. Kaiser, 'Aus den letzten Jahren des Beatus Rhenanus', *Zeitschrift für die Geschichte des Oberrheins* (1916) 30-52.

16. Adam, *op. cit.* 9-36, with full bibliography.

17. Dringenberg, an exceptionally gifted teacher, was on the staff at Sélestat from 1441 to 1477. He had very decided ideas on what was the right way to teach, and the Sélestat school was influenced by his method for many years after he had left: see Adam, *op. cit.* 12-14.

18. Adam, *op. cit.* 18-21.

19. Adam, *op. cit.* 77-83.

20. These literary societies, or small academies, first made their appearance towards the end of the fourteenth century in Italy, especially Florence. Among them were the academies of Acciaiuoli and Pomponio Leto, the Chorus Achademiae Florentinae, the academy of Cardinal Bessarion and the Accademia Liviana at Pordenone: see *Charta* 495. On the Stubengesellschaft at Sélestat see J. Gény, *Die Reichsstadt Schlettstadt und ihr Anteil an der social-politischen und religiösen Bewegungen der Jahre 1490-1536*, Freiburg 1900, 56.

21. Adam, *op. cit.* 22-23.

22. Adam, *op. cit.* 86.

23. Adam, *op. cit.* 86; G. Knod, 'Aus der Bibliothek des Beatus Rhenanus: Ein Beitrag zur Geschichte des Humanismus' in J. Gény and G. Knod, *Die Stadtbibliothek zu Schlettstadt*, Strasbourg 1889, Part II, 11-19, 47-55.

24. A. Horawitz, 'Die Bibliothek und Correspondenz des Beatus Rhenanus zu Schlettstadt', *Wiener Akademie der Wissenschaften* 78 (1874) 313-340; Adam, *op. cit.* 89.

25. Knod, *op. cit.* 81-85. On Rhenanus's relations with Cuno see Horawitz and Hartfelder, *op. cit.* 5, 30, 39, 43, 45-50, 56, 68, 72; Sicherl, *op. cit.* 169-170.

26. Pirckheimer was one of the great bibliophiles of the Renaissance. A patron of art and literature, a

166. A scholar deep in thought. From Justinus, Opuscula, *1500.*

Architecture. The present resting-place of Beatus Rhenanus's books is probably one of the most attractive libraries that have ever existed: it is the very epitome of a Renaissance humanist's library, done on a human scale and in the appropriate style. It consists of a single room, eight by four metres in size, with three stained-glass windows at one end. The library is entered by a double door in the centre of an elaborate wrought iron grille. Plain wooden bookcases line the two side walls, and the vaulted ceiling is decorated with polychrome arabesques. There is no furniture in the room apart from a pedestal on which there originally stood a head of Christ taken from a wood-carving of the Crucifixion; it has now been replaced by a bust of Johann Mentelin, the great Strasbourg printer of incunabula.[29]

167. The library in the 1970s.

Hellenist and an admirer of the ancient Greek and Roman civilizations in general, he built up an unrivalled library of the classics. One of his protégés was Albrecht Dürer, whom he commissioned to buy copies of all the Greek books he could find whenever he went to Italy to study Italian art. Subsequently Dürer executed a series of magnificent engravings to be used as frontispieces for these books. See E. Offenbacher, 'La bibliothèque de Willibald Pirckheimer', *La Bibliofilia* 40 (1938) 241-263.

27. See Knod, *op. cit.* 81-85; Adam, *op. cit.* 89.

28. Adam, *op. cit.* 75-85.

29. Johann Mentelin was born at Sélestat in 1410 and was living in Strasbourg by 1447. He set up his press in 1458 and ran it with impressive efficiency: according to the *Chronica Summorum Pontificum Imperatorumque* (Rome, 1474), he was printing three hundred pages a day. See *Charta* 58; Geldner I 55-57.

BIBLIOTHECA AVGVSTA

The Herzog August Library at Wolfenbüttel

CHAPTER TWENTY

Walking around Wolfenbüttel, a medium-sized town in Saxony, one has the feeling that for centuries the heart and soul of the place has been its library, the Bibliotheca Augusta. In point of fact the town has a long literary and cultural tradition, for it was there that the first theatre in Germany opened its doors and the first German newspaper was published (in 1609); but to this day its greatest pride is the library which was left to the town when the ducal court moved to nearby Brunswick in 1573 and which, within a few decades, was known throughout Europe as 'the eighth wonder'.[1]

The founder of the library was Duke Julius of Brunswick-Lüneburg, who held the title from 1568 to 1589 and transformed the medieval duchy into a modern state and a humanist centre. He supported the foundation of a university at Helmstedt, started his own printing press, introduced the church reforms being urged by the Protestants and opened his already well-stocked library to scholars from outside the court. In 1572 he promulgated a 'Liberey Ordnung' concerning the duties of the librarian and gave orders for all medieval manuscripts to be gathered in from the monasteries and cathedrals in the area and kept in his library.[2] His successor, Duke Heinrich Julius (*c.* 1589-1613), enlarged the library he inherited from his father and, being a writer and a knowledgeable music-lover, he brought a breath of internationalism into his court and the intellectual life of Wolfenbüttel.[3]

On the retirement of the librarian Leonhard Schröter in 1600, his successor Adam Leonicerus found the library sadly neglected, in a chaotic state and badly in need of proper organization.[4] A number of historic manuscripts were acquired, including the 165 codices of the theologian Matthias Flacius Illyricus,[5] a sixth-century Greek manuscript of works by John Chrysostom and two documents containing treaties signed by Charlemagne. On the death of Heinrich Julius in 1613 the library contained over 10,000 volumes, many of them comprising more than one work. In 1618 these were all given away by his successor Friedrich Ulrich to Helmstedt University, which returned them to Wolfenbüttel in 1814.[6]

The Herzog August Library takes its name from the illustrious and erudite Duke August of Brunswick-Lüneburg (1579-1666), who was appointed Rector of Rostock University at the tender age of sixteen and Rector of the famous University of Tübingen the following year.[7] He came into the title in 1635, when the duchy was under imperial military occupation and in a constant state of war, and it was nine years before he managed to recapture his castle at Wolfenbüttel. He then set off on an educational tour, after which he settled at Hitzacker, east of Lüneburg, surrounded by the books that his agents

168. The front door of the Herzog August Library.

had been collecting for him for years. By the time he eventually returned to Wolfenbüttel to take over the administration of the duchy in 1649, his collection had grown to 60,000 volumes, and by his death in 1666 it had more than doubled in size.[8]

Most of the books in Duke August's private library were in German and Latin, with a few in Italian, French and Greek. The great majority were published in his own time, but the existence of a number of historic incunabula, mostly illustrated, attests to the direction of his intellectual interests and his love of European literature. Thanks to the Duke's mania for collecting original material, many early Gothic bindings and

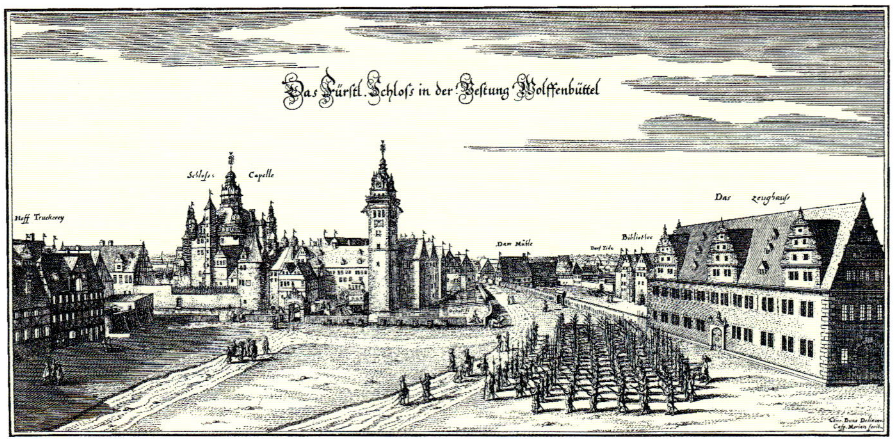

169. An 18th-century print of Wolfenbüttel.

damaged manuscripts illustrated with rare woodcuts, which would otherwise have perished, have been preserved for posterity. A typical case in point is the unique surviving copy of Ulrich Boner's *Der Edelstein*, printed at Bamberg by Albrecht Pfister in 1461, which was the first illustrated book printed with movable metal types.[9]

The books, which were kept in a separate building facing August's castle, were classified into twenty categories, within which they were arranged by size.[10] August regarded them as 'learned works' and spent his time reading them, meditating on their meaning and using them as works of reference for his own writings. He remained active and energetic to the end of his life, busying himself with the classification and study of his beloved books, but he never explained what it was that had first aroused his consuming interest in the written word. Nor did he write an autobiography, in which he might have set down his ideas about books and book lore. However, his belief in the importance of books is clearly apparent in the works he did write. In everything he did – whether as collector, author or ruler of his duchy – he kept a mass of notes recording all kinds of information, as if deliberately building up a legacy of learning for future generations to draw on, and by so doing he established his credentials as a humanist. His place as the leading bibliophile of his time is unchallenged, for he possessed copies of almost

1. See U. von Heinemann, *Die herzogliche Bibliothek zu Wolfenbüttel*, Wolfenbüttel 1894; A. Hobson, *Great Libraries*, London 1970, 202-211; P. Raabe, 'The Herzog August Library in Wolfenbüttel' in *Treasures of the Herzog August Library*, ed. P. Raabe, Wolfenbüttel 1984, VII-XV.

2. See Raabe, *op. cit.* VII; and, more generally, H. Bünting and J. Letzner, *Braunschweig-Lüneburgische Chronica*, Braunschweig 1772. Duke Julius was something of a martinet and his instructions to the librarian were very strict: he had to work in 'our Bibliotheca' every day, all the year round, and to be available at all times; he was to dust the books once a week; he was not to lend any books without written permission; and he was to refuse admittance to anyone who was armed or wearing a cape.

3. See Hobson, *op. cit.* 204; Raabe, *op. cit.* VII-VIII.

4. See A. Werner, 'J.A. Leonicerus (1557-?)' in P. Raabe (ed.),

170. Duke August as Rector of Tübingen University.

171. Psalter of King Matthias Corvinus (Cod. Guelf. 39 Aug. 4o): miniature by F.A. del Chierico on the title page.

172. Interior of the central hall of the library.

INPRIN
CIPIO.
ERAT.
VERBV̄.

every book printed in Europe in the sixteenth century and everything of any importance published in the seventeenth. For many years Duke August performed the librarian's duties himself and wrote out in his own hand nearly all of the impressive six-volume catalogue. The catalogue was kept on an ingenious 'book-wheel' which he had made for him at Augsburg.[11]

The way in which August amassed his treasures had nothing in common with the normal practice of contemporary princes, for whom books were some of the spoils of war to be looted from defeated enemies, often in large quantities. Very few of his books were acquired by force: they included three manuscripts belonging to Guarino da Verona that were taken by the imperial army at Mantua in 1630 and the manuscripts that August seized from the monasteries of St. Blasien in Brunswick and Marienthal near Helmstedt.[12] Many of his books were gifts from princes and prelates – such as a hundred volumes given to him by Cardinal Mazarin, with the latter's coat of arms imprinted on the cover – but the great majority were bought for him by an international network of

173. Duke August in his study, a scene with a highly esoteric atmosphere. Oil, 1656

Lexikon zur Geschichte und Gegenwart der Herzog August Bibliothek Wolfenbüttel, Wiesbaden 1992, 106.

174. J.A. Leonicerus. Woodcut from J.J. Boissard, Icones quinquaginta virorum illustrium, *Frankfurt 1598.*

5. See Hobson, *op. cit.* 221. Matthias Flach Francowitz (Illyricus) was an eminent Protestant theologian who was born at Albona in 1520 and died at Frankfurt-am-Main in 1575. He studied theology at Basel. In 1541 he was at Wittenberg, where he heard Luther and Melanchthon preaching. In Melanchthon he found a powerful patron, and it was due to their collaboration that the Lutheran interpretation of the Bible did not stifle the study of classical literature.

6. See Hobson, *op. cit.* 204.

7. By the time August completed his studies he already had a collection of 150 books: see Maria von Katte, 'The "Bibliotheca Augusta": Significance and Origin' in *Treasures...* 57. For more general information: Ead., 'Herzog August und die Kataloge seiner Bibliothek', *Wolfenbütteler Beiträge* 1 (1972) 168-199; Ead., 'Die Bibliotheca Selenica von 1586-1612: Die Anfänge der Bibliothek des

175. Priscianus (Cod. Guelf. 10 Aug. 4o): the second page of the dedicatory epistle, illuminated by Attavante degli Attavanti.

MARSILIVS FICINVS FLORETINVS PHILIPPO VALORI NOBILI ET MAGNANIMO VIRO S.D.

QVI PRECIPIT COGNOSCE TE IPSVM

Nos admonere uidetur ut animam cognoscamus. que quoniā ē media rerum omniū ē & omnia: hac itaq; cognita facile sumus omnia cogituri. Ego igitur ut animam ī primis assequerer p quam consequuturus omnia forem: ad philosophos non plebeos illos quidem sed egregios

agents whom he retained for the purpose. These agents were no ordinary booksellers or manuscript-hunters but persons of rank, often holding high positions, such as Philipp Hainhofer of Augsburg, H.J. von Blum (a diplomat in the imperial service), A. Wicquefort and the Jesuit priest Athanasius Kircher, who presented him with a Syriac Gospel book of the year 634.[13]

The oldest manuscript in the Wolfenbüttel library is the sixth-century Codex Agrimensorum describing Roman farming practices, which is written on parchment and illuminated with sketches in colour.[14] A fine example of tenth-century work is the Reichenau Lectionary (*Reichenauer Evangelistar* or *Perikopenbuch*), illuminated with priceless miniatures in the characteristic style of that period.[15] Manuscripts of the Burgundian school include numerous books of hours as well as a magnificent illuminated codex, formerly the property of the Duc de Berry, containing French translations of works by Boccaccio.[16] Perhaps the most highly prized items at Wolfenbüttel are the manuscripts from the

176. A 'book-wheel'. Illustration from A. Ramelli, Le diverse et artificiose machine, *Paris 1588.*

Herzogs August zu Braunschweig und Lüneburg', *Wolfenbütteler Beiträge* 3 (1978) 135-153.

8. At the age of 33 he possessed 4,000 books; by 1625, when he was 46, the number had grown to 25,000; and by the time of his death at the age of 86 it had risen to 135,000: see Maria von Katte, 'The "Bibliotheca Augusta"...' 57-58.

9. *GW* 4840; Geldner I 49-51.

10. The library occupied a rectangular room over the stables, with direct access from the castle, and the books were kept in shelves attached to the walls. The classification system comprised the following categories: Philosophy (subdivided into Ethics and Logic), Poetry, Rhetoric, Grammar, Music, Politics, Economics, Arithmetic, Geometry, Astronomy, Geography, Physics, Medicine, Warfare, Theology, History, Law and a miscellaneous section called Quodlibetica. For the first time each book bore a pressmark showing its proper position on the shelves, and August had the foresight to devise a numbering system that could be expanded indefinitely as each new accession came into the library. For example, if a new book on theology belonged between the volumes numbered 3 and 4, it was given the number 3.1. This made it possible for the catalogue to be kept up for another three hundred years without any serious problem arising.

11. August himself wrote the titles on the spines of his parchment-bound books and then entered them, with full particulars of publication, notes on the date, place and cost of purchase and other information about each book, in the library catalogue, which eventually filled four large-format volumes of several hundred pages each. Not until he had reached page 5,900 did he hand over the job to his secretary.

12. See Hobson, *op. cit.* 209.

13. See Hobson, *op. cit.* 209;

177. Woodcut of the Greeks with the wooden horse at Troy. From an edition of Virgil's Aeneid, *Leipzig, A. von Köln, 1494.*

ddit. S. Quasi debi
redditus his terris.
ra. Nauis quę ibi
i Virgiliū debes s
atticis reddas . in
ñ precar. DONA
Reddit. vsᵒ c̄ bono
.Nā quos occultā
nebris accœpat red
i. k Tersandrᵒ.
ynicis:& Argię filiᵒ.

Extulerat:fatisq; deūm defensus iniquis
Inclusos vtero danaos:et pinea furtim
Laxat claustra Sinon:illos patefactos ad auras
Reddit equus:lętiq; cauo se robore promunt.
Thersandrᵒ sthenelusq; duces:et dyrus vlisses:
Demissum lapsi per funē:athamasq; thoasq;:

l Sthēelus. S. Capanei:et Euadnes filius:
m Vlysses. S. Laertis:& Anthicne DONA. Vlysses & ipse dux intelligit.
n Toas C. filiᵒ Adremonis ex æcholia,

most famous Renaissance library of all, that of the Hungarian king Matthias Corvinus.[17] Out of all that vast collection of manuscripts by the best copyists and illuminators of the Renaissance, only 179 now remain: 45 of these are in Hungary, 32 in Vienna, 15 at Modena, 9 at Wolfenbüttel and the rest are scattered in libraries around the world.[18] Among the nine at Wolfenbüttel are: a Psalter given by Corvinus to his wife Beatrice, who was also a book-lover; two collections of letters by the eminent Neoplatonist Marsilio Ficino, who lived in Florence and kept up a regular correspondence with the Hungarian court; a codex that had belonged to Bartolomeo della Fonte (who went to Corvinus's court in 1498 and spent some time there helping to put the royal library in order) containing various historical and literary writings of his and the texts of his lectures at Florence University; and an extravagant panegyric congratulating Corvinus on his conquests, written by the papal secretary Alessandro Cortesio with the objective of winning the Hungarian king's support for the papacy's policy towards the Turks.[19]

One of the most noteworthy sections of the Herzog August Library is the collection of some 6,000 incunabula. Outstanding among them are the thirty-six-line Bible printed by Gutenberg *circa* 1458[20] and Albrecht Pfister's 1461 Bamberg edition of *Der Edelstein* by Ulrich Boner, already mentioned (see p. 394). Other examples of Pfister's work include a large number of leaflets with printed indulgences and the first German translation of the Bible, dating from Luther's time. A unique item which broke new ground in many respects when it was printed is the first book to come from the press of Adam Steinschaber: the first edition of the *Histoire de la belle Mélusine* by Jean d'Arras (Geneva, 1478), which was one of the first books printed at Geneva, the first illustrated book printed there and the first work ever printed in French.[21] This, the only complete copy of the 1478 edition now extant, was bought by Duke Julius in 1576. Many of the incunabula contain literary works by local writers, local folk-tales and romances, including books by Hans Folz and

179. An illuminated initial from the Reichenau Lectionary (fol. 5).

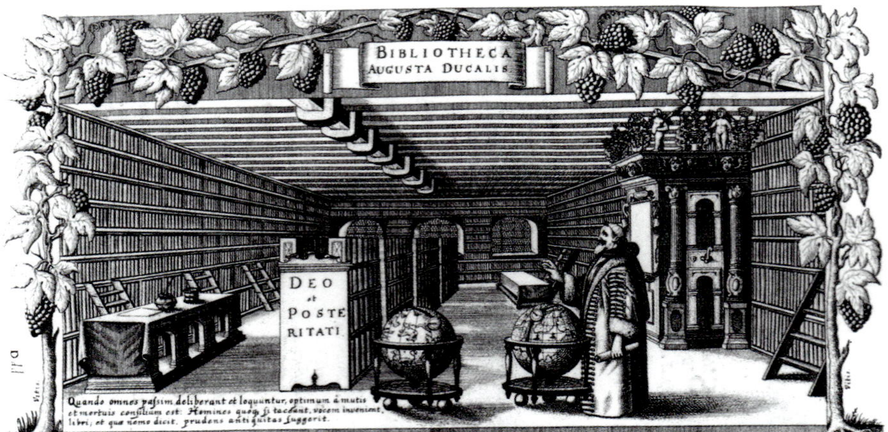

178. Duke August in his library. Engraving, 1650.

180. U. Boner, Der Edelstein, *Bamberg, A. Pfister, 1461.*

Raabe, 'The Herzog August Library...' IX-X.

14. See Raabe, 'The Herzog August Library...' X; M. Folkerts, 'Corpus Agrimensorum Romanorum' in *Wolfenbütteler Cimelien. Das Evangeliar Heinrichs des Löwen in der Herzog August Bibliothek* (Herzog August Library Exhibition Catalogues, No. 58), 1989, 28-32.

15. See Fedja Anzelewski, 'Reichenauer Perikopenbuch' in *Wolfenbütteler Cimelien...* 80-86.

16. See Raabe, *Lexikon...* 21.

17. See Ch. XXIII (pp. 447-463).

18. See J. Wieder, 'Les manuscrits Corviniens de la bibliothèque de Wolfenbüttel' in Raabe, 'The Herzog August Library...' 5.

19. See Wieder, *op. cit.* 6. The nine Corvinian manuscripts date from the last years of August's activity as a collector. They were illuminated at the studios of two famous Florentine miniaturists, Francesco di Antonio del Chierico and Attavante degli Attavanti.

20. On this Bible see H. Rei-

begryffen seynd· Eyn ander vrsach ist warū sy frey kunst genennet werden. das etwan alleyn die edlen freyen jüngling dise kunst lerneten· Aber die von dē böuel vnd vnedlen lernten die hantwerck vmb übung zů den wercken. wann übung des leybes ist dem gröbern volck bequemlicher· vnd übung des gemiets vñ rů des leibes gehört den edeln subtilen synnen als hugo spricht.

¶ Das· xxxv. capitel. von den zweien ersten freyē künsten· Gramatica vnd logica von irem vrsprung vñ vrsach warumb sy erfunden seynd· auch von irem lob vnd nutz· vnd zeletst von irem mißbrauch vñ vngemach·

SO wir in der gemaind von dē sybē künsten gesagt habent· so ist zimlich dz wir in sonderheit auch mit kurtzen worten von inen sagen· Vñ wellen von erst gramaticam vnd logicā berüren· darnach Rethoricā in dem andern Capitel· Sy werdendt auch

the famous first edition of the animal fable *Reineke Fuchs*, printed at Lübeck in 1498.[22]

Besides its splendid collection of early printed books, the library boasts 75,000 sixteenth-century editions and 120,000 of the seventeenth century. Clearly, then, it is much more than a repository of books evidencing the history and evolution of printing: indeed, it has a good cross-section of major works on philosophy, politics, religion and other branches of learning in German, Italian, English and French. These books provided local scholars and students with an invaluable reference

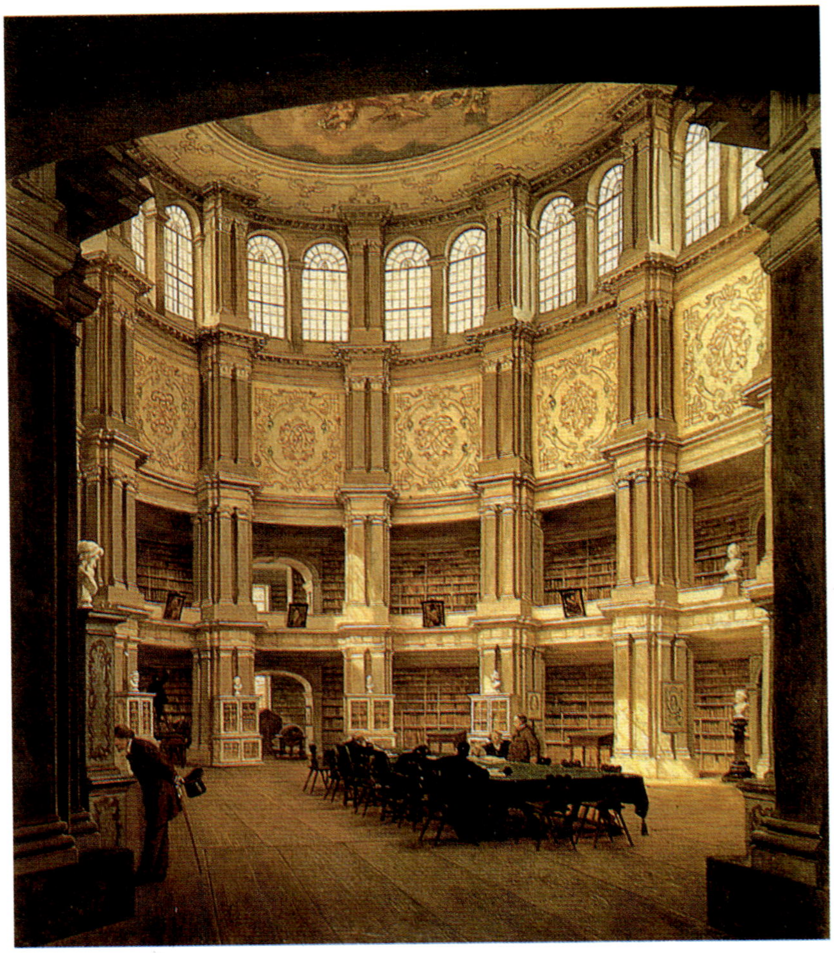

181. The domed central hall of the library as it was in 1887.

library, while many of them were typical of the humanist writings that helped to determine the direction of European thinking and so led to the Enlightenment. The Age of Reason itself is represented by 150,000 volumes, and two great luminaries of the Enlightenment, Leibniz[23] and Lessing,[24] actually served as librarians at Wolfenbüttel.

The library has a particularly fine cartography section including a number of unique Portuguese charts drawn on parchment in the sixteenth century, the great age of exploration, and embellished in colour.

nitzer, *Biblia deutsch. Luthers Bibelübersetzung und ihre Tradition* (Herzog August Library Exhibition Catalogues, No. 40), 1983.

21. See A. Lökkös, *Catalogue des incunables imprimés à Genève 1478-1500*, Geneva 1978, 14-17, No. 2.

22. J.C. Brunet, *Manuel du libraire et de l'amateur des livres*, IV, Paris (repr. Maisonneuve et Larose) 1966, 1224-1225.

23. Gottfried Wilhelm Leibniz, who was born at Leipzig in 1646 and died at Hannover in 1716, was one of the greatest geniuses of the modern era. His biographer, F. Hoefer (*NBG*

182. The library with the domed rotunda. After an engraving by A.A. Bech, c. 1766.

30 (1759) 465-500), suggests that Leibniz probably thought more profoundly than any other philosopher about the purpose and destiny of the human race with regard to work.

24. The well-known writer and philosopher Gotthold Ephraim Lessing, who was born at Kamenz, Saxony, in 1729 and died at Brunswick in 1781, did more than almost anyone else for the advancement of German literature.

25. See W. Milde, 'Die Kartensammlung' in Raabe, *Lexikon...* 91-92. The treasures of the Wolfenbüttel library were used as the basis for an exhibition in 1989 entitled 'Graecogermania', focussing on the various branches of learning in which German

183. Pseudo-Albertus Magnus, Compendium theologicae veritatis *[Strasbourg, Martin Schott, not before 1481] (515 Theol. 2).*

Wie ward meyster Jeronimus des hussen gesell außzgefürt vnd verbrannt da der husz verbrannt ward.

Other notable items are the maps of the Rhine by Kaspar Vogel (1555), a map of the world of 1570 and a magnificent map of Europe dated 1572.[25] The cartography section contains 4,500 items including thousands more maps of specialist interest and early terrestrial globes, such as Mercator's globe of 1541.[26]

Another notable feature of this glorious assortment of manuscripts and printed matter is the collection of prints of leading scholars and scientists from the Italian Renaissance to the Age of Enlightenment. This fascinating 'portrait gallery', comprising more than 40,000 prints, illuminates the close relationship that existed in those times between artists and intellectuals.[27]

In the Herzog August Library at Wolfenbüttel, that Ithaca of European scholars and of the humanist attitude towards the possession and use of books, the name of the founder, Duke Julius, is mentioned in an inscription carved on one of the interior doors, which offers the following advice to library users: 'If you come across something that does not entirely agree with your way of thinking, or something you find unacceptable, be calm about it and work on it quietly.'

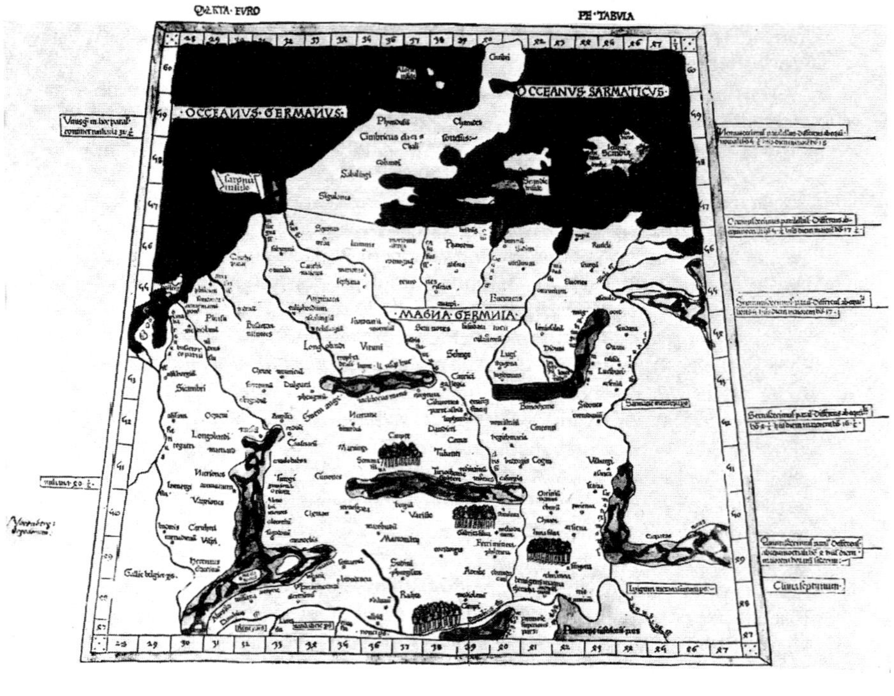

184. Map of the area that is now Germany in an edition of Ptolemy, Ulm 1482.

humanists drew on the knowledge of the ancient Greeks, such as geography and cartography. The twin pillars of those two sciences were Strabo and Ptolemy. Ptolemy was known in the West through Manuel Chrysoloras's manuscript of his *Cosmographia*, subsequently acquired by Palla Strozzi and translated into Latin, which was used as the basis for all the incunabular editions (p. 220). The maps were redrawn, with their Latin names added, by Francesco Lapaccini and Domenico di Lionardo Buoninsegni. The first scholars to take an interest in geography and cartography were humanists of Nürnberg, notably Regiomontanus, who set out to prepare an edition of Ptolemy's *Cosmographia*. This project never came to fruition, but his notes (translated into Latin) were included in the edition of the great bibliophile and Hellenist Willibald Pirckheimer, published at Strasbourg in 1525. The tradition started by Regiomontanus was continued by Martin Behaim, a native of Nürnberg who spent some years in the Netherlands before settling at the Portuguese court, where he joined the group of scientists working out the implications of the latest astronomical discoveries for navigators. Behaim informed them of Regiomontanus's findings and thus played a part in the construction of the first terrestrial globe, the Nürnberg globe of 1492: see 'Geographie und Kartographie' in *Graecogermania: Griechischstudien deutscher Humanisten. Die Editionstätigkeit der Griechen in der italienischen Renaissance (1469-1523)* (Herzog August Library Exhibition Catalogues, No. 59), 1989, 275-289.

26. See Raabe, 'The Herzog August Library...' XII.

27. *Ibid.*

185. Jean d'Arras, Histoire de la belle Mélusine, *Geneva, Adam Steinschaber, 1478.*

Comment melusine chait pasmee par terre pour la reproche que raymondin luy dist.

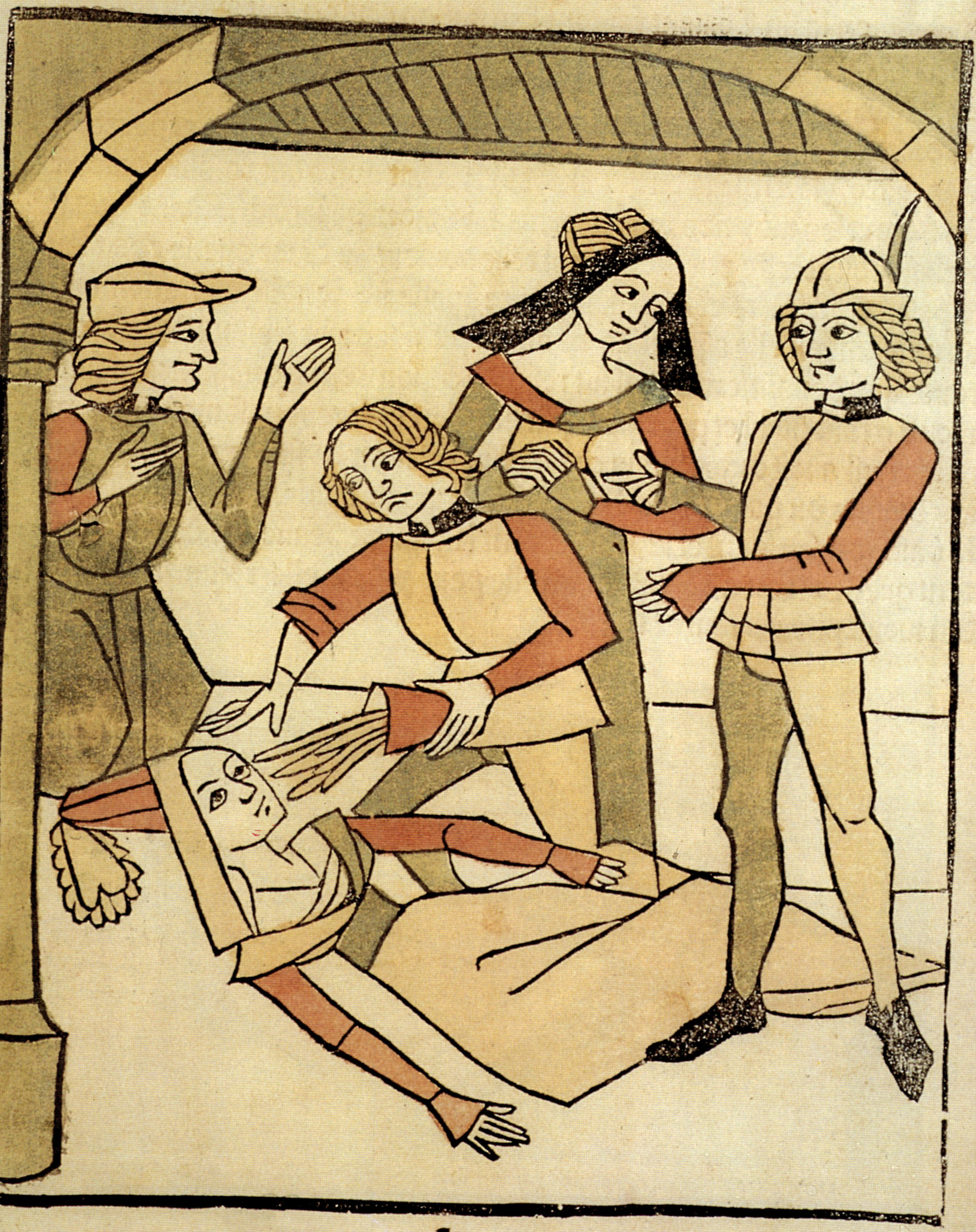

The Bibliothèque Nationale in Paris

CHAPTER TWENTY-ONE

Early in the sixteenth century Paris started to develop into a great humanist centre of the North, thus fulfilling the expectations of Petrarch, who had envisaged the city as a bastion of classicism where French scholars would once again immerse themselves in rhetoric and dialectics. It was at that time that the French royal library came into existence as such, although its origins go back tothe Middle Ages, to the private libraries of princes, statesmen and prelates in whom the meretricious attraction of collecting rarities was gradually superseded by a deeply-felt love of books.[1]

Pépin the Short (714-768), the energetic and indomitable king of the Franks, had a collection of manuscripts of no particular pretensions, like many other princes in the West. The first French ruler who can be credited with having formed a royal library was Charlemagne (742-814), the first Holy Roman Emperor. Although his own learning was merely superficial, he was keenly interested in the advancement of knowledge and gathered about him a circle of prestigious scholars as well as the most famous calligraphers and manuscript illuminators of the day. Charlemagne, himself a patron of literature, dearly wanted the Church to abandon its monopoly of learning and work towards the goal of wider education. The library he built up served as a model for his successors and also for other princely libraries in Europe, which now devoted more and more of their attention to the classics and contemporary writing.[2]

Charlemagne's biographer Einhard, who taught in the court school, also served as the Emperor's steward and was in charge of the royal library in the palace at Aix-la-Chapelle. In his *Vita Karoli*, Einhard states that when Charlemagne started his library in 780 he did so not as a mere collector of material things but because he was very interested in the classics and the writings of the Church Fathers. He enjoyed having historical and philosophical works read aloud to him with a small group of friends, his favourite being St. Augustine's *De civitate Dei*. He is known to have possessed several copies of the Bible and a number of historical works and poetry collections, including the *Silvae* of Statius, the *Cynegeticon* of Gratius, poems by Calpurnius Siculus and a manuscript of Nemesianus.[3]

Charlemagne remained strongly attached to humanistic ideals all his life, as attested by the provision he made in his will for the disposal of his library. Einhard, who was his executor, informs us that the Emperor wanted all his books to be sold on the open market and the proceeds given to the poor.[4] A gesture like that might have seemed natural enough in the Renaissance, but in the Middle Ages it was remarkably progressive. In the event, it appears that the Emperor's explicit instructions were not carried out to the letter: quite a number of manuscripts were kept in the court, or in the families of courtiers' relatives, and thanks to this dereliction of duty a good many of the manuscripts that Charlemagne had in his collection have been identified.

186. Paris. Woodcut from H. Schedel, Liber Chronicarum, *Nürnberg, Anton Koberger, 1493.*

CHAPTER 21
Bibliothèque Nationale, Paris

Whereas monasteries systematically collected valuable manuscripts and gradually built up large and well-stocked libraries, the collections of kings and princes lasted only as long as their owners were alive. Louis the Pious (Louis the Debonair), Charlemagne's son and successor, in general followed his father's example and amassed a collection of manuscripts, some of which he had copied for him by the best calligraphers while others were gifts from rulers in the West and the East. Angilbert de St. Riquier, for example, presented him with a copy of St.

187. St. John the Evangelist. Miniature in the Lorschen Evangeliar, Aachen, c. *810 (Cod. pal. lat. 50, fol. 67v).*

Augustine's *De doctrina christiana*, and ambassadors from the Byzantine Emperor Michael II the Stammerer in 827 brought with them a superb majuscule codex of works by Pseudo-Dionysius the Areopagite.[5] Writers and biblical exegetes gave copies of their works to Louis and to

1. See S. Balayé, *La Bibliothèque Nationale des origines à 1800*, Geneva 1988; A. Vernet (ed.), *Histoire des bibliothèques françaises. Les bibliothèques médiévales du VIe siècle à 1530*, Paris 1989, esp. 311-331 (= Denise Bloch, 'La formation de la Bibliothèque du Roi').

2. See K. Christ and A. Kern, 'Das Mittelalter' in F. Milkau and G. Leyh (ed.), *Handbuch der Bibliotheks-wissenschaft*, III, Wiesbaden 1953, 336-345; B. Bischoff, *Manuscripts and Libraries in the Age of Charlemagne*, tr. and ed. M. Gorman, Cambridge 1994, 56-75. Attempts to reconstruct Charlemagne's library have so far been unsuccessful except with regard to the Latin literature section, and even that with some reservations: see Bischoff, *op. cit.* 68-69. For more general information on the libraries and scriptoria of the period see É. Lesne, *Les Livres. Scriptoria et bibliothèques du commencement du VIIIe à la fin du XIe siècle* (=*Histoire de la propriété ecclésiastique en France*, IV), Lille 1938.

3. See Bischoff, *op. cit.* 56-58; *Einhardi Vita Karoli Magni*, ed. G. Waitz, Hannover 1911.

4. *PL* 97 60: 'Similiter et de libris, quorum magnam in bibliotheca sua copiam congregavit, statuit, ut ab his qui eos habere vellent, iusto pretio fuissent redempti, pretiumque in pauperibus erogatum.'

5. See B. Bischoff, 'Die Hofbibliothek unter Ludwig dem Frommen' in J.J.G. Alexander and M.T. Gibson (ed.), *Medieval Learning and Literature: Essays presented to Richard William Hunt*, Oxford 1976, 3-22; Bischoff, *Manuscripts and Libraries...* 76-92. Quite a body of legend is attached to this manuscript, which was regarded as a holy relic. In 827, on the eve of the feast of St. Denis (8th October), it was deposited at the Abbey of St. Denis on the orders of Louis the Pious, and within one night it was said to have healed nineteen sick persons. From that time on it was popularly believed that its author was St. Dionysius the Areopagite, the Athenian converted by St. Paul on the Areopagus in Athens, who was

his wife Judith, a woman of great learning who exerted a strong civilizing influence on the court from 819.[6]

Some time before 829 Louis the Pious engaged a monk from Lorsch named Gerward to be his librarian. Gerward was a member of the royal household from 814 and was subsequently given the title of *palatii bibliothecarius*. On Louis' death in 840, Gerward opened his will and discovered to his amazement that the Emperor had left instructions for his half-brother Drogo to prepare an inventory of his books and then give them away together with his personal effects (armour and clothes), thus following his father's example.[7]

From then until the time of King Charles V (the Wise), whose library was the most famous in France during the Middle Ages, the tradition initiated by Charlemagne was followed with little deviation. A clause in Charles the Bald's will stipulated that his collection of manuscripts was to be apportioned between his son and the abbeys of St. Denis and Compiègne.[8] And the sainted Louis IX (reigned 1226-1270), having taken the trouble to have a room fitted out for the storage and study of his books, eventually left them all to four monasteries: the Jacobin Monastery in Paris, Compiègne Abbey, the Franciscan Monastery in Paris and Royaumont Abbey.[9] This meant that Philip IV (the Fair) had to start a new collection from scratch, and only Jean II (the Good), who was crowned King of France in 1350, departed from the tradition to some extent by bequeathing certain manuscripts to two of his sons: some went to Jean, Duc de Berry, and a greater number to Charles V, who succeeded his father on the throne.[10]

Charles V (reigned 1364-1380) amassed a great collection of manuscripts in the course of his life. He was a convinced humanist at heart and took a serious interest in the education of his subjects, and indeed of the Christian world generally: he encouraged the translation into French of scholarly works which raised the intellectual standards of his time and he patronized Raoul de Presles, who made a French translation of St. Augustine's *De civitate Dei*.[11] The gifted poetess Christine de Pisan, a woman of Italian descent, was allowed free access to his books,[12] and Pierre Bohier rated him on a par with the Ptolemies (who possessed about 100,000 volumes) or Julius Caesar (who devoured all the books of every kind that he could lay his hands on), because Charles certainly did spend a great deal of time reading his books.[13]

In 1367 or 1368 Charles moved his library from the palace on the Île de la Cité to the top three floors of the Fauconnerie in the palace of the Louvre. He had all the walls panelled in walnut, put in heavy doors and brass window-bars for security and ordered lighting to be installed so that the library could be used in the evenings. Nor was this his only library, for he also had a good many books at his châteaux outside Paris (Beauté-sur-Marne, Vincennes).[14]

Charles's highly-developed artistic taste is also apparent in his choice

identified with the apostle of the Gauls who became the first bishop of Paris and founded the abbey. Abbot Hilduin had the text translated into Latin between 832 and 835, and innumerable copies of it were made thereafter. The original is now in the Bibliothèque Nationale (Par. gr. 437): see P. Lemerle, *῾Ο πρῶτος Βυζαντινός οὐμανισμός* (= *Le premier humanisme byzantin...*, tr. Maria Nystazopoulou-Pelekidou), Athens 1981, 22-24.

6. See F. von Bezold, 'Kaiserin Judith und ihr Dichter Walahfrid Strabo', *Historische Zeitschrift* 130 (1924) 377.

7. See K. Hampe, 'Zur Lebengeschichte Einhards', *Neues Archiv* 21 (1896) 611.

8. Balayé, *op. cit.* 2-3.

9. *Ibid.* 3.

10. On Jean II's library and his collections of manuscripts and miniatures see L. Delisle, *Recherches sur la librairie de Charles V*, I, Paris 1907, 326-336, and esp. pp. 327-328 on his bequests to his sons.

11. On Charles V's library see Delisle, *op. cit.* 1.

12. *Ibid.* 2-3. On her life and work see C.C. Willard, *The Writings of*

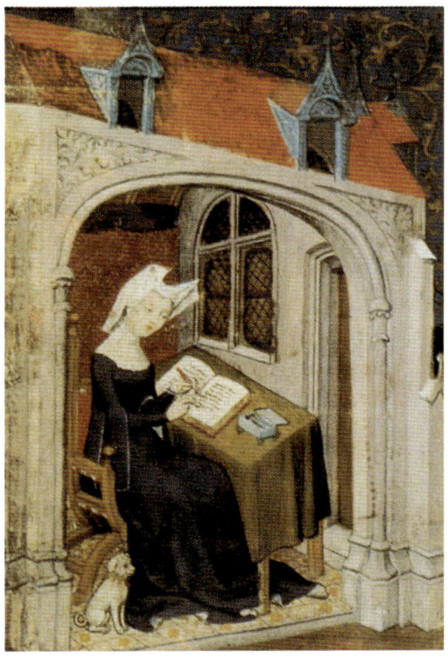

188. Christine de Pisan in her library. Miniature in Ms Harley 4431, British Library.

of calligraphers and miniaturists to enrich his library. They included such masters as Henri l'Uilier, copyist of *Le gouvernement des princes*,[15] Henri de Trevou, copyist of the second volume of the Bible in the French translation by Raoul de Presles, Jean l'Avenant, who had the title of *Scriptor librorum regis*, and the most famous of all, Raoulet d'Orléans, the calligrapher responsible for the little illuminated Bible given in 1362 to the Dauphin (the future Charles VI).[16] His collection included books in Latin as well as patristic writings in French translation and Greek classics in the original, and he commissioned Nicole Oresme to make new translations of Ptolemy and Aristotle. His special interest in Aristotle was due to his belief that he could learn from him how to be a good ruler of his country.[17]

Wishing to find someone with whom to share the pleasures and responsibilities of his superb book collection, Charles picked Gilles Mallet,[18] an energetic, honest, intelligent man with humanist leanings, and appointed him librarian. Mallet had entered the royal household in 1369, serving as a counsellor in daily contact with the King and holding a number of honorary positions at court. Many of the manuscripts in the royal library were acquired on his initiative and he compiled an inventory of the 917 codices in the collection, of which the original is lost but two copies survive, both dated 1380.[19] Mallet was kept on as librarian after the death of Charles V and held the post until he died in 1411.

Charles VI (1380-1422) was the first king to inherit the entire royal library on his accession. He took his responsibilities seriously and enlarged the collection by systematic purchases of manuscripts, but he failed to tighten up the efficiency of the library's lending policy. In fact he himself and Queen Isabeau were the main culprits: she, in particular, was in the habit of 'lending' manuscripts to friends of hers without making any attempt to ensure that they were returned.[20] April 1424 was a black month for the French royal library, as Garnier de Saint-Yon was instructed to prepare a catalogue listing the values of all the books that were to be sold to the Duke of Bedford, the English-appointed regent of France.[21] Bedford, a fanatical book-collector, had decided to enrich his library in England with the priceless manuscripts from the French royal library. He duly acquired all 843 of the manuscripts listed in the catalogue: most of them he shipped to England, and the rest he kept at his castle in Rouen.[22] Given his reputation as a bibliophile, there is no reason to suppose that he ever parted with any of his books during his lifetime; and so it came about that the collection built up by Charles V was eventually dispersed like those of his predecessors.

Meanwhile, in 1422, Charles VII had acceded to the French throne. His first concern, naturally enough, was to recover the French territories conquered by the English, which meant that he had no time to spare for re-creating the French royal library. Louis XI, who succeeded him in 1461, could hardly be described as a bibliophile, but he was certainly

Christine de Pisan, New York 1990.

13. *Ibid.* 3. Bohier's comments on Charles V are to be found in the preface to the *Vies des papes*, reprinted by Delisle, *op. cit.*, Appendix, XIII.

14. Delisle, *op. cit.* 8.

15. *Ibid.* 69.

16. *Ibid.* 69-70.

17. See F. Avril, *Bibliothèque Nationale. Manuscrits: La librairie de Charles V*, Paris 1968, 87-88 (Balayé, *op. cit.* 6-7).

18. Delisle, *op. cit.* 10-20.

19. The copies were made by Jean

189. Plotinus and St. Augustine. Miniature in a 15th-century manuscript of Raoul de Presles' French translation of De civitate Dei (Cité de Dieu), *fol. 289. Mâcon, Municipal Library.*

190. Petrarch, Des remèdes de fortune, *France (Paris?), shortly after 6th May 1503. Complimentary copy dedicated to King Louis XII (B.N., Ms Fr. 225).*

influenced by the humanist ideas spreading from Italy – especially from Florence, which was then the centre of the humanistic approach to learning and the arts – to such an extent that he was the first person to import Italian Renaissance books into France. In fact he was so taken with the new style of Florentine books that he engaged the services of copyists, translators and miniaturists (such as Jean Fouquet and Jean Bourdichon) for the expansion of the new royal library, and he appointed Laurent Paulmier as his new librarian.[23] In 1469 he confiscated ninety manuscripts from Cardinal Balue, who had fallen out of favour, and acquired part of the private library of his brother Charles de Guyenne.[24] On the death of Louis XI in 1483 his son Charles VIII inherited his books, and since then the French royal library has never been dispersed.

191. The devices of the French incunabular printers Jehan Alexandre and Martin Morin.

The invention of printing transformed the publishing scene in Europe and it rapidly became much easier for scholars and students in France, most of whom were far from wealthy, to acquire libraries of their own. In the thirty years of the incunabular period, from 1470 to 1500, French printing houses brought out about four thousand editions, thus ending the monopoly of the manuscript and opening the way for the large-scale growth of humanist libraries.[25] The first press to go into operation in Paris, and the first in France, was in the basement of the Sorbonne:[26] the university's interest in printing was stimulated partly by the existence of its fine library, founded in 1289 (which by the middle of the fourteenth century already boasted the remarkable number of approximately two thousand manuscripts), and more particularly by the

Blanchet in the year of Charles's death: see Delisle, *op. cit.* 23-25.

20. On Mallet's death in 1411 there were 188 volumes missing from the library, according to F. Avril (*op. cit.* 46). Delisle (*op. cit.* 131-132) lists the books that disappeared through the King's own negligence between 1380 and 1405 and those that were removed from the royal library by order of the Queen, who had a sizable collection of books of her own. See V. de Viriville, *La Bibliothèque d'Isabeau de Bavière, femme de Charles VI*, Paris 1858 (offprint from the *Bulletin du bibliophile* of 1858).

21. See Delisle, *op. cit.* 138-141. On the death of Charles VI there were still over 800 manuscripts in the royal library, in spite of the steady depletion of its stocks during his reign. When the Comte d'Angoulême was being held prisoner in London he happened to buy a book that had belonged to Charles V, with some notes in it which he recognized as being written in the King's handwriting (Ms Fr. 437).

22. Delisle, *op. cit.* 139.

23. According to the Abbé Jourdain, Louis XI gathered together the books that Charles V, Charles VI, Charles VII and he himself had kept in the various royal palaces and brought them all to Paris: see Jourdain's 'Mémoire historique sur la Bibliothèque du Roi', preface to *Catalogue des livres imprimés*, Paris 1739. Cardinal Jouffroy sent a number of manuscripts to the King from Rome and Florence, including a Latin translation of Strabo's *Geographia* copied at the famous scriptorium of Vespasiano da Bisticci (Lat. 4797).

24. See L. Delisle, *Le Cabinet des Manuscrits de la Bibliothèque Impériale: Étude sur la formation de ce dépôt*, I, Paris 1868, 79-83, 84-86.

25. See H.J. Martin, 'La naissance d'un médium' in *Le livre français, hier, aujourd'hui, demain*, Paris 1972,

192. Faustus Andrelinus, poem dedicated to François I. France (Paris?), spring of 1515. Complimentary copy dedicated to King François I (B.N., Ms Lat. 8397).

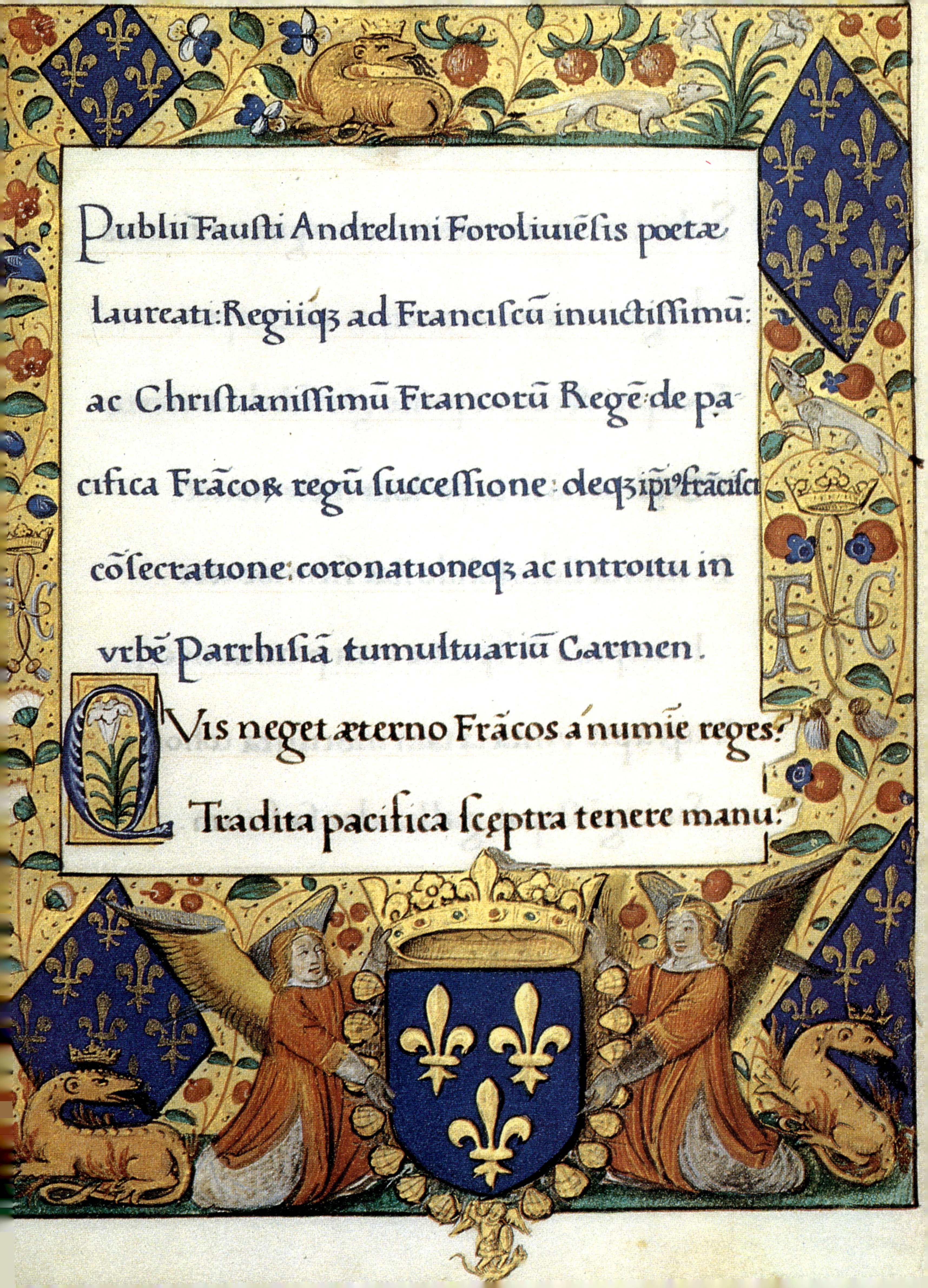

Publii Fausti Andrelini Foroliuiẽsis poetæ
laureati: Regiiq; ad Franciscũ inuictissimũ:
ac Christianissimũ Francorũ Regẽ de pacifica Frãcorum regnũ successione: deq; ipius Francisci
cõsecratione: coronationeq; ac introitu in
vrbẽ Parrhisiã tumultuariũ Carmen.

Quis neget æterno Frãcos a numĩe reges?
Tradita pacifica sceptra tenere manu?

Bibliothèque Nationale, Paris

towering personality of its Rector, Guillaume Fichet.[27]

Fichet, an admirer of the Platonist Cardinal Bessarion and a devotee of the Neoplatonist philosophy then being expounded by Marsilio Ficino and his fellow-humanist Johann Heynlin, invited three German printers to set up the first press in France. The first book brought out there was the *Epistolae* of Gasparino Barzizza, the celebrated teacher of Latin rhetoric, published in 1470.[28] The French were quickly won over to the new invention and printers of every nationality streamed out to all the major provincial cities of France, with the result that typography soon became an indispensable medium for the spread of learning. This is not to say that French noblemen who liked to collect works of literature and scholarship immediately turned their backs on manuscripts, but little by little they did start enriching their collections with printed books as well, showing a preference for those illustrated with elaborate miniatures after the Italian model.

The reign of Charles VIII (1483-1498) was marked by wars with Italy, especially after he came of age in 1491. On the pretext of assisting Ludovico il Moro, Duke of Milan, against the threat posed by Alfonso II of Naples, Charles invaded Italy with the ulterior motive of making himself King of Naples, claiming to have been granted the rightful title to the throne by the House of Anjou. Nor were his designs limited to the Italian peninsula, for he had bought the title to the imperial throne of Byzantium from Andreas Palaiologos and had ambitions of recovering the Christian lands conquered by the Turks.

On his victorious southward march in 1495 Charles captured Florence. The Medici he expelled as rulers of the city, but he went into ecstasies over their unrivalled collection of works of art, literature and scholarship. Most of the contents of their library had been removed to Venice for safe keeping,[29] so he had to be content with carrying off a few valuable manuscripts and illustrated printed books; but among them was an exquisite codex of works by Petrarch and sonnets by Dante, copied by Antonio Sinibaldi in 1476, that had belonged to Lorenzo de' Medici.[30] Most of the booty he took away with him from Italy was seized from the collections of the Aragonese kings of Naples, notably that of Alfonso the Magnanimous (1442-1458). Alfonso had built up his library after the death of Pope Nicholas V in 1455, when many of the latter's entourage of scholars moved to Naples and turned Alfonso's court into the greatest humanist centre in Italy: there Theodoros Gazis, George of Trebizond, Francesco Filelfo, Athanasios Chalkiopoulos, Lorenzo Valla, Poggio Bracciolini and many of the other Hellenists employed on the late Pope's ambitious projects continued work on their Latin translations of numerous Greek works which, either in manuscript or in printed form and suitably illustrated, ended up in the Neapolitan royal library.[31] Charles was guided round this treasure-house by the historian Paolo Emili, who advised him which manuscripts to take.

48-55; J.-M. Dureau, 'Les premiers ateliers français' in *Histoire de l'édition française*, I, Paris 1982, 162-175.

26. See R.H. Rouse, 'The Early Library of the Sorbonne', *Scriptorium* 21 (1967) 42-71, 226-251 (Pls. 5, 17, 18); R.H. and Mary A. Rouse, 'La bibliothèque du collège de la Sorbonne' in Vernet, *Histoire des bibliothèques françaises ... médiévales...* 113-123.

27. On Fichet, see: J. Philippe,

193. Ulrich Gering. Engraving by L. Bordan.

Guillaume Fichet, sa vie, ses oeuvres, Annecy 1892; A. Claudin, *The First Paris Press*, London 1989; F. Simone, 'Guillaume Fichet retore ed umanista', *Memorie della Reale Accademia delle Scienze di Torino*, 2nd ser., 69 (1939) 103-144; H.J. Martin, 'Les lectures de Guillaume Fichet et de Jean Heynlin d'après le registre de prêt de la bibliothèque de la Sorbonne', *Bibliothèque d'Humanisme et Renaissance* 17 (1955) 7-23, 145-153. For an extensive bibliography on Fichet's life and work see P.O. Kristeller, 'An Unknown Humanist Sermon on St. Stephen by Guillaume Fichet', *Mélanges Eugène Tisserant* 6 (1964) 459-497.

194. Binding of a codex of Petrarch's Trionfi *and other works. Florence, 1476, copied by A. Sinibaldi. This copy, which belonged to Lorenzo de' Medici, was given by the city of Florence to Charles VIII of France.*

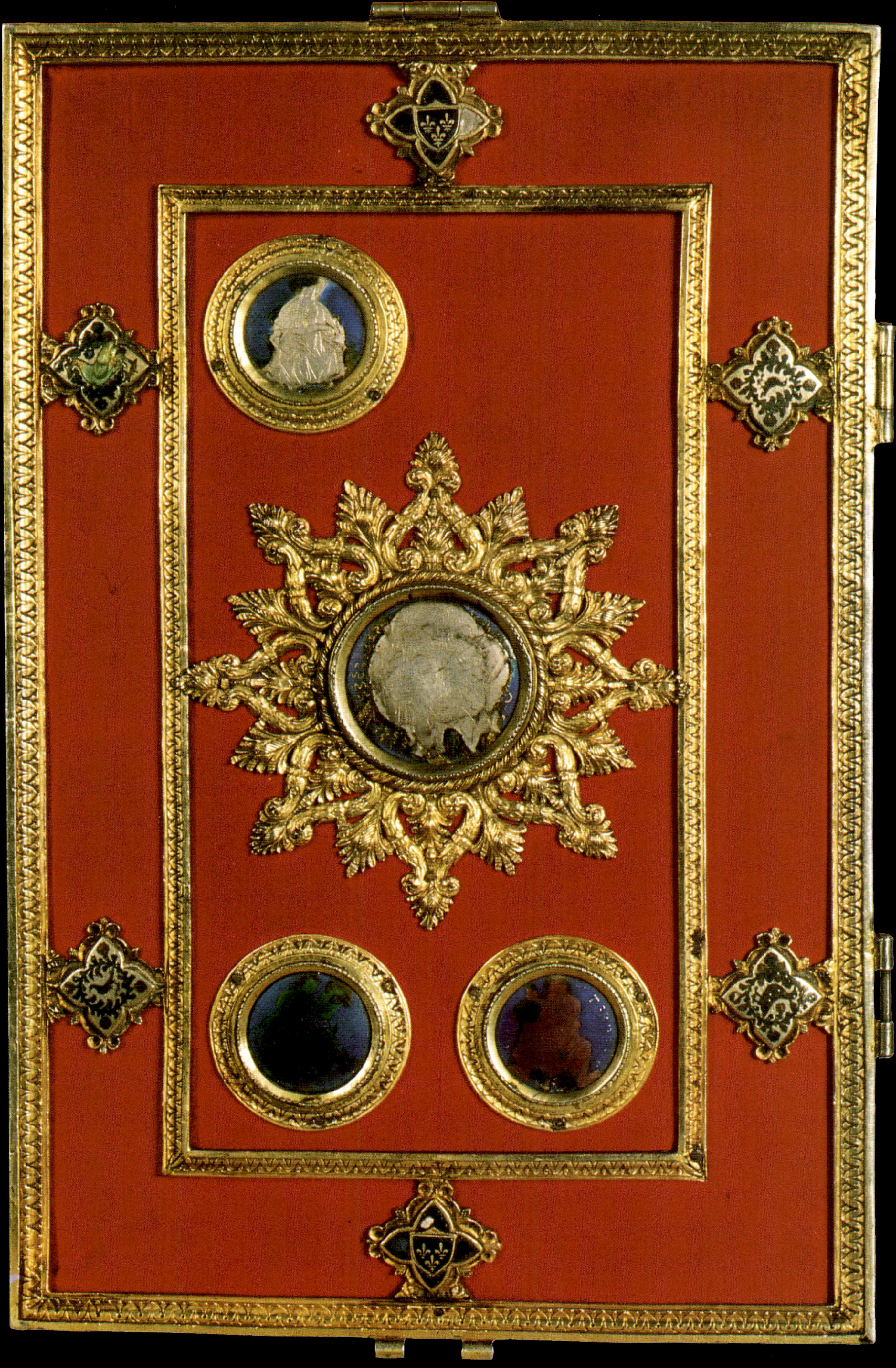

By the time he returned to Paris in 1496, Charles not only had with him a fabulous collection of valuable books and works of art but had also secured the services of Ianos Laskaris,[32] the cultural adviser to Lorenzo and Piero de' Medici, to work for him in Paris. However, Charles's untimely death at the age of twenty-seven prevented Laskaris from bringing his plans for the royal library to fruition. It is known that an inventory of Charles's household effects, compiled for his wife Anne of Brittany, listed 1,140 volumes looted from the Neapolitan royal library, but the inventory is lost and only 447 manuscript codices and 200 printed books can now be identified.[33] They include many that are of particular interest for what they tell us about the spread of humanism in France, for example 25 Greek manuscripts consisting mainly of religious works and two others (of the fourteenth and fifteenth centuries) containing tragedies by Sophocles and Euripides which had never before been available in France. The contents of Charles VIII's library, which had been kept at the château of Amboise, were not dispersed on his death but passed into the possession of his successor, Louis XII, who also inherited another, larger, family library.[34]

Louis XII (1498-1515) came to the throne at a time when the humanist movement was spreading throughout France, spearheaded by scholars at the French court and Italian humanists who were lured to cross the Alps by the information reaching them of the new spirit prevailing in Paris. Among the Frenchmen were Pierre de Courthardy, the brothers Guillaume and Guy de Rochefort and Robert Gaguin; among the Italians, Angelo Cato, Girolamo Balbi and Paolo Emili.[35] Paolo Emili went to Paris in 1483, at the invitation of Cardinal Charles de Bourbon, to study theology. The next year Girolamo Balbi arrived from Venice and four years after that, in 1488, two more Italians, Cornelio Vitelli de Cortone and Fausto Andrelini, added their contribution to the development of the humanistic outlook in Paris. Vitelli had spent fourteen years lecturing at Oxford, while Andrelini arrived from Rome fresh from his triumphs as the author of a collection of love poems entitled *Elegiae*.[36]

One who perfectly epitomizes the character of early French humanism is Jacques Lefèvre d'Etaples,[37] a scholar in the truest sense of the word, who was renowned for his industry. Lefèvre attended the lectures of Balbi and Andrelini, became acquainted with Paolo Emili, took lessons with Laskaris and eventually decided to devote himself to the renewal of philosophical thinking on the basis of the new interpretations of Aristotle combined with the study of Plato, whose ideas enthralled him. Having found where his interests lay, he travelled in Italy, spending some time in Florence, where he heard Poliziano, met and admired Ficino and was considerably taken with the humanistic views, religious beliefs and attitudes to scholarship developed by Pico della Mirándola.

It was because Louis XII was a scion of the House of Orléans that he inherited that family's library, which was built around the collection

28. On the edition of the *Epistolae*, see *BMC* VIII 2; Claudin, *op. cit.* 3-4.

29. See pp. 352.

30. See A. Chastel, *Art et humanisme à Florence au temps de Laurent le Magnifique*, Paris 1982; U. Baurmeister and M.-P. Laffite, *Des livres et des rois*, Paris 1992, 134-137.

31. See T. de Marinis, *La Biblioteca Napoletana dei Rè d'Aragona*, 4 vols., Milan 1947-1952, and *Supplemento*, 2 vols., Verona 1969.

195. Charles VIII of France. Engraving, 16th c.

32. See p. 346-348.

33. See Denise Bloch, 'La formation de la Bibliothèque du Roi' in Vernet, *Histoire des bibliothèques françaises ... médiévales...* 319. On 8th January 1499 Louis XII, having obtained an annulment of his marriage to Jeanne de France, married Anne of Brittany, and so the books that had belonged to Charles VIII and his queen, hitherto kept at Amboise, were moved to the royal palace at Blois.

34. Louis XII inherited the collection of the Dukes of Orléans, founded by Charles V's son Louis, who was

196. Claude de Seyssel, La victoire du roy contre les véniciens, *Paris, for Antoine Vérard, 1510 (Imprimés, Rés. Vélins 2776).*

Lexcellence & la felicite de la victoire q̄ eut le tres crestien roy de frãce loys. xii^e. de ce nom dit pere du peuple cõtre les Veniciẽs au lieu apelle agnadel pres la ville de carauas en la cõtree de giradade au pays de lõbardie Lan de grace mil cīq cẽs & neuf le. xiiii. iour de may. Cõposee p messire claude de seissel docteur en tous droictz / esleu de marseille / cõseiller & maistre des requestes ordinaires de lhostel dudit seigñr.

started by Charles V's son Louis, Duke of Orléans. Besides the many precious books bought in the French market, it had been enriched by manuscripts from private libraries in Milan, most notably that of the Visconti family, which came to Paris when Valentina Visconti married Duke Louis and brought her books with her as part of her dowry.[38] Louis XII also bought the fine collection of Louis de Bruges, the seigneur de la Gruthuyse, who had been an influential diplomat in the service of Dukes Philip the Good and Charles the Bold of Burgundy.[39] The King was wealthy enough to buy books on a large scale and have sumptuous illuminated manuscripts copied for him, with the result that his library was one of the best in fifteenth-century Europe. In 1499 Louis XII invaded Lombardy to secure his claim to suzerainty over Milan, and in the course of a two-year campaign he crushed the Milanese army; among the spoils he carried off was part of the famed Visconti-Sforza library from Pavia Castle.[40]

197. An engraving of Conrad Bade's print shop, which he used as his printer's mark.

The Sforza library, one of the greatest princely collections of the Italian Renaissance, was started by Galeazzo Visconti in the fourteenth century but also contained a number of volumes that had belonged to his predecessors. Nearly all the books in the library were virtually unknown in France: they included many manuscripts superbly illuminated by Italian miniaturists and 108 that had probably belonged to Petrarch. Among the latter were a commentary on St. Augustine by Petrarch, a translation of Homer, the *Natural History* of Pliny the Elder with notes

a great book-lover and started a library at his Paris residence in the Rue de la Poterne in 1393, at the age of twenty, by buying old manuscripts and systematically adding to his collection thereafter. See Delisle, *Le Cabinet des Manuscrits...* 98-104; P. Champion, *La librairie de Charles d'Orléans*, Paris 1910.

35. See A. Renaudet, *Préréforme et humanisme à Paris pendant les premières guerres d'Italie (1494-1517)*, Paris 1916, 118.

36. See Renaudet, *op. cit.* 122; R. Weiss, 'Andrelini, Fausto' in *DBI* 3 (1961) 138-141.

37. See Renaudet, *op. cit.* 130-135; G. Bedouelle, *Lefèvre d'Étaples et l'intelligence des écritures*, Paris 1976.

38. See Delisle, *Le Cabinet des Manuscrits...* 104-105; Élisabeth Pellegrin, *La bibliothèque des Visconti et des Sforza, ducs de Milan, au XVe siècle*, Paris 1955, and *Supplément*, Paris 1969.

198. Miniature by Lieven van Lathem in a manuscript of Les secrets d'Aristotes, *Bruges c. 1470 (B.N., Ms Fr. 562, fol. 7).*

199. In the royal library, c. 1488-1489. From an illuminated manuscript entitled La mer des histoires *made in honour of Charles VIII.*

by Petrarch and the *Commentaires sur les Psaumes* of Odon d' Asti.[41]

Louis XII, far from keeping his precious books hidden away under lock and key, was in the habit of displaying them proudly to visiting princes, ambassadors and men of letters. The man who probably did most to dissuade him from the vice of 'bibliotaphy' was Ianos Laskaris, whose expertise in the field of manuscripts and printed books was unrivalled. Laskaris wielded considerable influence at the French court, not only in matters relating to books and libraries. In the reign of Louis' predecessor, Charles VIII, he had been known as 'docteur des pays de Grèce' and had served as the royal adviser on eastern affairs; and when France was in difficulties with the Italian states after 1503, it was Laskaris whom Louis XII chose to send as his *ambassadeur par excellence* to strengthen French relations with Venice.[42]

One of Laskaris's claims to a place in the cultural history of France was his part in the reorganization of the royal library at Blois. Although the exact nature and extent of his contribution to the work is not known, the presumption must be that his knowledge and experience were considered essential for the cataloguing and arrangement of the manuscripts and printed books in the collection: it should not be forgotten that the library had recently been enlarged by the acquisition of the manuscripts which Charles VIII had carried off after his victorious campaign in Italy, the books seized by Louis XII from Pavia Castle, and the contents of the Visconti library, which were brought to Blois after the capture of Milan by the French in 1499. Moreover, the three years spent by Laskaris at Lorenzo de Alopa's press in Florence (1494-1496) had enabled him to form views of his own about printed books, which were carrying all before them in the Paris market.[43]

The distinguished French historian Claude de Seyssel visited the royal library at Blois several times and was full of admiration for its priceless treasures.[44] On one of his visits, perhaps in 1503, he offered to do whatever he could to enhance the King's enjoyment of his books, and so began his association with Laskaris: the latter agreed to translate Greek historical works into Latin, and Seyssel then put them into French for Louis XII to read. The fruits of their collaboration were French translations of *The History of the Successors of Alexander the Great* by Diodorus Siculus, Xenophon's *Anabasis* and Appian's *Roman History*.[45]

Following the death of Louis XII in 1515 and the accession of François I (1515-1547), France was the richest country in Europe, having made a strong recovery since the end of the Hundred Years' War. To say that the new king was a book-lover who carried on the tradition of his predecessors would be an understatement, for he was a man of profound intellect who founded the French royal library as such and the royal printing press.

From the very first years of his reign, François showed great interest in literature and the arts and created a thoroughly humanistic environ-

39. See J. van Praet, *Recherches sur Louis de Bruges*, Paris 1831.

40. Pellegrin, *op. cit.*

41. See Élisabeth Pellegrin, *Manuscrits de Pétrarque dans les bibliothèques de France*, Padua 1966.

42. See B. Knös, *Un ambassadeur de l'hellénisme – Janus Lascaris – et la tradition gréco-byzantine dans l'humanisme français*, Uppsala/Paris 1945; *Charta* 257-309.

43. On Laskaris's experience of printing and publishing, see *Charta* 272-288.

200. Ianos Laskaris. Engraving after an oil painting that belonged to Count Luigi Bossi of Milan: G. Roscoe, Vita e pontificato di Leone X, *VIII, Milan 1817, 48, 255.*

44. Claude de Seyssel (1450-1520) was in the service of Louis XII from 1498: see Knös, *op. cit.* 97-98.

45. See É. Legrand, *Bibliographie Hellénique, ou Description raisonnée des ouvrages publiés en grec par des grecs aux XVe et XVIe siècles*, I, Paris 1885, CLVIII. The only one of these

201. Dictys of Crete, De bello trojano, *Rome, early 14th c. Manuscript that belonged to Petrarch and was then acquired by the Aragonese kings of Naples (B.N., Ms Lat. 5690).*

quam auctores sunt eos qui de Samnitibus triumphasse
se Fabium exercitum in Apuliam processisse atque inde
magnas praedas egisse; nec discrepat quin dictator
eo anno A. Cornelius fuerit; id ambigitur belli-
ne gerendi causa creatus sit an ut, cum ludis
Romanis, quia L. Plautius praetor gravi morbo
forte implicitus erat, signum mittendis quadri-
gis daret functusque eo haud sane memorandi
imperii ministerio se dictatura abdicaret. Nec facile est aut rem rei aut auctorem auctori praeferre. Vi-
tiatam memoriam funebribus laudibus reor fal-
sisque imaginum titulis, dum familiae ad se quaeque
famam rerum gestarum honorumque fallente
mendacio trahunt; inde certe et singulorum gesta et publica monumenta rerum confusa. Nec
quisquam aequalis temporibus illis scriptor extat
quo satis certo auctore stetur.

Titi Livii ab urbe condita liber octavus explicit.
Incipit liber nonus feliciter.

Sequitur hunc annum no- *Cap. primum*
bilis clade Romana Cau-
dina pax T. Veturio Cal-
vino Sp. Postumio cons.
Samnites eo anno imperatorem
C. Pontium Herenni filium ha-
buerunt, patre longe prudentissimo natum, primum ipsum bellatorem ducemque. Is, ubi legati qui ad
dedendas res missi erant pace infecta redie-
runt, "Ne nihil actum" inquit "hac legatione cense-
atis, expiatum est quidquid ex foedere rupto irarum
in nos caelestium fuit. Satis scio, quibuscumque
diis cordi fuit subigi nos ad necessitatem deden-
di res quae ex nobis ex foedere repetitae fuerant,
iis non fuisse cordi tam superbe ab Romanis foederis expiationem spretam. Quid enim ultra fieri ad
placandos deos mitigandosque homines potuit
quam quod nos fecimus? Res hostium in praeda captas, quae belli iure nostrae videbantur,
remisimus; auctores belli, quia vivos non potui-
mus, perfunctos iam fato dedidimus; bona eo-
rum, ne quid ex contagione noxae remaneret penes nos,
Romam portavimus. Quid ultra tibi, Romane,
quid foederi, quid diis arbitris foederis debeo?
Quem tibi tuarum irarum, quem meorum suppli-
ciorum iudicem feram? Neminem, neque populum
neque privatum fugio. Quod si nihil cum po-
tentiore iuris humani relinquitur inopi, at ego
ad deos vindices intolerandae superbiae confugiam,
et precabor ut iras suas vertant in eos quibus
non suae redditae res, non alienae accumulatae
satis sint; quorum saevitiam non mors noxiorum,
non deditio exanimatorum corporum, non bona sequentia domini deditionem exsatient, pla-
cari nequeant nisi hauriendum sanguinem lani-
andaque viscera nostra praebuerimus. Iustum est
bellum, Samnites, quibus necessarium, et pia arma
quibus nulla nisi in armis relinquitur spes. Proinde cum rerum humanarum maximum momentum sit, quam propitiis rem, quam aversis agant
dis, pro certo habete priora bella adversus deos magis quam homines gessisse, hoc quod instat ducibus
ipsis dis gesturos." Haec non laeta magis quam
vera vaticinatus, exercitu educto circa Caudium castra quam potest occultissime locat. Inde ad Calatiam, ubi iam consules Romanos castra-
que esse audiebat, milites decem pastorum habi-
tu mittit pecoraque diversos alium alibi haud
procul Romanis pascere iubet praesidiis; ubi in-
ciderint in praedatores, ut idem omnibus sermo
constet, legiones Samnitium in Apulia esse, Luceriam omnibus copiis circumsedere, nec procul abesse
quin vi capiant. Iam is rumor ante de indu-
stria vulgatus venerat ad Romanos, sed fidem
auxere captivi eo maxime quod sermo inter
omnes congruebat. Haud erat dubium quin
Lucerinis opem Romanus ferret, bonis ac fi-
delibus sociis, simul ne Apulia omnis ad praesen-
tem terrorem deficeret. Ea modo qua irent con-
sultatio fuit. Duae ad Luceriam ferebant viae,
altera praeter oram Superi maris patens apertaque,
sed quanto tutior tanto fere longior, altera per
Furculas Caudinas brevior; sed ita natus locus
est: saltus duo alti, angusti silvosique sunt.

Sequitur hic. Cap. primum, in quo continetur exhortatio Pontii imperatoris Samnitum ad suos; inclusio Romanorum apud Caudium et exultatio Samnitum super Romanorum exercitum.

a. l. gessisse

Nota mirabile malitiam et magnam cautelam istius imperatoris Samnitum qua Romanos decepit.

Nota: xli capitulum [illegible]

ment around him, opening his doors to poets and painters, writers and printers. So enlightened was the atmosphere at his court that even Leonardo da Vinci was persuaded to leave Italy and settle in Paris under the king's personal patronage. François I came from a book-loving family and inherited a collection of books built up by Comte Jean d'Angoulême, a brother of Charles of Orléans.[46] No inventory of Louis XII's books was found on his death, but a catalogue of the Blois library drawn up in 1518 lists 1,626 volumes.[47] Theological works predominate but not overwhelmingly so, accounting for about one third of the total. The second-largest category comprises literary works, poetry and chival-

202. Greek-Latin dictionary belonging to Cardinal Charles de Bourbon. Manuscript copied by the Maître de Jacques de Besançon (B.N., Ms Gr. 55, fol. 1).

translations to be printed was *L'histoire des successeurs d'Alexandre le Grand* (Badius Ascensius, Paris, 1530): see P. Renouard, *Inventaire chronologique des éditions parisiennes du XVIe siècle (1501-1510)*, ed. Brigitte Moreau, II, Paris 1977, 404.

203. 'Portrait' of Josse Bade, 1494. See P. Renouard, J.B. Ascensius, *I, Paris 1908, 37.*

46. The fullest inventory of Jean d'Angoulême's books is to be found in G. Dupont-Ferrier, 'Jean d'Orléans comte d'Angoulême d'après sa bibliothèque', *Mélanges d'Histoire du Moyen Âge*, III, Paris 1897, 39-92.

47. See Balayé, *op. cit.* 27.

48. Laskaris also tried to establish Greek colleges modelled on that of Rome in other Italian cities, including Florence and Milan: see *Charta* 271.

49. Guillaume Budé, described by J.J. Scaliger as 'le plus grand grec de l'Europe', was one of the most eminent French classical scholars of his period and a profound believer in the ideals of humanism, which he followed even in the most trivial actions of his everyday life. His guiding principle was that it is breadth of learning, rather than eloquence, that makes the truly cultivated man. To defend Greek studies against a section of the French clergy, which denounced the views of the ancient Greeks as heretical, he wrote a treatise entitled *De Transitu Hellenismi ad Christianismum* in 1534 and dedicated it to François I (D.F. Penham, *De Transitu Hellenismi ad Christianismum*, New York (Columbia

ric romances; history comes in third place; there are about fifty volumes dealing with warfare, arithmetic and architecture; books on canon law and civil law represent barely ten per cent of the total; there are about eighty books on medicine and other sciences; and rather more than a hundred on philosophy.

In 1518 Laskaris, who was then living in Rome, revisited Paris bearing letters of recommendation from Pope Leo X addressed personally to François I, to explore the possibilities of opening a Greek college there.[48] His return sparked off a revival of interest in Greek literature in France, and Guillaume Budé, who was striving to promote Greek studies, found in him an invaluable ally.[49] Budé's first act was to persuade the King to transfer the royal library from Blois to Fontainebleau:[50] this was done not for reasons of mere ostentation but because by then a move was imperative, as the library premises at Blois were far too antiquated. And so François I's library found a new home in the royal palace of Fontainebleau, soon to become the most magnificent château in France after its renovation in 1528. The books were housed in a gallery directly below the one subsequently decorated by Rosso.[51] In about 1522 the King appointed Budé to the newly-created post of *Maître de la Librairie*, which he held until his death in 1540.[52] Budé was succeeded by Pierre de Chastel, a likable man who, as we shall see, was to be influential in giving the royal library a humanistic orientation.[53]

François' close association with Laskaris and Budé gave him the idea of building up a Greek library of his own, for which he mobilized a team of agents to look for Greek manuscripts in the East, and to a lesser extent in the West as well. The first person he sent out for this purpose was Gerolamo Fondulo, a former secretary of the philhellene Cardinal Salviati of Rome and a man whom Laskaris trusted absolutely. In 1529 Fondulo came back to Paris with some fifty manuscripts.[54] François then ordered his envoys in Venice – the names of Jean de Pins, Georges de Selve, Cardinal Georges d'Armagnac, Lazare de Baïf, François de Rossis and Guillaume Pellicier are mentioned[55] – to buy all the Greek manuscripts they could lay their hands on and to commission Greek scribes to copy others for his library. One of these envoys, probably Georges de Selve, brought to France an outstanding calligrapher from Crete named Angelos Vergikios (Ange Vergèce), who was given the job of copying Greek manuscripts for the royal library and was put in charge of the Greek collection.[56] The French ambassador in Constantinople, Antoine Rinçon, was instructed to look for manuscripts in the Ottoman Empire: he managed to obtain an introduction to the scholar Antonios Eparchos and bought thirty books from his private library, which Eparchos was willing to part with because he was so impoverished.[57] Meanwhile Chastel, who had travelled to Italy and the Middle East for the same purpose, enlisted the help of Pierre Gilles, Guillaume Postel

University) 1954). His most important work on Greek language and literature was *Commentarii Linguae Graecae*, printed by Josse Bade in Paris in 1529 (Renouard, *op. cit.* 239), which was a preliminary study for a full-scale Greek lexicon, the *Thesaurus Linguae Graecae*.

50. See Balayé, *op. cit.* 31. A Greek manuscript (B.N., Ms Gr. 1250) may have been given to François I by Laskaris at this time.

51. See P. Dan, *Trésor de merveilles de la maison royale de Fontainebleau*, Paris 1642, 98.

52. See Balayé, *op. cit.* 32.

53. *Ibid.* 32-35.

54. See Delisle, *Le Cabinet des Manuscrits*... 151.

55. See J. Irigoin, 'Les ambassadeurs à Venise et le commerce de manuscrits grecs dans les années 1540-1550' in *Venezia, centro di mediazione tra Oriente e Occidente, secoli XV-XVI. Aspetti e problemi*, II, Florence 1977, 399-413 and Pl. 2.

56. See P. de Nolhac, *Ronsard et l'Humanisme*, Paris 1921, 39.

57. See Delisle, *Le Cabinet des Manuscrits*... 157. On the purchase of Eparchos's codices see H. Omont, 'Catalogue des manuscrits grecs de Guillaume Pellisier, évêque de Montpellier, ambassadeur de François 1er à Venise', *Bibliothèque de l'École des*

204. King François I. Engraving from A. Thevet, Les vrais portraits et vies des hommes illustres, *II, Paris 1584.*

Bibliothèque Nationale, Paris

205. Guillaume Budé (1468-1540). Engraving by an anonymous artist.

and André Thevet. By 1552, after decades of collecting, the Fontainebleau library contained about 550 Greek codices, or perhaps more.[58]

François I cherished a dream of maintaining France's intellectual primacy in Europe by lavishing royal patronage on literature and education so as to breed a race of people capable of teaching the Christian faith and conforming to the law, not on the impulse of their own passions but in accordance with the principles of equality – in short, people who would be of service to the community at large.[59] With this object in view, and with the intention of creating a seat of learning comparable with the Museum founded by Ptolemy I in Alexandria, he founded the Collège Royal.[60] He also wished to raise the standard of Greek typography in the French court to the level attained by Aldus Manutius in Venice, and so in 1539 he engaged Conrad Neobar to take the matter in hand.[61] On Neobar's death the following year Robert Estienne, then *Imprimeur et libraire ès lettres hébraïques*, became responsible in practice for the printing of Greek books too, and he was officially appointed King's Printer in Greek in 1542.[62] That year marks the dawn of a new era for the printing of *editiones principes* of Greek classics and

Chartes 46 (1886) 13. See also Elli Yiotopoulou-Sisilianou, *'Αντώνιος ὁ Ἔπαρχος. Ἕνας Κερκυραῖος οὐμανιστής τοῦ ΙΣΤ' αἰώνα*, Athens 1978, 95-96. Eparchos first gave Rinçon a number of manuscripts as a gift to François I, who sent him 1,000 écus in payment for them.

58. See C. Astruc, *Byzance et la France médiévale*, Paris 1958, XXVII-XXVIII. Vergikios compiled a catalogue of the Greek manuscripts in 1544, listing the names of their donors or suppliers: this gives a total of 260, but by the end of François I's reign in 1547 the figure had risen to 400. A new catalogue compiled under Henri IV in 1552 lists 546 manuscripts. See also Omont, *op. cit.*

59. See Annie Parent, 'Les "Grecs du Roi" et l'étude du monde antique' in *L'art du livre à l'Imprimerie Nationale*, Paris 1973, 56-57.

206. Robert Estienne. Engraving from J. Verheiden, Af-beeldingen van sommighe in Godtswoort ervarene mannen..., *The Hague, B.C. Nienlandt, 1603, 56-57.*

60. See A. Lefranc, *Histoire du Collège de France*, Paris 1893.

61. The post of King's Printer in Greek was instituted by François I in 1539, and Conrad Neobar of Köln was its first holder. In that same year a hitherto unpublished commentary on Aristotle's *Rhetorica* was printed and dedicated to Georges de Selve.

patristic writings in the original, as well as other monumental works relevant to Greek studies, a high point being reached with the publication in 1544 of the *Ecclesiasticae Historiae* of Eusebius of Caesarea.[63] A new fount of Greek characters was cast, modelled on the handwriting of Angelos Vergikios: these types, of exquisite design and workmanship, were made by Claude Garamont, the greatest type-cutter and type-founder of his day.[64]

François I has so many claims to fame, not only for laying the foundations of the French royal library which later evolved into the Bibliothèque Nationale, but for all he did to develop the supranational humanistic spirit so characteristic of France in his reign, that even to summarize his achievements is quite beyond the scope of this book. It is perhaps fitting to close this chapter with an excerpt from the funeral oration delivered by Pierre de Chastel:

> Qui pourrait ne louer celuy qui a remis les aornemens de la Grèce en vie et en vigueur, la poësie, l'histoire, la philosophie, en son royaume; a faict chercher les livres, qui encore se cherchent par tout le monde, et faict tous les jours ressusciter autheurs et mémorables esperis qui estoyent il y a plus de mil ans ensepvelis?[65]

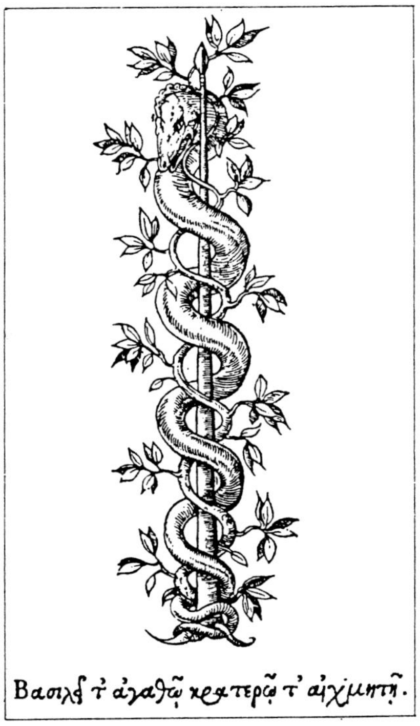

207. The device of the King's Printer in Greek. Eusebius Pamphili, Ecclesiasticae Historiae, *Paris 1544.*

208. Claude Garamont. Engraving, 1582.

See Elizabeth Armstrong, *Robert Estienne, Royal Printer: An historical study of the elder Stephanus*, Cambridge 1954, 118.

62. *Ibid.* 124-130.

63. *Ibid.* 131-138.

64. See P. Gusman, 'Claude Garamont, graveur des lettres grecques du roi, tailleur de caractères de l'Université (1480-1561)', *Byblis* 4 (1925) 85-95; Armstrong, *op. cit.* 51-52.

65. From P. Galland (ed.), *Petri Castellani vita*, Paris 1674, 221: see Balayé, *op. cit.* 43.

15 16 17 18 19
Maaß-Stab von 20 Wiener Klaffter oder 120 Schuh.

The Nationalbibliothek in Vienna

CHAPTER TWENTY-TWO

The man who changed the face of the Austrian Imperial Library (the Hofbibliothek) and spent thirty years of his life turning it from a private collection of the emperors' books into an organized library worthy of the *imperium* embodied in the Holy Roman Empire was the Dutch humanist and book-lover Hugo Blotius. Blotius took over the Hofbibliothek in 1575, at which time Emperor Maximilian II (1564-1576) possessed about 10,000 titles bound in 7,379 volumes, collected over a period of two centuries.

Hardly any records of the Hofbibliothek survive from before the time of Maximilian I, so its early history has to be reconstructed from secondary sources.[1] Duke Albrecht III of Austria (1365-1395) owned an evangelistary copied and illuminated in 1368 by Brünner Kanonikus, Pastor von Landskron and Johannes von Troppau: it is quite likely that he ordered it himself, considering what a fine collection of manuscripts he had. The priceless tenth-century codex known as the Palladius manuscript, recorded by Blotius in his catalogue of 1576, was probably one of Albrecht's acquisitions. Another person whose name is closely associated with the library is Emperor Frederick III (1440-1493), who, though not himself a scholar-prince like so many contemporary Italian rulers, nevertheless did much to promote literature and the arts in Austria. He was lucky enough to have at his disposal the great manuscript collection of his nephew Ladislaus Posthumus, who was Albrecht III's great-grandson and had inherited some valuable books of his. Frederick also acquired the magnificent library of Wenceslaus I (1378-1400), containing manuscripts with elaborate illuminations by the most famous miniaturists in Bohemia: more than 110 manuscripts from Frederick's collection have been identified in the Nationalbibliothek, including the Wenceslaus Bible, a number of imperial edicts and two volumes of astronomical writings.[2]

Frederick III marked some of his books – the oldest being Codex 2704, written in 1439 when he was still Duke of Austria – with a bookplate bearing the legend *AEIOU*, the meaning of which is still a mystery. Working out the hidden meaning of the five vowels presents a splendid challenge for lovers of riddles, and more than three hundred conjectures have been put forward so far. Jottings in the Emperor's private notebook suggest two possible interpretations, both similar in meaning: *Austriae est imperare orbi universo* ('It is Austria's destiny to rule the whole world') or *Als erdreich ist Oesterreich underthan* ('The whole earth is subject to Austria'). However, as Frederick was interested in oriental languages and had a leaning towards oriental mysticism, it is more than likely that the five vowels had some cabbalistic connotation.[3]

Frederick's only son was Maximilian I (1508-1519), the godson of that great Renaissance bibliophile Cardinal Bessarion.[4] Not only did Maximilian inherit a love of books from his godfather, but he was himself a talented writer, to judge by his autobiographical romances *Freydal*, *Theuerdank* and *Der Weisskunig*.[5] Maximilian I, who suc-

209. The exterior of the library. Engraving by Salomon Kleiner.

ceeded his father as King of the Romans in 1493 and as Emperor in 1508, was the first occupant of the Austrian throne to have any real humanistic leanings. He was on friendly terms with the scholars of his day and frequently sponsored research programmes with a scientific or humanistic slant. Even before he inherited his father's manuscripts he had acquired, through his two marriages, two priceless collections that came from the greatest manuscript centres of his time. By his marriage to Marie of Burgundy in 1473 the Habsburg dynasty came into possession of many superb specimens of Burgundian and Northern French miniature painting. These codices, valued in Maximilian's time at 100,000 guilders, represented about one eighth of Marie of Burgundy's personal fortune.[6] Although they belonged to Maximilian, they

210. Preliminary drawing of the Prunksaal. Engraving by J.A. Delsenbach, 1719.

1. The basic reference work for this chapter is J. Strummvoll (ed.), *Die Hofbibliothek (1368-1922)* (= *Geschichte der österreichischen Nationalbibliothek*, I), Vienna 1968. On the history of the library up to the Renaissance, see E. Trenkler, 'Die Frühzeit der Hofbibliothek (1368-1519)', *ibid.* 3-57.

2. See Trenkler, *op. cit.* 6. According to I. Mosel, the work of classifying and arranging the manuscripts was entrusted to two eminent scholars, Enea Silvio Piccolomini (the future Pope Pius II, a great bibliophile) and Georg Peurbach.

3. Most of the contents of Frederick's library are lost, and a good many manuscripts that were once thought to have belonged to him are no longer assigned to his collection. Of the sixty-nine codices he is known to have possessed, thirty-five deal with theology, ten with history, eight with mathematics, astronomy and medicine, and the other sixteen with miscellaneous other subjects: see Trenkler, *op. cit.* 6, 9-14; and esp. A. Lhotsky, 'Die Bibliothek Kaiser Friedrichs III', *Mitteilungen des Instituts für österreichische Geschichtsforschung* 58 (1958) 124-135. One of the masterpieces from his collection, the Wenceslaus Bible, is reproduced in O. Mazal (ed.), *Ein Weltgebaüde der Gedanken: Die Österreichische Nationalbibliothek*, Graz 1987, 61.

4. See Trenkler, *op. cit.* 10. Bessarion arrived in Vienna on 4th May 1460 on a diplomatic mission from the Vatican, with the object of persuading Frederick to give up his acquisitive designs on Hungarian territory. While there he was introduced by Nicolaus da Cusa to the humanist and astronomer Georg Peurbach and became friendly with the young Regiomontanus, who followed the Cardinal to Rome: see p. 326.

5. Cod. vindob. 2831, 2822 and n.s. 2645 respectively: see Trenkler, *op. cit.* 17. On Maximilian's love of books see T. Gottlieb, *Büchersammlung Kaiser Maximilians*, I, Leipzig 1900.

6. See Trenkler, *op. cit.* 15. The

211. The Prunksaal as it is today.

remained in Flanders for several decades. Some were brought to Vienna by his daughter Margaret and some others eventually reached the Hofbibliothek in the seventeenth century. In 1493, on his accession to the imperial throne, Maximilian married Bianca Maria Sforza, whose dowry included a representative selection of Italian manuscripts. The one collection of books that did not automatically pass into Maximilian's possession was that of his own father, as it was deemed to be Frederick's personal creation and his son's claim to it was a matter for negotiation. However, he did inherit the books that had belonged to his uncle Sigismund, even though the latter had made no provision for them in his will. Among them was the entire library of Georg von Liechtenstein, which had been brought to Innsbruck by Sigismund's father, Duke Frederick IV of Austria, after the capture of Trento. Maximilian managed to retrieve the manuscripts from Ladislaus Posthumus's collection, which had been dispersed, and thus he eventually realized one of his father's dearest wishes: that all the royal family's books should be concentrated in the hands of one person.[7]

Maximilian did not keep his books in a special room: like the princes of Italy and France in the early fifteenth century, he stored them in large and small leather-bound chests which accompanied him on his travels and went with him to his summer palace for his long vacations there. A document dated 7th February 1507 lists the documentary records and books in his possession, which were kept in two boxes in his castle at Wiener Neustadt. In a letter written some time between 1508 and 1513, when he was Emperor, he expressed his concern about the fate of the library of the late King Matthias Corvinus of Hungary: 'The Greek books must not be forgotten: it is in them that the flame of liberty is to be found. We shall decide what is to be done with them in negotiations with the King of Hungary.'[8]

Influenced by the tide of humanism flowing from Italy, Maximilian engaged Conrad Celtis, a humanist from Nürnberg, to be his librarian. Celtis, who was reputed to write the best poetry anywhere in Europe north of the Alps and was the first German poet to be honoured as such by the Emperor, had the good fortune to be befriended and taught by prominent Greek and Italian members of the humanist movement such as Giovanni Battista Guarino at Ferrara, Markos Mousouros at Padua and Pomponio Leto in Rome.[9] Celtis's contribution to the development of the Hofbibliothek cannot be assessed solely in terms of what he did as its librarian, as he was generally agreed to be one of the few Germans who worked as a true classical scholar in the Italian manner. Only a few years before his death in 1508 he described the imperial library as 'small, but enriched with Greek, Latin and exotic (Hebrew and Arabic) writers': he was referring to the manuscripts of Terence's plays, the German translations of Aesop's *Fables*, Aristotle's *Poetics* and many other works.[10]

library bequeathed to Marie of Burgundy by her father, Charles the Bold, contained not only his own books but also those of four earlier Dukes of Burgundy. On Maximilian's death this collection passed to his grandson, Emperor Charles V, and then to Charles's son, King Philip II of Spain, eventually becoming the nucleus of the Royal Library of the Netherlands, now known as the Library of King Albert I. See L. Delisle, *Le Cabinet des Manuscrits de la Bibliothèque Impériale: Étude sur la formation de ce dépôt*, I, Paris 1868, 68-71.

7. See Trenkler, *op. cit.* 15-16. On the Sforza library see Élisabeth Pellegrin, *La bibliothèque des Visconti et des Sforza, ducs de Milan, au XVe siècle*, Paris 1955.

8. See Trenkler, *op. cit.* 19. On the library of Matthias Corvinus see Ch. XXIII (pp. 447-463).

9. See Trenkler, *op. cit.* 22 ff. Conrad Celtis (1459-1508), after studying at Köln and Heidelberg, lectured on Platonic philosophy at various German universities. Although an able and resourceful man,

212. An engraving of Emperor Maximilian I (1459-1519).

213. Dioscorides. Constantinople, post 512 (Cod. vindob. med. gr. 1).

ΕΥΡΕϹΙϹ

Maximilian I died in 1519, and in accordance with his will ('My books and chronicles are to be carefully looked after, so that they will be there for my grandchildren to find') a large part of his library was moved from Vienna to Innsbruck. The next emperor was Maximilian's grandson Charles V (1519-1555), who was too preoccupied by the political and religious turmoil of the Reformation to take much interest in the imperial library. Charles was succeeded by his brother Ferdinand I (1558-1564), who was born at Alcalá in Spain and as a boy was fortunate enough to have Erasmus as his teacher. Although Ferdinand was well aware of the importance of books in his subjects' lives, he had no time to develop a policy of his own for the library, for it was only in 1531 that he was elected King of the Romans and he had to wait another quarter of a century and more before acceding to the throne of the Holy Roman Empire. His reign, marked by the rise of the Jesuits (who had opened a house in Vienna in 1551) and continuing strife between Catholics and Protestants, is widely regarded as the beginning of the history of the Hofbibliothek. No first-hand information about the library in Ferdinand's reign has come down to us, with the result that we can only draw inferences from the involvement of such scholars as Johannes Cuspinianus, Wolfgang Lazius, Kaspar von Niedbruck and Augerius Busbeck in the emperors' efforts to obtain new books.

Johannes Cuspinianus held a senior post in the imperial library and amassed an enormous collection of books of his own.[11] On his death in 1529 his books passed into the possession of the Viennese bishop Johann Fabri. Fabri, a prominent Reformer who made good use of his excellent library to support his religious convictions, bequeathed it on his death in 1541 to the Collegium Sancti Nicolai, which he had founded. However, it is clear from Blotius's catalogue of 1576 that some of the books which had belonged to Cuspinianus and Fabri were acquired by the Hofbibliothek.[12]

The man who did most to enrich the imperial library was Wolfgang Lazius, who, following the example of Poggio, combed the monastic libraries of Vienna and the surrounding country for rare manuscripts. Born in Vienna in 1514, he first studied medicine but soon went over to the humanities, and in 1536 he obtained a post at Vienna University as a lecturer in Classics. In 1547 he was appointed official historian to Ferdinand I and commissioned to write a history of the Empire and its peoples. In the course of his researches he made three long journeys (in 1548, 1549 and 1551), from which he brought back a fine haul of manuscripts to Vienna. His letters of recommendation from the Emperor opened all monastery doors and he purchased or was given a great many manuscripts; many more, too, he borrowed and never returned. Nowhere in his personal papers is there any suggestion that these were intended for the imperial library, which did not get them until after his death in 1565.[13]

214. An engraving of Conrad Celtis.

he never outgrew the influence of his Italian and Greek teachers. His dearest wish was that Germany should keep abreast of Italy in the rediscovery of the ancient world, and he was the first person to take a serious interest in his country's antiquities: in pursuit of that interest, he made a translation of Tacitus's *Germania* which attracted the attention of Enea Silvio Piccolomini and Nicolaus da Cusa. He also scoured the country to find manuscripts of medieval Germanic writers and discovered, among other things, the Latin epic *Ligurium* written in honour of Emperor Frederick I (12th c.). Celtis was a classicist who initiated a revival of German literature. In Vienna he founded the Societas Danubiana in imitation of the Societas Rhenana in Heidelberg, both of them being literary societies modelled on the Italian academies, especially the New Academy of Aldus Manutius in Venice. See H. Rupprich (ed.), *Der Briefwechsel des Konrad Celtis*, Munich 1934; L. Spitz, *Conrad Celtis, the German Arch-Humanist*, Cambridge Mass. 1957. On his relations with Aldus see M.J.C. Lowry,

215. King David, from a 6th c. manuscript of the Book of Genesis (Cod. vindob. gr. 31).

ΕΞΗΛΘΕΝ ΔΕ ΒΑΣΙΛΕΥΣ ΣΟΔΟΜΩΝ [illegible]
ΑΝΤΗΣΙΝ ΑΥΤΩ ΜΕΤΑ ΤΟ ΑΝΑΣΤΡ[illegible]
[illegible]ΤΗΣ ΚΟΠΗΣ ΤΩΝ ΒΑΣΙΛΕΩΝ ΕΙΣ ΤΗΝ
ΚΟΙΛΑΔΑ ΤΗΝ ΣΑΥΗ· ΚΑΙ ΜΕΛΧΙΣΕΔΕΚ ΒΑΣΙ
ΛΕΥΣ ΣΑΛΗΜ ΕΞΗΝΕΓΚΕΝ ΑΡΤΟΥΣ ΚΑΙ ΟΙΝΟΝ
ΗΝ ΔΕ ΙΕΡΕΥΣ ΤΟΥ ΘΥ ΤΟΥ ΥΨΙΣΤΟΥ ΚΑΙ
ΗΥΛΟΓΗΣΕΝ ΤΟΝ ΑΒΡΑΜ ΚΑΙ ΕΙΠΕΝ ΕΥΛΟΓΗ
ΜΕΝΟΣ ΑΒΡΑΜ ΤΩ ΘΩ ΤΩ ΥΨΙΣΤΩ ΟΣ ΕΚΤΙΣΕ
ΤΟΝ ΟΥΝΟΝ ΚΑΙ ΤΗΝ ΓΗΝ· ΚΑΙ ΕΥΛΟΓΗΤΟΣ Ο ΘΣ Ο
ΥΨΙΣΤΟΣ· ΟΣ ΠΑΡΕΔΩΚΕΝ ΤΟΥΣ ΕΧΘΡΟΥΣ ΣΟΥ
ΥΠΟΧΕΙΡΙΟΥΣ ΣΟΙ· ΚΑΙ ΕΔΩΚΕΝ ΑΥΤΩ ΔΕΚΑΤΗΝ
ΑΠΟ ΠΑΝΤΩΝ

Augerius Busbeck († 1592) was more closely associated with the Hofbibliothek than anyone else before Blotius. Like Lazius, he collected manuscripts for the Emperor: taking advantage of his position as ambassador in Constantinople from 1556 to 1562, he bought many valuable Greek manuscripts which he found in private and monastic libraries there, as well as books and manuscripts from the Corvinian Library, part of which had been dispersed in 1526.[14] Busbeck was Maximilian II's tutor and was also responsible for the imperial library. He accompanied Maximilian on his travels and stayed on in France from 1574 to supervise the administration of the property of Maximilian's daughter Elisabeth, who went back to Vienna on the death of her husband, King Charles IX of France.

Maximilian II became King of Bohemia in 1549 and Holy Roman Emperor in 1564. Soon after his accession to the Bohemian throne he took into his service a young diplomat with strong humanist leanings, Kaspar von Niedbruck. The bond that united them was neiher humanism nor an interest in the promotion of Greek literature, but theology. In particular, both of them were steadfast followers of Luther and resolute supporters of the cause of Matthias Flacius Illyricus, who had boldly set out to prove, on historical evidence, that the Lutheran Church was the only one properly entitled to call itself apostolic. Niedbruck bought books from the international book fair at Frankfurt and manuscripts from Prague and the Rhine valley. The manuscripts, before being handed over to the Hofbibliothek in Vienna, were copied at Regensburg for Flacius's private library.[15]

Another major contributor to the riches of the Hofbibliothek was Johannes Sambucus, who collected 565 Greek and Latin manuscripts including many that had belonged to eminent humanists such as Francesco Filelfo, Giovanni Pontano, Giorgio Antonio Vespucci, Guarino da Verona and Cardinal Bessarion.[16] From 1551 the library was assured of a guaranteed supply of new books as a result of the Ordinance of Montpellier, which required all printers holding the imperial franchise to give the Hofbibliothek one copy of every book they printed. Some years later, in 1558, Duke Albrecht of Bavaria persuaded Maximilian to buy the library of Johannes Albrecht Widmanstetter, a leading authority on Syria, before it was dispersed.[17]

From the time of Blotius's appointment as the official imperial librarian in 1575, the records of the Hofbibliothek cease to be fragmentary and the thousands of documents concerning proposals and ideas for its organization add up to an invaluable chronicle of library management. Hugo Blotius, born at Delft in 1534, was in the habit of translating his Dutch name of de Bloot ('naked') into Greek as *Gymnicus* with the epithet *Xylogaeus* ('Timberlander', a pun on the German *Hol(z)länder*). After attending the universities of Louvain and Orléans he travelled widely, going as far afield as Toledo in 1561, Basel (where a comedy he

The World of Aldus Manutius, Oxford 1979, 264-268; M. Sicherl, *Johannes Cuno, ein Wegbereiter des Griechischen in Deutschland*, Heidelberg 1978, 32.

10. See Trenkler, *op. cit.* 22; Gottlieb, *op. cit.* 32.

11. See Trenkler, *op. cit.* 27.

12. See F. Unterkircher, 'Vom Tode Maximilians I. bis zur Ernennung des Blotius (1519-1575)' in Strumvoll, *Die Hofbibliothek...* 61; and esp. H. Ankiwicz-Kleehoven, *Der Wiener Humanist Johannes Cuspinian*, Graz/Köln 1959.

13. See Unterkircher, *op. cit.* 62 ff. Lazius informs us that he started his library with thirty manuscripts,

216. The coat of arms of Wolfgang Lazius.

217. Illustrations from a copy of Dioscorides. Constantinople, post 512 (Cod. vindob. med. gr. 1).

had written was in production) in 1567, Strasbourg (where he lectured on ethics) in 1569, and finally Italy. Having visited the great centres of humanist studies at Padua, Rome, Naples and Venice, he returned to Vienna bearing fulsome letters of introduction from Aldus Manutius the younger to the doctor Johannes Crato.[18] These letters were to prove very useful for the advancement of his career: on the strength of them he was engaged as tutor to the son of the Hungarian Chancellor, Johann Listyus, and to Maximilian himself, and from 1572 to the son of Lazarus Schwendi, a general in the imperial army. In this way he acquired friends and protectors at court and in April 1575 he was given the post of imperial librarian, which moved him to write to his brother in an outburst of joy, 'O imperial library, o ornament of the Muses, o sweetness of my life, I salute thee. Thee I salute, the sole hope of my salvation.'[19]

At the time when the Emperor gave Blotius the key of the library with instructions to inspect all the books and compile a catalogue in duplicate, the books were kept in a small room in the Minorite Friary. The scene that met Blotius's eyes when he first entered the library gave him a shock that he never forgot, and in the introduction to his catalogue of 1575 he recorded the impression it had made on him: 'Dear God, what a state the library was in when we first saw it last July! How neglected and untidy it all appeared, how much damage had been done by insects and worms, and the whole place thick with cobwebs! When we opened the windows, which had been shut for months with no ray of sunlight ever penetrating the library, a fog of polluted air wafted out.'[20]

Blotius had ambitious plans for the Hofbibliothek and was confident that he would be able to create a 'library of mankind' surpassing all other royal libraries. From the moment of his appointment the destiny of the library was linked with his private life, and the vicissitudes of his family affairs had a direct impact on the library throughout his career. The post of imperial librarian brought in less money than he had expected and the Emperor did not honour his obligations: at one stage Blotius was owed three years' salary plus a further 600 guilders for extra work done on the library. Consequently he was forced to supplement his income with outside work, such as giving lessons in rhetoric, and it was only after his second marriage that he started to feel financially secure.[21]

One of Blotius's first acts after taking over as librarian was to advise the Emperor to draw up a set of library rules; yet, even though two assistants (*famuli*) were engaged in 1583 and the Emperor and his court were keen to develop and improve the library, its organization remained slipshod and not the slightest respect was shown for the value and importance of the manuscripts.[22] No particulars are known of the way the library was run in Blotius's time: we do not know, for example, whether or not it had fixed opening hours, who were allowed to use it or to borrow books, or whether it was possible for books to be read on the premises. According to Blotius's notes, it often happened that

acquired with great difficulty. These, and the manuscripts he garnered from libraries, monasteries and archives in Vienna, he used as the source material for his most important book, *Vienna Austriae: Rerum viennensium commentarii in quatuor libros distincti*, printed at Basel by J. Oporinus in 1546. See also H. Menhardt, 'Die Kärntner Bibliotheksreise des Wolfgang Lazius' in *Beiträge zur Geschichte und Kulturgeschichte Kärntens*, Klagenfurt 1936, 101-112.

14. See Unterkircher, *op. cit.* 71-73. Although Busbeck returned to Vienna in 1562, he kept the 274 Greek manuscripts he had collected in Constantinople for fourteen years before finally handing them over in 1576, in order to maximize his profit from the transaction. According to an entry dated 2nd March 1568 in the court accounts, he was paid the exorbitant sum of 200 guilders for binding the codices in the imperial library. One of the manuscripts he bought was the historic codex of Dioscorides' *De materia medica* (*Περί ὕλης ἰατρικῆς*), written in about 512 for Princess Juliana Anicia, a granddaughter of the Roman Emperor Valentinian III. This codex, which had been in the library of the Prodromos Monastery (the home of the Katholikon Mouseion: see pp. 168) since the end of the fourteenth century, had come into the possession of the Jewish physician of Sultan Süleyman the Magnificent, who sold it to Busbeck. *De materia medica* was written by Dioscorides in the first century A.D., but it is basically a digest of an earlier work by Cratenas, the physician to King Mithradates VI of Pontus (120-63 B.C.). On Mithradates' library and his interest in medicine see p. 101. At the front of this manuscript, on what would normally be the title page, is the oldest extant dedicatory illumination, showing Princess Juliana seated in solemn state with a cupid offering her a bound manuscript in token of the

218. Aristotle, from a manuscript of his Historia naturalis, *Rome 1457 (Cod. vindob. phil. gr. 64).*

ΤΕ
ΑΡΙϹΤΟΛΗϹ

manuscripts were lent out or taken away to Prague, where Rudolf II (1576-1602) had his court, without being returned to the library. In vain did Blotius protest to the Emperor about his habit of sending scribbled notes ordering manuscripts to be sent to him without acknowledgement of receipt: Rudolf showed no inclination to change his ways. Since he was powerless to put this chaotic situation to rights, and since it would seem that there were not in fact any facilities for serious study in the library, Blotius started lending the books out indiscriminately, mainly for the purpose of winning new friends in high places. In 1593 a three-man committee was formed to scrutinize the library's affairs, and before long it prepared a report on the state of the Hofbibliothek with comments on the way it was managed and the favours granted by Blotius to foreign visitors. The report has not survived, but evidently it was far from favourable to the imperial librarian and undermined Maximilian's confidence in him.[23]

Towards the end of the sixteenth century Blotius began to feel the strain of his ever-increasing workload and heavy responsibilities, and in 1595 he wrote: 'In my twenty years in the service of two emperors, Maximilian II and Rudolf II, in addition to my scientific and financial duties I have had to run round closing the windows whenever there is a rainstorm and opening them again to let in the sun, and to watch the servants when they sweep the floor. Since the discovery of the theft I have had to do these chores myself, and other dirty work too – I, a Doctor of Law and the keeper of the great Emperor's library!' Thoroughly disenchanted, he felt old before his time, and in 1597 he wrote despondently to his friend Hubertus Giphanius, 'I am old and decaying at sixty-four, and naked [*Bloot*], because I am not paid by the Emperor, nor do my tenants pay their rent.'[24] In 1600, on the death of his 'Inspector', Strein, his own position was upgraded, but he remarked ruefully, 'I await the arrival of another nobleman, half-educated and full of officious zeal.' Blotius's mistrust of the aristocracy was entirely justified. He was always lending library books in good faith to princes and court favourites and then being unable to get them back: no matter how often he reminded them, they coolly answered that the books had been lost, and if they had died in the meantime their relatives claimed to know nothing about the matter. Nevertheless he went on lending books out as before and continued to allow free access to the library on the principle that 'A library that keeps its doors closed is like a candle inside a barrel, which burns but gives no light.'[25] In the last years of his life he handed over most of the work of running the library to his successor Tengnagel, and in 1608 he died, having neither realized his ambitions for the library nor discharged his obligations to the emperors.[26] The truth is that he did not receive the support he expected for so responsible a job as that of organizing the Austrian imperial library in the early seventeenth century.

gratitude of the inhabitants of a Constantinopolitan suburb for her generosity in building a church for them in 512 or 513. See Eleni Kakoulidi, «Ἡ Βιβλιοθήκη τῆς Μονῆς Προδρόμου-Πέτρας στήν Κωνσταντινούπολη», *Ἑλληνικά* 21 (1968) 7-8. On the distinctive features of the manuscript see: J. Ebersolt, *La miniature byzantine*, Brussels 1926, 14 Pl. VII; G. Galavaris, *Ζωγραφική Βυζαντινῶν Χειρογράφων*, Athens 1995, 18, 35, 213.

15. See Unterkircher, *op. cit.* 67-69. Niedbruck never held the post of librarian of the Hofbibliothek, although he was well qualified to do so: apart from anything else, his duties in the diplomatic service of Maximilian II (from 1550) and Ferdinand I (from 1553) kept him away from Vienna for long periods. Niedbruck was born at Bolchen in 1525 and spent ten years as a student at various universities. He heard Calvin speak in 1539 and later became a follower of Melanchthon and Flacius Illyricus. He completed

219. Juliana Anicia between Magnanimity and Prudence. From Dioscorides. Constantinople, post 512 (Cod. vindob. med. gr. 1, fol. 6v).

220. Christ the Pantokrator in a Gospel book written by the monk Andreas in 1109 (Cod. vindob. suppl. gr. 164, fol. 5r).

+ Σὺ Χ(ριστ)ὲ πόθον καὶ σοῖς ζωηροῖς λογίοις· πολλὴν ὑπὸ σαρκὴν πε-
ράθρων ἀόρατον· ζάλην ἀμέτρου περὶ κοσμικὴν τοιαύ-
ταις τῶν ὁρατῶν καὶ φθειρομένων ἀρετῶν· ἐπὶ τῶν ἀδελφῶν στομένις τοῦ
κοινοῦ βίου, ὁμάδης καὶ σκώμματα ἐφέρησιν καὶ θλῖψιν· φεύδω τὸ ὕψος ὁ ἐρ-
γαστήρια· κόπον ὡς σίδηρος ὑπὲρ δύναμιν πᾶσαν· καὶ μόλις ἐξισχύσα-
τη ... ἀφηριζόμενος σοῦ γράψαι πᾶσαν· ταύτην τὴν βί-
βλον τὴν ... διαθήκην· καὶ ἐξύφαινα τὸν πόθον τῆς καρδίας· καὶ
... τῆς ψυχῆς μου τὸ φίλτρον· αὐτὸς οὖν φιλάνθρωπε καὶ
ὁ κριτὰς πρόσδεξαι ταύτην ... λύσιν τῶν κακῶν μου· ...
ὧν περ ἥμαρτον ἐν ὅλη τῆ ζωῆ μου· καὶ τάξον κἀμὲ μετὰ
τῶν ἐκλεκτῶν σου· τῶν ἠγαπηκότων σε ἐκ ψυχῆς ὅλης:—
εὐχέσθε τῷ γράψαντι ἀναγινώσκοντες:— + Ναὶ ... διὰ τὸν κ(ύριο)ν

Blotius set out his ideas on how the Hofibliothek ought to be run in a lengthy report to the Emperor dated 8th September 1579.[27] It is worth summarizing the main points of the report, because they are of great interest for the light they shed on contemporary library practice and some of them are still relevant today.

Writing in faultless Latin, Blotius starts with the assertion that not enough use has been made of the best way of enriching the library, because he was not kept informed by the Chancellery of the names of the printers who had been granted the imperial franchise (*Druckpriviligien*), with the result that printers often defaulted on their obligation to send copies of all their publications to the library. And even when books did reach the library by this route, the Emperor often gave them away to friends and members of the aristocracy, thus depriving the library of major works such as the quadrilingual Bible printed by Plantin in Antwerp. Other great obstacles to the smooth running of the library, as we have seen, were the non-existence of any kind of lending policy and the untrustworthiness of those who bought books for the Emperor, like Flacius Illyricus. In the second section of the report Blotius points out that it would be quite a simple matter for the library to be greatly enlarged: a regular allocation of funds would be needed for the purchase of books, a strict check would have to be kept on everything produced by printers holding the imperial franchise and a certain amount of money would need to be spent on the conservation of books and manuscripts and the painting and decoration of the library. In the third section, which is concerned with the qualifications required of the librarian, Blotius says that the ideal person for the job would work full-time in the library, with no outside employment; he would be a linguist; he would be honest, reliable, hard-working and careful; he would not be poor; he would not be superstitious; and he would be naturally studious, with a deep-seated love of books.[28] Finally, Blotius mentions his own qualifications, such as his erudition (he spoke six or seven languages), adding that he made regular trips to the international book fair at Frankfurt and to monasteries in Europe. In his view, the post of imperial librarian should be held by a nobleman: he cites the examples of the Vatican Library, whose librarian was a cardinal, and the Biblioteca Laurenziana, where the position was given to a member of the aristocracy.[29]

Architecture. More than a century was to pass after Blotius's death before the Hofbibliothek found premises in a building worthy of the quality and value of its contents and the power of the Austrian Empire under the Habsburgs. In 1722 Emperor Charles VI gave orders that the library was to be accommodated in the planned new building in the grounds of the riding school in the Hofburg, which was to be designed by Graf von Althan. Who actually designed the Library is another matter, for the extant sources are far from clear on the subject. All the

221. Medallion with an effigy of Hugo Blotius.

his studies in Italy, at the universities of Padua and Bologna. His early death in 1557 while on a diplomatic mission to Brussels prevented him from seeing the publication of the first volume of his monumental work *Magdeburger Centurien*, published in ten volumes between 1558 and 1574, for which he had amassed an unprecedented quantity of archival material. See V. Bibl, 'Niedbruck und Tanner: Ein Beitrag zur Entstehungsgeschichte den Magdeburger Centurien und zur Charakteristik König Maximilians II.', *Archiv für österreichische Geschichte* 85 (1898) 379-430.

16. See Trenkler, *op. cit.* 73. Sambucus, born at Tyrnau in 1531, spent ten years at universities in various parts of Europe (Ingolstadt, Strasbourg, Paris, Padua, Venice, Bologna). In 1557 he acquired friends at court and became a member of the royal household. His particular interests were philosophy, medicine and history. See H. Gerstinger, 'Johannes Sambucus als Handschriftensammler' in *Festschrift der Nationalbibliothek*, Vienna 1926, 251-400.

17. This regulation, probably proposed after the promulgation of the Ordinance of Montpellier, required all printers holding the imperial franchise to surrender three copies of every book they printed, of which one was destined for the Hofbibliothek.

18. See F. Unterkircher, 'Hugo

available evidence points to the conclusion that the designs were almost certainly drawn by the architectural firm of Johann Bernhard Fischer von Erlach and that the building was completed by his son, Joseph Emanuel.[30]

The first thing likely to strike an observant visitor is that the interior architecture and decoration of the library are in a different style from the exterior. The façade is in the French architectural style of the early eighteenth century and has none of the Baroque features typical of so many other buildings in Vienna.[31] The interior of the Great Hall is one of the most beautiful library interiors ever built. The Prunksaal, as the

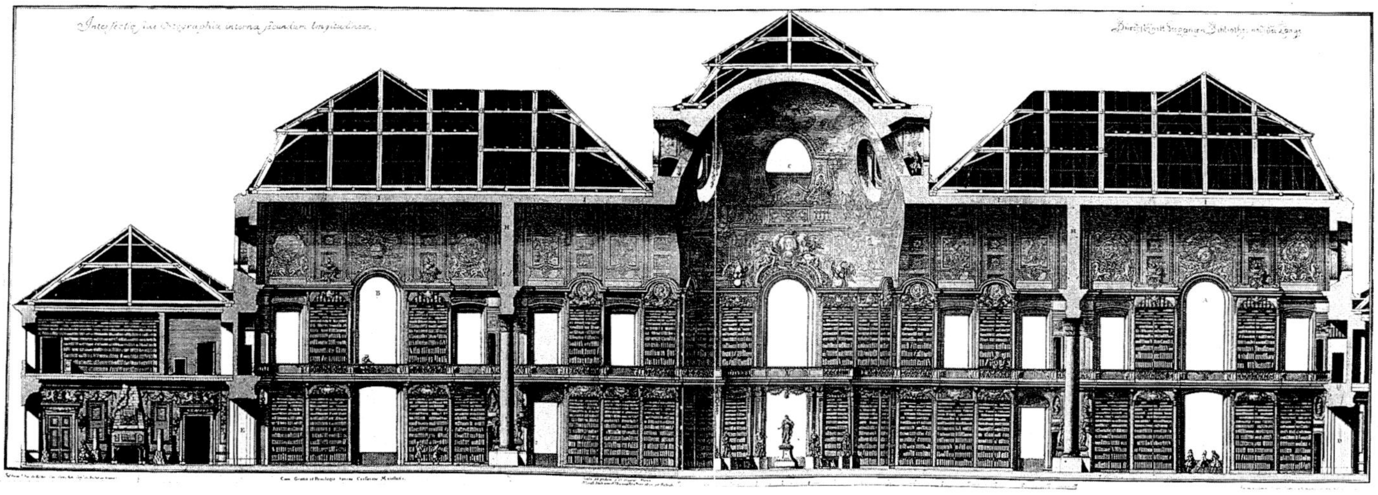

222. Side elevation of the Prunksaal. Drawing by Salomon Kleiner.

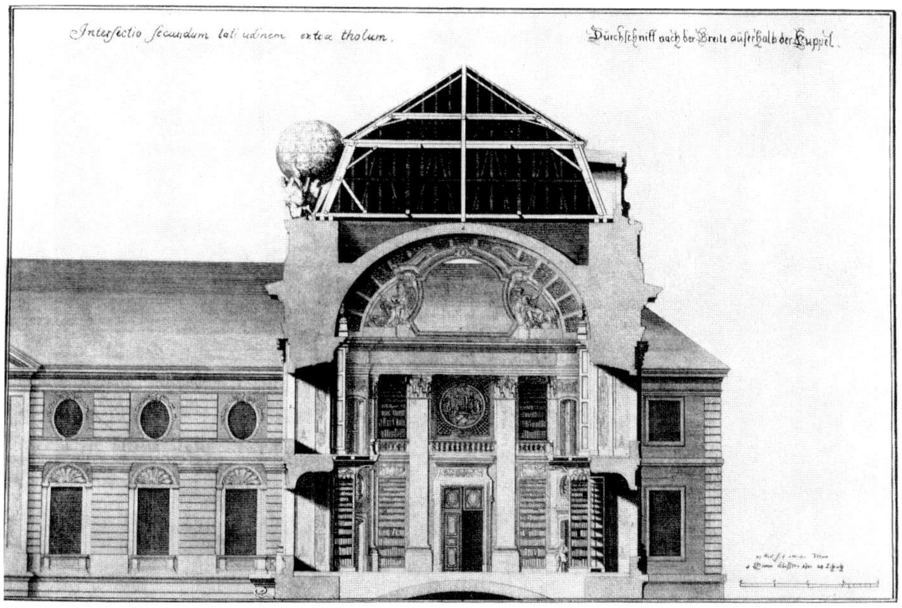

223. Vertical section of the Prunksaal. Drawing by Salomon Kleiner.

Blotius (1575-1608). Sein Leben' in Strumvoll, *Die Hofbibliothek...* 81-127. Blotius's writings about his work provide historians with a rich source of primary material relating to the library. He was someone who enjoyed writing, so the documents in question are numbered in thousands: historical and scholarly papers, catalogues, copious notes on points of librarianship, plans and proposals addressed to the Emperor, and innumerable letters to the friends and acquaintances all over Europe with whom he corresponded.

19. See Unterkircher, *op. cit.* 86.

20. *Ibid.* 87-88.

21. *Ibid.* 91.

22. *Ibid.* 92-93. Blotius enumerates the library assistants' duties in one of his letters. They were required to attend on the librarian, to look after his clothes and shoes and to have three or four hours of schooling daily for a year: once they had acquired the necessary education, they would have more time to devote to more specialized matters. Provided they had shown themselves capable of handling the manuscripts with proper care and respect, they were then allowed to use the Emperor's books without any restriction. In the 1590s, when Blotius moved house and was

Great Hall is usually known, is cruciform in plan, with a large dome over the crossing supported by a drum with eight large windows. The whole roof appears to be supported by two pairs of marble Corinthian columns standing in the aisle at an equal distance from the crossing. The shelving is on two levels, the ground floor and an upper gallery: it is all of solid wood, and the decorative carvings (capitals, ornamental brackets, palmettes, etc.) are gilded. An elaborately carved balustrade, made and decorated in the same way as the shelving, runs all along the upper gallery. Another feature of the interior of the Prunksaal, not found in otherwise similar monumental libraries such as those of Strahov Abbey in Prague and the Abbey of St. Gall in Switzerland, is the presence of numerous statues of Austrian emperors and princes positioned symmetrically around the hall.[32]

224. An 18th c. print of the library building, after a drawing by Salomon Kleiner.

The shelving visible from the floor of the Prunksaal, in which the carved and gilded ornamentation of the woodwork is well set off by the rich bindings of the books that fill every inch of the shelf space, conceals what amounts to a second, hidden, library. This is reached by way of sections of shelving that serve as secret doors, swinging open to reveal spiral staircases leading up to the gallery with yet more shelves of books lining the stairwells. The walls above the shelving, as well as the vaults and the interior of the dome, are painted with frescoes in a distinctive style, in colours reminiscent of the Italian Renaissance. As far as is known, the entire interior decoration scheme was designed and executed by Daniel Gran.[33]

living a long way away from the library, he decided to appoint one of the many assistants who had been trained during his time in office to be his official deputy with the title of Coadjutor. The successful candidate was required to be a linguist (with the emphasis on oriental languages), to be unmarried, to have a good memory and to be willing to work in the library for seven or eight hours a day without a break, for a salary of 100 guilders.

23. See Unterkircher, *op. cit.* 97. To be fair to Blotius, it has to be said that he had protested to the Emperor as early as 1576 about the absence of rules and regulations and the consequences of the disorganized state of the library. It was the Emperor himself who insisted on granting free access to the library to all comers and allowing anybody to read any manuscript they liked, and he then held Blotius responsible for any loss or damage that might occur. It need hardly be said that such laxity only encouraged all sorts of irregularities, and perhaps even thefts of books.

24· See Unterkircher, *op. cit.* 98.

25. *Ibid.* 99.

26. *Ibid.* We learn from a letter written by Tengnagel that in 1601 Blotius lent seven books to Elias Hutter, who lived in Nürnberg. At the next stocktaking it was discovered that the books had not been returned. Tengnagel found the books in Nürnberg and saw to it that they were brought back to the library, but he makes it clear that Blotius had not been guilty of any malpractice or negligence.

27. See Unterkircher, *op. cit.* 100.

28. 'Just as medicinal herbs and poisonous weeds grow together in a garden, just as poisons stand next to medicines in an apothecary's shop, so too a library should stock books about all branches of learning and all religions. A defender of the true faith should find in the library books by those who hold opposing views, so that he can draw his arguments from them. After all, such books were to be found in the Vatican Library and in monastic libraries in France and elsewhere: the works of Hus, Calvin,

Luther and Zwingli may have been kept separate, but they were there.'

29. See Unterkircher, *op. cit.* 101.

30. See W. Buchowiecki, *Der Barockbau der ehemaligen Hofbibliothek in Wien, ein Werk J.B. Fischers von Erlach*, Vienna 1957; W. Jaksch, Edith Fischer and F. Kroller, *Österreichischer Bibliotheksbau*, I: *Von der Gotik bis zur Moderne*, Graz 1992, 42-50.

31. See Buchowiecki, *op. cit.* 34-38.

32. See Buchowiecki, *op. cit.* 38-40, 45. The statues were not originally intended for the library: they had been commissioned by Emperor Leopold I from the sculptor Alberto Cormesina in 1696.

33. See Buchowiecki, *op. cit.* 49-55. The fresco adorning the drum of the dome gives an artist's impression of study sessions at the Athens school of philosophy. The themes of all the rest of the painted decoration are drawn from Greek mythology: some of the mythical characters are portrayed as personifications of natural phenomena.

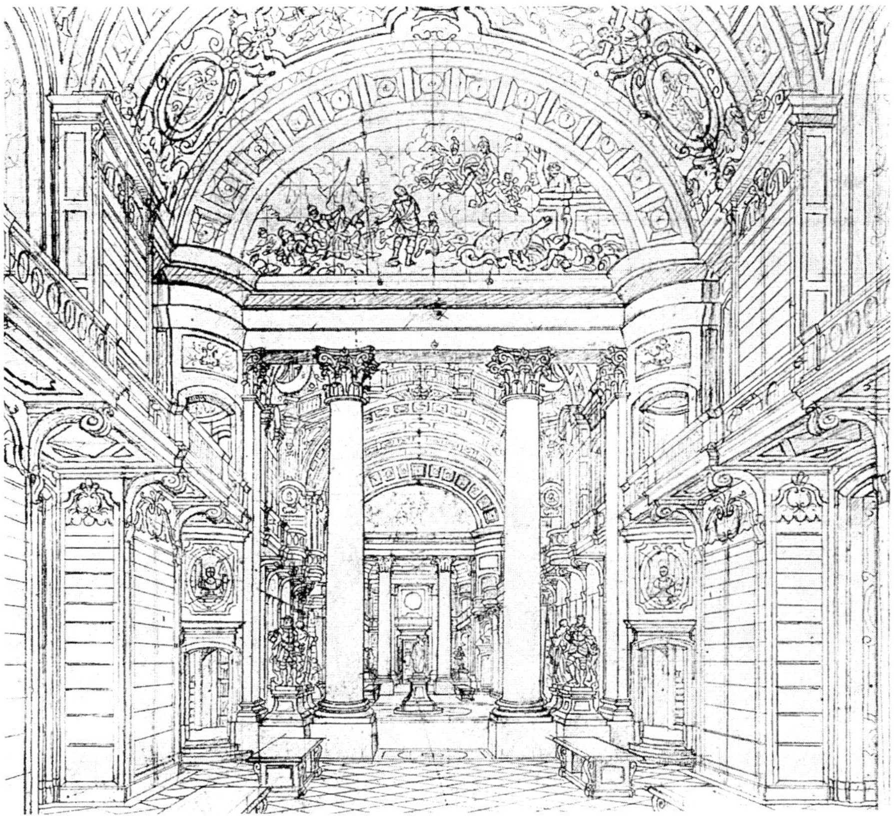

226. Perspective drawing of the Prunksaal by Salomon Kleiner.

225. Longitudinal section of the Prunksaal (Cod. vindob. 5853).

227. Cross-section of the dome of the Prunksaal. Drawing by Salomon Kleiner.

BVDA

The Corvinian Library

CHAPTER TWENTY-THREE

If Matthias Corvinus's library at Buda, the Bibliotheca Corvina, had survived with its priceless contents intact, it would have stood comparison with the most famous libraries in Italy, as it was by all accounts the biggest and best library of its day outside the Vatican.[1] Bartolomeo della Fonte's description of it as 'superior to any other prince's library' was probably no mere exaggeration inspired by humanist enthusiasm.[2]

Matthias Corvinus, the son of the great Hungarian hero János Hunyadi, was born at Kolozsvár (Klausenburg, now Cluj, in Romania) on 27th March 1433 and died in Vienna on 6th April 1490. He ascended the Hungarian throne at a time of great turbulence: when he succeeded King Ladislas V in 1458, aged only twenty-five, his first task was to create order out of the chaos created by the self-interested oligarchies of the aristocracy. He organized a disciplined army of mercenaries, appointed his own men to positions of power in court and in the Church, and threw himself into European politics, waging war against Bohemia and Austria. But at the same time, being a man of artistic sensitivity and taste, he created a climate that encouraged a flowering of literature in Hungary, with the result that soon his court was no whit inferior to the humanist circles of the Italian princes.[3]

The idea of starting the library did not originate with Matthias, nor was it he who decided on the Renaissance slant of its contents. The initiator of the project was the unsung hero János Vitéz.

János Vitéz was born in 1408 and came to the royal court of Buda as a young man in 1433, when King Sigismund of the House of Luxembourg was at the height of his power and prestige. He had taken Holy Orders and soon made a reputation for himself by his forceful personality, literary ability and efficiency.[4] Humanists were to be met with at Sigismund's court, and Buda had already been visited by Francesco Filelfo, Ambrogio Traversari and Antonio Loschi, all of whom dedicated books of theirs to Sigismund. But the man who really introduced the humanist way of life into the Hungarian court was Pier Paolo Vergerio the elder, who spent a quarter of a century working in Buda.[5] There he formed a close friendship with Vitéz, as a result of which Vitéz sent his nephew János Csezmiczei, better known as Janus Pannonius, to the humanist school of Guarino da Verona at Ferrara. One consequence of Pannonius's education at Ferrara was the establishment of cultural relations between that city and Buda, especially in the field of art, for Ferrara exerted a powerful influence on Hungarian manuscript illumination throughout the Renaissance.[6]

During the short reign of the boy king Ladislas V (1452-1457) Vitéz, as his Chancellor, systematically carried on the work he had started earlier. In 1454 he persuaded Ladislas to write to Alfonso I of Naples, asking him to send manuscripts to Buda, and he made the city of Várad (now Oradea, in Romania), of which he was the bishop, the centre of Hungarian intellectual life. After the accession of Matthias Corvinus, Várad retained its

228. Buda. Woodcut from Liber Chronicarum, *Nürnberg, A. Koberger, 1493.*

position of eminence and Vitéz continued to entertain foreign humanists. Travellers, scholars, miniaturists and other artists worked there, including the Frenchman Petrus Gallicus representing the world of Western European music.[7] Copyists played a prominent part in the city's intellectual life, and with their help Vitéz built up the first humanist library in Hungary, rightly regarded as the precursor of the Corvinian Library. Unfortunately very little of his collection survives, but thanks to his nephew Pannonius and Vespasiano da Bisticci, a Florentine chronicler and bookseller, we do have a fair idea of its size and the range of subjects it covered.[8] When Janus Pannonius was made Bishop of Pécs in 1459, he bade farewell to Várad in one of his most beautiful poems (for among his other accomplishments he was a fine poet), in which he sang the praises of his uncle's library, 'so full of many famous books from

229. Matthias Corvinus. Woodcut from P. Giovio, Elogia virorum bellica virtute illustrium, *Basel 1575.*

antiquity'.[9] And Bisticci, one of the most influential figures in the book trade in Italy, records that Vitéz made it one of his main goals in life to build up a library in which every branch of learning was represented.

Fewer than thirty of Vitéz's books have survived, and they, unfortunately, are not representative of the greater part of his collection. They include works by Victorius and Tertullian and perhaps a manuscript containing Ptolemy's *Cosmographia* in the Latin translation by Regiomontanus, all dating from the time when Vitéz was Archbishop of

1. The story of the Corvinian Library, now lost almost in its entirety, is a never-ending source of interest to book-lovers, not only because of the richness of its contents but also because of the circumstances that led to its dispersal. According to Johann Lomeier's historical study *De bibliothecis liber singularis*, Zutphen 1669, 'This hero [Corvinus], without regard to expense, founded a large library which contained more than fifty thousand printed and manuscript books.' Julius Pflugk, the first historian of the Corvinian Library, agrees with Lomeier ('The library is said to have consisted of fifty thousand volumes') and gives it as his opinion that this estimate cannot be far from the truth, as Peter Pázmány offered to buy it from the Turks for 200,000 florins (*Epistola ad Vitum a Seckendorf, praeter fata Bibliothecae Budensis, librorum quoque ultima expugnatione repertorum catalogum exhibens*, Jena 1686). In reality, however, the library must have been very much smaller: according to Csaba Csapodi in his detailed study entitled *The Corvinian Library: History and Stock*, Budapest (Akadémia Kiadó) 1973, 17-29, it could not have contained more than two thousand volumes.

The other question of interest to historians is what happened to the library. It is still not known whether the books were taken to Constantinople at Sultan Suleyman's orders, or whether most of them were destroyed when Buda was sacked by the Turks after their capture of the city in 1526, or whether the library survived intact at that time and the books were dispersed gradually thereafter. The sources are contradictory, and although the consensus of opinion in the German-speaking countries in the seventeenth century was that the library had been completely destroyed by the Sultan, Pál Enyedi, in his history of the Transylvanian war, wrote fulsomely of 'the library of

230. St. Jerome, Expositio Evangelii secundum Matthaeum *(Cod. vindob. lat. 930, fol. 1r).*

INCIPIT PRA
EFATIO SĀC
TI HIERONY
MI P̄BRI IN EXPO
SITŌE M EVAGE
LIIS SCDV MATTHEū

PLVRES
FVISSE
QVI EVAN
GELIA
SCRIP
SERIT

et Lucas Euangelista testatur dicens. qm quidem multi
conati sunt ordinare narrationem rerum que in nobis
complete sunt sicut tradiderunt nobis. qui ab initio ipi
uiderunt sermonem. et ministrauerunt ei. et perseue
rantia usq. in presens tempus monumenta declarant. q̄
aduersis auctoribus edita. diuersarum heresum fuere
principia. Vt est illud iuxta ægiptios & Thomam et
Mathiam et Bartholomeum. duodecim quoq. aplor
et basilidis atq. appelles. ac reliquor quos enumerare

Ex Augustissima Bibliotheca Caesarea Vindobonensi.

Esztergom, but nothing remains of the original works and Latin translations by the great Renaissance humanists such as Guarino da Verona, Poggio, George of Trebizond, Ioannes Argyropoulos[10] and Leonardo Bruni, with whom Vitéz was on friendly terms and corresponded regularly: those either perished owing to the total lack of interest of Vitéz's successors in the archdiocese of Esztergom, notably Johann Beckensloer, or else they were absorbed after his death into Corvinus's library, without any indication of their previous ownership, and shared the fate of that great collection.[11]

Vitéz and Pannonius exerted a powerful influence on King Matthias, especially in matters of scholarship and the arts, and it is no exaggeration to say that they were virtually joint rulers of the country.

231. Matthias Corvinus. From a manuscript of J.F. Marlianus Mediolanensis, Epistolarium *(Volterra, Biblioteca Guarnaci, Cod. lat. 5518.iv.49.3.7, fol. 5r).*

But Corvinus too was a great apostle of humanism and an outstanding personality in his own right. The following assessment of his character is by János Csontosi:

> King Matthias was a greatly gifted and very learned man of independent spirit, strong and born to govern; a prince with an extraordinary personality and a decided inclination for authority, a man of such remarkable individuality that he was able to assimilate, in a manner peculiar to himself, the Renaissance aspirations awakened in his soul by Vitéz and Janus Pannonius, in this way achieving results which far surpassed the original intentions of his instructors.[12]

Matthias Corvinus which still survives in its original location in Buda, without having been sacked, because guards had been set to protect it.' See Csapodi, *op. cit*. 72-90 ('The Decay of the Library').

As Csapodi points out (*op. cit.* 7), the literature on the Corvinian Library was already extremely extensive in 1942, when Klára Zolnai and Joseph Fitz compiled a 130-page list of all the relevant titles in their *Bibliographia Bibliothecae Mathiae Corvini*, Budapest 1942.

For more general information on the Library see Ilona Berkovits, *Illuminated Manuscripts from the Library of Matthias Corvinus*, Budapest 1963.

2. Bartolomeo della Fonte (Fontio, Fonzio) was one of Italy's leading Greek scholars who had studied under Ioannes Argyropoulos and Andronikos Kallistos. Owing to the jealousy of Poliziano he was more or less forced to leave Italy, whereupon he settled at Buda. He translated numerous Greek books into Latin and worked for a time as a proofreader at San Jacopo di Ripoli, the first printing press in Florence. See also *Charta* 197.

3. V. Frankói, *A. Hunyadiak és a Jagellók kora: A magyar nemzet története,* ed. Sándor Szilágyi, IV, n.d.

4. *VBV* I 319-326; V. Frankói, *Vitéz János esztergomi érsek élete*, Budapest 1879, 13; P. Ruzicska, *Storia della letteratura ungherese*, Milan 1963, 237-243; Berkovits, *op. cit*. 11.

5. *VBV* I 393; Berkovits, *op. cit*. 11.

Pier Paolo Vergerio, who was born at Capo d'Istria in 1370 and died in Hungary in 1444, was a member of a distinguished Italian family. He spent some time travelling round Italy, displaying his talents for philosophy, civil law, mathematics, rhetoric and Greek, which he had learnt from Manuel Chrysoloras. In Florence he studied under Francesco Zabarella, an expert in canon law, who liked him so much that he took him into his

232. Agathias, De bello Gothorum, *title page (fol. 1r). Budapest, National Széchényi Library.*

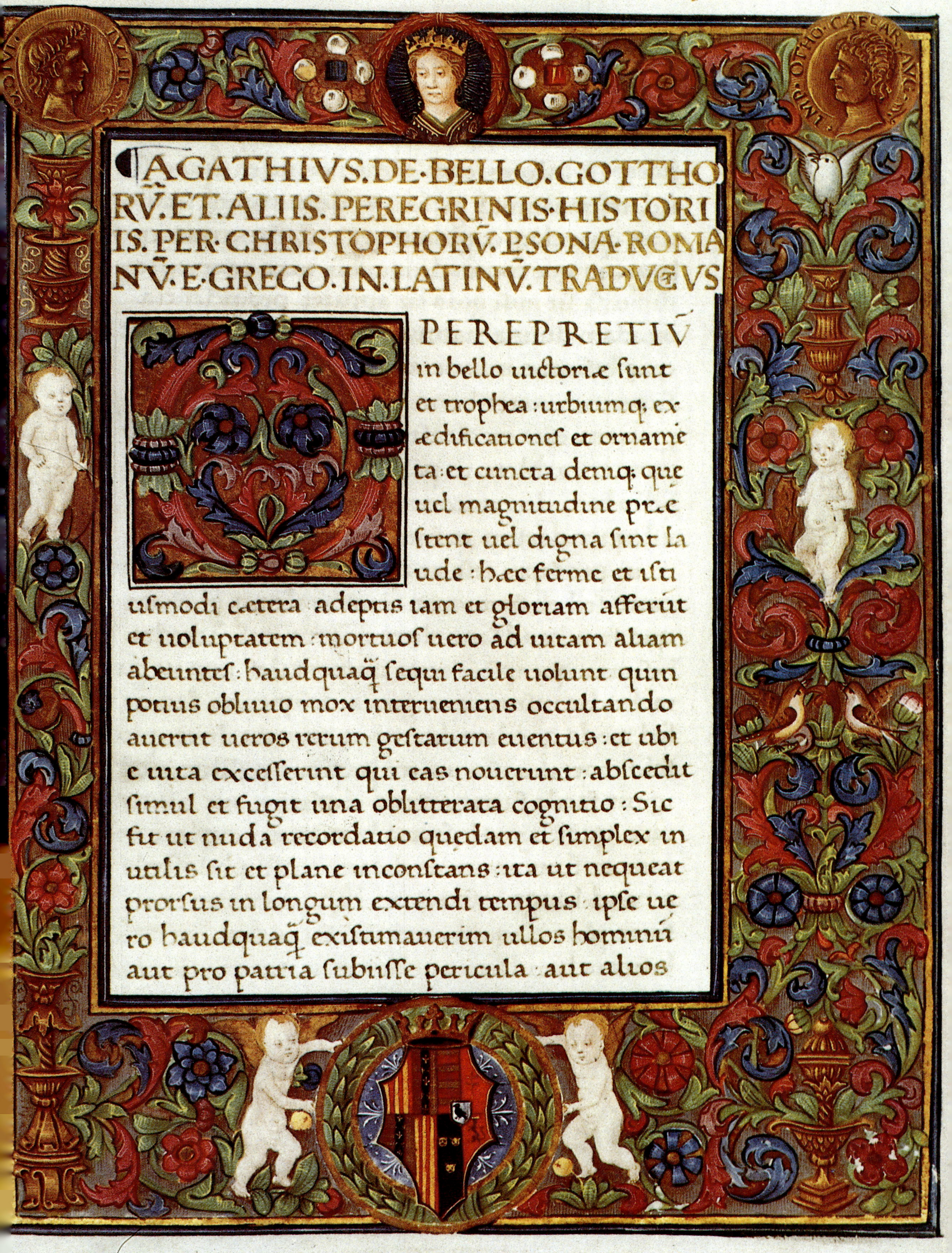

AGATHIVS.DE.BELLO.GOTTHO
RV.ET.ALIIS.PEREGRINIS.HISTORI
IS.PER.CHRISTOPHORV.PSONA.ROMA
NV.E.GRECO.IN.LATINV.TRADVCTVS

PEREPRETIV
in bello uictoriae sunt
et trophea: urbiumq; ex
aedificationes et ornamen
ta: et cuncta demq; que
uel magnitudine prae
stent uel digna sint la
ude: haec ferme et isti
usmodi caetera adeptis iam et gloriam afferũt
et uoluptatem: mortuos uero ad uitam aliam
abeuntes: haudquaq̃ sequi facile uolunt quin
potius obliuio mox interueniens occultando
auertit ueros rerum gestarum euentus: et ubi
e uita excesserint qui eas nouerunt: abscedit
simul et fugit una oblitterata cognitio: Sic
fit ut nuda recordatio quedam et simplex in
utilis sit et plane inconstans: ita ut nequeat
prorsus in longum extendi tempus: ipse ue
ro haudquaq̃ existumauerim ullos hominũ
aut pro patria subisse pericula: aut alios

Janus Pannonius, who did more than any other Hungarian to enrich Corvinus's library by purchases of books in Italy, had had a less privileged education than Vitéz, lacking the books that would have fostered his humanist interests. Bitterly conscious of this, he constantly urged King Matthias to build up an extensive library so as to lift his country out of its 'barbarian' condition.[13]

We do not know exactly when Corvinus started collecting books systematically, nor when his library was founded. Most probably he did not follow any clearly-defined plan: it was simply that his private collection gradually came to be thought of as a library when it became so big that it had to be arranged on a systematic footing.

The main source of books and manuscripts for the library was Italy. In the art of manuscript illumination and book illustration the predominant influence was Ferrara, and later Florence. The special relationship with Ferrara was cultivated by Janus Pannonius, who was introduced by another Hungarian, Andreas Pannonius, to the art studios and scriptoria in that city and studied the working methods of the gifted court miniaturist Guglielmo Giraldi. Ferrara was the first choice for most

employ. He went with Zabarella to Rome and in 1414 accompanied him to the Council of Konstanz, where he met his former teacher Chrysoloras for the last time. After Zabarella's death in 1417, Vergerio moved to Sigismund's court in Hungary and never returned to Italy. See L. Smith, 'Note cronologiche Vergeriane', *AVT* 10 (1920) 149-157; J. Huszti, 'Pier

233. Plautus, Comoediae. *Manuscript copied at Ferrara between 1465 and 1472 (Cod. vindob. 111, fol. 1r).*

234. János Vitéz. Miniature in Plautus, Comoediae *(Cod. vindob. 111, fol. 1r).*

235. Janus Pannonius. Miniature in Plautus, Comoediae *(Cod. vindob. 111, fol. 1r).*

236. Parchment binding made for Corvinus. Biblia *(Erlangen Univ. Library, Ms No. 6, Kötéstábla).*

XIII

young Hungarians going to study in Italy, largely because of the patronage offered by Andreas Pannonius, though Florence also attracted a good many, owing to the influence of Florentine humanists living at the court of Buda. Marsilio Ficino's Platonic Academy, the Chorus Achademiae Florentinae of Ioannes Argyropoulos, the Studium and the other open schools run by humanists in Florence all whetted the interest of Hungarian students, as Vasari attests.[14]

The year 1465 is a landmark in the history of Hungarian humanism. It was then that Janus Pannonius was appointed ambassador to Italy: his entry into Rome with an escort of three hundred horsemen opened the Italian humanists' eyes to the grandeur of Corvinus's court, and Vespasiano da Bisticci wrote fulsomely of the unrivalled splendour of the procession. Pannonius brought his diplomatic mission to a successful conclusion by obtaining the Pope's consent to the founding of a university at Pozsony (now Bratislava, in Slovakia) and the confirmation of Vitéz as Archbishop of Esztergom. He also took the opportunity to make personal contact with the members of Ficino's Academy in Florence and Pomponio Leto's Academy in Rome.[15]

But Pannonius was less interested in diplomacy, with all its pomp and ceremony, than in finding manuscripts. In the well-stocked bookshops of Rome he found what he was looking for, not only for himself but also for his uncle Vitéz, for King Matthias, for the library at Buda and probably for the new University of Pozsony as well. His passion for books made a deep impression on Bisticci, who wrote: 'He bought all the books he could find in Rome – books in Greek and in Latin, in all fields of study – and on arriving in Florence he went on buying all the Greek and Latin books available, regardless of their price.'[16] He went back to Buda taking Galeotto Marzio with him, and his new acquisitions aroused the admiration of scholars, especially Vitéz and Georgius Polycarpus, who could not conceal their impatience to borrow them.

The third man who was instrumental in building up the Corvinian Library, after Janus Pannonius and Vitéz, was Galeotto Marzio, who was appointed the first official Librarian (*Praefectus Bibliothecae Budensis*).[17] Marzio, who had paid a brief visit to Hungary in 1461, stayed there for about seven years from his arrival in 1465. As one of the representatives of Italian humanism in Buda, he made it his first concern to promote humanist studies, and only when he had satisfied himself in that respect did he take up his duties as Librarian. During his time in Buda, up to 1472, he saw the Library through its initial preparatory phase, which ended with two unpleasant events: the dismissal of Vitéz as Archbishop of Esztergom and the death of Janus Pannonius. Both were consequences of the revolt of the aristocracy against Corvinus, in which Vitéz was a ringleader and Pannonius also took part. Vitéz was imprisoned and Pannonius died in a castle belonging to the Bishop of Zagreb while fleeing to exile in Italy, but we do not know what became of their

Paolo Vergerios a magyar humanizmus kezdetei', *Filológiai Közlöny* (1955) 521-533.

6. *VBV* I 327-335; J. Huszti, *Janus Pannonius*, Pécs 1931; see also pp. 460-461 and n. 14.

Pannonius, born in 1434 in a little village near the confluence of the Drava and the Danube, was educated in Italy from 1447, first at Guarino's school in Ferrara and then at Padua, where he studied canon law. In 1451 he left Italy and went back to Hungary for about eight years (until 1458). Returning to Italy in 1460, he was consecrated Bishop of Cinquechiese by Pope Pius II. He fought with Matthias Corvinus against the Turks and died in Croatia in 1472.

7. J. Ábel, *Adalékok a humanismus történetéber Magyarországon*, Budapest 1880, 158-159; Id., 'Magyarországi humanisták és a Dunai Tudós Társaság', *Ért. MTA* 8 (1880) 8.

237. Ioannes Argyropoulos. Woodcut from N. Reusner, Icones, *Basel 1599.*

8. On Vitéz's library see: V. Frankói, *Vitéz János könyvtára*, Budapest 1878; Edit Hoffmann (ed.), *Régi magyar bibliofilek*, Budapest 1929.

9. *VBV* I 333; Berkovits, *op. cit.* 13; Huszti, *Janus Pannonius* 189. The third biggest library in Hungary at

238. Didymus Alexandrinus, Liber de Spiritu Sancto *(Pierpont Morgan Library, New York, Ms 496, fol. 2r).*

INCIPIT PRAEFATIO S HIERONYMI IN LIBRO S DIDYMI GRAECI MONACHI ALEXANDRINI DE SPIRITU SANCTO.
Dum in babilone uersarer et purpurate meretricis essem colonus et iure quiritium uiuerem uolui aliquid garrire de spiritu sancto et
MA
MA

books or just how many of them ended up in the Corvinian Library. A substantial part of Pannonius's collection – mostly Greek manuscripts – and some of the manuscripts belonging to Vitéz are known to have come into the Corvina's possession. These greatly enlarged the royal collection, which until then had numbered no more than 250 books, with the result that by 1472 it contained about five or six hundred volumes.[18]

This first phase in the history of the Corvinian Library, ending with the death of the two men primarily responsible for its conception, was followed by a period that was no less fruitful, though new books were now acquired through different channels. Matthias, deeply soured by the aristocracy's attempt to dethrone him and particularly shocked by the involvement of his beloved counsellors Vitéz and Pannonius, laid the blame for the whole episode on the Humgarian humanists *en bloc*, but he still did not give up the idea of creating a great library. In the nineteenth century Hungarian scholars were surprised to learn from Csontosi that Carlo Malagola, a professor at Bologna University, maintained that Corvinus 'bought the private library of Manfredini, Prince of Bologna, in about 1475.'[19]

Matthias's interest in humanist studies, and hence in his library, revived in 1476 following his marriage to Beatrice, the daughter of King Alfonso II of Naples. Beatrice, who was a book-lover and had a good collection of manuscripts of her own, brought all her books with her to Buda and, once there, supported every effort to promote humanist ideals. Her personal interest prompted Matthias to start buying books for his library again, on a substantial scale. Before long the gap left by the loss of Vitéz and Pannonius was filled by new Italian humanists such as Francesco Fontana, Giustiniano Cavitelli (a former diplomat from the court of Prince Ercole of Ferrara), Lucas Lupus from Milan, Gabriele Rangoni from Verona and Giovanni Leoncio.[20]

Corvinus's library also benefited from the king's contacts with Marsilio Ficino himself and other Florentine humanists, notably Francesco Bandini and Taddeo Ugoleto. In 1477 Ficino sent to his friend Bandini, then living in Buda, a manuscript of his containing the biography of Plato in Latin translation, with a preface by himself in which he wrote, 'I am not sending the Plato to Athens, because Athens has been destroyed, but rather to Pannonia which is under the enlightened rule of the great King Matthias, a man imbued with abundant power and wisdom, with which he will soon revitalize the temple of the almighty and wise Pallas.'[21] From then on Ficino was in fairly frequent contact with Buda, largely because Bandini set up a Neoplatonic Academy there in imitation of the Platonic Academy in Florence. Ficino's Latin translations, chiefly of Plato and the Neoplatonists, were well received in Bandini's circle, and before long these cultural ties were extended into the sphere of politics, as evidenced by Ficino's open letter to Matthias (*Exhortatio ad bellum contra barbaros*) appealing to him to

the time of the Renaissance, after those of Corvinus and Vitéz, was undoubtedly that of Janus Pannonius. Following the example of these three, many other Hungarians built up collections that were bigger and better than in any other country north of the Alps. However, it is hard to say exactly what Pannonius had in his library, because his books bear no distinguishing marks such as a bookplate, his coat of arms or marginal notes written in his own hand, with the result that many of his books were once thought to have belonged to Corvinus. A number of codices have now been identified as coming from Pannonius's collection: these include the *Bibliotheca* of Diodorus Siculus (Ö.N.B. Suppl. gr. 30), Marsilio Ficino's *Commentarium in Platonis Convivium de Amore* (Ö.N.B. Cod. lat. 2472), Plutarch's *De dictis regum et imperatorum* (Luph. Rep. I.80), Xenophon's *Cyropaedia* (Erlangen Univ., Ms 1226). See C. Csapodi, 'Les livres de Janus Pannonius et sa bibliothèque à Pécs', *Scriptorium* 28 (1974) 32-50.

239. An initial C framed by a miniature of a copyist or reader, in a manuscript containing George of Trebizond's Compendium grammaticae *(Budapest, National Széchényi Library, Clmae 428, fol. 1a)..*

240. B. Fontius, Opera *(Herzog August Bibliothek, Wolfenbüttel, Cod. 43. Aug. 2, fol. 1r).*

BARTHOLOMAEVS
FONTIVS
MATHIAE CORVINO
REGI ·S·

MATHIA

urbe fama: quemadmodum felicitate ac uirtute ualidas bello nationes domueras: et quacunque uictricia signa conuerteras perinde ut alter Mars ingentes hostium strages semper ediderās. Sed nondum quae longe potiora sunt armis cognoueramus: ut fortitudini animi & scientiae militari studium quoque uehemens

come to the aid of 'worthy Italy' when the Turks were threatening the Italian states.[22]

Ficino and Bandini undoubtedly played a major part in enriching Corvinus's library, but the man who did most to raise the standard of the books in the royal collection was Taddeo Ugoleto, the new Librarian. Ugoleto, who had excellent Latin and equally good Greek, travelled regularly around the libraries of Italy and monasteries further north, and thus he had a comprehensive knowledge of the books available in Western Europe. Little is known about his life in Buda, but we have ample information about his work on the reorganization of the library and the foundation of a scriptorium in Florence on Corvinus's orders. The scriptorium, which was managed by Naldo Naldi, employed four copyists and was a godsend to the bookseller Vespasiano da Bisticci,

241. Beatrice of Aragon and Matthias Corvinus. Relief. Berlin, National Museum.

who, by taking Vitéz's side against Corvinus, had so enraged the king that he flatly refused to buy any more books from him.[23]

For a library outside Italy, the Corvina was unusually well stocked with Greek manuscripts. Indeed, it had so many of them that Berascianus was probably right in saying that they could not all have been bought in Italy: some of them must have been sought out in the Greek homelands, especially Constantinople. As we have seen, Janus Pannonius bought Greek manuscripts both for himself and for Corvinus, Vitéz and others when he visited Florence, Rome and other cities in Italy as early as 1465. A letter from Pannonius to Vitéz, in jocular vein, makes it clear that he had some Greek manuscripts in his possession: 'Haven't I sent you enough already? All I have left are Greek books, you

242. George of Trebizond. Woodcut from N. Reusner, Icones, *Basel 1599.*

10. In about 1471 Pannonius had delivered to Argyropoulos (who may have been his Greek teacher) a letter from the King of Hungary inviting him to Buda to teach Greek on a regular basis. Argyropoulos declined, preferring to return to Rome and go on with his teaching there. See G. Cammelli, *I dotti bizantini e le origine dell' Umanesimo*, II: *Giovanni Argiropulo*, Florence 1941, 131-132.

The only Greek who maintained close contact with the Hungarian court was George of Trebizond (Georgios Trapezountios). His translations and the breadth of his learning won him a high reputation in humanist circles everywhere, though his argumentative nature often turned public feeling against him. On one occasion, for example, he wrote an open epistle entitled *Παντοτινή δόξα* to Sultan Mehmet II, urging him to make himself ruler of the whole world now that he had captured Constantinople, the 'Queen of Cities', and this created such a furore that George was imprisoned. However, his knowledge of astronomy and astrology caused scholars to overlook his personal faults. This was especially true in

243. Philostratus, Heroica *(Budapest, National Széchényi Library, Clmae 417, fol. 1v).*

DIVO MATTHIE COR
VINO: PRINCIPI INVI
CTISS: VNG: BOE: Q; RE
GI PHILOSTRATI HER
OICA: ICONES. VITE S
OPHISTARVM. ET EPIST
OLE AB ANTONIO BON
FINE TRADVCTE: ET IN
COR: BIBLIOTHECĀ RE
GIA IMPENSA RELATE

have taken all my Latin volumes. By Jove, it's lucky none of you know Greek, otherwise I wouldn't even have any Greek books left. When you learn Greek I shall study Hebrew, so that I can collect Hebrew books as well.' No doubt many of Pannonius's Greek books ended up in Corvinus's library and enabled Ugoleto (unlike his predecessor Marzio, who knew no Greek at all) to satisfy his love of Greek literature.[24]

The second phase in the history of the Corvina lasted some twelve years, from 1472 to 1485, during which time the Library was enlarged by the acquisition of at least five hundred new books (about 300 in Latin and 200 in Greek), at the most conservative estimate. Thus by about 1484 Corvinus's library contained approximately a thousand volumes.[25]

A major factor underlying the progress of the Library in this, its most fruitful period, was Corvinus's entry into Vienna at the head of an army of 8,000 men. The Hungarian king was in no way overwhelmed by the prestige and grandeur of Vienna, and he decided to keep the capital of his empire – and his library – at Buda. He commissioned Naldi to write a panegyric in praise of the Library and sent him on a mission to visit 'all the libraries in Europe', as Ugoleto records, to publicize the greatness of the Corvina and locate new sources for the further enrichment of the Library. This marks the beginning of a new phase in which the old manuscripts were replaced with new copies exemplifying the highest standards of Renaissance calligraphy and illumination.[26]

Matthias Corvinus had still greater ambitions for his library, and he told his closest advisers of his plans. In a letter written to Moreno a few months before the king's death, the Florentine humanist Bartolomeo della Fonte wrote, 'In this, as in so many other matters in the past, it is the King's desire to surpass all other monarchs, in other words to create the richest library in the world.'[27]

Corvinus had a great admiration for learned men and spared no expense to provide scholars with the books they needed to pursue their studies in every branch of learning. Nor was he put off by the obstacle of the Greek language: Greek texts were translated into Latin in Buda, mostly by Antonio Bonfini, who may have had some help from Ugoleto, although the latter spent most of his time in Florence.[28]

The marvel of printing presses and printed books came too late for Corvinus to be swept off his feet by the magic of it. Although the German master printer Andreas Hess set up a press in Buda and produced the first book to be printed there (*Chronica Hungarorum*) as early as 1473, thus making it possible for the king to spread humanist ideas more widely, the output of incunabula in Hungary was insignificant when compared with other countries in Europe, especially Italy.[29]

The sudden death of Matthias Corvinus in 1490, at the early age of forty-seven, left the Library still incomplete. However, it had some two thousand volumes on its shelves by that time, and so his ambitious plans for it were close to fulfilment. Already it was bigger and better than the

Hungary, where a keen interest was taken in the study of the stars and their influence on human affairs – so much so that Marzio Galeotto addressed Corvinus as 'Rex et astrologus' (see the preface to J. Ábel (ed.), *Irodalontörténeti Emlékek*, 2 vols., Budapest 1886-1890) and it is recorded that Vitéz would never embark on any new venture without first consulting the stars: see J. Monfasani, *George of Trebizond: A biography and a study of his rhetoric and logic*, Leiden 1976.

11. *VBV* I 321. On Beckensloer's treatment of the books see Berkovits, *op. cit.* 13.

12. J. Csontosi, 'A Korvina', *Pallas Nagy lexikon*, X, Budapest 1895, suppl., VI. (The translation is taken from Berkovits, *op. cit.* 13-14.)

13. In a letter to Marzio Galeotto, Pannonius excused himself for his neglect of his studies, which he said was 'due partly to my other business, partly to the circumstance that I could not obtain the necessary books in this barbarian country, nor did I find an appreciative audience which might have spurred on my ambition to learn': Huszti, *Janus Pannonius* 251. (The translation is taken from Berkovits, *op. cit.* 14.)

14. *VBV* I 328-329; G. Vasari, *Le vite de' più eccellenti pittori, scultori*

244. Marsilio Ficino. Woodcut from N. Reusner, Icones, *Basel 1599.*

ed architetti, con nuove annotazioni e commenti di Gaetano Milanesi, Florence 1878, III 334. See also G. Gombosi, 'Pannóniae Mihály és a renaissance Kezdetei Ferraraban', *Az Országos Magyar Szépmüvészeti Múseum Evkönyve* 6 (1929-1930) 91-108. On the art of manuscript illumination in Ferrara see Ilona Berkovits, *La miniatura nella corte di Mattia Corvino: Ferrara ed il Rinascimento ungherese*, Budapest 1941, 14.

15. Huszti, *Janus Pannonius* 231; Csapodi, *The Corvinian Library*... 41; Berkovits, *Illuminated Manuscripts*... 15-16. On Pomponio Leto's Academy 294.

16. J. Ábel, *Analecta ad historiam renascentium in Hungaria litterarum spectantia*, Budapest 1880, 225; Csapodi, *The Corvinian Library*... 41.

17. See Csapodi, *The Corvinian Library*... 43. For further information see Huszti, *Janus Pannonius* 216, 227.

18. Berkovits, *Illuminated Manuscripts*... 18. On the first period of the Library see Csapodi, *op. cit.* 40-45.

19. See Csapodi, *The Corvinian Library*... 46.

20. Berkovits, *Illuminated Manuscripts*... 18-19; A. Berzeviczy, *Beatrix Királyné*, Budapest 1908. On Beatrice's library see C. Csapodi, *Beatrix Királyné Könyvtára*, Muszle 1964, 201-224.

21. See Csapodi, *The Corvinian Library*... 47; J. Huszti, *Platonista törekvések Mátyás király udvarában*, Pécs 1925. The text of Ficino's preface is given in J. Ábel and I. Hegadüs, *Analecta nova*, Budapest 1903.

22. See the Introduction to the second volume of Ficino's *Epistolae*, 1482.

23. See Csapodi, *The Corvinian Library*... 48-49.

Naldi, whom Ficino called his greatest friend, was born in Florence in 1435 and died there *circa* 1500. Practically nothing would now be known about him if he had not been immortalized in the work of Ficino and Angelo Poliziano. He was a protégé of Lorenzo de' Medici and taught rhetoric, grammar and poetry at the Florence Studium. See A. della Torre, *Storia dell' Accademia Platonica di Firenze*, Florence 1902, 503-508, 668-681.

245. Alexander Cortesius, Laudes bellicae *(Herzog August Bibliothek, Wolfenbüttel, Cod. 85,I.1. Aug., fol. 3)*

libraries of the d'Este family at Modena, of Duke Federico da Montefeltro at Urbino, of King Alfonso in Naples, of the Medici in Florence and of any other ruler in Western Europe: only the Vatican Library could boast that it was still unsurpassed. All that remains of the Corvinus collection amounts to about two hundred books in various libraries around the world, that is to say one tenth of the total.[30]

The next king on the throne, Vladislas I, was a lightweight in comparison with the exuberant personality of his predecessor. The death of Matthias Corvinus marked the beginning of a decline in Hungary's political and cultural fortunes, culminating in the disastrous battle of Mohács (1526), where the Hungarian army was routed by the Turkish hordes. The Library was one of the many casualties: from then on it was more or less left to its fate and its contents were dispersed to the four winds.[31]

Architecture. If at least some ruins of Matthias Corvinus's palace had survived the siege of 1686 it might now be possible, using the evidence of contemporary descriptions, to locate the very spot that was chosen for the royal collecion of books. We do know from the writings of Naldo Naldi and Miklós Oláh that the library was near the palace chapel, and it seems somewhat improbable that a separate building was erected specifically to house it, as some historians have suggested. Assuming that there was no such building, the likeliest hypothesis is that the two rooms described by Naldi were on the first floor of the palace, with the Latin books in the larger room (about eight to ten metres long) and the Greek and oriental books in the smaller one. These were the two main rooms of the library, though it is quite possible that other, smaller rooms were used for keeping books and papers of lesser importance, as Oláh records.

The layout of the Corvinian Library did not follow the example of Italian libraries such as that of Cesena, for example, and later the Vatican or even the Laurenziana. There is a distinctively personal touch about its design, which is more reminiscent of a strongroom than a library. According to Naldi, the books were kept on shelves along the walls, with a curtain to protect them from dust. Below the shelves there was a row of cabinets in which the rest of the manuscripts were kept. A sofa for the use of the king stood between two of the windows, and there were a number of three-legged stools in the middle of the room. This was where King Matthias went when he wanted peace and quiet for contemplation or conversation with other humanists.

On the evidence available it is not possible to blame the disappearance of Corvinus's books on any one person or event. It may be that after the king's death humanists in his court borrowed manuscripts from the library, most of which they failed to return, and of course the library was sacked after the battle of Mohács: any manuscripts that were not ripped to pieces by looters interested only in the jewels and exquisitely-worked precious metals adorning the covers were carried off to Constantinople, now the capital of the Ottoman Empire, where they lay mouldering for centuries in damp cellars in the Sultan's palace. Some of them changed hands from time to time, and about a hundred were returned to Hungary by the Sultan in 1869 and 1873.

246. Matthias Corvinus. Woodcut from Constitutiones incliti regni Ungarie, *Leipzig* c. *1491.*

24. See Csapodi, *The Corvinian Library...* 49; Mária Kubinyi, *Libri manuscripti graeci in bibliothecis Budapestinensibus asservati*, Budapest 1956. For Pannonius's letter to Vitéz see M. Galeotto, 'De dictis et factis Matthiae' in J. Ábel (ed.), *Irodalontörténeti Emlékek*, II, Budapest 1890, 7-8. On Ugoleto see n. 28.

25. See Csapodi, *The Corvinian Library...* 51; Berkovits, *Illuminated Manuscripts...* 15.

26. See Csapodi, *The Corvinian Library...* 51-57.

Matthias Corvinus's library provided the impetus for the start of manuscript illumination in Buda and did much to keep miniaturists in business both there and in Italy. The manuscripts intended for the Corvina are works of great beauty displaying the highest artistic standards, in which we can recognize the hands of Attavante degli Attavanti, Giovanni Boccardi and Francesco di Antonio del Chierico, as well as many anonymous artists working in Buda. For examples of these illuminations and some typical bindings see Berkovits, *Illuminated Manuscripts...* Pls. 1-47. See also L. Vayer, 'Rapporti tra la miniatura italiana e quella ungherese nel trecento' in *La miniatura italiana tra Gotico e Rinascimento,* ed. Emanuela Sesti, I, Florence 1985, 3-33.

27. See Csapodi, *The Corvinian Library...* 55 (B. Fontius, *Epistolarum libri*, ed. Ladislaus Juhász, Budapest 1931, 36).

28. See Csapodi, *The Corvinian Library...* 46.

Information about his duties as Librarian is supplied by Ugoleto himself in his preface to *Opera Ausonij nuper reperta* (*BMC* VII 946), printed in 1499 at his brother Angelo's press in Parma. Taddeo mentions that he first had the idea of preparing an edition of Ausonius in the year when invited him to take charge of his collection of Greek and Latin books.

Ugoleto was perhaps better qualified for this post than anybody else: himself a highly cultured man and a collector of manuscripts, he fully deserved the title of *Musarum Cultor* bestowed on him by the anonymous engraver of a medallion (A. del Plato, *Librai e biblioteche parmesi del secolo XV*, Parma 1905). He travelled frequently to Florence to buy manuscripts for Corvinus, and his excellent relations both with the literary élite and with the Medici themselves, who evidently financed his purchases of manuscripts for Corvinus in some way, stood him in good stead. Evidence for the financial assistance given to Corvinus by the Medici is to be found in the Florentine State Archives (Ia. Cancelleria. – Signori Carteggio. Missive, Registri 51, c. 48): see A. de Hevesy, *La Bibliothèque du Roi Matthias Corvin*, Paris 1923, 52-53.

29. Proctor II 692; Geldner II 358. See also J. Fitz, 'König Matthias Corvinus und der Buchdruck', *GJ* 14 (1939) 128-137; and esp. J. Fitz, *A magyar nyomdászat, könyvkiadás és Könyvkereskedelem története a XV. században*, Budapest 1959.

30. See Csapodi, *The Corvinian Library...* 56-57, 25-29.

31. See Csapodi, *The Corvinian Library...* 57-62.

Kollarii Supplementorum Cod. XCVI.

247. Ioannes Zonaras, Ἐπιτομὴ ἱστοριῶν (Compendium of History) *(Vindob. hist. gr. 16, fol. 1r).*

The Library of Strahov Abbey

CHAPTER TWENTY-FOUR

The library of Strahov Abbey in Prague, famed for the beauty of its ornate Theology Hall and Philosophy Hall, was founded by monks of the Premonstratensian order, which for a long period was very strong in Bohemia and Moravia. The initial nucleus of the library dates from the foundation of the abbey in 1143, about ten years after the death of St. Norbert, founder of the order.

Norbert, a scion of an aristocratic family by the name of Genner, was born between 1080 and 1085 near Xanten, a town in Westphalia.[1] Attracted to the Church from a very early age, he first became a canon in the Order of St. Victorius at Xanten and was then given a position in the court of Archbishop Friedrich of Schwarzenburg in Köln. Before long he had risen to be a secretary in the imperial court, and he took an active part in the dispute between Pope Paschal II and Emperor Henry V. In 1115, following Henry's excommunication by the Pope, Norbert went back to his home town of Xanten. His beliefs and his whole outlook on life had undergone a drastic change: he renounced the world, buried himself in his studies, was ordained deacon and, at the age of about thirty, gave away all he possessed to the poor and set off across Europe as a penitent pilgrim. By the time he had travelled through France, Belgium and part of Germany, preaching the Catholic faith and castigating the priests for their dissolute way of life, he had gathered about him a band of followers, with whom he established a commune at Prémontré, in a remote area of northern France. On Christmas Eve, 1121, Norbert and his companions celebrated midnight mass and dedicated their lives to the Church of the Blessed Virgin and St. John the Baptist, and thus was the Premonstratensian order born. On 12th February 1126 Pope Honorius II issued the bull *Apostolicae disciplinae sectantes*, ratifying the foundation of the order, and Norbert was consecrated Archbishop of Magdeburg the same year. From then on he strove to preserve the way of life ordained by the Rule of the Premonstratensians and took an active part in the campaign for the conversion of the Baltic peoples to Christianity. Subsequently he was appointed Chancellor to the Holy Roman Emperor and became one of the most influential men in the Empire. After a visit to Rome to mediate in the dispute between Pope Innocent II and Antipope Anaclitus II, he fell ill and died at Magdeburg on 6th June 1134.

Strahov Abbey was founded, not on the initiative of the Premonstratensians themselves, but at the instigation of Jindřich Zdík, the Bishop of Olomouc and representative of the order in Bohemia and Moravia, who asked the abbot of Steinfeld, a Premonstratensian monastery in the Rhine valley, to send some monks to open a house in Prague.[2] The first monks arrived in Prague in 1140 and three years later, in 1143, they founded the Abbey of Mount Sion, commonly known as Strahov. Such was the extent of its influence on social and cultural life in Bohemia and Moravia that the abbey was from the outset an educational centre, an essential stopping-place for all the leading intellectuals and artists

248. Strahov Abbey. Drawing based on the frontispiece of A. Kubiček and D. Libal, Strahov, *Prague 1955.*

of the Empire. During the troubles of the ensuing centuries, however, it was impossible for Strahov to escape unscathed. In the Hussite wars it was repeatedly destroyed by fire, and at one stage it was abandoned for eighteen years.[3] Its present magnificent form dates from a period of rebuilding in Renaissance style, which started in 1586 at the instigation of Emperor Rudolf II and continued until the nineteenth century.[4]

Not many libraries in Europe can boast a continuous history going back more than eight hundred years, but in Prague both the Strahov and

249. Bishop Jeronym Hirnheim. Oil, 1689.

the Capitular Library date from the Romanesque period (mid twelfth century).[5] There are at least five codices from this period in the Strahov library, and four more in other libraries in Prague. All nine are written in the same hand, and all bear the inscription *Iste liber est ecclesie Syon, que et Strahov dicitur*: clearly they all come from the same scriptorium, probably founded by Bishop Zdík, who is believed to have given them to Strahov for the benefit of the monks in the newly-founded monastery and other Premonstratensian communities. Among them are the *Moralia* of Gregory the Great and two copies of St. Augustine's *De civitate Dei*, the

1. On Norbert see Kašpar Elm, *Norbert von Xanten, Adliger, Ordensstifter, Kirchenfürst*, Köln 1984. The existence of so many fine libraries in Premonstratensian monasteries is accounted for by the Rule drawn up by Norbert, which allows time for meditation and study. After 1124 the Premonstratensian order spread from France into Belgium, Westphalia, Bavaria, Saxony, the Netherlands, Italy, Greece and even Palestine. Norbert was canonized in 1582.

2. See A. Kubiček and D. Libal, *Strahov*, Prague 1955; F. and R. Maleček, *Strahov Praha* (a catalogue of the possessions of Strahov Abbey), Prague (Nakladetelstvi-Orion) n.d., 111.

3. The Hussite wars ensued from the martyrdom of Jan Hus, a lecturer at Prague University who campaigned to reform the lax morals of the Catholic Church and to eliminate the many abuses that were perpetrated in the name of the Papacy. After his death his followers waged a victorious war under the leadership of John Ziska, expelling and killing thousands of Germans as well as Catholics loyal to the Pope. After a time, however, the Hussite movement broke up into smaller groups such as the Calixtines, the Taborites and the Adamites, which themselves became further fragmented after Ziska's death. In 1457 the Taborites, who rejected all teaching not sanctioned directly by the Bible, divided into two splinter groups, the Union of Brothers and the Bohemian and Moravian Brothers, which spread as far as Poland. It is worth mentioning that they were active in the movement for the reunion of the churches and that they themselves wished to ally themselves with the Eastern Orthodox Church, mainly over the issue of papal supremacy, which they rejected.

4. See *Strahovská Knihovna. Památníku národního písemnictví, Historické sály, dějiny a růst fondů* (*The History and Collections of the Strahov Library*), Prague 1988, 168.

5. There are two other large Premonstratensian monasteries with fine libraries – Želiv Abbey and Teplá Abbey – dating back to the

twelfth and thirteenth centuries.

Želiv Abbey was founded in about 1140 by the Benedictines, but in 1149 the Bishop of Prague replaced the Benedictines with Premonstratensians from Steinfeld in Germany. The only building that has survived from the Romanesque period is the church: all the others, including the Baroque library, date from the seventeenth and eighteenth centuries. The books from the library were dispersed during the period of Communist rule, and it seems extremely unlikely that it will ever be possible to reconstitute the collection in all its former glory.

250. The coat of arms of the Premonstratensian order.

Teplá Abbey was founded by B. Hroznata, who gave away all he possessed to pay for its construction, joined the Premonstratensian order and died in prison in 1217; his daughter Vojslava founded a nunnery at Chotěšov. The church at Teplá, started in the Gothic style, was completed in the Baroque period. After the Hussite wars Teplá was the biggest monastery in Bohemia, and from the sixteenth century onwards it helped many other monastic communities to retain their autonomy. The abbey is best known for its Baroque library, decorated with magnificent frescoes similar to those in the Philosophy Hall of the library at Strahov. The most striking features of the Teplá library are the height of the ceiling, the large windows admitting plenty of daylight and the

first of which is the famous Hildebert Codex, one of the most spendid examples of twelfth-century Bohemian calligraphy.[6] Since some of these Strahov manuscripts have been discovered in other libraries, it would seem that the monks did not spend their lives confined to the monastic precinct: evidently some of the books were kept outside the abbey, especially after the catastrophic fire of 1258 and during the Hussite wars which led to the abandonment of the abbey from 1420 to 1438.

251. St. Norbert. Engraving reproduced in Kašpar Elm, Norbert von Xanten, *Köln 1984.*

Strahov Abbey and its library recovered their former glory and rose to new heights of splendour under Abbot Jan Lohelius (1586-1612), who went on to become Archbishop of Prague.[7] The buildings were renovated and the library reconstituted, and the new nucleus of books was enlarged by Lohelius's successor Kašpar Questenberg. Towards the end of the Thirty Years' War nineteen large boxes of books valued at 20,000 guilders, representing a large part of the total library stock, were carried off by the Swedish army.[8] In 1665, under Abbot Vincenc Frank, the library was further enriched by the purchase of the Freisleben collection from Johlava, at a price of 3,000 guilders. A few years later, through the generosity of Abbot Jeroným Hirnheim, a fine large room worthy of the abbey's prestige and splendour was built to house its books. This was the so-called Theology Hall, completed in 1671. When the books on the shelves were counted after Hirnheim's death in 1678, the total number of volumes was found to be 5,564.[9]

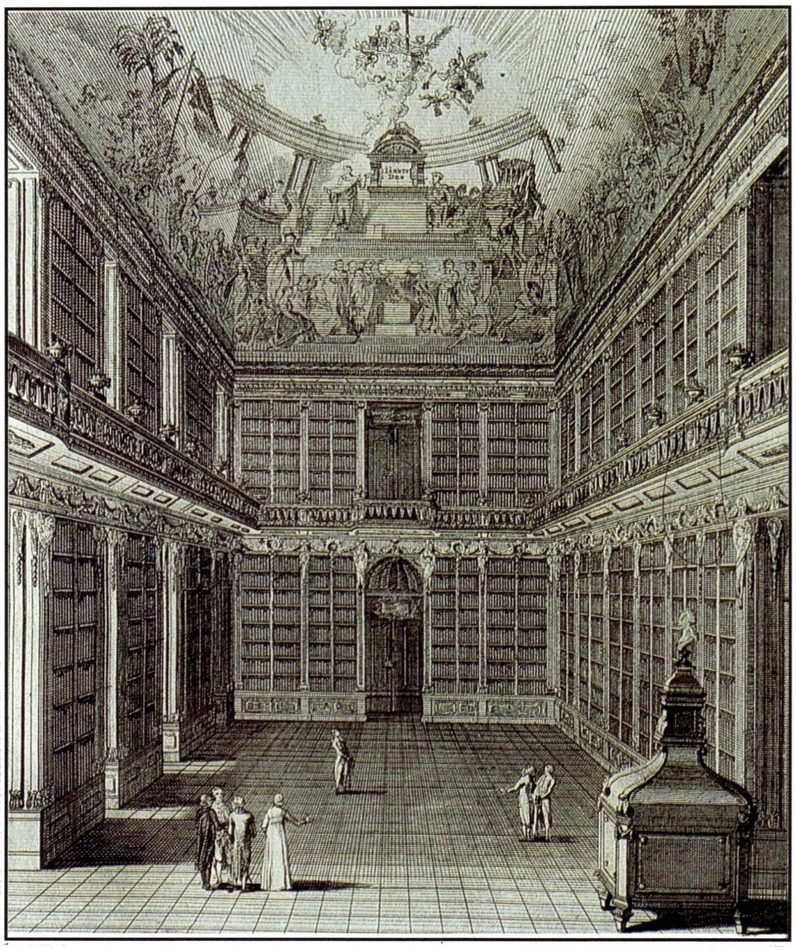

252. The interior of the Philosophy Hall. Engraving in A. Maulbertsch, Historico-Philosophica Descriptio ... Canonia Strahoviensi, *Prague 1797.*

From the end of the seventeenth century the Strahov library started expanding rapidly through gifts and bequests of books, and even of whole collections belonging to church dignitaries and professors at Prague University[10] such as Jiří Pontan of Breitenberg, Dean of St. Vitus's Cathedral, the jurist Jan K. Schambogen and the physicist Jan F. Löw of Erlsfeld. A new catalogue compiled in 1756 listed some 12,000 volumes, and the total was further enlarged by the acquisition of two large libraries – from the book-collector Jan Clauser in 1775 and the Chancellor of the Treasury Jan Heidl in 1780. By this time it was manifestly necessary to

two-tiered upper gallery creating the effect of a three-storied library. It is the second-biggest library in Bohemia, and its oldest manuscripts date from the ninth century. See B. Ardura and K. Dolista, *Prémontrés en Bohème, Moravie et Slovaquie*, Prague (Karlova University) 1993, 29-45.

6. See *Strahovská Knihovna...* 168.

7. *Ibid.*

8. What actually happened was that a battalion of Finnish soldiers serving under the Swedes took the books back with them to Turku along

253. Breviary for the use of Premonstratensians, Paris, Thielman Kerver, 1507.

with the rest of their spoils of war. The books were accidentally destroyed by fire in the early nineteenth century.

9. See *Strahovská Knihovna...* 168.

10. Prague University was founded in 1348 by Emperor Charles IV. Although attempts were made to establish a proper library for the students and teaching staff from the outset, nothing came of these efforts until the early seventeenth century;

254. The interior of the Philosophy Hall at Strahov Abbey.
255. The interior of the Theology Hall at Strahov Abbey.

Art, as well as documentary records from local archives in Bohemia.[12]

In 1950 the Strahov library contained about 130,000 volumes, including 3,000 manuscript codices and no less than 2,500 incunabula. There is also a large collection of early printed books (i.e. those printed in the early sixteenth century), including a representative selection of theological and secular works from presses all over Europe.[13] The oldest manuscript dates from the ninth century: it is the famous Strahov Evangeliary, probably written at Tours and illuminated in the second half of the tenth century, which is one of the most splendid pieces of work produced by the School of Trier during the reign of Otto I. Among the library's other rare treasures are a codex containing four

258. One of the frescoes by Siard Nosecký in the Theology Hall.

chronicles of Frederick Barbarossa's incursions into Italy, based on local sources, and a copy of the Venerable Bede's *Historia Ecclesiastica Gentis Anglorum* in the hand of the calligrapher monk Ansbert. A number of volumes are of particular interest to the Czechs: they include a codex of the *Chronicles* written by the followers of Cosmas Vincentia and Abbot Jarloch, which comes from Milevský Monastery, and a manuscript of the early Czech translations of John Mandeville's *Travels* and of *Tristan und Isolde*. The library also possesses historic translations of the Bible. The most richly illuminated manuscript is a copy of Albert von Sternberg's *Pontifex*, a folio codex on parchment dating from the reign of Charles IV.[14]

The Strahov collection of incunabula is the second biggest in Bohemia (after that of the State Library in Prague) and one of the finest in Europe.[15] It includes sixteen printed in Czech, of which seven are unique. Some of them come from the Plzeň press of Mikuláš Bakalář, such as Breidenbach's *Peregrinatio in terram sanctam* (1498) and *Life of Muhammad*, the *Life of Adam and Eve* (*c.* 1498) and the *Lucidár* (1498).[16] Other historic incunabula are a unique fragment of the earliest illustrated edition of Aesop's *Fables* (Prague, 1488) and the oldest extant

mat of his books. It was in 1507, too, that he went into partnership with Hieronymus Hölzel, a Nürnberg printer, and from then on a change was apparent not only in the visual style of his books but also in the type of works he selected for his list. In his early period Bakalář had been aiming

259. Mikulaš Bakalář's device (1507). Reproduction of the title page of Zdeněk Tobolka, Plzenský tiskař Mikuláš Bakalár, Písek 1927.

at the wider reading public and had chosen books that were educative and supported the values of the Counter-Reformation, Breidenbach's *Peregrinatio in terram sanctam* and *Life of Muhammad* being typical examples. These were short and inexpensive works designed to appeal to the readership he had in mind, as were his brief travel guides and his calendars, which sold very well. After he went into partnership with Hölzel, however, the influence of Renaissance Nürnberg became clearly apparent in the the artwork and the quality of paper and print in his books. Bakalář was one of the leading printers of the incunabular period in Czechoslovakia: of the thirty-one incunabula printed there, nine came from his press. See Leo Kohút, 'Das Werk des Wiegendruckers Mikuláš

260. The Strahov Evangeliary, the oldest manuscript in the abbey. 10th c.

261. Capricorn, from a parchment manuscript almanac. 15th c.

add on another room for the new accessions, and so the outstandingly beautiful and highly atmospheric Philosophy Hall came into being.

The dissolution of the Bohemian monasteries during the reign of Josef II dealt yet another blow to the Strahov library: many of its books were sold off to booksellers at giveaway prices.[11] However, this loss was soon offset, first by the acquisition of the libraries of two institutions

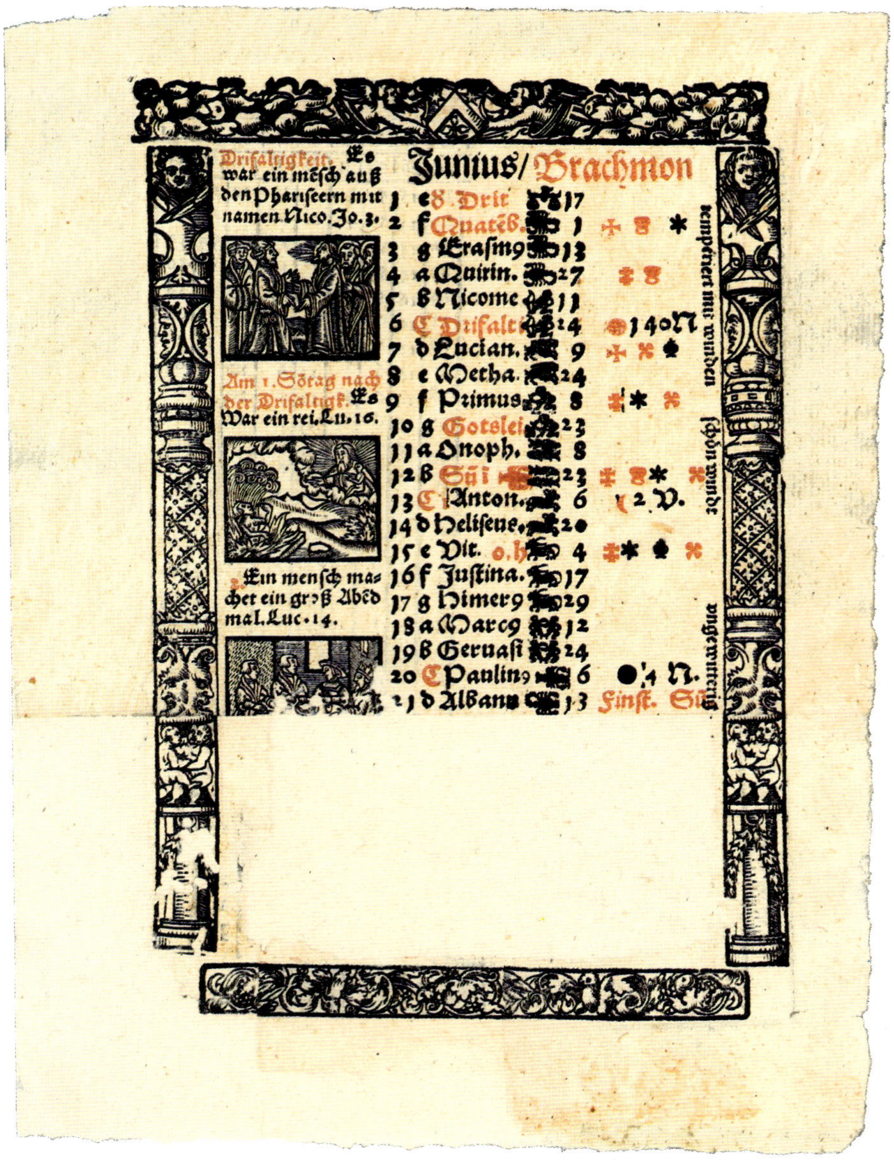

256. A page from a calendar printed at Prague. 16th c.

under the abbey's jurisdiction: St. Norbert's College and Milevský Monastery. Then in 1792 a very fine collection of Greek and Latin classics was bought from Josef von Riegger, and this was followed in 1798 by the acquisition of the private library of Antonin Strnad, the Director of the Prague Observatory. The enlightened Strahov librarian

however, there were some books in the university, mostly donated by professors, wealthy residents of Prague and other noblemen. In 1622 an imperial edict was issued handing over the control of the university to the Jesuits, and the 'Library of the Karolinum' (comprising all the libraries of the Jesuit colleges) was moved to the Klementinum. Thus two great libraries came into existence: that of the Jesuits (the *Biblioteca maior*) and the *Biblioteca minor*, which were amalgamated early in the eighteenth century to form a new library. This, like so many other libraries in Bohemia, was housed in a Baroque edifice, and its architecture and interior decoration are no less splendid than those of the great monastic libraries: the elaborate ceiling frescoes, the attractive two-tiered bookcases and the beautiful patterned floor create a bookish atmosphere similar to that of the Philosophy Hall in the Strahov library. See Petr Voit, *Pražské Klementinum*, Prague 1990.

11. Josef II, who succeeded Maria Theresa on the imperial throne of Austria, was a zealous reformer with high ideals for his country, and he wanted to eliminate anything that could be held to symbolize Bohemia's autonomy. His policy of suppressing the monasteries was an integral part of this programme.

12. See *Strahovská Knihovna*... 168-169.

13. See *Strahovská Knihovna*... 171. When the Strahov library became part of the Memorial Institute of the Nation's Writings, it entered a new period of rapid expansion. Before long its stock of 130,000 volumes had risen to 900,000, partly through the addition of some 400,000 volumes of monastic writings from various towns and abbeys in central and northern Bohemia. New acquisitions, such as the great collection of 50,000 volumes from the Karásek Gallery, sparked off a fresh round of donations from writers and thinkers such as the bibliophile J. Knytl and the poets V. Nezval and J. Hora. With the addition of major works of Czech literature of the eighteenth

and nineteenth centuries, the Strahov library became a fully representative museum of Czech writing.

14. Some of these manuscripts are remarkable for their very ornate and costly bindings made with velvet, gilded metal, rosettes inlaid with enamel palmettes, precious and semi-precious stones and even miniature reliefs of gilded embossed metal. Two such are the Strahov Evangeliary (9th-10th cent.) and the *Plenarium of St. George* (*c.* 1310). See Maleček, *Strahov Praha* 47, 86-87.

15. See *Strahovská Knihovna*... 170. Proctor ascribes the Prague incunabula to three anonymous printers: the 'Printer of the *Stratuum* (1478)', the 'Printer of the Bible (1488)' and the 'Printer of the New Testament (1497)'. The oldest dated book known to have been printed in Prague is the Bohemian Psalter of 1478: see A. Schubert, 'Die sicher nachweisbaren Inkunabeln Böhmens und Mährens von 1501', *ZB* 16 (1896) 51-61, 126-136, 176-185, 217-230. No book printed in Prague in the incunabular period bears a printer's name: see *BMC* III 808; Geldner II 352. For a fuller survey of Czech incunabula see P. Krasnopolski, 'Tschechische Inkunabeln', *Zeitschrift für Bücherfreunde*, n.s., 17 (1925) 95-102; Id., 'Prager Drucke bis 1620', *GJ* 4 (1927) 72-84.

16. Mikuláš Bakalář Štetina was typical of the incunabular printers of Bohemia and Slovakia. All that is known about his origins is that he was born in Hungary. He was educated at Krakow University but later, for reasons that we shall probably never know, he became interested in typography and worked as an assistant to a printer as yet unidentified. By 1493 he was living in Plzeň, where he was a prominent member of the local community. He set up a small print-shop in 1498, and with his family to assist him he did all the work involved in printing a book. The year 1507 marked the end of the first stage of his printing career: it was then that he started marketing his books himself, printing with more than one fount and varying the hitherto uniform for-

257. The library of Teplá Abbey.

Bohumír Jan Dlabač, a writer himself, added an impressive number of works by humanist and Bohemian nationalist authors and started making a systematic collection of newspapers and periodicals, which now offer an invaluable source of documentation for contemporary events. And in the early nineteenth century the library expanded rapidly. From 1801 onwards a number of avid collectors gave their books to Strahov, including the bibliographer Bartsch; in 1837 Václav Peutelschmidt donated his library of 9,000 volumes and in 1848 Jan Hauser, a priest from Peruc, did the same with his 8,000 volumes. Whenever a monk died his books went to the abbey library, and there was an unceasing inflow of new stock from institutions such as the Czech Academy of Science and

Art, as well as documentary records from local archives in Bohemia.[12]

In 1950 the Strahov library contained about 130,000 volumes, including 3,000 manuscript codices and no less than 2,500 incunabula. There is also a large collection of early printed books (i.e. those printed in the early sixteenth century), including a representative selection of theological and secular works from presses all over Europe.[13] The oldest manuscript dates from the ninth century: it is the famous Strahov Evangeliary, probably written at Tours and illuminated in the second half of the tenth century, which is one of the most splendid pieces of work produced by the School of Trier during the reign of Otto I. Among the library's other rare treasures are a codex containing four

258. One of the frescoes by Siard Nosecký in the Theology Hall.

chronicles of Frederick Barbarossa's incursions into Italy, based on local sources, and a copy of the Venerable Bede's *Historia Ecclesiastica Gentis Anglorum* in the hand of the calligrapher monk Ansbert. A number of volumes are of particular interest to the Czechs: they include a codex of the *Chronicles* written by the followers of Cosmas Vincentia and Abbot Jarloch, which comes from Milevský Monastery, and a manuscript of the early Czech translations of John Mandeville's *Travels* and of *Tristan und Isolde*. The library also possesses historic translations of the Bible. The most richly illuminated manuscript is a copy of Albert von Sternberg's *Pontifex*, a folio codex on parchment dating from the reign of Charles IV.[14]

The Strahov collection of incunabula is the second biggest in Bohemia (after that of the State Library in Prague) and one of the finest in Europe.[15] It includes sixteen printed in Czech, of which seven are unique. Some of them come from the Plzeň press of Mikuláš Bakalář, such as Breidenbach's *Peregrinatio in terram sanctam* (1498) and *Life of Muhammad*, the *Life of Adam and Eve* (c. 1498) and the *Lucidár* (1498).[16] Other historic incunabula are a unique fragment of the earliest illustrated edition of Aesop's *Fables* (Prague, 1488) and the oldest extant

mat of his books. It was in 1507, too, that he went into partnership with Hieronymus Hölzel, a Nürnberg printer, and from then on a change was apparent not only in the visual style of his books but also in the type of works he selected for his list. In his early period Bakalář had been aiming

259. Mikulaš Bakalář's device (1507). Reproduction of the title page of Zdeněk Tobolka, Plzenský tiskař Mikuláš Bakalár, Písek 1927.

at the wider reading public and had chosen books that were educative and supported the values of the Counter-Reformation, Breidenbach's *Peregrinatio in terram sanctam* and *Life of Muhammad* being typical examples. These were short and inexpensive works designed to appeal to the readership he had in mind, as were his brief travel guides and his calendars, which sold very well. After he went into partnership with Hölzel, however, the influence of Renaissance Nürnberg became clearly apparent in the the artwork and the quality of paper and print in his books. Bakalář was one of the leading printers of the incunabular period in Czechoslovakia: of the thirty-one incunabula printed there, nine came from his press. See Leo Kohút, 'Das Werk des Wiegendruckers Mikuláš

260. The Strahov Evangeliary, the oldest manuscript in the abbey. 10th c.

261. Capricorn, from a parchment manuscript almanac. 15th c.

20
1
3
4

printed calendar, for the year 1485, printed by Johann Alacraw at Vimperk (Winterberg).

Among the large collection of incunabula at Strahov are some from the very earliest period of typography: the *editio princeps* of Caesar's *De bello gallico* printed by Konrad Sweynheim and Arnold Pannartz, the first printers in Italy, at Subiaco Abbey in 1469; several books printed by the Frenchman Nicolas Jenson, who was the first to set up a press in Venice; and first editions of Greek and Latin classics from the famous printing house of Aldus Manutius; Hartmann Schedel's monumental *Liber Chronicarum*, printed by Anton Koberger at Nürnberg in 1493; and other books from the presses of great incunabular printers such as Gutenberg's assistant Peter Schöffer, Johann Senseschmidt, who worked at Nürnberg and Bamberg, and the renowned Leipzig printer Conrad Kachelofen.[17]

262. The imposing pile of Strahov Abbey. Coloured pen-and-ink drawing by J. Schimmel, late 18th c.

The majority of the books, representing a large proportion of all the European literature written from the sixteenth to the nineteenth century, are kept in two great rooms, the Philosophy Hall and the Theology Hall. The Philosophy Hall contains books on the subjects that were then taught at universities, namely philosophy, history, literature, geography, natural history, astronomy and mathematics. The Theology Hall also has books on European literature, but its greatest claim to fame is the huge collection of editions of the scriptures, from polyglot Bibles to small booklets about the New Testament. It also contains all the main writings of the Church Fathers and most of the literature of the Reformation.

Architecture. The oldest part of the Strahov library is the Theology Hall, built between 1670 and 1679 under Abbot Jeroným Hirnheim.

Bakalář-Štetina zu Pilsen', *GJ* (1966) 116-128.

17. See *Strahovská Knihovna*... 170. The Bohemian humanists were not unaffected by the upheavals in the educational world caused by the humanist movement in Italy. Sigismond Gelenius, for example, who was born in Prague in 1477 and died in Basel in 1544, studied at many of the major centres of learning in Italy, Germany and France, learnt several European languages and perfected his Greek and Latin in Italy. On his way back to Bohemia he stopped in Basel and there met Erasmus, who introduced him to Johann Froben, one of the great early printers of northern Europe, who took him on to the team of scholars working for his press. Gelenius translated and edited numerous classical and theological works for Froben. His most important work is entitled *Lexicon symphonum quatuor linguarum, Graecae scilicet, Latinae, Germanicae et Sclavinicae* (Basel, 1537). See P. Verrua, *Umanisti ed altri 'studiosi viri' italiani e stranieri di qua e di là dalle Alpi e dal Mare*, Geneva 1924, 97.

18. See *Strahovská Knihovna*... 172.

19. See *Strahovská Knihovna*... 174.

In the late seventeenth and eighteenth centuries, and especially during the Enlightenment, painting frescoes on the library ceiling of an imperial or other important monastery was not simply a matter of decorative art. The subjects depicted were meant to symbolize and draw attention to the intellectual interests of the person responsible for the work, who wanted the room to be dignified with pictorial representations of mythological and historical persons and events illustrating the high worth of human values and of the pursuit of true wisdom. What Abbot Mayer was trying to do in the Philosophy Hall at Strahov was to recreate the library of Louka u Znojma Abbey, not only by using the bookcases intended for it but also by reproducing its greatest artistic masterpiece, which was its ceiling fresco. That fresco, the idea for which had been conceived by Norbert Kerber in 1778, gave a 'historical account' of the intellectual development of the human race, featuring mythological scenes and historical figures and giving especial prominence to artists and scholars. The composition is deployed around two focal points, one at each end: Moses and Aaron with the Ten Commandments, symbolizing the transience of the Old Testament, are contrasted with St. Paul at the altar of the Unknown God on the Areopagus, preaching the eternal divine supremacy of Christ.

The artist commissioned to reproduce the composition and subject matter of the Louka fresco at Strahov was the great eighteenth-century Austrian painter Franz Anton Maulbertsch (1724-1796). After some time spent on discussions, tests and making preliminary sketches in miniature, the composition assumed its final form. The focal point is a relief of Adam teaching his sons to honour God, with Cain depicted as the first blasphemer rather than the archetypal fratricide. Adam stands out conspicuously against a black mountain range which symbolizes ignorance and the punishment of original sin, gazing at the light that radiates from civilized human society. Mankind is idealized in the forms of Deucalion and Pyrrha, who escaped the great flood and became the progenitors of the regenerated human race. The total chaos that ensues from giving free rein to one's natural instincts is represented by a centaur and a lecherous satyr in pursuit of a woman holding a tambourine. The scene of Alexander the Great and his horse Bucephalus is particularly interesting: Alexander is depicted not as a hero (as he usually is in Baroque frescoes) but as a personification of ambition and the lust for power, flaws of character that lead only to arrogance and the oppression of the weak. His example is presented as a warning against tyranny, a fate which would have overtaken many city-states had it not been for the philosophers, portrayed here in princely robes: first among them is Aristotle, followed by Diogenes in his tub,

Thereafter the stock of books grew so rapidly that less than fifty years later, in 1721, Abbot Marian Hermann had to expand the library. At the same time it seemed sensible to take the opportunity of redecorating the hall with new frescoes. The decision had to be taken quickly as there were not many years to go before 1727, when the abbey would be celebrating the centenary of the translation of the relics of St. Norbert from Magdeburg to Strahov. The artist eventually commissioned to do the frescoes was Siard Nosecký, who painted a series of compositions on subjects related to books, in panels framed by ornate Baroque stucco mouldings (1721-1726). The Theology Hall is an outstanding example of interior design effecting an ideal union between the style of the medieval monastic library and the style of the Baroque.[18]

263. The main room of the Klementinum library.

The Philosophy Hall of the Strahov library owes its existence to Abbot Wenceslaus Josef Mayer, a man whose many qualities included diplomacy and boldness of vision. Towards the end of the eighteenth century, at the very time when Emperor Josef II was launching his policy of suppressing the monasteries, Mayer embarked on the construction of a new wing for the Strahov library.[19] The new building, designed in the Neoclassical style by Ignatius Johann Pilliardi in 1783, was beautified with allegorical compositions in honour of Josef II by the sculptor Ignatius Francis Platzer. When it was learnt that the beautiful carved bookcases made by Johann Lahofer for the huge library of the Premonstratensian monastery at Louka u Znojma (Klosterbruck) were not going to be installed there, Abbot Mayer requested the Emperor's approval for the bookcases to be given to Strahov, or sold to it at a price that the abbey could afford. Eventually, after considerable structural alterations had been made to accommodate Lahofer's masterpieces of wood-carving, the Philosophy Hall was completed in 1794.

The Strahov library preserves a centuries-long tradition of caring for books. Its historic Theology and Philosophy Halls create a highly atmo-

265. The title page of the Life of Muhammad, Plzeň 1498.

264. More of the frescoes by Siard Nosecký in the Theology Hall.

Heraclitus lamenting the woes of human life, and Democritus, together with the sarcastic Phanias of Lesbos, mocking the folly of vanity. But the road to wisdom is not an easy one, largely because of the human greed for material goods: we are given the example of Crates, who, having lost all he possessed in a shipwreck, chose to devote his life to philosophy rather than expend his energies on amassing wealth all over again. The source of wisdom in Egypt is personified in the figure of the Sphinx, with the fathers of medical science – Asclepius, Hippocrates and Galen – clustered round her. Lawgivers and wise rulers, represented by Lycurgus and Solon, occupy a prominent place in the composition. Pythagoras is honoured for his mathematical knowledge. Wisdom, which finds practical expression in high-minded and just government, is symbolized in the person of Cleobulus, one of the Seven Sages of ancient Greece. The latter's daughter Cleobulina appears in the centre of a group of scientists: Thales, Archimedes and Anaxagoras. Two philosophers together occupy

266. Papal manuscript by Alberto di Štembank. Second half of the 14th c.

Dominica prima in adventu
domini officium ad missam.

Ad te levavi animam meam deus
meus in te confido non erubescam
neque irrideant me inimici mei et-
enim universi qui te expectant non
confundentur. Ps. Vias tuas domine
demonstra mihi et semitas tuas e-
doce me. Gloria. quod per totum adventum est observandum preter
festa andree nicolai concep-
tionis s. marie et s. thome

Excita quesumus domine
potentiam tuam et veni
ut ab imminentibus peccatorum
nostrorum periculis te mereamur
protegente eripi, et te liberante
salvari. Qui cum p. v. r. ii. s. marie que de beata maria. iii. de omnibus
sanctis Conscientias nostras que tres
collecte videlicet temporalis sancte
marie et de omnibus sanctis per totum
adventum usque ad vigiliam
nativitatis dicuntur tamen de sanctis que de
tempore minime omittitur. Nota
quando in aliis temporibus anni occurrunt in missa tres collecte.
tunc prima sub uno per dominum et alie
due sub uno per dominum concluduntur
Si autem quatuor. tunc prime due sub
uno per dominum et alie due sub uno
per dominum terminantur. Cum vero quinque
occurrunt. tunc in sequentibus tamen sub uno
per dominum et reliquis iiii sicut sub uno
per dominum sunt dicende. Et si sex oc-
currerint tunc prime due sub uno
per dominum et alie iiii tamen sub uno per dominum terminantur. Si vero septem occur-
rerint tunc i sub uno per dominum
et cetere sex sub uno per dominum concluduntur.
et hoc raro contingit nisi in festo
s. silvestri. festivis vero diebus
prima sit oratio festi cum oratione de
tempore sub una conclusione. deinde
alie due sequuntur. lectio epistole
beati pauli apostoli ad Romanos
Fratres. Scientes. xiii.
quia hora est iam nos de
sompno surgere. Nunc enim
propior est nostra salus quam cum
credidimus. Nox precessit. di-
es autem appropinquavit. Ab

spheric environment of rare distinction, while its priceless contents – the books themselves – epitomize the motto of the abbey's founder: *Ad omne bonum opus parati* ('Ready for every good work').

267. Imperio citation from Francis II to Joseph Mayer, Abbot of Strahov.

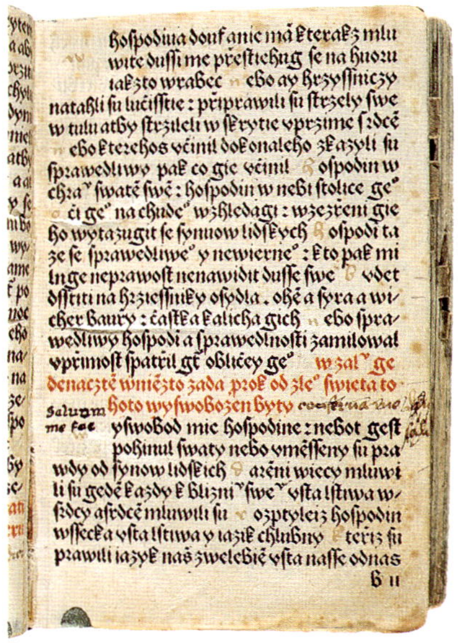

268. One of the first incunabula printed in Prague.

the topmost rung on the ladder of knowledge: Plato by virtue of his incisive logic and Socrates for his greatness of spirit. Here Socrates is immortalized at the moment when he is about to drink the hemlock. The funerary stele above his cell is intended to convey the idea that he does not stand for the doctrine of the transmigration of souls but for an afterlife of eternal happiness or punishment.

269. View of Venice from the travels of Bedrich di Donin in Italy. Early 17th c.

Si placeat uarios hominum cognoscere cultus,
Area longa patet Sancto contermina Marco,
Celsus ubi Adriacas Venetus Leo despicit undas.
Hic circum gentes cunctis ex partibus Orbis
Aethiopas, Turcos, Sclauos, Arabesq; Syrosq;
Inueniesq; Cypri, Cretæ, Macedumq; colonos,
Innumerosq; alios uaria Regione profectos.
Sæpe etiam nec uisa prius nec cognita cernes.

[illegible]

A·H·L·D·

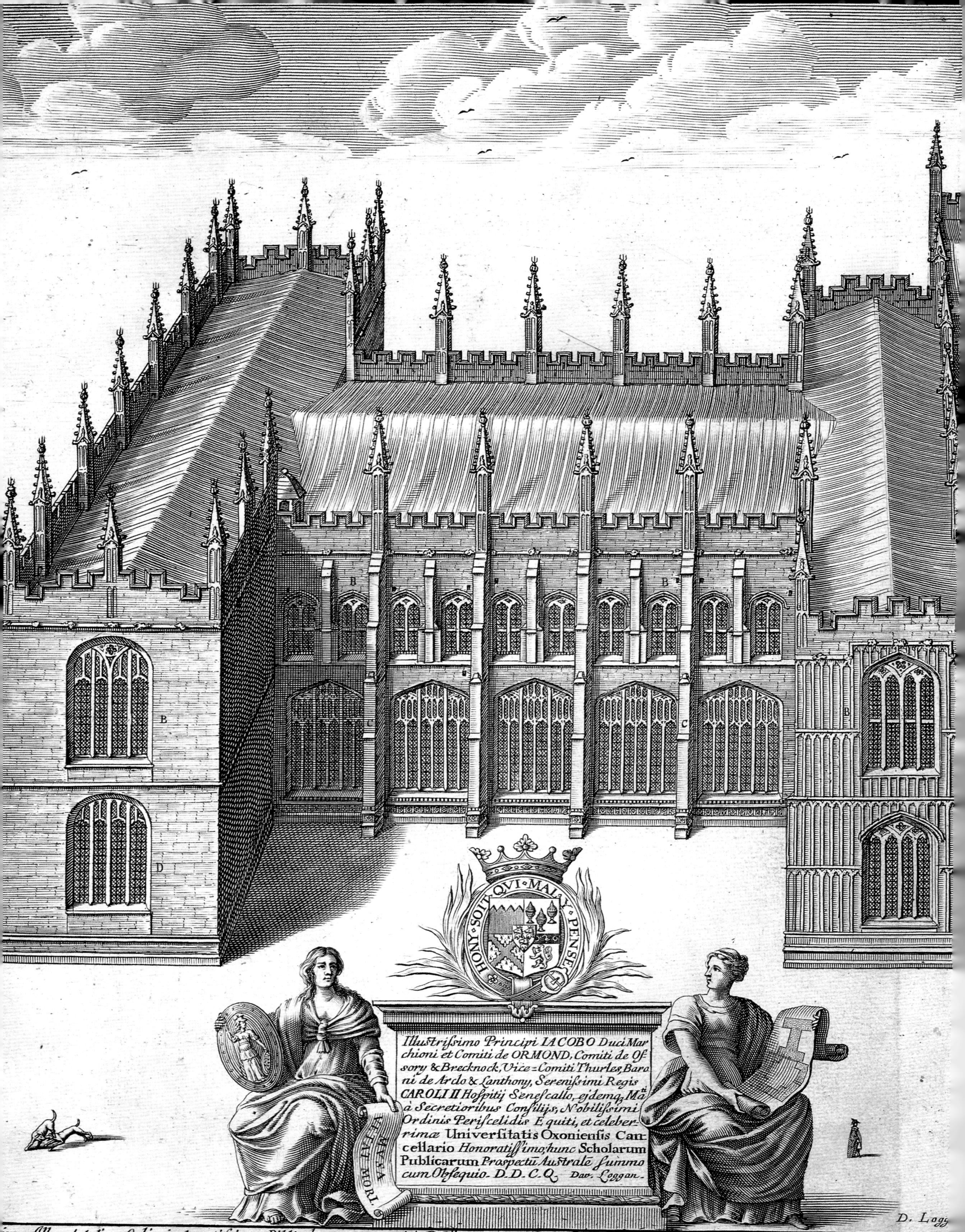

ima Illa et totius Orbis instructissima Bibliotheca quæ meritò Bodlejana nuncupatur in hanc quæ cernitur molē excreuit ab unicâ veteris Fun
idem Bibliotheca quicquid librorū possederit acceptū retulit Munificentiæ Humphredi Ducis Glocestrensis, et Joh: Tipetost Alumni Baliolensis, Q
ues Latinos Bibliothecæ moriens legauit. Postmodū (cùm Temporū virûmq; Injuriâ ita vastata fuerat ut libris direptis. et Pluteis ac Sedil
Aur. Qui à Serenissimâ Reginâ Elizabethâ in exteras Provincias sæpius legatus est, et apud fœderatos Belgas in Senatoriū Ord
n. 1600: hocq; et sequentibus annis Alij viri Literis & Nobilitate Illustres vel Libros vel Pecunias numeratas quotidie et affatim suppedit
teò ut totius Bibliothecæ Figura tunc Temporis literam T referre videretur. Et Hoc ipso Anno Honoratissimus simul ac Doctissimus Bodlei

The Bodleian Library

CHAPTER TWENTY-FIVE

The Bodleian Library of Oxford University, like other medieval and humanistic libraries, no longer exists in its original form. The present library owes its existence to a plan conceived by Sir Thomas Bodley, its founder, in 1598, but its origins go back to much earlier endeavours to set up college libraries in the University.

The initial nucleus of the Bodleian was a collection of books put togeth er for the use of students at the few colleges grouped round St. Mary's Church in High Street, Oxford, which then constituted the University. In 1320 Thomas Cobham, Bishop of Worcester, decided to make a home for these books by building an upper room to be used as a library over Convocation House, near St. Mary's Church, and he undertook to buy the furniture and fittings for the library himself. On his death, however, the situation took a turn for the worse: bad management of his estate left insufficient money for the building to be finished, and the creditors prevented his gift of manuscripts to the library from going through. The legal wrangle continued for about ten years, until 1337; the library was not finally built until thirty years after that, in 1367; and the furniture, that is the desks to which the books were chained, was not installed until 1410.[1]

This small collection of books was opened to humanist scholars through the munificence of Humfrey, Duke of Gloucester, a patron of literature who was firmly committed to humanist ideals. Duke Humfrey, as he is known, was the youngest son of King Henry IV. He was born in 1390 and created Duke by his brother Henry V in 1414. He may or may not have studied at Oxford, and in any case we do not know the name of the teacher who inspired him with his love of the classics, his keenness on the new learning and, above all, his passion for books. His liberal patronage of poetry and literature in general won him the sobriquet of 'Good Duke Humfrey', he donated money to the Divinity School at Oxford, and the gift of his private collection of at least 281 manuscript codices transformed the University Library, which until then had been quite small.[2]

The Duke's valuable collection has not survived. Duke Humfrey, the first large-scale English collector of humanist writings, had formed a close friendship with the Italian humanist Pier Candido Decembrio, who advised him on the purchase of manuscripts and also copied a representative selection of Greek and Latin works for him. In this way Duke Humfrey acquired Plato's *Republic*, the *Letters* of Pliny the Younger, poems by Dante, Petrarch and Boccaccio and a great many other ancient and medieval classics, none of which had been seen in England before.[3]

No better home could have been found for this splendid collection of manuscripts than a room in the Divinity School, the finest university building in England at the time and one of the most beautifully designed buildings of its period, especially in the way the tall, wide windows fit so harmoniously into its frontage. In 1444 it was decided to add another room over the Divinity School to house the precious books. However, time went by and

270. The Bodleian Library, after an engraving by David Loggan.

nothing was done, and had it not been for a generous donation of 1,000 marks from Thomas Kempe, the Bishop of London, which eventually made it possible for work to be put in hand, it is doubtful whether the project would ever have come to anything.[4]

The new library was opened to readers in 1488. It was laid out in the style typical of college libraries: symmetrically placed on either side of a central aisle, at right angles to the walls between the windows, were rows of double-sided lectern desks. The manuscripts were kept on shelves underneath the sloping desk-tops, to which they were chained. Unfortunately this beautiful library lasted a mere sixty-five years, the main reasons for its demise being a lack of real interest and a shortage of funds. Although the invention of printing made hitherto rare and expensive books available in large numbers at affordable prices, the

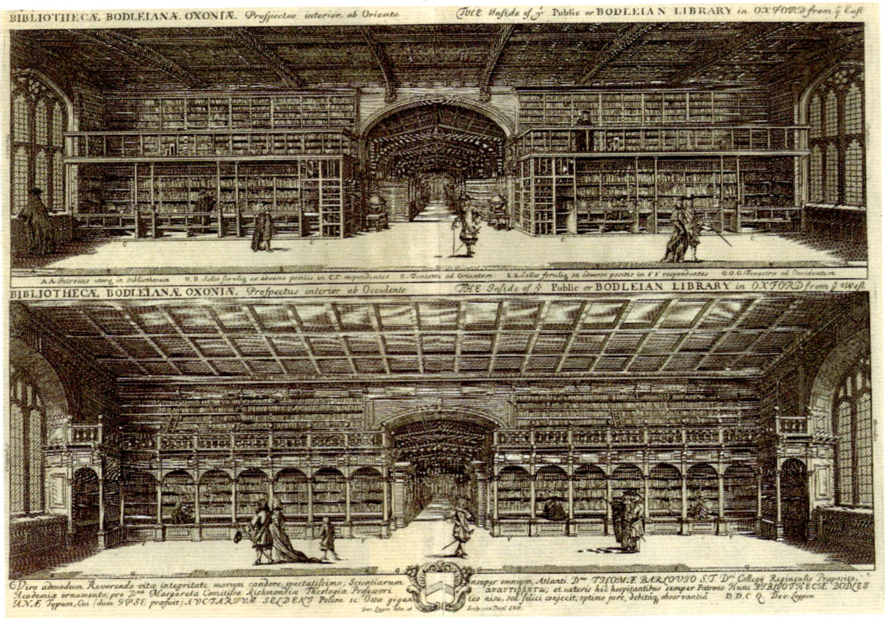

271. The interior of the Bodleian Library, after an engraving by David Loggan.

University authorities treated even the books they already had with appalling carelessness and disrespect.[5] They allowed indiscriminate borrowing, with the result that soon the library was just 'a great desolate room'. Then they started selling off manuscripts to bookbinders and even to tailors for the price of the vellum. By 1556 the room was empty of books and Congregation gave its permission for the desks – all that what was left in the library – to be sold to one of the colleges, Christ Church. This left Oxford University with no public library at all, and so it remained for the next forty-two years.[6]

Eventually, however, the library was resuscitated and named after Thomas Bodley, a man with a humanistic education to whom it was unthinkable that such a seat of learning as Oxford University should try

1. Under the library regulations drawn up by the University in 1367, Cobham's books were to be chained to the desks and admission was to be free to scholars and readers, but only 'at convenient times' (*temporibus opportunis*). It was also decided to sell off the most valuable books for a total of £40 or more, in order to raise enough money to pay a librarian. The relevant passage in the regulations is perhaps the earliest written ordinance laying down the duties of a university librarian in England. The University acquired outright ownership of Cobham's books in 1410 through the good offices of the Chancellor, Richard Courtenay: see J.W. Clark, *The Care of Books: An essay on the development of libraries and their fittings from the earliest times to the end of the eighteenth century*, Cambridge 1901, 151. On the history of the construction and architecture of the buildings surrounding St. Mary's Church see T.G. Jackson, *Church of St. Mary the Virgin, Oxford*, Oxford 1897, 90-106.

2. A. Hobson, *Great Libraries*, London 1970, 164; D. Rogers, *The Bodleian Library and its Treasures, 1320-1700*, Henley-on-Thames (Aidan Ellis) 1991, 11.

3. Pier Candido Decembrio was one of the luminaries of early Italian humanism and a very brilliant man. According to A. Corbellini, 'Appunti sull' Umanesimo in Lombardia', *Bollettino della Società Pavese di Storia Patria* 17 (1917) 5-13, he was born at Pavia in 1392 (according to others, in 1399) and died at Milan in 1477. His Greek teacher may have been the great Manuel Chrysoloras. He was the secretary of Pope Nicholas V and later held a similar post in the court of the Duke of Milan. Decembrio started translating Greek works into Latin for Pope Nicholas V. The first book he translated, Appian's *Roman History*, was followed by Plato's *Republic*, which he dedicated to Filippo-Maria Visconti, Duke of Milan. See M. Borsa, *Pier Candido*

272. The interior of Duke Humfrey's Library.

to function without a library. Bodley was born in 1544 at Exeter, a city with a tradition of humanistic studies and Greek teaching, into a Protestant family. In the reign of the Catholic Queen Mary Tudor his family emigrated to Geneva to escape persecution. Thomas, who was then twelve years old, had the opportunity there to broaden his intellectual horizons. He studied divinity with Calvin himself and Théodore de Bèze, Hebrew with Antoine Chevalier, and Greek language and literature with Filippo Beroaldo, who had succeeded Frangiskos Portos as Professor of Greek there.[7]

Returning to London on the accession of Elizabeth I, Bodley entered Magdalen College, Oxford, as an undergraduate. In 1563 he gained a fellowship at Merton College, where he continued his studies for the next twelve years. His Greek was so good that he also lectured on the subject, while at the same time he read widely in Natural Philosophy (i.e. natural sciences). He made a considerable name for himself in university circles, so much so that he was elected Proctor at the age of only twenty-five and appointed Public Orator soon after.[8] However, the Continent evidently held some kind of fascination for him and, being a man with political ambitions, he found that the pull of university life was no longer strong enough to keep him in England. In 1576 he set off to improve his general knowledge and linguistic skills by travel, visiting several countries and spending several years out of England. In 1585 he entered the diplomatic service. After a period spent travelling as Queen Elizabeth's representative to assist the Protestant cause in such countries as Denmark, France, Germany and the Netherlands, a mission which required delicate handling, he stayed on in the Hague. Bodley was unquestionably capable of rising to greater heights, but he had no taste for intrigues at Court and the manoeuvring for political influence among the great families of England, so in 1597 he retired from public life.[9]

On 23rd February 1598 he wrote to the Vice-Chancellor of Oxford University offering to resuscitate the University Library by restoring the premises at his own cost, donating his collection of books and manuscripts and endowing the foundation: 'I was to think, that my duty towards God, the expectation of the world, my natural inclination, & very morality, did require, that I should ... do the true part of a profitable member in the State: whereupon ... I concluded at the last to set up my Staff at the Library door in Oxford; being thoroughly persuaded, that ... I could not busy myself to better purpose, than by reducing that place ... to the public use of Students.'[10]

On 2nd March 1598 the legislative assembly of the University formally accepted Bodley's gift, and work started forthwith on the restoration of the library. Bodley's adviser in the project was Sir Henry Savile, an old friend from his time at Merton. By 1600 the restoration was complete but not enough progress had been made with the acquisition of books,

273. The library of Queen's College, Oxford, after an engraving by O. Jewitt.

Decembrio e l'Umanesimo in Lombardia, Milan 1893; E. Ditt, 'Pier Candido Decembrio', *Memorie del R. Istituto Lombardo di Scienze e Lettere* 24 (1931) 21-108. On his translations of Plutarch and Plato see V. Zaccaria, 'P.C. Decembrio traduttore di Plutarcho e di Platone', *IMU* 2 (1959) 194-195. Duke Humfrey, who had great confidence in Decembrio's judgment, commissioned him to buy books – mainly Latin classics – on a regular basis for an annual stipend of 100 ducats. Decembrio had hoped to be remunerated for his services by being given the freehold of the villa that had once belonged to Petrarch, but this request was ignored.

4. The Divinity School is an architectural gem, notable for the delicate tracery of the whole design and especially the vaulted ceiling, even though the overall effect is perhaps excessively ornate. The intersections of the ceiling ribs are ornamented with 455 bosses carved with the coats of arms or monograms of the benefactors mainly responsible for the construction of the School, Thomas Kempe and his uncle, Cardinal John Kempe, being prominent among them.

274. The Arts End of the Bodleian Library, showing the north window and the bookshelves of 1613.

and the opening of the library was therefore delayed for about two years so that the first impression should be worthy of the effort that had gone into it. When it was eventually opened on 2nd November 1602 there were 299 manuscripts and 1,700 printed volumes on its shelves. Bodley was knighted soon afterwards by James I and the library was called the Bodleian from that time on. Sir Francis Bacon, a friend of his, gave him a presentation copy of *The Advancement of Learning*, accompanied by a

275. Sir Thomas Bodley. Engraving from a portrait painting. From Mrs. R. Lane Poole, Catalogue of Portraits in the Bodleian Library, *71.*

letter in which he describes Bodley's library as 'an ark to save learning from deluge'. By the time the first printed catalogue of the Bodleian was published in 1605, three years after it opened, it contained about 6,000 volumes.[11]

Architecture. The invention of printing, and the resulting increase in the potential for the production and dissemination of books, led to radical changes in library design, which in the early Renaissance was still as it had been in the Middle Ages.[12] So the designers of the new library

5. Hobson, *op. cit.* 164; Rogers, *op. cit.* 9. On the layout of college libraries at Oxford (e.g. Corpus Christi, Merton) and Cambridge, and of other libraries elsewhere (e.g. the Chapter Library at Hereford), see Clark, *op. cit.* 171-198.

6. Hobson, *op. cit.* 166.

7. By far the best source of information on Bodley's childhood, youth and education is his own brief autobiography, which was first published at Oxford (printed by Henry Hall at the University Press in 1647): *The Life of Sir Thomas Bodley, the Honourable*

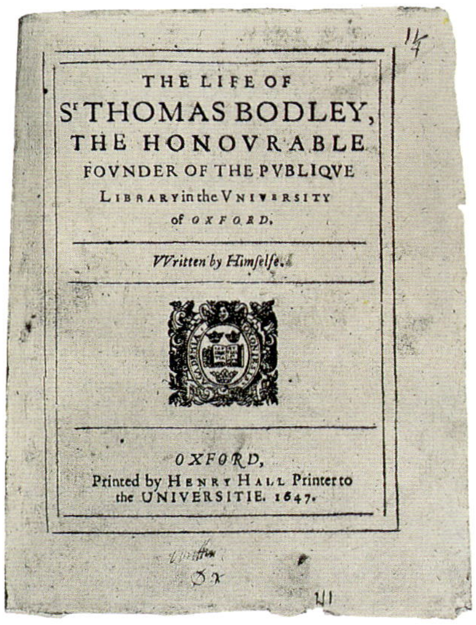

THE LIFE OF
Sr THOMAS BODLEY,
THE HONOVRABLE
FOVNDER OF THE PVBLIQVE
LIBRARY in the VNIVERSITY
of OXFORD.

Written by Himselfe.

OXFORD,
Printed by HENRY HALL Printer to the UNIVERSITIE. 1647.

276. The Life of Sr Thomas Bodley, *Oxford, Henry Hall (Printer to the University), 1647.*

277. St. Peter. Miniature in a Greek manuscript of the New Testament, Constantinople, early 12th c. (Auct. T. infra 1.10, fol. 292v).

278. Illuminated initial: King David enthroned, with harp. From the Ormesby Psalter, England (English school of the late 13th - early 14th c.) (Douce 366, fol. 10r).

279. Dante seated at his desk. Illuminated initial in a manuscript of the Inferno, *Venice, early 15th c. (Canon. ital., 107, fol. 1).*

280. An initial illuminated by Filippo Strozzi, from Pliny the Elder, Historia naturalis, *Venice, Nicolaus Jenson.*

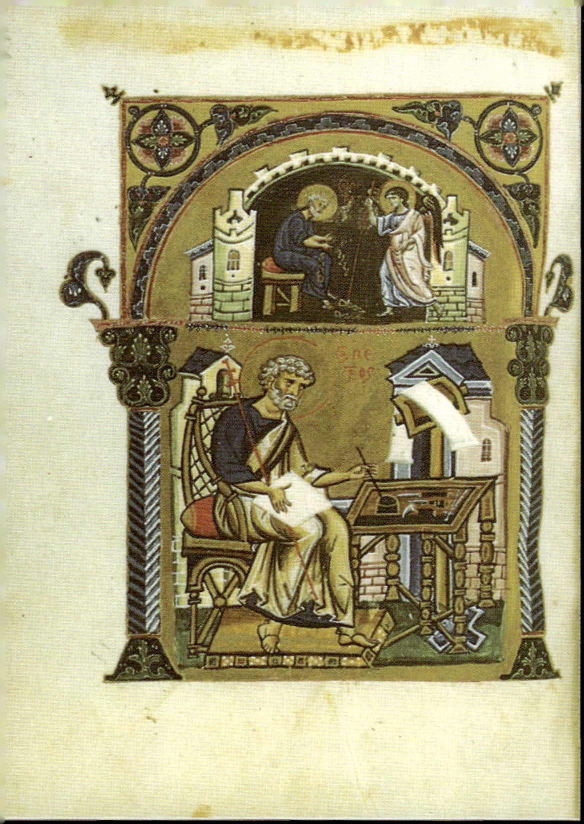

abiit in consilio impiorũ: ⁊ in uia
peccatorum non stetit: ⁊ in cathe
dra pestilentie non sedit
Sed in lege domini uoluntas eius: ⁊ i
lege eius meditabitur die ac nocte
Et erit tamquam lignum qd plã
tatum ẽ secus decursus aquarũ: qd
fructum suũ dabit in tempore suo.

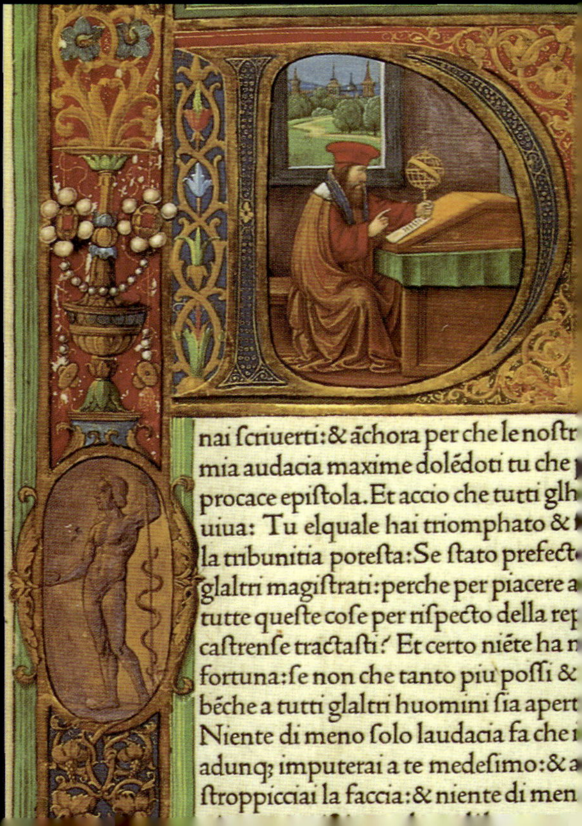
nai scriuerti: & ãchora per che le nostr
mia audacia maxime dolẽdoti tu che
procace epistola. Et accio che tutti glh
uiua: Tu elquale hai triomphato &
la tribunitia potesta: Se stato prefect
glaltri magistrati: perche per piacere a
tutte queste cose per rispecto della rep
castrense tractasti: Et certo niẽte ha n
fortuna: se non che tanto piu possi &
bẽche a tutti glaltri huomini sia apert
Niente di meno solo laudacia fa che
adunq; imputerai a te medesimo: & a
stroppicciai la faccia: & niente di men

borrowed a number of features from the layout that had come to prevail in college libraries in England in the sixteenth century. The scale of the room, as dictated by the dimensions of the Divinity School, was ideal for a well-organized, up-to-date university library laid out in accordance with the latest design principles. The windows, which were the main source of light, presented a problem, and so Bodley followed medieval practice in the positioning of the reading-desks but with some major improvements as regards the shelving of the books. The desks were still in pairs facing each other, but each pair was now attached to and sepa-

281. Manuel Philes, Bestiary. *A Greek manuscript copied by Angelos Vergikios, 1564, with illuminations possibly by his daughter.*

rated by a bookcase with shelves on both sides, which greatly increased the available shelf space. This carrel system had probably been first used at Merton College some ten years earlier. The final result produced by Bodley and his advisers was a distinctive new approach which conveyed something of the atmosphere of a medieval monastic library, here adapted to the Renaissance style that had evolved in Italian libraries while preserving the 'feel' of a functional library meeting the needs of a centre of learning such as Oxford University. The layout of the Bodleian served as a model for other university libraries in England for at least the next hundred years.[13]

282. The interior of the Bodleian Library. Anonymous drawing.

Founder of the Publique Library in the University of Oxford.

8. Bodley, *op. cit.* 3.

9. *Ibid.* 13.

10. *Ibid.* 14-15.

11. Sir Henry Savile, a man of great erudition who was successively Warden of Merton and Provost of Eton, rendered signal services to education and literature, most notably with his eight-volume edition of the works of St. John Chrysostom, which were printed in Greek at his own press at Eton (1610-1613). In 1619 Savile gave his Greek types to Oxford University. These types, not notable for their clarity, were greatly inferior to the famous *grecs du roi* of the French King François I, designed and cut by Claude Garamont after the script of Angelos Vergikios, which Savile had originally hoped to get. See N. Barker, *The Oxford University Press and the Spread of Learning, 1478-1978*, Oxford 1978, 10. The first book to be printed in Greek in England was the *Homilies* of John Chrysostom (with Latin

283. Aesop's Fables, *Strasbourg, Heinrich Knoblochtzer, c. 1481 (with English translation written in by hand).*

Verum eni potes pe[r] legatos a samys postulare &c. Wherfor it is necessarye that thou sende an ambassady unto the Samyens: that they will sende to the Esope: And that thou shalt pardonne & forgyve to them theyr offence.
Que si hec fecerit, i[n] tua manu samios habes/ ffor if thou mayst have Esope: they of Samye been in thy handes.
Tunc cresus hoc consilio suasus. And the kynge sodenly sent an ambassady to them of Samye &c
Viri samy cupio eqndem ad regis pedes me conferre my lordes of, it plesith me wel to goo toward the kynge
Set vobis prius fabulam narrare But or I goo thedre I woll tell yow a fable

Quo tempore aialia bruta ad vnu[m] conveniant In tyme whenne beestes cowde speke. lupi ouibus bellum intulerunt the wolves made warre ayenst the shepe. Igitur oues cum se a lupis tueri nequirent And because the shepe myght not kepe them ne hold them ayenst the wolves

Auxilium a canibus postulaverunt they demaunded helpe of the dogges.
Qui pro ouibus pugnantes lupos &c By the which the shepe made the wolves to turne bakwarde.
Tunc lupi cum se bello inferiores &c And because the wolves cowde not myght nat. yet ne have any pray, ne wynne no thynge vpon the shepe. because of the dogges that kepte them.
Pacem perpetuam offerunt ouibus per legatos the wolves sent an Ambassade vnto the shepe for to have perpetuell peace with them.
Modo unicam pacis conditionem recip[iant] ut canes &c And for to have peas. the wolves went and demaunded, that for to esshewe all suspection. the dogges shold be taken to the wolves. or elles distroyed for euer
Oues stolide lupis credentes &c And the shepe as fooles. for to have good peas and concorde. consentid to this demaunde
Igitur lupi occisis canibus &c And whanne al the dogges were slayne: the wolves toke vengeance on the shepe as apperith.
Decreuerunt: decreed. Determynde
Nullo pacto mitteretur sholde nott goo &c
Decreto samiorum non paruit Obeyed nott to the will of the samyens
Set una cum legato ad cresum &c But went with the ambassady toward the kynge
Coramque eo se presentauit And whanne he was come to the kynges courte &c
Indignabundus ait he was wroth and angry with hym selfe And seide as by that meanys

exeplū aliorū copias ɔtra samios trāsmittere. m regiꝰ nūctiꝰ impedimēto fuisset/ qui regi iq̄t. nunq̄ posses samo potiri. m esopꝰ. cuiꝰ ɔsilio samy vtūt² prius inde amoueatur. Verū eni potes ꝑ legatos a samys postulare. ꝙ si tibi transmittatur esopus. et g̃tias quasuis ⁊ tributorū remissionē ipsis indulges. quod si hoc faciūt. itua manu samios habes Tūc cresꝰ hͦ ɔsilio suasꝰ. quēdā ex ꝓceribꝰ samū legauit. Is cū samū applicuit. atq3 i ɔtione mā data regis exposuit. suasitq3 plebi. vt regi esopū trāsmitterent Esopꝰ in ɔtionē accitꝰ. ac regis sentenciā sētiēs ait Viri samy cupio eq̄dē ad regis pedes me cōfere. s3 vobis pꝛiꝰ fabulā narraē

QVo tempore animalia bruta ad vnū ɔueniebant. lupi ouibus bellū intulerunt. igit² oues cum se a lupis tueri nequirent. auxiliū a canibꝰ postulaŕt/ qui ꝓ ouibuꝰ pugnantes lupos dare terga vrgebant. Tunc lupi cū se bello inferiores ɔnoscerēt ꝓpter canes. pacē ꝑpetuā offerūt ouibꝰ ꝑ legatos. modo vnicam pacis ɔditionē recipiāt. vt canes ad oiez suspitionē belli tollēdā lupis custodiēdi tradātur/ oues stolide lupis credētes/ pacē cū lupis accepta ɔditioē firmaŕt. Igit² lupi occisis canibꝰ absq3 dificultate oues ꝑdide/rūt. Hāc fabulā cū dixit esopꝰ. sami vt esopꝰ nullo pacto mitteretur decreuerūt. ℂ At esopꝰ decreto samiorū nō paruit. s3 vna cū legato ad cresū regē nauigauit. corāq3 eo se presentauit/ cresus vero cū Esopū cōspexit indignabūdꝰ ait. hic ne auctor est. ꝙ sa-

hic ne auctor est Is this same he: for the syght of whom: that they of Samye wole nat obeye vnto me.
Maxime rex non vi nec coactus adsum &c Ha right dere sir & kynge magnyfyke. Certainly I am nott come before thy magestye by force. but of my good wil I am comen to the dygnytye so amesse of thy benyngnite. that thou shalt here what I shall say to the.
Datum ut copia fandi The kynge gave hym audience. And leve to say what he wold &c And thus he saide.
Homo quidam ... Whilis that other day was a man which chassyde the flyes. The whiche may take any thynge, the whiche seynge that he wolde have killed there.
Inquit locusta &c she prayed the fouler/ saynge, I pray ye that thou withoute cause wilte nat sle me

The books were arranged in alphabetical order, by authors, and a 'Table' or shelf-list was affixed to the end of each bookcase as a guide to readers. The manuscripts were shelved together with the printed books, not in a separate room, but the small-format books (octavos and the smaller quartos) were kept in 'Closets' and the rare books in locked cupboards known as 'the Archives'.[14]

Thomas Bodley realized that if he wanted to create a great library he would have to rely on gifts from others besides himself, and so in 1600 he opened a Register of Benefactors, in which it was soon considered an honour for one's name to be inscribed. The first name entered in the Register is that of Thomas Sackville, the Chancellor of the University at the time. Besides having their names recorded in the Register with a note of the titles of the books given by them or bought with their money, benefactors were commemorated by specially-made brass stamps bearing their coats of arms, which were impressed on the covers of the books so acquired. Among those whose gifts are evidenced by such stamps are Lord Hunsdon, Sir Robert Sidney, Sir Walter Raleigh and Sackville himself. Other benefactors included Lord Lumley (the High Steward of the University, who was perhaps the greatest English book collector of his time), William Camden, Sir Robert Cotton (a friend and adviser of Bodley's), Henry Savile and Thomas Allen (who gave an important collection of medieval manuscripts). To supplement the donations, many books were purchased from two London booksellers, John Norton and John Bill, a considerable number came from the Frankfurt Book Fair and some were bought on expeditions made for that purpose to Paris,

284. Another view of the Bodleian Library. Arts End is on the left, Duke Humfrey's Library in the background. Published by J.H. Parker in London, 1836.

translation), printed by Reginald Wolfe in 1543. Wolfe, who was born in Gelderland (then in Germany), went to England in 1530 and set up as a printer in 1542. He had the most complete stock of types in England, which may have come from the matrices of printers in Basel. See C. Clair, *A History of Printing in Britain*, London 1965, 81-82.

12. Hobson, *op. cit.* 167; Rogers, *op. cit.* 29, 42.

13. Although the output of incunabula in England does not compare with that of the great early centres of printing in Italy, Germany, France and elsewhere, at least 230 editions were printed in the four cities which had presses in the fifteenth century (London, Oxford, Westminster and St. Albans). Not one book in Greek or Hebrew was printed in England in the incunabular period, and only a few isolated editions of the classics: works by Phalaris, Aristotle (both in Latin translation), Cicero, Virgil, and some of Donatus's grammatical works (Proctor II 714-724). The first

285. The coat of arms of Oxford University, held by two angels. From John Scolar, Questiones super libros Ethicorum Aristotelis, *Oxford 1518.*

286. Theodoros Komnenos Doukas Synadenos and his wife Eudokia. From a Greek manuscript of the Typikon *(Rule) of the Convent of the Good Hope in Constantinople. Lincoln College, Oxford (gr. 35, fol. 8r).*

Seville and Rome. Authors and printers, too, gave copies of their books to the Bodleian for the furtherance of learning.[15]

Most of the books in the Bodleian Library were in Latin, including many by little-known writers of dubious merit such as Borrhaeus, Farinaceus and Menochius. Next in order of preference came books in Italian, followed by French, Spanish, Greek and Hebrew. The largest subject category was Theology; there were also sizable sections on Jurisprudence and Medicine, as well as books dealing with the two medieval divisions of the 'liberal arts', the Trivium (Grammar, Logic

287. Shelving and carrels in the Chapter Library at Hereford.

and Rhetoric) and the Quadrivium (Arithmetic, Geometry, Astronomy and Music). Bodley also showed a keen interest in oriental languages, making systematic purchases of Arabic and Hebrew manuscripts for the library, and he seriously considered sending a suitably-qualified scholar to the Ottoman Empire to investigate the possibility of buying works of oriental literature. In 1608 he asked Paul Pinder, an Oxford graduate who was then consul of the Company of English merchants in Aleppo, to collect books in Syriac, Turkish, Arabic, Persian or any other oriental language. One of his ideas was to build up a collection of Chinese literature, and by the time of his death in 1613 – although there was still no one in England who actually knew the language – the Library already contained forty-nine Chinese manuscripts.[16] The Bodleian also has a fine collection of Greek manuscripts, in most important respects the best in England. Its nucleus consists of 244 codices from the library of Francesco Barocci, acquired in 1629, plus twenty-nine from Sir Thomas Roe's collection and ninety-four donated by Archbishop Laud between 1635 and 1641. These fine holdings were enlarged by further purchases in the early decades of the nineteenth century.[17]

The person Bodley chose to look after all these valuable books and manuscripts and arrange and catalogue them was Thomas James,[18] a man particularly well qualified for the task. James, who came from a

press in Oxford was set up in 1478, ten years before the library over the Divinity School opened, by a German called Theodoric, known as Rood ('the Red'). It ran until 1485 and produced at least thirteen editions including Aristotle's *Logica* (in the Latin translation by Leonardo Aretino) and the *Epistles* of Phalaris: see Clair, *op. cit.* 52; Barker, *op. cit.* 2-4.

14. Rogers, *op. cit.* 23, 28.

15. Hobson, *op. cit.* 167.

16. Hobson, *op. cit.* 168; Rogers, *op. cit.* 28-29. For information on English book-collectors in general see Bernard Quaritch (ed.), *Contributions towards a Dictionary of English Book-Collectors, as also of some Foreign Collectors*, London 1969 (reprint of the edition of 1892-1921).

17. Rogers, *op. cit.* 84. Francesco Barocci (Barozzi) was born of aristocratic Venetian parents at Candia, Crete, on 9th August 1537, and died at Venice in 1604. He was taught Greek and Latin by Andrea Doni and later read philosophy and mathematics at the Studium in Padua. His main interest was the development of scientific thought, a subject which he

288. The device of Oxford University with the initials AC:OX (= Academia Oxoniensis). From J. Barnes, Academiae Oxoniensis Pietas, *Oxford 1603.*

289. Ioannes Argyropoulos teaching in the University of Constantinople. 15th c. (Barocc. 87, fol. 33v).

290. St. John the Evangelist and the hermit St. Luke of Stiri, from the Slavonic manuscript Gospels of Gavril, *written in Moldavia by the copyist Gavril in 1429 (Canon. gr. 122, fols. 235v, 144v)*

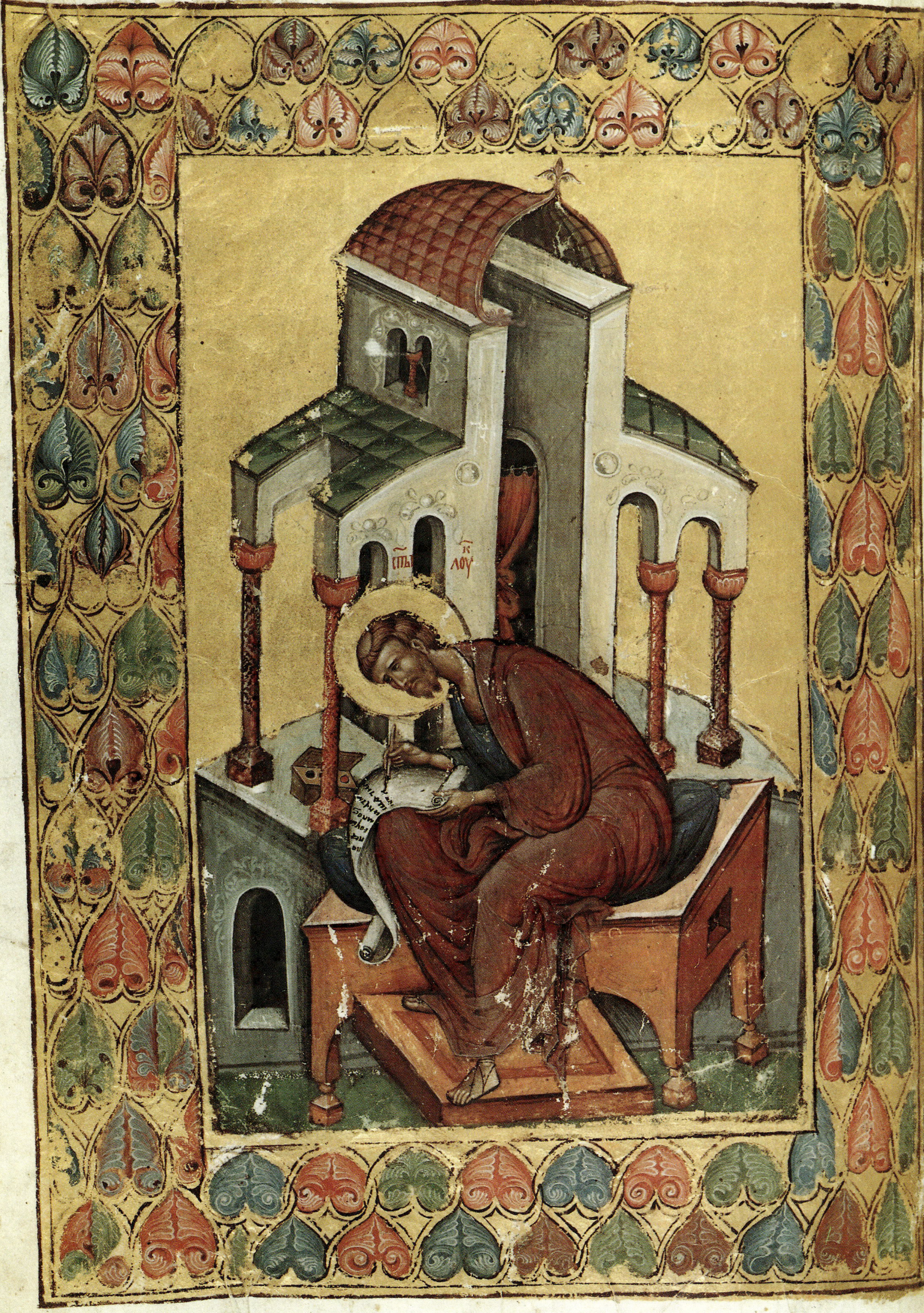
СТЫ
ЛОУК

similar background to Bodley, had been a scholar of Winchester and was now a Fellow of New College. A prodigious polymath and a stickler for scholarly accuracy, he edited the first English printing of a classic handbook of library management, Richard de Bury's *Philobiblon*, and, working in close co-operation with Bodley, he compiled the *Catalogue* of the Bodleian, one of the earliest library catalogues ever published. The *Catalogue* is basically an alphabetical list of the books and manuscripts in the library, classified according to the categories in which they were arranged on the shelves. Not content with this, James also started to compile a subject catalogue, which he never completed.[19]

291. Portrait of Thomas James, which hangs with other portraits of Bodley's Librarians in the Curators' Boardroom. Unsigned painting dated between 1620 (according to the evidence of the inscription) and 1629, the year of James's death.

pursued through profound study and criticism of ancient science modelled on Greek and Latin writers. To his nephew Giacomo Barocci (1562-1617) he bequeathed a collection of manu-

292. The device of Oxford University with the motto Sapientiae et felicitatis. *From J. Barnes,* A Catechism or Short Kind of Instruction, *Oxford 1588.*

scripts which was probably bought by an English bookseller and was presented to the Bodleian by the Earl of Pembroke in 1629. The original catalogue of the Barocci collection is in the Biblioteca Marciana (no. 1528) and was published by I.F. Tomasini in his book *Bibliothecae Venetae manuscriptae publicae et privatae...*, Utini 1650, 64, 66-91, 92. William Herbert, 3rd Earl of Pembroke, who gave the collection to the Bodleian, had bought it for £700: see H.O. Coye, *Catalogi codicum manuscriptorum bibliothecae Bodleianae, pars prima*, Oxford 1853, cols. 9-416. On the Barocci see *DBI* 6 (1964) 495-499, 508-509; Rogers, *op. cit.* 84, 88.

18. Rogers, *op. cit.* 44. Thomas James was born at Newport, Isle of Wight, in 1573(?) and died in 1629. He received the best education England had to offer, acquired a solid grounding in a wide range of subjects and was referred to by some of his contemporaries, with good reason, as a 'living library'. He spe-

By the time he died, Sir Thomas Bodley had secured enough endowments to cover running expenses and the cost of new acquisitions, thus making the library financially self-sufficient. Moreover, an agreement which Bodley negotiated in 1610 between Oxford University and the Stationers' Company in London ensured that his library would receive a steady supply of new books at no cost, for the Company undertook that one unbound copy of every new work printed by its members was to be given to the Bodleian Library, free, 'for ever'. This arrangement has been confirmed by successive Copyright Acts: to this day, the Bodleian is one of the six copyright deposit libraries in Britain.[20]

Sir Thomas Bodley died in 1613 and was given a state funeral in Merton College chapel. His qualities and his way of life were an inspiration to poets and philosophers such as Robert Burton, the author of *The Anatomy of Melancholy*.

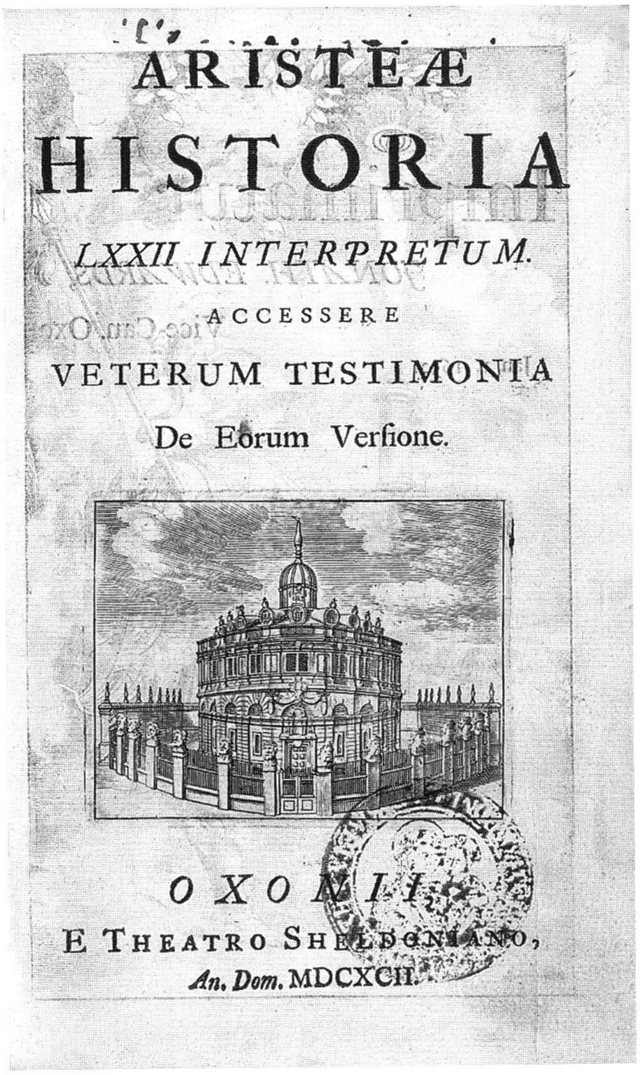

293. Aristeas, Historia, *Oxford, Sheldonian Theatre, 1692.*

cialized in palaeography and had a flair for picking out forged readings and interpolations in classical and postclassical texts. With the support of the university establishment, James undertook to examine the manuscripts in the possession of the Oxford and Cambridge colleges and compile a register of them. This duly appeared with the title of *Ecloga Oxonio-Cantabrigiensis*, London 1600. In 1620 poor health compelled him to resign as Bodley's Librarian, but his interest in academic work remained undimmed and he embarked on a campaign, probably with the help of a team of scholars, of combing through the writings of the Church Fathers in private and public libraries in England to correct textual errors introduced by Roman Catholic editors.

19. Hobson, *op. cit.* 167; Rogers, *op. cit.* 51.

20. Hobson, *op. cit.* 171; Rogers, *op. cit.* 51. In England the problem of literary piracy, payment of royalties and printers' privilege was not taken as seriously by the authorities as it was in Italy, France and Germany. However, efficient policing by the government and the limited output of books kept matters within bounds. Furthermore, the great English universities granted sole rights of a kind to their own presses and thus greatly reduced the opportunities for piracy.

ABBREVIATIONS

Arch. Class.	*Archivio Classico.*
AGGW	*Abhandlungen der Göttinger Gesellschaft der Wissenschaften.*
Anal. Boll.	*Analecta Bollandiana*, Brussels 1822- .
ASI	*Archivio Storico Italiano.*
AV	*Archivio Veneto.*
AVT	*Archivio Veneto Tridentino.*
BCH	*Bulletin de Correspondance Hellénique.*
BICS	*Bulletin of the Institute of Classical Studies.*
BMC	*Catalogue of Books Printed in the XVth Century now in the British Museum*, I-XII, London 1908-1985.
BMGS	*Byzantine and Modern Greek Studies.*
BSA	*Annual of the British School at Athens.*
BSR	*Papers of the British School at Rome.*
BZ	*Byzantinische Zeitschrift.*
Census	*Incunabula in American Libraries. A third census of fifteenth-century books recorded in North American collections*, ed. F.R. Goff, New York (Kraus/Reprint) 1973.
Charta	Staikos, K.S., *Charta of Greek Printing: The Contribution of Greek Editors, Printers and Publishers to the Renaissance in Italy and the West. Vol. I: Fifteenth Century*, Cologne 1998.
CIAG	*Commentaria in Aristotelem Graeca*, Berlin.
CSHB	*Corpus Scriptorum Historiae Byzantinae*, Bonn 1828- .
DBI	*Dizionario Biografico degli Italiani*, 1960- .
DOP	*Dumbarton Oaks Papers.*
EEBΣ	*Ἐπετηρίς Ἑταιρείας Βυζαντινῶν Σπουδῶν.*
EMA	*Ἐπετηρίς Μεσαιωνικοῦ Ἀρχείου.*
Eph	*Ἐκκλησιαστικός Φάρος.*
Fabricius	Fabricius, I., *Bibliotheca Graeca sive notitia scriptorum veterum graecorum*, 12 vols., Hamburg 1790-1809.
FGrHist	*Die Fragmente der griechischen Historiker*, ed. F. Jacoby, Berlin, Leiden, 1923- .
Firmin-Didot	Firmin-Didot, A., *Alde Manuce et l'Hellénisme à Venise*, Paris 1875.
Geldner	Geldner, F., *Die deutschen Inkunabeldrucker. Ein Handbuch der deutschen Buchdrucker des XV. Jahrhunderts nach Druckorten*, 2 vols., Stuttgart 1968-1970.
GJ	*Gutenberg Jahrbuch.*
GRBS	*Greek, Roman and Byzantine Studies.*
GW	*Gesamtkatalog der Wiegendrucke*, 8 vols., published by the Kommission für Gesamtkatalog der Wiegendrucke, repr. Stuttgart (A. Hiersemann) 1968.
H	Hain, L., *Repertorium bibliographicum in quo libri omnes ab arte typographica inventa usque ad annum MD. typis expressi ordine alphabetico vel simpliciter enumerantur vel adcuratius recensentur*, 2 vols., Stuttgart/Paris 1826-1838.

HBW	Milkau, F., and G. Leyh (ed.), *Handbuch der Bibliothekswissenschaft*, I, Wiesbaden 1952, III.1, Wiesbaden 1955.
IG	*Inscriptiones Graecae*, Berlin 1873– .
IMU	*Italia Medioevale e Umanistica.*
JHS	*Journal of Hellenic Studies.*
JRS	*Journal of Roman Studies.*
KRS	Kirk, G.S., J.E. Raven and M. Schofield, *Οἱ Προσωκρατικοί Φιλόσοφοι* (= *The Presocratic Philosophers*, 2nd edn., Cambridge 1983, tr. D. Kurtovik), Athens 1988.
Krumbacher	Krumbacher, K., *Ἱστορία τῆς Βυζαντινῆς Λογοτεχνίας* (= *Geschichte der byzantinischen Litteratur von Justinian bis zum ende des ostromischen Reiches (527-1453)*, Munich 1891, tr. G. Sotiriadis), 3 vols., repr. Athens (V. Grigoriadis) 1974.
MTA	*Magyar Tydományos Akadémia.*
MU	*Medioevo e Umanesimo.*
NAV	*Nuovo Archivio Veneto.*
NBU/NBG	*Nouvelle Biographie Générale depuis les temps le plus reculés jusqu'à nos jours*, 46 vols., Paris (Firmin-Didot Frères) 1852-1877.
OAME	Orlandi, G., *Aldo Manuzio, editore*, 2 vols., Milan 1976.
OCP	*Orientalia Christiana Periodica.*
PG	Migne, J.P., *Patrologiae Cursus Completus. Series Graeco-Latina*, vols. 1-161, Paris 1857-1866.
PL	Migne, J.P., *Patrologiae Cursus Completus. Series Latina*, vols. 1-122, Paris 1844-1855.
Pr	Proctor, R., *An Index to the Early Printed Books in the British Museum: From the invention of printing to the year MD. With notes of those in the Bodleian Library*, 4 vols., London 1898-1938; Supplement, London 1899.
Proctor	Proctor, R., *The Printing of Greek in the Fifteenth Century*, Oxford 1900.
RE	*Paulys Real-Encyclopädie der classischen Altertumswissenschaft*, ed. G. Wissowa et al., Stuttgart/Munich 1893-1978.
RIS	*Rerum Italicarum Scriptores.*
SIFC	*Studi Italiani di Filologia Classica.*
TAPA	*Transactions and Proceedings of the American Philological Association.*
TM	Centre de Recherche d'Histoire et Civilisation de Byzance, *Travaux et Mémoires.*
VBV	Vespasiano da Bisticci, *Le Vite*, ed. Aulo Greco, 2 vols., Florence (Istituto Nazionale di Studi sul Rinascimento) 1970-1976.
ZB	*Zentralblatt für Bibliothekswesen.*

BIBLIOGRAPHY

BIBLIOGRAPHY

El-Abbadi, M., *The Life and Fate of the Ancient Library of Alexandria*, Paris (UNESCO) 1990.

Ábel, J., *Adalékok a humanismus történetéber Magyarországon*, Budapest 1880.

— *Analecta ad historiam renascentium in Hungaria litterarum spectantia*, Budapest 1880.

— 'Magyarországi humanisták és a Dunai Tudós Társaság', *Ért. MTA* 8 (1880) 8.

— (ed.), *Irodalontörténeti Emlékek*, 2 vols., Budapest 1886-1890.

Ábel, J., and Hegadüs, I., *Analecta nova*, Budapest 1903.

Ackerman, J.S., *The Architecture of Michelangelo*, I-II, London, 1961.

Adam, P., *L'humanisme à Sélestat. L'école. Les Humanistes. La bibliothèque*, Sélestat (Imprimerie Stahl) 1987, 51-67.

Adler, Ada, *Suidae Lexikon* (= *Lexicographi Graeci*, XI), Stuttgart 1971.

Aesop: *The Medici Aesop*, with intro. by Everett Fahy and trans. by B. McTigue, New York 1989.

Ahrweiler, Hélène, 'L'histoire et la géographie de la région de Smyrne entre les deux occupations turques (1081-1317), particulièrement au XIIIe siècle', *TM* 1 (1965) 1-204.

— 'Sur la carrière de Photius avant son patriarcat', *BZ* 58 (1965) 348-363.

(see also Glykatzi-Ahrweiler)

Akominatos, Niketas: *see* Choniates

Alce, P.V., and d'Amato, A., *La biblioteca di S. Domenico in Bologna*, Florence 1961.

Alexander, J.J.G., and Gibson M.T. (ed.), *Medieval Learning and Literature: Essays presented to Richard William Hunt*, Oxford 1976.

Alexander, P.J., 'Church Councils and Patristic Authority: The Iconoclastic Councils of Hiereia (754) and St. Sophia (815)', *Harvard Studies in Classical Philology* 63 (1959) 493-505.

— *The Oracle of Baalbek*, Washington D.C. 1967.

Allen, T.W., 'The Origin of the Greek Minuscule Hand', *JHS* 40 (1920) 1-12.

Altman, C.B., *Khorsabad: The Citadel and the Town*, Chicago 1938.

Amatucci, A.G., *Storia della letteratura latina cristiana*, Turin 1955.

Amici, C.N., *Foro di Traiano: Basilica Ulpia e bibliotheche*, Rome 1982. (ROME)

d'Ancona, P., *La miniatura fiorentina*, Florence 1913.

André, J., *La vie et l'oeuvre d'Asinius Pollion*, Paris 1949.

André-Leickman, B., and Ziegler, C., *La naissance de l'écriture: cunéiforme et hiéroglyphes*, Paris 1982.

Angold, M., *A Byzantine Government in Exile: Government and society under the Laskarids of Nicaea (1204-1261)*, Oxford 1975.

Ankiwicz-Kleehoven, H., *Der Wiener Humanist Johannes Cuspinian*, Graz/Köln 1959.

Annuaire 1985: Spécial 500e anniversaire de la naissance de Beatus Rhenanus, Sélestat (Les amis de la bibliothèque humaniste de Sélestat) 1985.

Anzelewski, Fedja, 'Reichenauer Perikopenbuch' in *Wolfenbütteler Cimelien...* 80-86.

Ardura, B., and Dolista, K., *Prémontrés en Bohème, Moravie et Slovaquie*, Prague (Karlova University) 1993.

Arethae scripta minora, ed. L.G. Westerink, I, Leipzig 1968.

Armstrong, Elizabeth, *Robert Estienne, Royal Printer: An historical study of the elder Stephanus*, Cambridge 1954.

Arns, R.P.E., *La technique du livre d'après Saint Jérôme*, Paris 1953.

Arrigoni, E., 'Ecumenismo Romano-Cristiano a Bisanzio e tramonto del concetto di Ellade ed Elleni nell' impero d'Oriente prima del mille', *Nuova Rivista Storica* 55 (1971) 151.

Ashby, T., and Platner, S.B., *A Topographical Dictionary of Ancient Rome*, London 1929.

Astruc, C., *Byzance et la France médiévale*, Paris 1958.

— 'L'inventaire dressé en septembre 1200 du trésor de la bibliothèque de Patmos. Édition diplomatique', *TM* 8 (1981) 15-30.

— 'Les listes de prêts figurant au verso de l'inventaire du trésor et de la bibliothèque de Patmos dressé en septembre 1200', *TM* 12 (1994) 495-499.

Athanassiadi, Polymnia, 'Persecution and Response in Late Paganism: The evidence of Damascius', *JHS* 113 (1993) 1-29.

Avril, F., *Bibliothèque Nationale. Manuscrits: La librairie de Charles V*, Paris 1968.

Baatz, D., 'Fensterglas, Glasfenster und Architektur' in A. Hoffmann and E.L. Schwandner (ed.), *Bautechnik der Antike*, Berlin 1991, 1 ff.

Balayé, S., *La Bibliothèque Nationale des origines à 1800*, Geneva 1988.

Baldacchini, L., 'Dalla "libraria domini" alla biblioteca publica' in L. Baldacchini (ed.), *La Biblioteca Malatestiana di Cesena*, Rome 1992, 133-167.

Bandini, A.M., *Specimen litteraturae florentinae saeculi XV*, 2 vols., Florence 1747-1751.

Bardy, G., 'Les origines des écoles monastiques en Orient' in *Mélanges J. de Ghellinck*, I, Gembloux 1951, 293-309.

Barfucci, E., 'Vespasiano da Bisticci (1421-1498) e la sua bottega' in *Lorenzo de' Medici e la società artistica del suo tempo*, Florence 1964, 247-271.

Barker, N., *The Oxford University Press and the Spread of Learning, 1478-1978*, Oxford 1978.

Bataillon, L.J., Guyot, B.G. and Rouse, R.H. (ed.), *La production du livre universitaire au Moyen εge. Exemplar et pecia* (Actes du symposium tenu au Collegio San Bonaventura de Grottaferrata en mai 1983), Paris 1988.

Batiffol, P., 'Librairies byzantines à Rome', *Mélanges d'Archéologie et d'Histoire de l'École Française de Rome* 8 (1888) 297-308.

Baurmeister, Ursula and Laffite, Marie Pierre, *Des livres et des rois*, Paris 1992.

Bayer, E., 'Demetrius Phalereus', *Tübinger Beiträge zur Altertumswissenschaft* 36 (1942) 105 ff.

Bec, C., *Les marchands écrivains à Florence 1375-1434*, Paris 1967.

Beck, H.-G., *Kirche und theologische Literatur im byzantinischen Reich*, Munich 1959.

— 'Der Leserkreis der byzantinischen Volksliteratur' in *Byzantine Books and Bookmen: A Dumbarton Oaks Colloquium 1971*, Dumbarton Oaks 1975, 47-67.

Bedouelle, G., *Lefèvre d'Étaples et l'intelligence des écritures*, Paris 1976.

Bell, H.I., *Egypt from Alexander the Great to the Arab Conquest*, Oxford 1948.

Benakis, L.G., «Ἡ θεωρητική καί πρακτική αὐτονομία τῆς φιλοσοφίας ὡς ἐπιστήμης στό Βυζάντιο», *Ἀφιερωματικός τόμος στόν κ. Δεσποτόπουλο*, Athens 1991, 239-243.

Bentley, R., *Dissertation upon the Epistles of Phalaris*, London 1777.

Berbérian, H., 'Autobiographie d'Anania Širakači', *Revue des études arméniennes*, n.s., 1 (1964) 189-194.

Berger, S., 'De la tradition de l'art grec dans les manuscrits latins des évangiles', *Mémoires de la Société Nationale des Antiquaires de France* 52 (1891) 144-154.

Berkovits, Ilona, *La miniatura nella corte di Mattia Corvino. Ferrara ed il Rinascimento ungherese*, Budapest 1941.

— *Illuminated Manuscripts from the Library of Matthias Corvinus*, Budapest 1963.

Beroni, G., *La Biblioteca Estense e la cultura ferrarese ai tempi del duca Ercole I, 1471-1505*, Turin 1903.

Berschin, W., *Griechisch-lateinisches Mittelalter. Von Hieronymus zu Nikolaus von Kues*, Berne/Munich 1980.

— 'The Medieval Culture of Penmanship in the Abbey of St. Gall' in King and Vogler, *The Culture of the Abbey of St. Gall*, 69-80.

— 'Latin Literature from St. Gall' in King and Vogler, *The Culture of the Abbey of St. Gall*, 145-156.

Bertalot, L. and Campana, A., 'Gli scritti di Jacopo Zeno e il suo elogio di Ciriaco d'Ancona', *La Bibliofilia* 41 (1939) 356-376.

Berve, H., *Die Tyrannis bei den Griechen*, II, Munich 1966.

Berzeviczy, A., *Beatrix Királyné*, Budapest 1908.

Bethe, E., *Buch und Bild im Altertum*, Amsterdam 1964.

Beylié, L. de, *L'Habitation Byzantine: Recherches sur l'architecture civile des Byzantins et son influence en Europe*, Grenoble/Paris 1902.

Bezold, F. von, 'Kaiserin Judith und ihr Dichter Walahfrid Strabo', *Historische Zeitschrift* 130 (1924) 377.

Bibl, V., 'Niedbruck und Tanner: Ein Beitrag zur Entstehungsgeschichte den Magdeburger Centurien und zur Charakteristik König Maximilians II.', *Archiv für österreichische Geschichte* 85 (1898) 379-430.

Biblioteca Apostolica Vaticana, Florence (Nardini) 1985.

Biblioteca Marciana: Venezia, Florence (Nardini) 1988.

Biblioteca Medicea Laurenziana: Firenze, Florence (Nardini) 1986.

Bidez, J., 'Aréthas de Césarée, éditeur et scholiaste', *Byzantion* 9 (1934) 391-408.

— *Un singulier naufrage littéraire dans l'antiquité*, Brussels 1943.

Bieler, L., *Irland, Wegbereiter des Mittelalters*, Olten 1961.

— 'The Classics in Celtic Ireland' in R.R. Bolgar (ed.), *Classical Influences on European Culture, A.D. 500-1500*, Cambridge 1971, 45-49.

Bietak, M., 'Connections between Egypt and the Minoan World: New results from Tell el-Dab'a/Avaris' in *Egypt, the Aegean and the Levant: Interconnections in the second millennium B.C.*, London 1995, 19-28.

Bietenholz, P., *Basle and France in the Sixteenth Century*, Geneva 1971.

Bigi, E., 'Andronico Callisto' in *DBI* 3 (1961) 162-163.

— 'Aurispa, Giovanni' in *DBI* 4 (1962) 593-595.

Billanovich, G., *I primi umanisti e le tradizioni dei classici latini*, Freiburg 1953.

— 'Veterum vestigia vatum', *IMU* 1 (1958) 155-243.

Birt, T., *Das antike Buchwesen*, Berlin 1882.

Bischoff, B., 'Wendepunkte in der Geschichte der lateinischen Exegese im Frühmittelalter', *Sacri Eruditi, Jaarboek voor Godsdienstwetenschappen* 6 (1954) 189-279.

— 'Il monachesimo irlandese nei suoi rapporti col continente' in *Settimane di studio del Centro italiano di studi sull'alto medioevo*, IV, Spoleto 1957, 121-138.

— *Mittelalterliche Studien*, I-II, Stuttgart 1966-1967.

— *Lorsch im Spiegel seiner Handschriften*, Munich 1974.

— 'Die Hofbibliothek unter Ludwig dem Frommen' in Alexander and Gibson, *Medieval Learning and Literature*, 3-22.

— *Manuscripts and Libraries in the Age of Charlemagne*, tr. and ed. M. Gorman, Cambridge 1994.

Bischoff, B., Virginia Brown and J.J. John, 'Addenda to *Codices Latini Antiquiores*', *Mediaeval Studies* 54 (1992) 286-307.

Bittel, K., 'Untersuchungen auf Büyükkale', *Mitteilungen der Deutschen Orient-Gesellschaft* 91 (1958) 57-72.

Blanchard, A. and Bataille, A., in *Recherches de Papyrologie* 3 (1964) 161.

Blanck, H., *Τό βιβλίο στήν ἀρχαιότητα* (= *Das Buch in der Antike*, Munich 1992, tr. D.G. Georgovasilis and M. Pfreimter), Athens 1994.

Blemmydes: *Nicephori Blemmydae curriculum vitae et carmina*, ed. A. Heisenberg, Leipzig 1896.

Bloch, Denise, 'La formation de la Bibliothèque du Roi' in Vernet, *Histoire des bibliothèques françaises*, 311-331.

Blum, R., *La Biblioteca della Badia Fiorentina e i codici di Antonio Corbinelli*, Vatican City 1951.

Blum, W., *Georgios Gemistos Plethon: Politik, Philosophie und Rhetorik im spätbyzantinischen Reich (1355-1452)*, Stuttgart 1988.

Blumenthal, H.J., '529 and its Sequel: What happened to the Academy', *Byzantion* 48 (1978) 369-385.

Bodley, Thomas, *The Life of Sir Thomas Bodley, the Honourable Founder of the Publique Library in the University of Oxford*, Oxford (printed by Henry Hall at the University Press) 1647.

Bohmer, A. and Widmann, H., 'Von der Renaissance bis zum Beginn der Aufklärung' in *HBW* III.1 526-527.

Bohn, R., *Altertümer von Pergamon*, II, Berlin 1885.

Boissonade, J.F., *Anecdota Nova*, Paris 1844.

Bologna, P., *La stampa fiorentina del monastero di S. Jacopo di Ripoli e le sue edizioni*, Turin 1893.

Bonfante, Larissa, et al. (with contributions by J. Chadwick, B.F. Cook, W.V. Davies, J.F. Healey, J.T. Hooker and C.B.F. Walker), *La naissance des écritures: Du cunéiforme à l'alphabet* (= *Reading the Past: Ancient Writing from Cuneiform to the Alphabet*, London 1990, tr. Christiane Zivie-Coche), Paris 1994.

Bonfiglio Dosio, G., 'Il testamento di Novello Malatesta (9 aprile 1464)', *Romagna arte e storia* 8, 22 (1988) 11-18.

Boon, A., *Pachomiana latina*, Louvain 1932.

Bordreuil, Pierre (ed.), *Une bibliothèque au sud de la ville: Ras-Schamra-Ougarit VII*, Paris 1991.

Borges, J.L., «Τό τεῖχος καί τά βιβλία», *Διερευνήσεις* (= *Otras inquisiciones*, tr. A. Kyriakidis), Athens 1990.

Borsa, M., *Pier Candido Decembrio e l'Umanesimo in Lombardia*, Milan 1893.

Boselli, A.I., 'Le pitture della biblioteca dell'ex-convento dei benedettini in Parma', *Aurea Parma* 2 (1913) 167-172.

Botfield, B., *Praefationes et Epistolae Editionibus Principibus Auctorum Veterum Praepositae*, Cambridge 1861.

Bottéro, J., *Mésopotamie: L'écriture, la raison et les dieux*, Paris 1989.

Boyancé, C., 'Le culte des Muses chez les philosophes grecs', *Bibliothèque des Écoles Françaises d'Athènes et de Rome* 141 (1937) 329 ff.

Boyd, C.E., *Public Libraries and Literary Culture in Ancient Rome*, Chicago 1915.

Branca, V., *Tradizione delle opere di Giovanni Boccaccio*, Rome 1958.

Bréhier, L., 'Un patriarche sorcier à Constantinople', *Revue de l'Orient chrétien* 9 (1904) 261-268.

— 'L'enseignement classique et l'enseignement religieux à Byzance', *Revue d'histoire et de philosophie religieuses* 21 (1949) 34-69.

— *La Civilisation Byzantine*, III, Paris 1950.

Brizzi, G.P. and Verger, J. (ed.), *Le università dell' Europa. Le scuole e i maestri. Il Medioevo*, Milan 1994.

Brown, H.F., *The Venetian Printing Press*, London 1891.

Brown, P., 'The Rise and Function of the Holy Man in Late Antiquity', *JRS* 61 (1971) 80-101.

Browne, R.W., *A History of Classical Literature*, II: *A History of Roman Classical Literature*, London 1851.

Browning, R., 'Recentiores non Deteriores', *BICS* 7 (1960) 11-21.

— 'An Unpublished Funeral Oration on Anna Comnena', *Proceedings of the Cambridge Philological Society* 8 (1962) 1-12.

— 'Literacy in the Byzantine World', *BMGS* 4 (1978) 39-54.

— 'Further Reflections on Literacy in Byzantium' in *Τό Ἑλληνικόν* (festschrift in honour of S. Vryonis), I, New Rochelle N.Y. 1990, 69-84.

Bruce-Mitford, R.L.S., 'The Art of the Codex Amiatinus' (Jarrow Lecture), *Journal of the British Archaeological Association*, 3rd ser., 32 (1969) 1-25.

Brunet, J.C., *Manuel du libraire et de l'amateur des livres*, IV, Paris (repr. Maisonneuve et Larose) 1966.

Brunhölzl, F., 'Der Bildungsauftrag der Hofschule' in B. Bischoff (ed.), *Karl der Grosse, Lebenswerk und Nachleben*, II: *Das geistige Leben*, Düsseldorf 1965, 28-41.

Bryer, A. and Herrin, Judith (ed.), *Iconoclasm*, Birmingham 1977.

Buchowiecki, W., *Der Barockbau der ehemaligen Hofbibliothek in Wien, ein Werk J.B. Fischers von Erlach*, Vienna 1957.

Buchthal, H. and Belting, H., *Patronage in Thirteenth-Century Constantinople: An atelier of Late Byzantine book illumination and calligraphy*, Washington 1978.

Bude, E.G., *Armarium und Κιβωτός*, Berlin 1939.

Budge, E.A.W., *The Egyptian Book of the Dead (The Papyrus of Ani): Egyptian text, transliteration and translation* (London 1899), new edn., New York/London 1949.

Bünting, H. and Letzner, J., *Braunschweig-Lüneburgische Chronica*, Braunschweig 1772.

Burkert, W., 'La genèse des choses et des mots: Le papyrus de Derveni entre Anaxagore et Cratyle', *Études Philosophiques* 25 (1970) 443-455.

Bury, J.B., *A History of the Eastern Roman Empire from the Fall of Irene to the Accession of Basil I (8O2-67)*, London 1912.

Burzachechi, M., 'Ricerche epigrafiche sulle antiche bibliotheche del mondo greco', *Rendiconti dell' Accademia Nazionale dei Lincei* 18 (1963) 75-97 and 39 (1984) 307-331.

Butler, A.J., *The Arab Conquest of Egypt and the Last Thirty Years of the Roman Domination*, Oxford 1902.

Cagnat, M.R., 'Les bibliothèques municipales dans l'empire romain', *Mémoires de l'Institut National de France* 38 (1909) 1-26.

Calderini, A., 'Ricerche intorno alla biblioteca e alla cultura greca di Francesco Filelfo', *Studi Italiani di Filologia Classica* 20 (1913) 204-224.

Callegari, A., 'La casa del Petrarca in Arquà ed il suo ultimo restauro', *Atti e Memorie della R. Accademia di Scienze, Lettere ed Arti di Padova*, n.s., 11 (1924-1925) 211-257.

Callmer, C., *Antike Bibliotheken* (= Opuscula Archaeologica, III), Lund/Leipzig 1944.

Cameron, Averil, 'The End of the Ancient Universities', *Cahiers d'histoire mondiale* 10 (1966-1967) 653-673.

— 'The Last Days of the Academy at Athens', *Proceedings of the Cambridge Philological Society* 15 (1969) 7-29.

— *Agathias*, Oxford 1970.

Cammelli, G., *I dotti bizantini e le origini dell' Umanesimo*, I: *Manuele Crisolora*, Florence 1941; II: *Giovanni Argiropulo*, Florence 1941; III: *Demetrio Calcondila*, Florence 1954.

Camp, J.M., *The Athenian Agora*, London 1986.

Campana, A., 'Le biblioteche della provincia di Forl™. I: Cesena' in D. Fava (ed.), *Tesori delle biblioteche d'Italia: Emilia-Romagna*, Milan 1931, 3-43.

Camporeale, S.I., *Lorenzo Valla. Umanesimo e teologia*, Florence 1972.

Canart, P., 'Scribes grecs de la Renaissance', *Scriptorium* 17 (1963) 56-82.

— 'Démétrius Damilas, alias le "Librarius Florentinus"', *Rivista di Studi Bizantini e Neoellenici*, n.s., 14-16 (1977-1979) 281-347.

Canfora, L., *Ἡ χαμένη βιβλιοθήκη τῆς Ἀλεξανδρείας* (= *La biblioteca scomparsa*, Palermo 1986, tr. F. Arvanitis), Athens 1989.

Cantalamessa Carboni, G., *Biografia di Enoc d'Ascoli*, n.p. 1918.

Capasso, M., *Storia fotografica dell' officina dei papiri*, Naples 1983.

Carcopino, J., *Les secrets de la correspondance de Cicéron*, II, Paris 1947, 305-329.

Carmenati, M., 'Un diplomato naturalista del Rinascimento: Andrea Navagero', *NAV* 24 (1912) 164-205.

Cassiodorus, *Institutiones*, ed. R.A.B. Mynors, Oxford 1937.

Castellani, C., 'Il prestito dei codici manoscritti della Biblioteca di San Marco a Venezia nei suoi primi tempi e le conseguenti perdite dei codici stessi', *Atti del Imp. Reg. Istituto Veneto*, 7th ser., 8 (1896-1897) 311-377.

Castrifrancanus, A., *Oratio habita in funere Urbani Bellunensis*, Venice 1524.

Catrettoni, G., *Das Haus des Augustus auf dem Palatin*, Mainz 1983.

Cavallo, G., *Ricerche sulla maiuscola biblica*, Florence 1967.

— 'Il libro come oggetto d'uso nel mondo bizantino', *XVI. Internationaler Byzantinisten-Kongress*, Vienna 1981, 395-423.

— 'La cultura italo-greca nella produzione libraria' in V. Scheiwiller (ed.), *I Bizantini in Italia*, Milan 1986, 495-612.

— (ed.), *Libri editori e pubblico nel mondo antico*, Rome/Bari 1989.

— 'Le tavolette come supporto della scrittura: qualche testimonianza indiretta', *Bibliologia* 12, Turnhout 1992, 97-105.

Cecchi, A., *The Piccolomini Library in the Cathedral of Siena* (= *La Libreria Piccolomini nel Duomo di Siena*, Florence 1982, tr. A. McCormick), Siena 1991.

Cecchini, G., 'La quattrocentesca biblioteca del convento di S. Domenico di Perugia' in *Miscellanea di scritti vari in memoria di Alfonso Gallo*, Florence 1956, 249-254.

— *Sei biblioteche monastiche rinascimentali*, Milan 1960.

— 'Evoluzione architettonico-strutturale della biblioteca pubblica in Italia dal secolo XV al XVII', *Accademie e Biblioteche d'Italia* 35 (1967) 27-47.

Černý, J., *Paper and Books in Ancient Egypt*, London 1952.

Champion, P., *La librairie de Charles d'Orléans*, Paris 1910.

Chastel, A., 'Le platonisme et les arts de la Renaissance' in *Congrès de Tours et Poitiers ... 1953*, Paris 1954.

— *Art et humanisme à Florence au temps de Laurent le Magnifique*, Paris 1982.

Cheles, L., *The Studiolo of Urbino: An Iconographic Investigation*, Wiesbaden 1986.

Chevalier, J. and Gheerbrant, A., *Dictionnaire des Symboles*, III, Paris 1974.

Chiera, E., *List of Personal Names from the Temple School of Nippur*, Philadelphia 1916.

Choniates, Niketas Akominatos, *Ἱστορία*, ed. C.A. Fabrotus, Venice 1729.

— *Historia*, ed. J.L. van Dieten, 2 vols., Berlin 1975.

(see also Lampros)

Christ, K. and Kern, A., 'Das Mittelalter' in *HBW* III.1 336-345.

Christ, U., 'Die Bibliothek Reuchlins in Pforzheim', *ZB* 52 (1924).

Christes, J., *Sklaven und Freigelassene als Grammatiker und Philologen im antiken Roma*, Wiesbaden 1986.

Christie, R., *Selected Essays*, London 1902, 193-222 ('The Chronology of the Early Aldines').

Cioni, A., 'Bissoli, Giovanni' in *DBI* 10 (1968) 701-703.

Cipriani, M., 'Attavanti, Attavante' in *DBI* 4 (1962) 526-530.

Cirillo, D., *Il Papiro*, with intro. by M. Gigante, Naples 1983.

Clair, C., *A History of Printing in Britain*, London 1965.

Clark, A.C., 'The Reappearance of the Texts of the Classics', *The Library*, 4th ser., 2 (1921) 36.

Clark, J.W., *The Care of Books: An essay on the development of libraries and their fittings from the earliest times to the end of the eighteenth century*, Cambridge 1901.

Claudin, A., *The First Paris Press*, London 1989.

Clough, C.H., 'Cardinal Bessarion and the Greeks at the Court of Urbino', *Manuscripta* 8, 3 (1964) 160-171.

Clucas, L., *The Trial of John Italos and the Crisis of Intellectual Values in Byzantium in the Eleventh Century*, Munich 1981.

Coccia, E., 'La cultura irlandese precarolina – miracolo o mito?', *Studi Medievali*, 3rd ser., 8 (1967) 257-420.

Coggiola, G., 'Il prestito di manoscritti della Marciana dal 1474 al 1527', *ZB* 25 (1908) 47-50.

Cohn, L., 'Aristarchos' in *RE* 2 (1895) 862-873.

— *«Διονύσιος ὁ Θρᾷξ»* in *RE* 5 (1903) 977-983.

Colini, A., 'Foro del Pace', *Bollettino della Commissione Archeologica Communale di Roma* (1941) 15 ff.

Collura, P., *Studi paleografici: La precarolina e la carolina a Bobbio* (= Fontes Ambrosiani, 22), Milan 1943.

Comparetti, D. and Petra, G. de, *La villa ercolanese dei Pisoni*, Turin 1883.

Condoleon, N.M., «Ἀρχίλοχος καί Πάρος», *Ἐπετηρίς τῆς Ἑταιρείας Κυκλαδικῶν Μελετῶν,* τόμ. 5 (1965) 53-103.

Constantinides, C.N., *Higher Education in Byzantium in the Thirteenth and Early Fourteenth Centuries (1204 - ca. 1310)*, Nicosia 1982.

Conti, G., 'L'edificio: Architettura e decorazione' in L. Baldacchini (ed.), *La Biblioteca Malatestiana di Cesena*, Rome 1992, 57-118.

Conze, A., 'Die pergamenische Bibliothek', *Sitzungsber. Berliner Akad. für Wissenschaft* 53 (1884) 1257 ff.

Coppola, C., 'Contributo alla restituzione del testo della lettera a Tarasio, proemiale della "Biblioteca" di Fozio', *Rivista di Studi Bizantini e Neoellenici*, n.s., 12-13 (1975-1976) 129-153.

Corbellini, A., 'Appunti sull' Umanesimo in Lombardia', *Bollettino della Società Pavese di Storia Patria* 17 (1917) 5-13.

Corpus Inscriptionum Latinarum, Berlin 1962- .

Coulter, Cornelia C., 'Boccaccio and the Cassinese Manuscripts of the Laurentian Library', *Classical Philology* 43 (1948) 217 ff.

Courcelle, P., *Les lettres grecques en Occident de Macrobe à Cassiodore*, Paris 1948.

— *La Consolation de Philosophie dans la tradition littéraire. Antécédents et postérité de Boèce*, Paris 1967.

Coye, H.O., *Catalogi codicum manuscriptorum bibliothecae Bodleianae, pars prima*, Oxford 1853.

Crisci, E., 'La maiuscola ogivale diritta. Origini, tipologie, dislocazioni', *Scrittura* 9 (1985) 103-115.

Csapodi, C., *Beatrix Királyné Könyvtára*, Muszle 1964 (= 'La biblioteca di Beatrice d'Aragona, moglie di Mattia Corvino', *Italia ed Ungheria* (1967) 113-133).

— *The Corvinian Library: History and Stock*, Budapest (Akadémia Kiadó) 1973.

— 'Les livres de Janus Pannonius et sa bibliothèque à Pécs', *Scriptorium* 28 (1974) 32-50.

Csontosi, J., 'A Korvina', *Pallas Nagy Lexikon*, X, Budapest 1895.

Curris, A., *Ugarit (Ras Shamra)*, Cambridge 1985.

Dagron, G., 'L'empire romain d'orient au IVe siècle et les traditions politiques de l'hellénisme: Le témoignage de Thémistios', *TM* 3 (1968) 1-242.

Dain, A., 'La transmission des textes littéraires classiques de Photius à Constantin Porphyrogénète', *DOP* 8 (1954) 33-47.

— *Les manuscrits*, Paris 1964.

Dan, P., *Trésor de merveilles de la maison royale de Fontainebleau*, Paris 1642.

Darrouzès, J., 'Épistoliers byzantins du Xe siècle', *Archives de l'Orient Chrétien* 6 (1960) 22.

— 'Recherches sur les ΟΦΦΙΚΙΑ de l'Église Byzantine', *Archives de l'Orient Chrétien* 11 (1970) 337-351.

Davies, C.H.S., *The Egyptian Book of the Dead*, New York 1895.

Davies, W.V., 'Les hiéroglyphes égyptiens' in Bonfante et al., *La naissance des écritures*... 101-171.

De Fine Licht, K., 'Untersuchungen an den Trajansthermen zu Rom', *Analecta Romana* 7 (1974), suppl. 19, 1990.

Deimel, A., *Sumerische Tempelwirtschaft zur Zeit Urukaginas und seiner Vorgänger*, Rome 1931.

Delaruelle, E., 'La connaissance du grec en Occident du Ve au IXe siècle', *Mélanges de la Société toulousaine d'études classiques* 1 (1946) 207-226.

Delaruelle, L., 'Une vie d'humaniste au XVe siècle: Gregorio Tifernas', *Mélanges d'Archéologie et d'Histoire de l'École Française de Rome* 19 (1899) 9-33.

Delbouille, M., 'Apollonius de Tyr et les débuts du roman français', *Mélanges offerts à Rita Lejeune*, II, Gembloux 1969, 1184 ff.

Delehaye, H., 'Stoudion-Stoudios', *Anal. Boll.* 52 (1934) 64-65.

Delisle, L., 'Recherches sur l'ancienne bibliothèque de Corbie', *Mémoires de l'Institut National de France* 24 (1861) 267-342.

— *Le Cabinet des Manuscrits de la Bibliothèque Impériale. Étude sur la formation de ce dépôt*, I, Paris 1868.

— *Recherches sur la librairie de Charles V*, I, Paris 1907.

Delitzsch, F., *Assyrische Lesestücke*, Leipzig n.d.

— *Assyrische Grammatik*, Berlin 1906.

Della Torre, A., *Storia dell' Accademia Platonica di Firenze*, Florence 1902.

Delorme, J., *Gymnasion. Étude sur les monuments consacrés à l'éducation en Grèce*, Paris 1960.

— *Παγκόσμια Χρονολογική Ἱστορία* (= *Chronologie des civilisations*, tr. and ed. K. Dokou et al.), I, Athens 1989.

Delz, J., 'Ein unbekannter Brief von Pomponius Laetus', *IMU* 9 (1966) 417 ff.

Deraedt, D., *La politique monastique des empereurs de Nicée (1204-1261)* (unpublished dissertation, Louvain 1952).

Derenne, E., *Les procès d'impiété intentés aux philosophes au Vème et au IVème siècles*, Liège 1930.
Destrez, J., *La pecia dans les manuscrits universitaires du XIIIe et du XIVe siècle*, Paris 1935.
Deubner, O., *Das Asklepieion von Pergamon. Kurze vorläufige Beschreibung*, Berlin 1938.
Devreesse, R., *Introduction à l'étude des manuscrits grecs*, Paris 1954.
— *Les manuscrits grecs de l'Italie méridionale*, Vatican City 1955.
Dhorme, P., *La religion assyro-babylonienne*, Paris 1920.
Diehl, C., 'Le trésor et la bibliothèque de Patmos au commencement du XIIIe siècle', *BZ* 1 (1892) 488-525.
Diels, H., *Doxographi Graeci*, Berlin 1879.
— *Die Fragmente der Vorsokratiker*, ed. W. Kranz, Berlin 1951.
Dietz, K.M., *Protagoras von Abdeira: Untersuchungen zu seinem Denken* (doctoral dissertation), Bonn 1976.
Diller, A., 'Codices Planudei', *BZ* 37 (1937) 296-301.
— 'The Library of Francesco and Ermolao Barbaro', *IMU* 6 (1963) 253-262.
— 'Three Greek Scribes Working for Bessarion: Trivizias, Callistus, Hermonymus', *IMU* 10 (1967) 404-410.
Dini Traversari, A., *A. Traversari e i suoi tempi*, Florence 1912.
Dionisotti, C., 'Bembo, Pietro' in *DBI* 8 (1966) 133-151.
Diringer, D., *The Book Before Printing: Ancient, medieval and oriental*, New York 1982.
Ditt, E., 'Pier Candido Decembrio', *Memorie del R. Istituto Lombardo di Scienze e Lettere* 24 (1931) 21-108.
Dobroklonskij, A.P., *Prep. Feodor, ispovjednik i igumen Studijskij*, Odessa 1913.
Domeniconi, A., 'Ser Giovanni da Epinal, copista di Malatesta Novello', *Studi Romagnoli* 10 (1959) 261-282.
— 'I custodi della Biblioteca Malatestiana di Cesena dalle origini alla seconda metà del Seicento', *Studi Romagnoli* 14 (1963) 385-396.
— *La Biblioteca Malatestiana*, Cesena 1982.
Dorez, L., 'Un document sur la bibliothèque de Théodore Gaza', *Revue de Bibliothèques* 3 (1893) 385-390.
Dougherty, R.P., 'Writing upon Parchment and Papyrus among the Babylonians and Assyrians', *Journal of the American Oriental Society* 42 (1928) 109-135.
Driver, G.R., *Aramaic Documents of the Fifth Century B.C.*, Oxford 1954.
— *Semitic Writing from Pictograph to Alphabet*, London 1976.
Droysen, J.G., *Ἱστορία τῶν διαδόχων τοῦ Μεγάλου Ἀλεξάνδρου*, tr. and annotated by R.I. Apostolidis, 2 vols., Athens 1992.
Duft, J., *Die Lebensgeschichten der Heiligen Gallus und Otmar* (= Bibliotheca Sangallensis, 9), St. Gall/Sigmaringen 1988.
— 'The Contribution of the Abbey of St. Gall to Sacred Music' in King and Vogler, *The Culture of the Abbey of St. Gall*, 57-67.
— 'Irish Monks and Irish Manuscripts in St. Gall' in King and Vogler, *The Culture of the Abbey of St. Gall*, 119-128.
Duft, J., Gössi, A. and Vogler, W., *Die Abtei St. Gallen*, Bern 1986.
Duft, J. and Meyer, P., *The Irish Miniatures of the Abbey Library of St. Gall*, Olten/Bern/Lausanne 1954.
Duft, J. and Schnyder, R., *Die Elfenbein-Einbände der Stiftsbibliothek St. Gallen*, Beuron 1984.
Duneau, J.-F., 'Quelques aspects de la pénétration de l'hellénisme dans l'empire perse sassanide (IVe-VIIe siècles)' in *Mélanges René Crozet*, Poitiers 1966, 13-22.

Dupont-Ferrier, G., 'Jean d'Orléans comte d'Angoulême d'après sa bibliothèque', *Mélanges d'Histoire du Moyen Âge*, III, Paris 1897, 39-92.

Dureau, J.-M., 'Les premiers ateliers français' in H.J. Martin et al. (ed.), *Histoire de l'édition française*, I, Paris 1982, 162-175.

Düring, I., *Aristotle in the Ancient Biographical Tradition*, Göteborg 1957.

— *Ὁ Ἀριστοτέλης: Παρουσίαση καί ἑρμηνεία τῆς Σκέψης του* (= *Aristoteles. Darstellung und Interpretation seines Denkens*, tr. P. Kotzia-Panteli), 2 vols., Athens 1991-1994.

Dvornik, F., 'The Patriarch Photius in the Light of Recent Research' in *Berichte zum XI. Internationalen Byzantinisten-Kongress*, Munich 1958, III.2 1-56.

Dziatzko, K., *Untersuchungen über ausgewählte Kapitel des antiken Buchwesens*, Leipzig 1900.

Easterling, P.E. and Knox, B.M.W., *Ἱστορία τῆς Ἀρχαίας Ἑλληνικῆς* (= *The Cambridge History of Classical Literature*, I: *Greek Literature*, tr. N. Konomi, Ch. Grimba and M. Konomi), Athens 1994.

Ebersolt, J., *La miniature byzantine*, Brussels 1926.

Eggenberger, C., 'The Art of the Book in St. Gall' in King and Vogler, *The Culture of the Abbey of St. Gall*, 93-118.

Eichgrün, E., *Kallimachos und Apollonios Rhodios*, Berlin 1961.

Einhardi Vita Karoli Magni, ed. G. Waitz, Hannover 1911.

(Ekdotike Athenon), *Οἱ θησαυροί τοῦ Ἁγίου Ὄρους*, Athens 1973-1991.

Eleen, L., 'Crivelli, Taddeo' in *DBI* 36 (1988) 156-160.

Eleopoulos, N.X., *Ἡ Βιβλιοθήκη καί τό Βιβλιογραφικόν Ἐργαστήριον τῆς Μονῆς τοῦ Σπουδίου*, Athens 1967.

Elm, Kalpar, *Norbert von Xanten, Adliger, Ordensstifter, Kirchenfürst*, Köln 1984.

Engelbert, P., 'Zur Frühgeschichte des Bobbieser Skriptoriums', *Revue Bénédictine* 78 (1968) 220-260.

Erman, A., *Die Literatur des Aegypter*, Leipzig 1923 (Eng. trans. by A.M. Blackman, London 1927).

Eusebius of Caesarea, *Εἰς τόν βίον τοῦ μακαρίου Κωνσταντίνου βασιλέως*, ed. J.A. Heikel, I, Leipzig 1902.

Eustratiades, J., «Ἐπιστολαί Πατριάρχου Γρηγορίου τοῦ Κυπρίου», *Eph* 1-5 (1908-1910).

— *Γρηγορίου τοῦ Κυπρίου οἰκουμενικοῦ Πατριάρχου ἐπιστολαί καί μῦθοι*, Alexandria 1910.

Fabbri, P.G., 'Il signore, la libreria, la città' in L. Baldacchini (ed.), *La Biblioteca Malatestiana di Cesena*, Rome 1992, 15-54.

Fabroni, A., *Laurentii Medicis Vita*, II, Pisa 1784.

Falkenstein, A., 'Gilgamel' in *Reallexikon der Assyriologie*, 1957-1971, III 361.

Fanelli, V., 'I libri di messer Palla Strozzi (1372-1462)', *Convivium* 1 (1949) 57-73.

Fassulakis, S., *The Byzantine Family of Raoul-Ral(l)es*, Athens 1973.

Fava, D., *La Biblioteca Estense nel suo sviluppo, con il catalogo della mostra permanente*, Modena 1925.

Feger, R., in *RE* suppl. 8 (1956) 517-520.

Fehrle, R., *Das Bibliothekswesen im alten Rom*, Wiesbaden 1986.

Félibien, M. and Lobineau, G., *Histoire de la ville de Paris*, V, Paris 1725.

Ferrai, L.A., 'La biblioteca di S. Giustina di Padova' in G. Mazzatinti (ed.), *Inventario dei manoscritti d'Italia nelle bibliotheche di Francia*, II, Rome 1887, 569-573.

Ferrari, Mirella, 'Spigolature Bobbiesi', *IMU* 16 (1973) 1 ff.

Festugière, A.J., *Antioche païenne et chrétienne. Libanius, Chrysostomus et les moines de Syrie*, Paris 1959.

Février, J.G., *Histoire de l'écriture*, Paris 1984.

Fiocco, G., 'La casa di Palla Strozzi', *Memorie dei Lincei, Classe scienze morali*, ser. VIII, 5.7 (1954) 361-382.

— 'La biblioteca di Palla Strozzi' in *Studi di Bibliografia e di Storia in onore di Tammaro de Marinis*, II, Verona 1964, 289-310.

Fitz, J., 'König Matthias Corvinus und der Buchdruck', *GJ* 14 (1939) 128-137.

— *A magyar nyomdászat, könyvkiadás és Könyvkereskedelem története a XV. században*, Budapest 1959.

Flacelière, R., *Ό Δημόσιος καί Ἰδιωτικός Βίος τῶν Ἀρχαίων Ἑλλήνων* (= *La vie quotidienne en Grèce au siècle de Périclès*, Paris 1959, tr. G.D. Vandorou), Athens 1990.

Flocon, A., *L'univers des livres. Étude historique des origines à la fin du XVIIIe siècle*, Paris 1961.

Flodr, M., *Incunabula Classicorum*, Amsterdam 1973.

Florentis, Deacon Chrysostomos G., *Βραβεῖον τῆς Ἱερᾶς Μονῆς Ἁγ. Ἰωάννου τοῦ Θεολόγου Πάτμου*, Athens 1980.

Foffano, T., in *IMU* 12 (1969) 113-128.

Folkerts, M., 'Corpus Agrimensorum Romanorum' in *Wolfenbütteler Cimelien...* 28-32.

Follieri, Enrica, 'Un codice di Areta troppo a buon mercato: Il Vat. Urb. Gr. 35', *Archeologica Classica* 25-26 (1973-1974) 262-279.

Fonkitch, B.L., 'La bibliothèque de la Grande Lavra du Mont-Athos aux Xe-XIIIe siècles', *Palestinskij Sbornik* 80 (1967) 167-175.

Fontaine, J., *Isidore de Seville et la culture classique dans l'Espagne wisigothique*, 2 vols., Paris 1959.

Fontius, B., *Epistolarum libri*, ed. Ladislaus Juhász, Budapest 1931.

Forni, G.G., 'F. Petrarca scolare a Bologna', *Atti e Memorie della Academia Petrarca di Lettere, Arti e Scienze*, n.s., 37, Anni 1958-1964 (1965) 83-96.

Förster, R., *De antiquitatibus et libris manuscriptis Constantinopolitanis*, Rostock 1877.

Fournier, M., *Les Statuts et privilèges des universités françaises depuis leur fondation jusqu'en 1789...*, 4 vols., Paris 1890-1894.

Franceschini, G., *I Malatesta*, Varese 1973.

Franceschini, Marina de, *Villa Adriana, mosaici, pavimenti, edifici*, Rome 1991.

Frangiskos, E.N., «Οἱ σωζόμενοι κατάλογοι τῶν ἐντύπων τῆς Βιβλιοθήκης τῆς Μονῆς Ἁγ. Ἰωάννου τοῦ Θεολόγου Πάτμου», ἀνάτυπο ἀπό τά πρακτικά τοῦ Διεθνοῦς Συμποσίου μέ θέμα: *Ἱερά Μονή Ἁγ. Ἰωάννου τοῦ Θεολόγου - 900 χρόνια ἱστορικῆς μαρτυρίας (1088 - 1988)*, offprint from the *Proceedings of the International Symposium on 'The Monastery of St. John the Divine: Nine hundred years of historical testimony (1088-1988)', Patmos, 22-24 September 1988*, Athens 1989, 311-330.

Frangiskos, E.N. and Florentis, Ch.G., *Πατμιακή Βιβλιοθήκη: κατάλογος τῶν ἐντύπων (15ος - 19ος αἰ.)*, I-II, Athens 1993-1995.

Frankói, V., *Vitéz János könyvtára*, Budapest 1878.

— *Vitéz János esztergomi érsek élete*, Budapest 1879.

— *A. Hunyadiak és a Jagellók kora: A magyar nemzet története*, ed. Sándor Szilágyi, IV, n.d.

Frantz, Alison, *The Athenian Agora: Results of excavations conducted by the American School of Classical Studies at Athens*, XXIV: *Late Antiquity, A.D. 267-700*, Princeton 1988.

Fraser, P.M., 'Two Studies on the Cult of Sarapis in the Hellenistic World', *Opuscula Atheniensia*, III, Lund 1960, 11.6.

— *Ptolemaic Alexandria*, 3 vols., Oxford 1972.

Fuchs, F., *Die höheren Schulen von Konstantinopel im Mittelalter*, Leipzig/Berlin 1926.

Funaioli, H., *Grammaticae romanae fragmenta*, Leipzig 1907.

Gaeta, F., *Lorenzo Valla: Filologia e storia nell' Umanesimo italiano*, Naples 1955.

Galataziotou, Catia, *The Making of a Saint: The life, times, and sanctification of Neophytos the Recluse*, Cambridge 1991.

Galavaris, G., *Ζωγραφική Βυζαντινῶν χειρογράφων,* στή σειρά *Ἑλληνική Τέχνη*, Athens 1995.

Galeotto, M., 'De dictis et factis Matthiae' in Ábel, *Irodalontörténeti Emlékek*, II, 1890, 7-8.

Gallavotti, C., 'La custodia dei papiri nella villa suburbana ercolanese', *Bollettino dell' Istituto di patologia del libro* 2 (1940) 53 ff.

— 'La libreria di una villa romana ercolanese', *Boll. dell' Ist. di patologia del libro* 3 (1941) 129 ff.

Galletti, P.F., *Capena municipio de' Romani*, Rome 1756.

Galli, G., 'Gli ultimi mesi di vita della stamperia di Ripoli e la stampa del Platone', *Studi e ricerche sulla storia della stampa del Quattrocento* 20 (Milan 1942), repr. Nendeln, Liechtenstein (Kraus/Reprint) 1972, 159-184.

Gardiner, A.H., 'Die Klagen des Bauern' in *Literarische Texte des Mittleren Reiches*, I, Leipzig 1908.

— *Late Egyptian Stories*, Brussels 1932.

— *Egyptian Grammar, being an introduction to the study of hieroglyphs*, Oxford 1957.

Gargan, L., 'Il libro per l'università' in Brizzi, G.P., and J. Verger (ed.), *Le università dell' Europa. Le scuole e i maestri. Il Medioevo*, Milan 1994, 73-97.

Garin, E., 'Le traduzioni umanistiche di Aristotele', *Atti e Memorie dell' Accademia Fiorentina di Scienze Morali* 8 (1950) 1-50.

— *L'umanesimo italiano. Filosofia e vita civile nel Rinascimento*, Bari 1952.

— *Educazione umanistica in Italia*, Rome/Bari 1971.

Gaskoin, G.J.B., *Alcuin: His Life and His Work*, London 1903.

Geannakoplos, Th.D., «Ἡ βιβλιοπωλία κατά τούς βυζαντινούς χρόνους», *Ὁ Βιβλιόφιλος* 8 (1954) 111-113.

Geannakoplos, K.I., *Ἕλληνες λόγιοι εἰς τήν Βενετίαν: Μελέται ἐπί τῆς διαδόσεως τῶν ἑλληνικῶν γραμμάτων εἰς τήν δυτικήν Εὐρώπην (Greek scholars in Venice... tr. ch. G. Patrinelis),* Athens 1965.

Gény, J., *Die Reichsstadt Schlettstadt und ihr Anteil an der social-politischen und religiösen Bewegungen der Jahre 1490-1536*, Freiburg 1900.

Gény, J. and Knod, G., *Die Stadtbibliothek zu Schlettstadt*, Strasbourg 1889.

Gerstinger, H., 'Johannes Sambucus als Handschriftensammler' in *Festschrift der Nationalbibliothek*, Vienna 1926, 251-400.

Giannelli, C., *Codices vaticani graeci, 1485-1683*, Vatican City 1950.

Giannetto, Nella (ed.), *Vittorino da Feltre e la sua scuola. Umanesimo, Pedagogia, Arti*, Florence 1981.

Gibbon, E., *The History of the Decline and Fall of the Roman Empire*, II, London 1788.

Gilbert, F., 'Biondo, Sabellico and the Beginnings of the Venetian Official Historiography' in *Florilegium Historicale* (Essays presented to Wallace K. Ferguson), Toronto 1971, 276-293.

Gill, J., 'The Church Union of the Council of Lyons (1274) Portrayed in Greek Documents', *OCP* 40 (1974) 5-45.

Glenisson, J. (ed.), *Le Livre au Moyen Âge*, Paris 1988.

Glorieux, P., 'Études sur la *Bibliomania* de Richard de Fournival', *Recherches de théologie ancienne et médiévale* 30 (1963) 205-231.

Glykatzi-Ahrweiler, Hélène, *Ἡ πολιτικὴ ἰδεολογία τῆς Βυζαντινῆς Αὐτοκρατορίας* (= *L'idéologie politique de l'empire byzantin*, tr. Toula Drakopoulou), Athens 1977.

Godel, R., *Platon à Héliopolis d'Égypte*, Paris 1956.

Goldmann, A., 'Drei italienische Handschriften-Kataloge s. XIII-XV', *Centralblatt für Bibliothekswesen* 4 (1887) 142-155.

Gombosi, Gy., 'Pannóniae Mihály és a renaissance kezdetei Ferrarában', *Az Országos Magyar Szépmüvészeti Múzeum Evkönyve* 6 (1929-1930) 91-108.

Goossens, G., 'Introduction à l'archivéconomie de l'Asie Antérieure', *Revue d'Assyriologie* 46 (1952) 98-107.

Gori-Montanelli, L., *Brunelleschi e Michelozzo*, Florence 1957.

Gottlieb, T., *Büchersammlung Kaiser Maximilians*, I, Leipzig 1900.

Gouillard, J., 'Le Synodicon de l'Orthodoxie', *TM* 2 (1967) 56-71.

Grabar, A., *L'iconoclasme byzantin. Dossier archéologique*, Paris 1957.

Graecogermania: Griechischstudien deutscher Humanisten. Die Editionstätigkeit der Griechen in der italienischen Renaissance (1469-1523) (Herzog August Library Exhibition Catalogues, No. 59), 1989.

Graindor, P., *La guerre d'Alexandrie*, Cairo 1931.

Gregori, G. de, *Biblioteche d'Antichità, Accademie e Biblioteche d'Italia*, Rome 1937.

Grigioni, C., 'Matteo Nuti. Notizie bibliografiche', *La Romagna* 6, 8-9 (1909) 361-365.

— 'Per la storia della scultura in Cesena nel secolo XV', *La Romagna* 7, 10 (1910) 392.

Grumel, V., 'Jean Grammatikos et saint Théodore Studite', *Échos d'Orient* 36 (1937) 181-189.

Gubler, H.M., 'The Culture of Baroque Architecture at the Abbey of St. Gall' in King and Vogler, *The Culture of the Abbey of St. Gall*, 201-213.

Guilland, R., *Le Thômaïtès et le Patriarcat. Études de topographie de Constantinople byzantine*, II, Berlin/Amsterdam 1969.

Guillemain, B., *La cour pontificale d'Avignon (1309-1376). Étude d'une société*, Paris 1962.

Guillemin, A.M., *Le public et la vie littéraire à Rome*, Paris 1937.

Gusman, P., 'Claude Garamont, graveur des lettres grecques du roi, tailleur de caractères de l'Université (1480-1561)', *Byblis* 4 (1925) 85-95.

Guthrie, W.K.C., *The Greeks and Their Gods*, London 1950.

— *A History of Greek Philosophy*, 6 vols., Cambridge 1962-1981.

— *Οἱ Σοφιστές* (= *The Sophists*, Cambridge 1971, tr. D. Tsekourakis), Athens 1991.

Gutkind, C., *Cosimo de' Medici il Vecchio*, Florence 1940.

Haelst, J. van, 'Les origines du codex' in A. Blanchard (ed.), *Les débuts du codex*, Turnhout 1989, 13-35.

Hägg, T., 'Photius at Work: Evidence from the text of the Bibliotheca', *GRBS* 14 (1973) 213-222.

— *Photios als Vermittler antiker Literatur*, Uppsala 1975.

Halkin, F., 'Manuscrits galésiotes', *Scriptorium* 15 (1961) 221-227.

— 'La date de composition de la "Bibliothèque" de Photius remise en question', *Anal. Boll.* 81 (1963) 414-417.

Hampe, K., 'Zur Lebengeschichte Einhards', *Neues Archiv* 21 (1896) 611.

Hartmann, L.M., 'Johannicius von Ravenna' in *Festschrift für Theodor Gomperz*, Vienna 1902, 319-323.

Heb, J., 'König Matthias Corvinus und der Buchdruck', *GJ* (1939) 128-137.

Hecker, O., *Boccaccio-Funde*, Braunschweig 1902.

Heckethorn, C.W., *The Printers of Basle in the XV and XVI Centuries*, London 1897.

Heiberg, J.L., 'Der byzantinische Mathematiker Leon', *Bibliotheca Mathematica* (Stockholm), n.s., 1887, 33-36.

— 'Beiträge zur Geschichte Georg Valla's und seiner Bibliothek', *ZB* 16 (1896) 353-416.

Heidel, A., *The Gilgamesh Epic and Old Testament Parallels*, Chicago 1949.

Heinemann, U. von, *Die herzogliche Bibliothek zu Wolfenbüttel*, Wolfenbüttel 1894.

Hengel, M., *Judaism and Hellenism: Studies in their encounter in Palestine during the Early Hellenistic period*, London 1974.

Henry, P., *Plotin et l'Occident. Firmicus Maternus Victorinus, Saint Augustin et Macrobe*, Louvain 1934.

— (ed.), *Photius, Bibliothèque, texte établi et traduit*, 9 vols., Paris 1959-1991.

Herculaneum Fragments, 9 vols., Oxford 1889, and Facsimiles, Oxford 1891.

Hering, G., *Οἰκουμενικό Πατριαρχεῖο καί Εὐρωπαϊκή Πολιτική 1620-1638* (= *Ökumenisches Patriarchat und europäische Politik 1620-1638*, tr. D. Kurtovik), Athens 1992.

Hevesy, A. de, *La Bibliothèque du Roi Matthias Corvin*, Paris 1923.

Hilprecht, H.V., *Old Babylonian Inscriptions, chiefly from Nippur*, Philadelphia 1895.

Hobson, A., *Great Libraries*, London 1970.

Hoefer, F., 'Leibniz' in *NBG* 30 (1759) 465-500.

Hoepfner, W., 'Zu griechischen Bibliotheken und Bücherschränken' in *Sonderdruck aus Säule und Gebälk zu Struktur und Wandlungsprozeß griechisch-römischer Architektur*, Mainz 1996, 25-36.

Hoffmann, Edit (ed.), *Régi magyar bibliofilek*, Budapest 1929.

Holenstein, J., 'Zur Forschung über den Buchmaler Nikolaus Bertschi von Rorschach', *Zeitschrift für schweizerische Archäologie und Kunstgeschichte* 16 (1956) 75-98.

Holtz, L., 'Le Parisinus Latinus 7530, synthèse cassinienne des arts libéraux', *Studi Medievali*, 3rd ser., 16 (1975) 97-152.

Holzberg, N., 'Beatus Rhenanus (1485-1547). Eine biographisch-forschungsgeschichtliche Bestandsaufnahme zum 500. Geburtstag des Humanisten', *Annuaire 1985*, 19-32.

Horawitz, A., 'Beatus Rhenanus: Ein biographischer Versuch', *Wiener Akademie der Wissenschaften* 70 (1872) 189-244.

— 'Die Bibliothek und Correspondenz des Beatus Rhenanus zu Schlettstadt', *Wiener Akademie der Wissenschaften* 78 (1874) 313-340.

Horawitz, A. and Hartfelder, K. (ed.), *Briefwechsel des Beatus Rhenanus* (Leipzig 1886), repr. Hildesheim (G. Olms) 1966.

Hornsbostel-Hüttner, G., *Studien für römischen Nischenarchitektur*, Leiden 1979.

Hourmouziadis, N., *Ἕνας Ἀθηναῖος θεατής στά ἐν ἄστει Διονύσια*, Athens 1988.

Houston, G.W., 'A Revisionary Note on Ammianus Marcellinus 14.6.18: When did the Public Libraries of Ancient Rome Close?', *Library Quarterly* 58 (1988) 258 ff.

Howard, Deborah, *Jacopo Sansovino: Architecture and Patronage in Renaissance Venice*, New Haven/London 1975.

Hueber, F. and Strocka, V.M., 'Die Bibliothek des Celsus', *Antike Welt* 6 (1975) 3 ff.

Hülsen, C. and Jordan, H., *Topographie der Stadt Rom in Altertum*, Berlin 1907.

Hunger, H., *Reich der neuen Mitte: Der christliche Geist der byzantinischen Kultur*, Vienna/Köln 1965.

— *Βυζαντινή Λογοτεχνία: Ἡ λόγια κοσμική γραμματεία τῶν Βυζαντινῶν* (= *Die höchsprachliche profane Literatur der Byzantiner*, Munich 1978, tr. G.Ch. Makris et al.), 3 vols., Athens 1987-1994.

— *Ὁ κόσμος τοῦ Βυζαντινοῦ βιβλίου: Γραφή καί ἀνάγνωση στό Βυζάντιο* (= *Schreiben und Lesen in Byzanz. Die byzantinische Buchkultur*, tr. G. Vasilaros), Athens 1995.

Huszti, J., *Platonista törekvések Mátyás király udvarában*, Pécs 1925.

— *Janus Pannonius*, Pécs 1931.

— 'Pier Paolo Vergerios a magyar humanizmus kezdetei', *Filológiai Közlöny* (1955) 521-533.

Iamblichus, *De Mysteriis*, ed. G. Parthey, Berlin 1857.

Iliou, F., *Προσθῆκες στήν ἑλληνική βιβλιογραφία! Α΄ Τά βιβλιογραφικά κατάλοιπα τοῦ É. Legrand καί τοῦ H. Pernot (1515-1799)*, Athens 1973.

Impellizzeri, S., 'L'umanesimo bizantino del IX secolo e la genesi della *Bibliotheca* di Fozio', *Rivista di Studi Bizantini e Neoellenici*, n.s., 6-7 (1969-1970) 9-69.

Irigoin, J., 'Les premiers manuscrits grecs écrits sur papier et le problème du bombycin', *Scriptorium* 4 (1950) 194-204.

— *Histoire du texte de Pindare*, Paris 1952.

— 'Les débuts de l'emploi du papier à Byzance', *BZ* 46 (1953) 314-319.

— 'Survie et renouveau de la littérature antique à Constantinople', *Cahiers de civilisation médiévale* 5 (1962) 287-302.

— 'Les manuscrits grecs 1931-1960', *Lustrum* 8 (1962) 287-302.

— 'Les origines de la fabrication du papier en Italie', *Papiergeschichte* 13 (1963) 62-67.

— 'Centres de copie et bibliothèques' in *Byzantine Books and Bookmen: A Dumbarton Oaks Colloquium 1971*, Dumbarton Oaks 1975, 17-27.

— 'La culture grecque dans l'Occident latin du VIIe au XIe siècle' in *Proceedings of the Settimana di Spoleto "La cultura antica nell' Occidente latino dal VII all' XI secolo" (1974)*, Spoleto 1975, 425 ff.

— 'Les ambassadeurs à Venise et le commerce de manuscrits grecs dans les années 1540-1550' in *Venezia, centro di mediazione tra Oriente e Occidente, secoli XV-XVI. Aspetti e problemi*, II, Florence 1977, 399-413.

Izeddin, M., 'Un texte arabe inédit sur Constantinople byzantine', *Journal Asiatique*, 246 (1958) 453-457.

Jackson, H., 'Aristotle's Lecture-room and Lectures', *Journal of Philology* 35 (1920) 191-200.

Jackson, T.G., *Church of St. Mary the Virgin, Oxford*, Oxford 1897.

Jacobs, E., *Untersuchungen zur Geschichte der Bibliothek im Serai zu Konstantinopel*, Heidelberg 1919.

Jaeger, W., *Early Christianity and Greek Paideia*, Cambridge Mass. 1961.

— *Παιδεία: Ἡ μόρφωσις τοῦ Ἕλληνος ἀνθρώπου* (= *Paideia. Die Formung des griechischen Menschen*, tr. G.P. Verrios), III, Athens 1974.

Jaksch, W., Edith Fischer and F. Kroller, *Österreichischer Bibliotheksbau*, I: *Von der Gotik bis zur Moderne*, Graz 1992.

Janin, R., *Constantinople Byzantine*, II, Paris 1964.

— *La géographie ecclésiastique de l'empire byzantin*, I: *Le siège de Constantinople et le patriarcat oecuménique*, III: *Les églises et les monastères*, Paris 1969.

— *Les églises et les monastères des grands centres byzantins*, Paris 1975.

Jean, C.F., *Šumer et Akkad: Contribution à l'histoire de la civilisation dans la Basse-Mésopotamie*, Paris 1923.

— *La littérature des Babyloniens et des Assyriens*, Paris 1924.

Jensen, P., *Kosmologie der Babylonier*, Strasbourg 1890.

Johnson, R.R., *The Role of Parchment in Greco-Roman Antiquity* (dissertation), Los Angeles/Ann Arbor 1988.

Jones, T.B., 'Bookkeeping in Ancient Sumer', *Archaeology* 9 (1956) 16-21.

Jourdain, Abbé, 'Mémoire historique sur la Bibliothèque du Roi', preface to *Catalogue des livres imprimés*, Paris 1739.

Julian the Apostate: *Oeuvres de Julien*, I.2: *Lettres et fragments*, ed. J. Bidez, Paris 1924.

Jullien de Pommerol, Marie-Henriette, 'Livres d'étudiants, bibliothèques de collèges et d'universités' in Vernet, *Histoire des bibliothèques françaises*, 93-111.

Jüthner, J., 'Hellenen und Barbaren', *Das Erbe der Alten*, n.s., 8 (1923) 7 ff.

Kähler, H., *Hadrian und seine Villa bei Tivoli*, Berlin 1954.

Kaibel, G., 'Die Prolegomena *Περί κωμωδίας*, *Abhandlungen der Göttinger Gesellschaft der Wissenschaften*, n.s., 2.4 (1898) 4 ff.

— (ed.), *Comicorum Graecorum Fragmenta*, Berlin 1899.

Kaiser, H., 'Aus den letzten Jahren des Beatus Rhenanus', *Zeitschrift für die Geschichte des Oberrheins* (1916) 30-52.

Kakoulidi, Eleni, «Ἡ Βιβλιοθήκη τῆς Μονῆς Προδρόμου - Πέτρας στήν Κωνσταντινούπολη», *Ἑλληνικά* 21 (1968) 3-39.

Kampman, A.A., *Archieven en bibliotheken in het oude Nabije Oostern*, Schoten-Antwerpen 1942.

Kaplony, P., 'Ka' in *Lexikon der Aegyptologie*, III, 1980, col. 276.

Karapidakis, N.E., *Ἱστορία τῆς Μεσαιωνικῆς Δύσης (5ος - 11ος αἰ.)*, Athens 1996.

Karivieri, Arja, 'The So-called Library of Hadrian and the Tetraconch Church in Athens', *Papers and Monographs of the Finnish Institute at Athens* 1 (1994) 89-113.

Kaster, W.J.W. (ed.), *Scholia in Aristophanem* (in the series 'Prolegomena de Comoedia'), I, Groningen 1960, IV, Groningen/Amsterdam 1962.

— 'Scholium Plautinum plene editum', *Mnemosyne*, 4th ser., 14 (1961) 23 ff.

Katte, Maria von, 'Herzog August und die Kataloge seiner Bibliothek', *Wolfenbütteler Beiträge* 1 (1972) 168-199.

— 'Die Bibliotheca Selenica von 1586-1612: Die Anfänge der Bibliothek des Herzogs August zu Braunschweig und Lüneburg', *Wolfenbütteler Beiträge* 3 (1978) 135-153.

— 'The "Bibliotheca Augusta": Significance and Origin' in *Treasures*... 57-63.

Kenyon, F.G., *Books and Readers in Ancient Greece and Rome*, Oxford 1951.

Kessler, E., 'Das Problem des frühen Humanismus: Seine philosophische Bedeutung bei Coluccio Salutati', *Humanistische Bibliothek* I (1968).

King, James C., and Werner Vogler (ed.), *The Culture of the Abbey of St. Gall*, Stuttgart/Zürich 1991.

King, L.W., *The Seven Tablets of Creation*, 2 vols., London 1902.

Kleberg, T., 'Book Auctions in Ancient Rome?', *Libri* 22 (1973) 1 ff.

— 'La Grecia e l'epoca ellenistica' and 'Roma a l'epoca greco-romana' in G. Cavallo (ed.), *Libri editori e pubblico nel mondo antico*, Rome/Bari 1989, 27-39, 40-80.

Knithakis, G. and Soumbolidou, E., «Νέα στοιχεῖα διά τήν Βιβλιοθήκην Ἀδριανοῦ», *Ἀρχαιολογικό Δελτίο* 124.1 (1969) 107-117 (Pls. 54-57).

Knod, G., 'Aus der Bibliothek des Beatus Rhenanus: Ein Beitrag zur Geschichte des Humanismus' in Gény and Knod, *Die Stadtbibliothek zu Schlettstadt*, Part II, 11-19, 47-55.

Knös, B., *Un ambassadeur de l'hellénisme – Janus Lascaris – et la tradition gréco-byzantine dans l'humanisme français*, Uppsala/Paris 1945.

Koch, J. (ed.), *Artes liberales. Von der antiken Bildung zur Wissenschaft des Mittelalters*, Leiden/Köln 1959.

Kohút, L., 'Das Werk des Wiegendruckers Mikuláš Bakalárštetina zu Pilsen', *GJ* (1966) 116-128.

Kominis, A., *Πίνακες χρονολογημένων Πατμιακών κωδίκων*, Athens 1968.

Kougeas, S., *'Ο Καισαρείας 'Αρέθας καί τό ἔργον αὐτοῦ*, Athens 1913.

Kovacs, Maureen Gallery, *The Epic of Gilgamesh*, Stanford 1989.

Kramer, S.N., 'A New Library Catalogue from Ur', *Revue d'Assyriologie* 55 (1961) 169-176.

— *L'histoire commence à Sumer* (orig. published as *History Begins at Sumer*, London 1958), Paris 1986.

Krasnopolski, P., 'Tschechische Inkunabeln', *Zeitschrift für Bücherfreunde*, n.s., 17 (1925) 95-102.

— 'Prager Drucke bis 1620', *GJ* 4 (1927) 72-84.

Kriaras, E., «Μ. Ψελλός», *Βυζαντινά* 4 (1972) 55-128.

Kristeller, P., *Early Florentine Woodcuts*, London 1897.

Kristeller, P.O., *Renaissance Thought: The Classic, Scholastic and Humanist Strains*, New York/Hagerstown/San Francisco/London 1961.

— 'An Unknown Humanist Sermon on St. Stephen by Guillaume Fichet', *Mélanges Eugène Tisserant* 6 (1964) 459-497.

— 'Platonismo bizantino e fiorentino e la controversia su Platone e Aristotele' in A. Pertusi, (ed.), *Venezia e l'Oriente fra tardo Medioevo e Rinascimento*, Florence 1966, 103-116.

Kroll, W., 'Krates von Mallos' in *RE* 11 (1922) 1634-1641.

Kubiček, A., and D. Libal, *Strahov*, Prague 1955.

Kubinyi, Mária, *Libri manuscripti graeci in bibliothecis Budapestinensibus asservati*, Budapest 1956.

Kyrou, A., *Βησσαρίων ὁ Ἕλλην*, 2 vols., Athens 1947.

Labet, R., 'Gilgamesh' in *Religions du Proche-Orient asiatique*, Paris 1970, 145-226.

Labowsky, Lotte, 'Manuscripts from Bessarion's Library Found in Milan', *Medieval and Renaissance Studies* 5 (1961) 109-131.

— 'Bessarione' in *DBI* 9 (1967) 686-696.

— *Bessarion's Library and the Biblioteca Marciana: Six Early Inventories*, Rome 1979.

Ladas, G.G. and Hadjidimos, A.D., *Ἑλληνική βιβλιογραφία: Συμβολή στόν δέκατο ὄγδοο αἰώνα*, Athens 1964.

Laistner, M.L.W., *Christianity and Pagan Culture in the Later Roman Empire*, Ithaca N.Y. 1951.

Lambert, M., 'La naissance de la bureaucratie', *Revue Historique* 224 (1960) 1-26.

— 'Le premier triomphe de la bureaucratie', *Revue Historique* 225 (1961) 21-46.

Lambert, W.G., 'Gilgamesh in Literature and Art: The Second and First Millennia' in Ann Farkas et al., *Monsters and Demons in the Ancient and Medieval Worlds*, Mainz 1987, 37-52.

Lameere, W., *La tradition manuscrite de la correspondance de Grégoire de Chypre, patriarche de Constantinople (1283-1289)*, Brussels/Rome 1937.

Lampros, S., «Περί τῆς βιβλιοθήκης τοῦ Μητροπολίτου 'Αθηνῶν Μιχαήλ 'Ακομινάτου (1182-1205)», *'Αθήναιον* 6 (1877) 354-367.

— *Μιχαήλ 'Ακωμινάτου Χωνιάτου τά σωζόμενα*, I-II, Athens 1879-1880.

— *Ἀργυρουπούλεια*, Athens 1910.

Lampsidis, O., *Φιλολογικά εἰς τήν Χρονικήν Σύνοψιν Κωνσταντίνου τοῦ Μανασσῆ*, Athens 1951.

Lanciani, G., 'Degli antichi edificii componenti la chiesa di SS Cosma e Damiano', *Bollettino della Commissione Archeologica Communale di Roma* 10 (1882) 39 ff.

— *Pagan and Christian Rome*, London 1892.

Langdon, S., *Excavations at Kish*, I, Chicago 1924.

Langie, A., *Les bibliothèques publiques dans l'ancienne Rome et dans l'empire romain*, Fribourg 1906.

Laourdas, V., *Photios. Epistolae et Amphilochia*, 6 vols., Leipzig 1983-1988.

Lascaris Theodori, Ducae, Epistulae CCXVII, ed. N. Festa, Florence 1898.

Launey, M., 'Recherches sur les armées hellénistiques', *Bibliothèque des Écoles Françaises d'Athènes et de Rome* 169 (1949/50) 273, 1163.

Laurent, V., 'La correspondance inédite de Georges Babouscomitès' in the festschrift *Εἰς μνήμην Σπυρίδωνος Λάμπρου*, Athens 1935, 83-100.

Layard, A.H., *Discoveries among the Ruins of Nineveh and Babylon*, New York 1856.

Layton, Evro, 'Nikodemos Metaxas, the First Greek Printer in the Eastern World', *Harvard Library Bulletin* 15.2 (1967) 140-168.

— «Ἡ τεχνική τοῦ βιβλίου» in G. Hering (ed.), *Τό ἑλληνικό βιβλίο (1476-1830)*, Athens 1986, 291-292.

Lefebvre, G., *Grammaire de l'égyptien classique*, Cairo 1955.

— *Romans et contes égyptiens de l'époque pharaonique*, Paris 1988.

Lefranc, A., *Histoire du Collège de France*, Paris 1893.

Legrand, É., *Bibliographie Hellénique, ou Description raisonnée des ouvrages publiés en grec par des grecs aux XVe et XVIe siècles*, I, Paris 1885.

— *Bibliographie hellénique du dix-huitième siècle*, I, Paris 1918.

Lehmann, E., *Die Bibliotheksräume der deutschen Klöster im Mittelalter*, Berlin 1957.

Lehmann, P., *Erforschung des Mittelalters*, III, Stuttgart 1960.

Lemerle, P., *Ὁ πρῶτος βυζαντινός οὐμανισμός: Σημειώσεις καί παρατηρήσεις γιά τήν ἐκπαίδευση καί τήν παιδεία στό Βυζάντιο ἀπό τίς ἀρχές ὥς τόν 10ο αἰώνα* (= *Le premier humanisme byzantin...*, tr. Maria Nystazopoulou-Pelekidou), Athens 1981.

Lesky, A., *Ἱστορία τῆς Ἀρχαίας Ἑλληνικῆς Λογοτεχνίας* (= *Geschichte der griechischen Literatur*, Bern 1957/58, tr. A.G. Tsopanaki), Thessaloniki 1983.

Lesne, É., *Les Livres. Scriptoria et bibliothèques du commencement du VIIIe à la fin du XIe siècle* (= *Histoire de la propriété ecclésiastique en France*, IV), Lille 1938.

Levi, L., 'Cinque lettere inedite di Manuele Moschopoulos', *SIFC* 10 (1902) 61-63.

Levi d'Ancona, Mirella, *Miniatura e miniatori a Firenze dal XIV al XVI sec.*, Florence 1962.

Levison, W., *England and the Continent in the Eighth Century*, Oxford 1946.

Lewis, N., *L'industrie du papyrus dans l'Égypte gréco-romaine*, Paris 1934.

— 'The Non-Scholar Members of the Alexandrian Museum', *Mnemosyne* 16 (1963) 257-261.

Lexa, F., *La magie dans l'Égypte antique*, 3 vols., Paris 1925.

Lhotsky, A., 'Die Bibliothek Kaiser Friedrichs III', *Mitteilungen des Instituts für österreichische Geschichtsforschung* 58 (1958) 124-135.

Liebenwein, W., *Studiolo: Storia e tipologia di uno spazio culturale*, tr. A. Califano, Ferrara/Modena 1988.

Lindsay, W.M., *Notae Latinae*, Cambridge 1915.

Linforth, I.M., *The Arts of Orpheus*, Berkeley 1941.

Lökkös, A., *Catalogue des incunables imprimés à Genève 1478-1500*, Geneva 1978.

Lollini, F., 'Bologna, Ferrara, Cesena: I corali del Bessarione tra circuiti umanistici e percorsi di artisti' in P. Lucchi (ed.), *Corali Miniati del Quattrocento nella Biblioteca Malatestiana*, Milan 1989, 19-36.

Lomeier, J., *De bibliothecis liber singularis*, Zutphen 1669.

Lo Parco, F., *Aulo Gianno Parrasio*, Vasto 1899.

Lowe, E.A., *Codices latini antiquiores*, 2 vols. (with suppl.), Oxford 1934-1971.

— 'The *Script of Luxeuil*: A title vindicated', *Revue Bénédictine* 63 (1953) 132-142.

— *Palaeographical Papers*, II, Oxford 1972.

Lowry, M.J.C., 'Two Great Venetian Libraries in the Age of Aldus Manutius', *Bulletin of the John Rylands University Library of Manchester* 57 (1974) 128-166.

— *The World of Aldus Manutius: Business and Scholarship in Renaissance Venice*, Oxford 1979.

Lucas, A., *Ancient Egyptian Materials and Industries*, 4th edn. revised by J.R. Harris, London 1962.

del Lungo, I. (ed.), *Prose volgari inedite, poesie latine e greche edite ed inedite di A.A. Poliziano*, Florence 1867.

Macler, F., 'Extraits de la Chronique de Maribas Kaldoyo', *Journal Asiatique* (May-June 1903) 492 ff.

Maïer, Ida, *Les manuscrits d'Ange Politien*, Geneva 1965.

Makowiecka, Elzbieta, *The Origin and Evolution of Architectural Form of Roman Library* (in the series 'Studia Antiqua'), Warsaw 1978.

Malaguzzi, V., *La corte di Ludovico il Moro*, IV, Milan 1923.

Maleček, F. and R., *Strahov Praha* (a catalogue of the possessions of Strahov Abbey), Prague (Nakladetelstvi-Orion) n.d.

Mallett, Margaret, 'Writing in Early Byzantium' in *The Uses of Literacy in Early Medieval Europe*, Cambridge 1990, 156-185.

Maltezou, Chryssa, «Τά λατινικά ἔγγραφα τοῦ Πατμιακοῦ ἀρχείου», *Σύμμεικτα* 2 (1970) 349-378.

Manacorda, M.A., 'Scuola e insegnanti' in *Oralità, scrittura, spettacolo*, Turin 1983.

Manafis, K.A., *Αἱ ἐν Κωνσταντινουπόλει Βιβλιοθῆκαι. Αὐτοκρατορικαί καί Πατριαρχική καί περί τῶν ἐν αὐταῖς χειρογράφων μέχρι τῆς Ἁλώσεως (1453)*, Athens 1972.

Mancini, G., *Giovanni Tortelli cooperatore di Niccoló V nel fondare la Biblioteca Vaticana*, with supplement by Mgr. G. Mercati, Florence 1921.

Mandolfo, A., 'Alopa, Lorenzo' in *DBI* 2 (1960) 523.

Manetti, Giannozzo, *Vita Nicolai V*, in *RIS* III/2, 1734, 907-960.

Mango, C., 'The Availability of Books in the Byzantine Empire, A.D. 750-850' in *Byzantine Books and Bookmen: A Dumbarton Oaks Colloquium 1971*, Dumbarton Oaks 1975, 29-45.

— *Βυζάντιο: Ἡ Αὐτοκρατορία τῆς Νέας Ρώμης* (= *Byzantium: The Empire of New Rome*, London 1980, tr. D. Tsoungarakis), Athens 1990.

Mango, C. and Hawkins, E.J., 'The Hermitage of St. Neophytos and its Wall Paintings', *DOP* 20 (1966) 122 ff.

Manoussacas, M., «Ἡ ἀλληλογραφία τῶν Γρηγοροπούλων χρονολογουμένη (1493-1501)», *EMA* 6 (1956) 156-209.

— «Ἀρσενίου Μονεμβασίας τοῦ Ἀποστόλη ἐπιστολαί ἀνέκδοτοι (1521-1534)», *EMA* 8/9 (1959) 5-56, 208.

Mansi, J.D., *Sacrorum conciliorum nova et amplissima collectio*, 13 vols., Florence/Venice 1759-1798.

Maracchi Biogarelli, Berta, *La Biblioteca Medicea-Laurenziana nel secolo della sua apertura al pubblico (11 giugnio 1571)*, Florence 1971.

Marava-Hadjinikolaou, Anna and Toufexi-Paschou, Christina, *Κατάλογος Μικρογραφιῶν Βυζαντινῶν Χειρογράφων τῆς Ἐθνικῆς Βιβλιοθήκης τῆς Ἑλλάδος*, I, Athens 1978.

Marchini, G., 'Il San Marco di Michelozzo', *Palladio* 6 (1942) 113.

Margolin, Jean-Claude, 'Beatus Rhenanus et Boniface Amerbach: Une amitié de trente ans', *Annuaire 1985*, 157-175.

Marinatos, S., 'Some General Notes on the Minoan Written Documents, *Minos* 1 (1951) 39-42.

Marinis, T. de, *La Biblioteca Napoletana dei Rè d'Aragona*, 4 vols., Milan 1947-1952, and *Supplemento*, 2 vols., Verona 1969.

Mariotti, S., *Livio Andronico e la traduzione artistica*, Milan 1952.

Markopoulos, A., «Θεοδώρου Β΄ Λασκάρεως, Ἀνέκδοτον ἐγκώμιον πρός τόν Γεώργιον Ἀκροπολίτην», *ΕΕΒΣ* 36 (1968) 104-118.

— «Νέα στοιχεῖα γιά τή χρονολόγηση τῆς *Βιβλιοθήκης* τοῦ Φωτίου», *Σύμμεικτα* 7 (1987) 165-181.

Marrou, H.-I., 'Autour de la bibliothèque du pape Agapit', *Mélanges d'Archéologie et d'Histoire de l'École Française de Rome* 48 (1931) 124-169.

— *Saint Augustin et la fin de la culture antique* (thesis), Paris 1938.

— *Ἱστορία τῆς Ἐκπαιδεύσεως κατά τήν Ἀρχαιότητα* (= *Histoire de l'éducation dans l'antiquité*, Paris 1948, tr. Th. Fotinopoulos), Athens 1961.

Martin, H.J., 'Les lectures de Guillaume Fichet et de Jean Heynlin d'après le registre de prêt de la bibliothèque de la Sorbonne', *Bibliothèque d'Humanisme et Renaissance* 17 (1955) 7-23, 145-153.

— 'La naissance d'un médium' in *Le livre français, hier, aujourd'hui, demain*, Paris 1972, 48-55.

Martines, L., *The Social World of the Florentine Humanists, 1390-1460*, London 1963.

Martini, E., 'Demetrios von Phaleron' in *RE* 4 (1901) 2817-2841.

Marzi, D., 'Giovanni Gutenberg e l'Italia', *La Bibliofilia* 2 (1900-1901) 81-135.

Masai, F., *Pléthon et le platonisme de Mistra*, Paris 1956.

Masini, N., *Vita di Domenico Malatesta signore di Cesena*, BCM, Ms 45188 (16th c.), published by G.M. Muccioli in *Catalogus Codicum Manuscriptorum Malatestianae Caesenatis Bibliothecae*, II, Cesena 1784, 273.

Maspero, G., *Les contes populaires de l'Égypte ancienne* (Paris 1882), repr. Paris 1988.

— 'La mythologie égyptienne', *Revue de l'Histoire des Religions* 19 (1889).

— *The Dawn of Civilization: Egypt and Chaldaea*, tr. M.L. McClure, London 1894.

Massa Positano, L., 'Prolegomena et Commentarius in Plautum' in Kaster, *Scholia in Aristophanem*, IV/1 25, 92.

Masson, A., *Le décor des bibliothèques du Moyen εge à la Révolution*, Geneva 1972.

Mazal, O. (ed.), *Ein Weltgebaüde der Gedanken: Die Österreichische Nationalbibliothek*, Graz 1987.

McKerrow, R.B., *Printers' and Publishers' Devices in England and Scotland, 1485-1640*, London 1913.

McMurtie, C., *The Invention of Printing: A Bibliography*, New York 1936 (repr. 1962).

Medvedev, I., *Βυζαντινός οὐμανισμός, 14ος - 15ος αἰ.* (unpublished translation from the Russian by G. Beveratos, Leningrad 1967).

Megas, A.Ch., «Ὁ προουμανιστικός κύκλος τῆς Παδούης (Lovato Lovati - Albertino Mussato) καί οἱ τραγωδίες τοῦ Σενέκα», *Ἐπιστημονική Ἐπετηρίς Φιλοσοφικῶν Σπουδῶν* 11 (1967) 229-233 (English summary).

Meier, G., 'Geschichte der Schule von St. Gallen im Mittelalter', *Jahrbuch für Schweizerische Geschichte* 10 (1884) 33-127.

Meinardus, O., *Monks and Monasteries of the Egyptian Deserts*, Cairo 1962.

Menhardt, H., 'Die Kärntner Bibliotheksreise des Wolfgang Lazius' in *Beiträge zur Geschichte und Kulturgeschichte Kärntens* (Festgabe für Dr. Martin Wutte), Klagenfurt 1936, 101-112.

Mercati, G., 'Minuzie', *Bessarione* 38 (1922) 135-143.

— *Per la cronologia della vita e degli scritti di Niccol‰ Perotti, arcivescovo di Siponto*, Rome 1925.

Mergiali-Falangas, Sophia, *L'enseignement et les lettrés pendant l'époque des Paléologues*, Athens 1996.

Messa, L. and Ungaro, Lucrezia, 'Rilievi moderni e recostruzioni 1926-1986', *Archivio Classico* 41 (1989) 199-214.

Meyier, K.A. de, 'Scribes grecs de la Renaissance', *Scriptorium* 18 (1964) 258-266.

Middleton, J.H., *The Remains of Ancient Rome*, London 1892.

Miglio, M., 'Bussi, Giovanni Andrea' in *DBI* 15 (1972) 565-572.

Mignon, M., 'La maison de Pétrarque à Vaucluse', *Études italiennes* 9 (1927) 215-235.

Miklosich, F. and Müller, J., *Acta et diplomata graeca medii aevis sacra et profana*, 6 vols., Vienna 1860-1890.

Milanesi, G., *Le lettere di Michelangelo Buonarotti*, Florence 1875.

Milde, W., 'Die Kartensammlung' in Raabe, *Lexikon...* 91-92.

Miliarakis, A., *Ἱστορία τοῦ Βασιλείου τῆς Νικαίας καί τοῦ Δεσποτάτου τῆς Ἠπείρου (1204-1261)*, Athens 1898.

Mioni, E., 'Bessarione bibliofilo e filologo', *Rivista di Studi Bizantini e Neoellenici*, n.s., 5 (1968) 61-83.

— 'La biblioteca greca di Marco Musuro', *AV*, 5th ser., 93 (1971) 5-28.

— 'Bessarione scriba e alcuni suoi collaboratori' in *Miscellanea Marciana di Studi Bessarionei*, Padua 1976, 263-318.

— *Εἰσαγωγή στήν Ἑλληνική Παλαιογραφία* (= *Introduzione alla Paleografia Greca*, Padova 1973, tr. N.M. Panayotakis), Athens 1977.

Mitford, T.B., 'The Hellenistic inscriptions of Old Paphos', *BSA* 56 (1961) 1 ff.

Mohler, L., *Kardinal Bessarion als Theologe, Humanist und Staatsmann: Funde und Forschungen*, 3 vols., Paderborn 1923-1942.

Molho, A., 'Corbinelli, Antonio' in *DBI* 28 (1983) 745-747.

Momigliano, A., 'Cassiodorus and the Italian Culture of his Time', *Proceedings of the British Academy* 41 (1955) 207-245.

— *The Conflict between Paganism and Christianity in the Fourth Century*, Oxford 1963.

Monfasani, J., *George of Trebizond: A biography and a study of his rhetoric and logic*, Leiden 1976.

Monfrin, J. and Jullien de Pommerol, M.H., *La Bibliothèque pontificale à Avignon et à Peniscola pendant le Grand Schisme d'Occident et sa dispersion*, Rome 1989.

— 'La bibliothèque pontificale à Avignon au XIVe siècle' in Vernet, *Histoire des bibliothèques françaises*, 146-169.

Moraux, P., *Les listes anciennes des ouvrages d'Aristote*, Louvain 1951.

— *Der Aristotelismus bei den Griechen von Andronikos bis Alexander von Aphrodisias*, IV: *Die Renaissance des Aristotelismus im 1. Jhr. v. Chr.*, Berlin/New York 1973.

Morçay, R., 'La cronica del convento fiorentino di San Marco', *ASI* 81 (1913) 1-29.

Muccioli, G.M., *Catalogus Codicum Manuscriptorum Malatestianae Caesenatis Bibliothecae*, 2 vols., Cesena 1780-1784.

Müller, C.W. (ed.), *Oratores Attici*, 2 vols., Paris 1847-1848.

— 'Protagoras über die Götter', *Hermes* 95 (1967) 140-159.

Müller, K., 'Neue Mittheilungen über Janos Lascaris und die Mediceische Bibliothek', *Centralblatt für Bibliothekswesen* 1 (1884) 333-412.

Müller-Graupa, E., «Mouseion» in *RE* 16 (1933) 797-821.

Müntz, E., *Les arts à la cour des papes pendant le XVe et le XVIe siècle: Recueil des documents inédits*, III, Paris 1878.

Müntz, E. and Fabre, P., *La Bibliothèque du Vatican au XVe siècle*, Paris 1887.

Münzer, F., 'C. Calvisius Sabinus' in *RE* 3 (1899) 1411.

Musial, S., 'Beatus Rhenanus étudiant de philosophie à Paris (1503-1507)', *Annuaire 1985*, 271-279.

Nash, E., *Bildlexikon zur Topographie des antiken Rom*, II, Tübingen 1961.

Nauck, A. (ed.), *Tragicorum Graecorum Fragmenta*, Leipzig 1889.

Naville, É., *Das Aegyptische Todtenbuch der XVIII. bis XX. Dynastie*, Berlin 1886.

Newberry, P., *The Amherst Papyri*, London 1899.

de Niccolò, Paolo, 'Profilo storico della biblioteca Apostolica Vaticana' in *Biblioteca Apostolica Vaticana*, Florence 1985, 19.

Nicol, D.M., *The Byzantine Family of Kantakouzenos*, Washington 1968.

Nicolai, R., 'Le bibliotheche dei ginnasi', *Nuovi Annali della Scuola Speciale per Archivisti e Bibliotecari* 1 (1987) 17 ff.

Nielsen, I., *Thermae et balnea*, Aarhus 1990.

Nogara, A., 'Note sulla composizione e la struttura della Biblioteca di Fozio', I, *Aevum* 49 (1975) 213-242.

Nolhac, M.P. de, 'Inventaire des manuscrits grecs de Jean Lascaris', *Mélanges d'Archéologie et d'Histoire de l'École Française de Rome* 6 (1886) 251-274.

— *La bibliothèque de Fulvio Orsini*, Paris 1887.

— *Pétrarque et l'Humanisme*, 2 vols., Paris 1907.

— *Ronsard et l'Humanisme*, Paris 1921.

Norsa, M., *La scrittura letteraria greca*, Florence 1939.

Nystazopoulou-Pelekidou, Maria, *Βυζαντινά ἔγγραφα τῆς μονῆς Πάτμου*, Athens 1980.

Ochsenbein, P., 'Teaching and Learning in the Gallus Monastery' in King and Vogler, *The Culture of the Abbey of St. Gall*, 133-144.

Offenbacher, E., 'La bibliothèque de Willibald Pirckheimer', *La Bibliofilia* 40 (1938) 241-263.

Offenberg, A.K., 'The First Printed Book Produced at Constantinople (1493)', *Studia Rosentaliana* 3 (1969) 96-112.

Ogilvy, J.D.A., *Books Known to the English*, Cambridge Mass. 1967.

O'Gorman, J.F., *The Architecture of the Monastic Library in Italy, 1300-1600*, New York 1972.

Ohly, K., 'Stichometrische Untersuchungen', *ZB*, Beiheft 61 (1928) 88-89.

Oikonomides, N., 'Literacy in Thirteenth Century Byzantium: An example from western Asia Minor' in *Τό Ἑλληνικό* (festschrift in honour of S. Vryonis), I, New Rochelle N.Y. 1990, 253-265.

Oleroff, A., 'Démétrius Trivolis, copiste et bibliophile', *Scriptorium* 4 (1950) 260-263.

Olmstead, A.T., *Assyrian Historiography*, Columbia 1916.

Omont, H., 'Catalogue des manuscrits grecs de Guillaume Pellisier [*sic*], évêque de Montpellier, ambassadeur de François 1er à Venise', *Bibliothèque de l'École des chartes* 46 (1886) 13.

— 'Un premier catalogue des manuscrits grecs du cardinal Ridolfi', *Bibliothèque de l'École des chartes* (1888) 309 ff.

Oppenheim, A.L., 'A Note on the Scribes in Mesopotamia' in *Studies in Honor of Benn Landsberger*, Chicago 1965, 253-256.

Orcutt, W.D., *The Book in Italy*, London 1926.

— *The Magic of the Book: More reminiscences and adventures of a bookman*, Boston 1930.

Orlandi, G., *Aldo Manuzio editore. Dediche, prefazioni, note ai testi*, 2 vols., Milan 1976.

Orlandos, A.K., *Μοναστηριακὴ Ἀρχιτεκτονική*, Athens 1927.

— *Ἡ ἀρχιτεκτονικὴ καὶ αἱ βυζαντιναὶ τοιχογραφίαι τῆς μονῆς τοῦ Θεολόγου Πάτμου*, Athens 1970.

Padover, S.K., 'Byzantine Libraries' in Thompson (J.W.), *The Medieval Library*, 310-329.

Papachristodoulou, G.Ch., «Τό ἑλληνιστικό Γυμνάσιο τῆς Ρόδου: Νέα γιά τή βιβλιοθήκη του» in *Akten des XIII Internationalen Kongresses für klassischen Archäologie*, Mainz 1990, 500 ff.

Papadopoulos, J.B., *Théodore II Lascaris empereur de Nicée*, Paris 1908.

Papritz, J., 'Archive in Altmesopotamien: Theorie und Tatsachen', *Archivalische Zeitschrift* 55 (1959) 11-50.

Parent, Annie, 'Les "Grecs du Roi" et l'étude du monde antique' in *L'art du livre à l'Imprimerie Nationale*, Paris 1973, 56-57.

Parrot, M., *Mari, une ville perdue ... et retrouvée par l'archéologie française*, Paris 1936.

— *Mission archéologique de Mari*, II: *Les palais: Architecture*, Paris 1958.

Parsons, E.A., *The Alexandrian Library, Glory of the Hellenic World*, 3rd edn., New York 1967.

Parthey, G., *Das alexandrische Museum*, Berlin 1838.

Passadaios, A., *Ὁ Πατριαρχικός Οἶκος τοῦ Οἰκουμενικοῦ Θρόνου*, I, Athens 1995.

Pasquali, G., 'Biblioteca' in *Enciclopedia Italiana*.

Pastorello, Ester, *L'Epistolario Manuziano. Inventario cronologico-analitico 1483-1597*, Venice/Rome 1957.

Patrinelis, Ch.G., «Ἕλληνες κωδικογράφοι τῶν χρόνων τῆς Ἀναγεννήσεως», *Ἐπετηρίς τοῦ Μεσαιωνικοῦ Ἀρχείου* (1958-1959) 63-125.

Pellegrin, Élisabeth, *La bibliothèque des Visconti et des Sforza, ducs de Milan, au XVe siècle*, Paris 1955, and *Supplément*, Paris 1969.

— *Manuscrits de Pétrarque dans les bibliothèques de France*, Padua 1966.

Pelletier, A., 'Aristeae ad Philocratem epistula', *Sources Chrétiennes* 89 (1962).

Penham, D.F., *De Transitu Hellenismi ad Christianismum*, New York (Columbia University) 1954.

Pérez Martini, Immaculada, 'Y propos des manuscrits copiés par Georges de Chypre (Grégoire II) patriarche de Constantinople (1283-1289)', *Scriptorium* 46 (1992) 73-84.

Pernot, H., 'Hellénisme et Italie méridionale', *Studi italiani di filologia classica* 13 (1936) 161-182.

Perrot, G., and C. Chipiez, *A History of Art in Ancient Egypt*, tr. W. Armstrong, 2 vols., London 1883.

Pertusi, A., *Giorgio di Pisidia, poemi*, I: *Panegirici, epici* (= Studia Patristica et Byzantina, 7), Ettal 1960.

— ΕΡΩΤΗΜΑΤΑ: Per la storia e le fonti delle prime grammatiche greche a stampa', *IMU* 5 (1962) 321-350.

— (ed.), *Venezia e l'Oriente fra tardo Medioevo e Rinascimento*, Florence 1966.

— 'Gli inizi della storiografia umanistica nel Quattrocento' in A. Pertusi (ed.), *La storiografia veneziana fino al secolo XVI. Aspetti e problemi*, Florence 1970, 269-332.

— *Leonzio Pilato fra Petrarca e Boccaccio*, Venice/Rome 1979.

Petit, P., *Libanius et la vie municipale à Antioche au IVe siècle après J.-C.*, Paris 1955.

— *Les étudiants de Libanius*, Paris 1956.

— 'Recherches sur la publication et la diffusion des discours de Libanius', *Historia* 5 (1956) 479-507.

Petrarch: *Francesco Petrarca, Prose*, ed. G. Martellotti, Milan/Naples 1955.

Petrochilos, N., *Ρωμαῖοι καί Ἑλληνιμσμός. Μιά διαλεκτική σχέση*, Athens 1984.

Petrucci, A., *La scrittura di Francesco Petrarca*, Vatican City 1967.

Pettas, W., 'The Cost of Printing a Florentine Incunable', *La Bibliofilia* 75 (1973) 67-85.

Pfeiffer, H.F., 'The Roman Library of Timgad', *Memoirs of the American Academy in Rome* 9 (1931) 157 ff.

Pfeiffer, R., 'Conrad Peutinger und die humanistische Welt', *Augusta* (1955) 179-186.

— *Ausgewählte Schriften*, Munich 1960, 175-182 ('Humanitas Benedictina').

— *Ἱστορία τῆς Κλασσικῆς Φιλολογίας. Ἀπό τῶν ἀρχῶν μέχρι τοῦ τέλους τῶν ἑλληνιστικῶν χρόνων* (= *History of Classical Scholarship: From the beginnings to the end of the Hellenistic age*, Oxford 1968, tr. P. Xenos et al.), Athens 1972.

— *Ἱστορία τῆς Κλασσικῆς Φιλολογίας. Ἀπό τό 1300 μέχρι τό 1850* (= *History of Classical Scholarship: From 1300 to 1850*, tr. P. Xenos et al.), Athens 1980.

— 'Die Sophisten, ihre Zeitgenossen und Schüler im fünften und vierten Jahrhundert' in C.J. Classen (ed.), *Sophistik*, Reinbeck 1970, 170-219.

Pflugk, J., *Epistola ad Vitum a Seckendorf, praeter fata Bibliothecae Budensis, librorum quoque ultima expugnatione repertorum catalogum exhibens*, Jena 1686.

Philippe, J., *Guillaume Fichet, sa vie, ses oeuvres*, Annecy 1892.

Piazzesi, G., 'Le due biblioteche', *Archivio Classico* 41 (1989) 180 ff.

Pica, A., *Il gruppo monumentale di S. Maria delle Grazie in Milano*, Rome 1937.

Piccard, G., 'Carta bombycina, carta papyri, pergamena graeca. Ein Beitrag zur Geschichte der Beschreibstoffe im Mittelalter', *Archivalische Zeitschrift* 61 (1965) 46-75.

Piccolomini, Enea Silvio, *Intorno alle condizioni e alle vicende della Libreria Medicea privata*, Florence 1875.

Piganiol, A., *L'empire chrétien (325-395)*, Paris 1947.

Pigulevskaja, N., 'Istorija nisibijskoj Akademii, Istočiniki po istorii sirijskoj Školy', *Palestinskij Sbornik* 17 (80) (1967) 90-109.

Pinner, H.L., *The World of Books in Classical Antiquity*, Leiden 1948.

Pinto, Olga, 'Le bibliotheche degli Arabi nell' età degli Abbassidi', *La Bibliofilia* 30 (1928) 139-165.

Pintor, F., 'Per la storia della libreria medicea nel Rinascimento', *IMU* 3 (1960) 189-210.

Planoudes: *Maximi monachi Planudis epistulae*, ed. M. Treu, Breslau 1890.

Platina, Bartolomeo, *De vitis Pontificum Romanorum*, Köln 1573.

del Plato, A., *Librai e biblioteche parmesi del secolo XV*, Parma 1905.

Platthy, J., *Sources on the Earliest Greek Libraries with the Testimonia*, Amsterdam 1968.

Pohl, A., 'Bibliotheken und Archive im alten Orient', *Orientalia* 25 (1956) 105-109.

— 'Der Archivar und die Keilschriftforscher', *Orientalia* 29 (1960) 230-232.

Polemis, D.I., *The Doukai*, London 1968.

Pope, M., *BSA* 55 (1960) 200-210.

Portoghesi, P., 'La biblioteca laurenziana' in P. Portoghesi and B. Zevi (ed.), *Michelangiolo architetto*, Turin 1964, 209-350, 856-865.

Posener, G., Krieger, P. and de Cenival, J.-L., *The Abu Sir Papyri*, London 1968.

Posner, E., *Archives in the Ancient World*, Cambridge Mass. 1972.

Praet, J. van, *Recherches sur Louis de Bruges*, Paris 1831.

Pratesi, R., 'Antonio da Massa Maritima' in *DBI* 3 (1961) 555-556.

Preisendanz, K., 'Papyruskunde' in *HBW* I 192-196.

Pritchard, J.B., *Ancient Near Eastern Texts relating to the Old Testament*, 3rd edn., Princeton 1969.

Przychocki, G., 'Menander im Katalog der Patriarchalbibliothek zu Konstantinopel', *Bulletin International de l'Académie Polonaise des Sciences et des Lettres* 1-3 (1937) 28-34.

Psellos, Michael, *Chronographia*, ed. E. Renauld, I, Paris 1926.

Pütz, T., *De M. Tulli Ciceronis Bibliotheca* (dissertation), Münster 1925.

Quaritch, B. (ed.), *Contributions towards a Dictionary of English Book-Collectors, as also of some Foreign Collectors*, London 1969 (reprint of the edition of 1892-1921).

Raabe, P., 'The Herzog August Library in Wolfenbüttel' in *Treasures*... VII-XV.

— (ed.), *Lexikon zur Geschichte und Gegenwart der Herzog August Bibliothek Wolfenbüttel*, Wiesbaden 1992.

Radt, W., *Pergamon*, Köln 1988.

Rallis, G. and Potlis, M., *Σύνταγμα τῶν Θείων καί Ἱερῶν κανόνων τῶν τε Ἁγίων καί Πανευφήμων Ἀποστόλων, καί Ἱερῶν Οἰκουμενικῶν καί Τοπικῶν Συνόδων, καί τῶν κατά μέρους Ἁγίων Πατέρων*, 6 vols., Athens 1852-1859.

Ramboldi da Imola, B., *Commentum super Dantis Comediam*, ed. J.P. Lacaita, V, 1887.

Rapin, C., 'Les inscriptions économiques de la trésorerie hellénistique d'Ai Khanoum (Afghanistan)', *BCH* 107 (1983) 315-372.

— 'Les textes littéraires grecs de la trésorerie d'Ai Khanoum', *BCH* 111 (1987) 225-266.

Rashdall, H., *The Universities of Europe in the Middle Ages*, ed. F.M. Powicke and A. Emden, 3 vols, Oxford 1936.

Reale Accademia Ercolanese, *Herculanensium voluminum que supersunt*, Collectio prior, 9 vols., Naples 1793-1850, Collectio altera, 11 vols., Naples 1862-1876.

Regenbogen, O., 'Theophrastos' in *RE* suppl. 7 (1940) 1354-1562.

— «*Πίναξ*» in *RE* 20 (1950) 1409-1482.

Reinitzer, H., *Biblia deutsch. Luthers Bibelübersetzung und ihre Tradition* (Herzog August Library Exhibition Catalogues, No. 40), 1983.

Renaudet, A., *Préréforme et humanisme à Paris pendant les premières guerres d'Italie (1494-1517)*, Paris 1916.

Renouard, A.A., *Annales de l'imprimerie des Alde, ou Histoire des trois Manuce et de leurs éditions*, 3rd edn., Paris 1834.

Renouard, P., *Inventaire chronologique des éditions parisiennes du XVIe siècle (1501-1510)*, ed. Brigitte Moreau, II, Paris 1977.

Reumont, A., 'Enoche d'Ascoli', *ASI* 20 (1874) 188-190.

Reynolds, L.D. and Wilson, N.G., *Ἀντιγραφεῖς καί Φιλόλογοι: Τό ἱστορικό τῆς παράδοσης τῶν κλασικῶν κειμένων* (= *Scribes and Scholars: A guide to the transmission of Greek and Latin literature*, 2nd edn., London 1975, tr. N.M. Panayotakis), Athens 1981.

Rhodes, D.E., *Incunabula in Greece: A first census*, Munich 1980.

— (ed.), *La Stampa a Firenze 1471-1550: Omaggio a Roberto Ridolfi* (exhibition catalogue), Florence 1984.

Riché, P., *Éducation et culture dans l'Occident barbare, VIe-VIIIe siècles* (= Patristica Sorbonensia, 4), Paris 1962.

— *Les écoles et l'enseignement dans l'Occident chrétien de la fin du Ve siècle au milieu du XIe siècle*, Paris 1979.

Richter, Gisela, *The Portraits of the Greeks,* 3 vols., London 1965.

Ridolfi, R., 'La biblioteca del cardinale Niccol‰ Ridolfi', *La Bibliofilia* 31 (1929) 174-193.

— *La Stampa in Firenze nel secolo XV*, Florence 1958.

Riva, C., 'Gli inediti di Antonio Domeniconi', *Studi Romagnoli* 30 (1979) 69-83.

Robathan, Dorothe M., 'Libraries of the Italian Renaissance' in Thompson (J.W.), *The Medieval Library*, 509-588.

Robert, L., 'Notes d'épigraphie hellénistique', *BCH* 59 (1935) 421-425.

Roberts, C.H., 'The Codex', *Proceedings of the British Academy* (1954) 169-204.

— 'Books in the Graeco-Roman World and in the New Testament' in *The Cambridge History of the Bible*, I, Cambridge 1970, 48-66.

Roberts, C.H. and Skeat, T.C., *The Birth of the Codex*, London 1983.

Roberts, R.J., 'The Greek Press at Constantinople in 1627 and its Antecedents', *The Library*, 5th ser., 22 (1967) 13-43.

Robinson, R.P., 'De fragmenti Suetoniani de grammaticis et rhetoribus codicum nexu et fide', *University of Illinois Studies in Language and Literature* VI.4 (1922).

Rogers, D., *The Bodleian Library and its Treasures, 1320-1700*, Henley-on-Thames 1991.

Rohifs, G., *Scavi linguistici nella Magna Grecia* (in the series 'Collezione di studi meridionali'), Halle/Rome 1933.

Romanelli, G., 'Il progetto di Sansovino e lo scalone' in *Da Tiziano a El Greco. Per la storia del manierismo a Venezia, 1549-1590* (exhibition catalogue), Milan 1981, 277-285.

Romilly, Jacqueline de, *Les grands sophistes dans l'Athènes de Periclès*, Paris 1988.

— *'Αλκιβιάδης* (= *Alcibiadès*, tr. Athina-Babi Athanasiou and Katerina Miliaressi, Athens 1995.

Rose, H.J., *A Handbook of Greek Literature*, London 1948.

— *Ἱστορία τῆς Λατινικῆς Λογοτεχνίας* (= *A Handbook of Latin Literature*, London 1967, tr. K.Ch. Grollios), 2 vols., Athens 1978-1989.

Rosmini, C., *Vita di Francesco Filelfo da Tolentino*, 3 vols., Milan 1808.

Ross, W.B., 'Giovanni Colonna, Historian at Avignon', *Speculum* 45 (1970) 535-545.

Ross, W.D., *Plato's Theory of Ideas*, Oxford 1951.

Rossi, G.M., 'Barozzi' in *DBI* 6 (1964) 495-499.

Rostovtzeff, M., *Social and Economic History of the Hellenistic World*, Oxford 1941.

Rouse, R.H., 'The Early Library of the Sorbonne', *Scriptorium* 21 (1967) 42-71, 226-251.

Rouse, R.H. and M.A., 'The Book Trade at the University of Paris, ca. 1250-ca. 1350*' in Bataillon et al., *La production du livre universitaire...* 41-114.

— 'La bibliothèque du collège de la Sorbonne' in Vernet, *Histoire des bibliothèques françaises*, 113-123.

Rowe, A., 'The Discovery of the Famous Temple and Enclosure of Sarapis at Alexandria', Appendix to the *Annales du Service des Antiquités de l'Égypte*, Cahier No. 12, 1946.

Runciman, S., *Mistra, Byzantine Capital of the Peloponnese*, London 1980.

Rupprich, H. (ed.), *Der Briefwechsel des Konrad Celtis*, Munich 1934.

Rüsch, E.G., *Tuotilo – Mönch und Künstler. Beiträge zur Kenntnis seiner Persönlichkeit*, St. Gall 1953.

Ruzicska, P., *Storia della letteratura ungherese*, Milan 1963.

Sabbadini, R., *Centotrenta lettere inedite di Francesco Barbaro*, II, Salerno 1884.
— *Biografia documentata di G. Aurispa*, Noto 1890.
— 'Le scoperte di Enoche da Ascoli', *Studi italiani di filologia classica* 8 (1899) 119-131.
— 'Nuove notizie e nuovi documenti su Ognibene de' Bonisoli Leoniceno', *Antologia Veneta* 1 (1900) 12-26, 174-189.
— *Storia e critica di testi latini*, Catania 1914.
— *Il metodo degli Umanisti*, Florence 1922.
— *Le scoperte dei codici latini e greci nei secoli XIV e XV*, new edn. by E. Garin, Florence (Sansoni) 1975.
Sabellico, M.A., *Vita Pomponii Laeti*, Strasbourg 1510.
Sabellici Opera Omnia, Basel 1560.
Sacrae Congregationis de Propaganda Fide Memoria Rerum (1622-1700), I, Rome/Freiburg/Vienna 1971.
Sakkelion, I., *Πατμιακή Βιβλιοθήκη, ἤτοι Ἀναγραφή τῶν ἐν τῇ Βιβλιοθήκῃ τῆς κατά τήν νῆσον Πάτμον γεραρᾶς καί βασιλικῆς μονῆς τοῦ ἁγίου Ἰωάννου τοῦ Θεολόγου τεθησαυρισμένων χειρογράφων τευχῶν*, Athens 1890.
Salles, Catherine, *Lire à Rome*, Paris 1994.
Sanudo, M., *Diarii*, 3rd edn., ed. R. Fulin et al., XXXIV, Venice 1892.
Sapegno, N., 'Boccaccio, Giovanni' in *DBI* 10 (1968) 836-856.
Scapecchi, P., 'New Light on the Ripoli Edition of the *Expositio* of Donato Acciaioli' in D.V. Reidy (ed.), *The Italian Book 1465-1800: Studies presented to D.E. Rhodes on his 70th birthday*, London 1993, 31-33.
Schaeffer, C.F.A., 'La première tablette', *Syria* 33 (1956) 161-168.
Schatkin, M., *Critical edition of, and introduction to, St. John Chrysostom's 'De Sancto Babyla', contra Iulianum et gentiles* (dissertation), Fordham Univ., N.Y., 1-106.
Schawe, J., 'Der alte Vorderorient' in *HBW* I 1-50.
Scheil, V., *Une saison de fouilles à Sippar*, Paris 1902.
— *Les nouveaux fragments du Code de Hammurabi sur le prêt à intérêt et les sociétés*, Paris 1918.
Schipke, R., *Untersuchungen zur Herstellung und Verbreitung des Buches im lateinischem Westen zwischen dem 4. und 6. Jahrhundert* (dissertation), Berlin 1976.
Schmidt, F., *Die Pinakes des Kallimachos*, Kiel 1924.
Schmidt, Johanna, 'Patmos' in *RE* 18 (1949) 2174-2191.
Schmökel, H., 'Mesopotamia' in Schmökel, H. (ed.), *Kulturgeschichte des alten Orient*, Stuttgart 1964, 46.
Schneider, A.M., *BYZANZ*, Berlin 1936.
Schneider, N., 'Die Urkundenbehälter von Ur III und ihre archivalische Systematik', *Orientalia* 9 (1940) 1-16.
Scholderer, V., 'The Petition of Sweynheim and Pannartz to Sixtus IV', *The Library*, 3rd ser., 6 (1915) 186-190.
— 'Printers and Readers in Italy in the Fifteenth Century', *Proceedings of the British Academy* 35 (1949) 25-47.
— *Fifty Essays in Fifteenth- and Sixteenth-Century Bibliography*, ed. D.E. Rhodes, Amsterdam 1966, 74-89 ('Printing at Venice to the End of 1481').
Schott, S., *Les chants d'amour de l'Égypte ancienne*, Paris 1956.
Schubart, W., *Das Buch bei den Griechen und Römern*, Heidelberg 1962.
Schubert, A., 'Die sicher nachweisbaren Inkunabeln Böhmens und Mährens von 1501', *ZB* 16 (1896) 51-61, 126-136, 176-185, 217-230.

Schürer, E., *Geschichte des jüdischen Volkes in Zeitalter Jesu Christi (175 B.C. - A.D. 135)*, new English edn. revised by Pamela Vermes, I-III, Edinburgh 1987-1995.

Ševčenko, I., 'Observations sur les recueils des Discours et des Poèmes de Th. Métochite et sur la bibliothèque de Chora à Constantinople', *Scriptorium* 5 (1951) 279-288.

— 'The Imprisonment of Manuel Moschopoulos in the year 1305 or 1306', *Speculum* 27 (1952) 133-157.

— *La vie intellectuelle et poétique à Byzance sous les premiers Paléologues*, Brussels 1962.

— 'Theodore Metochites, the Chora and the Intellectual Trends of his Time' in P.A. Underwood (ed.), *The Kariye Djami*, IV, Princeton 1975, 19-91.

Sherwin-White, A.N., *The Letters of Pliny: A historical and social commentary*, Oxford 1966.

Sicherl, M., 'Die Editio Princeps Aldina des Euripides und ihre Vorlagen', *Rheinisches Museum für Philologie* 118 (1975) 205-225.

— *Handschriftliche Vorlagen der Editio Princeps des Aristoteles*, Mainz 1976.

— 'Die Musaios-Ausgabe des Aldus Manutius und ihre lateinische Übersetzung', *IMU* 19 (1976) 256-276.

— *Johannes Cuno, ein Wegbereiter des Griechischen in Deutschland. Ein biographisch-kodikologische Studie*, Heidelberg 1978.

— 'Die Editio Princeps des Aristophanes' in B. Hallen, (ed.), *Das Buch und sein Haus*, I: *Erlesenes aus der Welt des Büches*, Wiesbaden 1979, 189-231.

Simone, F., 'Guillaume Fichet retore ed umanista', *Memorie della Reale Accademia delle Scienze di Torino*, 2nd ser., 69 (1939) 103-144.

Simopoulos, K., *Ξένοι ταξιδιῶτες στὴν Ἑλλάδα, 333 μ.Χ.-1700*, 4 vols., Athens 1970-1975.

Simson, B., *Jahrbücher des fränkischen Reiches unter Ludwig dem Frommen*, II, Leipzig 1876.

Sisson, M.A., 'The Stoa of Hadrian at Athens', *BSR* 11 (1929) 50-72 (Pls. XVII-XXVII).

Skeat, T.C., 'The Use of Dictation in Ancient Book-Production', *Proceedings of the British Academy* 42 (1956) 179 ff.

Skoutariotes: *Theodori Scutariotae additamenta ad Georgii Acropolitae Historiam*, ed. A. Heisenberg, I, Leipzig 1903.

Skouteropoulos, N.M., *Ἡ ἀρχαία σοφιστική: Τά σωζόμενα ἀποσπάσματα* (fragments edited, translated into Modern Greek and annotated by N. M. Skouteropoulos), Athens 1991.

Smith, L., 'Note cronologiche Vergeriane', *AVT* 10 (1920) 149-157.

Somigli, C., *Un amico dei Greci*, Arezzo 1964.

Sommer, R., in *Hermes* 61 (1926) 389-422.

Sonderegger, S., 'German Language and Literature in St. Gall' in King and Vogler, *The Culture of the Abbey of St. Gall*, 161-184.

Spatharakis, O.I., *Corpus of Dated Illuminated Greek Manuscripts*, Leiden 1981.

Speck, P., 'Die kaiserliche Universität von Konstantinopel', *Byzantinisches Archiv* 14 (1974).

Speiser, E.A., 'Scribal Concept of Education' in Kraeling, C.H., and R.M. Adams (ed.), *City Invincible*, Chicago 1960.

Spetsieri-Horemi, Alkistis, 'Library of Hadrian at Athens: Recent finds', *Rivista di antichità* 4.1 (1995) 137-147.

Speyer, W., *Die literarische Fälschung im heidnischen und christlichen Altertum. Ein Versuch ihrer Deutung*, Munich 1971.

Spitz, L., *Conrad Celtis, the German Arch-Humanist*, Cambridge Mass. 1957.

Starr, R.F.S., *Nuzi*, I, Cambridge Mass. 1939.

Starr, R.J., 'The Used-Book Trade in the Roman World', *Phoenix* 44 (1990) 148 ff.

Steinacker, H., 'Die römische Kirche und die griechischen Sprachenkenntnisse des Frühmittelalters', *Mitteil. des Inst. für Oesterr. Geschichtsforschung* 62 (1954) 28-66.

Sternbach, L., 'Georgii Pisidae carmina inedita', *Wiener Studien* 14 (1892) 51-68.

Stone, Isabella, 'Libraries of the Greek Monasteries in Southern Italy' in Thompson (J.W.), *The Medieval Library*, 330-337.

Stotz, P., *Ardua spes mundi. Studien zu lateinischen Gedichten aus St. Gallen*, Bern/Frankfurt 1972.

Strahovská Knihovna. Památníku národního písemnictví, Historické sály, dějiny a růst fondů (*The History and Collections of the Strahov Library*), Prague 1988.

Strasburger, H., *Ptolemaios und Alexander*, Leipzig 1934.

Streck, M., *Aschurbanipal und die letzten assyrischen Könige bis zu Untergange Niniveh's*, Leipzig 1916.

Streeten, B.H., *The Chained Library*, London 1939.

Strocka, V.M., 'Römische Bibliotheken', *Gymnasium* 88 (1981) 298-329.

Strummvoll, J. (ed.), *Die Hofbibliothek (1368-1922)* (= *Geschichte der österreichischen Nationalbibliothek*, I), Vienna 1968.

Sturm, J., 'Vie de Beatus Rhenanus', *Annuaire 1985*, 17-18.

Tatakis, B., *Ἡ φιλοσοφία στό Βυζάντιο* (= *La philosophie byzantine*, Paris 1949, tr. Eva K. Kalpourdzi, edited and with bibliography updated by L.G. Benakis), Athens 1977.

Tcherikover, V., *Hellenistic Civilisation and the Jews*, Philadelphia 1959.

Testi, L., 'I corali miniati della chiesa di S. Giovanni Evangelista in Parma', *La Bibliofilia* 20 (1918-1919) 1-30, 132-152.

Theiler, W., *Porphyrios und Augustin* (= Schriften der Königsberger gelehrten Gesellschaft, 10), Halle 1933.

Theophanes, *Chronographia*, ed. C. de Boor, I, Leipzig 1883.

Thompson, H.A., 'The Libraries of Ancient Athens' in *Contributions to Aegean Archaeology: Studies in Honor of William A. McDonald*, Minneapolis 1985, 295-297.

Thompson, H.A. and Wycherley, R.E., *The Athenian Agora*, XIV, Princeton 1972.

Thompson, J.W. (ed.), *The Medieval Library*, Chicago 1939 (reprinted in 1965 with additions by B.B. Boyer).

— 'Libraries of Ancient Greece' in *Ancient Libraries*, Berkeley 1940, 17-25.

Thompson, R. Campbell, *The Epic of Gilgamesh*, Oxford 1930.

Thomsen, R., *Studien über dem ursprungliche Bau des Caesarforums* (= Opuscula Archaeologica, II), Lund/Leipzig 1941.

Thureau-Dangin, F., Genovillac, H. de and Delaporte, L., *Inventaire des tablettes de Tello conservées au Musée Impérial de Constantinople*, Paris 1910-1914.

Tigay, J.H., *The Evolution of the Gilgamesh Epic*, Philadelphia 1982.

Tolnay, C. de, 'La bibliothèque laurentienne de Michel-Ange', *Gazette des Beaux-Arts* 14 (1935) 95-105.

Tomasini, I.F., *Bibliothecae Venetae manuscriptae publicae et privatae...*, Utini 1650.

Tøsberg, J., *Offentlige bibliotheker: Romerriget i det 2. arhundrede e Chr.*, Copenhagen 1976.

Travlos, J., *Pictorial Dictionary of Ancient Athens*, Athens 1971.

Treadgold, W.T., *The Nature of the Bibliotheca of Photius*, Dumbarton Oaks 1980.

Treasures of the Herzog August Library, ed. P. Raabe, Wolfenbüttel 1984.

Trenkler, E., 'Die Frühzeit der Hofbibliothek (1368-1519)' in Strummvoll, *Die Hofbibliothek...* 3-57.

Triandi, Ismini, «Παρατηρήσεις σέ δύο ὁμάδες γλυπτῶν τοῦ τέλους τοῦ 6ου αἰώνα ἀπό τήν Ἀκρόπολη» in W. Coulson et al. (ed.), *The Archaeology of Athens and Attica under Democracy*, Oxbow Monograph 37, 1994, 83-91.

Tsantsanoglou, K., *Τό Λεξικόν τοῦ Φωτίου, Χρονολόγηση - Χειρόγραφη παράδοση* (*Ἑλληνικά,* suppl. 17), Thessaloniki 1967, 11-35.

Tsiknopoulos, I.P. (ed.), *Κυπριακά Τυπικά*, Nicosia 1969.

Tsirpanlis, Z.N., *Οἱ ἑλληνικές ἐκδόσεις τῆς "Sacra Congregatio de Propaganda Fide" (17 αἰ.): Συμβολή στή μελέτη τοῦ θρησκευτικοῦ οὑμανισμοῦ,* Athens 1974.

— *Εἰσαγωγή στή Μεσαιωνική Ἱστορία τῆς Δυτικῆς Εὐρώπης*, Thessaloniki 1996.

Tsourkas, C., *Les débuts de l'enseignement philosophique et de la libre pensée dans les Balkans. La vie et l'oeuvre de Théophile Corydalée (1570-1646)*, Thessaloniki 1967.

Tuillier, A., 'Recherches sur les origines de la Renaissance byzantine au XIIIe siècle', *Bulletin de l'Association Guillaume Budé*, 4th ser., 3 (1955) 73-76.

Turner, E.G., *Athenian Books in the Fifth and Fourth Centuries B.C.*, London 1952.

— *The Typology of the Early Codex*, Philadelphia 1977.

— *Ἑλληνικοί πάπυροι: Εἰσαγωγή στή μελέτη καί τή χρήση τῶν παπύρινων κειμένων* (= *Greek Papyri: An Introduction*, Oxford 1968, tr. G.M. Parasoglou), Athens 1981.

Turyn, A., *Studies in the Manuscript Tradition of the Tragedies of Sophocles*, Urbana 1952.

— *The Byzantine Manuscript Tradition of the Tragedies of Euripides*, Urbana 1957.

— *Codices Graeci Vaticani saeculis XIII et XIV scripti annorumque notis instructi*, Vatican City 1964.

— *Dated Greek Manuscripts of the Thirteenth and Fourteenth Centuries in the Libraries of Italy*, Urbana 1972.

— *Dated Greek Manuscripts of the Thirteenth and Fourteenth Centuries in the Libraries of Great Britain*, Dumbarton Oaks 1980.

Tzetzes: *Ioannis Tzetzae Historiae*, recensuit Petrus Aloisius M. Leone, Naples 1968.

— *Prolegomena to Aristophanes*, in Kaster, *Scholia in Aristophanem*, I xx.

Ulman, B.L., 'Petrarch's Favorite Books', *TAPA* 54 (1923) 21-38.

— 'Studies', *Philological Quarterly* 20 (1941) 213-217.

— 'The Humanism of Coluccio Salutati', *MU* 4 (1963) 3-11.

Ulman, B.L. and Stadter, P.A., *The Public Library of the Renaissance in Florence: Niccol%o Niccoli, Cosimo de' Medici and the Library of San Marco*, Padua 1972.

Unterkircher, F., 'Vom Tode Maximilians I. bis zur Ernennung des Blotius (1519-1575)' in Strummvoll, *Die Hofbibliothek...* 61-77.

— 'Hugo Blotius (1575-1608). Sein Leben' in Strummvoll, *Die Hofbibliothek...* 81-127.

Vakalopoulos, A., *Ἱστορία τοῦ νέου ἑλληνισμοῦ*, Thessaloniki 1973.

Valcanover, F., 'Profilo Artistico' in *Biblioteca Marciana: Venezia* 37-49.

Vasari, G., *Le vite de' più eccellenti pittori, scultori ed architetti, con nuove annotazioni e commenti di Gaetano Milanesi*, III, Florence 1878.

Vasiliev, A.A., 'Pero Tafur: A Spanish traveler of the fifteenth century and his visit to Constantinople, Trebizond and Italy', *Byzantion* 7 (1932) 75-122.

— *History of the Byzantine Empire, 324-1453*, 2 vols., Madison Wis. 1964.

Vast, H., *Le cardinal Bessarion*, Paris 1878.

Vayer, L., 'Rapporti tra la miniatura italiana e quella ungherese nel trecento' in *La miniatura italiana tra Gotico e Rinascimento*, ed. Emanuela Sesti, I, Florence 1985, 3-33.

Vecce, C., 'Il giovane Beato Renano e gli umanisti italiani a Parigi all' inizio del XVI secolo', *Annuaire 1985*, 134-140.

Verde, A.F., *Lo studio fiorentino 1473-1503. Ricerche e documenti*, 4 vols., Florence 1973 - Pistoia 1977.

Verger, J., *Les Universités au Moyen Âge*, Paris 1973.

— 'Les universités françaises au XVe siècle', *Cahiers d'histoire* 21 (1976) 43-66.

Verges, Noel des, 'Adrien', *NBU* 1 (1852) 302-326.

Vernarecci, A., 'La libreria di Giovanni Sforza, signore di Pesaro', *Archivio di storia patria per le Marche e per Umbria* (1886) 502, 518, 519.

Vernet, A., 'Du "Chartophylax" au "Librarian"' in *Vocabulaire du livre et de l'écriture au Moyen Âge* (Actes de la table ronde, Paris 24-26 septembre 1987), ed. Olga Weijers, Turnhout 1989, 155-167.

— (ed.), *Histoire des bibliothèques françaises. Les bibliothèques médiévales du VIe siècle à 1530*, Paris 1989.

Verrua, P., *Umanisti ed altri 'studiosi viri' italiani e stranieri di qua e di là dalle Alpi e dal Mare*, Geneva 1924.

Vianello, N., 'I libri del Petrarca e la prima idea di una pubblica biblioteca a Venezia' in *Miscellanea Marciana di Studi Bessarionei*, Padua 1976, 435-451.

Viriville, V. de, *La Bibliothèque d'Isabeau de Bavière, femme de Charles VI*, Paris 1858 (offprint from the *Bulletin du bibliophile* of 1858).

Visani, A., 'La biblioteca del convento di San Marco in Firenze', *L'Archiginnasio* 35 (1940) 275-285.

Vogel, Marie and Gardthausen, V., 'Die griechischen Schreiber des Mittelalters und der Renaissance', *ZB* (1909).

Vogler, W., 'Historical Sketch of the Abbey of St. Gall' in King and Vogler, *The Culture of the Abbey of St. Gall*, 9-24.

Voit, P., *Prazské Klementinum*, Prague 1990.

Volk, O., *Die byzantinischen Klosterbibliotheken von Konstantinopel...* (unpublished dissertation, Munich 1955).

Volpe, G., *Matteo Nuti architetto dei Malatesta*, Venice 1989.

Vranoussi, Era, «'Ανέκδοτος κατάλογος ἐγγράφων τῆς ἐν Πάτμῳ μονῆς (ΙΒ΄-ΙΓ΄ αἰ.)», *Σύμμεικτα Κέντρου Βυζαντινῶν Ἐρευνῶν,* 2 Athens 1966, 137-162.

— *Βυζαντινά ἔγγραφα τῆς μονῆς Πάτμου, Α΄ Αὐτοκρατορικά*, Athens 1980.

Vryonis, S., 'The Will of a Provincial Magnate, Eustathius Boilas (1059)', *DOP* 11 (1957) 263-277.

— *The Decline of Medieval Hellenism in Asia Minor and the Process of Islamization from the Eleventh through the Fifteenth Century*, Berkeley/Los Angeles/London 1971.

Vyver, A. van de, 'Cassiodore et son oeuvre', *Speculum* 6 (1931) 244-292.

— 'Les Institutiones de Cassiodore et sa formation à Vivarium', *Revue Bénédictine* 53 (1941) 59-88.

Walker, C.B.F., 'Le cunéiforme' in Bonfante et al., *La naissance des écritures*, 25-99.

Walker, G.S.M., *Sancti Columbani Opera*, Dublin 1957.

Wallach, L., *Alcuin and Charlemagne*, Ithaca N.Y. 1959.

Walser, E., *Poggius Florentinus. Leben und Werke*, Leipzig/Berlin 1914.

Ward, Avra, *Τό Ἔπος τοῦ Γκίλγκαμες*, Athens 1994.

Waterman, L., *Royal Correspondence of the Assyrian Empire*, Ann Arbor 1930.

Wehrli, F., *Die Schule des Aristoteles*, V-VI, Basel 1950-1952.

— 'Demetrios von Phaleron' in *RE* suppl. 11 (1968) 514-522.

Weidner, E.F., *Handbuch der babylonischen Astronomie*, I, Leipzig 1915.

Weiss, R., 'Andrelini, Fausto' in *DBI* 3 (1961) 138-141.

Weitemeyer, M., *Babylonske og assyriske arkiver og biblioteker*, Copenhagen 1955.

— 'Archive and Library Technique in Ancient Mesopotamia', *Libri* 6 (1956) 217-238.

Weitzmann, K., 'The Selection of Texts for Cyclic Illustration in Byzantine Manuscripts' in *Byzantine Books and Bookmen: A Dumbarton Oaks Colloquium 1971*, Dumbarton Oaks 1975, 69-109.

Weitzmann, K., Loerke, W.C., Kitzinger, E. and Buchthal, H., *The Place of Book Illumination in Byzantine Art*, Princeton 1975.

Wendel, C., 'Der Bibel-Auftrag Kaisers Konstantins', *ZB* 56 (1939) 165-175.

— 'Planudes', *BZ* 40 (1940) 406-445.

— 'Planudes als Bücherfreund', *ZB* 58 (1941) 82-84.

— 'Tzetzes' in *RE* 7A_2 (1948) 1959-2011.

— 'Die bauliche Entwicklung der antikes Bibliothek', *ZB* 63 (1949) 407-428.

— *Die griechisch-römische Buchbeschreibung verglichen mit der des vorderen Orients*, Halle 1949.

— 'Das griechisch-römische Altertum' (completed by W. Göber) in *HBW* III.1 51-144.

— *Kleine Schriften zum antiken Buch- und Bibliothekswesen*, ed. W. Krieg, Köln 1974.

Wendland, P., *Aristeae ad Philocratem epistula*, Leipzig 1900.

Werner, A., 'J.A. Leonicerus (1557-?)' in Raabe, *Lexikon...* 106.

West, M.L., *Hesiod: Theogony*, Oxford 1966.

— *Hesiod: Works and Days*, Oxford 1978.

Westermann, A., *Vitarum Scriptores Graeci*, Amsterdam 1845.

Whitehead, P.B. and Biasiotti, G., 'La chiesa di SS Cosma e Damiano', *Rend. Pont. Acc. d. Arch.*, 3rd ser., 3 (1924-1925) 83 ff.

Whittaker, J., 'Parisinus Graecus 1962 and Janus Lascaris', *Phoenix* (University of Toronto Press) 31 (1977) 239-244.

Wieder, J., 'Les manuscrits Corviniens de la bibliothèque de Wolfenbüttel' in *Treasures...* 1-22.

Wilamowitz-Moellendorff, U. von, *Antigonos von Karystos*, IV, Berlin 1881.

Wilberg, W., Theurer, M., Eichler, F. and Keil, J., *Die Bibliothek* ('Forschungen in Ephesos' 5.1), 2 vols., Vienna 1953.

Wilkins, E.H., *Petrarch's Later Years*, Cambridge Mass. 1959.

— *Life of Petrarch*, Cambridge Mass. 1961.

Willard, C.C., *The Writings of Christine de Pisan*, New York 1990.

Wilson, N.G., 'The Libraries of the Byzantine World', *GRBS* 8 (1967) 53-80.

— 'The Composition of Photius' *Bibliotheca*', *GRBS* 9 (1968) 451-455.

— 'Books and Readers in Byzantium' in *Byzantine Books and Bookmen: A Dumbarton Oaks Colloquium 1971*, Dumbarton Oaks 1975, 1-15.

— *Scholars of Byzantium*, Baltimore 1983.

— *From Byzantium to Italy: Greek Studies in the Italian Renaissance*, London 1992.

Winckelmann, J.J., *Sendschreiben von den Herculanischen Entdeckungen*, German edn., 1792.

Wiseman, D.J., 'Assyrian Writing-Boards', *Iraq* 17 (1955) 3-13.

Witt, R., *Coluccio Salutati and his Public Letters*, Geneva 1976.

Wittkower, R., 'Michelangelo's Biblioteca Laurenziana', *Art Bulletin* 16 (1934) 123-218.

Wolfenbütteler Cimelien. Das Evangeliar Heinrichs des Löven in der Herzog August Bibliothek (Herzog August Library Exhibition Catalogues, No. 58), 1989.

Woodhouse, C.M., *Gemistos Plethon: The last of the Hellenes*, Oxford 1986.

Woolley, C.L., *Excavations at Ur: A record of twelve years' work*, London 1954.

Xanthopoulos, K., *Συνοπτική ἔκθεσις τῆς πνευματικῆς ἀναπτύξεως τῶν νεωτέρων Ἑλλήνων ἀπό τῆς ἀναγεννήσεως αὐτῶν μέχρι τοῦδε*, Constantinople 1880.

Xanthopoulos, Nikephoros Kallistos, «Ἐκκλησιαστική Ἱστορία», *PG* 147 457B.

Yiotopoulou-Sisilianou, Elli, *Ἀντώνιος ὁ Ἔπαρχος - Ἕνας Κερκυραῖος οὐμανιστής τοῦ ΙΣΤ' αἰώνα,* Athens 1978.

Yourcenar, Marguerite, *Ἀδριανοῦ Ἀπομνημονεύματα* (= *Mémoires d'Hadrien*, tr. Ioanna D. Hadjinikoli), Athens 1975.

Zaccaria, V., 'P.C. Decembrio traduttore di Plutarcho e di Platone', *IMU* 2 (1959) 194-195.

Zakythinos, D., *Μεταβυζαντινά καί Νέα Ἑλληνικά*, Athens 1978.

Zardini, Eugenia, 'Sulla biblioteca dell'archivescovo Areta di Cesarea', *Akten des XI. Internationalen Byzantinisten-Kongresses, München 1958*, Munich 1960, 671-678.

Zazzeri, R., *Sui codici e libri a stampa della Biblioteca Malatestiana di Cesena*, Cesena 1887.

Ziegler, K., 'Photios' in *RE* 20 (1941) 684-724.

Zinner, E. von, 'Die wissenschaftlichen Bestrebungen Regiomontans' in *Beiträge für Inkunabelkunde*, n.s., 2 (1938) 89-103.

Zolnai, Klára, and J. Fitz, *Bibliographia Bibliothecae Mathiae Corvini*, Budapest 1942.

Zorzi, M., *La Libreria di San Marco. Libri, lettori, società nella Venezia dei Dogi*, Milan 1987.

Zuntz, G., *The Text of the Epistles: Corpus Paulinum*, London 1953.

INDEX

INDEX

TRANSLATOR'S NOTE ON THE SPELLING OF GREEK NAMES

Any book containing Greek proper names over the whole period from antiquity to the present day presents almost insuperable problems of transliteration. The general principles I have tried to follow are as follows:-

(1) Where a name is commonly known in a Latinized or anglicized form (e.g. Plato, Athens, Rhodes), that form is used.

(2) Greek names in antiquity and up to the end of the Heraclian dynasty of East Roman emperors (A.D. 711) are Latinized in the traditional way (e.g. Pisistratus, Thucydides, not Peisistratos, Thoukydides).

(3) From *c.* 711 until the emergence of the Greek independence movement (late eighteenth century) they are transliterated in accordance with the following system: α=a, β=b, γ=g, δ=d, ε=e, ζ=z, η=e, θ=th, ι=i, κ=k, λ=l, μ=m, ν=n, ξ=x, ο=o, π=p, ρ=r, σ=s, τ=t, υ=y (but αυ, ευ, ου = au, eu, ou), φ=ph, χ=ch, ψ=ps, ω=o.

(4) In the modern era they are transliterated phonetically (αυ=av or af, β=v, γι=y, ευ=ev or ef, η=i, μπ=b or mb, ντ=d or nd, φ=f, χ=ch or h). So too, in general, are Modern Greek authors' names in the footnotes and Bibliography, unless their works have been published in English with their names given in a different form.

Some inconsistencies and discrepancies are almost inevitable. For these we offer our apologies.

Aaron 479
d'Abbeville, Gérard 210, 212
Abbot, George, Archbishop of Canterbury 258
'Abd Allah bin Mohammad 260
'Abd al-Latîf 87
Abdera 34
Abusir 30
Academus 43
Academy: *see* Plato. For other academies, see under their names.
Acciaiuoli, Donato 228, 231, 344, 346
  academy of 390
Accorsi, Buono: his library 180
Achillaeus, Lucius Elpidius 85
Achillas 75, 76, 82, 84
Achilles Tatius 155, 175
Adalhard, cousin of Charlemagne 204
Adramyttenos, Emmanuel 179, 233
Adrian of Niridanus 198
Adrianople 125
Aegae, library of Macedonian kings 101
Aelbert 202
Aelia Capitolina: *see* Jerusalem
Aelian (Claudius Aelianus) 30, 35
Aemilius, Publius 101
Aemilius Paullus, Lucius 101, 102
  his library 101
Aeneas 197
Aeschylus 50, 221, 330
  his 'library' 36, 50
Aesculapius, Temple of, Rome: its library 112
Aesop 23, 175, 222, 234, 345
Agapitus I, Pope 192
Agathias, historian 153
Agathocles 42
Ahmet III, Sultan 262
Ai Khanoum 91, 94, 95, 96, 124
  library 95, 96, 124
Aix-la-Chapelle 409
Akataleptos Monastery: *see* Christos Akataleptos
Akkad, Akkadians 3, 4, 8
Akoimetoi (Acoemeti), Monastery of, Constantinople: its library 147
Akropolites, Georgios 175
Akropolites, Konstantinos 174
  his library 174
Alacraw, Johann 478
Alaparos 15
Albergati, Niccolò 285, 288, 290
Alberico di Porta Ravegnana 209
Albert I, King of Belgium, his library 432
Albertus Magnus 312
Albinus: *see* Alciun
Albizzi family 285
Albizzi, Luca degli 342
Albona 398
Albrecht III, Duke of Austria 429
Albrecht, Duke of Bavaria 436
Alcaeus 82
Alcalá 434
Alcibiades 35, 40, 53, 173, 344
  his library 35, 53, 173
Alcuin 202, 203, 204, 205
Aldhelm 198
Aldus Manutius 182, 227, 229, 231, 232, 233, 234, 278, 334, 336, 337, 379, 388, 426, 438, 478
  his academy 234
Aldine press 233-235
Aleppo 496
Aleria 228, 229
Alexander V, Antipope 182
Alexander, Bishop of Jerusalem: his library 132
Alexander, Cornelius ('Polyhistor') 111
Alexander of Aphrodisias 330
Alexander the Great 3, 14, 21, 41, 44, 45, 46, 57, 58, 59, 60, 66, 73, 84, 97, 196, 197, 479
  his copy of the *Iliad* 57
  supplies Aristotle with funds and books 57
Alexander of Pleuron 65, 67
Alexandria 46, 61, 62, 64, 65, 66, 67, 68, 69, 70, 72, 73, 74, 75, 76, 80, 81, 83, 84, 85, 86, 87, 88, 89, 91, 92, 93, 94, 97, 99, 100, 106, 108, 111, 112, 125, 126, 130, 132, 140, 141, 142, 143, 144, 146, 152, 153, 171, 196, 215, 228, 426

Alexandrian Library 57-89, 124, 142, 321
architectural layout 68
arrangement by literary genre 72
'books from the ships' 72
classification scheme 67, 68
its destruction 75-81
its directors 66-69
historical summary 81-88
Alexios I Komnenos, Byzantine Emperor 167, 267, 268
Alexis, comic playwright 52
his library 52
Alfonso I (the Magnanimous), King of Naples 416, 447, 461
his library 416
Alfonso II, King of Naples 416, 456
Allen, Thomas 494
Almadiano, Giovanni Baptista 225
Alopa, Lorenzo de 231, 232, 422
Aloros 15
Alsace 382, 384
Althan, Graf von 442
Amalasuntha, daughter of Theodoric 192
Amasis, Pharaoh 29
Amboise 418
Ambrose of Milan, St. 312
Amelon (Amillaros) 15
Amempsinos 15
Amendolara 302
Amenemhet I, Pharaoh 25
Amerbach, Bonifacius 386
Amerbach, Johann 380, 389
Amisus 48
Ammenon 15
Ammianus Marcellinus 69, 70, 80, 84, 112, 137
on the size of the Alexandrian Library 69, 70
on the burning of the Alexandrian Library 80
Ammonius, grammarian (*c.* 100 B.C.) 66, 69
Ammonius Hermeiou, Neoplatonist 87, 278
Amphion 61
'Amr ibn al-'Aç, Emir 77, 86
Anaclitus II, Antipope 465
Anacreon 32
Ananias of Shirak 151, 191
Anastasius I, Byzantine Emperor 139
Anastasius of Sinai 148
Anaxagoras of Clazomenae 32, 33, 35, 38, 140, 480
'one-drachma editions' of his works 33
Anaximander 29
Anaximenes of Lampsacus 93
Anaximenes of Miletus 29
Ancus Marcius, Roman king 97
Andrelini, Fausto 418
Andron of Alexandria 82
Andronicus Rhodius 47, 49, 52, 53, 54
Andronikos II Palaiologos, Byzantine Emperor 176, 260
Andronikos III Palaiologos, Byzantine Emperor 176
Andros 154, 170
Angehrn, Beda, Abbot of St. Gall 376
Angelopoulos, Constantine 263
Angelopoulos, Panayotis 263
Angelopoulos, Theodore 263
Angelos family 254
Angilbert de St. Riquier 410
d'Angoulême, Jean, Count 412, 424
Anjou, House of 416
Anna Comnena: *see* Komnene
Anna Dalassene 268
Anne of Brittany, Queen of France 418
Annius Postumus 111
Annu (On, Heliopolis) 22
'Anonymous teacher' and his library 163, 164
Ansbert, monk and calligrapher 474
Anthemocritus 36
Anthimos the Deacon 246
Antigonus of Carystus 92
Antigonus Gonatas, King of Macedonia 42, 60, 73
Antimachus 38, 124
Antinoe 83
Antinoupolis, district of Alexandria 125
Antioch 133, 141, 142, 143, 145, 150, 152
its library (Temple of Trajan) 124
Antiochus I 67, 73
Antipater of Tyre 92
Antisthenes 33
Antium 104
Antonio da Massa 179
Antony, St. 312
Antony, Mark (Marcus Antonius) 82, 92, 102, 103, 108, 110
and library of Pergamum 92
Antwerp 442
Apellicon 48, 101
his library 48
Aphthonius 65, 66, 85, 89, 94
description of Serapeum library 65, 85
Aphrodisias: its library 124
Apollinaris the Younger, Bishop of Laodicea 145
Apollo 95, 217
– Palatinus, Temple of, Rome 110, 112, 124
Bibliotheca [Templi] Apollinis 110
Apollodorus, client of Demosthenes 41
Apollodorus, grammarian (*c.* 100 B.C.) 66, 69
Apollodorus, endower of library on Cos 77, 91
Apollodorus of Athens, chronicler 82, 93
Apollodorus of Damascus 111, 116, 125
architect of Biblioteca Ulpia 111
and of Baths of Trajan 116
biog. 125
relations with Hadrian 125
Apollonides 88
Apollonius of Athens ('the Grammarian') 108
Apollonius Eidographus 66, 69
Apollonius Molo 102
Apollonius of Perge 155
Apollonius Rhodius 66, 67, 68, 75, 81, 230, 350
Apollonius of Tyana 114, 116
Apollonius of Tyre 196
Apollonopolis (Edfu) 26
Apostoles, Arsenios 179, 233
Apostoles, Michael 177, 178, 225, 226, 228, 330, 332
his library 225, 226
Apsinus 226
Aquileia 132
Aquilius Regulus, Marcus 108
Aquinas, Thomas 312
Aratus of Soli 63, 70, 73
Arbon Forest 359
Archagoras, son of Theodotus 34
Archimedes 76, 480
Architecture of libraries:
Athens 52-54
Byzantine Empire 182-186
Mesopotamia 11-12
Pergamum 94-96
Renaissance 235-237
Rome 112-120
Graeco-Roman 123-130
Archytas of Tarentum 33, 37, 42, 50
his library 42
relations with Plato 42
Areopagus, Athens 410
Arethas, Archbishop of Caesarea 139, 161, 162, 163, 171, 172, 278
his library 161-162, 164
production and selling costs of his books 161-162

his scribes 162
and their fees 162
his scriptorium 162
Aretino, Leonardo 496
Aretophilos, Athenian philosopher 346
Arezzo 295
Argiletum, district of Rome 108
Argyropoulos, Ioannes 177, 178, 180, 221, 222, 224, 228, 231, 302, 330, 344, 346, 350, 450, 454, 458
his library 180
Aristarchus of Samothrace 66, 69, 77, 81, 92, 93, 179, 221
Aristarchus of Tegea 98
Aristeas 59, 61, 64, 65, 66, 69, 71, 72, 74, 80
'Letter of Aristeas' 64-65
Aristides, Aelius 125, 162, 174
on the libraries of Athens 125
Aristion of Ceos 46
Aristippus of Cyrene 42
Aristogeiton 35
Aristomenes 35
Aristophanes 33, 34, 35, 36, 40, 63, 69, 84, 96, 99, 106, 108, 123, 171, 330
and the role of books 35
criticizes book production 35, 36
Aristophanes of Byzantium 66, 68, 72, 74, 75, 81, 91, 95
Aristotle 30, 31, 34, 35, 38, 39, 40, 41, 43, 44, 45, 46, 47, 48, 49, 52, 53, 57, 60, 61, 62, 63, 66, 70, 72, 74, 80, 81, 84, 94, 101, 118, 130, 141, 158, 161, 166, 175, 227, 235, 330, 339, 370, 379, 386, 412, 418, 479, 494
Corpus Aristotelicum 44
his library 43-45
catalogue of 44-45
classification of 44-45
and the Lyceum 43
his will 45
Arius Didymus 92
d'Armagnac, Georges, Cardinal 425
Armenian press, Constantinople 264
Arnoaldus, Beatus 389
Arpinum 102, 104
Arquà 216, 217
d'Arras, Jean 402
Arrian 59
Arsames, Persian satrap 54
Arsenios, Abbot of Patmos 270
Arsinoe 19, 59, 60
Artamytos, Mt. (monastery) 169
Artemis 29, 31, 45, 125, 270
Artemon of Cassandreia 93
Ascalon 44
Ascensius, Badius: *see* Bade
Asclepiades, Julius 83
Asclepius 94, 480
Ascoli: *see* Enoch
Asconius Pedianus 220
Asinius Pollio: *see* Pollio
Asklepieion library: *see* Pergamum
Assur 7, 14
Assurbanipal (Sardanapalos) 7, 12, 13, 14, 15, 16
his library 12-14
Assus 46, 47
Atedius Melior 105
Athanasios the Miracle-Worker, calligrapher 172
Athanasius, St. (of Alexandria) 246
Athena Polias 123
Athenaeum library, Rome 124
Athenaeus 29, 30, 73, 74, 196, 222
Deipnosophistai 29
his list of libraries 30
Athenagoras, Patriarch 262
his library 262
Athenion 48
Athenodorus 92
Athens 29, 30, 31, 33, 34, 35, 36, 38, 39, 41, 42, 43, 44, 45, 46, 47, 48, 49, 52, 57, 60, 61, 62, 67, 68, 70, 80, 82, 91, 92, 93, 97, 99, 101, 102, 103, 106, 108, 118, 123, 124, 143, 150, 167, 170, 194, 215, 219, 258, 278, 282, 410, 445, 456
Agora 35
library, according to Zosimus 44-45
public library 30
Athos, Mt. 169, 184, 278
Atrapes, Leon 226
Atrectus, bookseller 108
Atrium Libertatis, Rome 110, 111, 113, 124
Attalus I, King of Pergamum 59, 91, 92
Attalus III Philometor, King of Pergamum 48
Attavanti, Attavante degli 230, 344, 346, 348, 402, 462
Atticus, Titus Pomponius 48, 102, 103, 104, 106, 118
biog. 102-103
Cicero's publisher 103-104
correspondence with Cicero 103-104
his library 103-104
Augsburg 160, 375, 382, 389, 400
August, Duke of Brunswick-Lüneburg 393, 394, 398, 400, 402, 406
his library: *see* Wolfenbüttel
Augusta, Bibliotheca: *see* Wolfenbüttel
Augustine of Canterbury, St. 198
Augustine of Hippo, St. 184, 189, 198, 246, 312, 370, 420
his 'library' 184
the Morgan Augustine 197
Augustus (Gaius Julius Caesar Octavianus), Roman Emperor 82, 83, 84, 88, 92, 104, 110, 111, 112, 114, 142 (*see also* Octavian)
his library (Palatine Library) 110-111
architecture of 113-114
and the Sebasteion library 83, 124
Temple of, and library: *see* Tiberius
Aulus Gellius: *see* Gellius
Aurelia Eusebia, Byzantine Empress 142
Aurelian, Roman Emperor 84, 89
Aurispa, Giovanni 172, 177, 179, 221, 222, 285, 288, 306, 310, 321, 350
Ausonius, Decimus Magnus 463
Austria: *see* Nationalbibliothek
Autoreianos, Georgios or Arsenios 173
l'Avenant, Jean 412
Aventine Hill, Rome 147
Avignon 216, 218, 288, 292
papal library 216, 288

Baanes, calligrapher working for Arethas 161
Babouskomites, Georgios 169
Babrius 23
Babylon 7, 8, 9, 12, 15, 57, 58
Bacon, Sir Francis 490
Bactria 91, 95
Bade, Josse (Jodocus Badius, Badius Ascensius) 388, 424, 425
Badia Fiorentina, library of 221
Baebius Macro 109
Baebius Pamphilius 97
Baghdad 154, 159
Baïf, Lazare de 425
Bakalár štetina, Mikuláš 473-474
Balbi, Girolamo 418
Balue, Cardinal 414
Bamberg 402, 478
Bambyce (Hierapolis), Syria 154
Bandini, Francesco 456, 458
Barbaro, Ermolao, the Elder 179
Barbaro, Ermolao, the Younger 382
Barbaro, Francesco 224, 339, 342
Barbius 23
Bardanes Philippikos, Byzantine Emperor 246
Bardellone, Giacomo 234, 235

Barlaam of Calabria 254
Barnabas, calligrapher 144
Barocci (Barozzi), Francesco 496
Barocci (Barozzi), Giacomo 500
Barzizza, Gasparino 416
Basel 359, 379, 380, 382, 386, 389, 398, 478
Basil I, Byzantine Emperor 163
Basil the Great, St. 150, 175, 205, 276, 290
Basilica Aemilia, Rome 111
Basilica Julia, Rome 111
Basiliscus, Byzantine Emperor 142
Bassiano 233
bath-houses 112, 116, 117, 122, 124, 125 (*see also* libraries)
Battisti del Cinque 354
Baugulf, Abbot of Fulda 204
Beatrice of Aragon 402, 456
her library 456 (*see also* Matthias Corvinus)
Beaufort, Henry, Bishop of Winchester 296
Becchi, Gentile 346
Beckensloer, Johann 450
Bede 203
Bedford, Duke of 412
Behaim, Martin 406
Belhassim, Antonios 206
Belisarius, Byzantine general 192
Bellerophon 50
Bellon du Mans, Pierre 272
Belvedere, Cortile del, Vatican City 302
Bembo, Pietro 334
Benedict, St. 192, 194, 196
Rule of 194, 359, 360
Benedict of Aniane 360
Benedict Biscop 198
Benjamin, Patriarch 262
Bernhard, Abbot of St. Gall 370
Beroaldo, Filippo 488
Berossus 15, 58, 73
Babyloniaca 73
Berry, Duc de 400, 411
Bertschi, Nikolaus, miniaturist 375
Berytus (Beirut) 143
Bessarion, Cardinal 178, 225, 226, 228, 229, 290, 294, 296, 305, 306, 310, 312, 314, 321, 322, 324, 326, 328, 330, 332, 336, 337, 379, 390, 416, 429, 430, 436
academy of 225
his library 226 (*see also* Marciana)
his scriptorium 226
in Bussi's circle 229
Beyazit II, Sultan 346
Bèze, Théodore de 488
bibliokapelos: *see* booksellers
'Bibliolathas' 74
bibliophylax: in Alexandria 67, 74
in Byzantium (= librarian) 149, 246, 252
Biblioteca (Bibliotheca, Bybliotheca): *see under respective names*
Bibliothèque Nationale, Paris 409-427
Bilgamesh: *see* Gilgamesh
Bill, John, bookseller 494
Bion: his library 42
burns his books 42
Biondo, Flavio 225, 310
Birago, Lampugnino 229, 328
Bissoli, Giovanni 184
Bithynia 41, 150, 170, 267
Blachernai Palace, Constantinople 184
Blanchet, Jean 412
Blancini, Giovanni 328
Blarer, Diethelm, Abbot of St. Gall 375, 376
Blavart, Thomas: *see* Utrecht
Blemmydes, Nikephoros 168, 169, 170, 172
mission to locate manuscripts 169
Blessed Virgin and St. John the Baptist, Church of, Prémontré 465
Blois 422, 424, 425
Royal library 422, 424, 425
Blossius of Cyme 101, 102
Blotius, Hugo 429, 434, 436, 438, 440, 442, 443, 444
Blum, H.J. von 400
Bobbio, Abbey of 190, 197, 198, 204, 205
Boccaccio, Giovanni 217, 218, 312, 339, 400
Boccardi, Giovanni 462
Bodleian Library, Oxford 485-501
Bodley, Sir Thomas 485, 486, 488, 490, 492, 496, 500, 501
Boethius, Anicius Manlius Severinus 191, 192, 370
Boethus 53
Bohemia 436, 447, 463, 473
Bohier, Pierre 411
Boilas, Eustathios 175
Bolchen 440
Bologna 209, 210, 222, 227, 285, 288, 299, 312, 314, 322, 332, 382, 442
University 456
see also San Domenico
Bolzanio, Urbano 235
Bonfini, Antonio 460
Boniface VIII, Pope: his library 288
Bono, Giovanni 306
Book of the Dead 21
books:
endure for all time 24
their role: according to the sophists 33-34
according to Aristophanes, in the Greek world 34-36
in Mesopotamia and Classical Greece 4, 5, 6, 7, 9-12, 33-34
in the theatre 34-35
manufacture of 49-52
dimensions of papyrus roll 20
codices 154
written on sherds, shells and bones 42
of Prodicus 37
burning one's own books 34, 42, 43, 108
booksellers 35, 39
bybliopolae 35
librarii 104
itinerant 108
in Rome 108
in Constantinople 153-154
bookseller/publishers and their relations with authors 35, 41, 105
bookshops 35, 39, 108, 153, 154
in Argiletum, Rome 108
in Sigillaria, Rome 108
in Vicus Sandaliarus, Rome 108
in Vicus Tuscus, Rome 108
in Constantinople 153-154
taberna libraria 108
book trade 41
exports from Athens 41
scribes' remuneration 36, 51, 105-106
in Rome 105, 106, 108, 109
Borja, Alfonso de: *see* Calixtus III
Borrhaeus 496
Borsippa 14
Botticelli, Sandro 345
Boukoleon, Constantinople 184
Bourbon, Charles de, Cardinal 418
Bourdichon, Jean 414
Bracciolini: *see* Poggio
Bramante, Donato 336
Bratislava: *see* Pozsony
brevium (inventory) of Patriarchal library 250
Brindisi: *see* Brundisium
Bruchium, district of Alexandria 85, 88
Bruges, Louis de 420
Brundisium (Brindisi) 109
Bruni, Leonardo 180, 285, 340, 450
Brunswick 393, 398, 404

Brussels 442
Bucharest 278
Buda 447, 448, 450, 454, 456, 458, 460, 462
Budé, Guillaume 73, 384, 424, 425
Buonarroti: *see* Michelangelo
Buoninsegni, Domenico di Leonardo 342, 406
Burgundy 432
Burton, Robert 501
Bury, Richard de 500
Busbeck, Augerius 434, 436, 438
Bussi, Giovanni Andrea de 228, 229, 328

Caecilius, lawyer, convert to Christianity 134
Caesar, Julius 46, 75, 76, 77, 82, 83, 84, 86, 88, 89, 92, 99, 108, 109, 111, 117, 126, 130, 137, 218, 250, 411
and the Alexandrian Library 75-76, 88
and bilingual libraries 83, 110
Caesarea, Cappadocia 161
Caesarea, Palestine 85, 140, 141
Calabria 218, 370
Calderini, Domizio 233
Calenus, Fufius 110
Caligula, Roman Emperor 111
Calixtus III, Pope 294, 324
Callimachus 60, 65, 66, 67, 68, 74, 75, 81, 86, 92
aulicus regius bibliothecarius 65
his position in the Alexandrian Library 66
his catalogue of the Library 67-68
'A great book is a great evil' 75
Pinakes 67-68
classification of books by literary genre 67-68
Callinus: publishes Lycon's works 61
Calpurnius Siculus 409
Calvin, John 440, 444, 488
Calvisius (Calvisius Sabinus?) 92
Camaldolese Order 298, 342
Cambridge University, college libraries 490, 501
Camden, William 494
Camerino, Alberto da 224
Campana, Giovanni Antonio 225
Campania 190
Campesani, Benvenuto 215
Candia (Herakleion), Crete 332, 350, 496
Canterbury 198
Capitoline Library, Rome 124
Capitular Library, Prague 466
Capo d'Istria 450
Cappelli, Pasquino 219
Caracalla, Roman Emperor 83, 84, 112, 117
threatens to burn Aristotelians' books 84
library in Baths of Caracalla 112, 116
Carloman, Frankish ruler (son of Charles Martel) 359
Carneades 74
Cartagena 194
Carteromachus (Fortiguerra), Scipio 227
Carthage 82, 123, 130, 142, 152
Cassander 62
Cassiodorus, Flavius Magnus Aurelius 191, 192, 193, 194, 196, 370
and the Codex Amiatinus 193
Cassius Dio: *see* Dio Cassius
Cassius Eminas 97
Casus Sancti Galli, chronicle 364
Cato, Angelo 418
Cato, Marcus Porcius, 'the Censor' 100, 101, 190
Cato, Marcus Porcius, 'of Utica' 93, 102, 124, 190
Catrinello, Andrea 306, 312
Catullus, Gaius Valerius 108, 215
Catullus, Quintus Lutatius (Lutatius Daphnis) 108
Cavitelli, Giustiniano 456
Cebes 31
Celsus, Library of, at Ephesus 123, 126
Celtis, Conrad 234, 432, 434
Cencio: *see* Rustici
Ceolfrid 193
Ceos 40
Cephisodorus 44
Cesena 180, 222, 237, 305, 306, 310, 312, 314, 316, 318, 344, 354, 462 (*see also* Malatestiana)
Council of Ninety-Six 316
Cethegus, Cornelius Pompeius 97
Chalcedon: *see* Councils
Chalcis 45
Chalkiopoulos, Athanasios 225, 226, 290, 330, 416
Chalkokondyles, Demetrios 178, 180, 184, 231, 344, 346
his library 180
Chantzeris: *see* Samuel
Charlemagne, Holy Roman Emperor 198, 202, 204, 205, 288, 393, 409, 410, 411
Charles III, Holy Roman Emperor (= Charles II, King of France) 360
Charles V, Holy Roman Emperor 298, 432, 434
Charles VI, Holy Roman Emperor 412, 414, 442
Charles I (the Bald), King of France (= Charles II, Holy Roman Emperor) 326, 411, 432
Charles V (the Wise), King of France 411, 412, 414, 418, 420
his library 411, 412
Charles VI (the Foolish), King of France 412
Charles VII, King of France 414
Charles VIII (the Affable), King of France 231, 352, 414, 416, 418, 422
his library 416
Charles IX, King of France 436
Charles the Bold, Duke of Burgundy 420
Charles de Guyenne 414
Charles of Orléans 424
chartophylakion (record office) and *chartophylax* (archivist) of the Patriarchate 252
Chastel, Pierre de 425, 427
Cheops (Khufu), Pharaoh 25
Chevalier, Antoine 488
Chierico, Francesco di Antonio del 344, 402, 462
Chios 41
Choerilus 52
Choiseul-Gouffier, Comte de 272, 274, 278
Choniates, Michael 167, 171
his library 167, 171
Choniates, Niketas Akominatos 167, 168, 252
on the destruction of books in Constantinople (1204) 167
Chora, Monastery of, Constantinople 140, 170, 172, 176, 177
its library 176, 177
Chortasmenos, Ignatios, Metropolitan of Selymbria 321
Chortasmenos, Ioannes 177
Chorus Achademiae Florentinae 229, 390, 454
Chotesov, nunnery of 467
Choumnos, Nikephoros 170, 176
his dictum about books 170
Christ Church, Oxford 486
Christodoulos, St. 162, 163, 267, 268, 270, 276
his library 162, 163, 267-270

Christos Akataleptos, Monastery of, Constantinople 149, 170, 172, 174, 175
its library 174-175
Christosatur 151, 152
Chrysermus 67
Chrysippus 50, 141
Chrysokokkes, Georgios 177, 321
Chrysoloras, Manuel 177, 178, 180, 182, 219, 220, 224, 298, 339, 342, 346, 374, 406, 450
his library 180, 220, 222
teaches at Studium, Florence 220
Chrysostom: *see* John Chrysostom
Chrysoverghis: *see* Loukas
Chur-Rhaetia 372
Ciapino 354
Cicero, Marcus Tullius 41, 43, 48, 49, 52, 53, 61, 68, 85, 98, 100, 101, 102, 103, 104, 106, 108, 118, 124, 132, 150, 190, 212, 215, 216, 218, 219, 229, 234, 310, 374, 494
his library 102-104
and Aristotle's library 48, 49
on Demosthenes 104
Ciriaco d'Ancona 225, 226, 330
Citium, Cyprus 42
Clarke, Edward Daniel 278
classification, arrangement and storage of books:
in Mesopotamia 11-12
in the Alexandrian Library 67-68 (*see also* Callimachus [*Pinakes*])
in baskets 26
in bookcases 94
in storage jars 96
Claudius, Roman Emperor 83, 88, 89, 104, 112, 114
Clauser, Jan 468
Cleanthes of Assus, Stoic philosopher 42, 45, 141
Clearchus, Bithynian ruler 41
Clearchus, Prefect of Constantinople 142
Clearchus of Soli, Peripatetic philosopher 41, 95
Clemency, Mosque of 77
Clement VI, Pope 216, 288
Clement VII, Pope 339, 352, 354
Clement of Alexandria 20, 22, 84, 194
classification of hieroglyphics 20
Cleobulina 480
Cleobulus of Rhodes 480
Cleopatra VII 59, 75, 81, 82, 92
and the Pergamum library 82
Clitomachus 74
Clodius (P. Clodius Pulcher) 108
Cluny Abbey: its library 220, 221, 246
Cnidus: its library 124
Cobham, Thomas, Bishop of Worcester 485, 486
Coccio, Marco Antonio: *see* Sabellico
Collège Royal, Paris 73, 426
Collegium Sancti Nicolai, Vienna 434
Cologne: *see* Köln
Colonna, Caterina 314
Columban (Columbanus), St. 190, 198, 359
Compiègne Abbey 411
Comum (Como) 123
Congregation for the Propagation of the Faith 258, 260
Constantine I ('the Great'), Byzantine Emperor 85, 112, 130, 140, 141, 292
Constantine V Kaballinos, Byzantine Emperor 147, 250
Constantine VII Porphyrogennetos, Byzantine Emperor 164, 165, 166, 168, 170
his library (the Kamilas) 164
Excerpta 164
Constantine IX Monomachos, Byzantine Emperor 154, 165, 166
Constantinople 85, 125, 137, 140, 141, 142, 143, 146, 147, 148, 149, 151, 152, 154, 155, 158, 159, 160, 161, 162, 164, 165, 166, 168, 170, 171, 172, 174, 175, 176, 177, 178, 180, 181, 182, 184, 190, 191, 192, 194, 205, 219, 220, 222, 224, 235, 245, 250, 252, 254, 256, 258, 260, 262, 263, 264, 267, 278, 299, 310, 312, 321, 322, 324, 330, 346, 350, 375, 425, 436, 438, 448, 458, 462
Higher School (University) 144, 146, 148, 154, 185 (*see also* Katholikon Mouseion)
Imperial Library 141-143, 164-165
see also Oecumenical Patriarchate
Constantius II, Byzantine Emperor 85, 124, 139, 141, 142, 144, 145, 153, 165, 170, 181, 182
first imperial library in Constantinople 141-142
Contuggi, Matteo 306
Convenole da Prato 215
Convocation House, Oxford 485
Corbellini, Antonio 486
Corbie Abbey: its library 198, 204, 205
Corbinelli, Antonio 220, 221
Corinth 49, 123, 124, 170
its library 124
Coriolanus, Gaius Marcius 101
Coriscus 46
Cormesina, Alberto 445
Cornelia, mother of the Gracchi 102
Cornelius Alexander (Polyhistor) 111
Corpus Christi College, Oxford: its library 490
Cortesio, Alessandro 402
Corvinian Library 447-463
Corvinus, Matthias: *see* Matthias
Cos (Kos) 60, 77, 124, 268, 274
libraries 77, 124
Cosmas the Scholastic: his library 153
Cotignola 290
Cotton, Sir Robert 494
Councils of the Church:
First Ecumenical (Nicaea, 325) 246, 375
Laodicea (341-381) 153
Second Ecumenical (Constantinople, 381) 375
Third Ecumenical (Ephesus, 431) 148, 375
Fourth Ecumenical (Chalcedon, 451) 148, 375
Seville (619) 194
Toledo (633) 194
Sixth Ecumenical (Constantinople, 680-681) 246, 252
Quinisextum (Trullan, in Trullo) (Constantinople, 691/2) 153
First Iconoclastic (Hiereia Palace, 754) 250
Seventh Ecumenical (Nicaea, 787) 246, 252
Constantinople (867) 139
Nicaea (1208) 254
Lyon (1274) 175
Constantinople (1351) 254
Ferrara-Florence (1437-1439) 256, 285, 299, 322
Konstanz (1414-1417) 220, 290, 296, 374, 452
Courthardy, Pierre de 418
Cratenas, physician to Mithradates VI 438
Crates of Mallus, Stoic philosopher 91, 92, 93, 100, 101, 480
at the court of Pergamum 91-93
in Rome 100
Crates of Thebes, Cynic philosopher 480
Cratippus 93
Crato, Johannes 438
Creation Epic (Mesopotamia) 15
Cremona 302

Crete 3, 124, 225, 332, 346, 350, 425, 496
library 124
Crivelli, Taddeo 310, 312
Croton 31
Csezmiczei, János: *see* Pannonius
Csontosi, János 450, 456
Ctesias of Cnidus 52, 54
Cuno, Johannes 227, 380, 388
Cusa, Nicolaus da 229, 326, 328, 430, 434
Cuspinianus, Johannes 434
Cydas 66, 69
director of Alexandrian Library 66, 69
Cyprus 42, 60, 69, 70, 74, 77, 169
Cyrene 60, 67, 68
Cyril, St., Patriarch of Alexandria 85, 89, 246
Cyril I Loukaris, Patriarch 258
Cyrus, author of *Ecclesiastical History* 254
Cyzicus (Kyzikos) 125

Damasus, Pope 134
Damilas, Demetrios 231, 296
Dante Alighieri 312, 416
Daonos (Daon) 15
Datus, Augustinus 386
Decembrio, Pier Candido 485, 486, 488
Decembrio, Umberto 288
Decius, Flavius 143
Dedefhor, Prince 27
Deir el-Medina 23
Dekadyos, Ioustinos 179, 233
Delos 67
Delphi: its library 124
Demetrios I, Patriarch 282
Demetrius, bookseller 88
Demetrius, copyist 294
Demetrius the Cynic 49
Demetrius of Phalerum 46, 47, 60, 61, 62, 64, 65, 66, 70, 71, 72, 94
his role in the Alexandrian Library 60-62, 64, 65
Demetrius Poliorcetes 47, 61, 344
Demetrius of Troezen 86
Democides 32
Democritus 174, 480
Demophilus 99
Demosthenes 40, 41, 44, 49, 53, 93, 104, 141, 171, 174, 180
copies works of Thucydides 41
his autograph manuscripts 41
his 'library' 41, 49
Dertona: its library 124
Derveni papyrus 30, 32
Devaris, Matthaios 302, 346, 350
Deventer 388
Diagoras of Melos 38
Diana, Temple of, Rome 125
Didymoteichon 176, 254
Didymus of Alexandria 74
'Bibliolathas' 74
Didymus the Blind, exegetist 194
Dieuchidas of Megara 30
Dio Cassius (Cassius Dio Cocceianus) 76, 84
on the Alexandrian Library 76
on Caracalla 84
Dio Chrysostom (Dio Cocceianus) 106, 111, 151, 162, 226
Diocles, father of Euthydemus 34
Diocles, endower of library on Cos 77, 91
Diocles, grammarian (*c.* 100 B.C.) 66, 69
Diocletian (Diocles), Roman Emperor 83, 84, 85, 108, 131, 134
Edict *De pretiis* 108
Diodorus, Valerius 83, 88
Diodorus Siculus 26, 52, 76, 272
Bibliotheca 63, 76
Diodotus, Stoic philosopher 93, 102
Diogenes of Apollonia 32
Diogenes the Cynic 326, 479
Diogenes Laertius 30, 32, 34, 38, 44, 46, 47, 50, 51, 61, 62, 70, 86, 92
Dion of Syracuse 38
Dionysius I, ruler of Syracuse 37, 38, 42, 49
Dionysius, assistant in Cicero's library 103
Dionysius the Areopagite, St. 246, 410
Pseudo-Dionysius the Areopagite 246, 410
Dionysius Exiguus 194
Dionysius of Halicarnassus 40, 49, 93, 97, 167, 226
Dionysius of Magnesia 103
Dionysius the Thracian 48, 65, 72, 87, 143, 219
Dionysodorus, Flavius Marcius Se[verianus?] 83
Dionysus, Theatre of 36
Diophanes of Mytilene 102
Diophantus 154, 176, 330
Dioscorides (Dioscurides) 146, 177
Divi Traiani, Bibliothecae: see Trajan, library of
Divinity School, Oxford 485, 488, 492, 496
Djedkare-Isesi, Pharaoh 20
Dlabač, Bohumír Jan, librarian of Strahov 473
Dokeianos, Ioannes 226
Domitian, Roman Emperor 83, 105, 111
Domus Tiberianae, Bibliotheca 124
Donai, Robert de 212
Donatus, Aelius 133, 234, 494
Doni, Andrea 496
Dositheos Dorieus, Patriarch 321
Doukas, Demetrios 179
Doukas, Michael, historian 179
Doxapatres, Ioannes 174
Dringenberg, Ludwig 384, 390
Drogo, half-brother of Louis the Pious 411
Duauf 22
Dürer, Albrecht 235, 388, 389, 391
Dur-Sharrukin: *see* Khorsabad
Dyrrhachium 123, 124

Education: in Byzantium 143
in Middle Ages 192, 196, 202, 205, 208-210
Platonic 38-39
in Rome 101-102
Egyptian literature: its subject matter 23-24
Einhard, Frankish historian 198, 409
Eirenikos (Irenicus) 252
Elam, Elamites 3, 8, 9, 12
Eleazar, high priest of Jerusalem 64, 151
Elias of Alexandria 81, 93
Eliot's Court Press, London 258
Elisabeth, consort of Charles IX of France 436
Elizabeth I, Queen of England 488
Ematheia, near Ephesus 169
Emili, Paolo 416
Enheduanna 13
Enlightenment, Age of 406
Enlil 9
Ennana 27
Ennius, Quintus 98, 99, 100, 124, 190
Enoch, Alberto (Enoch d'Ascoli) 292, 299
Eparchos, Antonios: his library 425, 426
Ephesus, 29, 123, 124, 142, 168, 169, 375 (*see also* Celsus, Library of)
Ephraim, Archbishop of Antioch 246
Epicharmus 52, 238
Epicongylus 65
Epicurus 85, 118
Gardens of 85
Epidaurus: its library 124
Epimenides 30

d'Épinal, Jean (Johannes de Spinalo) 310, 312
Epiphanius of Salamis (Constantia), Cyprus 65, 73, 85, 89, 194
Epiros, Despotate of 167
Erasmus, Desiderius 235, 379, 380, 384, 388, 434, 478
Eratosthenes of Cyrene 48, 59, 60, 66, 68, 69, 73, 76
director of Alexandrian Library 68-69
Ercole, Prince of Ferrara 456
Eressus 50
Ergersheim, Martin 384, 390
Ermoupolis (Syros) 282
Esarhaddon 12
Escorial library 237
d'Este family 222, 461
Estienne, Robert 426
Esztergom 454
Etana, Myth of 13
Eton College: printing press 492
Euboea 45, 268, 270
Euclid (Euclides), mathematician 155, 161, 176, 184, 330
Euclides of Athens 30, 34
his library 30
Euclides of Megara 32
Eucratides 95
Eudemus 45
Eudocia, Byzantine Empress 145, 147, 163
Euedarachos (Euedoreschos) 15
Eugenius IV, Pope 285, 288, 305, 344
Euhemeria 83, 98
Euhemerus 98
Eumenes II, King of Pergamum 47, 69, 76, 81, 91, 92, 93
and Aristotle's books 47
and the Pergamum library 76, 81, 91, 92, 93
Eupolis 35, 106
Euripides 30, 36, 40, 50, 52, 98, 99, 330, 418
his library 40, 52
his scribe-cum-publisher 36
Eusebius, Bishop of Caesarea (Eusebius Pamphili) 85, 132, 140, 150, 245, 246, 254
Eustathios, Archbishop of Thessalonika 163, 302
Eustathius, Governor of Antioch 150
Euthydemus, son of Diocles 31, 32, 34, 49
his library 31-32
Eutyches, archimandrite 145
Eutychios, Christian Arab historian 80, 87
Evanthius 141
Exeter 488

Fabius Pictor, Quintus, 106
Fabri, Johann, Viennese bishop 434
Fabri, Johannes, benefactor of Sélestat library 384, 389
Faiyûm 85
Fantini, Fredolo 305
Fara 4, 13
Farinaceus 496
Faurndau, Monastery of 372
Fausta, wife of Constantine the Great 292
Faustina, Temple of, Rome 111
Favorino, Guarino 278
Feltre: *see* Vittorino
Ferdinand I, Holy Roman Emperor 434, 440
Ferrara 229, 310, 312, 314, 336, 432, 447, 452
Ferrara-Florence: *see* Councils
Ferrières, Abbey of 202
Festus, Sextus Pompeius: definition of library 53
Fichet, Guillaume 416
Ficino, Marsilio 231, 344, 379, 382, 402, 416, 454, 456, 461
Platonic Academy 454
Fidus Optatus 106
Fiesole 344
Filelfo, Francesco 177, 180, 184, 221, 285, 290, 294, 299, 306, 310, 344, 416, 436, 447
his library 180, 221
Filelfo, Gian Mario 179
Fischer von Erlach, Johann Bernhard 443
Fischer von Erlach, Joseph Emanuel 443
Flacius (Flach) Illyricus, Matthias 393, 398, 436, 440, 442
Flanders 432
Flavia Melitene: her library at Pergamum 94
Flavia Secundilla 123
Flavius Rogatianus, Marcus Iulius Quintianus 123
Florence 177, 180, 218, 219, 220, 221, 222, 224, 227, 229, 230, 231, 232, 234, 236, 238, 285, 296, 298, 299, 302, 314, 342, 344, 346, 350, 352, 354, 380, 382, 390, 402, 414, 416, 418, 422, 450, 452, 454, 456, 458, 463
Studium (University) 346, 454, 461
see also Laurenziana
Florentinus, priest in Jerusalem 133
Florentis, Chrysostomos 278, 283
Folz, Hans 402
Fondulo, Gerolamo 425
Fontainebleau 425, 426
Royal library 425, 426
Fontana, Domenico 238, 299
Fontana, Francesco 456
Fonte, Bartolomeo della (Bartholomaeus Fontius) 402, 447, 450, 460
Forma Urbis Romae 117
Foschi, Cristoforo 312
Fouquet, Jean 414
Fournival, Richard de 212
Francis, St. 305, 306
Franciscan Monastery, Paris 411
François I, King of France 231, 236, 334, 422, 425, 426, 492
his library 422, 425, 426
Frank, Vincenc, Abbot of Strahov 467
Frankfurt, international book fair 436, 442, 494
Fratres Communis Vitae 380, 388
Frederick I Barbarossa, Holy Roman Emperor 474
Frederick III, Holy Roman Emperor 324, 326, 429, 430, 432
his library 429-430
Frederick IV, Duke of Austria 432
Freisleben collection 467
Friedrich Ulrich, Duke of Brunswick-Lüneburg 393
Froben, Johann 380, 386, 388, 478
Fronto, Marcus Cornelius 197
Fufius Calenus 110
Fulda, Abbey of 204, 216, 360
Fust, Johannes 226

Gabrielli, Angelo 336
Gaguin, Robert 418
Gaisberg, Franz von, Abbot of St. Gall 374
Galen (Claudius Galenus) 59, 68, 70, 72, 74, 80, 81, 87, 92, 93, 330, 480
his library 74
his writings burnt 74
On My Own Books 74
on forgeries and pirated works 70, 80-81
Galeotto, Marzio 454, 460
Galesion, Mt. 162
Galileo (Galileo Galilei) 87

Gallicus, Petrus 448
Gallus (Gall), St. 198, 216, 359, 368, 370, 372, 374, 375, 376
Gallus, Gaius Cornelius 120
Garamont, Claude 427, 492
Garnier de Saint-Yon 412
Gaspare da Verona 233
Gaza 141, 143
Gazis, Theodoros 178, 180, 225, 229, 290, 328, 416
his library 180
Gebwiler, Gervais 382
Gebwiler, Hieronymus 379, 382, 384
Gedeon, scribe 226
Gelenius, Sigismond 478
Gellius, Aulus 70, 106, 108, 109, 196, 216, 229
Noctes Atticae 106
Gemistos (Plethon), Georgios 177, 178, 226, 305, 306, 321, 330, 384
Geneva 402
Gennep, Norbert: *see* Norbert, St.
George of Cappadocia 142, 152
his library 142
George of Cyprus: *see* Gregory II of Cyprus
George of Pisidia, deacon, chronicler and poet 174, 175, 245, 250
George of Trebizond 151, 152, 167, 178, 254, 290, 294, 298, 321, 416, 450, 458
Georgios, deacon, *chartophylax* of the Patriarchate 246, 250
Georgios Monachos, chronicler 146
Germanos I, Patriarch 146, 246, 250
Germanos II, Patriarch 168
Gerward, librarian to Louis the Pious 411
Gherardo di Giovanni 345
Ghirlandaio, Domenico 299
Gigl brothers 376
Gilgamesh (Bilgamesh), epic of 4, 7, 8, 12, 13
Gilles, Pierre 425
Giovanni, Cola di 296
Giovanni Bono, St. 306
Giphanius, Hubertus 440
Giraldi, Guglielmo, miniaturist 452
Gloucester, Duke of: *see* Humfrey
Glykas, Michael 144, 145, 158, 170, 181
Glykys, Ioannes 176
Gonzaga, Gian Francesco 222
Göppingen 372
Gordian II, Roman Emperor: his library 74
Gorgias (of Leontini) 39, 41
his teaching 41
Gozbert, Abbot of St. Gall 359, 360, 374, 375
Gracchus, Gracchi 101
Graff, Urs 388
Gran, Daniel 444
Greek college, Rome 298
Gregoras, Nikephoros 177
Gregoropoulos, Ioannes 179, 386
Gregory I ('the Great'), Pope 190, 191, 194, 198, 312, 370
Gregory II (George) of Cyprus, Patriarch 154, 169, 171, 173, 174, 175, 176, 254
his library 171, 174
Gregory V, Patriarch 262
Gregory of Nazianzos, St. 163, 276, 290
Gregory of Nyssa, St. 150, 205, 246
Gregory of Tours 197
Grimald, Abbot of St. Gall 360, 370
Grimani, Antonio, Doge 334
Grimani, Domenico, Cardinal 235, 336, 337
Grimani, Vettor 334, 337
Gritti, Andrea, Doge 336
Groote, Geert 388
Grottaferrata 339
Guarino, Giovanni Battista 379, 386, 432
Guarino da Verona 177, 179, 180, 181, 182, 294, 342, 398, 436, 447, 450, 454
his library 177, 180, 398
Guerra, Giovanni 302
Gugger von Staudach, Coelestin, Abbot of St. Gall 375, 376
Gundelfingen, Prince Heinrich von, Abbot of St. Gall 374
Gutenberg, Johann 226, 402, 478
Guyenne, Charles de: his library 414
gymnasium libraries 91, 124

Habsburg dynasty 430, 442
Hadrian, Roman Emperor 88, 94, 111, 123, 124, 125, 126, 130
his libraries:
at Athens 123, 124, 125
at Jerusalem 125
at Tibur 123, 124, 125, 126
Hagia Sophia, Church of, Constantinople 245, 250, 260, 268
Hagios Andreas, Monastery of, Constantinople 173
Hagios Chrysostomos, Monastery of, Cyprus 163
Hagios Demetrios tes Xyloportas, Church of, Constantinople 256
Hagios Georgios ton Manganon, Monastery of, Constantinople 163
Hague, the 488
Hainhofer, Philipp 400
Halicarnassus: library 124
Hammelburg 386
Hammurabi, Code of 8
Hannover 404
Harmodius 35
Harpocration 83, 88
Hartmut, Abbot of St. Gall 360, 370, 374
Hauser, Jan, priest from Peruc 473
Hecataeus of Abdera 62, 63, 64
Hecataeus of Miletus 63
Hegius, Alexander 388
Heidelberg 432, 434
Heidl, Jan 468
Heinrich Julius, Duke of Brunswick-Lüneburg 393
Heliopolis 22
Hellanicus of Lesbos 34
Helmstedt 393, 398
Henri IV, King of France 426
Henry IV, King of England 485
Henry V, King of England 485
Henry V, Holy Roman Emperor 465
Heraclea Pontica: its library 124
Heracles 37, 41, 52, 238
Heraclides Ponticus 38, 39
Heraclitus 29, 32, 33, 45, 174, 480
his 'library' 29, 32-33, 45
Heraclius, Byzantine Emperor 139, 144, 245
Herbert, William: *see* Pembroke, Earl of
Herculaneum 117, 118
its library 117-118
Hereford, Chapter Library 490
Hermann, Marian, Abbot of Strahov 479
Hermeias, ruler of Assus 46
Hermeias, *Ecclesiastical History* 254
Hermes Trismegistus 21
Hermippus, Alexandrian historian 38, 47, 73, 92
Hermippus of Smyrna 33, 86
Hermodorus 39, 219
Plato's publisher 39, 219
Hermogenes 174
Hermonymos Spartiates, Georgios 179, 379, 384
Hermonymos, Charitonymos 226
Herodotus 19, 29, 50, 51, 73, 290, 330
Herondas (Herodas) 62, 67
Herpyllis 45
Hersfeld Abbey 198, 216

Herzog August Library: *see* Wolfenbüttel
Hesep-ti, Pharaoh 22
Hesiod 30, 52, 58, 67, 141
Hess, Andreas 460
Hesychius of Alexandria 234
Hesychius of Miletus 74, 75
Heynlin, Johann 416
Hierocles, Neoplatonist 222, 330
Hierapolis, Egypt 67
Hierapolis, Syria: see Bambyce
hieratic: *see* scripts
hieroglyphics: *see* scripts
Hieronymus of Rhodes 33
Hilary, St. 133
Hilduin, Abbot of St. Denis 411
Hipparchus 62
Hippocrates 80, 81, 222, 296, 480
Hippolytus, St. 132
Hirnheim, Jeroným, Abbot of Strahov 468, 478
Hitzacker 393
Hofbibliothek, Vienna: *see* Nationalbibliothek
Hofmann, Crato 379, 384
Holbein, Hans 388
Holobolos, Maximos 174
Holy Apostles, Church of, Constantinople 256
Hölzel, Hieronymus 474
Homer 29, 34, 35, 46, 49, 52, 62, 63, 65, 67, 69, 72, 80, 92, 98, 99, 124, 141, 143, 174, 179, 217, 218, 231, 235, 276, 294, 346
  Alexander the Great's copy 46- 47
Honorius II, Pope 465
Hora, Josef 472
Horace (Quintus Horatius Flaccus) 98, 102, 105, 108, 120, 232, 234, 374
Hortensius Hortalus, Quintus 103
Horus, Temple of, Apollonopolis 26
'House of Books' 25 (*see also* Scribe)
'House of Wisdom', Baghdad 159
Hroznata, Blessed 467
Hroznata, Vojslava 467
Humfrey, Duke of Gloucester 485, 488
Hummelberg, Gabriel 375
Hummelberg, Michael 388
Hunsdon, Lord 494
Hurri 10
Hus, Jan, and Hussite wars 444, 466
Hutter, Elias 444
Hyginus, Gaius Julius 111
Hypatia, philosopher 88, 138
  her death 88

Iamblichus 166
Iasites, (Michael) 174
Ibn al-Kifti 87
Ibn an-Nadim 160
Ibycus 32
Iconium 267
Iconoclastic controversy 250
ideograms: *see* scripts
Ignatios, Patriarch 160, 163, 250, 256
Imola 219
Imperial Library, Vienna: *see* Nationalbibliothek
Ingolstadt University 442
Innocent II, Pope 465
Innsbruck 432, 434
Iobates, King of Libya 80
Iona, abbey and library 198
Irenaeus, St. 285
Irenicus: *see* Eirenikos
Isabeau, Queen of France 412
Isenrich, monk 364
Ishtar 13
Isidore, Abbot of Patmos 282
Isidore of Kiev, Cardinal 178, 326
Isidore of Pelusium 148
Isidore of Seville 70, 99, 194, 196
  Etymologiae 100
  and the Alexandrian Library 70
Isocrates 39, 40, 41, 42, 141, 276
  on the role of books 39-40
  his library 39-40
  his school 39-40
Italos: *see* John Italos
Iznik: *see* Nicaea

Jacobin Monastery, Paris 411
James I, King of England 490
James, Thomas, Bodley's Librarian 496, 500
Janiculum Hill, Rome
Jarloch, Abbot 474
Jarrow Abbey 186, 193, 198
Jean II (the Good), King of France: his library 411
Jeanne de France, Queen of France 418
Jemdet Nasr 4
Jenson, Nicolas 478
Jerome, St. 112, 130, 132, 133, 141, 152, 229, 312, 370
  his library 132-134
  publication of his works 132-134
Jerusalem (Aelia Capitolina) 64, 124, 125, 132, 147, 252, 267, 288
  library 132
Jesuits 472
  Jesuit libraries in Prague 472
Jewish press, Constantinople 262
Jihlava 468
Job, Book of 138
Johannes, Abbot of St. Gall 359
Johannes, copyist for Platina 294
John XXII, Pope 216, 288
John VIII Xiphilinos, Patriarch 165, 174
John X Kamateros, Patriarch 254
John III Doukas Vatatzes, Byzantine Emperor 168, 169
John VIII Palaiologos, Byzantine Emperor 222
John, Patriarch of Antioch 138
John, Metropolitan of Rhodes 268
John the Calligrapher, copyist for Arethas 161
John Chrysostom, St. 140, 143, 144, 150, 151, 153, 163, 184, 194, 246, 276, 290, 393
  his library 150
  his views on books 144, 150, 151
  his views on slavery 140
John Climacus 148
John of Damascus, St. 139, 174
John the Evangelist (John the Divine), St. 153, 176, 268
  the Apocalypse 153
John the Grammarian, Patriarch 147, 148, 250, 254
  'the Sorcerer Patriarch' 250
  scrutinizes books for the Iconoclasts 147, 250
John Italos 166, 167
  his trial for heresy 167
John Philoponus 77, 80, 87, 93
Josef II, Austrian Emperor 472, 480
Josephus, Flavius 33, 105
Jouffroy, Cardinal 414
Jourdain, Abbé 414
Jovian, Byzantine Emperor 145
Judaea 57
Judith, consort of Louis the Pious 411
Julian 'the Apostate', Byzantine Emperor 142, 145, 152
  his library 142
Juliana Anicia, Princess 438
Julius, Duke of Brunswick-Lüneburg 393, 394, 406
Julius Pollux: *see* Pollux
Juno Regina, Temple of, Rome 111
Jupiter Stator, Temple of, Rome 111
Justinian I ('the Great'), Byzantine Emperor 139, 143, 144, 145

his legal Code and its impact on books 143-144
Juvenal (Decimus Junius Juvenalis) 130, 204

Kachelofen, Conrad 478
Kallierges, Zacharias 179, 278, 298, 302, 354
Kallistos, Andronikos 178, 180, 222, 225, 226, 229, 290, 328, 330, 450
his library 180
Kamenz 404
Kamilas: *see* Constantine VII
Kanonikus, Brünner 429
Karásek Gallery library 472
Karolinum (Prague University) and its library 472
Karykes, Demetrios 168
Kastrenos, Demetrios 179
Katholikon Mouseion (University), Constantinople 170, 176, 180, 330, 438
its students and teachers 176, 180
Kavakes Ralles, Demetrios 306
Kayserberg 382
Kedrenos, Georgios 143, 182
Kefallinia (Cephalonia) 258
Kemly, Gall 374
Kempe, John, Cardinal 488
Kempe, Thomas, Bishop of London 486, 488
Kerber, Norbert 466, 478
Kheti 22
Khorsabad: temple of Nabu and library 11
Khufu: *see* Cheops
Khunanup 24
Kierher, Johannes 388
al-Kind, Arab scholar 159
Kirbet Qumran 124
Kircher, Athanasius 400
Kish 4
Klementinum, Prague 472
Klosterbruck: *see* Louka u Znojma
Knossos 50
Knytl, Josef 472
Koberger, Anton 478
kollema
Köln 229, 426, 432, 465
Kolozsvár (Klausenburg, Cluj) 447
Komnene, Anna 166
Alexiad 166
Komnenos dynasty 167 (*see also* Alexios I, Manuel I)
Königsberg 328
Konstanz (Constance) 359, 360, 374 (*see also* Councils)
Kontovlakas, Andronikos 380
Konya: *see* Iconium
Korais, Adamantios 278
Korydalleus, Theophilos 258
Kos: *see* Cos
Kosmas, hieromonk 225, 226
Krakow 473
Kritoboulos of Imbros, historian 179
Kuler, Mathias 310
Kydones, Demetrios 179
Kyriakidis, Panayotis 260
Kyzikos: *see* Cyzicus

Lactantius, Lucius Caecilius Firmianus 229
Lacydes 91, 92
Ladislas V, King of Hungary 447
Ladislaus Posthumus 429, 432
Laelius, Gaius ('the Wise') 99
Lagash (Tello) 7
Lahofer, Johann 480
Lampsacus 60
Landino, Cristoforo 344, 346
Landskron, Pastor von 429
Langres 193
Laodicea: its library 124
see also Councils
Lapaccini, Francesco 345, 406
Lapidus, Johann 389
Larcius Licinius 109
Larissa 169
Larnesius, Livius: his library 30, 74, 137
Laskaris family: *see also* Theodore I, Theodore II
Laskaris, Ianos 178, 222, 228, 230, 231, 232, 296, 298, 302, 334, 336, 346, 348, 350, 379, 382, 418, 422, 424, 425
his library 348
Laskaris, Konstantinos 178, 180, 225, 336
Lateran Palace and Library, Rome 288, 292
Latmos (Latros), Mt. 162, 267, 268
Laud, Archbishop: his Greek manuscript collection 496
Laurentum 120
Laurenziana, Biblioteca (Florence) 339-356
Lavra, the Great, Monastery, Mt. Athos 154
Lazius, Wolfgang 434, 436
Lefèvre d'Étaples, Jacques 379, 382, 386, 388, 418
Leibniz, Gottfried Wilhelm 404
Leipzig 478
Leo I ('the Great'), Pope 285
Leo X, Pope 296, 298, 302, 336, 352, 425
Leo III, Byzantine Emperor 144
'burnt down a library' 144
Leo IV, Byzantine Emperor 143
Leo V (the Armenian), Byzantine Emperor 144, 147, 250
Leo the Mathematician (Leo the Philosopher) 137, 154, 155, 158, 159, 169
his library 137, 154, 155
Leonardo da Vinci 424
Leoncio, Giovanni 456
Leoniceno, Niccolò 234, 336
Leoniceno, Ognibene 234, 235, 302
Leonicerus, Johann Adam 393
Leopold I, Holy Roman Emperor 445
Lesbos 45, 169, 480
Lessing, Gotthold Ephraim 404
Leto, Pomponio 229, 294, 302, 328, 332, 390, 432, 454
academy of 332, 454
Libanius 133, 142, 150, 151, 152
his library 150
marketing of his books 150
his copy of Thucydides 151
librarianship 67, 74, 149
libraries:
archival, in Egypt 25-26
archival, in Mesopotamia 4-6, 9-13
in bath-houses 116-117
bilingual libraries 83, 110, 112-113, 218-219, 246, 290, 346-347, 352
defined by Pompeius Festus 53
early Christian 132-133
gymnasium 91, 124
lighting of 117-118
of literature, in Mesopotamia 9-11
palace, in Mesopotamia 8-9, 12-13
parish
private:
in Classical Greece 30-31, 37-49
in Mesopotamia 10
in Rome 102-104
public: *see* Athens, Rome, Samos
of rhapsodists 30
school, in Sumer 4-6
tameia (library storerooms) 66
universal (world) library 14, 57, 58, 63, 73, 74, 75, 81, 88
librarii: *see* booksellers
libri lintei 98
Liechtenstein, Georg von: his library 432

Liechtenstein, Hermann de (Levilapis) 182
Liège 370
Linacre, Thomas 235
Lindisfarne Abbey: its library 198
Linus: his library 52
Linz 328
Listyus, Johann 438
Liutward, Bishop of Vercelli 370
Liviana, Accademia: *see* Pordenone
Livius Andronicus, Lucius 98, 99, 102
his 'library' 98
Livius Salinator, Marcus 98
Livy (Titus Livius) 76, 97, 190, 216, 229
and Alexandrian Library 76
Lohelius, Jan, Abbot of Strahov 467
Lombardy 285, 312
London 258, 414, 486, 494
Lonigo 234
Lorsch Abbey 204, 205, 411
its library 205
Loschi, Antonio 447
Loser, Gabriel 376
Louis IX, King of France (St. Louis) 411
Louis XI, King of France 210, 212, 326, 328, 412, 414
Louis XII, King of France 418, 420, 422, 424
his library 418-420
Louis, Duke of Orléans: his library 420
Louis de Bruges 420
Louis the German, Frankish King 360
Louis the Pious (Louis the Debonair), Frankish Emperor 359, 360, 410, 411
his library 410-411
Louka u Znojma (Klosterbruck) Abbey 478, 479, 480
Loukaris: *see* Cyril
Loukas Chrysoverghis, Patriarch 252
Louvain 436
Louvre, the, Paris
Lovati, Lovato 170, 215
Löw, Jan F. 468
Lübeck 404
Lucan (Marcus Annaeus Lucanus) 216, 234
Lucian (Loukianos) 49, 162, 190, 204, 222, 276, 374
on Demosthenes's books 49
To the Ignorant Book-Collector 49
Lucretius (Titus Lucretius Carus) 215, 216, 234, 386
Lucullus, Lucius Licinius 48, 52, 101, 104, 118
his library 48, 101, 104, 119
his coterie 48
a philhellene 48
Ludovico il Moro, Duke of Milan 416
Luke, Abbot of Chora Monastery 176
Luke, monk of Stylos 267
Lumley, Lord, High Steward of Oxford University 494
Lu-Nanna 13
Lüneburg 393
Lupus, Lucas 456
Lutatius Daphnis: *see* Catullus
Luther, Martin 382, 398, 402, 445
Luxembourg, House of 447
Luxeuil Abbey 197, 198
Lyceum (Peripatetic school), Athens 34, 43, 45, 46, 47, 53, 124
its library 45, 46, 47
Lycomachus 61
Lycon 61, 91, 92
his library 61
Lycophron of Chalcis 65, 67, 73, 330
Lycurgus, Athenian orator 43, 45, 72, 480
official copies of the great tragedians 44-43, 45-46, 72
Lydus, John: *see* John the Lydian
Lyon 108 (*see also* Councils)
Lyra, Nicolaus de 229
Lysimachus 91

Macario, Jacopo 306, 312
Macedonia, Macedonians 42, 45, 46, 57, 58, 61, 73, 84, 97
royal library: *see* Aegae
Macer, Gaius Licinius 98
Macer, Gnaeus Pompeius: organizes Augustus's library 110
Machairas Monastery, Cyprus 163
Macrobius, Ambrosius Theodosius 216
Maecenas, Gaius Cilnius 110
Maffei, Giuliano 225
Magdalen College, Oxford 488
Magdeburg 465, 482
Maglie, Giovanni Onorio de 296
Mainz 198, 229
Makarios, hieromonk 137
Makrotos, Ioannes 169
Malagola, Carlo 456
Malatesta, Cleopa 306
Malatesta, Novello 180, 222, 237, 305, 306, 310, 312, 314, 316, 318
Malatesta, Pandolfo 305
Malatesta, Sigismondo 305
Malatesta, Violante 312, 314
Malatestiana, Biblioteca (Cesena) 305-319
Malchus 142
Mallet, Gilles 412, 414
Mallus 92
Malmesbury Abbey: its library 198
Malpaghini, Giovanni (Giovanni da Ravenna) 220, 294
al-Mamûn, Caliph 155, 158
and 'House of Wisdom' 158
Manasses, Konstantinos 158, 170
Manetho 26, 58, 62, 67, 73
Aegyptiaca 67
Manetti, Giannozzo 285, 288, 290, 298, 339, 340
Manfredini, Prince of Bologna 456
Mangio, Benedetto 184
Manilius, Marcus 374
Mantua 234, 302, 324, 398
Convivium of 324
Manuel II, Patriarch 169
Manuel I Komnenos, Byzantine Emperor 252
Manuel II Palaiologos, Byzantine Emperor 169, 174, 179, 222
Manuel of Apollonia 226
Manutius: *see* Aldus
Mar Abas Katina 58
Marca d'Ancona 322
Marcellus, son of Octavia 110
Marcellus, author of work on mechanics 155
Marcellus, Irish missionary: *see* Moengal
Marcellus of Apamea 148
Marcian, Byzantine Emperor 146
Marciana, Biblioteca (Venice) 314, 321-337, 352, 500
Marco, Giovanni di 312
Marcus, Irish bishop 368, 372
Marcus Aurelius (Antoninus), Roman Emperor 162
Marduk 9, 10, 15
Hymn to Marduk 9
Margaret, daughter of Maximilian I 432
Margounios, Maximos 258
Mari 4, 9, 10
archival library 9-10
Maria Theresa, Empress of Austria 472
Marie of Burgundy 430, 432
Marienthal Monastery, near Helmstedt 398
Mark Antony: *see* Antony
Maroullos Tarchaniotes, Michael 179
Martial (Marcus Valerius Martialis) 105, 108, 111, 150, 190, 215, 232

Martinozzi, Niccolò 310
Mary Tudor, Queen of England 488
Marzio Galeotto: *see* Galeotto
Massimo, Pietro 229, 372
mastabas (private tombs) 21
Matthaios I, Patriarch 322
Matthaios II, Patriarch 256
Matthias Corvinus 226, 230, 402, 432, 447-463, (*see also* Corvinian Library)
Maulbertsch, Franz Anton 479
Maurice, Byzantine Emperor 144
Mavromatis, Neophytos 262
Maximilian I, Holy Roman Emperor 429, 430, 432, 434
Maximilian II, Holy Roman Emperor 429, 436, 438, 440
his library 436-442
Mayer, Wenceslaus Josef, Abbot of Strahov 478, 480
Mazarin, Jules, Cardinal 398
Medicea, Biblioteca: *see* Laurenziana
Medici family 222, 231, 232, 352, 416, 461
Medici, Cosimo de' ('il Vecchio') 180, 236, 285, 299, 312, 339, 344
his library 339
Medici, Giovanni di Bicci de' 339
Medici, Giovanni di Cosimo de' 299, 344
Medici, Giovanni di Lorenzo de' 298, 352 (*see also* Leo X)
Medici, Giulio de', Cardinal 352 (*see also* Clement VII)
Medici, Lorenzo de' (brother of Cosimo) 340, 344
Medici, Lorenzo de' ('the Magnificent') 180, 231, 340, 344, 346, 352, 416, 418, 461
his library 344-348
Medici, Piero di Cosimo de' (Piero I) 299, 344, 345
Medici, Piero di Lorenzo de' (Piero II) 348, 352, 418
Megaclides 34
Megalaros (Megalanos) 15
Mehmet II, Sultan 458
Melanchthon, Philipp 398, 440
Melissenos, Theodotos, Patriarch 250
Melissus, Gaius 110
librarian of Octavian Library 110
Melozzo da Forlì 299
Memnon 41
Memphis 30
Menander 36, 69, 75, 99
Menecleus of Barce 82, 93
Menedemus of Chalcis 73
Menes (Narmer) 21, 26
Menochius 496
Menon 45
Menophilus, assistant in Cicero's library 103
Mentelin, Johann 391
Mercator, Gerhardus (Gerhard Kremer) 406
Merton College, Oxford 488, 490, 492, 501
its library 490, 492
Mesarites, Nikolaos 168
Mesolonghi 278
Mesopotamia 3, 9, 16, 19
Messina 235, 336
Metaxas, Nikodemos 258, 262
Meteora 162
Methodios, St. 162
Metochites, Theodoros 176, 177
Mettius Epaphroditus, Marcus: his library 74
Michael II (the Stammerer), Byzantine Emperor 410
Michael III, Byzantine Emperor 256
Michael VIII Palaiologos, Byzantine Emperor 170, 174
Michael IV Autoreianos, Patriarch 254
Michelangelo (Michelagniolo di Lodovico Buonarroti) 336, 339, 352, 354
Michelozzi, Bernardo 180
Michelozzo di Bartolommeo 222, 236, 237, 238, 336, 339, 342, 344, 352, 354
Milan 180, 181, 184, 219, 227, 344, 420, 456, 486 (*see also* Santa Maria delle Grazie)
Miletus 29, 162, 267
Milevský Monastery 472, 474
Minephtah 27
Minori Osservanti, Order of 312 (*see also* Observant Order)
Minorite Friary, Vienna 438
Minucciano, Alessandro 184
Minucius Felix, Marcus 134
Mirándola, Pico della 235, 337, 382, 418
Mistras 177, 178, 179, 272, 305, 321
Mitanni 9
Mithradates I, King of the Parthians 95
Mithradates VI, King of Pontus 100, 101, 118, 438
his library 100-101, 119
Mnemon of Side 72, 81
Modena 402, 461
Moengal (Marcellus) 368, 372
Moglio, Pietro da 340
Mohács, battle of 462
Molo, Apollonius 102
Monasteriotes, Metropolitan of Ephesus 168
monastic libraries: the first in the East 146-150
Monopoli, Pietro de 302
Monte Cassino Abbey: its library 218
Montefeltro, Federico da, Duke of Urbino 222, 236, 285, 461
Montefeltro, Guido Antonio da 314
Montepulciano, Bartolommeo da 374
Montpellier, Ordinance of 215, 436, 442
Moravia 463
Morgan: *see* Augustine
Morosini, Pietro 328
Morosini, Tommaso, Latin Patriarch 254
Moschopoulos, Nikephoros 175
his library 175
Moschus, John: cost of his copy of New Testament 152
Mount Sion, Abbey of 465 (*see also* Strahov)
Mousouros, Markos 179, 221, 222, 233, 235, 332, 334, 379, 380, 432
his library 235
Mouzalon, Theodoros 176
Müller, Johann: *see* Regiomontanus
Murbach Abbey 198, 216, 382
Musaeus 63
Museum (Alexandria) 58, 59, 60, 61, 62, 63, 67, 68, 69, 70, 74, 81, 82, 83, 84, 85, 88, 89, 91, 126, 140, 228
its foundation 60-63
description of 60-63
funding of 63
its Superintendent (*Epistates*) 67
its members 63
'the Muses' birdcage' 63, 70
'new Museum' (Collège Royal so called) 426
Mussato, Albertino 215
Mylasa: its library 124
Mylius, Crato 389
Myra 42
Mystras: *see* Mistras

Nabu, temple of: *see* Khorsabad
Naevius, Gnaeus 99, 100, 190
Nafplion 282
Naldi, Naldo 298, 458, 460, 461, 462
Nannar, Temple of, at Ur 13
Naples 117, 118, 182, 217, 222, 227, 292, 298, 416, 438
Royal library 416

Naram-Sin 11
Narmer: *see* Menes
Nationalbibliothek (Imperial Library, Hofbibliothek), Vienna 429-445
Prunksaal 443-445
Naucellius 197
Naucratis 50, 69
Navagero, Andrea 332, 334
Nebbia, Cesare 302
Neferirkara, Pharaoh 26
Neleus: his library 30, 46, 47, 51, 93
Nemesianus 409
Neobar, Conrad 426
Neophytos, St., and his library 163, 164
Neophytos VII, Patriarch 262
Neoptolemus of Parium 120
Nepos, Cornelius 103
Nerli, Bernardo 231
Nero, Roman Emperor 83, 111, 114, 292
Nerva, Forum of, Rome 108
Netherlands, Royal Library of 432
New Academy of Aldus Manutius, Venice 235, 434
New College, Oxford 500
Newport, Isle of Wight 500
Nezval, Vitězslav 472
Nicaea 168, 169, 170, 174, 267, 322
Niccoli, Niccolò 179, 218, 219, 220, 224, 225, 236, 285, 288, 296, 339, 340, 342, 345, 350
his library 219-220, 340, 342
Nicholas I, Pope 256
Nicholas V, Pope (Tommaso Parentucelli) 225, 256, 285, 288, 290, 292, 294, 298, 306, 322, 324, 416, 486
his library 288-294
Nicholas I the Mystic, Patriarch 164
Nicholas III, Patriarch 268, 270
Nicocrates of Cyprus: his library 30
Nicomachus of Gerasa 159, 176
Nicomedia 85, 143, 150
Nicosia, Cyprus 163
Niedbruck, Kaspar von 434, 436, 440
Niger, Franciscus 386
Nika riots 148
Nikephoros, Patriarch 250
Nikephoros, Metropolitan of Laodicea 282, 375
Nikephoros 167
Niketas, *spatharios* 175
Niketas, bibliophile 350
Niketas David of Paphlagonia, 'the Philosopher' 160, 250
Nikolaidis, Pothitos 283
Nîmes: its library 124
Nimrud 7, 14, 16
Nineveh 7, 12, 13, 14, 15, 58
Nippur 4, 7, 8, 9
temple library 7
Nisibis 194
Nonianus 104
Nonnus of Panopolis 176
Norbert, St. 465, 472, 479
Norton, John, bookseller 494
Nosecký, Siard 479
Notker Balbulus 360, 368, 370, 375
Notker Labeo 372, 374
Noto 222
Numa Pompilius 97
Nürnberg, 324, 380, 386, 406, 432, 444, 474, 478
Nuti, Giovanni 312
Nuti, Matteo 222, 237, 306, 314
Nuzi 10
Nyssa: its library 123, 124, 142

Observant Order (of Franciscans) 312 (*see also* Minori Osservanti)
Ockham, William of 312
Octavia, sister of Augustus: library of (Octavian Library, *Bibliotheca Porticus Octaviae*, *Bibliotheca Templi Novi*) 110, 111, 112, 113
Octavian (Gaius Julius Caesar Octavianus) 103, 114, 124 (*see also* Augustus)
Octavian Library: *see* Octavia
Odoacer (Odovacar) 192
Oea (Tripoli): its library 124
Oecolampadius, Johannes 389
Oecumenical Patriarchate, Constantinople (the Phanar): its library 245-264
Oedipus 36
Oenopides 33
Oláh, Miklós 462
Olympiodorus on spurious works 93
Olympus, Mt. (in Bithynia) 13
Omar, Caliph 75, 77, 80, 89
and the Alexandrian Library 77, 80
omphalos of papyrus roll 50
On (city of): *see* Annu
Onesander, son of Nausicrates 69, 77
director of Alexandrian Library 70, 77
Onesicritus 47
Onesimus 50
Onomacritus of Athens 65
Opis, Mesopotamia 59
'Orchestra' (in Agora, Athens): concentration of bookshops 35
Oresme, Nicole 412
Origen 84, 88, 132, 140, 152, 194
his library 152
Orléans, House of 436
d'Orléans, Raoulet 412
Orosius, Paulus 80, 112, 350
Orpheus 29, 32, 33, 52
Orpheus of Croton 65
Orphic hymns 30
Orsini, Fulvio 350
Ostia 232, 339
Otfried of Weissenburg 360
Otiartes 15
Otmar, Abbot of St. Gall 359
Otto I, Holy Roman Emperor 474
Otto III, Holy Roman Emperor 190
Ovid (Publius Ovidius Naso) 104, 108, 111, 190, 229, 374
Oxford 485, 488, 490, 494, 496, 501
Oxyrhynchus 84

Pachomius 146, 148, 163
his Rule (*Typikon*) 146, 148, 163
Pacis, Bibliotheca [Templi]: *see* Vespasian, library of
Padua 170, 215, 216, 224, 227, 334, 336, 380, 382, 432, 438, 454, 496
Painted Stoa (*Poikile Stoa*), Athens 42
use of books in teaching there 42
Palaiologos, Andreas 416
Palaiologos, Theodoros II, Despot of the Morea 306
Palaiologos emperors: *see* Andronikos, John VIII, Manuel II, Michael VIII, Theodore II
Palatine Hill, Rome 110, 147
Palatine Library 83, 111, 113, 182
Palestine 132, 140, 146, 152, 245
Palmyra 84
Pammakaristos Convent, Constantinople 256
Pamphilus, teacher of Eusebius: his library 140, 152
Panaetius 92
Panayia ton Palation, Church of, Constantinople 256
Pannartz, Arnold 182, 229, 326, 478
Pannonius, Andreas 452, 454, 460
Pannonius, Janus (János Csezmiczei) 447, 448, 450, 452, 454, 456
Pantaenus, founder of Catechetic School at Alexandria 82
Pantaenus, Flavius Menander 123
Pantaenus, Titus Flavius, and his library 123, 124, 125

library regulations 129
Pantokratoros Monastery, Mt. Athos 256
paper, introduction of 154
bambykinos 154
Pardo, Giovanni 180
Parentucelli, Tommaso 285, 290, 312, 340 (*see also* Nicholas V)
Paris 39, 180, 182, 209, 210, 216, 217, 321, 359, 379, 382, 384, 386, 388, 409, 411, 414, 418, 420, 422, 425, 442, 494 (*see also* Bibliothèque Nationale)
Parma 202, 463 (*see also* San Giovanni Evangelista)
Parmenides 31
Parrasio, Giano 180, 181
Parthenius, chamberlain to Domitian 105
Paschal II, Pope 465
Patmian School 278
Patmos, Monastery of St. John the Divine 66, 149, 163, 184, 267, 268, 270, 272, 274, 278, 282, 283, 375, 376
its library 267-283
Patrae (Patrai): its library 124, 161
Patriarchal Press, Constantinople 258-262
Paul, St. 130, 147, 267, 410, 479
Paul I, Pope 288
Paul II, Pope 294
Paul, church elder (4th c.) 133
Paul, Bishop of Cirta: his library 134
Paul of Aegina 330
Paul the Deacon 193
Paulmier, Laurent 414
Pavia 321, 359, 486
Pázmány, Peter 448
Peace, Forum of, Rome 114
Peace, Temple of, and library, Rome 108, 114, 124
pecia system 209-210
Pellicier, Guillaume 425
Peloponnese 305
Pembroke, Earl of 500
Penteklesiotes, (Ioannes) 174
Pentheus 49
Pepi 22
Pépin, son of Charlemagne 202, 204
Pépin the Short, Frankish King 288, 409
Perdiccas 60
Pergamum 30, 48, 53, 69, 70, 72, 76, 81, 82, 91, 92, 93, 94, 95, 100, 106, 112, 125, 130, 142, 143, 144, 152
its library 91-95, 124
architecture of 94-95
Asklepieion library 124
and pseudepigraphy 93-94
Pergola, Jacopo da 306
Peribleptos Monastery, Constantinople 173
Pericles 34, 38, 41, 82
Peripatetic school: *see* Lyceum
Perotti (Perottus), Niccolò 225, 288, 290, 296, 312, 330
Persepolis 46
Perugia: *see* San Domenico
Petrarch (Francesco Petrarca) 192, 212, 215, 216, 217, 218, 219, 312, 322, 336, 339, 340, 409, 420, 422, 488
his library 215-217
Petronius (C. Petronius Arbiter) 296
Petros 167
Peurbach, Georg 326, 328, 330, 430
Peutelschmidt, Václav 473
Peutinger, Conrad 382, 389
Pfäfers, Monastery of 372
Pfister, Albrecht 394, 402
Pflugk, Julius 448
Pforzheim 379, 380
Phaedrus, Epicurean philosopher 102
Phakrases, Ioannes 176
Phalaris 494
Phanar, Constantinople 184, 256 (*see also* Oecumenical Patriarchate)
Phanias of Lesbos 480
Phanostratus 61
Pharos, Alexandria 64
Philadelphia (Amman): its library 124
Philanthropinos, Alexios 171
Philaretus, Jewish doctor 80
Philarges, Petros: *see* Alexander V
Philemon 99
Philetaerus of Tieum 91
Philetas 60, 62, 67, 69
Philip II, King of Macedon 60
Philip II, King of Spain 237, 432
Philip IV (the Fair), King of France 411
Philip the Good, Duke of Burgundy 420
Philip of Opus, publisher of Plato 39, 50
Philip of Side: his library 152
Philippi: its library 124
Philo Judaeus 102, 290
philobiblos 48
Philocrates 71
Philodemus of Gadara 118, 120
Philolaus of Croton 31, 33, 38, 296
as publisher 31
Philoponus: *see* John Philoponus
Philotimos of Constantinople 346
Photios I, Patriarch 41, 125, 137, 139, 153, 155, 158, 159, 160, 161, 162, 164, 198, 250, 256, 262
Bibliotheca (*Myriobiblos*) 155, 158, 159, 160
Lexicon 155
Photios II, Patriarch: his library 262
Piacenza: *see* San Sepolcro
Piadena 302
Picardie 382
Piccolomini, Enea Silvio 222, 238, 294, 305, 430, 434 (*see also* Pius II)
Pico della Mirándola, Giovanni 235, 337, 382, 418
Pilato, Leonzio 218, 324
Pilliardi, Ignatius Johann 480
Pinakes: *see* Callimachus
Pindar 67, 162, 278, 330
Pinder, Paul 496
Pins, Jean de 425
Pintoricchio (Pinturicchio), Bernardino 222, 238, 294
Pio, Alberto, Prince of Carpi: his library 235
Piraeus: its library 123
Pirckheimer, Willibald 235, 389, 390, 406
Pisa 222
Pisan, Christine de 411
Pisistratus: his library 30, 124, 194
Piso, Lucius Calpurnius 117, 118, 119, 120
his library 117-118
Pistoia 210
Pittacus 82
Pitton de Tournefort, J. 272
Pius II, Pope 324, 430, 454 (*see also* Piccolomini)
his library 430
Pius III, Pope 296
Planoudes, Maximos 154, 171, 172, 173, 175
Plantin, Christophe 442
Platina (Bartolomeo Sacchi) 294, 299, 302, 303
Plato 26, 31, 32, 33, 37, 38, 39, 40, 41, 42, 43, 44, 46, 50, 58, 63, 73, 98, 102, 104, 123, 141, 149, 158, 161, 163, 166, 174, 219, 229, 231, 272, 274, 278, 326, 330, 337, 376, 456, 482
Academy of 37, 39
his library 37-39
his 'unwritten doctrines' 39
on education 38
his attitude to books 38
the first book-collector 37-39
Arethas's manuscript of 161-162
Platon of Sakkoudion 148, 149, 162
Platonic Academy, Florence 339, 342, 454, 456

Platzer, Ignatius Francis 480
Plautius Lateranus 292
Plautus, Titus Maccius 65, 73, 99, 100, 190
the Plautine Scholium 65, 73
Pleiad, The 72
Plethon: *see* Gemistos
Pleuron 73
Pliny the Elder (Gaius Plinius Secundus) 20, 86, 97, 100, 108, 109, 110
describes manufacture of papyrus rolls 20
Pliny the Younger (Gaius Plinius Caecilius Secundus) 105, 108, 109, 119, 190, 386
Plotinus 166, 174, 189, 305, 330
Plousiadenos, Ioannes 226
Plutarch 34, 59, 82, 92, 93, 101, 118, 171, 172, 177, 310, 344, 389
Plzen 474
Poggio Bracciolini, Giovanni Francesco 219, 221, 285, 288, 290, 294, 339, 340, 374, 434, 450
Pogos, Ioannis 262, 264
Polemon of Ilium 93
Polion 83
Poliziano, Angelo Ambrogini 231, 296, 332, 334, 344, 346, 350, 379, 418, 450, 461
Pollio, Gaius Asinius 83, 99, 101, 103, 104, 110, 111, 112, 113
and library architecture 112-113
his library 112
Pollux (Polydeuces), Julius 35
Polybius, historian 42, 101, 177, 296, 330
Polybius, pupil of Hippocrates 80
Polycarpus, Georgius 454
Polycrates, ruler of Samos 29, 30, 31, 32, 60
his library 29
Polycrates, sophist 37
Pompeii 117
its library 124
Pompey (Gnaeus Pompeius) 99, 101
Pomponazzi, Pietro 334
Pomposa 215
Pontan, Jirí 468
Pontano, Giovanni 184, 436
popular reading matter in Egypt 23
Pordenone 390
Accademia Liviana 334
Porphyrion, Pomponius 294
Porphyry 39, 153, 155, 166, 189
Portos, Frangiskos 488
Postel, Guillaume 425
Postumus, Annius 112
Pothinus 75
Pozsony (Bratislava) University 454
Prague 238, 436, 440, 442, 444, 463, 465, 466, 468, 472, 473, 478
University 466, 468
Praxiphanes 75
Premonstratensians 465
Presles, Raoul de 411, 412
'Printer of the Bible (1488)' 473
'Printer of the New Testament (1497)' 473
'Printer of the *Statuum* (1478)' 473
Proclus 38, 166
Proclus, son of Xanthias 155
Prodicus of Ceos 36, 40, 104
Horae 37
'one-drachma lesson' 41
'fifty-drachma lecture' 37, 41
Prodromos, hermit (Bishop Kaloethes) 168, 169, 170
Prodromos (Petra) Monastery, Constantinople: its library 177, 488
Proetus 49
proof-readers 106
Propertius, Sextus 215
Protagoras of Abdera 34, 37, 38, 39, 40, 88, 104
his teaching method 34
his books burnt 34
Prudentius (Aurelius Prudentius Clemens) 235
Prusa 168
its library 124
Psellos, Michael 165, 166, 167
Pseudo-Dionysius, etc.: *see* Dionysius, etc.
Ψυχῆς Ἰατρεῖον ('Sanatorium of the Soul') 26, 66, 274, 283, 375
Ptolemy I Soter 58, 59, 60, 62, 73, 74, 81, 83, 87, 165, 172, 246
founder of Museum 61-62
Ptolemy II Philadelphus 47, 60, 61, 62, 63, 64, 65, 67, 70, 73, 76, 80, 81, 87, 142
Ptolemy III Euergetes 65, 68, 70, 81
Ptolemy V Epiphanes 68, 69, 91, 93
Ptolemy VI Philometor 64, 69, 81, 87
Ptolemy VII Neos Philopator 69, 81
Ptolemy VIII Euergetes II 26, 66, 76, 81
Ptolemy IX Soter II 69, 82, 91
Ptolemy XI Auletes 76
Ptolemy XII 75
Ptolemy (Claudius Ptolemaeus), geographer 155, 328, 330, 406, 412
Ptolemy el-Garib 51
Pyrrho 63
Pyrrhus I, King of Epirus 97, 98
Pythagoras 26, 31, 33, 37, 38, 50, 61, 63, 73, 80, 81, 238, 330
unwritten 'doctrines' 33

Queen's College, Oxford 488
Questenberg, Kašpar 467
Quintilian (Marcus Fabius Quintilianus) 105, 194, 220, 234
Quirinal Hill, Rome 103, 352
Greek press 298, 302

Raleigh, Sir Walter 494
Ramboldi da Imola, Benvenuto 218
Ramses II 27, 63, 66
his library 26
'sanatorium of the soul' 26
Rangoni, Gabriele 456
Ras Shamra (Ugarit): its library 10
Ratger, monk 364
Ratpert, monk 360, 370
Ravenna 190, 191, 328
Recanati, Giuseppe 234
recitationes 104
Regensburg 436
Regiomontanus (Johann Müller of Königsberg) 225, 326, 328, 406, 430, 448
Reichenau 198, 205, 216, 288, 359, 364
Reticius, Bishop of Autun 133
Reuchlin, Johann 379, 380
Rhachotis, district of Alexandria 65, 68
rhapsodists and their libraries 30
Rhenanus, Beatus (Bild von Rhynow) 375, 379, 380, 382, 384, 386, 389, 391
his library 379-391
Rhodes 41, 45, 68, 75, 82, 102, 124, 142
its library 124
Richbod, Abbot of Lorsch 205
Ridolfi, Niccolò, Cardinal 296, 302, 350
Riegger, Josef von 472
Rimini 305, 306
Rinçon, Antoine 426
Rinuccini, Alamanno 346
Ripoli, San Jacopo di 230, 231, 450
Ripon Abbey 198
Rochefort, Guillaume de 418
Rochefort, Guy de 418
Roe, Sir Thomas: his Greek manuscript collection 496
Romagna 322
Romano, Antoniazzo 299

Rome 30, 43, 48, 49, 52, 74, 76, 77, 82, 84, 88, 92, 93, 97, 98, 99, 100, 101, 102, 104, 105, 106, 109, 110, 111, 112, 113, 114, 116, 117, 119, 120, 123, 124, 125, 130, 132, 133, 134, 137, 147, 152, 180, 184, 190, 192, 194, 198, 202, 215, 220, 221, 222, 225, 227, 228, 229, 230, 233, 236, 250, 256, 267, 278, 288, 290, 292, 294, 296, 298, 302, 312, 321, 322, 324, 326, 328, 330, 332, 334, 336, 346, 350, 364, 380, 384, 414, 418, 425, 430, 432, 438, 452, 454, 458, 496
its public libraries 110-117
Ronsard, Pierre de 73
Rösch, Ulrich, Abbot of St. Gall 374, 375
Rossi, Roberto 339, 342
Rossis, François de 425
Rosso, Giovanni Battista 425
Rossos, Ioannes 225, 226, 330, 354
Rostock University 393
Rouen 412
Rovere, Francesco della: *see* Sixtus IV
Royaumont Abbey 411
Rudolf II, Holy Roman Emperor 440, 446
Rufinus, Italian theologian (4th c.) 132, 133
relations with St. Jerome 132
Rustici, Cencio de' 220, 374
Rusticus, deacon 148

Sabbas, monk of Stylos 267
Sabellico (Marco Antonio Coccio) 332, 334
Sacchi, Bartolomeo: *see* Platina
Sackville, Thomas 494
Saelwulf, monk 272
St. Albans: printing press 494
St. Antony of Padua, Friary of, Constantinople 312
St. Blasien, Monastery of, Brunswick 398
St. Catherine's Monastery, Mt. Sinai 146, 148
its library 148
St. Denis, Abbey of, near Paris 411
St. Gall, Abbey of, and its library 66, 198, 216, 359, 368, 370, 372, 374, 375, 376
St. George, Church of, Constantinople 256
St. John the Divine, Monastery of: *see* Patmos
St. Lawrence, Church of, Rome 134
Saint-Loup, Abbey of, Troyes 202
St. Mark, Library of: *see* Marciana
St. Mark's Basilica, Venice 167, 332, 344
St. Martin, Abbey of, Tours 203
St. Mary's Church, Oxford 485
St. Peter's Church, Rome 267, 288
its library 288
St. Petersburg 276
St. Riquier, Abbey of 410
St. Tryphon, Church of, Nicaea 169
St. Victorius, Order of, 465
St. Vitus's Cathedral, Prague 468
SS Cosma e Damiano, Church of, Rome 114
SS Sergius and Bacchus, Monastery of, Constantinople 147
Sainte-Foy, Convent of, Sélestat 390
Sakkara 22
Sallust (Gaius Sallustius Crispus) 234, 374
Salmydessus 41
Salomon III, Abbot of St. Gall 360, 368, 370
Salutati, Coluccio 219, 220, 232, 339, 340, 350
his library 340
Salviati family 352
Salviati, Cardinal 425
Salviatus, copyist 294
Sambucus, Johannes 436, 442
Sammonicus, Serenus 74
Samos 29, 30, 31, 60, 169
its public library 124
Samuel Chantzeris, Patriarch 260
'sanatorium of the soul': *see* *Ψυχῆς Ἰατρεῖον*
San Biagio, Francesco di 225
San Domenico, Monastery of, Bologna: its library 236, 237, 314
San Domenico, Monastery of, Perugia: its library 236, 314, 344
San Giovanni Carbonara, Monastery of, Naples 180
San Giovanni Evangelista, Monastery of, Parma: its library 236, 314, 344
San Jacopo di Ripoli: *see* Ripoli
San Marco, Monastery of, Florence 180, 236, 285
San Procolo, district of Bologna 210
San Sepolcro, Monastery of, Piacenza 236, 314
Sancti Nicolai Collegium, Vienna 434
Sansovino, Jacopo 238, 336, 337
Sala Sansovino (in Biblioteca Marciana) 337
Santa Giustina, Monastery of, Padua 224
Santa Maria degli Angeli, Monastery of, Florence 339
Santa Maria delle Grazie, Monastery of, Milan: its library 236
Santa Scholastica, Abbey of: *see* Subiaco
Santa Trinità, Church of, Florence 224
Santo Spirito, Monastery of, Florence 218
Sanudo, Marino 334
Sardanapalus: *see* Assurbanipal
Sargon I, Assyrian king 8, 13
Sargon II, Assyrian king 12
Sarzana 285
Sassoferrato 296
Sassolo da Prato 180
Satyrus: on Plato's books 38
Svile, Sir Henry 492, 494
Savona 222
Scaevola, Quintus Mucius, 'the Augur' 101
Scaliger, Joseph Justus 424
Scarperia, Jacopo da 178, 180, 182
Scepsis 46
Schambogen, Jan K. 468
Schedel, Hartmann 478
Schlettstadt: *see* Sélestat
Schöffer, Peter 226, 478
Scholarios, Georgios 177
schools 4, 5, 6, 9, 13
for royal scribes 13, 14, 22, 24, 25
'sons of the school' 5
of Livius Andronicus 98
'law schools' 8
Roman education 101-102
'father of the school' 5
philosophy schools in Athens 143-144
of Sphoracius 154
Schröter, Leonhard 393
Schürer, Matthias 389
Schwarzenburg, Friedrich von, Archbishop of Köln 465
Schwendi, Lazarus 438
Scipio, Publius Cornelius (son of S. Africanus Major) 101
Scipio Aemilianus, Publius Cornelius (Scipio Africanus Minor) 99, 101
Scipio Nasica, Publius Cornelius 99, 100
scribes (in Mesopotamia and Egypt) 5, 6, 9, 10, 16 (royal), 17, 23, 24, 25
Enheduanna 13
Shadanu
'Scribe of the House of Books' 26
scriptoria
of Bessarion 225-226
Monastery of Studius 148, 149, 150, 154, 171

scripts:
Assyro-Babylonian 3-4
cuneiform 3, 4, 5, 11
epistolographic or demotic (Egypt) 20-21
hieratic 20
hieroglyphic 20-21
ideographic 5-7
Linear A and B 50
linear hieroglyphic 20
lower-case script introduced in Byzantium 154
Sumero-Akkadian 4, 14
Scythinus of Teos 33
Sebasteion (Temple of Julius the God), Alexandria: its library 83, 124
Secundus, bookseller 108
Sedulius Scotus 372
Séez, Collège de 209
Sekoundinos, Nikolaos 290, 394
Sélestat (Schlettstadt) 379, 382, 384, 386, 389, 391
Humanist Library 379-391
Seleucus I Nicator 30, 58, 88, 91
recovers books looted from Athens library 30, 58
'burns all the books in the world' 58, 89
Selve, Georges de 425, 426
Seneca, Lucius Annaeus, the Younger ('the Philosopher') 118, 216
Sennacherib 12
his library 12
Senseschmidt, Johann 478
Septimius Severus, Roman Emperor 111
Septuagint: see Seventy
Serapeum (Temple of Serapis), Alexandria: its library 59, 64, 65, 66, 85, 88, 89, 94, 124, 137
'subsidiary' library 65-66, 90
Serapion, Abbot 137
Sergios, Patriarch 245
Seripandi, Cardinal 180
Servius 206
Servius Clodius: Cicero acquires his library 103
Sesostris I, Pharaoh 24
Seti II (Seti Minephtah), Pharaoh 26, 27
Seventy, the, and the Septuagint 64, 65, 73
Seville 194, 496
Seyssel, Claude de 422
Sforza, Alessandro 285, 290
Sforza, Bianca Maria 432
Sforza, Francesco, Duke of Milan 312
Sforza family library 432
Sgouropoulos, Demetrios 221, 222, 224, 225
Shamshi-Adad, Assyrian king 10
Shepseskaf, Pharaoh 26
Shuruppak 4, 58
Sidney, Sir Robert 494
Siena 222, 238, 294, 299
Sigeros, Nikolaos 216
Sighicelli, Gaspare 299
Sigillaria district, Rome 106, 108
Sigismund, King of Hungary and Holy Roman Emperor 447
Sigismund, uncle of Maximilian I 432
Signa, Martino da 218
Si Huang Ti, Chinese emperor 59
Silius Italicus 374
sillybos 103
Simmias of Thebes 31
Simplicius, Neoplatonist philosopher 278, 330
Sinai, Mt. 23 (*see also* St. Catherine's Monastery)
Sinaitis, Hilarion 262
Sinibaldi, Antonio 412
Sin-liqi-unninni, editor of Gilgamesh epic 13
Sintram, calligrapher 372
Sinuhe, Story of 24
Sippar: its libraries 4, 8
Siron, teacher of Virgil 118
Sixtus IV, Pope 229, 298, 312, 326, 384
Sixtus V, Pope 299
Skaranos, Demetrios: his library 180
Skenoures, Arsenios 268
Skoutariotes, Ioannes 226
Skoutariotes, Nikolaos 174
Skoutariotes, Theodoros 168, 170, 174
his library 174
Sligo, Marquis of 283
Smyrna 62, 124, 143, 168, 262
its library 124
Sneferu, Pharaoh 25
Societas Danubiana, Vienna 235, 434
Societas Rhenana, Heidelberg 434
Socrates 31, 32, 33, 35, 37, 38, 41, 42, 50, 58, 63, 81, 194, 482
his library 31-33
dialogue with Euthydemus 31-32
Socrates of Constantinople 152
Soli, Cyprus: its library 124
Solon 26, 30, 37, 63, 73, 480
Sophianos, Nikolaos 350
sophists and books 33-37
Sophocles 50, 84, 221, 330, 418
Sophron 38
his books 38
Sophronios, Patriarch of Jerusalem 252
Sorbon, Robert de 210, 212
Sorbonne 210, 414
Sosipater Charisius 125
Sositheus, Cicero's 'reader' 103
Sosius brothers, Horace's publishers 108
Sotades 98
Sozomenus 195
Speusippus 39, 44
Spézia, La 285
Spinalo, Johannes de: *see* d'Épinal
Squillace 192
Stagira 62, 105, 150, 204, 216
Statius, Publius Papinius
Steinfeld Abbey 465
Steinschaber, Adam 402
Stephanos, Metropolitan of Medeia 226
Stephanos, monk and *bibliophylax* 246
Stephanos, financial official 164
Stephen Uroš II (Stephen Milutin), King of Serbia 177
Stoa of Attalus, Athens 123
Stoa Poikile: *see* Painted Stoa
Stobaeus 64
Strabo 43, 44, 48, 51, 52, 53, 61, 62, 74, 88, 180, 229, 406
on Aristotle's library 43, 44
visits Alexandrian Library 62
description of the Museum 62-63
comment on Apellicon 48
Strahov Abbey (Abbey of Mount Sion), Prague, and its library 444, 463, 465, 466, 472, 473, 474, 478, 479, 480
Strasbourg 379, 382, 386, 391, 438, 442
Strato of Lampsacus 60, 61, 62, 74, 92
Strnad, Antonin 472
Strobilos 268
Strozzi, Barbo 224
Strozzi, Gianfranco 224
Strozzi, Lorenzo 224
Strozzi, Niccolò 224
Strozzi, Noferi 224
Strozzi, Onofrio 224
Strozzi, Palla 180, 220, 222, 224, 285, 406
his library 220, 222, 224
Strümpf, Johann 375
Stubengesellschaft (literary society): at Sélestat 384
Studium: *see* Florence
Studius, Monastery of, Constantinople 148-149, 150, 154, 162, 170, 274, 276
its library 149
its *Typikon* (Rule) 149

Stuttgart 380
Stylos, Monastery of 267
Subiaco Abbey (Santa Scholastica) 229, 328, 478
Suetonius (Gaius Suetonius Tranquillus) 83, 111
'Suidas': *see Souda*
Süleyman the Magnificent, Sultan 438, 448
Sulla, Faustus Cornelius: his library 49
Sulla, Lucius Cornelius 49, 101, 102, 104
his library 48, 49, 101
Sulpicius Rufus, Publius (Servius?) 102
Sultantepe 7
Susa: its library 124
Sweynheim, Konrad 182, 229, 326, 478
Sylo, Dominican friary of
Sylvester I, Pope 292
Symmachus, Aurelius Memmius 192
Synadenos, Ioannes Komnenos 175
his library 175
Synkellos, Georgios 67, 73
Syracuse 37, 38
Syropoulos, Silvestros 254

Tablets: *see* writing tablets
Tafur, Pero: visits library of Blachernai(?) Palace, Constantinople 170
Taio Monastery, Zaragoza 288
Tarasios, Patriarch 155, 159, 160
Tarchaniotes: *see* Maroullos
Tarentum 98
Tarsus 60, 147
Tashmetum 13
Tebaldi, Bartolo 342
Tegea 98
Tehiptilla family, archival library 40
Telephus, grammarian 92
Tell ed-Der 10
Tell el-Dab'a 54
Tello: *see* Lagash
Templi Augusti, Bibliotheca: *see* Tiberius
Templi Novi, Bibliotheca: *see* Octavia
Templum Pacis: *see* Peace, Temple of
Tengnagel, Sebastian 440, 444
Teos 48
Teplá Abbey 467
its library 467
Terence (Publius Terentius Afer) 99, 142, 204
Terentius, scribe 97
Tertullian (Q. Septimius Florens Tertullianus) 124, 132, 133, 290, 448
Thalassius, manager of Libanius's scriptorium 150
Thales of Miletus 29, 480
Thebes, Egypt 23
Themistius 141, 142, 153, 154
Theodora, Byzantine Empress 173, 181
Theodora Raoulaina and her library 174, 176
Theodore I Laskaris, Byzantine Emperor 167, 168, 252
Theodore II Laskaris, Byzantine Emperor 169, 170
Theodore II Palaiologos, Despot of the Morea 306
Theodore, Abbot of Pherme 138
Theodore Eirenikos, Patriarch 168
Theodore the Studite 147, 148, 149, 162, 163
his library 149
his monastic regulations 149
organization of the monastery 149
Theodore of Tarsus, Archbishop of Canterbury 197
Theodoretos, Abbot of Patmos 282
Theodoric the Great 192
Theodoric 'the Red' 496
Theodoros, legal adviser and notary to Oecumenical Patriarchate 226
Theodosius I ('the Great'), Byzantine Emperor 190
Theodosius II, Byzantine Emperor 143, 145, 147
Theognostos, Metropolitan of Perge 225, 226
Theon of Alexandria, Neoplatonist mathematician 155
Theophanes, chronicler 250
Theophanes of Mytilene 110
Theophilos, Byzantine Emperor 164
Theophilus, Patriarch of Alexandria 86, 89
Theophilus of Antioch 285
Theophrastus 19, 30, 34, 35, 43, 45, 46, 47, 51, 60, 61, 62, 63, 101, 130, 330
his library 45-46
leaves his books to Neleus 46
catalogue of his writings 46
his will 46
Theopompus of Athens 35
Theopompus of Chios 93
Thersites 49
Thessalonica (Thessalonika) 32, 123, 124, 142, 169
its library 124
Thévenot, Jean de 272
Thomaitis Triklinos, Constantinople 245, 252, 254
Thomas I, Patriarch 245
Thucydides 41, 44, 93, 141, 151, 290, 330
Thumb, Peter 375, 376
Thurii 38
Tiberianus, Junius 98
Tiberius, Roman Emperor 86, 102, 111
his library (*Bibliotheca Templi Augusti*) 111, 124
Tibullus, Albius 204
Tibur (Tivoli): Hadrian's villa and library 123, 124, 126
Tiglath-Pileser III, Assyrian king 12
Timaeus 42
mocked for his book-learning 42
Timgad: its library 123, 124, 142
Timon of Phlius 50, 70
describes Museum as 'the Muses' birdcage' 70
Timotheus, *The Persians*, papyrus of 30
Tiphernas, Gregorius 180, 182
Tiridates 163
Titus, Roman Emperor 83, 105, 111
Toderini, G., Abbot 262
Toledo 436
Tomi 103
Tommaso da Modena 186
Torre, Joachim della 180
Torresani d'Asola, Andrea 227
Tortelli, Giovanni 179, 288, 292, 294, 299
Tours 474 (*see also* St. Martin's Abbey)
Trajan, Roman Emperor 111, 112, 114, 123, 124, 130, 142
library of (*Bibliotheca Ulpia*) 111-112, 114, 130
its architecture 114, 119-120
library in Baths of Trajan 116
Trajan's Column 119
Traversari, Ambrogio 224, 298, 339, 340, 342, 447
Trebizond 151, 152, 167, 254, 321 (*see also* George of Trebizond)
Trento 432
Trevou, Henri de 412
Trier 133
School of 478
Trivizias, Georgios 225, 226
Trivolis, Demetrios 225, 226
Troad 46, 168, 169
Troppau, Johannes von 429
Tryphon, Quintilian's publisher 105
Tuotilo 360, 368

Turku, Finland 468
Turrecremata, Johannes de, Cardinal 229
Tusculum 104, 118
Tyana 116
Tychicus, teacher of Ananias of Shirak: his library 151, 152
typikon (Rule) of monasteries 146, 147
Tyrannio the Elder 48, 51, 52, 53, 74, 103, 118, 137
his library 48, 52, 74
Tyrnau 442
Tzangaropoulos, Georgios 226
Tzetzes, Ioannes 64, 65, 67, 69, 73, 74, 167
Prolegomena to Aristophanes 65

Udine 332
Udine, Giovanni da 332, 354
Ugarit: its alphabet 10 (*see also* Ras Shamra)
Ugoleto, Angelo 463
Ugoleto, Taddeo, librarian of Corvinian Library 184, 456, 458, 460, 463
L'Uilier, Henri 412
Ulm 180
Ulpia, Bibliotheca: *see* Trajan, library of
Ulpian (Domitius Ulpianus) 97
ummia (head of school) 5
Unas, Pharaoh 21
Ur 4, 7, 13
Urartu 9, 12
Urbino 222, 236, 285, 314, 336, 461
Urceo, Antonio 227
Urgel, Felix de 203
Uruk 4, 7
Utrecht, Tomaso da (Thomas Blavart) 310

Valascase, Armenian king 58
Valdarno 294
Valens, Byzantine Emperor 139, 142, 145, 246
decree concerning manuscripts (A.D. 372) 142
Valentinian III, Roman Emperor 190, 438
Valerius Cato 102
Valerius Flaccus, Gaius 220
Valerius Maximus 216, 234
Valerius Titanianus 83
Valla, Giorgio 235
his library 235
Valla, Lorenzo 288, 290, 292, 294, 302, 416
Valle, Niccolò de 229, 328
Várad (Oradea) 447, 448
Varro, Marcus Terentius 77, 93, 108, 110, 112, 196, 218
De bibliothecis 110
Vasari, Giorgio 344, 345, 454
Vasilios, manager of Patriarchal press 262
Vatican Library 285-303, 352
Vaucluse 216, 217
Vegetius 370
Velleius Paterculus 382
Venice 167, 184, 227, 229, 230, 231, 233, 235, 262, 272, 278, 282, 294, 298, 302, 322, 326, 330, 332, 334, 346, 386, 416, 422, 425, 426, 434, 438, 442, 478, 496
quasi alterum Byzantium 321
see also Marciana
Vercelli: cathedral library 219
Vergerio, Pier Paolo (the elder) 447, 450, 452
Vergikios, Angelos (Ange Vergèce) 425, 426, 427, 492
Verona 215, 332, 456
Vespasian, Roman Emperor 105, 109, 114
his library (Temple of Peace, *Bibliotheca [Templi] Pacis*) 111, 114
Vespasiano da Bisticci 310, 345, 414, 448, 454, 458
Vespucci, Giorgio Antonio 436
Vestinus, Lucius Iulius 88
Vettori, Pier 350
Vicenza 182, 215
Vicovaro 332
Victorius 448
Vicus Sandaliarus, Rome 108
Vicus Tuscus, Rome 108
Vienna 108, 234, 262, 282, 324, 326, 328, 402, 430, 432, 434, 436, 438, 440, 447, 460 (*see also* Nationalbibliothek)
Vigano 228
Vimperk (Winterberg) 478
Vincentia, Cosmas 474
Virgil (Publius Vergilius Maro) 104, 106, 120, 124, 190, 215, 216, 386, 494
Virginius Rufus 98
Visconti family library 420, 422
Visconti, Filippo-Maria, Duke of Milan 486
Visconti, Galeazzo 420
Visconti, Valentina 420
Vitalian, Pope 197
Vitelli de Cortone, Cornelio 418
Viterbo 330
Vitéz, János, Archbishop of Esztergom 448, 450, 452, 454, 456, 458
his library 447-448
Vitruvius (Marcus Vitruvius Pollio) 54, 95, 117, 118
on lighting of libraries 117
Vittorino da Feltre 228, 229, 234
Vivarium, Monastery of 192, 193, 194
its library 194
Vives, Ludovicus 72
Vladislas I, King of Hungary 462
Vogel, Kaspar 406
Volsinii: its library 124
Voltaire 274, 276, 278
Volterra 225
Vopiscus, Flavius 98
Vortoli, Antonio 272
Voulgaris, Evgenios 278

Wagner, Leonhard 375
Waldo, Abbot of St. Gall 359
Wannenmacher, Joseph 376
Wearmouth Abbey 193, 198
Weissenburg, Monastery of 360
Wenceslaus I, King of the Romans: his library 429
Westhuss, Johannes de 384, 390
Westminster: printing press 494
Wicquefort, Abraham 400
Widmanstetter, Johannes Albrecht 436
Wiener Neustadt 432
Wight, Isle of 500
Wilfrid, St. 198
Wimpfeling, Jakob 384, 390
Winchester 500
Winithar, monk 359, 364
Wittenberg 398
Wolfcoz, calligrapher 360
Wolfe, Reginald 494
Wolfenbüttel 393, 394, 400, 402, 404, 406
Herzog August Library (Bibliotheca Augusta) 393-406
writer's fame 24
writing tablets:
as notebooks 50
how made 49-50
gold plates 30
see also books
Württemberg 372
Würzburg 198, 205

Xanten, Westphalia 465
Xanthopoulos, Nikephoros Kallistos 254
Xenocrates 39
Xenophanes 31, 34
Xenophon 31, 33, 34, 41, 42, 49, 93, 101, 235, 272, 290
  on Socrates's library 31-33
Xerxes: loots Athens library 30, 58
Xiphilinos family library 174
Xiphilinos, John: *see* John VIII
Xiphilinos, Manuel 174
Xisourthos (Sisouthros, Sisithros) 15

Yannina 278
York 202

Zabarella, Francesco 450-452
Zacchi, Gaspar 332
Zagreb 454
Zanzolini, Antonio 312, 316
Zaragoza 288
Zdík, Jindrich, Bishop of Olomouc 465, 466
Zeliv Abbey 467
Zeno, Byzantine Emperor 143, 144
Zeno, Jacopo, Bishop of Feltre 290
Zeno of Citium 42, 68, 125
  working in Athens bookshop 42
  his library 42
  founder of Stoic school 42
Zeno the Eleatic 31
Zeno of Sidon 118
Zenobia, Queen of Palmyra 84
Zenodotus of Ephesus 62, 65, 66, 67, 68, 69, 72, 81
  director of Alexandrian Library 67
Zenodotus, grammarian (*c.* 100 B.C.) 67, 69
Zimri-Lim, Sumerian king 4
Ziska, John 466
Zonaras, Ioannes 143, 147, 153
Zopyrus, orator (3rd c. B.C.) 50, 93
Zopyrus of Heraclea 65
Zoroaster 73
Zosimus 44, 176
Zwingli, Huldreich 445
Zygomalas, Theodosios 256

«The Great Libraries» by Konstantinos Staikos was set by Mary Karava
in Times founts. Color separations by Tassos Bastas. The second
impression was printed by M. Toumbis S.A. under the
supervision of Stavros Yannopoulos in 2,000
copies on Zanters Mega matt 150 gr. paper,
and bound by V. Kypraios. Printed
in June 2001 for Kotinos S.A.

ΚΟΤΙΝΟΣ